Commercial Law

Ian Brown LL B, D Phil
Reader in Law,
Faculty of Law,
University of the West of England, Bristol

Butterworths
A Member of the LexisNexis Group

Members of the LexisNexis Group worldwide

United Kingdom	Butterworths Tolley, a Division of Reed Elsevier (UK) Ltd, Halsbury House, 35 Chancery Lane, LONDON, WC2A 1EL, and 4 Hill Street, EDINBURGH EH2 3JZ
Argentina	Abeledo Perrot, Jurisprudencia Argentina and Depalma, BUENOS AIRES
Australia	Butterworths, a Division of Reed International Books Australia Pty Ltd, CHATSWOOD, New South Wales
Austria	ARD Betriebsdienst and Verlag Orac, VIENNA
Canada	Butterworths Canada Ltd, MARKHAM, Ontario
Chile	Publitecsa and Conosur Ltda, SANTIAGO DE CHILE
Czech Republic	Orac sro, PRAGUE
France	Editions du Juris-Classeur SA, PARIS
Hong Kong	Butterworths Asia (Hong Kong), HONG KONG
Hungary	Hvg Orac, BUDAPEST
India	Butterworths India, NEW DELHI
Ireland	Butterworths (Ireland) Ltd, DUBLIN
Italy	Giuffré, MILAN
Malaysia	Malayan Law Journal Sdn Bhd, KUALA LUMPUR
New Zealand	Butterworths of New Zealand, WELLINGTON
Poland	Wydawnictwa Prawnicze PWN, WARSAW
Singapore	Butterworths Asia, SINGAPORE
South Africa	Butterworths Publishers (Pty) Ltd, DURBAN
Switzerland	Stämpfli Verlag AG, BERNE
USA	LexisNexis, DAYTON, Ohio

© Reed Elsevier (UK) Ltd 2001

A CIP Catalogue record for this book is available from the British Library.

ISBN 0 406 02434 0

Printed and bound in Great Britain by Butler & Tanner Ltd, Frome and London

Visit Butterworths LexisNexis *direct* at www.butterworths.com

Foreword

Forty years ago, I was busy writing the first edition of my *Commercial Law*, to be published by Butterworths. As I indicated in the Preface to my 6th edition (1988), my intention over the years was to make available an up-to-date basic textbook for Law Society and university students embarking on a study of commercial law or the most important parts of it.

I saw these important aspects as agency, sale of goods, hire-purchase and commercial credit, negotiable instruments, and insurance law.

Now, Dr Ian Brown has written a much more substantial, comprehensive work, expounding at length what are, arguably, the three key fields of commercial law – agency, sale of goods, and consumer credit. When Dr Brown was originally approached by the publishers, he was asked to prepare a 7th edition of my text, but it became apparent that his breadth of learning and research should not be constrained within the more concise limits of my editions.

Hence, this is a new book on the three chosen topics of commercial law, with a thorough study of the origins of agency and sale of goods law, and the more modern topic of consumer credit, the philosophy of the legal concepts involved, as well as a careful case law and statute-based interpretation of where the law now stands. Dr Brown has used Commonwealth and United States, as well as UK, sources to illustrate many of his themes. These countries have, after all, similar common law origins, our UK Sale of Goods Act 1893 was used as a model overseas, and we have shared many similar commercial developments and commercial instruments, like hire-purchase.

In the result, each of the three parts of Dr Brown's book has as much substance and material as major student texts on just one of the three topics. So, this is a comprehensive and detailed work, but it is a student book to be read, not just a reference book. The reader is taken through all aspects of the chosen subjects, providing a careful insight into the state of the law today, and how we got there. It is full of practical illustration of concepts and principles and, not of least importance for a student with a lot of serious endeavour to pursue, the text is very readable. The author reminds us how elegant and yet how rooted in its time was the Sale of Goods Act 1983. In the past 100 years or so, our law has moved a long way from the simple concept, ingrained in the common law, that 'one size fits all', ie that consumer sales were treated in the same way as commercial or mercantile transactions. For both, the legal assumption was that both parties had equality of bargaining power. Freedom of contract has always been such an important as well as emotive concept that the major qualifications to it by, for example, the Unfair Contract Terms Act, demonstrate how clearly we live in a world of change (see p 243).

Traditional common law concepts, like an agent's fiduciary duties to his principal, have displayed amazing adaptability and flexibility in, for example, the developing significance of 'Chinese walls', often so important in financial institutions, and firms of solicitors and accountants needing to avoid conflicts of interest (see p 117).

Since I mentioned readability, let me add that I do not just mean that the reader is gently and clearly led from one concept to the next, from the general rule to the particular and to the qualifications. I mean also the diversionary or humorous touch that can so often help to illuminate or remind one of the point at issue. A leading case on estate agents' remuneration is *Luxor (Eastbourne) Ltd v Cooper*, a House of Lords case in 1941, where the agreed estate agents' fee on the sale of cinemas was £10,000. Dr Brown neatly recalls that Lord Russell of Killowen was 'at pains to emphasise graphically that £10,000 was then the remuneration of a year's work by the Lord Chancellor' (see p 146).

Students will find this work of considerable help in the various courses of study of specific contracts that appropriately follow after they have acquired a basic knowledge of the general law of contract.

Lord Gordon Borrie QC
House of Lords
June 2001

Preface

Commercial law is a Protean subject and it is difficult, if not impossible, to ascertain its constituents and define its parameters. One consequence of this is that it has become commonplace for syllabuses in commercial law to treat the subject as a portmanteau: students take a cursory glance at many of its contents but are permitted a deeper scrutiny of none. Moreover, the legal curriculum is still dominated by the late 19th century ethos which, today, arguably means that the study of interests in real property is magnified and elevated. In contrast, commercial law rarely, if ever, figures as a compulsory subject in the undergraduate diet. It is incredible that, in the 21st century, a law student can graduate from an English university without, for example, any knowledge of the law relating to the sale of goods. It is equally unbelievable that the law of agency – a seminal, pervasive subject by any reckoning – is often compressed into one chapter in texts on the law of contract and, if it is examined in any greater depth, it is thought to be an esoteric field of study. It is plain that, at one extreme, syllabuses cannot contain every facet of commercial law and, at the other, that a handful of narrow, disjointed subjects should not be flung into the mixing pot with the contents labelled as commercial law. With these extremities in mind, it must be asked whether any areas within commercial law comprise that subject's bedrock.

As the content and scope of commercial law cannot be fixed with any degree of precision and differences of opinion will always exist as to its proper ambit (see Goode, 'The Codification of Commercial Law' (1988) 14 Mon LR 135, 141-143; Goode, *Commercial Law in the Next Millennium* (1998)), the location of its substratum may prove to be an arduous, or even a futile, task. It is suggested that the three mercantile areas considered in this text at least lay claim to be an important, integrated layer in the foundations of the subject, viz the law relating to agency, the sale of goods and consumer credit. A knowledge of these subjects is a pre-requisite to the understanding of other areas of commercial law but this trinity also has a satisfying congruity and a substantial interdependence. The principles of agency provide the key to unlock many of the concepts in the law relating to the sale of goods and the modern rules of consumer credit. It is difficult, for example, to appreciate the law on the transfer of title by a non-owner in the sale of goods without first having mastered the principles of apparent authority in agency. Indeed, the Sale of Goods Act 1979, s 21, is incomprehensible until 19th century agency doctrine is recognised as its rationale. Less obvious, but equally important, is the fact that agency explains some of the more esoteric rules on the passing of property in the sale of goods. The notion that the buyer may give his prior assent to the seller's subsequent appropriation of the goods as an act which passes the property in the goods to the buyer, begins to make sense only when it is realised that the buyer confers an authority on the seller to perform this act of appropriation – the seller becomes the buyer's agent for that purpose and the issue thus turns on the scope of his authority to perform the act in question. Even the structure and scope of the Consumer Credit Act 1974, s 56, is premised on the law of agency and is rendered meaningful only when the latter subject has been mastered. It will be apparent that this enumeration and scrutiny of hybridised rules could be augmented, but this must be the province of the text itself.

This book aims to provide a clear, practical account of the law, to explain the function and purpose of the rules which are examined and to place those rules in their historical and social context. The text is also critical of the law, where criticism is deserved, and suggestions are made for its reform. However, even when subjects are considered in some depth, a choice inevitably has to be made to jettison certain material. The text contains, for example, no separate consideration of either crimes or torts committed by agents and the topic of an agent's knowledge being imputed to his principal is also not included. Nevertheless, it is hoped that the book is cohesive throughout its subject areas and that it permits the reader a better understanding of the legal rules which are analysed. Sir Mackenzie Chalmers emphasised that 'a rule can never be appreciated apart from the reasons on which it is founded' (*Sale of Goods Act, 1893* (Introduction to the 1st edn, 1894) and, above all else, it is that precept which is followed throughout this book.

I am indebted to Lord Borrie QC and gratified that he has seen fit to write the foreword to the text. Lord Borrie is most often associated with his role as Director General of Fair Trading where his practical achievements, as the longest-serving Director thus far, were legion. However, Lord Borrie has also contributed much as an author and respected academic. My interest in commercial law was first kindled by the refreshing, critical approach adopted in *The Consumer, Society and the Law*, the book which Gordon Borrie wrote with Aubrey L Diamond in 1964 and which was published in four editions and numerous reprints. An undergraduate when first I read the book, I still remember how absorbing was the account of the buyer who asked for 'two nice fresh crabs for tea' (*Wallis v Russell* [1902] 2 IR 585) and how fascinating were the travails of the unfortunate purchasers of 'Golden Fleece' underpants (*Grant v Australian Knitting Mills Ltd* [1936] AC 85), a plastic catapult (*Godley v Perry* [1960] 1 WLR 9) and a bath bun which contained a large stone (*Chaproniere v Mason* (1905) 21 TLR 633). Quite dramatically, the law was animated and, equally intriguingly, complex legal principle was brought to bear on the everyday concerns of ordinary people. Although long out of print, *The Consumer, Society and the Law* still provides an immensely readable introduction to those drawn to commercial law, as does Lord Borrie's penetrating Hamlyn lecture, *The Development of Consumer Law and Policy – Bold Spirits and Timorous Souls* (1984). Amongst his many pursuits, Lord Borrie, ever a bold spirit, continues to monitor the pulse of the law.

Thanks must go to my colleague, Dr Adrian Chandler. Throughout he has bravely endured the onslaught of my interminable questions on the function and purpose of the law. Finally, although an edict of the publisher prevents authors from referring to any of its staff personally, I am also grateful to everyone at Butterworths who have been extraordinarily patient, efficient and attentive in transforming the manuscript into a completed book.

Ian Brown
1 June 2001

Contents

Chapter 8   The duties of the agent owed to his principal – Part 2: the agent's fiduciary duties   101

Chapter 9   The rights of the agent against his principal   142

Chapter 10   The relationship between principal and third party   165

PART TWO   THE SALE OF GOODS

Chapter 13   Introduction to the sale of goods   243

Chapter 14   The nature, definition and subject matter of the contract of sale   248

Chapter 15   The contract of sale distinguished from analogous contracts   276

Chapter 16   The passing of property in goods   294

Chapter 21 The duties of the seller relating to fitness for purpose of the goods and sales by sample   487

Chapter 38 The regulation of business activities   911

Table of statutes

Table of cases

PAGE

PAGE

PART ONE

The Law of Agency

CHAPTER 1

The conceptual basis and nature of agency

A definition of agency

Agency is concerned with those situations where one person acts for and on behalf of another. In sophisticated, commercial transactions, it is self-evident that individuals and, in particular, limited companies, may want to utilise the services of an agent who will transact business on their behalf. Today, agents are often specialists in particular fields who can find reliable third parties with whom the principal wishes to contract, thereby expediting business transactions and reducing costs. In commercial law, agency is thus concerned primarily with those situations where a contract is concluded between two parties (the principal and the third party) by the actions of an intermediary (the agent).

However, an agent need not be involved in negotiating complex, commercial contracts and an unpaid friend who purchases goods in a retail shop on behalf of another also acts as an agent in forming the contract for the sale of goods. As with much of English commercial law where broad, abstract principles are applied to disparate, practical business transactions, the common law of agency encompasses all undertakings where one person acts on behalf of another in the formation of a contract with a third party.

In the earliest and simplest transaction, the agent (A) would disclose the fact that he was acting for his principal (P) within certain limits and the third party (T) would want to contract with P. Here A would be acting as little more than a messenger or *nuntius* with no independent will. In such a setting, the fact that a contract was formed vicariously did not unduly stretch the notion of contract as based upon personal agreement, since A simply forged the link between the two consenting parties. The remedies available in the embryonic law of contract for breach of contract were certainly available to P and T. Agency has developed largely as a commercial notion and the common law has forged principles to meet mercantile demands whilst attempting to balance the interests of P and T and ensure that neither is prejudiced by the acts of A. When agency is examined in detail in later chapters, it will become evident that the earliest notion of a robotic, messenger agent, is now quite misleading as one of the enduring difficulties of modern agency relates to balancing the interests of P and T when A *exceeds* the actual authority which P has conferred upon him.

Although it is not a necessity, A will frequently have a contract with P in which A's functions are set forth and he will also normally be remunerated by P. Once A has brought P and T into a contractual relationship and been paid by P, A's task is complete and, usually, he will withdraw from the contractual arena thereby ceasing to have any liability either to P or T. The jigsaw puzzle of agency is only complete when the inter-connection of these three parties is understood and each facet of their union must be considered separately. However, the multi-faceted P–A–T relationship and the disparate range of functions which an agent may perform make agency a notoriously difficult concept to define with precision.[1] Nevertheless, the paradigm of agency can be delineated and then some of its features investigated in more detail:

> 'Agency is a *fiduciary relationship* which exists between principal and agent whereby each *consents* to the agent's acting on behalf of the principal, the agent then being said to possess an *authority* to affect the principal's *legal relations* with third parties.'

The relationship of P–A–T

THE AGENT HAS AUTHORITY TO AFFECT THE PRINCIPAL'S LEGAL RELATIONS WITH THE THIRD PARTY

The most important, central feature of agency is the concept of A's authority as it is this notion which enables A to affect P's legal relations with T. As will be seen in Chapter 2, A need not be appointed to act for P by *contract* nor need he possess contractual capacity but he must have *authority* from P, in some shape or form, if P's legal relations are to be altered. In the simplest example, A may be an unpaid, non-contractual agent who performs an undertaking for P, eg selling P's car for not less than £25,000, and this is sufficient to constitute an express agency relationship where A possesses an *actual* or *real* authority.

If A were always to act precisely within the authority actually conferred by P no difficulties would arise as regards A's acting beyond his authority but, at the same time, agency would have little practical, commercial utility. An agent must be able to manoeuvre in changeable, commercial conditions and thus take advantage of bargains which present themselves and are in P's best interests. Alternatively, A may be fraudulent in exceeding his authority and seeking to profit thereby but this may not be evident to a *bona fide* T who deals with A. It is thus clear that the law must cater for situations where A exceeds his actual authority and it is here that difficulties arise. Suppose that, in the above example, market conditions are such that A considers it to be in P's best interests to sell the car to a *bona fide* T for £20,000 – does T have a binding contract with P? If T wishes to sue P on this contract, on what basis may he enforce it where A lacks actual authority? Conversely, if P wishes to sue T, to what extent will the law allow him to do so? An outline of the types of authority which A may possess goes some way to answering these questions.

P confers actual or real authority on A

In the model situation, P will confer an *actual, express authority* on A by express words or possibly in writing. Such express authority may be brief and purely

---

1   See eg, the definition in the USA's *Restatement, Second, Agency* §1(1): 'Agency is the fiduciary relation which results from the manifestation of consent by one person to another that the other shall act on his behalf and subject to his control, and consent by the other so to act'. §1 is prefaced by the *caveat* that 'the brevity of a definition necessarily makes it an incomplete and inaccurate statement'.

oral (eg 'please sell my car for not less than £25,000') or, alternatively, P and A may intend that the authority with which A is endowed is both comprehensive and communicated formally to A in writing. In each of these examples, A will have an *actual, implied authority* to do 'whatever is necessary for, or ordinarily incidental to, the effective execution of his express authority in the usual way'.[2] In general, the more terse the express authority, the greater will be the width of the implied authority. For example, if A is expressly authorised to sell P's car he will have implied authority to demonstrate it and describe it to T. It will be evident from Chapter 2 that implied authority can be sub-divided and may derive from appointment to an office or position or it may emanate from custom in a particular market, for example. In the grant of express authority, P implicitly consents that A should possess an implied authority, which is, therefore, correctly regarded as part of actual authority.

As stated above, if no mechanism catered for situations where A exceeded his actual authority conferred by P, agency would have a severely limited ambit as A would then be a mere *nuntius* or messenger. Consequently, should A act *without authority* or *exceed* his authority, P may, within limits, choose to *ratify* and adopt A's act. Moreover, ratification is invaluable for T as he may wish to establish that P has ratified a contract and, thereby, T may secure a remedy against P. Indeed, ratification is arguably more important for T than for P, particularly as ratification can derive from *conduct*, eg P's conduct in keeping and selling goods delivered by T which had been ordered by A in excess of his authority. Ratification is regarded as equivalent to an antecedent authority and so it is also classified as a species of actual authority.

A has an apparent authority

The divisions of authority discussed so far are regarded as actual authority because in each instance the authority is *conferred* by P on A either before or after the act performed by A. Suppose, however, that A acts beyond his actual authority but appears, *from T's perspective*, to be acting with authority from P. This could happen where A is instructed to sell P's car for not less than £25,000 but A sells it to T for £22,500. Similarly, consider the situation where A is the credit manager of P's business but P has placed a private restriction on A's authority to grant credit. In the car example, everything may appear to be normal from T's viewpoint and, similarly, A may apparently be acting within his authority when granting credit to T which is, in fact, beyond the limit specified by P. Moreover, if the situation does appear to be normal, T will have no reason to suspect that A has exceeded his authority and, consequently, no thought of ascertaining any restriction on that authority. In these examples, may P refuse to ratify A's act and deprive T of any remedy against P? If P could do this, T would be left in a perilous and unacceptable position: he would have relied on the contract's coming into existence only to have the opportunity snatched from him. Consequently, there are situations where A may have no actual authority but may possess its antithesis, *apparent* authority. It cannot be stressed enough that apparent authority is available as a remedy only

---

2 *Bowstead & Reynolds on Agency* (16th edn, 1996), Art 27, para 3-018; *Pole v Leask* (1860) 28 Beav 562, 574 per Sir John Romilly MR: '...when an express authority is given, there is an implied authority combined with it to do all acts which may be necessary for the purpose of effecting the object for which the express authority is given' (affd (1862) 33 LJ Ch (NS) 155).

to T and is thus often referred to as 'agency by estoppel' – P is estopped from denying the appearance of authority which he has created in A. If P wishes to sue T he must ratify A's unauthorised act.

But what should be the criteria for the operation of an apparent authority which binds P to T? First, two diametrically opposed assertions should be considered as the possible bases of P's liability: (i) T has reasonably *relied* on the objective normality of the situation when dealing with A and so P should be liable or (ii) P should be liable only if he has voluntarily *created* the appearance of authority in A. It is plain that (i) looks at the situation from T's perspective whilst (ii) adopts P's viewpoint. In fact, English law attempts to amalgamate both (i) and (ii) and, consequently, the rule is that P must make a *representation*, by words or conduct, to T, that A has authority to act on P's behalf and T must *rely* upon that representation. Apparent authority is frequently referred to as the doctrine of 'holding-out' and P's representation (or holding-out) can be quite general in nature, eg P's appointment of A as the credit manager of P's business with P's acquiescence in A's continuing to act in that capacity.

It is important to emphasise that the first alternative above, T's reliance on appearances, unequivocally protects T whereas the second has a distinct bias in favour of P in its stipulating for his *creation* of the apparent authority. In complete contrast, many of the Civil law systems, and Germany in particular, were influenced by the writings of Rudolf von Ihering[3] and Paul Laband[4] in the middle of the 19th century and make a clear distinction between the internal P–A relationship and the external A–T relationship, emphasising that there is no necessary coincidence between the two[5] and that the smooth operation of commerce demands an agent with an extremely wide and virtually unimpeachable, external authority. The approach of the Civil law is thus arguably over-protective of T and, ideally, any legal system should strike a balance between the competing interests of P and T.

Does A have authority or power?

Hohfeld, the American jurist, was the first to argue precisely that 'the creation of an agency relation involves, *inter alia*, the grant of legal powers to the so-called agent, and the creation of correlative liabilities in the principal'.[6] The relationship of principal and agent was thus defined as one of 'power-liability' using Hohfeld's table of 'jural opposites' and 'jural correlatives'.[7] Hohfeld went on to emphasise that the term 'authority' was 'ambiguous and slippery in its connotation' and that it would be better to confine its use to the 'concrete

---

3   *His Jarbuch* I (1857) and II (1858).
4   *Die Stellvertretung bei dem Abschluss von Rechtsgeschäften nach dem Allgemeinen Deutschen Handelsgesetzbuch* (1866).
5   See Müller-Freienfels, 'Legal Relations in the Law of Agency: Power of Agency and Commercial Certainty' (1964) 13 Am J Comp L 193 and 341; 'Law of Agency' (1957) 6 Am J Comp L 165, 170-176; *Civil Law in the Modern World* (ed A N Yiannopoulos, 1965), Ch 4.
6   Hohfeld, *Fundamental Legal Conceptions as Applied in Judicial Reasoning*, (1919, 3rd printing, 1964) p 52.
7   Hohfeld, *Fundamental Legal Conceptions as Applied in Judicial Reasoning*, p 36. For an explanation of Hohfeld's analysis, see Dias, *Jurisprudence* (5th edn, 1985) Ch 2; *Salmond on Jurisprudence* (12th edn,1966) Ch 7; *Lloyd's Introduction to Jurisprudence* (6th ed, 1994) pp 390-392, 494-499; Corbin, 'Legal Analysis and Terminology' (1919) 29 Yale LJ 163. See further Radin, 'A Restatement of Hohfeld' (1938) 51 Harv L Rev 1141.

authorisation' between P and A rather than confuse it with 'the powers and privileges thereby created in the agent'.[8] Using this analysis, authority is purely the factual situation obtaining between P and A but power relates to the legal ability of A to affect P's legal relations with T. A may thus exercise his power by virtue of the authority given to him by P but he may still have power where he lacks such authority. Thus in cases of apparent authority, described above, A might be acting in contravention of the actual authority given by P but could, nevertheless, validly exercise his power and bind P to T. It is thus evident that A's authority can never be greater than his power. Although Hohfeld's analysis was adopted by commentators on agency[9] and enshrined in the USA's *Restatement*[10] it has never found overall favour in England: English law clings doggedly to the terminology of 'authority' in a variety of guises and this single concept is thus really an amalgam of authority and power.

While Hohfeld's reasoning is logical, it is somewhat clinical and invites the question of *when* such a power exists in A to affect P's legal relations. It is clear from what was said above that A may bind P by acts which are beyond A's actual authority, but does the notion of power assist in deciding the extent to which P is bound? If A's power is not necessarily traceable to his authority, what is its rationale and how may the boundaries of its operation be drawn? The answer given by Seavey[11] was that 'the existence and extent of the power is determined by public policy'. This is clearly somewhat indeterminate. Although it was criticised above, at least English law's view of apparent authority forges a causal link between P's holding-out of A and T's consequent reliance on the appearance of authority so created, arguably providing a more certain framework than either abstract notions of power or the Civil law's insistence that there is no necessary connection between the internal and the external aspects of agency.

Finally, the notion that A's power is determined by public policy lends weight to the views of some commentators that the consequences of agency are determined primarily by the law[12] rather than by the conduct and consent of the parties. The emphasis on the notion of power arguably aids a rational evaluation of apparent authority where P does not actually consent to A's having the relevant authority in that it is possible to assert that, although A does not have authority from P, he does have the requisite power to affect P's legal relations with T. But as stated above this approach sheds little light upon the extent of the power in question. The consensual basis of agency is considered separately, below.

A has the authority to affect P's legal relations with T

An agent is always a *representative* but there are many representatives who are not agents because they cannot affect P's legal relations with T. Powell[13] gave

---

8 Hohfeld, *Fundamental Legal Conceptions as Applied in Judicial Reasoning*, p 52.
9 See Seavey,'The Rationale of Agency' (1920) 29 Yale LJ 859; Corbin, 'The "Authority" of an Agent – Definition' (1925) 34 Yale LJ 788, 792-794; Montrose, 'The Basis of the Power of an Agent in Cases of Actual and Apparent Authority' (1938) 16 Can Bar Rev 757, 761-764; Falconbridge,'The Law of Agency' (1939) 17 Can Bar Rev 248, 251-252; Dowrick,'The Relationship of Principal and Agent' (1954) 17 MLR 24, 36-38.
10 See *Restatement, Second, Agency* §§ 6, 7, 8, 8A, and 12. However, §7 clearly mixes and confuses authority with power in specifying that 'authority is the power of the agent to affect the legal relations of the principal ...'
11 'The Rationale of Agency' (1920) 29 Yale LJ 859, 861.
12 See eg Fridman, *The Law of Agency* (7th edn, 1996), p 19.
13 *The Law of Agency* (2nd edn, 1961), p 4.

the examples of a Member of Parliament and a representative at a funeral or wedding, both of whom are clearly representatives but neither of whom are agents in that they lack the authority to affect P's legal position in relation to T.

This essential characteristic and function of affecting P's legal position may be crucial in deciding whether A is an agent. In *John Towle and Co v White*,[14] for example, A received cotton goods from the manufacturers, Towle & Co (P), in order to sell them in his 'cotton agency business'. The terms of business between A and P were that A could sell the goods at any price and on his own credit terms and for such goods sold A paid a fixed price to P but he did not give P any particulars of sale or name his customers. Moreover, A received the cotton in a 'grey state' and, at his own cost, had it dyed before sale thereby increasing its value by 25%. A was a member of a firm which carried on a separate business but all moneys from the cotton business were paid into an account of the firm. When the firm became financially embarrassed, P claimed the balance in the account on the basis that A was his agent. The House of Lords held that the proceeds of sale belonged to A as he was not an agent for P. Lord Selborne LC advanced three tests for deciding whether A was an agent: (i) Were the buyers of the goods liable to P in contract for the price of the goods? (ii) Could the buyers recover against P in contract for any defects in the goods? (iii) Could the dyer of the goods, employed by A, sue P for the costs of dyeing? As the answer to all these questions was in the negative, it meant that A was not an agent with authority to affect P's legal relations with others.[15]

Although A's authority to alter P's legal position with T is a central characteristic of agency proper, there is a class of 'canvassing' or 'introducing' agent who has no such authority and is typified by the estate agent who simply introduces P, the owner of the house, to T, its prospective purchaser, and the parties then contract *directly* with each other. Such agents owe fiduciary duties to their principals and are normally paid on a commission basis and, whilst the internal P–A relationship will thus be the same as in cases of agency proper, the external authority to affect P's legal position is absent. Moreover, the question of the 'commission agent's' indirect representation has received little attention in English law[16] but is an accepted feature in Civil law jurisdictions.[17] Here P may authorise A to act for him in buying goods, for example, on the basis that A will act in his own name as a *principal* with T. Again the internal aspects of agency between P and A are normal (P pays A by commission; A is a fiduciary) but the external features are missing in that A is not authorised to, and does not create privity of contract between P and T. It is the latter feature which distinguishes the 'commission agent' from the common law's unique recognition and development of the concept of the *undisclosed principal*. In English law, provided that A has actual authority to act on behalf of an undisclosed principal, it is possible for P to remain undisclosed and hidden from T (ie T thinks that A is a principal) yet P may nevertheless intervene to sue and be sued on the contract with T. The undisclosed principal's intervention in this manner is subject to limitations which are considered in detail in Chapter 10 and it is unclear whether or not the European notion of the commission agent is within the native, English doctrine.

---

14 (1873) 29 LT 78; affm *Ex p White, re Nevill* (1870) 6 Ch App 397.
15 See also *Garnac Grain Co Inc v HMF Faure & Fairclough Ltd* [1968] AC 1130n, 1137 (considered in Ch 2); *Weiner v Harris* [1910] 1 KB 285.
16 See Hill, 'The Commission Merchant at Common Law' (1968) 31 MLR 623.
17 See Müller-Freienfels, 'Comparative Aspects of Undisclosed Agency' (1955) 18 MLR 33.

THE RELATIONSHIP OF PRINCIPAL AND AGENT IS CONSENSUAL

Although there need be no *contract* between P and A defining their relationship,[18] the paradigm of agency is definitely premised upon the *consent* of both parties to its creation and, indeed, there is much support for the notion that consent is an essential characteristic of agency.[19] Certainly in the second half of the 19th century, consent, agreement and the grant of authority came to be the justifications for imposing liability upon P and the pervasive influence of the 19th century decisions still dominates today. However, it has been suggested by several commentators that an over-emphasis on consent is misleading and that, in many instances, agency arises by operation of law.[20] The basis of this argument is that P and A may have not manifested any *real* consent and that agency may arise *against* the wishes of P in cases of apparent authority. While this approach has much in its favour, it is arguable that it fails to make a proper distinction between real and implied consent and subjective and objective evaluations of factual relationships.[1] All types of authority can be rationalised in terms of consent by deploying an objective analysis. Thus in apparent authority, the principal's manifestation of consent is made to the third party and is formulated in terms of the principal's representing to the third party that his agent has the requisite authority. Moreover, it is equally feasible to justify cases of agency of necessity in terms of consent. Here A finds it necessary to act on behalf of P in a situation of emergency, eg P's horse is delivered at its destination by the railway but P is not there to collect it. Certainly where A has an actual authority from P, it is obviously arguable that P impliedly consents to A's having increased authority in such predicaments, these cases thus involving actual, implied authority rather than authority by operation of law.

Whether it is *desirable* to force all the categories of authority within the single notion of will theory and consent is another matter, as the process may be both strained and artificial. It is arguable that it may be appropriate in apparent authority, for example, to dispense with the idea of consent and recognise that an *imposition* of liability on P is easier to justify, along the lines of the employer's vicarious liability for the torts of his employees. Also, in cases of usual authority, where it is sometimes asserted that A has an authority assessed on the basis of

---

18 See Ch 2 for the rules relating to the creation of express agency.
19 See *Pole v Leask* (1862) 33 LJ Ch (NS) 155, 161 per Lord Cranworth: 'No one can become the agent of another person except by the will of that other person'; *Garnac Grain Co Inc v HMF Faure & Fairclough Ltd* [1968] AC 1130n, 1137 per Lord Pearson:'The relationship of principal and agent can only be established by the consent of the principal and the agent'. See also *Restatement, Second, Agency* § 1(1); *Bowstead & Reynolds on Agency* (16th edn, 1996) Art 1, para 1-001; Seavey, 'The Rationale of Agency' (1920) 29 Yale LJ 859, 863-864; Street, *The Foundations of Legal Liability* (1906), Vol II, *History and Theory of English Contract Law*, pp 432-433.
20 See Fridman, *The Law of Agency* (7th edn, 1996), pp 14-21; Markesinis and Munday, *An Outline of the Law of Agency* (4th edn, 1998), pp 5-6; Dowrick, 'The Relationship of Principal and Agent' (1954) 17 MLR 24, 24-28.
1   Lord Pearson in *Garnac Grain Co Inc v HMF Faure & Fairclough Ltd* [1968] AC 1130n, 1137, stressed that consent was vital to the agency relationship but that 'they [P and A] will be held to have consented if they have agreed to what amounts in law to such a relationship, even if they do not recognise it themselves and even if they have professed to disclaim it'. See also *Branwhite v Worcester Works Finance Ltd* [1969] 1 AC 552, 587, per Lord Wilberforce: '... the consent need not necessarily be to the relationship of principal and agent itself ... but may be to a state of fact upon which the law imposes the consequences which result from agency'. Both cases are considered in Ch 2.

what is objectively 'usual' in a trade or profession, it might be realistic to acknowledge that such an idea is based upon a public policy notion of 'inherent agency power', as in the USA.[2] Such questions are discussed later when the specific types of authority are considered.

THE RELATIONSHIP OF PRINCIPAL AND AGENT IS A FIDUCIARY RELATIONSHIP

Because of the trust reposed in A and his ability to affect P's legal relations, the law imposes strict *fiduciary duties* on A. During the 18th and 19th centuries, the Court of Chancery had jurisdiction over agency cases where A abused his position and the agent's duties were developed as an offshoot of the trustee-beneficiary relationship. The cases make it clear that these duties are imposed by the law and there is no question of their emanating from consent or the parties'common intent.[3] The overriding principle here is that A must not let his personal interest conflict with the duty owed to P, this general notion being capable of sub-division into the various individual duties which are considered in Chapter 8. In commercial agencies, it may sometimes be awkward to rationalise A's duty *vis-à-vis* P to rise above the morals of the market place with the fact that he functions within it and some decisions have to balance business efficacy and practice with duties of good faith in attempting to arrive at a just and reasonable conclusion.

LEGAL RELATIONS ARE CREATED BETWEEN THE PRINCIPAL AND THIRD PARTY AND THE AGENT THEN WITHDRAWS, HIS TASK BEING COMPLETED

If the arrangement between P–A–T goes to plan, A will have brought P and T into direct contractual relations and A will then withdraw from the scene as his role has been performed. However, A may be liable to T in certain situations which will be considered later[4] and, should A have acted without any type of authority whatever so that T has no contract with P and suffers loss thereby, A may be liable to T for *breach of warranty of authority*. This action is unique to agency and, as its title indicates, it is based upon A's warranting an authority which he does not possess. As A's liability for breach of warranty of authority is strict liability and is not premised upon negligence, it can act as an important life-line for T if he fails to establish any sort of authority in A.

SHOULD MORE EMPHASIS BE PLACED UPON THE AGENT'S ROLE?

A pervasive influence in English agency law is the emphasis which is placed upon A as the *alter ego* of P, this being summarised in the maxim *qui facit per alium facit per se*.[5] This notion is particularly evident in the early law in relation to A's appointment by deed (ie a power of attorney) in that such deeds were

2 See *Restatement, Second, Agency* §8A, considered in Chs 4 and 5 .
3 See eg *Gray v Haig* (1854) 20 Beav 219; *Parker v McKenna* (1874) 10 Ch App 96; *Armstrong v Jackson* [1917] 2 KB 822.
4 See Ch 11.
5 He who does something through another does it through himself.

construed particularly strictly in favour of P, thus maintaining the idea of the single identity of P/A. Similarly, as explained above, it is A's authority *conferred by P* which dominates English agency theory, this thread being traceable throughout all the types of authority. The strength of the concept of authority *and* the identity theory of P/A is exemplified in the doctrine of the undisclosed principal (referred to earlier) by which P has rights and liabilities under the contract with T, formed by A, even though the agency itself is not evident at all *provided that A has actual authority from P.* It is suggested that this concentration on A's authority derived from P and A's perceived role as a mere *nuntius* has made it difficult for English law to explain satisfactorily P's liability for A's unauthorised acts, for the law must trace A's authority backwards to some words or conduct of P from which the authority originates. As a consequence, the agent has often been portrayed as an acquiescent automaton.[6] Clearly the nature of agency demands the agent's subordination to his principal but, in a dynamic, corporate context, it may be apt to have more regard for the agent's position and function rather than concentrating purely on the extent of the authority actually or apparently conferred by P. In seeking to achieve the elusive balance between the interests of P and T, this re-alignment of perspective might equalise the scales in T's favour when A's apparent authority is evaluated. Moreover, as Reynolds[7] has pointed out, there can be situations where commercial expectations are that A should remain personally liable to T or have a dual function as an agent of P *and* a principal as regards T and it may also be appropriate to pay greater attention to A's position in these circumstances.

---

6   Eg Montrose, 'The Basis of the Power of an Agent in cases of Actual and Apparent Authority' (1938) 16 Can Bar Rev 757, 759: 'The term "agent" is only properly applicable to a person in connection with the relationship in which he stands to the principal, and ... that relationship is limited to acts to be done on the principal's behalf'.
7   'Agency: Theory and Practice'(1978) 94 LQR 224.

CHAPTER 2

Actual and implied authority

Actual, express authority

The commonest way in which the relationship of P and A is created is by express agreement: P appoints A as his agent and A, in turn, agrees to act on behalf of P. The agreement is often contractual but it need not be and a non-contractual agency is perfectly legitimate. This could occur where the agreement lacks consideration, eg P and A are friends and there is no question of payment for A's services,[1] or where one or both of the parties lack contractual capacity. In such cases of express appointment, A is said to have an *actual, express authority*. It should be emphasised that there are two areas of enquiry here. First, there is the question of the *creation* of the express contract or agreement and whether any formalities are required, for example. Second, there is the problem of interpreting and ascertaining the *scope* of the express authority so created. In *Freeman & Lockyer v Buckhurst Park Properties (Mangal) Ltd*,[2] Diplock LJ[3] said:

> 'An "actual" authority is a legal relationship between principal and agent created by a consensual agreement to which they alone are parties. Its scope is to be ascertained by applying ordinary principles of construction of contracts, including any proper implications from the express words used, the usages of the trade, or the course of business between the parties.'

FORMALITIES AND CAPACITY

The general rule is that no formalities are required for the appointment of an agent and his express authority may thus be contained in a deed, in writing or constituted by verbal agreement. This is so even if A is authorised to enter into a contract which is required to be in writing, eg a contract for the sale of land. There are exceptions to the general principle, most obviously the rule that where A is authorised to execute a deed on behalf of P, his authority must be contained in a deed, this being referred to as a power of attorney.[4]

---

1 Eg *Chaudhry v Prabhakar* [1988] 3 All ER 718; see Brown, 'The Gratuitous Agent's Liability' [1989] LMCLQ 148.
2 [1964] 2 QB 480.
3 [1964] 2 QB 480 at 502.
4 See *Berkeley v Hardy* (1826) 5 B & C 355; *Powell v London & Provincial Bank* [1893] 2 Ch 555; Law of Property (Miscellaneous Provisions) Act 1989, s 1, Sch 1 (amending the Powers of Attorney Act 1971).

In relation to the capacity of P and A, the rules are relatively uncomplicated. The general rule regarding P's capacity is that he can appoint an agent to enter into a contract on his behalf (or perform any other act) where he could lawfully enter into the contract or perform the act himself. Thus with principals who are infants, the modern view is that 'whenever a minor can lawfully do an act on his own behalf, so as to bind himself, he can instead appoint an agent to do it for him'.[5] As regards the capacity of A, the general rule is that, as his function is to contract on behalf of P, he need not have capacity to contract on his *own* behalf. It follows that infants, for example, are quite competent to act as agents. If the agency between P and the infant A is contractual then the infant's liability is dependent upon his capacity to contract as is any personal contractual liability which A may incur in relation to T. If, on the other hand, the agency is not contractual, the infant A has the identical non-contractual rights and duties of an agent with full capacity.

CONSTRUCTION AND INTERPRETATION OF ACTUAL, EXPRESS AUTHORITY

The express agreement between P and A may be purely oral, in writing or in the form of a deed when it is known as a power of attorney. Powers of attorney are construed particularly strictly and the authority conferred by the deed must be found 'within the four corners of the instrument either in express terms or by necessary implication'.[6] The courts are thus loath to extend the authority given on the basis that P should be protected and it should be stressed that this is contrary to the general rule concerning the construction of deeds which is that they be interpreted *against* the grantor.[7] In keeping with the policy of protecting P, general words are construed by reference to the *purpose* for which the authority is given.[8] In *Midland Bank v Reckitt*,[9] a clause in a power of attorney gave A, a solicitor, a right to draw cheques on P's bank account and apply the money for the purposes of P. There was also a clause providing that P 'ratifies and confirms and agrees to ratify and confirm whatsoever the attorney shall do or purports to do'. A drew cheques on P's account and paid them into his (A's) own, overdrawn account. A's bank was liable in conversion as the general words could not extend the authority given by the power.[10] Similarly, although the operative part of the deed may apparently confer authority in wide terms, it may be curtailed by the recitals in cases of ambiguity.[11] In *Danby v Coutts & Co*,[12] for example, the operative part of the deed conferred authority on A without duration but it was preceded by a recital that P was going abroad. It was held that A's authority was limited to the period of P's absence. Moreover, if authority given to perform specific tasks is followed by general words, the general words are limited to

---

5 *G (A) v G (T)* [1970] 2 QB 643, 652, per Lord Denning MR.
6 *Bryant, Powis & Bryant Ltd v La Banque du Peuple* [1893] AC 170, 177 per Lord MacNaghten.
7 See Stoljar, *The Law of Agency* (1961), pp 90-95.
8 See the restrictive decision in *Attwood v Munnings* (1827) 7 B & C 278, considered at length in Stoljar, *The Law of Agency* (1961), pp 92-95.
9 [1933] AC 1.
10 The clause could not be construed as ratification as it occurred *before* the act: see Ch 3 on ratification.
11 If there is no ambiguity in the operative part of the deed it will be dominant over the recitals, see *Rooke v Lord Kensington* (1856) 2 K & J 753.
12 (1885) 29 Ch D 500.

that which is necessary for the performance of the specific tasks. In *Hogg v Snaith*,[13] a power of attorney was given 'to demand and receive all moneys due to [P] on any account whatsoever and to use all means for the recovery thereof, to appoint attorneys to bring actions, and to revoke such appointments, *and to do all other business*'. It was held that 'all other business' must be limited to other business necessary for the recovery of the moneys.

Two reasons may be advanced in justification of these rules of strict interpretation which developed principally in the 19th century. First, it is obvious that a power of attorney is often professionally drafted and designed to limit precisely the scope of A's authority and, as such, it demands a strict interpretation. Second, powers of attorney were often employed in non-commercial situations where P was abroad or ill for long periods of time, for example, and it was arguably appropriate to interpret the power in P's favour. It does seem, however, that an unacceptable risk was often placed on T and Stoljar suggests that the stringent approach to interpretation opened a possibility of fraud 'for by appointing a general agent under a power of attorney, yet one suitably restricted in terms, the principal could expect handsome windfalls; for a third party would seldom trouble to consult the power if and where the agent appeared anyhow to have a general power to buy ...'[14] If this approach had been followed rigorously, the law would have failed to protect T and so it is important to emphasise that apparent authority might well govern the position in such situations thus allowing T a remedy.[15] Today, should A require an unfettered authority, the statutory form prescribed by the Powers of Attorney Act 1971, s 10 should be used as, under this provision, A can acquire authority which is limited only by P's incapacity to act through an agent.

Where A's authority is given in writing or orally it is interpreted much more liberally having regard to the relevant commercial background.[16] Certainly if there is ambiguity or uncertainty in the instructions given to A and he acts *bona fide* in accordance with one reasonable interpretation of them, he should be regarded as acting within his authority. In *Ireland v Livingston*,[17] a commission agent in Mauritius was authorised by P to buy 500 tons of sugar with 50 tons more or less being of no importance, P suggesting shipment to a variety of ports. It was held that shipment of 400 tons direct to London was a reasonable execution of the instructions and P could not refuse to accept the cargo on a falling market. Likewise in *Weigall & Co v Runciman & Co*,[18] A, a broker, received a telegram from a shipowner, P, asking him to 'fix steamer' on certain terms, which A took to be an instruction to demise (hire-out) one of P's vessels to T on those terms. P refused to hire-out a ship to the plaintiff arguing that he intended A to arrange the hire of a vessel *from* T. It was held that the defendant agent's interpretation was reasonable and hence he was not liable to the plaintiff. It should be emphasised however, that with modern communications it may be simple for A to obtain clarification of his instructions and, indeed, he may be in breach of duty if he fails to do so.

---

13 (1808) 1 Taunt 347.
14 Stoljar, *The Law of Agency* (1961), p 95.
15 Stoljar (*The Law of Agency* (1961), p 90) emphasises that 'a rule of strict construction, if generally applied, would have rendered the doctrine of apparent authority so much surplusage'.
16 See *Pole v Leask* (1860) 28 Beav 562, 574 per Sir John Romilly MR; *Freeman & Lockyer v Buckhurst Park Properties (Mangal) Ltd* [1964] 2 QB 480, 502 per Diplock LJ.
17 (1872) LR 5 HL 395.
18 (1916) 85 LJKB 1187.

IMPLIED AGREEMENT

A contract *or* an agreement between P and A may be impliedly created by their conduct and from a consideration of all the surrounding circumstances. *Bowstead & Reynolds* emphasises that no special rules peculiar to agency are involved here but, instead, 'the obvious proposition that contracts are not always expressly made, but often inferred by the court from the circumstances'.[19] Nevertheless, the difficulty lies in ascertaining *when* the law will acknowledge that the parties have impliedly created an agency relationship, recent decisions emphasising that it is difficult to predict when agency reasoning may be employed.[20]

At the outset it should be emphasised that the issue here is whether P and A have impliedly formed an *agency relationship* rather than the question of the creation of A's *authority*, although there is a fine line between the two notions and it is quite feasible for A's authority (express, implied or apparent) to emanate contemporaneously from the same acts which create the implied agency.[1] For example, in *Ashford Shire Council v Dependable Motors Pty Ltd*,[2] the appellants (P) wished to acquire a tractor and the shire clerk asked A to inspect one which the respondents (T) had for sale. A had recently been appointed as the shire engineer but had not yet taken up his duties at the date of the tractor's examination. In reliance on A's report, P purchased the tractor which was discovered to be unfit for its purpose. T argued that A was not P's agent and thus A's reliance on T's skill and judgement could not be imputed to P. The Privy Council held that A was being asked to anticipate his duties as shire engineer and to perform gratuitously what would have been his duty had his appointment commenced. Accordingly, A was acting as P's agent *and* was within his authority in disclosing to T the purpose for which the tractor was required. P was thus entitled to damages.

The litigation in *Garnac Grain Co Inc v HMF Faure & Fairclough Ltd*[3] illustrates the inherent difficulties in this context. A circle of four separate contracts was created, on the same day, for the sale of 15,000 tons of lard, viz, Allied sold to Gersony, Gersony to Garnac, Garnac to Faure and Faure to Allied. Allied was thus the first seller and would have been the last buyer in the circle but for their financial collapse and insolvency which meant that no delivery was made under any of the contracts. The contract between Garnac and Faure was disputed. Faure claimed damages for non-delivery but Garnac sought a declaration that they had lawfully rescinded the contract with Faure on the grounds that (i) they were induced to enter into it by fraudulent misrepresentations made by both Allied and Faure to the effect that Faure were not reselling to Allied and, (ii) in making the contract Faure acted as agents for Allied who was an undisclosed principal and the fraud of the principal meant that the contract had been properly rescinded and could not be enforced by the agents, Faure. At first instance,[4] Megaw J held that Faure had not made any fraudulent misrepresentation

---

19 *Bowstead & Reynolds on Agency* (16th edn, 1996), Art 8, para 2-030.
20 See, eg, the differences of opinion regarding the ascertainment of an agency relationship in *Moorgate Mercantile Co Ltd v Twitchings* [1976] QB 225, CA; revsd [1977] AC 890, HL.
1 See eg the (unsuccessful) arguments in *Branwhite v Worcester Works Finance Ltd* [1969] 1 AC 552 (below) that the dealer had apparent authority from the finance company by virtue of his possessing their hire-purchase forms and sufficient knowledge to complete them.
2 [1961] AC 336.
3 [1968] AC 1130n.
4 [1966] 1 QB 650.

but that Garnac must succeed on the second ground. The judge emphasised that Faure was acting as an agent for Allied and that if Faure could enforce the contract they would receive damages for breach of a contract which would not have been made but for the undisclosed principal's fraud. Faure, as agents, would then have to account to their principal, Allied, for the damages received but this would be unacceptable because 'the fraudulent principal would indirectly be entitled to enjoy the fruits of his own fraud'.[5]

The decision was reversed by the Court of Appeal[6] on the ground that there was no agency, either express or implied, between Faure and Allied and the effect of Allied's fraud did not therefore arise; the contract between Faure and Allied was thus a normal contract of resale. Accordingly, Faure could enforce the contract against Garnac.

The decision of the Court of Appeal was unanimously affirmed by the House of Lords,[7] on the basis that there was no evidence whatsoever of any agency between Faure and Allied. Lord Pearson evaluated the factors which were relevant in deciding when an agency relationship existed and developed three important points in his speech. First, the relationship of P and A can be established only by the *consent* of *both* parties given expressly or by implication from their words and conduct but that the parties will be held to have consented 'if they have agreed to what amounts in law to such a relationship, even if they do not recognise it themselves and even if they have professed to disclaim it'.[8] It is thus clear that an objective evaluation of consent[9] must be made and that an express disclaimer of agency will not prevail[10] if, on a consideration of all the facts, the agreement is properly construed as one of agency. Similarly, an express adoption of agency *terminology* does not necessarily categorise the relationship as one of agency if dominant facts prove otherwise.[11] Second, it is the parties' statements and acts at *the time of the alleged creation of the agency* which are *primarily* important, earlier words and conduct being less meaningful as 'historical background' and later words and conduct being of minor significance. Third, in relation to the *content* of the relationship, it should be asked what it is 'that the supposed agent is alleged to have done on behalf of the supposed principal'.[12] Applying these tests, Lord Pearson considered that, on the facts, there was no evidence that Faure and Allied had consented to the consequences of an agency relationship.

---

5   [1966] 1 QB 650 at 656.
6   [1966] 1 QB 650.
7   [1968] AC 1130n; see Fridman, 'Establishing Agency' (1968) 84 LQR 224.
8   [1968] AC 1130n at 1137.
9   See *Little v Spreadbury* [1910] 2 KB 658 (A client (P), by her conduct, induced her solicitor (A) to believe that he was authorised to compromise an action. It was held that she was bound by the compromise whether she intended to give the requisite authority or not and irrespective of whether she understood its terms).
10 See *Re Megevand, ex p Delhasse* (1878) 7 Ch D 511.
11 See *John Towle and Co v White* (1873) 29 LT 78, 79 where Lord Selborne LC stressed that 'the facts must speak for themselves, and if those facts show a state of things different to a simple arrangement between principal and agent, then the effect of these facts will not be altered simply because the language of agency has been used in a loose manner'. See also *Customs and Excise Comrs v Music and Video Exchange Ltd* [1992] STC 220.
12 [1968] AC 1130n, 1137. See also *John Towle and Co v White* (1873) 29 LT 78, 80, (discussed in Ch 1) for the tests employed in deciding, on the facts, whether an agency existed.

The question of when an agency relationship might be implied is also crucial in other areas of commerce. In hire-purchase transactions, for example, there is no clear rule at common law[13] regarding the possible agency of the dealer who arranges the credit. The basic mechanics of a paradigm hire-purchase transaction are that the customer/debtor approaches a dealer who has goods for sale and there will be a discussion regarding the possibility of credit. After bargaining between the parties regarding price (the customer may have existing goods to trade-in, for example), the dealer will produce forms which are supplied by the finance company/creditor. The customer and dealer will complete and sign the documentation thereby constituting an offer by the dealer to sell the goods to the finance company and an application for credit by the customer. If the finance company accepts the proposal, it purchases the goods from the dealer and, as the new owner of the goods, the company then grants credit to the customer who pays the requisite instalments of the price to the finance company. In this situation, should the dealer be regarded as (i) an independent contractor (ii) an agent acting on behalf of the customer/debtor or (iii) the agent of the finance company? Much may turn on the answers which are given to these questions, as illustrated by the decision in *Branwhite v Worcester Works Finance Ltd.*[14] The facts were largely as in the paradigm transaction described above. It was agreed that the price of the car which the customer wanted to buy would be £430 and £130 would be allowed for his existing car, the balance being payable by monthly instalments of £5. The customer signed the documentation in blank and the dealer said he would complete it and send it to the finance company. The customer then drove away in the new car and the dealer sold the customer's existing car to a buyer. In the documentation sent to the finance company, the dealer inserted the deposit correctly as £130 but he entered £649 as the cash price. The finance company accepted the proposal purchasing the car from the dealer for £649, paying £519 to the dealer and allowing him to keep the £130. When the customer saw the discrepancy in the figures in his copy of the agreement, he relied on the dealer to get them corrected and, in the meantime, he paid no instalments. The dealer did nothing and shortly afterwards he disappeared. Eventually the finance company repossessed the car and the customer then sued for the return of the £130 'deposit'. The House of Lords held that the finance company had received from the customer £130, albeit only in account and not in notes or by cheque, for a consideration which had wholly failed. Accordingly they were bound to repay £130 to him. Second, the House decided that the dealer did *not* receive the deposit as agent of the finance company and the finance company would thus not have to account for it to the customer. While acknowledging that the dealer can be the agent of the finance company in specific situations, the Law Lords emphasised that there is no general agency relationship between the parties and the dealer acts first and foremost on his own behalf. Lords Reid and Wilberforce dissented and considered that 'the established mercantile background of hire-purchase transactions'[15] whereby the dealer has a standing relationship with the finance company, led to the conclusion that the dealer was the finance company's agent. It seems undeniable that this is

---

13 The Consumer Credit Act 1974, ss 56, 57, 69 and 102 make the dealer the agent of the finance company in specific situations. Section 56 now applies to *Branwhite*'s facts, below.
14 [1969] 1 AC 552.
15 [1969] 1 AC 552 at 586, per Lord Wilberforce.

the average customer's perception of the transaction.[16] Referring to Lord Pearson's speech in *Garnac*[17] on the issue of consent, Lord Wilberforce said:[18]

> '... while agency must ultimately derive from consent, the consent need not necessarily be to the relationship of principal and agent itself (indeed the existence of it may be denied) but may be to a state of fact upon which the law imposes the consequences which result from agency. It is consensual not contractual. So interpreted, this formulation allows the establishment of an agency relationship in such cases as the present.'

In insurance contracts there is similarly doubt as to whether intermediaries are agents for the insured or the insurer. This is vitally important as regards knowledge which will be imputed to the insurance company if an agent acts on the company's behalf in completing a proposal form, for example. If, on the other hand, the agent is deemed to act on behalf of the insured, information received by the agent is not imputed to the insurance company and the insured might find the policy declared void for non-disclosure. The general rule is that only an agent under the direct control or employment of the insurer is an agent of the latter.[19] There is considerable doubt regarding the position of insurance brokers but some recent decisions have held certain brokers to be agents of the insurer[20] which clearly accords with reality in many situations, eg where the broker promises the insured that the policy is valid, as in *Stockton v Mason*.[1]

Actual, implied authority

It is rare that an express authority, even one which is detailed and explicit, will be sufficient to cope with all eventualities which A may face and thus it may be necessary to amplify that authority in order that A's mandate may be executed properly. The difficulty here is to determine the legitimate extent of such an amplification to which P would be deemed to consent and which would consequently be binding upon him. A's actual, implied authority extends to those acts which are 'necessary for, or ordinarily incidental to, the effective execution of his express authority in the usual way'.[2]

---

16 In *Branwhite*, Lord Morris of Borth-Y-Gest said that the customer trusted the dealer and thought him to be 'one of the governors' of the finance company (p 563).
17 [1968] AC 1130n.
18 [1969] 1 AC 552, 587.
19 See the cases stemming from *Newsholme Bros v Road Transport & General Insurance Co Ltd* [1929] 2 KB 356. There the answers in the proposal form, which were incorrect, were warranted to be true; an agent authorised by the insurers to *canvass for proposals* completed the proposal form and knew the true facts. He was held to be agent of the *proposer* with the result that the insurer could repudiate liability.
20 See *Stockton v Mason* [1978] 2 Lloyd's Rep 430; *Woolcott v Excess Insurance Co Ltd* [1979] 1 Lloyd's Rep 231.
 1 [1978] 2 Lloyd's Rep 430: see Lord Diplock's comments at pp 431-432.
 2 *Bowstead & Reynolds on Agency* (16th edn, 1996), Art 27, para 3-018. See also the definition of Eyre LCJ in *Howard v Baillie* (1796) 2 Hy Bl 618, 619: '... an authority of this nature necessarily includes medium powers, which are not expressed. By medium powers, I mean all the means necessary to be used, in order to attain the accomplishment of the object of the principal power ...'

Examples of actual, implied authority abound[3] but the facts of *Nelson v Raphael*[4] provide a strikingly graphic illustration of this notion. P, a motor trader, took T for a test drive in a Daf Variomatic car and, as P was going abroad on holiday, it was agreed that if T wished to buy the car, A would complete the sale and transfer the car to T. A, who was described as one of P's 'chaps', had such difficulty demonstrating the Daf's controls to T that T concluded that he would master the car's intricacies himself. Moreover, as he was clearly sceptical of A's driving ability, T considered it prudent to get out of the car and leave A in control of the vehicle. T's judgement was sound as, quite suddenly, the car careered out of P's driveway and collided with another car before hitting a tree. The Daf was an insurance write-off but P had the temerity to sue T for the price. The Court of Appeal held that T was not liable as A had implied authority to demonstrate the controls and P was thus responsible for A's negligence.

Perhaps the most important modern decision concerning actual, implied authority is *Hely-Hutchinson v Brayhead Ltd.*[5] Richards, the chairman of the defendant company (B Ltd), acted as *de facto* managing director with the consent of the board. The plaintiff was the managing director of Perdio Ltd which was in need of financial assistance. B Ltd was prepared to help and bought some of Perdio's shares with the eventual object of acquiring control of the company. The plaintiff agreed to put more money into Perdio if B Ltd would secure his position. Accordingly, Richards, on behalf of B Ltd and as chairman, signed two letters on B Ltd's note paper purporting to indemnify the plaintiff against loss which might result from his lending money to Perdio. As a result, the plaintiff advanced £45,000 to Perdio. Eventually the plaintiff sued B Ltd on the letter of indemnity but B Ltd denied liability arguing that Richards had no authority to sign the letters. At first instance, Roskill J considered that there was no 'implied authority in a chairman of a company, merely by reason of his office, to do what Mr Richards did'[6] but he held that Richards had apparent authority to bind B Ltd. The three judges in the Court of Appeal held that Richards had actual, implied authority 'from the conduct of the parties and the circumstances of the case'[7] but they did not disagree with Roskill J's finding of apparent authority. Lord Pearson[8] stressed that apparent and actual authority were 'not mutually exclusive' and, indeed, that the two types of authority often co-existed and coincided. It followed that the decision at first instance on apparent authority did not preclude the Court of Appeal's finding of actual, implied authority. Although the *scope* of these two types of authority may coincide,[9] there is, of

---

3   See, eg, *Mullens v Miller* (1882) 22 Ch D 194 (A authorised to find a purchaser for a house had implied authority to describe the property and state its value); *Sorrell v Finch* [1977] AC 728 (estate agent authorised to find a purchaser for a house did *not* have implied authority to receive a deposit from T on behalf of the vendor, P. P was thus not liable to return the deposit to T when A absconded); *Curtis v Barclay* (1826) 5 B & C 141 (A was authorised to receive and sell goods and pay himself a debt out of the proceeds. Held he had implied authority to commence proceedings against T who was wrongfully withholding the goods).

4   [1979] RTR 437.

5   [1968] 1 QB 549.

6   [1968] 1 QB 549 at 560.

7   [1968] 1 QB 549 at 584, per Lord Denning MR.

8   [1968] 1 QB 549 at 593.

9   In *Nelson v Raphael* [1979] RTR 437, Bridge LJ held (p 445) that A was 'acting fairly and squarely within the scope of his authority, whether one calls it implied or ostensible'.

course, no correlation between their *methods of creation*, as apparent authority is dependent on P's representation, made to T, that A has authority.

ACTUAL, IMPLIED AUTHORITY EMANATES FROM ACTUAL, EXPRESS AUTHORITY

It is crucial to stress that, as implied authority develops from A's actual, express authority and is a species of actual authority itself, it cannot extend to an act which is *prohibited* by the terms of the express authority. If, for example, A manages a retail shop he will have actual, implied authority to buy goods for resale but if P has instructed A expressly not to buy goods, he cannot possibly have actual, implied authority to do so. It is a non sequitur for A to assert that, although an act has been expressly prohibited by P, there is implied authority to perform it. This is patently the position where there is a clear and express prohibition but it must be stressed that there may well be a difference between *limiting* A's authority and *prohibiting* the performance of certain acts. Consider the case where P authorises A, a stockbroker, to sell his shares 'at the current market price'. Should A consider it in P's best interests to sell quickly at marginally less than the market price, he may well have a discretion to do so as part of his implied authority.[10]

In the example above of the retail shop and the express prohibition imposed by P on the purchase of goods, it is quite possible for A to have *apparent* authority to buy goods for the shop as apparent authority is not a type of actual authority and so it is not constrained by that notion.[11] As the manager of a retail shop, A may appear to T to have authority to buy goods and, assuming that T does not know of P's express prohibition and has no reason to think that it exists, he may be able to establish an apparent authority in A.

Finally, as actual implied authority is necessarily connected to actual, express authority, such an implied authority cannot exist in isolation. The force of this rule was illustrated recently in *The Choko Star*.[12] The established rule is that a master of a ship is an agent of the shipowner. The issue in *The Choko Star* was whether the master might have authority to enter into a contract of salvage on behalf of the *cargo-owners* when the ship took the ground and became stranded, there being no pre-existing, express agency between master and cargo-owner. Sheen J held that an implied authority could be established[13] as the cargo-owners must recognise that circumstances could arise during the voyage where the cargo had to be salved. The Court of Appeal reversed the decision and underlined the fact that actual, implied authority can only be an addition to express authority and cannot stand alone. Sheen J clearly considered that it was *reasonable* to endow the master with the requisite authority to act on behalf of the cargo-owner and, of course, this is a tempting conclusion to reach.[14] However, although Sheen

---

10 See, eg, the facts of *Keighley, Maxsted & Co v Durant* [1901] AC 240 (considered in Ch 3).
11 See *The Unique Mariner* [1978] 1 Lloyd's Rep 438 (considered in Ch 4)
12 *Industrie Chimiche Italia Centrale and Cerealfin SA v Alexander G Tsavliris & Sons Maritime Co, The Choko Star* [1990] 1 Lloyd's Rep 516.
13 [1989] 2 Lloyd's Rep 42.
14 The Merchant Shipping Act 1995, s 224(1), now gives the master authority to sign a salvage agreement.

J's conclusion beckons seductively, it cannot be sustained. Here the criterion of reasonableness is insufficient *per se*: unfettered implication must not be used as an invisible means to a certain end.[15]

---

15   See Brown, 'Authority and Necessity in the Law of Agency' (1992) 55 MLR 414; Munday, 'Salvaging the Law of Agency' [1991] 1 LMCLQ 1; Reynolds, 'Agency of Necessity' [1990] JBL 505.

CHAPTER 3

The doctrine of ratification

Introduction

In those situations where A lacks authority from P, ratification allows P to adopt and endorse A's acts and, in the majority of cases, it is a convenient commercial concept[1] for P, A and T. For example, an enterprising agent may wish to seize an opportunity which is presented and, without prior consultation with P, he may enter into a contract with T on behalf of P. Assuming that T wishes to contract with P, a subsequent ratification by P simply gives effect to the parties' intentions. Ratification thus acts as a curative[2] for A's initial lack of authority and it creates rights between P and T. As between P and A, ratification may similarly be crucial in that it will normally validate A's acts meaning that P may be liable to pay A remuneration or indemnify him against losses incurred in the transaction. Similarly, A is not normally liable to P for exceeding his authority as P usually ratifies voluntarily and thereby waives A's transgression.[3] If P chooses *not* to ratify, T has an action against A for breach of warranty of authority[4] which may thus act as T's safety net.

A striking feature of ratification is that it is retroactive in effect thereby becoming operative from the moment of *A's contracting with* T rather than the moment of P's ratification. It is obvious that the crucial period is that between A's transaction with T and P's subsequent ratification for it is during this interval that a change of circumstances might mean that P's back-dated ratification should be impermissible. It is important to clarify the issues as to when retroactive operation should be enforced or denied. In the majority of situations, T will have considered himself bound at the moment of entering into the contract with A and there will be no material change of circumstances causing hardship to T before ratification: here retroactivity correctly gives effect to the parties' intentions, as emphasised earlier. On the other hand, where

---

1 Lord Macnaghten described it as 'a wholesome and convenient fiction' in *Keighley, Maxsted & Co v Durant* [1901] AC 240, 247.
2 See *Koenigsblatt v Sweet* [1923] 2 Ch 314, 325, where ratification was categorised by Lord Sterndale MR as 'equivalent to antecedent authority'.
3 If P ratifies only to preserve his business reputation, for example, A might not be exonerated for breach of contract or duty: see *Suncorp Insurance and Finance v Milano Assicurazioni SpA* [1993] 2 Lloyd's Rep 225, 234-235 per Waller J.
4 See Ch 11.

the retrospective rule would cause detriment to T, it should not apply and several exceptions and modifications to the rule thus exist which, as will be seen later, are difficult to formulate. Different views exist regarding this 'detriment' and whether it should be defined in terms of a real or hypothetical disadvantage to T. For example, should T have the ability to withdraw from the contractual arena before P ratifies A's act? If retroactivity is the dominant, general rule, such a withdrawal should be impermissible unless there is other evidence of *actual* hardship to T. It is patently obvious, for example, that T's desire to renege on a bad bargain of his own making does not mean that retroactive ratification should be disallowed and, similarly, normal commercial risks which T must accept must be distinguished from situations where T is unfairly prejudiced by the retrospective ratification. This question is returned to later when retroactivity is examined in detail.

Finally, P's ratification may be express or implied (eg by P's conduct in accepting and then re-selling goods supplied by T). At first glance, it is tempting to surmise that the paradigm of ratification involves an avaricious P who snatches at beneficial opportunities proffered and expressly adopts A's unauthorised act but the position is often inverted – ratification can thus be equally beneficial for T when liability is imposed upon P in situations of presumed or implied ratification. Indeed it is arguable that this latter situation is the most frequent way in which ratification is enforced.[5]

Requirements of a valid ratification

At first sight, ratification appears to allow great scope for P's affirmation of unauthorised acts but the doctrine has been curtailed by the common law and is thus limited in scope. Some of the 19th century decisions clearly considered that the rules of ratification were too flexible and should be fettered but it is arguable that this was achieved at the cost of diminishing both commercial adaptability and practicality.[6]

THE PRINCIPAL MUST BE IN EXISTENCE AT THE TIME OF THE AGENT'S ACT

This requirement means that P must be a live human being or a juristic person at the date of A's act: A cannot act for a non-existent principal even if he knows that P will subsequently come into existence and then wish to ratify his act. The rule has caused difficulties where company promoters enter into contracts on behalf of companies which are in the course of formation as such companies do not exist as legal persons until incorporation. It follows

---

5 See Mechem, *Outlines of the Law of Agency* (4th edn, 1952, ed P Mechem), §§ 197-198: '... the various 'requirements' of ratification as given in the books, sound largely in terms of a principal who wishes in cold blood to become bound on a contract made in his name but by a purported agent who lacked authority to bind the purported principal ... this is quite unrealistic and, so, misleading ... rarely indeed is the principal trying to ratify; he is trying to escape from ratification'.
6 See *Keighley, Maxsted & Co v Durant* [1901] AC 240; *Watson v Swann* (1862) 11 CBNS 756, both considered later.

that the company cannot ratify the contract after the date of its formation and has neither rights nor liabilities on the contract.[7]

At common law, the legal position of the promoter (A) and the other party (T) was most unsatisfactory in that much turned on the terminology employed in the contract. In *Kelner v Baxter*,[8] the promoters contracted on behalf of a projected hotel company for the purchase of wine from T and, at the time of contract, both parties knew that the company had not been formed. The company was formed and the wine was delivered and consumed but, before payment was made, the company went into liquidation. Although the company could not be liable on the contract, it was held that the promoters incurred a personal liability thereby providing T with a much-needed remedy. In contrast, in *Newborne v Sensolid (Great Britain) Ltd*,[9] A did not purport to contract *on behalf* of the projected company but rather the contract was purportedly made by the *company itself* with A's signature being simply an authentication, ie 'Leopold Newborne (London) Ltd, Leopold Newborne'. It followed that, as the company was non-existent so was its purported contract, and neither the company (Leopold Newborne Ltd) nor Leopold Newborne personally could enforce the contract for the sale of tinned ham to T.

It was emphasised recently by Oliver LJ in *Phonogram Ltd v Lane*,[10] that the narrow, technical distinctions drawn in *Kelner* and *Newborne* with much turning on the form of A's signature, does not represent the true state of the common law. Instead, the law's task is to ascertain and evaluate the true intent of the parties. In other words, the question at common law is whether the contract is intended to be between the non-existent P and T, in which case the contract is a nullity, or between T and A personally, in which case rights and liabilities accrue under the contract. The recent decision in *Coral (UK) Ltd v Rechtman and Altro Mozart Food Handels GmbH*,[11] adheres to the view that the real intent of the parties must be established and that there is a material difference between a non-existent company and an existing company which has simply been misnamed. In the *Coral* case, a group of companies had been re-organised and A innocently refered to a subsidiary company (P) within the group by its previous trading name. A purported to contract on behalf of the subsidiary, P, in the contract for the sale of sugar to T, T never having been aware of the precise structure of the companies or the nomenclature used within the group. Potter J held that, following Oliver LJ's approach in *Phonogram*, the identity of the company within the group was not a matter of vital importance to T beyond the fact that T intened to contract with the appropriate corporate supplier within the group and, given that P admitted liability, it was inapt that A should be personally liable on the contract. Accordingly, P was liable on the contract.

The position at common law has been amended by legislation[12] and the current law is contained in the Companies Act 1985, s 36C(1)[13] which provides for the

---

7   *Kelner v Baxter* (1866) LR 2 CP 174; *Natal Land and Colonization Co Ltd v Pauline Colliery and Development Syndicate Ltd* [1904] AC 120. The company may enter into a new contract on the same terms as the pre-incorporation contract, in which case there is a novation.

8   (1866) LR 2 CP 174.

9   [1954] 1 QB 45.

10   [1982] QB 938, 945.

11   [1996] 1 Lloyd's Rep 235.

12   European Communities Act 1972, s 9(2); Companies Act 1985, s 36(4).

13   Inserted by the Companies Act 1989, s 130(4).

personal liability of A where the contract 'purports to be made by or on behalf of a company at a time when the company has not been formed'. There are three striking features of s 36C(1). First, the company still lacks the ability to ratify the contract and, even though the Jenkins Committee[14] recommended in 1962 that ratification should be possible, the suggestion has never been adopted. Second, the section does not (expressly) give A any *rights* under the contract but, almost certainly, the usual notion of contractual mutuality should apply. Third, liability under s 36C(1) is 'subject to any agreement to the contrary'. The fact that the operation of s 36C(1) can be abrogated by agreement seemingly allowed scope for A to evade liability by a qualified signature which purported to be that of the company itself, as in the *Newborne* case, above. However, it was made clear in *Phonogram Ltd v Lane*[15] that a contract which, under s 36C(1),[16] purports 'to be made by or on behalf of' a company will raise the presumption that A should be liable irrespective of whether he purportedly signed as an agent of the company or whether the contract was purportedly made with the company itself, with A's signature intended merely as authentication. Moreover, it was suggested in *Phonogram* that only a clear exclusion of personal liability would be sufficient to exonerate A from liability under s 36C(1).

More recent decisions have emphasised that s 36C(1) applies only to a contract purportedly made on behalf of a specific company at a time when that company *has not been formed*. It follows that s 36C(1) does not apply and A is not personally liable where the company exists but is in the process of changing its name, the contract in question being made in the new name before the certificate of incorporation in that new name has been issued,[17] nor is the section applicable where the company has existed but has been dissolved.[18] In these situations where s 36C(1) does not apply, the common law (as discussed above) is still of paramount importance.

THE PRINCIPAL MUST BE CAPABLE OF ASCERTAINMENT AT THE TIME OF THE AGENT'S ACT

The established rule is that not only must P be in existence, he must be identified in some way at the date of A's act, this notion thus limiting further the flexibility of ratification. Exactly what the process of 'ascertainment' or 'identification' entails is unclear but the purpose of the rule must be to enable T to appreciate with whom he is contracting via A. In *Watson v Swann*,[19] Willes J said that it was unnecessary for P to be named but that there should be such a description of him 'as shall amount to a reasonable designation of the person intended to be bound by the contract'.[20] In *Watson*, A was instructed to effect insurance cover on P's goods but being unable to do so, he declared the goods on the

14 (1962) Cmnd 1749, para 44.
15 [1982] QB 938.
16 In *Phonogram*, the Companies Act 1985, s 36(4) was applied but, in all material respects, that section was identical to the current s 36C(1).
17 *Oshkosh B'Gosh Inc v Dan Marbel Inc Ltd* [1989] BCLC 507; *Badgerhill Properties Ltd v Cottrell* [1991] BCLC 805 (company was in existence but had been described by an incorrect name).
18 *Cotronic (UK) Ltd v Dezonie* [1991] BCLC 721. For the most recent decision on s 36C(1), see *Braymist Ltd v Wise Finance Co Ltd* (2001) Times, 27 March.
19 (1862) 11 CBNS 756.
20 (1862) 11 CBNS 756 at 771.

back of his own policy which the underwriters then initialled. When P sued on the policy it was held that he must fail as the contract of insurance had not been made on his behalf and, indeed, at the date A took out the policy for himself, he did not know P.

Bowstead & Reynolds[1] asserts cogently that the rules of ratification follow those of *initial* authority and, as A need not name his principal where he has prior authority (eg 'bought for my P'), it is difficult to see why any further designation should be required for ratification – particularly when T is prepared to contract on the basis that P is not identified precisely. This was also the view expressed in *National Oilwell (UK) Ltd v Davy Offshore Ltd*[2] in the context of an insurance policy expressed to insure a named assured together with a class of others who were unnamed. Colman J considered that a member of the class who qualified as such at the date the policy was effected could ratify and sue on the policy provided that the named assured intended to create privity of contract with the insurers on behalf of the particular party. Moreover, in assessing this intention, the judge thought that the terms of the policy might be considered together with any contract between the principal assured and the co-assured and any other admissible evidence 'showing what was subjectively intended by the principal assured'.[3]

It is difficult to gauge the effect of this decision. The two extremities of the rule are clear in that an *undisclosed* principal cannot ratify (see below) and it is equally plain that P need not be *named*, but the important area between these extremities remains uncharted. The policy underlying this area of agency is that ratification must be confined within a boundary, but that boundary's perimeter is indistinct. The rule remains that ratification is impermissible where A does not have a principal in mind at the date of the transaction with T and only decides later to select one and allocate the contract to him – but where there is evidence that A had a principal in mind and intended, from the outset, that P should adopt the contract, he will be able to do so. It will thus be difficult, in practice, to distinguish between these two situations and it remains to be seen how this aspect of ratification will develop.

THE AGENT MUST PROFESS TO ACT AS AN AGENT FOR THE PRINCIPAL: AN UNDISCLOSED PRINCIPAL CANNOT RATIFY

Here A must *disclose to T* his intention *to act as an agent for P*, this stipulation thus being intertwined with the above requirement. The decision in *Wilson v Tumman*[4] illustrates this rule. There a sheriff wrongfully seized goods which were not the property of the judgment debtor. It was held that the execution creditor (P) could not be liable for the trespass as he could not ratify the sheriff's act which was performed under a public duty, not under the authority of P.

It is thus clear that, although an undisclosed P can sue and be sued where A acts within his *actual* authority, an undisclosed P cannot ratify A's unauthorised act. The leading authority for the rule is the decision of the House of Lords in

1 *Bowstead & Reynolds on Agency* (16th edn, 1996) Art 15, para 2-063.
2 [1993] 2 Lloyd's Rep 582, 593-597.
3 [1993] 2 Lloyd's Rep 582 at 597.
4 (1843) 6 Man & G 236.

Keighley, Maxsted & Co v Durant.[5] There A was authorised to buy wheat, on a joint account for himself and P, at a certain price. He entered into a contract to buy wheat in his own name, from T, marginally in excess of the price stipulated, intending and expecting that P would ratify but, nevertheless, P remained undisclosed to T. P subsequently purported to ratify but then refused to take the wheat. T resold the wheat at a loss and then sued P but it was held that he was not liable as A had not professed to make the contract on P's behalf.

The decision emphasised that it was unacceptable to have 'an intention locked up in the mind of the contractor, which he may either abandon or act on at his own pleasure, and the ascertainment of which involves an inquiry into the state of his mind at the date of the contract'.[6] It is often said that if the rule were otherwise, A could enter into contracts in the hope that a total stranger, entirely unconnected with the contract, might intervene and adopt it, this being unsatisfactory as lacking sufficient certainty and, indeed, not constituting ratification at all.[7] However, in *Keighley* A merely exceeded an existing authority given by an existing principal (their relationship bordered on a partnership), and thus the facts do not bear comparison with the situation where an ethereal and disembodied P, unconnected to A, might decide to intervene on the contract. Moreover, in *Keighley* it was T who wished to enforce the ratification against P. *Keighley* was really an attempt to curtail the doctrine of the undisclosed principal[8] by denying such a principal's right to ratify but, as emphasised above, if A does *not* exceed his authority and the other conditions for the undisclosed principal apply, P may intervene and take the benefit of the contract. Accordingly, on its facts, the case could easily have been regarded as one where A possessed actual, implied authority to exceed the price stipulated by P.[9]

The approach of the House of Lords in *Keighley* was, and remains, out of step with commercial reality and it is suggested that the reasoning of the majority (AL Smith LJ dissenting) in the Court of Appeal[10] was preferable. Collins and Romer LJJ considered that A's professing to act for P was superfluous as between P and A because A did not object to P's ratification and equally unnecessary as between P and T unless T could show that P's intervention made a material difference to the contract which T had envisaged. It was T who wished to enforce the contract in *Keighley* and so, far from being prejudicial, P's intervention and ratification would have been beneficial to T. As will be seen when the doctrine of the undisclosed principal is considered in detail,[11] there are few situations

---

5   [1901] AC 240. See also *Spiro v Lintern* [1973] 1 WLR 1002 which illustrates that, although T cannot establish ratification against P where P is undisclosed, T may nevertheless utilise the doctrine of *estoppel* thereby rendering P liable. Equally, where P is disclosed but the ratification is too weak to be established by T, P may be bound by virtue of estoppel, see *Worboys v Carter* [1987] 2 EGLR 1 (both decisions are discussed in Ch 4).

6   [1901] AC 240, 256 per Lord Davey.

7   In the Court of Appeal in *Durant & Co v Roberts and Keighley, Maxsted & Co* [1900] 1 QB 629, 645, Collins LJ emphasised that 'that would be, not ratification, but adoption, which our law does not admit'.

8   The undisclosed principal is considered in Ch 10; see in particular Rochvarg, 'Ratification and Undisclosed Principals' (1989) 34 McGill LJ 286.

9   Stoljar emphasised (*The Law of Agency* (1961), p 200) that the amount by which A exceeded the stipulated price was so minimal (authority to buy two kinds of wheat at 44s 3d and 45s 3d per quarter but actually bought at 44s 6d and 45s 6d per quarter) that the case could have been disposed of as one of actual, implied authority. P might then have been liable as an undisclosed principal.

10 *Durant & Co v Roberts and Keighley, Maxsted & Co* [1900] 1 QB 629.

11 See Ch 10.

where P's intervention results in material hardship to T. Indeed, if the general rule permitted ratification by an undisclosed principal then, provided T is protected by this latter requirement that no hardship must result, the ratification could only be advantageous to him in that he could sue either A (as a party to the contract) or P.

Finally, it must be stressed that, under this requirement that A must profess to act for P, it is the position from T's perspective which is crucial. In *Re Tiedemann and Ledermann Frères*,[12] A sold wheat to T on behalf of P but A had a secret and fraudulent intent to act for himself and purloin the proceeds of sale. T repudiated the contract as he suspected that A was making the contracts on his own behalf and he did not wish to deal with A for 'financial reasons'. It was held that P could nevertheless ratify the contract because, on the face of the transaction, A had purported to act for P.

P MUST HAVE THE CAPACITY TO ACT AS A PRINCIPAL (I) AT THE DATE OF THE AGENT'S ACT AND, (II) AT THE DATE OF RATIFICATION

Capacity at the date of A's act

If P was not competent to perform A's act at the time when A performed it, P cannot subsequently claim to ratify it. This means that infants and insane persons, for example, may not be able to ratify acts performed by agents just as they would have limited capacity to appoint agents in advance. *Boston Deep Sea Fishing & Ice Co v Farnham*[13] is a good example of such incapacity. A trawler owned by a French company was left in an English port during the Second World War, the company becoming an alien enemy as a result of the German occupation of France. The Boston company acted as manager/agent of the trawler without the French company's authority and the latter eventually purported to ratify the Boston company's acts. It was held that the ratification was impossible (and so A was not liable to tax on the profits made) as at the time of A's acting, P lacked the capacity to act as principal.

Incapacity also caused an enduring problem with limited companies in that acts which were *ultra vires* a company's memorandum of association were regarded as nullities and hence incapable of ratification even with the unanimous consent of the shareholders.[14] Although both the company and the third party could rely on the contract's being *ultra vires* in order to escape liability, it is arguable that most hardship was caused to the *bona fide* T who could thus be left without a remedy. Accordingly, the new rules implemented by the Companies Act 1989 are designed to abrogate the external operation of the *ultra vires* rule and thus validate transactions entered into by a company even though, technically, they are *ultra vires*.[15] The Companies Act 1985, s 35(1)[16] provides that the validity of an act done by a company 'shall not be called into question on the ground of lack of capacity by reason of anything in the company's memorandum'. It appears

---

12 [1899] 2 QB 66.
13 [1957] 1 WLR 1051.
14 See *Ashbury Railway Carriage and Iron Co Ltd v Riche* (1875) LR 7 HL 653.
15 As between the company and its directors, *ultra vires* acts are still impermissible and may lead to the latter being liable: see Companies Act 1985, s 35(3).
16 Inserted by the Companies Act 1989, s 108(1).

that this provision will not allow the company to rely on its own incapacity and neither may it be pleaded by T to evade liability.[17] Moreover, the Companies Act 1985, s 35(3) allows the company to ratify (by special resolution) any act or transaction which is *ultra vires* the company.[18] Because a company can only act through agents, it was not enough for the new provisions to remove objections relating to the *company's* capacity and thus the Companies Act 1985, s 35(A)1 removes any limitations upon the powers of directors and others to act on behalf of the company insofar as *bona fide* third parties are concerned.[19]

Capacity at the date of ratification

This aspect of capacity is, in some respects, unclear. Certainly if P is within the established categories of incapacity, ratification may be inoperative, eg P is insane or an alien enemy at the time of ratification. Here incapacity relates to the personal attributes of P and thus there may be a prohibition which renders ratification unlawful and contrary to public policy. Weight would be added to this conclusion if, for example, A's earlier unauthorised contract was partly executory and ratification imposed upon A a duty to perform an illegal act.

In cases which do not concern incapacity proper, it is unclear how far the notion of P's *inability* to ratify may extend and, of course, this question is inextricably bound-up with the retroactive operation of ratification (see below). It is usually said that the notion of P's inability to ratify explains the rule in insurance (marine insurance excepted) that P cannot ratify A's earlier unauthorised contract of insurance after a loss has occurred, this being justified on the basis that P could not himself lawfully insure after a loss.[20]

The early decision regarding the question of P's ability to ratify is *Bird v Brown*.[1] A, acting without authority on behalf of a seller of goods (P), gave notice of a stoppage in transit of goods on P's behalf. On arrival at their destination, the goods were demanded by the buyer's assignee in bankruptcy and should have been delivered into his possession but the master of the ship wrongfully refused to deliver the goods to the assignee. Instead, the goods were delivered to A, who also refused to deliver them to the assignee. A's original stoppage was subsequently ratified by P. It was held that ratification came too late to divest the assignees of their vested right to possession which had accrued when the transit ended at the port of destination and the freight had been tendered. Rolfe B held that the 'real question [was] whether the ratification ... after a conversion by [A], can have the effect of altering retrospectively the ownership of the goods, so as to prevent the plaintiffs [the assignees] from saying that the goods were theirs at the time of the conversion, which, if no subsequent ratification had occurred, certainly were theirs at that time, and would have so continued. We

---

17 Section 35(1) does *not* provide that companies shall have full and unlimited capacity so as to overrule *Ashbury Railway Carriage and Iron Co Ltd v Riche* (1875) LR 7 HL 653, but simply *prevents* either party from questioning a contract (or other 'act') on the ground of its being *ultra vires*.
18 Under s 35(3), such ratification does *not* affect the directors' liability for the *ultra vires* act unless there is a separate resolution to that effect.
19 Section 35(A)1 provides: 'In favour of a person dealing with a company in good faith, the power of the board of directors to bind the company, or authorise others to do so, shall be deemed to be free of any limitation under the company's constitution'.
20 *Grover & Grover Ltd v Mathews* [1910] 2 KB 401 (see below).
1 (1850) 4 Exch 786.

are of opinion that the ratification … had no such effect'.[2] This conclusion is not contentious but there is innate difficulty in understanding the meaning of Rolfe B's *obiter dictum* in *Bird* that the ratifying act 'must take place at a time, and under such circumstances, when [P] might himself have lawfully done the act which he ratifies'.[3]

In *Presentaciones Musicales SA v Secunda*,[4] the Court of Appeal stated recently that *Bird v Brown* was based primarily upon a refusal to divest the vested proprietary rights in the assignee in bankruptcy and that, accordingly, the decision is not founded upon the much wider notion of P's inability to ratify. Rolfe B's *dictum* was consequently censured as 'not a correct statement of the exceptions to the principles of ratification'.[5] This seems, with respect, to be correct; as discussed later, if retroactive operation is taken seriously, P can rarely be said to lack the *ability* to ratify.

It is also arguable that P may have lost the ability to perform the act in question at the time of ratification if ratification occurs outside an express time limit. In *Dibbins v Dibbins*,[6] it was held that an option to purchase shares, exercisable in three months and exercised by A in that time, without authority, could not be ratified by P after the expiry of the three months.

Bird and *Dibbins* are undoubtedly decisions which attempt to curtail the retroactive operation of ratification and they will be returned to later in this chapter. Having regard to the rule that ratification is backdated so as to take effect from the moment of A's act (and the application of this rule on the facts of *Secunda*) a generalised rule premised upon P's ability to ratify must now be very doubtful.

THE PRINCIPAL MUST HAVE FULL KNOWLEDGE OF ALL THE MATERIAL FACTS

P's ratification may have no effect if he can establish that he was ignorant of the *material* facts relating to it or that he acted under a mistake or because of A's misrepresentation. It is thus important to distinguish immaterial from material facts, the latter being limited to matters relating to the *substance* or *existence* of the obligation as opposed to its *values* or *inducements*.[7]

In *Savery v King*,[8] a son to whom a duty of disclosure was owed, purported to ratify a mortgage agreement (not made via an agent) which was prejudicial to him but it was held that the ratification was ineffective as he did not know that the transaction was voidable. Similarly, in *Banque Jacques-Cartier v Banque d'Epargne de Montreal*,[9] the defendant bank made a personal loan of money to the manager of the plaintiff bank. The loan was entered in the books of the plaintiff bank thereby representing it as a debtor in relation to the loan, and the plaintiff bank, in liquidation, only repudiated the loan nine months later. It was held that the new board of the bank had much to investigate and,

---

2 (1850) 4 Exch 786 at 798.
3 (1850) 4 Exch 786 at 799.
4 [1994] Ch 271.
5 [1994] Ch 271 at 284, per Roch LJ.
6 [1896] 2 Ch 348.
7 See the examples in the *Restatement, Second, Agency* § 91.
8 (1856) 5 HL Cas 627.
9 (1887) 13 App Cas 111.

consequently, there was no ratification by acquiescence as it did not have full knowledge of the facts. However, lack of knowledge is not a *carte blanche* for P, and he may be liable if he negligently accepts risks when ratifying without enquiring into the facts.[10]

Many of the earlier cases in this area involved A's levying unlawful distress and it seems that the courts tended to deny ratification as P's *tortious* liability was involved.[11] Consequently, *Bowstead & Reynolds* suggests that a 'blanket ratification'[12] may be more easily established in the contractual situation (eg P's receipt of goods) than in the tortious context as, objectively, P may be expected to know the true contractual position.

What sort of acts may be ratified?

The general rule is that all acts, whether lawful or unlawful, may be ratified, with the exception of acts which are *void* at their inception for some reason other than that they have not been authorised beforehand by P. It is clear therefore that A's contract, entered into without authority from P, may be ratified and is not regarded as a nullity.

In relation to unlawful acts, P's ratification may change an act wrongful against himself (eg an unauthorised sale of P's goods) or T (eg unauthorised distress of T's goods[13]) into a lawful act. Alternatively, upon ratification P may become liable for unlawful acts. This has most relevance as regards A's torts and the early cases on this topic are concerned with providing a remedy for T in the absence of an overall notion of vicarious liability. Consequently, many of the older decisions lack practical significance today and the question of ratification of torts which require personal fault is not of paramount importance in commercial law. Certainly P can be liable for the proprietary, strict liability torts of conversion[14] and trespass to goods but even here the ratification will frequently entail P's contractual liability or the ratification will itself amount to conversion.[15]

As regards void acts, the classic illustration is that considered earlier of companies which purport to enter into *ultra vires* contracts which cannot later be ratified.[16] This reasoning has been carried-over into other areas with decisions such as *Brook v Hook*[17] drawing a distinction between acts void *ab*

---

10 See *Fitzmaurice v Bayley* (1856) 6 E & B 868 (P wrote to A saying that he did not know what A had agreed to but that he would support him in all that he had done. Held that this was sufficient ratification); *Marsh v Joseph* [1897] 1 Ch 213.

11 Eg, *Freeman v Rosher* (1849) 13 QB 780 (without authority to distrain for rent, A wrongfully seized and sold a fixture and paid the proceeds to P who accepted them in ignorance of the full facts. Held that P had *not* ratified the trespass).

12 *Bowstead & Reynolds on Agency* (16th ed, 1996), Art 16, para 2-066.

13 See *Whitehead v Taylor* (1839) 10 Ad & El 210 (A, without authority after P's death, distrained (in P's name) goods belonging to T for rent due. Held that the executrix could ratify the distress and thus legalise A's acts).

14 See *Hillberry v Hatton* (1864) 2 H & C 822 (T's ship was stranded and was purchased unlawfully by A; P ratified the purchase in ignorance of the true position. It was held that P was liable in conversion); cf *Freeman v Rosher*, above.

15 See Stoljar, *The Law of Agency* (1961), pp 179-182, for a discussion of this topic.

16 See *Ashbury Railway Carriage and Iron Co v Riche* (1875) LR 7 HL 653.

17 (1871) LR 6 Exch 89.

initio and voidable acts, with only the latter being capable of ratification. In *Brook*, a forgery of P's signature on a promissory note was held to be illegal and a nullity and hence incapable of ratification,[18] but perhaps the best reason for denying efficacy to the ratification of forgeries is that, when forging P's signature, A seeks to act as the *principal* rather than the agent.[19] Moreover, the *Brook* distinction does not settle the issue of which acts are voidable rather than void. In *Danish Mercantile Co Ltd v Beaumont*,[20] for example, A's unauthorised commencement of proceedings was not regarded as a nullity and was thus capable of ratification. This seems a reasonable conclusion as A's acts were not *illegal*, as they were in *Brook*, and it is arguable that the ratification in *Danish Mercantile* cured a mere impediment. Although this aspect of ratification is clearly not of burgeoning significance, the law relating to it is in a most inconclusive state.

How ratification is effected and proved

Ratification may be either express or implied from P's words or conduct.

EXPRESS RATIFICATION

The general rule is that express ratification requires no particular form even if ratification of a written contract is involved,[1] but the execution of a deed can only be ratified by deed. Might it be possible for P to agree to ratify in advance? The scope of such a clause in a power of attorney whereby P agreed to ratify whatever his attorney should do, was considered in *Midland Bank Ltd v Reckitt*.[2] The court held that ratification in advance was not possible as it contradicted the essence of the notion itself and the clause could not be extended to cover acts done by A which were outside the purposes set out in the deed. Lord Atkin considered that the clause *might* amount to a promise to adopt acts done within A's apparent authority thereby strengthening T's position but, of course, in such a case T would have to know of the clause and rely upon it.[3]

---

18 But if P knows of the forgery and induces T to think that the signature is valid and/or delays in repudiating it, P may be estopped as against T. In *Greenwood v Martins Bank Ltd* [1933] AC 51, a wife (A) regularly forged her husband's (P) signature and drew money from his account applying it to her own use. On P's becoming aware of the forgeries, he was persuaded by A not to disclose the truth and he remained silent for eight months. When P finally said he would approach his bank, A committed suicide. P was unable to recover from the bank (T) the sums paid to A because he was estopped *not* because he had ratified.

19 See Powell, *The Law of Agency* (2nd edn, 1961), p 124, fn 2.

20 [1951] Ch 680. See also *Secunda* [1994] Ch 271, considered below.

 1 See *Soames v Spencer* (1822) 1 Dow & Ry KB 32. The justification is that, as the *initial authority* to execute a contract in writing need not be in writing, there is, similarly, no necessity for a written *ratification*.

 2 [1933] AC 1.

 3 Other possibilities arising from such a clause are: (i) a conferment of authority in wide terms (ii) evidence supporting an otherwise weak ratification (iii) a contractual offer made by P to both A and T capable of acceptance by an act in reliance upon it and, (iv) as an estoppel against P, if relied upon by A, in an action by P against A.

IMPLIED RATIFICATION

If P's conduct could not amount to implicit ratification, P would have an unparalleled and unfair advantage over T in that he could choose to ratify beneficial contracts and reject those which were disadvantageous, and this privilege would come with the bonus of retroactive operation. This would clearly be unacceptable and the fact that P may impliedly ratify A's acts is thus a most important remedy for T. In the abstract, virtually every act of P's could be regarded as implied ratification and so, to achieve a balance between P and T, safeguards must be imposed in order to protect P. Most prominently, if ratification is to bind him, P's words or conduct must be clear and so amount to unequivocal ratification, P must have *knowledge* of the position at the time of ratification and he must be able to *choose* whether or not to ratify so that unwanted benefits are not pressed upon him.

Acts which can amount to implied ratification are, for example, P's receipt of the purchase price of goods sold by A[4] or P's acceptance of goods bought by A. The problems arise on the borderline of positive and negative conduct in situations of P's silence, acquiescence and delay. It is suggested that the correct view is that *pure* silence will not normally amount to ratification because it is difficult to construe as meaningful[5] and, if T seeks to assert that P's silence amounts to ratification, he may be unable to establish that P has sufficient knowledge of the position.[6] When P does have such knowledge it is quite possible that silence and inactivity may constitute a valid ratification.[7] It is clear that P's delay in paying for goods supplied by T, his failure to return them, his use of them or an attempt to sell them may all be good evidence of ratification.[8] In *Prince v Clark*,[9] for example, P shipped goods to India and instructed the captain of the ship (A) to sell them and invest the proceeds according to P's instructions.

4 *Hunter v Parker* (1840) 7 M & W 322 (a shipmaster (A) sold the ship without P's authority and P's receipt of the purchase money with full knowledge of the facts was held to be ratification); Cf *The Bonita, The Charlotte* (1861) 1 Lush 252 (P's receipt of purchase money *without knowledge* was held not to be ratification).
5 See *Arctic Shipping Co Ltd v Mobilia AB, The Tatra* [1990] 2 Lloyd's Rep 51.
6 *Moon v Towers* (1860) 8 CBNS 611 (A caused an employee (T) to be arrested. P said that he would not interfere. The arrest was wrongful and T sued P in trespass. Held that there was insufficient evidence of any ratification 'direct or constructive'); *Banque Jacques Cartier v Banque d'Epargne de Montreal* (1887) 13 App Cas 111 (considered earlier); *Crampsey v Deveney* (1969) 2 DLR (3d) 161 (children who were joint tenants of land with their mother did not object until the time came for signing a deed transferring the land. Their silence did not amount to ratification of the mother's actions; also of importance was the fact that the children were ignorant of their interest in the land). Where P's inactivity/silence is relied on by T, there might be an estoppel raised against P on appropriate facts; this could provide T with a remedy against P if the technical requirements of ratification cannot be established (see *Spiro v Lintern* [1973] 1 WLR 1002, considered in Ch 4).
7 See *Suncorp Insurance and Finance v Milano Assicurazioni SpA* [1993] 2 Lloyd's Rep 225, 234-235 per Waller J.
8 *Smith v Hull Glass Co* (1852) 11 CB 897 (without authority, directors of a company (P) ordered goods which were necessary for the business of the company. Held that the 'contracts were afterwards sanctioned and adopted by the directors' (p 927, per Jervis CJ) where, to the knowledge of P, the goods were retained and used in the manufacturing process); *The Australia* (1859) 13 Moo PCC 132 (the master of a ship (A) made an unauthorised sale of it and the owner's (P) unreasonable delay of two years in not disavowing the sale was regarded as acquiescence and ratification even though he was dissatisfied with the sale (see pp 157-159, per the Right Hon Dr Lushington).
9 (1823) 1 B & C 186.

A sold the goods but invested the proceeds in unauthorised goods. A informed P of this by letter which P received on 29 May but he did not attempt to repudiate A's actions until 7 August. It was held that P must be regarded as having assented to the sale. It clearly behoves P to disavow A's acts promptly for, otherwise, he may be bound by an implied ratification.

An interesting example of implied ratification arose in the USA[10] in *Southern States Equipment Co v Jack Legett Co.*[11] P leased an air compressor from T for use in P's construction business and, when it was delivered, the site foreman, A, signed the rental agreement which provided, inter alia, that P should be liable for loss or damage to the equipment whilst it was in his possession. The compressor was stolen from P's building site. The trial court held that P was not liable as A had no authority to bind P for loss of the equipment but, reversing that decision, the appellate court held that P's prior 'pattern of conduct' in the rental contracts with T constituted an implied ratification of A's act. The evidence was thus that P had honoured many previous invoices of T's which had been signed by A and had contained these provisions and P was fully aware of the imposition of liability. Once P knew of the contract's terms, his continued silence and failure to object amounted to tacit consent to those terms. There is every reason to think that, on these facts, the same conclusion would be reached in English law.

As well as the requisite knowledge of the position, it is crucial that P should have a choice of whether or not to ratify and so a compulsory acceptance of A's unauthorised acts will not amount to ratification. In *Forman & Co Pty Ltd v The Liddesdale*,[12] A ordered that T should carry out extra repairs to P's ship, T knowing that A was thereby exceeding his authority. P sold the repaired ship but it was held that this did not amount to ratification as P had no choice but to retake his property from which he could not separate the repairs and this was 'not like the case of an acceptance of goods which were not previously the property of the acceptor'.[13] If the decision were otherwise, an unscrupulous T could always make P liable for unrequested and unwanted benefits but, on the other hand, it is undeniable that, in *The Liddesdale*, P acquired a ship of enhanced value and did not have to pay for the benefits received.[14]

It is implicit from the cases above concerning silence and delay that, provided there is some manifestation of ratification, P need not actually *communicate* it to T, although communication will be important evidentially. This seems correct in principle; as *Bowstead & Reynolds*[15] points out, ratification is a unilateral manifestation of will in the same way as a grant of initial, preceding authority. Finally, P cannot ratify the favourable parts of a transaction whilst disclaiming those parts that are unfavourable.[16] This is justified in that if the rule were otherwise P would have the ability to enforce a contract entirely of his own making. Adoption of part of the transaction should therefore be deemed to be ratification of the whole unless, of course, there are separate transactions which may be adopted.

---

10 For the USA's perspective, see Axelrod, 'The Doctrine of Implied Ratification – Application and Limitations' (1983) 36 Okla L Rev 849.

11 379 So 2d 881 (La App, 1980).

12 [1900] AC 190.

13 [1900] AC 190 at 204, per Lord Hobhouse.

14 See also the American decision in *Wing v Lederer* 222 NE 2d 535 (1966) (A's unauthorised employment of a tree surgeon was not ratified by P's (compulsory) retention of the benefits conferred).

15 *Bowstead & Reynolds on Agency* (16th edn, 1996), Art 17, para 2-072.

16 See *Union Bank of Australia v McClintock* [1922] 1 AC 240.

The effects of ratification

It was stated at the start of this chapter that ratification acts as a curative and, in general, it invests the parties with the same rights, duties and liabilities as if the act in question had been performed with prior authority. First, P and T will have an enforceable contract even if T has tried to withdraw before ratification, because ratification is retroactive in effect (see below). Second, A will no longer be liable to T for breach of warranty of authority[17] and will only be liable to T if he has taken on a personal liability. Third, A will not normally be liable to P for exceeding his authority[18] on the basis that P has voluntarily ratified and hence waived any breach of duty. It is arguable, however, that A should remain liable if P's ratification is necessitous in order to protect his own interests, eg to preserve his business reputation.[19] In *Suncorp Insurance and Finance v Milano Assicurazioni SpA*,[20] Waller J suggested[1] that the matter should be considered in two stages, viz has there been a valid ratification and has P waived the breach of duty *vis-à-vis* the agent. He considered that the facts will often lead to both a ratification of the transaction between P and T and an exoneration of A, but that there was no necessary correlation between these two notions. Fourth, A should have a right to remuneration[2] and indemnity[3] from P but the same arguments apply here regarding a necessitous ratification which might mean that A should forfeit these rights. Fifth, ratification of a single act does not give A any authority to do the same acts in the future.[4] Finally, the effects of the retroactive operation of ratification must be considered separately.

Retroactivity and ratification

THE GENERAL RULE OF RETROACTIVITY

Ratification is backdated to take effect from the moment of A's acting so that the position is as if A had been given a valid, antecedent authority. In the majority of cases a retroactive ratification is inoffensive, for T intends to contract with P and ratification thus gives effect to the parties' intentions. Nevertheless, it is clear that T is at the beck and call of P because he may elect *not* to ratify thus leaving T with only an action against A for breach of warranty of authority.

---

17 See *Spittle v Lavender* (1821) 2 Brod & Bing 452.
18 See *Smith v Cologan* (1788) 2 Term Rep 188n.
19 See *Restatement, Second, Agency* § 416 which provides that A remains liable if P 'is obliged to affirm the act in order to protect his own interests' or 'is caused to ratify by the misrepresentation or duress of the agent'.
20 [1993] 2 Lloyd's Rep 225.
 1 [1993] 2 Lloyd's Rep 225 at 234-235.
 2 *Keay v Fenwick* (1876) 1 CPD 745.
 3 *Hartas v Ribbons* (1889) 22 QBD 254.
 4 *Irvine v Union Bank of Australia* (1877) 2 App Cas 366 (directors of a company borrowed in excess of the amount allowed which act was subsequently ratified by a majority of the shareholders. It was held that this conferred no future authority to borrow in excess of their powers. The correct course was to comply with the articles of association and increase their borrowing powers). Cf *Restatement, Second, Agency* § 43 (2): 'Acquiescence by the principal in a series of acts by the agent indicates authorisation to perform similar acts in the future'. Might repeated ratification *which is known to T* be evidence of apparent authority?

The greatest controversy, however, surrounds T's position between contract and ratification. Might events occur within that period of time which would dictate that ratification should be disallowed? The true effect of retroactivity should mean that T is bound from the moment of contracting with A and it is clear from *Bolton Partners v Lambert*,[5] that the overall rule of retroactivity is a strong one meaning that, in general, T has no right of withdrawal before ratification. In *Bolton*, T made an offer to A, the managing director of a company, for the purchase of the company's premises. A, acting without authority, accepted on the company's (P) behalf. T then attempted to withdraw the offer but ten days later the company ratified A's acceptance. It was held that P's ratification operated retrospectively rendering T's attempted withdrawal invalid.

Bolton has been criticised both by commentators[6] and the judiciary[7] chiefly on the basis that the contract which was formed lacked mutuality: T was bound to P from the outset but P could opt not to ratify without consequence. Fry,[8] a vociferous critic of rectroactivity in this context, considered that every facet of the contract lacked *consensus*; P's consent was missing when, without authority, A accepted T's offer and, moreover, T withdrew his consent before P ratified. He also considered that T was in a less favourable position when making an offer to A than to an ordinary individual because, in the latter situation, T could revoke at any time before acceptance. Again, it has been asserted that, in favouring P, *Bolton* represents a perverse allocation of risk.[9] Finally, in the USA, the *Bolton* analysis is rejected in the *Restatement*[10] which does not permit ratification after T has withdrawn from the transaction.

As a rejoinder to these criticisms it must be asked why T should have a right of withdrawal in the *Bolton* situation when he considered that he was bound contractually from the moment of A's acceptance. Second, he was insufficiently concerned with A's authority to make any enquiries regarding its scope and, thirdly, he subsequently sought to renege on a bad bargain entirely of his own making. It is perhaps more realistic to assert that, quite literally, T got what he bargained for. Moreover, in general terms, retroactivity is supportable in that

---

5 (1889) 41 Ch D 295.
6 See Seavey, 'The Rationale of Agency' (1920) 29 Yale LJ 859, 886-892. Seavey thought that the *Bolton* reasoning was 'to worship the fiction of relation back as a transcendental shrine ... it creates an offer when none was intended and imposes upon a mistaken party an obligation not imposed upon an offeror' (p 891). See also Wambaugh, 'A Problem as to Ratification' (1895) 9 Harv L Rev 60; Tamaki, 'The Rule in Bolton v Lambert' (1941) 19 Can Bar Rev 733.
7 See *Fleming v Bank of New Zealand* [1900] AC 577 where the Privy Council reserved the right to reconsider *Bolton*; *Re Portuguese Consolidated Copper Mines Ltd* (1890) 45 Ch D 16, 21, per North J.
8 *Specific Performance*, Additional Note A.
9 See E M, 'Notes' (1889) 5 LQR 440 (T is placed at an 'undeserved disadvantage' ... if either party is to be prejudiced it should be P 'who is taking the benefit of his agent's misrepresentation').
10 See *Restatement, Second, Agency* § 88. There have been differing views regarding retroactivity in the USA decisions. *Dodge v Hopkins* 14 Wis 630 (1861) is an inversion of *Bolton*, viz, P's ratification is ineffective unless T assents to it. This view effectively eliminates the notion of ratification: P's 'ratification' thus constitutes *an offer* which T can accept or reject. The *Restatement's* position is thus a compromise between the extremes of *Bolton* and *Dodge* in that it views the original 'contract' between A and T as an offer from T to P which (like any normal offer) may be accepted by P but only before T's revocation occurs. It was cogently asserted by Powell (*The Law of Agency* (2nd edn, 1961), p 145) that the rule in the *Restatement* 'has the doubtful merit that what was sauce for the goose has become sauce for the gander'.

it secures certainty in business transactions and where, for example, there is some purely technical irregularity in a company secretary's authority such as the lack of 'a resolution or a quorum or a deed' the rule 'will keep alive the agreement between A and T pending its formal ratification by the company'.[11]

Exceptions and modifications to retroactivity

When *Bolton* is accepted as the general principle, care must be taken to ensure that T is not prejudiced by retroactivity. It was emphasised recently in *Presentaciones Musicales SA v Secunda*,[12] that the logic of the dividing line between retroactivity and its exceptions is not easy to detect but, regrettably, the court did not attempt to draw any such line. If a purely abstract analysis is employed, the time between A's contracting and P's ratification is erased as a result of retroactivity meaning that no exceptions in T's favour could be formulated for events which have occurred within that time-span. It is plain, however, that this analysis carries abstraction too far and it must be asked when T might argue successfully that P's ratification should be ineffective.

It is submitted that all exceptions to *Bolton* should be based solely upon prohibiting *identifiable* hardship accruing to T from a material change in circumstances, ie he must not be *worse off* as a result of retroactivity. But where T considers himself bound from the moment of contract, it is difficult to postulate many situations in which he could subsequently incur hardship which do not involve an inherent commercial risk. One clear situation of hardship would be where P indicates to T that he does not intend to ratify, T then relying on that fact and thereby incurring a detriment should P subsequently seek to ratify. Indeed, this was formulated as an exception to ratification by Lord Atkin in *McEvoy v Belfast Banking Co Ltd*[13] and it is arguable that such a notion, based upon estoppel, may be the true rationale of some of the other limitations on retroactive operation, most particularly the suggested rule that ratification must take place within a reasonable time. If P delays in ratifying T may rely on the fact that P does not intend to ratify and, provided that such reliance is reasonable, ratification might be denied to P if detriment has accrued to T as a consequence of the reliance. The modifications to *Bolton* must now be considered and some must clearly be re-appraised in the light of the *Secunda* decision.

THE TRANSACTION BETWEEN AGENT AND THIRD PARTY IS 'SUBJECT TO RATIFICATION'

It is quite possible for the transaction between A and T to be made expressly 'subject to ratification' in which case there is no binding contract unless and until ratification occurs and either party may withdraw before ratification.[14] Moreover, the contract may be *impliedly* subject to ratification, the decision in *Warehousing & Forwarding Co of East Africa Ltd v Jafferali & Sons Ltd*[15] giving

11 Stoljar, *The Law of Agency* (1961), p 191.
12 [1994] Ch 271.
13 [1935] AC 24, 45. P's refusal to ratify which is *uncommunicated* to T can nevertheless be reversed so that the eventual ratification is valid, see *Simpson v Eggington* (1855) 10 Exch 845.
14 See *Watson v Davies* [1931] 1 Ch 455.
15 [1964] AC 1.

considerable latitude to this notion. There the Judicial Committee of the Privy Council held that it was not clear that A had contracted subject to ratification but that where T has 'intimation of the limitation of the agent's authority neither party can be bound until ratification has been duly intimated to the other party to the contract'.[16] This decision appears to limit *Bolton* to those situations where T believed conclusively that A had authority and A's acceptance was, accordingly, unequivocal and unconditional.

Where T makes an offer to A which is accepted by A 'subject to ratification by P', and P opts to ratify at a later date, it seems inevitable that a head-on conflict would arise between the retroactive effect of *Bolton v Lambert* and the rule that an offer will lapse on the expiry of a reasonable period of time.[17] Assuming that P has the ability to ratify several months after T's offer has been made,[18] it seems impossible to decide whether *Bolton* or the rule on lapse would prevail. In any event, should T consider the ratification to be delayed unduly, the rules on lapse of the offer add an extra weapon to his armoury.

VESTED PROPRIETARY RIGHTS CANNOT BE DIVESTED

It was acknowledged in *Bolton*[19] that ratification will not be permitted if its effect would be to divest proprietary rights which had accrued before ratification. In *Bird v Brown*,[20] for example, A, acting without authority, gave notice of stoppage in transit of goods on behalf of the seller/P but the assignees in bankruptcy of the buyer claimed the goods on arrival and had the better right to possession than A. P eventually ratified the stoppage but it was held that it came too late to divest the assignees of their prior, proprietary right to the goods.

TIME LIMITS AND RATIFICATION

The issue of time in relation to ratification involves two separate questions. First, where there are no express time limits for the commencement of the contract (as in *Bolton*) or for the performance of any other act, may P choose to ratify at some unrestricted, future date and then rely upon retroactivity to cure the delay or, alternatively, must ratification occur within a reasonable time? Second, if there are such express time limits, may P ratify even though the stipulated time limit has expired?

Ratification within a reasonable time?

The question of a reasonable time must be considered first. There was no mention of time in *Bolton* although, on the facts, the ten days' lapse before ratification

---

16 [1964] AC 1 at 9-10, per Lord Guest.
17 *Ramsgate Victoria Hotel Co v Montefiore* (1866) LR 1 Exch 109.
18 The question of time limits and ratification is considered below.
19 (1889) 41 Ch D 295, 307 per Cotton LJ.
20 (1850) 4 Exch 786. See also *Donelly v Popham* (1807) 1 Taunt 1 (a naval commodore, without authority, appointed X as captain of a ship. When the issue arose of sharing prizes taken by the ship, it was held that even if the Crown ratified the appointment, the commodore and X could not share prizes taken *before* ratification as others would have vested proprietary rights in the prizes).

was almost certainly not an unreasonable delay. However, both *Re Portuguese Consolidated Copper Mines Ltd*[1] and *Metropolitan Asylums Board v Kingham & Sons*[2] accept that ratification must occur within a reasonable time and, if this exception is valid, it is arguable that its correct basis is estoppel, ie P's delay in ratifying induces T to believe that it will not occur and T relies on this position to his detriment.

Ratification and express time limits?

The problem posed by express time limits is also surrounded by doubt. The *Kingham* decision, above, added the qualification that the reasonable time can never extend beyond the time at which the contract is to commence and the decision thus subscribes to the view that ratification is ineffective outside express time limits. In *Kingham*, T submitted a tender to supply eggs to P, the supply to commence on 30 September. The tender was accepted by A, without authority, on 22 September. T purported to withdraw on 24 September as he had made an error in his pricing but P sought to ratify on 6 October. It was held that ratification was too late. The rule is often justified by asserting that T would not know what his position was on 30 September and, if the ratification had been allowed, it would have enabled P to create retrospectively a right of action for breach of contract. However, it should be stressed that the only material difference between *Kingham* and *Bolton* was the express date for the commencement of the contract in *Kingham* and the defendants in both cases had attempted to withdraw before ratification took place. It is certainly questionable therefore whether there was any hardship to T in *Kingham* but, rather, that he should have been liable for an anticipatory breach of contract and it seems likely that a modern court would view *Kingham* in the same light.

The idea that express time limits are mandatory is also evident in *Dibbins v Dibbins*.[3] There an option to purchase which was exercisable in three months was exercised by A, without authority, in that time but only ratified outside the three month period. It was held that the ratification was invalid. It is arguable that *Dibbins* was based principally upon the court's refusal to extend a period artificially by the operation of ratification but it is also possible to place the decision alongside *Bird v Brown* as founded upon the refusal to divest proprietary rights. These decisions do impose a degree of certainty upon the operation of ratification but it is essential to realise that, within the context of retroactivity, there is no *intrinsic* hardship to T if ratification is delayed or express time limits are exceeded. Such hardship can only arise when the delay induces T to act, or refrain from acting, in some way so that he would be prejudiced by the ratification. Thus in *Presentaciones Musicales SA v Secunda*,[4] P was able to ratify A's unauthorised commencement of proceedings against T, even though the ratification occurred outside the period prescribed by the Limitation Act 1980. Here T was none the worse off as a result of the ratification and, indeed, he would have gained a positive advantage had P's ratification been disallowed.

1 (1890) 45 Ch D 16.
2 (1890) 6 TLR 217.
3 [1896] 2 Ch 348.
4 [1994] Ch 271.

RATIFICATION IS DISALLOWED WHERE THE PRINCIPAL LACKS THE
ABILITY TO RATIFY

This is the extremely tenuous and indecisive notion that ratification 'must take place
at a time, and under circumstances, when [P] might himself have lawfully done the
act which he ratifies'.[5] This *dictum* from *Bird v Brown* apparently introduces the
notion of P's *ability* to ratify which is most difficult to ascertain and apply in this
context and was referred to earlier in this chapter. For example, is P unable to ratify
in the *Dibbins* situation where ratification occurs outside an express time limit? It
is indisputable that, as ratification is backdated, P cannot be said to lack the *ability*
to ratify when he does so outside a time limit. If it is thought appropriate to place
limits on P's ability to ratify outside express time-limits, they should not be premised
upon such an elusive and incorporeal notion as the 'ability' to ratify.

However, it appears that P's inability to ratify lies at the root of the rule in insurance
that P cannot ratify an unauthorised contract of insurance once he has been apprised
of the loss, because he could not himself validly insure at that date. In *Grover &
Grover Ltd v Mathews*,[6] P was insured with T and, several days before the fire policy
expired, A renewed it with T without consulting P. A few days after the annual policy
expired, there was a loss caused by fire and, on the same day, P ratified A's earlier
renewal. It was held that P could not ratify after the loss had occurred and the court
refused to follow the established rule in marine insurance[7] that ratification was
permissible after a loss. The marine rule was justified, as a matter of commercial
expedience, on the basis that both parties acknowledged that the loss might arise
before ratification and this possibility was thus a rudimentary characteristic of the
contract.[8] It is crystal-clear that the rule prohibiting ratification in insurance cannot
be premised upon hardship because there is rarely any detriment in the event of
ratification after the loss. The insurer is able to assess both the risk and the premium
at the date A contracts on behalf of P and ratification thus gives effect to the parties'
intentions. Indeed, modern decisions are beginning to recognise this obvious fact.[9]

The *Secunda*[10] case again exemplifies many of the difficulties connected with
the notion of ability to ratify. There solicitors, without authority, commenced
proceedings against T but, of course, all the technicalities and formalities
connected with the proceeedings were complied with lawfully. P ratified A's acts
but the ratification occurred outside the period prescribed by the Limitation Act
1980. As P could not have *commenced* proceedings at that time, had he lost the
ability to ratify A's act? It was held that *Bolton* applied to the *Secunda* facts and
A's act was thus validated by the ratification. The Court of Appeal clearly did
not think that the fact that P had exceeded the time limit had any particular
significance *per se* and, most importantly, there was an express criticism by Roch
LJ[11] of the *dictum* in *Bird v Brown* concerning P's lawful ability to ratify. The
Secunda decision is both logical and just. T was patently no *worse off* as a result
of the ratification and, indeed, he would have secured an unjustifiable bonus

---

5   *Bird v Brown* (1850) 4 Exch 786, 799, per Rolfe B.
6   [1910] 2 KB 401.
7   See *Hagedorn v Oliverson* (1814) 2 M & S 485.
8   See *Jardine v Leathley* (1863) 3 B & S 700.
9   See *Bedford Insurance Co Ltd v Instituto de Resseguros do Brasil* [1985] QB 966; *National
    Oilwell (UK) Ltd v Davy Offshore Ltd* [1993] 2 Lloyd's Rep 582.
10 [1994] Ch 271; see Brown, 'Ratification, Retroactivity and Reasonableness' (1994) 110
    LQR 531.
11 [1994] Ch 271 at 284: 'The conclusion that I have reached is that the dictum cited from
    Bird v Brown is not a correct statement of the exceptions to the principles of ratification'.

had ratification been denied. Furthermore, no proprietary rights were affected and, on the facts, any argument that P lacked the lawful ability to ratify was both unrealistic and untenable. After *Secunda*, the intangible notion that P might lack the ability to ratify has been exposed as flawed and deficient.

POSSIBLE MODIFICATIONS FROM DECISIONS WHICH PRECEDE *BOLTON*

Some commentators mention *Kidderminster Corpn v Hardwick*[12] and *Walter v James*[13] as exceptions to retroactivity but it should be emphasised that both these cases precede *Bolton* and must therefore be of doubtful significance. *Hardwick* is particularly controversial as the decision (which is not considered in *Bolton*) does not analyse agency principles and makes no mention of retroactivity. In *Hardwick*, T agreed to lease certain market stalls from P, a municipal corporation, but the contract was neither executed under P's common seal nor signed on his behalf by any person authorised under seal to do so. T could not provide sureties for the rent within the stipulated conditions and so he purported to withdraw. Later there was a ratification of the lease under P's common seal. P then determined the lease and, as P was able only to re-let the stalls at a loss, he sued T for damages for breach of contract. It was held that, as the contract was not under seal, T was not bound by it. Ratification is mentioned briefly in the decision and the view is expressed that, as it occurred after T had withdrawn from the contract, it came too late to be effective.[14] But the case simply does not consider the retroactive operation of ratification and it is therefore difficult to assert, as does Fridman,[15] that *Hardwick* establishes that P may not sue T for breaches of contract which occur before ratification. If this were the position, *Bolton* would be robbed of virtually all its practical significance as T would have the right of withdrawal in all but name.

In *Athy Guardians v Murphy*,[16] P could only contract under seal but A's authority was not given under seal and neither the original agreement nor its purported ratification was so made. T attempted to withdraw before ratification and it was held that he could do so and was not liable to P. *Hardwick* was followed and convincingly explained as a case where the agreement was invalid for reasons *other than A's lack of authority*, ie, the contract was not executed under P's common seal and there was thus *no contract* from which T could withdraw even though he purported to do so.[17] If there is no contract there is nothing for P to ratify, this reasoning being analogous to the notion considered earlier that a void act cannot be ratified. In *Bolton*, of course, it was emphasised that A's acceptance did constitute a contract subject only to its being shown that A had *authority*[18] – and that was provided by ratification. If the *Athy* analysis is correct, *Bolton* is limited to curing the lack of authority in A where the contract with T would, otherwise, be valid.

The *ratio* of *Walter v James* is obscure but it was accepted in *Bolton* as being a case where A and T agreed to rescind the transaction prior to ratification thus leaving

12 (1873) LR 9 Exch 13.
13 (1871) LR 6 Exch 124.
14 See Kelly CB at p 22; Pigott B at pp 22-23.
15 Fridman, *Law of Agency* (7th edn, 1996), p 102.
16 [1896] 1 IR 65.
17 This was the view of *Hardwick* which was followed on very similar facts in *Oxford Corpn v Crow* [1893] 3 Ch 535. Although *Crow* was decided after *Bolton*, like *Athy*, the decision did not apply the retroactive rule.
18 See (1889) 41 Ch D 295, 307-308 per Cotton LJ.

nothing for P to ratify. In *Walter*, A, without authority, paid P's debt to T but when T learnt of the lack of authority he repaid the money to A. This was done because both A and T realised that, as the payment was unauthorised, P would not have to reimburse A. When T sued P for the debt, P pleaded that T had been paid and purported to ratify A's earlier payment. Not surprisingly, it was held that the ratification was ineffective but here it was surely crucial that T had simply not been paid and a valid ratification would have meant that form could override substance with material hardship thereby accruing to T. However, it has been suggested[19] that *Walter* may have a wider significance: in cases where T subsequently discovers A's lack of authority, it may be possible to argue that he is entitled to withdraw rather than being obliged to wait and see if the transaction will be ratified. If this point is ever taken by the courts, *Bolton* will be further diminished in significance.

ARE THERE ANY WIDER CONTROLS ON RETROACTIVE OPERATION?

It will now be apparent that, unlike the USA,[20] English law has no overall principle which could deny ratification where there is a material change in circumstances between contract and ratification which might render ratification inequitable, eg destruction of the subject matter of the contract[1] or a dramatic rise in market prices favouring P. Again, it is arguable that such facts are irrelevant to the operation of retroactivity: provided that T assumes that he is bound from the moment of A's acceptance, these instances may be considered as part-and-parcel of the commercial risks which T must accept, just as he would have to in any contract where both the property and the risk pass to him immediately on contract. A prudent third party insures his property against loss. Moreover, it should always be remembered that a cautious and circumspect third party can specify that the agreement is 'subject to ratification' thereby preserving his right to withdraw before ratification occurs.

CONCLUSION

There are two irrefutable exceptions to retroactivity, viz T can withdraw his offer or acceptance before P's ratification provided that T contracted 'subject to ratification' and, second, P's ratification cannot divest accrued proprietary rights in another. Beyond this, there can be no *absolute* exceptions if retroactivity is the dominant rule. The *Secunda* decision has exposed as erroneous any generalised notion that P may lack the 'ability' to ratify and it has also demonstrated that a substantial lapse of time between A's act and P's ratification may be entirely inconsequential, even where ratification occurs outside an express time limit. Apart from the two inflexible rules, above, it is suggested that estoppel provides the unifying theme for any other exceptions to retroactivity: the question which should always be asked is whether T would incur an actual detriment and thus be worse off if retroactive ratification were permitted. Nine times out of ten, T will suffer no such detriment as a consequence of retroactivity but, instead, will get his just deserts.

---

19 *Bowstead on Agency* (15th edn, 1985), Art 18, pp 75-76 (the comment is absent in the current edition).
20 See *Restatement, Second, Agency* § 89: if the 'situation has so materially changed that it would be inequitable to subject [T] to liability', he has an election to avoid liability.
 1 Cf *Williams v North China Insurance Co* (1876) 1 CPD 757, 770 where Pollock B seemed to assume that, in a sale of goods, ratification would be impermissible where the goods had ceased to exist at the date of ratification.

CHAPTER 4

Apparent authority

The nature and context of apparent authority

Apparent authority means that P, by his representations *made to T*, creates an appearance of authority in A. P is therefore said to 'hold-out' A as possessing an authority to act on his behalf and will be estopped as against T where T has relied upon the apparent authority so created. P is thus bound by the apparent authority which he has instigated to the same extent as if A had actual authority and the fact that A lacks such actual authority is immaterial. Representation, appearance and reliance are thus the interlocking facets of apparent authority. In the simplest situation, P may inform T expressly that A has the requisite authority but, more commonly, the representation will involve P's *conduct*, eg P allows A to act as the manager of his business and T relies on this appearance of authority when he contracts with A.

APPARENT AUTHORITY DISTINGUISHED FROM OTHER TYPES OF AUTHORITY

Actual, express authority and apparent authority

It is most important to separate apparent authority from the other types of authority and, at the same time, appreciate their inter-relation. First and foremost, it should be emphasised that apparent authority is the antithesis of actual, express authority: actual authority emanates from the relationship between P and A *inter se* whereas apparent authority is founded exclusively on the *nexus* between P and T.[1]

Actual, implied authority and apparent authority

A may have actual, implied authority to do whatever is necessary for, or ordinarily incidental to, the execution of his actual, express authority. The *scope* of A's actual, implied authority may thus be co-extensive with his apparent

---

1 In *Freeman & Lockyer v Buckhurst Park Properties (Mangal) Ltd* [1964] 2 QB 480, 503, Diplock LJ emphasised that, in actual authority, T is a stranger to the relationship of P–A but that, in apparent authority, A is a stranger to the relationship of P–T.

authority because, where T relies on apparent authority, he is entitled to assume that A has the authority which would normally be implied between P and A. Thus in *Freeman & Lockyer v Buckhurst Park Properties (Mangal) Ltd*,[2] Diplock LJ said that actual and apparent authority 'generally co-exist and coincide'.[3] Moreover, the decision in *Hely-Hutchinson v Brayhead Ltd*[4] (considered in Chapter 2), illustrates that implied and apparent authority can be alternative grounds for the same decision.

Nevertheless, actual, implied authority and apparent authority should be separated both in terms of their basis and, in one crucial situation, their scope. There are two rudimentary points to emphasise here. First, actual, implied authority, emanating as it must from A's actual, express authority, can never exist in isolation and be self-sufficient.[5] Second, while actual, implied authority may expand and explain the express authority, it cannot extend to acts which have been *prohibited* by P. Apparent authority, on the other hand, is unfettered by private restrictions which P may place upon A's authority and may thus encompass such prohibited acts, provided, of course, that they are within A's apparent authority. For example, A, the manager of P's retail shop, might be prohibited from buying stock for the shop by P's private restriction on A's actual authority but this could not affect A's undoubted apparent authority to buy such goods from T.

The division between actual, implied authority and apparent authority was accentuated in *The Unique Mariner*.[6] A ship was stranded and the master (A) contacted his owners (P) who told him that arrangements had already been made for a salvage tug (T1) to be sent to render assistance. Quite by coincidence, another tug (T2) was in the area and offered its services to A. A signed a salvage agreement with T2. A could not have actual, implied authority to enter into the agreement with T2 as P had expressly told A to contract with T1, but it was held that A had apparent authority to bind P to the salvage agreement with T2.

Waugh v H B Clifford & Sons Ltd[7] also differentiates apparent from implied authority in the context of a solicitor's authority to compromise actions. Brightman LJ pointed out that if the terms of a compromise have been discussed between the parties and the defendant's solicitor then writes to the plaintiff's solicitor offering to compromise at £100,000, the defendant's solicitor would clearly have apparent authority to make the offer. It would not follow, however, that the defendant's solicitor would possess implied authority to offer this sum as the client might have restricted the sum on offer. Even so the apparent authority would be unaffected, thus binding the defendant to the compromise.

THE DIFFERENT CONTEXTS OF APPARENT AUTHORITY

Apparent authority may exist in several different contexts. In the commonest situation, A may exceed his actual authority but nevertheless act within an apparent

2 [1964] 2 QB 480.
3 [1964] 2 QB 480 at 502.
4 [1968] 1 QB 549.
5 See *Industrie Chimiche Italia Centrale and Cerealfin SA v Alexander G Tsavliris & Sons Maritime Co, The Choko Star* [1990] 1 Lloyd's Rep 516 (considered in Ch 2); Brown, 'Authority and Necessity in the Law of Agency' (1992) 55 MLR 414.
6 [1978] 1 Lloyd's Rep 438.
7 [1982] Ch 374.

authority thereby rendering P liable. As emphasised above, A may have apparent authority to perform an act which is prohibited by the terms of his express authority – in the simplest example, selling goods below a fixed price limit. Moreover, apparent authority may bind P in cases where A acts fraudulently for his own benefit and contrary to P's interests because any prohibition will often be unknown to T and, likewise, the fraud may not be evident to him.[8]

Second, and less commonly, apparent authority may create an *agency* where none existed before but it is obviously difficult to create all the incidents of agency where there is no existing relationship at all between P and A. There are, however, the 'impostor' cases where this has occurred. In *Barrett v Deere*,[9] A had a seat in P's counting house and he appeared to be part-and-parcel of P's business. He took payment of a debt from T, giving him a formal receipt in P's name but A was a swindler and a total stranger to the business, having seemingly walked in from the street. It was held that T's payment to A was binding upon P, even though A was not employed by P and had absconded with the money. Lord Tenterden CJ held that 'the debtor has a right to suppose that the tradesman has the control of his own premises, and that he will not allow persons to come there and intermeddle in his business without his authority'.[10] Where there is no existing relationship of principal and agent, it is more common to find that P has created apparent *ownership* in the other party: this could occur, for example, where an owner of goods (O) allows X to have possession of O's goods and documents of title to those goods and, even though O does not wish it, X sells the goods to a *bona fide* T. If, as a consequence of O's conduct and representations, X appears to be O, this is clearly a case of apparent ownership. It should be stressed that only rarely will O lose title to his goods by creating apparent ownership in another as, in order to preserve vested rights of ownership, the law's stipulations for the creation of such apparent ownership are particularly strict. If the rule were otherwise ownership would become illusory and a simple loan of goods to another would be a particularly hazardous venture. Although an apparent agent and an apparent owner might both possess the apparent power to transfer title in P's goods, for example, it should be stressed that agency, premised as it is on *authority* to act for P within certain limits, is the antithesis of *ownership*, which is unfettered by any concept of authority. These two notions nevertheless share common roots in the concept of holding-out.[11]

Third, A's actual authority may have ended but an apparent authority may nevertheless endure and upon which T may rely. This is particularly useful to T in those circumstances where he cannot possibly know that A's actual authority

8   See eg *Lloyd v Grace, Smith & Co* [1912] AC 716 (P, a solicitor, was liable to T when his managing clerk (A) defrauded a client (T) and disposed of T's property for his own benefit); see also *Trueman v Loder* (1840) 11 Ad & El 589; *Hambro v Burnand* [1904] 2 KB 10; *Uxbridge Permanent Benefit Building Society v Pickard* [1939] 2 KB 248; *Lloyd's Bank Ltd v Chartered Bank of India, Australia and China* [1929] 1 KB 40 (infra); *Canadian Laboratory Supplies Ltd v Engelhard Industries of Canada Ltd* (1979) 97 DLR (3d) 1.

9   (1828) Mood & M 200; see also *Galbraith and Grant Ltd v Block* [1922] 2 KB 155 (considered in Ch 22) and the USA decisions: *Kanelles v Locke* 12 Ohio App 210 (1919) (T arrived at a hotel and was met by A who appeared to be in charge but was an impostor. A registered T, took certain valuables from him and gave T a receipt in P's name. P was liable on the basis that his negligence enabled A's apparent authority); *Miltenberger v Hulett* 175 SW 111 (1915); *Hoddeson v Koos Bros* 135 A 2d 702 (App Div 1957).

10 (1828) Mood & M 200 at 202.

11 See eg, *Eastern Distributors v Goldring* [1957] 2 QB 600; *Pickering v Busk* (1812) 15 East 38. Apparent ownership and O's loss of title is considered in Ch 18.

has been terminated. In *Drew v Nunn*,[12] for example, a husband (P) gave his wife (A) authority to act on his behalf and held her out to the plaintiff tradesman (T) as clothed with that authority. P then went insane, his mental condition thereby terminating A's actual authority. During the period of P's insanity, A ordered boots and shoes from T who had no knowledge of P's mental state. P later recovered his reason and was held to be liable for the price of the goods supplied by T on the basis that A's apparent authority had continued during the period of P's insanity.

APPARENT AUTHORITY IS AVAILABLE AS A REMEDY *ONLY* TO THE THIRD PARTY

There has always been much debate as to whether apparent authority is based upon estoppel or upon an independent notion of authority.[13] The dominant view of modern English law is that apparent authority is a species of estoppel[14] and, of course, estoppel is primarily a rule of evidence which prevents one party from denying the existence of a certain state of facts. It is clear from the cases that apparent authority is available as a remedy only to T and, should P wish to sue T, he would have to ratify A's act. This should be relatively easy in that ratification will normally be inferred from lodging a counterclaim against T.

The recognition that estoppel is at the root of apparent authority undoubtedly leads to a constriction of P's liability from the outset: the first question asked is whether P is estopped by having *created* apparent authority by his representation made to T and not whether T has *relied* on a reasonable appearance of authority in A. T's reliance is thus a corollary of P's representation. Many would argue that this represents an inversion of priorities in that T's reasonable reliance should be the dominant factor to consider and that, by creating voluntarily the agency relationship, liability should be *imposed* upon P where his agent has exceeded his authority but this fact is not evident to T. It will be seen later that, within the notion of apparent authority, several mechanisms exist to protect P, not least the notion that A cannot hold himself out. Moreover, the rule that all apparent authority must be traceable to P is somewhat awkward and unrealistic in impersonal, modern commerce. In 1961, Stoljar[15] stressed that 'estoppel-theory perpetuates what is perhaps the basic error in agency law. It invites us to think that the making of the legal relation between P and T somehow depends on some direct communication from P to T. In fact, the interesting and important rules of modern agency are concerned not with what happens between P and T, but with what happens between A and T'. These issues are returned to later in this chapter.

---

12 (1879) 4 QBD 661; see also Ch 12 on termination of agency.
13 See Stoljar, *The Law of Agency* (1961), pp 25-30; Powell, *The Law of Agency* (2nd edn, 1961), pp 68-72; Spencer Bower and Turner, *Estoppel by Representation* (3rd edn, 1977), Ch IX; Fridman, *Law of Agency* (7th edn, 1996), pp 120-121; Mechem, *Outlines of the Law of Agency* (4th edn, by P Mechem, 1952), Ch V §§ 85-90; Cook, 'Agency by Estoppel' (1905) 5 Col L Rev 36; Ewart, 'Agency by Estoppel' (1905) 5 Col L Rev 354; Cook, 'Agency by Estoppel: A Reply' (1906) 6 Col L Rev 34; Seavey, 'The Rationale of Agency' (1920) 29 Yale LJ 859, 873-874.
14 See eg *Rama Corpn v Proved Tin and General Investments* [1952] 2 QB 147, 149-150 per Slade J; *Freeman & Lockyer v Buckhurst Park Properties (Mangal) Ltd* [1964] 2 QB 480, 503 per Diplock LJ; *Egyptian International Foreign Trade Co v Soplex Wholesale Supplies Ltd and P S Refson & Co Ltd, The Raffaella* [1985] 2 Lloyd's Rep 36, 41 per Browne-Wilkinson LJ.
15 *The Law of Agency* (1961), p 29.

IS THE THIRD PARTY PUT ON ENQUIRY?

It should be stressed that A must apparently possess authority and such authority clearly cannot exist if T has actual knowledge that A does not have the requisite authority or if there is anything unusual or extravagant in the way A acts in his dealings with T. In the latter situation, knowledge of A's lack of authority may be imputed to T who is then said to be 'put on enquiry' and consequently unable to rely on apparent authority. This question is examined more closely at the end of this chapter.

The historical background of apparent authority

It is clear that where A has exceeded his actual authority but acts within an apparent authority, the law faces a dilemma regarding which of the two innocent parties, P or T, should bear the loss. As with usual authority, discussed in Chapter 5, the difficulty here is to define the basis and scope of an authority which A may possess beyond his actual authority and which may bind P. Although the terms 'apparent authority', 'ostensible authority', 'agency by estoppel' and 'holding-out' convey the general tenor of this authority, the rationale of P's liability must be ascertained.

As commerce expanded and became more impersonal in the 19th century, it became clear that the *external* aspect of agency between A and T had to be faced squarely and rationalised. Agents were becoming more adventurous and were often entrepreneurs in their own right as well as acting as agents for various principals. What if A contravened his actual authority but this was not evident to a *bona fide* T who, for example, bought goods from A? *Pickering v Busk*[16] is a seminal decision illustrating the difficulties which confronted the law in the changing commercial practices at the start of the 19th century. In *Pickering*, P was the purchaser of hemp which was lying at certain wharfs in London. He had the hemp transferred in the wharfinger's books into the name of the broker (A) who effected the purchase for him and whose ordinary business was to buy and sell hemp. Without any actual authority and acting in his own name, A sold the hemp to the *bona fide* defendant, T, who shortly afterwards became bankrupt. P demanded the hemp from T's assignees in bankruptcy. It was held that P's transfer of the goods into A's name authorised him to deal with them and judgment was given for the defendant, T. Today this would be categorised as a case of apparent *ownership* (P was undisclosed and could make no representation regarding the apparent authority of A as an agent) but the arguments and judgments mix the terms 'implied authority', 'apparent authority', 'appearance of ownership' and P's 'enabling' the sale. Most importantly, Lord Ellenborough CJ's judgment did not separate apparent agency from apparent ownership; rather it was the fact that A *was* an apparent owner which clothed him with the apparent authority to sell the goods.[17] Most

---

16 (1812) 15 East 38.
17 This compendious notion was enacted in the Sale of Goods Act 1893, s 21(1) as an exception to the *nemo dat* rule, viz the owner of goods might 'by his conduct [be] precluded from denying the seller's authority to sell'. This wording remains unchanged in the Sale of Goods Act 1979, s 21(1) (see Ch 18).

significantly, his far-sighted judgment acknowledged the vulnerable position of T and that A's authority was not limited 'to his actual authority, the reality of which is afterwards to be tried by the fact'. Instead, A could bind P 'within the limits of the authority with which he has been apparently clothed by the principal'.[18] This was truly a dramatic innovation. Previous decisions had considered whether A might have an implicit discretion in the terms of his actual authority to exceed a price stipulated by P, for example, and the courts had begun to separate the implications of A's having either a 'general' or a 'special' authority.[19] But here the courts were doing little more than trying A's actual, internal authority 'by the fact'. In *Pickering v Busk* there was a realisation that A must be capable of possessing some sort of external authority if the new mercantile practices of the early 19th century were to flourish, and this seminal decision marks the inauguration of 'apparent authority'.

Many of the earliest apparent authority cases are characterised by the clear policy imperative of protecting T, the most famous statement to this effect being that of Ashurst J in *Lickbarrow v Mason*[20] where he exhorted that 'whenever one of two innocent persons must suffer by the acts of a third, he who has enabled such third person to occasion the loss must sustain it'. Certainly where the issue is the possible transfer of title in goods to a *bona fide* T,[1] such policy is justifiable (as many of the early decisions stress) on the basis of commercial utility which demands that T's reasonable reliance on appearances should be the primary consideration. But there is also a wider awareness in these early decisions that P should be responsible for A, some decisions framing this almost in terms that P comes under an obligation or owes a duty to T to control his agent.[2] The overall emphasis was thus that the owner of a business who received benefits from it should carry primary responsibility for any losses arising from its mismanagement.[3] Moreover, the early 19th century decisions are often content with broad notions such as 'implied' or 'general' authority, there being a distinct bias towards accentuating, for example, a 'general authority to sell' in A which, if not recognised, would be 'a fraud on the public'.[4] These pragmatic, commercial decisions reached the right conclusions with an absence of analytical soul-searching which was conspicuous in the Civil law systems during the same period

18 (1812) 15 East 38 at 43.
19 See the decisions condidered in Ch 5 (usual authority).
20 (1787) 2 Term Rep 63,70. See also *Pickering v Busk* (1812) 15 East 38, 43, per Lord Ellenborough CJ: 'Strangers can only look to the acts of the parties, and to the external indicia of property, and not to the private communications which may pass between a principal and his broker'; *Gillman v Robinson* (1825) 1 C & P 642, 643, *per* Best CJ: 'One of two innocent persons must suffer for the fraud of a third ... if [P] held out the party as his agent ... the defendant[P] is the one of the two innocent persons who ought to suffer'.
1 See Ch 18 where this topic is examined.
2 Eg 'The master at his peril ought to take care what servant he employs; and it is more reasonable, that he should suffer for the cheats of his servant, than strangers and tradesmen': *Anon* (1690) Holt KB 641, per Holt CJ. See also Holt CJ's comments in *Hern v Nichols* (1700) 1 Salk 289.
3 See, eg, *Smith v Hull Glass Co* (1852) 11 CB 897, 928 per Maule J; *Summers v Solomon* (1857) 7 E & B 879. In *Smith v M'Guire* (1858) 3 H & N 554, 561, Pollock CB said: 'It would be most inconvenient if a person could not go into a shop and purchase an article without first asking the shopman whether he has authority to sell it. It may be that he was merely employed to sweep the shop; but it would be absurd to apply to the general business of life the doctrine as to the necessity of ascertaining whether an agent is acting within the scope of his authority – indeed the business of London could not go on'.
4 *Whitehead v Tuckett* (1812) 15 East 400, 411 per Bayley J.

when European jurisdictions acknowledged the clear demarcation between the internal (P–A) and external (A–T) aspects of agency.[5]

It was a good deal later in the 19th century that the English courts, influenced by *laissez-faire* notions of freedom of contract, adopted the reasoning of estoppel wholeheartedly and began to dissect that notion into its clinical, component parts. Certainly by the middle of the 19th century, *laissez-faire* individualism was becoming the touchstone of liability[6] with a concomitant emphasis upon the notion that civil obligations were founded upon consent. P's *representation* and his *creation* of the apparent authority were the paramount considerations rather than T's *reliance* upon appearances, thus rationalising apparent authority with consensual theory. As a result, there was a contraction of P's liability. If the sentiments in *Lickbarrow v Mason*[7] adequately summarised the law at the start of the 19th century, then it is arguable that the Lord Chancellor's views in *Farquharson Bros & Co v King & Co*[8] were representative of the early 20th century. In *Farquharson*, P stored his timber with a dock company, authorising A to sign and send delivery orders to the company. A perpetrated a fraud in ordering timber to be transferred into an assumed name and then, using that alias, sold the timber to a *bona fide* T and ordered it to be delivered to T. The House of Lords held that P was not estopped and could recover the value of the timber from T. Disposing of the case tersely, the Earl of Halsbury LC emphasised that 'a servant has stolen his master's goods, and the question arises whether the persons who have received those goods innocently can set up title against the master ... I really do not understand what estoppel has to do with this case'.[9] A's fraud was thus elevated as the primary reason to exonerate P but the equally important fact, that P initiated the situation from which A's fraud emanated, was consequently subjugated as inconsequential. This was not the approach which had been taken by the majority in the Court of Appeal in *Farquharson*.[10] There it was accepted that P should be liable on the basis that he had *enabled* the fraud to be perpetrated but the Lord Chancellor[11] also denigrated this notion in forthright terms:

'In one sense every man who sells a pistol or a dagger enables an intending murderer to commit a crime; but is he, in selling a pistol or a dagger to some person who comes

---

5 Eg, the theories of Paul Laband and Rudolf von Ihering referred to in Ch 1. See Müller-Freienfels, 'Law of Agency' (1957) 6 Am J Comp L 165, 170-176; 'Legal Relations in the Law of Agency: Power of Agency and Commercial Certainty' (1964) 13 Am J Comp L 193, 197-202 and 341; *Civil Law in the Modern World* (ed A N Yiannopoulos), Ch 4. The author traces the dominance of the 19th century theories of Ihering and Laband in Civil law jurisdictions to the effect that a commercial agent had a fixed, general authority, not alterable by the *internal* restrictions of P. Laband considered that even T's *knowledge* of restrictions between P and A would not limit A's authority *vis-à-vis* T. An exception to A's all-embracing authority would only be admitted where there was collusion between A and T to cause loss to P.

6 See Lord Cranworth's (dissenting) speech in *Pole v Leask* (1862) 33 LJ Ch (NS) 155, 162 which emphasised the consensual basis of contractual liability, P's vulnerability and T's obligation to ascertain the validity of the agency. Lord Cranworth considered that if T had dealt with an authorised A on fifty occasions, it was not necessarily safe for T to rely on such authority on the fifty-first occasion.

7 (1787) 2 Term Rep 63.

8 [1902] AC 325.

9 [1902] AC 325 at 329 and 330.

10 [1901] 2 KB 697; see also *Canadian Laboratory Supplies Ltd v Engelhard Industries of Canada Ltd* (1979) 97 DLR (3d) 1.

11 [1902] AC 325, 332.

to buy in his shop, acting in breach of any duty? Does he owe any duty to all the world, as is suggested here, to prevent people taking advantage of his selling pistols or daggers in his business, because he does in one sense enable a person to commit a crime?'

It was seen earlier that, in English law, consent is the foundation of authority in agency. Consent, albeit assessed objectively, is also seminal within the operation of apparent authority: the standpoint of the modern law is that apparent authority emanates from P and must be attributed to the statements and acts of P. It is, undeniably, somewhat awkward to apply this reasoning in justification of P's liability within apparent authority when A has performed an act which is *prohibited* by the terms of his actual authority. In this situation, employing the most objective of yardsticks, P is deemed to consent to A's apparent authority. If consent and voluntary representation appear to be artificial bases for apparent authority, it must be asked whether there are any other means by which A's external, apparent authority might be rationalised and justified.

First, T might assert that as P has instigated the agency relationship for his own benefit, he should consequently shoulder the burden when A exceeds his actual authority but is within an apparent authority. Such a broad policy argument is analogous to the *imposition* of vicarious liability on an employer for the torts of his employees committed in the course of their employment. Although this reasoning had undoubtedly begun to emerge in the early decisions such as *Pickering v Busk*, it is arguable that the analogy with vicarious liability is misplaced: an imposition of liability is appropriate where T is an involuntary participant in an employee's torts but less so in the contractual, agency context, where T voluntarily enters into the transaction with a prior ability to assess risks and make choices.[12]

Second, it could be contended that the *bona fide* T's reliance upon appearances should be accorded maximum protection on the basis that apparent authority has no significant purpose if its scope is constricted in order to favour P. Again, T's simple reliance on appearances is, without more, too extreme a test which could render P liable where there is no chain of causation whatever between P and T, eg X, a thief, steals P's goods without P's fault or knowledge but, nevertheless, from T's perspective, the thief appears to be either P himself or P's agent authorised to sell the goods.

Third, English law might adopt something akin to the USA's wide theory of 'inherent agency power' which deliberately jettisons the established concepts and categories of authority. The *Restatement, Second, Agency* § 8A provides that:

> 'Inherent agency power is a term used ... to indicate the power of an agent which is derived not from authority, apparent authority or estoppel, but solely from the agency relation and exists for the protection of persons harmed by or dealing with a servant or other agent'.[13]

It is plain that English law subscribes to none of the possibilities outlined above, nor does it adhere to the Civil law's strict separation of internal from external authority. Should the scales be weighted in favour of P or T? Is it possible to formulate rules which strike a balance between P's and T's opposing interests

---

12 For worthwhile discussions regarding vicarious liability and apparent authority see Seavey, 'Agency Powers' (1948) 1 Okla L Rev 3; Mearns, 'Vicarious Liability for Agency Contracts' (1962) 48 Va L Rev 50; Bester, 'The Scope of an Agent's Power of Representation' (1972) 89 SALJ 49. See also Ch 5 on usual authority which considers the external aspect of A–T.
13 See the informative article by Fishman, 'Inherent Agency Power – Should Enterprise Liability Apply to Agents' Unauthorized Contracts?' (1987) 19 Rutgers L J 1.

and apportion the risks realistically? If both the American and Civil law notions arguably lead to T's over-protection, the modern English approach favours the preservation of ownership at the expense of commercial certainty. At the start of the 21st century, where P is frequently an impersonal, transnational corporation and the complexities of commerce are increasingly conducted through multi-layered agents, it is perhaps inappropriate that apparent authority is dogged by notions of consent, representation and estoppel. A bias towards an externalised perspective is certainly more advantageous to T but, in the modern corporate context, it is surely correct that, first and foremost, P should carry the burden of A's exceeding his authority, thereby arguably securing a fitting allocation of risk between the parties.

The recent decision of the Court of Appeal in *First Energy (UK) Ltd v Hungarian International Bank Ltd*,[14] considered below, clearly recognises that the protection of T should be dominant within the rules of apparent authority. Indeed, Steyn LJ's exhortation that 'the reasonable expectations of honest men'[15] must be protected echoes the sentiments in the early decisions on apparent authority which were discussed earlier. *First Energy* may lead to a resurgence of emphasis being placed upon T's reasonable reliance on appearances. In turn, instead of seeking to limit P's liability by accentuating the necessity for his unequivocal representation of apparent authority in A, there may be a re-assertion of the notion that P is primarily responsible for initiating the situation from which A's apparent authority springs.[16]

Conditions for the operation of apparent authority

Apparent authority is founded on P's voluntary representation that A has authority which is made to T and relied upon by him.[17] These requirements may now be sub-divided and analysed.

THE PRINCIPAL MUST REPRESENT THAT THE AGENT HAS AUTHORITY

Broadly, there are two types of representation which are found within apparent authority: P may either make a specific representation to T or, alternatively, put A in a position which carries a 'usual' authority, eg a bank manager or solicitor.[18] Not surprisingly, it is the second type which generates most problems throughout the conditions for the operation of apparent authority.

---

14 [1993] 2 Lloyd's Rep 194.
15 [1993] 2 Lloyd's Rep 194 at 196.
16 For modern statements to this effect see *Burt v Claude Cousins & Co Ltd* [1971] 2 QB 426, 450 per Sachs LJ; *Panorama Developments (Guildford) Ltd v Fidelis Furnishing Fabrics Ltd* [1971] 2 QB 711, 717 per Lord Denning MR; *Gurtner v Beaton* [1993] 2 Lloyd's Rep 369, 379 per Neill LJ.
17 For seminal decisions on the requirements and operation of apparent authority see *Rama Corpn v Proved Tin and General Investments* [1952] 2 QB 147; *Freeman & Lockyer v Buckhurst Park Properties (Mangal) Ltd* [1964] 2 QB 480; *Hely-Hutchinson v Brayhead Ltd* [1968] 1 QB 549.
18 See eg, *First Energy (UK) Ltd v Hungarian International Bank Ltd* [1993] 2 Lloyd's Rep 194, infra; *United Bank of Kuwait Ltd v Hammoud* [1988] 1 WLR 1051 (a solicitor giving undertakings as security for loans was within his apparent authority).

The general rule is that it is P who must make the representation regarding A's authority, for it is P who will be liable to T. It follows that A cannot make a representation regarding the existence or scope of his own authority because by so doing he would be holding-out himself as having the requisite authority to bind P: self-authorising agents are unacceptable in that they represent a negation of agency reasoning.[19] Although this rule seems to be straightforward in principle, it proves to be somewhat troublesome in application.

First, the requirement has the potential to cause difficulties where P is a limited company rather than a human being, because a company must necessarily act solely through its agents. In *Freeman & Lockyer v Buckhurst Park Properties (Mangal) Ltd*,[20] the second defendant (A), a director of Buckhurst Park Properties Ltd (BPP), appointed the plaintiff architects to do certain work. When the plaintiffs sued for their fees, BPP argued that A had no authority to bind the company. Although BPP's articles of association made provision for the appointment of a managing director, no one had been formally appointed but A had acted as such to the knowledge of the board of directors. It was held that BPP was liable as A had apparent authority to bind the company. Diplock LJ emphasised that, to render a company liable, the representation had to be made by someone who had *actual authority* to manage the company, this condition being fulfilled in *Freeman & Lockyer* as the board had represented that A possessed authority.

Second, it must be asked whether the rule denying A's ability to hold-out himself as having authority is a reasonable and practical one. The problem here really relates to A's possible *enlargement* of his existing authority and the extent to which T could or should be expected to enquire regarding its scope. Consider the example of a simple retail sale, given by Staughton J in *Armagas Ltd v Mundogas SA, The Ocean Frost*:[1] T asks for credit, A disappears for a moment but returns and then grants credit to T. Staughton J had no doubt that, from T's perspective, it would be implicit that A had obtained approval from his superior, even if he had not actually done so, and thus T's reliance on appearances would be reasonable. However, this view found no favour on appeal, the decision in *Armagas* being that an agent who lacked apparent authority to conclude a charterparty did not have apparent authority to notify T that approval of the transaction had been given by P.[2] The question is paramount where P is a large, impersonal corporation in that it is difficult for T to rely on any representation of P other than his installation of A in a position within the company hierarchy. If T deals with a 'senior manager' should he need to look beyond that fact and, even if T should be careful, is he able to make any sensible evaluation of A's authority? Surely there are circumstances where T must trust to A's outward appearances including A's statements or conduct regarding the extent of his authority?

---

19 See *A-G for Ceylon v Silva* [1953] AC 461; *British Bank of the Middle East v Sun Life Assurance Co of Canada (UK) Ltd* [1983] 2 Lloyd's Rep 9; *Armagas Ltd v Mundogas SA, The Ocean Frost* [1986] AC 717; *Re Selectmove* [1995] 1 WLR 474, 478 per Peter Gibson LJ.
20 [1964] 2 QB 480.
 1 [1985] 1 Lloyd's Rep 1, 15.
 2 [1986] AC 717. Robert Goff LJ emphasised that to decide otherwise would be illogical: A, lacking apparent authority to enter into a contract could *not* bind P by wrongfully asserting that he *had actual authority* but *would* bind P by a wrongful assertion that he had *obtained actual authority* from P.

These questions were answered largely in the negative in *British Bank of the Middle East v Sun Life Assurance Co of Canada (UK) Ltd.*[3] There the plaintiff bank was dealing with an agent of Sun Life who was a 'unit manager'. He gave a guarantee on behalf of Sun Life although he had no actual authority to do so, his authority being limited to transmitting proposals for life assurance and loans to higher officers of the company. As the document in question expressly provided for its signature by two representatives of Sun Life but was signed only by the unit manager, the plantiff bank wrote to the 'general manager' of Sun Life asking for confirmation of the unit manager's authority. A reply was received from a 'branch manager' who, without any actual authority, confirmed the first agent's authority. The House of Lords held that the branch manager did not have apparent authority to answer the letter; rather he had held-out himself as having authority.

It is tolerably clear that apparent authority can emerge from an assurance as to A's authority given either by P or by an agent with actual authority to give the assurance and, indeed, P was held to be liable on the basis of such a confirmation of authority in a Canadian decision[4] but the court was divided as to exactly which agent would be such a 'responsible corporate official' for the purpose of giving an assurance.[5] This surely emphasises that T cannot realistically be expected to differentiate between such officials and is unable make a reasoned judgement regarding their authority but, instead, must trust to reasonable, external appearances. However, once again, the rule emanating from *Sun Life* is one which conspicuously protects P.

The rigid and arguably unrealistic decision reached in *Sun Life* should be compared with the preferable conclusion arrived at in *First Energy (UK) Ltd v Hungarian International Bank Ltd.*[6] The plaintiff (T) sought credit facilities from the defendant bank (P) and dealt with its agent who was a 'senior manager' in charge of the Manchester office. A told T that he had no direct authority to sanction a credit facility. Credit was in fact granted to T but the parties never formalised an overall facility. T wanted more financing for his business and A wrote to T enclosing hire-purchase agreements, indicating that, on their completion, funds would be released to T. T completed the documentation but P refused any finance. It was held that, although A had no apparent authority to sanction the transaction himself, he did have apparent authority to sign letters on behalf of P communicating an offer to T, which T had accepted, and P was therefore bound by the contract. *Armagas Ltd v Mundogas SA, The Ocean Frost*[7] was distinguished: there T knew of A's limited authority and thus A could not enlarge his apparent authority by his *own* representations but, in *First Energy*, A clearly had apparent authority to communicate decisions, that authority emanating from the position of seniority in which P had placed A. The decision in *First Energy* emphasised the commercial realities of the situation in that T

3 [1983] 2 Lloyd's Rep 9.
4 *Canadian Laboratory Supplies Ltd v Engelhard Industries of Canada Ltd* (1979) 97 DLR (3d) 1.
5 The case concerned A's sale of goods to T and the members of the court differed as to whether a 'purchasing agent's' assurance to T could bind P, but all were agreed that an assurance by a 'Vice-President (Operations)' did bind P.
6 [1993] 2 Lloyd's Rep 194; see Brown, 'The Agent's Apparent Authority: Paradigm or Paradox?' [1995] JBL 360; Reynolds, 'The Ultimate Apparent Authority' (1994) 110 LQR 21.
7 [1986] AC 717.

should not be expected to question the apparent authority of a senior bank manager and thus 'the reasonable expectations of honest men [were] protected'.[8] The perspective adopted in *First Energy* is unquestionably that of T and the decision is remarkable for its forthright enunciation of policy reminiscent of the early decisions such as *Pickering v Busk*.[9] It is respectfully suggested that the decision is correct: the dilemma remains in where to draw the line regarding A's legitimate extension of his authority[10] but this is no more difficult than the general, innate problem regarding the scope of A's apparent authority.

THE PRINCIPAL'S REPRESENTATION MUST BE CLEAR AND UNEQUIVOCAL

P's representation can be express (oral or written) or implied from the circumstances and it is the notion of the implied representation which causes most difficulties. The general rule is clear: the representation must unequivocally accord with a grant of authority to A and if it is susceptible of several different interpretations it may be ineffective to bind P. In *Colonial Bank v Cady and Williams*,[11] for example, executors of a will signed blank transfers on the reverse of share certificates in order that the shares should be registered in their names. The broker to whom the certificates were sent, fraudulently filled in the blanks in his own name and deposited them with the plaintiff bank who took them, *bona fide*, as security for advances made to the broker. It was held that the conduct of the executors was equivocal as it was consistent either with an intention to sell or pledge the shares or to have themselves registered as owners. Accordingly, their conduct did not estop them from setting up their title as against the bank. Also, it was held that, on the facts, the bank should have enquired into the broker's authority. Lord Herschell considered, however, that an *owner's* delivery of a signed, blank transfer to a broker would constitute an estoppel for he 'must, presumably, have signed it with the intention at some time or other of effecting a transfer'.[12] The general rule which demands an unequivocal representation is clear but there is much uncertainty in fixing the boundaries of such a representation. Some attempt at categorisation can be made, however.

Course of dealing

The representation may be implied from a course of dealing with T and, indeed, the earliest cases were based upon this idea, ie if P *usually* sent his servant/agent to buy goods on credit terms from a tradesman and A went marginally beyond

---

8 [1993] 2 Lloyd's Rep 194 at 196, per Steyn LJ. See also *Shearson Lehman Bros Inc v Maclaine, Watson & Co Ltd* [1988] 1 WLR 16, 28 per Lord Bridge of Harwich: 'In the real world it seems to me that business would come to a standstill if persons who receive documents from clerks or secretaries, acting in the course of their employment, were not entitled to assume that those documents were sent with the authority of the employer, and if this is true of the ostensible authority of staff in such humble grades, it must equally be true of staff at higher levels'.

9 (1812) 15 East 38.

10 See also *Canadian Laboratory Supplies Ltd v Engelhard Industries of Canada Ltd* (1979) 97 DLR (3d) 1,10 where Laskin CJC subscribed to the view that A's representations regarding his authority might bind P; cf Fridman, 'The Self-Authorizing Agent' (1983) 13 Man LJ 1.

11 (1890) 15 App Cas 267.

12 (1890) 15 App Cas 267 at 286.

the price limit stipulated by P, for example, P would nevertheless be liable for the cost.[13] This simple example illustrates the essence of apparent authority in its striking a balance between P and T: T's safeguard is his entitlement to rely on the normality of the established course of dealing, whereas P would not be liable where, for example, A bought far in excess of stipulated prices or bought distinctly different goods from those usually bought.

Representations implied from P's conduct

It is clear that a representation can be made 'by conduct, that is, by permitting the agent to act in some way in the conduct of the principal's business with other persons'.[14] The most problematic situation is where P appoints A to a position which carries a usual authority, eg a managing director. It is arguable, on the one hand, that simply installing A in such a position is, without more, an example of actual, express authority but, on the other hand, it could be asserted that this is a sufficient representation of his authority to do acts commensurate with his position.[15] Certainly once A begins to act, there can be a representation in P's acquiescing in those acts but, of course, this fact must be known to T for apparent authority to exist. Assuming that appointing A to a position is a sufficient representation, the further difficulty lies in ascertaining the scope of the apparent authority so created, ie deciding which acts are usually performed by a 'senior manager' or any other designated agent, the facts of *First Energy*, considered above, being paradigmatic of these difficulties. The modern view is that the entirety of P's conduct and all the circumstances of the case must be considered, not simply A's position or title in isolation.[16]

Possession of property and documents of title

Allowing A to have possession of property and/or documents of title may be a sufficient representation of apparent agency *or* apparent ownership so that, despite any secret restriction imposed by P, A may validly dispose of the property to T. A prime illustration of such circumstances occurred in *Pickering v Busk*,[17] considered earlier. However, it is stressed consistently throughout the cases that merely entrusting A with possession of goods or documents of title is insufficient, *per se*, to create in him either apparent authority or apparent ownership. If the rule were otherwise, ownership would be illusory in that a bailee in possession of goods, for example, could sell them and create a good title in T. Some further

---

13 See eg, *Hazard v Treadwell* (1722) 1 Stra 506 (P sent A to buy goods on credit, P paying T at a later date. On the next occasion P sent A with cash but A bought the goods without paying T: P was liable for the cost; *Summers v Solomon* (1857) 7 E & B 879 (A had for several years managed P's shop, ordering goods from T in P's name for which P paid. A absconded and bought goods from T in P's name. P was liable for the price).

14 *Freeman & Lockyer v Buckhurst Park Properties (Mangal) Ltd* [1964] 2 QB 480, 503 per Diplock LJ.

15 See *Hely-Hutchinson v Brayhead Ltd* [1968] 1 QB 549, 583 per Lord Denning MR: 'When the board appoint one of their number to be managing director, they invest him not only with implied authority, but also with ostensible authority to do all such things as fall within the usual scope of that office'.

16 See *British Bank of the Middle East v Sun Life Assurance Co of Canada Ltd* [1983] 2 Lloyd's Rep 9; *Egyptian International Foreign Trade Co v Soplex Wholesale Supplies Ltd and P S Refson & Co Ltd, The Raffaella* [1985] 2 Lloyd's Rep 36, 45 per Kerr LJ; *Gurtner v Beaton* [1993] 2 Lloyd's Rep 369, 379 per Neill LJ.

17 (1812) 15 East 38.

act is needed before P loses title to T. In *Rimmer v Webster*,[18] for example, P gave A, a broker, a mortgage bond with instructions to sell it. A fraudulently induced P to execute transfers of the bond to A together with an acknowledgment of receipt of the purchase money by P, even though P had received nothing. A then obtained from T a loan of £1,000 on the security of the bond and executed a sub-mortgage of the bond to T producing the transfers as proof of title. It was held that P was bound by the sub-mortgage.[19]

Subsequent representations of P

It is clear from the decision in *Spiro v Lintern*,[20] that P's representations made *subsequently* to the contract may constitute an estoppel, although the representations may not, technically, create an apparent authority in A. In *Spiro*, P instructed his wife to find a purchaser for his house but he did not give her actual authority to sell. The wife agreed a sale to the plaintiff, T. P had done nothing to hold out his wife as his agent at this stage, but then P met T and did not demur at T's being the purchaser. Moreover, to the knowledge of P, T was allowed to do repairs to the house. P then gave his wife authority to sell in a power of attorney but she sold the house, at a higher price, to X. The Court of Appeal held that ratification of the contract was impossible as P had been undisclosed at the time of A's agreement with T[1] but that T could succeed on the basis of estoppel. This was because P knew of T's mistaken belief that P was obligated to sell the house to him and P had done nothing to disabuse T; P's failure to correct T's mistaken belief thus amounted to a representation that his wife had authority to sell and T had relied on that representation to his detriment.

Spiro v Lintern was followed in *Worboys v Carter*,[2] although in the latter case P was not an undisclosed principal. In *Worboys*, P was the tenant of a farm who got into dire financial straits which resulted in his receiving a custodial sentence for VAT fraud. P's wife consulted a solicitor and, as a result of this initiative, A, a surveyor, visited the farm and suggested that, in order to eradicate P's financial problems, P should assign the tenancy of his agricultural holding. A visited P in prison and, although A was given limited authority to act on P's behalf, he was never authorised to assign the tenancy. A nevertheless gained the impression that he did possess such authority and he agreed to assign the tenancy to T. P had hoped to avoid the loss of his tenancy throughout but he never protested to T, did not inform T of A's lack of authority and, in fact, allowed T to measure the rooms of the house for carpets and curtains. T also sold his own farm based upon the expectation that he would acquire the tenancy of P's farm. The Court of Appeal decided that (i) A had no actual authority to assign the farm to T (ii) P had done nothing to repudiate the contract with T but he never wished to be bound by it and so it was inapt to assert that he had ratified A's acts (iii) P was, however, estopped from denying the existence of a contract with T (following the decision in *Spiro*).

---

18 [1902] 2 Ch 163.
19 The transfer of title by virtue of apparent authority/ownership is considered fully in Ch 18.
20 [1973] 1 WLR 1002.
 1 See *Keighley, Maxsted & Co v Durant* [1901] AC 240 (considered in Ch 3).
 2 [1987] 2 EGLR 1.

Silence as a representation

It is plain from *Spiro v Lintern*, above, that P's silence can lead to his being estopped but *Spiro* is seemingly based upon estoppel as a discrete notion and cannot be regarded as authority for the proposition that P's silence may suffice to create an apparent authority in A. From T's point of view, it is largely irrelevant whether P is estopped or is bound by virtue of his creation of apparent authority in A, but these are distinctly separate notions.

Spiro acknowledged that silence might found an estoppel where 'a man is under a duty – that is, a legal duty – to disclose some fact to another and he does not do so'[3] and the notion of 'legal duty' was held to apply, on the facts, to P's duty to disclose to T that P's wife had acted without authority from P.[4] In *Moorgate Mercantile Co Ltd v Twitchings*,[5] the House of Lords confirmed that, at least in the context of loss of title to goods, an owner would not be estopped from asserting his title by silence or inaction as it is difficult to construe any representation from such colourless conduct. If silence is to acquire a positive content, Lord Wilberforce stressed that there must be a duty to speak or act in a particular way owed to the person prejudiced.

The requirement of a duty to speak is thus beyond doubt but the ambit of such a duty remains elusive. In the *Henrik Sif*,[6] Webster J could not discern 'the existence of any separate or pre-existing legal duty to speak'[7] on the part of P in *Spiro* and he thus thought that it was unclear whether such a legal duty was a necessity. Webster J preferred Lord Wilberforce's wider formulation in *Twitchings*[8] and, quoting from Lord Wilberforce's speech, he concluded that estoppel by silence or acquiescence arises where a reasonable man would expect that the person against whom the estoppel is raised, acting honestly and responsibly, would bring the true facts to the attention of the other party known by him to be under a mistake as to their respective obligations.[9]

The question came to the fore again in *The Tatra*,[10] where T alleged that P's silence prevented him from denying A's authority to enter into a binding contract with T. On the facts, Gatehouse J held that A had no actual authority from P and, as P had no intention of entering into a contract with T and did not know that A was purporting to act for him, P could not possibly have sufficient knowledge to raise any duty to speak and thus he was not estopped.

It is thus relatively clear that, where P comes under a duty to speak, his silence can suffice to establish an estoppel against him but, because of the technical requirements of apparent authority which demand an unequivocal representation on P's part, it is difficult to found such an authority on P's silence alone.

---

3 [1973] 1 WLR 1002, 1010 per Buckley LJ.
4 This approach was followed expressly in *Worboys v Carter* [1987] 2 EGLR 1 (see Woolf LJ at p 5, para K).
5 [1977] AC 890 (considered in Ch 18).
6 *Pacol Ltd v Trade Lines Ltd, The Henrik Sif* [1982] 1 Lloyd's Rep 456.
7 [1982] 1 Lloyd's Rep 456 at 465.
8 [1977] AC 890, 903.
9 Other decisions have emphasised the necessity for a duty to speak or follow a certain course of action, see: *The August Leonhardt* [1985] 2 Lloyd's Rep 28, 35 per Kerr LJ; *The Stolt Loyalty* [1993] 2 Lloyd's Rep 281, 289-291 per Clarke J
10 *Arctic Shipping Co Ltd v Mobilia AB, The Tatra* [1990] 2 Lloyd's Rep 51.

THE PRINCIPAL'S REPRESENTATION MUST BE MADE TO THE THIRD PARTY

It is obvious that the representation can be made to a particular T but it is also plain that it can be made to a wider group. In *Whitehead v Tuckett*,[11] Lord Ellenborough CJ spoke of a holding-out to the world[12] and, whilst this may have been acceptable for the conditions prevailing at the start of the 19th century, the notion of holding-out has been narrowed since that time. Perhaps Lord Lindley's view is preferable today in its stipulating that the holding-out must be to T 'or under such circumstances of publicity as to justify the inference that he knew of it and acted upon it'.[13] The rule that the representation must be unequivocal and the significance of P's installing A in some office or position is met again here. It is clear however from the cases already considered, that this may constitute a sufficiently proximate representation when T relies on A's usual authority.

Where P's representation is *negligent*, it is often said that P must owe a duty of care to T if he is to be bound by the representation,[14] but the circumstances from which such a duty might spring and the width of the class to which it might be owed, are both very unclear.

THE THIRD PARTY MUST RELY ON THE PRINCIPAL'S REPRESENTATION AND ACT UPON IT

There must be a causal link between P's representation and T's reliance upon it. In *Swan v North British Australasian Co Ltd*,[15] a registered owner of shares signed ten forms of transfer in order to allow his broker (A) to dispose of the shares but A used the forms to sell other shares, which he had stolen from P, to a *bona fide* T. It was held that apparent authority could not apply as the proximate cause of the loss was A's fraud, *not* P's conduct. Furthermore, on the facts, the court considered that P had not been negligent as he owed no duty of care in relation to A's execution of the forms. It follows that T cannot rely on apparent authority if, despite appearances, he does not believe that A had authority or if he chooses to rely on sources of information other than P. Moreover, T may *actually* know the extent of A's authority or be put on enquiry regarding it.

The requirement of the causal link between P and T provides a ready means by which the court may exclude P's liability: in cases such as *Swan* there is surely such a link in that P's conduct in voluntarily transferring the forms to A enables A's fraud. It is arguable therefore that there should only be a break in the chain if, for example, A found the forms in a dustbin and then perpetrated the fraud. A's fraud as the proximate cause of the loss is often accentuated, as in *Farquharson Bros & Co v King & Co*,[16] but such niceties are cold comfort to the *bona fide* T who reasonably relies on the apparent authority in A only to find that he has no remedy against P.

---

11 (1812) 15 East 400.
12 Speaking of the internal restrictions between P and A, Lord Ellenborough stressed that 'the world was not privy to that communication,' and unless T could rely on outward appearances 'in what a perilous predicament would the world stand in respect of their dealings with persons who may have secret communications with their principal' (pp 408 and 409).
13 *Farquharson Bros & Co v King & Co* [1902] AC 325, 341.
14 See eg, *Swan v North British Australasian Co Ltd* (1863) 2 H & C 175; *Mercantile Credit Co Ltd v Hamblin* [1965] 2 QB 242; *Moorgate Mercantile Co Ltd v Twitchings* [1977] AC 890.
15 (1863) 2 H & C 175.
16 [1902] AC 325; see also *Lloyd's Bank Ltd v Chartered Bank of Australia, India and China* [1929] 1 KB 40.

T must also act upon P's representation. The earliest cases demand only that the representation should be 'acted upon' by T[17] and although some of the later decisions speak of 'detriment' or 'disadvantage' to T,[18] it is clear that, today, this requirement is satisfied by T's entering into the contract with A on the faith of P's representation.[19]

Apparent authority and notice of A's lack of authority

If T has *actual* notice that A lacks authority, there can be no question of apparent authority or any reliance by T. Thus in *Overbrooke Estates Ltd v Glencombe Properties Ltd*,[20] P gave property to auctioneers (A) to sell, the sale catalogue specifying that A lacked authority to make or give any representations or warranties in respect of the property. T nevertheless asked questions of A, and A replied (incorrectly) that no compulsory purchase schemes would affect the property. It was held that the statements could not be within any apparent authority of A and T was consequently bound by the contract.

Unlike the law of real property, there is no established doctrine of constructive notice in commercial law.[1] This is because commercial transactions vary so dramatically in scale and content that it is impossible to apply a fixed standard to all of the disparate types encountered. Similarly, it is rarely practicable for T to make enquiries in commercial contracts and, in business, it may often be imprudent to do so. The speed and, often, informality of contracting, clearly militate against any detailed investigations. Finally, such enquiries are of limited *utility* in a contract for the sale of goods, for example, where there will often be no evidence of ownership and no document of title.

Although commercial law lacks a doctrine of constructive notice as such, there is the analogous notion of being 'put on enquiry' which, in this context, means that the court may deem that the circumstances were such that T should have known of A's limited authority or that his suspicions should have been aroused so that further enquiries would have been judicious. As apparent authority will vanish if T is put on enquiry, it is crucial to know when the court will consider that T should have enquired further.

The test is an objective one having regard to all the circumstances of the case.[2] As a general proposition, if A is acting within the usual authority of a person in that position, there is no duty on T to enquire but if the transaction is abnormal in any way T may be under an obligation to make enquiries. Much may turn, for example, on the status of A within an organisation and whether his acts are commensurate with his usual authority. In *Lloyd's Bank Ltd v Chartered Bank of India, Australia and China*,[3] A, an employee in a bank, was fraudulently drawing cheques on his principal and paying them into the defendant bank (T).

---

17 See eg, *Pickard v Sears* (1837) 6 Ad & El 469, 473 per Lord Denman CJ; *Freeman v Cooke* (1848) 2 ExCh 654, 663 per Parke B.
18 See eg, *Whitechurch (G) Ltd v Cavanagh* [1902] AC 117.
19 See *Freeman & Lockyer v Buckhurst Park Properties (Mangal) Ltd* [1964] 2 QB 480, 506 per Diplock LJ; *Arctic Shipping Co Ltd v Mobilia AB, The Tatra* [1990] 2 Lloyd's Rep 51, 59 per Gatehouse J.
20 [1974] 1 WLR 1335.
1 See *Manchester Trust v Furness* [1895] 2 QB 539.
2 See *Feuer Leather Corpn v Frank Johnston & Sons Ltd* [1981] Com LR 251.
3 [1929] 1 KB 40.

It was held that T was on enquiry because of the large sums involved having regard to A's position. Similarly, in *Midland Bank Ltd v Reckitt*,[4] a solicitor (A) had authority to draw cheques on his client's (P) account and apply the money for the purposes of P. A fraudulently drew cheques on P's account, signing them 'P by his attorney A', and paid them into his own account to meet an overdraft. A's bank was held to be on enquiry and liable in conversion as the form of the cheques showed that the money was not A's.[5] The fact that A is acting fraudulently and in his own interests is obviously a relevant factor to consider in deciding whether T is put on enquiry, although it is not by any means decisive as the fraud may not be apparent in any way if A is skilful in covering his tracks.

As regards dealings with agents of companies, the common law was that T had constructive notice of limitations imposed upon agents by the company's memorandum and articles of association[6] and other public documents which companies were required to deliver to the Registrar of Companies. This rule, when coupled with the notion that companies lacked capacity to enter into contracts if they were *ultra vires* the company, caused considerable hardship to third parties. The doctrine of constructive notice has been substantially amended by the Companies Act 1985, ss 35B and 711A(1) which provide that T is not bound to enquire as to whether a transaction is permitted by the company's memorandum (s 35B) and is not deemed to have notice of any matter merely because it is disclosed in a public document delivered to the Registrar of Companies (s 711A(1)). There is even wider protection given to T, when dealing in good faith with a company, in the Companies Act 1985, s 35 A(1)–(3) in that the power of its board of directors to bind it by an act or transaction (or to authorise other persons to do so) is deemed to be free of any limitations imposed by the company's memorandum and articles and T is not regarded as being in bad faith by reason only that he knows that an act is beyond the directors' powers. These amendments abrogate the external effect of the *ultra vires* doctrine allowing T to enforce the contract against the company. The new rules have not yet been worked-out by the courts in any detail and thus the 'indoor management rule'[7] may, in the interim, still have significance. This rule provides that if T deals in good faith with the board he is not affected by any internal, procedural defects of the company or a failure to comply with rules prescribed by the company's memorandum and articles for the conduct of business.

---

4   [1933] AC 1.
5   See also *Underwood (A L) Ltd v Bank of Liverpool & Martins* [1924] 1 KB 775 (the sole director of a company, who was also a main shareholder, paid cheques which were drawn in favour of the company into his own bank account. Held the bank was put on enquiry).
6   See *Ernest v Nicholls* (1857) 6 HL Cas 401.
7   The rule was established in *Royal British Bank v Turquand* (1855) 5 E & B 248.

CHAPTER 5

Usual and customary authority

Basis and classification of usual authority

There is much debate regarding the basis and legitimate scope of 'usual authority' in agency centring upon whether this type of authority can exist in its own right or whether it is simply an addendum and ornament to some of the established categories of authority. Moreover, confusion is generated by questions of terminology, as the term 'usual authority' is used in several different locations within the concept of authority.

Usual authority is primarily a sub-division of *actual, implied authority* and it thus emanates from and enlarges the scope of the actual authority which exists between P and A, as explained in Chapter 2. However, usual authority is also found within the notion of *apparent authority*. Before the scope of usual authority can be considered in detail, it is necessary to classify the differing contexts in which the nomenclature 'usual authority' is employed. It is scarcely surprising that usual authority appears in various guises as the term has a facile applicability in a broad range of situations and, like a notion of 'reasonableness', the perception of what is 'usual' can become over-extended.

USUAL AUTHORITY WITHIN ACTUAL, IMPLIED AUTHORITY

First, where A is appointed to a position which carries a usual authority, eg a managing director of a limited company, he impliedly possesses such usual authority unless P excludes it by informing A and T. Here A impliedly has the usual authority which is incidental to and necessary for the execution of his duties. In *Hely-Hutchinson v Brayhead Ltd*,[1] for example, Lord Denning MR said that when the board of directors appoints A as a managing director 'they thereby impliedly authorise him to do all such things as fall within the usual scope of that office'.[2] Similarly, in *Walker v Great Western Rly Co*,[3] it was held that a general manager of a railway company had implied authority to obtain medical assistance for a servant of the company but, in contrast, a

1 [1968] 1 QB 549.
2 [1968] 1 QB 549 at 583.
3 (1867) LR 2 Ex 228.

station master did not have such authority to obtain aid for an injured passenger in *Cox v Midland Counties Rly Co.*[4]

Second, an agent who belongs to an established trade, business or profession and is authorised to perform an act within the course of his business, impliedly has the usual authority to do whatever is incidental to and necessary for the execution of his duties. For example, a solicitor who is conducting litigation on behalf of his client (P) has implied authority to compromise the action provided that he acts *bona fide* and reasonably.[5] The cases within this classification are thus principally concerned with the practices employed by agents in the different professions and, as Powell[6] points out, their 'legal authority ... could in each case take up the space of a whole book'.

Thirdly, A has a usual or customary authority to act according to the reasonable and lawful usages of a place, market or business in which he is employed as an agent, eg the Stock Exchange. In *Robinson v Mollett*,[7] for example, a tallow broker (A) was authorised to buy tallow on behalf of P and he alleged a custom in the trade to buy, in his *own name*, both *before and after* the order of P, sufficient tallow to allot to several principals. P refused to accept the goods which A had bought in his own name and so A sold them and sued P for the difference in price but it was held that A must fail. He had no implied authority to buy in his own name and P was not bound by such a custom of which he had no knowledge for its effect 'convert[ed] a broker employed to buy, into a principal selling for himself'[8] thereby involving A in a conflict between his duty to P and his own interest as a buyer and seller of the tallow. In conclusion, it is clear that there may often be an overlap between the categories of usual authority delineated above and it should be emphasised that these divisions share the common root of actual, implied authority.

USUAL AUTHORITY WITHIN APPARENT AUTHORITY

'Usual authority' is also utilised in *apparent authority*[9] when P's representation or holding-out involves appointing A to a position which carries a usual authority, eg a senior bank manager.[10] In *Panorama Developments (Guildford) Ltd v Fidelis Furnishing Fabrics Ltd*,[11] for example, a company secretary (A) hired cars from the plaintiffs ostensibly as transport for customers visiting the defendant company's (P) factory but, in reality, he used the cars for his own purposes and the hire charges were never paid. A had ordered the cars on the company's notepaper and signed as 'company secretary'. P argued that the older decisions established that company secretaries have only a humble role with no authority to make contracts on behalf of a company. The Court of Appeal held that a

---

4 (1849) 3 Exch 268.
5 See eg *Re Newen* [1903] 1 Ch 812; *Waugh v H B Clifford & Sons Ltd* [1982] Ch 374.
6 Powell, *The Law of Agency* (2nd en, 1961), p 42.
7 (1874) LR 7 HL 802. See also eg *Cropper v Cook* (1868) LR 3 CP 194; *Scott and Horton v Godfrey* [1901] 2 KB 726; *Bailey (E) & Co Ltd v Balholm Securities Ltd* [1973] 2 Lloyd's Rep 404.
8 (1874) LR 7 HL 802, 838 per Lord Chelmsford.
9 See Ch 4.
10 See Steyn LJ's comments in *First Energy (UK) Ltd v Hungarian International Bank Ltd* [1993] 2 Lloyd's Rep 194, 201.
11 [1971] 2 QB 711.

modern company secretary had a greater authority than at the end of the 19th century and, as he was now more than 'a mere clerk',[12] he had apparent authority to hire transport and bind the company; hiring vehicles in this way was regarded as standard administrative procedure for a company secretary in the 20th century. It is thus clear that a managing director, for example, may possess actual, implied (usual) authority and apparent authority at the same time and the extent of the two authorities may coincide. But what is the position if P *withdraws* such usual authority from A but does not inform T? In the face of such an express prohibition, A cannot have an *actual, implied* authority and so it is frequently asserted that, in such a case, A must be within an apparent authority if T is to succeed against P. However there is a possibility that usual authority may exist as a species of authority in its own right, separate from both actual, implied authority and apparent authority.

USUAL AUTHORITY AS AN INDEPENDENT CATEGORY

Finally, it is arguable that there is an independent category of usual authority which neither emanates from A's actual authority as an implied authority nor exists as part of apparent authority but, instead, is based upon an external, objective assessment of the authority which agents possess by virtue of their belonging to a trade, business or profession. This authority would thus *attach* to agents of the character, type or class in question. It would also bind P in those situations where he had attempted to exclude it from A by a private restriction, provided that T could establish that he was unaware of the restriction on this usual authority and was not put on enquiry by any suspicious circumstances rendering the authority 'unusual'. Such a classification of usual authority would entail an externalised view of agency analogous to the Civil law theories which separated internal from external authority or the USA's notion of 'inherent agency power'.[13] Whether such an independent category of usual authority does exist is considered later in this chapter. Its origins can arguably be traced to the early cases concerning A's 'general authority', as many of the decisions cannot satisfactorily be said to rest exclusively upon actual or apparent authority and are considered next.

The historical background of usual authority

The somewhat obsessive categorisation above is a 20th century phenomenon with which the early decisions were not pre-occupied. As commerce began to expand and become more impersonal, there was a need to ascertain the degree of external authority which A might possess and upon which T might reasonably rely, beyond the boundaries of A's *actual* authority to which P expressly consented. The tension is evident in the developing law between the

---

12 [1971] 2 QB 711 at 716, per Lord Denning MR. See also Staughton LJ's comments in *United Bank of Kuwait Ltd v Hammoud* [1988] 1 WLR 1051,1063, that he preferred to consider modern expert evidence regarding 'the ordinary authority of a solicitor' rather than referring to 'elderly decisions'.
13 See Ch 4 on apparent authority.

internal P–A relationship (with P's asserting the restrictions on A's authority) and the external A–T relationship (with T's asserting his justifiable reliance upon usual practices/appearances). Several points emerge from the courts' quest to explain and rationalise A's external authority and the decisions disclose a gradual and necessary progression from a simple consideration of the internal aspect of agency (P–A) to an evaluation of the external aspect (A–T).

As discussed in Chapter 1, the Civil law systems insisted on the rigid separation of the internal and external aspects of agency. Although there was clearly an awareness of this division in the common law, it was never acknowledged as precisely as in the Civil law. Instead, the late 18th and early 19th century decisions on apparent authority, discussed in Chapter 4, demand unequivocally that T's interests must be protected before those of P and the cases embody a robust commercial realism. Later in the 19th century, P's liability in apparent authority was explained, somewhat uncomfortably, in terms of his creating and consenting to A's having such an authority. This perspective consequently sees the internal and the external aspects of agency as a single, unbroken thread which leads back to P – a view which means that some fictionalising is clearly necessary in explaining A's external authority, especially where it is held to encompass acts which have been expressly prohibited by P.

The roots of usual authority are to be found in decisions which pre-date the inductive cases on apparent authority but they are part of the same quest to explain and rationalise A's external authority. Once agents became a recognised facet of mercantile law, there was a natural aspiration to chart the functions of different *categories* of agent. Consequently, many early cases sought to ascertain the practices and scope of authority possessed by the various commercial agents which began to emerge as a new phenomenon in the rapidly developing commerce from the end of the 17th century onwards, eg factors and brokers.[14] A prominent feature in this classification process was the important and pervasive distinction between 'general' and 'special' agents.[15] Paley[16] emphasised that a general agent was empowered 'to bind his employer by all acts within the scope of his employment, and that power cannot be limited by any private order or direction *not known to the party dealing with the agent*'. On the other hand, a special agent was one 'who is employed about one specific act, or certain specific acts only, [and] does not bind his employer, unless his authority be strictly pursued; *for it is the business of the party dealing with him to examine his authority*'.[17] In order to illustrate these types of agent, Paley[18] explained that if P kept livery stables and instructed his agent to sell a horse and not to give any warranty regarding it but A nevertheless warranted its soundness, P would be liable as A was within his general authority. But P would not be liable if he sent a stranger to a fair to sell a horse with express instructions not to give warranties

---

14 See Stoljar, *The Law of Agency* (1961), Chs 10 and 11; Munday,'A Legal History of the Factor' (1977) 6 Anglo-Am LR 221.
15 The notion of 'general authority' begins to appear at the end of the 17th century and extends through the 18th into the early 19th centuries: see eg *Boulton v Arlsden* (1697) 3 Salk 234; *Thorold v Smith* (1706) 11 Mod Rep 87, 88 per Holt CJ; *Nickson v Brohan* (1712) 10 Mod Rep 109, 110 per Parker CJ; *Fenn v Harrison* (1790) 3 Term Rep 757; *Runquist v Ditchell* (1799) 3 Esp 64; *Whitehead v Tuckett* (1812) 15 East 400.
16 *A Treatise on the Law of Principal and Agent* (3rd edn, 1833).
17 *A Treatise on the Law of Principal and Agent*, pp 199-202 (emphasis added).
18 *A Treatise on the Law of Principal and Agent*, p 203.

for here A would have only a particular authority. The separation of general from particular agents had only a limited potential for development, however, and a moment's reflection reveals two flaws in this analysis. First, the process by which agents were to be alloted to either of the categories was indistinct and, certainly from T's point of view, A's status might be far from obvious. Second, when commerce increased in complexity, volume and pace, it became quite unrealistic to demand that T should make positive enquiries of A in order to ascertain his authority. In *Hicks v Hankin*,[19] for example, P objected that A had gone beyond the stipulated price in purchasing malt and, as A was a special agent, P was not bound. It was held that A had a discretion to exceed the prices fixed by P and was thus not in the category of a special agent. P was therefore bound by A's purchase from T.

The notion that A could possess 'general authority' was thus a significant feature in the assessment of his his external authority: if apparent authority was premised on P's holding-out, the ascertainment of general authority necessitated an objective scrutiny of A's status and position. At the start of the 19th century, the problems inherent in an increasingly impersonal pattern of commerce were exemplified in *Whitehead v Tuckett*,[20] a progressive decision which was also seminal in the development of A's objective, external authority. In *Whitehead*, brokers (A) in Liverpool bought and sold sugar on behalf of wholesale grocers in Bristol (P). When the market was low, A had an unlimited authority regarding quantity and price but, at other times, P imposed a check on prices. A's authority was contained in letters from P in which the sugar market and its prices were discussed in some detail, P's instructions being rather ambivalent overall. The dispute concerned 50 hogsheads of sugar sold by A, *in his own name*, to the plaintiff (T), below the minimum price stipulated by P in the correspondence. Some sugar had been delivered to T but the remainder was at A's warehouse at the time of A's bankruptcy. P had not been paid by A and so he refused to deliver the remaining sugar to T on the basis that a broker had only a special, not a general, authority and, as such, he had exceeded his authority specified in the letters. It was held that A's sale was valid as he had a general authority and P's letters gave him a wide discretion. A verdict was thus found for the plaintiff, T.

Several crucial points emanate from the judgments in *Whitehead*. First, it is arguable that the decision was based upon A's actual, implied authority as emphasis was placed upon the width of A's discretion/authority expressed in P's letters. That would be a facile interpretation. The far-sighted judgments clearly accepted that what really mattered was the general authority as understood by T. Bayley J's short judgment is the most sophisticated in that it instantly recognises the external role of 'common brokers for the sale of sugars' and that it would be 'a fraud on the public' if the validity of the sale to T were denied.[1] The decision was thus so crucial precisely because it took the first, faltering steps towards acknowledging that an objective evaluation should be made of A's authority, rather than simply enunciating the subjective, actual authority possessed by differing types of agent (this being the argument urged by P's counsel). It is evident, however, that the judges had not then resolved the precise basis of P's liability in this situation. Second,

---

19 (1802) 4 Esp 114.
20 (1812) 15 East 400.
 1 (1812) 15 East 400 at 411.

as P was undisclosed, modern legal analysis would deny that *Whitehead* could be a case of apparent authority in A, for an undisclosed principal cannot make any representation to T regarding agency. Finally, and most controversially, it is arguable that A was expressly prohibited from selling at the price obtained[2] and that, consequently, this could not be a case of actual, implied authority. This analysis would leave *Whitehead* as a decision based upon an independent, externalised category of usual authority as exemplified in *Watteau v Fenwick*, considered below. The modern preference is, undoubtedly, to deny the existence of usual authority as a discrete division of authority and to compress all cases within either actual or apparent authority, the latter category consequently encompassing all situations where A acts in contravention of his actual authority. It must now be asked whether it is possible and prudent for usual authority to exist as an independent category of authority.

The enigma of *Watteau v Fenwick*: is there an independent category of usual authority?

The difficulty here is to decide whether A might bind P where he has neither actual authority (of any type) nor apparent authority to perform the act in question. Might A possess some form of usual authority stemming from his *position* as an agent or emanating from the very *fact* that an agency exists? Situations where this type of usual authority might need to be invoked are rare: A would have to perform an act prohibited by P thus excluding any category of actual authority but A's apparent authority should arguably provide a broad enough framework in which to assess P's potential liability. At the outset therefore, there should be no eager embrace of usual authority as a general panacea for curing a host of problems, for such a notion may be neither necessary nor practicable.

The case at the eye of the storm is *Watteau v Fenwick*.[3] There the owner of a beerhouse, Humble (A), transferred it to the defendant firm of brewers (P) but A remained as P's manager, the licence being in A's name and his was the name painted over the door. It was agreed between P and A that A would have no authority to buy any goods for the business except bottled ales and mineral waters, all other goods being supplied by P. A nevertheless ordered cigars and Bovril for the business from the plaintiff (T) who, upon discovering P's existence, sued P to recover the price of the goods delivered. It was argued that, as A possessed no actual authority of any sort, P could only be liable on the basis of apparent authority, but that an appearance of authority could not possibly be substantiated as P was undisclosed and was unable to perform any acts which held out A as his *agent*. Despite this argument, judgment was given for the plaintiff (T). Wills J decided that:

> 'The principal is liable for all the acts of the agent which are within the authority usually confided to an agent of that character, notwithstanding limitations, as between the principal and the agent, put upon that authority. It is said that it is only so where there has been a holding out of authority ... But I do not think so'.[4]

---

2 P's instructions to A were indecisive. Lord Ellenborough CJ was not prepared to find 'any general prohibition' against a sale or 'absolute limitation' on the terms of sale (p 408) and Le Blanc J thought it 'unnecessary' to consider the situation of an agent's exceeding his authority (p 411). The two other judges did not mention the point.
3 [1893] 1 QB 346.
4 [1893] 1 QB 346 at 348-349.

The judge relied on an analogy with the law relating to dormant partners (which is now recognised as incorrect[5]) and the earlier, unclear decision in *Edmunds v Bushell and Jones*.[6] There was thus no phalanx of previous, unequivocal authority supporting the *Watteau* reasoning and the decision has been followed only once, on almost identical facts, in *Kinahan & Co v Parry*.[7] Moreover, *Watteau* has not found favour in Canada,[8] has been doubted in Australia,[9] and was criticised recently in England by Bingham J as 'a somewhat puzzling case' which he would be 'extremely wary of applying'.[10] On the other hand, in many significant USA decisions where A had no actual or apparent authority, the courts have applied similar principles to those of *Watteau*,[11] and its reasoning has been adopted wholeheartedly in the USA's *Restatement*, with the notion of 'inherent agency power'. The *Restatement, Second, Agency* § 8A provides:

> 'Inherent agency power is a term used...to indicate the power of an agent which is derived not from authority, apparent authority or estoppel, but solely from the agency relation and exists for the protection of persons harmed by or dealing with a servant or other agent'.[12]

A CRITIQUE OF *WATTEAU*

In view of the divergent opinions above, the merits and demerits of the *Watteau* doctrine must be considered.

---

5 See Powell, *The Law of Agency* (2nd edn, 1961), pp 76-77.
6 (1865) LR 1 QB 97. In *Edmunds*, A carried on P's business in A's name. Although P had forbidden A to draw or accept bills of exchange, A accepted a bill and it was held that P was liable on it. The short judgments contain references to both apparent authority and A's being 'an ostensible principal' (p 100). It is impossible to ascertain the precise basis of liability in this decision but it does not set forth unequivocally any independent notion of usual authority.
7 [1910] 2 KB 389. The decision was reversed on the ground that there was no evidence that the whisky supplied was for P's use and not for A personally: [1911] 1 KB 459.
8 Two decisions refused to follow *Watteau*: *McLaughlin v Gentles* (1919) 51 DLR 383 (Supreme Court of Ontario) and *Sign-O-Lite Plastics Ltd v Metropolitan Life Insurance Co* [1990] 73 DLR (4th) 541 (British Columbia Court of Appeal); see Fridman, 'Case Comment' (1991) 70 Can Bar Rev 329. *McLaughlin* preferred to follow the decision of the Privy Council in *Miles v McIlwraith* (1883) 8 App Cas 120, where there was no hint of any reasoning analogous to that in *Watteau*.
9 See *International Paper Co v Spicer* (1906) 4 CLR 739 (High Court of Australia).
10 *Rhodian River Shipping Co SA v Halla Maritime Corpn, The Rhodian River* [1984] 1 Lloyd's Rep 373, 379-380.
11 See eg, *Thurber & Co v Anderson* 88 Ill 167 (1878) (P placed his son (A) in charge of his grocery store and saloon but ordered him not to make any purchases. A ordered imported ale and cigars from T, by mail, in P's name. It was held that P was liable because 'by permitting another to hold himself out to the world as his agent, the principal adopts his acts ...' (p 169)); *Hubbard v Tenbrook* 124 Pa 291 (1889) (A managed P's business as an apparent owner but with instructions not to buy goods on credit; P was liable to T when A nevertheless bought goods in disregard of the limitation. Mitchell J said: 'A man conducting an apparently prosperous and profitable business obtains credit thereby, and his creditors have a right to suppose that his profits go into his assets for their protection in case of a pinch or an unfavorable turn in the business. To allow an undisclosed principal to absorb the profits, and then when the pinch comes, to escape responsibility on the ground of orders to his agent not to buy on credit, would be a plain fraud on the public. No exact precedent has been cited. None is needed.'); *Kidd v Thomas A Edison, Inc* 239 F 405 (SDNY); affd 242 F 923 (2d Cir 1917).
12 See also *Restatement, Second, Agency* §§ 140, 161 comment a, 194, 195.

Should A's authority be based on actual and apparent authority only?

The primary criticism of *Watteau* is that there is neither scope nor need in agency doctrine for anything other than actual and apparent authority.[13] Historically, this appears to be too narrow an appraisal; as seen in *Whitehead v Tuckett*,[14] the current categories of authority were not always so entrenched. For its adherents, this criticism really rests on A's having no *acceptable* authority because, in view of the prohibition on his buying goods for the business, A's actual authority was non-existent and P did not hold-out A as his agent. However, *Watteau* recognises this fact and clearly considers that A's authority stems from the agency relationship itself and that, in apportioning risks and liability, it is unacceptable to allow an undisclosed principal to contract via A *and* take advantage of the secret limitation on A's authority should it suit him to do so. If the *Watteau* approach were to be followed generally, this type of authority in agency would correspond to vicarious liability in tort, A's usual authority thus being substituted for the employee's 'course of employment'. Here, the analogy with vicarious liability is apt because that notion is not dependent upon the *victim's* knowledge of whether or not the employee is within the scope of his employment and, equally important, the employer can be vicariously liable for the employee's acts which he had expressly prohibited. Certainly many commentators see a connection between *Watteau* and vicarious liability[15] and, in the USA, the fusion of these notions is the foundation and justification of 'inherent agency power'.[16] Although many of the early English agency decisions in this context favoured an externalised view of A's authority with P's concomitant responsibility for A, this is not the overall course which has been followed by the law.[17]

Does *Watteau* expose P to 'unlimited responsibility'?

It has been suggested that *Watteau* exposes the undisclosed principal 'to the prospect of unlimited responsibility'.[18] Again, this broad criticism must be treated with caution. As Seavey[19] pointed out, P's liability for A's unauthorised acts ultimately rests on public policy. It is arguably appropriate policy that P, the instigator and beneficiary of the agency relationship, should be liable in the

---

13   See *Bowstead & Reynolds on Agency* (16th edn, 1996), pp 109 and 418; Cf Powell (*The Law of Agency* (2nd edn, 1961), pp 73-78) and Stoljar (*The Law of Agency* (1961), pp 55-59) both of whom supported *Watteau* unequivocally. See generally Montrose, 'Liability of Principal for Acts Exceeding Actual and Apparent Authority' (1939) 17 Can Bar Rev 693.
14   (1812) 15 East 400.
15   See Seavey, 'The Rationale of Agency' (1920) 29 Yale LJ 859, 880-881; Seavey, 'Agency Powers' (1948) 1 Okla L Rev 3, 10-20; Mearns, 'Vicarious Liability for Agency Contracts' (1962) 48 Va L Rev 50; Wright, 'The American Law Institute's Restatement of Contracts and Agency' (1936) 1 U Toronto LJ 17, 40-47; Treitel, *The Law of Contract* (10th edn, 1999), p 663; *Anson's Law of Contract* (27th edn, 1998), p 630.
16   See *Restatement, Second, Agency* § 8A (quoted supra); see also Fishman, 'Inherent Agency Power – Should Enterprise Liability Apply To Agents' Unauthorized Contracts?' (1987) 19 Rutgers LJ 1 (the author considers that inherent agency power 'does not provide sufficient benefits to outweigh the confusion which has resulted from its application' and that the classification of P's liability as 'enterprise liability' is unwarranted; consequently, he concludes that the traditional rules of authority strike a correct balance between P and T).
17   But see Lord Wilberforce's comments in his dissenting speech in *Branwhite v Worcester Works Finance Ltd* [1969] 1 AC 552, 587: 'It may be that some wider conception of vicarious responsibility other than that of agency, as normally understood, may have to be recognised in order to accommodate some of the more elaborate cases which now arise when there are two persons who become mutually involved or associated in one side of a transaction'.
18   Fridman, *Law of Agency* (7th edn, 1996), p 75.
19   'The Rationale of Agency' (1920) 29 Yale LJ 859, 861.

Watteau situation – certainly T's perception is that there is no need to make enquiries regarding the existence or scope of A's authority or position. Care must be taken, however, with broad arguments of risk allocation and public policy because both the imposition and denial of liability may have negative effects. Montrose[20] emphasised that if P is broadly liable, commerce might be restricted because of the fear of employing agents but, in the absence of P's liability, commerce might likewise be impeded because of a reluctance to deal with agents.

It could be argued, however, that *Watteau* should correctly be regarded as a relatively limited decision and that the controversy which it has always courted has served only to elevate and extend its *ratio decidendi*. Accordingly, the decision might properly be confined to situations where A manages the business of an undisclosed principal and to goods which are usually supplied for that business.[1] It is clear that an undisclosed principal cannot ratify A's unauthorised contracts[2] and thus T cannot allege ratification against P in the *Watteau* situation. It would be grossly unfair if P could evade liability when, as in *Watteau*, T's claim was for goods delivered 'over some years'.[3] It follows that, as an undisclosed principal cannot hold-out A as his agent, the *Watteau* notion of usual authority is the only way in which the innocent tradesman can make the undisclosed principal liable for the unauthorised acts of A. If *Watteau* is thus reined-in, the decision does not by any means implicate P in 'unlimited responsibility' for A.

Is *Watteau* premised upon apparent *ownership*?

As *Watteau* cannot be premised upon apparent authority in A,[4] it has been argued by some commentators that it is justifiably based on the idea that P created *apparent ownership* in A.[5] The cases where an owner may lose title to his goods by creating

---

20 'Liability of Principal for Acts Exceeding Actual and Apparent Authority' (1939) 17 Can Bar Rev 693,711-712.

1 The claim was successful for cigars and Bovril which 'would usually be supplied' but the claim for 'other articles' was disallowed: *Watteau v Fenwick* [1893] 1 QB 346, 346 and 348. See also *Kinahan & Co v Parry* [1910] 2 KB 389, a decision in which *Watteau* was followed; on appeal ([1911] 1 KB 459) it was held that P, an hotel owner, could not be liable for whisky bought by his manager (A) without his authority because it could not be established that the whisky had been bought for use in the hotel rather than for A's personal use; *Jerome v Bentley & Co* [1952] 2 All ER 114, 116 (Donovan J emphasised that *Watteau* could not apply to private individuals who carried on 'no calling at all' but that 'beerhouse managers are a well-known class of agent [to whom] it is easy to apply the phrase "the authority usually confided to an agent of that character"'.

2 *Keighley, Maxsted & Co v Durant* [1901] AC 240.

3 There is no indication in *Watteau* that P might sue on the contract, eg for non-delivery of the goods. See Ferson, 'Bases for Master's Liability and for Principal's Liability to Third Persons' (1951) 4 Vand L Rev 260, 280 who argues that *Watteau* is correct purely on the basis that P used/sold the goods supplied by T and, following such an act of dominion over the goods, P should be 'deemed bound in a contract to pay the invoice price'.

4 Goodhart and Hamson, 'Undisclosed Principals in Contract' [1932] 4 CLJ 320, 336, describe *Watteau* as an 'excellent example of a pure estoppel by conduct'. This was castigated by Wright (1935) 13 Can Bar Rev 116, 120: 'Naturally there was no apparent authority ... as the fact of agency was unsuspected ... Such an unwarranted use of "estoppel" seems difficult to justify'.

5 Mechem, *Outlines of the Law of Agency* (4th edn, 1952), pp 114-116; Hornby, 'The Usual Authority of an Agent' [1961] CLJ 239; Conant,'The Objective Theory of Agency: Apparent Authority and the Estoppel Of Apparent Ownership' (1968) 47 Neb L Rev 678; Tettenborn, 'Agents, Business Owners and Estoppel' [1998] 57 CLJ 274 (the author contends that *Watteau* is not premised upon agency principles but on P's representation that P and A were the same legal entity and thus existed as one business enterprise. This view has something in common with the notion in the USA of 'inherent agency power' (see the *Restatement, Second, Agency* § 8A, as that concept similarly renounces any connection with authority in agency).

apparent ownership[6] in another would therefore be extended to situations where P instals A as apparent owner of his business. As a general proposition, there must be a stronger case for making P liable where he has installed A as the apparent owner of his business than where he has permitted A merely to control his business as an apparent agent. If P deliberately chooses to remain undisclosed and run his business under the disguise of an apparent owner he must surely be deemed to accept the inherent and extensive risks of such a venture. This analysis is superficially attractive but, as emphasised cogently by Hetherington,[7] it affords no logical basis for limiting what the apparent owner of a *business* may do. The author emphasised that, in this context, apparent ownership 'suggests that whether the apparent owner buys cigars or sells the tavern (which the "owner of the business" may surely do), the principal should be bound'.[8]

However, the decision in *Lloyds and Scottish Finance Ltd v Williamson*[9] stresses the risks inherent in apparent ownership and, more importantly, its juristic basis has much in common with *Watteau*. The plaintiff owner (O) of a Jaguar saloon car delivered it to a car dealer (D) with instructions to sell it at any price D could obtain, with the proviso that D should account to O for £625. D sold the car on terms that the buyer (B) should pay the price to a third party (T), to whom D was indebted. Both B and T were *bona fide* and had no reason to suspect that D was not the owner of the car. O's argument was that the payment of the price to a third party (T) instead of paying it to the seller of the car (D), meant that the sale was not in the ordinary course of business of a mercantile agent and thus B should obtain no title to the car under the Factors Act 1889. The Court of Appeal held that B obtained a good title to the car. D was authorised to sell as an apparent owner/principal and not as an agent or factor and thus whether the sale was in the ordinary course of business was relevant only to the *bona fides* of the buyer. Moreover, the court stressed that the decision was *not* based upon estoppel or apparent authority but, instead, it was premised upon the common law concept of apparent ownership and the doctrine of the undisclosed principal.

Can *Watteau* be justified as part of the doctrine of the undisclosed principal?

Although *Bowstead & Reynolds*[10] concludes that, as in apparent authority, the *Watteau* remedy is available only to T, this would not necessarily be so if *Watteau* were to be regarded as a species of actual authority, based upon an externalised notion of usual authority. Using this analysis, P would be able to intervene on the contract as an undisclosed principal and sue and be sued within the existing and conventional rules of that doctrine, ie A must have actual authority from P and none of the other limitations on the undisclosed principal's intervention must be applicable. This view would, again, demand that the notion of actual authority be extended to cover the *Watteau* situation as it is beyond doubt that an agent for an undisclosed principal must act within his actual authority.[11]

---

6 See Ch 18 where this topic is considered in depth.
7 'Trends in Enterprise Liability: Law and the Unauthorized Agent' (1966) 19 Stanford L Rev 76.
8 (1966) 19 Stanford L Rev 76 at 110.
9 [1965] 1 WLR 404.
10 *Bowstead & Reynolds on Agency* (16th edn, 1996), Art 78, p 419.
11 *Keighley, Maxsted & Co v Durant* [1901] AC 240.

It has also been suggested that *Watteau* is justifiable because, on the facts of the decision, A would have had apparent authority had there been no veil obscuring P from view.[12] This encapsulates the overall spirit and intent of Wills J's judgment in *Watteau* as the judge was adamant that, in cases where P is undisclosed, a secret limitation on A's authority must not prevail and deprive T of a remedy. However, the suggestion that A ought to possess apparent authority or would have possessed it in different circumstances does not, of course, justify the decision within the orthodox rules of agency.

Is the *Watteau* reasoning too vague and elusive?

Finally, it is alleged that 'the supposed doctrine is too vague to be satisfactorily employed'[13] and it must be admitted that the breadth of the rule militates against its certain application. That an agent might possess an externalised, usual authority, was a notion which could be applied successfully to commercial agents in the 18th and 19th centuries but, in modern, corporate commerce, it is difficult to assert that agents have any 'usual' authority based upon an objective assessment of their *type or class*. For example, in *Hely-Hutchinson v Brayhead Ltd*,[14] Roskill J considered that there was no 'implied authority in a chairman of a company, merely by reason of his office, to do what Mr Richards did ... I do not think that mere status, derived from the holding of a particular office such as chairman or managing director or chief executive, of itself implies an authority which would not otherwise exist'.[15]

That being said, there is innate common sense in the distinction between general and special agents at least as a starting point from which to develop rules[16] and, as explained above, usual authority exists as a notion elsewhere within authority where it is neither criticised nor ascertainment of its scope thought to be insurmountable. But in those other instances usual authority is merely an adjunct to A's actual authority or a component of apparent authority[17] and does not exist in the somewhat amorphous way envisaged in *Watteau*, where P was undisclosed.

---

12 Kerr, *The Law of Agency* (1972), pp 194-195.
13 *Bowstead & Reynolds on Agency* (16th edn, 1996), p 418; see also p 109 ('too vague to serve as a systematic basis for the formation and prediction of legal decisions'); Hornby, 'The Usual Authority of an Agent' [1961] CLJ 239, 246-248.
14 [1968] 1 QB 549.
15 [1968] 1 QB 549 at 560.
16 Seavey considered that there was 'considerable business sense in the classification' ('The Rationale of Agency' (1920) 29 Yale LJ 859, 883), the distinction is preserved in the *Restatement, Second, Agency* §3 and Stoljar thought it 'an indispensable concept provided it is tied up with apparent authority' (*The Law of Agency* (1961), p 49). Cf *Bowstead & Reynolds on Agency* (16th edn, 1996), Arts 29 and 30; Powell, *The Law of Agency* (2nd edn, 1961), pp 30-31. Although Powell supported *Watteau* (see pp 73-78) he considered that 'clear-cut distinctions between general and special agents, even if they are capable of being made (which is doubtful), tend only to over-simplify and thereby to confuse the issues which are involved in particular cases' (p 31).
17 In *Egyptian International Foreign Trade Co v Soplex Wholesale Supplies Ltd and PS Refson & Co Ltd, The Raffaella* [1985] 2 Lloyd's Rep 36, 45 Kerr LJ emphasised that, in apparent authority, the 'label' given to A within a company is of limited value in ascertaining his authority. See also the cases on apparent authority in Ch 4.

CONCLUSION

The *Watteau* concept of usual authority is regarded by many as unacceptable when it is applied in the situation of an undisclosed principal. However, given the existence of the doctrine of the undisclosed principal there is, as Mechem[18] suggested, no unreasonable extension of it in 'holding that if a principal actually puts forward an agent to act as an ostensible principal in a certain position, he should be held responsible for all the acts which such a position usually and naturally justifies, regardless of what his private instructions may have been. The doctrine of necessary and usual powers does not rest upon estoppel'. It is plain, however, that if this reasoning were to take root in English law, there would have to be an acceptance of the broad theory that P is primarily responsible for A's acts.

Without doubt, *Watteau* represents an under-developed form of vicarious liability in agency law. The elaboration of such an externalised, usual authority, could ameliorate the less attractive aspects of apparent authority which are over-protective of P but, again, this would entail a shift of emphasis in that T's reliance on reasonable appearances would have to assume much greater significance than it does now. The decision in *Watteau v Fenwick* may be just, reasonable and meritorious, but it simply cannot be allocated a place within current orthodoxy and it thus persists within agency law as a peripheral mutation.

18   'The Liability of an Undisclosed Principal' (1910) 23 Harv L Rev 590, 599-601.

CHAPTER 6

Agency of necessity

Introduction

Agency of necessity refers to those situations in which a person is met with an emergency where the property or other interests of another are endangered and it thus becomes necessary to act on behalf of that other in order to preserve his property or other interests. How should the law view A's allegedly necessitous action? Broadly speaking there are two alternative approaches to necessity either one of which the law could adopt.

The first is to encourage A's initiative by authorising his reasonable actions in an emergency, possibly going further and imposing a *duty* on him to act responsibly in such crises. It can scarcely be doubted that, within an *existing* agency, most principals would welcome such a rule which provides a rational basis for the protection of their interests by A, the person best-fitted to make a reasoned, balanced decision on their behalf.

Second, it is possible to limit drastically the definition of an emergency to extreme cases and then impose rigorous conditions on the operation of A's authority to act for P in such crises. This approach guards P against unscrupulous agents who might seek to justify their actions in the name of necessity, but there is a danger that the law may become too zealous in guarding P's interests with the consequence that A is characterised as little more than an automaton. By and large, English law adopts this second alternative, consequently exhibiting a conspicuous bias in favour of protecting ownership and effectively divorcing legal from moral obligation.

Agency of necessity is a commodious compartment containing an assortment of situations connected only by the notion of necessitous action.[1] The rules of agency of necessity are derived primarily from the authority of the shipmaster to act in emergencies as agent of the shipowner and cargo owners in order to preserve the ship and her cargo. Its origins are also to be found in the notion that the acceptor of a bill of exchange for the honour of the drawer has an entitlement to be reimbursed by the person for whom he pays. The rules have been extended to carriers by land and apply, with less certainty, to other bailees. The deserted wife's right to pledge her husband's credit for necessaries to support

---

1 See Williston, 'Agency of Necessity' (1944) 22 Can Bar Rev 492; Treitel, 'Agency of Necessity' (1954) 3 U Western Aust L Rev 1.

herself was, formerly, classed as agency of necessity and, currently, agency arising from cohabitation is within this category.

Finally, a person may assume an obligation on behalf of another in an emergency or preserve that other's property in such a situation, eg a man repairs his absent neighbour's house when the roof is damaged in a gale. Here the repairer would know the neighbour but there may also be instances where one person acts on behalf of a stranger in attempting to save that stranger's property from adversity, eg a man finds straying cattle and feeds and stables them. These situations correspond to that of *negotiorum gestio* in Roman law where the *gestor* who acted voluntarily to preserve the property of another in emergencies had a right to reimbursement for expenses incurred or damage suffered in performing the service. In marked contrast to the ethical Roman law, English law treats the *gestor* as an intermeddler and generally denies him any compensation for his services. The English perception is summarised in Bowen LJ's notorious admonition that 'liabilities are not to be forced upon people behind their backs, any more than you can confer a benefit upon a man against his will'.[2] The tenor of this comment has a significance beyond *negotiorum gestio*, however, as it is arguable that Bowen LJ's statement characterises English law's approach to agency of necessity generally.[3] There can be little doubt that the law conscientiously guards against any undue extension of the notion for fear that, under the guise of necessity, A's authority might become all-embracing thus making him, in effect, a principal. Accordingly, the law has developed stringent conditions for successfully establishing an agency of necessity, these being considered later.

The historical development of agency of necessity

The most prolific source of agency of necessity is that of the shipmaster's authority. In order to preserve the ship or her cargo in an emergency the master may sell,[4] hypothecate[5] or jettison[6] the cargo. He has similarly wide powers in relation to the ship and may sell,[7] hypothecate[8] or enter into a salvage agreement regarding the vessel.[9]

---

2   *Falcke v Scottish Imperial Insurance Co* (1886) 34 Ch D 234, 248; see Zimmermann, *The Law of Obligations* (1990), pp 435-436, where it is suggested that this approach 'reflects the traditional individualism and the reserved mentality of the English people' but that the Roman principle was 'a prime example of the sober sense of realism with which the Roman lawyers were able to attune law and social ethics to each other and, more specifically, to balance the individualistic interest in not having one's affairs interfered with and the interests of society in encouraging ethically desirable activities on behalf of others'.

3   See *Sachs v Miklos* [1948] 2 KB 23 (considered later) where Lord Goddard CJ commenced his judgment by stating: 'This action appears to be a warning against doing a friendly act. Its moral is: never do anything for anybody when asked without going to solicitors and having a formal agreement drawn up' (p 34).

4   *Australasian Steam Navigation Co v Morse* (1872) LR 4 PC 222.

5   *The Gratitudine* (1801) 3 Ch Rob 240

6   *The Gratitudine* (1801) 3 Ch Rob 240; *Burton v English* (1883) 12 QBD 218.

7   *The Australia* (1859) 13 Moo PCC 132.

8   *The Karnak* (1869) LR 2 PC 505.

9   *The Renpor* (1883) 8 PD 115.

The maritime cases are a specialised group where, by any standards, there is often a real emergency. However, the argument that A's actions are justifiable as a consequence of his being placed in a necessitous situation is clearly one that is capable of wide application and it was inevitable that the courts would eventually have to decide whether the notion of 'necessity' might legitimately be extended beyond the established categories of emergency and develop as a broad principle within the rules of authority in agency. A watershed was reached in *Hawtayne v Bourne*,[10] when the court had to consider the possible extension of the shipmaster cases to an alleged emergency on dry land. In *Hawtayne*, a manager of a mine (A) was placed in an invidious position: in order to avoid a threat by unpaid miners to seize and sell the materials and equipment belonging to a mine (warrants of distress had been obtained), A borrowed money, on behalf of P, from the plaintiff bank and paid the arrears of wages. It was held that A had no authority to bind P, Parke B refusing to extend the shipmaster and bills of exchange cases.[11] The court was clearly concerned that A's authority should not be enlarged to the extent that he became, in effect, the principal, and emphasised that, on the facts, A could and should have contacted P before borrowing the money.

The decision in *Gwilliam v Twist*[12] was just as restrictive as that in *Hawtayne*. In *Gwilliam*, the drunken driver (A) of the defendant's (P) omnibus was prevented from driving by a policeman, the driver then authorising a passer-by, who happened to be a former employee of the defendant, to drive the bus the quarter of a mile to the depot. The plaintiff was injured through the negligence of the substitute driver. It was held that, as P could have been contacted, there was no necessity for A to employ the substitute driver and P was not liable, Lord Esher MR reaffirming that agency of necessity was 'confined to certain well-known exceptional cases'.[13] These important yet confining decisions ensured that agency of necessity would remain tethered and never develop into a broad and useful notion as an expansion of the agent's authority.[14]

Despite this narrowness of approach, agency of necessity made some progress and was successfully extended to carriers by land although many of the cases were decided upon the basis of implied authority in an existing agency relationship and were consequently free of the emotionally charged connotations of 'necessity'. The first decision concerning carriers by land is one where A entered into a contract in his own name to preserve P's property and then sought reimbursement from P. In *Great Northern Rly Co v Swaffield*,[15] a station master was held to have authority to make a contract for the stabling of a horse when its owner did not arrive to collect it and, having paid the livery charges, the station master was able to recover the amount of such charges from the owner. The *Swaffield* decision was significant in that the shipmaster cases were extended

---

10 (1841) 7 M & W 595, 598.
11 See also Parke B's restrictive views in *Cox v Midland Counties Rly Co* (1849) 3 Exch 268 (a stationmaster was unable to bind the railway company by contract to provide surgical attention for an injured passenger).
12 [1895] 2 QB 84.
13 [1895] 2 QB 84 at 87.
14 Commenting upon *Hawtayne*, Lord Chorley considered that 'the green shoots of this promising doctrine were glared upon with Medusa-like effect by Parke B, archpriest of the legalistic school, and withered' ('Liberal Trends in Present-Day Commercial Law' (1939) 3 MLR 272, 275).
15 (1874) LR 9 Exch 132.

expressly to cover this terrene situation. Similarly, in *Sims & Co v Midland Rly Co*,[16] a quantity of butter was sent by rail to the plaintiffs (P) with no time specified in the consignment note during which delivery should take place. During the transit there was a strike of railway workers and the defendants could not send the butter on to its destination. The station master at Sharpness found that the butter was 'oozing away' in the August heat and, acting on the instructions of the defendants, he sold the butter. In an action to recover damages for breach of contract to deliver the goods, it was held that the defendants were not liable. The decision in *Sims* was that the strike had to be considered in calculating what was a reasonable time for delivery and so the reasoning was not based upon agency of necessity. However, Scrutton J opined that, although it would be rare for the conditions of agency of necessity to exist in carriage by land, the necessity rules were applicable to such carriers. Accordingly, if the question had fallen to be decided on the facts of *Sims*, the judge thought it essential to consider 'whether there was a real business necessity for the sale in view of the probable duration of the strike and the nature of the goods, and whether it was possible from a business point of view to communicate with the consignees and obtain their instructions before the sale'.[17]

The importance of communication with P was reiterated in *Springer v Great Western Rly Co*,[18] where tomatoes belonging to the plaintiff (P) and in course of transit were delayed by a strike. As they were deteriorating and 'half cooked',[19] they were sold by the defendants (A). It was held that communication with P was possible on the facts and it was A's duty to do so. As P would have collected the goods had he been informed of the position, A was liable in damages. In relation to carriers by land, it is likely that such emergencies are considered as arising only in relation to perishable goods and livestock and will not be extended[20] although, in principle, goods other than perishables may be equally subject to calamities as the cases below illustrate.

Beyond carriers by land, it is difficult to assess how far agency of necessity may extend but there seems little doubt that bailees and consignees of goods are within its ambit. In *Prager v Blatspiel, Stamp and Heacock Ltd*,[1] both P and A were fur merchants, P in Bucharest and A in London in possession of P's skins. Because of the First World War it became impossible for A to send the skins to P or to communicate with him and, accordingly, A sold them. After the armistice, P repudiated the sale and sought damages in conversion. In a trenchant and lucid judgment, McCardie J stressed that the object of the law was to 'meet, so far as it can, sets of fact abnormal as well as usual. It must grow with the development of the nation. It must face and deal with changing or novel circumstances. Unless it can do that it fails in its function and declines in its dignity and value. An expanding society demands an expanding common law'.[2] Consequently, he

16   [1913] 1 KB 103.
17   [1913] 1 KB 103 at 112.
18   [1921] 1 KB 257.
19   [1921] 1 KB 257 at 265, per Bankes LJ, quoting the defendant's traffic agent.
20   This was the view of Lord Goddard CJ in *Sachs v Miklos* [1948] 2 KB 23, 35-36 adding that 'the court should be slow to increase the classes of those who can be looked upon as agents of necessity in selling or disposing of other people's goods without the authority of the owners'.
 1   [1924] 1 KB 566.
 2   [1924] 1 KB 566 at 570. In *Jebara v Ottoman Bank* [1927] 2 KB 254, 270, Scrutton LJ was critical of McCardie J's judgment, cautioning against expanding the doctrine of necessity 'without clearly defining the limits, if any, of its expansion'.

applied the rules of agency of necessity to the facts of the case but concluded that there was no necessity to sell the furs: on a rising market, they could and should have been stored until the end of the war and this would have resulted in only minimal deterioration in their condition.

Similarly, in *Tetley & Co v British Trade Corpn*,[3] the defendant banker (A) in Batum received a quantity of tea and spices from the plaintiff (P) in London with instructions to deliver the goods to T and collect payment but, because of local disturbances and the British military's evacuation of Batum, A feared that the goods might be looted. Accordingly he shipped them to Constantinople and stored them there. It was held that communication with P, while possible, was of doubtful utility on the facts because of the length of time it would have taken and, accordingly, A had acted reasonably as an agent of necessity, was not liable in conversion and could recover the costs of the removal. A did not recover the warehousing charges however, as the goods had been stored for two months before P had been informed of the position.

The decision in *Sachs v Miklos*[4] provides an interesting contrast to the cases above. In *Sachs*, A agreed to store P's furniture free of charge in her home but A then lost touch with P because he failed to let A know of his whereabouts. The lodgers which boarded in A's house were a source of income for A and, after storing the furniture for three years, A decided that she needed the space which was taken up by the furniture. After several unsuccessful attempts to contact P by telephone and letter, A sold the furniture at auction. P materialised some eighteen months after the sale and demanded the furniture from A who tendered the £15 received at auction but, as the furniture had risen in price, P decided to sue A in conversion. The court considered that the steps taken by A in attempting to communicate with P were reasonable and it was unnecessary to 'hunt London for him and make elaborate enquiries'.[5] Nevertheless, it was held that A was liable in conversion. The court decided that there was no emergency compelling the sale which was made principally for A's benefit in that she wanted to use the rooms in her house. Lord Goddard CJ was emphatic that the categories of agency of necessity should remain limited[6] and he was reluctant to extend the rules to a gratuitous bailee, but he managed to curtail investigation of the wider issue of such extension by denying that any emergency existed on the facts of the case. He distinguished the *Sachs* situation from one 'where the house had been destroyed and the furniture left exposed to thieves and the weather'[7] which, by inference, appeared to be what the judge considered the remote threshold of an emergency in this situation.[8]

Most recently, companies which provide breakdown services and have recovered stolen vehicles on instructions from the police, have sought to recover

3 (1922) 10 Ll L Rep 678.
4 [1948] 2 KB 23.
5 [1948] 2 KB 23 at 34, per Lord Goddard CJ.
6 [1948] 2 KB 23 at 36.
7 [1948] 2 KB 23 at 36.
8 See also *Munro v Wilmott* [1949] 1 KB 295 (car left with a gratuitous bailee who was liable in conversion for its sale but was entitled to an allowance for improvements made); Cf *Coldman v Hill* [1919] 1 KB 443 (a bailee of cattle was liable for failing to take reasonable steps to recover them and not informing the owner or the police of their theft. Scrutton LJ considered that a bailee who could not obtain instructions from the owner in time might act 'as agent of necessity on behalf of and at the expense of the owner, taking the steps which a reasonable owner would take in defence of property' (p 456). See also the Torts (Interference with Goods) Act 1977, ss 12, 13 and Sch 1.

the removal and storage charges from the owners of the cars on the basis of agency of necessity.[9] The claims have been rejected because it could not be said that necessity compelled the recovery of the vehicles without the authority of their owners. Rather, the companies were simply complying with a request from the police and, consequently, their intent was not to preserve the owners' property. It is thus clear that, in the 21st century, the courts remain reluctant to extend the boundaries of agency of necessity.

Classification of agency of necessity

It is extremely difficult to find a connecting path through the maze of disparate factual situations which constitute agency of necessity. This task is complicated by the fact that the common law in this area has developed in a singularly utilitarian and pragmatic way and the judiciary has been disinclined to enunciate the *basis* of agency of necessity. There are three possible foundations upon which agency of necessity might be constructed. First, it is arguable that authority to act is granted by the law in specific situations but such a basis, rooted in public policy, is particularly unhelpful as an organising principle for necessity cases. Second, some of the decisions are premised upon A's actual, implied authority to cope with an emergency. If this approach is adopted, the question is simply whether or not A's implied authority can extend to the steps which he has taken to resolve the emergency. Such an enquiry can take place only within existing agency relationships where A has an actual authority upon which an implied authority can be grafted. Third, many cases consider that A's authority must be circumscribed severely on the basis that it emanates solely from the necessity itself. This view means that the necessity itself generates the authority and dictates its scope. It must be stressed that the three possible bases of agency of necessity can all be traced in the decisions, but no single basis can be identified as dominant.

In analysing the law, it is proposed to follow the twofold division suggested by Lord Diplock[10] viz, (i) cases of agency proper where A enters into a contract with T, on behalf of P, consequently binding P contractually to T and (ii) situations where a person acts for another and subsequently seeks reimbursement or an indemnity from him. This classification aids clarity of exposition but entails some anomalies, as discussed later.

CASES OF AGENCY PROPER: THE AGENT ENTERS INTO A CONTRACT WITH THE THIRD PARTY ON BEHALF OF THE PRINCIPAL

An immediate sub-division should be made of this category, distinguishing two quite separate situations, viz:

(a) A is an agent with *pre-existing authority from P* and is impliedly granted an extended authority to cope with the emergency and
(b) A person who is *not an existing agent* becomes an agent by virtue of the emergency in which he is embroiled.

---

9 See *Surrey Breakdown Ltd v Knight* [1999] RTR 84; *Lambert v Fry* [2000] 10 CL 11.
10 *China-Pacific SA v Food Corpn of India, The Winson* [1982] AC 939, 958.

Although this cleavage is not always recognised in the cases, it is an important one from which several fundamental matters of principle emanate.

A is an agent with pre-existing authority: might he have implied authority to deal with the emergency?

As this situation involves an extension of an existing agency, A's authority to take appropriate action may be part of his *actual, implied authority*.[11] Indeed, the origin of the shipmaster's authority to act in emergencies on behalf of the shipowner was arguably based upon actual, implied authority as being necessary for and *ordinarily incidental* to the execution of his express authority. Thus, as Parke B explained in *Hawtayne v Bourne*,[12] 'the law provides for that which is common, not for that which is unusual; on that principle it is that the master of a ship has authority to charge his owners, because ships are ordinarily exposed to casualties'.[13] It is arguable therefore that the master's actual, implied authority is adequate to cover the pragmatic, commercial definition of an 'emergency'[14] and that agency of necessity would apply only to those cases where he performs an act *outside* the scope of his implied authority.

Moreover, apart from the shipmaster's authority, there are numerous 'necessity' cases which are based upon implied authority and make no mention of the stringent conditions for the operation of agency of necessity. In *Walker v Great Western Rly Co*,[15] for example, a general manager of the defendant company was held to have authority 'incidental' to his employment to bind the company to pay for surgical attendance on a servant of the company injured in an accident on the railway. Likewise, in *Langan v Great Western Rly Co*,[16] a sub-inspector of railway police had authority to pledge the credit of the defendant for the board of injured passengers at a nearby inn, medical attendance given to them and other comforts provided, including brandy.[17]

11 See *Restatement, Second, Agency* § 47 which is headed 'Inference of Authority to Act in an Emergency', the comment to which emphasises that this authority is created 'by the principal's consent'.
12 (1841) 7 M & W 595, 598.
13 See also *Beldon v Campbell* (1851) 6 Exch 886, 889, per Parke B; *Grant v Norway* (1851) 10 CB 665, 687, per Jervis CJ; *The Unique Mariner* [1978] 1 Lloyd's Rep 438 (the master (A) of a stranded ship has actual, implied authority to accept, on behalf of the shipowner (P), the services of a salvage tug or, if such authority has been restricted by P, A may nevertheless have apparent authority).
14 Eg Sir Montague Smith's definition of 'commercial necessity' in *Australasian Steam Navigation Co v Morse* (1872) LR 4 PC 222, 230 as *not* being 'irresistible compelling power' but instead 'the force of circumstances which determine the course a man ought to take'.
15 (1867) LR 2 Exch 228.
16 (1873) 30 LT 173.
17 See also *Montaignac v Shitta* (1890) 15 App Cas 357 (A had authority under a power of attorney to borrow money for the purpose of carrying on the business entrusted to him. Held that he had implied authority to borrow money from a native financier in Lagos when the business was 'under the necessity of raising funds' (per Lord Herschell, p 361)); *Poland v John Parr and Sons* [1927] 1 KB 236 (In order to protect his employer's property from theft, A struck the plaintiff, a suspected thief. Held A had 'implied authority' in this 'emergency' to hit the plaintiff (per Bankes LJ, at 241) and his employer was therefore liable for the injury to the plaintiff); *Gokal Chand-Jagan Nath v Nand Ram Das-Atma Ram* [1939] AC 106 (A accepted part payment in cash from T who was financially embarrassed. Held that A had authority and a duty to obtain the best possible bargain for P and, as he had done that, he was not liable to P).

As implied authority springs from actual authority, only an agent with actual authority at the time of the emergency may possess implied authority to act for P. This point was emphasised recently in *The Choko Star*.[18] Not long after setting sail for Italy, *Choko Star* took the ground in the River Parana in Argentina and became stranded. The master signed a salvage agreement on behalf of the shipowners and the cargo-owners and the ship was refloated. The cargo-owners contended that the master had no authority to engage salvors on their behalf but they paid their share of the salvage reward and then claimed restitution of the amount from the salvors. At first instance, Sheen J held that the master had actual, implied authority to contract on behalf of the shipowners *and* the cargo-owners but the decision was reversed by the Court of Appeal. It was stressed that, whilst the master is the agent of the shipowner and may have implied authority to act on his behalf, there is no pre-existing agency between the master and the cargo-owner and it was thus impossible for the master to have any implied authority *vis-à-vis* the cargo-owner. Accordingly, in relation to the cargo-owner, the master's authority could arise only under the conditions of an agency of necessity and, on the facts, those conditions were not met as the master was able to contact the cargo-owners.[19]

It is evident that an existing agent may thus have implied authority to cope with an emergency and yet, as will be seen below, there are instances where an existing agent has had to fulfil the stringent conditions of agency of necessity in order successfully to bind P to T. This is a most unsatisfactory position as it is unclear when either type of authority may be applied to the facts and which classification of authority might have priority over the other. It does seem that the modern approach in this area is that, even within a pre-existing agency, the strict stipulations of agency of necessity may be applicable where A acts as a literal agent in seeking to make a contract on behalf of P, and this view was clearly the one which was favoured in the decision of the House of Lords in *China-Pacific SA v Food Corpn of India, The Winson*.[20]

A has no pre-existing agency relationship with P

In all the cases where A has acted as an agent proper and sought to enter into a contract with T on behalf of P, there has been a *pre-existing relationship* of some sort between the parties (eg bailment) and, in most of them, a pre-existing *agency* can be identified. The relevance of the pre-existing relationship was accentuated in *Jebara v Ottoman Bank*,[1] where Scrutton LJ suggested that an expansion of agency of necessity was 'less difficult when the agent of necessity develops from an original and subsisting agency ... but the position seems quite different when there is no pre-existing agency, as in the case of a finder of perishable chattels or animals'.[2]

As emphasised above, those who intervene in emergencies on behalf of strangers are likely to be classified separately, and often somewhat uncharitably, as intermeddlers. More significantly, it will usually be extremely difficult, if

---

18   *Industrie Chimiche Italia Centrale and Cerealfin SA v Alexander G Tsavliris & Sons Maritime Co, The Choko Star* [1990] 1 Lloyd's Rep 516; see Brown, 'Authority and Necessity in the Law of Agency' (1992) 55 MLR 414; Munday, 'Salvaging the Law of Agency' [1991] 1 LMCLQ 1.
19   The Merchant Shipping Act 1995, s 224(1), now gives the master authority to sign a salvage agreement in relation to the cargo.
20   [1982] AC 939 (considered below).
1   [1927] 2 KB 254.
2   [1927] 2 KB 254 at 271.

not impossible, to apply the conditions of agency of necessity to the intermeddler as the rules are premised on there being an identifiable principal at the time of the emergency. The primary question which is asked by the courts is whether or not A could have contacted P because, if he could so contact P, there is no emergency. This question thus tends to assume the pre-condition of there being a principal/agent relationship in existence when the catastrophe occurs and, while the 'stranger's' identity might be known to the intermeddler, there will be no agency in existence in such cases. Of course, where one person saves goods which belong to a total stranger it is arguable that some notion of agency of necessity should arise precisely because there is no contactable principal but, overall, this logic has not commended itself to English law.

In summary, it is clear from *The Choko Star* that, where there is no pre-existing agency, it is possible to gain authority in an emergency to act as a literal agent for P *only* where the conditions relating to agency of necessity are fulfilled.

Conditions for the operation of agency of necessity where the agent seeks to enter into a contract on behalf of the principal

From the cases above it is possible to glean the conditions which must exist for agency of necessity. It is tolerably clear that these rules do not apply where the issue is decided solely upon the basis of implied authority and the extent to which they may apply to those cases where A seeks reimbursement from P is uncertain. On the other hand, the rules do apply to the cases of agency proper where A seeks to enter into a contract on P's behalf in an emergency, as defined below.

IT MUST BE COMMERCIALLY IMPOSSIBLE FOR THE AGENT TO COMMUNICATE WITH THE PRINCIPAL

Some decisions specify that communication with P must be impossible[3] or, put another way, the fact that A cannot communicate with P *is* the necessitous situation. As elsewhere in agency of necessity, there is a considerable divergence of opinion as to whether it must be literally impossible for A to contact P. Certainly the decision in *John Koch Ltd v C & H Products Ltd*[4] takes a very restrictive view of this issue. There A had negotiated a sale of quick-frozen fish from T to P but was in doubt as to whether P could find a ship in order to perform the contract on time. A thus sought instructions from the defendant company (P Ltd). A could not contact the person (S) who controlled P Ltd and was 'the only man who matter[ed]'[5] in the company but he was in communication with the company's employees, although none of them had any authority to make a decision. Acting in P's best interests, A cancelled the contract and sought to recover from P all sums which had been paid on its behalf. Sellers J held[6] that A's inability

---

3 *Gwilliam v Twist* [1895] 2 QB 84, 88 per A L Smith LJ; *Prager v Blatspiel, Stamp and Heacock* [1924] 1 KB 566, 571 per McCardie J.
4 [1956] 2 Lloyd's Rep 59.
5 [1956] 2 Lloyd's Rep 59 at 61, per Singleton LJ.
6 [1956] 1 Lloyd's Rep 302.

to contact S meant that he was an agent of necessity and thus he could recover from P the amounts paid. The Court of Appeal[7] held that A was in breach of contract and could not be an agent of necessity as, on the facts, A could contact P and there was no emergency. The court held, however, that no damage had resulted from the breach and A could recover the amounts from P which had been paid on its behalf.

The notion that communication must be impossible is almost certainly overly-confining and, in an age of instantaneous communications, a strict adherence to the rule would virtually negate the doctrine of agency of necessity. Moreover, many of the leading cases stipulate, in different ways, for the lesser requirement of difficulty or impracticability of communication.[8] In *Springer v Great Western Rly Co*,[9] Salter J stated that communication had to be 'commercially impracticable'[10] and Scrutton LJ questioned whether it was 'commercially impossible to communicate'[11] with P. Similarly, in the (restrictive) decision in *Gwilliam v Twist*,[12] Lord Esher MR asked whether there was 'an opportunity to consult'[13] with P.

It is suggested that the question of communication with P, rather than being a pre-condition of agency of necessity, should simply be one factor in deciding whether A faced an emergency and whether, having regard to all the circumstances, his actions were reasonable. Indeed this approach was adopted in *Tetley & Co v British Trade Corpn*[14] (considered above) where, in deciding that A was an agent of necessity, Bailhache J stressed the impracticability of communicating with P and that any cable sent to him would not have been answered in less than 15 days.[15] In *The Choko Star*,[16] Sheen J made several telling points regarding the ease and speed of modern communications, emphasising that in many situations the shipmaster *can* communicate with the cargo-owners but this very fact compounds his difficulties. What is he to do if some owners order one course of action while others demand its opposite? If ownership of the cargo has changed during the voyage, whom should the master contact? Sheen J considered that these questions indicated that the master was the person best fitted to make a decision regarding salvage and there is much to commend this more liberal approach to the problems engendered by communication.[17]

---

7   [1956] 2 Lloyd's Rep 59.
8   See *The Australia* (1859) 13 Moo PCC 132 (considered below).
9   [1921] 1 KB 257.
10   [1921] 1 KB 257 at 262.
11   [1921] 1 KB 257 at 267-268; see also *Sims & Co v Midland Rly Co* [1913] 1 KB 103, 112 where Scrutton J stipulated that it must be 'practically impossible to get the owner's instructions in time'.
12   [1895] 2 QB 84.
13   [1895] 2 QB 84 at 87. See also *Restatement, Second, Agency* §47 which provides that communication should be 'impracticable'.
14   (1922) 10 Ll L Rep 678.
15   See also *Walker v Great Western Rly Co* (1867) LR 2 Exch 228; *Langan v Great Western Rly Co* (1873) 30 LT 173 where there is no mention in either case of possible communication with P but, instead, there was a 'necessity ... for what may be called instantaneous action' (*Langan*, p 176 per Bramwell B).
16   [1989] 2 Lloyd's Rep 42, 46-47.
17   In *China-Pacific SA v Food Corpn of India, The Winson* [1982] AC 939, 961 Lord Diplock considered that impossibility of communication *might* still be vital in cases of agency of necessity proper but *where a bailee was seeking reimbursement of his expenses in storing goods*, inability to communicate with the owner was *not* a condition precedent to his recovery; instead it was sufficient if the bailee had asked for instructions but the owner 'failed to give any instructions when apprised'.

Finally, it has never been ascertained whether A could be an agent of necessity where P has expressly refused to countenance A's proposed actions. The general rule which stipulates that it must be at least impracticable for A to contact P if he is to be constituted an agent of necessity would indicate that such an express prohibition would exclude any possibility of authority, but the position is unclear.[18] As mentioned earlier, the true basis of agency of necessity has never been ascertained with any certainty. If agency of necessity is premised upon P's implied consent to A's acting in necessitous circumstances, P's express prohibition would exclude any possibility of such an agency arising but if A's authority springs from the necessity itself, P's prohibition might be to no avail.[19]

THE AGENT'S ACTION MUST BE NECESSARY IN THE CIRCUMSTANCES

This involves the concept of an emergency being sufficiently serious so that there is a necessity for A to act in the way that he does. In *Phelps, James & Co v Hill*,[20] Lindley LJ defined necessity in the context of the shipmaster's need to put into port in bad weather in order that the ship could be repaired:

> 'By "possible" and "necessary" is meant reasonably possible and reasonably necessary, and in considering what is reasonably possible or reasonably necessary every material circumstance must be taken into account – eg, danger, distance, accommodation, expense, time, and so forth. No one of these can be excluded'.

Thus as long as A's choice of action is a reasonable one, it need not be the *only* possible course open to him. In *The Australia*,[1] a vessel was despatched by her owner from San Fancisco to Hong Kong where it was soon found that, if she were to be made seaworthy, the extensive repairs which were needed would exceed the ship's value. The master could not defray the expenses himself nor could he raise money on the bottomry of the ship and, to make matters worse, the vessel incurred many debts and liabilities while in Hong Kong. Consequently, the ship was sold by the master. It was held that the necessity which the law contemplated was not 'an absolute impossibility of getting the vessel repaired'[2] but, instead, if the ship could not be sent upon her voyage without such repairs as no prudent man would venture, that constituted a necessity which justified the master in selling. The argument that the master might have contacted the owner was dismissed because the shortest space of time for such communication was four months and the expenses incurred during that period would 'eat up the whole value of the ship'.[3]

In *Australasian Steam Navigation Co v Morse*,[4] Sir Montague Smith emphasised that 'the word "necessity", when applied to mercantile affairs ... cannot of course mean an irresistible compelling power' and that when A 'adopts the

---

18 See *Chapman v Morton* (1843) 11 M & W 534, where it was held that A could not be an agent of necessity where P had 'directly repudiated his acting as their agent' (per Parke B, p 541) but this view was doubted by Evans J in *Graanhandel T Vink v European Grain & Shipping Ltd* [1989] 2 Lloyd's Rep 531, 533. Also, in *Tetley & Co v British Trade Corpn* (1922) 10 Ll L Rep 678, A acted contrary to the last instructions of P and was nevertheless held to be an agent of necessity.
19 See Brown, 'Authority and Necessity in the Law of Agency' (1992) 55 MLR 414.
20 [1891] 1 QB 605, 610-611.
1   (1859) 13 Moo PCC 132.
2   (1859) 13 Moo PCC 132 at 144, per the Right Hon Dr Lushington.
3   (1859) 13 Moo PCC 132 at 157, per the Right Hon Dr Lushington.
4   (1872) LR 4 PC 222, 230.

course which, to the judgment of a wise and prudent man, is apparently the best for [P], it may be properly be said of the course so taken, that it was, in a mercantile sense, necessary to take it'. It is thus clear that A's opinion regarding the necessity is irrelevant but it is sufficient if a reasonable man would conclude there to be a necessity. Moreover, as Lord Simon[5] explained, the time for determining whether there is a necessity is when the supposed emergency becomes apparent.

THE AGENT MUST ACT *BONA FIDE* IN THE PRINCIPAL'S BEST INTERESTS

It was clear in *Prager v Blatspiel, Stamp and Heacock*,[6] for example, that A was neither *bona fide* nor acting in P's best interests in selling the furs which were rising in price, McCardie J concluding that A was 'dishonest'.[7] Similarly, in *Sachs v Miklos*,[8] an important factor in the decision was that the sale of P's furniture was made for A's benefit.[9] Reference should also be made to *The Winson*, considered below, where Lord Simon considered this requirement of A's *bona fides* and motive.

Situations where a person acts for another and subsequently seeks reimbursement or an indemnity from him

As mentioned at the start of this chapter, these cases are analogous to *negotiorum gestio* in Roman law and, strictly speaking, are not cases of agency in that 'A' does not seek to affect 'P''s legal relations with T. Rather, he seeks reimbursement from P or, if sued by P, he may wish to establish that his intervention was not wrongful. Consequently, these are principally cases of restitution and only an outline of this area is appropriate here.[10]

There are well-established instances where reimbursement is allowed, the most notable being salvage,[11] where the salvor voluntarily assists or saves a vessel in distress and may claim a reward, and the acceptance of a bill of exchange by a person not liable on it, for the honour of the drawer, whereby the acceptor is entitled to be reimbursed by the person for whom he pays. Another example concerns the

---

5   *China-Pacific SA v Food Corpn of India, The Winson* [1982] AC 939, 965.
6   [1924] 1 KB 566.
7   [1924] 1 KB 566 at 574.
8   [1948] 2 KB 23; see also *Tronson v Dent* (1853) 8 Moo PCC 419.
9   See also *Lambert v Fry* [2000] 10 CL 11 (a company which acted on the instructions of the police and recovered stolen cars could not claim reimbursement from the car's owner as the company's intent and motive was to comply with the request from the police. In order to succeed, the company would have needed to have acted, at least partly, with the intent of preserving the owner's property).
10 See Goff and Jones, *The Law of Restitution* (5th edn, 1998) Chs 17 and 18; Burrows, *The Law of Restitution* (1993) Ch 8; Dawson, 'Negotiorum Gestio: The Altruistic Intermeddler' (1960) 74 Harv L Rev 817; Birks, 'Negotiorum Gestio and the Common Law' [1971] CLP 110; Marasinghe, 'The Place of Negotiorum Gestio in English Law' (1976) 8 Ottawa L Rev 573; McCamus, 'Necessitous Intervention: The Altruistic Intermeddler and the Law of Restitution' (1979) 11 Ottawa L Rev 297; Aitken, 'Negotiorum Gestio and the Common Law: A Jurisdictional Approach' (1988) 11 Sydney LR 566; Rose, 'Restitution for the Rescuer' (1989) 9 OJLS 167.
11 See *Kennedy's Law of Salvage* (5th edn, 1985); Brice, *Maritime Law of Salvage* (1983).

stranger who buries a deceased person when there is a necessity to do so (eg the whereabouts and identity of the personal representatives are unknown) and who is entitled to be indemnified by the person responsible for the funeral,[12] this situation being very close to the *actio funeraria* in Roman law.

However, as emphasised at the start of this chapter, Bowen LJ's dictum in *Falcke v Scottish Imperial Insurance Co*[13] sets the tone of English law regarding any possible development of a generalised restitutionary doctrine of necessitous intervention. Thus a stranger who intervenes to preserve another's property has no general right to reimbursement and does not have even a lien on the property.[14] In *Binstead v Buck*,[15] for example, a finder of a dog who fed it for twenty weeks was unsuccessful in a claim against the owner for the cost. Likewise in *Nicholson v Chapman*,[16] where a person who rescued logs from a river and refused to surrender them unless he was paid was held not to be a salvor nor entitled to a lien and, accordingly, was liable in conversion. Sometimes however, decisions may be said to have applied *negotiorum gestio* by sleight of hand.[17]

In *China-Pacific SA v Food Corpn of India, The Winson*,[18] issues were raised which were relevant both to reimbursement and agency of necessity proper. The defendant was the sole owner of a cargo of wheat on board the vessel *Winson* when she became stranded in the South China Sea. The master signed a salvage agreement, on behalf of the shipowner and cargo-owner, for the plaintiff to provide salvage services. It was not disputed that the circumstances *at that time* entitled the master to act as agent of necessity for the cargo-owner. The cargo was carried to Manila where the salvors, having no premises of their own, personally contracted for its storage with third parties. The cargo-owners had been informed of the proposal for storage and had raised no objections. The dispute arose because the cargo-owners would pay the salvor's expenses only from the date of the shipowner's abandonment of the voyage but refused to pay those which were incurred earlier. The House of Lords held that the salvor's services in relation to the cargo had ceased upon arrival at Manila but they had become gratuitous bailees of the goods and, having a duty to look after those goods, they had a correlative right to charge the cargo-owner for expenses reasonably incurred in the storage. It was suggested that the right to reimbursement could arise more easily where the parties had an existing

---

12 See eg *Jenkins v Tucker* (1788) 1 Hy Bl 90 (a father paid for his married daughter's funeral as her husband had left her, sometime earlier, to live in Jamaica; it was held that the father could recover the funeral expenses from the husband); *Rogers v Price* (1829) 3 Y & J 28 (an undertaker, who did not know the identity of the deceased's executor at the time of the funeral, recovered expenses from the executor).

13 (1886) 34 Ch D 234, 248.

14 See also *Surrey Breakdown Ltd v Knight* [1999] RTR 84, 88 per Sir Christopher Staughton; *Lambert v Fry* [2000] 10 CL 11 (in both cases, car breakdown companies acting on instructions from the police to recover stolen cars, could not claim reimbursement from the owners of the cars).

15 (1776) 2 Wm Bl 1117.

16 (1793) 2 Hy Bl 254.

17 See eg *Schneider v Eisovitch* [1960] 2 QB 430 (the plaintiff was injured in a car accident caused by the defendant's negligence and her damages included an amount representing expenses incurred by a relative in rendering unrequested but reasonably necessary services to her); *Munro v Wilmott* [1949] 1 KB 295; *Greenwood v Bennett* [1973] QB 195 (in both cases *bona fide* improvers of cars were held entitled to an allowance for work done when the cars were returned to their owners); Matthews, 'Freedom, Unrequested Improvements, and Lord Denning' [1981] 40 CLJ 340.

18 [1982] AC 939.

relationship such as bailment and that the rigorous conditions of agency of necessity should apply *only* where A sought to enter into a contract on behalf of P thereby binding P to T.

In the three courts in which *The Winson* was heard, there was a remarkable difference of opinion regarding the possibility that the salvor might be an agent of necessity proper. At first instance,[19] Lloyd J considered that the test of necessity was not always the impossibility of communicating with P but, instead, could be the inability to obtain proper instructions (here the cargo-owners had remained silent). The Court of Appeal[20] would not accept that the owner's failure to give instructions constituted a necessitous situation on the facts although, in the House of Lords, Lord Diplock[1] agreed with Lloyd J's conclusion and considered that the Court of Appeal's view was wrong. The Court of Appeal also thought that there was no emergency when the cargo *arrived at Manila* and that it would be insufficient for the salvor simply to show a necessity at the time of the signing of the salvage agreement, a point with which Lord Simon[2] agreed in the House of Lords. Finally, Lord Simon[3] considered that the salvors had not acted *entirely* for P's benefit in that a significant reason for storing the cargo was to maintain their lien on it, but he thought that if A acts from mixed motives, it may be sufficient if he acts *primarily* for P's benefit.

The Winson reaffirms the strict conditions of agency of necessity and subscribes to the view that, even within an existing agency, authority to enter into a contract on P's behalf in an emergency will be difficult to establish as the conditions of necessity must be complied with. However, the decision specifies that a right to reimbursement may be more easily construed from the general principles applicable to the relationship between the parties. It is respectfully suggested that this reasoning is anomalous. First, it is most unclear why the situation where a person seeks reimbursement from another should be separated decisively from that where he enters into a contract on behalf of another. Second, it is curious that an existing agent with an actual authority to act for P has to establish the conditions of agency of necessity in order to make a contract on P's behalf in an emergency, while much less strict, elusive requirements apply to a person who is *not* an existing agent but who has a 'pre-existing relationship', when he contracts personally and then seeks reimbursement from P. This is surely somewhat unorthodox in that it subjugates the agent's authority and elevates the 'pre-existing relationship'.

Finally, although the notion of a 'pre-existing relationship' is nebulous at best, it is arguable that the approach of the House of Lords may lead, seemingly unintentionally, to an acceptance and widening of the notion of reimbursement in situations of *negotiorum gestio*.

19 [1979] 2 All ER 35.
20 [1981] 1 QB 403.
 1 [1982] AC 939, 961.
 2 [1982] AC 939 at 965.
 3 [1982] AC 939 at 965-966.

CHAPTER 7

The duties of the agent owed to his principal – Part 1: the agent's duties of performance

Introduction

In many instances the principal-agent relationship is formal and contractual, meaning that both the extent of A's express authority and his rights and duties are specified in a written contract. In other cases there may be a purely oral contract but, in both situations, there will be a remedy for breach of contract if there is a failure to perform under the terms of the contract. However, as emphasised in Chapters 1 and 2, there is no requirement that the principal-agent relationship be contractual and the gratuitous agent also owes duties to P although, as will be seen, the foundations and extent of the gratuitous agent's liability have always been contentious issues. It is always necessary to ascertain whether the agency is contractual or gratuitous, for much depends upon this distinction.

The fiduciary nature of the principal-agent relationship has provided fertile ground for equity's imposition of duties of loyalty based upon the confidential, special union of principal and agent. These fiduciary duties are considered in the next chapter but the duties of performance, which are considered in this chapter, are not considered to be fiduciary in nature as, usually, neither an actual nor a possible conflict of interest arises where, for example, A fails to execute P's orders promptly. Indeed, it was stressed recently by Millett LJ that 'it is obvious that not every breach of duty by a fiduciary is a breach of fiduciary duty'.[1] It is equally obvious that there is an intermediate zone between, at one end of the spectrum, the mundane duties of performance and, at the opposite end, the elevated fiduciary duties premised on good faith and loyalty. Certainly P may contend that A is in breach of a fiduciary duty in attempt to secure equitable remedies. Should the court decide to impose a constructive trust upon A in favour of P, the benefits to P of a proprietary claim are immense in that A will be divested of all ill-gotten gains, but establishing that A is in breach of a fiduciary duty may also be crucial should P seek to circumvent the periods of limitation and the rules concerning remoteness of damage, for example.

The court undeniably interpreted the notion of fiduciary duty in generous terms in the Canadian decision in *Laskin v Bache & Co Inc*.[2] A, a stockbroker,

---

1 *Bristol & West Building Society v Mothew (t/a Stapley & Co)* [1996] 4 All ER 698, 710.
2 (1971) 23 DLR (3d) 385.

bought shares on P's behalf but failed to provide her with the share certificates. The shares began to fall in value and P lost an opportunity to sell them because she did not have the certificates. A had prevaricated throughout, telling P that it was only 'a matter of time' before the certificates were delivered but he had, in fact, accepted a 'fail ticket' in lieu of the certificates at the date of purchase. The acceptance of a 'fail ticket' by a buying broker meant that he no longer had the right to require delivery of the share certificates by the selling broker on a specific date and thus he simply accepted the selling broker's undertaking to do his best to make delivery. A did eventually secure the share certificates and P instructed him to sell the shares. When sued by P, A argued that P's loss was too remote as the parties could not have contemplated, as a consequence of the breach, the loss which P suffered in being unable to sell the shares. Alternatively, A contended that at some point P must have realised that the certificates would not be delivered and that she should then have sold her shares to mitigate her loss. P's submission was that A was in breach of fiduciary duty and that she should thus be compensated in equity, the common law's rules on remoteness of damage thus being immaterial. Arnup J A held that A's failure to carry out P's instructions, his failure to tell P that he had taken a 'fail ticket' and the consistent advice given to her that delivery of the certificates was imminent, were all breaches of A's fiduciary obligations and had a causal connection with her loss. Accordingly, A was obligated in equity to make good that loss.

The same approach to the duties of performance was followed in *Fine's Flowers Ltd v General Accident Assurance Co of Canada*.[3] There P, the owner of an extensive horticultural business, relied on A, an insurance agent, to obtain 'full coverage' against losses under an insurance policy. A obtained coverage against a wide range of business risks but not that which occurred, viz damage to plants caused by a failure of the heating system. The Ontario Court of Appeal held that A was liable in breach of contract and negligence, but the court also approved the reasoning in *Laskin's* case and thus considered that A might be liable for breach of fiduciary duty.

These questions regarding the boundary between contractual and fiduciary duties have not been broached in the English decisions but the current indications are that it is unlikely that English law would wish to extend the notion of fiduciary obligation in commercial agencies to cover instances of negligence or breach of contract.[4] It is as well to heed the recent warning that 'the word "fiduciary" is flung around now as if it applied to all breaches of duty by solicitors, directors of companies and so forth. But ... "fiduciary" means of or pertaining to a trust or trusteeship. That a lawyer may commit a breach of the special duty of a trustee, eg, by stealing his client's money [or] by entering into a contract with the client without full disclosure ... is clear. But to say that simple carelessness in giving advice is such a breach is a perversion of words'.[5]

---

3 (1977) 81 DLR (3d) 139.
4 See *Re Goldcorp Exchange Ltd* [1995] 1 AC 74 (considered in Ch 16).
5 *Girardet v Crease & Co* (1987) 11 BCLR (2d) 361, 362 per Southin J.

The agent's duties of performance

THE CONTRACTUAL AGENT'S DUTY TO PERFORM THE TRANSACTION WHICH HE HAS UNDERTAKEN

A contractual agent must perform under the terms of his contract and not exceed his authority for, otherwise, he will be liable in damages.[6] The general rule is strict: provided P's instructions are clear and unequivocal, A must obey them precisely. In *Bertram, Armstrong & Co v Godfray*,[7] A was instructed to sell shares when they reached a certain price and it was held that he had no discretion to wait until the shares went higher. Likewise, in *Volkers v Midland Doherty Ltd*,[8] A, a stockbroker, was told by P to buy certain shares 'at the market price first thing in the morning'. At the opening of the market next day (7am), A could have bought the shares but refrained from doing so until he consulted with the salesman with whom P usually dealt. A considered that he was acting in P's best interests in seeking advice on the wisdom of the purchase. Trading in the shares was suspended at 8.45 am, P's order was never placed and by the time that trading resumed, the shares had more than doubled in price. It was held that A was liable to P for the loss of profits.

Other illustrations of this duty are to be found in the rule that a solicitor or barrister who is instructed not to compromise an action will be liable in breach of contract if he does compromise it even if he considers such a settlement to be in P's best interests.[9] Thus even if P's instructions are rash, A will not be liable for loss resulting from the execution of positive yet injudicious orders.[10]

However, the strict rule of performance must be defined having regard to the terms and context of A's authority and it is thus quite possible for A to exercise a discretion by virtue of his actual, implied authority. For example, a solicitor who has no instructions to the contrary may agree to the settlement of an action if he considers it to be in P's best interests.[11] Moreover, A may be under a duty to warn and advise P in cases where he thinks P's instructions are imprudent and loss may result from their execution. Finally, should P's instructions be ambiguous, A will not be liable for breach of contract if he honestly and reasonably chooses to act on one of the interpretations[12] and A need not obey instructions which entail the performance of an illegal act.[13]

---

6 *Turpin v Bilton* (1843) 5 Man & G 455 (A failed to insure P's ship and was liable in damages when the vessel was lost); *Ferrers v Robins* (1835) 2 CM & R 152 (A, an auctioneer, sold goods on behalf of P and, contrary to P's instructions, accepted a bill of exchange from the buyer. A was liable to P when the buyer defaulted).
7 (1830) 1 Knapp 381.
8 (1985) 17 DLR (4th) 343.
9 *Fray v Voules* (1859) 1 E & E 839; *Swinfen v Lord Chelmsford* (1860) 5 H & N 890.
10 *Overend, Gurney & Co v Gibb* (1872) LR 5 HL 480.
11 *Re Newen* [1903] 1 Ch 812.
12 *Ireland v Livingston* (1872) LR 5 HL 395. If A realised or should have realised that the instructions were ambiguous, he may be under a duty to obtain clarification from P where it is possible to do so. See Ch 2 where *Ireland* is considered.
13 *Cohen v Kittell* (1889) 22 QBD 680 (A not liable in damages for failing to place bets which P had instructed him to make).

THE CONTRACTUAL AGENT'S DUTY TO EXERCISE DUE CARE AND SKILL IN EXECUTING HIS AUTHORITY

Clearly the first duty relating to precise performance must be qualified by this second duty which demands that A must perform his authority with due care and skill. A's duty to act with due care and skill may be sub-divided into its various aspects.

First, A must execute his instructions with reasonable dispatch having regard to all the circumstances of the case[14] and he must not delay unreasonably in communicating material facts to P. In *Proudfoot v Montefiore*,[15] P's cargo was lost but A deliberately refrained from telling P promptly of the loss by sending a letter to P rather than telegraphing him. A was thereby acting under the misguided impression that this would help P in successfully insuring the cargo. As he had not received A's letter, P duly insured the cargo but it was held that A's duty was to have telegraphed and the insurance effected by P was void for non-disclosure of a material fact. A's knowledge of the facts was thus attributed to P.[16]

Second, as regards A's standard of care, he must exercise such care and skill as is usual for an agent in his business or professional position. In *Metropolitan Toronto Pension Plan v Aetna Life Assurance Co of Canada*,[17] Rosenberg J stressed that 'in the case of an agent who is paid for his services, a higher standard is exacted than in the case of an agent acting without reward ... if he is an agent following a particular trade or profession ... he must then show such skill as is usual and requisite, in the business for which he receives payment'.[18] It should be emphasised, however, that A need act only *bona fide* in P's best interests and with a reasonable degree of care and skill and, provided that he meets the requisite standard of care, he cannot be liable for errors of judgement. Consequently, this duty does not mean that A becomes a guarantor of the success of his endeavours. In *Moore v Mourgue*,[19] for example, P instructed A to insure a cargo but did not specify any terms or nominate an insurer. A, acting *bona fide*, insured with underwriters who employed an exclusion clause in the contract, the cargo being lost in circumstances which fell within the clause. It was held that, although A could have insured the cargo elsewhere without such a clause, he was not liable to P as he had exercised his discretion *bona fide*.

Third, in relation to the contractual agent there is the issue of whether remedies must be pursued in contract. As will be seen below, the gratuitous agent's liability to P arises necessarily by virtue of a tortious duty of care but the old view was that, when a contract existed between the parties, it fixed their rights and duties and was the true measure of their bargained-for, allocation of risks. It was thus impossible to sustain a separate action in tort.[20] Recent decisions have allowed

---

14 *Barber v Taylor* (1839) 5 M & W 527 (P instructed A to buy a quantity of cotton and send P the bill of lading. Upon the arrival of the goods, A failed to release the bill for several days and was held to be in breach of contract for not releasing the bill within a reasonable time – on the facts, within 24 hours).
15 (1867) LR 2 QB 511.
16 See also *Volkers v Midland Doherty Ltd* (1985) 17 DLR (4th) 343 (considered above).
17 (1992) 98 DLR (4th) 582.
18 (1992) 98 DLR (4th) 582 at 597.
19 (1776) 2 Cowp 479. See also *Morten v Hilton, Gibbes & Smith* [1937] 2 KB 176n.
20 See eg, *Clark v Kirby-Smith* [1964] Ch 506; *Bagot v Stevens, Scanlon & Co Ltd* [1966] 1 QB 197.

actions in tort and contract for the negligent performance of undertakings[1] and it is clear that a contractual agent may now also be liable in negligence. The matter has practical significance in relation to the measure of damages and the different periods of limitation in tort and contract actions. The cause of action in tort does not accrue until the damage has been suffered whereas in contract time begins to run from the moment that the breach occurs; it might thus be possible to sustain an action in tort when a claim in contract has become time-barred. Indeed, in *Henderson v Merrett Syndicates Ltd*,[2] the House of Lords held that where a plaintiff has concurrent remedies in contract and tort he may choose the remedy which is most advantageous to him, unless his contract precludes him from so doing.

THE GRATUITOUS AGENT'S DUTIES OF PERFORMANCE

As the gratuitous agent has no contract with P, the duties of performance which he owes to P are tortious in nature but, because he is not rewarded by P for his services, fixing the boundaries of his liability is a controversial issue. That the gratuitous agent should, in some circumstances, owe a duty of care when executing his authority cannot seriously be disputed. It is more difficult, however, to specify exactly when such a duty of care should arise and then fix accurately the standard of care which A must exhibit.

Being free from the restraints of contractual obligation, it seems that the gratuitous agent should not be liable for failing to commence performance of the work entrusted to him. It is thus often asserted that the gratuitous agent could not be liable for nonfeasance[3] but would be liable in misfeasance if he negligently failed to complete work which he had started. In *Wilkinson v Coverdale*,[4] for example, A was liable when he undertook gratuitously to effect an insurance policy for P but was so negligent in performing the task that P could recover nothing on the policy when his house burnt down. To the modern observer this distinction between nonfeasance and misfeasance looks obscure in that both involved negligent omissions with, ironically, the greater omission of nonfeasance going unpunished.

Equally criticisable, however, were the different standards of care which applied to gratuitous and contractual agents. A gratuitous agent had to show only the degree of care and skill which he would exercise in his *own* affairs (unless he held himself out as possessing certain skills when he would have to meet the standards of one with such skills) and would be liable only for 'gross negligence'.[5] This subjective test of liability, involving a lesser standard of care than that demanded

---

1 See *Esso Petroleum Co Ltd v Mardon* [1976] QB 801; *Midland Bank Trust Co v Hett, Stubbs & Kemp* [1979] Ch 384.
2 [1995] 2 AC 145.
3 See *Coggs v Bernard* (1703) 2 Ld Raym 909; *Elsee v Gatward* (1793) 5 Term Rep 143; *Balfe v West* (1853) 13 CB 466. Cf *Restatement, Second, Agency* § 378 which provides that the gratuitous A who has undertaken to perform an act for P in circumstances where P has relied on the promise in not appointing another A, owes a duty of care to P to perform the act or give sufficient notice to P that he will not perform thus enabling P to engage a substitute.
4 (1793) 1 Esp 74.
5 These subjective standards are traceable to early bailment cases, see eg *Coggs v Bernard* (1703) 2 Ld Raym 909.

of a contractual agent, meant that P's choice of agent to perform the task in question entailed an acceptance of the risk that the agent might be inept. In *Shiells v Blackburne*,[6] for example, a general merchant (A) undertook, without payment, to enter P's goods with his own at the Custom House but owing to A's error both parcels of goods were entered under the wrong denomination of goods and were seized. It was held that A had not held himself out as possessing any speciall skills in this regard and, as he had acted *bona fide* to the best of his ability, he was not liable to P.

It is not easy to justify these distinctions between contractual and gratuitous agents particularly when it is remembered that a nominal consideration can transform a gratuitous agency into a contractual one with a concomitant, elevated standard of care. The stringent fiduciary duties also apply to both categories of agent. Moreover, the modern law of tort has developed general, objective standards of reasonable care and it would be anomalous if agency were to retain comparative, subjective standards as the yardstick of liability. Against such considerations, however, is the innate feeling that, as A is unpaid, he should not be subjected to duties which are too burdensome.

These issues were considered recently in *Chaudhry v Prabhakar*.[7] P, a young woman who had recently passed her driving test, asked A, a close friend, to find a reliable car for her to buy. There was no question of A's being paid for this service. A inspected a Volkswagen Golf and noticed that the bonnet had been 'crumpled' but he recommended that P should buy the car from the second defendant, a panel beater. P duly purchased the car but a few months later it became apparent that it had been in a bad accident and had been poorly repaired consequently being unroadworthy. The Court of Appeal held that A was liable in negligence and rejected the notion that A's standard of care was to be measured subjectively by the degree of care shown in his own affairs. Rather it should be an objective standard being 'that which may reasonably be expected of him in all the circumstances'.[8] The relevant circumstances were thus whether or not A was paid, the degree of reliance which P placed upon A and the extent of A's actual or professed skill.

It must be emphasised that, in *Chaudhry*, counsel for A conceded that A owed a duty of care and, in the absence of such a concession, it is by no means clear when a duty of care might arise. Indeed, May LJ doubted that the concession was correct and considered that the imposition of tortious duties was inappropriate in *Chaudhry* where, on his interpretation of the facts, a friend performed a favour for another in a purely social context. Furthermore, it should be stressed that, in *Chaudhry*, A did not buy the car on behalf of P but only recommended that P should purchase it and thus there was no agency in the orthodox sense. Consequently, it remains to be seen whether *Chaudhry* is applicable in cases of agency proper and, even assuming that it does apply to gratuitous agents, there is still much doubt as to when the circumstances demonstrate the requisite voluntary assumption of responsibility on the part of the gratuitous agent in order to ground liability in tort.

---

6 (1789) 1 Hy Bl 158.
7 [1989] 1 WLR 29; see Brown, 'The Gratuitous Agent's Liability' [1989] LMCLQ 148.
8 [1989] 1 WLR 29 at 34, per Stuart-Smith LJ.

THE DUTY NOT TO DELEGATE

The general rule is that A must not delegate his authority or appoint a sub-agent[9] unless he has express[10] or actual, implied authority[11] from P to do so. The rule is justified in that A is already a delegate in whom P has reposed confidence and it is totally inappropriate for A to perform vicariously – *delegatus non potest delegare*. It is thus obvious that A 'has no right without notice to turn his principal over to another of whom the principal knows nothing'[12] but equally obvious that exceptions to this general rule must exist. Whether A may delegate is thus determined by the nature and scope of his authority and it is clear that, unless A is prohibited from delegating the task in question, he will have actual, implied authority to delegate in the following situations.

Where the act performed is purely ministerial

Although as a general rule A cannot delegate his substantive authority to another, it is patently obvious that there are numerous administrative and clerical mundanities which must necessarily be performed by others such as secretaries and clerks. *Bowstead & Reynolds* states emphatically that these are not instances of delegation.[13] This view is supported in a decision where A was authorised to endorse P's name to a bill of exchange but A directed her daughter to do so; Williams J said that 'the daughter was to be considered merely as her mother's instrument, not her delegate'.[14] Similarly, in *Parkin v Williams*,[15] P gave a power of attorney to her sister and a solicitor which contained an express power to sell land and execute all the necessary transfers of sale. The solicitor and the sister decided that certain land should be sold by auction and an auctioneer was given the necessary authority to sell. Eventually the auctioneer signed a memorandum of sale on behalf of the vendor but P objected that she had not agreed to any sale. It was held that, although the power of attorney contained no express power to delegate the signing of contracts, the signing by the auctioneer was a 'mechanical act' only and was within the implied authority conferred under the power.

In other cases, the issue will turn on whether the task in question is truly ministerial or whether it entails A's personal skill, discretion or confidence, in which case A must not delegate performance of complex duties to a sub-A. In *Rossiter v Trafalgar Life Assurance Association*,[16] the defendants (P) appointed A as their agent in Sydney with authority to grant life assurances and a sub-A effected a life assurance policy on T's life. Some six weeks after the insurance commenced, T, a naturalist, was murdered by 'native savages' while he was on an expedition to the Percy Islands. P denied liability on the policy arguing that

9 See eg *Cockran v Irlam* (1814) 2 M & S 301; *Solly v Rathbone* (1814) 2 M & S 298; *Catlin v Bell* (1815) 4 Camp 183.
10 An unauthorised delegation may be ratified: *Keay v Fenwick* (1876) 1 CPD 745.
11 See *De Bussche v Alt* (1878) 8 Ch D 286, 310-311 per Thesiger LJ, where there is an enunciation of the situations in which A has implied authority to delegate.
12 *Cockran v Irlam* (1814) 2 M & S 301, 303 per Lord Ellenborough.
13 *Bowstead & Reynolds on Agency* (16th edn, 1996), Art 36, para 5-003.
14 *Lord v Hall* (1848) 2 Car & Kir 698.
15 [1986] 1 NZLR 294.
16 (1859) 27 Beav 377.

A had no power to delegate his authority and that he was not bound by any policy in respect of which A had not exercised his judgement and discretion. It was held that P was liable on the policy and the appointment of the sub-A was considered to be 'regular and within the clear duty and province of the agent of the office in order to obtain insurances'.[17] Similarly, in *Allam & Co Ltd v Europa Poster Services Ltd*,[18] solicitors (sub-A) acting for A issued notices terminating licence agreements and it was held that the service of the notices was valid as such a ministerial act involved no confidence or discretion.[19]

Where delegation is usual in A's trade or profession provided that the usage is not unreasonable or inconsistent with A's express authority

This is simply an elaboration of part of A's actual, implied authority derived from the customary usages of a place, market or business.[20] In *Solley v Wood*,[1] for example, the court approved the practice of country solicitors employing town agents.

Where P is aware at the time of the creation of the agency that A intends to delegate and P does not object

In *Quebec and Richmond Railroad Co v Quinn*,[2] a company (P) was incorporated by an Act of the Canadian Legislature to build a railroad in Canada, an English contractor (A) being employed to do the work. A appointed a sub-A to construct the railroad and, in the course of construction, Quinn's land was compulsorily acquired. The dispute centred upon who should pay the compensation awarded to Quinn by arbitrators. Quinn sued P for the amount but P pleaded that the sub-A had no authority to bind the company and should not have referred the matter to arbitration. It was held that P was liable as 'they gave their powers to individuals who they knew would exercise them only by deputy',[3] and P also realised that the sub-A was acting in the name of P.

Where A's authority is such that it is necessary to execute it wholly or partly by means of a sub-agent

The *Quebec*[4] case, above, is also an illustration of this exception to the general rule and, in an American decision,[5] A was a an insurance agent who had responsibility for such a wide geographical area that the court considered that it was clearly intended that he could employ others to help him with the work.

---

17 (1859) 27 Beav 377 at 383, per Sir John Romilly MR.
18 [1968] 1 WLR 638.
19 See also *Re Deutsch* (1976) 82 DLR (3d) 567 (a Consul (A) as administrator of an estate was held to be entitled to appoint a sub-A actually to administer the deceased's estate); *McCann (John) & Co v Pow* [1974] 1 WLR 1643 (estate agents could not delegate their function to another firm of estate agents).
20 See Ch 2.
 1 (1852) 16 Beav 370.
 2 (1858) 12 Moo PCC 232.
 3 (1858) 12 Moo PCC 232 at 265, per the Right Hon T Pemberton Leigh.
 4 (1858) 12 Moo PCC 232.
 5 *Insurance Co of North America v Thornton* 130 Ala 222, 30 So 614 (1901).

Where from the conduct of P and A it may reasonably be presumed that their intention was that A should delegate his authority

In *De Bussche v Alt*,[6] A was authorised to sell a ship in India, China or Japan at a certain price but, as he could not sell the ship himself, he obtained P's consent to employ a sub-A in Japan to do so. The sub-A in fact purchased the ship himself and resold it to T at a profit. It was held that A had express authority to appoint the sub-A and privity of contract was created between P and the sub-A so that the latter was liable to account for the profit made. But the court went further, holding that the case was 'pre-eminently one in which the appointment of substitutes at ports other than those where the agent himself carries on business is a necessity, and must reasonably be presumed to be in the contemplation of the parties'.[7]

Where in the course of A's performing his authority unforeseen emergencies occur which necessitate his delegating certain tasks to another[8]

See *De Bussche v Alt* discussed above.

The effects of delegation

UNAUTHORISED DELEGATION

The effects of an unauthorised delegation are relatively clear: A will be liable to P for breach of duty and, generally, the acts of the sub-A will not bind P. Similarly, P is not liable to the sub-A for commission[9] and the sub-A has no lien against P.[10] However, it is important to stress that, even if P has expressly forbidden A's delegation, T may have a remedy against P as he may be able to rely on apparent authority in A to delegate if such authority would normally be part of A's actual, implied authority. An unauthorised delegation may also be ratified by P.[11]

AUTHORISED DELEGATION

Where the delegation is authorised, there is, somewhat paradoxically, much uncertainty regarding both the nature and effects of the legal relationships which are created. The doctrine of privity of contract assumes significance here and there is also considerable uncertainty as to whether tortious liability may be incurred in some of the relationships which are created.

---

6 (1878) 8 Ch D 286.
7 (1878) 8 Ch D 286 at 311, per Thesiger LJ; see also *Re Deutsch* (1976) 82 DLR (3d) 567 (a foreign Consul (A) who was given a power of attorney in the will of a deceased person was held able to appoint a sub-A to administer the estate, on the basis that this was the probable intent of the donor of the power).
8 *De Bussche v Alt* (1878) 8 Ch D 286; Cf *Gwilliam v Twist* [1895] 2 QB 84 (see Ch 6).
9 *Schmaling v Thomlinson* (1815) 6 Taunt 147.
10 *Solly v Rathbone* (1814) 2 M & S 298.
11 *Keay v Fenwick* (1876) 1 CPD 745.

The position between P and T

First, regarding the position between P and T, it is beyond doubt that if the appointment of the sub-A is authorised beforehand or is subsequently ratified by P, the acts of the sub-A will bind P. Thus P may be bound by a contract made by the sub-A,[12] may acquire knowledge through him[13] and commencement of proceedings by the sub-A may be valid.[14] P is bound in these instances where A has *authority* to delegate to the sub-A, irrespective of whether *privity of contract* is created between P and the sub-A.

Once it is admitted that the acts of the sub-A may bind P, it would seem natural to assert that, if there is no privity between P and the authorised sub-A but P is nevertheless bound by that sub-A's acts, there must be a principal-agent relationship between P and the sub-A. This is not the general rule, however, and the most convincing explanation of why P is bound by the authorised sub-A's acts is provided by Mechem[15] who considered that P's liability here was not premised on the notion that the sub-A became P's direct agent but, instead, P was bound 'by the act of his own agent who, in this instance, is (properly) doing the act through the subagent'.

The position between P and the sub-A

Second, when the P– sub-A nexus is evaluated, the possibility of privity of contract between them assumes great significance. It is quite possible, of course, for A to create both privity of contract and an agency between P and the sub-A, as in *De Bussche v Alt*, provided that A has the requisite authority to do so and the parties intend that legal relations be created. In fact, privity was achieved in *De Bussche* with a minimum of effort.[16] However, it was emphasised in *Calico Printers' Association v Barclays Bank*,[17] that the creation of privity of contract between P and the sub-A is not a concomitant of A's authority to delegate but, instead, privity requires 'precise proof'.[18] Wright J held that P must not only contemplate the appointment of the sub-A but also that he must authorise[19] A to create privity of contract between P and the sub-A.

Plainly, much must turn on the facts and the detailed relationship between the parties: should P be in immediate contact with the sub-A, for example, it

---

12   *De Bussche v Alt* (1878) 8 Ch D 286.
13   *Re Ashton, ex p McGowan* (1891) 64 LT 28.
14   *Solley v Wood* (1852) 16 Beav 370.
15   Mechem, *Outlines of the Law of Agency* (4th edn, 1952, ed P Mechem), p 51.
16   See also *Powell & Thomas v Evan Jones & Co* [1905] 1 KB 11 where *De Bussche* was followed. The sub-A was employed, with the assent of P, to procure an advance of money to P. The sub-A was regarded as a fiduciary and liable to account to P for bribes paid by T who advanced the money but the court considered that there was 'abundant evidence' (p 18, per Collins MR) of privity of contract between P and sub-A. Mathew LJ thought that, on these facts, 'the ordinary course of business...is that [the sub-A] takes the position of agent to the principal' (p 22).
17   (1931) 145 LT 51 (the plaintiff (P) appointed Barclays Bank (A) to collect the price of goods sold abroad. A appointed a local sub-A to collect the price and to warehouse and insure the goods if the buyer did not take delivery. The sub-A failed to insure and the goods were destroyed by fire. Held that (i) no privity existed between P and sub-A (ii) sub-A was not liable in negligence and, (iii) A would normally be liable but was protected by an exclusion clause in his contract with P).
18   (1931) 145 LT 51 at 55, per Wright J.
19   *Bowstead & Reynolds on Agency* (16th edn, 1996), Art 36, para 5-010 suggests that, because of this decision, A's authority to delegate 'will not readily be implied'.

should be much easier to establish a *direct* appointment by P of the sub-A.[20] Moreover, it must surely be crucial to ask what *function* the sub-A is performing and, to this end, several factual situations can be separated.[1] First, A may have authority to appoint the sub-A as an agent to P. This would mean either that A has brought P and the sub-A into a contractual relationship or that A has the authority to appoint the sub-A as P's agent. In both cases the logical conclusion must be that the sub-A has become P's agent. Second, A may have authority to appoint a substitute for himself to the extent that A does not perform the undertaking at all. Third, A may have authority to appoint a sub-A *in addition* to himself to perform some part of the original undertaking. In the first two situations, it is arguable that privity between P and the sub-A is apt whereas the latter relationship seems to be a case of delegation proper where A should remain liable for the default of his sub-A, the consequences of privity between P and the sub-A consequently being misplaced.

It is thus apparent that an authority in A to delegate does not, without more, create privity of contract between P and the sub-A. Thus, in general, A remains liable to P for the execution of his undertaking and is answerable for the default of the sub-A whom he has appointed. In turn, the sub-A must answer to A. For example, in *Stewart v Reavell's Garage*,[2] P took his 1929 model Bentley car to the defendant's garage (A) to have the brakes repaired. The brake drums needed relining by a specialist and, to P's knowledge, A did not undertake such work. P suggested a firm who would do the work but, on receiving their quotation for the price, both P and A considered it to be too costly. Consequently, A suggested that another firm (sub-A) known to them should do the work, their quotation being less costly. P assented to this arrangement. The work done by the sub-A was faulty with the result that, on applying the brakes, P's Bentley veered off the road and overturned. Sellers J held that A remained liable for the sub-A's defective work even though it was performed with P's express consent. Another instance of the general rule that A remains liable for the acts of the sub-A occurs where the sub-A receives money on behalf of P. It is clear that this is sufficient to make A accountable to P just as if A had received the money himself.[3]

It must always be remembered that, should A be liable to P for the acts of the sub-A in this way, he can seek redress from the sub-A who is answerable to A as

---

20 See *Muller (W H) & Co v Lethem* [1928] AC 34, 47-48 per Viscount Cave LC; *Schwensen v Ellinger, Heath, Western & Co* (1949) 83 Ll L Rep 79.
1 See Powell's rigorous dissection of the possible factual situations which can arise here (*The Law of Agency*, (2nd edn, 1961), pp 307-311).
2 [1952] 2 QB 545; *Meyerstein v Eastern Agency Co Ltd* (1885) 1 TLR 595 (P employed A to transmit shipping documents in relation to a consignment of goods shipped from Hamburg to Shanghai and to forward them to P's Shanghai correspondent, there to be sold at the best possible price. A forwarded the goods to another firm (sub-A) who pledged them with a Bank in return for an advance. Held that there was no privity between P and sub-A and A was liable for the acts of the sub-A); *Ecossaise Steamship Co Ltd v Lloyd, Low & Co* (1890) 7 TLR 76 (P employed Glasgow shipbrokers to find a charterer for his ship who had a 'first-class signature'. With P's approval, the Glasgow brokers communicated P's requirements to London shipbrokers (A) who, in turn, communicated with a Paris firm of shipbrokers. The Paris brokers effected a charter with a firm which did not exist and P suffered a loss. Held that P had authorised the Glasgow firm to delegate to the London brokers who thereby became P's agent and, as such, A remained liable for the Paris firm, who the court considered to be the agent for the *charterer* and not P's agent).
3 *Matthews v Haydon* (1796) 2 Esp 509; *National Employers' Mutual General Insurance Association Ltd v Elphinstone* [1929] WN 135; *Balsamo v Medici* [1984] 1 WLR 951.

A's agent. The law's approach is justified by two intertwined reasons. First, A should not be able to slough-off his liability to P simply by appointing a sub-A. Second, there is the (circuitous) justification that the general rule is that no privity of contract is created between P and the sub-A. However, it is arguably a harsh result to make A liable for the defaults of the sub-A where delegation is *authorised* and A has not been negligent in appointing the sub-A. This was the view taken by Atkin LJ in *Thomas Cheshire & Co v Vaughan Bros & Co*,[4] where he suggested that, in some circumstances, A might not be liable where he 'used reasonable care in the selection of the sub-agent'.[5] Of course, where A is authorised to delegate and is not negligent in selecting the sub-A, there is a greater likelihood that privity might be created between P and the sub-A such that A would not be liable to P.

Finally, when there is no privity of contract between P and sub-A, none of the incidents of contract are applicable to their relationship. P is thus not liable to the sub-A for remuneration[6] nor does the sub-A have any duty to account to P[7] and he is not liable to P for money had and received.[8] In *New Zealand and Australian Land Co v Watson*,[9] P, a land owner in New Zealand, shipped wheat to England and employed a factor (A) to sell it. With authority from P, A regularly employed a broker (sub-A) to sell the goods and, when he received the proceeds of sale, the sub-A accounted to A. The proceeds of sale were still in the sub-A's hands when A became bankrupt and was indebted to the sub-A. P sued the sub-A for the proceeds but it was held that he must fail as there was no privity of contract between them, and the sub-A was not liable to account to P.[10]

Might the sub-A be liable to P in negligence?

In 1931, Wright J stated that he knew of 'no English case in which a principal has recovered against a sub-agent for negligence'[11] but this assertion was made just prior to the decision in *Donoghue v Stevenson*[12] which initiated the modern development of the tort of negligence. Certainly bailors have maintained actions in tort against sub-bailees where there has been physical loss or damage to the bailor's goods[13]

---

4   [1920] 3 KB 240.
5   [1920] 3 KB 240 at 259. See also *Re J Mitchell* (1884) 54 LJ Ch 342 (A was liable to the beneficiaries of a will for money entrusted to a solicitor who embezzled it. Here A was negligent in paying money to the solicitor with knowledge of the latter's bankruptcy but Chitty J emphasised that A would be exempt from liability had he properly performed his duty and, for example, paid the money to a bank which had failed).
6   *Schmaling v Thomlinson* (1815) 6 Taunt 147.
7   *Lockwood v Abdy* (1845) 14 Sim 437.
8   *Cobb v Becke* (1845) 6 QB 930; *Robbins v Fennell* (1847) 11 QB 248 (both cases of country solicitors (A) employing town agents(sub-A) to whom their clients' (P) money was remitted; in neither case was the sub-A liable to the client for money had and received). The client's remedy here is against A. It is arguable that a modern court would decide these issues as part of the law of restitution.
9   (1881) 7 QBD 374.
10 The court was also emphatic that no fiduciary relationship existed between P and the sub-A and, if one existed, it was between A and the sub-A.
11 *Calico Printers' Association v Barclays Bank* (1931) 145 LT 51, 55 (P failed to recover against the sub-A for negligently failing to insure P's goods as there was held to be no privity of contract between the parties and the sub-A was not liable in negligence).
12 [1932] AC 562.
13 See *Morris v C W Martin & Sons Ltd* [1966] 1 QB 716; *Lee Cooper v C H Jeakins & Son Ltd* [1967] 2 QB 1; *Moukataff v British Overseas Airways Corpn* [1967] 1 Lloyd's Rep 396.

and in *Junior Books Ltd v Veitchi Co Ltd*,[14] a sub-contractor was liable in negligence to the owner of premises in which he did work even though the negligence caused purely economic loss.

After *Junior Books*, there was a marked disinclination to allow damages in negligence for financial loss, this view being well illustrated by *Balsamo v Medici*.[15] There an Italian owner (P) of a vintage car asked his friend Medici (A), a car dealer, to sell it on his behalf in England, the proceeds of sale to be remitted to P's mother-in-law who was in England. A successfully sold the car at auction but had to return to Italy before the sale's completion and, without authority from P, he appointed a sub-A to collect and transmit the money to Mrs Zecchi, P's mother-in-law. The sub-A thought that he was acting for A, had no knowledge of P and did not know that Mrs Zecchi was P's mother-in-law. The sub-A was apparently duped by an impostor who pretended to be Mrs Zecchi's representative and this resulted in the sub-A's paying the proceeds of sale in cash to that person who then promptly disappeared. A was insolvent and so it was important for P to seek a remedy against the sub-A. Walton J held that, although A was clearly liable to account to P, it was beyond doubt that the sub-A was not liable so to account and, also, was not liable in negligence. The judge chose to follow the bailment cases mentioned above and would have allowed the claim against the sub-A only where there was physical loss or damage to P's property. P's claim thus failed as he could not show that the money in the sub-A's hands 'was actually [P's] money'. If, on the other hand, P had been able to prove such a proprietary interest, the judge considered that the position would be precisely the same as if the sub-A 'had thrown away stamps or coins belonging to [P]'.[16] It is respectfully suggested that the decision is correct as P neither authorised nor knew of the sub-delegation at the time it was effected and, likewise, it could not be said that P relied on the sub-A to perform the task of collecting and transmitting the money.

However, in *Henderson v Merrett Syndicates Ltd*,[17] Lloyd's 'indirect names' successfully maintained an action in negligence against sub-agents with whom they had no privity of contract. The basis of the House of Lords' decision was that the sub-agents had assumed responsibility to perform professional services for the names who had, in turn, relied on the provision of those services. There was thus a sufficiently proximate relationship between the parties to give rise to a duty of care to exercise reasonable skill and care within the principle expounded in *Hedley Byrne & Co Ltd v Heller & Partners Ltd*.[18] It is thus clear that *Hedley Byrne* liability may exist on appropriate facts but it is difficult to predict when there will be sufficient proximity between P and the sub-A upon which to ground such liability.

Conclusion

It is evident that the legal relationship of principal and sub-agent is convoluted and inexact. Agency is a consensual subject and, irrespective of contract or tort,

---

14 [1983] 1 AC 520.
15 [1984] 1 WLR 951. See Whittaker, 'Remedies for Economic Loss against a Sub-Agent' (1985) 48 MLR 86; Reynolds, 'Tort Actions in Contractual Situations' (1985) 11 NSULR 215.
16 [1984] 1 WLR 951 at 960.
17 [1995] 2 AC 145.
18 [1964] AC 465.

there should, in principle, be no obstacle to the sub-A's being constituted P's direct agent on appropriate facts, particularly as the sub-A has been held to be a fiduciary and thus liable for secret profits[19] and, as detailed above, the acts of the authorised sub-A will bind P. This is certainly the position adopted in the USA[20] where, although the sub-A is generally not liable to P for breach of contract, he is liable 'for failing to pay over anything received for the principal, for careless handling of the principal's affairs, for negligent failure after undertaking to act, and for any violation of fiduciary duty'.[1] These duties are balanced by P's duty to indemnify the sub-A.[2]

19   *Powell & Thomas v Evan Jones & Co* [1905] 1 KB 11 (there was also considered to be sufficient evidence of privity between P and the sub-A on the facts).
20   See *Restatement, Agency, Second* (*Appendix*, reporter's note to § 5, pp 32-36); see also Seavey, 'Sub-Agents and Sub-Servants' (1955) 68 Harvard LR 658.
1   *Restatement, Agency, Second*, p 34.
2   *Restatement, Agency, Second*, p 35.

CHAPTER 8

The duties of the agent owed to his principal – Part 2: the agent's fiduciary duties

Introduction

The notion of the fiduciary relationship[1] is an enlargement of the law of trusts proper, the paradigm principal and agent relationship being fiduciary in nature in that P reposes confidence in A and trusts him to perform his undertaking with honesty and integrity. Moreover, as A acts on P's behalf and has the power to affect P's legal relations, it is fitting that P's vulnerable position be protected by the notion of fiduciary obligation. Fiduciary relations are thus 'founded on the highest and truest principles of morality'[2] meaning that fiduciaries must operate 'at a level higher than that trodden by the crowd'.[3] As will be seen later in this chapter, such exalted statements of principle translate into a series of practical duties which demand that A must work altruistically for P. It should be stressed at the outset that the fiduciary duties are not dependent on there being a contract between P and A and they apply with equal force in gratuitous agencies.

During the 18th and 19th centuries, the Court of Chancery extended its jurisdiction to the principal-agent relationship and developed the rigorous fiduciary duties which A owes to P. An agent is thus regarded as a status-based fiduciary along with the other established relationships of trustee/beneficiary, company director/company, solicitor/client and partner/co-partner, the central feature of these relationships being that, without further enquiry, they are regarded as being fiduciary in nature. The nucleus from which all the individual

---

1 See especially Dowrick, 'The Relationship of Principal and Agent' (1954) 17 MLR 24, 28-32; Sealy, 'Fiduciary Relationships' [1962] CLJ 69; Jones, 'Unjust Enrichment and the Fiduciary's Duty of Loyalty' (1968) 84 LQR 472; Finn, *Fiduciary Obligations* (1977); Shepherd, *The Law of Fiduciaries* (1981); Shepherd, 'Towards a Unified Concept of Fiduciary Relationships' (1981) 97 LQR 51; *Equity and Commercial Relationships* (ed Finn, 1987); *Equity, Fiduciaries and Trusts* (ed Youdan, 1989); Flannigan, 'The Fiduciary Obligation' (1989) 9 OJLS 285; Finn, 'Fiduciary Law and the Modern Commercial World' in *Commercial Aspects of Trusts and Fiduciary Obligations* (ed McKendrick, 1992), Ch 1; Mason, 'The Place of Equity and Equitable Remedies in the Contemporary Common Law World' (1994) 110 LQR 238; Sealy, 'Fiduciary Obligations, Forty Years On' (1995) 9 JCL 37; Austin, 'Moulding the Content of Fiduciary Duties' in *Trends in Contemporary Trust Law* (ed Oakley, 1996); Millett, 'Equity's Place in the Law of Commerce' (1998) 114 LQR 214.
2 *Parker v McKenna* (1874) 10 Ch App 96, 118 per Lord Cairns LC.
3 *Meinhard v Salmon* 164 NE 545 (1928), 546 per Cardozo CJ.

fiduciary obligations emanate is that A must not let his personal interest conflict with the overriding duties owed to P. Moreover, it will become clear when the substantive duties are examined, that A must not put himself in a position where there is a *possibility* of a conflict of interest and duty.[4] Elevated standards are thus demanded of A who must act selflessly in P's best interests and, in the absence of disclosing the true position, must never profit from the agency relationship. In the middle of the 19th century, the fiduciary's situation was authoritatively depicted by Lord Cranworth LC in *Aberdeen Rly Co v Blaikie Bros:*[5]

> 'And it is a rule of universal application, that no one, having [fiduciary] duties to discharge, shall be allowed to enter into engagements in which he has, or can have, a personal interest conflicting, or which possibly may conflict, with the interests of those whom he is bound to protect. So strictly is this principle adhered to, that no question is allowed to be raised as to the fairness or unfairness of a contract so entered into. It obviously is, or may be, impossible to demonstrate how far in any particular case the terms of such a contract have been the best for the interest of the cestui que trust, which it was possible to obtain. It may sometimes happen that the terms on which a trustee has dealt or attempted to deal with the estate or interests of those for whom he is a trustee, have been as good as could have been obtained from any other person– they may even at the time have been better. But still so inflexible is the rule that no inquiry on that subject is permitted.'

In the USA, the position is summarised more succinctly, but less eloquently, by the *Restatement, Second, Agency* § 387:

> 'Unless otherwise agreed, an agent is subject to a duty to his principal to act solely for the benefit of the principal in all matters connected with his agency.'

AGENTS, FIDUCIARY DUTIES AND COMMERCE

There are two quintessential features in the classical exposition of the rules of fiduciary obligation. First, there are many statements in the older decisions that the fiduciary principles are inflexible and must be applied rigidly. For example, an agent may be in breach of fiduciary duty where there is a possibility that, in the future, his personal interest might conflict with the duty owed to P, even though P may have benefited from A's actions.[6] Second, it is clear that fiduciary duties are *imposed* upon the parties rather than being the product of an imputed, common intent.[7] This strictness of approach often appears rather heavy handed today and, for better or worse, modern agency law inclines toward the view that the fiduciary duties should be both pliable and applied with discretion. There are certainly several prominent difficulties caused by the interpolation of fiduciary duty into commercial agencies.

Exalted, altruistic fiduciary duties may sometimes be difficult to square with the activities of commercial agents. Commerce is an activity which, after all, has the quest for profit as its *raison d'être* and it is an exacting duty which demands that, although A functions within the market place on behalf of P, he

---

4 See *Boardman v Phipps* [1967] 2 AC 46.
5 (1854) 1 Macq HL 461, 471-472.
6 See *Boardman v Phipps* [1967] 2 AC 46.
7 See Dowrick, 'The Relationship of Principal and Agent' (1954) 17 MLR 24, 31.

must rise above its morals in his dealings with P.[8] In 1914, A V Dicey[9] commented on the juxtaposition of commercial pratice and absolute morality:

'Even at the present day the Courts maintain, or attempt to maintain, rules as to the duty of an agent towards his employer which are admitted by every conscientious man to be morally sound, but which are violated every day by tradesmen, merchants, and professional men, who make no scruple at giving or accepting secret commissions ... here, at any rate, the morality of the Courts is higher than the morality of traders or of politicians'.

A further concern is that the widely varying types of commercial agent and the different functions which they perform mean that it is difficult to fix accurately the scope of the fiduciary duties and dispense decisively the appropriate remedies for their breach. Many questions are obvious yet difficult to answer succinctly. Might the full panoply of fiduciary duties be inapplicable to some agents? Is it always apt to apply fiduciary duties to those agents who act gratuitously on P's behalf? Should P have proprietary or personal remedies for breach of the fiduciary duties? These difficulties can only be resolved by applying the fiduciary duties flexibly to appropriate agency situations rather than enforcing those duties indiscriminately simply because agency is regarded as a status-based fiduciary relationship. A degree of uncertainty is, however, the concomitant of flexibility. In *Re Coomber*,[10] Fletcher Moulton LJ cautioned against the notion of a standardised fiduciary relationship with remedies applied mechanically and automatically:

'Fiduciary relations are of many different types; they extend from the relation of myself to an errand boy who is bound to bring me back my change up to the most intimate and confidential relations which can possibly exist between one party and another where the one is wholly in the hands of the other because of his infinite trust in him ... in some minds there arises the idea that if there is any fiduciary relation whatever any of these types of interference is warranted by it. They conclude that every kind of fiduciary relation justifies every kind of interference. Of course that is absurd. The nature of the fiduciary relation must be such that it justifies the interference.'[11]

---

8 In *Meinhard v Salmon* 164 NE 545 (1928), 546 Cardozo C J emphasised that 'many forms of conduct permissible in a work-a-day world for those acting at arm's length, are forbidden to those bound by fiduciary ties'.

9 *Law and Public Opinion in England During the Nineteenth Century* (2nd edn, 1914), p 368.

10 [1911] 1 Ch 723.

11 [1911] 1 Ch 723 at 729. See also *Boardman v Phipps* [1967] 2 AC 46, 123 per Lord Upjohn: 'Rules of equity have to be applied to such a great diversity of circumstances that they can be stated only in the most general terms and applied with particular attention to the exact circumstances of each case'; *New Zealand Netherlands Society Oranje Inc v Kuys* [1973] 1 WLR 1126, 1129-1130 per Lord Wilberforce: 'The obligation ... not to allow a conflict to arise between duty and interest, is one of strictness ... Naturally it has different applications in different contexts ... but the precise scope of it must be moulded according to the nature of the relationship'; *Hospital Products Ltd v United States Surgical Corpn* (1984) 156 CLR 41, 97 per Mason J: 'The fiduciary relationship, if it is to exist at all, must accommodate itself to the terms of the contract so that it is consistent with, and conforms to, them. The fiduciary relationship cannot be superimposed upon the contract in such a way as to alter the operation which the contract was intended to have according to its true construction'; *Securities and Exchange Commission v Chenery Corpn* 318 US 80, 85-86 (1943) per Justice Frankfurter: 'To say that a man is a fiduciary only begins the analysis: it gives direction to further inquiry. To whom is he a fiduciary? What obligations does he owe as a fiduciary? In what respect has he failed to discharge those obligations? And what are the consequences of his deviation from duty?'; Lehane,'Fiduciaries in a Commercial Context' in *Essays in Equity* (ed PD Finn, 1985), Ch 5.

Similarly, in *Boardman v Phipps*,[12] Lord Upjohn considered that 'the facts and circumstances must be carefully examined to see whether in fact a purported agent and even a confidential agent is in a fiduciary relationship to his principal. It does not necessarily follow that he is in such a position (see *Re Coomber*)'.[13] In short, while agency is clearly classifiable as a fiduciary relationship, the content and intensity of A's duties and the range of P's remedies may vary with the structure and subject-matter of the agency relationship at issue.[14] Certainly equity's most stringent rules are more aptly applied to express trustees than agents for two conspicuous reasons. First, the trust has a more certain factual content and form than many agency relationships and the beneficiary is frequently in a more exposed position than P. Second, the beneficiary has little control over the trustee, the latter having both legal title to, and control of the trust property, whereas P does not usually vest the title to property in A and, by and large, he retains effective control of A's activities.

Finally, there are undoubted difficulties generated by the general rule that, where P and A have a contract, they may exclude or limit the fiduciary duties by contract terms. Again it is apparent that there is something of a conflict here. It is one thing for the law to apply the duties with discernment having regard to adversarial, commercial conditions, but quite another to grant the parties free rein to exclude the fiduciary duties on the basis that they do not harmonise with their contractual undertakings. Should the fiduciary duties dominate contractual undertakings or vice-versa? In *Kelly v Cooper*,[15] the Privy Council decided that the needs of commerce and the nature of estate agency meant that the fiduciary duties could be configured according to the contractual situation to hand. Lord Browne-Wilkinson[16] considered that 'agency is a contract made between principal and agent ... like every other contract, the rights and duties of the principal and agent are dependent upon the terms of the contract between them, whether express or implied'. The emphasis here is that fiduciary duties are necessarily subjugated to contract terms but, with respect, it is suggested that this represents an inversion of priorities. Fiduciary obligation is founded on the vulnerability of one of the parties thus causing him to place reliance upon the other and, in turn, this justifies equity's protective jurisdiction. Rather than accepting that the duties are freely excludable the primary question should surely be whether it is reasonable for the parties to exclude or modify, by the use of contract terms, the foundations of loyalty and confidence upon which the relationship is built.[17] Moreover, while accepting that the fiduciary duties might properly be excluded by express terms, it is quite a different proposition to allow, as did *Kelly*, that the fiduciary duties are capable of modification by *implied* terms of the contract. It is interesting to note that, at the other extreme, new Regulations[18] which implement an EC Directive[19] imply

---

12   [1967] 2 AC 46, 127.
13   The celebrated passage from *Re Coomber* [1911] 1 Ch 723, warning against standardised fiduciary relations, was set-out earlier.
14   See *Kelly v Cooper* [1993] AC 205 (considered below).
15   [1993] AC 205 (considered below).
16   [1993] AC 205 at 213-214.
17   See also *Jirna Ltd v Mister Donut of Canada Ltd* (1971) 22 DLR (3d) 639; affd 40 DLR (3d) 303; *Midcon Oil & Gas Ltd v New British Dominion Oil Co Ltd* (1958) 12 DLR (2d) 705, both considered below.
18   The Commercial Agents (Council Directive) Regulations 1993 (SI 1993/3053 as amended by SI 1993/3173) became operative on 1 January 1994, for existing and subsequent agreements.
19   EC Commercial Agents Directive 86/653/EEC.

certain duties of good faith into specialised, commercial agency relationships and provide that the obligations created are not excludable.[20]

BUSINESS COMPETITOR OR FIDUCIARY?

As a general proposition, it is indisputable that where A has the power to affect P's legal position, the agency is fiduciary in nature.

Apart from the established categories of fiduciary relationship and those situations where the parties choose to add fiduciary duties to their contractual undertakings, there is a recalcitrant, contemporary difficulty as to whether some commercial relationships entered into between apparent equals might properly be characterised as fiduciary in nature or, at least, as being subject to appropriate fiduciary duties. The problem here is whether the contract *itself* may generate fiduciary duties. There is a tendency to assert that the unconscionable conduct of the defendant justifies equity's intervention but it must always be borne in mind that a mercantile contract may provide adequate safeguards and remedies for the injured party and so a fiduciary relationship may be inapt where the parties accept the cut-and-thrust of commerce. This was the eventual view taken in the important Australian decision in *Hospital Products Ltd v United States Surgical Corpn*,[1] considered below. On the other hand, fiduciary obligations have been held to exist in some commercial relationships where there is no great disparity of bargaining strengths.[2] The contention that a fiduciary relationship exists is primarily of significance in relation to the proprietary remedies which are sought. For example, the imposition of a remedial, constructive trust places the injured party in an incomparably superior position in that his entitlement to profits made by the fiduciary may far exceed any claim in damages for breach of contract and may also mean that the fiduciary is stripped of assets to the possible detriment of his general creditors who have no say in the matter.

---

20 The Regulations, which are couched in very broad terms, apply to *self-employed* commercial agents (not gratuitous agents) with *continuing authority* to negotiate the *sale or purchase* of goods on behalf of P (reg 2((1)) and they impose a non-excludable general duty of good faith on A *and* P. P must provide A with all necessary documentation and information relating to the goods which A requires to perform the agency and must inform A of any anticipated downturn in the volume of business (regs 3, 4 and 5). See Reynolds, 'Commercial Agents Directive' [1994] JBL 265; Davey, J and Randolph, F, *Guide to the Commercial Agents Regulations* (1994).

1 (1984) 156 CLR 41 (High Court of Australia).

2 See *United Dominion Corpn v Brian Pty Ltd* (1985) 157 CLR 1 (High Court of Australia); *LAC Minerals Ltd v International Corona Resources Ltd* (1989) 61 DLR (4th) 14 (Supreme Court of Canada). In *LAC*, the plaintiff (P), an entrepreneurial mining company which was in need of finance to support exploration, owned mining rights on certain land where it was drilling exploratory holes. The defendant (D), a better established mining company, approached P with a view to a partnership/joint venture and P revealed the results of the drilling from which it was clear that the adjacent property was likely to have mineral deposits and that P was seeking to acquire that property. While negotiations between P and D were still in progress, D put in a successful, competing bid for the land and developed the mining itself. Held that D was in breach of a duty not to misuse confidential information and the appropriate remedy was the imposition of a constructive trust upon D. While there was unanimity as to D's liability, the judgments in *LAC* vary considerably regarding the relevance of fiduciary relationships and duties in commerce and there are some forceful statements that fiduciary duty has a distinct role to play in commerce, eg 'It is simply not the case that business and accepted morality are mutually exclusive domains' (p 44, per La Forest J).

In some of the newly-developing and somewhat ill-defined relationships such as franchising and distributorship, it is difficult to predict whether the courts will consider that agency principles and accompanying fiduciary duties are pertinent to the facts or, alternatively, decide that the business relationship is entered into between equals dealing at arm's length. In this context, the decision in *Hospital Products Ltd v United States Surgical Corpn*[3] is a seminal one. There the plaintiff (P) granted to the defendant (D) the exclusive right to distribute in Australia certain surgical products which were manufactured by P, but D intended to use this contractual relationship as the foundation to establish itself as a manufacturer of similar products in direct competition with P. Once D had the capacity to make its own goods, it suspended the orders for P's products, terminated the contract with P and supplied the customers with its own products. P contended that fidiciary duties amplified the contractual relationship and so, in addition to D's liability for breach of contract, D held its business on constructive trust for P. The Court of Appeal of New South Wales[4] held that the contract contained an express term that D would promote P's products and an implied term that D would not perform acts which were detrimental to the market for P's products. Consequently, D was obliged to act in P's best interests. The High Court of Australia unanimously rejected the finding of an implied term and, by a majority, held that no fiduciary obligations should be imposed on D because the contract was entered into between equals dealing at arm's length and, from the outset, D had intended to profit legitimately from the relationship. Consequently, D was held not to be a constructive trustee but was liable in damages for breach of contract.

Similarly, in *Jirna Ltd v Mister Donut of Canada Ltd*,[5] the dispute concerned a franchise relationship under which the plaintiff could use the defendant's trade name and manufacturing processes but was obliged to buy materials from suppliers approved by the defendant franchisor at prices negotiated by the defendant. The franchise agreement stated that the parties were to be independent contractors and that 'no partnership, joint venture or relationship of principal and agent is intended'. The defendant received a rebate from the suppliers based upon the volume of supplies bought by the franchised dealers and the plaintiff argued that the defendant was liable to account for the rebate on the basis that it was a secret profit. At first instance, it was held that this was more than a vendor-purchaser relationship; rather it was a fiduciary relationship which precluded the defendant from making a secret profit. The decision was reversed on appeal[6] on the basis that the court must give full effect to the express intentions of the parties[7] who had no disparity of bargaining power and were equals dealing at arm's length.[8]

This issue will remain contentious because it is clear that 'the category of cases in which fiduciary duties and obligations arise from the circumstances of

---

3 (1984) 156 CLR 41.
4 [1983] 2 NSWLR 157.
5 (1970) 13 DLR (3d) 645.
6 (1971) 22 DLR (3d) 639; affd 40 DLR (3d) 303.
7 See also *Midcon Oil & Gas v New British Dominion Oil Co* (1958) 12 DLR (2d) 705 (the parties intended to exploit jointly a gas field, the contract declaring that no agency or partnership relationship was created. The Supreme Court of Canada implemented the contract terms and refused to find a fiduciary relationship between the parties).
8 See also Brown, 'Franchising – A Fiduciary Relationship' (1971) 49 Texas L Rev 650.

the case and the relationship of the parties is no more "closed" than the categories of negligence at common law'.[9] That being said, the intrusion of fiduciary obligation into routine commercial transactions has always been viewed with apprehension by English law[10] and, most recently, the decision in *Re Goldcorp Exchange Ltd*,[11] exemplifies the comprehensive refusal to admit equitable doctrine into a contract for the sale of goods.

REMEDIES FOR BREACH OF FIDUCIARY DUTY

There are numerous remedies available for breach of fiduciary duty but, just as the intensity and scope of the duties are contentious issues throughout varying factual relationships, it comes as no suprise that there is correlative apprehension and uncertainty regarding the appropriate remedies for the various breaches of duty. The range of potential remedies is vast: damages may be awarded for breach of contract or liablity may arise in tort; the transaction tainted by breach of duty may be set aside and an order made that the fiduciary must account for profits or restore specific property. Again, the court may grant an injunction restraining breaches of duty and a fiduciary may often be liable for money had and received.

Equity's dominant strategy is to impose duties on fiduciaries which are analogous to those of a trustee. In many instances, proprietary remedies are available for breach of duty and, consequently, where A is in breach of duty and profits thereby, he may hold the benefits on constructive trust for P so that the money or property involved *belongs* to the latter. This proprietary remedy should be contrasted with a personal remedy which makes A liable, by way of *obligation*, to pay money to P. It may often be of no concern to P whether a remedy is personal or proprietary but the proprietary claim does possess several conspicuous advantages: (i) P will have the remedy of tracing money or property which was received by A but which is in the hands of T (ii) P is entitled to the profits from his money or property (iii) the equitable doctrine of laches applies to P's claim instead of the periods prescribed by the Limitation Acts (iv) P's property will not be available to A's creditors in the event of A's bankruptcy and, (v) if A mixes P's money with his own, P may be entitled to the entire fund if A is unable to prove which part is his.

It will already be apparent that A may be in breach of the fiduciary duties where he has made an undisclosed gain in the course of the agency, even though no *loss* is caused thereby to P. This could apply, for example, where A has taken a bribe from a third party,T, but the terms of P's contract with T are more beneficial to P than could be obtained elswhere. In the context of bribes taken by agents, it is now clear that the maxim that 'equity looks on as done that which ought to be done' is applied with such rigour that A's illicit profits are treated as belonging to P and are held by A on constructive trust for P.[12] The wider issue of whether proprietary remedies should always be available to P where A has profited in breach of duty is a vexed and much-

---

9 *Laskin v Bache & Co Inc* (1971) 23 DLR (3d) 385, 392 per Arnup JA.
10 See *Re Wait* [1927] 1 Ch 606 (considered in Ch 16).
11 [1995] 1 AC 74 (considered in Ch 16).
12 See *A-G for Hong Kong v Reid* [1994] 1 AC 324 (considered later in this chapter).

debated topic.[13] It is sometimes asked whether proprietary remedies should be restricted to those cases where P has suffered a *loss* of property with a consequential gain made by A, and concern is often expressed for the creditors of the insolvent agent if the property is withdrawn from them and awarded to P.[14] That being said, it is difficult to see how A's creditors can complain where the 'proprietary remedy merely withdraws from the insolvent's estate an asset which it was never meant to have'[15] and it is surely better that P should receive a windfall than allowing either the rogue fiduciary or his creditors to secure an ill-gotten gain. Moreover, at the heart of the fiduciary duties lies the aim of deterring corruption and the rules are not premised simply on compensatory principles. In 1874, James LJ[16] stressed the cardinal rule that A is prevented from asserting that a profit could not have been obtained by P:

> 'The rule is an inflexible one, and must be applied inexorably by this court, which is not entitled, in my judgment, to receive evidence, or suggestion, or argument, as to whether the principal did or did not suffer any injury in fact, by reason of the dealing of the agent; for the safety of mankind requires that no agent shall be able to put his principal to the danger of an inquiry such as that'.

Although this statement encapsulates late 19th century morality expressed in compellingly florid terms, Lord Templeman's speech in *A-G for Hong Kong v Reid*,[17] set the same tone at the end of the 20th century. Indeed, after *Reid's* case, it is arguable that proprietary remedies are available automatically for breach of fiduciary duty.

WHEN DOES THE AGENT HOLD PROPERTY AS A TRUSTEE?

Apart from profits made in breach of duty, it is of cardinal importance to know when A holds money or property as a trustee or, alternatively, when such money or property is regarded as belonging to A but subject to a duty to pay it to P. This has particular relevance where A becomes insolvent while in the possession of property gleaned from the agency and thus deriving from either P or T. *Bowstead & Reynolds*[18] stresses that, although it is difficult to generalise, the situations where a trust has been held to exist fall largely into two broad categories, viz (i) where money or property has been specifically entrusted to A by P to hold for P's benefit or to use for a specific purpose; and (ii) where money or property has been handed to A by T to hold or convert into specific property for the benefit of P.

The facts of *Burdick v Garrick*[19] provide a prime illustation of these principles. A solicitor in London (A) held a power of attorney from P in America to sell P's

---

13   See especially Youdan, 'The Fiduciary Principle: The Applicability of Proprietary Remedies' in *Equity, Fiduciaries and Trusts* (ed Youdan, 1989); Gummow, 'Unjust Enrichment, Restitution and Proprietary Remedies' in *Essays on Restitution* (ed Finn, 1990), Ch 2.
14   See Goode, 'Property and Unjust Enrichment' in *Essays on the Law of Restitution* (ed Burrows, 1991), Ch 9; Goode, 'The Recovery of a Director's Improper Gains: Proprietary Remedies for Infringement of Non-proprietary Rights' in *Commercial Aspects of Trusts and Fiduciary Obligations* (ed McKendrick, 1992).
15   Millett, 'Bribes and Secret Commissions' [1993] Restitution L Rev 7, 17.
16   *Parker v McKenna* (1874) 10 Ch App 96, 124-125.
17   [1994] 1 AC 324; *Reid's* case is considered later in this chapter.
18   *Bowstead & Reynolds on Agency* (16th edn, 1996), para 6-043.
19   (1870) 5 Ch App 233; see also *North American Land and Timber Co v Watkins* [1904] 1 Ch 242; affd [1904] 2 Ch 233.

English property and invest the proceeds in P's name. A received interest from the investments and paid it into his firm's account. P died intestate and some eight years later his widow filed a bill against A for an account. It was held that A held the money in trust for P and thus the Statute of Limitations was no bar to the suit. Sir GM Giffard LJ stressed that ' this was a very special power of attorney, under which the agents were authorised to receive and invest, to buy real estate, and otherwise to deal with the property; but under no circumstances could the money be called theirs; under no circumstances had they the least right to apply the money to their own use, or to keep it otherwise than to a distinct and separate account; throughout the whole of the time that this agency lasted the money was the money of Mr Garrick, and not in any sense theirs'.[20]

It does seem that, currently, the matter is approached 'more functionally and [the courts] ask whether the trust relationship is appropriate to the commercial relationship in which the parties find themsleves; whether it was appropriate that money or property should be, and whether it was, held separately, or whether it was contemplated that the agent should use the money, property or proceeds of the property as part of his normal cash flow in such a way that the relationship of debtor and creditor is more appropriate'.[1] This 'functional' approach was evident in the recent decision in *Triffit Nurseries v Salads Etcetera Ltd*.[2] The defendant (A) marketed and distributed vegetables, including the produce of Triffit Nurseries (P), and remitted the proceeds of sale to P. Much of the produce was sold to supermarkets (T) and it was clear that A acted merely as a commission agent for P and never obtained title to the vegetables. A went into administrative receivership with amounts outstanding in respect of sales of P's vegetables to T. The receivers got in the outstanding moneys from T and regarded the sums obtained to be part of A's assets which were subject to a debenture in favour of A's bank. P, on the other hand, considered that the money belonged to him, contending that the cessation of A's business ended A's authority to act for P and the relationship of debtor and creditor also ceased. Accordingly, P argued that any money obtained for produce after the cessation of A's business was held on trust for P. The Court of Appeal held that (i) there was no general principle that a person whose business was to act as an agent in turning to account the property of P was not entitled to keep the proceeds of P's property after he had ceased to carry on business (ii) the agency was not terminated automatically on the appointment of receivers but, even if it had been thus determined, that could not by itself alter A's rights and those of its receivers to seek outstanding sums due from customers and P's claim could only succeed if the circumstances were such that it would be wholly unconscionable for the receivers to oppose the claim, and (iii) immediately before receivership the customer's debts were assets of A which were charged to the bank and the appointment of receivers and the cessation of trading could not alter that. It followed that the customer's debts were not P's property nor were they held on trust for P.

Classification of the agent's fiduciary duties

A's duties may now be classified and examined separately but it is important to realise that it is not possible to put the duties into water-tight compartments and

---

20 (1870) 5 Ch App 233 at 243.
1 *Bowstead & Reynolds on Agency* (16th edn, 1996), para 6-043.
2 [2000] 2 Lloyd's Rep 74.

there may be an overlap of several duties in any one set of facts. The Law Commission[3] recently summarised the duties which a fiduciary owes to his beneficiary in four broad rules viz, (i) the no conflict rule: A must not place himself in a position where his own interests conflict with his duty to P (ii) the no profit rule: A must not profit from his position at the expense of P (iii) the undivided loyalty rule: A must not place himself in a position where his duty towards one P conflicts with his duty owed to another P (iv) the duty of confidentiality: A must not use confidential information acquired in the course of the agency for his own benefit or for the benefit of a third party. These classifications embody all the issues relevant to A's fiduciary duties but the duties must now be sub-divided and considered in detail.

THE AGENT'S DUTY TO MAKE A FULL DISCLOSURE WHERE HE HAS A PERSONAL INTEREST

This duty lies at the heart of the fiduciary relationship. A cannot enter into any transaction where his personal interest might conflict with his overriding duty of impartiality to P *unless* P has full knowledge of the all the facts and the extent of A's interest and then chooses to assent to A's course of action. As P must have the opportunity of preventing A's actions, A's disclosure must be full and precise and the burden of proving it lies on A.[4] For example, in *Imperial Mercantile Credit Association v Coleman*,[5] A was a director of a company and a stockbroker who arranged for the sale of shares to the company, in which he was interested as a stockbroker, taking a commission on the sale. The company's articles required that a director who dealt with the company should 'declare his interest'. The other directors knew A to be a broker and he told them that he had an 'interest' – while they knew that this meant commission they did not know its amount. It was held that A should have declared the *nature* of his interest and that he was liable to account to the company for the whole amount of the commission.

Likewise, it is insufficient for A to make a partial disclosure which would put P on enquiry[6] and any custom which allegedly allows A to put his interest above his duty is prima facie unreasonable and will be ineffective in the absence of P's consent.[7] Moreover, as a fiduciary in whom P has reposed trust and confidence, A is almost certainly under a duty to disclose his own breaches of duty,[8] thus setting the seal on the severity of the rule of disclosure.

A's duty to act solely for the benefit of P and make a full disclosure of any self-interest is central to all the other fiduciary sub-duties (eg A must not exploit P's confidential information for his own gain or take a bribe from T) but it finds its clearest application in those situations where A deals with P, viz, A is instructed to sell P's property but A buys it himself or A is instructed to buy property on P's behalf but chooses to sell his own property to P. It should be emphasised that

---

3 *Fiduciary Duties and Regulatory Rules* (Law Com No 236, Cm 3049, 1995), para 1.4.
4 *Dunne v English* (1874) LR 18 Eq 524.
5 (1873) LR 6 HL 189.
6 *Dunne v English* (1874) LR 18 Eq 524 (it was insufficient for A to inform P that 'several persons' were interested in buying P's mine when A was one of the persons).
7 See *Robinson v Mollett* (1875) LR 7 HL 802 (considered in Ch 5).
8 See the decisions concerned with employment: *Horcal Ltd v Gatland* [1983] IRLR 459; affd [1984] IRLR 288 without reference to this issue; *Sybron Corpn v Rochem Ltd* [1984] Ch 112; *Nottingham University v Fishel* [2000] IRLR 471.

there is no *prohibition* on A's dealing with P in this way, the rule being that the transaction will be valid provided that A discloses any personal interest and does not take unfair advantage of the position. In *McPherson v Watt*,[9] A, a Scottish attorney, bought houses from two clients, the purchases being apparently for A's brother but A was the real buyer. The House of Lords held that as A had not disclosed his interest he could not obtain specific performance of the contract. Where a solicitor wishes to purchase property from a client, it is thus essential for him to ensure that the client has independent advice or the transaction will be tainted.[10] Likewise, in *Armstrong v Jackson*,[11] P instructed A, a stockbroker, to buy shares in a certain company. A pretended to buy in the open market but, in fact, sold his own shares to P. Six years later, the shares had dramatically fallen in price and it was held that P could rescind the transaction and recover all sums paid to A, the decrease in the value of the shares and the lapse of time[12] being no bar to rescission. McCardie J stressed that 'a broker who is employed to buy shares cannot sell his own shares unless he makes a full and accurate disclosure of the fact to to his principal, and the principal, with a full knowledge, gives his assent to the changed position of the broker. The rule is one not merely of law but of obvious morality'.[13]

In these situations where A has dealt with P, A may assert that the contract is fair in that P has been charged the market price and that A had no intent to defraud, but it is clear that in the absence of full disclosure this is immaterial and P may nevertheless rescind the contract.[14]

Duration of the duty of disclosure

There is no doubt that the requirement of disclosure may subsist after A has ceased to be P's agent but the duty's existence and duration will depend upon the circumstances of the case, the type of agent involved and, most importantly, whether confidence still exists between P and A.[15] A director's fiduciary duty owed to his company does not necessarily terminate when he ceases to be a director but, at the same time, he must eventually be freed from the obligations owed to the previous company.[16] Similarly, a solicitor's duty of disclosure may last longer than that of a stockbroker who has a more impersonal relationship with P. In *McMaster v Byrne*,[17] P owned shares in a company and granted X an option to purchase them for $30,000. X assigned the option to A who was the

---

9 (1877) 3 App Cas 254.
10 See *Spector v Ageda* [1973] Ch 30, where Megarry J suggested that a solicitor should not act for a client in these circumstances.
11 [1917] 2 KB 822.
12 P was ignorant of the fraud throughout.
13 [1917] 2 KB 822 at 823-824; see also *Lucifero v Castel* (1887) 3 TLR 371 (P authorised A to buy a yacht for himself but A bought the yacht himself and resold it to P at a profit without any disclosure of the position. It was held that A was in breach of duty and could recover from P only the price he had paid for the yacht although he did recover the agreed commission).
14 *Gillett v Peppercorne* (1840) 3 Beav 78; *Bentley v Craven* (1853) 18 Beav 75; *Aberdeen Rly Co v Blaikie Bros* (1854) 1 Macq 461;
15 See *Carter v Palmer* (1842) 8 C & Fin 657(A had been P's counsel for a long time and had acquired intimate knowledge of P's property. After the agency had ended, A bought some of P's property and made a profit but the House of Lords held that A must account to P); *Allison v Clayhills* (1907) 97 LT 709.
16 See *Island Export Finance Ltd v Umunna* [1986] BCLC 460.
17 [1952] 1 All ER 1362.

company's solicitor and had, formerly, been P's solicitor. A exercised the option at a time when negotiations were in progress for the take-over of the company (A being fully aware of the proposed take-over) and, as a result, he sold the shares for $127,000. It was held that a confidential relationship still existed between P and A and thus A should have disclosed the position to P before buying the shares.

The *McMaster* case should be contrasted with *Christoforides v Terry*.[18] There, P employed A, a broker, to make speculative purchases of cotton for him and P became heavily indebted to A owing to a fall in cotton prices. As P could not reimburse A, A closed the account in accordance with the terms of his agency and called upon P to indemnify him against the loss but P refused. A then sold the cotton which he had bought on P's behalf and immediately re-purchased it at the same price. A got into financial difficulties and assigned his property for the benefit of his creditors. An action to enforce the claim for indemnity was brought by the trustee of the deed of assignment but P resisted the claim on the ground that A had committed a breach of duty. It was held that, as A had validly terminated the agency and the method of resale ensured that A would not make a secret profit, this was an acceptable procedure and so A was entitled to an indemnity from P.

It is beyond doubt, however, that A cannot assert that his *own* breach of duty terminates the agency thereby leaving him free of the duty of disclosure in subsequent transactions for this would provide him with a clinical means of evading his fiduciary duties. In *Regier v Campbell-Stuart*,[19] P instructed A to give her particulars of any house suitable for purchase by P. A found such a house and, through a nominee, X, bought it for £2,000, the purchase money being furnished by A. A then purported to buy it from X for £4,500 and offered it to P for £5,000, pointing out that this would allow A a profit of £500. P duly purchased the house for £5,000. It was held that A might terminate the agency relationship by selling his own property to P but that if he concealed material facts and fraudulently obtained an advantage for himself, his duties to P had not ended and he was accordingly liable to account to P for the secret profits obtained.

In conclusion, it is impossible to state with precision when A might be free of the duty of disclosure and consequently able to deal with P at arm's length. Certainly the decision in *Nordisk Insulinlaboratorium v Gorgate Products Ltd*[20] indicates that the termination of an agency may be crucial and that duties do not endure *ad infinitum*. In *Nordisk*, P deposited insulin with an English bank in 1939 but, on P's becoming an enemy alien in 1940, the insulin was sold to A who had been P's selling agent before the war, A then reselling the goods at a profit. At first instance, Vaisey J held that A was liable to account to P for the profits made as 'the fiduciary nature of an agency is, to my mind, far too deeply seated to be shaken and destroyed as easily as the defendants would seem to have supposed'.[1] That decision was reversed, the Court of Appeal holding that A's earlier agency had been to sell liquid insulin but it was crystallised insulin which had been deposited with the bank and, once that deposit had been effected,

---

18 [1924] AC 566.
19 [1939] Ch 766. See also *McLeod and More v Sweezey* [1944] 2 DLR 145 (P was induced by A's fraud to terminate the agency, A then making a secret profit from information obtained while he was P's agent. A was held liable to account to P for the profit made).
20 [1953] Ch 430.
 1 [1953] Ch 430 at 435.

the agency was at an end and A was not under any fiduciary duty to P. The court also considered that the agency had never been confidential in nature as A had at no time acquired any secret knowledge regarding the insulin. Lord Evershed MR questioned whether, assuming that there had been fiduciary duties owed by A which were contractual in origin, they would cease when P became an enemy alien or whether a 'residuary obligation'[2] in equity might subsist, but he came to no definite conclusion. The nature of the contract between P and A and its duration can thus only be relevant factors amongst many in assessing whether A has sloughed-off his duties owed to P.[3]

Remedies where A has dealt with P in breach of duty

Where A has dealt with P and failed to make a full disclosure, P has several remedies. First, P may choose to rescind the contract and it does not matter that the price charged by A was fair or at the market value. Likewise, it is no bar to rescission that the contract between P and A has been executed or that the property has depreciated in value,[4] but P must commence proceedings within a reasonable time of discovering the truth or he will be held to have acquiesced.[5] Moreover, P may set aside the contract even where A purchased the property in question *before* he became P's agent.[6]

Alternatively, should P wish to affirm the contract (or be obliged to affirm as a bar to rescission applies, eg the property has been conveyed to T) the general rule is that he can claim the profit made by A or damages for breach of contract. In *Bentley v Craven*,[7] A was a partner in a firm of sugar refiners and also an independent wholesale grocer who speculated in sugar. He bought sugar and sold it to the firm making a considerable personal profit (although the sale was at the fair, market price) without disclosing the position. It was held that the firm was entitled to the profit made by A. Similarly, in *De Bussche v Alt*,[8] the authorised sub-A who was employed to sell P's ship at a minimum price, bought it himself at that price and resold it at a large profit. It was held that, although rescission was impossible, the sub-A was liable to account to P for the profit made on the resale.

However, where P does not seek rescission (or cannot obtain it because a bar to rescission applies) but instead wishes to recover the profit made by A, some of the decisions draw a crucial distinction between two situations, viz (i) A, an existing agent of P, is instructed to acquire property for P and must thus find a suitable vendor, but A secretly buys property from T and then resells it to P at a profit and, (ii) A secretly sells property to P which A owned *before* the date of

---

2 [1953] Ch 430 at 442.
3 See *Keppel v Wheeler* [1927] 1 KB 577 (P instructed A to offer a block of flats for sale. A received an offer from T, subject to contract, and communicated it to P who accepted. Before contracts were exchanged, A received a higher offer from T2. Believing that his duty to P was discharged, A did not tell P of this offer but, instead, arranged a sale from T to T2 and obtained commission on that sale. A sued P for commission on the original sale to T; P counterclaimed for the difference between the price paid by T and the price paid by T2 to T. It was held that A was entitled to commission as he acted *bona fide* but he was liable in damages to P for breach of duty. A was still P's agent and should have told him of the better offer).
4 *Armstrong v Jackson* [1917] 2 KB 822.
5 *Wentworth v Lloyd* (1863) 32 Beav 467.
6 See *Armstrong v Jackson* [1917] 2 KB 822 (facts considered earlier).
7 (1853) 18 Beav 75.
8 (1878) 8 Ch D 286.

the agency and makes a profit on the sale to P. In (i), A is liable to account for the profit because, at the date he buys the property, he buys on P's behalf and therefore holds it on trust for P[9] but in (ii), as A did not purchase the property originally on P's behalf, he is not liable for the profit and the normal remedy is rescission.[10] If P chooses to affirm the contract or rescission is barred for any reason, eg *restitutio in integrum* is impossible, P's only remedy will be damages *if* any loss has been sustained.[11] Moreover, P may lose that right if his affirmation is such that he abandons his rights against A.

The leading decision concerning these issues is *Re Cape Breton Co.*[12] There certain coal areas were purchased for £5,500 by six people, one of whom was A, the legal estate being vested in X and this trust remaining undisclosed. Two years later, a company was formed for the purpose of acquiring the property and A was one of the first directors. X agreed to sell the coal areas to the company for £42,000 but A did not disclose that he was a part-owner of the property. When the company was wound up, the shareholders agreed to sell the property (with full knowledge of A's interest) at much less than the company had paid. Subsequently, a contributory took out a summons to make A liable in misfeasance but it was held (Bowen LJ dissenting) that, since the company had decided to affirm the contract with full knowledge of the facts, A could not be personally liable in damages and that a claim for the difference between the price at which A originally bought the property and the price paid by the company could not be sustained, as A was not a fiduciary at the date he acquired the property and could not be treated as having bought it on behalf of the company.

Re Cape Breton Co was approved by the Privy Council in *Burland v Earle*[13] where the rule was widened in that there the director (A) purchased the property in question *while he was a director* but, on a subsequent sale of it to the company (P), A was allowed to retain the profit made because, at the time of the original purchase, he had no 'commission or mandate ... to purchase on behalf of the company'[14] and so he could not be regarded as a trustee of the property purchased. Lord Davey stressed that 'a person of a more refined self-respect and a more generous regard for the company of which he was president [might] have been disposed to give the company the benefit of his purchase'[15] but that he was under no legal obligation to do so.

These decisions are justified on two grounds. First it is said that it is difficult to assess the profit made by A on the sale to P and, second, that if the court were to intervene, this would 'force on the vendor [A] a contract to sell at another price'.[16] Neither justification is convincing for, as Bowen LJ stressed in his dissenting judgment in *Re Cape Breton Co*,[17] where the property has a market value, eg shares, the profit would be assessed as the difference between the market value of the shares at the time they were sold by A to P and the price at which they were in fact sold. It should not, therefore, be an insuperable difficulty to

---

9 *Tyrrell v Bank of London* (1862) 10 HL Cas 26.
10 *Re Cape Breton Co* (1885) 29 Ch D 795; affd *sub nom Cavendish-Bentinck v Fenn* 12 App Cas 652.
11 *Jacobus Marler Estates Ltd v Marler* (1913) 85 LJPC 167n.
12 (1885) 29 Ch D 795.
13 [1902] AC 83.
14 [1902] AC 83 at 98, per Lord Davey.
15 [1902] AC 83 at 99.
16 [1902] AC 83 at 99, per Lord Davey.
17 (1885) 29 Ch D 795, 806-810.

arrive at a fair estimate of the true value of property which has no market value at the time of the sale and to decide otherwise enables A to 'pocket the illegitimate profit which he makes upon a picture or a gem when he may not do so in the case of shares'.[18] Regarding the issue of the making of a new contract between the parties, Bowen LJ argued strongly that, compelling A to disgorge the profit obliged him to 'return something which he ought not to have' and so it was 'not altering the contract, [but] only insisting upon an incident which equity attaches to it'.[19]

The analysis in *Re Cape Breton Co* and *Burland v Earle* probably does not extend beyond the facts of those cases and, at least in the context of a company promoter's duties, the decisions do not appear extreme. A promoter is not an agent of the company before it is formed because a company which is not in existence canot act as a principal[20] and, moreover, a promoter is not normally treated as a trustee of the future company.[1] It is only when a promoter acts with the company in mind that he becomes a fiduciary in relation to it. Accordingly, it is crucial to decide when the promotion commences. Although one of the first acts of a company promoter will be to enter into contracts with a view to reselling property to the company, this does not necessarily mean that the promotion has commenced and he will owe no fiduciary duty to the company when it is ultimately formed.[2]

However, in the general context of agency, *Re Cape Breton* does not attune with the stringency of the rule in *Boardman v Phipps*.[3] If the Draconian rule in *Boardman* succeeds in its deterrent effect, it is tempered by the reasoning in that case which allows that A might be granted an award of expenses if appropriate. So, for example, should A be obliged to account to P in the situation of *Re Cape Breton Co*, he might be permitted an allowance[4] for his investment in the property concerned. Certainly, where P has chosen freely to affirm the contract, as did the company in *Re Cape Breton Co*, this appears to be a just outcome. However, in those cases where P cannot rescind the contract for some reason beyond his control, eg *restitutio in integrum* is impossible, it is surely imperative that he be able to claim the profit from A.[5]

---

18 (1885) 29 Ch D 795 at 810, per Bowen LJ.
19 (1885) 29 Ch D 795 at 809.
20 *Kelner v Baxter* (1866) LR 2 CP 174.
 1 *Omnium Electric Palaces Ltd v Baines* [1914] 1 Ch 332.
 2 *Erlanger v New Sombrero Phosphate Co* (1878) 3 App Cas 1218, 1234 per Lord Cairns LC. Similarly, the promoter owes no duty if the contract with the original seller provides that a company will be formed and the property resold to it (*Re Coal Economising Gas Co, Gover's Case* (1875) 1 Ch D 182) and even if completion is deferred until the company is formed and has raised sufficient capital to pay the original seller (*Re Leeds and Hanley Theatre of Varieties Ltd* [1902] 2 Ch 809). If promoters have invited the public or other investors to subscribe for shares *before* they make purchases of property which are subsequently sold to the company, the promotion of the company will have commenced and the promoters will be liable for profits made on the resale: see *Ladywell Mining Co v Brookes* (1887) 35 Ch D 400, 411 per Cotton LJ
 3 [1967] 2 AC 46 (considered later in this chapter).
 4 But see *Guinness plc v Saunders* [1988] 1 WLR 863, CA; on appeal [1990] 2 AC 663, HL where it was said that this sort of allowance will be rare.
 5 See the discussion of this line of cases in *Cook v Evatt (No 2)* [1992] 1 NZLR 676; Watts, 'Accounting for Profits – Fiduciaries Required to Disgorge in New Zealand' [1992] LMCLQ 439. See also the discussion of *Re Cape Breton* by Nolan, 'Conflicts of Interest, Unjust Enrichment, and Wrongdoing' in *Restitution Past, Present and Future: Esays in Honour of Gareth Jones* (eds Cornish, Nolan, O'Sullivan and Virgo, 1998), Ch 7, pp 109-117.

Disclosure where A acts for two principals

The cases considered above are instances where A's *own* interests conflict with a duty owed to P, but the rule of disclosure also prevents A from putting himself in a position where his duty to one principal is inconsistent with his duty to the other. This will often arise where A acts for both parties in the same transaction, eg a solicitor acting for vendor and purchaser in the sale of real property, this being a dangerous practice[6] which can clearly lead to a conflict of duties. A must obtain the informed consent of both principals[7] to his acting in this dual way but obviously such a prior consent will not absolve A if he does eventually find himself in a position where his duties to both principals conflict.[8] In *North and South Trust Co v Berkeley*,[9] an insurance broker (A) who was the agent of the assured (P) was instructed by the insurers to obtain an assessor's report in connection with a claim made by the assured under his policy of insurance. It was held that A was in breach of duty to P in acting for the insurers without P's consent but that P was *not* entitled to see the report which A obtained while acting for the insurers.

What if A acts for two principals in two *separate* transactions where the duties owed to each principal conflict – is A entitled to keep the two agencies separate? This situation arose in *Kelly v Cooper*[10] where estate agents (A) accepted instructions to sell the houses of two adjacent house owners (P1 and P2) in Bermuda. The prospective buyer offered to buy P2's house and, on the same day, made an offer for P1's house. The buyer bought both houses but P1 alleged that A should have told him of the buyer's interest in P2's house, this being material information in that the possible dual sale presented the buyer with an unusual opportunity and might have led to P1's house having an enhanced value. It was thus arguable that A had, in breach of his fiduciary duty, placed himself in a position where his duty of disclosure owed to P1 was in conflict with his duty of confidentiality owed to P2 *and* that there was a conflict between A's personal interest in securing commission for selling both houses and his duty of disclosure to P1. The Privy Council dismissed P1's claim in a somewhat imperious manner deciding that, although the attempted simultaneous purchase of both houses was a material fact which could have affected the price of P1's house, the proposed purchase of P2's house was confidential information acquired in the course of that agency and could not be disclosed to P1. Accordingly, A was held to have acted with propriety. Lord Browne-Wilkinson concluded that (i) the scope of the fiduciary duties were to be defined by the terms of the contract of agency (ii) it was impossible to imply into an estate agent's contract either a term that he should disclose confidential information acquired in the course of another agency or a term preventing him from acting for rival vendors and, (iii)

---

6   The practice is consistently condemned, see *Moody v Cox and Hatt* [1917] 2 Ch 71, 91 per Scrutton LJ; *Spector v Ageda* [1973] Ch 30, 47 per Megarry J.

7   See *Clark Boyce v Mouat* [1994] 1 AC 428, where the Privy Council held that a solicitor could act for both parties in a transaction, even where their interests might conflict, *provided* he obtained informed consent from them both. 'Informed consent' was held to mean consent given in the knowledge that there is a conflict between the parties and that, as a result, the solicitor may be disabled from disclosing to each party the full knowledge which he possesses regarding the transaction or may be disabled from giving advice to one party which conflicts with the interests of the other. *Clark* was applied recently in *Taylor v Schofield Peterson* [1999] 3 NZLR 434.

8   See *Moody v Cox and Hatt* [1917] 2 Ch 71, 81 per Lord Cozens-Hardy MR.

9   [1971] 1 WLR 470.

10   [1993] AC 205.

there *was* an implied term that he should be able to act for rival vendors and keep confidential the information obtained.

Kelly is controversial and criticisable.[11] It is submitted that A should have sought the consent of both P1 and P2 to reveal the buyer's interest to the other, terminating at least one agency in the absence of their dual consent. Moreover, the reasoning in *Kelly* is dictated solely by contractual principles when agency is not necessarily contractual in nature but, that apart, it is hardly satisfactory to demand that fiduciary duties should be defined by reference to the parties' contract and then perform that task by means of *implied*, rather than express, terms. The decision elevates contractual undertakings while subjugating fiduciary duties to the exigencies of commerce and, consequently, it is suggested that its reasoning should be treated with caution.

Chinese walls

Finally, the question of A's acting for two principals where his duties might conflict is relevant in the financial services sector and particularly after the abolition of single capacity trading on the Stock Exchange. For example, two departments of the same bank might be advising two different, competing clients, eg one department is advising a company regarding an unwanted take-over bid while the other department is advising the bidder. Many financial institutions in the City of London utilise 'Chinese walls',[12] these being strict demarcation barriers which prevent the movement of information between different departments of the same organisation and thus prevent conflicts of interest from arising. Chinese walls are also very important for solicitors and accountants. A large firm of solicitors may find that one department is acting for a client while a separate department is acting for another client with an opposing interest. Unless the consent of both clients is obtained, there is an inherent conflict of interest in this situation. The likelihood of such conflicts has increased as organisations have merged and grown in size meaning that it is quite possible for one firm to be the only specialist in its particular field. However, if a firm of solicitors can construct successfully a Chinese wall between the two departments in question, the potential conflict of interest will be contained.

The efficacy of Chinese walls has been considered recently by the House of Lords in *Bolkiah v KPMG*.[13] There the respondents, a firm of accountants, were auditors for an investment agency which was established to manage the assets of the Government of Brunei. The appellant, Prince Jefri Bolkiah, was the chairman of the agency in 1996 and, at that time, he was involved in extensive litigation. KPMG provided forensic accounting services for the appellant and, during the course of the litigation, the firm had access to highly confidential information concerning the extent and location of the appellant's assets. The litigation was settled in March 1998 and, at about the same time, the appellant

11 See Brown, 'Divided Loyalties in the Law of Agency' (1993) 109 LQR 206; Reynolds, 'Fiduciary Duties of Estate Agents' [1994] JBL 147; see also the consideration of *Kelly* in *Fiduciary Duties and Regulatory Rules*, Law Com No 236, Cm 3049 (1995), paras 3.24-3.36.

12 The origin of this phrase is obscure but it is suggested that Chinese walls are constructed to prevent the overhearing of 'Chinese whispers'. Apart from being the name of a well-known children's game, the derivation of the latter phrase appears to be as enigmatic as the former.

13 [1999] 2 AC 222.

was removed from his position as chairman of the agency. In June 1998, the Government of Brunei began an investigation into the activities of the agency during the period when the appellant had been its chairman and retained KPMG to investigate the whereabouts of certain assets which, it was suggested, had been used by the appellant for his own benefit. KPMG attempted to protect the appellant's confidentiality by constructing Chinese walls and ensuring that the employees who assisted with the appellant's litigation were not the same employees who worked on the agency's investigation. Nevertheless, the appellant commenced an action for breach of confidence aginst KPMG and sought an injunction restraining the firm from acting for the agency. The House of Lords allowed the appeal and granted an injunction. The House emphasised that, where the court's intervention is sought by a *former* client, as in *Bolkiah*, the court's jurisdiction is not based upon a conflict of interest as there is none. The fiduciary relationship existing between solicitor[14] and client comes to an end with the termination of the retainer and, thereafter, the duty to the former client is a continuing duty to preserve the confidentiality of information imparted during the subsistence of the solicitor-client relationship. In a speech with which the other Law Lords agreed, Lord Millett stressed that the duty to preserve confidentiality is unqualified – the duty is to keep the information confidential, not merely to take all reasonable steps to do so. Accordingly, the House of Lords rejected the more lenient approach adopted by the Court of Appeal in *Bolkiah* and evident in earlier decisions,[15] that the court will not intervene unless it is satisfied that there is a reasonable probability of real mischief. Instead, the House of Lords adopted the much stricter approach that the court should intervene 'unless it is satisfied that there is no risk of disclosure. It goes without saying that the risk must be a real one, and not merely fanciful or theoretical. But it need not be substantial'.[16]

If the court considers that there is a risk of disclosure, the second stage of the enquiry relates to the adequacy of the protective measures taken by the firm in question. In *Bolkiah*, Lord Millett emphasised that, once the former client has established that the defendant firm is in possession of information imparted in confidence and that the firm is proposing to act for another party with an interest adverse to his in a matter to which the information is or may be relevant, the evidential burden shifts to the defendant firm to show that there is no risk that the information will come into the possession of those now acting for the other party. Accordingly, Lord Millett concluded that there is no rule of law that Chinese walls are insufficient to eliminate that risk but that such barriers 'need to be an established part of the organisational structure of the firm, not created ad hoc and dependent on the acceptance of evidence sworn for the purpose by members of staff engaged on the relevant work'.[17] Consequently, the Chinese walls in *Bolkiah* were held to be inadequate information barriers.

In the light of this exacting decision, it is clear that it will be difficult to build effective Chinese walls and, most particularly, it seems that it will be almost impossible to do so, *ad hoc*, once the conflict has arisen within the organisation. That being said, there were particular difficulties in *Bolkiah* as the work involved a large number of employees who rotated from project to project within the firm

---

14 It was conceded by KPMG that an accountant who provides litigation support services must be treated in the same way as a solicitor.
15 See *Rakusen v Ellis, Munday & Clarke* [1912] 1 Ch 831.
16 *Bolkiah v KPMG* [1999] 2 AC 222, 237 per Lord Millett.
17 [1999] 2 AC 222 at 239.

and, significantly, the Chinese walls were constructed in an attempt to separate employees within a *single* department who were accustomed to working with each other. Where the firm is smaller and the matters less complex, effective Chinese walls are clearly attainable and, indeed, have been successfully constructed post *Bolkiah*.[18]

In its Consultation Paper, the Law Commission[19] suggested that effective Chinese walls demanded several organisational arrangements, viz (i) the physical separation of the relevant departments in order to insulate them from each other (ii) educational programmes to emphasise the importance of not divulging confidential information (iii) strict, well-defined procedures for coping with the situation where it is felt that the wall should be crossed (iv) monitoring of the efficacy of the wall by compliance officers and (v) disciplinary sanctions where the wall has been breached. In the Law Commission's final report,[20] the recommendation is that there should be legislation giving protection to firms which operate established Chinese wall arrangements and thus a firm would be protected from liability where (i) information is withheld from a customer pursuant to a Chinese wall arrangement (ii) a firm places itself in a position where its own interest on one side of the wall conflicts with a duty owed to a customer of a department on the other side of the Chinese wall but neither department knows of the firm's conflicting interest and, (iii) a firm owes conflicting duties to the customers of different departments on different sides of a Chinese wall but neither department is aware of the conflict.

THE AGENT'S DUTY NOT TO USE THE PRINCIPAL'S PROPERTY OR CONFIDENTIAL INFORMATION ACQUIRED IN THE COURSE OF THE AGENCY IN ORDER TO ACQUIRE A BENEFIT FOR HIMSELF

If A uses P's property in order to obtain a benefit for himself without disclosing the position to P and obtaining P's consent, he is accountable for the profit to P.[1] Because A holds tangible property belonging to P, this duty is the paradigm of a trustee's duties being extended to an agent. For example, in *Shallcross v Oldham*[2] a shipmaster was authorised to use the vessel to the best advantage but as he could not procure a remunerative cargo, he purchased a cargo of coal on his own account and charged himself the proper freight. It was held that he must account to the owners for the profit made on the sale of the cargo and not simply for the reasonable freight. Similarly, in *Reid-Newfoundland Co v Anglo-American Telegraph Co Ltd*,[3] a telegraph company agreed with a railway company to erect a 'special wire' which was only to be used in connection with the railway and was not to be used to transmit 'commercial messages' except for the benefit and account of the telegraph company. In fact, the railway company used the wire for their own

---

18 See *Re Solicitors' Firm* [2000] 1 Lloyd's Rep 31 (Timothy Walker J held that a firm of solicitors successfully established a Chinese wall because (i) *before* any question of conflict arose, there was clear departmental and physical separation (ii) there was no cross-pollination between the two departments and the two individuals in charge of the respective cases had never met one another or been into each others' offices (iii) only hard copies of documents were stored in the respective departments of those concerned).

19 *Fiduciary Duties and Regulatory Rules* 1992 (Law Com CP, No 124).

20 *Fiduciary Duties and Regulatory Rules* 1995 (Law Com No 236, Cm 3049).

1 See *Phipps v Boardman* [1965] Ch 992, 1018-1019 per Lord Denning MR.

2 (1862) 2 John & H 609.

3 [1912] AC 555.

business purposes but were held accountable to the telegraph company for all profits made which were held in trust for the company.

Likewise, if A has received information in confidence from P in the course of his agency he will not be allowed to profit from it without P's consent.[4] The basis of this fiduciary duty is traceable to 'the broad principle of equity that he who has received information in confidence shall not take unfair advantage of it'[5] and there is no need to ground the agent's duty in an express or implied contract to preserve confidentiality, as in the decisions concerning employees.[6] Indeed, the dominant inclination in *Boardman v Phipps*[7] was that confidential information is the property of P[8] and if A profits illicitly from its use he will hold any gains as a constructive trustee for P. However, the assertion that information is property does not make it any easier to decide when information is confidential, what the scope of A's liability should be in this context and what defences might be available to A where confidential information has been imparted in breach of duty.

A wide range of information is capable of being classified as confidential but it is extremely difficult to define a 'trade secret' as the possibilities are limitless.[9] An intransigent problem with both agents and employees lies in differentiating P's confidential information, which obviously belongs to P, from A's skill, experience and knowledge gained legitimately in the agency, which are inseparable from A and clearly belong to him.[10] In *Island Export Finance Ltd v Umunna*,[11] Hutchison J stressed that a director could not be liable to account to his former company for exploiting information gained solely in his position as a director but which amounted to his 'general fund of knowledge and … stock-in-trade'.[12] Much may thus turn on the nature of the agency, the practices of the trade or industry concerned and the information itself.[13]

---

4 See Finn, *Fiduciary Obligations* (1977), Ch 19; Goff and Jones, *The Law of Restitution* (5th edn, 1998) Chs 33 and 34; Gurry, *Breach of Confidence* (1984); Jones, 'Restitution of Benefits Obtained in Breach of Another's Confidence' (1970) 86 LQR 463.

5 *Seager v Copydex Ltd* [1967] 1 WLR 923, 931 per Lord Denning MR. See also *Coco v A N Clark (Engineers) Ltd* [1969] RPC 41; *Moorgate Tobacco Co Ltd v Philip Morris Ltd (No 2)* (1984) 56 ALR 193.

6 See eg, *Faccenda Chicken Ltd v Fowler* [1987] Ch 117. Where A is also an employee of P's, a duty of confidentiality may arise from an express or implied term of the contract of employment.

7 [1965] 1 Ch 992, CA; affd [1967] AC 46, HL.

8 Lords Hodson (p 107) and Guest (p 115) thought that information was property; Viscount Dilhorne (pp 89-90) that 'some information … can properly be regarded as property'; Lord Cohen (p 102) thought it 'not property in the strict sense of that word' and Lord Upjohn (pp 127-128) that it is not property 'in any normal sense' but 'equity will restrain its transmission to another'. See also *A-G v Guardian Newspapers Ltd* [1987] 1 WLR 1248 where Sir Nicolas Browne-Wilkinson V-C spoke of the personal obligation of confidence giving rise to a property right; cf *Breen v Williams* (1996) 186 CLR 71 (High Court of Australia did not consider information to be property); Palmer and Kohler, 'Information as Property' in *Interests in Goods* (eds Palmer and McKendrick, 2nd edn, 1998), Ch 1.

9 In *Faccenda Chicken Ltd v Fowler* [1987] 1 Ch 117, 138, Neill LJ said: 'It is clearly impossible to provide a list of matters which will qualify as trade secrets or their equivalent. Secret processes of manufacture provide obvious examples, but innumerable other pieces of information are *capable* of being trade secrets, though the secrecy of some information may be only short-lived'.

10 See eg, *Stevenson, Jordan & Harrison Ltd v MacDonald and Evans* [1952] 1 TLR 101; *Faccenda Chicken Ltd v Fowler* [1987] Ch 117.

11 [1986] BCLC 460.

12 [1986] BCLC 460 at 482.

13 See eg *Nordisk Insulinlaboratorium v Gorgate Products Ltd* [1953] Ch 430; *Kelly v Cooper* [1993] AC 205 (both considered earlier).

Once information has passed into the public domain it cannot, as a general rule, be regarded as confidential for 'ideas ... once released and however released into the open air of free discussion ... cannot for ever be effectively proscribed as if they were a virulent disease'.[14] Nevertheless, in some situations there may be a fiduciary obligation not to republish information which has been made public and the duty to preserve confidentiality may extend to third parties to whom the information has been transmitted. In *Schering Chemicals Ltd v Falkman Ltd*,[15] the plaintiff engaged Falkman (F) to train its executives in deflecting criticism of the plaintiff's marketing of a pregnancy testing drug which had been withdrawn from the market. F was given detailed information regarding the drug and agreed to preserve its confidentiality. F employed Elstein (E), a television journalist, who acquired the same information regarding the drug from the training courses organised by F but most of the information was also available from public sources. E never gave an express undertaking of confidentiality and subsequently he approached a television company with a proposal for a documentary about the drug. The Court of Appeal (Lord Denning MR dissenting on the basis that the information was publicly available) granted an injunction to restrain the showing of the film. Shaw LJ's judgment was based squarely on breach of fiduciary duty, emphasising that 'even in the commercial field, ethics and good faith are not to be regarded as merely opportunist or expedient'.[16]

There are two cases which illustrate graphically A's abuse of confidential information. In *Lamb v Evans*,[17] the proprietor of a trades directory employed canvassers to obtain advertisements from traders which would be included in the directory, but he discovered that the canvassers were proposing to assist in the production of a rival journal after their agreements with him had ended. It was held that the canvassers were not entitled to use the information gained while in the plaintiff's employment for the purposes of the rival publication. The decision in *Peter Pan Manufacturing Corpn Ltd v Corsets Silhouette Ltd*[18] exemplifies A's abuse of confidence and P's concomitant remedies. English licensees of patents for brassières were shown new designs, in confidence, by the American manufacturers. The English company made use of the information in the design of their own brassières and terminated their licence from the American company. It was held that the plaintiffs could obtain an injunction to restrain the manufacture and sale of the brassières, an account of profits from garments already sold and an order for delivery up or destruction of the offending articles.

THE AGENT'S DUTY NOT TO TAKE ADVANTAGE OF HIS POSITION IN ORDER TO ACQUIRE BENEFITS FOR HIMSELF

This duty is very wide and does not entail A's use of P's property in order to make illicit gains but instead involves A's profiting from the agency itself without P's consent. As with the other duties, full disclosure of the facts will exonerate

---

14 *A-G v Guardian Newspapers Ltd* [1987] 1 WLR 1248, 1321 per Lord Oliver.
15 [1982] QB 1.
16 In *A-G v Guardian Newspapers Ltd* [1987] 1 WLR 1248, 1319, Lord Oliver suggested that only rarely might information in the public domain be subject to a duty of confidentiality.
17 [1893] 1 Ch 218.
18 [1964] 1 WLR 96.

A. It is difficult to frame this broad duty precisely but if the benefit is acquired by A in the course of his agency (or arises because A holds himself out as acting for P) and its retention would be inconsistent with A's undertaking to P, A must account to P for the profit made. Many of the cases in this area concern company directors, the general rule being that, as fiduciaries, they cannot retain any benefit acquired in the conduct of the company's business unless there is an explanation to, and approval of such gains by the shareholders.

The duty is frequently said to originate in *Keech v Sandford*[19] where property had been leased to a trust and, on the termination of the lease, the landlord refused to renew the lease to the trustee in his capacity as such. The trustee accordingly renewed the lease for himself but the court decided that he held the benefit of the lease on trust for the beneficiary. It is most important to stress the deterrent effect of the rule which was held to apply even though the trustee acted in good faith, there was no loss to the trust and no unjust enrichment of the trustee. This stringent approach, evident in many 19th century decisions,[20] is clearly based on guarding against temptation and the *likelihood* of the fiduciary's personal gain. As will be seen below, the penal nature of this duty is accentuated further in that A must disgorge any profit despite the fact that P has *benefited* from A's actions and even though the profit is made as a result of A's own skill and enterprise. The overall policy is thus clear but a measure of categorisation helps to clarify this wide-ranging duty.

Flagrant breaches of duty

As A must account to P for profits made in situations where P suffers no loss, it follows that if A flagrantly and dishonestly profits at P's expense, the courts will promptly castigate A and likewise order him to account. In *Cook v Deeks*,[1] three directors of a railway construction company obtained for themselves a contract to build a railway line to the exclusion of the company and concealed the position from the fourth director. It was held that they had used their position to exclude the company whose interests came first and thus they held the contract for the benefit of the company.

It is hardly surprising to find that the courts are particularly strict where there is a dishonest abuse of position and corrupt wrongdoing.[2] *Reading v A-G*[3] is one example of such corruption. Reading was a sergeant in the British Army who was paid £20,000 for his assistance in the smuggling of illicit spirits and/ or drugs in Cairo. His uniformed presence on lorries carrying these goods meant that they were not searched by the police. Reading was tried and convicted by a court-martial on a charge of conduct prejudicial to good order and military

---

19　(1726) Sel Cas Ch 61.
20　See eg *Ex p James* (1803) 8 Ves 337; *Ex p Bennett* (1805) 10 Ves 381; *Benson v Heathorn* (1842) 1 Y & C Ch Cas 326; *Hamilton v Wright* (1842) 9 Cl & Fin 111; *Aberdeen Rly Co v Blaikie Bros* (1854) 1 Macq 461; *Parker v McKenna* (1874) 10 Ch App 96.
1　[1916] 1 AC 554.
2　In *LAC Minerals v International Corona Resources* (1989) 61 DLR (4th) 14, 51-52, La Forest J stressed that 'allowing the defendant to retain a specific asset when it was obtained through conscious wrongdoing may so offend a court that it would deny to the defendant the right to retain the property. This situation will be more rare, since the focus of the inquiry should be upon the reasons for recognising a right of property in the plaintiff, not on the reasons for denying it to the defendant'.
3　[1951] AC 507; see also *A-G v Goddard* (1929) 98 LJKB 743 (Crown could recover bribes received by a police officer).

discipline and the military authorities, on behalf of the Crown, seized the balance of money in Reading's bank account. Reading audaciously petitioned for its return but it was held that he could not recover it as it had been obtained by abuse of his position. A striking feature of *Reading* was that the army sergeant could not be classified as a true fiduciary;[4] moreover, although the Crown had suffered no actual loss (the gain was at T's expense) and the money had been earnt directly from a criminal act, it was held that the Crown could retain it.

Other situations: might an advantage or profit ever belong to A?

In cases where there is no blatant disregard of P's interests, it may be debatable whether the gain is made in the course of the agency and whether its retention is inconsistent with A's undertaking to P. The early decisions considered that it was both impossible and undesirable to investigate what information A had obtained from the agency or what use he had made of it[5] and it is plain that if this deterrent rule were to be relaxed complications would ensue in fixing the boundaries of the duty. Might there be situations where A does not have to make a disclosure to P as the profit made is a legitimate one, arising from a transaction outside the scope of his fiduciary relationship with P? Many of the decisions in this area concern the fiduciary duties of company directors and involve what is referred to in the USA as the 'corporate opportunity' doctrine[6] – a broad notion which entails a decision as to when an opportunity or an advantage should fall to the company in question rather than being exploited personally by a director.[7] The leading English decisions must be considered first and it is fair to say that they apply the narrow, deterrent rule with ferocious zeal.

In *Regal (Hastings) Ltd v Gulliver*,[8] the plaintiff company (Regal) owned a cinema and wished to extend its operations by acquiring two further cinemas with a view to the eventual sale of all three. The scheme was to be furthered by forming a subsidiary company which Regal intended to control and which would acquire the other two cinemas. The landlord of the cinemas was prepared to offer a lease of them but required that the directors should personally guarantee the rent unless the paid-up capital of the subsidiary was at least £5,000. As the directors were loath to give such guarantees and Regal did not have sufficient money to subscribe further, the directors subscribed personally for the remainder of the capital. The proposed sale of the cinemas did not occur and, eventually, the directors sold all their shares in both companies, making a profit on the shares in the subsidiary. Regal, now controlled by the new purchasers of the shares, sued the former directors to recover the profit. The House of Lords held that the directors had placed themselves in a position where their personal interests conflicted with their duties owed to Regal and, as they had obtained the profit by using their position as directors, they were accountable for it to Regal, even after it had been sold. Lord Macmillan thought that there was a liability to account

---

4 But in the HL he was so classified by Lord Normand.
5 In *Ex p Bennett* (1805) 10 Ves 381, Lord Eldon LC emphasised that 'the safest rule is, that a transaction, which under circumstances should not be permitted, shall not take effect ... as if ever permitted, the inquiry into the truth of the circumstances may fail in a great proportion of the cases'.
6 See Anon, 'Corporate Opportunity' (1961) 74 Harv L Rev 765.
7 See Austin, 'Fiduciary Accountability for Business Opportunities' in *Equity and Commercial Relationships* (ed Finn, Sydney, 1987), Ch 8.
8 [1967] 2 AC 134n, [1942] 1 All ER 378.

for the profit once it was proven that 'what the directors did was so related to the affairs of the company that it can properly be said to have been done in the course of their management and in utilisation of their opportunities and special knowledge as directors'.[9] The lower courts had exonerated the directors, emphasising their *bona fides* and the absence of any conspiracy to divert a valuable investment from Regal to themselves but the House of Lords unequivocally rejected this 'misapprehension'[10] – although the directors had 'entered into the transaction lawfully, in good faith and indeed avowedly in the interests of the company ... that does not absolve them from accountability for any profit which they made, if it was by reason and in virtue of their fiduciary office as directors that they entered into the transaction'.[11] The strength of the *Regal* decision is shown by the fact that recovery of the profits by the the company would benefit only the new purchasers who recovered an 'unexpected windfall'[12] in the reduction of the price which they had paid for the shares but, as Lord Porter[13] explained, this was an immaterial consideration in the light of the dominant rule that a fiduciary must not profit from his position.

The *Regal* decision was influential in the leading case of *Boardman v Phipps*.[14] There a will created a trust which included a shareholding in a private company which was not prospering. The solicitor (B) acting for the trust, and a beneficiary, (P), decided that it would benefit the trust if they acquired control of the company and they proceeded to do that by buying sufficient shares with their own money. B and P made a partial, informal disclosure, telling the two active trustees (the third being senile) of the position and no objections were raised. During the extensive negotiations, B and P gained knowledge of the company and acquired confidential information which assured them that the investment was sound. The outcome was that both B and P *and* the trust made considerable profits from the dealing in the shares. The House of Lords nevertheless held that B and P were accountable to a beneficiary for a proportion of the profit corresponding to his share in the trust fund but they were allowed to retain 'liberal'[15] expenses which were incurred in the take-over of the company.

It is a well-established principle that, despite the fiduciary's breach of duty, the court has a discretion to compensate him for time and energy expended in the deft administration of property or management of a business[16] and this conclusion is often justified on the basis of the maxim that 'he who seeks equity must do equity'. Consequently, an order for an account of profits is perceived as restitutionary rather than penal. It is, however, somewhat uncomfortable to juxtapose an allowance of compensation with a breach of duty even if the infraction at issue is only slight. There is also considerable uncertainty as to

---

9   [1967] 2 AC 134n, 153.
10   [1967] 2 AC 134n at 144, per Lord Russell of Killowen.
11   [1967] 2 AC 134n at 153, per Lord MacMillan.
12   [1967] 2 AC 134n at 157, per Lord Porter.
13   [1967] 2 AC 134n at 157.
14   [1967] 2 AC 46, HL; [1965] 1 Ch 992, CA; [1964] 1 WLR 993 (Wilberforce J).
15   [1967] 2 AC 46, 104 per Lord Cohen.
16   See *Yates v Finn* (1880) 13 Ch D 839; *Re Jarvis* [1958] 1 WLR 815; *Re Duke of Norfolk's Settlement Trusts* [1982] Ch 61; *O'Sullivan v Management Agency & Music Ltd* [1985] QB 428 (the contract between the plaintiff and his manager, the defendant, was set aside on grounds of undue influence but the latter was nevertheless entitled to remuneration, expenses and a 'fair profit'. Dunn LJ stressed that the plaintiff's success was 'phenomenal' (p 458) during the years when he was managed by the defendant); *Re Berkeley Applegate Ltd* [1989] Ch 32; *Warman International Ltd v Dwyer* (1995) 69 ALJR 362 (below).

when the court will exercise its discretion in the fiduciary's favour.[17] Certainly a more exacting approach was evident in *Guinness Plc v Saunders*,[18] where the House of Lords took the view that only rarely would remuneration be awarded to a fiduciary in this way. In the principal speeches delivered, both Lord Templeman and Lord Goff of Chieveley considered that the allowance made in *Boardman* was correct[19] as there the beneficiaries took the profits which resulted from Boardman's work and, had that work not been done, it would have been necessary to employ an expert to earn the profits. Nevertheless, Lord Goff warned that the award of an allowance should be restricted to cases where it could not have the effect of *encouraging* a conflict of interest and duty.[20]

In the *Boardman* litigation, all three courts were in agreement that B and P had acted in some fiduciary capacity, perhaps as 'self-appointed agents',[1] and thus they had purported to act for the trust, at least at the start. The majority in the House of Lords considered that B and P obtained the information which enabled them to profit from their position as fiduciaries and Lords Hodson and Guest did not doubt that the information became trust property.[2] Lords Cohen and Hodson went further in justifying the decision by stipulating that B's interest *might* conflict with his duty in the *future* if he were consulted by the trustees to advise on an application to the court to seek approval for a purchase of the shares by the trust.[3] In forceful, dissenting speeches, both Viscount Dilhorne and Lord Upjohn considered that the purchase of the shares was outside the ambit of the agency. Viscount Dilhorne pointed out that there could be no conflict of interest and duty as one of the trustees had made it clear that the trust was *opposed* to buying the shares and thus B and P acted solely on their own behalf.[4] The dissentient Law Lords could thus see no parallel with *Boardman's* facts and those in *Regal* as, in the latter case, the directors became the owners of shares which were to have been the property of the Regal company. It is thus plain that the Law Lords in the majority and minority were diametrically opposed: the majority was prepared to speculate upon a hypothetical breach of duty and impose a penal liability on the fiduciaries, whereas the minority emphasised the fiduciaries' *bona fides*, the enhancement in value of the trust property, and the speculative risk taken by B and P in investing their own money in shares which the trustees never contemplated buying.

---

17 See *Phipps v Boardman* [1965] Ch 992, 1020 per Lord Denning MR: 'If the defendant has done valuable work in making the profit, then the court in its discretion may allow him a recompense. It depends on the circumstances. If the agent has been guilty of any dishonesty or bad faith, or surreptitious dealing, he might not be allowed any remuneration or reward'.

18 [1990] 2 AC 663.

19 [1990] 2 AC 663 at 693-694 per Lord Templeman; p 701 per Lord Goff.

20 [1990] 2 AC 663 at 700-702. Cf *Estate Realties Ltd v Wignall* [1992] 2 NZLR 615 where, in a closely reasoned judgment, Tipping J allowed expenses to a fiduciary in breach of duty, preferring the approach in *O'Sullivan's* case (supra) to that of Lord Goff in *Guinness*. The judge likened the allowance of expenses to rescission of a contract 'subject to fair and reasonable accounting between the parties' (p 631).

1 See [1964] 1 WLR 993, 1007 per Wilberforce J; [1965] Ch 992, 1017 per Lord Denning MR; [1967] 2 AC 46, 87 per Viscount Dilhorne.

2 [1967] 2 AC 46, 107 and 115 per Lords Hodson and Guest respectively. See earlier for a consideration of this head of liability.

3 [1967] 2 AC 46 at 103-104 and 111, per Lords Cohen and Hodson respectively. As Finn (*Fiduciary Obligations* (1977)) emphasises, this is 'remarkable,' for 'a person who has not been asked to advise, but who might be asked to, puts his interest into conflict with a duty he has not undertaken' (p 245). Moreover, if he *had* been asked to advise, B might have either declined or declared his interest.

4 [1967] 2 AC 46 at 76 and 88.

In *Industrial Development Consultants Ltd v Cooley*,[5] the defendant (A) had been the managing director of the plaintiff company (P) and had conducted negotiations on behalf of P with the Eastern Gas Board. Subsequently, a representative of the Gas Board approached A saying that he would not deal with P but would contract with A personally. A falsely told P that he was ill and was allowed to resign immediately. A then promptly entered into a contract with the Gas Board. P subsequently claimed from A the profits emanating from the contract. A's defence was that (i) the information he exploited was received in his personal capacity and there could be no fiduciary obligation to transmit it to P and, (ii) P could not have obtained the contract as the Gas Board would not have contracted with P. Both defences were rejected, Roskill J stressing that A had only one capacity which was the managing director of the plaintiff company and, as he had received information in that capacity, he had a duty to pass it on to the company. The case is thus important both for this *positive* aspect of A's duty and because it illustrates that A cannot simply terminate the agency and then assert that he is at liberty to exploit an opportunity which belongs to his former principal.[6]

Analysis and criticism of the deterrent rule

The sledgehammer rule, exemplified by *Boardman*, is clearly criticisable in its failure to discriminate between two extremes: on the one hand, profit made by a dishonest agent, who is unjustly enriched at P's expense and, on the other, profit made by an honest agent, at the expense of a third party, with a resultant benefit to P.[7] Should the law adhere to *Boardman's* prophylactic rule or undertake an equitable evaluation of the relevant issues? This dilemma uncovers several possibilities. First, a complete prohibition of profiteering agents protects principals absolutely but provides a disincentive to efficient and adept administration consequently diverting entrepreneurial talent in other directions.[8] Second, an indulgent approach might engender better management but encourage profiteering opportunities to the principal's possible detriment. Third, and most likely, a lenient approach might encourage bad management *and* provide a smoke screen for A to cover his illicit practices, eg, on the facts of *Regal*, the directors might not work conscientiously for the company and its subsequent inability to proceed with the venture might then be regarded as sanctioning the directors' personal profit.

In refusing to follow the deterrent rule, it is suggested that the court reached the wrong conclusion in *Peso Silver Mines Ltd v Cropper*.[9] The plaintiff company (Peso) was formed to take over a group of silver mining claims in the Yukon, the defendant being one of the first directors. Peso was soon converted to a public company and rapid expansion put such a strain on its finances that it was unable to buy further claims which were offered for sale by a third party. Six weeks later, Peso's original directors and the company's geologist formed a private company to exploit these new claims. Control of Peso passed to Charter Oil Co

---

5   [1972] 1 WLR 443; see Prentice, 'Directors' Fiduciary Duties – The Corporate Opportunity Doctrine' (1972) 50 Can Bar Rev 623.

6   See also *Island Export Finance Ltd v Umunna* [1986] BCLC 460, 480 per Hutchison J.

7   See Jones, 'Unjust Enrichment and the Fiduciary's Duty of Loyalty' (1968) 84 LQR 472.

8   See the economic analysis of Bishop and Prentice, 'Some Legal and Economic Aspects of Fiduciary Remuneration' (1983) 46 MLR 289.

9   (1966) 58 DLR (2d) 1 (Supreme Court of Canada).

Ltd, Peso then demanding that the defendant should account for profits made. The Supreme Court of Canada dismissed the claim on the basis that the board had acted in good faith towards Peso in rejecting the offer to sell the claims and any subsequent dealing with the property by a director was not in the course of the execution of his office. Both plaintiff and defendant relied on *Regal* (ie the defendant was either within or without his office of director) but the court felt that *Peso's* facts were distinguishable from those in *Regal*: once the board had reached the decision, in good faith, not to purchase the new claims, the company had no interest in them whereas, in *Regal*, the cinemas were wanted by the company but could not be obtained and this crucial element produced the conflict of interest and duty.

In *Peso*, there were detailed, instructive judgments in the British Columbia Court of Appeal,[10] the majority taking the view that the complexities of corporate structure meant that it was not 'enlightened'[11] to extend the rules on fiduciary duties. In a powerful dissenting judgment, Norris J A considered that such complexities *increased* the need for vigilance lest fraud could be perpetrated and camouflaged by a complex corporate structure ie, the smoke screen notion referred to above. He thus considered that it was enough for Peso to prove that the defendant director *could* have acquired the information in his office, rather than the majority approach which, taking a very narrow view of *Regal*, demanded that he must *only* have acquired it in that capacity. It is suggested that the dissenting judgment is correct and that the reasoning of the majority in *Peso* provides a clinical means for directors to usurp their fiduciary duties.[12] It is, of course, the argument that an opportunity is *unavailable* to P and can therefore be exploited by A which is so dangerous in its simultaneously facilitating and justifying A's actions. If the argument had been allowed on the facts of *Cooley*, for example, (ie T would never have dealt with P) the notion of a conflict of interest and duty appears to evaporate allowing a *carte blanche* to unscrupulous agents for the abandonment of their duties. The *Peso* notion of *bona fide* rejection does little to defuse this danger.

A significant advance was made in the decision in *Canadian Aero Service Ltd v O'Malley*.[13] The plaintiff company (Canaero) was engaged in topographical mapping and two directors (M and Z) did extensive work on aerial mapping of Guyana, the idea being that Canaero would gain the contract. M and Z subsequently formed a separate company and obtained the contract in direct competition with Canaero. Canaero claimed an account of profits from M and Z but its action failed at first instance and in the Ontario Court of Appeal[14] on the basis that M and Z obtained the contract by exercising their own skill and knowledge rather than abusing any confidential information, and the opportunity of securing the contract arose only when they had terminated their

---

10 (1966) 56 DLR (2d) 117 (BCCA).
11 (1966) 56 DLR (2d) 117 at 154-155, per Bull JA.
12 See Beck, 'The Saga of Peso Silver Mines: Corporate Opportunity Reconsidered' (1971) 49 Can Bar Rev 80. The author cogently criticises *Peso* as being indistinguishable from *Regal*: 'Peso was in exactly the same position as the Regal company – it wanted the property but could not finance the purchase' (p 101). He also considers that a court 'should not set itself the task' of delving into the *bona fides* of directors (p 102). See also Prentice, 'Regal (Hastings) Ltd v Gulliver – The Canadian Experience' (1967) 30 MLR 450.
13 (1973) 40 DLR (3d) 371; see Beck, 'The Quickening of Fiduciary Obligation: Canadian Aero Services v O'Malley' (1975) 53 Can Bar Rev 771.
14 (1972) 23 DLR (3d) 632.

employment with Canaero. A unanimous Supreme Court of Canada held that M and Z must account; they could not spend years developing an opportunity for the company and then seize it for themselves when it came to fruition. This seemed to be a somewhat obvious case of breach of duty but, in a broadly based judgment, Laskin J balanced the need for exemplary behaviour from directors with a modernised notion of fiduciary duty in corporate commerce. He thus deliberately shunned any absolute, dogmatic rule, but emphasised that the standards of loyalty to which directors should conform must be tested by many factors which could not be listed exhaustively – he nevertheless enumerated some of the relevant factors[15] viz, the position/office held; the nature of the corporate opportunity, its ripeness and specificity; the director's relation to the opportunity; the amount of knowledge possessed by the director, the circumstances in which it was obtained and whether it was special or confidential.

Uncertainty is undoubtedly engendered by the range of factors specified in *Canadian Aero Services* and, in its favour, such a criticism cannot be levelled against *Boardman's* deterrent rule. However, it is perhaps time for equity's inflexible prohibition to bend in favour of the more reasoned and equitable solution presented by *Canadian Aero Services* and this seems to be the approach which has been followed in recent decisions. In *Queensland Mines Ltd v Hudson*,[16] the defendant, Hudson (A), while acting as managing director of Queensland Mines Ltd (P), started negotiations with the Tasmanian Government for the issue of exploration licences for the mining of iron ore. The financial collapse of one of P's shareholders left it without working capital and so A took the licences in his own name, resigned as managing director and formed a company to carry out the mining. A made a full disclosure to the board of P which decided to renounce any interest in the licences and assented to A's pursuing the matter on his own account. The Privy Council held that A was not liable to account to P. At first instance, the judge had followed the strict, deterrent approach and insisted that a fiduciary must not act in a way in which he is *exposed* to temptation but the Privy Council took a more lenient approach in holding that each case must be examined on its facts[17] to see if there is, in fact, a conflict of interest. Likewise, in *Island Export Finance Ltd v Umunna*,[18] the plaintiff (P) alleged that the defendant, an ex-director (A), had diverted to himself a maturing business opportunity and must account to P. In dismissing P's claim, Hutchison J approved and applied the *Canadian Aero Services* reasoning and held that (i) the opportunity was not a maturing one for P (ii) P was not pursuing the opportunity when A resigned (iii) A's resignation was not prompted by a desire to gain the opportunity for himself and, (iv) A had not exploited any confidential information which he acquired as a director but, instead, had simply used his knowledge of the particular market in question.

In the recent decision in *Warman International Ltd v Dwyer*,[19] the High Court of Australia also took a more liberal approach in relation to remedies for breach of fiduciary duty. There the defendant, Dwyer (A), who was clearly in breach of duty in dishonestly diverting a business opportunity from the plaintiff company (P) and incorporating two companies to exploit the advantage gained, was held

---

15   (1973) 40 DLR (3d) 371 at 391.
16   (1978) 52 ALJR 399; see 'Recent Cases' (1978) 52 ALJ 574; Sullivan, 'Going It Alone – Queensland Mines v Hudson' (1979) 42 MLR 711.
17   (1978) 52 ALJR 399 at 401 and 404 per Lord Scarman.
18   [1986] BCLC 460.
19   (1995) 69 ALJR 362.

liable to account to P for two years' profits. While it was stressed that the liability of a fiduciary to account did not depend upon any loss being suffered by the person to whom the obligation was owed or the fact that the latter could not have earnt the profit himself, the court considered that the assessment of the award was often extremely difficult in practice and the outcome could depend upon a number of factors. Thus, the court drew a distinction between cases where A acquired a specific asset and those in which a business had been acquired and operated by A; in the former case it would be apt to make A account for the asset and all profits gained but, where A had operated a business, it was thought equitable, in some circumstances, to allow A to retain some of the profits. In particular, this was thought to be appropriate where the profits resulted from A's own efforts, skill and property, and consideration might also properly be given to what was lost by P. In *Warman*, the two years' profits for which A had to account (the trial judge had awarded four years' profits plus the payment of a purchase price for goodwill) thus reflected his own involvement in the new business and the fact that the third party with whom A collaborated was about to terminate its contract with P and, even without A's machinations, that contract would probably have survived no longer than one year. Above all, the court's reasoning was that A's liability to account should not be turned into a vehicle for P's unjust enrichment and, while there can be no precise formula for reaching equilibrium between P and A, it is difficult to find fault with such a rational viewpoint.

THE AGENT'S DUTY NOT TO MAKE A SECRET PROFIT OR TAKE A BRIBE

SECRET PROFITS

A secret profit is any financial advantage which A receives in the execution of his agency over and above the amount to which he is lawfully entitled. A cannot retain any such profit unless there is a full disclosure to P of all the facts and P consents to the profit. There are thus many examples of secret profits in the sub-duties considered earlier, eg where A is employed to buy property for P and does so but charges P more than he paid for it.[20] There are several general issues regarding secret profits which must be accentuated. First, A will be liable to account to P for the secret profit despite an absence of fraud or bad faith on A's part.[1] Second, the duty not to profit applies even where A is not being paid a commission by P,[2] ie A is a gratuitous agent. Third, although A will have to account for the profit made, he *may* be able to claim remuneration from P, provided A has not been fraudulent.[3]

BRIBES

A secret profit may arise without any active intervention or connivance by a third party but a bribe is limited to situations where A secretly receives money or property, in the course of his agency, from T, who is dealing with P or seeks

---

20 See eg *Lucifero v Castel* (1887) 3 TLR 371 (considered earlier in this chapter).
1 *Boardman v Phipps* [1967] 2 AC 46.
2 *Turnbull v Garden* (1869) 38 LJ Ch 331.
3 See *Hippisley v Knee Bros* [1905] 1 KB 1; *Keppel v Wheeler* [1927] 1 KB 577; *Boardman v Phipps*, supra. See Ch 9 where remuneration is considered in detail.

to deal with P.[4] P has various remedies against both A and T which will be considered later, the primary remedy being the recovery of damages *or* the amount of the bribe from *either* A or T. As with the other fiduciary duties, P's informed consent will legitimise what would otherwise be a bribe.

The definition of a bribe

The three constituents of a bribe were underscored in *Industries & General Mortgage Co Ltd v Lewis*,[5] viz, (i) T, the briber, makes the payment to A (ii) T makes the payment knowing that A is acting as P's agent and, (iii) T does not disclose to P that he has made the payment to A.[6] It is obviously not uncommon to find that both T and A are dishonest, T thus bribing A with the corrupt purpose of securing an advantage in dealings with P.[7] However, the terseness and simplicity of the above constituents of a bribe should be noted: the law's policy is to discourage bribery and thus, in the civil law, once a bribe has been made, there need be no proof of A's actual corruption and it cannot avail either A or T to prove that A acted consistently in P's best interests.[8] Likewise, it is not a pre-requisite of a bribe that P should sustain any loss.[9] In the light of a bribe, the law assumes that the worst consequences may ensue and there is no further investigation to be made. In *Hovenden & Sons v Millhoff*,[10] Romer LJ[11] was emphatic that:

'First, the court will not inquire into the donor's motive in giving the bribe, nor allow evidence to be gone into as to the motive. Secondly, the court will presume in favour of the principal and as against the briber and the agent bribed, that the agent was influenced by the bribe; and this presumption is irrebuttable.'

The law's net is thus cast widely and it is clear that T is regarded as party to A's breach of duty when he knows that A is acting for P at the date of the bribe or discovers it later and still enters into a contract with P, for example.[12]

Bribes encompass commission paid by T to A for introducing business to T[13] and payments that are *promised* to A[14] as well as those paid to him. A bribe

---

4   See the succinct definitions in *Hovenden & Sons v Millhoff* (1900) 83 LT 41, 43, per Romer LJ; *Anangel Atlas Compania Naviera SA v Ishikawajima-Harima Heavy Industries Co Ltd* [1990] 1 Lloyd's Rep 167, 171 per Leggatt J. The broad definition of a secret profit technically encompasses a bribe and some of the earlier cases fail to differentiate the two situations.
5   [1949] 2 All ER 573, 575 per Slade J.
6   It is sufficient that there is *no disclosure to P*, ie a bribe does not have to be hidden by elaborate subterfuge to qualify as such. It is thus no defence to argue that P could have discovered it – see below re disclosure.
7   Eg *Shipway v Broadwood* [1899] 1 QB 369 (P agreed to buy a pair of horses from T provided they were passed as sound by a veterinary surgeon (A) employed by P. T bribed A in order that he would certify the horses as sound but it was held that T could not recover the price of the horses).
8   *Harrington v Victoria Graving Dock Co* (1878) 3 QBD 549.
9   In *Industries & General Mortgage Co Ltd v Lewis* [1949] 2 All ER 573, 578 Slade J stressed that the law presumes that P 'has suffered damage to at least the amount of the bribe'.
10 (1900) 83 LT 41.
11 (1900) 83 LT 41 at 43.
12 *Grant v Gold Exploration and Development Syndicate Ltd* [1900] 1 QB 233.
13 *Powell & Thomas v Evan Jones & Co* [1905] 1 KB 11 (a sub-A was employed to secure an advance of money to P. The money was advanced by a company, T, who paid the sub-A a secret commission for introducing the business to the company. It was held that the sub-A had to account to P for the commission).
14 *Grant v Gold Exploration and Development Syndicate Ltd* [1900] 1 QB 233. In the situation of a promised but unpaid bribe, A cannot be liable for money had and received as he has received none but, as *Grant's* case makes clear, the money could be recovered from T either in an action for damages for deceit or, less certainly, for money had and received (see remedies, below).

may take any form such as a gift of shares in a company,[15] and, indeed, 'any surreptitious dealing between one principal and the agent of the other principal is a fraud on such other principal, cognizable in this Court'.[16] It will be abundantly clear that, in order to constitute a bribe, it is not a requirement that the payment should be made by T to induce a contract between P and T, a fact accentuated recently in *Petrotrade Inc v Smith*.[17] There it was stated that a secret payment is just as corrupt in the absence of any such contract and 'to focus on the possible outcome of the payment is to misapprehend the key distinguishing feature of a corrupt payment, namely that the making of it gives rise to a conflict of interest on the part of the agent'.[18]

There is scant authority on the question of tips and gratuities paid to agents. In *The Parkdale*[19] a shipmaster received three payments totalling £45 from consignees of cargo *after* their cargoes had been unloaded and it was held that he could keep this 'little present'.[20] A facile interpretation would be that this result is justified where the amount is promised and paid once the relevant contract has been completed but this somewhat naive approach overlooks too easily the fact that later payment may be the result of an earlier dishonest agreement and/or that it may influence future dealings. Similarly, as the law cannot enter into relative evaluations of the *amounts* paid to agents, it is suggested that such gratuities should be classified as bribes in those situations where T secures a general influence in his favour.[1]

Finally, it should be stressed that there is a perimeter to the seemingly boundless definition of a bribe. Because the rules stipulate that it is immaterial that A was not influenced by the bribe and did not actually act corruptly as a result of its having been made, it is often assumed that all payments which T makes to A are bribes. That is not the legal position. In *Rowland v Chapman*,[2] Buckley J emphasised that, where there *is* a conflict of interest and duty the law does not enquire whether A has been influenced but, if there is no such conflict, the payment will *not* be a bribe.[3] In *Rowland*, A was an agent for his six co-purchasers in the purchase of land, the purchase money being provided in seven equal shares, but there was an arrangement that A was to receive a commission from the vendor on the price of £18,000. For every £100 reduction in the price of the land, A lost 30s in commission from the vendor but his interest as a purchaser was to buy

---

15 *Re Morvah Consols Tin Mining Co (McKay's Case)* (1875) 2 Ch D 1 (a director of a company (A), when contracting on behalf of the company (P) with T, received from T 600 fully paid-up shares in the company. It was held that A had to account to the company for the highest value borne by the shares during the period they were held by him); see also *Re Caerphilly Colliery Co (Pearson's Case)* (1877) 5 Ch D 336.
16 *Panama and South Pacific Telegraph Co v India Rubber, Gutta Percha, and Telegraph Works Co* (1875) 10 Ch App 515, 526 per James LJ.
17 [2000] 1 Lloyd's Rep 486.
18 [2000] 1 Lloyd's Rep 486 at 490, per David Steel J.
19 [1897] P 53.
20 [1897] P 53 at 58-59, per Gorell Barnes J; see also *Meadow Schama & Co v C Mitchell & Co Ltd* (1973) 228 Estates Gazette 1511, discussed above.
1 See *Smith v Sorby* (1875) 3 QBD 552n (T paid A a gratuity in order to secure influence generally and A was subsequently influenced in T's favour in making a contract with T on behalf of P. Held that the contract was voidable at P's option even though the gratuity was not paid with direct reference to that contract).
2 (1901) 17 TLR 669.
3 See also *Anangel Atlas Compania Naviera SA v Ishikawajima-Harima Heavy Industries Co Ltd* [1990] 1 Lloyd's Rep 167, 171, where Leggatt J stressed that the 'key' to determining whether or not the payment was a bribe was whether or not the payment 'gives rise to a conflict of interest'; *Petrotrade Inc v Smith* [2000] 1 Lloyd's Rep 486.

the land as cheaply as possible. Consequently, for every £100 reduction in price, A gained one seventh as a purchaser, ie approximately £14, but he lost 30s, the net result being that he gained £12 10s on every reduction of £100. As A's duty to his co-purchasers and his personal interest were the same, there was no conflict of interest and the co-purchasers could not rescind the contract as a result of the payment.

The fact that there must be a conflict of interest also explains the decision in *Meadow Schama & Co v C Mitchell & Co Ltd*.[4] There P instructed an estate agent (A) to find premises in the West End of London for purchase by P. After A found such premises, P started to 'squeeze out' A by employing another agent who had been instructed to sell P's existing property and with whom P wished to secure favourable terms by paying one commission on the sale of his existing property and the purchase of the new premises. Consequently, A arranged with the estate agents who were acting for the vendor of the West End premises that they would pay A £600 commission if A did not obtain commission from P. Contracts were exchanged on the premises, P refused A commission and A did not receive the £600. The Court of Appeal reversed the judge's decision that A was disentitled to commission from P because he had colluded in the arrangement for a secret commission of £600. Lord Denning MR stressed that A's commission had been earnt, P had repudiated it and A had done nothing adverse to P; Megaw LJ added that A was not in a position to commit a breach of duty.

Disclosure and bribes

It is clear that 'the real evil is not the payment of money, but the secrecy attending it'[5] and so, in relation to disclosure of what would otherwise be a bribe, the general rule is that P must have full, prior knowledge of the facts and thus give his informed consent to A's retention of the payment.[6] Consequently, it is insufficient for A to argue that P had an 'opportunity of discovering the existence of [the] commission'.[7] Similarly, it is inadequate for T to argue that he thought A would disclose the bribe to P[8] or that A assured him that disclosure had been made to P[9] if that was untrue and P did not know. Presumably this argument would apply, *a fortiori*, to deprive A of a defence where he argues that T promised to disclose the payment, but there is no direct authority on this point. However, where P knows of the payment and consents to it, he cannot subsequently claim the amount from A.[10]

There is some doubt, however, concerning P's knowledge and consent in this context. In *Great Western Insurance Co v Cunliffe*,[11] it was usual for underwriters

---

4   (1973) 228 Estates Gazette 1511.
5   *Shipway v Broadwood* [1899] 1 QB 369, 373 per Chitty LJ.
6   In *Bartram and Sons v Lloyd* (1904) 90 LT 357, 359-360, Romer LJ said that the 'disclosure should be such as fairly to bring home to the mind of [P] a proper appreciation of the facts so as to put him to his election'. On the facts, P had not been informed of A's commission at the inception of the agreement.
7   *Temperley v Blackrod Manufacturing Co Ltd* (1907) 71 JP Jo 341, 342 per AT Lawrence J.
8   *Grant v Gold Exploration and Development Syndicate Ltd* [1900] 1 QB 233, 248-249 per Collins LJ.
9   See *Taylor v Walker* [1958] 1 Lloyd's Rep 490, 513 per Havers J.
10 *Anangel Atlas Compania Naviera SA v Ishikawajima-Harima Heavy Industries Co Ltd* [1990] 1 Lloyd's Rep 167
11 (1874) 9 Ch App 525.

to allow insurance brokers (A) a 12% discount calculated on yearly profits for punctual payment of premiums in addition to a normal 5% commission on each reinsurance. P, a marine insurance company in New York, employed A for settling claims, for which A received remuneration from P, and for effecting reinsurances, but no remuneration was fixed by P for the latter work. P made no enquiry as to the remuneration paid by the underwriters and A disclosed only the 5% commission, but he received the 12% commission for over eight years. Eventually P discovered the 12% commission but did not object for a further two years. It was held that P could not recover the amount from A. *Cunliffe* was followed in a second decision[12] which established that if P knows that A is remunerated by T but does not enquire further he must accept that A is paid whatever is usual and cannot subsequently object on the ground that he was unaware of the *extent* of the remuneration. It is arguable that these cases are out-of-step with the strict rule that, in the absence of P's fully informed consent, all benefits obtained by A in transacting business for P belong to P even if P could not have obtained them himself.[13] It is thus possible that the *Cunliffe* line of cases is based upon particular business usage but, in reality, it seems that the decisions attempt to draw a distinction between, on the one hand, advantages which correctly belong to P and, on the other, remuneration paid by T which enables A to earn his living.[14]

Remedies where A has been bribed

If the bribe had been paid in money, the early 19th century cases established that, in equity, A must account to P for the sum[15] but the action later became classified as one at common law for money had and received by A for the use of P.[16] Sub-agents are similarly liable to P despite the fact that there is no privity of contract between P and the sub-A.[17] The remedy is available even though P has suffered no loss[18] and could not have obtained the sum himself.[19] Most importantly, *the briber, T, is also liable jointly and severally with A*. It is one thing for P to recover the bribe from A, who is a fiduciary, but quite another to justify the recovery of the bribe from T. Nevertheless, the decisions clearly

---

12 *Baring v Stanton* (1876) 3 Ch D 502.
13 See eg *Queen of Spain v Parr* (1869) 39 LJ Ch 73 (insurance A ordered to credit P with a 10% discount given by the insurer for prompt payment of premiums in cash); *Copp v Lynch* (1882) 26 Sol Jo 348 (solicitor made to account to his client for a commission paid by the insurance company on the premium of the client).
14 In *Rowland v Chapman* (1901) 17 TLR 669 (facts above), Buckley J stressed that the co-purchasers (P) knew that A 'was not a gentleman who was likely to work for nothing' and that, as no commision was paid by them, it was probably paid by T. Also, that A 'certainly took no steps to conceal the receipt of the commission' and, as A told P's solicitors (who were acting in the sale) of the commission, their knowledge bound P. Accordingly, there was sufficient disclosure even though it was not 'in plain and direct terms'.
15 *Fawcett v Whitehouse* (1829) 1 Russ & M 132.
16 *Mahesan v Malaysia Government Officers' Co-operative Housing Society Ltd* [1979] AC 374.
17 *Powell & Thomas v Evan Jones & Co* [1905] 1 KB 11.
18 *Reading v A-G* [1951] AC 507 (considered earlier in this chapter).
19 *Boston Deep Sea Fishing and Ice Co v Ansell* (1888) 39 Ch D 339 (a director (A) of a company (P), received a bribe in the form of a dividend on shares which he held in another company (T). It was held that P could succeed against A for money had and received even though, as a non-shareholder, the company (P) was not entitled to a dividend).

acknowledge T's liability for money had and received even though the money is paid to A and (probably) in situations where T promises to pay A but does not actually do so.[20] It is clearly rather awkward to assert that T is liable for money had and received when he has paid it to A but, at least in the instances where T sells property to P and overcharges P by the amount of the bribe paid to A, the modern cases state that P may *recover* the bribe from T on a restitutionary basis.[1]

Alternatively, P can claim damages against A in the tort of deceit for any loss suffered and, again, *the briber, T, is also liable jointly and severally with A.*[2] This action is advantageous where the loss exceeds the bribe and, if there is any doubt regarding the action for money had and received where the money is merely promised by a dishonest T, a claim in deceit could certainly be maintained against A and T in such a situation. It has never been clear whether this is a conventional action in deceit with the burden of proof on P[3] or, alternatively, whether the irrebuttable presumption that bribery has occurred means that the dishonesty of A and T need not be established. The latter view was dominant in the earlier cases with the addition that the damages would be presumed to be at least the amount of the bribe[4] but Lord Diplock's observations in *Mahesan's*[5] case incline toward damages in tort being 'the actual loss which [P] has sustained as a result of entering into the transaction in respect of which the bribe was given'.[6] It is suggested that *Mahesan* establishes that actual loss must be established but that the other elements of fraud are irrebuttably presumed.[7]

It had long been assumed, following *obiter dicta* in *Salford Corpn v Lever,*[8] that these remedies were *distinct and cumulative* so that, for example, P might obtain the amount of the bribe from A *and* sue T in damages, with no diminution in the damages against T as a consequence of P's having recovered the bribe from A. P would thus recover twice the amount of his loss but this was regarded in *Salford* as an acceptable deterrent against bribery.[9]

---

20 *Salford Corpn v Lever* [1891] 1 QB 168; *Grant v Gold Exploration and Development Syndicate Ltd* [1900] 1 QB 233; *Hovenden and Sons v Millhoff* (1900) 83 LT 41; *Mahesan v Malaysia Government Officers' Co-operative Housing Society Ltd* [1979] AC 374.

1 See *Armagas Ltd v Mundogas SA, The Ocean Frost* [1985] 1 Lloyd's Rep 1, 20 per Staughton J; *Arab Monetary Fund v Hashim* [1993] 1 Lloyd's Rep 543, 564-565 per Evans J.

2 *Mahesan v Malaysia Government Officers' Co-operative Housing Society Ltd* [1979] AC 374.

3 See *Grant v Gold Exploration and Development Syndicate Ltd* [1900] 1 QB 233, 243-244 per A L Smith LJ.

4 See *Hovenden & Sons v Millhoff* (1900) 83 LT 41; *Grant v Gold Exploration and Development Syndicate Ltd* [1900] 1 QB 233; *Industries & General Mortgage Co Ltd v Lewis* [1949] 2 All ER 573.

5 *Mahesan v Malaysia Government Officers' Co-operative Housing Society Ltd* [1979] AC 374, 382-383.

6 [1979] AC 374 at 383.

7 Both Staughton J in *Armagas Ltd v Mundogas SA* [1985] 1 Lloyd's Rep 1, 19, and Leggatt J in *Anangel Atlas Compania Naviera SA v Ishikawajima-Harima Heavy Industries Co Ltd* [1990] 1 Lloyd's Rep 167, 170, considered that *Mahesan* did not affect the irrebuttable presumption in relation to dishonesty and corruption.

8 [1891] 1 QB 168; see also the *Hovenden* and *Grant* cases, above.

9 Sir Frederick Pollock thought that 'the morality of the law is, much to the benefit of the world, decidedly above the morality of ordinary mercantile life as regards the duties of agents', although he did comment that a double recovery of damages by P 'almost amounts to an absurdity' (Notes, (1891) 7 LQR 99). The *Mayor of Salford* principle may also have been influenced by the then current rule that judgment against one tortfeasor released the others and it was thus essential to separate A's liability from that of the briber, T.

However, in *Mahesan v Malaysia Government Officers' Co-operative Housing Society Ltd*,[10] the Privy Council refused to follow the *Salford* principles on the basis that they were 'in conflict with basic principles of English law as they have been developed in the course of the present century'.[11] In *Mahesan*, T conspired with A for the purchase of land and its resale to the defendant housing society (P), making a net profit of $443,000 after spending $45,000 on the eviction of squatters. T gave A a bribe of $122,000 and then absconded, leaving A to face the wrath of P. In the High Court of Malaysia, A was convicted of criminal offences of corruption, sentenced to seven years in prison and ordered to pay a penalty of $122,000 to P but P's claim for damages was disallowed. In the Federal Court of Malaysia, P succeeded in his claim for the bribe of $122,000 *and* damages assessed at $443,000 *and* the criminal penalty of $122,000. The Privy Council reversed that decision pointing out the swingeing consequences of triple recovery against A. Accordingly, it was held that as against A and the briber, T, P has *alternative* remedies viz, (i) an action for money had and received against A (or T) for the amount of the bribe *or* (ii) an action for damages for fraud against T (or A) for the actual loss sustained. The court considered that P would have to elect between these alternatives but need not do so before the time of judgment and, as P would have opted for the larger amount, he was awarded damages of $443,000.

The *Mahesan* decision harmonises with the orthodox notion that damages are compensatory in nature and, consequently, it has been censured for its slackening of the deterrent rule[12] but, certainly on the facts, it would be difficult to countenance any other outcome. Moreover, the fact that P may claim the larger of the two amounts when coupled with the other remedies available to him (eg refusal to pay A commission) means that there is still considerable punitive force in the bribery rules.

Bribes are held on constructive trust for P

Formerly it was the law that, where T bribed A but P had no pre-existing proprietary right to the money at the date of payment, A did not hold the amount of the bribe on trust for P. In principle, this seemed somewhat perverse in the context of the strict rules of fiduciary duty but, in practice, the remedies outlined above would suffice except where A was insolvent or had invested the bribe and then a proprietary remedy would arguably be apt.

The leading decision on bribes was *Lister & Co v Stubbs*,[13] where the court held that a constructive trust did not arise on A's receipt of the bribe. There A invested the bribes largely in the purchase of land and P claimed to follow the money into the investments, moving for an injunction to restrain A from dealing with them or an order directing him to bring them into court. It was held that relief would not be granted as the relationship between P and A was one of debtor and creditor, not that of trustee and *cestui que trust*. The court's reasoning was that, as P had no pre-existing proprietary right to the

---

10 [1979] AC 374.
11 [1979] AC 374 at 379-380 per Lord Diplock.
12 Tettenborn, 'Bribery, Corruption and Restitution – The Strange Case of Mr Mahesan' (1979) 95 LQR 68, 73; see also Needham, 'Recovering the Profits of Bribery' (1979) 95 LQR 536.
13 (1890) 45 Ch D 1; see also *Metropolitan Bank v Heiron* (1880) 5 Ex D 319.

money paid by T to A, it was not P's money so as to make A a trustee of it and, although A had to account for such a bribe, the error should not be made of 'confounding ownership with obligation'.[14] The court thus took an extremely pragmatic view of the position and considered that the consequences of imposing a trust were overly burdensome in that, if A became bankrupt, the property acquired by him with the bribe money would be awarded to P and withdrawn from the unsecured creditors. Moreover, bearing in mind that *Lister* was heard in 1890, it is quite astonishing that the utilitarian view of commercial morality which was adopted was such that the court considered it would be unfair if P 'could compel [A] to account to [him], not only for the money with interest, but for all the profits which he might have made by embarking in trade with it'.[15]

It is principally the perceived injustice to A's creditors which has led some to support *Lister*,[16] and, indeed, it has been suggested that the creditors have a better claim to protection than P as they have parted with property against a promised payment from A, whereas P may not have parted with anything and may have lost nothing.[17] However, it is submitted that the better view is that the 'proprietary remedy merely withdraws from the insolvent's estate an asset which it was never meant to have'.[18] Moreover, it is suggested that *Lister* was particularly unsatisfactory in that it was responsible for the unacceptable irony that a *bona fide* agent who profited from his position was a constructive trustee of the profits made (eg Boardman in *Boardman v Phipps*) whereas a dishonest agent who took bribes had merely to account to P for the amount of the bribe and, by astute investment, might profit extensively from his breach of duty.[19]

In *A-G for Hong Kong v Reid*,[20] the Privy Council refused to follow *Lister*. In *Reid*, the defendant worked in the legal service of the Government of Hong Kong and, in breach of his fiduciary duty as a Crown servant, accepted bribes (NZ $2.5m) to obstruct the prosecution of criminals. He invested the money in properties in New Zealand. Reid was sentenced to eight years' imprisonment and ordered to pay the Crown $2.5m, but none of that sum

---

14   (1890) 45 Ch D 1 at 15, per Lindley LJ. *Lister* did not affect the overall rule that a trustee who appropriates trust property holds it as a constructive trustee. The decision also distinguished *Re Canadian Oil Works Corpn (Hay's Case)* (1875) 10 Ch App 593 (vendors of property to a company gave part of the purchase price to a director) and thus a constructive trust was imposed where the bribe emanated from the beneficiary's property. Moreover, a constructive trust arose where the bribe was in the form of property, not money, see *Re Morvah Consols Tin Mining Co (McKay's Case)* (1875) 2 Ch D 1; *Re Caerphilly Colliery Co (Pearson's Case)* (1877) 5 Ch D 336 (company directors received fully paid-up shares in the companies as a bribe from T).

15   (1890) 45 Ch D 1; see also *Islamic Republic of Iran Shipping Lines v Denby* [1987] 1 Lloyd's Rep 367 where *Lister* was followed.

16   See Birks, *An Introduction to the Law of Restitution* (1985), p 388; Goode, 'Ownership and Obligation in Commercial Transactions' (1987) 103 LQR 433,441-445; Goode, 'Property and Unjust Enrichment' in *Essays on the Law of Restitution* (ed Burrows, 1991), p 231; Birks, 'Obligations and Property in Equity: *Lister v Stubbs* in the Limelight' [1993] LMCLQ 30.

17   Goode, supra, (1987) 103 LQR 433, 444-445.

18   Millett, 'Bribes and Secret Commissions' [1993] Restitution L Rev 7, 17.

19   See Maudsley, 'Proprietary Remedies for the Recovery of Money' (1959) 75 LQR 234, 243-245; Youdan, 'The Fiduciary Principle: The Applicability of Proprietary Remedies' in *Equity, Fiduciaries and Trusts* (ed Youdan, 1989); Millett, 'Bribes and Secret Commissions' [1993] Restitution L Rev 7 (*Lister* is roundly condemned).

20   [1994] 1 AC 324.

was ever paid. The appellant thus claimed that the titles to the properties were held on constructive trust for the Crown. Delivering the advice of the Privy Council, Lord Templeman evaluated the leading decisions extending from *Keech v Sandford* to *Boardman v Phipps*, his conclusion being that *Lister* was inconsistent with the notions that (i) a fiduciary must never benefit from his own breach of duty (ii) he should account for a bribe as soon as he receives it and, (iii) equity regards as done that which ought to be done. Accordingly, the Privy Council decided that a fiduciary who took a bribe held it and any property acquired therewith on constructive trust for his beneficiary. Lord Templeman stressed that 'bribery is an evil practice which threatens the foundations of any civilised society'[1] and the imposition of a constructive trust is thus an effective disincentive to engage in such corrupt practices.[2] The fact that A now holds any property representing the bribe on constructive trust for P means that, if the property depreciates in value, the fiduciary has to pay the difference between that value and the initial amount of the bribe to the beneficiary and, likewise, should the property appreciate in value the fiduciary cannot retain any profits. Where this proprietary remedy is successfully invoked, certain other advantages accrue to P. First, the equitable doctrine of laches applies to his claim rather than its being time-barred by the periods prescribed by the Limitation Act. Second, should A become insolvent, his unsecured creditors would not share in the property representing the bribe, this being justified by Lord Templeman on the basis that 'the unsecured creditors cannot be in a better position than their debtor'.[3] Finally, it is now also clear that all bribes are subjected to a constructive trust, no matter how the bribe is constituted and irrespective of its source[4] thus eradicating the *Lister* inconsistency regarding whether or not P had a pre-existing proprietary right to the bribe. Similarly, *Reid* erases the former injustice that a *bona fide* agent who profited from his agency was subjected to a constructive trust whereas a dishonest agent who had been bribed might merely have to account to P.

All that being said, *Reid* has been criticised on the basis that the maxim that 'equity looks on as done that which ought to be done' is normally applicable only to contracts which are specifically enforceable and where it can thus be deemed that specific property has transferred to the claimant. The objection that is raised is thus that A's obligation to account for a bribe is not in any sense equatable with an obligation to grant a proprietary interest in a specific asset where there is a consensual relationship between the parties.[5]

Further criticism has stressed that the reasoning of the Privy Council did not distinguish between (i) P's claim to property which he has lost, ie A has extracted

---

1 [1994] 1 AC 324 at 330.
2 Cf Cornish, 'The Principal Questions' in *The Frontiers of Liability* (ed Birks, 1994), Vol I, p 80, who argues that a proprietary remedy should not be employed in insolvency to give preference over ordinary creditors and, before property is deemed to belong to P rather than A, it must be shown that this will act as 'a properly aimed punitive measure'.
3 [1994] 1 AC 324 at 331; see also Millett, 'Bribes and Secret Commissions' [1993] Restitution L Rev 7, 17 who argues that sympathy for the plight of the creditors of an insolvent fiduciary is misplaced in that 'allowing a proprietary remedy merely withdraws from the insolvent's estate an asset which it was never meant to have'.
4 [1994] 1 AC 324 at 331, per Lord Templeman.
5 See Oakley, 'The Bribed Fiduciary as Constructive Trustee' [1994] 53 CLJ 31; Gardner, 'Two Maxims of Equity' [1995] 54 CLJ 60, 60-63.

P's property wrongfully or intercepted property[6] which, but for the conduct of A, P would have received and (ii) P's claim to profits which A has wrongfully made, ie A has made a personal gain in the execution of the agency. It has become prosaic to assert that a proprietary remedy should be available only in situation (i) where P's loss is A's direct gain[7] but it is submitted that the rule of equity, which should not be be attenuated, has always been that the profits made in situation (ii) *belong* to P, on the basis that they would have accrued to P but for A's breach of duty. If the process of attentuation is allowed to commence, it inevitably follows that equity's rules are subjected to elaborate dissection in the search to justify the availability of proprietary remedies in particular cases. This, of course, undermines the central tenet of equity in this context that 'the court will presume in favour of the principal and as against the briber and the agent bribed'.[8] It is submitted that, certainly in the context of bribes, the decision in *A-G for Hong Kong v Reid* is long overdue.

P's additional remedies where A is bribed

P has yet more remedies where A takes a bribe. A will forfeit his right to commission from P and, unlike some of the decisions concerning secret profits, here the courts seem unwilling to exercise any discretion in A's favour.[9] A may also lose his right to indemnity.[10] Furthermore, P may dismiss A without notice[11] and it is apparent from the cases considered earlier that A and T may be guilty of a criminal offence.[12] Any contract entered into with the briber, T, is voidable at P's option: P may therefore rescind the contract and recover any money paid[13] and he may do this even if he had terminated the contract earlier

---

6 See eg, *Cook v Deeks* [1916] 1 AC 554. Care must be taken, in all but the most obvious cases, to ensure that property would have accrued to P had A not intervened.

7 See Goode, 'Property and Unjust Enrichment' in *Essays on the Law of Restitution* (ed Burrows, 1991), Ch 9; Oakley, 'The Bribed Fiduciary as Constructive Trustee' [1994] 53 CLJ 31; Pearce, 'Personal and Proprietary Claims against Bribees' [1994] LMCLQ 189; Uff, 'The Remedies of the Defrauded Principal after Attorney-General for Hong Kong v Reid' in *Corporate and Commercial Law: Modern Developments* (eds Feldman and Meisel, 1996), Ch 13; *Halifax Building Society v Thomas* [1996] Ch 217, 228-229 per Peter Gibson LJ; McCormack, *Proprietary Claims and Insolvency* (1997), Ch 5,'Fiduciaries, Bribes and Constructive Trusts'; Goode, 'Proprietary Restitutionary Claims' in *Restitution Past, Present and Future: Essays in Honour of Gareth Jones* (eds Cornish, Nolan, O'Sullivan and Virgo, 1998), Ch 5 (here the author suggests cogently that the two central reasons underpinning the decision in *Reid*, viz (i) equity looks on as done that which ought to have been done, and (ii) A's creditors cannot stand in a better position than A himself, are circular arguments in that they presuppose the existence of P's proprietary claim).

8 *Hovenden & Sons v Millhoff* (1900) 83 LT 41, 43 per Romer LJ.

9 *Salomons v Pender* (1865) 3 H & C 639; *Boston Deep Sea Fishing & Ice Co v Ansell* (1888) 39 Ch D 339; *Andrews v Ramsay & Co* [1903] 2 KB 635; *Harrington v Victoria Graving Dock Co* (1878) 3 QBD 549 (A's commission was denied even though he had not acted corruptly as a result of the bribe and P's interests were unaffected). See Ch 9.

10 *Stange & Co v Lowitz* (1898) 14 TLR 468; *Nicholson v J Mansfield & Co* (1901) 17 TLR 259 (both cases concerned secret profits of stockbrokers).

11 *Bulfield v Fournier* (1895) 11 TLR 282; *Boston Deep Sea Fishing & Ice Co v Ansell* (1888) 39 Ch D 339.

12 See in particular the Prevention of Corruption Acts 1906 and 1916, ss 1 and 2 respectively.

13 *Panama and South Pacific Telegraph Co v India Rubber, Gutta Percha, and Telegraph Works Co* (1875) 10 Ch App 515; *Re a Debtor* [1927] 2 Ch 367; *Taylor v Walker* [1958] 1 Lloyd's Rep 490.

on insufficient grounds being unaware of the bribery.[14] If it is too late to rescind, he may bring the contract to an end for the future.[15]

In *Logicrose Ltd v Southend United Football Club Ltd*,[16] the court considered the question of P's rescission in the light of his retention of the bribe. It was held that P could recover the bribe from A whether he elected to affirm or rescind the contract with T, following reasoning in an earlier decision that the bribe belonged to P.[17] There could thus be no assertion that P's retention of the bribe amounted to affirmation of the contract. Similarly, although rescission involved the return of benefits obtained under the contract, the court accepted that the bribe was money paid *otherwise* than under the contract and it did not have to be returned.

Finally, in all cases thus far the bribe has been paid or offered by T himself or paid or offered in situations where an agent of T is authorised to make it and it may therefore be imputed to T. What is the position if a bribe is offered by an agent of T without T's knowledge? In *Armagas Ltd v Mundogas SA*,[18] the Court of Appeal considered that, in these circumstances, tortious, vicarious liability reasoning should be applied, ie T is liable in damages when A has acted in the course of his employment, this approach being regarded as appropriate in view of the tortious liability of T in damages where he is the briber.[19]

THE AGENT'S DUTY TO KEEP THE PRINCIPAL'S PROPERTY SEPARATE FROM HIS OWN, MAINTAIN PROPER ACCOUNTS AND RECORDS AND PAY OVER MONEY HELD TO THE USE OF THE PRINCIPAL

As a general rule, A must not mix his money or property with that of P and if such a mixing means that it is impossible to ascertain the respective shares, the court will presume that the entire fund belongs to P.[20] The onus of proof is on A to show which part of the fund is his. This obligation arises only where money or property is beneficially owned by P because A will then be in the position of a trustee.

It is not entirely clear when A will be regarded as a trustee[1] and, in some instances, the court may decide that the relationship of P and A is one of debtor and creditor in order that A's commercial activities are not overly-restricted. In *Henry v Hammond*,[2] for example, the plaintiff average adjuster who was acting on behalf of foreign insurers, instructed the defendant shipping agent to sell the cargo of a salved vessel and pay all claims and expenses in relation to it. After the sale, £96 remained in A's hands which appeared in his balance sheets for

---

14 *Alexander v Webber* [1922] 1 KB 642.
15 *Armagas Ltd v Mundogas SA* [1986] AC 717, 742-743 per Robert Goff LJ.
16 [1988] 1 WLR 1256.
17 *Grant v Gold Exploration and Development Syndicate Ltd* [1900] 1 QB 233, 251 per Collins LJ.
18 [1986] AC 717.
19 The court followed the decision of the Supreme Court of Canada in *Barry v Stoney Point Canning Co* (1917) 55 SCR 51. In *Armagas*, Robert Goff LJ reserved the question ([1986] AC 717, 745) whether rescission (as opposed to damages) might be appropriate and available to P where the bribe offered to A was one for which T was *not* vicariously liable (eg made by a stranger) on the basis that, although T would be innocent, it would still be inequitable to hold P to the contract thus procured by bribery.
20 *Lupton v White* (1808) 15 Ves 432.
 1 See the consideration of this issue earlier in this chapter.
 2 [1913] 2 KB 515.

four years as a debt due from him. Nearly thirty years later, the plaintiff brought an action to recover the amount arguing that A had made himself an express trustee of the sum so that the Statute of Limitations did not apply. The court held that this was an ordinary commercial transaction which did not require A to keep the amount separate from his other moneys and, accordingly, he was not an express trustee and the Statute of Limitations provided a good defence to the claim. Certainly where A is instructed to purchase land or take a lease for P and does so in his *own* name he will become a trustee of it for P.[3]

A must also keep accurate accounts of all transactions entered into on P's behalf and be ready to produce them at all times for, otherwise, the court will 'presume everything unfavourable to him'.[4] P has the action of account as the procedure by which A is made to render an account.[5] An account is settled where P has approved it and the general rule is that it will not be re-opened. However, where A has been guilty of fraud and over-charging the rules are stringent and, in such a situation, accounts have been re-opened for the previous twenty-five years,[6] lapse of time being no defence.

A is similarly under a duty to produce for P all records and documents relating to P's affairs. In *Yasuda Fire & Marine Insurance Co of Europe Ltd v Orion Marine Insurance Underwriting Agency Ltd*,[7] it was held that A's records must be available to P even after the termination of the agency. There A acted as an underwriting agent for P and an express term of the agency contract entitled P to inspect A's records relating to insurance business transacted on behalf of P. P terminated the agreement and A alleged that, as the agreement had been terminated by repudiatory breach, he was under no obligation to perform any part of the agreement. Colman J held that an agency relationship could exist independently of any contract between the parties and P was entitled to a continuing access to A's records unless the right was excluded by the contract. The express term in the contract between P and A did not exclude that right and P's right to inspect the records had not been discharged. It is clear that, on the termination of the agency, P is only entitled to take delivery of documents which have been prepared by A on P's behalf and the court will differentiate documents directly connected with the agency from those belonging to A.[8]

Whenever A holds money to the use of P, he must pay it over to P. Thus an action for money had and received will lie where A received money on P's behalf or money is entrusted to A for a particular purpose which he has not carried out or where A has made a secret profit.[9] The action cannot be maintained until A has received the money or has been credited with it in his own account with T, unless there is some fault on A's part, eg A sells goods and neglects to collect the proceeds from T.[10] If sued for money had and received, A may set-off all expenses

---

3   *Lees v Nuttall* (1829) 1 Russ & M 53; *Atkins v Rowe* (1728) Mos 39 (lease).
4   *Gray v Haig* (1854) 20 Beav 219, 226 per Romilly MR.
5   For the history of this action see Fifoot, *History and Sources of the Common Law* (1952), pp 268-277; Stoljar, *The Law of Agency* (1961), pp 299-300.
6   *Stainton v Carron Co* (1857) 24 Beav 346.
7   [1995] QB 174.
8   See eg *Chantrey Martin v Martin* [1953] 2 QB 286.
9   As a general rule, where A holds money which belongs in law or equity to P, any interest earned on it belongs to P and where A receives money in breach of duty, he must pay interest on it from the date of his default.
10   *Varden v Parker* (1798) 2 Esp 710; *Hunter v Welsh* (1816) 1 Stark 224.

reasonably incurred in the agency.[11] It is striking that P may succeed in an action for money had and received even where A received the money from T in a transaction which was void or illegal, eg if A is employed to make bets and wins, P may recover the winnings from A even though the betting transaction is void.[12] this does not apply, however, if the relationship between P and A is illegal[13] on the basis that, as both parties are equally at fault, the court will not assist P.

11 *Dale v Sollet* (1767) 4 Burr 2133.
12 *De Mattos v Benjamin* (1894) 63 LJQB 248; *Tenant v Elliott* (1797) 1 Bos & P 3 (a broker who effected an illegal insurance for P received payment on a loss under the policy from the underwriter and was held liable to P for money had and received).
13 *Harry Parker Ltd v Mason* [1940] 2 KB 590 (P employed A to place £12,000 on a horse called 'Another Greek' in a race at Nottingham. P relied on A's representations that the bet could be made without affecting the horse's starting price by implementing a complex scheme using youths on bicycles who would place some bets with street bookmakers and the remainder with bookmakers throughout the country. This scheme involved two illegalities, viz using street bookmakers and placing a sham bet on another horse to deceive the public. In fact, A had never placed the bet although 'Another Greek' was unplaced in the race. It was held that P could not recover the money as it had been handed to A for an illegal purpose).

CHAPTER 9

The rights of the agent against his principal

Introduction

It will be noticed that, although there is a voluminous amount of law concerning the strict duties which A owes to P, this chapter does not delineate any correlative duties which P owes to A – instead, A has certain *rights* which he may enforce against P. In English law, it has always been assumed that P needs protection from A's abuse of his position but not vice versa: the matters dealt with below are described, at best, as P's liabilities. Moreover, the law's strict rules for the implication of terms into contracts, which emphasise that such terms must be both obvious and necessary to give business efficacy to the undertaking, have not aided any evolution of P's duties of good faith.[1] Nevertheless, recent Regulations[2] which implemented an EC Directive[3] stipulate that, in the relatively limited context of 'commercial agencies',[4] P owes a general, non-excludable duty of good faith to A.[5] The 1993 Regulations apply also to commercial agents' rights in relation to remuneration, these being referred to where relevant in this chapter.

Remuneration

THE SOURCES OF REMUNERATION

From A's perspective, remuneration is probably the most important aspect of the agency relationship but the dominant rule is that A has no general right to remuneration for services rendered to P: it is perfectly acceptable for agency to be gratuitous and consensual in nature. Consequently, A is entitled to remuneration *only* if there is an express or implied term to that

---

1 Cf *Restatement, Second, Agency* §§ 432-437. See generally Burrows, 'Contractual Co-operation and the Implied Term' (1968) 31 MLR 390.
2 Commercial Agents (Council Directive) Regulations 1993 (SI 1993/3053 as amended by SI 1993/3173).
3 Dir 86/653 (18 December 1986, OJ L382/17).
4 See Ch 12, on the termination of agency, for the definition of a 'commercial agent'.
5 Regs 4 and 5; see Ch 12 where the 1993 Regulations are considered in more detail.

effect in his contract[6] or, if there is no contract, A may have a right to claim in restitution on a *quantum meruit*.

Express terms

If there are express terms in the contract between P and A, the general rule is that it is not possible to imply terms which are inconsistent with the express provisions. In *Kofi Sunkersette Obu v Strauss & Co Ltd*,[7] an express term of A's contract provided for remuneration of 'a monthly sum of fifty pounds' and commission 'which I have agreed to leave to the discretion of the company'. The Privy Council held that only the sum of £50 per month was payable and it could not determine the rate of commission as this would entail making a new contract for the parties and transferring to the court a discretion which was vested in P.[8]

Implied terms

If there are no express terms as to remuneration, a term relating to it will be implied only where the court is satisfied that the parties intended that A should be remunerated.[9] However, in professional and commercial agencies, P's request that A should act for P, followed by A's rendering of services to P, leads to a presumption that remuneration was intended, unless there are indications to the contrary.[10]

Where it is possible to imply a term, the normal rules apply regarding the implication of such terms.[11] A term may be implied on the grounds of business efficacy or to give effect to the intentions of both parties, for example. In *Way v Latilla*,[12] A undertook to supply P with information relating to African gold mines and concessions and alleged that there was an agreement for P to give him a share in the mines and reasonable remuneration. The House of Lords held that there was no concluded agreement regarding the share but that an employment contract existed between the parties and, as the surrounding circumstances indicated that it was not to be gratuitous, a term was implied as to reasonable remuneration which was fixed having regard to the earlier

---

6 The contract itself may be implied, of course, and P's request and A's subsequent performance should usually give rise to such a contract. The implied contract may, in turn, contain implied terms as to reasonable remuneration.
7 [1951] AC 243.
8 See also *Taylor v Brewer* (1813) 1 M & S 290 (A agreed to accept 'such remuneration as should be deemed right' and was held entitled to no remuneration under the contract); *Re Richmond Gate Property Co Ltd* [1965] 1 WLR 335 (no implied term possible where the company's articles stipulated for 'such remuneration as the directors may determine').
9 *Reeve v Reeve* (1858) 1 F & F 280.
10 *Miller v Beale* (1879) 27 WR 403. In relation to self-employed 'commercial agents' (see Ch 12), the Commercial Agents (Council Directive) Regulations 1993, reg 6, provides that, in the absence of any agreement as to remuneration, such an agent is entitled to the remuneration that commercial agents appointed for the goods forming the subject of his agency are customarily allowed in the place where he carries on his activities or, in the absence of such customary practice, he is entitled to reasonable remuneration taking into account all aspects of the transaction.
11 See generally *Liverpool City Council v Irwin* [1977] AC 239. See also the Supply of Goods and Services Act 1982, s 15, which provides that where the consideration for the supply of services is not determined by the contract, is left to be determined in a manner agreed by the contract, or determined by a course of dealing between the parties, there is to be an implied term for the payment of a reasonable charge.
12 [1937] 3 All ER 759.

negotiations between A and P. In determining an amount, the courts may consider the customs of A's profession or trade and, for example, the scale of charges fixed by a professional body but A cannot simply point to such a scale and be remunerated accordingly. Rather he must show that the scale was incorporated expressly or impliedly into the contract and if he relies on a customary implication, the custom must be certain, notorious and reasonable.[13]

Quantum meruit

Finally, where there is no contract between P and A but A has rendered services which were accepted freely by P with full knowledge of the position, the court may award A reasonable remuneration on the restitutionary basis of *quantum meruit*. Although some decisions refer to *quantum meruit* in relation to claims under an implied term of a contract, the restitutionary remedy is better confined to situations where, for a variety of reasons, there is no contract. For example, the original contract may have been rescinded,[14] P and A may have agreed to fix the remuneration at a later date but failed to reach agreement,[15] the contract might not have sufficient certainty of terms and thus be unenforceable[16] or the contract may lack the requisite formalities as in *Craven-Ellis v Canons Ltd*.[17] There a company director's contract of appointment was void as he had never obtained the qualification shares as stipulated in the company's articles of association but, having rendered services to the company, he was able to recover remuneration on a *quantum meruit* basis.

THE AGENT'S REMUNERATION MUST HAVE BEEN EARNT: THE PRECARIOUS POSITION OF THE COMMISSION AGENT

Has the event occurred upon which remuneration is payable?

Assuming that there is an express or implied term entitling A to remuneration, he must nevertheless earn it in the sense that the event upon which payment depends must have occurred. If a contractual agent is paid a fixed salary, he will be entitled to remuneration if he abides by the terms of his contract with P and only rarely will such terms provide for payment by reference to *results* produced by A. However, most agents are paid on a commission basis for results achieved, most commonly for some completed transaction which they have secured for P.

In deciding whether A has performed the task upon which remuneration depends, the terms of the agency contract should be examined first in order to ascertain (i) the precise event which gives rise to remuneration and (ii) whether that event has occurred. It may be a relatively straightforward task to discern whether or not A has completed the task he was engaged to perform. In *Lockwood v Levick*,[18] for example, A introduced buyers to manufacturers (P) and was paid

---

13 See eg, *Wilkie v Scottish Aviation Ltd* 1956 SC 198.
14 *Faraday v Tamworth Union* (1916) 86 LJ Ch 436 (the contract was rescinded by A as a result of P's innocent misrepresentation. A was able to recover reasonable remuneration on a *quantum meruit*).
15 *Loftus v Roberts* (1902) 18 TLR 532.
16 See *Scammell v Ouston* [1941] AC 251; *Jaques v Lloyd D George & Partners Ltd* [1968] 1 WLR 625.
17 [1936] 2 KB 403.
18 (1860) 8 CBNS 603.

commission on 'all goods bought'. It was held that A was entitled to commission where he found a buyer who gave an order which was accepted by P, even though P was unable to supply the goods to the buyer. Erle CJ emphasised that 'the plaintiff performed all the service for which he was employed; and the defendant had the option of delivering the goods and so making profit'.[19]

Many of the cases on remuneration concern estate agents and the perennial difficulty of deciding when such agents acquire a vested right to commission. The distinct stages in a sale of real property ((i) introduction of a potential buyer (ii) agreement 'subject to contract' and (iii) exchange of contracts and completion) and the unfettered ability of both parties to resile from the agreement before the exchange of contracts, has prompted a desire in estate agents to claim a vested right to commission at an early stage in the negotiations. However, the commission agent's predicament is that he is paid only on the accomplishment of a task and where, for example, P engages an estate agent to sell his property, he clearly desires a completed, rather than an aborted sale, of that property. McCardie J[20] stressed that:

> 'It is a settled rule for the construction of commission notes and the like documents which refer to the remuneration of an agent that a plaintiff cannot recover unless he shows that the conditions of the written bargain have been fulfilled. If he proves fulfilment he recovers. If not, he fails. There appears to be no halfway house, and it matters not that the plaintiff proves expenditure of time, money and skill.'

The indulgent view is that this is a harsh approach: A is in an invidious position as he may expend much time and effort in attempting to conclude a contract only to be thwarted at the final hurdle for any number of reasons (eg T does not materialise to contract with P; T or P decides not to proceed at the last minute). The opposing, sceptical view, stresses the fact that A comes under no *obligation* to find T, that he may do little or no work in attempting to find T without legal consequence, and that he accepts the business risk of failing to complete his assignment. These conflicting perspectives must now be considered in more detail.

The decision in *Luxor (Eastbourne) Ltd v Cooper*

The leading decision on the commission agent's remuneration is *Luxor (Eastbourne) Ltd v Cooper*.[1] A company (P) appointed A to find a purchaser for certain cinemas at not less than £185,000, in return for £10,000 payable to A from the sale price on completion. A introduced T who offered, subject to contract, £185,000 for the cinemas but P decided not to proceed with the sale. A claimed the commission or damages for breach of an implied term that the company

---

19 (1860) 8 CBNS 603 at 609. Where the Commercial Agents (Council Directive) Regulations 1993 apply (see Ch 12), reg 10(1) stipulates that commission is 'due' upon whichever of the following events is the earliest: (i) P has executed the transaction (ii) P should, according to his agreement with T, have executed the transaction or, (iii) T has executed the transaction. 'Execution' is intended to mean 'performance' under the contract rather than *concluding* a contract. A final limit is provided by reg 10(2), which cannot be derogated from, in that 'commission shall become due at the latest when the third party has executed his part of the transaction or should have done so if the principal had executed his part of the transaction, as he should have'. Reg 10(2) would mean, for example, that should P refuse to deliver goods in breach of contract or supply defective goods so that T does not pay, P must nevertheless pay A his remuneration.

20 *Howard Houlder & Partners Ltd v Manx Isles Steamship Co* [1923] 1 KB 110, 113-114.

 1 [1941] AC 108.

would not, without just cause, act so as to prevent his earning the commission. The House of Lords held that A's rights depended solely on the express terms of the contract and both of A's claims were rejected. Commission was not payable as the stipulated result, the completion of the sale, had not occurred, and it was *unnecessary* to give business efficacy to the contract to imply a term that P would not deprive A of the opportunity to earn commission. The issues of (i) A's vested right to commission and, (ii) the possibility of an implied term not to deprive A of commission, must be considered separately.

Luxor and A's vested right to commission

On this issue, the House took the sceptical view outlined above, underlining the fact that there is no correlation between the estate agent's contract to sell property and a contract of employment, as the estate agent does not get paid for work done but, instead, he is remunerated for results achieved in a completed sale. This point is accentuated as A's commission is payable from the proceeds of sale of the property. Similarly, the fact that A might fail to complete the sale was regarded as an inherent, business risk which he freely accepted. In *Luxor*, the ample remuneration on offer accurately reflected A's gamble, Lord Russell of Killowen being at pains to emphasise graphically that £10,000 was then the 'remuneration of a year's work by a Lord Chancellor'.[2] Although it is not expressly articulated in *Luxor*, the normal commission contract is regarded as unilateral in nature with a concomitant right of P to revoke his offer of payment at any time before A accepts the offer by securing a completed sale. It is apparent from *Luxor* that, on the facts, a 'completed sale' would take place at the moment a binding contract was completed between P and T (ie, exchange of contracts), A then having a vested right to commission.[3]

Luxor and the implied term not to deprive A of commission

It should be emphasised that, prior to *Luxor*, the courts had shown a willingness to protect A by deploying the notion that P came under a duty not to prevent A from earning commission. Such a duty was first expressed in *Prickett v Badger*,[4] where A found a purchaser for P's property but P was unable to convey the property for lack of title. A recovered on a *quantum meruit* for work done. Similarly, in *Inchbald v Western Neilgherry Coffee, Tea and Cinchona Plantation Co*,[5] A agreed to sell the shares of P company for an immediate commission and further payment of £400 when all the shares were allotted. The company had been formed to purchase a tea estate but its owner later refused to sell so it was decided to wind up the company before the shares were sold. The court acknowledged that the company had *bona fide* reasons for liquidation but that A could recover some commission. The court thus balanced A's risk that the company might be wound up against the company's guiltless actions in preventing the earning of A's commission and awarded A £250 (£400 less £150 to reflect A's risk). Willes J thought that A should succeed against P where P 'prevents or makes it less probable that he should receive

2 [1941] AC 108 at 126.
3 [1941] AC 108 at 126 per Lord Russell of Killowen; p 142 per Lord Wright.
4 (1856) 1 CBNS 296.
5 (1864) 17 CBNS 733.

[commission]'.[6] This reasoning culminated in the decision in *Trollope (G) & Sons v Martyn Bros*[7] where P withdrew from the sale of his property when the negotiations were still 'subject to contract' but A nevertheless obtained damages against P. The Court of Appeal held that P should be liable to A if he *unreasonably* withdrew from the negotiations.

This line of authority came to a dead-stop in *Luxor* when the House of Lords expressly overruled *Trollope*, pointing to the innate uncertainty of deciding whether or not P's withdrawal was unjust and unreasonable, and the other decisions came under heavy fire.[8] After such a comprehensive assault, it must be asked whether A has *any* redress where P withdraws from the transaction and deprives him of commission.

The overriding emphasis in *Luxor* was that P had an unfettered and legitimate right to resile when the agreement with his purchaser was 'subject to contract' and thus he could not possibly be subject to an implied term, *vis-à-vis* A, not to withdraw from the negotiations.[9] Such an implied term was not obviously necessary to give business efficacy to the contract and it could not be the intention of *both* parties that it should exist. Indeed, if there were to be an implied term to that effect, it would make the subsidiary undertaking to pay commission to A more important than the primary contract for the sale of the property itself.

Moreover, *Luxor* stressed that other important issues militated against the possibility of an implied term. First, where P employed several estate agents, it could not sensibly be argued that a resulting sale to T, arranged by one A, would render P liable in damages to the other agents for preventing their earning of commission.

Second, Viscount Simon LC[10] pointed to other intractable problems regarding the possibility of an implied term: suppose an offer to buy made by T who is introduced by A is immediately bettered by a second offer from another T introduced by a second A, would P be bound to reject the second offer or accept it only with the consequence of paying two commissions? If the terms of the agency contract were that A should find a tenant for P's house, would P be bound to accept the first tenant introduced by A? The thrust of the Lord Chancellor's rhetorical questions was clear and, indeed, the overall inutility of the implied

---

6 (1864) 17 CBNS 733 at 741.
7 [1934] 2 KB 436.
8 *Luxor* stressed that *Prickett* should be regarded as limited to its facts (p 121, per Viscount Simon LC; p 127, per Lord Russell of Killowen; p 147, per Lord Wright; p 156, per Lord Romer) and Lord Wright thought that *Inchbald* was incomprehensible unless it could be considered as 'analogous to a case of wrongful dismissal' (p 147). *Luxor* also re-affirmed that an express contractual provision for remuneration and the absence of any actual benefit received by P, excluded A's claim on a *quantum meruit* (p 125, per Lord Russell of Killowen; pp 140-141, per Lord Wright).
9 There is a difficulty here which is usually ignored. If the undertaking between P and A is *unilateral* in nature (this point *not* being argued in *Luxor*) and leads to a binding contract only when A has *completed* his task, it would mean that, during performance, there is no contract into which any term could be implied. Where a measure of protection is available to A, it should perhaps be classified as an implied, collateral *contract* not to revoke. Also, it is unclear the extent to which modern decisions concerning unilateral contracts, which suggest that the offeree should be protected from the offeror's revocation once the offeree has commenced performance, might apply to A (eg *Errington v Errington and Woods* [1952] 1 KB 290; *Ward v Byham* [1956] 1 WLR 496; see also *United Dominions Trust (Commercial) Ltd v Eagle Aircraft Services Ltd* [1968] 1 WLR 74; *Daulia Ltd v Four Millbank Nominees Ltd* [1978] Ch 231). See also Murdoch, 'The Nature of Estate Agency' (1975) 91 LQR 357, 369-375.
10 [1941] AC 108, 116.

term in this context cannot be disputed. For example, in *French & Co Ltd v Leeston Shipping Co Ltd*,[11] a shipbroker (A) who had procured a charterparty for 18 months under which he was entitled to 2½% commission on hire paid and earnt, alleged that the shipowner (P) was in breach of an implied term not to deprive A of commission by selling the ship after only four months of the charter had run. The House of Lords refused to imply such a term observing that it was unnecessary to do so as the contract functioned perfectly without it and the proper course of action for a prudent A would have been to provide for his needs by express stipulation.

Although *Luxor* appeared to close every door on the hapless agent, *dicta* in that decision left one door ajar in suggesting that the position might be different where P withdrew *after* a binding contract had been entered into between P and T,[12] because then P would be at fault and it might be possible to imply a term in the agency contract that P should not deprive A of the opportunity of earning commission.[13] On such facts, a term was implied successfully in *Alpha Trading Ltd v Dunnshaw-Patten Ltd*.[14] There the seller/P wished to sell cement and A introduced T, a potential buyer. A binding contract was entered into between P and T, A's remuneration being payable upon the 'mutual *performance*' of the contract between P and T, but P did not deliver the cement and thus failed to perform under that contract. The claim for remuneration under the agency contract could not succeed as there had been no performance of the main contract of sale but the Court of Appeal held that it was 'necessary to imply a term which prevents [P] from playing a dirty trick on the agent with impunity after making use of the services provided by that agent'.[15] Accordingly, A was awarded damages of $25,000, being equivalent to the amount of commission which would have been payable under the contract.[16] The *Alpha* case thus turns on P's wrongful act in breach of contract with T and is not comparable with *Luxor* or *French* where both principals legitimately exercised their rights and were not in breach of contract to T.[17]

---

11 [1922] 1 AC 451.
12 See Lord Wright's comments at pp 141-142 and pp 149-150. See also *obiter* statements to the same effect in *George Trollope & Sons v Martyn Bros* [1934] 2 KB 436, 445 per Scrutton LJ (dissenting) and *Dennis Reed Ltd v Goody* [1950] 2 KB 277, 285 per Denning LJ.
13 If a binding contract has been formed between P and T, A will often have a vested right to commission under the *express* terms of the agency contract as the formation of a binding contract with T is usually the event upon which remuneration is payable.
14 [1981] QB 290; see Carter, 'The Life of an Agent in Commerce is a Precarious One' [1982] 45 MLR 220.
15 [1981] QB 290 at 306, per Templeman LJ.
16 See also *Moundreas (George) & Co SA v Navimpex Centrala Navala* [1985] 2 Lloyd's Rep 515; *Orient Overseas Management and Finance Ltd v File Shipping Co Ltd, The Energy Progress* [1993] 1 Lloyd's Rep 355 (a term was implied that the defendant owners of *Energy Progress* would not agree to a premature termination of the charter-party by substituting a new vessel for *Energy Progress* thereby depriving the plaintiff managers of the vessel of a bonus payable 'on the termination of the charter by effluxion of time'. Gatehouse J acknowledged that a commission broker could not normally prevent an owner of property from disposing of it and depriving the broker of commission (*French & Co Ltd v Leeston Shipping Co Ltd* [1922] 1 AC 451) but the fact that the managers accepted this risk as one event which would deprive them of their bonus did not mean that they accepted the risk of losing the bonus because of a consensual, early termination of the charter-party).
17 Where the Commercial Agents (Council Directive) Regulations 1993 apply (see Ch 12), reg 11 provides that A's right to commission can be extinguished only where the contract between P and T 'will not be executed' *and* that fact is 'due to a reason' for which P is 'not to blame'. Reg 11(2) provides that, where the right to commission is extinguished, A must refund any commission which he has received. The wording here is elusive: What is

Similarly, if A cannot perform his task without the active co-operation of P, it was acknowledged in *Luxor*[18] that it might be possible to imply a term that the necessary co-operation should be forthcoming. The Lord Chancellor's example in *Luxor* was that P's compliance as a sitter would be required in a contract for A to paint P's portrait and, at least in that situation, it seems clear that the implication could be justified under general principles in that it would be necessary to give business efficacy to the contract.[19]

Finally, although the primary concern is that A may be placed in a disadvantageous position regarding commission where P defaults in the performance of the contract with T, it is plain that A may be equally disadvantaged where T defaults. Might A have any remedy in this situation? It is, of course, P who promises to pay A commission and thus A has neither control over, nor any remedy for, T's breach of contract with P. Similarly, as Denning LJ[20] pointed out in relation to estate agency, if the purchaser/T of property defaults, the vendor/P is not bound to sue for specific performance or damages simply to enable the estate agent to earn commission. The question of T's breach arose in *Marcan Shipping (London) Ltd v Polish Steamship Co, The Manifest Lipkowy*.[1] P agreed to buy a vessel from the seller, T, and A was to receive a commission to be deducted from the proceeds of sale when paid to T. By virtue of a collateral undertaking between T and A, T agreed that the commission should be deducted from the price. A binding contract was completed between P and T but T failed to deliver the vessel. A contended that there was an implied term in the collateral agreement with T that T would not fail to perform the contract and deprive A of commission. The

---

encompassed by 'blame'? Is P to be blamed in the *Luxor* situation? Although P has a legitimate right to withdraw in the *Luxor* situation, if the transaction were within the Regulations, might he be in breach of the duty of good faith in reg 4 and therefore be sufficiently at fault for the requirement of 'blame'? Reg 11 must mean, however, that P cannot refuse to pay A commission where the failure to 'execute' (perform) the contract is the result of P's *breach of contract*, as in the *Alpha* case. Alternatively, P need not pay A commission where the contract will not be executed because T is in breach of contract or is insolvent, for example.

18 [1941] AC 108, 118 per Viscount Simon LC; p 148 per Lord Wright.

19 See *Mackay v Dick* (1881) 6 App Cas 251 (a steam-powered 'digging machine' was sold on condition that it should be capable of excavating at a specified rate on the buyer's (B) land. B wrongfully refused to provide facilities for a proper trial and (without argument as to the correct remedy) he was held liable for the *price* of the machine); *Colley v Overseas Exporters* [1921] 3 KB 302; *Mona Oil Equipment & Supply Co Ltd v Rhodesia Rlys Ltd* [1949] 2 All ER 1014; *Bournemouth & Boscombe Athletic Football Club v Manchester United Football Club* (1980) Times, 22 May (footballer transferred for a fee part of which was payable after he had scored 20 goals; before the goals were scored, the player was omitted from the first team. The club was held to be in breach of contract as it had failed to provide the player with a reasonable opportunity of scoring the goals). In *Luxor*, Lord Wright stressed that P's act which prevents A from fulfilling a condition on which his right to payment depends must be *wrongful* and, in the *Mona Oil* case (supra), Devlin J thought that 'in the light of the decision in *Luxor*' use of the implied term 'could now with advantage be restricted to the exceptional case' (p 1016). For example, no term could be implied that P should remain in business in order to give A the opportunity of earning commission: see *Rhodes v Forwood* (1876) 1 App Cas 256; *Lazarus v Cairn Line of Steamships Ltd* (1912) 106 LT 378 (considered in Ch 12). In *Mackay v Dick* (supra), B was liable for the price, the position thus being assessed as if the condition had been fulfilled and the goods had been sold to B. However, as Sir Guenter Treitel suggests (*The Law of Contract* (10th edn, 1999), p 62), the appropriate remedy for breach of the subsidiary obligation not to prevent occurrence of a condition should be damages, thereby allowing for the possibility that the condition might not have occurred even if there had been no breach.

20 *Dennis Reed Ltd v Goody* [1950] 2 KB 277, 285.

1 [1989] 2 Lloyd's Rep 138.

Court of Appeal held that the undertaking between T and A imposed no *obligation* on T to answer for the commission – instead it was simply the *machinery* for the transfer of the commission to A. Moreover, a term in the collateral agreement between T and A to the effect that A would be remunerated by T if T defaulted in the performance of the main contract could not be implied, either from the point of view of business efficacy or as a term which the parties must obviously have intended. Bingham LJ thought that it was 'by no means obvious ... that the sellers [T] would have intended to pay nearly a quarter of a million dollars ... to the other party's agents even if, albeit through their own fault, they never received any proceeds of the sale of the vessel'.[2]

Express terms in estate agents' contracts

Most of the litigation on express terms has concerned estate agents and the various clauses drafted by them but it is clear that the estate agent's contract involves no special rules and the normal estate agency undertaking is regarded as unilateral in nature.[3] After *Luxor's* onslaught on their position, estate agents devised clauses which sought to secure their commission at some time before exchange of contracts. However, the overall emphasis is that the courts impute an intention to the parties that commission should 'be payable in the event of an actual sale'[4] and that any other construction of the contract would require 'clear and unequivocal language'.[5] This theme is repeated time and again by the judges and although the plethora of cases cannot be considered here in detail,[6] the key decisions disclose the tenor of the law. It cannot be over-emphasised that whether or not the event has occurred upon which remuneration is payable involves a question of construction and interpretation of each contract's terms. In *Luxor*,[7] Lord Wright said:

> 'I deprecate in general the attempt to enunciate decisions on the construction of agreements as if they embodied rules of law. To some extent decisions on one contract may help by way of analogy and illustration in the decision of another contract, but, however similar the contracts may appear, the decision as to each must depend on the consideration of the language of the particular contract, read in the light of the material circumstances of the parties in view of which the contract is made. '

If the contract provides that A must 'find a purchaser' the courts have demanded that commission is due only when a binding contract to purchase results[8] and if T withdraws after contract and before completion no commission is payable as T is no longer a 'purchaser'.[9] In an attempt to avoid this construction, estate agents sought commission on the introduction of a third party who was 'ready, willing and able to purchase' but, despite the courts' initial acceptance of this wording,[10] it was made clear in two restrictive decisions[11] that if T's offer was

---

2 [1989] 2 Lloyd's Rep 138 at 144.
3 *Luxor (Eastbourne) Ltd v Cooper* [1941] AC 108, 124 per Lord Russell of Killowen.
4 *Midgley Estates Ltd v Hand* [1952] 2 QB 432, 435-436 per Jenkins LJ.
5 *Luxor (Eastbourne) Ltd v Cooper* [1941] AC 108, 129 per Lord Russell of Killowen.
6 See Ash, *Willing to Purchase* (1963); Murdoch, *Law of Estate Agency and Auctions* (3rd edn, 1994); Murdoch, 'The Nature of Estate Agency' (1975) 91 LQR 357.
7 *Luxor (Eastbourne) Ltd v Cooper* [1941] AC 108, 130.
8 See eg, *McCallum v Hicks* [1950] 2 KB 271 ('find someone to buy').
9 *James v Smith* (1921) [1931] 2 KB 317n.
10 See eg *Bennett & Partners v Millett* [1949] 1 KB 362.
11 *Graham and Scott (Southgate) Ltd v Oxlade* [1950] 2 KB 257; *Dennis Reed Ltd v Goody* [1950] 2 KB 277.

in any way conditional, as in the normal offer 'subject to contract', this would mean that he was not 'willing' to purchase.

However, a radical change of approach was evident in *Christie Owen & Davies Ltd v Rapacioli*.[12] There P instructed A to help him find a purchaser for his business at a price of £20,000, commission being payable if A 'effected an introduction either directly or indirectly of a person ... ready willing and able to purchase [for £20,000] or any other price'. A introduced T whose offer of £17,700 was accepted 'subject to contract' and a draft contract was prepared and signed by T but P decided not to proceed. The Court of Appeal held that A was entitled to commission because T was willing to contract with P, on terms acceptable to P, until the moment of P's withdrawal. The court also recognised (contrary to the view in *Luxor*) that P might have to pay two commissions – the first to the agent who had introduced a willing purchaser/T to whom P did not sell, and the second to the agent who introduced the ultimate purchaser/T. The case has been criticised[13] in that P may dispute the terms of the sale until contracts are exchanged and 'willingness' can therefore be established conclusively only by a *completed* contract because, until contract, there is merely a temporary willingness which might be varied.[14]

Arguably A's safest course is to avoid any emphasis on the *conclusion* of the contract and T's status as a *completed purchaser*.[15] For example, in *Drewery and Drewery v Ware-Lane*,[16] A's terms were that commission was due when a 'prospective purchaser' signed A's 'purchaser's agreement' and the vendor signed A's 'vendor's agreement'. Both documents were signed, both were 'subject to contract' but the prospective purchaser was unable to obtain a mortgage and therefore never entered into a contract to purchase. It was held that the phrase 'prospective purchaser' did not require that the purchaser be ready, willing or able but that, instead, he had merely to contemplate the purchase in good faith. As that condition had been fulfilled, A was entitled to commission.

Where A is appointed 'sole agent' it is indisputable that he is granted a measure of protection in that P will be liable in damages if he sells the property through another agent.[17] However, in the absence of an express prohibition, P will not be so liable if he sells the property privately to a purchaser unknown to A.[18] If, however, A is given a sole and *exclusive* right to sell, P could be liable in damages for breach of contract if he privately negotiates a sale during the period of the agency.[19] Sole agency undertakings are usually thought to be bilateral contracts,

---

12 [1974] QB 781.
13 See *Bowstead & Reynolds On Agency* (16th edn, 1996), Art 58, pp 290-292.
14 The notion that T must be 'irrevocably willing' had been clearly expressed by Denning LJ in *McCallum v Hicks* [1950] 2 KB 271, 276, and *Dennis Reed Ltd v Goody* [1950] 2 KB 277, 287-288, but his comments were expressly disapproved in *Rapacioli*.
15 But there are dangers in emphasising the *possibility* of purchase: in *Jaques v Lloyd D George & Partners Ltd* [1968] 1 WLR 625 commission was payable should A be 'instrumental in introducing a person willing to sign a document capable of becoming a contract to purchase at a price, which at any stage in negotiations has been agreed by [P]' but it was held that this clause was too uncertain to be enforced.
16 [1960] 1 WLR 1204.
17 *Hampton & Sons Ltd v George* [1939] 3 All ER 627.
18 *Bentall, Horsley and Baldry v Vicary* [1931] 1 KB 253; *Sadler v Whittaker* (1953) 162 Estates Gazette 404.
19 See *Chamberlain and Willows v Rose* (1924) 47 TLR 101, summarised in *Bentall, Horsley and Baldry v Vicary* at [1931] 1 KB 253, 261; *Brodie Marshall & Co (Hotel Division) v Sharer* [1988] 19 EG 129; *Property Choice Ltd v Fronda* [1991] 2 EGLR 249; cf *Harwood v Smith* [1998] 1 EGLR 5 (considered below).

consideration being present in A's express or implied promise to use his best efforts to sell P's property in return for P's promise not to sell via another agent.[20] It has been suggested that P's withdrawal of the property from the sole agent could be a breach of the undertaking[1] but the better view must be that only a sale of the property through another agent would amount to such a breach.

Estate Agents Act 1979

The Estate Agents Act 1979 seeks to regulate standards within the business of estate agency but the Act and Regulations made under it contain several provisions which are crucial to the remuneration of estate agents. Under s 18 of the 1979 Act and Regulations made in 1991,[2] certain written information regarding remuneration must be given by the estate agent to P *before*[3] he 'enters into a contract' with the estate agent under which the latter 'will engage in estate agency work on behalf of the client'. If this is not done, A will not be able to enforce the contract without special leave of the court.[4] Although the Act uses the terminology of contract, it does not alter the general rule that estate agency normally involves the formation of a unilateral contract so that no contract is complete until, as a general rule, a binding contract for the sale of the property has been entered into. Consequently, it has been suggested that this provision may be of doubtful utility.[5] However, where there is a sole agency or sole selling rights, the contract will usually be bilateral in nature and this problem should thus not arise.

Regulation 5 of the 1991 Regulations demands that the terms 'sole agency', 'sole selling rights' and 'ready, willing and able to purchase' must be explained by A (before the contract for agency work is entered into) and, most significantly, the exact words of explanation are provided in the Schedule to the Regulations.[6]

---

20 *Christopher (E) & Co v Essig* [1948] WN 461; *Mendoza & Co v Bell* (1952) 159 Estates Gazette 372; Cf Murdoch, 'The Nature of Estate Agency' (1975) 91 LQR 357, 373-375, who argues that sole agencies are unilateral in nature but that the court will readily imply a collateral contract not to revoke.

1 *Glentree Estates Ltd v Gee* (1981) 259 Estates Gazette 332, 336 per Ewbank J.

2 The Estate Agents (Provision of Information) Regulations 1991 (SI 1991/859) made under s 30 of the 1979 Act.

3 See reg 3(1) ('when communication commences between the estate agent and the client or as soon as is reasonably practicable thereafter provided it is a time before the client is committed to any liability towards the estate agent').

4 See Estate Agents Act 1979, s 18(5).

5 See Reynolds [1980] JBL 39, 41.

6 **(a) Sole selling rights:** 'You will be liable to pay remuneration to us, in addition to any other costs or charges agreed, in each of the following circumstances –
   – if unconditional contracts for the sale of the property are exchanged in the period during which we have sole selling rights, even if the purchaser was not found by us but by another agent or by any other person, including yourself;
   – if unconditional contracts for the sale of the property are exchanged after the expiry of the period during which we have sole selling rights but to a purchaser who was introduced to you during that period or with whom we had negotiations about the property during that period'.
   (b) Sole agency: 'You will be liable to pay remuneration to us, in addition to any other costs or charges agreed, if at any time unconditional contracts for the sale of the property are exchanged—
   – with a purchaser introduced by us during the period of our sole agency or with whom we had negotiations about the property during that period; or
   – with a purchaser introduced by another agent during that period'.
   For the explanation in the Schedule of 'ready, willing and able purchaser', see below.

It should also be stressed that these 'explanations' provide that A is entitled to actual commission/remuneration (rather than damages) in all the situations specified. Anti-avoidance measures in reg 5(2) further stipulate that any terms used by A which have 'a similar purport or effect' to the three specified terms in reg 5 must also be explained using the statutory form which can be amended if necessary.

The question of 'sole selling rights' under the Regulations was considered recently in *Harwood v Smith*.[7] There A had sole selling rights, within reg 5(1)(a), for the sale of P's nursing home. During the currency of the agency, but without any intervention by A, P answered an advertisement from a prospective purchaser, T, who was hoping to purchase a nursing home. P exchanged contracts with T two days *after* the agency had formally ended. In relation to sole selling rights, para (a) of the Schedule to the Regulations provides that remuneration is payable to A 'if unconditional contracts for the sale of the property are exchanged after the expiry of the period during which we have sole selling rights but to a purchaser who was introduced to you during that period or with whom we had negotiations about the property during that period'. The Court of Appeal held that the wording of para (a) was unclear but a reasonable client would understand it to apply only to introductions made by A rather than introductions made by anyone else and, accordingly, A was not entitled to remuneration.

The definition in para (c) of the Schedule to the Regulations of a purchaser who is a 'ready, willing and able purchaser' is that he is 'prepared and is able to exchange unconditional contracts for the purchase of your property'. Most significantly, it is also provided in para (c) of the Schedule that:

'You will be liable to pay remuneration to us, in addition to any other costs or charges agreed, if such a purchaser is introduced by us in accordance with your instructions and this must be paid even if you subsequently withdraw and unconditional contracts for sale are not exchanged, irrespective of your reasons'.

In principle, this provision is most favourable to estate agents as the common law's view is that use of the word 'purchaser' indicates that T becomes a purchaser only when contracts are exchanged[8] whereas the Regulations do not demand that the transaction reaches this stage. There has been no reported decision on para (c) and its scope is thus unclear but it should be stressed that P's liability turns on his *withdrawal* from the agency contract and, where P is disinclined to sell his property, he should thus take care to avoid an express withdrawal. Estate agents are, nevertheless, faced with the unpalatable fact that para (c) attempts to impose liability on P under the subsidiary, agency contract, when he has an unfettered right to withdraw from the primary transaction relating to the sale of the property at any time until there is an exchange of contracts.

THE AGENT MUST BE THE EFFECTIVE CAUSE OF THE TRANSACTION

Where A's commission is payable on the happening of an event, A must show not only that the event has occurred but that he was the effective cause of its

---

7 [1998] 1 EGLR 5.
8 See the cases cited earlier and *Davis v George Trollope & Sons* [1943] 1 All ER 501 (held that 'willing buyer' means a person who actually becomes a buyer).

happening.[9] It is plain that A will not be entitled to commission if he has not contributed at all to the event which has transpired[10] but the position is less clear where he has been only partially successful in bringing about the desired result or if he has played only a small part in causing it to happen. The notion of effective cause is not precisely defined in the cases but a consideration of some of the decisions illustrates the problems of causation involved.

In *Green v Bartlett*,[11] an estate agent and auctioneer was employed by P to sell the island of Herm by auction or otherwise. At auction, the property was not sold but, having attended the auction, T approached A and was given P's name. T eventually bought the island directly from P. It was held that A was entitled to commission as the ultimate sale was the direct consequence of A's initial efforts to sell the property.[12] This is undoubtedly a just result but it is difficult to predict with any degree of precision when A's initial efforts can be said unequivocally to engender the eventual transaction for which he claims commission. Suppose A completes his authority in introducing T to P but the parties enter into further dealings over a period of years. Might A have a right to commission in perpetuity? What if the transactions subsequently entered into were not of a *type* contemplated by A's original authority?

Green v Bartlett should be contrasted with the decision in *Tribe v Taylor*.[13] P required additional capital for his business and promised A 5% commission should he find a suitable third party who would inject new capital. A introduced T who lent P £10,000 and A received his commission. Several months later, P and T entered into a partnership and T invested a further £4,000 in the business. It was held that A was not entitled to commission on the £4,000 as this was the outcome of negotiations for the partnership to which A was a stranger.

Although it is plain that the chain of causation was held to be linked to A in *Green* and broken in *Tribe*, it is impossible to articulate the principle underlying the cases with any more precision and, overall, the courts are driven to make a rather rough-and-ready evaluation of effective cause.[14] It is clear that a *novus actus interveniens* will deprive A of commission and, using this analysis, it is

---

9 Where the Commercial Agents (Council Directive) Regulations 1993 apply (see Ch 12), reg 7(1) provides that: 'A commercial agent shall be entitled to commission on commercial transactions concluded during the period covered by the agency contract – (a) where the transaction has been concluded as a result of his action; or (b) where the transaction is concluded with a third party whom he has previously acquired as a customer for transactions of the same kind'. Reg 7(1) thus embodies the notion of effective cause. Under reg 7(1) the transaction must be '*concluded*' and this conflicts with reg 2(1) where the commercial agent is defined as having authority 'to *negotiate* the sale or purchase of goods'. Reg 7(1)(b) refers specifically to the issue of 'repeat orders' where T places further orders with P, during the currency of the agency, without A's intervention (see reg 8, below, for post-termination orders). See also reg 7(2) which dilutes the notion of effective cause in that A is entitled to commission on transactions concluded during the agency 'where he has an exclusive right to a specific geographical area or to a specific group of customers and where the transaction has been entered into with a customer belonging to that area or group'.

10 See *Howard Houlder & Partners Ltd v Manx Isles Steamship Co Ltd* [1923] 1 KB 110; *Shackleton Aviation Ltd v Maitland Drewery Aviation Ltd* [1964] 1 Lloyd's Rep 293 (both considered in Ch 12).

11 (1863) 14 CBNS 681.

12 See also *Nahum v Royal Holloway and Bedford New College* [1999] EMLR 252.

13 (1876) 1 CPD 505.

14 Eg Stoljar considered (Stoljar, *The Law of Agency* (1961), p 313) that the courts seek to limit A's commission to 'his first and major act'. Although this is arguably correct, it is somewhat vague as a practical test.

possible to distinguish *Green* from the not dissimilar facts of *Taplin v Barrett*.[15] In *Taplin*, A introduced T to P as a prospective purchaser of P's property but no agreement was reached between them. P subsequently sold the property at auction and T was the purchaser. Here the property was sold and sold to T, but it was indisputable that the auctioneer's act was the effective and proximate cause of the sale, not A's initial introduction.[16]

The decision in *Coles v Enoch*[17] graphically illustrates the problems inherent in establishing whether A is the effective cause of the transaction in question. P, the owner of a shop which was suitable for conversion into a pin-table arcade, agreed to pay A commission if A could find a tenant for the shop. A telephoned M, a manufacturer of pin-tables, as he considered M might be a possible tenant but M said he wanted to consult his partner. T, who was sitting in M's office, overheard the conversation and asked M for the shop's address but M would say only that it was 'in Victoria', adding that, if he did not take the lease he would give T further details. Without any further communication with anyone, T went to Victoria, found the shop and arranged a lease directly with P. At first instance,[18] it was held that A was entitled to commission as there was an unbroken chain of causation between A and T. Thus, in pursuit of a tenant, A had discussed the possibility of a lease with M, M had approached T as a possible tenant and had given T information which resulted in T's leasing the premises. The Court of Appeal[19] reversed the decision and, treating M as A's sub-agent, held that M's deliberate withholding of the address conclusively snapped the chain of causation leading to A and thus T's acts were the effective cause of the ensuing transaction.[20]

Where agents are in competition with one another to secure one sale, the question will often arise as to which agent is the effective cause of the sale. In *Bartlett v Cole*,[1] P employed A to sell his café and A introduced T who needed to obtain a loan before he could buy. Consequently, T went to A2 in search of a lower priced business. A2, who also had P's business on his books, assured T of finance and told him to employ a solicitor. A2 provided no finance but T's solicitor arranged it successfully and T bought P's property. It was held that A's original introduction would have been successful had it not been for the finance difficulties and, consequently, the elimination of those difficulties made A's introduction the effective cause of the sale. It seems clear therefore, following the principles of causation outlined above, that the tendency is to allow commission to the first agent who introduces T *unless* there is an obvious

15 (1889) 6 TLR 30.
16 See also *Toulmin v Millar* (1887) 58 LT 96 (A, employed to lease an estate, procured a tenant, T, who subsequently bought the estate without any further intervention by A. Held that A was not entitled to commission on the sale); *Hodges & Sons v Hackbridge Park Residential Hotel Ltd* [1940] 1 KB 404 (A, employed to find a purchaser for an hotel at a specific price, brought it to the attention of the War Office who failed to reach agreement with P. Ultimately, the War Office compulsorily acquired the hotel at a lesser price and against the wishes of P. Held that A was not entitled to commission as he had been employed to find a ready and willing purchaser and secure a *voluntary* sale at a price acceptable to P).
17 [1939] 3 All ER 327.
18 [1939] 1 All ER 614.
19 [1939] 3 All ER 327.
20 Powell asks, but does not answer (*The Law of Agency* (2nd edn, 1961), p 338) what the position would have been had T been in A's office while A communicated full particulars to M, T then leasing the shop without saying anything to A.
1 [1963] EGD 452; see also *John D Wood & Co v Dantata* [1987] 2 EGLR 23.

breakdown of negotiations between P and T which effectively breaks the chain of causation and enables A2 to claim the commission. Indeed, *Taplin v Barrett*, above, is such a case.[2]

However, it was suggested recently in *Lordsgate Properties Ltd v Balcombe*,[3] that two agents might be entitled to commission on the *same* transaction if both were instrumental in causing the sale or different contracts entitled each agent to commission for different reasons. The first possibility seems remote and has not been applied in any decision but the second situation arose in *Lordsgate* and both agents obtained commission where A was instructed to 'introduce an applicant who purchased' the property but A2 had only to be 'instrumental in negotiating a sale'.

Finally, in some agency relationships where A relies very heavily on commission, he may claim remuneration after the agency has terminated for business introduced prior to termination, this being the issue of commission on 'repeat orders' or 'renewals'.[4] A's entitlement to commission turns on the construction of the agency contract, the older cases inclining to the view that no commission would be payable after termination (especially where the contract was for a specified period) unless the contract unequivocally provided for it.[5] The modern approach, exemplified in *Sellers v London Counties Newspapers*,[6] is that continuing commission may be payable if that is the intention of the parties, such intention being found more readily where A is an independent contractor rather than an employee.[7] Virtually all the cases on this topic concern the interpretation of express terms and it is clear that an implied term allowing continuing commission will be difficult to establish.[8]

---

2   See also *Anscombe & Ringland Ltd v Watson* [1991] 2 EGLR 28; *Chesterfield & Co Ltd v Zahid* [1989] 2 EGLR 24. Both were cases where negotiations between P and T (introduced by A) had broken down but A2 revived the parties' flagging interest in the sale and successfully claimed commission. In *Chasen Ryder & Co v Hedges* [1993] 1 EGLR 47, Staughton LJ suggested that if A introduced T first and a purchase followed, it might well be inferred that A was the effective cause, the evidential burden then shifting to A2 to displace the inference but A2 would not necessarily have to show that 'the interest aroused by the first introduction ha[d] evaporated'.

3   [1985] 1 EGLR 20, per Drake J.

4   For a detailed consideration of this topic see Powell, *The Law of Agency* (2nd edn, 1961), pp 364-369.

5   Eg, *Nayler v Yearsley* (1860) 2 F & F 41; *Gerahty v Baines & Co Ltd* (1903) 19 TLR 554; *Marshall v Glanvill* [1917] 2 KB 87.

6   [1951] 1 KB 784.

7   See the two 'independent contractor' cases where A successfully claimed commission after termination: *Bilbee v Hasse & Co* (1889) 5 TLR 677; *Levy v Goldhill & Co* [1917] 2 Ch 297.

8   Where the Commercial Agents (Council Directive) Regulations 1993 apply (see Ch 12), reg 8 provides that A is entitled to commission on transactions concluded after the agency has terminated if '(a) the transaction is mainly attributable to his efforts during the period covered by the agency contract and if the transaction was entered into within a reasonable period after that contract terminated; or (b) in accordance with the conditions mentioned in regulation 7 above, the order of the third party reached the principal or the commercial agent before the agency contract terminated'. Reg 9 provides for the situation where the incoming A claims commission under reg 7 *and* commission is payable to the previous, outgoing A under reg 8 – the rule is that the incoming A is *not* entitled to commission 'unless it is equitable because of the circumstances for the commission to be shared between the commercial agents'. There is thus a bias in favour of the outgoing A and particularly as no situation is envisaged in which he would receive nothing.

NO REMUNERATION IN CASES OF MISCONDUCT AND BREACH OF DUTY OR IN RESPECT OF UNLAWFUL OR WAGERING TRANSACTIONS

As a general rule, A is entitled to remuneration only where the transaction is expressly or impliedly authorised or is ratified by P.[9] Should A's authority be revoked prior to his performing an act which would entitle him to remuneration, he might have other remedies (eg breach of contract) but he will *not* be entitled to remuneration.[10]

Similarly, A is not entitled to remuneration in respect of transactions where he commits a breach of duty which is sufficiently serious to justify P's repudiation of the obligation to pay A. Alternatively, A's breach may be regarded as a repudiation which P may accept. Where A is in serious breach of duty, P may terminate the agency without notice but commission which has been earnt previously and is due at the date of breach must be paid.[11] It is not easy to decide, however, when such a gross breach of duty has occurred. Any breach of the fiduciary duties should arguably lead to loss of remuneration[12] but, where A is in good faith,[13] the courts clearly preserve a discretion to award him remuneration. In *Hippisley v Knee Bros*,[14] an auctioneer who was employed to sell goods received discounts from printers and advertisers but, acting *bona fide*, he charged P the full amount. It was held that he must account to P for the discounts but the court held that he was entitled to commission as he was in good faith and the receipt of the discount was incidental to the main function of selling the goods. Similarly, in *Keppel v Wheeler*,[15] A was allowed commission as 'an agent might quite properly claim his commission, and yet have to pay damages for committing a bona fide mistake which amounts to a breach of duty'.[16] Moreover, transactions may be regarded as severable so that fraudulent dealings may be separated from those that are honest and in relation to which commission may be payable.[17] P may also waive A's breach of duty[18] but waiver is not implied from the fact that P accepts the benefit of the transaction negotiated by A or recovers the bribe which was paid to A.[19]

9 *Marsh v Jelf* (1862) 3 F & F 234 (an auctioneer who was instructed to sell property by auction sold it by private contract and was not entitled to commission).
10 *Campanari v Woodburn* (1854) 15 CB 400.
11 *Boston Deep Sea Fishing & Ice Co v Ansell* (1888) 39 Ch D 339.
12 See *Keppel v Wheeler* [1927] 1 KB 577, 592 per Atkin LJ. Agents were disentitled to commission in: *Salomons v Pender* (1865) 3 H & C 639 (secret profit); *Boston Deep Sea Fishing & Ice Co v Ansell* (1888) 39 Ch D 339 (bribe); *Andrews v Ramsay & Co* [1903] 2 KB 635 (bribe): 'a principal is entitled to have an honest agent, and it is only the honest agent who is entitled to any commission', per Lord Alverstone CJ, at p 638; *Harrington v Victoria Graving Dock Co* (1878) 3 QBD 549 (A's commission was denied even though he had not acted corruptly as a consequence of the bribe and P's interests were unaffected).
13 See *Boardman v Phipps* [1967] 2 AC 46 (considered in Ch 8) where the *bona fide* A was allowed generous expenses even though in breach of duty; cf Lord Goff's warning in *Guinness plc v Saunders* [1990] 2 AC 663, 700-702, that such allowances should be restricted to cases where they cannot have the effect of encouraging a conflict of interest and duty.
14 [1905] 1 KB 1. See also *Keppel v Wheeler* [1927] 1 KB 577 where A obtained commission as he was *bona fide*.
15 [1927] 1 KB 577.
16 [1927] 1 KB 577 at 588, per Bankes LJ.
17 *Nitedals Taendstikfabrik v Bruster* [1906] 2 Ch 671.
18 *Harrods Ltd v Lemon* [1931] 2 KB 157.
19 *Andrews v Ramsay & Co* [1903] 2 KB 635.

Many of the agency cases on unlawful transactions and commission concern the statutory requirements for the conduct of certain professions: unlicensed and unqualified professional agents may be unable to recover remuneration.[20] Also, in accordance with the normal rules on illegal contracts, A cannot recover remuneration for any transaction which is *ex facie*, or to his knowledge, unlawful, or is unlawful by virtue of a statute which imposes strict liability.[1] Before 1892, commission was recoverable by agents employed to make wagers[2] but the law was changed by the Gaming Act 1892, s 1, which provides that remuneration is irrecoverable in respect of any contract or agreement rendered null and void by the Gaming Act 1845.

Indemnity

THE NATURE AND SOURCES OF INDEMNITY

In the execution of his authority, A may incur liabilities, losses and expenses. The general rule is that he has a right to be indemnified against such liabilities and to have reimbursed any money which he has paid. A can enforce this right directly or by exercising his right of lien. Moreover, if A is sued by P, he has a right to set-off the amount of the liabilities and expenses incurred. It is necessary to consider briefly the sources of indemnity and its juristic basis as these dictate the extent of A's claim to be indemnified.

Where the agency is contractual, there will be either an express or implied term relating to indemnity (unless excluded by the contract) which extends to all liabilities incurred or payments made by A whilst acting within his express and implied authority. A's right of indemnity is thus extensive and covers the disbursements which both P *and* A are legally bound to make. For example, in *Adams v Morgan & Co*,[3] A sold a business to P and managed it on his behalf for a specific period, A having an express term in his contract relating to indemnity. It was held that A could be indemnified for supertax which he had to pay on the profits of the business even though P, a corporation, was not liable for the tax. Furthermore, the width of this notion allows A an indemnity for payments which could not have been *enforced* but regarding which A was under a moral or professional duty to pay. In *Rhodes v Fielder, Jones and Harrison*,[4] P revoked A's authority to pay fees to counsel but A nevertheless paid them. It was held that A was entitled to an indemnity from P because, although counsel could not have sued for the fees, A would have been guilty of professional misconduct had he refused to pay. Moreover, A obtained an indemnity where, although under a liability, he had incurred

---

20 See eg The Solicitors Act 1974, s 25(1).
 1 See eg *Stackpole v Earle* (1761) 2 Wils KB 133 (no remuneration for procuring the sale of public offices); Cf *Haines v Busk* (1814) 5 Taunt 521 (A effected a charter-party on P's ship which was illegal as certain licences had not been obtained. As A did not know of the absence of the licences and was under no duty to obtain them, it was held that he could recover remuneration).
 2 *Knight v Fitch* (1855) 15 CB 566.
 3 [1924] 1 KB 751.
 4 (1919) 89 LJKB 15.

no losses[5] and for a payment made as a result of his exercising his judgement reasonably and *bona fide*.[6]

Where A is not a contractual agent, his claim is restitutionary in nature and, consequently, his right to indemnity is generally thought to be much narrower than in a contractual agency. A's claim is thus confined to reimbursement of payments made by A (i) under compulsion of law (ii) which P has the ultimate liability to pay and (iii) from which P obtains a benefit by the discharge of a liability.[7] In *Brook's Wharf and Bull Wharf Ltd v Goodman Bros*,[8] the defendant stored ten packages of squirrel skins which he had imported from Russia in the plaintiff's bonded warehouse from where they were stolen without any fault on the part of the plaintiff. Although the defendant remained liable to pay duty on the skins, he declined to pay anything on non-existent goods and the plaintiff was compelled under statute to pay the duties. The plaintiff succeeded in his action to recover from the defendant the amount paid because the defendant had the primary obligation to pay the duties and, if the plaintiff had not been reimbursed, the defendant would have been unjustly enriched at the plaintiff's expense.

A right to indemnity also exists in equity. Although a trustee is not in general entitled to any remuneration, he has a right to be indemnified against his out-of-pocket expenses. Accordingly, provided that A may seek equity's protection (eg as a trustee), the scope of his right to indemnity may be wider than in restitution.[9]

Finally, where A is authorised to transact business at a particular place or in a particular market (eg the Stock Exchange), he is entitled to be indemnified according to the customs and usage of the place or market,[10] subject to the general rule that P will not be bound by any unreasonable custom unless he had knowledge of it when he granted A's authority.

SITUATIONS WHERE THE AGENT HAS NO RIGHT TO INDEMNITY

First and foremost, it is perhaps self-evident that A will have no right to an indemnity where the transaction concerned is unauthorised and has not been ratified by P, except where A can claim reimbursement on a restitutionary basis and does not have to rely on a contractual right to indemnity. In *Warwick v Slade*,[11] for example, P successfully revoked A's authority to effect a policy of insurance but A nevertheless effected it and paid the premiums. It was held that A had no right to be indemnified by P.

---

5 *Lacey v Hill, Crowley's Claim* (1874) LR 18 Eq 182 (a stockbroker (A) incurred liabilities on P's behalf and subsequently made a composition agreement for the debts. The balance had not been claimed by the creditors but P had to indemnify A to the full extent of the liabilities incurred on his behalf).

6 *Pettman v Keble* (1850) 9 CB 701(A, acting *bona fide*, compromised an action brought against him in respect of a contract entered into on P's behalf. P was aware of the action but gave A no instructions. A was entitled to an indemnity even though, on the facts, the plaintiff/T could not have succeeded in the action). See also *Frixione v Tagliaferro & Sons* (1856) 10 Moo PCC 175.

7 See Goff and Jones, *The Law of Restitution* (5th edn, 1998), Ch 15.

8 [1937] 1 KB 534; see also *The Pindaros* [1983] 2 Lloyd's Rep 635.

9 See Snell, *Equity* (29th edn, 1990), pp 257-259.

10 See eg, *Reynolds v Smith* (1893) 9 TLR 494.

11 (1811) 3 Camp 127; see also *Bowlby v Bell* (1846) 3 CB 284.

Second, there is no right to be indemnified where the loss or liability is incurred as a consequence of A's negligence, insolvency, breach of duty or default. A simple illustration of this rule is evident in *Lage v Siemens Bros & Co Ltd*,[12] where A was negligent in not declaring a quantity of cable wire to the Customs in Brazil and, consequently, he incurred a fine. It was held that he could not obtain an indemnity from P as he was in breach of duty. Within this heading, A may lose his right to indemnity because of his own insolvency which is not caused by the activities undertaken on behalf of P. In *Duncan v Hill*,[13] P instructed A, a stockbroker, to buy shares and carry them over to the next account. Before settlement of that account, A became insolvent and was declared a defaulter with the consequence that he incurred a loss on the sale of P's shares. P was not bound to indemnify A as the loss was not caused by the execution of his authority on behalf of P but because of his own insolvency.

Third, A cannot claim to be indemnified for expenditure incurred in relation to the performance of P's illegal instructions or A's own illegal conduct. This rule applies only where A knows that the transaction is illegal or where it is *ex facie* unlawful. Accordingly, an election agent who acted corruptly in making illegal payments to canvassers while campaigning on behalf of a candidate in the election was unable to recover the amounts paid from the candidate[14] and a broker who effected an insurance on a voyage which was illegal could not recover from P the amount of the premiums paid.[15] If, on the other hand, A can prove his innocence or that P misled him as to the nature of the transaction, he may not lose his right to indemnity. In *Adamson v Jarvis*,[16] A, an auctioneer, sold goods on P's behalf but only after he had completed the sale and handed the proceeds to P did he discover that P had no title to the goods. When the real owner compelled A to pay him the full price of the goods, it was held that A could obtain an indemnity from P as the transaction was not obviously illegal and A had no notice of P's lack of title. As mentioned earlier, although in many professions an unqualified agent, who thus acts illegally, may not recover remuneration from P, he may nevertheless obtain an indemnity.[17] Where P and A are joint tortfeasors and A is sued, he can recover a contribution from P under the Civil Liability (Contribution) Act 1978, s 1(1), the amount of the contribution being left to the discretion of the court.

Finally, there is no right to reimbursement for expenses or losses incurred in relation to wagering transactions. This has not always been the rule: following the general principle outlined above that indemnity is available for payments which neither P nor A could be *compelled* to make but which might entail serious consequences if not paid, A could recover an indemnity where he paid lost bets on P's behalf.[18] The position was changed by the Gaming Act 1892, s 1, which disallows A's right to indemnity in respect of gaming and wagering transactions rendered null and void by the Gaming Act 1845.

---

12 (1932) 42 Ll L Rep 252.
13 (1873) LR 8 Exch 242.
14 *Re Parker* (1882) 21 Ch D 408.
15 *Ex p Mather* (1797) 3 Ves 373 ('If a man is employed to buy smuggled goods; if he paid for the goods and the goods come to the hands of the person, who employed him, that person shall not pay for the goods': per Loughborough LC, p 373).
16 (1827) 4 Bing 66.
17 See *Smith v Lindo* (1858) 5 CBNS 587 (an unlicensed broker bought shares on behalf of P and was able to recover the price of the shares but unable to recover any commission).
18 *Read v Anderson* (1884) 13 QBD 779.

Lien

THE NATURE OF THE POSSESSORY LIEN

A possessory lien is a right to retain possession of the goods or chattels of another until the satisfaction of a debt or other obligation owed by that other. A's right to a lien is therefore principally a lever by which he may seek to enforce his rights to remuneration and indemnity.

There are two types of possessory lien. First, a *particular lien* is the right to retain possession of another's goods or chattels until all claims are met in relation to those particular goods or chattels. Second, a *general lien* is a right to retain possession until a general balance of account is settled or until the satisfaction of debts or obligations incurred independently of the goods or chattels which are retained. All agents have particular liens, general liens not being favoured by the law but nevertheless available to bankers, marine insurance brokers, solicitors and stockbrokers.

A possessory lien confers a right to retain possession only and does not give A a right to sell except where trade usage or statute permit; in fact, a sale will destroy the lien rendering A liable in conversion. Once the lien attaches, it constitutes an immediate right to possession and it follows that P cannot sue in conversion as he has no immediate right to possess the goods and, should P or T wrongfully remove the goods, A may sue either in conversion. But A cannot acquire more extensive rights in the goods than those of P at the time when the lien attached and A's claim will thus be subject to all rights and equities of third parties which were in existence at that time.[19]

THE AGENT'S ACQUISITION OF A LIEN

First, it is clear that a lien can attach only to goods and chattels and choses in action which are represented by documents, eg share certificates, insurance policies and bills of exchange. *Bowstead & Reynolds*[20] emphasises that references to liens over money should correctly be explained in terms of A's right of set-off if sued by P.

Second, if A is to have a lien, he must possess the goods either actually or *constructively* and thus they are sufficiently in his possession if he holds a document of title to the goods or they are held by a third party specifically on A's behalf.[1] It is equally clear that A may not have the right to possession even though the goods are in his custody and control. In *Hoggard v Mackenzie*,[2] a Scottish firm (P) of lace manufacturers appointed A as the manager and assistant of their branch in London. A had control and management of the business; he engaged employees, drew cheques and kept the key of the warehouse containing the goods. It was also expressly agreed that A should have a lien on all goods

---

19 See eg, *Peat v Clayton* [1906] 1 Ch 659.
20 *Bowstead & Reynolds on Agency* (16th edn, 1996), Art 67, para 7-076.
 1 See *Bryans v Nix* (1839) 4 M & W 775 (cargo delivered to a barge-master by P with instructions to hold the cargo for A); *McCombie v Davis* (1805) 7 East 5 (goods held by A's employee specifically on A's behalf).
 2 (1858) 25 Beav 493.

consigned to him for sale. On P's bankruptcy, A claimed to have a lien on the goods for £14,734 which was outstanding on bills of exchange which A had accepted for P. It was held that, although A had 'absolute command and control' over the goods, as long as the goods 'remained in the warehouse in London, in the name of the bankrupts, and at their establishment carried on entirely by their servants ... that possession was the bankrupts', and that as long as they remained there, [A] could not alter that position'.[3]

Third, A's possession must be obtained lawfully in the course of his agency and so he will have no lien where possession is obtained by misrepresentation or without the requisite authority.[4]

Fourth, A must obtain possession in his capacity as an agent and thus he will not have a lien where goods are deposited with him simply for safe custody as a bailee.[5] In *Dixon v Stansfield*,[6] for example, a factor had acted for P on several occasions but, on the occasion in question, he was instructed by P to take out an insurance policy on P's goods. It was held that A had no lien on the policy in respect of other services performed as a factor as he did not acquire the policy in his capacity as a factor.

Finally, there must be no express or implied agreement between P and A which is clearly inconsistent with the right of lien[7] and the goods must not be delivered to A for a special purpose inconsistent with the exercise of a lien.[8]

THE AGENT'S LOSS OF LIEN

Perhaps the most obvious way for a lien to be extinguished is where P correctly tenders the amount owing and A either accepts or refuses the tender.

Second, A may waive his right to the lien either expressly or impliedly. An implicit waiver can occur where A's conduct indicates an abandonment of the lien or his actions are inconsistent with the lien's continuance. In the leading decision in *Boardman v Sill*,[9] brandy was stored in the defendant's (D) cellars and warehouse rent was due on it. When the plaintiff demanded the brandy, D refused to deliver it and stated that it was his own property. He later contended that he had a lien on the brandy for the rent but it was held that the brandy had been detained on an entirely different ground from the supposed lien and, as no demand for rent had been made by D, he must be taken to have waived his lien,

---

3 (1858) 25 Beav 493 at 499-500, per Sir John Romilly MR.
4 *Taylor v Robinson* (1818) 2 Moore CP 730 (A, a factor, bought goods from S, on behalf of P, and P paid S a rent for the goods to remain on S's premises. Without any authority, A removed the goods to his own premises at roughly the same time as P became bankrupt. Held that P's possession continued and A had no lien).
5 *Muir v Fleming* (1822) Dow & Ry NP 29 (insurance policy left with A for safe custody conferred no general lien for advances made to the assured).
6 (1850) 10 CB 398.
7 *Re Bowes, Strathmore v Vane* (1886) 33 Ch D 586 (a life insurance policy was deposited at a bank with a memorandum charging it with overdrafts up to a stated amount. Held that this agreement excluded the banker's general lien on the policy); Cf *Fisher v Smith* (1878) 4 App Cas 1 (held that an agreement for monthly settlement of an insurance broker's (A) account did not exclude A's lien on policies in his possession for unpaid premiums).
8 *Brandao v Barnett* (1846) 12 Cl & Fin 787 (certain bills were deposited at a bank in a locked box, the key being left with the customer. The bills were then entrusted to the bank with instructions to obtain interest on them, exchange them for new bills and deposit them in the box. Held that the banker's lien did not extend to the bills which had been deposited with him for a special purpose inconsistent with a general lien).
9 (1808) 1 Camp 410n.

if he had one.[10] The facts of *Forth v Simpson*[11] are illustrative of a different method of waiver. There the holder of a lien on three stabled racehorses allowed their owner to take them out and race them without restriction and it was held that these actions were inconsistent with the lien's continuation.

Third, A's lien will evaporate where he parts with possession of the goods over which he has a possessory lien. If the lien is to be lost in this way, A's parting with possession must be voluntary. In *Sweet v Pym*,[12] A delivered the goods which were subject to the lien on board ship to be conveyed on account and at the risk of P. Unsurprisingly, it was held that A had lost his lien which could not be revived by stoppage in transit. Moreover, the lien will not be affected if the party obtaining possession did so by fraud or forcibly without A's consent.[13] In this situation, the lien will continue and A may sue in conversion whether he is in possession or not and even if he has regained possession by using a trick.[14]

As explained above, A's possession is not affected by the fact that a third party (eg a bailee or employee) holds the goods on his behalf. Moreover, A's parting with possession may be accompanied by acts which show that his lien is expressly or impliedly reserved. In *Albermarle Supply Co Ltd v Hind & Co*,[15] a garage had a repairer's lien on taxi cabs but allowed their owner to take them out daily to ply for hire on condition that the cabs continued 'in pawn' and were returned to the garage each night. The Court of Appeal held that the terms of the agreement between the owner and the garage indicated that the lien should not be lost when the cabs were taken out by their owner. Likewise, it is clear that A may reserve his lien and transfer possession of a chattel to P so that P can sell it and account for the proceeds to A.[16] Even A's unilateral reservation of his lien in circumstances where the other party did not agree to it has been held to preserve the lien.[17]

---

10 See also *Weeks v Henry Goode* (1859) 6 CBNS 367 (the plaintiff demanded a lease from the defendant, Henry Goode, an attorney. The defendant attorneys had a lien over the lease for work done for the plaintiff. Henry Goode declined to give up the lease until rent due to Phillip Goode was paid but he added that it 'was more Phillip's business than his own' and that, as Phillip was not in, he (Henry) would either return the lease that day or write a letter to the plaintiff declining to return it. The plaintiff received neither lease nor letter and issued a writ the following day. It was held that the lien had been waived by the assertion of a right to detain the lease upon another ground and the court found for the plaintiff).

11 (1849) 13 QB 680; see also *Hatton v Car Maintenance Co Ltd* [1915] 1 Ch 621 (the defendant garage maintained the plaintiff's car and provided a chauffeur, the car being kept at the garage when the plaintiff was in London but she could take it out without restriction. Held that (i) the garage did not have a lien for amounts due from the owner under the agreement because they maintained the car rather than repairing/improving it (ii) even if a lien had existed, it would have been lost by the arrangement under which the owner could take the car out as and when she pleased); Cf *Albermarle Supply Co Ltd v Hind & Co* [1928] 1 KB 307 (infra) where, on very similar facts to *Forth* and *Hatton*, parting with possession was accompanied by an agreement which preserved the lien.

12 (1800) 1 East 4.

13 *Wallace v Woodgate* (1824) Ry & M 193; *Dicas v Stockley* (1836) 7 C & P 587.

14 See *Bristol (Earl) v Wilsmore* (1823) 1 B & C 514.

15 [1928] 1 KB 307.

16 See *North Western Bank Ltd v Poynter, Son & Macdonalds* [1895] AC 56 (a pledgee returned a bill of lading to the pledgor 'as trustee' so that the pledgor could obtain delivery of the goods, sell them on the pledgee's behalf and account for the proceeds in satisfaction of the debt. Held that the pledgee's security was not affected and they were entitled to the proceeds of sale of the cargo as against the general creditors of the pledgor).

17 *Caldwell v Sumpters* [1972] Ch 478 (a vendor of property changed her solicitor during negotiations. The former solicitor (S1) surrendered deeds, over which he had a lien, to the new solicitor (S2) with a reservation that they were held to S1's order. S2 wrote to S1 refusing to agree to those terms but did not offer to return the deeds. Held that S1's lien continued and that if S2 did not agree to the terms he should have demanded that the deeds be taken back).

LIEN OF SUB-AGENTS

Where privity of contract is created between P and sub-A, the latter becomes an agent of P and should have all the normal rights against him, including lien. The rule is equally clear in the opposite situation where A has no actual or apparent authority authority to appoint the sub-A in that the latter will have no right of lien against P.[18]

But what is the position where A has authority to delegate a task to the sub-A without creating privity of contract with P? If P is disclosed, the sub-A can have a lien against P on the basis that *both* parties are aware of the position and P can be regarded as having contemplated the sub-A's lien. The sub-A can thus exercise against P any lien which the sub-A would have had against A if A had been the owner of the goods. This lien against P will be limited to claims arising from the performance of the authority which is properly delegated to the sub-A and it cannot be defeated by any settlement between P and A to which the sub-A is not a party.[19] As against A, the sub-A has the rights of an agent against his principal as that is the normal relationship between them.

Where P is undisclosed, the above reasoning cannot apply as the sub-A will not be aware of P but, nevertheless, it is well-established that where delegation is authorised, the sub-A has a lien against the undisclosed principal.[20] Again, the sub-A may exercise the lien that would have been available against A had he been the true principal. The rationale of this rule appears to be that the undisclosed principal intervenes on the contract of A subject to equities already in existence.

---

18   *Solly v Rathbone* (1814) 2 M & S 298; see Ivamy, 'Liens of Sub-Agents' (1951) 18 The Solicitor 101.
19   *Fisher v Smith* (1878) 4 App Cas 1 (A, with authority from P, employed an insurance broker (sub-A) to effect a policy for P. P paid A the premium due but it was held that the sub-A nevertheless had a lien on the policy for premiums he had paid and for which he was liable). See also *Ex p Edwards* (1881) 8 QBD 262.
20   *Mann v Forrester* (1814) 4 Camp 60.

CHAPTER 10

The relationship between principal and third party

Introduction

The pivotal feature in deciding whether P and T are bound contractually relates to the nature and extent of A's authority, the different types of authority having been considered in earlier chapters. It is now necessary to add to the question of A's authority a consideration of the different categories of *principal* which exist, as this may be a crucial factor in fixing the liability of the parties.

The paradigm agency has a *disclosed*, *named* principal but, in commercial contracts, it is quite common to find a disclosed but *unnamed* principal, eg 'bought on behalf of my principal'. By and large, the same considerations apply to these two categories as P's existence, and hence the fact of an agency, have been made known to T. It follows that both the named and unnamed principal fall within the classification of the disclosed principal.[1] However, English law acknowledges the *undisclosed principal* where both P's existence and identity are hidden, T's perception being that A is the only contracting party. Within certain limits, which are considered later, the undisclosed principal may intervene on the contract made between A and T and sue and be sued.

The disclosed principal

If P is disclosed, he can sue and be sued on the contract made by A where A has actual authority or P ratifies A's unauthorised act. Similarly, a disclosed P may create apparent authority in A, but whilst P may be liable to T on a contract entered into within the scope of A's apparent authority, P cannot sue on such a contract unless he ratifies it. Ratification will normally be inferred from bringing a counterclaim against T but the other limitations surrounding ratification may be relevant. In a disclosed agency, A is generally not liable to T on the contract but he may be liable to T for breach of warranty of authority where he has exceeded his authority and P has not ratified the contract (see Chapter 11).

---

1 There can be difficulties with the unnamed principal as it may be unclear with whom T contracts: might T consider that A is liable when he does not know P's identity or, alternatively, does he run the risk that redress must be sought from P whomsoever he is? See the cases, infra, where it is unclear whether A acts on his own account or for a principal, and the question of A's personal liability in Ch 11.

The general rule above that the disclosed P may sue and be sued is not applicable in cases of deeds and negotiable instruments. P may not sue or be sued on any deed, even if it is said to be executed on his behalf, unless he is named as a party to it and it is executed in his name. Similarly, this rule on *naming* P means that an undisclosed principal cannot sue or be sued on a deed and such a principal cannot be liable on a negotiable instrument (see below). In *Schack v Anthony*,[2] a shipmaster executed a charterparty by deed in his own name 'as agent for the owners' but the owners could not sue on the contract for the freight as they were not parties to the deed. There are exceptions to this rule however. First, where A contracts by deed in his own name but is a trustee for P, equity will allow P to enforce the contract[3] and, second, by virtue of the Law of Property Act 1925, s 56(1),[4] P may be entitled to sue on A's deed. Third, there is the Powers of Attorney Act 1971, s 7(1),[5] the effect of which is unclear.[6] The section is designed to alter the old rule that the holder of a power of attorney should sign in P's name and use P's seal but the section has the potential to abrogate the common law rule that P must be named as a party in the deed. The decision in *Harmer v Armstrong*[7] indicates that it does not have this effect and the better view is that the holder of a power of attorney may execute a deed in his own name but that P should be mentioned in the body of the deed and A should state that he acts on behalf of P.

As negotiable instruments may come into the hands of those who have no knowledge of the original circumstances of their issue, and as such persons ought to be able to rely on the face of the instrument, there are provisions in the Bills of Exchange Act 1882 which relate to A's signature on bills of exchange, promissory notes and cheques. Section 23 provides that P cannot be liable on any negotiable instrument unless his signature appears on it, but s 91(1) provides that it is unnecessary that P signs with his own hand if his signature is written by some person by or under his authority. P is thus bound if A acts within the course of his authority and signs the instrument with P's name. In other cases, s 26(1) provides that if A signs in a representative character he is not personally liable but this must be clear and not simply have words added which describe him as an agent. Section 25 provides that such a signature by procuration operates as notice to T that A has a limited authority to sign and P will only be bound if A is acting within his authority.

---

2   (1813) 1 M & S 573. See also *Re International Contract Co, Pickering's Claim* (1871) 6 Ch App 525 (P not liable where the deed was in A's name)
3   *Harmer v Armstrong* [1934] Ch 65.
4   'A person may take an immediate or other interest in land or other property, or the benefit of any condition, right of entry, covenant or agreement over or respecting land or other property, although he may not be named as a party to the conveyance or other instrument'.
5   Section 7(1) provides: 'The donee of a power of attorney may, if he thinks fit (a) execute any instrument with his own signature and, where sealing is required, with his own seal, and (b) do any other thing in his own name, by the authority of the donor of the power; and any document executed or thing done in that manner shall be as effective as if executed or done by the donee with the signature and seal, or, as the case may be, in the name, of the donor of the power'.
6   See *Bowstead & Reynolds on Agency* (16th edn, 1996), Art 79; Powell, *The Law of Agency* (2nd edn, 1961), pp 178-180.
7   [1934] Ch 65.

The doctrine of the undisclosed principal

As mentioned in the introduction to this chapter, English law recognises the concept that an undisclosed principal may intervene on the contract made between A and T and have both rights and liabilities under that contract. The unadorned statement that, C, a third party, may intrude on a contract made between A and B is startling to the modern lawyer raised upon notions of privity of contract, but the undisclosed principal's right to intervene is both ancient and entrenched. Technically, the rules concerning the undisclosed principal do not infringe the axiom of privity as P does not become a party to the contract between A and T.[8] It cannot be stressed enough that A and T have a binding contract and, within certain parameters, the undisclosed principal may *intervene*[9] on that contract. T thus has an immediate safeguard in that he may choose to proceed against either A or P. Moreover, in most impersonal, commercial contracts, the revelation of P is immaterial to T: in a contract for the sale of goods, for example, the identity of the seller is often of little significance to T. It follows that the application of the rules concerning the undsclosed principal do not entail any contortion of logic. It will be apparent that P and T have no direct contract where P is undisclosed. Instead, P's right of intervention is coupled with T's right to sue either A or P and thus a contract is created in all but name. Finally, as P's intervention on the contract between A and T is the source from which the rules of the undisclosed principal emanate, there is no need for any cumbersome assignment of rights from A to P which, in the absence of the undisclosed principal doctrine, would clearly be needed.

The undisclosed principal can first be observed in the law reports during the early 18th century[10] when executory contracts for the sale of goods were rare, the normal contract of sale being executed with immediate payment and delivery. Many of the early cases concern the role of *factors*, a species of agent which has long since disappeared from commercial life. Factors were mercantile agents entrusted by P with the possession of goods in order to sell them on P's behalf and who were able to make immediate delivery to T and receive payment in cash from T from which commission was deductible. With this method of contracting, neither P nor T was concerned as to the existence or identity of the other: A delivered the goods to T and would be liable to T if he gave any warranty on them and, similarly, A collected the price from T and accounted for it to P. This system worked well unless the factor became bankrupt in which event he might not account to P for the price and so, increasingly, P began to intervene in bankruptcies. The earliest decisions established that the proceeds from the sale did not belong to the estate of the bankrupt factor.[11] The second stage of

---

8   At least two modern decisions appear to be premised on the fact that the undisclosed P has a contract with T, thus being in conformity with the position where P is dislclosed (see *Keighley, Maxsted & Co v Durant* [1901] AC 240; *Said v Butt* [1920] 3 KB 497), but this is incorrect and unsustainable.
9   P's intervention on the contract of A and T was re-affirmed as the basis of the undisclosed principal doctrine in *Welsh Development Agency v Export Finance Co Ltd* [1992] BCLC 148, 173 per Dillon LJ, and 182 per Ralph Gibson LJ.
10 See the superb account by Stoljar, *The Law of Agency* (1961), pp 204-211.
11 See eg *Burdett v Willett* (1708) 2 Vern 638; *Garrat v Cullum* (1709) Bull NP 42; *Copeman v Gallant* (1716) 1 P Wms 314.

development was to allow the undisclosed principal's recovery directly against T[12] and this was followed by an acknowledgment of T's right to sue the undisclosed principal.[13]

It was mentioned earlier that a cursory glance at the undisclosed principal doctrine might suggest that it is anomalous and potentially unjust in its allowing the intervention of a principal who was not contemplated in the original undertaking between T and A. However, the early cases point to the opposite conclusion. Clearly justice was served in the bankruptcy cases by P's having the right to be paid by T rather than proving in A's bankruptcy. Moreover, whether A or P received the proceeds of sale must have been immaterial to T in such conspicuously impersonal, commercial contracts. The undisclosed principal doctrine enshrines commercial good sense provided that the law guards against the imposition upon T of an unwanted stranger whose presence involves a material alteration to the contract's substance. It was primarily in the latter half of the 19th century and the early 20th century that the undisclosed principal's intervention appeared anomalous as difficult to square with the notion of privity of contract and the consensual basis of contractual undertakings[14] but, fortunately, the pragmatic English doctrine has survived to be admired in Europe[15] where an outcome similar to that in the English decisions can be achieved only by A's assignment of his rights to P.

Limitations on the operation of the undisclosed principal doctrine

THE AGENT MUST ACT WITHIN HIS ACTUAL AUTHORITY

The rules on ratification stipulate that P must be 'ascertainable'[16] at the date of A's contracting with T, and the decision in *Keighley, Maxsted & Co v Durant*[17] accentuated that an agent for an undisclosed principal must act within his *actual* authority, thus putting beyond doubt the rule that an undisclosed principal cannot ratify his agent's unauthorised contract with T. There were two, somewhat groundless anxieties, which underpinned the decision of the House of Lords in *Keighley*. The first was that it was unacceptable for agents to enter into contracts with third parties in the hope that a principal might materialise and adopt the contract and, secondly, the Law Lords clearly considered that the doctrine of the undisclosed principal did not harmonise with the notion of privity of contract.

---

12 See eg *George v Clagett* (1797) 7 Term Rep 359.
13 See eg *Snee v Prescot* (1743) 1 Atk 245, 248, where Lord Hardwicke LC considered that T's right to sue P was well-established and had 'been often so settled at Guildhall'; *Nelson v Powell* (1784) 3 Doug KB 410.
14 See *Armstrong v Stokes* (1872) LR 7 QB 598, 604, per Blackburn J; *Keighley, Maxsted & Co v Durant* [1901] AC 240; *Dunlop Pneumatic Tyre Co Ltd v Selfridge & Co Ltd* [1915] AC 847, 864 per Lord Parmoor; Pollock, 'Notes' (1887) 3 LQR 358; Atiyah, *The Rise and Fall of Freedom of Contract* (1979), pp 496-501.
15 See Müller-Freienfels, 'The Undisclosed Principal' (1953) 16 MLR 299, 300-303; 'Comparative Aspects of Undisclosed Agency' (1955) 18 MLR 33.
16 *Watson v Swann* (1862) 11 CBNS 756.
17 [1901] AC 240; see Rochvarg, 'Ratification and Undisclosed Principals' (1989) 34 McGill LJ 286.

However, the rules of the undisclosed principal doctrine are premised upon A's having an *existing* principal at the date that A contracts with T and so the first possibility of the illusory P would, in any event, be outside the scope of those rules. Likewise, the undisclosed principal doctrine pre-dates modern notions of privity of contract and the stipulations which curtail P's intervention provide more than adequate safeguards for T.

As emphasised in Chapter 3, *Keighley's* rule is far too restrictive. On the facts of the case, A marginally exceeded his existing, actual authority and the position was hardly synonymous with that where an agent has no authority whatever from any principal. Moreover, it was convincingly stated in the Court of Appeal in *Keighley*[18] that, as the undisclosed principal doctrine is accepted and such a principal is allowed to intervene on the contract, there is no sound reason to demand that A should have a *prior* authority, for T is unaware of both P's existence and any *concept* of authority in A. Assuming that A has initial authority to act on behalf of an undisclosed principal, it is thus very difficult to see why ratification by such a principal should be disallowed. Nevertheless, the decision of the House of Lords in *Keighley* is now ingrained in English law and it effectively limits the scope of the undisclosed principal doctrine.

The doctrine of the undisclosed principal is also restricted in that such a principal cannot create any apparent authority in A as, of necessity, a principal who is undisclosed is incapable of performing any acts holding-out A as his *agent* to T. The rather nebulous concept of usual authority recognised in *Watteau v Fenwick*[19] does, however, apply to the undisclosed principal and, as the undisclosed principal can neither ratify an unauthorised contract nor create apparent authority in A, *Watteau* prevents his being unjustly enriched at T's expense. As in cases of apparent authority, *Watteau* may be available as a remedy only to T.

It should also be stressed that the notion of apparent *ownership* may mean that the undisclosed principal is bound by unauthorised dispositions of his property[20] made by A. However, as this notion involves a representation that A is an owner, it is not strictly connected with agency. Nevertheless, as discussed in Chapters 4 and 5, *Pickering v Busk*[1] is the clearly recognisable foundation of both apparent authority and apparent ownership.

While it is plain that, in general, A must have actual authority to act for his undisclosed principal, the range of situations to which the undisclosed principal doctrine may apply is unclear. Moreover, the precise nature of the authority which must be conferred on A has never been established with certainty. First and most prominent, at least in the cases, are those instances where P authorises A not to disclose him but, nevertheless, endows A with authority to enter into a contract on his behalf with T. Second, in order to secure his own position, A may not disclose P (eg, because A does not want T to deal directly with P in the future[2]) and P may acquiesce in this practice. Both these situations are within the undisclosed principal doctrine but it is uncertain whether the rules apply to a third possibility where the undisclosed principal gives A authority to act for

18 [1900] 1 QB 629.
19 [1893] 1 QB 346; see Ch 3.
20 See Ch 18 for a consideration of apparent ownership and the sale of goods.
 1 (1812) 15 East 38; see Stoljar, *The Law of Agency* (1961), Ch 5.
 2 The undisclosed principal rules apply even where A acts contrary to express instructions from P and does not disclose P; see *Ex p Dixon, Re Henley* (1876) 4 Ch D 133.

him but does not intend to intervene on the contract with T, eg, A, acting as a principal himself, buys goods from T but then deals as an agent *vis-à-vis* P and not as an independent seller of the goods to P. This is the European notion of the self-employed 'commissionaire' or 'commission agent' in an indirect agency. Most of the European jurisdictions recognise the agency aspect of this relationship (ie P–A) but P cannot intervene on the contract between A and T and so he has neither rights nor liabilities under it. *Bowstead & Reynolds*[3] points out that there is no clear authority as to whether or not this type of agency is within the rules of the undisclosed principal in English law. It is, however, not uncommon to find this method of commercial arrangement in England and it is sometimes used by 'confirming houses' who act for overseas customers in buying goods from sellers in the home market. It is likely that the indirect agency is characterised, in English law, as involving two separate contracts of sale meaning that A acts as a principal in *both* contracts.[4] Nevertheless, this perspective disregards the foundations of the undisclosed principal in that factors in the 18th century dealt precisely as in the third situation.

MIGHT THE TERMS OF THE CONTRACT BETWEEN THE AGENT AND THE THIRD PARTY EXCLUDE THE UNDISCLOSED PRINCIPAL?

Where there is an express term of the contract between A and T that A is the only party to it, the undisclosed principal cannot intervene[5] and such a clause is the most effective way to exclude an undisclosed principal. However, the position is less clear where there is no express term. When P is undisclosed A must necessarily contract as a principal but certain decisions acknowledge that A might impliedly contract as the *real and only* principal. There is also some old authority that, with written contracts, parol evidence may be inadmissible to prove the undisclosed principal's existence.

The early cases established that an undisclosed principal could intervene even where a written contract resulted between A and T[6] and parol evidence regarding P's existence was admitted on the basis that such evidence did not *contradict* the writing. Thus, in *Higgins v Senior*,[7] Parke B stressed that the parol evidence 'does not deny that [the contract] is binding on those whom, on the face of it, it purports to bind; but shews that it also binds another'.[8] However, in *Humble v*

---

3 *Bowstead & Reynolds on Agency* (16th edn, 1996), Art 78, para 8-072. See also Reynolds, 'Practical Problems of the Undisclosed Principal Doctrine' [1983] CLP 119.
4 The common law could adopt one of three possibilities: (i) the rules are as in the European model, viz A contracts with T as a principal but there is an internal P–A relationship (ii) the rules of the undisclosed principal apply and it is irrelevant that A is not authorised to enter into a contract with T on behalf of P (iii) the relationship is not one of agency but, instead, there are watertight, separate contracts between P–A and A–T and A deals as a principal in both.
5 *United Kingdom Mutual Steamship Assurance Association v Nevill* (1887) 19 QBD 110.
6 *Bateman v Phillips* (1812) 15 East 272; *Wilson v Hart* (1817) 7 Taunt 295.
7 (1841) 8 M & W 834.
8 (1841) 8 M & W 834 at 844. It was made clear in *Higgins* that the undisclosed principal could intervene where the contract required a written memorandum under the Statute of Frauds even though A had signed the memorandum without any reference to the agency. The undisclosed principal cannot sue or be sued on a deed however and cannot be liable upon a negotiable instrument (see above).

Hunter,[9] a decision which regrettably is magnified out of all proprtion,[10] the court accepted that the undisclosed principal's intervention might be disallowed as being inconsistent with the terms of the written contract. There A signed a charterparty on behalf of P, the shipowner, but A described himself as 'owner' of the chartered vessel. It was held that P could not sue T for unpaid freight: the undisclosed principal doctrine could not apply where 'the agent contracts as principal; and he has done so here by describing himself as 'owner' of the ship'.[11]

It must be asked whether the reasoning in *Humble* is logical and sustainable. The decision clung obdurately to the need for privity of contract between A and T and thus Lord Denman CJ emphasised that 'you have a right to the benefit you contemplate from the character, credit and substance of the party with whom you contract'.[12] This is undeniable, but the decision overlooks the fact that the essence of the undisclosed principal doctrine is that A *does* remain liable to T, who may thus obtain the benefits specified. Moreover, if A's *character* is important to T, he can protect himself by a term in the contract with A to the effect that that A is the only contracting party and, even in the absence of such a contract term, P may be prevented from intervening where A's personality is the predominant factor which induced T to contract with A (see later). It is plain that, if *Humble's* stress on privity and the notion that A 'contracts as a principal' were followed to a logical conclusion, the undisclosed principal doctrine would be eradicated in that an agent acting for an undisclosed principal must, necessarily, contract in his own name as a principal. Similarly, as both Powell[13] and Stoljar[14] pointed out, *Humble's* privity argument is capable of applying to all contracts, not just those in writing. Although it is easy to find fault with the reasoning in *Humble*, the decision was given strong support in *Formby Bros v Formby*[15] where it was justified as resting upon the parol evidence rule. In *Formby*, T agreed to build two houses for A who signed the written contract as 'proprietor'. It was held that parol evidence was inadmissible to prove that the undisclosed principal was liable as this would contradict the written contract.[16]

Humble has been followed in other decisions[17] but it has more often been criticised and distinguished. The leading modern decision is *Fred Drughorn Ltd v Rederiaktiebolaget Trans-Atlantic*,[18] where *Humble* came perilously close to being overruled. In *Drughorn*, A was described in a charterparty as 'charterer' and the House of Lords held that this characterisation of A was not in absolute terms so as to convey the impression that A was the only party to the contract. Accordingly, the undisclosed principal's intervention was not thwarted. Lord

9 (1848) 12 QB 310.
10 See Stoljar's condemnation of *Humble* (*The Law of Agency* (1961), p 223): 'As so often, we seem confronted with that strange phenomenon in the law, that a rule based on confusion and of no practical worth somehow always manages to survive'.
11 (1848) 12 QB 310 at 315, per Lord Denman CJ.
12 (1848) 12 QB 310 at 317.
13 *The Law of Agency* (2nd edn, 1961), p 155.
14 *The Law of Agency* (1961), p 221.
15 (1910) 102 LT 116.
16 See Landon, 'Parol Evidence and Undisclosed Principals' (1945) 61 LQR 130 and (1946) 62 LQR 20.
17 *Rederiaktiebolaget Argonaut v Hani* [1918] 2 KB 247; *Fawcett v Star Car Sales* [1960] NZLR 406.
18 [1919] AC 203.

Sumner stressed that the contract 'states that [A] charters, and so he does; but it does not say that he is not chartering for others, and if that is what he has done in fact the law allows them to prove it'.[19] Viscount Haldane distinguished and explained *Humble* on the basis that there A made an assertion of title to property[20] and it thus became a term of the contract that he should contract as owner, but where *contractual* rights were involved, such as the hiring of a ship, it was 'business common-sense'[1] that A should be able to contract for an undisclosed principal. Although *Humble* and *Formby* were not overruled, Lord Shaw added that 'the time may arise'[2] when both decisions might have to be reviewed by the House.

In the light of the *Drughorn* decision, *Humble* must be explained on the basis that A may contract, expressly or impliedly, as the only principal. However, even if this is accepted as the rationale of *Humble*, most subsequent decisions have regarded A's description in the contract to be sufficiently equivocal with the consequence that the undisclosed principal can be admitted with rights and liabilities under the contract.[3] It must follow inexorably that, where A signs the contract in his own name without any other embellishment, he cannot be regarded as impliedly contracting as the real and only principal because it is impossible to ascertain whether he is a principal or an agent and the undisclosed principal must therefore be admitted.

In summary, the reasoning that T's protection must be secured by adhering to privity of contract between T and A is fallacious as A remains liable to T, and there is clearly no absolute rule prohibiting the admissibility of parol evidence.[4] Moreover, only a remnant of the rule remains that A may have expressly or impliedly contracted, in writing or otherwise, as the real and only principal, thus precluding the undisclosed principal's intervention. That this latter rule has a severely restricted ambit has been underscored by recent cases. The decisions in

---

19   [1919] AC 203 at 209.
20   This view had been taken in *Humble* itself by Wightman J (p 316).
 1   [1919] AC 203 at 207, per Viscount Haldane.
 2   [1919] AC 203 at 207. See also *Killick & Co v WR Price & Co and Lingfield Steamship Co Ltd* (1896) 12 TLR 263, 264, where Lord Russell CJ 'gravely doubted whether [*Humble*] would be recognised as an authority at the present time'.
 3   *Danziger v Thompson* [1944] KB 654 (A contracted as 'tenant' and the undisclosed principal (A's father) was admitted and liable for the rent); *Epps v Rothnie* [1945] KB 562 (A, describing himself as 'landlord', let a house to T. The undisclosed principal, the owner of the house, successfully brought proceedings to recover possession. Scott LJ thought (p 565) that *Humble* and *Formby* should no longer be regarded as good law); *O/Y Wasa Steamship Co Ltd & NV Stoomschip Hannah v Newspaper Pulp and Wood Export Ltd* (1949) 82 Ll L Rep 936 (the undisclosed principal was admitted where A was described in a charterparty as 'disponent owner'); cf *Collins v Associated Greyhound Racecourses Ltd* [1930] 1 Ch 1 (A applied for shares and the undisclosed principal was not allowed to rescind the contract as 'the articles ... contain the usual provision that the company shall be entitled to treat the registered holder of any shares as the absolute owner thereof ... and the application imports that it is made by [the agents] as the real and only principals' (p 19, per Luxmoore J)). See below for further consideration of *Collins*.
 4   The argument regarding the parol evidence rule had originally been rejected in *Wilson v Hart* (1817) 1 Moore CP 45. See also *Finzel, Berry & Co v Eastcheap Dried Fruit Co* [1962] 1 Lloyd's Rep 370, 375, per McNair J: '... it is clear law to-day that a person who has concluded a contract in his own name may prove by parol evidence that he was acting for an undisclosed principal unless he has contracted in such terms as to show that he was the real and only principal, and that it was really a question of the construction of the particular contract which determined whether parol evidence was admissible to prove that some person other than the party named in the written contract was, in fact, the true principal'.

both *The Astyanax*[5] and *Siu Yin Kwan v Eastern Insurance Co Ltd*,[6] have stressed that the modern approach to the undisclosed principal doctrine is to look at all the surrounding circumstances in assessing the intentions of the parties. In *Siu Yin Kwan*, a shipping agent (A) acted on behalf of shipowners (P) in obtaining insurance against claims by members of the ship's crew but A acted in his own name and was described in the policy as the insured. The insurers argued that they had contracted solely with A and thus P could have no rights under the policy. The Privy Council held that there was nothing in the proposal form or policy which expressly or by implication excluded the undisclosed principal's right to sue and that, following *Drughorn*, even if A had been named as the employer of the crew it would not necessarily have prevented P's intervention in such an 'ordinary commercial contract'.[7] *Siu Yin Kwan* thus epitomises the pragmatic, commercial nature of the undisclosed principal rules and it is respectfully suggested that the decision's rational conclusion cannot be faulted.

MIGHT THE THIRD PARTY ASSERT SUCCESSFULLY THAT EITHER THE AGENT'S OR THE PRINCIPAL'S IDENTITY IS SUFFICIENTLY IMPORTANT TO EXCLUDE THE UNDISCLOSED PRINCIPAL?

It is clear that there are some contracts which are are sufficiently personal to exclude the intervention of the undisclosed P. For example, a contract which involved A's peronal skills and attributes (eg a contract for A to paint T's portrait) could not be performed by an undisclosed principal. Where T considers that identity is a material issue, he may argue that he wished to contract only with A and that P should not be admitted or he may assert that he would not have contemplated any dealings with P had he known the real position. The decisions in which personality has been material in barring P's intervention are all somewhat unsatisfactory and they establish no overall rule. It is plain that, by and large, issues such as payment and delivery are crucial in commercial undertakings rather than the *identity* of the parties and thus only rarely can personality, *per se*, be material in the formation and performance of business contracts.

A particularly clear situation where T desires to contract solely with A is where T has a right of set-off against A. In *Greer v Downs Supply Co*,[8] A owed T a debt of £17, T agreeing to buy timber from A to the value of £29 on the basis that the debt would be set-off against the price of the goods, ie T would pay only £12 for the timber. A told T that he had started his own business but, in

---

5 *Asty Maritime Co Ltd and Panagiotis Stravelakis v Rocco Giuseppe & Figli, SNC, The Astyanax* [1985] 2 Lloyd's Rep 109 (A, described as 'disponent owner' chartered a vessel to the defendant (T), the object of the arrangement being to avoid an Argentinean tax on freight which would otherwise have been payable by the plaintiff shipowners (P), a company registered in Cyprus. It was held that the undisclosed principal could not enforce the charterparty against T (P's loss was more than that of the nominal disponent owner). The court considered 'disponent owner' to be a neutral phrase but the surrounding circumstances showed the clear commercial purpose (shared by all the parties) of avoiding tax and A was thus a principal in his own right, not a mere nominee.
6 [1994] 2 AC 199; see Reynolds, 'Some Agency Problems in Insurance Law', Ch 4 in *Consensus Ad Idem, Essays on the Law of Contract in Honour of Guenter Treitel* (1996, ed F D Rose), pp 92-95.
7 [1994] 2 AC 199 at 208, per Lord Lloyd of Berwick.
8 [1927] 2 KB 28. See also *Campbellville Gravel Supply Ltd v Cook Paving Co Ltd* (1968) 70 DLR (2d) 354, which, on almost identical facts, followed *Greer*.

fact, A was employed by the plaintiff, P, and P sued T for the cost of the timber. It was held that P must fail and could not intervene as T had contracted with A solely to obtain the set-off. The judgments are most indecisive but Scrutton LJ considered that sometimes T contracts with A for 'reasons personal to the agent ... to the exclusion of his principal'.[9]

There are *dicta* to the same effect in *Collins v Associated Greyhound Racecourses Ltd*[10] where the startling conclusion was reached that a contract to take shares in a company was a type of contract in which the personality of A was crucial thereby disallowing P's intervention as a shareholder. Lawrence LJ thought that 'a contract to become a member of a company is, in my opinion, one of that class of contracts in which an undisclosed principal cannot insist on taking the place of a party apparently contracting on his own account',[11] and Lord Hanworth MR said that 'the contract between the company and [A] was one in which importance attached to the personality of the persons with whom the company were contracting'.[12]

Probably the most contentious decision in this context is that in *Said v Butt*.[13] P had made serious and unfounded charges against T, the managing director of a theatre company, but P wished to attend the first performance of a play at the theatre. As his application for a ticket had been refused by T, P employed A to buy a ticket without disclosing that it was for P. On arrival at the theatre, P was refused admission. He sued T for procuring a breach of contract with the theatre company and, in order to succeed, he had to establish a binding contract with the company, but it was held that P had no such binding contract and thus T could not be liable for causing any breach of it. McCardie J proceeded on the basis that, in undisclosed principal cases, a contract is made between *T and P* and thus this contract was affected by a mistake regarding the identity of P.[14] However, the essence of the undisclosed principal doctrine is that a contract is made between *T and A* upon which P may intervene: the correct question should thus have been whether the contract with A was sufficiently personal to exclude P, as it was held to be in *Greer* and *Collins*.[15] Although McCardie J was at pains

---

9   [1927] 2 KB 28 at 35.
10   [1930] 1 Ch 1.
11   [1930] 1 Ch 1 at 36.
12   [1930] 1 Ch 1 at 33. Commenting on *Collins*, Goodhart and Hamson, ('Undisclosed Principals in Contract' [1932] 4 CLJ 320, 355) state that it is 'abundantly clear that a contract to take shares in a company is impersonal, in the sense that the benefit may be assigned'. In *Collins*, it was P who sought to rescind the contract when only he, not A, had relied on the misrepresentation in the company's (T) prospectus. It was thus thought that *T's rights against A* should not be prejudiced by the intervention of P, as they would be if P could rescind where A, being ignorant of the misrepresentation, could *not* have done so.
13   [1920] 3 KB 497.
14   Even accepting that mistake is applicable in *Said*, the modern approach to that notion (as opposed to older ideas of lack of consensus which McCardie J chose to apply) would cause difficulties as: (i) It is insufficient for T to argue negatively that he did not want to deal with P. T would have had to show that identity was material and that he did not want to contract with A but with some other person, this being impossible in *Said* as there was no other person with whom T wished to deal, and (ii) T was *not* mistaken regarding A's identity and the transaction was face-to-face. If an operative mistake were to be allowed on *Said's* facts, a capricious or unscrupulous party might always avoid his obligations with ease.
15   See Glanville Williams, 'Mistake as to Party in the Law of Contract' (1945) 23 Can Bar Rev 380, 406-409, who supports *Said* on the basis that (i) using the notion of 'fair dealing', P should not be able to enforce the contract when either he or A knows that T would not contract with him and (ii) an undisclosed principal *is* party to the contract as he can sue and be sued upon it. Argument (i) has also been adopted by Treitel, *The Law of Contract* (10th edn, 1999), p 675.

to stress that a play's first night is a special event with a selected audience, there was no evidence that T positively relied on any personal trait of A as member of such a select group.

A more objective, commercial approach, is to argue that P's intervention is only prevented where the benefit of a contract is not assignable or where its burden cannot be vicariously performed. As mentioned above, in a contract stipulating that A will paint T's portrait it would be unacceptable for P to intervene as the real artist and 'equally unthinkable, is the proposition that a stranger could be brought forward as the principal in a contract to remove an appendix ... or play third base'.[16] Where the assignment analogy is adopted, there are few commercial contracts where P could not intervene. It is thus arguable, for example, that a contract for the purchase of a theatre ticket is clearly an impersonal, assignable contract[17] where the undisclosed principal should be permitted to intervene. This approach is borne out in many of the cases. In *Nash v Dix*,[18] T wished to sell a Congregational chapel but turned down P's offer to buy it as P was a member of a committee of Roman Catholics who intended to use the building as a place of worship. P therefore asked A, the manager of a mineral water company, to attempt to buy the building and, if A was successful, P agreed to buy it from A allowing him £100 profit. A admitted that T's perception was that A was buying the property for the mineral water company but A made no statement to that effect and there were no restrictions on the use of the building. On discovering the true position, T refused to complete on the ground that A was buying as an agent for P. North J held that A could obtain specific performance but that he was not acting as an agent for P; instead, A was acting on his own account with a view to reselling at a profit. The judge also held there to be no misrepresentation on A's part as T 'did not care a straw who [he was] contracting with'.[19] Although A was found not to be acting as an agent in *Nash*, the case illustrates the assignment argument perfectly: in a simple sale of land the identity of the purchaser is immaterial and, as the purchaser could buy and resell to another without restriction or assign the benefit of the contract to any person who could obtain specific performance, there can be no valid reason to exclude an undisclosed principal's intervention.

Certainly this objective approach was adopted unequivocally in *Dyster v Randall & Sons*.[20] T, a firm of auctioneers, had employed P but he had left in circumstances which meant that T would not do business with him. P (at this stage an undischarged bankrupt) wished to acquire plots of land that T was developing and he therefore employed A to buy the plots on his behalf as an undisclosed principal. P then began to build bungalows on the land without adhering to certain stipulations in the contract between A and T, eg to submit plans of any buildings to T. Still being unaware of P's part in the dealings, T drew A's attention to the lack of plans. A thereupon revealed the true position and, as completion of the purchase had not occurred, A and T purported to cancel

---

16 Mechem, *Outlines of the Law of Agency* (4th edn, 1952), pp 110-111.
17 See Goodhart and Hamson, 'Undisclosed Principals in Contract' [1932] 4 CLJ 320, 349, who suggest, somewhat unrealistically, that *Said* could be justified in that a purchase of a theatre ticket is a contract the benefit of which is unassignable. This reasoning means that anyone who buys a ticket for another would have to disclose his principal or at least his agency.
18 (1898) 78 LT 445.
19 (1898) 78 LT 445 at 449.
20 [1926] Ch 932.

the contract to buy the land. P then sued for specific performance and succeeded as the agreement was held not to be one 'in which any personal qualifications possessed by [A] formed a material ingredient, but is a simple agreement for sale of land in consideration of a lump sum to be paid on completion'.[1]

The application of the assignment analogy was illustrated recently in *Siu Yin Kwan v Eastern Insurance Co Ltd*,[2] the facts of which were considered earlier. There it was argued that, as the general rule is that insurance does not run with the property insured but is a *personal* contract, the contract of insurance could not be enforced by the undisclosed principal. While the Privy Council accepted that a contract of motor insurance, for example, was personal and could not be assigned, it was held that the identity of the employer in *Siu* was a matter of indifference to T, the insurer, and provided the proposal form gave the relevant information, the undisclosed principal's identity was immaterial to the insurer when assessing the risk.

It is apparent from these cases that, where there is no duty of disclosure, A's mere non-disclosure of P's existence is not a misrepresentation, even where A knows that if disclosure were made, T would not enter into the contract, as in *Dyster*.[3] However, A's *active* misrepresentation provides T with a defence if he is sued on the contract by P. In *Archer v Stone*,[4] specific performance was refused because T asked A specifically whether he was acting for P or his nominees and A replied, falsely, in the negative. There can, of course, be a misrepresentation by conduct and this raises the difficult issue of possible misrepresenation by the suppression of information: might there be situations where A's truthful elevation of his own position suppresses the fact that he is acting for an undisclosed principal to such an extent that a false impression is created which amounts to a misrepresenation? In *Nash v Dix*, considered earlier, the court thought that either A's (truthful) description of himself as 'Manager of the Epping Natural Mineral Waters Company Ltd' was not a misrepresentation or, alternatively, that it was a misrepresentation but T had not been induced by it as he was unconcerned as to the identity of the purchaser of the property. Consequently, although the general rule is undoubtedly that A has no duty to disabuse T and rescue him from his own misconceptions, it is impossible to embellish the rule with any further detail. It is possible, of course, that A's self-characterisation might be such as to bring the case within the *Humble v Hunter* reasoning, meaning that A impliedly contracted as the real and only principal.

The final question in relation to personality is whether P, when sued by T, might have the defence that T contracted with A personally and would not have dealt with P had he known the true position. There is no authority on this issue and it is arguable

---

1   [1926] Ch 932 at 938, per Lawrence J. See also *Smith v Wheatcroft* (1878) 9 Ch D 223 (A entered into negotiations for the purchase of land from T but he then became P's agent and the agreement was completed for the undisclosed principal. T argued that A had misrepresented that he wanted the land for his own use and knew that T did not want to sell to P. Specific performance was granted as no personal considerations entered into the contract. It is unclear from the decision but it seems that neither A nor P knew that T would not deal with P).
2   [1994] 2 AC 199.
3   Lawrence J stated specifically that non-disclosure was not misrepresentation (p 939) but that the position would be different if 'some personal consideration formed a material ingredient'. See also Goodhart and Hamson, 'Undisclosed Principals in Contract' [1932] 4 CLJ 320, 349, who considered that, in *Said v Butt*, A represented by conduct that he alone had an interest in the contract and that no one else would occupy the theatre seat. As Powell emphasised (*The Law of Agency* (2nd edn, 1961), p 161), this is most unlikely.
4   (1898) 78 LT 34.

that both P and T must be treated equally. However, there must surely be a difference here between (i) situations where P authorised A to conceal the agency in order that P may gain some advantage from the concealment as an undisclosed principal and (ii) circumstances where A was ordered to disclose P but A contravened his authority and did not do so. In situation (i) it would be unfair to allow P the defence of personality but it would almost certainly be equitable for the defence to be available to P in situation (ii). It should always be remembered that T has a remedy against A on the contract but in situation (i) it would be unjust for P to deny his liability where, for example, A is insolvent.

Defences available to the principal and third party

WHERE THE PRINCIPAL SUES THE THIRD PARTY

The general rule is that, as A normally exits the scene leaving a contract between P and T, T has all the defences that he would have had against P if P had made the contract himself. Hence T has all the defences arising *from the contract itself*, eg illegality, fraud or misrepresentation by A,[5] and he may commence proceedings for rescission and restitution.[6] A's act must, of course, be within his actual or apparent authority or it will not affect P but where it is within such authority, it does not matter that A is acting fraudulently for his own benefit or that P is unaware of A's acts.[7] Where there is fraud by P himself, this will also provide T with a defence.[8]

Similarly, T has all the defences *available against P personally*, eg a set-off against P, but he cannot utilise defences which are *personal to A* and *unconnected* with the contract, eg a set-off against A personally.

The same rules should apply where P is *undisclosed* with the addition that, as the contract is initially made between A and T, T should not be prejudiced by P's intervention. Logically therefore, T should be able to plead against P all personal defences which he had against A, eg a set-off against A personally, which were accrued before he became aware of P's existence. However, some cases on set-off indicate that this may not be the position unless P has misled T in some way (see below).

WHERE THE THIRD PARTY SUES THE PRINCIPAL

P, whether disclosed or undisclosed, has all the defences against T *arising from the contract itself formed via A*, eg fraud or misrepresentation of T, and all

---

5 Eg, *Mullens v Miller* (1882) 22 Ch D 194 (A misrepresented the value of property he was selling and specific performance was refused).

6 Eg, *Reese River Silver Mining Co Ltd v Smith* (1869) LR 4 HL 64 (T, induced by misrepresentation of the directors of a company to take shares in the company, was entitled to rescission); *Refuge Assurance Co Ltd v Kettlewell* [1909] AC 243.

7 *Biggs v Lawrence* (1789) 3 Term Rep 454 (a partner sold goods which, to his knowledge, were packed for smuggling. It was held that the firm could not recover the price of the goods from T even though the other partners were unaware of the illegality); *Apthorp v Neville & Co* (1907) 23 TLR 575.

8 See *Garnac Grain Co Inc v HMF Faure and Fairclough Ltd* [1966] 1 QB 650 (considered in Ch 2).

defences *personal to P himself*, eg P's infancy or a set-off in favour of P. However, P cannot plead defences which are *personal to A himself*, eg a set-off in favour of A. In *Collins v Associated Greyhound Racecourses Ltd*,[9] the undisclosed principal was unable to rescind a contract for misrepresentation when only he, and not A, relied on the untrue statement. As suggested earlier, the decision may be justified in that T must not be deprived of a remedy against A in the undisclosed principal situation, unless it is clear that A would have had the defence against T, and it would have been unavailable to A as he had not been influenced by the misrepresentation.

Settlement with the agent

Settlement involves those situations where, for example, T has sold goods to P and P pays A for the goods or, vice-versa, where P has sold goods to T and T pays the price of the goods to A. In many agency situations, it is obviously a common occurrence that P or T will settle with A and consider such payment to be a discharge of the obligation owed. It is thus imperative to decide whether P and T may thus settle with A and effectively discharge their obligations or whether a second payment might be necessary should A abscond with the money, for example. Two simple diagrams should clarify this notion of settlement:

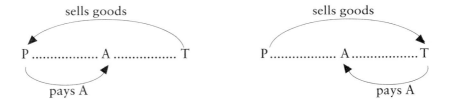

The general rule regarding settlement is clear: as A normally departs from the contractual arena leaving a contract between P and T, *neither* party is discharged by settling with A but, as will be seen, it is arguable that this rule should be qualified where there is an undisclosed principal. There is much vacillation in the cases but a pattern can be discerned if settlement is divided into its components.

WHERE THE PRINCIPAL SETTLES WITH THE AGENT

The general rule above applies and P is not discharged by a payment made to A or an adjustment of his accounts with A. This is justified in that the transaction between P and A is of no concern to T and a debtor (P) must seek-out his creditor (T) and pay him. In *Kymer v Suwercropp*,[10] T sold coffee to brokers, A, who

9   [1930] 1 Ch 1.
10 (1807) 1 Camp 109; see also *Stewart v Hall* (1813) 2 Dow 29.

bought on behalf of P. P paid A who then became insolvent. Lord Ellenborough CJ held that T could succeed against P for the price as 'a person selling goods is not confined to the credit of a broker who buys them; but may resort to the principal on whose account they are bought'.[11]

However there are inroads upon this general rule where P's payment to A may be a good discharge of the debt owed to T thus barring T's recourse to P. The decisions reveal two distinct approaches and an attempt to reconcile and amalgamate them.[12]

The estoppel approach: has T induced P to settle with A?

T's words or conduct may have led P to conclude that he should pay A and, if P does then pay A, it would be most unfair to make him pay again. In this situation, P would be relying on T's representations and there would be consequent hardship and detriment should he have to pay again, in which case T would be estopped from claiming the money from P. It must therefore be determined what sort of words or conduct on T's part would generate such an estoppel.

In *Kymer v Suwercropp*,[13] Lord Ellenborough CJ considered that if T 'lets the date of payment go by, he may lead [P] into a supposition, that he relies solely on [A]; and if in that case the price of the goods has been paid to [A], on account of this deception, [P] shall be discharged'.[14] Similarly, in *Wyatt v Hertford*,[15] Lord Ellenborough CJ stressed that if T chose to take a security from A and gave A a receipt as though he had been paid, P would be discharged if he then paid A in reliance on these facts, even though A's security failed.[16]

It seems that T's delay in seeking payment from P is insufficient, *per se*, to bar T's claim. In *Davison v Donaldson*,[17] T sold beef to A, a managing owner of a ship, and repeatedly sought payment from A but did not obtain it. P, a co-owner of the ship, settled with A two months after the goods were supplied and again two years later. It was more than three years later that T sought payment from P (A then being bankrupt) and it was held that T should succeed against P. Nevertheless, all three judges thought T's delay in seeking payment was capable of misleading P and could amount to a representation that T had been paid by

---

11 (1807) 1 Camp 109 at 112.
12 See Mechem, 'The Liability of an Undisclosed Principal' (1910) 23 Harv L Rev 513, 520-530.
13 (1807) 1 Camp 109.
14 (1807) 1 Camp 109 at 112.
15 (1802) 3 East 147.
16 See also *Heald v Kenworthy* (1855) 10 Exch 739 where Parke B emphasised that P's settlement with A did not discharge P unless 'the conduct of [T] would make it unjust for him to call upon [P] for the money; as for example, where [P] is induced by the conduct of [T] to pay [A] the money on the faith that [A and T] have come to a settlement on the matter, or if any representation to that effect is made by [T] either by words or conduct ... but ... there is no case of this kind where [T] has been precluded from recovering, unless he has in some way contributed either to deceive [P] or to induce him to alter his position' (p 746); *Irvine & Co v Watson* (1880) 5 QBD 414 (which strongly supports the *Heald* reasoning).
17 (1882) 9 QBD 623; see also *Irvine & Co v Watson* (1880) 5 QBD 414 (A bought oil, on behalf of P, from T, the terms being 'cash on or before delivery'. T delivered the oil without insisting on pre-payment and P, not realising that T had not been paid, settled with A. It was held that T's not insisting upon pre-payment did not mislead P into paying A and P was thus liable); *Everett v Collins* (1810) 2 Camp 515.

A or show that T elected to look to A for payment.[18] Finally, it should be stressed that some of the cases do focus upon this fact of T's *electing* to look to A for payment[19] and this is one feature to consider in deciding this issue.

It would, of course, be difficult to apply this estoppel notion to an *undisclosed* principal as it is awkward to assert that T can make any representations to a principal of whom he has no knowledge. Hence, it cannot realistically be said that T elects to look to A or delays in seeking payment from P when he does not know of P's existence. The estoppel notion can apply, however, once the undisclosed principal is revealed to T.[20]

Prejudice accruing to P: is P unfairly prejudiced by having to pay twice?

This is a broader notion which focuses upon P's position and asks whether it might be inequitable to make P pay again. This approach is traceable primarily to *dicta* in *Thomson v Davenport*[1] to the effect that it *might* be unjust to make P pay T where P had first settled with A but, on the facts, P had not settled with A and the decision was that justice required that P must pay T.[2] This outcome is hardly surprising: where T has *not* induced P to settle with A, as discussed in the first line of reasoning above, it is plain that T has a legitimate claim to be paid by P and P should not be able to argue that there is any hardship or prejudice in thus settling his debt owed to T. Consequently, in *Heald v Kenworthy*,[3] the court considered that estoppel reasoning was the only sound basis upon which P might refuse payment and many of the older decisions were rationalised and explained by the court on that footing.

However, this broader notion of P's being unfairly prejudiced could apply to the *undisclosed principal* because, as emphasised earlier, it is extremely difficult to assert that T has made any representations to a party of whom he is unaware. In *Armstrong v Stokes*,[4] for example, an undisclosed principal paid A in good faith, according to the normal practice between P and A, *before* T discovered

18 See *Hopkins v Ware* (1869) LR 4 Exch 268 (A, a solicitor, paid P's debt by means of his own cheque and the creditor/T failed to present it until four weeks had elapsed when it was dishonoured and A had absconded. A had funds of P's at the time the cheque was forwarded to T and, in the interim, P had paid A an extra amount to cover the cheque. There was a reasonable chance of the cheque's being paid if it had been presented speedily. It was held that P was discharged); *Smethurst v Mitchell* (1859) 1 E & E 622 (T delayed in not suing P for nine months, during which time P settled with A. P was held to be discharged).

19 See *Smethurst v Mitchell* (1859) 1 E & E 622 (considered in election, below); *Smith v Ferrand* (1827) 7 B & C 19.

20 Eg *Smethurst v Mitchell* (1859) 1 E & E 622.

 1 (1829) 9 B & C 78. See also *Railton v Hodgson* (1804) 4 Taunt 576n and *Smyth v Anderson* (1849) 7 CB 21: both decisions acknowledge, in the broadest terms, that it might be 'unfair' and 'unjust' to make P pay for the goods again. In *Smyth*, T sold goods to A who was acting on behalf of a foreign P in Bombay. P made remittances to A and, at the time of A's insolvency, A was indebted to P. T knew of P from the invoice and certainly he knew of P at the date that he sought payment from A. It was held that T could not recover against P as he (T) had looked to A and had got what he 'considered an advantage, viz the security of [A]' (per Maule J, p 41).

 2 The decision is based primarily upon election, ie did T's debiting A with the price of the goods amount to an election to proceed only against A? P was *unnamed* at the date of purchase and the court held that (i) T was under no obligation to ascertain P's identity and, (ii) T was not exercising a choice by charging A as he had insufficient information to debit anyone else and could thus proceed against P when he was named.

 3 (1855) 10 Exch 739.

 4 (1872) LR 7 QB 598.

P's existence. A became insolvent without having paid T but it was held that P need not pay again as this would be unjust. Blackburn J expressly rejected the attempt which was made in *Heald* to draw the two lines of reasoning together.[5] However, two important, later decisions,[6] severely criticised *Armstrong* and unequivocally reinstated the *Heald* reasoning.

Conclusion

In conclusion, the estoppel analysis is dominant and is clearly appropriate to the disclosed principal, but should there be a different rule for the undisclosed principal based upon the rule in *Armstrong v Stokes*? *Bowstead & Reynolds*[7] supports the *Armstrong* reasoning in relation to the undisclosed principal arguing that, as T deals exclusively with A and does not expect P to be accountable, P's duty is simply to ensure that A has sufficient funds and so if T is prejudiced it is because of his misplaced trust in A. This is a persuasive argument but it appears to side-step the primary fact that the undisclosed principal knows that he owes a debt to T which surely cannot be sloughed-off simply because P pays A: it is, after all, a simple enough task for P to ask A whether T has been paid. Secondly, the reasoning in *Armstrong* turns on the fact that T did not know of the existence of P when P paid A in good faith and this analysis thus makes the undisclosed principal's liability dependent upon the *knowledge of T* as to whether or not there is a principal. As noted above, P's liability should surely turn on the state of his (P's) knowledge and whether he knows that T has a claim against him.[8] Finally, it is arguable that, as instigator of his own concealment, the undisclosed principal should be in no better position than the disclosed principal and that, by settling with A, P erroneously trusts his chosen agent and should therefore bear the loss himself in the *Armstrong v Stokes* situation.

WHERE THE THIRD PARTY SETTLES WITH THE AGENT

The general rule also applies in this converse situation in that T must pay his creditor, P, and T is not discharged by a payment made to A. However, the rule must immediately be qualified as A may have actual or apparent authority to accept payment from T. In *International Sponge Importers Ltd v Andrew Watt & Sons*,[9] A, a travelling salesman, sold sponges on behalf of P and the monthly statement of account which was sent to T contained a warning that cheques should be crossed and made payable to P and that no receipt was valid unless on P's printed form. T nevertheless paid A in cash and, on this occasion, A appropriated the money. It was held that T was discharged by his payment to A. At first sight the decision looks surprising as it is tempting to ask what more P could have

---

5   The decision seems based upon the desire to restrict the undisclosed principal doctrine in not allowing T 'an unexpected godsend' (p 604) against P.

6   *Irvine & Co v Watson* (1880) 5 QBD 414; *Davison v Donaldson* (1882) 9 QBD 623

7   *Bowstead & Reynolds on Agency* (16th edn, 1996), Art 82, para 8-105; Reynolds, 'Practical Problems of the Undisclosed Principal Doctrine' [1983] CLP 119, 133-135. See also Mechem, *Outlines of the Law of Agency* (4th edn,1952), §§ 184-186, where this approach is advocated.

8   This was the view of Bramwell LJ in *Irvine v Watson* (1880) 5 QBD 414, 417-418; see also Higgins, 'The Equity of the Undisclosed Principal' (1965) 28 MLR 167, 175-178.

9   [1911] AC 279.

done to limit A's authority and alert T to the limitation. The decision must be viewed, however, in the light of the previous dealings which had taken place as, in those dealings, T had paid for the sponges by cheques made payable to A and P had always entrusted A with the custody and delivery of the goods. As A could collect money due on the account, the House of Lords held that it was reasonable for T to assume that A could 'make even better terms for his employers by taking cash – rather than postponed terms of payment'.[10] Without such business practice, the courts are loath to find any authority in A to receive payment[11] but if the money is accepted by P, it should be stressed that he may have ratified the transaction and T will then be discharged.

Where there is an *undisclosed* principal, logic demands that T should be able to settle with A as, in so doing, he pays the only visible creditor. There is clear and ancient authority that, as long as T does not know of P's existence, T can safely pay A and is discharged from liability.[12] However, in *Drakeford v Piercy*,[13] T paid A before discovering P's existence but it was held that this did not discharge T unless P had misled T in some way, eg by giving A possession of the goods to be sold so that he appeared to be an owner and thus authorised to receive payment. Technically, it is difficult to see how an undisclosed principal may mislead T and why such extra considerations should be relevant when T has paid A in good faith, but *Drakeford* followed a line of cases concerning set-off, which clearly seek to protect P, and will be considered next.

The third party's right of set-off against the agent

The situation which commonly arises here is that A owes a personal debt to T and T chooses to contract with A so that he can set-off the debt against the price of goods supplied by A. If P sues T for the price of the goods sold to T via A, may T claim to set-off against P the amount of the debt owed by A? T may also have settled with A for the price of the goods less the amount of the set-off and so the questions of set-off and settlement often go hand-in- hand. A simple diagram illustrates the position:

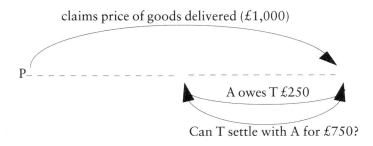

claims price of goods delivered (£1,000)

P

A owes T £250

Can T settle with A for £750?

10   [1911] AC 279 at 288, per Lord Shaw of Dunfermline.
11   See *Linck, Moeller & Co v Jameson & Co* (1885) 2 TLR 206 (T was not justified in paying A merely because P had authorised such payment in one previous transaction); *Butwick v Grant* [1924] 2 KB 483 (A acted for P in selling coats to T on one isolated occasion, P sending the goods to T with an invoice bearing P's name. T's payment to A was held not to be a good discharge).
12   *Coates v Lewes* (1808) 1 Camp 444 per Lord Ellenborough: '… in this case the person employed to sell, himself acted as a principal, and the plaintiffs knowing this, authorised his mode of dealing, and all its consequences'; *Curlewis v Birkbeck* (1863) 3 F & F 894.
13   (1866) 14 LT 403.

The position regarding set-off is governed by whether P is disclosed or undisclosed.[14]

THE DISCLOSED PRINCIPAL AND THE THIRD PARTY'S RIGHT OF SET-OFF

With the disclosed principal, the rule is straightforward and it follows the general rule in settlement, discussed above: T knows that P is his creditor and he must therefore pay P in full irrespective of any personal debt owed by A to T, and T will not be discharged by settling with A unless A had actual or apparent authority to receive the payment.

It is, of course, not uncommon in a disclosed agency that the parties may settle accounts between themselves for debts owed. P may thus be indebted to A and P may authorise A to accept settlement from T and pay himself his own debt from the amount paid by T. In addition, A's own debt to T may be written off in the settlement of accounts between A and T. For example, if P sells goods to T at a price of £5,000, P owes A £1,000 and A owes T £1,000, A may be authorised to accept £4,000 from T, which must then be transmitted to P, thereby settling all the accounts between the parties.[15]

THE UNDISCLOSED PRINCIPAL AND THE THIRD PARTY'S RIGHT OF SET-OFF

A moment's thought reveals that the rule that set-off is not available to T where P is disclosed should be reversed in the undisclosed principal situation. This is because T contracted with A assuming him to be acting on his own account and thus, when P is revealed and sues T, T should have all the defences which are personal to A, including the right of set-off. Regrettably, the law has not adopted this straightforward strategy and there are two different approaches to the problem of set-off in relation to the undisclosed principal which must be considered.

T normally has the right of set-off against the undisclosed principal

This is the logical, general rule outlined above and favours T's position in allowing him the right of set-off. It is premised upon the notion that the undisclosed principal intervenes subject to the equities in existence at that time,[16]

---

14 See Derham, 'Set-Off and Agency' [1985] 44 CLJ 384.
15 See *Barker v Greenwood* (1837) 2 Y & C Ex 414.
16 See *Ramazotti v Bowring and Arundell* (1859) 7 CBNS 851, 856, per Erle CJ: 'I am of opinion that the undisclosed principal, adopting the contract made by his agent, must adopt in omnibus, and, if it were coupled with an agreement that the defendant should have a right to set off a debt due to him from the agent, the principal must take the contract subject to that agreement of set-off'. In *Turner v Thomas* (1871) LR 6 CP 610, Willes J explained that the undisclosed principal's intervention subject to the set-off was 'founded on principles of common honesty' in that 'one who satisfies his contract with the person with whom he has contracted ought not to suffer by reason of its afterwards turning out that there was a concealed principal' (p 613); see also *Montgomerie v United Kingdom Mutual Steamship Association Ltd* [1891] 1 QB 370, 372, per Wright J.

and P is thus normally subject to T's right of set-off. Indeed, in 1785 Lord Mansfield CJ considered this rule to have been 'long settled'.[17]

T has the right of set-off *only* where the undisclosed principal is at fault in misleading T

The second line of decisions favours P's position and demands that, if he is to be subject to T's set-off, P must do something *more* than simply remaining undisclosed. The cases in this second group demand that P must have been at *fault* in misleading T in some way if he is to be saddled with T's set-off.

The first decision clearly adopting this approach was *Baring v Corrie*,[18] where a broker (A) sold 50 hogsheads of sugar to T on behalf of an undisclosed principal and, A being bankrupt, P sued for the price. T claimed to set-off an amount owed by A but the claim was rejected. The court drew a crucial distinction between factors and brokers. Factors sold goods on their own account as independent merchants and sometimes acted for undisclosed principals but, in both these situations, the factor had possession of the goods. Brokers, on the other hand, did not have possession of the goods and ought not to sell in their own names. In *Baring*, T knew that the brokers acted sometimes as agents and at other times as independent merchants but, as T had 'negligently abstained'[19] from making any enquiries of the brokers, he was not entitled to the set-off.

The *Baring* decision unequivocally protected P,[20] and was responsible for the notion that, if P were to be subject to the set-off, he would have to mislead T by, for example, entrusting A with possession of the goods as a 'proprietor'.[1] The hallmark of approval was given to this view by the House of Lords in *Cooke & Sons v Eshelby*,[2] where the majority considered that it was premised upon estoppel.[3] There T admitted that he had no particular belief as to whether A was acting on his own account or on behalf of a principal and, as P's conduct could thus not have induced T to think that A was acting on his own account, T had no right of set-off against P.

The rationale of *Baring v Corrie* seems to be that A's authority as a broker was to act for a *disclosed* principal who would thus not be subject to T's set-off and, as A acted outside his authority in not disclosing P, it was unfair to burden P with the set-off unless he had in some way contributed to A's acting as an unfettered principal. This conclusion was fortified by T's failure to enquire meaning that the balance tipped against T rather than P. However, the estoppel reasoning which *Baring* engendered is, for several reasons, extremely difficult

---

17 *Rabone v Williams* (1785) 7 Term Rep 360n, followed in *George v Clagett* (1797) 7 Term Rep 359 (both cases concerned factors).
18 (1818) 2 B & Ald 137.
19 (1818) 2 B & Ald 137 at 145, per Abbott CJ.
20 Abbott CJ stressed that, if T had succeeded in his claim 'it would not be safe for any merchant ever hereafter to employ a broker' (p 144).
1 (1818) 2 B & Ald 137 at 145, per Bayley J, who expanded upon the requirements for the imposition of liability on P, viz: Did P enable A to appear as proprietors of the goods and to practise a fraud on T? Did A actually practise a fraud? Did T use use due care to avoid such fraud? In *Baring*, all these questions were answered against T.
2 (1887) 12 App Cas 271; followed in *Cooper v Strauss & Co* (1898) 14 TLR 233.
3 Lord FitzGerald doubted estoppel as the rule's true basis (p 283) but, on the facts, he thought it sufficient that P had not misled T. The estoppel reasoning is also advanced in *Drakeford v Piercy* (1866) 14 LT 403, per Blackburn J; *Montagu v Forwood* [1893] 2 QB 350, 355, per Bowen LJ; *Fish v Kempton* (1849) 7 CB 687, 691, per Wilde CJ.

to sustain. First, it is surely correct that T should have the right of set-off where he knows of no party other than A and does not suspect that one exists and, from T's point of view, any further gloss demanding that A appear as 'proprietor' or 'principal'[4] is immaterial. Second, as T may have contracted with A purely and simply to obtain the set-off, it is surely perverse and unfair to make his rights dependent on P's fault.[5] Third, it is awkward, at best, to assert that an *undisclosed* principal may hold-out A to T and that T is able to rely on the representations of someone of whom he has no knowledge. Fourth, the cases are vague regarding the nature of the conduct which would amount to such a holding-out: P's entrusting A with the possession of the goods is regarded as crucial in the early cases which distinguish factors from brokers and it seems that this is sufficient in itself.[6] In one case,[7] P had specifically instructed A, a factor, to disclose the agency and A disobeyed, but P was nevertheless subject to the set-off on the basis that 'the very fact of entrusting your goods to a man as a factor ... is *prima facie* authority from you to him to sell in his own name'.[8]

Is T ever put on inquiry?

It should be emphasised that, using either approach outlined above, T may be put on inquiry that A is in fact acting for a principal. Under the first approach, such knowledge would deprive T of his set-off because there would be no equity in T's favour. Under the second approach, T's knowledge of a principal would mean that P's conduct could not be said to mislead T into thinking that A acted entirely for himself as an owner.

It is necessary that T should realise only that there may be *an agency*[9] rather than the identity of P, but the facts which might put T on inquiry are infinitely variable and no clear pattern emerges. It is clear from the cases discussed above that, certainly in a sale of ascertained goods supposedly owned by A at the date of contract, the fact that A lacks physical possession of the goods and/or their

---

4　In *Cooke & Sons v Eshelby* (1887) 12 App Cas 271, 275, Lord Halsbury LC asserted that 'the ground upon which all these cases have been decided is that the agent has been permitted by the principal to hold himself out as the principal'. But it is surely reasonable to conclude that this occurs, of necessity, where A acts for an undisclosed principal.

5　If P is *not* at fault under this line of cases, T may be able to argue that he contracted with A solely to obtain the set-off and P's intervention is barred on grounds of identity or as being inconsistent with the express or implied terms of the contract: see *Greer v Downs Supply Co* [1927] 2 KB 28 (considered earlier).

6　Contrast this with the related doctrine of apparent ownership where entrusting another with bare possession of goods is clearly insufficient to raise an estoppel against the owner: see Ch 18.

7　*Ex p Dixon, Re Henley* (1876) 4 Ch D 133.

8　(1876) 4 Ch D 133 at 137, per Brett JA. Sealy and Hooley, *Text and Materials in Commercial Law* (2nd edn, 1999), state (p 174) that estoppel reasoning cannot apply where A disobeys P's instructions and acts in his own name. With respect, this is difficult to accept. As P is undisclosed, this an unconventional application of estoppel but there seems to be no reason why A's contravention of P's instructions should have any more relevance here than in apparent authority, where such a contravention may not be operable in restricting A's authority. Indeed, Fridman suggests (*Law of Agency*, 7th ed 1996, pp 269-270) that estoppel reasoning might best be confined to cases where A disobeys P's instructions and does not disclose him indicating, presumably, that other facts such as P's giving A possession of the goods would be sufficent to estop P and subject him to the set-off.

9　*Baring v Corrie* (1818) 2 B & Ald 137; *Semanza v Brinsley* (1865) 18 CBNS 467; *Mildred, Goyeneche & Co v Maspons, Y Hermano* (1883) 8 App Cas 874.

indicia of title may be vital as an indication that T is put on inquiry. T might also be alerted by A's occupation,[10] the surrounding circumstances[11] and the information in the contractual or other documents.[12]

Conclusion

It is clear that, generally, the undisclosed principal should be subject to T's set-off and the first approach, outlined above, is the only one which can logically be supported. Consequently, it is suggested that the undisclosed principal's intervention should always be subject to the equities in existence at that time and this rule should be coupled with the notion that T might be put on inquiry regarding the existence of a principal. As Professor Reynolds[13] suggests, the most cogent reason to deprive T of the set-off is not that P is at fault but, rather, that *T could be expected to realise* that there might be a principal behind A. If T then chooses to proceed with the contract, he must surely be deemed to accept the risk that he might not obtain the set-off.

The doctrines of merger and election

Where there is an undisclosed principal, A remains personally liable on the contract and there may be situations with a disclosed principal where T enters

10   In *Moore v Clementson* (1809) 2 Camp 22, T had express knowledge of the agency but Lord Ellenborough considered (p 24) that T's 'general knowledge' of A as a *factor* was insufficient to abrogate T's set-off because factors normally sold goods of undisclosed principals and their own goods; Cf *Baring v Corrie* (1818) 2 B & Ald 137, 144, where Abbott CJ accepted that there was a *duty* to inquire where A had a dual capacity as *broker* and independent merchant; *Dresser v Norwood* (1864) 17 CB (NS) 466 (T's own agent (a broker) knew that A was a factor selling goods on behalf of a P and the knowledge was imputed to T thus depriving him of a set-off against the factor).
11   *Maanss v Henderson* (1801) 1 East 335 (A was an English subject who, in time of war, was instructed to effect an insurance policy on P's ship. P was a neutral foreigner and A effected the policy in his own name, this being A's normal practice with A's usual broker (T). A did inform T that the property was neutral. A got into financial difficulties and stopped payment to T and, at that time, A was indebted to T. A loss was incurred under the policy and the question was whether T had a lien on the policy for the amounts owed by A. Lord Kenyon CJ held T had sufficient indication that A was acting as an agent and not on his own account and thus T had no lien for the amounts owed by A).
12   Eg *Pratt v Willey* (1826) 2 C & P 350 (A sold coal in his own name but P was named as seller on a ticket which accompanied the coal. Held that T should have enquired further and not dealt with A as a principal; accordingly he had no right of set-off); *Cooper v Strauss & Co* (1898) 14 TLR 233 (Kennedy J held that, on the evidence available, A, a factor who sold hops, had informed the buyer, T, of the agency and thus T had no right of set-off. However, the judge did not think that a sale note reading 'Sold for and on account of', with no name of any P inserted, was sufficient to convey notice of an agency to T, as factors sometimes dealt on their own account and sometimes acted for principals); *Ex p Dixon, Re Henley* (1876) 4 Ch D 133 (on a bill of exchange drawn upon T for the price of goods delivered, the words 'Agents for [P]' were printed in pale blue ink with the wording partly obscured by A's name. Held to be insufficient notice to T of an agency and thus T did have the right of set-off. Brett JA (p 138) accepted that, if the wording had been legible, T would have had notice); cf *Greer v Downs Supply Co* [1927] 2 KB 28 (T raised the question with A that a different supplier's name (ie P) appeared on a letter sent in reply to his order. A gave the excuse that the name was his trade name. Held that T may have had constructive notice of the agency but he did not have actual notice and he was thus *not* deprived of the set-off as its availability was the only reason he had contracted with A).
13   'Practical Problems of the Undisclosed Principal Doctrine' [1983] CLP 119, 122-125.

into the contract with A on such terms that A is personally liable on it.[14] As *both* A and P are liable to T in these situations, it might be assumed that their liability would be joint and several (ie T could sue either A or P or both together, subject, of course, to T's being unable to recover twice) but this is not the position which English law has adopted. Instead, the law considers that there is only one obligation and that the liability of A and P is treated as an *alternative* liability. In such cases, the doctrine of election is said to apply by which T cannot sue both A and P but must choose one or the other and, certainly where a judgment is obtained against either A or P, T's right to proceed against the other is barred by virtue of the concept of merger. Moreover, an act short of judgment may be held to evince an intent on T's part to look to one party only and thus constitute a conclusive act of election.

If this much is accepted, the rational mind baulks at the strikingly robotic way in which these concepts are applied: T loses his right to proceed against the second party where his proceedings against the first party have been commenced in ignorance of there being such a second party and even where judgment against the first party remains unsatisfied. Here, it cannot be asserted that T has 'elected' to pursue one party and abandon his claim against the other because his actions are borne of ignorance rather than informed choice.

It is becoming increasingly evident that, where both A and P are liable, it is difficult to sustain the general rule that their liability should be cast in the alternative. In the New Zealand decision in *Fowler (L C) & Sons Ltd v St Stephen's College Board of Governors*,[15] the concepts of election and merger were castigated vigorously. Following the view originally put forward by Professor Reynolds,[16] Thomas J considered that 'election' is misnamed and should correctly be regarded as an example of waiver or estoppel. This would mean denying a mechanical application of election; rather, T might be barred from proceeding against one party only because his actions are sufficiently unambiguous to show a waiver of his rights against that party. The requirements of estoppel would thus have to be present and T's decision not to proceed against one party would have to be based upon full knowledge of all the facts. The judge then emphasised that election and merger have no relevance where liability is joint and several, as each party is liable on his separate promise as well as his joint promise. More importantly, he considered that even where liability was a joint liability so that there was only one cause of action against P and A, the notion of election should be treated with caution. Speaking of such joint liability, Thomas J expressed the view that:

'The plaintiff is not then obliged to sue one or the other; he or she may sue both. It is open to him or her to discontinue against the one and sue the other or to amend the proceeding by adding the other. The action of suing one to the exclusion of the other may add some credence to the claim that the plaintiff has waived his right to sue the other person. But it will not be decisive. The answer will still depend on the circumstances of the case and whether the plaintiff made a deliberate and unequivocal election based on a full knowledge of all the relevant facts'.[17]

Thomas J further opined that obtaining judgment against one party should not bar a claim against the other by virtue of the notion of merger and, to decide

---

14 See Ch 11.
15 [1991] 3 NZLR 304.
16 Reynolds, 'Election Distributed' (1970) 86 LQR 318.
17 [1991] 3 NZLR 304 at 309.

otherwise, is 'an irony which would discredit the law'.[18] In conclusion, the judge considered that election and merger had some credence where P is undisclosed, meaning that on the principal's revelation T could and should decide to proceed against either A or P, but that it would still be possible in some undisclosed principal situations for both A and P to be liable on the contract. It is difficult to fault this analysis but it could not presently be adopted in English law having regard to the weight of authority against it.

As mentioned earlier, the law on settlement and set-off is entangled with the idea of election. Consider, for example, the situation where (i) T has sold goods to A (ii) T has then claimed payment from A and, (iii) as a consequence, P has settled with A. Should A then abscond with the money, for example, P might be discharged from the obligation to pay again. In this example, apart from the possibility that T had by his conduct induced P to settle with A, a further factor contributing to P's discharge might be that T had elected to look exclusively to A and exonerate P from liability. It might thus be asserted that the true basis for the discharge of P is that, by his conduct, T had waived his rights to proceed against P and had truly abandoned any claim against him.

It is important to establish what theoretical justification exists for these doctrines of merger and election. One fact is abundantly clear: merger and election apply only where both A and P are liable on the contract and, consequently, these principles have no relevance in the paradigm case where A contracts as an agent on behalf of P and A incurs no personal liability to T on the contract.[19]

WHERE JUDGMENT IS OBTAINED AGAINST EITHER THE AGENT OR THE PRINCIPAL: THE NOTION OF MERGER

One rule is undisputed in relation to both the disclosed and undisclosed principal: where T *obtains judgment* against A, T may not proceed against P despite the fact that the judgment against A remains unsatisfied and, in cases of the undisclosed principal, where T obtains judgment in ignorance of the fact that there is a principal.[20]

In relation to the undisclosed principal, the rule was put beyond doubt in *Kendall v Hamilton*,[1] a leading case on joint debtors. The appellants successfully sued a debtor but, the judgment remaining unsatisfied, they discovered and sued a second debtor, but it was held that they must fail as there was legally only one debt and judgment against the first debtor extinguished the liability of the second.

In *Kendall*, the House of Lords supported the rule in two different ways. First, Earl Cairns LC took the view that there was only one obligation and that as the appellants had obtained judgment against one party 'they exhausted their right of action, not necessarily by means of any election ... but because the right of action which they pursued could not, after judgment obtained, co-exist with a right of action on the same facts against another person'.[2] The Lord Chancellor

---

18 [1991] 3 NZLR 304 at 311.
19 *Fowler (L C) & Sons Ltd v St Stephen's College Board of Governors* [1991] 3 NZLR 304.
20 *Priestly v Fernie* (1865) 3 H & C 977.
 1 (1879) 4 App Cas 504; Lord Penzance dissented, describing the rule as 'unbending and indiscriminate' (p 530). See also *Scarf v Jardine* (1882) 7 App Cas 345 (a seminal decision on election in relation to partnership).
 2 (1879) 4 App Cas 504 at 515.

added that this was certainly the position in relation to an undisclosed principal.[3] This theory is often explained in terms of merger,[4] ie where T has obtained judgment on one cause of action, that cause of action is merged in the judgment. Certainly where T sues A in ignorance of their being an undisclosed principal, this rule cannot be based upon the idea of election as T does not know of P's existence and thus, being totally insensible as to the true position, T cannot exercise any choice regarding which party to sue.

Second, Lord Blackburn[5] considered that the liability of the newly discovered debtor was a bonus for which the appellants had never bargained but, having destroyed that remedy by earlier obtaining judgment, they could not complain of their 'bad luck'.[6] Where T has obtained judgment against A and subsequently discovers the undisclosed principal, there is some credence in the 'bonus' theory because T originally considered that he had made only one contract with A and, while he also has a remedy against the undisclosed principal, he must elect between the parties at some stage. At least in relation to joint debtors, the *Kendall* rule has been abrogated by statute[7] and so the 'one obligation theory' in relation to A and P begins to look dubious. However, the current position is that the liability of the undisclosed principal and agent must be viewed as an alternative liability and so the *Kendall* reasoning is still pertinent in the law of agency.

The concept of merger also applies to the disclosed principal in those situations where both A and P are liable on the contract and T obtains judgment against one.[8] In the modern decision in *Barrington v Lee*,[9] P instructed two estate agents, A1 and A2, to sell his house. T, a prospective purchaser, made an offer subject to contract and paid a deposit to both agents. The sale did not proceed and although A1 returned the deposit A2 did not. T obtained an unsatisfied judgment against A2 and this was held to bar any subsequent action against P.[10] Where P is disclosed, judgment against one party can be more convincingly regarded as conclusive evidence of election as there are two visible parties but, as cogently argued in *Bowstead & Reynolds*,[11] the *reason* for the existence of the rule is more difficult to justify in cases of the disclosed principal than in instances of the undisclosed principal. As T knows of P, there is no question of P's liability being a 'bonus' as explained in *Kendall*, and where T bargains for the liability of both A and P as a safeguard to ensure satisfaction, it is surely both unjust and contradictory to demand that an unsatisfied judgment against one should bar a claim against the other.

---

3 (1879) 4 App Cas 504 at 514-515.
4 See eg *King v Hoare* (1844) 13 M & W 494, 504, per Parke B: '... the cause of action is changed into matter of record, which is of a higher nature, and the inferior remedy is merged in the higher'; *Debenham's Ltd v Perkins* (1925) 133 LT 252, 254 per Scrutton LJ; *Marginson v Ian Potter & Co* (1976) 136 CLR 161, 169 per Gibbs and Mason JJ.
5 (1879) 4 App Cas 504, 544.
6 (1879) 4 App Cas 504, 544.
7 See the Civil Liability (Contribution) Act 1978, s 3.
8 *Morel Bros & Co Ltd v Earl of Westmorland* [1904] AC 11; *R M K R M (Firm of) v M R M V L (Firm of)* [1926] AC 761.
9 [1972] 1 QB 326.
10 It should be stressed that P is no longer liable on these facts for the return of the deposit (see *Sorrell v Finch* [1977] AC 728) but *Barrington* is still valid on the question of merger.
11 *Bowstead & Reynolds on Agency* (16th edn, 1996), Art 84, para 8-117.

THE DOCTRINE OF ELECTION

Election proper should be confined to cases of the disclosed principal where both A and P are liable to T and cases of the undisclosed principal where T discovers the existence of the principal before he pursues any course of action. In these cases, T is able to choose between proceeding against A or P and 'election' is given its literal meaning. Although the law acknowledges that acts which fall short of judgment are capable of amounting to election,[12] very few of the decisions have held that such acts do amount to an unequivocal, binding election.

There are several requirements for a valid election. First, T must have full and actual[13] (not constructive) knowledge of the facts and realise that there are two persons between whom he must elect. In *Longman v Hill*,[14] T did some bill-posting for the 'Irish Exhibition', a group of individuals which later became incorporated, T then issuing a writ against the company for amounts owed to him. It was held that T could still succeed against the individuals and had made no definitive election to exonerate them from liability.

Second, T's election must clearly and unequivocally show that he has abondoned his claim against one of the parties and that he looks exclusively to the other[15] and it must be made voluntarily.[16] In *Calder v Dobell*,[17] A was authorised to buy cotton on behalf of P and told not to disclose him. T did not wish to sell to A personally and thus A disclosed P's name. Bought and sold notes were then exchanged between A and T and T invoiced the goods to A who refused to accept them in a falling market. It was held that these acts were no bar to his ultimate action against P. Likewise, the following facts have all fallen short of election: debiting A,[18] demanding payment from A,[19] receiving part-payment from A,[20] taking a bill of exchange from A,[1] proving in A's bankruptcy[2] or pursuing a claim in arbitration,[3] and serving a writ on P.[4]

---

12 See the cases reviewed in *Clarkson, Booker Ltd v Andjel* [1964] 2 QB 775.
13 *Dunn v Newton* (1884) Cab & El 278.
14 (1891) 7 TLR 639. In *Pyxis Special Shipping Co Ltd v Dritsas & Kaglis Bros Ltd, The Scaplake* [1978] 2 Lloyd's Rep 380, 385, Mocatta J held that, when T started arbitration proceedings against A, he did not know that 'the defendants [P] were possessed of far more substantial means than [A]'. T's acts were thus not performed with full knowledge of the facts and he could proceed against P.
15 *Clarkson, Booker Ltd v Andjel* [1964] 2 QB 775, 794, per Russell LJ.
16 *Fowler (L C) & Sons Ltd v St Stephen's College Board of Governors* [1991] 3 NZLR 304.
17 (1871) LR 6 CP 486.
18 *Thomson v Davenport* (1829) 9 B & C 78; *Calder v Dobell* (1871) LR 6 CP 486.
19 *Calder v Dobell* (supra); *Eastman v Harry* (1875) 33 LT 800; *Beigtheil & Young v Stewart* (1900) 16 TLR 177 (demanding payment of P); *Chestertons v Barone* (1987) 282 Estates Gazette 87 (estate agent submitting account to (an originally undisclosed) P did not bar proceedings against the solicitor (A) acting for P).
20 *Ex p Pitt* (1923) 40 TLR 5.
 1 *Robinson v Read* (1829) 9 B & C 449.
 2 *Curtis v Williamson* (1874) LR 10 QB 57.
 3 *Pyxis Special Shipping Co Ltd v Dritsas & Kaglis Bros Ltd, The Scaplake* [1978] 2 Lloyd's Rep 380.
 4 *Clarkson, Booker Ltd v Andjel* [1964] 2 QB 775; cf *Cyril Lord Carpet Sales Ltd v Browne* (1966) 111 Sol Jo 51 (T issued a summons against A for the price of carpets supplied to P's hotel but T made no attempt to commence proceedings against P until six months later and then, realising that A was resident in America, P's name was substituted for A's name on the summons. CA held that T had unequivocally decided to pursue his remedy against A and his claim against P thus failed. *Clarkson* was distinguished in that there the plaintiff had been careful to preserve his rights against both defendants in correspondence. See the criticism of *Cyril Lord* in Reynolds, 'Election Distributed' (1970) 86 LQR 318, 342-343; *Chestertons v Barone* [1987] 1 EGLR 15 (May LJ considered (p 17) that election could rarely be established without the commencement of legal proceedings).

Third, the decision in *Smethurst v Mitchell*[5] is that, with an undisclosed principal, T must make his election within a reasonable time of discovering P, nine months delay being held to be unreasonable on the facts. It should be stressed that, in *Smethurst*, the delay induced P to think that T looked only to A and, consequently, P settled with A. Thus the salient point of the decision was that, by his conduct, T was estopped from claiming against P whose position had changed for the worse.

Conclusion

Election has been convincingly criticised in the USA[6] and, as discussed earlier, election and merger have been censured in a recent New Zealand decision.[7] The leading English authority on agency emphasises[8] that, apart from the merger cases, there are only two decisions concerning the undisclosed principal in which there has been held to be a binding election[9] and both are explainable as estoppel cases where, after discovering P, T's conduct had induced P to settle with A, consequently barring T's action against P. Thus apart from the cases where T has obtained judgment against A, Professor Reynolds would only disallow T's claim against the undisclosed principal in such estoppel situations where P has been induced to act to his prejudice by T's conduct. As regards the disclosed principal, he argues that many of the cases are based upon formation of contract rather than election, this being borne out by the 19th century decisions on invoicing and debiting of one party[10] and, accordingly, he would also apply estoppel reasoning to disclosed principal situations as the only justification for denying T's remedy against P.[11]

---

5 (1859) 1 E & E 622.
6 See Clayton, 'Election between the Liability of an Agent and his Undisclosed Principal' (1925) 3 Texas L Rev 384; Merrill, 'Election between Agent and Undisclosed Principal: Shall We Follow the Restatement?' (1933) 12 Nebraska L Bull 100; Sargent and Rochvarg, 'A Reexamination of the Agency Doctrine of Election' (1982) 36 U of Miami LR 411.
7 See *Fowler (L C) & Sons Ltd v St Stephen's College Board of Governors* [1991] 3 NZLR 304.
8 Reynolds, 'Election Distributed' (1970) 86 LQR 318
9 *MacClure v Schemeil* (1871) 20 WR 168; *Smethurst v Mitchell* (1859 1 E & E 622.
10 Eg *Addison v Gandassequi* (1812) 4 Taunt 574 (P, a foreign merchant, was in England to select goods to be sent to Lima. T showed goods to P at A's office, P haggling over the price and indicating the market in which he sold. T subsequently received an order from A, the goods then being invoiced and debited to A. A became bankrupt. It was held that T understood the position and thus had chosen to contract with A, not P); *Calder v Dobell* (1871) LR 6 CP 486 (above).
11 See the critical comments of Thomas J in *Fowler (L C) & Sons Ltd v St Stephen's College Board of Governors* [1991] 3 NZLR 304 who considered that election was really founded upon waiver and, in *Pyxis Special Shipping Co Ltd v Dritsas & Kaglis Bros Ltd, The Scaplake* [1978] 2 Lloyd's Rep 380, 385, Mocatta J's emphasis upon the fact that P was not prejudiced by T's first proceeding against A.

CHAPTER 11

The relationship between agent and third party

Introduction

Where A enters into a contract on behalf of a disclosed principal, the general rule is that A does not become a party to the contract and he acquires no rights or liabilities under it: the essence of agency is that a contract is completed between P and T. Undoubtedly T will often incorrectly assume that A is personally liable but, provided it is clear that A has contracted for and on behalf of P, A does not become liable to T on any contract. In *Wakefield v Duckworth*,[1] for example, A, a solicitor, ordered photographs from T on behalf of his client, P. Although T alleged that A was liable to pay, it was held that T's only recourse was to P as he knew that the solicitor was acting for a P.[2] The position would, of course, be different if A were to pledge his personal credit.[3] A is still not liable on the contract with T where he has no authority to conclude it on P's behalf,[4] although, as will be seen later, he may be liable to T for *breach of warranty of authority* in such a situation, ie on the warranty that he possesses the requisite authority to act on P's behalf.

It is, nevertheless, quite possible for A to incur personal liability to T on the contract and one obvious situation where A is personally liable is when he acts for an undisclosed principal. However, A may also contract personally when acting for a *disclosed* principal, the nature and extent of his liability being dependent upon the intentions of the parties as manifested in the terms of the contract, the relevant surrounding circumstances and any pertinent and provable custom. Stoljar[5] emphasised that confusion was introduced into the question of the parties' liability at the end of the 18th and beginning of the 19th centuries by the theory of election[6] which was responsible for the notion that liability was alternative, ie where A acts for a disclosed principal, there is *either* a contract between P and T *or* one between A and T, but there could

---

1 [1915] 1 KB 218.
2 See also *Royle v Busby & Son* (1880) 6 QBD 171 (solicitor not liable for sheriff's fees merely because he lodged a writ at the sheriff's office on behalf of a judgment creditor).
3 *Newton v Chambers* (1844) 13 LJQB 141.
4 'I think in no case where it appears that a man did not intend to bind himself, but only to make a contract for a principal, can he be sued as principal, merely because there was no authority': *Lewis v Nicholson* (1852) 18 QB 503, 511 per Lord Campbell CJ.
5 *The Law of Agency* (1961), pp 235-238.
6 See Ch 10.

not be a duality of relationships between P and T *and* A and T. In essence, there is no reason why there should not be two such relationships (as in cases of the undisclosed principal) and some recent decisions have favoured this view[7] but it is difficult to know when this interpretation might be adopted[8] and, overall, where A undertakes liability, the prevailing attitude is that he is solely liable to T, to the exclusion of P.

The contractual liability of the agent

LIABILITY ON CONTRACTS UNDER SEAL

Where A is party to a deed and executes it in his own name, he will be personally liable on it, *even* where he is described in the deed as acting on behalf of a *named* P.[9] This question was considered in Chapter 10 in relation to deeds and P's rights and liabilities, ie P may *not* sue or be sued on any deed, even if it is said to be executed on his behalf, unless he is named as a party to it and it is executed in his name. Thus if A wishes to escape liability he must execute the deed as P's deed in this way.[10]

LIABILITY ON NEGOTIABLE INSTRUMENTS

If A's signature does not appear on the instrument, he will not be personally liable[11] and, likewise, he will not incur liability where he signs clearly indicating his *representative* capacity, the paradigmatic form being that A acts 'for and on behalf of' P. However, if A merely adds *descriptive* words indicating nothing other than his character as an agent, he will be personally liable.[12] Lord Ellenborough CJ stipulated succinctly that, to avoid liability, A must indicate plainly that he is 'a mere scribe'.[13] Particularly strict rules apply to signatures by officers of companies under the Companies Act 1985, s 349(4).[14]

7   Eg *International Rly Co v Niagara Parks Commission* [1941] AC 328, 342 per Luxmoore LJ; *Bridges & Salmon Ltd v The Swan (Owner), The Swan* [1968] 1 Lloyd's Rep 5.
8   See Reynolds, 'Personal Liability of an Agent' (1969) 85 LQR 92.
9   *Cass v Rudele* (1692) 2 Vern 280 (A contracted by deed, on behalf of P, to buy certain houses and pay £800 for them. Held that A was personally liable to pay that sum); *Hancock v Hodgson* (1827) 12 Moore CP 504 (directors of a company contracted by deed to buy a mine and were held personally liable for the price even though the deed recited that they were acting on behalf of the company).
10 See also the Powers of Attorney Act 1971, s 7(1).
11 Bills of Exchange Act 1882, s 23.
12 Bills of Exchange Act 1882, s 26(1).
13 *Leadbitter v Farrow* (1816) 5 M & S 345, 349.
14 This section provides that if an officer of a company or a person on its behalf signs or authorises to be signed on behalf of the company any bill of exchange, promissory note, endorsement, cheque or order for money or goods in which the company's name is not mentioned in legible characters, he is liable to a fine and is personally liable on the instrument unless payment is made by the company. The original purpose of this section was to ensure that T was not misled into thinking he was contracting with an organisation having unlimited liability when, in fact, he was dealing with a limited company: see *Atkin v Wardle* (1889) 5 TLR 734; *Durham Fancy Goods Ltd v Michael Jackson (Fancy Goods) Ltd* [1968] 2 QB 839; *Jenice Ltd v Dan* [1993] BCLC 1349.

LIABILITY WHERE THE AGENT ACTS ON BEHALF OF A FOREIGN PRINCIPAL

A strong presumption of fact used to exist that if A, in England, contracted on behalf of a foreign principal, disclosed or undisclosed, A assumed personal liability and had no authority to pledge the foreign principal's credit by creating privity of contract between P and T.[15] Thus only A could sue and be sued on the contract. The idea that A should be personally liable was based upon the difficulties inherent with foreign trade in an era of poor communications over long distances. As a seller of goods, T would often be unwilling to extend credit to someone who was not subject to the same law as himself and he might face interminable difficulties in locating a foreign debtor;[16] conversely, the foreign principal would also benefit from the certainty of the position.

The status of the presumption began to weaken in later cases[17] and in *Teheran-Europe Co Ltd v S T Belton (Tractors) Ltd*,[18] the Court of Appeal held that the presumption no longer existed but that the existence of a foreign principal might be one factor to consider in assessing the intent of the parties. Interestingly, Diplock LJ said that the presence of a foreign principal could be important in determining whether the mutual intent of T and A 'was that the agent should be personally liable to be sued as well as the principal'.[19] This indicates that, on appropriate facts, *both* A and P might be liable instead of the previous position that A was exclusively liable.

LIABILITY WHERE THE AGENT ACTS ON BEHALF OF A
NON-EXISTENT PRINCIPAL

Where A purports to act on behalf of a principal who is non-existent or fictitious, A may be personally liable on the contract, the situation commonly arising where A acts for a company which has not been registered or for an unincorporated association such as a club or society which has no legal personality. As they are not legal persons, neither the unregistered company nor the unincorporated association can be bound contractually. This question was considered in Chapter 3 in relation to the ratification of pre-incorporation contracts. It will be remembered that considerable difficulties were caused because it was most unclear when A might be liable: although he could be personally liable on the contract where he purported to act as an agent for an unformed company (as in *Kelner v Baxter*[20]) the contract might be a nullity where it was purportedly that of the non-existent company itself, with A's signature being simply an authentication (as in *Newborne v Sensolid (GB) Ltd*).[1]

---

15 *Paterson v Gandasequi* (1812) 15 East 62 (see Ch 10); *Smyth v Anderson* (1849) 7 CB 21; *Elbinger Act für Fabrikatur von Eisenbahn Material v Claye* (1873) LR 8 QB 313; *Hutton v Bullock* (1874) LR 9 QB 572. See Hudson, 'Agents for Foreign Principals' (1966) 29 MLR 353; Stoljar, *The Law of Agency* (1961), pp 238-242.
16 See *Armstrong v Stokes* (1872) LR 7 QB 598, 605 per Blackburn J.
17 Eg *Brandt (H O) & Co v Morris & Co* [1917] 2 KB 784; *Maritime Stores Ltd v H P Marshall & Co Ltd* [1963] 1 Lloyd's Rep 602.
18 [1968] 2 QB 545 (foreign P had the right to sue T for alleged breach of implied conditions relating to the quality/fitness of the goods).
19 [1968] 2 QB 545 at 558.
20 (1866) LR 2 CP 174.
 1 [1954] 1 QB 45.

In many of the non-existent principal cases where T is unaware of the true position, A's liability might better be justified as resting upon breach of warranty of authority although, as will be seen later, there is a difficulty here as damages recoverable from A are assessed on the basis of T's recourse to P, and so they would be nominal where the non-existent company has no funds. Alternatively, A's liability in deceit or negligence would be a realistic possibility. In any event, in relation to limited companies, the position has been greatly improved by the Companies Act 1985, s 36C(1)[2] which provides for the personal liability of A where the contract purports to be made 'by or on behalf of a company' which has not been formed.

Similarly, A may be personally liable where he purports to contract on behalf of an unincorporated association which has a fluctuating membership and no legal personality[3] but much will necessarily turn on the facts and the construction of the contract.[4] In these situations, T frequently knows the status of the association as the supposed principal. It is thus arguable that he is deemed to know that the club or society has no legal existence and so, if A purports to act on behalf of the club, he does not warrant any authority and cannot be liable for breach of warranty of authority. A finding that the agent is personally liable may thus reflect the true intent of the parties.

LIABILITY WHERE THE AGENT IS PROVED TO BE THE REAL PRINCIPAL

There are *dicta* in some older cases[5] supporting the notion that, where A purports to contract as an agent but is, in fact, the principal, he may be personally liable on the contract. The cases are, however, hardly conclusive and were decided at the time when A was thought to be personally liable where he was unauthorised, this being the view before the action for breach of warranty of authority was established. It was realised later that A could not be liable on the contract unless he had undertaken personal liability and thus, as *Bowstead & Reynolds*[6] stresses, if A purports to act for a principal (whether named or unnamed) but has no authority from P and in reality acts for himself, A should correctly be liable for breach of warranty of authority or in tort. However, the action for breach of warranty of authority has profound limitations as damages are based on T's recourse to P and so A's personal liability on the contract has an attractive simplicity from T's perspective.

Undoubtedly there is an inclination to accept the view that A may be personally liable on the contract where, in reality, he is acting for himself. The cases here are abstruse, to say the least. In *Gardiner v Heading*,[7] it was unclear whether A was acting as an agent and, although T clearly considered that he was so acting, A was held to be personally liable on the contract. In *Gardiner*, a builder (T)

---

2 Inserted by the Companies Act 1989, s 130(4).
3 *Bradley Egg Farm Ltd v Clifford* [1943] 2 All ER 378.
4 See eg *Jones v Hope* (1880) 3 TLR 247; *Steele v Gourley* (1887) 3 TLR 772; Lloyd, *Law of Unincorporated Associations* (1938); Warburton, *Unincorporated Associations: Law and Practice* (1986).
5 See *Railton v Hodgson* (1804) 4 Taunt 576n; *Jenkins v Hutchinson* (1849) 13 QB 744; *Carr v Jackson* (1852) 7 Exch 382; *Adams v Hall* (1877) 37 LT 70.
6 *Bowstead & Reynolds on Agency* (16th edn, 1996), Art 110, para 9-085.
7 [1928] 2 KB 284.

had done work for the Finance Guarantee Company (FGC) on the orders of A, a director of the company. As T had not been paid, he went to the offices of FGC and A told T that he had 'another job' for him; A then took T to the premises where the work was neeeded. As the building work progressed, T made out the estimates to FGC and A did not object. Finally, T was told to paint the name 'Metropolitan Housing Corporation Ltd' (MHC) on the front of the premises. On completion of the work, T sought payment from FGC but he was told by another director of that company that the work had not been done for FGC but, instead, had been ordered for MHC, a company in which A held one share. T tried repeatedly to obtain payment from A and eventually succeeded in an action against him. Scrutton LJ[8] considered that the situation was analogous to that of the undisclosed principal who can be sued when discovered: it followed that here A could be sued when he was revealed as the real principal. Romer J[9] added that A had ordered the work and 'just as he did not say he was an agent, so he did not say he was a principal. But in law he contracted so as to make himself prima facie liable personally'.

A was also personally liable in the curious case of *Hersom v Bernett*.[10] There T bought peppermint oil from A who purported to act for an undisclosed principal. In fact, the oil had been stolen and had to be surrendered to the real owner and so T sued A to recover the price paid to A. A then pleaded that his principal was named Williams but the court rejected that plea as false and it was held that A was personally liable. Roxburgh J said that, where A has given false evidence as to his principal, he should not be allowed to assert that the principal is someone else 'but must thereafter be treated as having no principal; or, in other words, as being himself the principal'.[11] As emphasised by *Bowstead & Reynolds*,[12] these two propositions are not equivalent and, although it is the first which seems correct, in *Hersom* the court appeared to apply the second. There is also authority that A may *sue* on the contract when he is shown to be the real principal, this question being considered later when A's contractual rights are examined.

LIABILITY ON WRITTEN AND ORAL CONTRACTS

Written contracts

Whether A has contracted personally on written contracts (other than deeds and bills of exchange) is a question of the intent of the parties to be deduced from the terms of the written agreement as a whole. The decisions promulgate the rule, originally formulated in relation to deeds and negotiable instruments, considered earlier, that A's *descriptive* signature is binding upon him personally whereas A's *representative* signature will exonerate him from liability and bind P. Moreover, the parol evidence rule has exerted a pervasive influence in its not allowing the admission of extrinsic evidence to contradict the writing. Certainty is engendered by both the parol evidence rule and the supposition that A's unqualified signature should bind him personally, and this was obviously a prime requirement in many of the situations discussed above where T needed to rely

---

8 [1928] 2 KB 284 at 290.
9 [1928] 2 KB 284 at 292.
10 [1955] 1 QB 98.
11 [1955] 1 QB 98 at 103.
12 *Bowstead & Reynolds on Agency* (16th edn, 1996), Art 110, para 9-086.

on the liability of the person designated in a deed or a negotiable instrument which was transferable, for example. However, in the case of other written contracts, the application of technical and often arbitrary distinctions regarding the form of A's signature may mean that the true intent of the parties is obscured. By and large, the decisions have espoused a robust, mercantile pragmatism but, at the same time, they have generated a plethora of over-subtle distinctions.

The basic rule is that A will be deemed to have contracted personally if he signs the contract in his own name without any qualification, unless a contrary intention is manifest elsewhere in the document. In *Parker v Winlow*,[13] a memorandum of a charter-party was expressed to be made between 'Captain Parker ... and G W Winlow, agent for E Winlow & Son' and was signed by G W Winlow without any qualification. It was held that G W Winlow was personally liable even though he named his principal because 'mere words of description attached to the name of a contractor, such as are used here, saying he is agent for another, cannot limit his liability as contractor'.[14] The warning was given that 'mercantile men ... must use restrictive words, as if they sign per procuration, or use some other words to express that they are not to be personally liable'.[15] It is thus clear that, even though the fact of an agency is obvious, A can nevertheless be personally liable.

The courts have subsequently sought to apply the distinction between descriptive and representative signatures and words. In *Gadd v Houghton*,[16] fruit brokers (A) in Liverpool gave T the following sold-note: 'We have this day sold to you on account of James Morand & Co, Valencia, 2000 cases Valencia oranges'. Although the brokers signed the contract without any qualification, it was held that the words 'on account of' showed an intention to make P liable and the brokers were thus not liable for non-delivery of the fruit. James LJ considered that 'when a man says he is making a contract "on account of" someone else ... he uses the very strongest terms the English language affords to shew that he is not binding himself, but is binding his principal'.[17]

Gadd's case was approved by the House of Lords in *Universal Steam Navigation Co Ltd v James McKelvie & Co*[18] where a charterparty of a steamer was expressed to be made 'between T H Seed & Co Ltd, agents for the owners, and James McKelvie & Co, Charterers'. The contract was signed 'For and on behalf of James McKelvie & Co (as agents). J A McKelvie'. The owners were aware at the time the charter-party was signed that McKelvie & Co were not the actual charterers but were acting as agents for their principal in Rome. It was held that, although McKelvie & Co were described as charterers in the body of the charter-party, they were not liable for demurrage as they had signed 'as agents'. Viscount Cave LC held that these words clearly showed that McKelvie & Co had no intention of being personally bound and 'unless they had that meaning, they appear to me to have no sense or meaning at all'.[19]

The *Gadd* and *McKelvie* decisions make a rational evaluation from which it is hard to dissent, but the distinctions drawn between representative and

---

13 (1857) 7 E & B 942.
14 (1857) 7 E & B 942 at 949 per Crompton J.
15 (1857) 7 E & B 942 at 949 per Crompton J.
16 (1876) 1 Ex D 357.
17 (1876) 1 Ex D 357 at 359.
18 [1923] AC 492.
19 [1923] AC 492 at 495.

descriptive signatures are difficult to apply in practice and there is little consistency in the cases. It is clear that an agent may be personally liable where he is merely described as such, ie 'A, agent', either by the form of his signature or in the body of the contract,[20] yet *McKelvie's* case acknowledges that the phrase 'as agents' appended to A's signature is indicative that A is not bound.[1] The more recent decisons arguably endorse a stricter approach than that in *McKelvie's* case and illustrate that A must be cautious if he is to avoid liability. In *The Virgo*,[2] a clause on the first page of a charter-party referred to the defendant agents as 'charterers' of the vessel while clause 31 provided that the vessel was chartered 'on behalf and for account of General Organization for Supply Goods Cairo', but there were no words attached to the signature of the defendants to indicate their status as anything other than a principal. At first instance, it was held that the defendants were not personally liable for demurrage for, otherwise, no 'worthwhile meaning'[3] could be attributed to clause 31, but the decision was reversed by the Court of Appeal. It was emphasised that, taking the contract as a whole, the intention was that the defendants should be personally liable and, although no general rule applied to the weight to be given to wording according to its *location* in a contract, it would be remarkable if clause 31 (which was a rider clause) were dominant over the earlier clause where the defendants were clearly described as charterers.

The same conclusion was reached in *The Frost Express*.[4] There the plaintiff agents were managers of a pool of vessels owned by various shipowners. The

---

20 *Parker v Winlow* (supra); *Bridges & Salmon Ltd v The Swan (Owner),The Swan* [1968] 1 Lloyd's Rep 5, 13 per Brandon J. Powell emphasises (*The Law of Agency*, 2nd edn, 1961, p 249) that a signature 'AB, agent' is 'simply a description of AB and is as ineffective, by itself, to exclude his liability as if he had signed "AB, grocer"'. In *Sika Contracts Ltd v B L Gill and Closeglen Properties Ltd* (1978) 9 BLR 11, Gill, an engineer, entered into a contract with the plaintiff for the repair of beams in premises owned by the second defendant. Gill signed the acceptance for the quotation in his own name adding 'Chartered Civil Engineer'. Kerr J acknowledged that, in practice, it was unusual for a professional man to add 'as agent only' to his signature but Gill was nevertheless held to be liable; the fact of his acting in a professional capacity did not exclude his personal liability.

1   In *McKelvie*, Lord Sumner doubted (p 501) that when 'agents' was added to the signature it should be construed as being merely descriptive because 'one's signature is not the place in which to advertise one's calling, nor is "agent" ordinarily used to describe a trade, as "tailor" or "butcher" would be'. But he admitted that 'when people add "agent" to a signature to a contract, they are trying to escape personal liability, but are unaware that the attempt will fail'. He added that in construing the words 'as agents', a distinction should be drawn between 'and as agents' and 'only as agents' – only the latter construction would exclude A's liability.

2   *Tudor Marine Ltd v Tradax Export SA, The Virgo* [1976] 2 Lloyd's Rep 135; see also *Pyxis Special Shipping Co Ltd v Dritsas & Kaglis Bros Ltd, The Scaplake* [1978] 2 Lloyd's Rep 380 (A was named in a charter-party as charterer and the contract was signed by A without qualification but also signed on the reverse by P and clause 29 provided that 'freight and demurrage will be guaranteed by the actual charterers, [P]' and, again, this was signed by P. It was held that P was liable as a contracting party); *Jugoslavenska Linijska Plovidba v Hulsman (t/a Brusse & Sippel Import-Export), The Primorje* [1980] 2 Lloyd's Rep 74 (negotiations started for the shipment of goods, the charterers described as '[A] on account of Indonesian Government'. In fresh negotiations for a different vessel, the statement regarding the Indonesian Government was not repeated, several telexes and the charter-party described A as charterer and A never objected, but the charter-party was not signed by A. It was held that A was personally liable).

3   [1976] 2 Lloyd's Rep 135 at 141, per Mocatta J.

4   *Seatrade Groningen BV v Geest Industries Ltd, The Frost Express* [1996] 2 Lloyd's Rep 375.

agents chartered *Frost Express* to the defendants and in box 3, which was headed 'Owners/Place of business', it was A's name which was typed with the qualification 'as agents to Owners or as Disponent Owners'. In the box which was headed 'Signature (Owners)', the managing director of the plaintiff agents had signed his name without any qualification. The cargo of bananas was improperly refrigerated and it was alleged that A had undertaken personal liability on the contract. At first instance, it was held that A was not liable: Gatehouse J held that parol evidence was admissible to resolve the ambiguity in box 3 and that evidence indicated that the defendants knew that A was merely the manager of a pool of vesels. The mutual intent of the parties was thus that A contracted as an agent for the vessel's owner. The Court of Appeal reversed that decision and held that it was 'clear beyond doubt'[5] that A was liable; the qualification 'as agents' in box 3 did not exclude A's personal liability in view of the fact that his signature was unqualified.

It is plain from the decisions considered above that specific formulae cannot be regarded as prescriptive: the question of A's liability depends upon an objective assessment of the parties' intentions and the construction of the entirety of the written contract in dispute.[6] Many of the decisions undoubtedly turn upon upon fine distinctions but, as Stoljar[7] stresses, many of the older cases were often concerned only superficially with stereotyped wording. The real problem was whether A could sue T for non-delivery of goods and obtain his commission where P was a foreign buyer and would take no direct action[8] or, alternatively, whether A should be liable on a charter-party for demurrage where P was foreign and thus difficult to proceed against.

Parol evidence in relation to written contracts

When written contracts are being construed, the question of the admissibility of extrinsic evidence is of paramount importance. Might A escape liability by establishing that, although the written contract indicates that he is personally liable, parol or other extrinsic evidence indicates that he was acting purely as an agent? The general rule is that extrinsic evidence cannot be adduced to *contradict* the written contract, thereby deleting A and relieving him of liability as a contracting party. In *Higgins v Senior*,[9] A, the defendant, acted on behalf of P in selling 1,000 tons of iron to the plaintiff, T, but the sold note made no mention of P and was signed 'John Senior & Co, William Senior'. No iron was ever delivered and Parke B held that A was personally liable. It is clear from the decision that extrinsic evidence may be adduced to *add* P's liability to that of A (eg P is undisclosed) as this does not entail any contradiction of the written terms. In any event, the parol evidence rule applies only where the parties' intention is that their contract be contained *exclusively* in the writing and it follows that

---

5 [1996] 2 Lloyd's Rep 375 at 378, per Evans LJ.
6 See eg *Bridges & Salmon Ltd v The Swan (Owner), The Swan* [1968] 1 Lloyd's Rep 5, 12 per Brandon J.
7 *The Law of Agency* (1961), pp 255-256.
8 See *Brandt (H O) & Co v H N Morris & Co Ltd* [1917] 2 KB 784, where A bought oil for P in the USA, the bought-note stipulating that A bought 'for and on behalf of' P, although there was nothing in the body of the contract limiting A's rights as a principal. It was held that A could maintain an action for damages for non-delivery, this conclusion being aided by the fact that, in time of war, the destination of the goods had to be indicated.
9 (1841) 8 M & W 834.

extrinsic evidence is admissible where they do not intend the document to articulate the entirety of the contractual undertakings.[10]

Moreover, where A contracts in writing in a representative capacity as an agent only, extrinsic evidence is admissible to clarify[11] the contract and resolve any ambiguity. It would thus be possible to establish the identity of P because this would not contradict the written terms. It should be noted that, in *The Frost Express*,[12] the Court of Appeal held that the contract was unambiguous both as to the identity of A and the fact that he undertook personal liability and so extrinsic evidence was inadmissible as an aid to construction.

Finally, even though A contracts as an agent, evidence of a custom or usage is admissible to show that A is personally liable, provided that the custom or usage is neither inconsistent with, nor repugnant to, the express terms of the written contract. For example, in *Hutchinson v Tatham*,[13] A signed a charter-party 'as agent to merchants' and it was held that, although A did not intend to contract personally, evidence was admissible to prove a custom that, if A did not name his principal within a reasonable time, he would be personally liable. Here the custom was not inconsistent with the written contract as P still carried the primary liability but A could become liable if he did not identify his principal.

Oral contracts

In the case of oral contracts there can, of necessity, be no argument relating to the parol evidence rule and the question of whether A contracted personally is largely a question of fact: the terms of the contract must be examined and their effect ascertained. The facts of the *The Swan*[14] epitomise the difficulties which are encountered. A fishing vessel was owned by J D Rodger (JDR) who formed a company (JDR Ltd) to hire it from him and operate it. Orders were given to the plaintiffs by JDR to repair the vessel, these instructions being partly oral and partly in writing on the company's notepaper and signed 'JDR Director'. The plaintiff's account was sent to the company which could not pay and so JDR was sued. It was held that, although JDR contracted as an agent for JDR Ltd, when a shipowner discussed repairs with a ship-repairer it was natural to assume that the shipowner accepted personal liability unless the contrary were made clear and, as JDR had not done that, he was personally liable. Here JDR had not expressly referred to himself as an agent and his signature was merely descriptive but, on the other hand, the plaintiff repairer had sent his bill to the company. Accordingly, Brandon J considered the case to be 'somewhat near the borderline, with strong arguments available either way'[15] but the fact of JDR's being a shipowner tipped the balance against him.

---

10 *Rogers v Hadley* (1861) 2 H & C 227 (parol evidence was admissible to show that bought and sold notes did not contain the entire contract between the parties. Wilde B said that 'in order to establish a written contract it is necessary to prove, not merely that a certain paper bears the signatures of the parties, but that in so signing they made a contract' (p 256)).
11 *McCollin v Gilpin* (1881) 6 QBD 516.
12 *Seatrade Groningen BV v Geest Industries Ltd, The Frost Express* [1996] 2 Lloyd's Rep 375 (considered ante).
13 (1873) LR 8 CP 482.
14 *Bridges & Salmon Ltd v The Swan (Owner), The Swan* [1968] 1 Lloyd's Rep 5.
15 [1968] 1 Lloyd's Rep 5 at 13.

It is a difficult question to decide whether A might be liable where P is *unnamed* but the fact of an *agency* is disclosed. With contracts wholly in writing, this would be one factor to consider, along with those discussed above, in deciding whether A might be personally liable. However, where the agency is disclosed, it is arguable that the general rule that A contracts on behalf of P should be dominant in both written and oral contracts, on the basis that T intends to contract with P whoever he may be,[16] unless T can prove otherwise and establish A's liability. Nevertheless, it is equally clear that the opposite view might be tenable in some situations on the basis that P's being unnamed might lead to the presumption that T looks primarily to A as the identified and trusted party. The litigation in *The Santa Carina*[17] illustrates these two perspectives. Both the plaintiffs and defendants were brokers and members of the Baltic Exchange, the plaintiffs' main function being to act as an agent in supplying bunkers and fuel to ships throughout the world. The defendants telephoned the plaintiffs and the latter agreed to supply fuel oil to *Santa Carina*, knowing that the defendants were acting as agents for charterers of the vessel. The invoices were sent to the defendants and, eventually, the plaintiffs commenced proceedings against the defendants. At first instance,[18] Mocatta J was influenced by the cases on written contracts and held that, although it was clear that the defendants were agents, they were personally liable as they had not indicated that they were to be free of liability. The decision was reversed by the Court of Appeal on the basis that, as the defendants were known to be agents,[19] it was for the plaintiffs to prove that they should be personally liable and this they had failed to do. Lord Denning MR considered that (i) the cases on written contracts could not apply rigidly to oral contracts and (ii) there can be situations where A does not name P and, because P's credit and standing are unknown to T, T may look to A for personal liability but, in other cases, T looks to P, whoever he may be, the facts of *The Santa Carina* clearly falling into the latter category.[20] Overall, this approach does not fit happily with the earlier decision in *The Swan*, but the general tenor of the law seems to be that, with both named and unnamed principals, A is not to be personally liable unless there is precise evidence to the contrary.[1]

---

16 *Teheran-Europe Co Ltd v S T Belton (Tractors) Ltd* [1968] 2 QB 545, 555 per Diplock LJ.
17 *N & J Vlassopulos Ltd v Ney Shipping Ltd, The Santa Carina* [1977] 1 Lloyd's Rep 478.
18 [1976] 2 Lloyd's Rep 223.
19 *The Santa Carina* extends the notion of the unnamed P to situations where the fact of A's agency gives notice of a P. The normal unnamed P entails A's express reference to the existence of a P, eg 'bought for my P'.
20 The *Restatement, Second, Agency* § 321 takes a middle course between the extremes represented in *The Santa Carina* and provides that, where P is unnamed, A is liable (unless otherwise agreed) as a party to the contract. The inference is that A is liable *together* with P. See Reynolds, 'Practical Problems of the Undisclosed Principal Doctrine' [1983] CLP 119 where it is asserted that *The Santa Carina's* reasoning exonerates A in some cases where he might properly be regarded as undertaking liability and thus the author suggests that the *Restatement's* rule be adopted in England.
 1 Eg *Wilson v Avec Audio-Visual Equipment Ltd* [1974] 1 Lloyd's Rep 81, 83 per Edmund Davies LJ: 'It requires clear and precise evidence of a very special relationship before an agent can be rendered personally liable in respect of a contract entered into on behalf of his principal'.

The contractual rights of the agent

When A contracts in a representative capacity on behalf of P, the basic rule follows that of A's liability and, generally, A cannot sue on the contract.[2] However, where the intention of the parties is that A should be party to the contract, he clearly has both rights and liabilities under it.

In *Short v Spackman*,[3] the plaintiff brokers (A) were authorised to buy Greenland whale oil on behalf of P and employed an oil broker to act for them. The defendant seller of the oil was unwilling to sell to A but, on being told that A was acting for an unnamed principal, he agreed to sell to A, the bought note stating 'Bought for Messrs Short, Brown and Bowyer' (the plaintiff brokers) 'of Mr W F Spackman' (the defendant). Under a general authority from P, A then re-sold the oil to Buck & Co but, when informed of this, P renounced the sale. The defendants did not deliver the oil and A had to pay a sum of money to Buck & Co in settlement. The defendants contended that P's repudiation of the contract and A's acquiescence therein terminated the engagement between themselves and A but it was held that, as A had contracted personally with the defendants he could sue them, and P's repudiation of the contract did not affect the position.

Apart from the rule that A may be party to the contract with T, as in *Short* above, there are also some specific situations where A is entitled to sue on the contract. First, where P is undisclosed A is both personally liable and entitled to sue on the contract and, although P may intervene, the general rule is that his intervention must not prejudice T's right to sue A if he so wishes.[4]

Second, there are numerous cases on factors and auctioneers which establish that these agents can sue the buyer of the goods, T, for the price, the old cases being justified on the basis of such agents having 'special property' in the goods or a lien over them.[5] The more modern tendency is to explain the auctioneer's right to sue on the basis that he enters into a collateral contract with T.[6] Although the cases on factors are redundant in this context, the auctioneer's right to sue still prevails and applies even though he has been paid a sum sufficient to cover his commission.[7] It is now accepted that, in relation to other agents, A's having a *routine* interest in the contract's completion, eg the earning of commission, is insufficient, *per se*, to allow him to sue upon it.[8]

---

2   Eg *Fawkes v Lamb* (1862) 31 LJQB 98 (a broker who signed a contract note in a representative capacity had no right to sue the buyer for the price); *Fairlie v Fenton* (1870) LR 5 Exch 169 (a broker had no right to sue the buyer for not accepting the goods).

3   (1831) 2 B & Ad 962.

4   *O'Herlihy v Hedges* (1803) 1 Sch & Lef 123.

5   'An auctioneer has a possession, coupled with an interest, in goods which he is employed to sell, not a bare custody like a servant or shopman ... [and] also a special property in him, with a lien for the charges of the sale, the commission, and the auction duty, which he is bound to pay': *Williams v Millington* (1788) 1 Hy Bl 81, 84 per Lord Loughborough CJ. In *Williams*, A sold goods for a named P on P's premises. T bought goods at the sale and paid part of the price but, for the remainder, T claimed to set-off a debt owed to him by P. It was held that, as A had paid P in full for the goods, he could recover the full price of the goods from T.

6   See *Benton v Campbell, Parker & Co Ltd* [1925] 2 KB 410, 416 per Salter J.

7   *Chelmsford Auctions Ltd v Poole* [1973] QB 542 (T bought a car at auction for £57, A's commission being £3.50. T paid a deposit of £7 and thus A's claim was satisfied but it was held that, as A had paid P from his own funds, A could recover the balance of the price from T).

8   Eg *Fairlie v Fenton* (1870) LR 5 Exch 169.

Can A sue on the contract when he has purported to act as an agent but is shown to be the real principal?

In essence, it seems theoretically incorrect and potentially unjust to T if A is allowed to change his character to that of a principal. This was clearly the view of Lord Ellenborough CJ in *Bickerton v Burrell*,[9] where the main ground of the decision was that A could not undergo instant mutation and become the principal, but some judgments questioned whether A might do so if he gave *notice* to T of the true position. By borrowing from the pragmatism of the undisclosed principal, it could thus be argued that A should be able to change character to that of a principal and sue T, provided that no hardship accrues to T. The latter approach seems dominant and there is clear authority that A may sue T (i) where identity is not a material factor in the contract's formation and A gives notice to T that he is the real principal before any action is commenced or, (ii) where the contract has been partly performed by T with full knowledge that A is the real principal. In *Rayner v Grote*,[10] A purported to sell goods on behalf of a *named* principal in a *written* contract. T, the buyer, accepted and paid for part of the goods having had notice that A was the real principal. It was held that A could sue T for non-acceptance of the remainder of the goods. Alderson B emphasised that A's change of status to that of a principal would not be permitted where 'the skill or solvency of the person who is named as the principal [is] a material ingredient in the contract'[11] and suggested that, as a general rule, A should not be permitted to sue where the contract is executory and wholly unperformed or where it is partly performed by T without knowledge of who is the real principal.[12]

Although there are adequate safeguards here for T, A's permitted change of character contradicts the normal rule of agency that T contracts with the named principal. Similarly, it is difficult to see how the rule could apply where the terms of the contract exclude A from being a party to it and, where the contract is in writing, the parol evidence rule will be contravened as the contract terms are *contradicted* by the deletion of the named principal and the substitution of A as the real principal. Moreover, in many of these cases where A's status changes, T should be able to plead misrepresentation. However, if A were *not* allowed to sue, it would often mean that T would be unjustly enriched as he would not have to pay for goods delivered (eg on the facts of *Rayner v Grote*).

Where P is *unnamed*, the general rule follows the named principal situations and A can intervene and reveal himself as the real principal. Here it is clearly difficult for T to allege that P's identity was important to him at the date of contract and thus A's revelation as P can rarely be prejudicial to T. This notion is allowed considerable latitude in the cases. In *Schmaltz v Avery*,[13] it was held that A could reveal himself as P and sue on a charter-party where it was expressed to be made between 'G Schmaltz & Co (agents for the freighter)' and the defendant shipowner.

---

9   (1816) 5 M & S 383, 386.
10   (1846) 15 M & W 359.
11   (1846) 15 M & W 359 at 365.
12   This approach was followed in *Gewa Chartering BV v Remco Shipping Lines Ltd, The Remco* [1984] 2 Lloyd's Rep 205 (A, the chartering broker of a firm, chartered a vessel from the owners who were given the impression that the charterers were a large trading group known to the owner's broker. It was held that the firm for which A acted could not enforce the contract; the identity of the other contracting party and responsibility for the payment of freight were material to the owners).
13   (1851) 16 QB 655.

The court accepted that the opposite conclusion might be reached should P's identity be material to T, but that such a consideration could apply only to a named principal. Accordingly, A was allowed to prove that he was the freighter on the basis that P's identity was a matter of indifference to the defendant, T, who did not even bother to enquire who P was. Moreover, the court thought that A's intervention did not contradict the written contract as he could be considered as 'filling two characters, namely those of agent and principal'.[14]

Schmaltz was followed in *Harper & Co v Vigers Bros*,[15] where commercial pragmatism was undoubtedly over-extended. A shipbroker (A) entered into a charter-party with the defendant (T) for the supply of a vessel to be named later. A was said to be acting 'by authority of and as agents for the owners' and the freight was specified. In fact, A had no principal and had not arranged for a vessel to carry the cargo but, instead, he was attempting to speculate on freight charges and obtain brokers' fees, ie if A could only secure a ship at more than the specified freight he would pay the difference himself and so lose money but, if he obtained a ship at a lower rate than that specified in the contract, he would keep the difference. A later chartered a ship at a lower rate from shipowners, A being described as 'agents for charterers' and T's name being inserted as charterer. Again A was acting as a principal and not on behalf of T. Eventually a dispute arose as to the freight which was payable, T arguing that the lower rate was payable, but then A revealed himself as principal and claimed the higher rate. It was held that A should succeed (although his costs were disallowed) even though Pickford J conceded that if T had known the true position he would probably not have made the contract.

It is doubtful whether these cases would be followed today[16] and many of the criticisms of the named principal situation are applicable to the unnamed principal, although the identity notion has significantly less force. However, even where P is unnamed, T should surely be able to argue successfully that his contract is with P and it is unacceptable to make his protection dependent upon possible hardship which, as the facts of *Harper* show, may be difficult to establish.

The agent's liability for breach of warranty of authority

THE BASIS OF THE AGENT'S LIABILITY

A may represent, by words or conduct, that he has authority to act on P's behalf when he lacks such authority. If T is induced by A's representation to act in a way in which he would not have done but for the representation, A is deemed to warrant that the representation is true and will be liable to T for any loss caused. Moreover, A can be liable for breach of warranty of authority even where he acts in good faith under the mistaken impression that he has authority from P.

At the start of the 19th century, some cases decided that if A had no authority from P he would be personally liable on the contract[17] but it was soon realised that A could not be liable contractually unless he had contracted personally and

14 (1851) 16 QB 655 at 663 per Patteson J.
15 [1909] 2 KB 549.
16 See the criticism in *Hill Steamship Co Ltd v Hugo Stinnes Ltd* 1941 SC 324; see also *Sharman v Brandt* (1871) LR 6 QB 720.
17 *Thomas v Hewes* (1834) 2 Cr & M 519, 530n; *Jones v Downman* (1842) 4 QB 235n; *Downman v Williams* (1845) 7 QB 103.

thus undertaken such liability.[18] Where A fraudulently claimed to have authority and thereby caused loss to T, he could be liable in deceit[19] and if liability for negligent misrepresentation had developed in the 19th century, it is arguable that A would have been liable to T only in deceit or for negligently failing to exercise reasonable care in ascertaining whether or not he had authority. However, A's liability on a separate, implied warranty of authority was firmly established in *Collen v Wright*[20] as a stringent liability which was applicable to the *bona fide*, innocent agent. There a land agent agreed to lease a farm to T for twelve and a half years but P refused to execute the lease and proved that A had, albeit unknowingly, exceeded his authority. It was held that A was liable for breach of warranty of authority and his innocence provided no defence for it did not alleviate the inconvenience and damage sustained by T.

There has been much discussion as to the basis and nature of A's liability for breach of warranty of authority. Although, in essence, this liability could be classified as either contractual or tortious, the late 19th century was characterised by an unwillingness to extend the conspicuously limited remedy in the tort of deceit[1] and a generalised liability for negligent misstatement was initiated only in the 20th century with the momentous decision in *Hedley Byrne & Co Ltd v Heller & Partners Ltd*.[2] Accordingly, as A's liability is strict, it is usually said to be based upon contract,[3] A's undertaking being classified as a collateral contract and unilateral[4] in nature, ie A offers to warrant his authority and T accepts by entering into a contract with P or, as will be seen below, by entering into a transaction with another party.

THE AGENT'S LIABILITY IS STRICT

After the decision in *Yonge v Toynbee*,[5] it could not be doubted that A's liability was strict. There a solicitor (A) was instructed by a client (P) to defend an action

18 *Jenkins v Hutchinson* (1849) 13 QB 744. Lord Campbell CJ stressed in *Lewis v Nicholson* (1852) 18 QB 503, 511, that if A were to be personally liable 'this absurdity would follow, that, if [A], professing to have but not having authority from [P], made a contract that [P] should marry [T], [T] might sue [A] for breach of promise of marriage, even though they were of the same sex'.
19 *Polhill v Walter* (1832) 3 B & Ad 114.
20 (1857) 7 E & B 301; affd 8 E & B 647.
 1 *Derry v Peek* (1889) 14 App Cas 337; Brown and Chandler, 'Deceit, Damages and the Misrepresentation Act 1967, s 2(1)' [1992] LMCLQ 40.
 2 [1964] AC 465.
 3 *Lewis v Nicholson* (1852) 18 QB 503, 511 and 515 per Lord Campbell CJ and Crompton J respectively; *Yonge v Toynbee* [1910] 1 KB 215, 228 per Buckley LJ; *Edwards v Porter* [1925] AC 1 per Lords Atkinson (p 23) and Sumner (p 46); *Benton v Campbell* [1925] 2 KB 410, 415 per Salter J; *Penn v Bristol and West Building Society* [1997] 3 All ER 470, 476-477 per Waller LJ.
 4 See *Collen v Wright* (1857) 8 E & B 647, 657-658 per Willes J: 'The obligation arising in such a case is well expressed by saying that a person, professing to contract as agent for another, impliedly, if not expressly, undertakes to or promises the person who enters into such contract, upon the faith of the professed agent being duly authorised, that the authority which he professes to have does in point of fact exist. The fact of entering into the transaction with the professed agent, as such, is good consideration for the promise'; *Rasnoimport V/O v Guthrie & Co Ltd* [1966] 1 Lloyd's Rep 1, 13 per Mocatta J. See also Radcliffe, 'Some Recent Developments of the Doctrine of *Collen v Wright*' (1902) 18 LQR 364, 368-369; Seavey, 'The Rationale of Agency' (1920) 29 Yale LJ 859, 885-886; Wedderburn, 'Collateral Contracts' [1959] CLJ 58, 68.
 5 [1910] 1 KB 215.

which was at that time threatened, and afterwards commenced, against P. Before commencement of the action, P was certified as insane and A's authority was thus terminated but, in ignorance of the insanity, A continued with the action. It was held that the plaintiff (T) could recover the costs of the action from A. The court approved *Collen v Wright*[6] and the decisions which had sought to restrict A's liability to situations where he was negligent[7] were criticised and regarded as wrong. It is clear from *Yonge* that A's liability extends to situations where P has died or where a company has been dissolved,[8] for example.

THE BREADTH OF THE AGENT'S LIABILITY

It is beyond doubt that A's liability has a considerable breadth and scope but it must be emphasised that, despite its width, A is liable only for warranting that he has *authority* from P; as will be seen later, he does not warrant P's solvency, honesty or the fact that P will perform the contract with T.

In *Firbank's Executors v Humphreys*,[9] the plaintiff (T) agreed to construct a railway line for a company (P) and was to be paid in cash but, as P could not pay, T agreed to accept debenture stock in lieu of cash. The defendants (A), who were directors of the company, issued certificates for the debenture stock but, unknown to them, all the debenture stock that the company had power to issue had been already issued and that which T received was valueless. The company subsequently went into liquidation. On behalf of the defendants (A), it was argued that the debentures were issued in fulfilment of a contract which was *binding* upon P whereas, in cases such as *Collen v Wright*, A professed to enter into a contract on behalf of P which was *invalid* as against P. Nevertheless, it was held that the defendants were liable on the implied warranty that they had authority to issue valid debenture stock.[10] Lord Esher MR considered that A can be liable for breach of warranty of authority where he has asserted

---

6 (1857) 7 E & B 301; affd 8 E & B 647.
7 *Smout v Ilbery* (1842) 10 M & W 1 (a husband (P) had dealt with a butcher (T). P went to China and subsequently died. T continued to supply goods to P's wife (A), both T and A being ignorant of the death. It was held that A was not liable to T); *Salton v New Beeston Cycle Co* [1900] 1 Ch 43 (a solicitor (A) was authorised to defend an action on behalf of a company (P) but his authority was determined by the dissolution of the company shortly before trial. Neither A nor the plaintiff (T) knew this fact until after the trial. It was held that A should not be liable in the absence of negligence but, as A knew of the last meeting of the company on the day of the trial, he was put on enquiry as to its dissolution and was liable to T for costs subsequently incurred).
8 *Yonge v Toynbee* [1910] 1 KB 215, 227-228 per Buckley LJ.
9 (1886) 18 QBD 54.
10 See also *Richardson v Williamson* (1871) LR 6 QB 276 (T lent £70 to a building society (P) receiving a certificate of deposit signed by the directors (A). P had no borrowing powers as no rule had been made allowing the building society to borrow. It was held that the directors were liable on an implied warranty that they had authority to borrow); *Weeks v Propert* (1873) LR 8 CP 427 (directors of a company issued a debenture bond when the company had exhausted its borrowing powers and were held liable on an implied warranty that they had authority to issue a valid debenture); *Chapleo v Brunswick Building Society* (1881) 6 QBD 696 (directors of an unincorporated building society held-out the secretary as having authority to borrow in excess of the amount prescribed by the building society's rules. The secretary borrowed in excess of this amount and absconded with the money. It was held that, although they were not fraudulent, the directors were liable to the lender on an implied warranty of authority).

incorrectly that he has the authority of P and thereby 'induces another person to enter into *any transaction* which he would not have entered into but for that assertion'.[11]

The *Firbank* approach was followed by the House of Lords in *Starkey v Bank of England*.[12] There a broker (A), acting in good faith, asked the Bank of England to transfer consols (Government securities) to a purchaser but the power of attorney under which A acted contained the forged signature of one of the two brothers who jointly owned the consols (P). After the death of the brother who had perpetrated the forgery, the remaining brother obtained restitution from the Bank and the House of Lords held that, as A had impliedly warranted his authority to transfer the consols, he must indemnify the Bank. In *Starkey*, the transaction into which the Bank was induced to enter was not with the supposed principal but this was regarded as immaterial, the Earl of Halsbury LC[13] stressing that the crucial question was whether there was a contractual warranty between A and T rather than the issue of whether an abortive contract followed as a consequence of A's representation.

The *Starkey* and *Firbank* decisions undoubtedly extended the notion of implied warranty of authority and were criticised[14] at the time. Those decisions are now beyond doubt, however, and the rule that an (invalid) contract need not result with P as a consequence of A's warranty was followed most recently in *Penn v Bristol and West Building Society*.[15] There Waller LJ[16] accentuated the fact that, although T must provide consideration for A's warranty of authority by acting in reliance on it, that consideration need not entail a contract with P but could be supplied by T's entering into a transaction with a third party. In *Penn*, a husband perpetrated a mortgage fraud in relation to a house which he owned jointly with his wife and forged her signature on documents. The wife was unaware of the fraud which was to consist of the purported sale of the house and the receipt of money in the form of a mortgage loan from the defendant building society. A solicitor (A), who mistakenly believed that he had authority from the wife (P) to negotiate the sale of the house, was liable to the defendants for breach of warranty of authority for the loss suffered as a consequence of relying on A's warranty.

The significant decision in *Rasnoimport V/O v Guthrie & Co Ltd*,[17] extended further the ambit of A's warranty. There a consignment of bales of rubber was shipped under a bill of lading which stated that there were 225 bales and was

---

11 *Firbank's Executors v Humphreys* (1886) 18 QBD 54, 60 per Lord Esher MR (emphasis added).
12 [1903] AC 114; affirming *Oliver v Bank of England* [1902] 1 Ch 610, CA.
13 [1903] AC 114 at 117-118.
14 Radcliffe, 'Some Recent Developments of the Doctrine of *Collen v Wright*' (1902) 18 LQR 364. Radcliffe argued that the essence of the implied warranty was a bargained-for, collateral contract (ie in consideration of T's entering into the main contract with P, A promises that he has authority from P) whereas these cases extended A's liability to his gratuitous statements which prejudiced T. He thus thought that, in *Firbank*, the directors were merely performing a ministerial act in relation to an *earlier* bargain and, in *Starkey*, the brokers were demanding that the Bank fulfil its statutory duty. An adoption of this analysis would mean that the plaintiff (T) did not provide consideration for A's promise in either of these situations.
15 [1997] 3 All ER 470; see also *Bristol and West Building Society v Fancy & Jackson (a firm)* [1997] 4 All ER 582; *Brooks & Co v Mortgage Corpns plc* (1999) 77 P & CR 355.
16 [1997] 3 All ER 470 at 474-477.
17 [1966] 1 Lloyd's Rep 1; see Reynolds, 'Warranty of Authority' (1967) 83 LQR 189.

signed by A on behalf of the shipowners. When the vessel arrived at Liverpool, there were only 90 bales, the remainder having been appropriated by third parties before loading. The plaintiffs (T), indorsees of the bill of lading who had paid for 225 bales, originally sued the owners for breach of contract but that action was stayed[18] and T then commenced proceedings against A for breach of warranty of authority. A argued strongly that, even if he had warranted his authority, he had not warranted anything to T, a mere indorsee of the bill of lading with whom he had not dealt directly. Mocatta J held that A was liable and adopted a unilateral contract analysis, thereby treating A's signature as an offer to the world analogous to the celebrated offer in *Carlill v Carbolic Smoke Ball Co.*[19] The implied warranty of authority was thus given by A 'to all whom [he] could reasonably foresee would become such indorsees and became actionable by such persons on proof of their having acted in relaince upon the warranty and having suffered damage thereby'.[20] A may thus be liable to all whom he can reasonably foresee will know of the warranty and act in reliance upon it. Of course, there will not be many situations in which the warranty's reach is so extended and, in *Penn v Bristol and West Building Society*,[1] Waller LJ thought that 'outside the ambit of bills of exchange or bills of lading, it may be difficult to contemplate the offer or promise of a warranty of authority being given to such a wide number of people'.[2]

Finally, it is evident that A may be liable for breach of warranty of authority where his representation is that another person has the requisite authority, eg company directors representing that the company secretary has authority to bind the company.[3]

The breadth of A's strict liability means, as Stoljar[4] emphasises, that A becomes 'a virtual insurer not only of the continued existence, sanity or capacity of his principal, but also of the fact that his principal's shares or other documents are not forged or valueless'. However, in one situation there is statutory protection for A: where he acts under a power of attorney which, unknown to him, has been revoked, he will not be liable to T for breach of warranty of authority.[5]

REBUTTAL OF THE WARRANTY: WHEN IS THE THIRD PARTY NOT MISLED?

The strictness of A's liability is mitigated by the law's acknowledgment that there are situations where the waranty is not implied or it may be the case that T is not misled and thus cannot sue on any warranty.

First, A may expressly[6] or impliedly disclaim authority in which case he is not liable to T. A may impliedly disclaim authority by informing T of facts from

---

18 Probably because of *Grant v Norway* (1851) 10 CB 665, which decided that a shipmaster had no actual authority to sign, as agent for the shipowner, a bill of lading for goods which had not been shipped *and* he lacked apparent authority to do so as T would know that he did not have such authority.

19 [1893] 1 QB 256.

20 [1966] 1 Lloyd's Rep 1,13 per Mocatta J.

 1 [1997] 3 All ER 470.

 2 [1997] 3 All ER 470 at 476.

 3 See *Chapleo v Brunswick Building Society* (1881) 6 QBD 696 (directors held-out a secretary as having authority to borrow); *Cherry & M'Dougall v Colonial Bank of Australasia* (1869) LR 3 PC 24.

 4 *The Law of Agency* (1961), p 264.

 5 Powers of Attorney Act 1971, s 5 (1).

 6 *Halbot v Lens* [1901] 1 Ch 344.

which it would be unreasonable to construe any warranty – Buckley LJ's example in *Yonge v Toynbee*[7] being A's statement that P was abroad and he was unsure whether he was still living. Where the facts are equally within the knowledge of A and T in this way, T can be said to rely on his own assessment of the risk and cannot make A answerable for breach of warranty of authority.[8]

Second, T may actually know that A does not have authority or be taken to know of a lack of authority or limitations upon its operation. In *Lilly, Wilson & Co v Smales, Eeles & Co*,[9] a shipbroker signed a charter-party 'by telegraphic authority'of the charterer 'as agent'. Owing to a mistake made by officials in the transmission of the telegram, the rate of freight offered was higher than the charterer intended. It was proved that this form of signature was known in commerce as negating the implication of any further warranty by A than that he had received a telegram which, if correct, authorised such a charter as he was signing. A was thus not liable for breach of warranty of authority. Similarly, lapse of time after the initial grant of authority might mean, in certain circumstances, that T should realise that A's authority has ceased.[10] It is tolerably clear that the situations in which T must be taken to know of A's lack of authority are rare. In *Rasnoimport V/O v Guthrie & Co Ltd*,[11] it was argued that, as *Grant v Norway*[12] established that T is taken to know that a shipmaster has no actual or apparent authority to sign for goods not shipped so as to bind P, T must also be taken to know that A does not warrant his authority in that respect. Mocatta J rejected this contention because to transpose cases concerning apparent authority to breach of warranty of authority 'would seriously weaken the effect of the doctrine laid down in *Collen v Wright*'.[13] Moreover, it appears that T has no duty to inquire regarding A's authority but there is a surprising dearth of case law regarding this question. Powell[14] suggested that T owes no such duty just as a person to whom a misrepresentation is made is not bound to inquire into its truth and this view seems to be borne out by *Rasnoimport*.[15] Commenting on the cases in which directors have impliedly warranted their authority to borrow money, Mocatta J[16] stressed that T did not fail on the ground that the directors' powers might have been discovered by examining the company's memorandum and articles of association.

---

7 [1910] 1 KB 215, 227.
8 In *Yonge v Toynbee* [1910] 1 KB 215, 227-228, Buckley LJ considered this to be a possible *ratio* of *Smout v Ilbery* (1842) 10 M & W 1 (ante), ie whether P was alive was a fact equally within the knowledge of both A and T. See also *McManus v Fortescue* [1907] 2 KB 1 (an auctioneer (A) knocked down property to T below the reserve price but the conditions of sale specified that each lot was subject to a reserve. A refused to sign a memorandum rendering the sale enforceable against the vendor but T's action for breach of warranty of authority failed as he had knowledge of A's lack of authority to sell below the reserve price).
9 [1892] 1 QB 456; see also *Suart v Haigh* (1893) 9 TLR 488.
10 See *Dillon v Macdonald* (1902) 21 NZLR 45 (Stout CJ considered that, where an estate agent showed T his written authority, T thus becoming aware of its date, he could not maintain an action for breach of warranty of authority if the agency then ended through lapse of time).
11 [1966] 1 Lloyd's Rep 1.
12 (1851) 10 CB 665.
13 [1966] 1 Lloyd's Rep 1, 11.
14 *The Law of Agency* (2nd edn, 1961), p 256.
15 [1966] 1 Lloyd's Rep 1.
16 [1966] 1 Lloyd's Rep 1 at 11.

Third, there will be no warranty where A's representation is one of law rather than fact. The position here is that, if all the facts are known to T and whether A has authority is a matter of law to be deduced from those facts, T is presumed to know the law and thus cannot make A liable if he (T) reaches the wrong conclusion. In other words, T's error regarding the law is distinguishable from A's plain misrepresentation of fact. The reasoning employed here is very similar to that in the cases considered earlier where the pertinent facts were within the knowledge of both A and T. Factual representations should be considered first. In *Richardson v Williamson*,[17] directors of a building society represented that they had power to borrow money when in fact no rule had been made to sanction borrowing. T had lent money to the society and the directors were liable on an implied warranty that they had authority to borrow on behalf of the society. Similarly, in *Cherry & M'Dougall v Colonial Bank of Australasia*,[18] directors gave authority to a manger to overdraw an account but they could borrow money only when consent had been obtained from the shareholders and, in fact, no such consent had been obtained. The directors were liable to the bankers on the implied warranty that they had authority to overdraw.

In both the foregoing cases, the requisite procedures which allowed the directors to borrow had simply not been complied with and it is relatively easy to classify such representations as being factual in content. Likewise, a statement that a borrowing limit has not been exceeded is one of fact.[19] In contrast, in *Rashdall v Ford*,[20] T wished to advance money on debentures and he applied to a railway company, the secretary of which offered him a company bond stating that the company could not yet issue debentures. T advanced the money and received a Lloyd's bond whereby the company acknowledged the debt and covenanted to pay interest. The company got into difficulties, the payment of interest ceased and T was advised that the bond was valueless. It was held that the directors were not liable on an implied warranty of authority as the validity of the bond was a question of law and not fact.[1]

The leading decision in *Beattie v Lord Ebury*[2] illustrates that some statements are not classifiable as representations of fact upon which any warranty of authority could be based. There directors, on behalf of a company, opened an account with a bank and sent a letter requesting the bank to honour cheques signed by two directors and the secretary. The account became heavily overdrawn and negotiations took place as to security for the debt owed, the directors transferring to two of the bank's managers, in trust for the bank, £20,000 preference shares and £10,000 in debentures. The bank obtained judgment against the company which was only partially satisfied and then it sought to make the directors liable on two grounds. First, it was asserted that the directors' original letter represented that they had power to overdraw the account and that the company would pay and, as the company had defaulted, the directors should be

---

17 (1871) LR 6 QB 276.
18 (1869) LR 3 PC 24.
19 See *Weeks v Propert* (1873) LR 8 CP 427.
20 (1866) LR 2 Eq 750.
 1 See also *Eaglesfield v Marquis of Londonderry* (1878) 38 LT 303; affirming 35 LT 822 (directors issued stock described as No 1 Preference Stock incorrectly believing that they had power to issue stock which ranked with No 1 Preference stock already issued and T shared that belief. It was held that the directors were not liable as their representation was one of law).
 2 (1872) 7 Ch App 777; affd LR 7 HL 102.

liable on their warranty. Second, the argument was pressed that the directors had represented that the shares and debentures were fully paid-up. It was held (reversing the decision of Sir James Bacon VC) that the bank must fail on both grounds: first, the letter contained no representation whatever that the directors might overdraw the account and, second, no representation had been made that the shares and debentures were fully paid-up but only that, when they were taken up by the public, the money paid for them would go to the bank. Sir G Mellish LJ held that the directors' original letter contained nothing more than the standard information required when opening a bank account and thus there was no representation of fact regarding the directors' authority 'except that they were directors of the railway company'.[3] Moreover, the judge stressed that (i) there was every likelihood that the directors did have authority to bind the company, particularly as the bank successfully sued the company, ie the directors would only be liable for breach of warranty of authority where the company was *not* bound and, (ii) even if there had been a warranty by the directors, the bank had not sustained any loss as they had had every possible remedy against the company. He concluded that 'from the beginning to the end Mr Beattie knew the whole circumstances of this railway company just as much as the directors themselves knew them; that there was no concealment from him, and that there was no deception in point of fact, and no mistake in point of fact'.[4]

MEASURE OF DAMAGES FOR BREACH OF WARRANTY OF AUTHORITY

Damages are assessed according to the orthodox principles of the law of contract and so T can recover from A the loss which was the natural and probable consequence of A's lack of authority. Where P repudiates the contract which A purported to make on his behalf, this loss is the amount of damages which could have been recovered against P if the contract had been authorised and he had refused to perform it, together with the costs and expenses incurred in relation to legal proceedings which were commenced against P. In this way, T will be placed in the same position as if the warranty had been true. Thus, in *Simons v Patchett*,[5] A, purporting to act for P, agreed to buy a ship from T but P repudiated the contract. T could only sell the ship at a lower price which, acting reasonably, was the best price he could obtain and so the measure of damages recoverable against A was the difference between the contract price and resale price. Following general principles of contract law, the fact that T has contracted to re-sell the property to X, and is liable on that contract, will be regarded as too remote a loss to recover from A,[6] unless A knows of the proposed sub-sale.[7]

A lucid example of the correct measure of damages is provided by *Re National Coffee Palace Co, ex p Panmure*.[8] P instructed A, a broker, to apply for fifty £1

---

3 (1872) 7 Ch App 777, 804.
4 (1872) 7 Ch App 777, 810 per Sir G Mellish LJ.
5 (1857) 7 E & B 568; see also *Richardson v Williamson* (1871) LR 6 QB 276 (directors of a building society represented that they had authority to borrow on behalf of the society and T lent £70. The measure of damages against the directors was thus £70 plus interest at the agreed rate).
6 *Spedding v Nevell* (1869) LR 4 CP 212.
7 *Rugg (C H) & Co Ltd v Street* [1962] 1 Lloyd's Rep 364.
8 (1883) 24 Ch D 367.

shares in a certain named company but, by mistake, A obtained an allotment of shares in another company with a similar name. At that time, the company in which P had become a shareholder had a large number of unallotted shares which the court considered were unsaleable. The company was soon wound up and P succeeded in having his name removed from the list of contributories as he had not authorised the application for the shares. It was held that the liquidator was entitled to recover from A the amount which the company had lost on the contract with P which, P being solvent and the shares unsaleable, was the sum of £50 payable for the shares.

The costs of T's legal proceedings against P can also be recovered against A provided they were reasonable and the fact that they might be commenced was in the contemplation of the parties.[9] Frequently, T will have attempted to sue P, but should T be sued by A or P, he can recover the costs of defending the action.[10] However, T will be unable to recover costs if he unreasonably continues with the action against P after it has been proved that A had no authority.[11]

Difficulties arise for T where P is insolvent. As the measure of T's loss is his recourse to P, the damages would be only nominal where P is insolvent because, in a successful action against P, T 'might not recover a shilling'.[12] The principle is further justified in that A does not warrant P's honesty, financial stability or solvency.[13] Moreover, T's damages will also be nominal where no contract could ever arise between P and T[14] and the same limitation should apply where P is a company which has not been formed and therefore lacks

---

9 *Hughes v Graeme* (1864) 33 LJQB 335 (T succeeded against A for the costs of a suit for specific performance against P as well as the value of the lost contract); *Spedding v Nevell* (1869) LR 4 CP 212.

10 *Yonge v Toynbee* [1910] 1 KB 215 (A, a solicitor, continued proceedings against T even though his authority had ended); *Pow v Davis* (1861) 1 B & S 220.

11 See *Godwin v Francis* (1870) LR 5 CP 295 (A, one of five joint owners of land, represented to T that he had authority to sell the land on behalf of his co-owners (P) and contracted to sell it to T. P repudiated the contract and sold the land at a higher price to X. T sued P for breach of contract and continued the action after P had sworn answers to interrogatories that A had no authority. In T's action against A for breach of warranty of authority, it was held that the measure of damages was (i) the costs of investigating the title (ii) the costs of the action up to the time that the answers to the interrogatories had been received (iii) the difference between the contract price and market price of the land, the price on the re-sale to X being taken as the market price, but (iv) T's loss on the re-sale of horses bought to stock the land (without notice to A and before investigation of the title) was too remote and irrecoverable).

12 *Re National Coffee Palace Co, ex p Panmure* (1883) 24 Ch D 367, 372 and 375 per Brett MR and Bowen LJ respectively.

13 'The fact is, that an agent does not promise that his principal shall carry out the contract, but only that he shall be bound by it': *Re National Coffee Palace Co, ex p Panmure* (1883) 24 Ch D 367, 375 per Bowen LJ.

14 *Heskell v Continental Express Ltd* [1950] 1 All ER 1033 (a seller of goods (T) to a foreign buyer had to arrange for their shipment. He procured cargo space for the goods but did not enter into a contract of carriage and, unknown to T, the goods were not dispatched. T nevertheless applied for a bill of lading which was negligently issued by A, the shipowner's (P) broker. T paid damages to the buyer for non delivery of the goods and then sued A for breach of warranty of authority to issue the bill of lading. It was held that T could not have recovered against P even if the bill had been issued with P's authority as only the receipt of the goods on behalf of the shipowner would have concluded the contract of carriage. Accordingly, as this had not happened, there was no contract of carriage and the bill was a nullity. T's rights on the bill were thus totally unaffected by A's lack of *authority* and he could recover nothing against A).

funds.[15] If possible in these situations, it would clearly be to T's advantage to maintain an action against A in tort, thereby circumventing the issue of the recourse to P as the measure of the loss.

Finally, it is often canvassed whether A can be liable for breach of warranty of authority where he has no actual authority but only apparent authority. Theoretically, it is arguable that A should be liable as he lacks actual authority but, practically, the fact that P could be liable to T would mean that T could establish no loss[16] and there are *dicta* that there is no breach of warranty of authority where A has apparent authority.[17] The same arguments would apply to cases where P subsequently ratifies A's act but with arguably more force having regard to the retrospective operation of ratification, although it has been pointed out[18] that T might incur expense should P initially refuse to ratify.

15 It is apparent that some of the older company cases, considered earlier, do not adhere strictly to this notion in that A is liable for breach of warranty of authority where the proposed contract is *ultra vires* the company. Such a contract would be a nullity even if authorised by P and so no loss could be established.
16 See *Drew v Nunn* (1879) 4 QBD 661 (A was held to have apparent authority to bind P when A's actual authority ended on P's insanity). *Drew* was not considered in *Yonge v Toynbee* [1910] 1 KB 215 (see termination in Ch 12).
17 *Rainbow v Howkins* [1904] 2 KB 322.
18 *Bowstead & Reynolds on Agency* (16th edn, 1996), Art 107, para 9-066.

CHAPTER 12

The termination of agency

Introduction

Just as the rules regarding the creation of authority affect all the parties in the agency relationship, the consequences of the termination of authority may resonate throughout the nexus of principal, agent and third party. First, there is the *internal* aspect of how A's actual authority may be ended as between P and A by the acts of the parties themselves and, second, there is the issue of when A's authority may be ended by operation of law. Third, there is the *external* question of the effect of termination on the relationship between P and T. Where T has no knowledge of the termination he may be entirely unaffected by it because, although A's actual authority may have ended, his apparent authority to bind P may endure.[1] Finally, there are some very specialised situations where A has an interest which is secured by the terms of the agency and his authority is consequently regarded as irrevocable.

A consistent and fundamental theme permeating the rules of termination at common law is the notion that the agency can be ended by either party without the other's consent. Taken to the extreme, A's authority might be validly terminated, without any notice being given to A, leaving him with no remedy against P. This startling conclusion reflects the underlying commercial nature of many agency relationships insofar as A and P accept the right of mutual regression without obligation, this position being vividly illustrated in *Luxor (Eastbourne) Ltd v Cooper.*[2] In general, A's authority is not equatable with a contract of employment but, instead, is directly comparable to an opportunistic venture which possesses the inherent risks of success or failure. That being said, some decisions have considered that the agency relationship in dispute involves mutual respect and obligation, although it is not by any means clear when this approach will be adopted as opposed to the austere, pragmatic analysis evinced in *Luxor*. Most recently, the Commercial Agents (Council Directive) Regulations 1993,[3] considered later

---

1 It should also be stressed that A's fiduciary duties owed to P may endure even though the agency has been terminated. See also *Yasuda Fire & Marine Insurance Co of Europe Ltd v Orion Marine Insurance Underwriting Agency Ltd* [1995] QB 174 (P's right to inspect A's records held to exist after termination of the agency; see Ch 8).
2 [1941] AC 108 (considered in Ch 9).
3 SI 1993/3053 as amended by SI 1993/3173.

in this chapter, have made make radical changes regarding A's compensation or indemnity when 'commercial agencies' are terminated. In the relatively narrow sphere in which the Regulations operate, 'commercial agencies' are drawn much closer to contracts of employment in that the agent is perceived as the weaker party in need of protection from the acts of a stronger, dominant principal. Under the Regulations, a 'commercial agent' may be entitled to compensation where, for example, a fixed-term agency contract expires without any fault on P's part – this being, hitherto, an uncontemplated proposition in English law.

The concepts outlined above are diverse and sometimes diametrically opposed to one another. However, attempts at rationalising the rules on termination are certain to falter, not least because the widely varying types of agency which are encountered and the disparate legal principles applicable to them mean that it is almost impossible to locate any unifying theme. The common law's rules on termination of agency have developed in a conspicuously utilitarian and *ad hoc* manner, leaving a patchwork of precepts and premises stitched together somewhat inexactly.

Termination by the acts of the parties

BY AGREEMENT

As A's authority may be created by agreement between P and A, it is axiomatic that it may be terminated in the same way. It is thus plain that the agreement may be discharged voluntarily by the parties. Equally evident is the fact that the agreement may expressly prescribe the duration of A's authority and, if the authority is not conferred expressly for a specific period of time, it will expire after the lapse of a reasonable period of time. These rules appertain simply to the express or implied terms of the agreement. It is also important to stress that, in interpreting the agency agreement, customs of particular trades or places may be established which dictate the duration of A's authority.[4]

The decision in *Danby v Coutts & Co*[5] illustrates these principles. There the operative part of a power of attorney appointed A1 and A2 to be P's attorneys without expressly limiting the duration of their powers but it was preceded by a recital that P was going abroad and wanted attorneys to act for him during his absence. It was held that the recital controlled the operative part of the deed and thus the attorneys' authority was limited to the period of P's absence. Accordingly, P was not bound by fraudulent transactions which the attorneys perpetrated after his return to England.

In construing the agreement between the parties it may often be clear that, where A has been appointed to execute a particular transaction, the completion

---

4 Eg *Lawford & Co v Harris* (1896) 12 TLR 275 (stockbrokers (A) were instructed to sell shares for P at a fixed price and did so at the end of the current account. The shares then increased in value and P successfully argued that the sale was unauthorised as, by custom, A's authority ended on the expiration of the current account); *Dickinson v Lilwal* (1815) 4 Camp 279 (a custom was succesfully established to the effect that a broker's authority expired at the end of the day on which it was given).
5 (1885) 29 Ch D 500.

of that transaction marks the end of his authority. In *Blackburn v Scholes*,[6] for example, Lord Ellenborough held that as soon as a broker had sold goods on behalf of P he was *functus officio* and the terms of the contract of sale could not be altered without a fresh grant of authority from P.

BY THE PRINCIPAL'S REVOCATION OR THE AGENT'S RENUNCIATION

It is a basic tenet of agency that either P or A may end the agency relationship without the consent of the other. Subject to certain exceptions considered later, the rule is forceful in that P may revoke A's authority by giving notice to A before the authority has been completely exercised or A may renounce it by giving notice to P which is accepted.

The general principle of revocation is graphically illustrated in *Hampden v Walsh*.[7] There P and T each deposited £500 with a banker (A) who was to act as stakeholder in respect of a wager between P and T as to whether or not the earth was flat. A decided that T had satisfactorily demonstrated the earth's curvature by proving the convexity of Bedford Level Canal but, before A paid the money to T, P demanded its return. A nevertheless paid the wager to T but it was held that P had revoked A's authority before it had been completed and he could thus recover the money from A.

The rule of unfettered revocation applies even where the original authority is given for consideration,[8] by power of attorney[9] and even if it is expressed to be irrevocable,[10] because something more is needed for true irrevocability.[11] Moreover, the revocation may be oral even where the original authority was by deed or in writing.[12] The rule permitting revocation is said, somewhat unconvincingly, to be 'necessary'[13] and it is further supported by the fact that contracts of agency, together with other relationships for the provision of personal service, are not enforceable by a decree of specific performance.[14]

It is thus evident that the revocation or renunciation may terminate the agency between P and A. It may also mean that A's actions on P's behalf are rendered ineffective and that A loses his rights to future remuneration and indemnity, for example. However, it is vital to set this matter of the abrupt termination of authority in its proper context: the revocation or renunciation cannot prejudice *other* rights

6 (1810) 2 Camp 341; see also *Bell v Balls* [1897] 1 Ch 663 (an auctioneer had no authority to sign a memorandum of the sale one week after the sale); *Gillow & Co v Lord Aberdare* (1892) 9 TLR 12 (an estate agent was employed to let or sell a house and, having let it, he found a purchaser. It was held that he had no authority to do so and he was not entitled to commission on the sale).

7 (1876) 1 QBD 189; see also *Gibson v Minet* (1824) 2 Bing 7 (P authorised a banker (A) to hold £400 at the disposal of T. P countermanded A's authority but A nevertheless paid the money to T. Held that A's authority could be revoked provided that he had not paid the money to T and thus P could recover the money from A); *Warlow v Harrison* (1859) 1 E & E 309 (P held able to revoke an auctioneer's authority at any time before the fall of the hammer).

8 *Doward, Dickson & Co v Williams & Co* (1890) 6 TLR 316.

9 *Walsh v Whitcomb* (1797) 2 Esp 565; *Frith v Frith* [1906] AC 254.

10 *Vynior's Case* (1609) 8 Co Rep 81b.

11 Irrevocable agencies are considered later in this chapter.

12 *R v Wait* (1823) 1 Bing 121.

13 'The proper conduct of the affairs of life necessitates that this should be so': *Frith v Frith* [1906] AC 254, 259 per Lord Atkinson.

14 *Chinnock v Sainsbury* (1860) 30 LJ Ch 409.

which subsist between P and A. The termination may thus be in breach of contract rendering one party liable in damages even though it is effective in ending A's actual authority. Moreover, P or A may have rights which *accrued* before termination, eg P may sue A for breach of duty or A may seek remuneration or indemnity in relation to pre-termination acts. Also, as discussed in Chapters 7 and 8, A's fiduciary obligations may subsist after the termination of his authority. When A's authority has been terminated, he may be liable to T for breach of warranty of authority if he continues to act as though he were authorised and he will be unable to claim remuneration or indemnity from P in respect of such post-termination acts.

Finally, and arguably more important than all the repercussions above, A's *apparent* authority may continue after the termination of his actual authority until T has notice that the authority has ended. Despite the termination of A's actual authority, it is thus quite possible that P may have a binding contract with T by virtue of A's enduring apparent authority.

Is notice required to terminate A's authority?

There are two distinct questions here. First, if P wishes effectively to end A's authority must he notify A of the termination? Second, if A seeks to renounce his authority must he inform P of that fact? Although these are fundamental and rudimentary questions, they cannot be answered conclusively.

The general rule is that, as between P and A, A's authority does not end until he receives actual notice of the revocation from P. In *Re Oriental Bank Corpn, ex p Guillemin*,[15] for example, money was paid into the Mauritius branch of a bank after proceedings to wind up the company had commenced in London but before the officers of the Mauritius branch had notice of the proceedings. It was held that, in the absence of notice, there had been no valid revocation of the bank officials' authority and thus the applicants were not entitled to have their money refunded as on the footing of a void transaction but could merely prove for the amount in the winding up, *pari passu* with the other creditors. Chitty J considered that the authority 'was not revoked in point of fact. It was, however, contended on behalf of the applicants that it was revoked in law by the mere appointment of the provisional liquidator. I cannot accede to that argument. I think the authority was not revoked until notice of the appointment reached the island. Unquestionably advice is required in order to terminate the authority of an agent where the revocation is by act of the principal'.[16]

The fact that P must give notice to A if he is successfully to end A's authority was accentuated by the facts in *Simpson (Robert) Co v Godson*.[17] There P had a charge account with the plaintiff department store upon which his wife (A) was expressly authorised to make purchases. Bills were sent regularly to A and were paid by P. P informed the store that he wished to close the account but he did not notify A of this fact and A subsequently made purchases on the account. The Ontario Court of Appeal held that, as no notice of termination had been given to A, her actual authority remained intact and so P was liable for the purchases made by her. The decision must be correct because P's notification to the store would end any apparent authority in A and it would be unjust if A were personally liable for the purchases on the ground that her

15 (1884) 28 Ch D 634.
16 (1884) 28 Ch D 634 at 640.
17 [1937] 1 DLR 454.

actual authority had ended. It is surely not unreasonable to demand that P should inform A if he wishes to end A's actual authority.[18]

Despite these decisions and the explicit statement of principle by Chitty J in *Re Oriental Bank*, above, there is old authority that there can be an implied revocation by an act of P's which is inconsistent with the agency's continuation and which comes to A's notice.[19] Moreover, in some cases it may be implied from the nature of the agency that no notice is required and this certainly seems to be the general position with estate agents.[20] Yet again, there is thus a wide divergence in the rules and it is unwise to state conclusions peremptorily.

As regards A's renunciation of his authority, *Bowstead & Reynolds*[1] considers that it does not terminate A's authority unless P accepts that it does so and, if it is thus accepted, P may be released from the duty to give any notice to A of the termination of his authority. Where A commits a repudiatory breach of duty, eg taking a bribe, the USA's *Restatement*[2] suggests that his authority would terminate automatically, but the English perspective is that such a breach merely entitles P to end A's authority.

Although notice to A may end his actual authority, it is important to stress again that A's *apparent* authority will continue until T has notice of the revocation and, therefore, T may have a remedy against P on this basis (see later).

NOTICE AND COMPENSATION ON THE TERMINATION OF THE AGENT'S AUTHORITY

The aspect of notice considered above relates to the communication of an *effective termination* of A's authority as between P and A. It must not be

18 The case was criticised by Wright (1937) 15 Can Bar Rev 196. He stressed that, until A receives notice of the termination of his authority, he can bind P to T provided that T *also* does not know of the termination. If, on the other hand, T does know of the termination, A should not be able to bind P. Accordingly, Wright's view was that the store could not render P liable after the account had been closed and the store knew that P did not *consent* to any contractual liability. Wright's solution was that (i) A should have been liable to the store and (ii) A would then have recourse against P.

19 *Smith and Jenning's Case* (1610) Lane 97; *Anon* (1700) 12 Mod 409. Both cases concern P's conduct which was held to terminate A's authority in a power of attorney; in the second case, A's authority to collect a debt from T was countermanded by P's commencement of proceedings against T.

20 See *Nelson (E P) & Co v Rolfe* [1950] 1 KB 139 (P instructed two estate agents (A1 and A2) regarding the sale of his property. A1 introduced T1 and P agreed to sell to T1 although no binding contract was concluded. A2 then introduced T2 but P refused to sell to T2 and the property was eventually sold to T1. The CA held that A2 was entitled to commission on the terms of the agency (to introduce a person 'able, ready and willing to purchase'). The court accepted however that the contract was subject to the implied terms that no commission would have been payable if (i) A2's authority had been revoked or (ii) the property had been either conveyed to T1, or a binding contract to sell to T1 had been concluded *without A2's knowledge*. The decision was followed in *Dickson (A A) & Co v O'Leary* (1979) 254 Estates Gazette 731 (CA) where A1 introduced T1 and contracts were exchanged between P and T1. It was held that A2 was not entitled to commission for introducing T2 as the right to commission was subject to an implied term that no commission is payable where the property has already been sold. These decisions apparently make a distinction between termination and revocation: P may seemingly *terminate* A2's agency by selling the property even though no notification is given to A2 but, if he wishes validly to *revoke* A2's authority, he must communicate his revocation to A2. Moreover, on certain facts, P can clearly be liable to A1 and A2 for two commissions: see Ch 9.

1 *Bowstead & Reynolds on Agency* (16th edn, 1996), Art 119, para 10-004; Art 122, para 10-023.

2 *Restatement, Second, Agency* Comment on §112.

confused with the question of A's dismissal and whether he may have a *right* to a period of notice under a contract with P and a concomitant *remedy* against P for his failure to give the requisite notice. It is this question which must now be considered.

While it is indisputable that the termination of A's authority may be valid and effective *per se*, A may be entitled to a remedy against P, eg for breach of an express or implied term of the contract. The availability of such a remedy depends upon the wide variety of possible agency relationships which run the gamut from formal, contractual agencies to informal, gratuitous undertakings. Moreover, the Commercial Agents (Council Directive) Regulations 1993, considered later, introduce the 'commercial agent' into the range of agencies recognised by English law and such an agent has a full panoply of remedies which he may pursue in the event that his authority is terminated. The assortment of agencies which exist should thus be delineated.

First, where A is an employee as well as an agent, he will be entitled to the statutory and common law remedies available in employment, eg unfair dismissal or wrongful dismissal in breach of contract.

Second, an agent who is paid by commission is often regarded as having no affiliation whatever with an employee. As emphasised at the start of this chapter, where A is promised a commission in the event of his securing a completed transaction on P's behalf, there is a strong tendency to say that he accepts the risk of receiving no compensation for work done in attempting to complete the task and that he also acknowledges that P may withdraw from the relationship, without consequence, before such completion.[3] It is arguable that commission agencies are based upon P's offer of a unilateral contract to A which is accepted by A only when the task in question is completed and P should thus be able legitimately to withdraw his offer at any time before A's acceptance. Certainly P's unfettered right of revocation is upheld in the standard estate agency relationship where A does not have a sole or exclusive agency.[4] There is an enduring debate in the law of contract regarding possible restrictions on the right of the offeror to withdraw his offer of a unilateral contract and often methods are sought to protect the offeree, eg by implying an obligation not to revoke once the offeree has commenced performance of the act in question.[5] Where a measure of protection has been available to the offeree, it may be justified on the basis that he confers a tangible benefit on the offeror prior to the conclusion of the unilateral contract and, moreover, the offeree's reliance on the offer may be significant – certainly he cannot be said freely to acknowledge the risk of revocation. All three factors of benefit conferred, reliance incurred, and absence of risk were pronounced in the domestic dispute in *Errington v Errington and Woods*.[6] But such an analysis will be unnecessary and inapt in many commercial agency relationships where there is neither a benefit conferred upon P nor evidence of detrimental reliance by A. On the contrary, the likelihood of revocation is a

3 See *Luxor (Eastbourne) Ltd v Cooper* [1941] AC 108 (considered in Ch 9).
4 See *Luxor (Eastbourne) Ltd v Cooper* [1941] AC 108; *Nelson (E P) & Co v Rolfe* [1950] 1 KB 139; *Dickson (A A) & Co v O'Leary* (1979) 254 Estates Gazette 731; Murdoch, 'The Nature of Estate Agency' (1975) 91 LQR 357.
5 Eg *Errington v Errington and Woods* [1952] 1 KB 290; *Ward v Byham* [1956] 1 WLR 496; *United Dominions Trust (Commercial) Ltd v Eagle Aircraft Services Ltd* [1968] 1 WLR 74; *Daulia Ltd v Four Millbank Nominees Ltd* [1978] Ch 231. As discussed in Ch 9, it should be impossible to imply a *term* that P will not revoke as, until A completes the task, there is no *contract* into which such a term can be implied.
6 [1952] 1 KB 290.

risk which is accepted openly by both parties: *Luxor (Eastbourne) Ltd v Cooper*[7] is the antithesis of the *Errington* case. There are numerous other decisions concerning commission agents in which it has been held that A's authority may be withdrawn summarily.[8] These decisions do not articulate any unilateral contract reasoning but indicate that the commission agent's position is not analogous to that of an employee where compensation for wrongful dismissal would be appropriate.[9] Certainly there is no perception in these cases that A suffers any detriment solely by virtue of P's withdrawal and, consequently, no tendency to limit P's right of revocation or award compensation to A where he has not been given any notice of termination.

Third, there is the question of non-contractual agencies. Where A has no contract with P nor is it *ever* intended that a contract will be entered into between them, P cannot be liable in breach of contract and A can be dismissed wthout P's incurring any liability, unless A has rights under the principles of restitution.

Fourth, A may be a 'commercial agent' within the Commercial Agents (Council Directive) Regulations 1993, which are considered later. If so, A is well-protected from possible abuse by P as the situations in which compensation or indemnity are payable on termination of the agency are clearly delineated.

Finally, A may have a bilateral contract with P where he provides consideration, eg A promises to use his best efforts to sell goods on P's behalf, and such a contract will often make express provision for termination. Overall, the question of termination in bilateral contracts turns upon whether or not the contract has a specific duration and these two types of contract must now be considered separately.

Contracts of indefinite duration

Where there is a bilateral contract of indefinite duration containing no express provision for termination, ascertainment of the parties' true intent may not be an easy task. It is unclear whether some of the commission agent cases referred to above might be classifiable as instances of bilateral contracts and, to the extent that they are so classifiable, they are authority for the proposition that there can be termination without notice where there is no express provision in the contract relating to termination. It is, however, almost inconceivable that a court would interpret a truly bilateral contract in this way.

At the other extreme, it is possible that, in the absence of an express provision regarding termination, the provisions of the contract may indicate that it is permanent and not terminable (except by breach or frustration). Although this seems an implausible proposition, it was the conclusion which was reached by the House of Lords in *Llanelly Rly and Dock Co v London and North Western Rly Co.*[10] There two railway companies entered into an agreement for the defendant company to have running powers over the plaintiff's lines, a chief consideration for the agreement being a loan of £40,000 to the plaintiff. The

---

7 [1941] AC 108.
8 *Alexander v Davis & Co* (1885) 2 TLR 142; *Henry v Lowson* (1885) 2 TLR 199; *Motion v Michaud* (1892) 8 TLR 253; affd 8 TLR 447; *Joynson v Hunt & Son* (1905) 93 LT 470; *Levy v Goldhill & Son* [1917] 2 Ch 297.
9 See *Motion v Michaud* (1892) 8 TLR 253; affd 8 TLR 447; *Levy v Goldhill & Son* [1917] 2 Ch 297.
10 (1873) 8 Ch App 942; affd LR 7 HL 550.

contract was acted on for four years but then the plaintiffs gave three months notice to determine it. The House of Lords held that there was a presumption that the contract was perpetual and irrevocable and the plaintiff had not discharged the burden of proving otherwise.[11]

However, the conferment of a perpetual benefit in return for consideration is hardly a common occurrence and, as Goff LJ emphasised in *Staffordshire Area Health Authority v South Staffordshire Waterworks Co*,[12] the large loan which was advanced to the plaintiff was a pivotal feature of the *Llanelly* decision. Moreover, as a general proposition, it is incredible that the parties to a commercial agency would envisage that their obligations should be binding in perpetuity. In *Martin-Baker Aircraft Co Ltd v Canadian Flight Equipment Ltd*,[13] the court considered that an agreement whereby the plaintiff manufacturers of aircraft ejection seats permitted the defendant company to 'manufacture, sell and exploit' its products on the American continent, and which had no provision for determination, should not be approached with any presumption in favour of permanence. McNair J suggested that 'if there is any presumption at all, it would seem to me to be a presumption the other way'[14] and, on the true construction of the contract, the parties could not have intended such a commercial agreement to be permanent; rather it was held to be determinable unilaterally on giving reasonable notice, which the court fixed at one year. The judge added that he had 'little doubt that the law merchant would regard a contract for sale of 100 tons of coal monthly at a fixed price, no period being specified, as a contract determinable on reasonable notice'.[15]

Martin-Baker Aircraft Co Ltd v Murison,[16] is also an important decision on the question of reasonable notice. The plaintiffs also appointed Murison (A), a director of Canadian Flight Equipment Ltd, to be 'sole selling agent for all their products ... on the North American Continent' and A promised to use his best endeavours in promoting the sale of the products and not to sell, or have any interest in any competitors' goods. Payment was to be by commission on orders received *and* there was an express provision allowing either party to determine the agreement summarily for failure to remedy a breach within fourteen days or in the event of liquidation. It was held that the agreement was not a pure agency agreement of the type exemplified in the commission agency cases and was thus not determinable summarily. The court considered that A had to expend time and money in performing the contract and was subject to restrictions which meant that this relationship approximated more closely to a contract of

---

11 See Carnegie, 'Terminability of Contracts of Unspecified Duration' (1969) 85 LQR 392.
12 [1978] 1 WLR 1387, 1401 (in the *Staffordshire Area Health* case, an agreement entered into in 1929 between the defendant water company (D) and the plaintiff health authority (P) provided that (i) D would 'at all times hereafter' supply to P 5,000 gallons of water per day free of cost (ii) P would 'at all times hereafter' be at liberty to take from the mains any further quantity needed, and (iii) payment therefor would be 7d for each 1,000 gallons so supplied. There was no express provision for termination or for any variation in the charge. Having regard to the great increases in water rates, D sought to terminate the agreement on giving six months' notice. Although Foster J held that the agreement was binding 'forever or in perpetuity', the Court of Appeal held the agreement was determinable on giving reasonable notice).
13 [1955] 2 QB 556.
14 [1955] 2 QB 556 at 577.
15 [1955] 2 QB 556 at 577.
16 [1955] 2 QB 556.

employment and was thus determinable on reasonable notice, again fixed at one year.[17] This conclusion was not affected by the provision for summary dismissal which McNair J considered to be merely a restriction upon the right of summary dismissal, which right always exists in certain circumstances, even in a contract ordinarily determinable by notice.

Contracts of definite duration

Where the contract provides that A should act on P's behalf for a specific period of time, the obvious conclusion would be that the contract must subsist for that period and that A would be entitled to damages should it be determined prematurely. There are decisions which reach this conclusion but others which subscribe to the view that P may legitimately end the agency by simply ending his business activities.

The decisions which allow P to terminate the agency without compensating A should be considered first. In *Rhodes v Forwood*,[18] P owned a colliery and it was agreed that, for seven years, or as long as A should continue in business at Liverpool, A should be the sole agent at Liverpool for the sale of P's coal. After four years, P sold the colliery and A then sought damages for loss of commission. The House of Lords held that P was not in breach of any express term of the contract as the agreement did not stipulate that P should *send* any coal to Liverpool for any specified period of time. Moreover, it was held that there could be no implied term binding P to keep the colliery. As Lord Chelmsford[19] pointed out, if P might legitimately not send any coal to Liverpool and thereby disable the agreement, there could be no difference if he chose to disable himself from performing the contract by selling the colliery.[20] The same approach has been followed in cases where P has disposed of the agency's subject matter. In *Lazarus v Cairn Line of Steamships Ltd*,[1] for example, A was appointed for three years

---

17 See also *Bauman v Hulton Press Ltd* [1952] 2 All ER 1121 (journalist who was held entitled to reasonable notice (six months) obtained damages for loss of salary and remuneration); *Decro-Wall International SA v Practitioners in Marketing Ltd* [1971] 1 WLR 361(defendants who distributed the plaintiff's goods entitled to one year's notice).
18 (1876) 1 App Cas 256.
19 (1876) 1 App Cas 256 at 268.
20 See also *Re English and Scottish Marine Insurance Co, ex p Maclure* (1870) 5 Ch App 737 (A agreed to act for five years as an insurance agent for P. Held P not liable for loss of A's commission when the company was voluntarily wound-up after 18 months); *Hamlyn & Co v Wood & Co* [1891] 2 QB 488 (defendant brewers agreed to sell grain to the plaintiffs for a term of ten years but the brewery was sold five years later: no implied term could be established that the business should not be sold); *Northey v Trevillion* (1902) 7 Com Cas 201(A was appointed for ten years as the sole buying agent for a firm in India and was not entitled to damages on the firm's dissolution); *Re R S Newman Ltd, Raphael's Claim* [1916] 2 Ch 309 (managing director appointed for one year not entitled to loss of commission on goods sold and loss of an option to take shares when a compulsory winding-up order was made four months after his appointment); *Leak v Charles & Sons Ltd* (1948) 92 Sol Jo 154 (A had no claim to commission where P agreed to pay him post-termination commission for nine months but P sold his business within three months); *Cowasjee Nanabhoy v Lallbhoy Vullubhoy* (1876) LR 3 Ind App 200 (a partnership appointed one of the partners as sole agent for life to buy and sell on behalf of the partnership on a commission basis; the partnership was dissolved but A was not entitled to any compensation); cf *Brace v Calder* [1895] 2 QB 253 where retirement of some of the partners, causing a dissolution, entitled A to damages for wrongful dismissal but here there was probably a contract of employment.
1 (1912) 106 LT 378. See also *French & Co Ltd v Leeston Shipping Co Ltd* [1922] 1 AC 451 (shipbrokers (A) employed to effect a charter of a steamship procured a charter for 18 months, commission being payable on hire paid and earnt under the charter-party. P sold

as the passenger agent for P's line of steamers but it was held that he had no claim for lost commission when P sold the vessels in his line five months later. An habitual theme permeating these decisions is that, where no *express* promise is made to continue the business upon which A's commission depends, A runs the risk that P may exercise his legitimate right to dispose of it and it is thus unnecessary for the business efficacy of the contract to imply a term to the contrary. Moreover, some cases question whether the agency is analogous to a contract of employment or whether it is a 'mere contract of agency with no service or subordination' meaning that there is 'no implied contract that the agent is to be supplied with the means of earning his commission'.[2]

In the second line of cases, A has been allowed a remedy where P terminates the agency. In *Turner v Goldsmith*,[3] P, a shirt manufacturer, agreed in writing to employ A as 'agent, canvasser and traveller' for five years and A promised to do his utmost to sell the goods 'manufactured or sold' by P. After two years, P's factory was burnt down and he did not resume business. It was held that A was entitled to damages for breach of contract. *Rhodes v Forwood* was distinguished as, in *Turner*, there was an express agreement to employ A for five years and the court considered that P did not fulfil the agreement unless he sent A a reasonable amount of samples to enable him to earn his commission. P argued that the contract was subject to an implied term that the obligation should cease if the factory ceased to exist. This argument did not prevail, however, as the contract applied to goods *sold* by P as well as those manufactured by him.

How may the *Turner v Goldsmith* line of cases be separated from those represented by *Rhodes v Forwood*? In the broadest sense, it is apparent that there is injustice to A if he is not compensated for the loss of the agency.[4] Moreover, the injustice of the situation is accentuated where a strong element of mutuality in the agreement is detected by the court[5] thereby clearly distancing such decisions from both *Rhodes v Forwood* and those cases considered earlier where

the vessel to the charterer after four months. A's claim for commission during the remainder of the contract failed as no implied term could be established that P would not end the charter-party by the sale of the ship); *Howard Houlder & Partners Ltd v Manx Isles Steamship Co Ltd* [1923] 1 KB 110 (shipbrokers (A) negotiated a charter-party with commission to be paid on hire earnt (as in *French*, supra) and granting the charterer an option to purchase the vessel for £125,000. The vessel was actually sold for £65,000 but it was held that A was not entitled to lost commission under the charter-party nor on the sale price of the vessel as he had taken no part in the new bargain); *Houlder* was followed on almost identical facts in *Shackleton Aviation Ltd v Maitland Drewery Aviation Ltd* [1964] 1 Lloyd's Rep 293 (charter and subsequent hire-purchase of aircraft by T without A's intervention. Held A was not entitled to any commission on the sale price).

2 *Northey v Trevillion* (1902) 7 Com Cas 201, 203, per Phillimore J; *Bauman v Hulton Press Ltd* [1952] 2 All ER 1121.

3 [1891] 1 QB 544.

4 See *Re Patent Floor Cloth Co Ltd* (1872) 26 LT 467(A was appointed for three years as a 'commission traveller' and was held entitled to damages for lost commission on the voluntary winding up of the company eight months later. Bacon VC considered (p 468) that a decision to the contrary would be 'monstrous', 'in the highest degree unreasonable' and 'wholly inequitable and unjust').

5 At first instance in *Reigate v Union Manufacturing Co (Ramsbottom) Ltd* [1918] 1 KB 592 (see fn 6, below), Bailhache J stressed that A had 'bought his agency' whereas in *Rhodes v Forwood*, there was no consideration moving from A to P which was executed (cf Bankes LJ at p 602). See also *Warren & Co v Agdeshman* (1922) 38 TLR 588 where, in awarding damages to A for the premature termination of a three year contract, Coleridge J emphasised the mutual obligations owed by P and A and that P was in breach of the obligation to supply A with samples. After such a breach, it would be unreasonable to allow P to terminate the contract thereby ending A's claim to damages *and* then get the benefit of the customers introduced by A.

A is viewed as a bare commission agent with (possibly) only P's offer of a unilateral contract underpinning the agency. Some decisions are plainly premised upon the presence or absence of an implied term regarding the continuance of the agency, ie it is an implied term that the agency should endure for the specified period or, putting the matter another way, it is *not* possible to imply a term that P might terminate the agency.[6] Other cases explain that A may be entitled to a 'continuing benefit'[7] while some emphasise the strength of the express promise made by P, meaning that arguments relating to implied terms are subjugated in the face of the unqualified, express provision.[8]

Termination by operation of law

Subject to certain exceptions considered later, A's *actual* authority may be terminated automatically by events which incapacitate either P or A, no matter whether the authority is conferred by deed and even if it is expressed to be irrevocable. These events must be considered separately.

DEATH OF THE PRINCIPAL OR AGENT

The death of either A or P terminates A's authority. In the case of A's death, the rule is justified in that the relationship of P and A is one of trust where A's personality is often crucial,[9] there being no possibility that A's personal representative could perform the undertaking as a substitute for A. The rule extends to joint agents where only one dies.[10]

6 *Turner v Goldsmith* [1891] 1 QB 544; *Mutzenbecher v La Aseguradora Española* [1906] 1 KB 254 (A was appointed as the exclusive insurance agent for P for five years but his authority was revoked after one year. Held that there was an implied term that P would not do anything to prevent A from acting as such during the agreed term); *Reigate v Union Manufacturing Co (Ramsbottom) Ltd* [1918] 1 KB 592 (A subscribed for £1,000 in shares in the defendant company (P) and was appointed for seven years as sole selling agent for P in the UK, India and the Colonies. One year later the company was wound up and eventually sold. Held that A was entitled to damages as an express term of the contract was that it would subsist for seven years and a term could not be implied that P might terminate the agency by ceasing to carry on the business).
7 *Lazarus v Cairn Line of Steamships Ltd* (1912) 106 LT 378, 380 per Scrutton J.
8 See *General Publicity Services Ltd v Best's Brewery Co Ltd* [1951] 2 TLR 875 (the defendants (D) agreed to display 'tariff booklets' in their hotel 'in the course of our business over a period of three years'. The booklets were supplied free of charge by the plaintiffs (P) and, as well as containing the hotel's tariff, they contained advertisements for businesses in the town where the hotel stood. After two years, D sold the hotel and the purchasers refused to display the booklets. Held that P was entitled to damages for breach of an express term and the obligation was unqualified. It was thus impossible to imply a term that the agreement would end if the defendants sold the hotel. This decision followed the approach of Scrutton J in *Lazarus v Cairn Line of Steamships Ltd* (1912) 106 LT 378, 380, viz, if there is an express term giving the plaintiff a right to a continuing benefit, the courts will not imply a term that the plaintiff's right shall cease on events not expressly provided for). See also *Re Premier Products Ltd* [1965] NZLR 50 (a company agreed to supply an association of master painters with paint for five years but went into voluntary liquidation before the contract expired. Held that no term could be implied that the company should remain in business simply to perform the contracts but that this was an unqualified obligation and the company was in breach of it).
9 *Farrow v Wilson* (1869) LR 4 CP 744.
10 *Adams v Buckland* (1705) 2 Vern 514.

P's death terminates A's actual authority[11] and thus A cannot sue for remuneration or indemnity in relation to acts performed after P is dead, even if he is unaware of the death.[12] Moreover, if he continues to act for P, he may be liable for any loss caused to the estate.[13] It seems likely, however, that P's estate cannot be bound under the principles of apparent authority (see below) and thus if A continues to warrant that he has P's authority, he will be liable to T for breach of warranty of authority.[14]

It is often asserted that P's executors may ratify a contract which was made by A on behalf of the deceased P but the two cases relied upon are doubtful. In the first,[15] although ratifcation was allowed, it is arguable that the contract was made on behalf of the executors and, in the second,[16] ratification was not established. Moreover, if ratification were allowed, it would appear to contradict one of the primary rules of that doctrine, viz, A must act for a principal who is in existence at the date of A's act.

The dissolution of a limited company is generally equivalent to the death of a human principal or agent and, on dissolution, the authority of the company's agents will cease[17] and the same rule applies where P or A is a partnership and there is a change in the partnership caused by death or retirement, for the partnership has technically changed its form and become a new one.[18] In *Triffit Nurseries v Salads Etcetera Ltd*,[19] both the judge at first instance and the Court of Appeal considered that the appointment of a receiver did not end the authority of a company to act as an agent automatically and for all purposes. Similarly, the cessation of A's business does not constitute an automatic termination of the agency relationship. 'Cessation of business' was said to be 'an uncertain concept at the best of times … [and] I do not think it is a satisfactory concept for addition to the list of causes of automatic determination of an agency relationship'.[20]

INSANITY OF THE PRINCIPAL OR AGENT

The insanity of either A or P terminates A's authority. A's insanity means that he is no longer capable of acting for P, while the ending of A's authority upon P's insanity seems to owe much to the older notion of the single identity of P and A. Thus in *Drew v Nunn*,[1] it was explained that 'where such a change occurs as to the principal that he can no longer act for himself, the agent whom he has appointed can no longer act for him'.[2] As with death, it is A's actual authority

11 *Wallace v Cook* (1804) 5 Esp 117; *Drew v Nunn* (1879) 4 QBD 661, 665, per Brett LJ.
12 *Pool v Pool* (1889) 58 LJP 67 (a solicitor was unable to recover costs incurred after P's death even though he had no knowledge of the death); *Campanari v Woodburn* (1854) 15 CB 400 (A was employed to sell a painting for P and, unaware of P's death, he sold the painting to T. Held that P's personal representative was not liable to A for the commission).
13 *Re Overweg, Haas v Durant* [1900] 1 Ch 209.
14 *Yonge v Toynbee* [1910] 1 KB 215, 227-228, per Buckley LJ.
15 *Foster v Bates* (1843) 12 M & W 226.
16 *Campanari v Woodburn* (1854) 15 CB 400.
17 *Salton v New Beeston Cycle Co* [1900] 1 Ch 43 (authority of the company's solicitor was determined on dissolution, even though he was unaware of it).
18 Eg *Tasker v Shepherd* (1861) 6 H & N 575 (on the death of one of two partners, the suvivor was under no obligation to employ A for the remainder of his specified term).
19 [1999] 1 Lloyd's Rep 697; affd [2000] 2 Lloyd's Rep 74 (considered in Ch 8).
20 [1999] 1 Lloyd's Rep 697, 700 per Longmore J.
 1 (1879) 4 QBD 661.
 2 (1879) 4 QBD 661 at 666, per Brett LJ.

which is terminated on insanity and thus any transaction will be void for lack of authority rather than voidable at the option of the insane person which would be the position with two parties contracting directly. In principle, there seems to be no objection to P's ratifying the unauthorised transaction should he regain his sanity.[3] Unlike death, however, *Drew v Nunn*[4] establishes that an insane principal may be bound by virtue of apparent authority (see later).

BANKRUPTCY OF THE PRINCIPAL OR AGENT

As a general rule, P's bankruptcy determines A's actual authority as bankruptcy is treated as incapacity and P's property is vested in the trustee in bankruptcy,[5] property being defined as including obligations.[6] It is thus usually asserted that, as bankruptcy is analogous to death, there can be no apparent authority where P is bankrupt, but statutory protection[7] is available to T. A's bankruptcy may similarly end his actual authority but termination does not follow automatically and much may depend on the terms of A's appointment.[8] There should thus be no objection in principle to a bankrupt *agent's* having apparent authority to act on behalf of P.

FRUSTRATION

A's actual authority may be ended by the occurrence of an event which frustrates the contract of agency or renders the agency or its objects unlawful or impossible to perform. In *Marshall v Glanvill*,[9] for example, A was conscripted for military service and sued P for damages for loss of commission but it was held that performance of the contract was impossible and thus no commission was payable. Similarly, the outbreak of war rendering P or A an enemy alien may end the agency relationship[10] but this is not an absolute rule and much depends upon whether continuation of the agency would benefit the enemy country.[11]

The effects of termination as regards the third party: apparent authority may endure

Where P has held-out A to T as having authority to act on his behalf, he will be bound by A's acts even though A's actual authority has been determined, provided

---

3 Provided that the contract entered into by A on P's behalf was not void: on regaining sanity, P may ratify a contract which, if entered into by him when incapacitated would be classifiable as a *voidable* contract.
4 (1879) 4 QBD 661.
5 *Dawson v Sexton* (1823) 1 LJOS Ch 185; 'Upon bankruptcy the trustee becomes the principal': *Drew v Nunn* (1879) 4 QBD 661, 666, per Brett LJ.
6 Insolvency Act 1986, ss 306 and 436.
7 Insolvency Act 1986, s 284(4) and (5).
8 *McCall v Australian Meat Co Ltd* (1870) 19 WR 188; *Hudson v Granger* (1821) 5 B & Ald 27.
9 [1917] 2 KB 87.
10 Eg *Stevenson (H) & Sons Ltd v Aktiengesellschaft für Cartonnagen-Industrie* [1918] AC 239 (A agreed to act as sole agent for a German company but the agreement was held to be determined by the outbreak of war).
11 See *Hangkam Kwingtong Woo v Liu Lan Fong* [1951] AC 707, 719, per Lord Simonds.

that T had no notice of the termination of authority. This notion was accepted in the early law[12] and is an application of the normal rules of apparent authority in that P's termination of A's authority is equivalent to any other secret limitation on his authority and, as long as it remains secret, it cannot be binding upon T. In *Trueman v Loder*,[13] for example, P had employed A for three years and he was 'universally known' to represent P at the time that P revoked A's authority. A then contracted to sell tallow to T, intending to make the contract on his own account, but T did not know that and thought that A represented P. Lord Denman CJ held that, as T had no notice that A's authority had been terminated, P was liable for non-delivery of the tallow. The general principle is established in both commercial transactions[14] and domestic situations where, in the absence of any notification to T, the apparent authority of wives or mistresses to order necessary goods, may persist after termination of their actual authority.[15] Moreover, the principle extends to P's creation of apparent *ownership*. In *Curlewis v Birkbeck*,[16] P sent horses to A, a licensed horse dealer, for sale in A's own name but, unknown to the buyer, T, P revoked A's authority to sell and to receive the price. T paid the price to A and it was held that the payment was good as against P because T had not received notice of the revocation of authority.

While it is plain that A may possess apparent authority after his actual authority has ended, it is unclear from the cases how long that apparent authority may endure. As between P and A may there may be no doubt that A is *functus officio*, but how long may A's apparent authority subsist? Following the general principles of apparent authority, much would depend upon the nature of P's holding-out and whether he makes a specific representation to T or, alternatively, appoints A to a position which carries a usual authority. In the former situation, a time-scale might be inferred from the representation itself but, in the latter

---

12 *Anon v Harrison* (1700) Holt KB 460 (a servant had authority to draw bills of exchange in his master's name and was then dismissed. Holt CJ held that the bills would bind the master if drawn 'so little time after, that the world cannot take notice of his being out of service; or if he were a long time out of his service, but that kept so secret, that the world cannot take notice of it').

13 (1840) 11 Ad & El 589.

14 *Aste v Montague* (1858) 1 F & F 264 (a livery-stable keeper (A) who had been P's coachman and continued to wear his livery ordered corn in P's name. P was liable to T for the price as he had not notified T of the termination of the employment); *Stavely v Uzielli* (1860) 2 F & F 30; *Pole v Leask* (1862) 33 LJ Ch (NS) 155; *Marsden v City and County Assurance Co* (1865) LR 1 CP 232 (an insurance policy, effected through a local agent of the defendant (P), provided that notice of loss had to be given to a 'known agent of the company'. P subsequently transferred the business to another company but, being unaware of the change, T notified A who made his report to the new company. Held that the notice was valid); *Scarf v Jardine* (1882) 7 App Cas 345 (a firm of two partners dissolved, one retired and the other carried on the business with a new partner. The new firm ordered goods from T which T supplied without any notice of the change. T sued the new firm but, on their bankruptcy, he sued the retired partner, Scarf (A). Held that, in principle, A was liable because, in the absence of any notification to T, the original partner had 'apparently continuing authority' (p 357, per Lord Blackburn) to bind A but that, having elected to proceed against the firm, T could not proceed against A); *Willis, Faber & Co Ltd v Joyce* (1911) 104 LT 576 (an underwriter (P) was liable on policies effected by his agent after revocation of A's authority because no notice of termination was given to T); *Morgan v Lifetime Building Supplies Ltd* (1967) 61 DLR (2d) 178.

15 *Ryan v Sams* (1848) 12 QB 460 (separation of P and his mistress (A); P was held liable to a tradesman (T) who, being unaware of the true position, did work to A's order after the separation); *Drew v Nunn* (1879) 4 QBD 661; *Debenham v Mellon* (1880) 6 App Cas 24, 33, per Lord Selborne LC.

16 (1863) 3 F & F 894.

situation, it is arguable that the apparent authority should continue until T has notice of the termination. This was the view of Lord Cranworth in his (dissenting) speech in *Pole v Leask*[17] where he considered that the burden would be on P to show that A's authority had been determined in cases of a 'general continuing agency' or where A 'fills some character from which such a general agency may be presumed'. Moreover, the Supreme Court of Canada[18] has recently held that a sales manager (A) of a large corporation had apparent authority to conclude a contract for the sale of goods even though his actual authority had been curtailed by a superior in the corporation. The court rejected the argument that T was under an obligation to inquire as to the extent of A's actual authority at the date of the contract; rather, the onus was on P to notify T of the limitation on A's authority.

Although T was under no positive duty to make inquiries on the facts of the Canadian decision, it must be asked whether T is ever put on inquiry and thus should realise that A's authority has terminated. The familiar question within apparent authority as to when T might be put on inquiry relates primarily to the possible *extent* of A's authority and, in *Willis, Faber & Co Ltd v Joyce*,[19] Scrutton J stressed that different considerations would apply where the issue was the possibility that A's authority had been *determined*. Consequently, although it was 'common knowledge'[20] that any agency might be terminated and any partnership deed might provide for termination, it was an untenable argument that such knowledge would put T on inquiry. If T were to be put on inquiry by such 'common knowledge', it would mean that the cases demanding that T be given notice of the withdrawal of authority were wrongly decided and, indeed, it could be argued that T would be perpetually on inquiry when dealing with an agent.

That being said, it is clear that situations can exist where T is put on inquiry. In *Stavely v Uzielli*,[1] P instructed his groom (A) to pay the farrier (T) who attended to P's horses in cash and not to pledge his credit. T had normally been paid in cash apart from one occasion when P settled T's account by cheque. T had submitted no accounts for payment for four years by which time A had died. P denied any authority in A to give credit. Erle CJ stressed that, although A had been held-out as having authority to pledge P's credit, the lapse of time during which T submitted no accounts could indicate that T realised that A lacked authority to give credit. Accordingly, the jury's verdict was that T's claim must fail.

Can A have apparent authority when P is incapacitated?

As apparent authority is postulated upon P's consent to a continuing representation, it is arguable that, if he is incapacitated, apparent authority in A should not continue. Lord Ellenborough's question encapsulates the difficulty:

---

17 (1862) 33 LJ Ch (NS) 155, 162; see also Powell, *The Law of Agency* (2nd edn, 1961), pp 399-400.
18 *Rockland Industries Inc v Amerada Minerals Corpn of Canada Ltd* (1980) 108 DLR (3d) 513.
19 (1911) 104 LT 576.
20 (1911) 104 LT 576 at 577.
 1 (1860) 2 F & F 30; see also *Re Parks, Canada Permanent Trust Co v Parks* (1956) 8 DLR (2d) 155 (T had constructive notice of P's insanity).

'How can a valid act be done in the name of a dead man?'[2] The same argument is clearly applicable to bankruptcy, as P's property is vested in the trusteee in bankruptcy who becomes the new principal. Moreover, this argument can be forcefully asserted where P is insane and clearly unable to evince any consent or make any representations to T. This was always the view of Powell[3] who differentiated between cases of P's voluntary termination of A's authority coupled with a failure to inform T and cases of involuntary termination as with insanity. In the latter case, he argued strongly that P was unable to give notice to T and should not therefore be held responsible.

The law on this question is in an inconclusive state. In *Drew v Nunn*,[4] P held-out his wife (A) to T, a tradesman, as having authority to pledge his credit and P then became insane. A subsequently ordered boots and shoes from T which T supplied, being unaware of the insanity. On regaining his sanity, P refused to pay for the goods but it was held that he was liable to T on the basis that, while he was sane, he had held-out A as having authority which had not been countermanded. The decision appears to conflict with *Yonge v Toynbee*,[5] where a solicitor, who continued proceedings on behalf of P in ignorance of the fact that P had become insane, was held liable to T in breach of warranty of authority, A's authority thus being terminated absolutely by the insanity irrespective of any notice to T.

There is here the habitual difficulty in apparent authority of deciding whether it is just to protect P or T, but with the added complication of an incapacitated principal where it might be argued that the interests of the insane, for example, should predominate.[6] *Drew v Nunn* was unequivocally based upon the need to protect T, Bramwell LJ emphasising that 'insanity is not a privilege, it is a misfortune, which must not be allowed to injure innocent persons'.[7] Brett LJ[8] went further in suggesting that he would apply the same principle where P makes a representation which is acted on after his death. However, *Blades v Free*[9] established that no authority subsisted after P had died even though T did not know of the death, but the decision is an early one which makes no express mention of apparent authority.

The modern approach almost certainly favours *Drew v Nunn*, this contention being supported by the fact that statutory protection is available to T in cases of bankruptcy.[10] It is difficult to disagree with Seavey who stressed that the result of the automatic termination of A's actual authority without any continuing apparent authority was 'shockingly inequitable, including as it does the liability of an innocent agent, deprived of his power without his fault, to respond upon his warranty of authority to the third person'.[11]

---

2 *Watson v King* (1815) 4 Camp 272, 274.
3 *The Law of Agency* (2nd edn, 1961), pp 403-404; see also Wade, (Book review) (1924) 40 LQR 111, 112.
4 (1879) 4 QBD 661. See also *Re Parks, Canada Permanent Trust Co v Parks* (1956) 8 DLR (2d) 155, where apparent authority endured after P's insanity but T was held to have constructive notice of the incapacity.
5 [1910] 1 KB 215 (considered in Ch 11).
6 See Müller-Freienfels, *Civil Law in the Modern World* (ed A N Yiannopoulos, 1965), Ch 4, pp 111-117.
7 (1879) 4 QBD 661, 668.
8 (1879) 4 QBD 661, 668.
9 (1829) 9 B & C 167 (P, who had cohabited with A for some years, went to the East Indies and subsequently died. Held that P's executor was not bound to pay for necessary goods supplied to A by a tradesman, T, after P's death but before the parties knew of the death).
10 See the Insolvency Act 1986, s 284(4) and (5).
11 'The Rationale of Agency' (1920) 29 Yale LJ 859, 893.

Limits on the termination of the agent's authority

IRREVOCABLE AUTHORITY[12]

Where A is given authority by deed or for valuable consideration in order that he may effect a security or protect an interest, his authority is irrevocable without his consent, as long as the security or interest remains in existence. Where an authority is irrevocable as defined here, it does not end on the death,[13] insanity or bankruptcy of P[14] and, where P is a company, its winding up or dissolution does not determine the authority.

This notion of irrevocability is somewhat elusive and abstract but its essence is that the authority and A's interest are entwined and inseparable and, here, A's authority 'is given for the purpose of being a security'.[15] A's normal authority is exercised in the management of P's business and there is thus a presumption that P may terminate the authority and manage his own affairs. In contrast, an irrevocable authority is exercised for A's benefit and in his own interest and thus *Bowstead & Reynolds* emphasises that such an authority should be regarded as 'a device for conferring a property interest ... rather than as a conferring of authority'.[16] For example, in *Gaussen v Morton*,[17] P was indebted to A and, in order to discharge the debt, gave A a power of attorney authorising him to sell certain land. Lord Tenterden CJ held that this 'was not a simple authority to sell and surrender the premises, but an authority coupled with an interest; for [A] was to apply the proceeds in liquidation of a debt due to himself'[18] and thus the authority could not be revoked.

It is clear, however, that the authority must be given explicitly to secure a *particular* interest of A's or confer such a benefit upon him and the fact that A has a *routine* interest in the performance of the authority, such as the payment of a salary, commission or the exercise of a lien, is insufficient to render the authority irrevocable. For example, in *Taplin v Florence*,[19] P authorised A to sell goods on P's premises but he then revoked A's authority and physically and forcefully ejected him from the premises. A argued that he had incurred expenses in preparing for the sale and had both a licence and an agreement with P to be on the premises to sell the goods, neither of which could be terminated except

---

12 See *Making Commercial Law, Essays in Honour of Roy Goode* (ed Cranston, 1997), Ch 10, Reynolds, 'When is an Agent's Authority Irrevocable?'
13 *Carter v White* (1883) 25 Ch D 666 (P owed A money and gave him a bill of exchange, accepted by himself, but leaving the drawer's name blank. P died before A had added the drawer's name but it was held that A could complete the bill after P's death).
14 *Alley v Hotson* (1815) 4 Camp 325 (P owed A money and, before going overseas, he gave A a power of attorney and ordered T to pay A the proceeds of sale of certain goods which had been consigned to T. T sent the proceeds to A but, before A received them, P commited an act of bankruptcy. Held that A could still apply the proceeds of sale in satisfaction of the debt).
15 *Smart v Sandars* (1848) 5 CB 895, 918, per Wilde CJ.
16 *Bowstead & Reynolds on Agency* (16th edn, 1996), Art 120, para 10-007; see also *Restatement, Second, Agency* § 138: 'A power given as security is a power to affect the legal relations of another, created in the form of an agency authority, but held for the benefit of the power holder or a third person and given to secure the performance of a duty or to protect a title ...'.
17 (1830) 10 B & C 731.
18 (1830) 10 B & C 731 at 734.
19 (1851) 10 CB 744; see also *Doward, Dickson & Co v Williams & Co* (1890) 6 TLR 316.

by mutual consent. Moreover, A asserted that he had an auctioneer's special property[20] in the goods and therefore a right to enter P's premises to deal with them. The court held that none of these arguments prevailed to render the authority irrevocable; A was simply a selling agent who had no interest in the subject-matter of the agreement as it is defined in the notion of irrevocability.

Although *Taplin* was a relatively straightforward case, the matter may not always be entirely clear-cut. In *Frith v Frith*,[1] A had been appointed attorney over an estate by two deeds which authorised him to enter into possession of the estate and manage it. P sought possession of the estate but A refused, arguing that the authority was irrevocable as he had given a personal guarantee, with P's consent, to a mortgagee of the estate, to pay the mortgage debt on the day of redemption. It was held that A was simply a manager with a fixed salary and the power of attorney contained no reference to any special interest created by the guarantee and it was not intended to be dependent on the continuance of such an interest. Accordingly, A's authority was held to be revocable. Similarly, in *Smart v Sandars*,[2] P consigned a quantity of wheat to a factor (A) for sale and A advanced money to P on the credit of the goods. P then instructed A not to sell but he nevertheless sold the goods and argued that his authority to sell had become irrevocable by the failure of P duly to repay the advances. It was held that A's authority was revocable and, although the making of an advance could be good consideration for an agreement that the authority to sell should become irrevocable, there was no such agreement on the instant facts. *Smart* also illustrates the rule that the authority and security must be created contemporaneously and the fact that A *subsequently* acquires an interest in the property is immaterial.

REVOCABILITY WHERE THE AGENT HAS INCURRED A PERSONAL LIABILITY TO THE THIRD PARTY

Where A incurs a personal liability to T in the execution of his authority, P cannot purport to revoke A's authority and thereby obviate his right to reimbursement or indemnity in relation to the liability. In *Chappell v Bray*,[3] A, the part-owner of a ship, was authorised by the other part-owners to repair the ship and he entered into a contract with T to lengthen the vessel. Subsequently, one part-owner said that he would not be answerable for the repairs but the work was completed and A paid T. It was held that A could recover the requisite proportion of the money from the defendant part-owner as 'an authority cannot be revoked if it has passed an interest and has been executed'.[4] The rule is not limited to those situations where A incurs a legal liability but extends to circumstances where A incurs a liability which could not be legally enforced but which ought to be discharged to avoid other loss to A or injury to his reputation, eg liability to pay a wagering debt on P's behalf[5] or barrister's fees.[6] Although this principle is often said to turn on irrevocability, it is perhaps better classified as an instance

---

20 See Ch 11.
1 [1906] AC 254.
2 (1848) 5 CB 895.
3 (1860) 6 H & N 145.
4 (1860) 6 H & N 145 at 152, per Wilde B.
5 *Read v Anderson* (1884) 13 QBD 779.
6 See *Rhodes v Fielder, Jones & Harrison* (1919) 89 LJKB 15 (considered in Ch 9).

of A's having certain vested rights once the authority has been executed, no act of P's then being able to deprive A of such rights.[7]

POWERS OF ATTORNEY AND PROTECTION FOR THE AGENT AND THIRD PARTY

Various statutory provisions modify the common law considerably in relation to revocability and powers of attorney.

First, the Powers of Attorney Act 1971, s 4, provides for irrevocability by largely reiterating the common law rules discussed above. Thus where a power of attorney is expressed to be irrevocable and is given to secure a proprietary interest of the donee of the power (A), or the performance of an obligation owed to the donee, then so long as the donee has that interest, or the obligation remains undischarged, the power is irrevocable. The statutory provision is narrower than the common law in two respects: the authority must be given in the form of a deed and it is only irrevocable where it is expressed to be so.

Second, protection is available under the 1971 Act for A and T where a power of attorney is capable of revocation and has been revoked. By s 5(1), the donee of the power (A) who acts in pusuance of it when it has been revoked does not incur any liability (either to the donor or any other person) if at that time he did not know it had been revoked. This section thus absolves A from any possible breach of duty owed to P, and for liability to T for breach of warranty of authority. Similarly, s 5(2) provides that where the power has been revoked and T deals with the donee without knowledge of the revocation, the transaction will be as valid as if there had been no revocation. This section clarifies the rules of apparent authority in the context of powers of attorney and other sections strengthen T's position futher. By s 5(3), where a power of attorney is expressed to be irrevocable and to be given by way of security, then, unless T knows that it was not given by way of security, he is entitled to assume that the power is incapable of revocation except by the donor with the consent of the donee and he will be treated as having knowledge of the revocation *only* if he knows that it has been revoked in that manner. Finally, by s 5(4), where T deals with A in ignorance of the power's revocation, it will be conclusively presumed in favour of T that he did not know of the revocation of the power if (i) the transaction between P and T was completed within twelve months of the date on which the power came into operation, or (ii) T makes a statutory declaration before or within three months after the completion of the transaction that he did not know of the power's revocation at the material time. It is apparent from s 5(5) that 'revocation' in the Act includes death, insanity and bankruptcy.

The Enduring Powers of Attorney Act 1985 provides further protection where P becomes insane.[8] Where such an enduring power has been created, A must register the instrument creating the power if he considers that P is becoming mentally incapable and s 1(1)(a) provides that subsequent insanity does not revoke the power. Following the pattern of the 1971 Act, there are provisions in the 1985 Act protecting A and validating the transaction for T, where the provisions of the Act have not been followed correctly.[9]

---

7 See Powell, *The Law of Agency* (2nd edn, 1961), p 395.
8 See *The Incapacitated Principal*, Law Com No 122, Cmnd 8977 (1983); Cretney, *Enduring Powers of Attorney; A Practitioner's Guide* (3rd edn, 1991); Munday, 'The Capacity to Execute an Enduring Power of Attorney in New Zealand and England' [1989] 13 NZULR 253.
9 See ss 1(3) and 9.

Termination under the Commercial Agents (Council Directive) Regulations 1993

In the light of the foregoing analysis of the law relating to the determination of A's authority, these Regulations[10] impose radical new rules regarding the termination of the authority of 'commercial agents'.[11] The 1993 Regulations implemented an EC Directive[12] and are premised upon the concept that, where a commercial agent has expended time and money in establishing a profitable customer-base for P in the buying or selling of goods, it would be unjust for P to terminate the agency and intervene to deal directly with those customers or another agent unless he compensates the commercial agent. The Regulations go further than this, however, and are not based upon P's *fault* in terminating the agency: as will be seen below, A may be entitled to 'compensation' where, for example, a fixed-term agency has simply run its course. The Regulations recognise that the clientèle which the commercial agent has assiduously established and the concomitant business goodwill which has accumulated, amount to invaluable assets for P. It is thus plain that these 'commercial agencies' are the antithesis of the one-off, perilous venture, exemplified in *Luxor (Eastbourne) Ltd v Cooper*.[13] Instead, the Regulations are rooted in the notions of good faith and fair dealing[14] and seek to reach equilibrium regarding the rights and duties of P and A within a continuing, commercial agency. The 1993 Regulations apply only to the internal P-A relationship[15] and therefore they have no bearing whatever on A's external authority.

WHO IS A 'COMMERCIAL AGENT'?

The Regulations apply *only* to paid,[16] 'commercial agents', who act on P's behalf in the buying or selling of goods. Regulation 2(1) provides the general definition of a 'commercial agent':

> 'In these Regulations–
> "commercial agent" means a self-employed intermediary who has continuing authority to negotiate the sale or purchase of goods on behalf of another person (the "principal"), or to negotiate and conclude the sale or purchase of goods on behalf of and in the name of that principal.'

This species of agent has been imported from European law and, hitherto, the 'commercial agent' was neither understood nor recognised in English law. Indeed, in 1977, the Law Commission reported that it was 'unable to identify such a social group in England'.[17] This can be accounted for in that it has never been customary for English law to classify *agents* and *agencies* and allot special rules

---

10 SI 1993/3053, as amended by SI 1993/3173. Guidance Notes on the Regulations are published by the DTI.
11 See Davey and Randolph, *Guide to the Commercial Agents Regulations* (1994); Saintier, 'New Developments in Agency Law' [1997] JBL 77.
12 Dir 86/653 (18 December 1986, OJ L382/17).
13 [1941] AC 108.
14 See regs 3, 4 and 5, detailing the rights and duties of P and A.
15 Reg 1(2).
16 The commercial agent need not be paid by *commission*: see reg 6(3).
17 (*Report on the Proposed EEC Directive on the Law Relating to Commercial Agents*, Law Com No 84 (1977), para 19).

to the various categories and sub-categories. Instead, the common law has fashioned broadly-based rules which apply to all situations where one person has authority to represent another and affect his legal position. However, litigation is revealing that there are now more self-employed intermediaries within the classification of commercial agents than was thought at first and the facts of *Tamarind International Ltd v Eastern Natural Gas (Retail) Ltd*,[18] considered later, exemplify the role of such agents in modern commercial conditions. The ever-increasing privatisation and deregulation of industry and commerce has spawned many relatively small, specialised companies, which cling like barnacles to the resultant, fractured structure of the modern commercial corpus.

It should be stressed that only those agents who are engaged in the sale and purchase of goods *on behalf* of their principals are within the Regulations. Consequently, the Regulations do not apply to distributors of goods, franchisees and independent contractors who may often be referred to as 'agents' but who are, in fact, buyers and sellers of goods in their own right with no semblance of an agency in existence.[19] This point was emphasised in the recent decision in *AMB Imballaggi Plastici SRL v Pacflex Ltd*.[20] There Pacflex purchased goods from AMB and re-sold them to purchasers with Pacflex adding their own 'mark-up' of over 5% and invoicing the purchasers themselves. AMB had been prepared, originally, to do business on a conventional agency basis with Pacflex in the sense that Pacflex would negotiate contracts between AMB and the purchasers of the goods and then be remunerated on a commission basis. This method of trading had, however, never been adopted, and Pacflex chose to re-sell the goods after adding their own mark-up as the most profitable way of doing business. The Court of Appeal had no hesitation in deciding that Pacflex never purported to negotiate on behalf of AMB and, emphatically, could not be said to have any 'continuing authority' to do so. Accordingly, Pacflex could not be classified as a commercial agent of AMB.

Moreover, in *Garry Parkes v Esso Petroleum Co Ltd*,[1] it was stressed that the agent must 'negotiate' the relevant contracts if he is to be classified as a commercial agent under reg 2(1). There the agent sold Esso motor fuel and was paid a commission on the volume sold at the pumps but, as the price was fixed by Esso, the court held that the agent concluded the sale as an agent but he did not 'negotiate' it and was thus not to be regarded as a commercial agent.

The requirement that the commercial agent's authority must be a 'continuing' one is clearly a significant factor and so an agent authorised to enter into a single transaction, for example, would not be within the Regulations. There is some uncertainty in the stipulation that the commercial agent must be 'self-employed' in that it is unclear whether this phrase was intended to embrace a company or a partnership, but it would be unnecessarily limiting if the Regulations were confined to natural persons. Moreover, in *Tamarind International Ltd v Eastern Natural Gas (Retail) Ltd*,[2] a limited company was, without argument on the point, held to be a commercial agent.

As the agent can have authority within reg 2(1) 'to *negotiate* the sale or purchase of goods', it is uncertain whether this might apply to 'canvassing' or

---

18   [2000] 26 LS Gaz R 35.
19   See Ch 15 where, in relation to the sale of goods, agency is distinguished from sale.
20   [1999] 2 All ER (Comm) 249.
 1   [1999] 1 CMLR 455.
 2   [2000] 26 LS Gaz R 35.

'introducing' agents who locate and introduce customers to P but do not enter into contracts on P's behalf.[3] There seems to be no reason, in principle, to exclude such agents from the Regulations and, provided that this type of agent has a continuing authority from P, he appears to be as worthy of the protection conferred by the Regulations as the agent who happens to enter into contracts on P's behalf. This conclusion is arguably reinforced by the capacious words used in the Schedule to the Regulations when delineating the functions of a 'commercial agent' (see below) in that reference is made to that agent's 'representative activities' and to his 'procuring a transaction'.[4]

Finally, under reg 2(1) the commercial agent must act 'on behalf of and *in the name of*' the principal and, while the paradigm of a disclosed, named principal is within this wording, it must surely be indisputable that it could not apply to an agent who acts for an undisclosed principal as, necessarily, such an agent acts in his *own* name.

The commercial agency must not be a secondary activity

Regulation 2(4) stipulates that the Regulations do not apply to persons whose activities as commercial agents are to be considered 'secondary' and the Schedule to the Regulations seeks to clarify, with a mixture of positive and negative requirements, whether or not an agent's role is primarily that of a commercial agent.

Paragraph 1 of the Schedule provides that, where the primary purpose of the arrangement with P is *other* than as set out in para 2 of the Schedule, the activities of the commercial agent are to be considered as secondary only. The positive indications that A is a commercial agent contained in para 2 can be summarised, viz (a) the business of P is the sale or purchase of goods of a 'particular kind' and (b) the goods concerned are such that – (i) transactions are 'normally individually negotiated and concluded on a commercial basis' and (ii) procuring a transaction on one occasion is likely to lead to a further transactions in the same goods with that customer in the future or to transactions in those goods with other customers in the same geographical area and that, accordingly (iii) it is in P's commercial interests in developing the market in the goods to appoint a representative to such customers with a view to that representative's devoting 'effort, skill and expenditure from his own resources' to that end.

Paragraph 3 goes on to provide criteria which indicate positively when A's activities are primarily those of a commercial agent, the absence of such criteria being an indication to the contrary viz (i) P is the 'manufacturer, importer or distributor of the goods' (ii) the goods are 'specifically identified' with P in the market in question rather than, or to a greater extent than, with any other person (iii) A devotes 'substantially the whole of his time to representative activities' (whether for one principal or several whose interests do not conflict) (iv) the goods are 'not normally available in the market in question' other than by means of A and (v) the arrangement is described as one of commercial agency.

Paragraph 4 lists three facts indicating that the arrangement is *not* primarily a commercial agency, viz (i) promotional material is supplied direct to potential

---

3   In relation to real property, estate agents are the paradigm of this type of representative but their lack of 'continuing authority' would exclude them from the Regulations.
4   Cf reg 7(1) which provides that A is entitled to commission on contracts '*concluded*' as a result of A's actions (see Ch 9).

customers (ii) persons are granted agencies without reference to existing agents in a particular area or in relation to a particular group and (iii) customers normally select the goods for themselves and merely place their orders through an agent.

Finally, para 5 provides that the activities of two species of agent are presumed *not* to fall within the definition of a commercial agent unless the contrary is proven, viz (i) mail order catalogue agents for consumer goods and (ii) consumer credit agents.

It should also be noted that reg 2(1)(i), (ii) and (iii) exclude three other agents from the category of commercial agents, viz (i) officers of a company or association who are 'empowered' to bind the company or association, (ii) partners 'authorised' to bind fellow partners, and (iii) persons acting as insolvency practitioners as defined in the Insolvency Act 1986, s 388. Likewise, reg 2(2) provides that the Regulations do not apply to (i) commercial agents whose activities are unpaid (ii) commercial agents when they operate on commodity exchanges or in the commodity market and (iii) the Crown Agents.

In *AMB Imballaggi Plastici SRL v Pacflex Ltd*,[5] Waller LJ forcefully criticised the criteria in the Schedule to the Regulations relating to the primary and secondary activities of the commercial agent. He stressed that, for the purposes of making the decision as to whether or not such activities are secondary, the Schedule contemplates an assessment of the agent's arrangement with the principal rather than assessing the agent's activities as a commercial agent in comparison with his *other* business activities. Moreover, the judge thought that paras 3 and 4 'provide no assistance as to what is being compared with what'[6] for the purpose of distinguishing primary from secondary activities, his conclusion being that clarification of the Regulations was needed as a matter of urgency.

Without explicit reference to the *Pacflex* decision, Morison J considered whether an agent's activities were 'secondary' in *Tamarind International Ltd v Eastern Natural Gas (Retail) Ltd*.[7] Following the deregulation of the gas and electricity supply industries, the defendants (ENG) began to market gas and electricity by means of self-employed intermediaries whose task was to persuade existing customers of British Gas to take their supply from ENG. It was not disputed that the agents were commercial agents within the Regulations but it was contended that their activities were 'secondary' within reg 2(4). Morison J rejected the argument that, in determining whether an agent's activities were secondary, a comparison had to be drawn between the amount of time spent on the commercial agency and the business generated thereby and the time spent on other, non-agency activities. Instead, he considered that the court should look at the nature of the commercial bargain between the principal and agent and that this approach reflected the purpose of the Directive. He also refused to accept that 'goods of a particular kind' in para 2(a) of the Schedule to the Regulations meant unique or special goods because, if accepted, this interpretation would emasculate the Regulations. Consequently, Eastern's gas did not cease to be 'goods of a particular kind' simply because it was no different from British gas.

Having regard to the factors stipulated in the Schedule to the Regulations, the judge considered that (i) the decision to employ these specialist agents was taken because other marketing techniques had been unsuccessful (ii) all the agents were exclusively devoted to serving ENG's interests (iii) the agents were carefully controlled as to their conduct in selling ENG's contracts and promoting its image (iv)

---

5   [1999] 2 All ER (Comm) 249.
6   [1999] 2 All ER (Comm) 249 at 254.
7   [2000] 26 LS Gaz R 35.

remuneration was a commission for each contract a customer was persuaded to enter into (v) Eastern's gas was not generally available in the market otherwise than through the agents (vi) the agents were allocated a geographical area on an exclusive basis (vii) although some promotional material was sent to potential customers by ENG, the selling effort was made largely by the agents (viii) the sale of Eastern gas to one customer was likely to lead to further sales to other customers through the process by which the existing customer was asked to give 'leads' to other potential customers (ix) ENG had received a substantial measure of future goodwill because the successful marketing of the gas meant that ENG might derive long-term benefits from their agents' efforts. Accordingly, the agents' activities were held to be within the Regulations and could not possibly be regarded as secondary activities.

MINIMUM PERIODS OF NOTICE FOR THE TERMINATION OF THE COMMERCIAL AGENCY

Regulations 14 and 15 stipulate that notice is required for the termination of contracts concluded for an indefinite period of time and thus resolve, at least in the context of commercial agents, the indecision which the common law exhibits on this issue. Regulation 15 provides that, where the agency contract is concluded for an indefinite period, either party may terminate it by notice of one month for the first year of the contract, two months for the second year commenced and three months for the third year commenced and subsequent years. A and P *cannot* agree on shorter periods but they can agree on longer periods; in the latter case, the notice to be observed by P must not be shorter than that observed by A. Moreover, unless otherwise agreed, the end of the period of notice must coincide with the end of a calendar month.

Regulation 14 is exacting in providing that an agency contract for a fixed period, which continues to be performed by P and A after the period has expired, 'shall be deemed to be converted' into an agency contract for an indefinite period and thus be subject to the same periods of notice as in reg 15. It is unclear whether reg 14 can be varied by agreement; unlike reg 15, there is no express provision that reg 14 cannot be derogated from.

ENTITLEMENT TO COMPENSATION OR INDEMNITY ON THE TERMINATION OF THE AGENCY

Most significantly, regs 17 and 18 contain broad provisions which relate to A's indemnity or compensation on the termination of the agency. These provisions are central to the Regulations and the overall object of the Directive that A should be compensated when he has suffered damage on termination of the agency and P is left with an accrued and continuing benefit in the form of a profitable customer-base.

Regulation 19 provides that regs 17 and 18 cannot be derogated from to 'the detriment' of A 'before the agency contract expires'. There is no room for manoeuvre regarding this express prohibition as illustrated in the recent decision in *Ingmar GB Ltd v Eaton Leonard Technologies Inc.*[8] There P was a company incorporated in California and A was appointed as its commercial

---

8   Case C-381/98; [2001] All ER (EC) 57.

agent in the United Kingdom, a clause in their contract providing that it was to be governed by the law of the State of California. After termination of the contract, A brought an action seeking payment of commission and compensation under reg 17. The High Court held that the Regulations did not apply but, on appeal, the Court of Appeal stayed the proceedings and referred the matter to the Court of Justice of the European Communities. That court held that the aim of the Directive was to protect commercial agents, particularly after termination of their contracts, and thus it was essential that P could not evade the provisions of the Directive by the simple expedient of a choice-of-law clause. Accordingly, the court ruled that the Directive had to be applied where A carried on his activities in a Member State even though P was established in non-member country.

When is compensation or indemnity payable?

Regulation 17(1) provides:

> 'This regulation has effect for the purpose of ensuring that the commercial agent is, after the termination of the agency contract, indemnified in accordance with paragraphs (3) to (5) below or compensated for damage in accordance with paragraphs (6) and (7) below.'

Accordingly, it is the 'termination of the agency contract' which is the trigger for compensation and indemnity. In *Moore v Piretta PTA Ltd*,[9] it was argued that this phrase should relate only to the contract governing the relationship of P and A at the date of termination and that where P and A enter into a series of contracts, the court should be concerned only with the last contract in time. It was held, however, that the phrase 'the agency contract' means simply 'the agency'.

The Regulations introduce no-fault compensation to this area of the law of agency and, in some situations, P is deemed to bear the risks which ensue from events outside his control which constitute, nevertheless, a 'termination of the agency'. A's death would fall within this category. This approach has been culled from Europe and, in particular, from German law. 'Termination' consequently encompasses a wide variety of situations which can be categorised, although the list is not exhaustive:

(a) where P commits a repudiatory breach of the agency contract which A accepts;[10]
(b) on termination of contracts of indefinite duration where the periods of notice in reg 15 have been complied with;
(c) in contracts of definite duration which have simply expired;
(d) under reg 17(8) where termination results from A's death;
(e) under reg 18(b)(ii) where A terminates the contract 'on grounds of ... age, infirmity or illness ... in consequence of which he cannot reasonably be required to continue his activities';[11]

---

9 [1999] 1 All ER 174.
10 See *Page v Combined Shipping and Trading Co Ltd* [1997] 3 All ER 656 (considered below).
11 Reg 18(b)(ii) is somewhat startling in that it appears to let A fix the date of his retirement *and* be compensated in situations which are, by any standards, loosely defined, but which must be considered as falling short of circumstances which would frustrate the contract.

(f) following (d) and (e) above, it seems likely that A would be entitled to compensation or indemnity when the contract is frustrated,[12] in which case the award might be more favourable to A than under the rules of frustration.

Although both indemnity and compensation apply on termination of the agency, the commercial agent is entitled to an indemnity *only* if there is an agreement to that effect between P and A and so indemnity is considered after the primary remedy of compensation has been evaluated.

The nature of the compensation

The commercial agent's overall right to compensation (and indemnity) is set-out in reg 17(1), above. Further detail is then furnished in reg 17(6) and the 'deeming' provision in reg 17(7) (a) and (b). Regulation 17(6) provides:

'Subject to paragraph (9) and to regulation 18 below, the commercial agent shall be entitled to compensation for the damage he suffers as a result of the termination of his relations with his principal.'

Although an English lawyer associates 'damage suffered' with P's *wrongful* act, it must be re-emphasised that this is not necessarily the case under the scheme of no-fault compensation which the Regulations impose. However, where the termination is wrongful, the Court of Appeal considered that A may claim compensation under the Regulations in augmentation of any damages at common law.[13]

Some guidance is imparted on the nature of the compensation by the 'deeming' provisions in reg 17(7) which enunciate *particular* cases where 'damage' occurs to A. Regulation 17(7) provides:

'For the purpose of these regulations such damage shall be deemed to occur particularly when the termination takes place in either or both of the following circumstances, namely circumstances which–
  (a) deprive the commercial agent of the commission which proper performance of the agency contract would have procured for him whilst providing his principal with substantial benefits linked to the activities of the commercial agent; or
  (b) have not enabled the commercial agent to amortise the costs and expenses that he had incurred in the performance of the agency contract on the advice of his principal.'

The compensation payable to A under regs 17(6) and 17(7) was considered in *Page v Combined Shipping and Trading Ltd.*[14] In January 1995, the plaintiff (A) entered into an agency agreement with the defendant company (P) which provided that he would buy and sell commodities on P's behalf for a minimum period of four years, his remuneration to be half the net profit received. When only five months of the contract had expired, P informed A that its South African parent company had decided to cease trading. A then terminated the agreement on the ground that P's conduct amounted to a repudiatory breach of contract and he claimed compensation for damage suffered under regs 17(6) and 17(7). At first instance, Wright J considered that the terms of the agency contract permitted P to operate it so that A would have earnt no remuneration and,

---

12 Although reg 16 preserves the common law rules on discharge of contract by breach and frustration.
13 See *Duffen v Frabo SpA* (1998) Times, 15 June.
14 [1997] 3 All ER 656.

accordingly, he held that A had lost nothing by the premature termination and had no case for compensation under the 1993 Regulations. The Court of Appeal reversed that decision and held that, even if Wright J's 'rather extravagant'[15] interpretation of the contract was correct, A was entitled to compensation under reg 17(6) based upon the commission which he would have earnt if the contract had continued to be performed in the normal manner throughout its remaining term of some three and a half years. Millett LJ[16] had no doubt that 'proper performance' in reg 17(7)(a) meant 'normal performance', this interpretation being aided by the fact that the word 'normal' was employed in the wording of several versions of the Regulations in other languages.

The nature of the compensation payable by P was again considered in *Duffen v Frabo SpA*,[17] where the 'damage' suffered by A was considered within the context of the familiar rules of causation. There A was the defendant's (P) exclusive commercial agent in the UK for the promotion and sale of P's products which were supplied to the plumbing trade. A was remunerated on a commission basis and was also paid a retainer of £4,000 per calendar month 'for and in respect of each of 36 calendar months' following the date of the agreement 'whether or not this agreement shall have previously terminated'. Disputes arose between A and P and, pursuant to a term of the agreement, A terminated the contract and sought, *inter alia*, compensation under the 1993 Regulations. Judge Hallgarten QC held that, first, compensation should be payable up to the earliest date when the agreement might have expired and, although it was permissible to look beyond that date, it would be inapt to do so in the instant case as A had acted as P's agent only for some 2½ years. Second, the judge stressed that the 'deeming' provision in reg 17(7)(a) 'only comes into play to the extent that [P] can be said to have benefited from [A's] prior efforts'. This benefit would normally be comprised of customers procured by A combined with P's ability to continue to deal with those customers without having to pay commission to A. On the facts, however, A had introduced no new customers to P and had been less than successful in nurturing existing customers. Third, the retainer of £4,000 per month served amply to amortise any costs which A might have incurred and so reg 17(7)(b)[18] could not assist A. Accordingly, the right approach was to consider what net earnings might have accrued to A had he remained P's agent during the relevant period, *without* taking into account the common law concepts of avoided loss and mitigation. The judge concluded that, without the retainer, the agency was not profitable nor would it have become profitable in its final year of operation. It followed that, under the Regulations, A was unable to show that he suffered 'damage' as a result of the termination of the agency.

While the conclusions in these decisions must be correct, it is more awkward to apply reg 17(7)(a) to a fixed-term contract which has expired or where A has received the prescribed period of notice under a contract of indefinite duration. In these situations, it is difficult to see that performance has been anything other than 'proper' meaning that A is 'deprived' of nothing and has thus suffered no 'damage' which would entitle him to compensation. However, the Regulations as a whole are not premised upon P's fault and so this appears to be fallacious reasoning. Presumably reg 17(7)(a) could apply where, for example, on the

15 [1997] 3 All ER 656 at 659, per Staughton LJ.
16 [1997] 3 All ER 656 at 661; see also Staughton LJ's more guarded approach at pp 660-661.
17 [2000] 1 Lloyd's Rep 180.
18 Reg 17(7)(b) is considered below.

expiration of a fixed-term agency, there is a causal link between A's work in establishing a profitable customer-base which has not come to fruition in terms of actual orders for P, and commission payable to A from customer's orders which P secures after the termination of the agency.[19] In other cases of termination after the prescribed period of notice or where a fixed-term contract has expired, it might be apt to limit compensation to unamortised costs and expenses under reg 17(7)(b), as being the only head of damage which A has suffered.

Regulation 17(7)(b) is narrower than reg 17(7)(a) in that, under the former, A must have incurred costs and expenses on *P's advice* and the circumstances of the termination mean that A has been unable to amortise or extinguish those costs.[20] The English lawyer accepts innately that a commission agent often runs the risk that expense and work done may be in vain but, once again, this perspective must be adjusted to accept the view that the commercial agency involves good faith and fair dealing in a co-operative, risk-sharing venture. It is nevertheless unclear how P's 'advice' is to be construed and what weight is to be attached to such guidance.

As mentioned earlier, reg 19 provides that the compensation provisions cannot be derogated from to 'the detriment' of A 'before the agency contract expires'. In the light of the overall tenor of the Directive and the Regulations, it is difficult to see why derogation should be permitted *after* the expiry of the contract. Finally, under reg 17(9), A will lose his entitlement to compensation if he does not notify P within one year following termination of his intention to pursue his entitlement.

In summation, compensation is based upon the 'damage' which A suffers on termination of the agency, meaning that he must incur a *loss*, although this is not necessarily as a result of P's breach of contract.[1] While A must suffer a loss, there is no *overall* requirement in the compensation principle enunciated in reg 17(6) that P should be left with a corresponding *benefit* on the termination of the agency. However, the deeming provision in reg 17(7)(a) clearly links A's loss of commission to the 'substantial benefits' which P gains and, in *Duffen v Frabo SpA*,[2] it was held that reg 17(7)(a) operated only where P could be said to have benefited from A's prior efforts.

Indemnity

The Directive allowed countries to choose between a scheme of indemnity or compensation and Great Britain opted for compensation; consequently, reg 17(2) provides that 'except where the agency contract otherwise provides, the commercial agent shall be entitled to be compensated rather than indemnified'.

If there is an agreement for indemnity, reg 17(3) stipulates that A is entitled to it 'if and to the extent that (a) he has brought the principal new customers or has significantly increased the volume of business with existing customers and the principal continues to derive substantial benefits from the business with such customers; *and* (b) the payment of this indemnity is equitable having regard to all the circumstances and, in particular, the commission lost by the commercial

---

19 See also reg 8 which provides for post-termination commission (see Ch 9) but requires a closer causal link than that suggested in this example.
20 See *Duffen v Frabo SpA* [2000] 1 Lloyd's Rep 180, considered above, where the flat-rate 'retainer' paid to A allowed him to amortise any costs incurred.
 1 It seems likely that A comes under an obligation to mitigate his damage but there is no reference to this in the Regulations; see *Duffen v Frabo SpA*, considered above.
 2 [2000] 1 Lloyd's Rep 180.

agent on the business transacted with such customers'. In *Moore v Piretta PTA Ltd*,[3] it was argued that 'brought the principal new customers' in reg 17(3)(a) must mean that A had actually 'introduced' customers to P, but it was held that this was too restrictive an interpretation and that the phrase meant simply that A had been 'instrumental in obtaining the business of new customers' for P.

One crucial difference between compensation and indemnity is that the amount of the indemnity is limited by reg 17(4) to 'a figure equivalent to an indemnity for one year calculated from the commercial agent's average annual remuneration over the preceding five years and if the contract goes back less than five years the indemnity shall be calculated on the average for the period in question'.

It will be noticed that the requirements in reg 17(3) (a) and (b) are *not* phrased as alternative requirements and so both must be complied with. It was noted above that the compensation principles do not necessarily depend upon any benefit accruing to P on termination of the agency. The indemnity principles in reg 17(3) demand, however, that P has continued to derive benefits from new or existing customers *and* that the indemnity payment is equitable in the circumstances.[4] If, for example, the termination meant that P was unable to carry on business and A promptly secured a remunerative commercial agency with another principal, it is difficult to see that any indemnity would be payable.

Finally, reg 17(5) provides that 'the grant of an indemnity ... shall not prevent the commercial agent from seeking damages'.[5] Once they have been adopted, the indemnity provisions cannot be derogated from (reg 19) but, under reg 17(9), A will lose his entitlement to indemnity if within one year following termination of his agency contract he has not notified his principal that he intends pursuing his entitlement.

Situations where no compensation or indemnity is payable

Regulation 18 stipulates that indemnity or compensation is not payable in certain situations, viz (a) where P terminates the agency because of A's default which would justify immediate termination or (b) where A has terminated the contract *unless* such termination is justified (i) by circumstances attributable to P (ie P's repudiatory breach) or (ii) on grounds of A's age, infirmity or illness, in consequence of which he cannot reasonably be required to continue his activities. Finally, A will lose the right to compensation or indemnity under reg 18, para (c) where he has, with the agreement of P, assigned his rights and duties under the contract to another person. This latter exception is presumably based upon the fact that A has obtained 'compensation' in the form of the purchase price received for the agency.

---

3 [1999] 1 All ER 174.
4 See the guidance given in *Moore v Piretta PTA Ltd* [1999] 1 All ER 174, 181-182.
5 A could thus seek damages for breach of contract, for example.

PART TWO

The Sale of Goods

CHAPTER 13

Introduction to the sale of goods

The Sale of Goods Acts 1893 and 1979

Codification and consolidation of the law

Although the contract for the sale of goods is one of the earliest and most important forms of commercial contract, the modern law of sale dates from the end of the 19th century. In 1888, Sir Mackenzie Chalmers drafted the Sale of Goods Bill which Lord Herschell introduced in the House of Lords in order that it might be evaluated and criticised. In 1891, the Bill was re-introduced in the Lords but questions arose as to its applicability in Scotland. After amendments by a Select Committee of the House of Commons, the Bill eventually became law as the Sale of Goods Act 1893.[1] The Act's long title was 'An Act for codifying the Law relating to the Sale of Goods' and its effect was to distil the principles of the common law in a lucid and comprehensive code[2] which was very advanced for its time. This is evidenced by the fact that the Act has been adopted as a model in most of the British Commonwealth jurisdictions and was also the basis of the USA's Uniform Sales Act 1906 until that legislation was replaced[3] in 1952 by the Uniform Commercial Code which differs in many respects from the 1893 Act.[4] Moreover, the provisions of the 1893 Act remained entirely unchanged in the United Kingdom until 1954 when s 4[5] was repealed. Thereafter successive amendments were made to the 1893 Act and the law has now been consolidated in the Sale of Goods Act 1979 (hereafter referred to as the SGA) although the 1979 Act cannot be regarded as a self-sufficient code because other important statutes, such as the Unfair Contract Terms Act 1977, now play an important role in the sale of goods. However, the overall plan and much of the wording of

---

1 The SGA 1893 came into operation on 1 January 1894.
2 Most strikingly referred to as 'the Code' throughout Atkin LJ's judgment in *Re Wait* [1927] 1 Ch 606, 625-641. See Chalmers, 'The Codification of the Law of Sale' (1891) 12 Journal of the Institute of Bankers 11; 'Codification of Mercantile Law' (1903) 19 LQR 10; Rodger, 'The Codification of Commercial Law in Victorian Britain' (1992) 109 LQR 570.
3 In all States except Louisiana.
4 See Gilmore, 'On the Difficulties of Codifying Commercial Law' (1948) 57 Yale LJ 1341; Corbin, 'The Uniform Commercial Code – Sales; Should it be enacted?' (1950) 59 Yale LJ 821; Williston, 'The Law of Sales in the Proposed Uniform Commercial Code' (1950) 63 Harv L Rev 561.
5 Section 4 demanded, inter alia, that contracts for the sale of goods over £10 in value should be supported by a note or memorandum in order to be enforceable.

the 1893 Act remain lucid and intact in the 1979 legislation and this surely distinguishes the work of Chalmers as an extraordinarily astute and enduring feat of draftsmanship.

Commercial law was revolutionised at the end of the 19th and beginning of the 20th century when the great codified mercantile statutes were enacted.[6] These statutes possessed 'the advantages of a code and something else as well ... a happy mean has been found between the excessive rigidity of the continental commercial codes and the pathless wilderness of precedent which was formerly the characteristic of our mercantile law'.[7] It may well be time for an entirely new codification of the sale of goods as the Law Commissions have warned that there is a limit to which the 1979 Act can be 'patched'[8] and amended. Indeed, it was suggested recently by the Chairman of the Law Commission that the time is ripe for a generalised codification of English commercial law.[9]

Changing conditions and amendments to the SGA

The draftsman of the 1893 Act would have no difficulty in deciphering the 1979 Act but he would undoubtedly be surprised at the changed conditions in modern society and the adoption of new business practices, both of which have led to considerable amendments to the original Act. There were two predominant features of the 1893 Act which characterised it as a creature of its time.

First, the new code drew virtually no distinction between the different types of sale which could exist and took little account of the scale of the transaction or the status of the parties. Thus, purely commercial sales (eg a sale of raw materials between manufacturers of goods), sales made between a commercial seller and a private buyer of goods (eg a sale of a pint of beer in a public house) and purely private sales (eg a contract between neighbours for the sale of a horse) were all treated alike.[10] In 1893, it was envisaged that the Act would apply primarily to sales of goods between traders who possessed roughly equal bargaining power and, of course, the 'consumer' began to figure as an entity only in the 20th century.

Second, the Act reflected the consensual nature of the contract of sale in that most of its provisions could be excluded or modified by the contrary intent of the parties.[11] In the 20th century, there was a conspicuously rapid growth in the inequality of bargaining power between large corporations and 'consumer' buyers and both an ability and willingness of the stronger party to abuse its dominant bargaining strength by, for example, the extensive use of unfair exclusion clauses

---

6   Viz, the Bills of Exchange Act 1882, Partnership Act 1890, Sale of Goods Act 1893 and Marine Insurance Act 1906.
7   Gutteridge, 'Contract and Commercial Law' (1935) 51 LQR 91, 117.
8   *Sale and Supply of Goods* (Law Com No 160, Scot Law Com No 104, Cm 137, 1987), para 1.15.
9   Arden, 'Time for an English Commercial Code?' [1997] 56 CLJ 516; see also Goode, 'The Codification of Commercial Law' (1986) 14 Monash LR 135.
10   The implied terms relating to merchantable quality and fitness for purpose in the SGA 1893, s 14, applied only in cases of a business seller, however.
11   'Sale is a consensual contract, and the Act does not seek to prevent the parties from making any bargain they please' (Chalmers, *Sale of Goods Act 1893*, Introduction to the first edition (1894)); see the SGA 1893, s 55 which acknowledged the parties' freedom to conclude their own contract. Certain areas of the Act were (and are) incapable of variation, however, eg the rule in s 16 that no property can pass in unascertained goods until the goods are ascertained.

in the contract of sale. Moreover, during the last century there was a revolutionary change in the nature of the complex goods which were bought routinely by consumer buyers with, often, total reliance placed by such consumers on pre-packaged goods bought for use and consumption from supermarkets. These dramatic changes could not have been foreseen at the end of the 19th century. Today, although freedom of contract is still a basic principle which is espoused by the 1979 Act, it is a notion which has been fettered.[12] For example, the Unfair Contract Terms Act 1977, s 6, provides that, in consumer contracts, the implied conditions in the SGA, ss 13-15 (relating to the description, quality and fitness for purpose of the goods) *cannot* be excluded or restricted by reference to any contract term and, indeed, it is a criminal offence, in the course of a business, to purport to display notices and advertisements or use contract terms which are void by virtue of the 1977 Act.[13] The implied condition of satisfactory quality in the SGA, s 14, has also been broadened to include elements such as the safety, freedom from minor defects and the durability of goods, thereby seeking to raise the standard of quality which a consumer buyer legitimately expects at the start of the 21st century.

Despite these changes, it remains a pronounced feature of English law that, overall, the principles relating to the sale of goods are of general application and there is no decisive separation of commercial sales from consumer sales. English law's rejection of a distinct consumer code has been defended by Reynolds[14] on the basis that the better approach is to modify general rules of law to take account of special consumer problems. This is one acknowledged technique of English law but, with respect, the approach advocated by Reynolds places immense and perhaps unwarranted[15] faith in the common law's willingness to adapt to changed social conditions. Moreover, it seemingly overlooks the difficulty that statutory modification is often a laborious process borne of much injustice to litigants. Once it is recognised that there are specialised consumer *problems* it is difficult to see why there should not be separate, coherent rules designed to solve them. A collation of such rules in an exclusive consumer code would surely be desirable in promoting certainty in the law and as an important step in seeking to inform consumers of their rights. Indeed, domestic commercial law is, more than ever, in need of unification. EC Directives show no sign of abatement and are frequently implemented by Regulations in the form of statutory instruments which amend existing UK legislation but which receive very little publicity when promulgated. Moreover, such Regulations are often made with little regard for the scope of the existing legislation, thus producing an overlapping, rather than an interlocking, set of rules. The original statutory instrument is frequently followed by amending Regulations resulting in a statutory patchwork which is both abstruse and inaccessible. After the common law has assiduously embroidered the patchwork, the modern legal system is surely only marginally less arcane than the early forms of action. It is submitted that separate commercial and consumer codes are long overdue.

---

12 See the SGA 1979, s 55(1).
13 See the Consumer Transactions (Restrictions on Statements) Order 1976 (SI 1976/1813, as amended by SI 1978/27).
14 See 'The Applicability of General Rules of Private Law to Consumer Disputes' in *Law and the Weaker Party, An Anglo-Swedish Comparative Study* (ed Anderman, 1982), Vol II, p 91 (see also the comment on Reynolds's essay by Hellner, ibid, p 111).
15 Even modern decisions can exhibit a marked resistance to acknowledge the consumer's separate needs: see eg *Bernstein v Pamson Motors (Golders Green) Ltd* [1987] 2 All ER 220.

The construction of codifying and consolidating statutes

As the 1893 Act was a codifying statute, it must be asked how far it is permissible to consider the earlier common law when construing such legislation. In theory, the correct approach is to disregard the earlier law and treat the Act as having wiped the slate clean. In *Bank of England v Vagliano Bros*,[16] Lord Herschell[17] said that 'the proper course is in the first instance to examine the language of the statute and to ask what is its natural meaning, uninfluenced by any considerations derived from the previous state of the law, and not to start with inquiring how the law previously stood'.[18] He went on to say that resort could be had to the previous law where, for example, the Act was unclear or where words are used in the Act which have previously acquired a technical meaning.

In reality, the matter is far less clear-cut and it is commonplace to find references in the decisions to 19th century case law particularly where it is clear that the Act was based upon a particular decision or line of decisions. Lord Herschell's reasoning clearly seeks to avoid confusion and secure certainty but it is suggested that his clinically technical view of a codified Act cannot be sustained as it would mean approaching the law blindfolded, or at least in blinkers. Certainly Chalmers did not see the Code as divorced from its antecedents, rather he considered that 'our common law is rich in the exposition of principles, and these expositions lose none of their value now that the law is codified. A rule can never be appreciated apart from the reasons on which it is founded'.[19] Consequently, he considered the correct approach to be that, as the propositions from the cases had become sections of the Act, 'each case ... must be tested with reference to the Act'.[20] Moreover, slavish adherence to Lord Herschell's technical method must mean that, eventually, the Code will become rigid and thus stultify the law's development. In 1972, Lord Diplock[1] cautioned that 'unless the Sale of Goods Act 1893 is to be allowed to fossilise the law and to restrict the freedom of choice of parties to contracts for the sale of goods to make agreements which take account of advances in technology and changes in the way in which business is carried on today, the provisions set out in the [Act] ought not to be construed so narrowly as to force upon parties ... promises and consequences different from what they must reasonably have intended'.

Divergent approaches are still evident in relation to the interpretation and construction of the SGA 1979. In 1973, a new s 14(6) was introduced[2] into the 1979 Act which, for the first time, provided a statutory definition of 'merchantable quality'. In two decisions of the Court of Appeal, both in 1987, diametrically opposed views were expressed on the issue of construing s 14(6). In the first decision,[3] Mustill LJ[4] considered that it was unwise to consult cases prior to 1973, as s 14(6) was a clear and self-sufficient statement of the law

---

16 [1891] AC 107; a decision on the Bills of Exchange Act 1882, another of the Codes drafted by Chalmers.
17 [1891] AC 107 at 144-145.
18 See also, to the same effect: *Bristol Tramways etc, Carriage Co Ltd v Fiat Motors Ltd* [1910] 2 KB 831, 836 per Cozens-Hardy MR.
19 Chalmers, *Sale of Goods Act 1893*, Introduction to the first edition (1894).
20 Chalmers, *Sale of Goods Act 1893*, Introduction to the first edition (1894).
 1 *Ashington Piggeries Ltd v Christopher Hill Ltd* [1972] AC 441, 501.
 2 By the Supply of Goods (Implied Terms) Act 1973, s 3.
 3 *Rogers v Parish (Scarborough) Ltd* [1987] QB 933.
 4 [1987] QB 933 at 942.

but, in the second case,[5] Lloyd LJ[6] thought that it was impossible to appreciate the change brought about by the new definition without first looking at the earlier law and he then evaluated the leading decisions from both the (early) 19th and 20th centuries and also appraised the views of prominent academics. The notion of 'merchantable quality' has been replaced in the SGA by that of 'satisfactory quality' and the SGA, s 14, both defines 'satisfactory quality' and specifies aspects to be considered in appropriate cases when applying the new quality standard. No doubt the same problem as to the construction of s 14 will surface when the meaning and scope of 'satisfactory quality' is considered by the judiciary. It is respectfully suggested that the reflective, considered approach of Lloyd LJ is the preferable one and the law can only benefit from such a thorough survey of the historical development of a statutory provision. In the same case, Lloyd LJ considered that there were good reasons why the court should have been referred to the relevant Law Commission reports and, after the House of Lords' ruling[7] allowing the courts, in certain circumstances, to refer to *Hansard* and other Parliamentary material, Lloyd LJ's contextual approach must surely be the correct one.

The relationship of the SGA with the common law and equity

The SGA codfies only the specialised rules concerned with the sale of goods and the Act is set in the context of the general law of contract. The SGA does not seek to be a self-standing, comprehensive Code on the sale of goods. Accordingly, the SGA s 62(2) provides:

> 'The rules of the common law, including the law merchant, except in so far as they are inconsistent with the provisions of this Act, and in particular the rules relating to the law of principal and agent and the effect of fraud, misrepresentation, duress or coercion, mistake, or other invalidating cause, apply to contracts for the sale of goods.'

It has never been decided whether 'common law' in s 62(2) means 'case law', in which case it would include the rules of equity or, alternatively, whether 'common law' is used in its technical sense as excluding the rules of equity. There seems little doubt that, today, it is implicit that the rules of equity are applicable to the sale of goods and it has been tacitly assumed in numerous cases that equitable remedies are available.[8]

---

5 *M/S Aswan Engineering Establishment Co v Lupdine Ltd* [1987] 1 WLR 1.
6 [1987] 1 WLR 1 at 6.
7 *Pepper (Inspector of Taxes) v Hart* [1993] AC 593; *Melluish (Inspector of Taxes) v BMI (No 3) Ltd* [1996] AC 454.
8 See eg *Rose (F E) Ltd v W H Pim & Co Ltd* [1953] 2 QB 450 (rectification); *Goldsmith v Rodger* [1962] 2 Lloyd's Rep 249 (innocent misrepresentation).

CHAPTER 14

The nature, definition and subject matter of the contract of sale

The formation of contracts for the sale of goods

The Statute of Frauds 1677, s 17, provided stringent controls on the enforceability of contracts for the sale of goods where those goods were of the value of £10 or more. Such contracts could be enforced only where there was a note or memorandum of the bargain made and signed by the parties to be charged or their agents. Section 17 admitted two exceptions to this general rule: first, where the buyer had accepted the goods and actually received them and, second, where he had given 'something in earnest to bind the bargain, or in part payment'. The Statute had been passed after the Restoration in order to constrain fraud and perjury but its emphasis on form undoubtedly meant that many were enabled to escape liability unjustly because plaintiffs could not produce written evidence of their wholly executory contracts. The Statute's provisions generated much litigation and many technical, rather dreary, legal distinctions with little conceptual importance. The Statute was, nevertheless, of immense practical significance and, for example, Blackburn[1] devoted the first 122 pages of his authoritative treatise on the sale of goods solely to cases on the Statute of Frauds. In terms of its impact on the evolution of the law, Atiyah[2] has suggested that the Statute impeded the acknowledgment and development of the wholly executory contract and that contemporary lawyers did not necessarily perceive the statutory requirement of writing as primarily evidentiary in nature. Almost certainly, the Statute's provisions were otiose by the end of the nineteenth century but, in 1893, the Sale of Goods Act, s 4, embodied s 17 of the Statute of Frauds. Furthermore, although in 1937 the Law Revision Committee[3] recommended that s 4 be repealed, it was not until 1954 that this occurred.

The SGA 1979, s 4(1), now provides that 'subject to this and any other Act, a contract of sale may be made in writing (either with or without seal), or by word of mouth, or partly in writing and partly by word of mouth, or may be implied from the conduct of the parties'. Consequently, there are no formalities of any sort prescribed in relation to the formation of contracts for the sale of goods under the 1979 Act.

---

1 *Contract of Sale* (2nd edn, 1885).
2 Atiyah, *The Rise and Fall of Freedom of Contract* (1979), pp 206-207; see also Simpson, *A History of the Common Law of Contract* (1975), pp 612-620.
3 *Sixth Interim Report* (1937), Cmnd 5449.

Moreover, the common law relating to offer and acceptance in contract formation applies to the sale of goods[4] and, likewise, the SGA, s 3 provides that 'capacity to buy and sell is regulated by the general law concerning capacity'. It is not proposed to enter into any further consideration of offer and acceptance or the limited capacity of minors in the law relating to the sale of goods, as these matters are commonly covered in texts concerned with the law of contract. The issue of fixing the price of the goods in contracts of sale is considered at the end of this chapter.

Rights of cancellation in contracts for the sale of goods

It has long been the law in relation to consumer credit agreements that the debtor has a right to cancel agreements which are signed off trade premises[5] but, until recently, there was no such 'cooling-off period' in relation to contracts for the sale of goods which were concluded away from business premises. The ever-burgeoning demands of consumer protection have resulted in several important rights given to the consumer buyer to cancel such contracts for the sale of goods and it is pertinent to consider, briefly, these rights of cancellation. The rationale of the 'cooling-off period' is much the same as in consumer credit agreements in that the consumer buyer may be subjected to unfair pressure when a 'doorstep seller' makes an unsolicited call at the consumer's home. Equally important is the fact that, where the trader's visit is unsolicited, the consumer has no opportunity to compare either the trader's goods or his terms of business with those on offer elsewhere.

CONSUMER PROTECTION (CANCELLATION OF CONTRACTS CONCLUDED AWAY FROM BUSINESS PREMISES) REGULATIONS 1987[6]

These Regulations, which implemented an EC Directive,[7] are aimed at curbing some of the worst excesses of 'doorstep selling'. Under the Regulations, 'consumers'[8] are granted a seven-day 'cooling-off period' during which there is a right to cancel an agreement for the supply of goods[9] or services costing more than £35 and entered into during an unsolicited visit by a 'trader'[10] to the consumer's home (or the home of another person) or the consumer's place of work.

Types of contract within the Regulations

As reg 3(1) provides that the Regulations apply to contracts 'for the supply by a trader of goods or services to a consumer', it will be apparent that the Regulations

---

4 See also the SGA, s 62(2).
5 See Ch 33.
6 SI 1987/2117; as amended by SI 1988/958; SI 1998/3050.
7 Council Directive 85/577/EEC (dated 20.12.1985).
8 Defined in reg 2(1) as a person 'other than a body corporate, who, in making a contract to which these Regulations apply, is acting for purposes which can be regarded as outside his business'.
9 Reg 2(1) provides that 'goods' has the meaning given by the SGA, s 61(1).
10 'Trader' is defined in reg 2(1) as 'a person who, in making a contract to which these Regulations apply, is acting for the purposes of his business, and anyone acting in the name or on behalf such a person'. 'Business' is not defined explicitly but reg 2(1) provides that it includes 'a trade or profession'.

extend far beyond sales of goods to many situations where 'cold-calling' and high-pressure salesmanship are rife, eg contracts for building repairs and maintenance and those relating to the installation of double-glazing and burglar alarms/security devices.

Under reg 3(2), certain contracts are excepted from the operation of the Regulations, viz (i) contracts for the construction, sale, and rental of immovable property (contracts for the repair of real property or the incorporation of goods within real property *are* within the Regulations) (ii) contracts for the supply of food, drink or other goods intended for current consumption by use in the household and supplied by regular roundsmen (iii) contracts for the supply of goods or services concluded on the basis of a trade catalogue which is readily available to the consumer to read in the absence of the trader before the conclusion of the contract, where there is to be 'continuity of contact' between the trader and the consumer and where both the catalogue and contract are accompanied by a prominent notice indicating that the consumer has a right to return the goods or otherwise cancel the contract within a period of not less than seven days of receipt of the goods (iv) insurance contracts and many contracts for financial services (v) contracts which do not require the consumer to make *total* payments (eg including VAT) exceeding £35 or contracts under which credit is provided (within the meaning of the Consumer Credit Act 1974) not exceeding £35 (other than a hire-purchase or conditional sale agreement), and (vi) under reg 4(2), contracts which are cancellable under the Consumer Credit Act 1974.[11]

The Court of Justice of the European Comunities has recently decided[12] that the Directive[13] did not apply where a son gave a guarantee to a bank regarding his father's liabilities under an overdraft facility. An employee of the bank had visited the father's home and, in the course of that visit, the son furnished the guarantee. The son was acting as a consumer but the father's overdraft related to his business as a builder and so the father was acting in a commercial capacity and definitely not as a consumer. It was held that the Directive (and certainly the English Regulations which implement it) applies only to bilateral contracts under which a trader supplies goods or services to a consumer and the guarantee in question was, from the guarantor's point of view, a unilateral obligation with no goods or services being supplied directly to him. The court considered that a major difficulty in extending the Directive to such contracts was that no provision was made therein for the fate of the principal contract if the guarantee should be cancelled, and this supported the conclusion that the Directive was not intended to apply to undertakings such as guarantees.

In which situations do the Regulations apply?

It is the notion of the 'unsolicited visit' which must be considered first. As mentioned earlier, reg 3(1) provides that the Regulations apply to an unsolicited visit by a trader to 'the consumer's home or to the home of another person[14] or

---

11   See Ch 33 where it is stressed that the Regulations could apply to certain contracts which are not regulated agreements within the Consumer Credit Act 1974, eg where the credit advanced is more than £25,000.

12   *Bayerische Hypothetken-Und Wechselbank AG v Dietzinger* [1998] 1 WLR 1035.

13   Council Directive 85/577/EEC.

14   Art 1(1) of the Directive applies only where the visit is to the consumer's home or that of *another consumer* (see *Bayerische Hypothetken-Und Wechselbank AG v Dietzinger* [1998] 1 WLR 1035, above, where the Directive could not apply as the visit was made to the father's home and he was not a consumer). The English Regulations are *not* limited in this way.

to the consumer's place of work'. The definition of an 'unsolicited visit' was tightened by the 1998 Regulations.[15] Traders sought to evade the Regulations by making an unsolicited preliminary visit or contacting the consumer by phone. If, during the course of the first visit or telephone conversation, the consumer agreed to a second visit, the trader would then assert that the consumer had acquiesced in his making the second visit which was, therefore, not unsolicited. This deceitful practice has been eradicated by the amended definition of an 'unsolicited visit' in the 1998 Regulations. Regulation 3(3) provides that an unsolicited visit is a visit by a trader (whether or not he is the trader who supplies the goods or services) 'which does not take place at the express request of the consumer' and includes 'a visit by the trader which takes place after he, or a person acting in his name or on his behalf, telephones the consumer (otherwise than at the consumer's express request) and indicates during the course of the the telephone call (either expressly or by implication) that he, or the trader in whose name or on whose behalf he is acting, is willing to visit the consumer'. A visit is also to be regarded as unsolicited where it is 'a visit by a trader which takes place after he, or a person acting in his name or on his behalf, visits the consumer (otherwise than at the consumer's express request) and indicates during the course of that visit (either expressly or by implication) that he, or the trader in whose name or on whose behalf he is acting, is willing to make a subsequent visit to the consumer'.

It must also be stressed that the Regulations apply to those contracts entered into (i) during a visit to the consumer's home or place of work or to the home of another person, made at the *express request* of the consumer, where the goods or services to which the contract relates are *other* than those concerning which the consumer requested the visit, provided that when the visit was requested the consumer did not know, or could not reasonably have known, that the supply of those other goods or services formed part of the trader's business activities (reg 3(1)(b)) or, (ii) during an excursion[16] organised by the trader away from premises on which he is carrying on any business (whether on a permanent or temporary basis) (reg 3(1)(d)). Moreover, reg 3(1)(c) is careful to stipulate that the contract need not actually be entered into away from business premises; instead, it is sufficient if the *offer* is made by the consumer during the trader's visit (or excursion) and the contract is completed at a later date. The consumer might, for example, be induced to make an offer by signing an order form for goods during the trader's visit. If, several days after his visit, the form is signed and accepted by the trader at his business premises and is then posted to the consumer, the resultant contract is within the Regulations.

Cancellation of the contract

Regulation 4(1) provides that no contract within the Regulations shall be enforceable against the consumer unless the trader has delivered to the consumer notice in writing in the prescribed form[17] indicating the right of the consumer to cancel the contract. Under reg 4(4), the notice must be delivered to the consumer at the time when the contract is entered into during the trader's visit (or excursion)

---

15 SI 1998/3050.
16 This means, for example, a boat or coach excursion organised by the trader where customers are induced to enter into contracts. This practice is prevalent in Europe but, as yet, it is uncommon in the UK.
17 See reg 4(3) and (4) and the Schedule to the Regulations, Parts I and II.

or, alternatively, at the time the consumer makes the offer to the trader during the visit (or excursion). The consumer may then cancel the contract 'within the period of 7 days following the making of the contract' by serving written notice on the trader which can be expressed in any way and need not comply with the prescribed form of cancellation which is delivered to the consumer by the trader (reg 4(5)).

It should be noted that the consumer has seven days in which to cancel the contract following 'the *making* of the contract' and so, in those cases where the consumer makes an offer to the trader, the seven days commence from the time that the trader *accepts* the offer. Moreover, reg 4(7) provides that a notice of cancellation posted by the consumer within the seven day cancellation period shall be deemed to have been served at the time of posting, whether or not it is actually received.

The principal, 1987 Regulations, made no provision for criminal liability but the 1998 Regulations amended the principal Regulations[18] so that a trader is guilty of an offence if he enters into a contract which is within the Regulations, but fails to deliver to the consumer the requisite notice of cancellation (reg 4A). Regulation 4B adds a defence of due diligence and reg 4C provides for the liability of persons other than the principal offender in specific circumstances (eg where a corporation is criminally liable, the corporate veil can be lifted meaning that a director or secretary may also be guilty of an offence). In relation to the criminal liability under the Regulations, a duty to enforce reg 4A is imposed on weights and measures authorities and powers are conferred enabling officers to require the production of information and to seize evidence.

There can be no contracting-out of the Regulations and, under reg 10(1), a contract term is void if, and to the extent that, it is inconsistent with a provision for the protection of the consumer contained in the Regulations.

Effects of cancellation

The overall effects of cancellation are that the consumer is entitled to be repaid money paid before cancellation (reg 5(1))[19] and he has lien on goods in his possession for any sum which is repayable (reg 5(2)) but, subject to the lien, he must return any goods which he has received and, in the meantime, he must retain possession of the goods and take reasonable care of them (reg 7(1)).

Under reg 7(3), the consumer is not bound to deliver the goods except at his own premises and in pursuance of a written request signed by the trader and served on the consumer either before, or at the time when, the goods are collected. If the consumer *delivers* the goods (whether at his own premises or elsewhere) to any person upon whom a notice of cancellation could have been served, or where he *sends* the goods at his own expense to such a person, he is discharged from any duty to retain possession of the goods or restore them to the trader (reg 7(4)). Furthermore, under reg 7(5), where the consumer has delivered the goods within reg 7(4), his obligation to take care of the goods is at an end and, where he sends the goods to another within reg 7(4), he is under a duty to take reasonable care to see that they are received by that other and not damaged in transit but, in other respects, his duty to take care of the goods is at an end. Finally, reg 7(6) places limits on the length of time during which the consumer's duty of care

---

18   See regs 4A–4H.
19   Reg 6 (as amended by SI 1988/958) provides for the repayment of credit.

subsists in that, if the trader requests the return of the goods from the consumer during the period of twenty one days following the cancellation and the consumer unreasonably refuses or unreasonably fails to comply with the request, his duty to retain posession and take reasonable care of the goods continues until he delivers them or sends them to the trader. If, however, the consumer does not receive a request for the return of the goods in the twenty one day period, his duty to take reasonable care of the goods ends on the expiration of the twenty one days.

Regulation 8 concerns the situation where the trader agreed to take goods in part-exchange. The part-exchange goods must be returned to the consumer within ten days, beginning with the date of cancellation, in substantially the same condition as when they were delivered. If the trader fails to return the goods, the consumer is entitled to recover a sum equal to the part-exchange allowance and the consumer can use the lien he has over the contract goods in his possession to enforce these obligations.

Under reg 7(2), there are four categories of goods which the consumer does not have to restore, viz (i) perishable goods (ii) goods which by their nature are consumed by use and which, before the cancellation, were so consumed (iii) goods supplied to meet an emergency, and (iv) goods which, before the cancellation, had become incorporated in any land or thing not comprised in the cancelled contract. Although the consumer does not have to return goods within these categories, he does have to pay for them and for the provision of any services in connection with the supply of the goods in accordance with the cancelled contract.

CONSUMER PROTECTION (DISTANCE SELLING) REGULATIONS 2000[20]

These Regulations, which implement the EC Directive on 'distance selling'[1] apply to 'distance contracts' for goods or services to be supplied to a 'consumer'[2] by a 'supplier'.[3] The central idea of a distance contract is thus that the parties never make face-to-face contact up to, and including, the moment at which the contract is concluded. A principal target of the Regulations is those mail order companies which take payment from the consumer and then fail to deliver the goods for an unconscionable period of time. The Regulations should improve dramatically the consumer's ability to put pressure on such companies to deliver the goods as the consumer is given a right to cancel distance contracts and be reimbursed without charge. Some of the detail in the Regulations must be examined but, as they are both lengthy and complex, it is impracticable to analyse every aspect of them here.

What is a 'distance contract'?

Under reg 3(1), a 'distance contract' means any contract concerning goods or services concluded between a supplier and a consumer 'under an organised

---

20 SI 2000/2334.
1 *Protection of Consumers in Respect of Distance Contracts* (Directive 97/7/EC, May 1997).
2 Defined in reg 3(1) as 'any natural person who, in contracts to which these Regulations apply, is acting for purposes which are outside his business'.
3 Defined in reg 3(1) as 'any person who, in contracts to which these Regulations apply, is acting in his commercial or professional capacity'.

distance sales or service provision scheme run by the supplier who, for the purpose of the contract, makes exclusive use of one or more means of distance communication up to and including the moment at which the contract is concluded'. It is thus imperative to know what is meant by 'means of distance communication' and this is also defined in reg 3(1) as 'any means which, without the simultaneous physical presence of the supplier and the consumer, may be used for the conclusion of a contract between those parties'. Schedule 1 provides an indicative list of means of distance communication, eg letter, telephone (with or without human intervention), facsimile machine, electronic mail, catalogue, radio and television. It thus plain that the Regulations apply to contracts entered into via the Internet.

Prior information requirements

Regualtion 7(1) provides that the supplier must provide to the consumer certain information 'in good time prior to the conclusion of the contract'. It is not practicable to refer to this information here but reg 7(1) provides that all the significant features of the undertaking should be detailed, eg the identity of the supplier; a description of the main characterisics of the goods; the price of the goods; the right to cancel the contract, and the arrangements for delivery. In addition, reg 8(1) specifies that the supplier shall provide this information 'in writing or in another durable medium which is available and accessible to the consumer' prior to the conclusion of the contract and, in any event, not later than the time of delivery where goods are concerned. Certain other detail regarding the right of cancellation and its exercise must be provided under reg 8(2).

Right of cancellation

The Regulations allow the consumer a 'cooling-off' period for cancellation during which he can give a notice of cancellation to the supplier (reg 10)). The notice must be 'in writing or in another durable medium' (reg 10(3)) but it can be expressed in any way which indicates an intent to cancel. Regulation 10(4) and (5) provide a list of situations in which the notice of cancellation is to be treated as having been 'properly given'. In the case of contracts for the supply of goods, reg 11 provides that the cancellation period begins with the day on which the 'contract is concluded' and ends 'on the expiry of seven working days beginning with the day after the day on which the consumer receives the goods'. Where, however, the supplier has not complied with the information requirements in reg 8, regs 10(3) and (4) extend the cooling-off period. Under reg 13, certain contracts are exempted from the cancellation provisions, the most relevant here being goods made to the consumer's specifications, contracts for the supply of audio or video recordings or computer software which have been 'unsealed' by the consumer, contracts for the supply of newspapers, periodicals or magazines and contracts for the supply of goods 'the price of which is dependent on fluctuations in the financial market which cannot be controlled by the supplier'.

Performance of the contract; right to be reimbursed and return of the goods

Where the consumer cancels the contract he must be reimbursed, free of charge, within a maximum period of thirty days (reg 14) and, under reg 17, the consumer is under a duty to retain the goods and take reasonable care of them in the period prior to cancellation. On cancellation, he must restore the goods to the supplier and, in the meantime, he must retain possession of them and take reasonable care of them. Regulation 17 provides further detail on the re-delivery of the goods to the supplier. Regulation 19 provides that, 'unless the parties agree otherwise' the contract must be performed within thirty days beginning with the day after the day the consumer sent his order to the supplier and, where the supplier is unable to perform the contract, substitute goods or services may be offered if the conditions in reg 19 are met.

The nature and purpose of the contract of sale

It is plain that the purpose of a sale of goods is to transfer ownership in those goods to B in return for the price of the goods being paid to S. This is encapsulated in the definition in s 2(1), below, where it will be noticed that ownership is referred to as 'the property in the goods'.[4] Quite naturally, English law regards the transfer of ownership in the goods from S to B as the quintessence of the contract of sale and, should S fail to give a good title to the goods so that no property passes to B, B may recover any money paid under the contract on the basis of a total failure of consideration and no allowance is made in S's favour for any use and enjoyment of the goods that B may have had.[5]

It is crucial to understand at the outset the difference between an 'agreement to sell' goods and a completed 'sale' of those goods, and appreciate the consequences which ensue from these separate concepts. Life can truly be breathed into many of the issues raised here only when the classification of goods which is adopted in the SGA is understood and the rules on the passing of property in goods are appreciated.[6] The SGA, s 2, sets-out in skeletal form, the types of agreement which are commonly encountered and certain rudimentary notions which must be grasped before further progress can be made in the Act. Section 2 provides:

(1) A contract of sale of goods is a contract by which the seller transfers or agrees to transfer the property in goods to the buyer for a money consideration, called the price.
(2) There may be a contract of sale between one part owner and another.
(3) A contract of sale may be absolute or conditional.
(4) Where under a contract of sale the property in the goods is transferred from the seller to the buyer the contract is called a sale.
(5) Where under a contract of sale the transfer of the property in the goods is to take place at a future time or subject to some condition later to be fulfilled the contract is called an agreement to sell.
(6) An agreement to sell becomes a sale when the time elapses or the conditions are fulfilled subject to which the property in the goods is to be transferred.

---

4 The SGA, s 61(1), provides that '"property" means the general property in goods, and not merely a special property'.
5 See *Rowland v Divall* [1923] 2 KB 500.
6 See Ch 16.

The difference between 'an agreement to sell' and 'a sale'

It will be observed that, most confusingly, s 2 refers to 'a contract of sale', 'an agreement to sell' and 'a sale'. Although three phrases are utilised here there are, in fact, only two distinct concepts to grasp. The essential point is that the SGA divides the 'contract of sale' into two categories, viz 'an agreement to sell' and 'a sale'.[7]

First, *an agreement to sell* is merely a contract under which S and B have agreed that the transfer of property in the goods to B is to take place at a future time or subject to some condition later to be fulfilled (see s 2(5)). It follows that, as a general rule, the agreement to sell generates contractual remedies only and so, should either party default, the other may sue in damages for breach of contract. Where, for example, S fails to deliver goods the property in which remains vested in him, B does not have any rights based upon ownership or possession and he has no equitable title to the goods, although he may have a remedy for breach of contract.

Second, *a sale* of goods occurs when the property in the goods is conveyed from S to B but it must be stressed that no *form* is required for the passing of property in the sale of goods. Consequently, a contract for the sale of *specific* goods can have a dual function as a contract and a simultaneous conveyance of the property in the goods to B. This could happen, for example, in a contract for the sale of a specific car which B has inspected, S and B having reached a complete agreement with no outstanding conditions to be performed.[8] Here B becomes the owner of the car at the moment of the formation of the contract (see s 2(4)). Alternatively, an agreement to sell *unascertained goods* (eg 100 bags of wheat from a larger quantity stored in a warehouse) could not act as an instantaneous conveyance of the property in the goods to B for the simple reason that the goods must be physically ascertained before B can *own* them. In an agreement to sell ten bottles of whisky from a case containing twelve bottles, it is self-evident that the ten bottles must be separated before they can be said to belong to B and this rule is even stronger where neither a bulk is identified nor a source of supply is specified, eg an agreement to sell 10 tons of barley. Consequently, in such an agreement the passing of property in the goods must take place 'at a future time or subject to some condition later to be fulfilled' (see s 2(5)) or it will be converted into a sale at a later date when property passes to B after a lapse of time or when certain conditions are fulfilled (see s 2(6)). As a sale passes the property in the goods to B, it confers proprietary rights upon him in addition to contractual rights and so, for example, if a third party were to seize the goods, B could commence proceedings in tort for wrongful interference with the goods. Similarly, the general rule in the SGA, s 20 is that B carries the risk of loss or damage to the goods once the property in them has passed to him.

Possession and the passing of property

It is striking that the practical concerns of S and B in relation to delivery of the goods and payment for them are not essential features in the distinction between an agreement to sell and a sale which passes the property in the goods to B. In English law, it is the intent of the parties manifested in the terms of their contract

---

7   See also the SGA, s 61(1), which provides that '"contract of sale" includes an agreeement to sell as well as a sale'.
8   See the SGA, s 18, r 1.

which is dominant and determines when property in the goods passes to B. It is quite possible, for example, for property in specific goods to pass to B on contract under the SGA s 18, r 1, even though he has neither paid for the goods nor obtained physical possession of them. This fact is emphasised in s 61(1) which provides that '"sale" includes a bargain and sale as well as a sale and delivery'.

It will be apparent that there is no necessary correlation between physical possession and ownership in English law. It follows that, while delivery of the goods to B may be a pivotal factor in determining ownership, it is not a pre-requisite to the passing of property. Instead, property may have passed to B meaning that delivery is a condition to be performed under the contract between S and B, albeit an important, practical one. Physical possession is, nevertheless, often a crucial factor in the transfer of title by a non-owner[9] and here, the *bona fide* buyer's claim to acquire good title from such a non-owner often turns on the fact of physical possession in the latter and his ability to make delivery to the buyer.

Pollock and Wright[10] considered that possession has three separate elements, viz (i) physical control (ii) legal possession as the state of being a possessor in the eye of the law and (iii) the right to possess. This classification is reflected in the types of possession which are recognised in the sale of goods but care must be taken to separate ownership, possession and custody, although none of these concepts has been defined with any degree of precision in English law. It has famously been asserted that English law has 'never worked out a completely logical and exhaustive definition of "possession"'[11] and, more recently, it was stressed that 'the English law of ownership and possession, unlike that of Roman law, is not a system of identifying absolute entitlement, but of priority of entitlement'.[12]

It is self-evident that there can be *de facto* possession coupled with custody and control. This is not necessarily indicative of ownership, however, as a person may have custody of goods and yet assert no rights over them beyond his actual custody. Alternatively, the person who has ownership of the goods and exercises custody and control clearly has both legal possession and the right to possess the goods. An owner may also have the right to possess goods which are physically in the custody of another[13] such as an employee or agent. The right to possess goods may also exist where the goods have been wrongfully converted by another or where, for example, a buyer has paid the price of the goods under the contract but has not succeeded in obtaining delivery of them.

The meaning of 'goods'

The SGA, s 61(1) provides:

' "Goods" includes all personal chattels other than things in action and money, and in Scotland all corporeal moveables except money; and in particular "goods" includes emblements, industrial growing crops, and things attached to or forming part of the land which are agreed to be severed before sale or under the contract of sale and includes an undivided share in goods.'

---

9 See Ch 18.
10 Pollock and Wright, *An Essay on Possession in the Common Law* (1888), pp 26-27.
11 *United States of America v Dollfus Mieg et Cie SA and Bank of England* [1952] AC 582, 605 per Viscount Jowitt.
12 *Waverley Borough Council v Fletcher* [1996] QB 334, 345 per Auld LJ.
13 See eg *Great Eastern Rly Co v Lord's Trustee* [1909] AC 109.

In the widest sense, it is plain from s 61(1) that the SGA applies to personal property and not real property; the enquiry here thus relates to the sub-divisions of personalty which are within the ambit of the SGA. There is also a modern debate as to whether 'goods' is a pertinent classification for certain types of property such as computer programs and human body parts.

'Personal chattels other than things in action and money'

It has become somewhat archaic to refer to moveable goods as 'chattels' and, although chattels are primarily regarded as a species of goods, the word has always been of imprecise ambit both in normal use and legal nomenclature.[14] The law distinguishes between personal chattels and real chattels and, in modern terminology, the latter primarily comprises leasehold interests in land which, of course, are not the concern of the SGA.

Personal chattels are subdivided into choses in possession and choses in action and the latter category is not within the statutory definition of 'goods'. Choses in action are 'all rights and incorporeal things, not being chattels real or choses in possession, which make up personalty'[15] and so debts, bills of exchange, bills of lading, shares and other securities, trade marks, patents, and insurance policies, are outside the SGA definition of 'goods'. Likewise, intangibles such as information are not classifiable as 'goods' but remedies may exist, of course, where someone profits illicitly from the use of confidential information.[16] This leaves only the category of choses in possession within the definition in s 61(1). Crossley Vaines[17] defined choses in possession as 'corporeal things, tangible, movable and visible' and the author went on to stress that 'they are, of course, always in the possession of someone, if "possession" is taken to mean an immediate right to posssession. Even a cigarette stub thrown away in the street remains in the possession of the smoker, in as much as he has the right to recover it; though probably if asked, he would say that he had abandoned it'.

'Money' is excluded from the statutory definition in s 61(1) because s 2(1) specifies that the consideration for the purchase of the goods must be money; the goods and their *price* are thus contrasted. Nevertheless, it is plain that money can sufficiently change its character and become 'goods' so that it can be bought and sold within the SGA: a coin, for example, might thus be sold as goods where it has curiosity value or is a collector's item[18] or has ceased to be legal tender.[19] This may also be the position where foreign money is bought because it will usually not be legal tender in the country where it is delivered and the rate of exchange is variable; these factors may indicate that the money has transmuted into 'goods', but there is no clear authority.

---

14 In *Robinson v Jenkins* (1890) 24 QBD 275, 279, Fry LJ opined that 'chattels is one of the widest words known to the law in its relation to personal property'.

15 Crossley Vaines, *Personal Property* (5th edn, 1973), p 11.

16 See eg *Boardman v Phipps* [1967] 2 AC 46.

17 *Personal Property* (5th edn, 1973), p 11.

18 *Moss v Hancock* [1899] 2 QB 111 (a £5 Jubilee gold piece which was a current coin but had a curiosity value greater than its face value was stolen from its owner and sold for £5 to a dealer in curios. The thief was convicted and, under the Larceny Act 1861, an order was made for the coin's restitution. The court thus seemed to consider that the coin was sold rather than being transferred as currency).

19 *R v Thompson* [1980] QB 229.

Goods and land

The definition of 'goods' in s 61(1) separates goods from land by providing that '"goods" includes emblements, industrial growing crops, and things attached to or forming part of the land which are agreed to be severed before sale or under the contract of sale'. But when a contract provides, for example, that crops or minerals shall be severed from the land and removed, it is not always clear whether this is a sale of goods or the creation of an interest in the land itself.[20]

Things growing on land are classically divided into *fructus naturales* (ie things growing naturally on the land such as timber or grass) and *fructus industriales* (ie crops such as potatoes or wheat which do not grow naturally but are cultivated by the industry of man). The right to 'emblements' was, strictly, the right given to a tenant at the determination of his estate to take annual, growing crops which yield a profit[1] (eg potatoes) but the SGA clearly intends a sale of such emblements to be within the classification of *fructus industriales*. Industrial crops were always regarded as chattels because they were the product of man's industry and were independent of the land on which they were grown; a sale of such crops was, consequently, not treated as creating an interest in land.[2] On the other hand, *fructus naturales* were regarded as part of the land until severance and an agreement granting B an interest in them before severance was regarded as creating an interest in land. Only where *fructus naturales* were to severed before sale or very soon afterwards,[3] would the contract be regarded as one for the sale of goods. It seems that these distinctions are now largely theoretical as regards the SGA and, today, most sales of growing crops will be classified as contracts for the sale of goods as, under the broad wording of s 61(1), S and B must necessarily contemplate that the crops will be severed 'before sale or under the contract of sale'[4] and it probably does not matter how long a delay there is before severance is effected.[5] Nevertheless, the statutory definition of 'land' is also extensive and many such transactions could be regarded as creating interests in land.[6] In the situation where B agrees to buy

---

20 See Hudson, 'Goods or Land?' (1958) 22 Conv 137.
1 See *Graves v Weld* (1835) 5 B & Ad 105.
2 *Evans v Roberts* (1826) 5 B & C 829.
3 *Marshall v Green* (1875) 1 CPD 35 (standing timber to be cut by B and removed immediately was held not to create an interest in land).
4 See eg *Waimiha Sawmilling Co Ltd v Howe* [1920] NZLR 681 (agreement for the sale of 'millable timber' on land (which included standing timber and cut logs). B had an irrevocable right for 17 years to enter the land and cut and remove the timber. This was held to be a sale of goods with a licence to enter the land and not a lease. See Cooper J's comments (pp 689-690) that the SGA definition of 'goods' was designed to 'get rid of the subtleties' as to whether S or B severed the crops from the land and that 'the sole test appears to be whether the thing attached to the land has become by agreement goods by reason of the contemplation of the severance from the soil'.
5 *Kursell v Timber Operators and Contractors Ltd* [1927] 1 KB 298 (contract for the sale of timber of a specific height to be cut over a period of 15 years was a sale of goods). But if B is given a right or discretion to enter land and cut timber and there is no *obligation* that he do so, the contract will not be one for the sale of goods, see *Egmont Box Co Ltd v Registrar-General of Lands* [1920] NZLR 741.
6 Suppose, for example, B is given by contract a right to take the annual crop of S's field for a period of ten years. The Law of Property (Miscellaneous Provisions) Act 1989, s 2, demands that a contract for the sale or other disposition of an interest in land should be made in writing and signed by or on behalf of each party. The 1989 Act does not define 'land' but it is likely that the definition in the Law of Property Act 1925, s 205(1)(ix) will apply, ie 'land' includes '... an easement, right, privilege or benefit in, over or derived from land'. It is arguable, therefore, that the above example could be a contract within s 2 of the 1989 Act and thus required to be in writing. Perhaps the best view is that such a contract is within the SGA *and* the 1989 Act.

land together with the growing, industrial crops, it is a question of construction as to whether the crops are regarded as part of the land or are sold separately as goods.[7] A pertinent fact might be, for example, that a separate price was agreed for the goods.[8]

A sale of minerals or gravel from land, for example, poses further difficulties particularly as these things are not simply attached to the land but, until extraction, are indisputably part of the land itself. Consequently, it is only by the process of abstraction that minerals can acquire the status of goods.[9] Minerals which have been extracted by the landowner/S may clearly be sold as goods or there may be an agreement that S will abstract them and property will pass to B at a later date. However, where B is to take the minerals himself the arrangement may bear more resemblance to the grant of a *profit à prendre*. In *Morgan v Russell & Sons*,[10] a lessee of a plot of land agreed to sell to B slag and cinders which lay on the ground but were not in definite or detached heaps and B was to be allowed to enter the land to remove the slag. The lessor prevented B from entering the land and B sued the seller/lessee in damages. It was held that this was not a sale of goods but a sale of an interest in the land itself and the fact that the *quantity* to be sold was indefinite was regarded as significant by Lord Alverstone CJ.[11] Overall it does seem that, in *Morgan*, B was permitted an interest in the cinders as part of the land rather than there being a sale of cinders as distinct goods.[12] Nevertheless, the decision lays down no hard-and-fast rule and it is quite possible under the wording of s 61(1) that a sale of minerals to be extracted by B can amount to a sale of goods. In *Amco Enterprises Pty Ltd v Wade*,[13] for example, there was an agreement that B would enter S's land and remove all sand, gravel and stone and pay for it in a fixed period of time. This was held to be a contract for the sale of goods in which the parties had agreed that B should sever the goods from the land.

There are arguably fewer problems, in relation to the sale of goods, with the question of 'fixtures', ie things attached to the land so that they become part of the land.[14] When goods are thus attached to the land, they become the property of the owner of the land by the process of accession, but it can often be difficult to decide when chattels have become affixed to the land in this way, the issue being primarily one within the law of real property. It is usually said that two factors are significant in the decision as to whether or not a chattel has become a fixture, viz the degree of annexation to the land and the object of the

---

7 See *English Hop Growers v Dering* [1928] 2 KB 174 (on the facts, a crop of hops which was almost ready for harvest was regarded as *fructus industriales* and so not part of the land). The problem seemingly does not arise with *fructus naturales* which are regarded as part of the land, see *Saunders v Pilcher* [1949] 2 All ER 1097.

8 See *Mayfield v Wadsley* (1824) 3 B & C 357; cf *English Hop Growers v Dering* [1928] 2 KB 174 where no separate price was agreed for the crop.

9 *Port v Turton* (1763) 2 Wils 169; *Wilkinson v Proud* (1843) 11 M & W 33.

10 [1909] 1 KB 357.

11 [1909] 1 KB 357 at 365.

12 See also *Mills v Stokman* (1967) 116 CLR 61 (sale of slate contained in rubble quarried from the land and dumped on one side as useless; the pile was either never severed from the land or it had been abandoned after severance and had thus become part of the land. Held an agreement allowing B to enter the land and take the slate was not a contract for the sale of goods but a grant of a *profit à prendre*).

13 [1968] Qd Rep 445.

14 See Bennett, 'Attachment of Chattels to Land' in *Interests in Goods* (eds Palmer and McKendrick, 2nd edn, 1998), Ch 11.

annexation.[15] In the recent decision in *Elitestone Ltd v Morris*,[16] the dispute concerned bungalows which had been built before 1945 and, although they rested on concrete foundation blocks in the ground, the bungalows could be removed only by demolition and thus did not fall within the category of 'mobile homes'. The plaintiffs were the freehold owners of the land who wished to develop the site and argued that the bungalows were chattels but the defendant occupiers of the bungalows resisted the claim for possession on the the ground that their homes were fixtures meaning that they were tenants from year to year who were protected by the Rent Act 1977. The House of Lords held that, as the bungalows could only be enjoyed in situ and were not removable, they had become part and parcel of the land and the absence of physical attachment to the land was irrelevant.[17] Certainly when fixtures are severed from the land (eg a building is demolished) they return to the status of goods and it is clear from the wording of s 61(1) that, where such severance is contemplated, and performed by either S or B, the contract will be one for the sale of goods.

The discussion above has focused upon whether or not the contracts in question related to 'goods' but it should be stressed that, if the contract is one for the sale of goods, it is almost beyond doubt that no property in those goods can pass before severance has taken place. As will be seen in Chapter 16, the entire apparatus of the SGA relating to the passing of property in all types of goods depends upon those goods being physically identified rather than merely being described and individualised in the contract and this must particularly be so where minerals are part of the land prior to severance.[18]

Computer software

There has been controversy for some time as to the legal status of computer software and the information which it contains.[19] The computer disks themselves are clearly goods and so is the computer hardware[20] but beyond this prosaic rule lies much uncertainty. There can be no doubt that the disks themselves are sold to the buyer but the copyright in the software remains vested in its author who licenses the buyer to load the software into his computer.

In *St Albans City and District Council v International Computers Ltd*,[1] the defendants supplied the plaintiff council with a computerised database for the

---

15 *Holland v Hodgson* (1872) LR 7 CP 328, 334 per Blackburn J.
16 [1997] 2 All ER 513.
17 The House of Lords considered that the twofold distinction between chattels and fixtures was apt to be unclear and it was better to adopt a threefold classification for objects brought onto land as being either (i) chattels (ii) fixtures, or (iii) part and parcel of the land itself, with objects within categories (ii) and (iii) being regarded as part of the land.
18 See, in particular, *Kursell v Timber Operators and Contractors Ltd* [1927] 1 KB 298; Cf Gow, *The Mercantile and Industrial Law of Scotland* (1964), p 80, who argues that severance is unnecessary as 'the indispensable and sole requirement of a conveyance is that the goods be individualised'.
19 See Carr and Arnold, *Computer Software: Legal Protection in the United Kingdom* (2nd edn), pp 143-146; Napier, 'The Future of Information Technology Law' [1992] 51 CLJ 46, 55-56; Macdonald, 'The Council, the Computer and the Unfair Contract Terms Act 1977' (1995) 58 MLR 585, 588-591.
20 *Toby Constructions Products Pty Ltd v Computa Bar (Sales) Pty Ltd* [1983] 2 NSWLR 48 (sale of an entire computer system including hardware and software was held to be a sale of goods).
1 [1996] 4 All ER 481.

purposes of calculating the community charge but the software was defective. One issue raised in the decision was whether the contract for the supply of software was subject to an implied term relating to its quality or fitness for purpose. In the Court of Appeal, Sir Iain Glidewell considered[2] that a computer disk containing a program was within the definition of 'goods' in the SGA, s 61(1): a sale of such a defective disk would thus be a sale of goods and S would be in breach of the SGA implied terms as to quality and fitness for purpose. However, he also thought that the program *itself* was not 'goods' and, as the program was simply transferred from the defendant's disk into the plaintiff's computer, there was no sale (or hire) of goods and no statutory implication of terms as to quality and fitness for purpose. The contract was, however, subject to an implied term at common law that the program would be reasonably fit for its purpose.

In the USA, a pattern may be emerging that a sale of standardised computer software is a sale of goods whereas a contract to design/write a program for a particular customer should be treated as a contract for services[3] and this latter point has been accepted by the English Court of Appeal.[4]

These decisions display an understandable desire for certainty in their attempt to shoehorn agreements for the supply of software into the established categories of contracts for the sale of goods or contracts for the supply of goods or services. However, a different approach was evident in the Scottish decision in *Beta Computers (Europe) Ltd v Adobe Systems (Europe) Ltd.*[5] There B ordered from S standard software in order to upgrade his existing system and the package was delivered in a 'shrink-wrap' which showed that it was subject to strict end user licence conditions, viz 'Opening the Informix SI software package indicates your acceptance of these terms and conditions'. B did not open the package and sought to return it to S who refused to take it back and sued for the price. S's claim was straightforward: B had placed an unconditional order for identified software and had been supplied with the product which he had ordered. S thus argued that he was not concerned with the conditions of use imposed by Informix, the owners of the intellectual property in the computer program, and that he was not in any sense an intermediary for Informix. B, on the other hand, contended that acceptance of the licence conditions was an implied condition suspensive of their agreement and that he was, consequently, entitled to reject the software. Lord Penrose held that the supply of proprietary software for a price was a single contract *sui generis*, although it did contain elements of nominate contracts such as the sale of goods and the grant of a licence. An essential feature of the transaction was, however, that the supplier undertook to make available to the purchaser both the medium on which the program was recorded and the right of access to, and the use of, the software. It followed that there could be no *consensus ad idem* until the conditions of use stipulated by the copyright owner were produced and accepted by the parties and this could not occur earlier than the moment at which those conditions were tendered to the purchaser. In any event, whether the tender of the software subject to conditions of use was regarded as a breach of a previously unconditional contract, or as being subject to an implied suspensive condition entitling the buyer to reject it if the conditions of use of the software

---

2   [1996] 4 All ER 481 at 493.
3   See *Triangle Underwriters Inc v Honeywell Inc* 604 F 2d 737 (1979).
4   *Salvage Association v CAP Financial Services Ltd* [1995] FSR 654.
5   1996 SLT 604.

were unacceptable, or as being made when there was no concluded contract, the buyer was entitled to reject the software.

In *Beta Computers*, Lord Penrose emphasised that the order of software was neither an order for the supply of disks as such nor an order for the supply of information as such. Rather, the subject of the contract was 'a complex product comprising the medium and the manifestation within it or on it of the intellectual property of the author'.[6] Consequently, Lord Penrose was not attracted by the argument that software supplied on a physical medium should be categorised rigidly as physical property like a book or a record. Moreover, he considered that the rights of the parties should not depend on the *medium* of supply because that would mean that 'the dominant characteristic of the complex product, in terms of value or of the significant interests of parties, would be subordinated to the medium by which it was transmitted to the user in analysing the true nature and effect of the contract'.[7] These difficulties thus led to the conclusion that the supply of proprietary software for a price was a contract *sui generis* which could not adequately be understood if expressed wholly in terms of any of the nominate contracts such as the sale of goods.

Cadavers and body parts

The general rule at common law has always been that there can be no right of property in a corpse or any part of a dead body[8] and, according to Coke, this principle originates in the notion that cadavers belonged solely to the Ecclesiastical jurisdiction.[9] The fact that a dead body was *res nullius* meant that the removal of bodies from graves was not theft, although it could amount to the common law misdemeanour of trespass.[10] Moreover, the absence of proprietary rights in a corpse when coupled with the overall Ecclesiastical influence led to the pervasive rule that it would be both inapt and impossible for human corpses or parts thereof to be traded as commercial chattels. However, there is clearly a difference between corpses which are to be buried or cremated and body parts which are preserved for anatomical use, for example. In the latter context, the decision in *Doodeward v Spence*[11] has been an influential one. There the plaintiff's father had purchased at auction a foetus with two heads which had been stillborn in 1868 and the plaintiff had been prosecuted for exhibiting it for gain; after the prosecution the foetus remained in a museum at Sydney University. The plaintiff sued in detinue for the return of this macabre object. The High Court of Australia held (Higgins J dissenting) that there could be property in a human body if it was lawfully altered with the object of preserving it for the purposes of medical or scientific examination and thus the plaintiff had a right to possession of the foetus as his property: only those entitled to have the body buried had a better right to possession. The *Doodeward* approach has been followed in recent English decisions[12] and it is

---

6 1996 SLT 604 at 608.
7 1996 SLT 604 at 609.
8 *Haynes' Case* (1614) 12 Co Rep 113; *Handyside's Case* (1749) 2 East PC 652; *Williams v Williams* (1882) 20 Ch D 659; *Dobson v North Tyneside Health Authority* [1996] 4 All ER 474; *R v Kelly* [1998] 3 All ER 741; see Scott, *The Body as Property* (1981); Matthews, 'Whose Body? People as Property' (1983) 36 CLP 193.
9 3 Co Inst 203; Coke considered that the cadaver was *caro data vermibus* and as *nullius in bonis*, it belonged only to the Ecclesiastical cognisance.
10 *R v Lynn* (1788) 2 Term Rep 733; *R v Sharpe* (1857) Dears & B 160.
11 (1908) 6 CLR 406.

clearly imperative that proprietary rights be recognised in preserved skeletons and anatomical specimens and that their status as 'goods' be acknowledged so that they can be bought and sold.

The law is somewhat unclear as to the position regarding human tissue,[13] eg organ transplants and the supply of blood, but certainly the sale of human organs and other commercial dealings in them is prohibited by the Human Organ Transplants Act 1989.[14] It is indisputable that human tissue can be stolen and there have been convictions for the theft of urine and blood collected for the purposes of testing alcohol level.[15] In the USA, there have been several decisions regarding the provision of blood transfusions and whether such transactions are classifiable as sales of goods. In one prominent case,[16] a private patient in a hospital received a blood transfusion contaminated with jaundice viruses which could not be detected by any tests and his account showed that a separate sum had been charged for the blood. He contended that the blood had been sold to him and that the sale therefore contained the strict liability provisions as to quality in New York sale of goods legislation, but it was held that the contract was one for the supply of services and that there could be liability only in negligence which, on the facts, had not been proved. There is, however, American authority supporting the opposite view that the supply of blood by a blood bank constitutes a sale of goods.[17] This divergence of opinion has led to the enactment of legislation in the USA to the effect that the provision of blood is a supply of services, thereby avoiding strict liability where, for example, AIDS has been contracted from a blood transfusion.[18] Although there is no definitive English authority on this question, the matter may often have little practical significance in that the Supply of Goods and Services Act 1982 contains implied terms relating to quality and fitness analogous to those in the SGA.[19]

An undivided share in goods

Goods are tangible objects and thus it is usual to think of their sale in terms of B's payment of the price in return for S's delivery of the goods. It is also not uncommon for several buyers to become owners in common of goods thereby holding the goods in undivided shares (eg quarter shares in a racehorse or boat). It seems that such ownership in common with undivided shares expressed in fractions has always been permissible,[20] but the original SGA in 1893 did not expressly provide any framework for co-ownership. The only reference to co-ownership in the SGA 1893 was in s 1(1) which now appears as s 2(2) and provides that 'there may be a contract of sale between one part owner and another'. It appears that this wording was designed to clarify the point that a sale could

---

12 See *Dobson v North Tyneside Health Authority* [1996] 4 All ER 474; *R v Kelly* [1998] 3 All ER 741 (appellants guilty of theft of 35 body parts from the Royal College of Surgeons).

13 See Magnusson, 'Proprietary Rights in Human Tissue' in *Interests in Goods* (eds Palmer and McKendrick, 2nd edn, 1998), Ch 2.

14 See also the Human Tissue Act 1961 and the Human Fertilisation and Embryology Act 1990.

15 *R v Welsh* [1974] RTR 478; *R v Rothery* [1976] RTR 550.

16 *Perlmutter v Beth David Hospital* 123 NE 2d 792 (1955).

17 *Belle Bonfils Memorial Blood Bank v Hansen* 579 P 2d 1158 (1978).

18 *McKee v Cutter Laboratories Inc* 866 F 2d 219 (1989).

19 See Bell, 'The Doctor and the Supply of Goods and Services Act 1982' (1984) 4 Legal Studies 175.

20 See *Marson v Short* (1835) 2 Bing NC 118.

exist *between* part-owners as certain doubts hovered over such a transaction. First, the sale of an undivided share in goods did not harmonise perfectly with the central definition of a sale of goods in s 2(1) as being a sale of 'the property'[1] in 'goods'. Second, it was unclear whether a person could purchase a share in his *own* goods as the normal presumption is that seller and buyer must be different persons.[2] Third, these reservations lead inescapably to the conclusion that an undivided share in goods might be more aptly classified as a sale of an abstract chose in action.[3] Fortunately, these uncertainties have been expunged and the law is now both clear and logical. The SGA s 61(1) has been amended[4] and now provides that 'goods' includes 'an undivided share in goods'. Section 61(1) also extends the definition of 'specific goods' to include 'an undivided share, specified as a fraction or percentage, of goods identified and agreed on as aforesaid'. A sale of a quarter share in a racehorse, for example, is now indisputably within the SGA as a sale of specific goods and ownership in common of such goods has been put on a rational footing.

Similar difficulties arise in relation to a sale of unascertained goods (eg five buyers each agree to buy 100 tons of wheat from a bulk of 1,000 tons in a warehouse) as no ownership in unascertained goods can transfer to B until the goods are ascertained. In the latter example, this can occur only when 100 tons are separated for each buyer from the bulk of 1,000 tons and thus identified as the contract 'goods' so that 'the property' might pass to the buyers. Although this is logical in that it is impossible for B to have bought goods unless he can physically identify them as his, might the buyers in the above example acquire ownership of undivided shares in the bulk of 1,000 tons? Until recently, English law had set its face against such a possibility at the cost of obvious injustice. If, for example, B had paid the whole price of the goods to S and S became insolvent before the property in the goods passed to B, B was limited to a a claim in damages for breach of contract or for the return of the price but he had no legal or equitable interest in the goods themselves. As an unsecured creditor, it is self-evident that such claims would usually be fruitless.

However, it is now also possible, under the (stringent) conditions imposed by the SGA, s 20A, for property in an undivided share of an identified bulk of goods to transfer to B so that B becomes an owner in common of the bulk with, for example, the seller and other buyers (eg B1 and B2 each agree to buy 1,000 gallons of oil from S's cargo of 10,000 gallons aboard a named vessel, and both pay S in advance for the goods). The question of co-ownership of goods is considered in detail in Chapter 16 when the rules concerning the passing of property are analysed.

1 Especially as 'property' is defined in s 61(1) as 'the general property in goods, and not merely a special property'.
2 See Chalmers, *Sale of Goods Act 1979* (18th edn, 1981), p 78.
3 For example, a line of cases concerned with the supply of liquor to members of members' clubs (eg *Graff v Evans* (1882) 8 QBD 373; *Davies v Burnett* [1902] 1 KB 666; *Trebanog Working Mens' Club and Institute v Macdonald* [1940] 1 KB 576) had taken the view that the liquor was the joint property of the members and the supply of a drink to a member in return for its price was not a retail sale for the purposes of the licensing Acts: no bargain/contract existed to buy the goods, instead each member had a right to have drink supplied at a certain price by virtue of his membership of the club to which he subscribed. Also, in *Re Sugar Properties (Derisley Wood) Ltd* [1988] BCLC 146, Mervyn Davies J treated shares in a racehorse as choses in action for the purposes of the Bills of Sale Act 1878.
4 By the Sale Of Goods (Amendment) Act 1995, following the recommendations of the Law Commissions, see *Sale of Goods Forming Part of a Bulk*, (Law Com No 215; Scot Law Com No 145 (1993)).

Miscellaneous items

There are other items which are almost certainly not classifiable as 'goods' for the purposes of the SGA although they may be referred to as 'commodities', 'things' or 'articles' in other statutory definitions. These comprise electricity and other forms of energy, living animals in the wild state,[5] the various types of intellectual property, and information. Moreover, although the definition of 'goods' in s 61(1) includes ships and the construction/sale of new vessels is clearly within the SGA rules on the passing of property, the transfer and ownership of ships is regulated by statute[6] and so the SGA rules do not apply in isolation.

The price of the goods

'A money consideration called the price'

Section 2(1) specifies that the consideration in a contract of sale of goods must be 'a money consideration, called the price' and, of course, it is equally valid for B actually to pay this money consideration or simply promise to pay it and thus be allowed credit.[7] However, where the goods are transferred for a consideration other than money, eg goods are exchanged for the provision of accommodation, the contract is not one for the sale of goods but will be a contract of barter or exchange. If *no* valuable consideration is given for the transfer of property in the goods, there will be a gift but there cannot be a sale. In stipulating that the consideration must be a price in money, English law defines the contract of sale of goods in narrow terms unlike, for example, American law, which stipulates that 'the price can be made payable in money or otherwise'[8] meaning that, in the USA, a contract of barter is treated as a contract of sale.

Gifts and promotional offers

The borderline separating sales from gifts can be indistinct, as illustrated in *Esso Petroleum Co Ltd v Customs and Excise Comrs*.[9] Esso devised a sales promotion scheme whereby a coin bearing the likeness of one of the English footballers selected for the 1970 World Cup was offered free to motorists who bought four gallons of petrol. Esso's extensive advertising stated that the coins were 'Going Free at your Esso Action Station now' and thirty different coins were available for the collector. The question for decision was whether the coins were being 'sold' and were accordingly chargeable to purchase tax. Pennycuick V-C held that the coins had

---

5　Dead wild animals can be sold as goods as can wild animals when lawfully placed in captivity. A grant by a landowner of hunting rights is a disposition of an interest in land or a *profit à prendre*.

6　See the Merchant Shipping Act 1995.

7　S and B can agree that the price is payable in any currency, see *Miliangos v George Frank (Textiles) Ltd* [1976] AC 443. If goods are paid for by credit card, the sale is within the SGA (see *Re Charge Card Services Ltd* [1987] Ch 150, 164 per Millett J: '... the true consideration in the contract of supply is the price, to be satisfied by the cardholder, by means of the card if he wishes'. The point was not considered on appeal: [1989] Ch 497).

8　UCC, s 2-304(1); a provision similar to this had been proposed by Chalmers in the draft Bill of the SGA but it was rejected later, see Chalmers, *The Sale of Goods* (1st edn, 1890), p 87.

9　[1976] 1 WLR 1.

been sold but the Court of Appeal reversed that decision and held that they were distributed as gifts and thus no tax was payable. In the House of Lords, the opinions expressed ran the gamut of possibilities. Viscount Dilhorne and Lord Russell agreed with the Court of Appeal's analysis that the coins were gifts and no contract had been formed between the parties as there was no intent to create legal relations. This finding of lack of intent was influenced by the fact that the coins had little intrinsic value. Lord Simon and Lord Wilberforce concluded that the relationship was contractual but was not a sale; instead there were two contracts, viz (i) a contract for the sale of the petrol and (ii) a collateral contract for the supply of a coin with every four gallons of petrol bought. The coins were thus not transferred for a money payment but were transferred in consideration of the motorist's entering into a contract for the sale of petrol. Lord Fraser was alone in taking the sensibly pragmatic view that there was a sale of the coin together with the petrol in a single transaction. The outcome of the case was that the coins had not been sold and were consequently exempt from tax.

If the transaction is a gift, it has been stressed above that there is no sale and the SGA does not apply. Moreover, if there is no *contract* whatever between the parties, the donee can have no contractual remedy against the donor. In *Esso*, three of the five Law Lords considered that the relationship was not a gift and so, today, the *Esso* transaction would almost certainly be within the Supply of Goods and Services Act 1982, s 1(1), as 'a contract under which one person transfers or agrees to transfer to another the property in goods'. As such, the transferee could seek the protection of the implied terms in the 1982 Act relating to quality and fitness for purpose should the goods prove defective.[10] It is now routine marketing practice to find promotional 'free gifts' included within packets of goods which are sold (eg breakfast cereals), attached to the principal goods or included in larger sized goods (eg '200ml bottle free with 500ml bottle'; '30% extra free') or goods are often sold on the basis of obtaining extra goods as a 'gift' (eg 'Buy 2 get 1 free'). It would surely be unreasonable to apply the collateral contract analysis in *Esso* to these types of transaction. At a technical level, the 'free' goods are often inseparable from the principal goods (eg 'gifts' in breakfast cereals) and are often both inseparable and of the same type as the principal goods (eg '30% extra breakfast cereal in this pack free'); the collateral contract argument is thus harder to sustain than in *Esso*. More importantly, the essence of many of these sales is that B receives a discount on the price: nobody would contend that a 30% discount on the price would preclude the transaction from being a sale and the position is no different where B obtains an extra amount of goods 'free'. Consequently, it is suggested that such sales will be regarded as single contracts for the sale of goods.[11] This conclusion is reinforced in that the

---

10 The report of the Law Commission which led to the 1982 Act declined to examine the law relating to gifts (see *Implied Terms in Contracts for the Supply of Goods* (Law Com No 95, 1979), para 32).

11 See *Esso* [1976] 1 WLR 1, 7-8 per Lord Fraser. See also *Imperial Tobacco Ltd v A-G* [1981] AC 718 (cards which might include a winning number were supplied 'free of charge' in packets of cigarettes. The issue was whether this was a lottery and this depended upon whether there had been a payment or contribution by participants to a fund from which prizes were drawn. HL held the scheme was a lottery as buyers of cigarettes secured a chance to win a prize and buyers bought the packet of cigarettes *and* the card); *A-G v L D Nathan & Co Ltd* [1990] 1 NZLR 129 (buyers of 2kg of beef in supermarkets received a 'free' bottle of wine at the checkout; the question was whether this was a sale of liquor without a licence. The CA of New Zealand held this was a single sale of beef and wine and Lord Fraser's approach in *Esso* was followed).

implied conditions relating to quality and fitness for purpose in the SGA, s 14 apply to 'goods supplied under the contract' and 'free gifts' would thus come within this wording, particularly where the 'gift' supplied is bargained-for rather than being an unwanted and hazardous extra.[12]

Barter

The paradigm contract of barter occurs where the goods of one party are simply *exchanged* for the goods of the other party without any *valuation* being placed on the goods. However, the contract will be one of barter where goods are exchanged for work done,[13] board and lodging[14] or any other valuable consideration.[15] The SGA does not apply to contracts of barter; instead, the contract is within the Supply of Goods and Services Act 1982, s 1(1), as 'a contract under which one person transfers or agrees to transfer to another the property in goods' and the implied terms of the 1982 Act relating to the quality and fitness for purpose of the goods apply to the barter. In cases of defective goods, it will often be immaterial whether the contract is classified as barter or sale as there are broad, statutory implied terms applicable to both types of contract, but there are other crucial issues which turn on the division into either sale or barter.

In a barter of goods, the innocent party who has not received the anticipated goods in exchange cannot sue for the value of the goods which he has delivered (ie as a 'price').[16] Instead his remedy is to sue for unliquidated damages for non-delivery of the promised goods and those damages will equal the value of the goods which have not been delivered. Moreover, there is no definitive authority on the passing of property (and risk) in a contract of barter and it is thus unclear whether property and risk can pass at the moment of contract as in a sale of specific goods or whether delivery is necessary: opinion on this issue points in both directions.[17]

It is the element of exchange which is the essence of a contract of barter but not all transactions comprise either simple exchange or obvious sale and, if money is an *ingredient* of the transaction, it may be regarded as a sale of goods. In

12 See *Wilson v Rickett Cockerell & Co Ltd* [1954] 1 QB 598 (unwanted 'free' detonator supplied with a quantity of Coalite was 'goods supplied' within s 14). This was the view of the Law Commissions (see *Exemption Clauses, Second Report* (Law Com No 69; Scot Law Com No 39; (1975), para 35).
13 *Garey v Pyke* (1839) 10 Ad & El 512 (introduction of customers to a tailor in exchange for clothes).
14 *Keys v Harwood* (1846) 2 CB 905 (furniture in exchange for board and lodging).
15 Barter is encountered in international trade. Countries with developing economies which lack hard currency and credit facilities may seek to exchange their goods for the goods exported from the industrialised economies; see Schmitthoff, 'Countertrade' [1985] JBL 115.
16 *Harrison v Luke* (1845) 14 M & W 139.
17 See *Cochrane v Moore* (1890) 25 QBD 57; *Pearce v Brain* [1929] 2 KB 310; *Koppel v Koppel* [1966] 1 WLR 802; *Widenmeyer v Burn, Stewart & Co Ltd* 1967 SC 85 (agreement between a German company and a Scottish company for the exchange of specific stocks of 1962 grain whisky for specific stocks of 1964 grain whisky, all the whisky lying in bond in Glasgow. No physical delivery of the whisky was contemplated. Held that, following Scots common law, the risk in bartered goods passed when the contract was perfected by the receipt of a delivery note by the German company's agent. The risk was thus on the German company when, a few hours after the receipt of the note, a wall in the warehouse accidentally collapsed and some of the whisky was lost); *Flynn v Mackin and Mahon* [1974] IR 101(Walsh J assumed that property in bartered goods passed only on physical delivery/ exchange of the goods); Smith, 'Exchange or Sale?' (1974) 48 Tulane L Rev 1029.

Aldridge v Johnson,[18] S agreed to exchange 32 bullocks for 100 quarters of barley from B's granary. The bullocks were valued at £192 and the barley at £215 and it was agreed that the difference of £23 would be paid in cash. B took delivery of the bullocks and S sent B 200 sacks to be filled with the barley. 155 of the sacks had been filled when B instructed that they be emptied back into bulk and S then learnt that B was about to be declared bankrupt. S claimed 100 quarters of barley from B but it was held that only property in the barley in the 155 sacks had passed to S. The court appeared to treat this as a case of reciprocal sales in that the value of *both* the bullocks and the barley had been ascertained in terms of money and then set-off against each other with the balance payable in cash. If this element of bilateral valuation had been missing, however, and the bargain had been a simple exchange of goods for other goods, it could not have been a contract of sale.[19] Accordingly, in *Flynn v Mackin and Mahon*,[20] the contract was held to be one of barter where S agreed to supply a new car in return for B's old car and a cash sum, with a cash value being attributed to *neither* car. The court considered that the contract would have been a sale if a price had been fixed for the new car and, in lieu of that price, S had agreed to take the old car and a cash sum.

Where B wants to buy a new car, it is now routine for him to deliver his existing car to a car dealer in 'part-exchange' for the new car. The dealer does not, of course, go through the process of paying B a price for his car only to have B repay it with an extra sum for the new car; instead, the parties fix a notional price for the existing car which is set-off against the price of the new car. Surprisingly, the legal status of part-exchange is unclear: the better view is that part-exchanges of vehicles, as described above, are not contracts of barter[1] but two interpretations of the transaction are possible. First, where a value is attributed in money to both the new and existing cars, there may be reciprocal contracts of sale with a set-off of prices, as in *Aldridge*, above.[2] This dissection into two sales would mean that property and risk in both cars could pass at the moment of contract under the SGA s 18, r 1. Second, there may be one contract for the sale of the new car coupled with an ancillary arrangement that if B delivers the existing car, an agreed allowance will be made on the price of the new car. If B does not deliver the car, S may then sue for the price. Here there is only one sale of the new car because the consideration for the existing car is not a price in money but a partial release of a debt. Property in the existing car would thus pass to S on delivery and not on the formation of the contract. *Benjamin*[3]

---

18 (1857) 7 E & B 885.
19 If the contract may be performed either by the delivery of goods *or* the payment of money, it appears to be a sale of goods: see *South Australian Insurance Co v Randell* (1869) LR 3 PC 101 (S had the option of receiving goods) *Messenger v Green* [1937] 2 DLR 26 (B had the option of delivering goods).
20 [1974] IR 101.
 1 See *Hands v Burton* (1808) 9 East 349; *Forsyth v Jervis* (1816) 1 Stark 437; *Sheldon v Cox* (1824) 3 B & C 420; *Bull v Parker* (1842) 12 LJQB 93; *Saxty v Wilkin* (1843) 11 M & W 622 *Keys v Harwood* (1846) 2 CB 905; *Flynn v Mackin and Mahon* [1974] IR 101; Cf *Implied Terms in Contracts for the Supply of Goods* (Law Com No 95, 1979), para 48, where the view was expressed that part-exchanges of vehicles were contracts of barter.
 2 See also *Flynn v Mackin and Mahon* [1974] IR 101; *Davey v Paine Bros (Motors) Ltd* [1954] NZLR 1122 (two vehicles valued at the *same* price and then exchanged came within the New Zealand SGA).
 3 *Benjamin's Sale of Goods* (5th edn, 1997), para 1-039; see also Goode, *Hire Purchase Law and Practice* (2nd edn, 1970), pp 304-305, who considers that the part-exchange buyer 'has an option to satisfy the monetary obligation in part by tender of goods'.

subscribes to this second interpretation and it gains support from *Dawson (G J) (Clapham) Ltd v H & G Dutfield*,[4] the only English decision on part-exchange of vehicles. There S agreed to sell two second-hand lorries to B for £475 and take two other lorries valued at £225 from B in part-exchange plus £250 in cash. B's existing lorries were to be delivered in one month. B paid the cash but failed to deliver the lorries and it was held that S should succeed for the balance of the price (£225) as a debt due to him. Hilbery J[5] stressed that 'there were not two purchases but only one transaction ... the concluded bargain was the sale of a Leyland and a Saurer for £475 and as part of the purchase and sale there was an agreement to allow £225 for two lorries if they were delivered within a month'. Overall, it is suggested that this second interpretation of part-exchange agreements accords with normal expectations in that B considers that he is satisfying part of the price of the new car by delivering his existing car.

Finally, it must be asked what the position is where B uses a coupon, voucher or label in part-payment for goods (eg '£1 off next purchase') or obtains goods in *exchange* for such a voucher without any money payment (eg 'Obtain one bottle free upon presentation of this voucher'). It is submitted that the first situation, where money does change hands, amounts simply to a sale of goods at a discounted price[6] and this situation corresponds with that of 'free' gifts attached to the principal goods which, it was suggested earlier, should also be contracts of sale. The second situation of an exchange of coupons for goods appears to be the paradigm of barter as there is no money payment at all, but this does not correspond with the view taken in *Davies v Customs and Excise Comrs*.[7] There customers of a retail draper bought 'checks' from the Provident Clothing & Supply Company and exchanged the checks for goods supplied by the draper. The customers were charged normal retail prices but, upon the draper's presentation of the checks to Provident, the latter redeemed them at their face value less 13¾ per cent. The Customs and Excise claimed there had been a sale by the draper to the customers at the full, retail price and that VAT was payable on that price but the draper contended that VAT was payable only on the lower cash sum paid to him by Provident. Delivering the judgment of the Divisional Court, Lord Widgery CJ held that there was a sale of goods by the draper to the customers and that 'the customer who presents the Provident check is paying cash and not consideration other than cash'.[8] Accordingly, VAT was payable on the cash price paid by the customer. This is a very awkward decision and it has been said that it can be justified only on the (unlikely) basis that both S and B contemplated that, if Provident did not pay

---

4   [1936] 2 All ER 232.
5   [1936] 2 All ER 232 at 233 and 234.
6   See *Buckley v Lever Bros Ltd* [1953] 4 DLR 16 (promotional offer of a plastic apron and twelve clothespegs in return for 50 cents and two box tops from soap powder. One of the pegs snapped in use and B was struck in the eye. Wells J assumed this was a sale of goods and B recovered damages for breach of the implied terms relating to quality in the (Ontario) SGA); cf *Chappell & Co Ltd v Nestlé Co Ltd* [1960] AC 87 (promotional offer of a gramophone record in return for 1s 6d and three chocolate wrappers. The issue of whether this was sale or barter did not arise directly but Lord Reid doubted (p 109) that it was a sale. He said:'... [the] price can only include money or something which can be readily converted into an ascertainable sum of money, therefore anything like wrappers which have no money value when delivered cannot be part of the consideration').
7   [1975] 1 WLR 204.
8   [1975] 1 WLR 204 at 206.

S, the latter could claim the price from the buyer.[9] It is difficult to resist the conclusion that such exchanges of coupons for goods should be within the Supply of Goods and Services Act 1982.[10]

Fixing the price in contracts of sale

The SGA, s 8 (1) provides that:

'The price in a contract of sale may be fixed by the contract, or may be left to be fixed in a manner agreed by the contract, or may be determined by the course of dealing between the parties.'

The Roman law of sale insisted that some overt act of delivery of possession was necessary to transfer the property in goods to B and that a sale of goods had to be for a *fixed* price in money. As Blackburn[11] stressed in 1885, these principles are alien to English law which, on both these rules, takes the opposite view: a contract for the sale of goods may act as a simultaneous conveyance of the property in the goods to B and the absence of a fixed price in an otherwise *complete* bargain does not necessarily suspend the passing of property to B. In many commercial transactions, S and B may be reluctant to enter into a long-term contract at fixed prices but may prefer to have some machinery which couples prices to market fluctuations, for example, and also a scheme allowing for the time and mode of payment to be varied. Here it may be indisputable that S and B have a finalised agreement and the basic rule in s 8(1) accords with commercial practice in allowing certain matters to be left for future resolution without vitiating the agreement.[12] Some early decisions,[13] criticised by Blackburn[14] as based upon the Civil law rather than native principles, had held that where S was to weigh or measure specific goods in order to ascertain the price, property would not pass until the weighing etc, was completed. Blackburn thought that weighing or measuring might be necessary in order to ascertain the goods themselves or put them into a deliverable state 'but where ... there is nothing unascertained except the money value of the price, and yet the goods are held not to be bargained and sold , there seems little to be said, except that such are the decisions'.[15] Nevertheless, it was these principles of English law which Chalmers sought faithfully to reproduce in the SGA and thus s 8 presupposes that a contract of sale has been concluded but the price is left to be fixed, and the rule concerning S's weighing or measuring of the goods in order to ascertain their price was enacted in the SGA, s 18, r 3.[16]

---

9 Chalmers, *Sale of Goods Act 1979* (18th edn, 1981), p 82.
10 The exchange of trading stamps for goods, made prominent by Green Shield Stamps, is regulated by the Trading Stamps Act 1964 (as amended by the Supply of Goods (Implied Terms) Act 1973, s 16, and the Consumer Credit Act 1974, Sch 4); see Cranston, *Consumers and the Law* (2nd edn, 1984), pp 342-343.
11 *Contract of Sale* (2nd edn, 1885), p 242.
12 See *Valpy v Gibson* (1847) 4 CB 837, 864 per Wilde CJ.
13 *Hanson v Meyer* (1805) 6 East 614; *Zagury v Furnell* (1809) 2 Camp 240; *Simmons v Swift* (1826) 5 B & C 857.
14 *Contract of Sale* (2nd edn, 1885), p 243.
15 *Contract of Sale* (2nd edn, 1885), p 243.
16 See Ch 16.

Provided that the contract of sale has been concluded, S and B are permitted considerable latitude as regards the fixing of the price. As emphasised above, it is possible for the property in the goods or the risk to pass to B before the final calculation of the price and, if this becomes impossible because the goods have perished, the court must do its best to estimate a fair price based on the value of the goods at the date of their loss.[17] The price can be fixed by a third party (see s 9, below) and the contract may even provide that one of the parties should determine the price and this is binding provided that he has exercised his discretion in good faith.[18] Moreover, the price can be fixed by reference to some occurrence which is external to the contract, eg the market price at the time of delivery.[19] Finally, it is possible for the price to be determined by the course of dealing between the parties.[20]

If the price is indeterminate, might the agreement fail for uncertainty?

The rule that the price may be left open in a concluded contract might be thought to contain an inherent contradiction because the absence of a fixed price could indicate that the parties have not formed a binding contract in the first place. If the price is left to be fixed at some time in the future, S and B run the risk that their agreement may be void as lacking both certainty of terms and intent to create legal relations.[1] The cardinal rule is that the parties make their own bargain but it can be enforced by the courts only if it is intelligible. In *May and Butcher v R*,[2] an agreement for the sale of tentage provided that the price, dates of payment and manner of delivery should be agreed 'from time to time' but the House of Lords held that the agreement was incomplete and unenforceable as amounting to nothing more than an agreement to agree in the future.[3] Nevertheless, there was a marked change of approach in the decision in *Hillas & Co Ltd v Arcos Ltd*,[4] where the House of Lords emphasised that the courts strive to uphold bargains wherever possible and will not be too astute in seeking defects in undertakings which are drafted in good faith by businessmen. Accordingly, in *Hillas*, an option for B to buy more timber from S in the future

---

17 *Castle v Playford* (1872) LR 7 Ex 98; *Martineau v Kitching* (1872) LR 7 QB 436 (for the facts, see Ch 24 on risk and Ch 16 on the passing of property).
18 *May and Butcher v R* [1934] 2 KB 17n, 21 per Viscount Dunedin.
19 *Charrington & Co Ltd v Wooder* [1914] AC 71 (provision in a lease for the supply of beer to publican at 'the fair market price' was held to be enforceable).
20 See *Agip SpA v Navigazione Alta Italia SpA* [1984] 1 Lloyd's Rep 353.
 1 If it is agreed that the price shall vary depending upon the happening of an event, the bargain may be regarded as a wager and declared void: see *Brogden v Marriott* (1836) 3 Bing NC 88 (S sold B a horse for £200 if he trotted 18 miles within the hour but for 1s if he failed. Held bargain was void); *Rourke v Short* (1856) 5 E & B 904 (dispute between S and B as to the price of rags, with T to decide the issue. If S was right the price would be 6s per cwt but if B was right, 3s per cwt. T decided in favour of S but B refused to pay 6s. Held agreement was void). These cases are premised on the fact that the variation in price is so great in relation to the market value of the goods that the transaction is a wager but this will not apply if the event can legitimately affect the value of the goods thereby justifying the difference in price.
 2 [1934] 2 KB 17n.
 3 See also *Scammell (G) & Nephew Ltd v Ouston* [1941] AC 251 (agreement to acquire goods 'on the understanding that the balance of the purchase price can be paid on hire-purchase terms over a two year period'. HL held this could not be a binding contract as it was too vague to be enforced).
 4 (1932) 147 LT 503.

was held to be enforceable even though it was couched in vague terms with no particulars of the kind of timber to be delivered or its method of shipment. The House of Lords held that, having regard to the parties' previous dealings, there was sufficient intent to be bound and the uncertainty could be resolved by examining the certain terms of the principal contract of sale and the normal practice in the timber trade.

Although the *Hillas* validation principle is now the dominant one, the lengths to which the courts will go in the resolution of uncertainty and ambiguity remain unclear.[5] Certain precepts are, however, well-established. The courts are particularly disposed to clarify imprecise and incomplete bargains where machinery, criteria or formulae are provided in the contract to resolve uncertainty,[6] eg an arbitration clause. Moreover, a meaningless clause can be deleted if it adds nothing to an otherwise complete agreement.[7] In those cases where the contract is partially[8] or fully executed,[9] it is desirable to uphold the bargain and an assertion of uncertainty is particularly implausible where the goods have been delivered and used. It follows that, where the courts are satisfied that there is substantial agreement between S and B, it may be possible to infer that a reasonable price is payable. In *Foley v Classique Coaches Ltd*,[10] for example, S owned a petrol station and adjoining land and he agreed to sell the land to B, who intended to use it for his motor coach business. The sale was made subject to B's entering into another agreement with S for the purchase of all his petrol for the coach business from S 'at a price to be agreed by the parties in writing and from time to time' and the contract provided that any disputes should be referred to arbitration. The land was conveyed and the petrol agreement acted upon for three years but then B argued, *inter alia*, that no agreement as to the price of the petrol had ever been concluded in writing. The Court of Appeal held that the contract was sufficiently certain to be enforceable and that, under the principle of *The Moorcock*,[11] a term should be implied into the agreement that B must pay a reasonable price for the petrol. Apart from the fact that the contract had been acted upon for several years, it was important that the petrol agreement was linked to the sale of the land and B no doubt paid a price for the land which reflected the fact that he was to buy all his petrol from S.

A reasonable price for the goods where no price is fixed

The SGA, s 8(2) provides:

> 'Where the price is not determined as mentioned in subsection (1) above the buyer must pay a reasonable price.'

---

5 See eg *Kleinwort Benson Ltd v Malaysia Mining Corpn Bhd* [1989] 1 WLR 379; *Walford v Miles* [1992] 2 AC 128.
6 See eg *Brown v Gould* [1972] Ch 53; *Sudbrook Trading Estate Ltd v Eggleton* [1983] 1 AC 444; *Queensland Electricity Generating Board v New Hope Collieries Pty Ltd* [1989] 1 Lloyd's Rep 205; cf *Ignazio Messina & Co v Polskie Linie Oceaniczne* [1995] 2 Lloyd's Rep 566.
7 *Nicolene Ltd v Simmonds* [1953] 1 QB 543.
8 *Sykes (F & G) (Wessex) Ltd v Fine Fare Ltd* [1967] 1 Lloyd's Rep 53.
9 *British Bank for Foreign Trade Ltd v Novinex Ltd* [1949] 1 KB 623; *Mack & Edwards (Sales) Ltd v McPhail Bros* (1968) 112 Sol Jo 211; *Trentham (G Percy) Ltd v Archital Luxfer Ltd* [1993] 1 Lloyd's Rep 25.
10 [1934] 2 KB 1.
11 (1889) 14 PD 64.

The SGA, s 8(3) adds:

> 'What is a reasonable price is a question of fact dependent on the circumstances of each particular case.'

Although B must pay a reasonable price where the contract has been executed and he has accepted the goods (on the footing that it would be unjust to allow his retention of the goods without payment) it is unclear whether a reasonable price is payable where the contract is executory.[12] Where property has passed to B and the contract is executory in the sense only that delivery has not been made, it seems likely that a reasonable price would be payable by him.[13] The reasonable price is usually ascertained by reference to the current market price at the time and place of delivery but this is not necessarily the sole test.[14] It is also important to stress that S may sustain a claim in quasi-contract for a reasonable price where the goods have been delivered but the contract is, for example, void for uncertainty or unenforceable.[15]

Price to be fixed by the valuation of a third party

It is quite acceptable for S and B to agree that the price shall be fixed by a third party (T) and, when the price is determined by T, S and B are bound by it. The SGA, s 9 allows for the situation where, in an agreement to sell goods, T is unable to arrive at a valuation of those goods. Section 9 provides:

> '(1) Where there is an agreement to sell goods on the terms that the price is to be fixed by the valuation of a third party, and he cannot or does not make the valuation, the agreement is avoided; but if the goods or any part of them have been delivered to and appropriated by the buyer he must pay a reasonable price for them.
> (2) Where the third party is prevented from making the valuation by the fault of the seller or buyer, the party not at fault may maintain an action for damages against the party at fault.'

Section 9 harmonises with general principles of the law of contract in that T's determination of the price is a condition precedent to the operation of the contract and, consequently, a failure of the condition means that the contract is avoided. Moreover, where the default of one party has prevented the condition from being realised, he is liable for breach of an implied term that he would not so act.[16]

It follows that, where the valuation fails under s 9(1) and the contract is avoided, neither S nor B can have have a remedy against the other[17] but any money or property transferred will have to be restored. Moreover, s 9(1) also provides that, if the valuation fails and the goods or any part of them have been delivered to and appropriated by the buyer he must pay a reasonable price for

12 *Acebal v Levy* (1834) 10 Bing 376, 382 per Tindal CJ.
13 *Hoadly v M'Laine* (1834) 10 Bing 482; *Hall v Busst* (1960) 104 CLR 206, 243-244 per Windeyer J; cf Menzies J at p 234 and the doubts of Fullager J at p 222; *Wenning v Robinson* (1964) 64 SRNSW 157, 161-162 per Walsh J; 167 per Asprey J.
14 *Acebal v Levy* (1834) 10 Bing 376, 383 per Tindal CJ.
15 See *Rose & Frank Co v J R Crompton & Bros Ltd* [1925] AC 445.
16 *Southern Foundries v Shirlaw* [1940] AC 701, 717 per Lord Atkin
17 *Thurnell v Balbirnie* (1837) 2 M & W 786; *Cooper v Shuttleworth* (1856) 25 LJ Ex 114 (two valuers to be appointed, one by each party; valuer appointed by defendant did not make the valuation. Held that plaintiff had no action against defendant); *Firth v Midland Rly Co* (1875) LR 20 Eq 100 (valuation was 'of the essence of the agreement' and the death of the valuer meant that it could not be enforced).

them. However, where there is an express contractual provision regarding valuation, it seems that the courts would be unable to imply term that a reasonable price should be paid in the event of the valuation's failure within s 9.[18] Moreover, T cannot be sued by either party if he has been appointed as a valuer but does not make the valuation; only if T contracted to do so can he be liable in damages.[19]

As a general rule, the parties are bound by the valuation unless there is fraud or collusion[20] or it can be proven that the valuation proceeded on the wrong basis or principle.[1] If the valuer, T, has been negligent or fraudulent he may be liable to either party who suffers loss as a result.[2]

Section 9(2) provides for the situation where T is prevented from making the valuation by the fault of S or B and, for example, that would be the position where S refuses to allow T to examine the goods so that the latter cannot make the valuation.

18 Section 9 is based upon the appointment in the contract of a named valuer, T. Where, under the terms of the contract, T is *to be appointed* at a later date but the *machinery* for such appointment breaks down, it has been held by the HL that the court can substitute its own machinery in order to fix a fair and reasonable price: *Sudbrook Trading Estate Ltd v Eggleton* [1983] 1 AC 444 (option to purchase land with two valuers to be appointed, one by each party. The landlord refused to appoint a valuer); see also *Re Malpass* [1985] Ch 42 (refusal of designated valuer to make the valuation. Here the court added the qualification that the machinery must be subsidiary and inessential). It remains to be seen whether this reasoning can apply to the sale of goods.
19 *Cooper v Shuttleworth* (1856) 25 LJ Ex 114.
20 *Campbell v Edwards* [1976] 1 WLR 403, 407 per Lord Denning MR.
 1 *Wright (Frank H) (Constructions) Ltd v Frodoor Ltd* [1967] 1 WLR 506; *Burgess v Purchase & Sons (Farms) Ltd* [1983] Ch 216.
 2 *Arenson v Casson Beckman Rutley & Co* [1977] AC 405.

CHAPTER 15

The contract of sale distinguished from analogous contracts

The SGA 1893, s 4, demanded that, in contracts for the sale of goods of the value of £10 and above, written evidence of the contract or part performance of it was necessary as a condition of enforceability. This requirement of formality, based upon the Statute of Frauds 1677, continued until the middle of the 20th century[1] and was one vital reason to distinguish contracts of sale from analogous bargains for which there was no prescribed form. Moroever, after the enactment of the SGA 1893, contracts for the sale of goods contained statutory implied terms relating to title, quality and fitness for purpose of the goods. Whilst the common law fashioned similar implied terms in analogous contracts (eg work and materials and hire of goods), the source and scope of the implied terms was obviously another important reason to distinguish sales from related transactions. The Supply of Goods and Services Act 1982 drew contracts for work and materials, barter, hire, and the supply of services within its boundaries and the 1982 Act introduced statutory implied terms relating to those contracts which are modelled on the SGA implied terms. Statutory intervention in recent years has thus led to a more rational scheme regarding the statutory implied terms in analogous contracts and the possible exclusion of those terms but it goes without saying that the SGA 1979 applies only to contracts for the sale of goods. Many principles which are well-established in the SGA, eg the rules for the passing of property in goods, are unclear in some of the related contracts, eg barter. Consequently, it is crucial to understand the basic rules of the transactions which resemble sale.

GIFT AND BARTER

Both of these transactions were examined earlier under the requirement that B's consideration in a contract for the sale of goods must be a price in money and, of course, no price is payable where there is a gift of goods or where goods are exchanged for other goods, as in a contract of barter. It will be remembered that 'free gifts', promotional offers and part-exchange transactions all cause problems of definition which were considered earlier.

---

1 SGA 1893, s 4, was repealed by the Law Reform (Enforcement of Contracts) Act 1954.

A gift of goods is based upon agreement: the donor and donee must intend to transfer ownership in the goods to the latter.[2] If a gift of goods is not made by deed, there must be either actual or constructive[3] delivery of the goods in order to perfect the gift at common law and it follows that, in the absence of a deed, a promise to make a gift of goods is unenforceable.[4] Gifts, even those made by deed, are not within the Supply of Goods and Services Act 1982.[5]

Contracts of barter are, however, drawn within the 1982 Act.[6] The great innovation of the 1982 Act was its provision of the statutory implied terms applicable to barter (ss 2, 3, 4 and 5)[7] and so, in cases of defective goods, it may be immaterial whether the contract is one of sale or barter. However, all the other aspects of barter, such as the rules on the passing of property in bartered goods, must be culled from the common law as discussed earlier.

CONTRACTS FOR WORK AND THE SUPPLY OF MATERIALS

It may often be difficult to distinguish a contract for the sale of goods from a contract where work and services are dominant and the supply of goods or materials is an auxiliary aspect of the contract.[8] How should one classify a contract to paint a portrait or an order for a bespoke suit from a Savile Row tailor? On a more mundane level, is the fitting of an exhaust to a car a contract for the sale of goods or one for the supply of a service where the goods are deemed to be an ancillary and subsidiary feature? When written evidence was required under the Statute of Frauds for the enforceability of contracts for the sale of goods and any implied terms applicable to contracts for work and materials had to be drawn from the common law, spurious distinctions might be made between contracts of sale and those for work and materials. It is difficult to resist the conclusion that contracts were often allotted to either of the two categories on the basis of whether or not it was just to impose liability upon the defendant. Today, problems of categorisation are less decisive because the Supply of Goods and Services Act 1982, ss 1 and 12 apply to contracts for work and materials and the Act provides that a contract may be one for 'the transfer of goods' within s 1 where services are also provided[9] and, likewise, a contract may be one for 'the supply of a service' within s 12 where goods are also transferred or bailed under the contract.[10] As the 1982 Act also introduced implied terms which were

---

2 See Crossley Vaines, *Personal Property* (5th edn, 1973), Ch 13; Bell, *Modern Law of Personal Property* (1989), Ch 10.
3 *Lock v Heath* (1892) 8 TLR 295 (symbolic delivery of one chair perfected the gift of all the donor's furniture).
4 *Irons v Smallpiece* (1819) 2 B & Ald 551; *Cochrane v Moore* (1890) 25 QBD 57; *Re Cole* [1964] Ch 175.
5 See s 1(2)(d).
6 See s 1(1).
7 As amended by the Sale and Supply of Goods Act 1994; see the Unfair Contract Terms Act 1977 for the restrictions on the ability to exclude the implied terms.
8 See *Implied Terms in Contracts for the Supply of Goods* (Law Com No 95, 1979), paras 56-66; Bartholomew, 'Contracts for the Sale of Goods and Contracts for Work and Labour' (1961) 35 ALJ 65; Samek, 'Contracts for Work and Materials and the Concept of Sale' (1962) 36 ALJ 66.
9 See s 1(3).
10 See s 12(3).

applicable to contracts for work and materials, the distinction between these contracts and contracts for the sale of goods may often be quite immaterial in cases where there is poor workmanship and/or the installation of defective goods. For example, where a plumber repairs a central heating system and fits new parts, a dissatisfied customer may now claim that the new parts were faulty or unsuitable in breach of the 1982 Act's implied terms relating to quality and fitness for purpose or that the plumber installed them incorrectly and was thus in breach of the Act's implied term that he would perform the service with reasonable care and skill. It would, of course, be possible for the customer to establish a breach of both of these implied terms.

There are, nevertheless, pertinent reasons to differentiate contracts for the sale of goods from contracts for work and the supply of materials. The SGA rules on the passing of property and risk in goods and the exceptions to the *nemo dat* rule[11] do not apply to the latter contracts. Moreover, the parties' remedies in the event of a breach of contract may differ substantially in the two categories of contract. In two recent decisions of the House of Lords concerning ship building contracts,[12] it has been held that there is a distinction to be drawn between a simple sale of existing goods and a sale of goods which entails manufacture and delivery of the goods: the latter case has elements of simple sale *and* the supply of services in that S must manufacture the goods. Consequently, where B has paid part of the purchase price in advance and then defaults in paying future instalments, for example, he is unable to recover the payments made even though he never obtains delivery of the goods under the contract. This is because there is not a total failure of consideration on such facts: the manufacture of the goods involves expense on S's part and B's advance payments must be regarded as contributing towards that manufacture. On the other hand, in a simple sale of goods there is only the price of the goods and their delivery to consider and, where the goods are not delivered, S cannot claim to retain any pre-payments as there is patently a total failure of consideration. This controversial matter is dealt with in more detail when S's remedies are considered.[13]

Differentiating a contract of sale from a contract for work and materials

It is open to the parties to categorise their contract as either one for the sale of goods or one for the supply of work and materials and thereby arrive at an apt allocation of risk but, where this is not done, the court must decide the category into which the contract falls. Most recently, the courts have been prepared to accept hybrid transactions and thus in the *Hyundai* and *Stocznia* decisions mentioned earlier, shipbuilding contracts were regarded primarily as contracts for the sale of goods with some elements of the obligation to be drawn from contracts to supply services in that the ship had to be *built* by S instead of simply being *sold* by him. Apart from this new hybridisation, it has always been assumed that the contract is either one of sale or one for work and materials and certain established principles can be delineated.

---

11 See *Dawber Williamson Roofing Ltd v Humberside County Council* (1979) 14 BLR 70 (considered in Ch 18).
12 *Hyundai Heavy Industries Co Ltd v Papadopoulos* [1980] 1 WLR 1129; *Stocznia Gdanska SA v Latvian Shipping Co* [1998] 1 WLR 574.
13 See Ch 27.

First, where the work done entails the installation or affixing of materials belonging to the person doing the work on the land or chattel of the person for whom the work is done so that the materials become *a fixture*, the contract is almost certain to be classified as one for work and materials. In such a case, property in the materials passes to the person for whom the work is done by accession when they are added to his property. The distinction must thus be drawn between goods sold and delivered as such with a subsidiary agreement for installation, this being a sale of goods (eg the sale of a washing machine to be plumbed-in), and those cases where the installation itself passes the property and the chattel becomes a fixture, this being a contract for work and materials (eg the supply and installation of a sunken bath in a bathroom). In *Tripp v Armitage*,[14] for example, Bennett (B) agreed to build a hotel for the defendant (D) and other parties had contracted for painting, glazing and ironwork. Before his bankruptcy, B had brought window frames onto the site and these were approved by the clerk of works employed by D. B then took the window frames away in order to fit them with pulleys. B's assignees in bankruptcy claimed the frames and it was held that property in them had not passed to D. The court considered this to be a contract to do work and so property in the frames would have passed to D only if they had been fixed to the freehold.[15] There are numerous examples under this heading which have been regarded as contracts for work and materials.[16] As stated above, if the contract in these situations is to be construed as one for the sale of goods, the intent of the parties and the principal aim of the contract must be to enter into a contract for the sale of goods with a supplementary undertaking that S will, for example, install those goods in B's premises. Here the division between sale and a contract for work and materials may often be indistinct but, for example, a contract to manufacture, deliver and install a large hopper for animal feed was regarded as a sale of goods,[17] as was a contract for S to supply and erect an electrical storage battery.[18] Similarly, the court considered that the contracts were for the sale of goods where S agreed to sew and lay a large fitted carpet for B,[19] and where he agreed to make and erect a tombstone for B.[20]

14 (1839) 4 M & W 687.
15 See also *Young and Marten Ltd v McManus Childs Ltd* [1969] 1 AC 454.
16 Supply and installation of machinery or equipment in buildings: *Buxton v Bedall* (1803) 3 East 303; *Appleby v Myers* (1867) LR 2 CP 651; *Sydney Hydraulic & General Engineering Co v Blackwood & Son* (1908) 8 SRNSW 10 (supply and installation of a lift in premises); *Aristoc Industries Pty Ltd v R A Wenham (Builders) Pty Ltd* [1965] NSWR 581 (supply and installation of lecture theatre seats); fit new parts to cars: *Stewart v Reavell's Garage* [1952] 2 QB 545; *Myers (G H) & Co v Brent Cross Service Co* [1934] 1 KB 46; supply machinery for a ship and alter the engines: *Anglo-Egyptian Navigation Co v Rennie* (1875) LR 10 CP 271; cf *Slater v Finning Ltd* [1997] AC 473 (installation of camshaft in a fishing vessel treated as a sale of goods); construction of an elaborate, revolving cocktail cabinet in the wall of a house: *Brooks Robinson Pty Ltd v Rothfield* [1951] ALR 909.
17 *Parsons (H) (Livestock) Ltd v Uttley Ingham & Co Ltd* [1978] QB 791 (carriage charges were an additional £15; Lord Denning MR considered (p 800) that the contract might better be regarded as divisible into (i) a sale of the hopper, and (ii) the erection of it.
18 *Pritchett & Gold and Electrical Power Storage Co Ltd v Currie* [1916] 2 Ch 515.
19 *Head (Philip) & Sons Ltd v Showfronts Ltd* [1970] 1 Lloyd's Rep 140; see also *Love v Norman Wright (Builders) Ltd* [1944] KB 484 (contract to supply and fit black-out curtains and rails was contract for work and materials).
20 *Wolfenden v Wilson* (1873) 33 UCQB 442.

Second, it may be possible to identify the skill of the person doing the work as the dominant feature of the contract so that it is substantially one for work and skill with the goods supplied as a supplementary feature of the undertaking. A good example is provided by *Dodd v Wilson and McWilliam*,[1] where the defendant veterinary surgeon inoculated the plaintiff's cattle with a serum to prevent mastitis but many of the herd became sick as a consequence. The defendant had bought the serum from the third party seller who had, in turn, bought it from the fourth party manufacturer. It was held that the contract between plaintiff and defendant was not one for the sale of goods but was one for work and materials in which there was an implied term as to the reasonable fitness of the serum for its purpose. On the other hand, there were clearly contracts of sale between the defendant and the third party and the third party and fourth party manufacturer. Likewise, contracts were regarded as predominantly for the provision of professional services rather than the sale of goods where an engineer devised and constructed a machine for the curving of metal tubing to be used on life-buoys of which the defendant was a patentee,[2] where an architect drew up a plan[3] and where graphic designers prepared artwork and advertising posters.[4] In contrast, it has been held that there was a sale of goods where a lunch of whitebait was prepared and sold in an hotel[5] and where a chemist compounded and sold a prescription drug.[6] The supply of meals illustrates the difficulties in this context: the provision of fish and chips to be eaten in the street might properly be regarded as a sale of goods but where dinner at The Savoy is cooked by a *cordon bleu* chef, the transaction must surely be closer to one for the supply of services.

Third, there is the question of goods to be manufactured from materials supplied (i) totally by the customer (ii) totally by the manufacturer or (iii) from an amalgam of the customer's and the manufacturer's materials. Where the customer for whom the work is done supplies *all* the materials which are to be made into new goods, it is normal to treat the contract as one for work and materials. It would be difficult to construe such a contract as one for the sale of goods unless property in the materials were transferred to the manufacturer with a subsequent sale of the new goods to the customer/supplier of the materials. In the converse situation where the manufacturer supplies the totality of the materials, it would thus seem logical to assert that the contract will be one for the sale of goods. There is authority to this effect[7] but it is not an absolute rule

---

1   [1946] 2 All ER 691.

2   *Grafton v Armitage* (1845) 2 CB 336 (the contract was not for the *delivery* of the machine. Coltman J stressed (pp 341-342): 'If this had been a contract … to make a machine for the defendant, the proper remedy would have been an action for goods sold and delivered, or an action for not accepting the machine … but here it appears that the plaintiff was merely employed to use his skill in devising a mode of carrying out the defendant's invention').

3   *Gibbon v Pease* [1905] 1 KB 810. See also the view that the drafting of a deed by an attorney is a contract for work and materials: *Grafton v Armitage* (1845) 2 CB 336, 339 per Erle J; *Lee v Griffin* (1861) 1 B & S 272, 277-278 per Blackburn J.

4   *Art Direction Ltd v USP Needham (NZ) Ltd* [1977] 2 NZLR 12.

5   *Lockett v A M Charles Ltd* [1938] 4 All ER 170.

6   *R v Wood Green Profiteering Committee* (1920) 89 LJKB 55 (the court considered this to be a sale with the cost of labour being an important element in fixing the price). The supply of drugs or appliances to a member of the public under the National Health Service is not a sale of goods and there is no *contract* with the chemist as the patient has a statutory right to demand the drug on payment: *Pfizer Corpn v Ministry of Health* [1965] AC 512. The Supply of Goods and Services Act 1982 cannot apply to the NHS supply of drugs but an injured patient might have a remedy under the Consumer Protection Act 1987.

7   See *Lee v Griffin* (1861) 1 B & S 272 (below).

and, in one case, a contract to paint a portrait was held to be one for work and materials. This question is considered in more detail below. The third situation arises where the maker of the new goods adds his own materials to those of the customer and this raises more difficult issues. Such a contract was treated as one for the sale of goods in *Dixon v London Small Arms Co Ltd*,[8] where S agreed to make rifles for the Crown with the price being settled minus the cost of the steel barrels and stocks which the Crown supplied to S. The House of Lords held that S was not a servant or agent of the Crown but was a private contractor under a contract for the sale of goods. As such, S was liable for infringing the plaintiff's patent and was not entitled to any Crown privilege. It is possible to view the contract as one for the sale of goods where the customer, B, intends to transfer property in his materials to S, the manufacturer, and the completed goods are then sold to B. It is arguable that this occurred in *Dixon* but this turn of events is comparatively rare. Certainly where the principal materials are supplied by the customer, it is normal to construe the contract as one for work and labour with the property in the materials supplied by the manufacturer passing to the customer by accession.[9]

Finally, the thread woven through all the cases above is the possibility of interpreting the contract as one for work and materials with the goods and materials supplied as a subsidiary element or, alternatively, construing the transaction principally as a sale of goods for a price with an attendant element of work to be performed. The notion that the 'substance' or 'essence' of the contract is either sale or work and materials is traceable to two significant decisions in the middle of the 19th century.[10] However, if the contract is *solely for the creation of goods* it is much more difficult to categorise it as decisively within one or other of these groupings: where the contract is one for a portrait to be painted, the artist's skill and the delivery of the finished article are inseparable and of equal importance. The issue of categorisation arose in *Lee v Griffin*[11] where, in a contract to make and fit a set of ivory 'artificial teeth' for a patient who died before they could be fitted, it was held that the dentist could not succeed against the patient's executor for work done and materials provided. It was held that the contract was for the sale of goods and, in the absence of writing, it was unenforceable. The court considered that 'where the contract is for a chattel to be made and delivered it clearly is a contract for the sale of goods'[12] and that 'the substance of the contract was for goods sold and

---

8   (1876) 1 App Cas 632.
9   See *Scott Maritimes Pulp Ltd v B F Goodrich Canada Ltd* (1977) 72 DLR (3d) 680 (contract to fit a rubber cover on a roller weighing 12 tons which squeezed water from wood pulp. Held this was a contract for work and labour, title in the rubber passing to the customer by accession). This is probably the position where a publisher prints an author's manuscript: *Clay v Yates* (1856) 1 H & N 73; see also the comments to this effect in *Lee v Griffin* (1861) 1 B & S 272; cf *Deta Nominees Pty Ltd v Viscount Plastic Products Pty Ltd* [1979] VR 167, 182-183 per Fullagar J: 'What the customer wants is a completion of the contract by the delivery ... of the completely new article of goods, the book; until the printer performs that obligation he has not performed his contract ... It is in my respectful opinion illogical to treat as relevant the consideration that the creative work embodied in the customer's manuscript is the "principal property" ... The "principal property" in the first hovercraft may just as easily be said to be that industrial property which is the brilliant idea of a patentee, but the contract for the manufacture and delivery of the first hovercraft itself must unquestionably have been a contract for the sale of goods'.
10 *Grafton v Armitage* (1845) 2 CB 336; *Clay v Yates* (1856) 1 H & N 73.
11 (1861) 1 B & S 272.
12 (1861) 1 B & S 272 at 275, per Crompton J.

delivered'.[13] Blackburn J rejected a comparative valuation test to determine whether the goods or the work done had the greater monetary value and, in case there might be any doubt as to the force and scope of his ruling, he was explicit in stating that a sculptor sells his completed work even though the valuation of his skill far exceeds the value of the marble used. It is self-evident that in a contract to create a thing, there will nearly always be a delivery of goods to the customer under the contract and so, taken literally, Blackburn J's reasoning would construe all such transactions as sales of goods. This seems rather simplistic and virtually all-embracing but, nevertheless, the breadth of Blackburn J's analysis was accepted unequivocally in a leading Australian decision[14] and there are many other instances where goods have been manufactured from materials belonging to S which, often without argument, have been accepted as sales of goods.[15]

The issue of classification arose again in *Robinson v Graves*,[16] where the defendant commissioned the plaintiff artist to paint a portrait of a woman, agreeing to pay 250 guineas for it, but repudiated the contract before the portrait was completed. The Court of Appeal held that this was a contract for work and labour and not for the sale of goods, the reasoning of the court being that the 'substance of the contract ... is that the skill and labour have to be exercised for the production of the article and that it is only ancillary to that that there will pass from the artist to his client ... some materials in addition to the skill involved'.[17] Accordingly, although there was an absence of writing necessary for the enforceability of a contract of sale, the plaintiff recovered damages which were assessed at £200. It has been cogently observed[18] that when a portrait is painted what passes to the client is not 'some materials' but a completed picture and that, accordingly, the decision in *Robinson v Graves* cannot be reconciled with that in *Lee v Griffin* and, furthermore, that the solution to this problem involves a choice between the competing and yet arbitrary rules in those cases.

SALE DISTINGUISHED FROM AGENCY

Where a buyer asks another to obtain goods for him or, conversely, where a seller asks another to dispose of goods for him, it has to be asked if that other is a contracting party in his own right or whether he is an agent acting on behalf

---

13 (1861) 1 B & S 272 at 278, per Blackburn J.
14 *Deta Nominees Pty Ltd v Viscount Plastic Products Pty Ltd* [1979] VR 167, 181-186 per Fullagar J.
15 *Isaacs v Hardy* (1884) Cab & El 287 (picture dealer (B) engaged an artist to paint a particular scene. B's object was to acquire something which he could sell in his business. Cf *Robinson v Graves* [1935] 1 KB 579); *Re Blyth Shipbuilding Co Ltd* [1926] Ch 494 (contract to build a ship; but contrast the hybrid analysis in *Hyundai Heavy Industries Co Ltd v Papadopoulos* [1980] 1 WLR 1129; *Stocznia Gdanska SA v Latvian Shipping Co* [1998] 1 WLR 574); *Cammell Laird & Co Ltd v Manganese Bronze & Brass Co Ltd* [1934] AC 402 (construction of a ship's propeller); *Newman v Lipman* [1951] 1 KB 333 (photograph taken by street photographer in Trafalgar Square); *Marcel (Furriers) Ltd v Tapper* [1953] 1 WLR 49 (bespoke mink jacket costing £950); *Ashington Piggeries Ltd v Christopher Hill Ltd* [1972] AC 441 (food for mink compounded by S); *Deta Nominees Pty Ltd v Viscount Plastic Products Pty Ltd* [1979] VR 167 (construction/delivery of a tool for making plastic drawers and drawers themselves).
16 [1935] 1 KB 579.
17 [1935] 1 KB 579 at 587, per Greer LJ.
18 *Benjamin's Sale of Goods* (5th edn, 1997), para 1-047.

of his principal. Here, sale and agency are distinct and incompatible relationships and the contrast between them cannot be over-emphasised: where one person acts as an unfettered seller or buyer *vis-à-vis* the other party the relationship cannot be one of agent and principal. In a straightforward commercial sale of goods, the relationship is competitive and adversarial as profit and loss are the *raison d'être* of commerce but, if one party acts as the agent of the other, a fiduciary relationship is created based on trust, good faith and confidentiality.

B asks A to obtain goods: B (P)<......A<......T

S asks A to dispose of goods: S (P)......>A......>T

There are principally two situations to consider in differentiating sale from agency. First, where B asks A to obtain goods for him, A could acquire the goods from T and sell them to B in his capacity as a seller or, alternatively, he might be an agent acting on B's behalf in obtaining the goods from T. Second, where A disposes of goods for S, there is the same problem as to whether he is a buyer of the goods from S meaning that A may sell them to T without restriction or, alternatively, whether A acts an agent in selling the goods on behalf of S to T. The consequences of A's being either an unrestricted seller or an agent owing strict duties to his principal are the same in both these situations.

Accordingly, if A acts as a seller of the goods (to T or B, see the diagram above): (i) he normally agrees in absolute terms to sell the goods at a price and he is obviously free to make a profit on the sale (ii) where A buy the goods and then resells them, there will be two, separate contracts of sale and (iii) A is answerable to his buyer for defects in the goods and the other obligations of the SGA apply between A and his buyer, eg the passing of property in the goods. Of course, A will also have a separate contract with his seller and so, should the goods prove defective with the consequence that A has paid damages to his buyer, A may seek redress from his seller.

Alternatively, where A is an agent in the archetypal sense of that term in that he acts on behalf of a disclosed principal[19] in buying or selling the goods: (i) he must have authority to buy or sell the goods on behalf of his principal (ii) his duty is ordinarily to use due diligence in acquiring or disposing of the goods (iii) he must obtain the best possible price for his principal and he cannot make any gain on the transaction unless he discloses the profit to his principal and obtains his consent to its retention (iv) he will normally obtain remuneration from the principal in the form of commission (v) privity of contract is established between the parties via A as the agent, so that there is only one contract of sale between them (vi) as A is an agent, he is not normally answerable for defects in the goods and (vii) the measure of damages for breach of A's duties may be different from the measure for breach of a contract of sale.

When does one party act as an agent for the other?

The question of whether or not the relationship is one of agency turns on the construction of the agreement and similar considerations apply to both the situations discussed above where A acquires or disposes of the goods. Although

---

19   Within limits, A may also act for an *undisclosed* principal (P) in buying or selling goods and such a P may intervene on the contract made between A and T. T can also elect to sue *either* A or P (see Ch 10).

the courts may be guided by the nomenclature used in any agreement, it is the substantive relationship between the parties which must be analysed and thus terminology is not decisive as 'there is no magic in the word "agency" [and] it is often used in commercial matters where the real relationship is that of vendor and purchaser'.[20] A manufacturer of goods, for example, may often market and sell his goods through an 'exclusive' or 'sole' agent but this label may be misleading. In *Lamb (W T) & Sons v Goring Brick Co*,[1] the defendant (D) appointed the plaintiff (P) for three years as 'sole selling agents of all bricks and other materials manufactured' at the brick works but, before the three years had elapsed, D informed P that they would sell their own materials in future. It was held that D was liable for breach of contract. If P had been an agent, this liability would not have existed as D could have sold his own goods during the continuation of the agency.[2] In *Lamb*, P was thus a buyer of the goods from D and had been granted a monopoly to sell those goods; D was consequently liable for wrongfully revoking it.

The principal distinction between buyers and sellers in their own right and agents, turns on the question of the profit which can be made and retained. Where, for example, A seeks to dispose of goods for P and the contract between them controls A's activities closely, imposes an obligation on A to account to P for the prices realised and specifies that he be remunerated by a pre-arranged commission, the relationship is almost certainly one of principal and agent.[3] In contrast, where the element of control is less evident in that, for example, A is permitted to alter the goods before selling them and is free to make and retain whatever profit he pleases on a sale to T, the indications are that he is a buyer for resale, possibly on a sale or return basis, but not an agent.[4]

These are only broad guidelines,[5] however, and the substantive relationship must be scrutinised in every case. For example, A may be closely controlled by P in that P fixes the resale price but A may nevertheless be a buyer for resale in his own right. In *Michelin Tyre Co Ltd v Macfarlane (Glasgow) Ltd*,[6] the respondent (R) was a 'stockist or agent' for the sale of Michelin tyres (M). The terms of the agreement were that (i) tyres were consigned to R at wholesale prices, they remained the property of M until payment by R and, until then, were held 'on behalf of' M (ii) R advertised the tyres at his premises and agreed to sell them only at M's fixed retail prices (iii) R agreed to pay for tyres as soon as they were sold and to keep-up the stock of tyres (iv) R was to insure the tyres at his own cost and (v) R was stated to be the 'stockist or agent' for M's tyres in the Michelin Guide to the British Isles. The House of Lords held (Viscount Haldane

---

20 *Ex p White, re Nevill* (1870) 6 Ch App 397, 399 per Sir W M James LJ; affd sub nom *John Towle & Co v White* (1873) 29 LT 78.
1 [1932] 1 KB 710; see also *Potter v Customs and Excise Comrs* [1985] STC 45 ('Tupperware' distributors held to be buyers of the goods, not agents).
2 *Bentall, Horsley & Baldry v Vicary* [1931] 1 KB 253 (estate agent appointed as 'sole agent' to sell; P did not incur liability in selling the property himself).
3 See *Weiner v Harris* [1910] 1 KB 285 (considered in ch 16). In *Ex p Bright, re Smith* (1879) 10 Ch D 566, Jessel MR held that there was nothing to prevent an agent's being remunerated by his retaining the surplus profit over and above the price which will satisfy the principal and that 'the amount of commission does not turn the agent into a purchaser' (p 570).
4 *Ex p White, re Nevill* (1870) 6 Ch App 397; affd sub nom *John Towle & Co v White* (1873) 29 LT 78 (considered in Ch 1).
5 See also the guidelines in the *Restatement, Second, Agency* § 14 J as to whether A is an agent or buyer for resale.
6 1917 2 SLT 205.

and Lord Parmoor dissenting) that M never envisaged becoming party to every contract of sale that R entered into and the absence of any provision that M should be given particulars of each sale and the fact that R did not have to account to M for the prices realised on a sale but had only to pay the wholesale price, meant that R was not an agent for M but a seller on his own account.

Moreover, although remuneration by commission is often emblematic of agency, it may sometimes be payable to a buyer for resale. In *Kelly v Enderton*,[7] Kelly (K) granted Enderton & Co (E & Co) an option to buy land and also agreed to pay them commission on the sale. E & Co exercised the option in favour of S but K sought to rescind the transaction on the basis that S was a clerk in E & Co's office and that the real purchaser was thus E & Co who, being agents to sell, were disqualified from purchasing the property themselves. The Privy Council held that E & Co were not agents as the option had been granted to them in plain terms and the payment of commission was, on the facts, consistent with their exercise of that option. Lord Dunedin[8] stressed that the commission was payable to E & Co on their finding a purchaser for the property or on their being purchasers in their own right. Likewise, in *Gannow Engineering Co Ltd v Richardson*,[9] the defendant (D) was granted 'sole selling rights' of the plaintiff's (P) machines in New Zealand and was entitled to 'commission' of 10% 'by way of deduction from the actual invoiced value' of the goods. Other important features of the relationship were that (i) the sale prices were not fixed by P (ii) payment for the goods sold was made by D or his agent and *not* by the customer who bought the machines in New Zealand and (iii) in some cases D installed the machines and charged for this service. D sold the machines at prices in excess of P's invoice price but it was held that he was not liable to account for the profits as this was not a principal/agent relationship but, instead, was one of vendor and purchaser. Myers CJ considered that 'just ... as there is no magic in the term "agent"... there is no magic in the mere use of the term "commission"' and, having regard to the context of the agreement, he held that 'its real meaning is "discount" or "rebate"'.[10]

Finally, the foundations which underpin reservation of title clauses are constructed on the buyer's having a dual capacity in that he is an independent buyer of the goods from the seller *and* he acts as an agent for the seller when he sells the goods. Consequently, S and B may agree that property in the goods will remain in S until B pays for the goods and, should B resell the goods before payment, he will be obliged to account to S for the proceeds of sale as an agent and fiduciary acting on behalf of S.[11] The question of Romalpa clauses is considered separately[12] but it should be stressed that, in relation to such clauses, the courts have often resisted forcefully the notion that a relationship of buyer and seller can transmute into one turning upon agency and fiduciary duty simply by affixing suitable labels to the parties and specifying certain consequences.[13] This may be both inapt and unjust if the substantive relationship comprises combative, commercial parties who are dealing at arm's length.

7 [1913] AC 191.
8 [1913] AC 191 at 195.
9 [1930] NZLR 361.
10 [1930] NZLR 361 at 367.
11 *Aluminium Industrie Vaassen BV v Romalpa Aluminium Ltd* [1976] 1 WLR 676.
12 See Ch 17.
13 See *Re Bond Worth Ltd* [1980] Ch 228.

SALE DISTINGUISHED FROM BAILMENT

The orthodox definition of a bailment is a delivery of a thing by one person (the bailor) to another (the bailee) for a specific and limited purpose, on terms that the bailee will re-deliver that thing to the bailor or, as directed by the bailor, deliver it to a third party, once the specific purpose has been achieved.[14] Commonplace bailments include the deposit of goods for cleaning, repair, storage, custody and, also, a simple hire of goods for use. The bailment may thus be principally for the bailor's benefit (eg storage of goods) or for the bailee's benefit (eg hire of goods for use).

The essence of bailment is the transfer of *possession* of a chattel to the bailee who becomes entitled to possessory remedies (eg conversion and trespass) against third parties and sometimes against the bailor himself. It is apparent that *property* in the goods does not pass to the bailee on delivery although in certain bailments property in the goods may ultimately pass to the bailee, eg hire-purchase and sale or return. Bailment is usually consensual (apart from involunatry bailments and those premised upon the finding of goods) and it is often contractual. The contractual bailment where the bailee pays money to the bailor for the use of goods is the nearest bailment to a contract for the sale of goods but it is separated decisively from sale in that the bailee obtains possession only whereas, of course, the object of a sale is to transfer the 'general property' in the goods to the buyer. In those cases where it is intended that property in the goods should pass to the recipient *on contract* in return for a price in money, there is patently a sale of goods within the SGA, s 2(4). Likewise, where the buyer obtains possession of the goods but property is to pass at some future time, there will be an 'agreement for sale' within s 2(5) and, at least where B obtains possession pursuant to the agreement to sell, B's possession will be that of a buyer in possession rather than a bailee.[15] That being said, bailment can co-exist with a contract of sale if that is the parties' intent and bailment is certainly a feature of Romalpa clauses and sale or return transactions where, in both cases, B can be a bailee of the goods in the period before property in the goods passes to him. Indeed, the SGA, s 20 acknowledges that either S or B may be a 'bailee or custodier' of the goods of the other party during the course of the contract of sale.

Bailment and mixtures: does bailment necessitate the return of the bailor's goods?

It has always been a central tenet of bailment that the bailee should re-deliver or otherwise deal with the *identical* goods which had been bailed and, accordingly, if the recipient of the goods had an obligation to re-deliver an equivalent amount of the same goods or completely different goods, the contract would be one of barter. The distinction between the return of the identical goods in bailment and the the transfer of property for value was accentuated in *South Australian Insurance Co v Randell*.[16] There the course of business was for farmers

---

14   See Paton, *Bailment in the Common Law* (1952), Ch 1; Crossley Vaines, *Personal Property* (5th edn, 1973), Ch 6; Palmer, *Bailment* (2nd edn, 1992), pp 131 et seq.

15   See SGA, s 25(1) and Factors Act 1889 s 9 (considered in ch 18). Under these sections it may be unimportant that B obtains possession of the goods as a bailee *provided* that the relationship of buyer and seller subsists.

16   (1869) LR 3 PC 101.

to deposit their corn with a miller who mixed it with other corn in large hutches and held it on terms that the farmers could at any time demand re-delivery of an equal quantity of corn of comparable quality to that delivered or the market price on the day of demand. The Privy Council held that this was not a bailment as each farmer's corn did not have to be stored separately and, indeed, there was no requirement that the miller should re-deliver the corn from any specific source. Instead, there was a transfer of property for value to the miller who could thus make a claim regarding the corn on an insurance policy which covered his own property.[17]

Where, as in *Randell*, a person transfers possession of his goods on terms that other goods may be returned to him, it is often fitting that he should not retain any *proprietary* rights in the goods deposited but should have only personal rights against the transferee. However, this notion appears to be on the wane after the decision in *Mercer v Craven Grain Storage Ltd*.[18] There the three plaintiff farmers (P) became members of a grain marketing scheme which involved depositing grain with the defendant (D) for storage, all the grain being mixed and held in a commingled bulk from which D could sell quantities of grain from time to time. The terms of the contract between P and D provided that the grain deposited should remain the property of P until it was sold on his behalf by D. P deposited 2,200 tonnes of wheat with D with instructions that it was not to be sold below £160 per tonne but nearly all of it was sold below that price. P was not paid and D became insolvent. P demanded the return of their wheat from D and subsequently sued D in conversion. D's principal argument was that this could not be a bailment as P's grain was mixed with other grain in a fluctuating bulk and, as it was impossible to identify P's grain separately, P could have no proprietary rights in the grain. Against this contention, there was the contract term that property in the grain was to remain in P until a sale was effected by D. The House of Lords held unanimously that P retained their proprietary rights in the grain. This meant that title remained in the farmers who were interested in the bulk at any given time in proportion to their respective tonnages and D was guilty of conversion if it allowed the bulk to become so depleted that the balance remaining was insufficient to satisfy P's demands. This decision thus recognises that there can be a bailment where bailor and bailee acknowledge that the bailor will not regain possession of the actual goods bailed because the bailee is authorised to substitute other goods for those delivered by the bailor.

At common law, it is undoubted that proprietary rights in goods can survive where those goods are mixed with other goods[19] and the *Mercer* decision rests on the notion that the bailors become tenants in common (co-owners) of the goods comprised in the mixture. The clear advantage to the bailor is that, as he retains property in the goods, he does not assume the risks attendant upon the bailee's insolvency but, on the other hand, the bailor does carry the risk that his goods might be accidentally destroyed (a risk against which he can insure). Tenancy in common is also the strategy adopted by the newly-inserted ss 20A and 20B of the SGA 1979 by virtue of which buyers who agree to buy specified amounts of goods from an identified bulk of goods become co-owners

---

17 See also *Chapman Bros v Verco Bros & Co Ltd* (1933) 49 CLR 306 (on very similar facts to *Randell*, the High Court of Australia reached the same conclusion); *Crawford v Kingston* [1952] 4 DLR 37.

18 [1994] CLC 328; see Smith, 'Bailment with Authority to Mix – and Substitute' (1995) 111 LQR 10.

19 See *Indian Oil Corpn v Greenstone Shipping SA (Panama)* [1988] QB 345.

of undivided shares in the bulk before there has been any separation of the goods from the bulk.[20] It is unclear, however, when the *Mercer* analysis will apply and no guidance as to future application was given by the House of Lords in that decision. Although it is explicit that co-ownership arises under the conditions prescribed by the SGA, ss 20A and 20B, it is most unclear when co-ownership will result at common law. In *Mercer*, although there was no express stipulation regarding co-ownership, P expressly consented to the mixing of the goods and there was an express term reserving property in the goods to himself until they were sold. In other modern decisions, however, co-ownership has been held to exist where there was an unforeseen and wrongful act of mixing goods[1] and where the court considered that the parties' implicit, common intent was that such a relationshp should exist, the co-owners being buyers of goods which were commingled.[2] Consequently, it is difficult to ascertain the role of the parties' intent in the formation of tenancies in common.[3] Moreover, the utility of the proprietary rights created in *Mercer* appear to be limited in that, on the facts of that case (and under the SGA, ss 20A and 20B), the bailor's and the buyer's proprietary rights will be lost where the bulk is totally depleted so that nothing remains and this might also be the position even if the bulk is immediately and fully replenished with substitute goods.

Bailment and manufactured goods

It is also important to consider the role of bailment in cases where goods are to be manufactured. It will be remembered that the question of whether a contract is one for the sale of goods or one for work and materials was considered earlier in relation to goods supplied by a customer to a manufacturer who works on them in some way and produces a finished article which is then re-delivered to the customer for a charge.

Where the principal materials/goods are supplied by the customer, it is normal for the manufacturer to be a bailee of the goods and for property in them to remain with the customer throughout the process of manufacture. The subordinate goods contributed by the manufacturer will vest in the customer by accession. Overall, therefore, the contract is one where the customer's goods are bailed to the manufacturer on the basis that they will be changed in some way by the work and materials of the manufacturer.

Problems also arise with bailment in relation to reservation of title clauses (Romalpa clauses) and manufactured goods. Under a Romalpa clause, S supplies goods to B and reserves property in the goods until B's obligations (principally payment for the goods supplied) are discharged.[4] One of the principles employed in reservation of title clauses is that of bailment and, in the *Romalpa* decision itself, a crucial concession made by B was that the relationship between S and B was one of bailment during the period in which money was owing to S for the goods supplied. In the situation where B subsequently sells the goods in their unaltered state to T, it is clear that B can be a bailee in the period between his

---

20 See Ch 16.
1   *Indian Oil Corpn v Greenstone Shipping SA (Panama)* [1988] QB 345.
2   *Re Stapylton Fletcher Ltd* [1994] 1 WLR 1181 (considered in Ch 16).
3   See Birks, 'Mixtures' in *Interests in Goods* (eds Palmer and McKendrick, 2nd edn, 1998), Ch 9.
4   Reservation of title is considered in Ch 17.

receiving the goods and their resale to T.[5] Here the notion of bailment remains intact as there is a realistic possibility that S might re-take the goods from B because of his failure to pay the price under the terms of the Romalpa clause. Greater difficulty is generated, however, where the goods supplied by S are to be used by B in a manufacturing process from which new goods will emerge with the consequence that S's goods will lose their original identity. It is obviously arguable that, where S and B intend that the goods supplied by S shall be consumed immediately in the manufacturing process *before* B's obligation to pay arises, the parties cannot truly intend that those goods should ever be recoverable by S. In *Borden (UK) Ltd v Scottish Timber Products Ltd,*[6] S supplied resin to B knowing that it would be consumed in the manufacture of chipboard some two days after delivery to B, even though the period of credit allowed to B was much longer than that. Bridge LJ thought it impossible that this relationship could amount to a bailment; rather it was a contract of sale and purchase and, consequently, S lost title to the resin when its identity was merged in the chipboard. It is, of course, no easy task to decide when S's goods have lost their identity in this way but, overall, the courts have been willing to equate loss of identity with a change in form.[7]

SALE DISTINGUISHED FROM PLEDGE

A pledge (or pawn) is a bailment of goods or their documents of title by a debtor/pledgor to his creditor/pledgee, the pledgee keeping possession of the goods or documents of title until the debt is discharged. The pledgee thus has effective security for the loan which he has made to the pledgor. Delivery of the goods, either actual or constructive,[8] is necessary for a valid pledge and so there can be no pledge of choses in action, such as shares.[9] It follows that the pledge has a limited ambit as a form of security and, as the pledgee must have possession of the goods, it is largely inapt for use in business, as assets used daily in commerce, eg machinery, obviously cannot be pledged. The Consumer Credit Act 1974, ss 114-122, regulate pledges provided the credit granted does not exceed £25,000.

A pledge differs from other bailments and possessory liens in that the pledgee has a right at common law to sell the goods if the pledgor defaults on the re-payment of the debt but, if he does sell the goods, he must pay any surplus money realised on the sale to the pledgor. It is thus said that the pledgee has a 'special property' in the goods in contrast with an outright sale of goods where, under the SGA, s 2, the buyer obtains 'general property'. Moreover, by the SGA, s 62(4), the provisions of the Act do not apply to pledges. The pledgee's special property allows him to sue third parties in tort for wrongful intereference with the goods and, should the pledgor dishonestly retake the goods, he may be guilty of theft. The pledgor retains

---

5 *Aluminium Industrie Vaassen BV v Romalpa Aluminium Ltd* [1976] 1 WLR 676; *Clough Mill Ltd v Martin* [1984] 3 All ER 982, 987 per Robert Goff LJ.
6 [1981] Ch 25.
7 See eg *Re Peachdart* [1984] Ch 131 (loss of title when the leather S supplied was cut into pieces to be made into handbags); *Chaigley Farms Ltd v Crawford, Kaye & Grayshire Ltd* [1996] BCC 957 (loss of title when livestock were slaughtered at an abattoir); see Ch 17.
8 *Dublin City Distillery Ltd v Doherty* [1914] AC 823.
9 *Harrold v Plenty* [1901] 2 Ch 314.

the general property in the goods and he may transfer it to a third party, subject to the rights of the pledgee. In this latter case, the contract is one for the sale of goods and not the assignment of a chose in action and so the third party may tender the amount due to the pledgee and either obtain possession of the goods or recover damages in conversion.[10]

SALE DISTINGUISHED FROM A MORTGAGE OF GOODS

Where there is a legal mortgage of goods, the general property in the goods is transferred from the debtor/mortgagor to the creditor/mortgagee in order to secure a debt. In a pledge of goods, the creditor has possession of the goods as effective security but, in a mortgage of goods, the mortgagor normally remains in possession of the goods. A mortgage of goods is thus apt where an owner wishes to raise money on the security of goods but does not or cannot give the lender of the money possession of the goods, eg goods and chattels used in the course of a business.

A mortgage resembles a sale of goods only in that, in a mortgage, the general property in the goods passes from the mortgagor to the mortgagee. There is one crucial and obvious difference between a mortgage and a sale: in a sale, the buyer becomes the absolute owner of the goods and the seller has no further interest in them whereas, in a mortgage, the mortgagor has a right of redemption and may thus have the property in the goods transferred back to him upon payment of the debt to the mortgagee. The relationship of the parties during the currency of the mortgage is that of debtor and creditor and, by the SGA, s 62(4), the provisions of the SGA do not apply to mortgages.

As the mortgagor usually remains in possession of the goods, there is a considerable risk to third party creditors because the mortgagor often appears to be an absolute owner of the goods free from any encumbrances when in, fact, property in the goods is vested in the mortgagee. Such creditors might consequently be misled by this possession into making an inaccurate assesment of the mortgagor's creditworthiness and find that their apparent rights of security in relation to the goods are worthless. As Lord Blackburn[11] explained, there were twin hazards for third parties in that the mortgage might be a sham and a deliberate attempt to defraud third party creditors or, alternatively, it might be a genuine transaction which would cause equal hardship to such third parties leading to assertions that the transaction was a sham. In both cases there was thus apt to be 'a great quantity of perjury ... fighting and expense'.[12] Consequently, ever since the first Bills of Sale Act 1854, legislation has demanded that, in mortgages or charges of personal property under which the mortgagee has no possession, the document effecting the transaction should be in a particular form and *registered* so that third parties have notice of the existence of the mortgage. Moreover, as well as the hazards to third party creditors, there is a danger to impecunious *debtors* who, in mortgaging their goods, could be trapped into signing documents with harsh and unreasonable provisions as to the rate of interest charged, for example.[13] The imposition of stringent requirements in the

---

10   *Franklin v Neate* (1844) 13 M & W 481.
11   *Cookson v Swire* (1884) 9 App Cas 653, 664.
12   *Cookson v Swire* (1884) 9 App Cas 653, 664.
13   See *Manchester, Sheffield and Lincolnshire Rail Co v North Central Wagon Co* (1888) 13 App Cas 554, 560 per Lord Herschell LC.

Bills of Sale Acts regarding the form and registration of such mortgages thus also protect the debtor and deter such sharp practice.

The Bills of Sale Acts 1878 and 1882 attempt to control the problems outlined above. A bill of sale is simply a document by which the property in goods is transferred from one party to another. It is not required in a straightforward sale of goods as the contract itself can pass the property in specific goods and there is usually physical delivery of the goods to the buyer.[14] Accordingly, bills of sale are needed in those situations where the seller of the goods remains in possession of the goods after transferring the property in the goods to another – here the party without possession clearly requires a document which is evidence of his title to the goods. It is this situation to which the Bills of Sale Acts 1878 and 1882 apply. By imposing requirements as to the registration of bills of sale, the 1878 Act sought to prevent creditors being defrauded by a secret transfer of the goods to another and, by insisting that bills of sale comply with detailed rules regarding their form and content, the 1882 Act was designed to prevent the needy mortgagor/grantor of a bill of sale from being entrapped into signing documents which he might not understand and thereby committing himself to an imprudent transaction. In short, the 1878 Act was designed to protect third parties while the 1882 Act was an early example of consumer protection.

The 1878 Act applies to absolute bills of sale *otherwise* than by way of security for the payment of money[15] and the amending Act of 1882 applies to bills of sale given by way of security for money lent where the creditor does not have possession of the goods. The 1882 Act is particularly stringent in its requirements and failure to comply with its provisions means that the bill of sale is void as against all creditors *and* the parties to the mortgage, although the lender of the money can recover the loan, with reasonable interest only, in an action for money had and received.[16] If a company creates a charge over goods then, under the Companies Act 1985, ss 395 and 396, it must also be registered at the Companies' Registry and, if it is not so registered, it will be void against the liquidator or administrator and any creditor of the company.

The requirements of form and registration under the Bills of Sale Acts are cumbersome and time-consuming and so alternative methods of granting security have been sought. The obvious concern here is that, if these alternative arrangements are readily accepted by the courts, the Bills of Sale Acts would also be easily circumvented and undermined. For example, there is a difficulty with hire-purchase agreements where an existing owner of goods sell them to a buyer and then immediately enters into a hire-purchase agreement which hires the goods back to him. The arrangement may well be a sham designed to avoid the Bills of Sale Acts, the real function of the transaction being to secure a loan. The task of the courts is thus to ascertain the true intent of the parties[17] and so the arrangement might be invalidated as being an unregistered

14 A registered ship can be transferred only by a bill of sale in the statutory form: see the Merchant Shipping Act 1995.
15 An absolute bill of sale which is *not* given by way of security is a rarity but it could arise where there is an absolute sale but it is simply inconvenient for the seller to grant immediate possession of the goods, eg in the sale of a factory and equipment where the seller is permitted to use the equipment for a period of time.
16 See *Davies v Rees* (1886) 17 QBD 408; *North Central Wagon Finance Co Ltd v Brailsford* [1962] 1 WLR 1288.
17 *North Central Wagon Finance Co v Brailsford* [1962] 1 WLR 1288, 1292 per Cairns J.

bill of sale[18] or, alternatively, it could be upheld as a genuine agreement.[19] By and large, the courts follow a liberal approach and where the agreement has been struck-down, there has usually been an initial and deliberate intent to evade the Bills of Sale Acts and conceal the real nature of the agreement. In *Re Watson,*[20] for example, Watson (W) wished to obtain a loan of money on the security of her furniture and it was arranged with Love (L) that W would sell the furniture to L and then W would hire it back under a hire-purchase agreement which entitled L to seize the furniture if W defaulted in making payments. W subsequently became bankrupt. It was held that the transaction was simply and actually one where W wished to obtain an advance of money on the security of goods and, as such, the agreement constituted a bill of sale which should have been registered under the Bills of Sale Acts. As there had been a failure to register, the purported transfer of the property in the goods to L was void as against W's creditors and her trustee in bankruptcy was entitled to seize the furniture and divide it amongst W's creditors. Lord Esher MR considered that the true intent of the parties was, from the outset, to evade the Bills of Sale Acts by executing documents which 'affect to be one thing when they really mean something quite different, and which are not true descriptions of what the parties to them are really doing'.[1]

It is clear that this is an unsatisfactory area of the law which tends to function on an *ad hoc* basis. There is now a pressing need for a new, all-embracing system for the registration of all non-possessory security devices and the latest recommendations for such a scheme are those of the Diamond review.[2]

SALE DISTINGUISHED FROM HIRE-PURCHASE, CONDITIONAL SALE AND CREDIT-SALE

A hire-purchase agreement is a contract under which the owner of goods hires them to the hire-purchaser and grants him an option to purchase them at the end of the period of hire. It follows that (i) property in the goods remains in the owner during the currency of the agreement (ii) the hire-purchaser has the status of a bailee, and (iii) he is under no obligation to exercise the option to purchase at the end of the hire period. Hire-purchase thus conveniently grants credit to the hire-purchaser while providing the owner with security in that, subject to many statutory controls, he may repossess the goods if the hire-purchaser defaults in paying the price in instalments.

In a conditional sale, the contract provides that property in the goods will not pass to B unless some condition is fulfilled and, most commonly, the condition is that the price of the goods must be paid in full. The conditional sale is thus almost identical in *purpose* to a hire-purchase contract, as the seller's security lies in the fact that the property in the goods remains vested in him until the

---

18   See eg *Re Watson, ex p Official Receiver in Bankruptcy* (1890) 25 QBD 27; *Polsky v S & A Services* [1951] 1 All ER 1062n; *North Central Wagon Finance Co v Brailsford* [1962] 1 WLR 1288.

19   See eg *Yorkshire Wagon Co v Maclure* (1882) 21 Ch D 309; *Staffs Motor Guarantee Ltd v British Wagon Co Ltd* [1934] 2 KB 305;*Welsh Development Agency v Export Finance Co Ltd* [1992] BCLC 148.

20   (1890) 25 QBD 27.

 1   (1890) 25 QBD 27 at 37.

 2   *A Review of Security Interests in Property* (HMSO 1989, DTI).

price is paid. The conditional sale is currently something of a hybrid and so the Consumer Credit Act 1974 controls aspects of the contract in the same way as a hire-purchase contract but, for example, the implied terms relating to quality and fitness for purpose are drawn from the SGA.

In a credit-sale, although B is granted credit on the price of the goods, property in the goods will pass to him either on contract or delivery and this is therefore an outright sale of goods. Again, the Consumer Credit Act 1974 regulates the formation and formalities of credit-sale agreements but, in other respects, credit-sales are governed by the Sale of Goods Act 1979.

In *Lee v Butler*,[3] it was held that a person who was in possession of goods under a conditional sale agreement had 'agreed to buy' the goods within the Factors Act 1889, s 9,[4] and could thus transfer a good title to the third party by virtue of that section, even though the seller still owned the goods. The format of the conditional sale thus failed to provide the seller with effective security for the unpaid price. However, two years after *Lee v Butler*, two important decisions of the House of Lords allowed the hire-purchase agrement to flourish. First, in *McEntire v Crossley Bros*,[5] it was held that hire-purchase agreements were not within the Bills of Sale Acts 1878 and 1882[6] as those Acts applied only where an *owner* of goods granted to another party a charge over goods and a right to seize them, whereas in hire-purchase it was the *hirer* who granted this right to the owner of the goods. Secondly, in *Helby v Matthews*,[7] the House of Lords ruled that a hirer under a hire-purchase agreement was not a person who had 'agreed to buy' the goods as he had merely an option to buy but was not under an *obligation* to do so. Accordingly, the hirer could not transfer good title to a third party and the owner's security remained intact.

Today, the SGA, s 25(2) provides that a buyer under a conditional sale is not to be regarded as a buyer in possession and, under s 25(2)(b), where a conditional sale agreement is a consumer credit agreement within the Consumer Credit Act 1974, it is regarded as serving the same function as hire-purchase as the buyer is allowed instalment credit terms. Consequently, today there is virtually no difference in purpose between conditional sale and hire-purchase agreements.

3 [1893] 2 QB 318.
4 A virtually identical provision is contained in the SGA, s 25.
5 [1895] AC 457.
6 See above, where these Acts are considered in relation to mortgages of goods.
7 [1895] AC 471.

CHAPTER 16

The passing of property in goods

The classification of goods

The purpose of a contract for the sale of goods is to transfer the 'general property'[1] in the goods from S to B and, in the vernacular, this can be taken to mean the transfer of 'ownership' in such goods. The rules relating to the passing of property in goods to B depend upon the classifications of goods in the SGA and it is thus vital to delineate the various categories of goods which are recognised.

First, the distinction is made between *existing* goods and *future* goods and, secondly, there is the separation of *specific* goods from *unascertained* goods. At first glance these categories seem to be self-explanatory, but there can be several permutations of the different classifications of goods. A simple example explains the basic notions. B may agree to buy the red, Honda Accord car which is parked in his drive and which he has inspected. Here the contract would be for existing, specific goods and property in the car could pass to B immediately on contract. On the other hand, B might agree to buy from S, a new, red Honda Accord to be delivered from the Honda factory two months later. Assuming that the car has to be manufactured at the factory, the agreement is one for future, unascertained goods and no property in the car can transfer to B until a brand-new, red Honda Accord is selected and earmarked in some way as B's car. This latter example is an agreement to sell future, unascertained, generic goods and S can supply any new red, Honda Accord, because it will have the requisite characteristics of the *genus*. It is thus plain that, in a contract to sell unascertained goods, the rule that the goods must be ascertained and identified before property in them can pass to B is justified and explained because it is simply not possible to say which goods are B's before the moment of ascertainment. In an agreement to sell one bottle of port from a box containing two bottles, no property can pass in the port until one bottle is selected as being B's property and this will apply, *a fortiori*, where no bulk has been specified as that from which the goods must be selected or no source of supply has been identified at all. Although with unascertained goods this process of ascertainment and earmarking is necessary for the passing of property, it is possible for B to become a *tenant in common* of a specified bulk of goods provided the conditions in the SGA, ss 20A and 20B

---

1 Section 61(1) provides that 'property' means 'the general property in goods, and not merely a special property'.

are satisfied. It cannot be stressed enough that such co-ownership does not mean that B acquires property in the goods; instead he has an *interest* in an undivided share of the bulk. Co-ownership is considered in detail later in this chapter.

It should be emphasised that the moment to categorise the goods is at the *date of contract*. An agreement for the sale of 100 sheep from a flock of 101 sheep is an agreement to sell unascertained goods and the contract does not change character and become one for specific goods when 100 sheep are identified and placed in a pen for B, although when this has been done the sheep will be referred to as 'ascertained goods' and, as indicated above, property in them may thereupon pass to B under the rules relating to unascertained goods. It is now necessary to examine these categories of goods in more detail.

EXISTING AND FUTURE GOODS

Both these types of goods are defined in the SGA, s 5(1), and the definition given there of future goods is repeated in the SGA, s 61(1). Section 5 provides:

'(1) The goods which form the subject of a contract of sale may be either existing goods, owned or possessed by the seller, or goods to be manufactured or acquired by him after the making of the contract of sale, in this Act called future goods.
(2) There may be a contract for the sale of goods, the acquisition of which by the seller depends on a contingency which may or may not happen.
(3) Where by a contract of sale the seller purports to effect a present sale of future goods, the contract operates as an agreement to sell the goods'.

Existing goods

As existing goods are those 'owned or possessed' by S, they could be either specific (eg the Doulton vase in S's hand) or unascertained (eg a bottle of beer from a crate containing twelve bottles in S's cellar) and, as explained above, consequences flow from this distinction as regards the passing of property. B cannot acquire property in the bottle of beer until, at the earliest, it is separated from the other bottles, but property in the Doulton vase could transfer to B immediately on contract.

Future goods

In the SGA, s 5(1), 'future goods' are defined as goods which must be 'manufactured or acquired', these two categories possessing significant differences. Goods to be manufactured, grown, or born of livestock must, of necessity, be future goods, these examples sharing the characteristic that the goods must come into existence in the future. It goes without saying that an agreement to sell future goods will often unequivocally concern unascertained goods (eg 500 gallons of beer to be brewed by S the following month). However, goods which are physically *in existence* but which S must *acquire* are also within the classification of future goods even though they seem, at first glance, to be closer to the category of existing goods (eg a Jaguar E type car which S intends to buy from a third party (T) and sell to B).

Where the goods which S intends to buy from T are owned and possessed by T, they could, at least in theory, be categorised as future/specific goods (eg the *only* Sheraton chair owned by T). This question is theoretical because no property in such goods can pass on contract and, for all practical purposes, the agreement will be treated as one for the sale of unascertained goods.[2] The agreement would certainly be one to sell future/unascertained goods where, for example, S must acquire from T 'a Doulton vase', as a generic object, T owning a collection of such vases.

Also within the category of future goods which are in existence but which must be acquired by S, would be goods which are to become S's property by succession or ownership of land, for example.

The SGA, s 5(3) emphasises that future goods can be the subject of a contract of sale but the contract can operate only as an *agreement* to sell. This is because 'a person cannot by deed, however solemn, assign that which is not in him – in other words, there cannot be a prophetic conveyance'.[3] In a contract for the sale of future goods, it is thus clear that the *property* in the goods cannot pass to B immediately: instead it can pass to B only at some time in the future according to the parties' intentions.[4]

The SGA, s 2(3) specifies that 'a contract of sale may be absolute or conditional' and, with future goods, the question arises whether the obligations of S and B are conditional on the goods coming into existence or being acquired by S or, alternatively, whether the obligation of one party or the other is absolute. Everything depends on the intention of S and B. Section 5(2) appears to contemplate the situation where the obligations of both S and B are contingent on S's acquiring the goods or their coming into existence and, if the condition is not fulfilled, neither party will be liable.[5] Alternatively, S may unconditionally contract to sell future goods and, if he cannot deliver them on the specified date, he will be liable for non-delivery; if he is also unable to give a good title to the goods, he will be in breach of s 12(1) (implied condition of title). Likewise, B may unconditionally contract to pay the price of the goods whether they come into existence or not and, as B accepts the risk of the event's failing to occur, he is said to buy a *spes* (a chance). This contract does not fall foul of the rules on wagering contracts, as S stands to gain the same amount regardless of the event's failure or success.[6]

---

2 Cf Chalmers, *Sale of Goods* (18th edn, 1981), p 271: 'It is clear that "future goods," even though particularly described, do not come within the definition of specific goods, but for most purposes would be subject to the same considerations as unascertained goods'. This would seem to be too wide an assertion; arguably the comment relates to the *passing of property* in future goods.

3 *Belding v Read* (1865) 3 H & C 955, 961, per Pollock CB.

4 At common law, before the SGA 1893, a distinction was drawn between future goods in which S had a 'potential property', meaning the expected increase in something *already owned* by S (eg wool from sheep owned by S) and future goods in which he did not have such property. Potential property could be the subject of an immediate grant or assignment (see *Petch v Tutin* (1846) 15 M & W 110) and not simply the subject of an agreement to sell. Although this distinction has *not* survived the SGA, it is arguable that in cases akin to those of potential property, property in the goods might pass to B on their coming into existence without any further appropriation (see later) but all now depends on the intent of S and B.

5 See eg *Lovatt v Hamilton* (1839) 5 M & W 639 (sale of 50 tons of palm oil to arrive per *Mansfield*, in the case of non-arrival or the vessel's not containing so much after delivery of former contracts, the contract to be void. On arrival, *Mansfield* had only 7 tons applicable to B's contract. In an action for non-delivery, held that B must fail as the arrival of the goods in *Mansfield* was a condition precedent and the contract was entire so B was not entitled to the 7 tons); see also *Howell v Coupland* (1876) 1 QBD 258 (below) which, it has been said (*Re Wait* [1927] 1 Ch 606, 630-631 per Atkin LJ; *Sainsbury (H R & S) Ltd v Street* [1972] 1 WLR 834, 837 per MacKenna J), is preserved after 1893 as an instance of a contingent sale under s 5(2).

6 See *Ellesmere v Wallace* [1929] 2 Ch 1.

SPECIFIC AND UNASCERTAINED GOODS

'Specific goods' are defined in the SGA, s 61(1) as 'goods identified and agreed on at the time a contract of sale is made and includes an undivided share, specified as a fraction or percentage, of goods identified and agreed on as aforesaid'. Although unascertained goods are not defined in the SGA, the phrase must refer, inferentially, to goods *not* identified and agreed on at the time a contract of sale is made.

Specific goods

Specific goods must be 'identified and agreed on' at the moment the contract of sale is entered into by S and B (the reference in s 61(1) to the 'undivided share' is considered below). Specific goods must thus be designated at the time of contract so that there can be no substitution of other goods for the specific goods which S and B have agreed upon (eg the Wedgwood vase in B's hands – not even an identical vase in S's hands will suffice). The contract itself may *identify* the goods to the extent that there is no ambiguity or room for substiution and then the goods will be specific, eg the 100 bags of barley in S's warehouse, the warehouse being named and no more than 100 bags of barley being stored in it at the date of contract. It is plain that the definition of 'specific goods' is very limiting: if there are 101 bags of barley in the latter example, the goods cease to be specific and the contract becomes one for the sale of unascertained goods.

In the examples above the specific goods are 'identified and agreed on' to the extent of being individualised as a *physical fact*. Might the definition in s 61(1) be extended to other situations where the goods are *described* specifically in the contract? It was suggested above that, at least in theory, future goods could be classified as specific goods where S agrees to sell goods to B that are presently owned and possessed by T (eg the only Sheraton chair owned by T) but here the goods are in existence.[7] A further problem is thus whether the goods have to be in existence to be specific. It is clear that an agreement to sell 'the *entire* crop of barley to be grown on S's farm next season' does mean that the goods are 'identified and agreed on' in the sense of the unambiguous description in the contract, even though the goods are not in existence at the moment of the contract's formation. Moreover, in the pre-Act decision in *Howell v Coupland*,[8] a sale of 200 tons of potatoes from a crop to be grown on particular land belonging to S was treated as a sale of specific goods to the extent that, when the crop was blighted by disease and failed, the contract was held to be frustrated. However, it has been clear since the decision in *Re Wait*[9] that an unascertained portion of a larger bulk cannot be specific goods (thereby ruling-out the potatoes in *Howell* as specific goods[10] after 1893). Similarly, it is suggested that the example given above of the entire crop of barley to be grown on S's farm next season would not be a contract for the sale of specific goods as the overriding modern emphasis is that the *goods* should be physically and factually specific at the time of

---

7 The decision in *Varley v Whipp* [1900] 1 QB 513 proceeds on the basis that the sale of a second-hand reaping machine, owned by T at the date of contract between S and B, was a contract for the sale of specific goods.
8 (1876) 1 QBD 258.
9 [1927] 1 Ch 606 (see below).
10 See *Re Wait* [1927] 1 Ch 606, 630-631 per Atkin LJ; *Sainsbury (H R & S) Ltd v Street* [1972] 1 WLR 834.

contract. In *Kursell v Timber Operators and Contractors Ltd*,[11] Sargant LJ[12] stressed that 'in order that goods may be specific they must in my view be identified and not merely identifiable ... for the purpose of the passing of the actual property in goods ... a present identification of the goods as specific goods appears to be required by the statute'.

It is vital to stress, however, that irrespective of any juggling with abstract definitions, the salient feature is that where the goods are not owned by S, or are not in existence at the time of contract, property in those goods cannot pass to B at the *moment of contract*. In these situations, the contract must operate as an agreement to sell the goods under s 5(3) and the property will pass at some future time when the goods become ascertained. There seems little doubt, therefore, that such contracts will be treated for all practical purposes as agreements to sell unascertained goods.[13]

An undivided share in specific goods

Section 61(1) also defines specific goods as 'an undivided share, specified as a fraction or percentage, of goods identified and agreed on as aforesaid'. This wording was added to s 61(1) in 1995[14] as the result of the Law Commissions'[15] recommendations which stressed that a sale of an undivided share in goods, expressed as a *fraction or percentage* (eg a one third share of a horse or boat; 50% of the cargo of wheat aboard a named vessel) was possible under the existing law, the buyer becoming owner in common with the other owner or owners, who may include the seller. However, the Law Commissions considered that the other issues surrounding the sale of such a fraction of goods should be clarified. First, it was thought that a sale of an undivided share in goods expressed as a fraction should be regarded as a sale of *goods* rather than a dealing in an incorporeal right or a chose in action. Accordingly, the definition of 'goods' in s 61(1) now includes 'an undivided share in goods'. Second, it was emphasised that a sale of an undivided share in goods expressed as a fraction should be regarded as a sale of *specific*, rather than unascertained goods for, otherwise, the rules on the ascertainment of goods could lead to absurd results where it was never intended to divide and deliver the respective shares: property in a third of a racehorse, for example, could pass to B only if the animal were dissected into three parts. Third, the Law Commissions acknowledged that, recognising an undivided share in goods expressed as a fraction as specific goods, involved diluting the definition of such goods but felt that the 'share is identified and agreed on, as clearly as it ever can be while remaining an undivided share, if the goods in which it is a share are identified and agreed on'.[16] Fourth, it was stated that,

---

11 [1927] 1 KB 298.
12 [1927] 1 KB 298 at 314.
13 It may be that such 'future/specific' goods can be treated as specific for some purposes, eg as regards the rules of mistake and frustration in ss 6 and 7: see Ch 24. The narrow definition of specific goods also causes problems where B seeks specific performance as, under the SGA, s 52, specific performance is available only where the goods are 'specific or ascertained', eg specific performance is not technically available where S agrees to sell all his future output of raw materials to B and is B's sole supplier: see Ch 29.
14 By the Sale of Goods (Amendment) Act 1995, s 2(d).
15 *Sale of Goods Forming Part of a Bulk* (Law Com No 215, Scot Law Com No 145, 1993), paras 2.4-2.6; 5.3-5.7.
16 *Sale of Goods Forming Part of a Bulk* (Law Com No 215, Scot Law Com No 145, 1993), para 2.6.

with this type of sale,'the Act's provisions based on possession or physical delivery will simply disapply themselves and the intentions of the parties will prevail'.[17] This is true most particularly where the parties do not intend that their respective shares in the goods will ever be divided or delivered (eg shares in a living racehorse). But as the new definition applies to 50% of the cargo of a named ship, for example, the parties' intent will usually be that the cargo is separated and delivered. If so, the rules in the SGA, ss 27-37 concerning delivery and performance would be applicable to the cargo example, as the Law Commissions acknowledged.[18]

It is thus clear that there can be a sale of an undivided share, specified as a fraction, of specific goods and that this is a sale of goods. The only reference in the SGA to a sale by a part owner is in s 2(2), viz 'there may be a contract of sale between one part owner and another' and this provision was probably inserted to accentuate the point that such transactions were sales rather than dealings in incorporeal rights. The position now must be that a sale of an undivided share or *part* of it is within the SGA as a sale of goods.[19]

Unascertained goods

As mentioned earlier, there is no definition in the SGA of either 'unascertained' or 'ascertained' goods. There are, however, three principal classifications of unascertained goods, viz:

(i)   generic goods, ie goods belonging to a *genus* or family of goods all sharing the same characteristics (eg 100 tons of wheat; a new Ford Mondeo car);
(ii)   goods not yet in existence but which have to be manufactured or grown by S (eg 50 tons of plums from next season's crop; a ship to be built by S);
(iii) a part, unsegregated at the time of contract, from a specified bulk (eg 10 litres of port from a cask containing 100 litres in S's cellar; 70cl of whisky from a butt in S's warehouse containing a larger, unspecified amount).

The factor which these classifications have in common is that the goods cannot be *physically identified* and so their *individuality* cannot be established at the

---

17 *Sale of Goods Forming Part of a Bulk* (Law Com No 215, Scot Law Com No 145, 1993), para 5.5. For example, it was thought that the rules on 'deliverable state' in s 18 will be inapplicable to the sale of 'an undivided share which, as such, is never in a deliverable state and cannot be delivered ... in the case of a sale of an undivided share everything depends on the intention of the parties' (para 5.6). Section 18, rules 1 and 3 would seem to be inapplicable to both a half share in a racehorse and 50% of a cargo as the goods would not be in a deliverable state at the date of contract, but it would appear that s 18, r 2 could apply to the cargo example; see below.

18 *Sale of Goods Forming Part of a Bulk* (Law Com No 215, Scot Law Com No 145, 1993), para 5.7.

19 Even after the 1995 amendments, Goode argues (*Commercial Law* (2nd edn, 1995, p 205)) that, to qualify as a contract of sale, the transferor must intend to transfer the 'totality' of his interest as this is what is meant by 'general property' in s 61(1). Goode thus considers that neither of the following would be a sale of goods: (i) a transfer by a sole owner of goods of part only of his interest to create ownership in common and (ii) a transfer by a part-owner of part of his interest. With respect, this seems most unlikely after the 1995 amendments. Transaction (i) must be at the heart of co-ownership and transaction (ii) is necessary so that part-owners can adjust the proportions in which their shares are held. Once the notion of infinite divisibility is recognised and the undivided share classified as 'goods', a sale of a fraction of the share is no different from a sale of part of the physical goods.

date of contract. This means that the goods can be designated in the contract by *description* only. Nevertheless, categories (i) and (ii) comprise wholly unascertained goods in that, in the example above, *any* 100 tons of wheat of the contract description can be delivered to B, whereas in category (iii) S is bound to sell goods which are drawn from the specified bulk. The SGA is often criticised for failing to make this distinction and it is self-evident that category (iii) has greater affinity with an agreement to sell specific goods than an agreement to sell unascertained goods – *a fortiori* if the bulk is small, eg 10 bottles of whisky to be drawn from a particular case of twelve identical bottles. Consequently, the goods in category (iii) are sometimes referred to as quasi-specific goods. At least some of the difficulties associated with sales from a specified bulk have been remedied by the newly-inserted ss 20A and 20B of the SGA[20] which allow that, in certain circumstances, there can be co-ownership of goods in an unsegregated bulk.

As mentioned earlier, the distinction between specific and unascertained goods is crucial as regards the passing of property: property in specific goods may pass to B on contract but no property in unascertained goods can pass to B until, at the earliest, the goods are ascertained and their individuality is established. Consider a contract for the sale of 5 bags of wheat from 100 bags in S's warehouse: until 5 bags are separated from the 100 and thereby become 'ascertained' goods, it is impossible for B to establish exactly which goods form the subject-matter of the contract and thus it would be equally impossible for *property* in any goods to pass to B before separation. In an agreement to sell unascertained goods, physical ascertainment of the goods thus entails a process by which the contract-goods are selected, segregated or completed. Thereafter, the question is one of intent and the parties may fix any moment for the passing of property in the ascertained goods from S to B.

As this rule on ascertainment is premised upon commercial practicalities, it has always been a consistent theme of the common law but, before the SGA 1893, the categories of specific and unascertained goods were not separated as decisively as they are today[1] and, in equity, there could be a transfer of an equitable interest in future property. This meant that as soon as property identifiable as the subject matter of the contract was acquired by the transferor, the transferee's equitable interest would attach to the property and be good against all except a *bona fide* purchaser for value of the legal title.[2] The extent to which the principles of equity applied to the ordinary sale of unascertained goods was never clear but the notion that future property could be assigned was finally rejected in *Re Wait*,[3] a seminal decision which emphasises the

---

20 Inserted by the Sale of Goods (Amendment) Act 1995.
1   Eg in *Whitehouse v Frost* (1810) 12 East 614, S sold to B 10 tons of Greenland oil from a cistern containing 40 tons and it was held that property in the goods thereupon passed to B without any severance of the oil (see also Le Blanc J's justification of *Whitehouse* in *Busk v Davis* (1814) 2 M & S 397). *Whitehouse* was overruled by *Laurie and Morewood v Dudin & Sons* [1926] 1 KB 223. See also the earlier reference to 'potential property' (above, fn 4).
2   See *Holroyd v Marshall* (1862) 10 HL Cas 191(an occupier of a mill mortgaged the chattels in the mill to his landlord with a covenant that all chattels added to the mortgaged goods or substituted for them should also be subject to the mortgage. HL held that as soon as new chattels were placed in the mill an equitable title in them vested in the mortgagee without any further action being necessary); *Tailby v Official Receiver* (1888) 13 App Cas 523.
3   [1927] 1 Ch 606.

consequences of the distinction between specific and unascertained goods. On 20 November, Wait agreed to buy 1,000 tons of wheat ex *Challenger*, which was to be shipped from the USA, the vessel being expected to load in December. On 21 November, he agreed to sell 500 tons of the wheat to B. The wheat was shipped in bulk on 21 December and a bill of lading for 1,000 tons was forwarded to Wait. On 5 February, whilst *Challenger* was at sea and before any separation or appropriation of the 500 tons, B paid the price to Wait. Wait went bankrupt on 24 February. *Challenger* arrived at Avonmouth on 28 February and Wait's trustee in bankruptcy claimed to be entitled to the 1,000 tons, whilst B claimed specific performance under s 52 or, alternatively, that the contract had operated as an equitable assignment allowing him a beneficial interest in the 500 tons. It was held that specific performance was not available as (i) the goods were neither specific nor ascertained and (ii) B had no equitable rights over the goods. B could thus prove only as an unsecured creditor in Wait's bankruptcy. Lord Hanworth MR thought that, even if the equitable rule had survived the SGA, there was insufficient identification of the goods for it to operate, but Atkin LJ considered that the equitable rule was simply inapplicable to a sale of part of a specified whole. He thought the matter was beyond dispute after the SGA 1893 because the Act's rules on the passing of property were 'complete and exclusive statements of the legal relations both in law and equity'.[4] It is thus clear that, while an agreement for the sale of real property makes the vendor a trustee for the purchaser, an agreement for the sale of unascertained goods vests no equitable ownership in B. In fact, B has no real rights at all under such an agreement and has only personal, contractual rights.[5] Recent decisions[6] have confirmed that, without a shadow of doubt, no equitable title can pass to B in a simple contract for the sale of unascertained goods merely by the contract itself.

It is one thing to insist that no property in unascertained goods can pass to B until they become ascertained but quite another to deny that B can have any sort of legal *interest* in unascertained goods as a tenant in common, ie a co-owner, with the other buyers. *Re Wait* is an example of the injustice which arose from the rule that B could not acquire such an interest in unascertained goods even where he had paid the price in full and it is this question which has been partially addressed by the two new sections of the SGA (ss 20A and 20B).

A summary of the new law is that where B has *paid* for some or all of a specified *quantity* of goods forming part of an *identified bulk*, he will obtain an undivided share in the bulk as a tenant in common with S and any other buyers – the facts of *Re Wait* are thus definitely within the new law. The SGA, ss 20A and 20B are considered later when the passing of property in unascertained goods is evaluated in detail.

---

4 [1927] 1 Ch 606 at 636. Sargant LJ dissented and thought that B had an equitable right or lien over the wheat. He stressed that, in many of the cases, it was precisely because the legal property had not passed that it was often necessary to invoke equity to make the contract effective (p 647).

5 The position is exactly the same where, in an agreement to sell specific goods, no property has passed to B on contract.

6 See *Leigh and Sillavan Ltd v Aliakmon Shipping Co Ltd, The Aliakmon* [1986] AC 785, 812 per Lord Brandon; *Re London Wine Co (Shippers) Ltd* [1986] PCC 121; *Re Stapylton Fletcher Ltd* [1994] 1 WLR 1181; *Re Goldcorp Exchange Ltd* [1995] 1 AC 74.

The consequences of the passing of property

As mentioned earlier, the purpose of a contract for the sale of goods is to transfer the 'general property' in the goods from S to B which, in general terms, can be taken to mean 'ownership'. Before a consideration of the rules regarding the *time* at which such a transfer may occur, several general observations should be made regarding the effects of the passing of property.

Property and possession

A prominent feature of English law is that there is no necessary connection between the passing of property and B's obtaining physical possession of the goods. Property may pass to B before the goods are delivered to him or, alternatively, S may retain property after the goods have been delivered to B. Of necessity, the separation of property from possession means that a party in possession may dispose of goods when he does not own them and, as will be seen later in this chapter, the SGA has made provision for this eventuality.

Certainly the failure to link property with possession is contrary to common expectations and, in particular, might be disadvantageous to a consumer buyer if he does not realise that he can be the owner of the goods before he has taken delivery of them. On the other hand, modern commerce could not function if S had first to acquire physical possession of the goods and then deliver them to B before property in them could pass to B.

Risk and frustration

Under the SGA, s 20(1), unless otherwise agreed, the goods remain at S's risk until the property in them is transferred to B but, when the property has been transferred to B, the goods are at B's risk irrespective of whether or not delivery has been made to him. The same observations regarding possible disadvantage to consumers apply under this rule and B should make sure that he has the necessary insurance cover at the appropriate time – B has an insurable interest in the goods at his risk, even if property has not passed to him.[7] Where the property in specific goods is still in S, the contract is capable of being frustrated if the goods perish (s 7) but once property has passed to B on a completed sale, frustration is no longer applicable.

Price

Under the SGA, s 49, the passing of property to B means that S is entitled to sue B for the price of the goods but, if it has not passed, S can only maintain an action for damages for non-delivery under the SGA, s 50.

Delivery and payment

The passing of property to B does not automatically give him the right to possess the goods as the SGA, s 28 provides that, unless otherwise agreed, delivery and

---

7 See *Inglis v Stock* (1885) 10 App Cas 263.

payment are concurrent conditions. B may thus claim possession where he is ready and willing to pay the price or can establish that S has granted him credit. Moreover, an unpaid seller of goods who is in possession of them, may have a lien over them for the price even though property has passed to B (s 41) or a right to stop the goods in course of transit to B and retain them until tender or payment of the price by B (ss 44-46). Similarly, where S is unpaid and has exercised his right of lien or stoppage, he can resell the goods and transfer a good title in them to a third party (s 48(2)).

Seller and buyer in possession

As property and physical possession are divorced in English law, there may often be a sale or other disposition of the goods by a party who has possession of them but no property in them. Thus property may have passed to B but S may have been left in possession of the goods (eg B agrees to buy a specific bed at a retail shop and S agrees to deliver it to B one week later). In this example, should S sell and deliver the bed to a *bona fide* B2, he will acquire title to it (see the SGA, s 24/Factors Act 1889, s 8), English law thereby rejecting the alternative, but impracticable solution, that B and B2 become tenants in common of the bed. Alternatively, property in the goods may remain in S but he may allow B to have possession of them (eg B agrees to buy a car from S and pays by cheque, S allowing B to drive away in the car immediately). Here B might be a swindler whose cheque is dishonoured but, should B sell and deliver the car to a *bona fide* B2, B2 will acquire title to it (see the SGA, s 25/ Factors Act 1889, s 9).

Damage to, or wrongful interference with, the goods

Where goods are damaged en route to B or delivered to the wrong person, the question of the passing of property may be relevant in deciding who should be the proper plaintiff in any action against a third party who has caused the loss. As regards claims in tort, if the plaintiff is to sue the third party he must show either that property had passed to him and he was the legal owner of the goods or that he had a right to possession of the goods at the time of loss, damage or misdelivery. The right to possession, of course, does not necessarily depend on the passing of property but may depend on payment. The difficulties which can arise are illustrated by the decision in *The Aliakmon*.[8] B agreed to buy a consignment of steel coils which were carried by sea on terms that risk passed to him on shipment but that S retained both property in the goods and the right to possession until payment by B. The coils were damaged en route by the carrier's careless stowage. The House of Lords held that the carrier owed no duty of care to B as B had neither property in the goods nor a possessory title at the material time, even though the goods were at B's risk. The actual decision in *The Aliakmon* would now be different as a result of the Carriage of Goods by Sea Act 1992 but the general principle of the decision remains intact and B could find himself in this position where goods are carried by land. Again, it is clearly imperative that B should insure goods which are at his risk.

---

8 *Leigh & Sillivan Ltd v Aliakmon Shipping Co Ltd, The Aliakmon* [1986] AC 785.

Insolvency

The passing of property is crucial where either S or B becomes bankrupt or goes into receivership or liquidation. First, the question of S's insolvency must be considered. If S becomes insolvent whilst either specific or ascertained goods are still in his possession, B may claim the goods *if* the property in them has passed to him and he will have this right to the exclusion of S's other creditors. Where the property had not passed to B at the date of S's insolvency, B was formerly in an unfortunate position because, even if he had paid the whole price to S, he was limited to a general claim as a creditor for breach of contract. This was a particularly acute problem where B bought goods from bulk with no ascertainment ever being effected, as in *Re Wait*,[9] but the position has been much improved with the enactment of ss 20A and 20B of the SGA which permit co-ownership of identified bulks in certain situations (see later).

Second, there is the issue of B's insolvency. If B becomes insolvent and S still has possession of the goods and is unpaid, he can exercise his lien or stop the goods in transit. If B becomes insolvent after obtaining possession and does not pay for the goods, then *if* property has passed to B, the goods belong to his estate leaving S to claim as an unsecured creditor. However, if property remains in S he can recover back the goods from B by asserting his proprietary right and thereby gain priority over B's other creditors. It has become increasingly common for S to employ a reservation of title clause to protect himself against B's insolvency, such a clause typically providing that risk shall pass to B on delivery but that property shall not pass until the full price is paid to S and, if B defaults in payment, S shall be entitled to recover possession of the goods. The difficult question of an extended reservation of title clause will be considered later. Here S may sell raw materials which are processed by B and resold and the difficulty concerns the extent to which S may claim the manufactured goods or the proceeds of their sale.

The time at which property passes from the seller to the buyer

At this stage, it is convenient to re-assemble several salient principles which permeate the rules on the passing of property.[10] First, property and possession are separated so that B may own goods which he does not physically control or possess. Second, English law allows the contract of sale to act as such in creating rights *in personam* between S and B and as a simultaneous conveyance of the property in the goods to B thus creating rights *in rem*. Where the contract passes the property immediately it is referred to as 'a sale' (see s 2(4)) thus distinguishing a sale from an 'agreement to sell' where property passes at some time after contract (see s 2(5)). As property may pass on contract, it follows that no particular significance is attached to delivery as passing property to

---

9   [1927] 1 Ch 606 (see earlier).
10 See generally Smith, *Property Problems in Sale* (1978), Chs II and III; Lawson, 'The Passing of Property and Risk in Sale of Goods – A Comparative Study' (1949) 65 LQR 352; Battersby and Preston, 'The Concepts of "Property", "Title" and "Owner" used in the Sale of Goods Act 1893' (1972) 35 MLR 268.

B. This is in marked contrast to Roman law which made a crucial distinction between contract and conveyance with the consequence that property could not be transferred to B without some act of delivery.[11] Third, as no *form* of conveyance is required and delivery is not crucial, it is the *intention* of the parties which governs the moment at which property passes from S to B. Fourth, no property in unascertained goods can pass until, at the earliest, the goods are ascertained but property in specific goods can pass on contract. Fifth, the SGA recognises that the intent of S and B regarding the passing of property may not be expressed in crystal-clear terms and so, most unusually for English law, the SGA has a set of presumptive rules analogous to a code which prescribe the moment at which property passes to B but which apply *only* where no conclusive intention can be culled from either the contract between S and B or the relevant surrounding circumstances.

The matters specified above are mirrored in the three central sections of the SGA which apply to the passing of property. First, s 16 provides:

'Subject to section 20A below[12] where there is a contract for the sale of unascertained goods no property in the goods is transferred to the buyer unless and until the goods are ascertained.'

Second, s 17 specifies:

'(1) Where there is a contract for the sale of specific or ascertained goods the property in them is transferred to the buyer at such time as the parties to the contract intend it to be transferred.

(2) For the purposes of ascertaining the intention of the parties regard shall be had to the terms of the contract, the conduct of the parties and the circumstances of the case.'

Finally, s 18 goes on to list the presumptive rules for the passing of property (see below) which apply 'unless a different intention appears,' ie these rules can be excluded by S and B's manifestation of a contrary intent. Once this overall plan is appreciated, it is logical to consider the rules on the passing of property according to whether the goods are specific or unascertained.

Passing of property in specific goods

Section 17 contains the governing rule in stipulating that property in specific goods may pass at such time as the parties intend. In *Varley v Whipp*,[13] Channell J considered that it was 'impossible to imagine a clause more vague than this, but I think it correctly represents the state of the authorities when the [1893] Act was passed'.[14] However, where no clear intent of S and B regarding the question of the passing of property can be established, s 18 rr 1-4 dictate the various times when property will pass in specific goods.

11 See Blackburn, *Contract of Sale* (2nd edn, 1885), pp 242-267; Fifoot, *History and Sources of the Common Law, Tort and Contract* (1949), pp 226-229.
12 Section 20(A) was inserted by the Sale of Goods (Amendment) Act 1995 and applies to sales from an identified bulk (see later).
13 [1900] 1 QB 513, 517.
14 See Blackburn, *Contract of Sale* (2nd edn, 1885), Part II, Chs I and II.

SECTION 18, RULE 1

Rule 1 provides:

> 'Where there is an unconditional contract for the sale of specific goods in a deliverable state the property in the goods passes to the buyer when the contract is made, and it is immaterial whether the time of payment or the time of delivery, or both, be postponed.'

Rule 1 embodies the central and ancient[15] notion of English law that property in specific goods may pass to B immediately on contract irrespective of payment or delivery. *Tarling v Baxter*[16] is a leading 19th century decision illustrating this rule. S agreed to sell to B a particular hay stack standing on land belonging to S's brother, with payment to be made one month after contract and no hay to be removed until the price had been paid. Before the price was due the hay stack was destroyed by fire but it was held that B must pay the price as the property in the goods had passed to him on contract. Clearly the essence of r 1 is that this immediate conveyance can occur only if no conditions are attached to the contract which suspend the passing of property to B and the goods are both specific and in a deliverable state. These factors must now be examined.

Unconditional contract

This phrase is meant[17] to indicate that there must be no condition *precedent* to the passing of property between S and B, eg a condition that the goods must pass certain tests prescribed by B before property passes to him. It is arguable that a condition *subsequent*, where B can return the goods to S if certain conditions are not met, would be within r 1, as here property would pass immediately to B but might *revest* in S on the operation of the condition. B's subjecting the goods to some test or gaining the approval of T to the suitability of the goods might also be the subject of a condition subsequent.

It is clear that, if r 1 is to be excluded by a conditional contract, the condition must suspend *the passing of property* and r 1 itself specifies that the fact that payment and delivery are to occur later does not necessarily postpone the passing of property until that time. However, an express clause reserving property to S until payment by B would obviously be a condition precedent to the passing of property and thus a 'conditional contract' which would oust the operation of r 1. Until the condition is fulfilled, the contract is effective as an agreement to sell but not as a sale of the goods.[18] Such a reservation of the right of disposal by S is recognised in the SGA, s 19(1).[19]

---

15 See Fifoot, *History and Sources of the Common Law: Tort and Contract* (1949), p 228.
16 (1827) 6 B & C 360; see also *Spartali v Benecke* (1850) 10 CB 212; *Sweeting v Turner* (1871) LR 7 QB 310; *Seath v Moore* (1886) 11 App Cas 350, 370 per Lord Blackburn.
17 Some early decisions had seemingly interpreted 'unconditional contract' as meaning that the contract must contain no conditions in the sense of basic stipulations. This was because the original SGA 1893, s 11(1)(c)(amended by Misrepresentation Act 1967, s 4(1)), deprived B of the right to reject goods for breach of condition where the contract was 'for specific goods, the property in which has passed to the buyer'. Potentially, B would thus have been unable to reject specific goods where property passed on contract under r 1. The strained interpretation in the cases thus meant that virtually all contracts were 'conditional', thereby preserving B's right to reject: see *Varley v Whipp* [1900] 1 QB 513; *Ollett v Jordan* [1918] 2 KB 41; *Leaf v International Galleries* [1950] 2 KB 86.
18 See SGA 1979, s 2(5) and (6).
19 See Ch 17.

Specific goods

The meaning of 'specific goods' was considered earlier and it will be remembered that the SGA, s 61(1) defines specific goods as 'goods identified and agreed on at the time a contract of sale is made and includes an undivided share, specified as a fraction or percentage, of goods identified and agreed on as aforesaid'. The latter part of s 61(1) relating to an 'undivided share' in specific goods was added to the section recently[20] and the Law Commissions' views on this question were considered earlier when the definition of 'specific goods' was analysed. The extended definition in s 61(1) means, for example, that a contract for the sale of a half share in a yacht is now a contract for the sale of specific goods, as is a contract for the sale of 50% of the cargo of wheat aboard a named vessel.

The requirement that goods must be 'identified and agreed on at the time a contract of sale is made' was considered in *Kursell v Timber Operators and Contractors Ltd*.[1] S agreed to sell to B all the timber of a certain height in a particular Latvian forest, B having 15 years in which to cut the timber. Six days after the contract, the Latvian Assembly passed a law under which the forest became the property of the Latvian State. It was held that no property passed to B under r 1 as the goods were neither identified nor agreed upon at the time of contract: it was not every tree in the forest which was sold to B but only those complying with certain measurements and the measurements had not been made at the date of contract. Sargant LJ stressed that the contract was ambiguous but that B was probably entitled to cut the timber which grew to the requisite height in the 15 years after contract and thus the goods were not specific at the date of contract.[2] He also considered that, even if the alternative interpretation were adopted and B could cut only the timber which had reached the requisite height at the date of contract, the goods would still be 'merely identifiable' rather than 'identified' factually as specific goods.[3] It is plain that *Kursell* defines 'specific goods' very narrowly. This can lead to surprising results: in a retail sale of goods to a consumer where B examines goods at the counter and agrees to buy identical, packaged goods from stock, the goods will not be specific at the date of contract and r 1 cannot apply. In this retail example the agreement is, in fact, an agreement to sell unascertained goods.

As mentioned earlier, even if future goods which are not in existence or not owned by S at the date of contract *can* be specific goods within the SGA definitions (Sargant LJ's judgment in *Kursell* militating against this view), it is apparent that no *property* in them can pass at the date of contract.

Deliverable state

Under the SGA, s 61(5), 'goods are in a deliverable state when they are in such a state that the buyer would under the contract be bound to take delivery of them'. In *Kursell*, it was held that the timber was not in a deliverable state until B had severed it as he could not 'be bound to take delivery of an undetermined

---

20 Inserted by the Sale of Goods (Amendment) Act 1995, s 2(d).
1 [1927] 1 KB 298.
2 Lord Hanworth MR also accepted this conclusion but based his judgment on the fact that the terms of the contract thus indicated a contrary intention (under s 17) to the immediate passing of property on contract.
3 [1927] 1 KB 298 at 314.

part of a tree not yet identified'.[4] Similarly, in *Underwood Ltd v Burgh Castle Brick and Cement Syndicate*,[5] S agreed to sell a condensing engine to B to be delivered free on rail in London. At the date of contract, the 30 ton engine was embedded in a concrete floor at S's premises in Millwall and it had to be detached from its base and dismantled by S before it was in such state that it could be delivered on rail. While it was being loaded onto a truck, it was damaged by S, and B refused to accept it. It was held that the property had not passed to B at the date of the accident and thus the risk was still on S. Property could not pass under r 1 as, at the date of contract, the engine was affixed to the freehold and could not be in a deliverable state in which B was bound to accept it until it was dismantled. Most importantly, Bankes LJ held that deliverable state does not depend upon the 'mere completeness of the subject matter in all its parts' but rather 'on the actual state of the goods at the date of the contract and the state in which they are to be delivered by the terms of the contract'.[6]

Again, the extended definition of 'specific goods' in s 61(1) should be mentioned here. A contract for the sale of 'an undivided share, specified as a fraction or percentage, of goods identified and agreed on' can apply to disparate contracts such as the sale of a half share in a live racehorse or 20% of a cargo aboard a named ship. In the latter example, the parties will certainly intend that the goods are separated after contract and then delivered to B and thus r 1 is inapplicable as the goods are not in a deliverable state at the date of contract. The same result would seem to follow in the former racehorse example, especially as the parties never intend to dissect the horse, and so their shares will never be either in a deliverable state or delivered.[7]

Factors indicating a contrary intention and ousting r 1

As specified by ss 17 and 18, the presumption in r 1 may be ousted by evidence of contrary intent which must be evident *at the date of contract* or r 1 will lock into place and property will pass to B. In *Dennant v Skinner and Collom*,[8] a car was knocked down at auction to B, a swindler, who had given a false name and address. B asked to take away the car in return for a cheque and was allowed to do so after signing a document in which it was agreed that the title to the car should not pass to B until his cheque had been honoured. B sold the car to T who sold it to the

---

4 [1927] 1 KB 298, 312, per Scrutton LJ.
5 [1922] 1 KB 343.
6 [1922] 1 KB 343 at 345; see also *Head (Philip) & Sons Ltd v Showfronts Ltd* [1970] 1 Lloyd's Rep 140 (S agreed to sell, stitch together and lay a large carpet for B. The carpet was delivered to B but stolen before it was laid. Mocatta J held that the carpet was not in a 'deliverable state' under s 18, r 5(1) at the date it was stolen, as there was further work to be completed by S, ie the laying of the carpet. No property had passed to B and the risk was thus still on S); cf *Pritchett & Gold and Electrical Power Storage Co Ltd v Currie* [1916] 2 Ch 515 (delivery to B of the components and materials of an electrical battery which were to be assembled by S, was held to be an unconditional appropriation of goods in a deliverable state under s 18, r 5(1)).
7 This was the view of the Law Commissions (*Sale of Goods Forming Part of a Bulk*, Law Com No 215, Scot Law Com No 145, 1993, para 5.6). Cf *Benjamin's Sale of Goods* (5th edn, 1997), para 5-024A, where it is suggested that 'if the parties intend that the undivided share is to remain permanently undivided, for example, where a half share in a racehorse is sold to each of A and B, [rule 1] could apply'. This argument is not elaborated upon but it is presumably based upon the fact that the undivided shares *are* in a deliverable state as nothing further is to be done to them.
8 [1948] 2 KB 164.

defendant. B's cheque was dishonoured. It was held that, under r 1, property passed to B on the fall of the hammer and there was no agreement to the contrary at that time. Accordingly, the defendant acquired a good title to the car.[9]

The most frequent example of contrary intent excluding r 1 is where S and B provide expressly that no property is to pass to B until payment by him. Under s 19(1), S may 'reserve the right of disposal' until certain conditions are fulfilled, eg payment of the price, and such provisions are now commonplace in Romalpa clauses.[10]

Most importantly, there may be situations where, in accordance with s 17, it may reasonably be inferred that the parties intend that property should pass only on payment. In *Ward (R V) Ltd v Bignall*,[11] S and B agreed a price of £850 for two cars which S had for sale and B paid a deposit of £25. He went to his bank to obtain the balance of £825 in cash but then had second thoughts regarding the purchase and tried to persuade S either to accept a lower price or to sell only one of the cars, which entreaties S refused. The decision focused upon S's damages for non-acceptance but, in the course of his judgment, Sellers LJ[12] said that the fact that B had agreed to buy the cars and paid £25 cash 'goes but a little way to establishing that the parties intended the vehicles then and there to become the buyer's property'. He emphasised that payment was to be in cash rather than by cheque, B had not seen the log books and that no arrangements had been made for the insurance or delivery of the cars. Diplock LJ[13] was more direct in stressing that 'the governing rule is ... in section 17, and in modern times very little is needed to give rise to the inference that the property in specific goods is to pass only on delivery or payment'. Similarly, in *Lacis v Cashmarts*[14] it was held that in a 'cash and carry' shop or a supermarket, property passes only on payment of the price and it seems likely that this is the position in most modern retail sales to a consumer. It is thus apparent that, although r 1 specifies that 'it is immaterial whether the time of payment or the time of delivery, or both, be postponed,' the absence of payment and delivery may be crucial in indicating that r 1 does not apply.

As the general rule under s 20(1) is that risk passes with property, an obvious inference to be drawn from a specific clause in the contract placing the risk on B is that the property has passed to him. Equally, such a provision allocating risk to S may be indicative that he has retained property in the goods, but much here depends on the facts and no definite conclusions can be drawn from such a provision in relation to the passing of property.[15] Similarly, an obligation to insure placed on one party may show that risk has passed to him[16] but, again,

---

9 There are three interesting features of *Dennant*: (i) It seems that after property has passed under r 1, the parties may agree that it can revest in S but it is clear that something more is needed than the agreement in *Dennant* that no property should pass until B's cheque is met (see Hallett J at p 172) (ii) On the facts, the defendant could arguably have acquired title by virtue of the SGA, s 25(1)/Factors Act, s 9 (buyer in possession) but this was not pleaded (iii) There could be no question of an operative mistake of identity on the facts and Hallett J considered *Dennant* to be indistinguishable from *Phillips v Brooks* [1919] 2 KB 243.

10 See Ch 17.

11 [1967] 1 QB 534.

12 [1967] 1 QB 534 at 541.

13 [1967] 1 QB 534 at 545.

14 [1969] 2 QB 400.

15 See *Martineau v Kitching* (1872) LR 7 QB 436, 454 per Blackburn J; *The Parchim* [1918] AC 157; *Carlos Federspiel & Co SA v Charles Twigg & Co Ltd* [1957] 1 Lloyd's Rep 240, 255 per Pearson J.

16 *Allison v Bristol Marine Insurance Co Ltd* (1876) 1 App Cas 209, 229 per Blackburn J.

it does not indicate conclusively that property is vested in that party. For example, in *Re Anchor Line (Henderson Brothers) Ltd*,[17] B took over a berth in Glasgow formerly occupied by S and agreed to buy a coaling crane belonging to S on terms that (i) the purchase price of £4,000 was 'deferred' (ii) until completion of the purchase, annual payments were to be made in respect of interest and depreciation, the latter payments to be deducted on completion, and (iii) B was to have 'entire charge of and responsibility for the crane in every respect'. Before completion, B went into liquidation and the dispute was whether property in the crane had passed to B on contract. It was held that the intention was that property would pass to B only on completion/payment of the price and the clause allocating responsibility to B indicated that property had *not* passed under r 1, as the clause would be unnecessary if r 1 applied.

As mentioned earlier, the extended definition of 'specific goods' in the SGA, s 61(1) to include 'an undivided share, specified as a fraction or percentage, of goods identified and agreed on', will mean that r 1 is inapplicable to contracts for the sale of specific goods within this definition. B may thus agree to buy a half share in a living racehorse or 50% of the cargo of wheat aboard a named vessel, but it does seem that the goods will not be in 'deliverable state' at the date of contract in either case. The rules on intent in s 17 will govern the passing of property in such a share in specific goods.[18]

Finally, where there is a contract for the sale of land together with specific goods, the normal inference is that property in the goods is intended to pass only on conveyance and r 1 is thus rebutted,[19] even where a separate price has been agreed for the goods.

SECTION 18, RULE 2

Rule 2 provides:

> 'Where there is a contract for the sale of specific goods and the seller is bound to do something to the goods for the purpose of putting them into a deliverable state, the property does not pass until the thing is done and the buyer has notice that it has been done.'

This rule was based upon the common law in the 19th century and particularly the decision in *Rugg v Minett*.[20] There B bought specific casks of turpentine at auction and, before delivery to B, S was to top-up the casks so that they all contained equal amounts as described in the auction catalogue. Only some of the casks were filled up when an accidental fire destroyed them all and none was delivered. It was held that property passed to B in all the casks which were filled up before loss because nothing further remained to be done to them by S under the contract to put them into a deliverable state. Accordingly, B had to pay only for the casks which were filled up and at his risk. The leading modern application of r 2 is the decision in *Underwood Ltd v Burgh Castle Brick and Cement Syndicate*[1] (considered earlier) where the condensing engine which was

---

17 [1937] Ch 1.
18 See *Sale of Goods Forming Part of a Bulk*, Law Com No 215, Scot Law Com No 145, 1993, para 5.5. See the comment above where 'deliverable state' under r 1 is considered.
19 *Neal v Viney* (1808) 1 Camp 471; *Stamps Comr v Queensland Meat Export Co Ltd* [1917] AC 624.
20 (1809) 11 East 210; see also *Acraman v Morrice* (1849) 8 CB 449 (below).
 1 [1922] 1 KB 343.

the subject of the contract of sale was damaged by S while it was being loaded onto a railway truck. Scrutton and Atkin LJJ applied r 2 in holding that, at the time of the loss, the property in the goods had not passed to B.[2]

'Specific goods' and 'deliverable state' have the same meaning in r 2 as that considered earlier and under r 1. Again, the extended definition of specific goods in the SGA, s 61(1), relating to 'an undivided share, specified as a fraction or percentage, of goods identified and agreed on', would seem to be pertinent within r 2 where the contract is, for example, for the sale of 20% of the cargo aboard a named ship. Here the parties will usually intend that the goods are separated after contract and then delivered to B and thus r 2 may be applicable where S 'is bound to do something to the goods for the purpose of putting them into a deliverable state'.

S is bound to do something to the goods for the purpose of putting them into a deliverable state

Rule 2 applies only where the obligation to put the goods into a deliverable state is placed on S and it seems that B cannot perform the tasks which it is S's duty to perform. In the (pre-Act) decision in *Acraman v Morrice*,[3] the course of business was for B to inspect S's felled trees and mark the portions which he required and S would then cut off the rejected portions and deliver the goods to B. At the time of S's bankruptcy, the timber had been marked and paid for by B but the rejected portions had not been severed. B cut off the rejected parts himself and carried the rest away but it was held that the property had not passed to him.

It should be stressed that the act which S performs is for the purpose of putting the goods into a *deliverable state* and the *passing of property* to B is suspended until the act is done. It is arguable, therefore, that the act in question must be a primary obligation under the contract of sale rather than merely an ancillary commitment. For example, if S agrees to service a car or shoe a horse before delivery to B, these acts may be insufficient to postpone the passing of property, although this will always be a question of the construction of the agreement and there can be no dogmatic rule one way or the other.[4] Again, should S sell the components of a machine and agree to assemble and install it for B, property might pass to B on delivery of the various parts: here it would clearly be arguable that the goods were in a deliverable state and only a subsidiary act remained to be performed by S after delivery.[5]

---

2 Bankes LJ considered that the parties' intent was that the engine should be in a deliverable state and thus no property should pass to B until the engine was safely loaded on a truck.

3 (1849) 8 CB 449.

4 See eg *Hinde v Whitehouse* (1806) 7 East 558 (auction sale of specific lots of sugar stored in a bonded warehouse with duties to be paid by S. Held sale was complete and risk was on B when the sugar was destroyed in a fire before any delivery to B. NB r 2 specifies that S is bound to do something *to the goods* which suggests that they must be *physically* dealt with in some way); Cf *Anderson v Ryan* [1967] IR 34 (B paid S the total price (£225) of a car immediately but S was to do repairs costing £22. Held no property passed until B paid £22 and took delivery).

5 See eg *Pritchett & Gold and Electrical Power Storage Co Ltd v Currie* [1916] 2 Ch 515 (S agreed to sell an electrical battery to B and S was to assemble it on T's premises; the materials/parts for the battery were sent by rail to B but S failed to erect the battery and B finally assembled it himself at T's home. Held this was not a sale of a completed battery but, instead, a sale of the component parts with a *supplemental* obligation that S should erect the battery. Delivery of the parts to B was thus an unconditional appropriation to the contract of goods in a deliverable state under s 18, r 5, and property thereupon passed to him. Here the goods were *unascertained* but the same reasoning could apply to a contract for the sale of specific goods under r 2).

In most situations where goods are to be manufactured by S the contract is one for unascertained goods but it is clear that r 2 applies to a contract for the sale of a *designated* chattel in the course of manufacture where property will not pass until the goods are in a deliverable state and B has notice of that fact.[6]

B has notice that the thing has been done

This requirement of notice was not part of the common law but was introduced by the SGA 1893 and it must be stressed that the requirement is that B 'has notice'. As S need not *give* notice to B, this probably means that B must have actual (rather than constructive) knowledge which may arguably emanate from his own observations or those of his agent.

SECTION 18, RULE 3

Rule 3 provides:

> 'Where there is a contract for the sale of specific goods in a deliverable state but the seller is bound to weigh, measure, test, or do some other act or thing with reference to the goods for the purpose of ascertaining the price, the property does not pass until the act or thing is done and the buyer has notice that it has been done.'

Rule 3 applies only to those situations where *specific* goods are in a *deliverable state* but S has to determine their *price* by a process of weighing, measuring or testing them or doing some other act or thing with reference to them, eg S agrees to sell a particular sack of coffee at £x per pound, S to weigh the coffee to ascertain the total price payable. The rule thus has a limited scope and it should be stressed that in many situations analogous to those envisaged by r 3, the contract will be one for *unascertained* goods, eg B agrees to buy 10 gallons of beer at £x per gallon and S has to draw off the 10 gallons from a 30 gallon barrel.

Rule 3 codifies the common law in the early 19th century and particularly the decision in *Hanson v Meyer*.[7] There B agreed to buy all the starch lying in a certain warehouse at £6 per cwt. although the exact weight was unknown to S and B at the date of contract. S gave B a note which directed the warehouseman to weigh and deliver the starch to B but, when the weighing and delivery was only partially completed, B went bankrupt. S was unpaid and he countermanded the order to deliver the remainder of the starch. It was held that B's assignees must fail in an action of trover as the weighing was a condition precedent to B's right to take possession.

---

6 Eg *Laidler v Burlinson* (1837) 2 M & W 602 (S agreed to complete a ship in his yard and B paid S in advance, although he was not obliged to do so. S went bankrupt before the vessel's completion. Held that no property passed to B until completion and S's assignees in bankruptcy were entitled to the ship).

7 (1805) 6 East 614; *Zagury v Furnell* (1809) 2 Camp 240 (sale of 289 bales of goatskins with five dozen in each bale at 57s 6d per dozen. It was a custom of the trade for S to count the skins before delivery but, before counting, all the bales were destroyed by fire. Held no property passed to B and the goods were at S's risk); *Simmons v Swift* (1826) 5 B & C 857 (S agreed to sell to B 'the bark stacked at Redbrook at £9 5s per ton'; held that no property passed to B until the bark had been weighed and the price ascertained); *Logan v Le Mesurier* (1847) 6 Moo PCC 116 (sale of a raft of red pine timber consisting of 50,000 feet more or less at 9½d per foot; the greater part of the timber was lost in a storm. Held no property passed to B and money paid could be recovered back).

Obligation of S to weigh, measure, test, etc

Under r 3, it is S who must perform the requisite act for ascertaining the price and neither B's weighing[8] nor that of a third party[9] attracts the operation of r 3. Again, it must be emphasised that S's weighing or testing etc, must be the act which suspends the passing of property to B and it was said in *Tansley v Turner*[10] that merely adding-up separate items which had been measured previously was too trifling an incident to postpone the passing of property. This is a question of the construction of the agreement but where the goods have to be counted in order to ascertain the price, the counting may well be the crucial act upon which the passing of property depends.[11] As with r 2, r 3 provides that B must have notice that the weighing etc, has been done and this must have the same meaning as under r 2.

Rule 3 has been criticised as having an uncertain place in English law. Blackburn[12] thought that the principle upon which r 3 was based had been 'somewhat hastily adopted from the civil law' where great emphasis was placed upon a sale for a *certain* price in money but no such stress had been evident in English law[13] until the start of the 19th century. Rule 3 can therefore be rebutted relatively easily by a contrary intent. In *Swanwick v Sothern*,[14] S gave B a delivery order for a specific quantity of oats being the total quantity in a particular bin in W's warehouse and asked W to 'weigh them over' and charge S any expense. B paid for the oats which were transferred to B in W's books but there was no weighing over. It was held that the sale was for a bin of oats for a certain sum and that the weighing was not part of the contract but was only for B's satisfaction. Accordingly, property in the oats passed to B when they were transferred to him in W's books. Indeed, it will often be a natural inference that the contract of sale is complete before the weighing or testing which may thus

---

8 *Turley v Bates* (1863) 2 H & C 200 (S sold a heap of clay to B at 2 shillings per ton, B to weigh the clay at T's premises. Held property passed to B on contract).

9 *Nanka-Bruce v Commonwealth Trust Ltd* [1926] AC 77 (S consigned 160 bags of cocoa to B at 59s per load of 60lbs. B was to resell the cocoa to merchants who were to check the weight and B would pay S according to the weight so checked. On the occasion in question B sold the cocoa to T and delivered the consignment notes to him. T credited B with the purchase price against a large debt which B owed to T. The Privy Council held that the checking of the weights by the merchants was not a condition precedent to the passing of property to B. On the contrary, the sale to B was a completed sale and so T obtained title to the goods. The checking of the weight was simply a means to satisfy the merchants that they had what they bargained for).

10 (1835) 2 Bing NC 151 (sale of timber at 1s 7½d per cubic foot, the felled trees having been marked and measured, all that remained was the completion of a statement showing the total price).

11 See Lord Alverstone CJ's example in *R v Tideswell* [1905] 2 KB 273, 277: if S agreed to sell to B a whole flock of sheep at so much a head and left A to count them and A and B fraudulently arranged that the count should be 25 whereas it was really 30, there would be no larceny as property would have passed to B before the fraudulent agreement. But if S sold as many sheep as B wanted, A and B arranging the count at 25 but 30 were delivered, B would be guilty of larceny of 5 sheep 'as to which there was no contract of sale'.

12 *Contract of Sale* (2nd edn, 1885), p 175. The author stressed that it was often clearly intended that the weighing should be done before B took *possession* but 'that is quite a different thing from intending it to be done before the vesting of the property'.

13 See *Martineau v Kitching* (1872) LR 7 QB 436, 449-451 per Cockburn CJ, who refused to acknowledge a general rule that property should not pass until the price was ascertained – such a rule would 'militate against principle' and was 'inconsistent with common sense and convenience' (p 450). Cockburn CJ preferred a rule based simply on intent.

14 (1839) 9 Ad & El 895.

be simply an administrative and corroborative act to be completed but not an incident which arrests the passing of property.[15]

SECTION 18, RULE 4

Rule 4 provides:

> 'When goods are delivered to the buyer on approval or on sale or return or other similar terms the property in the goods passes to the buyer:–
> (a) when he signifies his approval or acceptance to the seller or does any other act adopting the transaction;
> (b) if he does not signify his approval or acceptance to the seller but retains the goods without giving notice of rejection, then, if a time has been fixed for the return of the goods, on the expiration of that time, and, if no time has been fixed, on the expiration of a reasonable time.'

Rule 4 codifies the common law during the 19th century[16] and its essence is that there is an agreement[17] between S and B that B shall have possession of the goods for a trial period before any property in the goods passes to him. B thus has an option to buy the goods and may elect to buy them under r 4, para (a), or he may choose to reject the goods. Similarly, under r 4, para (b), if B has not rejected the goods, property can pass to him by the lapse of a fixed time or on the expiration of a reasonable time. A contract can be one for sale or return either where B intends to keep the goods himself or where he intends to sell them to a third party.[18] Goods may be delivered on 'other similar terms' within r 4 where they are, for example, 'on approbation'[19] or 'on trial'[20] but the underlying nature of the transaction must relate to B's

---

15 See *Kershaw v Ogden* (1865) 3 H & C 717(B agreed to buy 4 specific stacks of cotton waste at 1s 9d per pound and to send his own sacks and packer to remove them. B sent 81 sacks into which the 4 stacks were put. Two days later, 21 sacks were weighed and taken to B's warehouse but were then returned the same day as being of inferior quality. The other sacks were not weighed. Held that property in all 81 sacks had passed to B); *Martineau v Kitching* (1872) LR 7 QB 436 (sale of specific sugar loaves at 47s per cwt, some of which B left in the possession of S; approximate payment was made in advance of delivery and was subject to adjustment on delivery depending upon weight. A fire destroyed the sugar before B took delivery. The majority did not decide whether property had passed to B, the decision being that the contract's terms (at S's risk for two months, the loss occurring after two months) put the risk on B (but it seems clear that, if it had been necessary to decide whether or not property had passed, the decision would have been that it had passed to B before weighing/delivery). Only Cockburn CJ held that property had passed to B. In a forceful judgment, he stressed that intention was the dominant principle in English law for determining the passing of property and here the true intent of S and B was that property passed to B before the final price was ascertained on delivery; the purpose of the weighing was simply to see if the amount had been accurately ascertained.
16 See eg *Humphries v Carvalho* (1812) 16 East 45; *Elphick v Barnes* (1880) 5 CPD 321; *Blanckensee v Blaiberg* (1885) 2 TLR 36 There is virtually no evidence in the 19th century of B's 'adopting the transaction', as in r 4(a), apart from *Swain v Shepherd* (1832) 1 Mood & R 223, 224, where Parke J refers to the goods being 'received and adopted'.
17 Rule 4 does not apply to *unsolicited* goods. An involuntary bailee is under no obligation to return the goods or communicate with his bailor and cannot be forced into a binding contract as a result of his own silence in not rejecting the goods (see *Felthouse v Bindley* (1862) 11 CBNS 869). See also The Unsolicited Goods and Services Acts 1971 and 1975.
18 See *Poole v Smith's Car Sales (Balham) Ltd* [1962] 1 WLR 744, 748 per Ormerod LJ.
19 *Blanckensee v Blaiberg* (1885) 2 TLR 36.
20 *Ellis v Mortimer* (1805) 1 Bos & PNR 257.

option to purchase.[1] The fact that B is fraudulent in inducing S to deliver goods to him on sale or return will only render the transaction voidable, not void,[2] and thus B will be able to pass a good title to a third party by selling or pledging the goods within r 4(a) before S avoids the sale or return transaction.

Para (a): B signifies his approval to S or adopts the transaction

Few problems have arisen where B signifies his 'approval or acceptance' to S whereupon the property passes to B but difficulties have been caused by the provision that B may do 'any other act adopting the transaction'.[3] An obvious example of such an act occurred in *Astley Industrial Trust Ltd v Miller*.[4] B, a car dealer, had a new car on sale or return from the manufacturer and he then applied for, and received, the log-book from the local authority; Chapman J held that this was an act adopting the transaction.

In less obvious cases, it may be unclear whether B has adopted the transaction and, very soon after the SGA 1893, the law had to face the problem which arose where B pledged the goods with a third party. It is arguable that, in 1893, the draftsman of the SGA did not consider that a pledge of the goods would be an act 'adopting the transaction' as pledging the goods is not normally contemplated under the sale or return contract. Nevertheless, it was established in 1897 that B's pledge of the goods adopted the transaction, meaning that the property in the goods passed to him and thence to the third party pawnbroker. In *Kirkham v Attenborough*,[5] S was a manufacturing jeweller who let B have jewellery on sale or return. B pledged it with the defendant pawnbroker as security for an advance. S claimed the return of the goods or their value from the pawnbroker. The Court of Appeal held that property in the goods passed to B when he pledged the goods and Lord Esher MR did not doubt that this was an adoption, adding that 'any act which is consistent only with his being the purchaser is sufficient'.[6] The defendant thus acquired a good title to the jewellery. It should be stressed that, in the *Kirkham* situation, S's only remedy is against B for the price of the goods and where B is dishonest and has absconded, or is insolvent, the remedy is notional.

In *Kirkham*, the court held that B adopted the transaction by pledging the goods despite the fact that, theoretically, he could have redeemed them from the pawnbroker. Adoption was thus based upon B's pledge being 'inconsistent

---

1   A buyer on sale or return is thus *not* a person who has 'bought or agreed to buy' under the Factors Act 1889 s 9/SGA, s 25(1): see *Percy Edwards Ltd v Vaughan* (1910) 26 TLR 545. In *London Jewellers Ltd v Attenborough* [1934] 2 KB 206, 215, Scrutton LJ thought that, where B has goods on sale or return, although he is not a buyer in possession initially, he might become such a buyer when he exercises his right to sell. This view has not gained acceptance.
2   *London Jewellers Ltd v Attenborough* [1934] 2 KB 206 (B obtained jewellery on sale or return by fraudulently representing that he had a customer to whom he could sell it, his intention from the start being to pledge it. The pledgee acquired a good title under r 4(a)).
3   The wording of r 4 was described in *Kirkham v Attenborough* [1897] 1 QB 201 as 'unfortunately chosen' (per Lord Esher MR, p 203) and 'difficult to construe' (per Lopes LJ, p 204)
4   [1968] 2 All ER 36.
5   [1897] 1 QB 201; followed in *London Jewellers Ltd v Attenborough* [1934] 2 KB 206.
6   [1897] 1 QB 201 at 203.

with his free power to return [the goods]'.[7] This notion is even wider than the formulation that B's act may demonstrate that he is to be treated as a purchaser and it is rather awkward in this context. At the heart of the matter is the question of whether or not B has opted to buy the goods and his inability to return them does not speak volumes regarding their *purchase*: B might correctly be liable for loss of the goods or their destruction but this has little to do with his being a buyer of those goods. That being said, it is indisputable that the *Kirkham* rules have the potential to characterise B's most trivial acts in relation to the goods as indicative of his ownership.

Adoption of the transaction was considered again in the difficult case of *Genn v Winkel*.[8] There S, a diamond merchant, delivered diamonds to B on sale or return terms on 4th January and, on the same day, B delivered them on sale or return to B2. On 6th January, B2 delivered the stones to B3 (probably on sale or return) but B3 lost them. At first instance and in the Court of Appeal it was held that the property in the diamonds passed to B and thus he was liable for the price but the judges gave different reasons for arriving at this conclusion. At first instance, Scrutton J based his decision fairly and squarely on *Kirkham* and B's adoption of the transaction 'by doing something inconsistent with his power to return the goods – namely, handing them to another person who had the power as against him to retain them for a reasonable time while he saw whether he could sell them'.[9] In the Court of Appeal, Vaughan Williams LJ decided that B was responsible for the conduct of those who subsequently obtained possession through his act and the fact that B could not return the goods clearly resulted from his own act. B thus fell within the *Kirkham* adoption principles which the judge did not think were limited to a *deliberate* intention on the part of B to adopt the transaction. Fletcher Moulton and Buckley L JJ did *not* accept that an immediate delivery by B to B2 on sale or return was necessarily an act of B's adopting the transaction because B could still get the goods back from B2 before an unreasonable period had elapsed and return them to S. But both judges thought that, because B2 waited two days before passing the goods on to B3, B2's act amounted to an adoption of the transaction between himself and B and thus B was deemed to have sold the goods to B2. In this convoluted way, B was regarded as having adopted the first transaction with S as he 'must be deemed to be so dealing with the goods as to make it impossible for him to return them to [S]'.[10] The reasoning of the majority thus makes a very awkward amalgam of r 4, paras (a) and (b),[11] as the decision is seemingly based upon both adoption and retention.[12] It is suggested that the judgment of Vaughan Williams LJ is preferable as broadly

---

7   [1897] 1 QB 201 at 203, per Lord Esher MR. Similarly, Lopes LJ thought that B's pledging the goods meant that 'he no longer has the free control over them so as to be in a position to return them' (p 204).

8   (1912) 107 LT 434.

9   (1912) 107 LT 434 at 436.

10   (1912) 107 LT 434 at 438, per Buckley LJ.

11   This view arguably stems from Lopes LJ's judgment in *Kirkham*, who also mixed the two notions of adoption and retention, viz 'If the recipient of the goods retains them for an unreasonable time he does something inconsistent with the exercise of his option to return them, and thereby adopts the transaction' (p 204).

12   Two features emerge from this decision – (i) The arguments on unreasonable lapse of time are unconvincing as B2 waited only two days before transferring the goods to B3. The crucial factor was surely the loss of the goods, meaning that B could not return them within a reasonable time; and (ii) The majority's reasoning turns on the fact that buyers on sale or return have a right to keep the goods for a reasonable period of time, eg if 14 days is a reasonable period on the facts and B waits 7 days before transferring the goods to B2 on

based on agency principles in B's being responsible for the acts of his agent, B2, as a result of which property must be regarded as having passed to B.[13]

There is no direct authority on whether B's excessive use of the goods could amount to an act adopting the transaction and, while it seems indisputable that it could, B's immoderate use of a car (a car dealer who drove the car 1,600 miles in 3 months) was not regarded as an adoption in a leading, modern decision.[14]

Para (b): B's retention of the goods

Property will pass to B under para (b) on the expiration of a fixed time for the return of the goods or, if no time is fixed, on the expiration of a reasonable time. The SGA, s 59 provides that what is a reasonable time is a question of fact, and time begins to run from the moment when B receives the goods.[15] The act of retention must be B's act and not, for example, a seizure of the goods by a sheriff in an execution against B's property, for then B cannot exercise any choice regarding the retention.[16]

It appears from the decision in *Marsh v Hughes-Hallett*,[17] that express time limits are construed strictly thus giving S a measure of protection against dishonest and unscrupulous buyers. In *Marsh*, S let B have possession of his horse on January 22 for one week for 5 guineas and, if satisfied with the horse, B was to pay £65. On January 29, B wrote to S that he had been unable to test the horse adequately and he requested an extension of the time limit. S replied that the 7 days had elapsed and he considered the horse sold. It was held that property passed to B on the expiry of the 7 days.

The question of the lapse of a reasonable time was considered in *Poole v Smith's Car Sales (Balham) Ltd*.[18] At the end of August, S left a Vauxhall Wyvern car with B, a car dealer, on sale or return terms, B having authority to sell it for not less than £325. From October, S kept asking for the return of the car and, finally, on 7 November, he demanded either its return within three days or the payment of £325. The car was returned at the end of November. S refused to accept it as it had been driven 1,600 miles and was in a badly damaged condition having met with an accident while being used, without authority, by B's

---

sale or return, B2 has a *right* to keep the goods, as against B, for 14 days and, as S could demand them back in 7 days from the date of the transfer to B2, B's act must be one adopting the transaction. But this assumes that B has a right to keep the goods for a reasonable period of time and this is not at all clear: everything would seem to turn on the status of the legal relationship when goods are delivered on sale or return (see later). If B is allowed to have the goods for 7 days, does he have a *contractual* right to retain the goods for that period? If not, the goods would have to be returned on demand.

13 Vaughan Williams LJ also based his decision on retention (B could not return the goods in a reasonable time) and adoption (B's act was adoption as it meant that he could not return the goods). See also the pre-Act decision in *Ray v Barker* (1879) 4 Ex D 279 (B had diamond earrings on sale or return and he delivered them to a woman who said she could find a purchaser but, instead, she pledged them and absconded. Held that property passed to B as he could not return the goods in a reasonable time. This reasoning seems preferable to wrestling with the notion of 'adoption').

14 *Poole v Smith's Car Sales (Balham) Ltd* [1962] 1 WLR 744, 751 per Willmer LJ.

15 *Jacobs v Harbach* (1886) 2 TLR 419 (on 10 April, S sent to B a medicinal remedy for horses, on sale or return for six months, which B received on 16 April. Held the six months ran from 16 April).

16 *Gibson v Bray* (1817) 8 Taunt 76; *Re Ferrier* [1944] Ch 295.

17 (1900) 16 TLR 376.

18 [1962] 1 WLR 744.

employees. Bearing in mind the rapid deterioration of second-hand car values in the autumn, the Court of Appeal held that more than a reasonable time had elapsed, the property in the car had therefore passed to B and he was liable for the price of £325.

Notice of rejection

Property will pass to B under r 4, para (b), if B retains the goods 'without giving notice of rejection'. It follows that B may reject the goods within the appropriate time limits before property has passed to him and it is likely that rejection also applies to para (a).

The form of the notice of rejection and its effects have been clarified recently by the decision in *Atari Corpn (UK) Ltd v The Electronics Boutique Stores (UK) Ltd*.[19] There S argued that a notice would be effective only if B described the rejected goods precisely and had them physically available for collection at the time of the notice. This argument was rejected by the Court of Appeal as being commercially impracticable where, as in *Atari*, B had goods distributed among several retail shops. It was also stressed that S's argument confused the two different notions of the actual notice of rejection and B's obligations after rejection. It was held that the notice must unequivocally reject the goods but it was sufficient if the goods to be rejected were described generically[20] and/or in such other way as to enable individual identification later by some objective means. The goods would thus have to be physically available at the time of collection by S. It was also held that the effect of the notice was to determine the sale or return contract and S was then entitled to immediate possession of the goods. Thereafter, B's delay in returning the goods might render him liable for wrongful interference under the terms of the contract.[1] If B does reject and delivers the goods to S, he is entitled to the return of any deposit paid.[2] Moreover, S and B may agree that B can reject the goods only by returning them to S.[3]

There is clear authority that, should B want to reject the goods, he may indicate that he simply does not wish to exercise his option to purchase them and so he need not demonstrate that the goods are unsatisfactory or unfit for their purpose, for example. In *Berry and Son v Star Brush Co*,[4] B received a machine for making brushes on sale or return for 21 days and rejected it within that period because, although it was 'satisfactory in every way,' B feared industrial unrest if the machine were introduced. It was held that B's *bona fide* rejection was valid and he was not confined to rejection by reason only of defects in the machine. The requirement that B must be *bona fide* has never been considered in later decisions but it clearly places *some* limit on his right of rejection.

A further issue regarding rejection arose in *Bradley and Cohn Ltd v Ramsay and Co*.[5] There B had a parcel of black opals on sale or return at a price of

---

19 [1998] QB 539.
20 On the facts, unsold 'Atari Jaguar' stock was sufficient identification.
 1 See also *Ellis v Mortimer* (1805) 1 Bos & PNR 257, 259 per Chambre J.
 2 *Hurst v Orbell* (1838) 8 Ad & El 107.
 3 *Ornstein v Alexandra Furnishing Co* (1895) 12 TLR 128 (contract provided that furniture had to be returned to S; B rejected immediately but refused to return it unless the carriage were paid by S. B finally returned it but it was held that property had passed to him as he had kept the furniture beyond a reasonable time).
 4 (1915) 31 TLR 603.
 5 (1911) 28 TLR 13; affd 106 LT 771.

£750 and he offered S £300 for them. S decided to refuse B's offer but before S could reply, B sold the opals to the defendant for £300. S obtained judgment against B for the price of £750 but this remained unsatisfied as B was adjudicated bankrupt. S consequently sought the return of the opals, or their price, from the defendant. At first instance, Phillimore J considered that B had made a counter-offer which amounted to a rejection of the original sale or return terms and, thereafter, no property in the opals could vest in him. However, on a procedural point, it was held that the judgment obtained against B was accepted by S and amounted to a legal transfer of the goods to B; as a consequence the defendant's title was fed meaning that S could not recover against him. The Court of Appeal considered that, whilst a counter-offer could terminate the sale or return relationship, it did not necessarily do so[6] although Buckley LJ[7] held that, on the facts, B's counter-offer was an outright rejection of the sale or return terms. In any event, the Court of Appeal held that the judgment against B, in which he consented, amounted to an affirmation of his property in the goods and the action against the defendants could not succeed.

Nature of the sale or return transaction

The question of B's right to reject, for any reason, before the end of the trial period and the correlative issue of whether S may withdraw the goods from B during that period, depend upon the legal nature of the sale or return transaction and the character of B's possession during the interval before property passes to him or he rejects the goods. Surprisingly, these primary, functional issues have never been resolved satisfactorily.

If B is a bailee with an option to purchase on the statutory terms, it is arguable that the goods must be returned to S on demand. One possible interpretation of the relationship is thus that S makes an offer to sell to B which B may choose to accept but, following general principles, S may revoke his offer at any time before B's acceptance, even though the offer is said to be open for a specific period.[8]

Alternatively, it is possible to argue that B's promise to consider the purchase of the goods amounts to sufficient consideration moving from him so that S's offer must be kept open for the specified period.[9] Certainly in the early decision in *Ellis v Mortimer*,[10] B was held to be entitled to enjoy the goods during the entire trial period. There B had a horse on trial for one month at a price of 30 guineas if he decided to buy it but, after a fortnight, he told S that he liked the horse but not the price and, accordingly, S asked B to return it. B kept the horse for a further ten days but returned it within the month. S's action for the price failed. The majority[11] held that B had a contract for a month's trial which was not affected by his notification that the price did not suit him;[12] he might thus legitimately change his mind and decide to buy the horse, although he could

---

6 See (1912) 106 LT 771, 774 per Kennedy LJ.

7 (1912) 106 LT 771 at 775.

8 The counter-offer analysis in *Bradley and Cohn Ltd v Ramsay and Co* (1911) 28 TLR 13; affd 106 LT 771 (see above), would arguably support this view.

9 See *Bainbridge v Firmstone* (1838) 8 Ad & El 743.

10 (1805) 1 Bos & PNR 257.

11 Chambre J held that the contract had been 'entirely determined' (p 259) and that B could have been liable in trover.

12 Today, might B be held to have adopted the the transaction, under r 4(a), by keeping the horse for ten days after S's request to return it?

determine the contract before the expiry of the month if he chose. Lord Esher MR[13] likewise took the view that B could return the goods to S but that 'the person who has entrusted them to another cannot demand their return, and his only remedy is to sue for their price or value'. Most recently, Phillips LJ[14] agreed wth this *obiter dictum* and expressed the opinion that S makes an irrevocable offer to B to sell the goods but that B has a right to reject the goods before property passes to him.[15] This analysis is open to the objection that it does not establish a *contract* between S and B prior to the passing of property and so there is no contract into which any terms could be implied regarding, for example, the loss of, or damage to, the goods. It might also be an implied term that S could not demand the return of the goods before the contractual period had run its course, or even that B should keep the goods for the entire period of trial if their premature return might result in adverse publicity for S. It would certainly be desirable to establish that S and B have a contractual relationship in the sale or return period as this would add both certainty and fluidity to the law.[16]

Risk of loss or damage

One solution to the problem of which party should bear the risk of loss or damage would be to put the risk on the party in possession of the goods, but English law has not followed this course. The combination of r 4 and s 20(1), which specifies that risk passes with property, mean that B is not liable for accidental loss or destruction of the goods provided that the loss occurs before the property passes to him under r 4. Clearly, B is not to be regarded as an insurer for S. In *Elphick v Barnes*,[17] B had a horse on eight days trial but it died on the third day without fault of either party. It was held that the horse was still at S's risk and he could not maintain an action for the price. It was most important that there was an accidental loss of the horse and Denman J[18] stressed that if the loss of the goods had occurred through B's fault he 'would have been liable as much as if he had kept them an unreasonable time'.[19] This principle, linking fault with lapse of time, would apply where the goods are lost or destroyed by someone for whom B is responsible as B's inability to return the goods would necessarily mean that he kept them for an unreasonable time.[20] Where neither B nor those for whom he is responsible are at fault in damaging the goods, it appears that they may be *returned* within the fixed (or reasonable) time and it is likely that, following *Elphick*, S would have to accept the goods and B would not be liable.

---

13   *Kirkham v Attenborough* [1897] 1 QB 201, 203.
14   *Atari Corpn (UK) Ltd v Electronics Boutique Stores (UK) Ltd* [1998] QB 539. The other judges did not discuss this point.
15   See also *Janesich v George Attenborough & Son* (1910) 102 LT 605, 607 per Hamilton J: '... it is of the essence of a contract of sale or return that [B] shall have the right for the stipulated period to keep the goods'. *Genn v Winkel* (1912) 107 LT 434 (see above) seems to accept this view as Fletcher Moulton and Buckley LJJ refer to the 'contract' of sale or return and that, in the chain of sale or return transactions from B-B2-B3, B2 and B3 had the 'power' or 'right' to retain the goods for a reasonable time: this reasoning would surely apply with more force if there is an *express* trial period.
16   See Brown, 'The Sale of Goods and Sale or Return Transactions' (1998) 114 LQR 198.
17   (1880) 5 CPD 321.
18   (1880) 5 CPD 321 at 325.
19   This was also the view of Willmer LJ in *Poole v Smith's Car Sales (Balham) Ltd* [1962] 1 WLR 744, 753.
20   *Genn v Winkel* (1912) 107 LT 434, 437, per Vaughan Williams LJ.

Where B negligently damages the goods, his liability is obscure. If property has not passed to B it is impossible to assert that S could refuse to take back the goods and sue for the price; instead, it seems apt to allow B's return of the goods subject to his liability in damages. As mentioned earlier, B's precise legal status during the period of sale or return is unclear. If he is a contractual bailee, he is liable for negligence and carries the burden of proving that the goods were lost or damaged without his fault[1] but if he is classified as a gratuitous bailee he is liable only for 'gross negligence'. The modern tendency is to reject subjective standards of care in negligence[2] but, in sale or return, B is unquestionably classified as a bailee[3] and so this status must be relevant in assessing the requisite standard of care which he must exhibit. Of course, if B negligently damages the goods, it is open to the courts to construe his conduct as an act of adoption under r 4(a). In view of the decision in *Elphick* and the general rule that risk is linked with property, it is not surprising that the sale or return agreement will often provide expressly that the goods are at B's risk during the trial period and that he is liable for the price if they are damaged.[4] Alternatively, this may be the position by virtue of a trade custom.[5]

It is evident that r 4 draws no distinction between the various types of transaction where goods are delivered 'on approval or on sale or return or other similar terms' but these transactions often perform differing functions. A delivery of goods on approval terms is frequently made so that the prospective buyer, sometimes a private consumer, may test the goods in order to ascertain their fitness for his purpose. In other sale or return transactions, the prospective business buyer is able to acquire a stock of goods where he is unwilling or unable to make a capital outlay, the goods thus being acquired for the express purpose of resale to sub-buyers. In the USA, the Uniform Commercial Code follows this distinction and provides[6] that goods are at S's risk where they are on approval (eg to a consumer) but at B's risk in sale or return transactions (eg B, a retailer, acquires his stock on sale or return terms). This simplifies the law considerably and makes the issue as to whether S or B should insure a clear-cut one.

Finally, although considerable emphasis is always placed upon S's rights when B damages the goods, it should be stressed that, should the goods cause injury to B during the trial period, he can have no recourse to the implied conditions of the SGA relating to satisfactory quality and fitness for purpose because no property in the goods has passed to him.

Factors indicating a contrary intention and ousting r 4

It is plain that S must choose his sale or return buyer with care in view of the position regarding damage to the goods and the fact that B may make an

---

1 See eg *Houghland v R R Low (Luxury Coaches) Ltd* [1962] 1 QB 694.
2 See eg *Chaudhry v Prabhakar* [1989] 1 WLR 29 (considered in Ch 7), where the old, subjective standards of care in negligence were rejected in assessing a gratuitous agent's liability in negligence; see Brown, 'The Gratuitous Agent's Liability' [1989] LMCLQ 148.
3 See *Atari Corpn (UK) Ltd v Electronics Boutique Stores (UK) Ltd* [1998] QB 539: 'bailee' (Phillips LJ); 'contractual bailee' (Auld LJ).
4 *Bianchi v Nash* (1836) 1 M & W 545 (musical box on trial to B with the express stipulation that B should pay the price if it were damaged; S recovered the price).
5 See *Bevington v Dale* (1902) 7 Com Cas 112 (furs delivered to B on approval, with invoice, were stolen by burglars. A custom of the trade put the risk on B and S could recover the invoice price).
6 See Articles 2-327(1) and (2).

unauthorised disposition of the goods to a third party (T) and transfer good title to T.[7] In the latter situation, S has no remedy against T and it is cold-comfort that S may sue B for the price if B is a swindler who has absconded or is unable to pay. It may be that the effects of the decision in *Kirkham v Attenborough*,[8] relating to the adoption of the transaction, were not envisaged by the draftsman of the SGA[9] but it is hardly surprising that S often alleges that r 4 is excluded by a contrary intent. In some of the decisions, it is arguable that the courts have been too willing to infer such a contrary intent which ousts r 4 and have thereby coddled S at the expense of the *bona fide* T.

First, r 4 will not apply where the contract specifies some event other than those in r 4 as a condition of the passing of property to B. Most commonly, such a condition precedent is that no property passes to B until the goods are paid for. In *Weiner v Gill*,[10] S delivered jewellery to B, a retail jeweller, on terms of a memorandum stating 'On approbation. On sale for cash only or return. Goods had on approbation or on sale or return remain the property of [S] until such goods are settled for or charged'. The Court of Appeal held that a subsequent pledge did not pass the property in the goods to the defendant pawnbroker as the terms of the memorandum showed clearly that property should not pass to B until he paid for the goods or was debited with the price by S.[11]

Second, the contract may be one of agency rather than sale or return. In *Weiner v Harris*,[12] Weiner (P) a manufacturing jeweller, had been accustomed to send jewellery to a retail jeweller (A) on identical terms to those in *Weiner v Gill* above, but the terms were changed as follows: (i) goods 'on sale or return' were to be entered in a book kept by P; A acknowledged that the goods were P's property until paid for by A; (ii) goods were not to be kept as A's own stock; (iii) A's remuneration for selling the goods was to be one half of the profit; and (iv) after a sale A was to remit to P the cost price and half the profit. A pledged some of the jewellery with the defendant. It was held that the relationship between the parties was one of principal and agent, one dominant reason for this being that A was *remunerated* for selling the goods rather than being an owner/purchaser in his own right.[13] However, A was clearly a

---

7   See the discussion in *London Jewellers Ltd v Attenborough* [1934] 2 KB 206.
8   [1897] 1 QB 201(see above).
9   Where S lends goods to B so that B may assess their suitability, it is a cardinal principle of *nemo dat* that such possession does not enable B to transfer title to T. It is somewhat startling, therefore, that if B has the goods for the same purpose, but on sale or return terms, he may instantly sell them to T and transfer good title under r 4. This result is achieved without B's having a mercantile agency under the Factors Act 1889. See Taylor, 'Goods on Sale or Return and the Nemo Dat Rule' [1985] JBL 390.
10   [1906] 2 KB 574.
11   The same conclusion was reached in *Percy Edwards Ltd v Vaughan* (1910) 26 TLR 545 (B had a pearl necklace on terms that he would 'return it or the cash for it on October 18th'. B pledged the necklace on 13 October. Held that S could recover the necklace from the defendant pawnbroker as property was not intended to pass to B before payment) and *Kempler v Bravingtons Ltd* (1925) 133 LT 680 (diamonds on sale or return on terms that 'the goods ... remain my property until charged by me').
12   [1910] 1 KB 285.
13   See also *Ex p White, re Nevill* (1870) 6 Ch App 397; affd sub nom *John Towle and Co v White* (1873) 29 LT 78 (see Ch 1) (the fact that B paid S a fixed price for the goods and could retain whatever profit he made on sales indicated that the relationship was *not* one of agency but was sale or return. S was not therefore entitled to the profits made by B).

mercantile agent within the Factors Act 1889, s 2(1), and thus the defendant obtained a good title by virtue of that provision.[14]

Third, the intent of S and B may be that property in the goods passes *immediately* to B subject to a condition subsequent that property may revest in S if the goods do not meet with B's approval. A modern example of such a condition subsequent is a purchase of clothes in a retail shop with the proviso that they may be returned if they do not fit. Rule 4 would not apply in this situation and, although property here passes to B at the time of contract, an old and somewhat controversial decision appears to establish that the risk of accidental damage to the goods during the trial period would fall on S.[15]

Finally, it is possible that B might not hold the goods on sale or return terms but, instead, the parties' intent might be to create a bailment with a power to sell or otherwise dispose of the goods and this would mean that property would not pass to the bailee under the terms of r 4.[16]

Passing of property in unascertained goods

The basic steps towards the passing of property in unascertained goods were outlined at the start of this chapter where, also, there was an analysis of the different types of unascertained goods which are recognised in the SGA. It may be helpful to recap briefly: s 16 emphasises that no property in unascertained goods may pass to B unless and until the goods are ascertained but, once they are ascertained, s 17 provides that the property in them may pass at such time as S and B intend.

Again it must be stressed that there is thus a crucial difference between a contract for the sale of specific goods (which may act as a simultaneous conveyance of the property in the goods to B) and an agreement to sell unascertained goods (which cannot convey the property in the goods instantly). In a contract for the sale of unascertained goods, 'common sense dictates that the buyer cannot acquire title until it is known to what goods the title relates'[17] meaning that 'a contract to sell unascertained goods is not a complete sale, but a promise to sell'.[18] The reforms concerning co-ownership introduced by the SGA, ss 20A and 20B, do not alter this basic rule demanding ascertainment of the goods: B may now acquire a *proprietary, undivided share* of goods in an identified bulk but no *property* in the goods can pass to him in the absence of ascertainment.

---

14 *Weiner v Harris* indicates that the FA 1889, s 2(1), is not to be circumvented by a provision that property remains in S but what would be the position if the express terms were that B was in possession as a bailee and not as a mercantile agent? Presumably the FA, s 2(1), was not pleaded in *Weiner v Gill* as B (a retail jeweller) delivered the goods to B2 (a dealer in jewellery) on sale or return and thus the goods could not be in the possession of B2 with the consent of the owner (S); see Ch 18 for detail.

15 See *Head v Tattersall* (1871) LR 7 Exch 7 (horse bought on Monday at an auction, said to have been hunted with the Bicester hounds, but the contract contained a condition that it could be returned on Wednesday if it did not match its description. B returned it within the stipulated time but it had been injured without fault on his part. Held that B could nevertheless return the horse and that depreciation of a chattel ought to fall on the person who is owner of it (ie S)). See also Ch 24 (on risk) and Ch 23 (on rejection).

16 See the discussion in *Whitehorn Bros v Davison* [1911] 1 KB 463.

17 *Re Goldcorp Exchange Ltd* [1995] 1 AC 74, 90 per Lord Mustill.

18 *Badische Anilin und Soda Fabrik v Hickson* [1906] AC 419, 421 per Lord Loreburn LC.

There are several other striking features of agreements to sell unascertained goods which should be accentuated, viz:

(i)   It is immaterial to the issue of passing of property that B may have paid the purchase price in full before any ascertainment of the goods, this being prejudicial to B where S became insolvent before ascertainment but beneficial to S's creditors who obtained a windfall as a consequence of the lack of ascertainment.[19] Moreover, at common law, the notion of co-ownership was guarded jealously and the fact that several buyers had paid for the goods which constituted an identified bulk did not generally result in their being co-owners of that bulk.[20]

(ii)   Although property cannot pass to B in unascertained goods, the risk may pass to him where there is an identified bulk[1] and the contract frequently provides that the goods are at his risk (s 20(1), linking risk and property, applies 'unless otherwise agreed').

(iii) The lack of property in B may prevent his suing in tort for loss or damage to the goods.[2]

(iv)   It is impossible for S and B to contract-out of s 16 and allow property to pass to B before any ascertainment.[3]

When do the goods become 'ascertained'?

It is plain that the process of ascertainment is not as rigorous as that envisaged by 'unconditional appropriation' of the goods to the contract under s 18, r 5, considered later. Nevertheless, ascertainment demands that the goods be physically identified and their individuality established as the goods which are the subject-matter of the contract. For example, in *Thames Sack and Bag Co Ltd v Knowles & Co Ltd*,[4] the contract was for the sale of ten bales of Hessian bags on terms that the bags were ready for immediate delivery and an invoice was sent to B, after contract, which gave the specific numbers and marks of the bales from which the ten were to be taken. B did not pay promptly in accordance with the contract and S refused to deliver the bags. Sankey J held that S was entitled to cancel the contract and that, in any event, the goods were not ascertained and so specific performance could not be ordered under the SGA, s 52. It is difficult to conceive that the location of the unascertained goods could be *identified* any more precisely than this but, of course, the ten bales to be sold had not been separated from the remainder. It will be remembered that the goods were similarly held to be unascertained in *Re Wait*,[5] where Atkin LJ[6] considered that '"ascertained" probably means identified in

---

19 See *Re Wait* [1927] 1 Ch 606 (considered earlier). The co-ownership provisions in the SGA, ss 20A and 20B, now apply to the facts of *Re Wait*.
20 See *Laurie and Morewood v Dudin & Sons* [1926] 1 KB 223; *Re Wait* [1927] 1 Ch 606; *Karlshamns Oljefabriker v Eastport Navigation Corpn, The Elafi* [1982] 1 All ER 208.
1   See *Sterns Ltd v Vickers Ltd* [1923] 1 KB 78 (considered in Ch 24). B has an insurable interest in goods at his risk: see *Inglis v Stock* (1885) 10 App Cas 263.
2   See *Leigh and Sillivan Ltd v Aliakmon Shipping Co Ltd, The Aliakmon* [1986] AC 785.
3   *Karlshamns Oljefabriker v Eastport Navigation Corpn, The Elafi* [1982] 1 All ER 208, 212 per Mustill J.
4   (1918) 88 LJKB 585.
5   [1927] 1 Ch 606.
6   [1927] 1 Ch 606 at 630.

accordance with the agreement after the time a contract of sale is made, and I shall assume that to be the meaning'.[7]

The *Thames Sack and Bag* case is an archetypal, unsophisticated agreement for the sale and delivery of unascertained goods. In the 20th century, goods became infinitely more complex than in the 19th century and businesses grew to be transnational in scale. Moreover, with the advent of computers, it became possible to store and collate vast amounts of material capable of revealing instantly the physical whereabouts of goods anywhere in the world. Nevertheless, it remains an indelible fact that goods are physical objects and where the contract is one for the sale of unascertained goods, the passing of property is contingent on ascertainment of the goods, no matter how accurately their location is catalogued and described. This rudimentary principle was most pronounced in *Re Stapylton Fletcher Ltd*.[8] S was a vintner who entered into contracts to sell wine to buyers and also to store it for them indefinitely at a charge. Cases of wine of the same type/vintage which had been ordered by several buyers were mixed in stacks in a 'customers' reserve area', but different types/vintages were never mixed in the same stack. Although the cases were not identified with the buyers' names, S had a detailed and efficient index system which recorded all the buyers and the number of cases allocated to each. In the absence of any further physical ascertainment of the bottles of wine to the various buyers, no property in the goods could pass to them. Nevertheless, on S's insolvency, it was held that there had been sufficient ascertainment of the goods, under s 16, for a *tenancy in common* to exist at common law. Consequently, under s 17, property in the ascertained goods passed to the buyers as co-owners, this being their implied, common intent. Judge Paul Baker QC considered that, as the goods were to be stored by S, ascertainment was achieved by the segregation of the goods from S's trading stock and there was no compelling reason why, on such facts, each buyer's cases had to be separated from the stacks of wine.[9] It was stressed earlier that co-ownership is now a recognised aspect of the sale of goods and, provided certain conditions are met, B can acquire an undivided, proprietary share of goods in an identified bulk under the SGA, ss 20A and 20B. In the absence of ascertainment, however, B is limited to such a proprietary *share* and property in the physical goods cannot pass to him.

Once the goods become ascertained, property in them may then pass to B according to the parties' intent at any moment they specify, eg at the moment of actual ascertainment,[10] on delivery to B or at some time after delivery.[11] It should be stressed that property *may* pass once the goods are ascertained but, in order to do so, the parties' common intent must be clear as to the moment at which property is to pass.[12] However, as in the case of agreements to sell specific goods,

---

7 See also *Healy v Howlett & Sons* [1917] 1 KB 337 and *Laurie and Morewood v Dudin & Sons* [1926] 1 KB 223 on the meaning of 'ascertainment' (both considered later).
8 [1994] 1 WLR 1181.
9 [1994] 1 WLR 1181 at 1199-1200.
10 *Reeves v Barlow* (1884) 12 QBD 436 (contract to build houses which provided that building materials brought onto land should become the landowner's property. Held that 'the moment the goods were brought upon the premises the property in them passed in law ... no further performance of the contract was necessary, nor could be enforced' (per Bowen LJ, p 442).
11 *Armitage v John Haigh & Sons Ltd* (1893) 9 TLR 287 (contract for S to 'deliver and set up' machines in B's mill to be paid for three months after delivery. Hearing of B's impending bankruptcy, S took away the machines. Held property in the machines had not passed to B at the date of S's seizing them as they had not been 'set up' to function properly).
12 But see *Wait and James v Midland Bank* (1926) 31 Com Cas 172 (below), where such *common* intent seemed to be absent.

S and B often fail to fix the moment that property will pass to B. If no clear intent is evident regarding the moment of the passing of property, s 18, r 5(1) locks into place and specifies that property will pass only when the goods are 'unconditionally appropriated to the contract'. Rule 5(2) deals with appropriation by delivery and r 5(3) and (4) embody the rule of appropriation by exhaustion. Now that the SGA, ss 20A and 20B provide for co-ownership of goods held by S in bulk, it is necessary to consider contracts to sell an unsegregated part of an identified bulk as a separate topic.

SECTION 18, RULE 5

Rule 5(1) provides:

> 'Where there is a contract for the sale of unascertained or future goods by description, and goods of that description and in a deliverable state are unconditionally appropriated to the contract, either by the seller with the assent of the buyer or by the buyer with the assent of the seller, the property in the goods then passes to the buyer; and the assent may be express or implied, and may be given either before or after the appropriation is made.'

Rule 5(1) codifies the common law[13] which existed before the SGA 1893. The meaning of 'unascertained or future goods' and 'deliverable state'[14] were considered earlier in this chapter. There are two decisive features of r 5(1). First, the goods must be *unconditionally appropriated* to the contract by either S or B and, second, either S or B must *assent* to that appropriation made by the other party. Rule 5(2) sets down one fundamental way in which goods can be appropriated, viz the seller delivers the goods to the buyer or to a carrier for the purpose of transmission to the buyer. The two elements of appropriation and assent must now be evaluated separately.

APPROPRIATION OF THE GOODS UNDER RULE 5(1)

What does 'unconditional appropriation' entail?

The cardinal elements in r 5(1) are those of 'unconditional appropriation' and 'assent' to that appropriation. In the decision in *Wait v Baker*,[15] Parke B considered that 'appropriation' could be understood in different senses, but he emphasised that the central postulate regarding that notion is that 'property does not pass until there is a bargain with respect to a specific article, and everything is done which, according to the intention of the parties to the bargain, was necessary to transfer the property in it'.[16]

It was this axiom which Sir MacKenzie Chalmers, the draftsman of the SGA, sought to embody in r 5(1) but it is plain from Parke B's statement in

---

13 See eg *Rohde v Thwaites* (1827) 6 B & C 388; *Aldridge v Johnson* (1857) 7 E & B 885 (both considered below); *Wait v Baker* (1848) 2 Exch 1.
14 See the earlier consideration of this phrase in s 18, rr 1, 2 and 3 and, in particular: *Pritchett & Gold and Electrical Power Storage Co Ltd v Currie* [1916] 2 Ch 515; *Head (Philip) & Sons Ltd v Showfronts Ltd* [1970] 1 Lloyd's Rep 140.
15 (1848) 2 Exch 1.
16 (1848) 2 Exch 1 at 9.

Wait v Baker that the concept of appropriation may be somewhat elusive both in nature and application. Indeed, although he codified the common law faithfully, Chalmers's preference was that delivery should be the determining factor for the passing of property in r 5(1). Delivering a lecture in 1890 on the Sale of Goods Bill, he said that 'the other rules work well and intelligibly enough, but if delivery were substituted as the test in rule 5, I think that the law would be greatly simplified, while very few cases would be differently decided to what they are now. The preliminary controversy would be saved, while the result would remain practically the same'.[17] This assertion was present even in the last edition of Chalmers's book,[18] where it was suggested that 'if the decisions be carefully examined, it will be found that in every case where the property has been held to pass, there has been an actual or constructive delivery of the goods to the buyer'.[19] It is doubtful, however, whether the substitution of 'delivery' for 'appropriation' in r 5(1) would have made the law any clearer because, assuming that *constructive* delivery would be permissible, this is at least as elusive and impenetrable a notion as that of appropriation.

An 'unconditional appropriation' means that the goods must be identified as those which are the subject matter of the contract and it involves an overt act of one party irrevocably earmarking ascertained goods to the contract in question. The question of assent to the appropriation will be considered later but suffice to say at this stage that, as the appropriation is the act which passes the property in the goods, it must be done with the prior or subsequent assent of the other party. It should be noted that the appropriating act can be performed by either S or B: in the most straightforward example, S will appropriate the goods and B will then assent to the appropriation.

It cannot be stressed enough that unconditional appropriation entails an *irrevocable* act identifying the goods to which there is *mutual* assent of S and B: a mere selection of goods by one party which is revocable and which does not attach the goods to the contract will not constitute unconditional appropriation under r 5. Where, for example, S selects goods from bulk and intends that they be delivered to B in performance of the contract, the goods are undoubtedly 'ascertained' and thus property could then pass from S to B under ss 16 and 17 if that is their intent. In this example, the law does not consider the goods to have been irrevocably and unconditionally appropriated as belonging to B because S might choose to sell the designated goods to B2 and simply select other, identical goods from his stock for B.[20] The process of unconditionally appropriating the goods with assent under r 5 thus means that the goods are finally identified *and* agreed upon by both parties as the subject-matter of the contract so that nothing remains to be done and the property in the goods may then pass to B.

The emphasis upon *unconditional* appropriation means that property must pass by the appropriating act and not upon the occurrence of some other event

---

17 'The Codification of the Law of Sale' (1891) 12 Journal of the Institute of Bankers 11, 18.
18 *Sale of Goods Act 1979* (18th edn, 1981).
19 *Sale of Goods Act 1979* (18th edn, 1981), p 151 (this passage was approved by Pearson J in *Carlos Federspiel & Co SA v Charles Twigg & Co Ltd* [1957] 1 Lloyd's Rep 240, 255-256).
20 *Carlos Federspiel & Co SA v Charles Twigg & Co Ltd* [1957] 1 Lloyd's Rep 240, 255 per Pearson J.

such as payment.¹ Under s 19(1), S may, by the terms of the contract or the appropriation, 'reserve the right of disposal' of the goods until certain conditions are fulfilled, eg payment or tender of the price.² It follows that the paradigm of unconditional appropriation is that given in r 5(2), viz S delivers the goods to B or to a carrier for transmission to B and S does *not* reserve the right of disposal.

The application of 'unconditional appropriation' in the decisions

The stages along the road to unconditional appropriation were considered in *Wardar's (Import and Export) Co Ltd v W Norwood & Sons Ltd*.³ S had 1,500 cartons of kidneys in cold storage in London and sold 600 of them to B. S gave B's carrier a delivery note authorising him to collect 600 cartons and, when the carrier arrived at the cold store, 600 cartons had already been placed on the pavement. B's carrier handed over the delivery note and the cartons were loaded into the carrier's lorry. When the cartons arrived at B's premises in Glasgow the kidneys were unfit for human consumption. There was no evidence that the kidneys had deteriorated before the carrier loaded them. The Court of Appeal held that there was an unconditional appropriation of the goods passing the property to B when the delivery order was handed over to the cold store (which was S's agent). At that moment, the cold store acknowledged that the goods belonged to B and, as the goods deteriorated subsequently, the risk fell on B and he was liable for the price.

The decision in *Carlos Federspiel & Co SA v Charles Twigg & Co Ltd*,⁴ considers the meaning of appropriation in some detail. S agreed to sell a quantity of bicycles to B, an importer in Costa Rica, B paying for the goods in advance. The bicycles were packed at S's premises and marked with B's name. Moreover, S informed B of the shipping marks of the consignment and that the goods had been registered for shipment, although the goods never left S's premises. S then became insolvent, and the receiver refused to deliver them to B. It was held that no property in the goods had passed to B. Pearson J pointed out that (i) the setting apart or selection by S of the goods which he *expects* to use in performance of the contract is not enough for appropriation because S can change his mind and use those goods in performance of some other contract (ii) appropriation involves an intent to attach the contract irrevocably to the goods (iii) appropriation will generally be the last act to be performed by S and, on the facts, this would have been actual shipment of the goods.

The decision in *Hendy Lennox (Industrial Engines) Ltd v Grahame Puttick Ltd*,⁵ makes an interesting contrast with *Twigg's* case. The agreement was to sell generator sets to B which were set-aside at S's premises and marked with B's name. Staughton J held that the generators were only appropriated to the contracts when S sent B an invoice and delivery note with the serial numbers of

---

1 See eg *Godts v Rose* (1854) 17 CB 229 (S agreed to sell to B five tons of oil 'to be free delivered and paid for in fourteen days'. S had oil lying at a wharf and told the wharfinger to transfer certain casks into B's name and he then sent his clerk to B's counting house with a transfer order which was to be exchanged for a cheque. B obtained the transfer order but refused to give a cheque and thus the clerk informed the wharfinger not to deliver the oil. Despite this the oil was delivered to B but it was held that, in the absence of payment, no property in the goods passed to him).
2 See Ch 17.
3 [1968] 2 QB 663.
4 [1957] 1 Lloyd's Rep 240.
5 [1984] 1 WLR 485.

the generators. At that stage, S was no longer free to substitute other generators for those which had been earmarked and all that remained was for B to take delivery.

Appropriation of future goods

It will be remembered that future goods are defined in s 61(1) as 'goods to be manufactured or acquired by the seller after the making of the contract of sale'. There was a strong presumption at common law[6] that property in future goods to be manufactured by S passed to B only when the goods were completed and appropriated to the contract by S with the assent of B[7] and this presumption is, of course, embodied in r 5(1). Moreover, the courts are equally reluctant to infer that the parties intended there to be an appropriation and passing of property in the *materials* used in the construction of the goods before they become part of the fabric of those goods.[8]

The decision in *Reid v Macbeth and Gray*[9] is a pronounced example of this reluctance. A contract for the construction of a ship provided in clause 4 that 'the vessel as she is constructed ... and all materials from time to time intended for her [wherever situated] shall immediately as the same proceeds become the property of [B]'. Before the ship was completed S became bankrupt and various iron and steel plates were lying at railway stations, the plates having been passed by a Lloyd's surveyor and marked with the position each was to occupy in the ship. The House of Lords held that the plates were still the property of S. Lord Davey stressed that clause 4 meant that the materials would become B's property only when they became part of the structure of the ship and that 'there is only one contract – a contract for the purchase of a ship. There is no contract for the sale or purchase of these materials separatim'.[10]

The presumption in r 5 can give way in the face of a different intention of the parties and Lord Watson emphasised in *Seath & Co v Moore*,[11] that it was possible to frame a contract so that, at any stage in the construction of a ship, the property in it could pass to B and that subsequent additions would become B's property by accession. Certainly property in a vessel passed to B before its completion in *Re Blyth Shipbuilding and Dry Docks Co Ltd*.[12] There the shipbuilding contract provided for the payment of the price in instalments and the work was supervised by B's surveyor. Clause 6 of the contract further provided that property in the vessel should pass to B on payment of the first instalment.

---

6 It was emphasised earlier that the equitable notions of 'potential property' and equitable assignments of future goods did not survive the SGA 1893.
7 *Mucklow v Mangles* (1808) 1 Taunt 318 (contract to build a barge with the price paid in advance: B's name was painted on the stern before completion but two days after completion the barge was seized by the sheriff under an execution. Held no property passed to B); *Atkinson v Bell* (1828) 8 B & C 277 (B ordered two machines to be built by S which were packed in boxes and S wrote to B asking what method of delivery was required. S then went bankrupt. Held that no property passed to B and S failed in an action for the price); *Laidler v Burlinson* (1837) 2 M & W 602 (contract to complete a ship, B voluntarily paying his ¼ share of the price in advance. S then went bankrupt. Held that property in the incomplete ship remained in S and S's assignees were entitled to it); cf *Carruthers v Payne* (1828) 5 Bing 270.
8 *Seath & Co v Moore* (1886) 11 App Cas 350, 381 per Lord Watson.
9 [1904] AC 223.
10 [1904] AC 223 at 232.
11 (1886) 11 App Cas 350, 380.
12 [1926] Ch 494.

After payment of two instalments, S went into receivership. It was held that property in the incomplete ship passed to B but materials in the yard which had not been incorporated in the vessel had not passed to B. Here there was an express term as to the passing of property but, in the absence of such a term, it is difficult to *infer* an intent that property should pass to B before completion. In *Seath*,[13] Lord Watson considered that such an intent ought to be inferred from a provision that B should pay an instalment of the price at a particular stage of construction and, further, that the price was duly paid and that, before the stage was reached, the work was regularly inspected by B or his agent. In this way, property in the incomplete vessel could pass to B. It has been stressed, however, that these facts are not conclusive and it must always be asked 'what the contract really means'.[14]

Future goods are also defined as goods to be *acquired* by S and, again, the rule is strict in demanding that only the completion of the delivery to B will suffice as an act of unconditional appropriation. In *Flynn v Mackin and Mahon*,[15] S agreed to supply B with a new, blue Vauxhall Viva car which S was to acquire from T, a motor dealer. Whilst S was driving the Vauxhall to B for the purpose of delivering it, S was involved in an accident with the plaintiff who was badly injured. The plaintiff sought to establish that property in the car had passed to B and S was driving it as B's agent. On the facts, the court held that the agreement between S and B was one of barter or exchange and was not an agreement for the sale of the goods. However, Walsh J considered that, if the agreement had been within the SGA, there would have been no unconditional appropriation of the car by S's driving it to B to deliver it. This was because there was nothing in the contract between S and B to prevent S from selling the car to a third party while he was *en route* to B's home. Although this occurrence would be unlikely, it was nevertheless possible and permissible. S's obligation was simply to sell a new, blue Vauxhall Viva and, if he had sold the first car, he could have supplied B with another car which fitted that description.

APPROPRIATION BY DELIVERY UNDER RULE 5 (2)

Appropriation by delivery is covered specifically in r 5(2) which provides:

> 'Where, in pursuance of the contract, the seller delivers the goods to the buyer or to a carrier or other bailee or custodier (whether named by the buyer or not) for the purpose of transmission to the buyer, and does not reserve the right of disposal, he is to be taken to have unconditionally appropriated the goods to the contract.'

13 (1886) 11 App Cas 350, 380.
14 *Sir James Laing & Sons Ltd v Barclay, Curle & Co Ltd* [1908] AC 35, 43 per Lord Loreburn LC (construction of ships with price paid in instalments and under the superintendence of B's agent but with a provision that delivery was not to be complete until the ships passed certain trials. Held that no property passed before completion and trials took place); *McDougall v Aeromarine of Emsworth Ltd* [1958] 1 WLR 1126 (construction of a yacht with provision that property in it and all materials would pass on payment of the first instalment. Held no property could pass at that time as construction had not commenced and the materials had not been identified).
15 [1974] IR 101.

Rule 5 (2) is simply a particular application of r 5(1) in providing that delivery of the ascertained goods to B or to a carrier is the archetypal, unconditional appropriation, and the rule codifies the common law before the SGA 1893.[16]

It is essential to emphasise that the goods must become ascertained by the delivery and, if so, they are deemed to be unconditionally appropriated to the contract, but a delivery of *unascertained* goods to a carrier cannot pass the property to B under r 5(2). In *Healy v Howlett & Sons*,[17] S, a fish exporter carrying on business in Ireland, agreed to sell to B 20 boxes of 'hard, bright mackerel'. S despatched 190 boxes of mackerel by rail, instructing the railway officials at Holyhead to deliver 20 of the boxes to B and the remaining 170 boxes to two other consignees. The train arrived late at Dublin and the consignment missed the boat to Holyhead. Consequently, the fish deteriorated before they were earmarked at Holyhead. It was held that the property in the goods could not pass to B before the boxes were earmarked and thus the fish was still at S's risk at the time it deteriorated. Accordingly, B was not liable for the price. Ridley J[18] considered that, if delivery to the carrier in Ireland were to have passed the property, 'each box ought to have been marked with the name of its consignee' but S had not done this as he did not want rival exporters poaching his customers. The rule in *Healy* may be helpful to consumer buyers where, for example, an independent carrier has 15 identical beds on his lorry which are to be delivered to 15 buyers in one day but the lorry is involved in an accident *en route* to the first buyer. It is very likely that the beds in the lorry would be unascertained goods and thus the property and risk would not have transferred to the buyers at the date of the accident.

The most obvious application of r 5(2) is where there is a delivery of the ascertained goods to B or his agent[19] and there will then be an unconditional appropriation of the goods to that contract. If the *ascertained* goods are in the possession of a third party, T, (eg a warehouseman) delivery occurs when T attorns to B, thereby acknowledging that he holds the goods on B's behalf.[20] There must be an attornment, however, and if T merely *receives* a delivery order and does not separate the goods from bulk, no property will pass to B.[1]

---

16 See eg *Dutton v Solomonson* (1803) 3 Bos & P 582, 584, per Lord Alvanley; *Ogle v Atkinson* (1814) 5 Taunt 759 (B sent his own ship for the goods and S delivered them on board. Held property passed immediately to B); *Fragano v Long* (1825) 4 B & C 219 (hardware despatched by S marked with B's initials and insured on his account. Held property passed when the goods left S's warehouse and B could sue the defendant who damaged the goods while they were being put on board a ship); *Re Wiltshire Iron Co* (1868) 3 Ch App 443 (S placed iron in railway trucks and sent invoices to B, the trucks being moved to the line of the GWR, and then a winding-up order was made against S. Held property had passed to B).

17 [1917] 1 KB 337.

18 [1917] 1 KB 337 at 343.

19 *Ogle v Atkinson* (1814) 5 Taunt 759 (B sent his own ship for the goods which were delivered to the captain as B's property. Held property passed absolutely on delivery on board the ship).

20 See *Wardar's (Import and Export) Co Ltd v W Norwood & Sons Ltd* [1968] 2 QB 663 (considered above).

1 *Laurie and Morewood v Dudin & Sons* [1926] 1 KB 223 (T held 618 quarters of maize belonging to S. S sold 200 quarters to B and B resold them to B2 giving B2 a delivery order which he lodged with T. Before any severance from bulk had occurred, S stopped delivery as he was unpaid. Held no property had passed to B).

When ascertained goods are delivered to a carrier, s 32(1)[2] must be considered in tandem with r 5(2). Under s 32(1), delivery of the goods to a carrier for transmission to B is prima facie deemed to be delivery to B and so the combined effect of r 5(2), ss 32(1) and 20(1) (risk passes with property) is that property in the goods and risk normally pass to B when they are delivered to the carrier. The justification of these rules is that, in engaging the carrier, S acts as an agent for B, and the carrier then becomes the agent of B.[3] However, s 32(1) provides that this is only the 'prima facie' rule and it will not apply where the terms of the contract or appropriation provide that the carrier is S's agent and, in this case, property and risk normally pass when the goods are actually delivered to B or his agent.[4] The carrier will usually be regarded as S's agent where S agrees to deliver the goods at a particular *place*, the intent of the parties then being that no property should pass until delivery at that place.[5]

The underlying assumption of the general rule on delivery to a carrier is that B is deemed to have authorised S to pass the property in this way[6] and this is reflected in the wording of r 5(2) that delivery to B or to the carrier must be 'in pursuance of the contract'. It follows that the goods must be despatched by the authorised mode and in the time fixed by the contract.[7] But it should be noted that r 5(2) does not expressly refer to B's deemed assent to the appropriation: the assumption that B does assent is undoubtedly apt in many commercial sales but it is clearly inapt in modern consumer sales where the rule means that, for example, the posting of goods to a consumer who has ordered them from a catalogue passes the property and risk to B. This outcome would arguably follow from the decision in *Badische Anilin Und Soda Fabrik v Basle Chemical Works, Bindschedler*,[8] where B, a business buyer, ordered goods from S in Switzerland to be sent by post with B's paying the postal charges. The goods were manufactured according to an invention protected by an English patent and the disputed issue was whether S had 'made, used, exercised or vended' the invention within the ambit of the UK patent. The House of Lords held that S had not done so as the contract of sale was completed by the delivery of the goods to the Post Office in Switzerland. The Post Office was thus B's agent and property passed to B when the goods were delivered to the Post Office in Switzerland. The central issue in this business sale was whether the patent had been infringed and it is very likely that, in consumer sales, the court would infer a contrary intent under ss 17 and 32(1), so that property and risk would pass to B on delivery at his home. Nevertheless, it is suggested that the SGA should be amended to that effect.

Rule 5(2) will be inapplicable where S has, by the terms of the contract or the appropriation, 'reserved the right of disposal' (eg a condition that no property passes to B until payment). Similarly, in the case of cif contracts, the inference

2 See Ch 24 on the question of risk, where s 32(1) is considered in more detail.
3 *Wait v Baker* (1848) 2 Exch 1, 7, per Parke B.
4 *Wait v Baker* (above); *Badische Anilin Und Soda Fabrik v Basle Chemical Works, Bindschedler* [1898] AC 200, 207, per Lord Herschell; *Harrison v Lia* [1951] VLR 470.
5 See *Dunlop v Lambert* (1839) 6 Cl & Fin 600, 621 per Lord Cottenham LC; *Calcutta and Burmah Steam Navigation Co v De Mattos* (1863) 32 LJQB 322, 328 per Blackburn J; *Badische Anilin Und Soda Fabrik v Basle Chemical Works, Bindschedler* [1898] AC 200, 207, per Lord Herschell.
6 See *James v Commonwealth* (1939) 62 CLR 339, 377, where Dixon J, referring to a contract for the sale of unascertained goods by description, considered that 'the terms of the contract import the prior assent of the buyer' to S's appropriation by delivery to the carrier.
7 See eg *Aron (J) & Co Inc v Comptoir Wegimont* [1921] 3 KB 435.
8 [1898] AC 200.

that property passes on shipment is usually rebutted as S holds the documents against the price and the parties' intent is thus that property passes on the unconditional transfer of the bill of lading.

ASSENT TO THE APPROPRIATION UNDER RULE 5(1)

It was emphasised earlier that an act of appropriation by one party will not pass the property in the goods under r 5(1) unless the appropriation is accompanied by the *assent* of the other party. Appropriation entails an overt act earmarking the goods to the contract but assent relates to the vital process of *agreement* by which property in the goods passes from S to B. The assent can come from either S or B.[9] Moreover, it may be express or implied and given before or after the appropriation is made. The question of assent will be considered according to the difficulties which commonly arise, most problems ensuing from B's assent.

Subsequent assent of B

This is the commonplace situation where S designates certain goods as those which he intends to attach to the contract and then informs B that they have been appropriated. If B subsequently assents to the appropriation, expressly or by conduct, property in the goods passes to B at the moment of assent, even though the goods have not been delivered to him. In *Rohde v Thwaites*,[10] for example, B agreed to buy 20 hogsheads of sugar from a bulk in S's warehouse: 4 hogsheads were delivered to B and S then filled and appropriated the other 16 and gave notice to B to take them away, which B promised to do. It was held that property thereupon passed to B and S could recover the price from B. The same reasoning applies to goods manufactured by S when B is told that they are completed and B approves them.[11]

B's assent in *Rohde* was express but assent can be implied from conduct as where B gives instructions for an insurance policy to be effected on the goods,[12] where he is informed that goods are shipped aboard a certain vessel and he retains the bill of lading,[13] or where he pays the price after notification that the goods are ready for delivery.[14] Moreover, the tender of the delivery

---

9 The assent need not be given by S or B personally but may be given by an agent, see *Campbell v Mersey Docks and Harbour Board* (1863) 14 CBNS 412, 415 per Erle CJ and 416 per Willes J.

10 (1827) 6 B & C 388.

11 *Elliott v Pybus* (1834) 10 Bing 512 (B ordered a machine to be made by S. On completion, he acknowledged that it was made according to order, made a part-payment and requested S to deliver it. B then refused to pay the agreed price. Held that property had passed to B and S succeeded for the price); *Wilkins v Bromhead* (1844) 6 Man & G 963 (S built a greenhouse for B and informed B of its completion; B sent the price and asked S to keep the greenhouse until sent for. S's assignees in bankruptcy seized the greenhouse. Held property had passed to B); *Donaghy's Rope and Twine Co Ltd v Wright, Stephenson & Co Ltd* (1906) 25 NZLR 641.

12 *Sparkes v Marshall* (1836) 2 Bing NC 761 (B was informed by S that barrels of oats were shipped aboard *Gibraltar* and B showed his assent by insuring the oats. Held B could sue on the policy when the ship was lost).

13 *Alexander v Gardner* (1835) 1 Bing NC 671 (200 firkins of butter to be shipped in October were not shipped until November but B waived any objection and retained the invoice and bill of lading. In December the ship was wrecked. Held property had passed to B).

14 *Wilkins v Bromhead* (1844) 6 Man & G 963; *Elliott v Pybus* (1834) 10 Bing 512 (above).

note and its acceptance by the cold store in *Wardar's*[15] case (above) amounted to an appropriation by S with B's assent.

It also clear that assent may be inferred from silence as in *Pignataro v Gilroy*.[16] There the contract was for the sale of 140 bags of rice with delivery to be taken in 14 days. B sent S a cheque and asked for a delivery order which S sent for 125 bags lying at a wharf and told B that the remaining 15 bags were ready for collection at S's premises. S asked that B should send for the 15 bags 'at once' as he (S) was short of room. B did not seek delivery of the 15 bags until a month had elapsed during which time they had been stolen. It was held that B's assent must be inferred from the month's silence and thus he was liable for the price. Rowlatt J held that B's position was precisely the same as if he had written saying he would remove the goods, ie the position in *Rohde*.

Prior assent of B

Here B expressly or implicitly assents beforehand to S's later appropriation of the goods – again property will pass to B on appropriation without any delivery to him. For example, in *Pletts v Beattie*,[17] B signed an order for beer which contained an express assent to its later appropriation by S at the brewery. S selected six bottles of ale at the brewery, one of which was labelled with B's name and address, and placed them in a box with other bottles similarly labelled for other buyers. The ale was paid for on delivery at B's house. It was held that the sale/appropriation took place at the brewery and S could not be convicted of selling alcoholic liquor at a place where he was not authorised to do so by his licence.

It was stated in *Jenner v Smith*,[18] that B's assent is actually an *authority* which is conferred on S, as B's agent, to pass the property by appropriation and therefore it should always be asked whether the authority has been given and whether it has been exercised in accordance with its terms. The stipulated terms might be, for example, that delivery should be made to a carrier and property would thus not pass before then.[19]

As usual, the problematic cases are those where it is alleged that B has implicitly authorised the later appropriation by S. In *Aldridge v Johnson*,[20] B agreed to buy 100 quarters of barley out of a bulk of 200 quarters which he had seen and of which he approved, and it was agreed that B should send 200 sacks for the barley which S would fill and despatch to B by railway. S duly filled 155 sacks but could not arrange transport by rail, although B urgently requested delivery on several occasions. Almost two weeks after the contract, on the eve of S's bankruptcy, S emptied the sacks back into the bulk. It was held that, by inspecting the barley and sending the sacks, B had assented[1] to S's appropriation

---

15   [1968] 2 QB 663.
16   [1919] 1 KB 459; cf *Atkinson v Bell* (1828) 8 B & C 277(S made machines for B, told B that they had been completed and asked B what method of delivery was required. Some six weeks later, S was declared bankrupt and B had not replied. Held no property passed to B as he had expressed no assent).
17   [1896] 1 QB 519.
18   (1869) LR 4 CP 270.
19   The authority to appropriate given by B may also be revoked by B in which case B repudiates the contract and S's remedy is in damages for non-acceptance: *Ginner v King* (1890) 7 TLR 140.
20   (1857) 7 E & B 885.
 1   The majority was also prepared to find *subsequent* assent of B in his pressing for delivery after the sacks were filled; Crompton J questioned whether B knew that the sacks had been filled and he therefore doubted any subsequent assent.

and property in the barley in the 155 sacks had passed to B when they were filled. Accordingly, S's assignee in bankruptcy was liable in conversion.

Aldridge was followed on similar facts in *Langton v Higgins*,[2] where B agreed to buy all the oil of peppermint to be distilled from the crop of peppermint grown by S that year. S asked B to send bottles for the oil and these he filled, labelling them with their weight and then making out invoices. B had bought the oil of peppermint from S in this way for many years. Before the bottles were delivered to a carrier to take to the railway, S sold and delivered some of them to the defendant. It was held that property in the oil in the bottles passed to B when the bottles were filled and the defendant was thus liable in conversion.

Aldridge and *Langton* must be treated with caution as the notion of prior assent has limited application. For example, in many agreements for the sale of unascertained goods it could be argued that B necessarily assents beforehand to a later appropriation by S or, where goods are to be manufactured by S, that their completion is an act of appropriation to which B naturally assented at the date of contract. But it is clear that this is not the law and logic determines that, in agreements to sell unascertained goods by description, B should normally make a *subsequent* assent to an appropriation by S, and this is particularly so in the case of future goods. The decision in *Jenner v Smith*[3] made it clear that the prior authority conferred on S to appropriate the goods will rarely be *implied*. Thus, unless B *expressly* assents beforehand, as in *Pletts v Beattie*, above, most of S's acts which are preparatory to delivery such as packing and labelling goods, would seem to require a subsequent assent of B if they are to be acts of unconditional appropriation passing the property to B.[4] This is borne out by the approach adopted in *Carlos Federspiel & Co SA v Charles Twigg & Co Ltd*,[5] considered earlier, where only an actual shipment of the goods would have amounted to the final, decisive act of appropriation.[6] It has also been said that, until there is a subsequent assent, the law preserves the right of S to sell the goods to a third party and B is unable to complain if he receives other goods within the stipulated time.[7] It was crucial that, in *Aldridge*, B had inspected and approved the barley beforehand[8] and, in most situations, it is arguably both inapt and difficult to establish B's prior assent[9] apart from those cases where B is deemed to have authorised the appropriation by delivery under r 5(2).

2 (1859) 4 H & N 402.
3 (1869) LR 4 CP 270.
4 See also *Noblett v Hopkinson* [1905] 2 KB 214 (on Saturday, B ordered at a public house, half a gallon of beer to be delivered next day but paid for immediately. The beer was drawn and put in a bottle overnight. Held there was no appropriation to which B assented on Saturday and S committed an offence of selling the beer on Sunday. *Pletts v Beattie* was distinguished as, in *Pletts*, there was an express, prior assent of B).
5 [1957] 1 Lloyd's Rep 240, 255, per Pearson J: 'An appropriation by the seller, with the assent of the buyer, may be said always to involve an actual or constructive delivery'.
6 Certainly, as Chalmers suggested (*Sale of Goods*, 18th edn (1981), p 151), all the cases on appropriation where property has passed to B have involved an actual or constructive delivery to B. *Aldridge* and *Langton* are both classifiable as cases of constructive delivery (in *Langton*, Pollock CB held (p 408) that putting the oil into the bottles 'was the same thing as delivering it to [B]').
7 *Mucklow v Mangles* (1808) 1 Taunt 318, 319, per Heath J.
8 It is unclear whether the quasi-specificity of the goods in *Langton* (*all* the crop) may have influenced the issue of B's prior assent.
9 Cf *Re Stapylton Fletcher Ltd* [1994] 1 WLR 1181 (see later). S sold cases of wine to B and stored them for him indefinitely. Judge Paul Baker QC (sitting as a High Court judge) considered that '[B's] assent to any appropriation of specific cases without consultation can be safely inferred' (p 1198).

Assent of S

This relates to the relatively uncommon situation where B makes the
appropriation with the assent of S which is given either before or after the
appropriation is made. Very few problems have arisen with B's appropriation
and no cases are directly in point. This is because B's appropriation is a rarer
occurrence than S's appropriation and, when B selects goods from a bulk belonging
to S, the appropriation will frequently involve a decisive act of actual delivery
to B.[10] Moreover, it will often be the case that B selects goods from S's stock
before contract so that the resulting contract will be one for the sale of *specific*
goods to which r 5 has no application, eg B selects an item of clothing from a
rail in a retail shop and pays for it at the cash till. This would still be the case
where, for example, B is allowed to pick fruit or vegetables in S's fields and pay
for the amount selected on leaving.

RULES 5(3) AND 5(4): THE NOTION OF APPROPRIATION BY EXHAUSTION

In *Wait and James v Midland Bank*,[11] it was accepted that there could be an
ascertainment of goods by 'exhaustion'. Although this sounds recondite, all that
is required is that the sale and delivery of goods from a bulk, for example, has
left, as the entirety of the bulk, exactly the quantity of goods which B had agreed
to buy. In this case, it may well be the intent of the parties that property in those
goods has passed to B by the process of exhaustion which has taken place.

In *Wait and James*, S had sold to B a quantity of wheat from bulk in a
warehouse at Avonmouth. B took delivery of part of the wheat but deposited
delivery orders in respect of the remaining 850 quarters with the defendant
Bank by way of pledge. S sold off the wheat in the warehouse to other buyers
until only 850 quarters remained. When B became insolvent, both S (who was
unpaid) and the Bank claimed the wheat. Roche J held that the property had
passed to B as it had become ascertained by exhaustion and thus the Bank's
security was valid as against S. This reasoning was based purely on ss 16 and
17 and the intent of the parties but, while S presumably intended that property
in the remaining 850 quarters should pass to B, it was not at all clear that this
was B's intent as he appeared to be unaware of S's methods for the disposal of
the wheat.

The decision in *The Elafi*[12] extended the *Wait and James* concept of exhaustion
to a situation where all the contracts of sale became united in a single buyer.
There B agreed to buy from S 6,000 tons of copra from a cargo of 22,000 tons
aboard *Elafi*. The remainder of the cargo was to be sold to other buyers. It then
transpired that more than 22,000 tons had been loaded and the surplus of 500
tons was sold to a third party who immediately resold it to B. The vessel discharged
some of the cargo for the other buyers at Rotterdam and Hamburg and the cargo
remaining on board consisted of the 6,000 tons and the surplus and it was thus

---

10 See *National Coal Board v Gamble* [1959] 1 QB 11 (B's carrier collected coal from a
    colliery where his lorry was loaded from a hopper and then went to a weighbridge where
    S issued a ticket giving the weight of the load for the purpose of ascertaining the price.
    Held that the intent was that property would pass only when the coal was weighed).
11 (1926) 31 Com Cas 172.
12 *Karlshamns Oljefabriker v Eastport Navigation Corpn, The Elafi* [1982] 1 All ER 208.

all destined for B. During discharge of B's consignment in Sweden, some of the copra was damaged by water entering a hold as a result of the shipowner's negligence. Mustill J held that, after the prior deliveries to the other buyers, property passed to B by exhaustion as he could then say that *all* the copra remaining on board was his. Accordingly, B had property in the copra at the time it was damaged and could claim against the shipowners in tort.

The effect of these decisions has been confirmed by the insertion[13] in the SGA, s 18 of a new r 5(3) and 5(4) which provide:

> '(3) Where there is a contract for the sale of a specified quantity of unascertained goods in a deliverable state forming part of a bulk which is identified either in the contract or by subsequent agreement between the parties and the bulk is reduced to (or to less than) that quantity, then, if the buyer under that contract is the only buyer to whom goods are then due out of the bulk–
> (a) the remaining goods are to be taken as appropriated to that contract at the time when the bulk is so reduced; and
> (b) the property in those goods then passes to that buyer.
>
> (4) Paragraph (3) above applies also (with the necessary modifications) where a bulk is reduced to (or to less than) the aggregate of the quantities due to a single buyer under separate contracts relating to that bulk and he is the only buyer to whom goods are then due out of that bulk.'

It should be stressed that r 5(3) applies only to a contract for the sale of a *specified quantity* of unascertained goods forming part of an *identified bulk*, eg 1,000 bags of barley from the remaining 1,500 bags in S's barn. B need not pay the price of the goods in advance for r 5(3) to operate but, if B has paid in advance, he fulfils the requirements of the SGA, s 20A, relating to co-ownership, and property in an undivided share in the bulk passes to B who thus becomes an owner in common of the bulk. If the bulk of 1,500 bags is then reduced to 1,000 bags (or less) because of sales to other buyers, for example, and B is the only buyer entitled to goods from the bulk, the property in the quantity of barley remaining thereupon passes to B by exhaustion (confirming *Wait and James*). Under r 5(4), it is immaterial that B is entitled to the remainder of the bulk by virtue of more than one contract (confirming *The Elafi*).

Rule 5(3) specifies that the contract must be for 'the sale of a specified quantity of unascertained goods in a *deliverable state*' but it is unclear *when* the goods must be in such a state. A first reading would suggest that the goods should be in a deliverable state at the time the contract is entered into, but this would be a superfluous requirement for r 5(3) and so it is likely that the goods need be in a deliverable state only at the moment that 'the remaining goods are to be taken as appropriated' (r 5(3)(a)) to the contract, ie when the bulk is reduced and property passes to B. This interpretation would accord with r 5(1) in that there the goods must be in a deliverable state when they are unconditionally appropriated to the contract.

Rules 5(3) and (4) do not apply where there is a contrary intention and so it may not be uncommon for S and B to intend that property is to pass only on delivery or S may have employed a retention of title clause suspending the passing of property until payment by B. Again, in the situation envisaged by r 5(4), the parties may intend that the goods be appropriated to the separate contracts before property is to pass, meaning that r 5(4) would be excluded.

---

13 Inserted by the Sale of Goods (Amendment) Act 1995, s 1(2).

Contracts to sell an unsegregated part of a bulk

The rule that no property in unascertained goods can pass to B unless and until they have been ascertained must now be considered in relation to sales from bulk stores (eg 100 tons of barley from a cargo of 1,000 tons aboard a certain vessel). It was emphasised earlier, when the decision in *Re Wait*[14] was considered, that it is immaterial to the issue of passing of property that B may have paid the purchase price in full before any ascertainment of the goods. This is particularly harsh on B where S becomes insolvent before any ascertainment takes place for then B is abandoned to fate as an unsecured creditor and the goods may be resold with the proceeds of sale used to pay S's secured creditors. This difficulty has been addressed in the SGA, ss 20A and 20B[15] but, before any analysis of these new provisions, it is necessary to examine the perennial difficulties caused by contracts to sell quantities of goods from bulk stores.[16]

When B has paid in full for unascertained goods, he will often consider that he has a proprietary interest in them but, as the following cases illustrate, this misconception may be a costly one. In *Re London Wine Co (Shippers) Ltd*,[17] S agreed to sell to several buyers quantities of wine of specified types, all of which was lying in bond in different locations and was held to S's order. When B ordered the wine, he received a detailed invoice and, when he paid, he received a 'certificate of title' which described the wine, its vintage and quantity, and stated that B was 'the sole and beneficial owner'. However, there was never any physical segregation or appropriation of the wine unless B took delivery. S became insolvent and the bank, which had a floating charge on S's assets, appointed a receiver. The receiver's claim that no property in the wine had passed to the buyers was upheld by Oliver J as there was never any ascertainment of the goods. Moreover, arguments based on the creation of a trust in favour of the buyers were dismissed as, even if there were sufficient intent to create a trust, it would be impossible to establish that a certain number of cases of wine were held on trust when the bulk from which the wine would be drawn was itself unascertained, being described simply as 'lying in bond'. The judge was thus not prepared to regard 'lying in bond' as being an identified source from which the goods should be selected; rather, S was free to fulfil the contracts from any source, eg importing further wine of the same description. This uncertainty regarding the bulk also meant that it was impossible to assert that property had passed to some buyers by exhaustion or that others, who had bought the entire stock of one type of wine, could be tenants in common. Oliver J also rejected the argument that there was an equitable assignment of quantities of wine for which B had paid or that there could be specific performance of the contracts (thus following *Re Wait*). Finally, the notion that

---

14 [1927] 1 Ch 606; see also the earlier consideration of *Laurie and Morewood v Dudin & Sons* [1926] 1 KB 223; *Healy v Howlett & Sons* [1917] 1 KB 337.
15 Inserted in the SGA by the Sale of Goods (Amendment) Act 1995.
16 See generally Nicol, 'The Passing of Property in Part of a Bulk' (1979) 42 MLR 129; Goode,'Ownership and Obligation in Commercial Transactions' (1987) 103 LQR 433; Goode, *Proprietary Rights and Insolvency in Sales Transactions* (2nd edn, 1989); McKendrick, 'The Passing of Property in Part of a Bulk' in *Interests in Goods* (eds Palmer and McKendrick, 2nd edn, 1998), Ch 16.
17 [1986] PCC 121.

the buyers might acquire an interest by estoppel[18] was dismissed on the basis that, in this context, estoppel does not actually pass the property to B and thus the real title of the bank could not be affected.

A similar set of facts arose in *Re Goldcorp Exchange Ltd.*[19] S dealt in precious metals and bullion and, by means of pamphlets, newspapers and oral assurances given to customers, he promoted in explicit terms the safety of dealing with him. Over 1,000 buyers in New Zealand entered into contracts to buy gold from S, as an investment, on the basis that S would store their bullion but that delivery could be taken on seven days' notice. On payment, B was given a certificate 'certifying' his 'ownership' and S promised to hold sufficient stocks of gold to meet 'all commitments'. The gold was described as being held by S on a 'non-allocated basis' which was said to mean that 'you receive a certificate of ownership rather than the metal', the metal being 'stored in a vault on your behalf'. Apart from a handful of cases, there was never an appropriation of gold to any contract but, more importantly, S's stocks were not maintained at a sufficiently high level to meet 'all commitments'. A bank had a floating charge over S's assets and, on S's insolvency, it was discovered that there was not even sufficient gold to satisfy the bank's secured debt. The Privy Council rejected every argument which the majority of the buyers advanced in an attempt to gain priority over the bank, viz (i) the contract was classified as one for the purchase of unascertained, generic goods and thus no property could pass to B until the goods were ascertained but this had never been done; (ii) the collateral promises made in S's brochures did not constitute a declaration of trust by S in favour of B in relation to the current stock of bullion so as to transfer title to B in that bullion, as this would have restricted S's dealings with his general stock; (iii) arguments that S was estopped from denying B's title were to no avail because there was no fixed, existing bulk[20] from which a 'title' could be created by such a deemed appropriation but, in any event, an estoppel would not bind the bank which had a real title; (iv) B had no equitable interest in after-acquired bullion (ie bullion bought after the formation of the original contracts) as it was impossible to say that such later acquisitions of bullion by S related to any particular contracts;[1] (v) no trust attached to the after-acquired bullion, nor could S be either a fiduciary or bailee in relation to it as these notions were inconsistent with the actual position that S's stock could fluctuate in the normal course of business and, allowing that these possibilities could exist, an insuperable problem was that S

---

18 It was seen earlier that where the bulk is in the possession of T (eg a warehouseman) the acceptance by T of a delivery order given by S to B or the transfer of the goods in T's books to B will *not* pass the property where the goods are unascertained (see *Laurie and Morewood v Dudin & Sons* [1926] 1 KB 223). However, if S gives a delivery order to B or B gives a delivery order to his sub-B, a *confirmation* of the delivery order by S or T may estop them from denying that property has passed. But there must be a representation by words or conduct that B has a right to the goods and B must be prejudiced by a refusal to deliver the goods. Estoppel does *not pass the property* in the goods to B but he may maintain an action for wrongful interference if the goods are not delivered to him and S is then precluded from establishing an unpaid seller's lien. See eg *Knights v Wiffen* (1870) LR 5 QB 660; Blackburn, *Contract of Sale* (2nd edn, 1885), pp 190-196 and the cases there cited.

19 [1995] 1 AC 74.

20 In *Re Goldcorp*, Lord Mustill thought there was such an identified bulk in *Knights v Wiffen* (1870) LR 5 QB 660, ie the entire stock of barley in S's granary.

1   It was emphasised (pp 95-96) that the old decisions, headed by *Holroyd v Marshall* (1862) 10 HL Cas 191 (see earlier), were based upon after-acquired property being unequivocally identified with the contract in question.

had broken his promise and failed to maintain an adequate stock of bullion to which a proprietary interest could attach; (vi) the purchase price paid by B could be spent by S as he wished and the purchase moneys were thus not impressed with a trust in B's favour entitling him to trace the moneys into S's assets nor was S a fiduciary as regards such purchase moneys; and (vii) as B had never rescinded the contract of sale, it was too late to argue that misrepresentation or mistake rendered the transaction ineffectual entitling B to a proprietary right over S's assets which was superior to S's other creditors and, even if S had misrepresented the position, the purchase moneys became S's property and rescission could not entitle B to such a proprietary right.

Re Goldcorp epitomises both S's dominance at B's expense and the paramountcy of the bank's security. The Privy Council considered that there was insufficient disparity between the bank's commercial interest and the consumer buyers' interests to justify intervention on the latter's behalf. But the rigid legal rule that physical ascertainment of goods is a pre-condition for the passing of property should surely not have been allowed to obscure the obvious injustice which was sanctioned in *Re Goldcorp*.[2] The Court of Appeal of New Zealand[3] had held that, although B had no proprietary rights in the bullion, there was a fiduciary relationship between S and B, meaning that S held the purchase moneys on trust for the purpose of setting aside and holding sufficient bullion to meet B's demands. B thus retained a beneficial interest in the purchase moneys which could be traced into S's general assets in priority to the bank's charge. It is submitted that this enlightened decision was correct recognising as it did that '[S] held itself out as a trusted and expert dealer in bullion and as being in a position to assist members of the public to engage in investment in precious metals. It was an unsophisticated clientele being attracted to an unregulated market by representations of assurance and trust'.[4] In commerce, it is clear that the facile creation of fiduciary relationships must not become the universal panacea for perceived injustice, but the Privy Council entirely disowned principles premised upon good faith. Accordingly, Lord Mustill's distillation of the position was that 'customers put faith in the company, and ... their trust has not been repaid. But the vocabulary is misleading; high expectations do not necessarily lead to equitable remedies'.[5]

Despite the approach in *Re Goldcorp*, a remedy was forged for B within the existing law in the decision in *Re Stapylton Fletcher Ltd*.[6] Again S was a vintner who entered into contracts to sell wine to customers and then to store it for them indefinitely at a charge. When S received an order and wine was paid for, it was physically removed from S's trading stock and placed in a 'customers' reserve area'. There cases of wine of the same type and vintage which had been ordered by several buyers were mixed in stacks, but different types and vintages of wine were never mixed in the same stack. An index existed for each stack recording the different buyers and the number of cases allocated to each and a separate card was kept for each customer recording his total allocation of wines in the

---

2   Cf McKendrick, 'Unascertained Goods: Ownership and Obligation Distinguished' (1994) 110 LQR 509.
3   *Liggett v Kensington* [1993] 1 NZLR 257; see Scott, 'The Remedial Constructive Trust in Commercial Transactions' [1993] LMCLQ 330.
4   [1993] 1 NZLR 257 at 282, per Gault J.
5   [1995] 1 AC 74, 98.
6   [1994] 1 WLR 1181.

warehouse. On S's insolvency, the receivers sought directions from the court as to whether property in the wines had passed to the buyers. It was held that, as the wine was segregated in a special area (clearly distinguishing *Stapylton's* facts from *Re London Wine*) and the stacks contained cases or bottles of identical wine, the goods were ascertained for the purposes of s 16 and property could pass by 'common intention'[7] under s 17. Accordingly, the buyers were held to have acquired property in the goods as tenants in common.[8] However, other buyers who had bought wine *en primeur* (ie direct from the vineyards) fell foul of the rules on ascertainment as, although this wine was subject to a contract for its sale to S, it remained part of the generic stock of the vineyards and there was no ascertainment of any of it. Judge Paul Baker QC also reaffirmed the approach of *Re London Wine*, that a sale of goods does not, *per se*, create equitable rights and that estoppel is extremely limited in this context.

Co-ownership under the SGA, sections 20A and 20B

In 1993, the Law Commissions[9] recommended reform of the SGA, s 16, so that in a contract for the sale of a *specified quantity* of unascertained goods forming part of an *identified bulk*, a buyer who has *paid* for all or some of the contract goods should obtain an *undivided, proprietary share in the bulk* and thus become a tenant in common of the whole amount. The notion of a tenancy in common or co-ownership is well illustrated in *Re Stapylton Fletcher Ltd*, above. The Law Commissions' recommendations were enacted in the Sale of Goods (Amendment) Act 1995 with most of the reforms being contained in the newly-inserted ss 20A and 20B of the SGA 1979. Overall, the Law Commissions considered that the law was in need of reform as it did not synchronise with commercial practice in that B often considered that he acquired property in goods in a bulk before ascertainment and this misconception was shared by banks which accepted bills of lading in relation to part of a cargo as security for advances of money to B.

When the goods are separated from the identified bulk, property in the ascertained goods may then pass to B according to the ordinary rules considered earlier in this chapter and so the notion of B's undivided share is of an 'interim nature'[10] until such ascertainment or appropriation occurs. Nevertheless, B's proprietary share in the bulk should protect him in cases of S's insolvency and enable him to sue a carrier in tort if the goods are negligently damaged whilst being carried in bulk. Moreover, B may agree to resell all or part of the contract

---

7 [1994] 1 WLR 1181 at 1200, per Judge Paul Baker QC.
8 Following *Indian Oil Corpn Ltd v Greenstone Shipping SA (Panama)* [1988] QB 345 (shipowners mixed their own oil with oil they had been chartered to transport, ownership in common being held to result; see Brown, 'Admixture of Goods in English Law' [1988] LMCLQ 286). It is far from clear when co-ownership will result at common law but it is evident from *Stapylton* that the parties' intent regarding its creation need not be express. A singular difficulty in sales of goods from bulks is the difficulty in inferring any intent regarding co-ownership when the buyers have agreed to buy a specific quantity of goods rather than a *share* in the bulk. See Goode, 'Ownership and Obligation in Commercial Transactions' (1987) 103 LQR 433 ; Birks, 'Mixtures' in *Interests in Goods* (eds Palmer and McKendrick, 2nd edn, 1998), Ch 9.
9 *Sale of Goods Forming Part of a Bulk* (Law Com No 215; Scot Law Com No 145; 1993).
10 *Sale of Goods Forming Part of a Bulk* (Law Com No 215; Scot Law Com No 145; 1993), para 4.1.

goods to a sub-buyer[11] while the goods are in the bulk and, provided the conditions of s 20A are met, the sub-buyer will acquire property in an undivided share in the bulk and become an owner in common. There are three broad conditions for the operation of ss 20A and 20B which must now be considered, viz a contract for the sale of a *specified quantity* of goods, from an *identified bulk* to a *pre-paying* buyer.

Specified quantity of unascertained goods

Section 20A(1) applies only to a contract for the sale of a 'specified quantity of unascertained goods' forming part of an identified bulk and it appears that the quantity can be specified in any manner, eg weight, number or measurement. This means, for example, that contracts for the sale of 200 tons of wheat from a cargo aboard a certain vessel or 100 litres of oil from an identified storage tank containing 500 litres, are both within s 20A.

However, the sale of a share in an identified bulk expressed as a *fraction or percentage* is *not* within s 20A. The Law Commissions considered that contracts for the sale of shares in an identified bulk, expressed as fractions or percentages, were both possible under the existing law and were rarer than sales of specified amounts from a bulk. The position is put beyond doubt by the SGA, s 61(1), which now specifies that sales of an 'undivided share, specified as a fraction or percentage of goods' which are 'identified and agreed on' at the time the contract of sale is made, are sales of *specific* goods (eg 10% of a specific racehorse; half of the barley in an identified silo).[12] Similarly, the sale of the *whole* of a bulk, under one contract, to several buyers, is a sale of specific goods, the buyers becoming owners in common: examples given by the Law Commissions included the sale of a table to a husband and wife or a parcel of diamonds sold to a consortium of buyers.[13]

In relation to s 20A and 20B, it must be asked what the position is where the bulk is not in existence at the date of contract. It will be seen below that, by s 20A(1)(a), the bulk can be 'identified either in the contract or by *subsequent agreement* between the parties' and so, in a contract to sell a specified quantity of goods which do not yet exist (eg 2,000 tonnes of next season's barley) the parties may, for example, subsequently identify 5,000 tonnes of such barley in a warehouse from which they agree that the 2,000 tonnes shall be drawn, and this undertaking is within s 20A.

Where the bulk is not in existence at the date of contract, some contentious situations can be envisaged. It is clear that a contract for the sale of '30% of the barley to be grown on S's farm next season' is a contract for the sale of unascertained goods to which s 20A could not apply as the 30% does not constitute a 'specified quantity' of goods. What is the position where the quantity in the future bulk is *estimated* but the amount is designated as a fraction or percentage (eg half of the wheat to be grown next season on S's farm, estimated overall production being 50,000 tonnes)? Again, this latter example would appear to be outside s 20A. More precisely, the quantity in the future bulk might be *specified* but the amount might

---

11   The SGA, s 2(2), provides that there 'may be a contract of sale between one part owner and another' and so the sub-buyer can be an existing co-owner of the bulk.
12   The definition of 'specific goods' was considered earlier in this chapter.
13   See *Sale of Goods Forming Part of a Bulk* (Law Com No 215, Scot Law Com No 145, 1993), paras 2.4-2.6; 5.3-5.7.

be designated as a fraction or percentage (eg 10% of the cargo of 1,000 tonnes of wheat to be shipped next January on the *Challenger*). It is clearly arguable that the latter example ought to be within s 20A: the specified percentage can be converted to a 'specified quantity' by a simple calculation whereas, of course, this is impossible where the extent of the bulk has not been specified.

Identified bulk

Section 20A(1)(a) applies only to a contract for the sale of a specified quantity of unascertained goods when 'the goods or some of them form part of a bulk which is identified either in the contract or by subsequent agreement between the parties'. Section 61(1) defines 'bulk' as 'a mass or collection of goods of the same kind which (a) is contained in a defined space or area; and (b) is such that any goods in the bulk are interchangeable with any other goods therein of the same number or quantity'. The definition in s 61(1) demanding that the goods in the bulk must be 'interchangeable' with any other goods therein means that the bulk must be comprised of fungible goods, ie every particle or unit is indistinguishable from every other particle or unit. This obviously applies to bulks comprised of barley or petrol of the same quality, for example, but it is unclear how great the degree of difference in the goods must be before they cease to be interchangeable. Much here will depend on the parties' intent and business practice, however.

It is plain that warehouses, store rooms, storage tanks and compounds will be identified bulks and examples given by the Law Commissions included a cargo of wheat in a named ship and a heap of coal in the open at a specified location. The Law Commissions stressed, however, that the definition was not intended to include S's general trading stock. The new Act would thus not change the outcome of either *Re London Wine* or *Re Goldcorp*, a central feature of both decisions being that S was at liberty to sell his existing stock and satisfy his buyers from any available source. Undoubtedly the stacks of wine in *Re Stapylton Fletcher*,[14] which were segregated from S's general trading stock, would be an identifiable bulk within the new provisions but, again, it was unclear in *Stapylton* whether S was under an *obligation* to draw the buyers' wines from the stacks and, if he was not so obliged, the bulk would not be identifiable in that sense. In future disputes, much will depend on the interpretation given to the notion of the 'identified bulk' but it seems likely that the new provisions will have little effect outside the established field of commodity trading.[15] It should be stressed that, while the bulk must be identified, there is no requirement that the *amount* of goods in the bulk should be known, although this will be important when the shares of the co-owners are determined.

It will be noticed that, under s 20A(1)(a), the bulk may be 'identified either in the contract or by subsequent agreement between the parties'. The contract could thus be one for future, unascertained goods and it is permissible that, several months later, S and B may fix the identified bulk from which the goods are to be drawn. It should be noted here that the bulk must be 'identified in the *contract* or by

---

14 [1994] 1 WLR 1181.
15 The Law Commissions considered that the 'identified bulk' could occasionally apply in consumer sales, eg a consumer might buy and pay for a length of carpet forming part of a roll identified in the contract (*Sale of Goods Forming Part of a Bulk*, Law Com No 215, Scot Law Com No 145, 1993, para 4.3).

subsequent *agreement*' and thus there must be an agreement on this issue and it would be insufficient, without more, for S to *inform* B of the identified bulk.

It is arguably immaterial that goods are regularly withdrawn from the bulk and new goods are added so that the bulk's content constantly fluctuates: the modern view is that the notion of co-ownership can still be sustained where the additions are inadvertent or even wrongful.[16] However, the co-owners' *proprietary* rights will be lost where the identified bulk has been totally exhausted so that nothing remains, eg the entire bulk is sold to a third party who takes delivery[17] and it is debatable whether proprietary rights can survive where the bulk has been depleted totally and then replenished fully. It is probably of no consequence that the goods in the bulk are mixed with other goods of a different description *provided* that the goods are identifiable and separable (eg cattle mixed with horses in a stable). But it is very unclear whether proprietary rights can survive if S alters irreversibly the quality of the goods in the bulk (eg an addition of superior or inferior oil to a tank of oil) or the nature of those goods (eg leather skins are made into briefcases).[18]

Pre-paying buyer

The new provisions apply only where 'the buyer has paid the price for some or all of the goods which are the subject of the contract and which form part of the bulk' (s 20A (1) (b)). The reason for thus confining the reforms was that buyers who have not paid are not unduly prejudiced by the existing law in that they cannot be made to part with their money except in exchange for the goods (under the SGA, s 28, payment and delivery are concurrent conditions). Moreover, the Law Commissions thought that extending the new law to buyers who had not paid could cause practical difficulties for S's insolvency officer. For example, buyers who had not paid might be unwilling to pay in full if there were a risk that they might not receive their full quantity of goods but if all the buyers have paid in advance the insolvency officer can simply ask them to remove their goods.

None of the other rules in the SGA stipulate that payment is a pre-condition for the passing of property and there may be problems with the new provisions when resales are considered. Suppose that B agrees to buy 500 litres of wine from an identified bulk of 5,000 litres and B then resells it to B2 before any payment to S or ascertainment of the wine. If B2 has paid B and then S becomes insolvent, B2 has no proprietary interest and the receiver could resell the goods, B2 then being limited to a claim for non-delivery against B, which could be a nugatory right if B is also insolvent.

Section 20A(1)(b) applies where B has paid the price for 'some' of the goods and the section provides further that such part-payment shall be 'treated as payment

---

16   See *Indian Oil Corpn v Greenstone Shipping SA (Panama)* [1988] QB 345; *Mercer v Craven Grain Storage Ltd* [1994] CLC 328; *Re Stapylton Fletcher Ltd* [1994] 1 WLR 1181; see Birks, 'Mixing and Tracing' (1992) 45 CLP 69; Birks, 'Mixtures' in *Interests in Goods* (ed Palmer and McKendrick, 2nd edn, 1998), Ch 9.

17   Where this occurs and the third party acquires title to the goods (see below), it is very unlikely that a co-owner could trace successfully into the proceeds of sale of the goods: see *Re Goldcorp Exchange Ltd* [1995] 1 AC 74.

18   The Romalpa cases where the unpaid seller has lost title by virtue of a consensual arrangement for such altered goods must surely be inapt in the context of co-ownership where the pre-paying buyer does not thus consent to the change.

for a corresponding part of the goods' (s 20A(6)) and that, where there is part-payment, 'any delivery to the buyer out of the bulk shall ... be ascribed in the first place to the goods in respect of which payment has been made' (s 20A(5)). For example, if B agrees to buy 1,000 litres of oil from a tank containing 2,000 litres, makes a pre-payment of 50% of the price and takes delivery of 300 litres, he is taken to have paid for the 200 litres yet to be delivered.

The time when property in an undivided share passes to B

Provided the three broad conditions above are satisfied then, 'unless the parties agree otherwise' (s 20A(2)), property in an undivided share in the bulk is transferred to B and he becomes an owner in common of the bulk (s 20A(2) (a) and (b)). Property in the undivided share will thus pass to B, at the earliest, when the bulk is identified and B has made the pre-payment. The definition of 'delivery' in the SGA, s 61(1) has been modified and extended to be applicable to the new co-ownership provisions and now specifies that delivery includes 'such appropriation of goods to the contract as results in property in the goods being transferred to the buyer'. There is no requirement that the goods should be in a deliverable state for B to own an undivided share as this is an unnecessary requirement for the concept of ownership in common.

B's undivided share

Section 20A(3) provides that 'the undivided share of a buyer in a bulk at any time shall be such share as the quantity of goods paid for and due to the buyer out of the bulk bears to the quantity of goods in the bulk at that time'. Thus, if B has agreed to buy 500 tonnes of wheat from 1,000 tonnes and has paid for the goods in advance, provided that there are 1,000 tonnes in the bulk, B will own an undivided share of half of the 1,000 tonnes. Where there are fluctuations in the bulk, eg by accidental loss and intentional, partial deliveries from it, B's undivided share will necessarily alter. Thus, in the above example, if S were to deliver 250 tonnes of the 1,000 tonnes to B2 who has pre-paid, the bulk being thereby reduced to 750 tonnes, B's share will be increased to two thirds of the bulk (ie 500 tonnes out of 750 tonnes). However, should the bulk be reduced to 500 tonnes or less, B would cease to have an undivided share and property in the goods would pass to him by exhaustion under s 18, r 5(3) (considered earlier), this rule having been inserted in the SGA by the 1995 Act.[19]

Similar adjustments are made if the bulk contains more or less than was originally thought. Thus, if S thinks that the bulk contains 900 litres of oil and sells 100 litres to B and 200 litres to B2, both of whom have pre-paid, if the bulk contains 1,000 litres B owns one tenth, B2 owns two tenths, and the remainder belongs to S. If, on the other hand, the bulk contains 800 litres, B owns one eighth, B2 owns two eighths, and the remainder belongs to S.

Rules to facilitate normal trading

It is the normal rule that co-owners must consent to any division of the co-owned property[20] but, under ss 20A and 20B, co-ownership of the identified bulk is not

19 See the Sale of Goods (Amendment) Act 1995, s 1(2).
20 See the Law of Property Act 1925, s 188.

intended to prevent further sales from S's remaining share or to prevent delivery of the contract-quantities to the co-owners. In order to facilitate dealings with the bulk, s 20B(1) provides that an owner in common 'shall be deemed to have consented to – (a) any delivery of goods out of the bulk to any other owner in common of the bulk, being goods which are due to him under his contract; (b) any dealing with or removal, delivery or disposal of goods in the bulk by any other person who is an owner in common of the bulk in so far as the goods fall within that co-owner's undivided share in the bulk at the time of the dealing, removal, delivery or disposal'.

Overall, the buyers are thus deemed to consent to a system which functions on a first-come, first-served basis and s 20B(2) and (3) provide that co-owners are under no obligation to compensate other co-owners who receive less than their share: such unsatisfied buyers have only a contractual claim against S for short delivery and will thus have only notional rights where S is insolvent. The Law Commissions rejected any other scheme as being too complex, eg on S's insolvency, a scheme by which buyers who had taken delivery could be subjected to an adjustment exercise requiring them to compensate co-owners who had received less than their share or giving the court a broad discretion to order an equitable adjustment. However, the new provisions do not affect any contractual arrangements between co-owners as to adjustments between themselves (s 20B(3)(b)).

Several problems can arise with dealings from the bulk. First, in the course of normal deliveries from the bulk some buyers may receive less and some more than their share and, in the latter case, if B keeps the excess he must pay for it at the contract rate by virtue of the SGA, s 30(3).

Second, there may be several co-owners and the aggregate of their shares may *exceed* the amount of the bulk. To cope with this situation, s 20A(4) provides that the share of each buyer shall be 'reduced proportionately so that the aggregate of the undivided shares is equal to the whole bulk'. Thus, if four buyers each agree to buy 250 tonnes of wheat from a silo thought to contain 1,000 tonnes but which contains only 800 tonnes, each buyer's share shall be reduced proportionately so that he will own one quarter of the actual bulk, ie 200 tonnes each.

Third, the provisions as to deemed consent in s 20B(1)(a) and (b) apply only to other persons' dealings with the goods 'in so far as the goods fall within that co-owner's undivided share in the bulk' and thus the co-owners do not consent to over-sales by S to *new* buyers, ie selling the same goods twice. Where S is dishonest, this will obviously be a difficulty but the new rules make no provision for such an eventuality. The Law Commissions suggested that such a new buyer might acquire an interest in the bulk by virtue of the SGA, s 24 (seller in possession) and thus, where S transfers a document of title to this new buyer (eg a delivery order[1]) he would become a co-owner in the bulk with the shares of all the co-owners consequently being reduced proportionately. However, if the new buyer were actually to take delivery of the full amount of goods under his contract, it is arguable that he would obtain title to those goods under the combined operation of s 24 and s 18, r 5(2), so that the shares of the remaining co-owners would then be reduced proportionately. An alternative in this situation would be that, after the new buyer has taken delivery, property could pass by exhaustion under s 18, r 5(3) to a single, remaining buyer, who would thus own the entirety of the bulk and, in the event of his receiving short delivery, he could seek redress only from S.

---

1   See the Factors Act 1889, s 1(4).

Risk, loss and damage to the goods

There is no express provision in the new Act dealing with the transfer of risk but there are two enigmatic references to that notion which are of little help in determining the legal position. First, the Law Commissions[2] considered that B is entitled to delivery of goods which conform with the contract in quantity and quality, and this arguably implies that risk should remain with S until actual delivery to B. Second, this recommendation was implemented in even more elusive terms by s 20B(3)(c) which provides that nothing in ss 20A or 20B shall 'affect the rights of any buyer under his contract'. It is arguable that the thrust of this provision is simply to stress that B's normal rights are unaffected by ss 20A and 20B, eg his right to sue for non-delivery of the goods.

The parties may, and often will, provide expressly for the transfer of risk but, if there is no such provision in their contract, the general rule in s 20(1) is that risk passes with property and thus it is tempting to conclude that B may carry the risk from the moment he acquires an undivided share in the bulk. For several reasons, it is suggested that this is the most logical conclusion. First, it is well-established that unascertained goods may be at B's risk. In *Sterns Ltd v Vickers Ltd*,[3] B agreed to buy 120,000 gallons of white spirit from 200,000 gallons stored in a tank and received a delivery order for the goods. It was held that risk transferred to B even though there was no separation of the spirit from the bulk and property in the goods had *not* passed to him. *Sterns* is based upon the notion that, where B has a delivery order for the goods and complete control over their delivery, it is apt that risk should transfer to him at that moment. This argument should therefore apply with more force where B is a co-owner under the new provisions. Second, although no property in the goods themselves passes to B when he becomes a co-owner, B acquires a proprietary share in the bulk and the objective of the contract has been realised. Thirdly, when S has been paid in full for the goods and B has secured a proprietary share which he may sell without restriction, it would be an untenable conclusion that risk remains with S. This is fortified in that B's proprietary interest enables him to maintain an action in tort against a third party who damages the goods while they remain in bulk and protects him in the event of S's insolvency.

Assuming that goods in the bulk can be at B's risk before ascertainment, there is the obvious difficulty of how the loss is to be shared amongst the co-owners. The Law Commissions[4] suggested that risk of partial destruction rested with S so long as the quantity destroyed was within the quantity retained by him and so any goods retained by S are deemed to be destroyed first. If, for example, the bulk amounts to 100,000 tonnes of coal and S has agreed to sell 30,000 tonnes to B, the loss of 70,000 tonnes should be immaterial for B: S's goods are deemed to be destroyed first and he can still supply B with 30,000 tonnes of coal. A reasonable inference from the Law Commissions' suggestion is that, after S's share has been destroyed, the buyers would suffer a loss proportionately according to their shares in the bulk. Such a proportional loss would also seem to be the position where S does not retain any part of the bulk but sells shares in its entirety to several buyers. This seems the only viable possibility for, otherwise,

2 *Sale of Goods Forming Part of a Bulk*, (Law Com No 215; Scot Law Com No 145; 1993), para 4.34.
3 [1923] 1 KB 78 (considered in Ch 24).
4 *Sale of Goods Forming Part of a Bulk*, (Law Com No 215; Scot Law Com No 145; 1993), para 4.14.

S would have to deliver the full amount of goods to the first buyers to take delivery and then distribute the remainder of the goods *pro rata* amongst the other buyers. It may happen, of course, that damaged or defective goods are discovered only *after* ascertainment and delivery to B and then it seems that B has a claim only against S, as the co-ownership rules have rejected any notion of compensation among co-owners or any process of adjustment of shares amongst them after delivery.

If the conditions in s 20A are not complied with (eg no payment in advance by B) so that no proprietary share in the bulk is acquired and risk has *not* transferred to B, the destruction of the bulk could frustrate the contract, although the SGA, s 7 could not apply as that section covers only agreements to sell specific goods. Similarly, s 6, which provides that the contract will be void where the goods have perished at the time of contract, applies only to specific goods but, where the entire bulk has been destroyed at the time of contract, the parties could be discharged from their obligations by the rules of mistake or because the existence of the goods is an implied condition precedent which has not been fulfilled.

CHAPTER 17

Reservation of title clauses

Introduction

A reservation of title clause[1] in a contract for the sale of goods is a device by which, notwithstanding delivery of the goods to B, S retains title in them until he is paid in full by B. The purpose of such a clause is to give S a measure of protection in the event of B's insolvency as S has no proprietary right to retake the goods simply because he has not been paid. In the event of B's insolvency, preferential creditors (eg the Inland Revenue) and secured creditors (eg a Bank with a floating charge over B's assets) rank in priority to the unsecured creditors and the latter group, including S, frequently receives nothing. S is invariably left as a paralysed onlooker when the goods which he supplied to B are sold by a receiver to meet the claims of other creditors.

Contracts for either the simple hire or hire-purchase of goods provide effective and established methods by which S can reserve title in the goods but those contracts contemplate that the goods may be returned to S in the event of B's failure to meet his obligations and B is certainly not entitled to sell the goods during the currency of the contract. They are thus an inapt form of security where S supplies raw materials to B and B's business involves the manufacture and resale of new products. In many extended reservation of title clauses, B will have express authority to resell the goods and confer a good title on a sub-buyer and, even where such a sale is prohibited by S, a *bona fide* sub-buyer of the goods from B may very well acquire title to the goods under one of the exceptions to the *nemo dat* rule. The extent to which S may claim from B the proceeds of the sale of the goods when such a sub-sale is made is considered later. Similarly, many reservation of title clauses allow B to assimilate the goods in a manufacturing process from which new goods will emerge but whether S may claim ownership of the new goods is an obdurate and abiding difficulty of such clauses.

---

1 See generally Parris, *Effective Retention of Title Clauses* (1986); Goode, *Proprietary Rights and Insolvency in Sales Transactions* (2nd edn, 1989), Ch V; Wheeler, *Reservation of Title Clauses* (1991); Davies, *Effective Retention of Title* (1991); McCormack, *Reservation of Title* (2nd edn, 1995); Worthington, *Proprietary Interests in Commercial Transactions* (1996), Ch 2; McCormack, 'Title Retention and the Company Charge Registration System' in *Interests in Goods* (ed Palmer and McKendrick, 2nd edn, 1998), Ch 28.

The principle that S may retain title until the fulfilment of some condition is, however, not a new one. The SGA 1893, s 19 promulgated the notion of 'reservation of the right of disposal' and, currently, the SGA 1979, s 19(1) provides:

> 'Where there is a contract for the sale of specific goods or where goods are subsequently appropriated to the contract, the seller may, by the terms of the contract or appropriation, reserve the right of disposal of the goods until certain conditions are fulfilled; and in such case, notwithstanding the delivery of the goods to the buyer, or to a carrier or other bailee or custodier for the purpose of transmission to the buyer, the property in the goods does not pass to the buyer until the conditions imposed by the seller are fulfilled'.

In a contract for the sale of specific goods, a term of the contract may thus reserve to S the right of disposal, most commonly until the goods are paid for. If the contract is one for unascertained goods, it will be noticed that s 19(1) provides that either the terms of the contract *or* the appropriation itself may similarly reserve the right of disposal. When appropriating unascertained goods to the contract, it seems that S may *unilaterally* reserve the right of disposal and this will prevent property passing to B even if the reservation is in breach of contract.[2] Such unilateral reservation has frequently arisen in contracts for the sale of goods to be carried by sea where S desires some security against B's insolvency. An established method of achieving this is for the bill of lading to be made out to the order of S or his agent instead of to the order of B, and then the property in the goods shipped remains in S until he indorses the bill of lading to B and the price is paid or tendered. The SGA, s 19(2) expressly recognises and provides for this situation.[3]

In other contexts, 'simple' reservation of title clauses, under which S retains title in specific goods until payment, have long been regarded as lawful and practical devices. In *McEntire v Crossley Bros Ltd*,[4] B agreed to acquire an 'Otto' gas engine from S on terms that it should remain S's property until B had paid the full price of £240 in instalments. In fact, the contract characterised the parties as 'owner and lessor' and 'lessee' but provided that the engine would become B's property as 'purchaser' on completion of the instalments. Other clauses covered the care of the engine by B, the marking of it to indicate S's ownership and B's undertaking not to remove it from its installation without S's consent. Moreover, provision was made for S to retake the engine in the event of B's default or bankruptcy. After paying one instalment, B was adjudicated bankrupt. In the House of Lords, the assignees in bankruptcy argued that S had nothing more than a charge on the engine for the unpaid price and, as such, the charge was void for non-registration under the Bills of Sale Acts 1878 and 1882. The

---

2 See *Wait v Baker* (1848) 2 Exch 1; *Gabarron v Kreeft* (1875) LR 10 Exch 274; Bradgate, 'The Post-contractual Reservation of Title' [1988] JBL 477.

3 Section 19(2) provides: 'Where goods are shipped, and by the bill of lading the goods are deliverable to the order of the seller or his agent, the seller is prima facie to be taken to reserve the right of disposal'. NB this is a prima facie rule only and may thus be displaced by contrary intent.

4 [1895] AC 457; see also *Re Shipton, Anderson & Co and Harrison Bros & Co* [1915] 3 KB 676 (S sold a specific parcel of wheat in a warehouse in Liverpool on terms of 'payment cash within seven days against transfer order'. The wheat was requisitioned by the Government under emergency powers. Held S had reserved the right of disposal under the SGA, s 19 until payment by B and, as property had not passed to B, the contract was frustrated and S was excused from performance).

House of Lords held that the intent of the parties was that property in the engine had never passed to B, this being a question which 'the law permits them to settle ... for themselves by any intelligent expression of their intention'.[5] It is regrettable that, in many instances, the courts have failed to heed this direction: numerous decisions have paid lip-service to the task of upholding the parties' true intent while, at the same, effectively negating it.

The *Romalpa* decision

The full impact of reservation of title was not felt until the litigation in *Aluminium Industrie Vaassen BV v Romalpa Aluminium Ltd.*[6] There, S, a Dutch company, sold to B, an English company, a quantity of aluminium foil some of which B intended to use in its manufacturing process. B took delivery of the foil but never paid in full; subsequently B became insolvent and a receiver was appointed by B's banker under powers contained in a debenture. At that date, B owed S over £122,000 and the receiver held a quantity of foil which was in its original, unmixed state, and having a value of £50,235. Prior to insolvency, B had also sold some of the foil to third parties and the receiver kept the proceeds from that sale (£35,152) in a separate account. S claimed an order for delivery up of the unmixed foil and a declaration that they were entitled to the money held in the separate account on the basis that they could trace the proceeds of the sales into that account.

S's claims were based upon clause 13 of the contract which, somewhat crudely translated from the Dutch,[7] provided that (i) ownership of the foil transferred to B only when B had paid all that was owing to S (ii) until the date of payment B had, if S desired, to store the foil in such a way that it was clearly identifiable as S's property (iii) articles/objects manufactured from the foil were to become S's property as 'surety' for full payment by B (iv) until payment B must keep the manufactured articles for S in B's capacity as 'fiduciary owner' and, if required by S, B should store the articles in such a way that they could be recognised as such, and (v) B was entitled to sell and deliver the manufactured articles to third parties, in the ordinary course of business, on condition that, if S required, and B had not fully discharged its indebtedness to S, B should 'hand over' to S the claims B might have against such third parties. Most importantly, B conceded that while money was owing to S the foil was held by B as a bailee for S but B also contended that, after the foil was re-sold to third parties, the relationship between S and B was purely one of debtor and creditor. If accepted, this argument would have meant that, after such a sale, there could be no possibility of fiduciary relations between S and B allowing S to trace into the bank account. It should also be noted that the contract provided only for the sale of *articles/objects* made from the foil and thus did not contemplate the sale of original, unmixed foil. The Court of Appeal held that (i) the original, unmixed foil, which was held by the receiver, remained S's property and S was entitled to an order for its delivery up and (ii) a right should be implied that B might sell the unmixed foil as well as articles made from it and thus S was able to trace and claim the proceeds of the sub-sales in priority to both the general body of B's creditors and the bank as secured creditor.

---

5 [1895] AC 457 at 467, per Lord Watson.
6 [1976] 1 WLR 676.
7 Reservation of title clauses had long been used in Europe, see Pennington, 'Retention of Title to the Sale of Goods under European Law' (1978) 27 ICLQ 277.

The reasoning in *Romalpa* was based squarely upon acceptance of the notion that reservation of title is legitimate and, on the facts, was achieved by the fiduciary relationship which was created between the parties with the availability of the concomitant, equitable remedy of tracing. Roskill LJ elaborated upon the relationship and explained that there was no objection to B's having a dual capacity: when B resold the foil to the third party he sold as a *principal* in relation to the third party but as an *agent* for S. In his capacity as a principal, B could pass the property in the goods to the third party[8] but, in his capacity as an agent for S, B was accountable to S. Only at first instance in *Romalpa* was there a brief mention of the argument that a charge had been created which was void for non-registration[9] but Mocatta J regarded this contention as superfluous where S *retained* title: the proceeds of sale belonged in equity to S and a charge was thus not contemplated.

Sellers of goods promptly began to employ 'Romalpa' clauses in their contracts, much to the consternation of the banks which had previously relied on the supremacy of fixed and floating charges. Unsurprisingly, receivers and liquidators retorted with arguments against Romalpa clauses which have centred upon four principal grounds. First, it may be argued that the clause has not been successfully integrated as a term of the contract. As explained earlier, in relation to unascertained goods S may unilaterally impose a simple reservation of title *after* contract at the date of appropriation[10] but there is little doubt that complex, extended reservation of title clauses, must be incorporated as terms of the contract if they are to be effective.[11] Second, it may be asserted that, as a question of construction, the clause does not effectively permit reservation of title by S. Romalpa clauses have been cast in many differing forms and much may turn upon their precise draftsmanship; in retrospect, the judgments in *Romalpa* interpreted clause 13 leniently but, as will be seen later, subsequent decisions have been severe and exacting in their interpretation of Romalpa clauses. Third, the courts have clearly favoured the argument that, in the commercial context of Romalpa clauses, it is difficult to establish fiduciary relations between S and B and this has proved a potent weapon with which to defeat such clauses: it is one thing for the parties to apply the labels of agency, bailment and fiduciary duty to their adversarial, arm's length dealings but quite another to establish that those substantive relationships exist. Fourth, a widely accepted argument in post-*Romalpa* decisions has been that the clause gives rise to a charge created by B within the Companies Act 1985, s 396(1), which is void against the liquidator or any creditor (and thus a receiver) of the company for non-registration under the Companies Act 1985,

---

8   At first instance, Mocatta J considered that B could pass the property in the goods as a buyer in possession under the SGA, s 25(1).

9   At that time, void for non-registration under the Companies Act 1948, s 95.

10   Apart from analysing the dealings in terms of counter-offer and acceptance (see eg *Butler Machine Tool Co Ltd v Ex-Cell-O Corpn (England) Ltd* [1979] 1 WLR 401), there is no direct authority regarding, for example, an invoice on which S rubber-stamps a Romalpa clause.

11   See *John Snow & Co Ltd v DBG Woodcroft & Co Ltd* [1985] BCLC 54 (S established that, in accordance with general principles, its clause was an integral term of the contract for the sale of timber to B. Boreham J held that, as Romalpa clauses are now commonplace, they do not have to be specifically drawn to B's attention and thus do not require 'Lord Denning's red ink treatment' (p 60). However, the clause in *John Snow* was a simple reservation of title).

s 395(1).[12] It is often asserted that a Romalpa clause should be regarded as a registrable charge because, in effect, it creates a security interest in S. This argument is furthered in that there is no mechanism for the registration of Romalpa clauses and thus they are invisible to parties dealing with B. Such invisibility has implications for the accounting treatment of goods which are bought and sold subject to Romalpa clauses[13] and poses problems for banks wishing to lend money to B in that it is difficult accurately to evaluate the extent of B's assets. However, after the decision in *Clough Mill Ltd v Martin*[14] (see below), the charge argument has been discredited where the intent of the parties is patently that *title* is retained by S in the original, unchanged goods delivered to B. Once this basic proposition is accepted, it follows that B is not the owner of the goods and thus unable to grant a charge over them.

There are several distinct objectives of Romalpa clauses and the extent to which the variously-worded clauses succeed in attaining these objectives can now be considered. The difficulties may be sub-divided, viz (i) S reserves title to the original, unmixed goods delivered to B (ii) S claims products manufactured from the goods delivered to B and (iii) S claims the proceeds of sale from a resale by B.

The seller claims ownership of the original, unmixed goods

In this situation, where the clause reserves title in the original, identifiable goods until payment is made by B for those goods, there is no doubt that it is effective and, indeed, this point was conceded in *Romalpa* itself. It cannot be stressed enough, however, that S's goods must literally be unchanged and identifiable if this conclusion is to be reached. The matter was put beyond doubt in *Clough Mill Ltd v Martin*[15] where it was emphasised that there is nothing objectionable in S's simple reservation of title to the original goods supplied and that a court must give effect to the true intent of the parties. There S supplied yarn to B on terms that risk should pass to B on delivery but that 'ownership of the material shall remain with the seller, which reserves the right to dispose of the material until payment in full for all the material has been received by it'. B became insolvent before paying for all the yarn and S notified the receiver that it wished to repossess the unused yarn, which B had not paid for, but the receiver refused. At first instance,[16] it was held that the purpose of the clause was to provide security for the payment of the purchase price and thus property passed to B subject to a charge in favour of S but that the charge was void against the receiver for non-registration. The decision was reversed by the Court of Appeal. It was stressed that B had never acquired any title to the yarn and, under the SGA, s 19(1), S was able to assert legal title to yarn which B had not paid for

---

12 In the case of an unincorporated buyer, the argument is that the charge should be registered under the Bills of Sale Acts 1878 and 1882.
13 See Eastaway, 'Romalpa: Accounting, Tax and other Financial Implications' (1978) NLJ 439; Davies, *Effective Retention of Title* (1991), pp 120-123.
14 [1985] 1 WLR 111.
15 [1985] 1 WLR 111.
16 [1984] 1 WLR 1067.

and which was identifiable and unused. As B had never acquired any title to the goods, he was never in a position to confer a charge and so the question of whether it was void for non-registration did not arise. The unassailable logic of this approach was affirmed by the House of Lords in *Armour v Thyssen Edelstahlwerke AG*,[17] where it was re-emphasised that title never passes to B in the simplest form of reservation of title under consideration here.[18]

It is significant that the clause in *Clough Mill* referred unequivocally to S's reservation of 'ownership' and so the court distinguished *Re Bond Worth Ltd*,[19] where S sought to retain 'equitable and beneficial ownership' until full payment by B or until resale in which case S's 'beneficial entitlement' would attach to the proceeds of sale. There it was held that an equitable charge had been created in favour of S which was void for non-registration. There was no doubt regarding S's ownership in the *Armour* case, as the clause provided that 'all goods delivered by us remain our property (goods remaining in our ownership)' and draftsmen should clearly be at pains to avoid any terminology which smacks of that in *Re Bond Worth Ltd*.

Retention of title until payment in full and the 'all accounts' clause

The simplest Romalpa clause retains ownership only in those goods for which B has not paid. However, the clause may go further in stipulating that S reserves title until all goods supplied by him under the contract have been paid for[20] or, further still, until B settles all outstanding accounts, this term being referred to as an 'all accounts' or 'all moneys' clause.[1] As discussed later, these clauses should help to resolve S's practical difficulties in identifying and separating the goods which have not been paid for because, under such a provision, he can retake all the goods in B's possession.

In *Clough Mill*, the clause in question retained ownership 'until payment in full for all the material has been received ... in accordance with the terms of this contract' and the validity of this provision was appraised because it is clear that B might have paid in part and, when S exercises his right of repossession, he might be retaking goods for which B has already paid. If S should then resell the goods, questions arise concerning (i) whether account must be taken of the part-payment already received in deciding how much S should be entitled to sell and (ii) if S does resell, whether he is accountable to B in respect of the part-payment already received or in respect of any profit made on the resale by reason of a rise in market prices. Robert Goff LJ suggested that, if the contract between S and B is still subsisting rather than having been determined by S's acceptance of B's repudiation, it would be possible to imply a term that S should resell sufficient goods for the payment of the outstanding

---

17 [1991] 2 AC 339.
18 It appears that receivers and liquidators are, finally, allowing S's repossession of identifiable, unmixed goods: see *Re Weldtech Equipment Ltd* [1991] BCLC 393, 394 per Hoffmann J; *Compaq Computers Ltd v Abercorn Group Ltd* [1991] BCC 484, 488 per Mummery J; *ICI New Zealand Ltd v Agnew* [1998] 2 NZLR 129 (considered below, where it was common ground that S could recover the unchanged plastic pellets in B's possession).
19 [1980] Ch 228.
20 See *Re Bond Worth Ltd*, above; *Re Peachdart Ltd* [1984] Ch 131.
 1 See *Romalpa* (ownership transferred when B 'met all that is owing'); *Borden (UK) Ltd v Scottish Timber Products Ltd* [1981] Ch 25 (property passed to B when '(a) the goods the subject of this contract; and (b) all other goods the subject of any other contract ... have been paid for in full'); *Armour v Thyssen Edelstahlwerke AV* [1991] 2 AC 339 (see below).

price only, the remainder to be available to B for the purposes of the contract. If, in breach of the term, S should sell more than was necessary, he would have to account for the surplus to B. This equitable solution would thus mean that part-payments were taken into account and S could not retain any profits on a resale. If, on the other hand, the contract is determined by S's acceptance of B's repudiation, S could resell as an owner uninhibited by any contractual restrictions although he would have to repay any part of the price already paid by B because this sum would be recoverable by B on the ground of failure of consideration. S could, nevertheless, claim damages from B for any loss caused by B's repudiation and set-off that claim against his liability to repay B. Alternatively, Robert Goff LJ suggested that, if there were the necessary intent to create a trust, S could be held to retain title as a trustee thus applying the proceeds of sale in discharge of the outstanding balance of the price and then holding any surplus on trust for B. Sir John Donaldson MR suggested a simpler solution but one that must be premised on the contract's continuing in existence. He considered that 'until' in the phrase 'until payment in full' connoted 'not only a temporal but also a quantitative limitation'.[2] S could thus continue to sell the goods until he was paid in full but if, thereafter, he continued selling he would be accountable to B for having sold goods which, upon full payment having been received, were B's goods.

The second type of clause mentioned above, where S attempts to reserve title until all *accounts* are settled, is more controversial in that it attempts to reserve ownership in the goods supplied until another debt, incurred under some other contract, is discharged. In seeking to reserve ownership in goods until some extraneous debt has been paid, this type of clause begins to resemble the creation of a security interest rather than a pure retention of title. It has thus been cogently argued that it should be regarded as creating a charge not least because, if S retakes goods which B has paid for in full in order to settle an outstanding debt under a separate contract, S would immediately have to refund the price of those goods to B on the basis of failure of consideration and this would defeat the object of the clause.[3] Similarly, where B has a running account with S and always owes a certain amount, the 'all accounts' clause means that title in the goods supplied will, seemingly, never vest in B, although this should not affect the title of third parties where the goods are resold. Although there was an 'all accounts' clause in *Romalpa*, the point was not argued and, likewise, *Clough Mill* did not decide upon the efficacy of such a provision. However, in *Armour v Thyssen Edelstahlwerke AG*,[4] the clause retained title 'until all debts owed to us including any balances existing at relevant times – due to us on any legal grounds – are settled' and the House of Lords expressly approved the 'all accounts' provision[5] but expressly chose not to evaluate the situation where goods which have been partially paid for are retaken by S.

---

2 *Clough Mill Ltd v Martin* [1985] 1 WLR 111, 126.
3 See Goodhart and Jones, 'The Infiltration of Equitable Doctrine into English Commercial Law' (1980) 43 MLR 489, 508; Goodhart, 'Clough Mill Ltd v Martin – A Comeback for Romalpa?' (1986) 49 MLR 96; Cf Goode, *Proprietary Rights and Insolvency in Sales Transactions* (2nd edn, 1989), p 101, who, supporting *Clough Mill*, argues that S may 'impose any conditions he wishes for the transfer of ownership to his buyer'.
4 [1991] 2 AC 339.
5 See also *John Snow & Co Ltd v DBG Woodcroft & Co Ltd* [1985] BCLC 54 (clause was upheld where title was retained until B 'has met all the indebtedness to the seller').

S must be able to identify the goods which he repossesses as his property

Thus far in the consideration of Romalpa clauses, S has sought to retake unmixed goods, which are readily identifiable as his, under the terms of a simple reservation of title clause. Wherever possible, S should identify his goods by serial numbers or use appropriate packaging/labelling and have an express provision, such as that in *Romalpa*, that B must store the goods so that they are recognisable as S's property. However, if the 'all accounts' clause is effective (see earlier), this should help S as he can retake *all* his goods in B's possession and does not have to search only for those which have not been paid for.

It is clear from the decision in *Hendy Lennox (Industrial Engines) Ltd v Grahame Puttick Ltd*[6] that S's goods do not lose their identity where they are attached to other property but can be detached without damage either to the goods or property. In *Hendy Lennox*, S supplied diesel engines to B which were to be incorporated in 'diesel generating sets' but which could be detached in 'several hours' by removing bolts and connections, both the engines and generating sets remaining intact. Accordingly, Staughton J held that the proprietary rights of S to the engines were unaffected by this incorporation as 'they just remained engines, albeit connected to other things'.[7] The facts of *Hendy Lennox* were straightforward in relation to the incorporation and removal of the engines but, in many situations, there will be considerable argument as to whether S's goods can retain their identity after separation and whether B's property might be damaged thereby.

In other cases, where S supplies anonymous, small goods such as nuts and bolts, he may be faced with, and deterred by, the receiver's contention that the goods cannot be identified.[8] Where S's goods have been mixed with B's goods or those belonging to other suppliers, the 'whole matter is far from being within the domain of settled law'[9] and so it is necessary to examine the different forms which an admixture or annexation of goods may take,[10] using as a rough guide at least some of the permutations recognised in Roman law.[11]

Goods incorporated in real property or annexed as a fixture

It is settled law that if goods are incorporated in real property they become part of the realty and, likewise, if goods are annexed to land and cannot be severed without substantial damage to the goods or the realty, the goods become fixtures in the ownership of the landowner. There can be an effective provision in the contract that S can enter the land and retake his goods and such clauses can be found in hire-purchase contracts where, for example, heavy machinery has to be affixed to the land or a building in order to function.[12] In Romalpa cases, S

---

6   [1984] 1 WLR 485.
7   [1984] 1 WLR 485 at 494.
8   See Wheeler, *Reservation of Title Clauses* (1991), pp 133-135.
9   *Sandeman & Sons v Tyzack and Branfoot Steamship Co Ltd* [1913] AC 680, 695 per Lord Moulton.
10 See *Crossley Vaines on Personal Property* (5th edn, 1973), Ch 19; Matthews, 'Proprietary Claims at Common Law for Mixed and Improved Goods' [1981] CLP 159; Worthington, *Proprietary Interests in Commercial Transactions* (1996), Ch 6, paras 6.2.2-6.3.
11 See Leage, *Roman Private Law* (3rd edn, 1964, ed Prichard), pp 178-187; Borkowski, *Textbook on Roman Law* (2nd edn, 1997), pp 187-194.
12 See Guest and Lever, 'Hire-Purchase, Equipment Leases and Fixtures' (1963) 27 Conv 30.

might thus retake loose building materials, for example, but a reservation of title clause would be ineffective where such materials have become incorporated as part of a building.[13]

Admixture of goods without loss of identity

Perhaps the commonest mixture in the context of Romalpa clauses is where S's goods are mixed with B's (or another seller's) identical goods so that they are indistinguishable from B's goods but have not lost their physical identity or changed form, eg where S's wine is mixed with B's wine of the same type and quality. This commingling of goods, corresponding to the Roman classification of *confusio*,[14] must be a frequent occurrence in sales of commodities, eg S's wheat is mixed with B's wheat, or where B stores identical goods from various sellers in a warehouse from which deliveries are made to sub-buyers.

The general rule of English law is that, where the mixing is made with the consent of the parties or by accident, ownership in common results but, if the mixing is *wrongful*, the entirety of the goods will belong to the innocent party with no obligation to account to the wrongdoer.[15] This rule is justified in that it is the wrongdoer who has prevented identification of the goods and the rule's stringency both guarded against and deterred fraud and enabled the innocent party to retake his goods without fear of liability in tort. Nevertheless, the punitive nature of the rule meant that the innocent party might benefit substantially where the proportion of his goods was minimal in comparison with that of the wrongdoer. Accordingly, as recognised in *Indian Oil Corpn Ltd v Greenstone Shipping SA (Panama)*,[16] a just solution might often be that of ownership in common where the contributions in the mixture can be ascertained with a degree of accuracy. There the defendant shipowners chartered their vessel for the carriage of oil from Russia to India and mixed some of their own oil, already on board the vessel, with that which was to be shipped to India. The plaintiff receivers of the oil in India claimed the entire cargo. Staughton J found no conclusive evidence of wrongdoing on the part of the shipowner and held that there was ownership in common of the mixed oil. In cases of wrongdoing, the judge emphasised that the old, punitive rule was a rough and ready one more suited to times when accurate measurements could not be made. Thus, even in situations of wrongdoing, it would be unjust to award the entire mixture to the innocent party when his share could be ascertained precisely, such a measurement often being feasible in modern conditions and certainly attainable on the facts of *Indian Oil*. However, Staughton J limited this rule to cases where the mixed goods were substantially of the same nature and quality and stressed that any uncertainty

---

13 See *Trust Bank Central Ltd v Southdown Properties Ltd* (1991) 1 NZ Conv C 190, 851 (S lost title to joinery incorporated as a fixture in real property); Wylie, 'Reservation of Ownership: A Means of Protection for Unsecured Creditors of Bankrupt Builders' (1978) 42 Conv 37.

14 The Roman classification recognised *commixtio* as a mixture where separation was possible, eg black beads mixed with white beads, and here ownership would remain unchanged.

15 See *Ward v Aeyre* (1615) 2 Bulst 323; *Lupton v White* (1808) 15 Ves 432; *Buckley v Gross* (1863) 3 B & S 566, 574-575 per Blackburn J; *Spence v Union Marine Insurance Ltd* (1868) LR 3 CP 427, 437-438 per Bovill CJ; *Sandeman & Sons v Tyzack and Branfoot Steamship Co Ltd* [1913] AC 680, 695 per Lord Moulton.

16 [1988] QB 345; see Brown, 'Admixture of Goods in English Law' [1988] LMCLQ 286.

regarding quantity should be resolved in the innocent party's favour. Similarly, the innocent party could claim damages for any loss suffered in respect of quality or otherwise, by reason of the admixture.

The reasoning in *Indian Oil* is logical but it is unclear where the burden of proof lies regarding the quantities of goods in the mixture and the extent to which any 'uncertainty' should be resolved in the innocent party's favour. The onus should surely be on the wrongdoer to prove that the innocent party's goods are not in the mixture because the innocent party is obviously at a grave disadvantage if he must try to establish the precise quantity of his goods in the mixture. Indeed, it is difficult to see how S could ever achieve this where B has mixed several quantities of anonymous goods, such as nails or screws, and regularly resells quantities of those goods from the mixture. If this is the position, a separate storage provision in a Romalpa clause would be of no avail to S as, although B's mixing would then be wrongful, S would be unable to discharge the burden of proof and B would profit from his wrongdoing.

Admixture of goods with loss of identity

There is only sparse authority in English law relating to a mixture which causes the mixed goods to lose their separate identity so that a new product results, this classification corresponding to the Roman *specificatio*, eg wine made out of grapes. One view is that, following the rules on commingling without loss of identity and subject to the notion, discussed above, that a wrongdoer may lose his interest in the goods, the parties here become tenants in common of the new product according to the respective proportions of their goods contained in that product.[17]

It is suggested that the view which is likely to gain universal acceptance is that, where the new thing cannot be reduced to its original constituents then, provided the maker of that new thing is *bona fide*, he becomes its owner even though none of the materials used were his.[18] This conclusion has certainly been reached in several of the Romalpa cases involving goods manufactured by B, both where S has sought to claim ownership of manufactured products under an express contract term[19] and where he has not utilised a such a provision.[20] Where the mixture is wrongful, the new product might belong to S in its entirety or, alternatively, if B were to acquire ownership of the new thing, S and any other former owners of the goods would have actions in conversion or wrongful interference against the maker of the thing.

Accession: goods become annexed to other goods

This is the situation where goods are attached or annexed as accessions to other, more substantial goods, thus corresponding to the Roman category of *accessio*, eg writing added to parchment. The basic rule of *accessio* was that the accessions

---

17 See *Farnsworth v Federal Taxation Comr* (1949) 78 CLR 504, 510 per Latham CJ; *Coleman v Harvey* [1989] 1 NZLR 723; Goode, *Proprietary Rights and Insolvency in Sales Transactions* (2nd edn, 1989), p 92.

18 See *International Banking Corpn v Ferguson Shaw and Sons* 1910 SC 182 (B, in good faith, bought from S a quantity of oil which belonged to O. B made lard from the oil. Held the lard belonged to B); Smith, *Property Problems in Sale* (1978), p 204.

19 *Clough Mill Ltd v Martin* [1985] 1 WLR 111.

20 *Borden (UK) Ltd v Scottish Timber Products Ltd* [1981] Ch 25.

became the property of the owner of the principal thing but it cannot be said conclusively that this rule has been adopted by English law. There are two major difficulties in any question of accession, viz deciding, first, which thing *is* principal and which accessory and, second, determining *when* sufficient annexation has taken place to amount to accession and thereby vest ownership of the whole in the owner of the principal thing.[1] The principal thing is probably that which is greater in value[2] but there was no consistency on this rule in Roman Law and often an essential 'identity' test was posited so that, for example, painting on a tablet belonged to the artist.[3]

There is equal uncertainty regarding the question of when annexation has taken place. S's goods could be annexed to B's principal goods meaning that title in the entirety of the goods would pass to B and thus it is crucial to know when such an annexation takes place or, alternatively, whether S's goods could legitimately be separated from B's principal goods and retaken. Several tests have been advanced to decide this issue[4] but they all turn on whether the accessory is severable from the principal chattel. The test of 'injurious removal' seems to have gained most acceptance. Under this test the owner of the principal thing acquires title to the accessory *only* if its separation from the principal thing would cause serious damage to, or destruction of, the whole. For example, if S's engine[5] or tyres[6] can be detached from B's car without damaging the car, S can recover his goods, this rule being applied in the *Hendy Lennox*[7] decision, considered earlier. Other variants on this test are that of 'separate existence'[8] (ownership by accession applies only where the accessory has ceased to have a separate existence and has become integrated in the principal thing) and 'destruction of utility'[9] (ownership by accession applies only where removal of the accessory destroys the utility of the principal thing). All of these tests are elusive and equivocal: it is quite possible, for example, to reach the conclusion that a car's tyres become an integral part of the vehicle meaning that, under the third test, its utility would be destroyed if they were removed.[10] Finally, it has been suggested[11] that an analogy be drawn with fixtures to land (considered earlier) and thus an examination should be made of the degree and purpose of the annexation, ie goods attached to the principal thing would be treated as accessions to it unless it could be proved that they were not intended to be permanent.

1 The issue is important in hire-purchase where it is common for the goods to be improved by the debtor/hirer's addition of accessories; see Goode, *Hire-Purchase Law and Practice* (2nd edn), Ch 33.
2 See *Crossley Vaines on Personal Property* (5th edn, 1973), p 432; French Civil Code, Art 569, views the largest in value as the principal thing or the largest in volume if the values are roughly equal.
3 See Justinian, *Digest* 41. 1. 9. 2.
4 For a detailed consideration see Guest, 'Accession and Confusion in the Law of Hire-Purchase' (1964) 27 MLR 505.
5 See *Rendell v Associated Finance Pty Ltd* [1957] VR 604.
6 *Bergougnan v British Motors Ltd* (1929) 30 SRNSW 61; *Thomas v Robinson* [1977] 1 NZLR 385.
7 [1984] 1 WLR 485.
8 See *Lewis v Andrews and Rowley Pty Ltd* (1956) 56 SRNSW 439 per Manning J (dissenting).
9 See eg *Regina Chevrolet Sales Ltd v Riddell* (1942) 3 DLR 159.
10 This was the conclusion reached in *Regina* (above): tyres thus became part of a truck by accession as they were 'integrated and harmonised' (p 162, per MacDonald JA).
11 See Guest, 'Accession and Confusion in the Law of Hire-Purchase' (1964) 27 MLR 505, 509.

In the Romalpa situation, there is clearly a danger that S may lose title to B by accession and thus, wherever it is appropriate for the type of trading involved, S should insert an express term in the contract prohibiting the incorporation of his goods into B's principal chattel. If B breaches that term, his actions should be regarded as wrongful with the possibility that he would forfeit his interest to the entirety of the goods under the principles considered earlier. Alternatively, where B might annex his goods to S's principal chattel, S should consider an express term providing that the annexed goods become his and, although this might be the position under the common law rules of accession, title to the annexed goods would transfer to S under the express term in those instances where the degree of annexation would be insufficient under the common law. Such an 'attachment clause' is common in hire-purchase contracts and has been held to be effective in Australia.[12]

The seller claims products manufactured from the goods delivered to the buyer

It is clear from the foregoing analysis that S may recover his unmixed goods which are still in their original form and identifiable. Moreover, if the contract is *silent* regarding admixture or annexation of the goods, S's rights will depend on the principles considered earlier.

If, however, B's manufacturing process entails the consumption and loss of identity of S's goods, the general rule is that S's title to those goods is also lost. Consequently, it is crucial to know when this loss of individuality and character occurs. In *Borden (UK) Ltd v Scottish Timber Products Ltd*,[13] S supplied resin to B for use in making chipboard and reserved ownership of the resin until all goods supplied to B had been paid for in full, but the clause did not attempt to give S any rights in the finished chipboard. S knew that the resin would lose its physical identity within two days of delivery to B but the period of credit which was granted to B was much longer than this. S sought the right to trace the resin into the chipboard and thus claim a share of it. The Court of Appeal held that, once the resin was used in manufacture, it ceased to be a separable constituent of the chipboard and, as it had lost its identity, S's title to it was extinguished. S could thus not claim any property in the chipboard or in the proceeds of its sale and no term could be implied that S had any interest in, or charge over, the completed chipboard. It was stressed that, should S's claim be upheld, there would be intractable difficulties in quantifying the proportion of the chipboard which S could properly claim as attributable to his resin. Moreover, *Borden* effectively banished the idea that B could be a bailee of S's goods where the contract authorised B to consume the goods in the manufacturing process *before* B's obligation to pay arose. Bridge LJ[14] stressed that 'where it was never intended

---

12 See *Akron Tyre Co Pty Ltd v Kittson* (1951) 82 CLR 477 (plaintiff (P) let a vehicle to the hirer who fitted tyres to it but subsequently removed them and sold them to the defendant (D) who refused to deliver them to P. Held P could maintain an action against D in conversion).
13 [1981] Ch 25.
14 [1981] Ch 25 at 35.

that the resin should be recovered, either in its original or in its altered form' it was 'quite impossible to say that this was a contract of bailment'.[15]

The *Borden* reasoning was extended in *Re Peachdart Ltd*[16] to a situation where, to a certain extent, S's goods remained identifiable after the manufacturing process. There S supplied B, a manufacturer of handbags, with quantities of leather and the retention of title clause was modelled on the original terms in *Romalpa*. At the date of receivership, S claimed, *inter alia*, ownership of quantities of unused leather and completed and partly-completed handbags. It was conceded that S had title to the unused leather but S also argued that a specialist leather worker could identify a skin even after it had been made into a handbag. Vinelott J distinguished *Romalpa* as there the aluminium foil had not been used in any manufacturing process and had to be stored separately. Accordingly, it was held that the parties must have intended that once B appropriated a piece of leather and began to turn it into a handbag, it ceased to be the property of S. Instead, S had a charge on the handbags which, on the facts, was held to be void for non-registration.

The *Peachdart* approach was followed most recently in *Chaigley Farms Ltd v Crawford, Kaye & Grayshire Ltd*[17] where S, a farmer, supplied livestock to B, an abattoir, on terms that title in the 'livestock' and 'goods' was reserved to S until payment was made by B. Garland J held that there was an effective retention of title so long as the animals were alive but that, when they were slaughtered, S's title was extinguished. The judge refused to give an 'extended meaning'[18] to 'livestock' and 'goods' even though he acknowledged that the parties might have intended the Romalpa clause to extend to carcasses and, likewise, there were no problems in identifying the goods as S was B's sole supplier of animals.[19] Similarly, in *ICI New Zealand Ltd v Agnew*,[20] S supplied plastic pellets to B which B used to make transparent plastic containers, the contract providing that S retained 'ownership of the goods' until payment in full was received. S argued that (i) the pellets had not lost their original identity by being made into containers (ii) no other materials were used in the manufacturing process and (iii) that process could be reversed thus returning the containers to pellets. None of these arguments found favour with Henry J who decided that the pellets were used to make a product 'completely different in form'[1] from the pellets themselves, an argument graphically illustrated to the Court when the pellets were placed inside one of the containers. Accordingly, it was held that S had lost ownership in the pellets. The judge considered that this conclusion was unassailable as S had made express provision for goods which were manufactured from the pellets (see below), thus drawing a distinction between the goods which were the subject of the sale, ie the pellets, and the products resulting from the manufacturing proces, ie the containers.

---

15 In *Clough Mill Ltd v Martin* [1985] 1 WLR 111, 116, Robert Goff LJ emphasised that bailment can exist where the goods remain unchanged pending sale by B or consumption in his manufacturing process.
16 [1984] Ch 131.
17 [1996] BCC 957.
18 [1996] BCC 957 at 963.
19 Cf *Re Weddell New Zealand Ltd* (1996) 5 NZBLC 104,055 (on facts similar to *Chaigley Farms*, a more elaborate clause preserved S's title after slaughter even where the meat had been packed into cartons).
20 [1998] 2 NZLR 129.
 1 [1998] 2 NZLR 129 at 134.

A specific provision that ownership of manufactured products vests in S

In *Borden*, Bridge LJ[2] suggested that if S wished to acquire rights over the finished product he could do so only by express contractual stipulation but the two other judges opined that, if S were to have an interest in the completed chipboard, B would have to create a charge over it as security for the payment of debts incurred and, on the facts, the charge would be void for non-registration. The charge argument certainly prevailed in the earlier decisions. In *Re Bond Worth Ltd*,[3] S supplied raw acrilan which was to be woven into carpets by B but the provision that S was to have 'equitable and beneficial ownership of the products' was held to create a charge over the carpets which was void for non-registration. Likewise, in *Re Peachdart Ltd*,[4] even though there was a (lucid) clause by which S sought to retain ownership of the finished handbags and provided that B should act as a fiduciary for S in relation to such products, it was held that a charge was created over the complete and incomplete handbags.

The decisions above were premised on the fact that the manufactured products vested in B so that B might then create a charge over his own goods, but this assumption was questioned in *Clough Mill Ltd v Martin*.[5] There S supplied yarn to B which was to be made into fabric and the contract provided expressly that if any of the yarn was incorporated in other goods before payment, 'the property in the whole of such goods shall be and remain' with S until payment was made. In the Court of Appeal, both Robert Goff and Oliver LJJ considered (obiter) that, in principle, there was no reason why such a clause should not vest ownership of new products in S but both they and Donaldson MR thought that, in practice, the provision would more often give rise to a charge on the manufactured product in favour of S. This conclusion was based upon the fact that B will have borne the manufacturing costs of the new products and both B and other sellers may have contributed raw materials which are components of those new products. If S were to gain ownership of the newly manufactured goods he would thus receive a windfall profit of the full value of the new goods and this could not normally be the parties' true intent. Moreover, this conclusion was aided by the fact that other suppliers might have similar clauses vesting ownership of the new goods in themselves and the prospect of several suppliers claiming the goods was not at all sensible. This approach has been followed in several subsequent decisions where S has laid claim to new products. The clause in question has thus been held to create a charge over the new goods which was void for non-registration where a repairer of machines claimed ownership of any machine into which parts supplied by him had become incorporated.[6] Likewise, an unregistered charge resulted where S supplied cardboard sheets to B and claimed ownership of the cardboard boxes which were manufactured by B,[7] and where S supplied cloth which was made into dresses by B.[8]

It thus seems that only in rare circumstances might a 'new products' clause vest ownership of those new goods in S. However, in *Clough Mill*, Sir John Donaldson MR[9] suggested that 'if the incorporation of the yarn in, or its use as

---

2   [1981] Ch 25, 42.
3   [1980] Ch 228.
4   [1984] Ch 131.
5   [1985] 1 WLR 111.
6   *Specialist Plant Services Ltd v Braithwaite Ltd* [1987] BCLC 1.
7   *Modelboard Ltd v Outer Box Ltd* [1993] BCLC 623.
8   *Ian Chisholm Textiles Ltd v Griffiths* [1994] 2 BCLC 291.
9   [1985] 1 WLR 111, 125.

material for, other goods leaves the yarn in a separate and identifiable state, I see no reason why [S] should not retain property in it'. This view found favour in *Modelboard Ltd v Outer Box Ltd*,[10] even in those situations where B had added value to the goods by his labour and materials but, in *Modelboard*, the evidence was sparse regarding the process to which S's cardboard had been subjected by B and, having regard to the terms of the contract, a charge was held to exist. Moreover, the opinion was expressed in *Ian Chisholm Textiles Ltd v Griffiths*,[11] that it was not impossible for S to claim manufactured products provided very clear words specified that S *retained* title in the supplied goods and that title in the new goods *transferred* to him.

In conclusion, it is arguable that S may claim title to manufactured products provided that (i) the contract terms are unequivocal to that effect (ii) S's goods remain 'identifiable' and a 'new' product[12] has not resulted (here the work done/skill exercised by B would be important) (iii) B supplies no materials of his own or, perhaps, trivial, inexpensive items only, and (iv) only S's materials are incorporated in the goods and none from other suppliers. In particular, requirement (ii) is far from clear, and much doubt remains regarding this aspect of Romalpa clauses.

S claims a *proportion* of the new products equal in value to B's indebtedness?

In *Kruppstahl AG v Quitmann Products Ltd*,[13] the draftsman sought to avoid the problems discussed above by utilising a provision that S and B were to hold the new product jointly in the ratio of S's invoice value of the goods to those of B's goods but Gannon J held that this was a registrable charge as S was expressly acknowledging that he had only a limited interest in the new goods, that interest being confined to securing B's indebtedness for the price of the goods supplied by S.

In *ICI New Zealand Ltd v Agnew*,[14] S seemingly modified his Romalpa clause in order to address the windfall profit argument raised in *Clough Mill*. In *Agnew*, clause 10.2 of the contract provided that 'ownership of that proportion of the new products equal in value to the total sum owing to [S] shall on manufacture immediately vest in [S] absolutely and not by way of charge'. While Henry J acknowledged the *obiter dicta* in *Clough Mill* that, in principle, ownership of new products could vest in S, he considered clause 10.2 to be unworkable because (i) separate and continuing identification of the manufactured goods would be required to implement the provision (ii) there was no prohibition on B's incorporation of other materials in the manufacturing process and possibly materials from other sellers who used Romalpa clauses (iii) ownership of the

10 [1993] BCLC 623, 632-633 per Michael Hart QC (sitting as a Deputy Judge of the Chancery Division).
11 [1994] 2 BCLC 291, 299-301 per David Neuberger QC (sitting as a Deputy Judge of the High Court).
12 See *Pongakawa Sawmill Ltd v New Zealand Forest Products Ltd* [1992] 3 NZLR 304 (S supplied logs to B who converted them into sawn timber for sale; the New Zealand Court of Appeal held that S could claim the timber as the goods retained their identity); *Armour v Thyssen Edelstahlwerke AG* [1991] 2 AC 339 (S retained title where B cut the steel supplied into strips and the loss of identity point was not argued). See also Matthews, 'Specificatio in the Common Law' (1981) 10 Anglo-American L Rev 121; Whittaker, 'Retention of Title and Specification' (1984) 100 LQR 35.
13 [1982] ILRM 551.
14 [1998] 2 NZLR 129 (facts considered earlier).

new product did not relate to the price of the goods used to manufacture the individual product and no provision was made for the transfer of the new products to B once the amount owing to S was discharged and (iv) as B was allowed credit, S would never receive payment in full and B would never obtain title to the new product. Accordingly, it was held that the true meaning and effect of clause 10.2 was to create a floating charge over the new product and, being unregistered, it was void as against the liquidator.

The seller claims the proceeds from a resale by the buyer of the goods supplied

B may often sell the goods to a sub-buyer before payment is made to S and he may be expressly authorised to do so, as in *Romalpa* itself. Even if such a sub-sale is prohibited, the sub-buyer may acquire title to the goods under one of the exceptions to *nemo dat*. Most obviously, B might have apparent authority to sell the goods or sell them as either a buyer in possession under the SGA, s 25(1)/ Factors Act 1889, s 9,[15] or as a mercantile agent within the Factors Act 1889, s 2(1). As S will be unable to recover the goods from the sub-buyer, he may often try to claim the proceeds of the sub-sale but a Romalpa clause does not automatically impose upon B an obligation to account to S for the proceeds of sale of the goods in which title is retained by S and something more is needed if B is to be accountable to S in this way.

It will be recalled that, in *Romalpa*, it was conceded that B held the foil as a bailee until all money owing had been paid and the reservation of title clause both referred to B as 'fiduciary owner' of any goods manufactured from the foil until payment was made and required that, until payment, such goods be stored in such a way that they could be recognised as S's goods. However, B was expressly authorised to sell any manufactured goods (although it was *unmixed* foil which was sold) and thus he contended that, once such a sale had taken place, the relationship between S and B was that of debtor and creditor. Although the contract in *Romalpa* did not provide expressly that S could claim the proceeds of sale, it was held that the purpose of the reservation of title clause and the intent of the parties was to create a fiduciary relationship between S and B with the result that B was accountable to S for the proceeds of sale of the goods. This meant that the legal title to the proceeds vested in B but the beneficial ownership of such proceeds vested in S who, consequently, had the right to trace them in accordance with the principles in *Re Hallet's Estate*.[16] It was also significant in

---

15 Under ss 9/25(1), the sub-buyer would acquire title only on a *sale* by B and not under an *agreement* to sell which would be the position if B agreed to sell to the sub-buyer employing a Romalpa clause in that agreement: see *Re Highway Foods International Ltd* [1995] 1 BCLC 209. Also it seems that, in the absence of *actual* notice of a Romalpa clause, the sub-buyer's knowledge that Romalpa clauses are universally employed in the particular business concerned will be insufficient to constitute notice of S's rights under ss 9/25(1). In order to be outside the protection of ss 9/25(1), the sub-buyer may have to know of the Romalpa clause *and* that S has not been paid: see *The Saetta* [1993] 2 Lloyd's Rep 268; cf *Re Interview Ltd* [1975] IR 382 (sub-buyer knew of the Romalpa clause; held he was not in good faith, he had notice of S's rights and was not protected under any exception to *nemo dat* in the Factors Act or the SGA).

16 (1879) 13 Ch D 696.

Romalpa that the receiver had kept the proceeds of sale in a separate account and thus there was no question of different moneys becoming mixed.

Although there is a somewhat obscure right to trace at common law,[17] it has always been assumed that the finding of a fiduciary relationship in *Romalpa* was both pivotal to that decision and essential for any future claim to trace in equity but, startlingly, no other claim by S to proceeds of sale has been successful. By and large, subsequent decisions have restricted *Romalpa's* field of operation so drastically that, currently, it is difficult to see how a successful claim to proceeds might be established.

The process of confinement began with *Re Bond Worth Ltd*.[18] There a clause provided that 'our beneficial entitlement shall attach to the proceeds of resale or to the claim for such proceeds', arguably indicating conclusively that B had legal title to the goods while S retained the beneficial interest and, thereby, cementing the fiduciary relationship. Slade J held that, during the subsistence of the Romalpa provision, B was entitled to use any moneys from a resale for his own purposes and mix those moneys with his own in the ordinary course of business. He thus considered this unfettered right of B to be irreconcilable with a fiduciary relationship but, instead, to be indicative simply of B's position as a debtor. The judge added that, in *Romalpa*, the fact of a bailment relationship had been conceded, B was a 'fiduciary owner', a provision for separate storage existed and the proceeds of sale had been segregated by the receiver.

The restriction of *Romalpa* continued in *Hendy Lennox (Industrial Engines) Ltd v Grahame Puttick Ltd*,[19] where Staughton J held that, as between S and B, S's proprietary claim to the engines in question was not lost by their incorporation in generating sets but, as some of the generating sets had been sold to sub-buyers and property in the goods had passed to those buyers, the dispute centred principally upon whether S might successfully claim a share of the proceeds of sale representing the engines in the generating sets. It was held that S's claim must fail. As well as reiterating some of the factors which had been emphasised in *Bond Worth*, viz there was no separate storage provision and no mention was made of 'fiduciary owners', Staughton J stressed that S's conditions provided only for repossession of the engines and, on the basis that the expression of one thing is the exclusion of the other, this militated against an implied right to the proceeds of sale. Most importantly, the agreement that B should have at least one month's credit was held to neutralise any fiduciary relationship and any implied obligation to keep the proceeds of sale in a separate account.

Hendy Lennox was followed in *Re Andrabell Ltd*,[20] where S supplied travel bags to B which were resold by B in the ordinary course of its business as a retailer and the proceeds paid into B's general bank account where they were mixed with other moneys. B went into liquidation still owing money to S but it was held that S's claim to the proceeds of resale must fail. As the clause provided solely and simply that ownership of the goods should not pass to B until payment had been received by S, the familiar litany of points which distinguished *Andrabell's* facts from *Romalpa* was, here, quite rightly enunciated. In the light of such a terse, rudimentary clause, the relationship of S and B could scarcely

---

17 See Pearce, 'A Tracing Paper' [1976] 40 Conv 277; Goode, 'The Right to Trace and Its Impact in Commercial Transactions – I' (1976) 92 LQR 360; Khursid and Matthews, 'Tracing Confusion' (1979) 95 LQR 78.
18 [1980] Ch 228.
19 [1984] 1 WLR 485.
20 [1984] 3 All ER 407.

be seen as fiduciary in nature but, instead, was deemed to be that of business creditor and debtor.

Although the decision in *Clough Mill Ltd v Martin*[1] breathed new life into the simple reservation of title clause, later decisions have sustained the hostile approach to S's claims for the proceeds of a resale and, indeed, these decisions have questioned the correctness of *Romalpa* itself . In *Pfeiffer (E) Weinkellerei-Weineinkauf GmbH & Co v Arbuthnot Factors Ltd*,[2] S supplied wine to an English importer, B, on terms of a 'property reservation clause' and B resold quantities to sub-buyers on credit terms. B then entered into a factoring agreement under which it assigned to the defendant debts owed to B by the sub-buyers of the wine. The sub-buyers paid the defendant but B failed to pay all it owed to S and thus S claimed to be the beneficial owner of the proceeds of the sub-sales and argued that the defendant's title to the debts assigned under the factoring agreement was subordinate to S's prior equitable title. Phillips J held that (i) where B was permitted to resell the goods in the normal course of business, the normal implication was that he did so on his account and not as a fiduciary (ii) the clause in question detailed the nature of the interests which S was to have by way of security in respect of debts created by sub-sales and its terms were inconsistent with a fiduciary relationship (iii) by agreeing to the provisions of that clause, B had thus created a charge over its book debts which was void for non-registration. The conclusion that S had only an unregistered charge was sufficient to decide in favour of the defendant but Phillips J added that the priority of interests between S and the defendant depended upon the order in which notice of their interests had been given to the sub-buyer; as the defendant had been the first to give notice, he had priority over S's interest.

Phillips J again took a narrow view of the law in *Tatung (UK) Ltd v Galex Telesure Ltd*.[3] There S employed two sets of conditions, the first specified that proceeds of sale belonged to S absolutely and the second obliged B to keep the proceeds of resales in a separate account for S's benefit. Phillips J stressed that this complex clause was the source of the parties' obligations rather than the equitable principles which might have applied in the absence of an express provision and, accordingly, a charge had been created over the proceeds of sale. In order to accentuate his restricted view of the law, the judge concluded by questioning the correctness of the first instance decision in *Romalpa* that no registrable charge had been created.[4]

The *Pfeiffer* decision was followed, on almost identical facts, in *Compaq Computer Ltd v Abercorn Group Ltd*.[5] However, the Romalpa clause in *Compaq* was much better drafted than that in *Pfeiffer* in providing, *inter alia*, that (i) S's goods should be stored separately so that they were identifiable; (ii) B held the goods as 'bailee and agent'; (iii) B had to account to S as bailee or agent for the full proceeds of resale; and (iv) B had to keep a separate account of such proceeds. Despite these provisions, Mummery J held that a charge was created over the proceeds of resale because S's interest in the proceeds was limited to the amounts owing by B and was determinable on B's payment of the outstanding debt. This denial of a fiduciary relationship in the face of such a clear provision and the

---

1　[1985] 1 WLR 111.
2　[1988] 1 WLR 150.
3　(1989) 5 BCC 325.
4　(1989) 5 BCC 325 at 337.
5　[1991] BCC 484.

imposition on the parties of the 'true construction'[6] of their relationship virtually abrogates successful claims to the proceeds of resale. It is somewhat paradoxical, therefore, that the proposals for reform in the Diamond Review (see later) do not consider that S's claim to proceeds should be viewed as creating a charge.

In the light of the decisions above, it remains to be asked whether a claim to resale proceeds might ever succeed. In order to have any chance of success, S must certainly integrate in the contract all the terms that were present in the *Compaq* case and some other provisions. First, there must be a provision for separate storage/identification of S's goods, second, a declaration that B is a fiduciary and, third, B should be designated as a fiduciary in making the resale and should be obliged to keep proceeds of resale entirely separate from his own moneys. A primary difficulty is whether S should attempt to claim the full proceeds of sale including all profits made by B. Here S is in a cleft-stick. The obligation to account for all the proceeds is more fitting to a fiduciary relationship proper and was the position in *Romalpa* itself, but there is a danger that this provision may be interpreted as commercially unrealistic and not representative of the true intent of both parties, in which case a charge might be held to exist. If, on the other hand, S allows B to keep profits and limits the obligation to account purely to the outstanding indebtedness to S, this may be construed as militating against a fiduciary relationship and, again, be indicative of a charge in the context of a debtor-creditor relationship.[7] Finally, there is the question of a period of credit allowed to B and whether he may use resale proceeds in his own business during that period. It may well be held that a period of credit is inconsistent with a fiduciary relationship and S's interest in the proceeds[8] but 75 days' credit was allowed in *Romalpa* and, while this was regarded as a formidable obstacle to the duty to account, it was held that the express terms of the contract must be followed. Even if S's contract terms are impeccably drafted, there are still great practical difficulties inherent in any claim for proceeds. It may, for example, be very difficult for S to identify the proceeds where his goods have been sold to sub-buyers along with other goods. Likewise, B will often have paid any proceeds into his general (often overdrawn) account. More often, there are rarely any moneys available to S but, instead, merely a succession of debts left unpaid by the sub-buyers.

Claims to the proceeds of resale of manufactured goods?

The same obstacles as those above apply to S's claim for the proceeds of resale of manufactured or mixed goods. In the current state of the law, it seems indisputable that such a claim would be construed as vesting the proceeds in B subject to charge in favour of S, as it is likely that S's goods may have been 'consumed'[9] and B's labour/skill in making the goods and the contribution of his (and possibly other suppliers') materials, are also factors which militate strongly in favour of a charge.[10]

6 [1991] BCC 484 at 496, per Mummery J.
7 See *Re Andrabell Ltd* [1984] 3 All ER 407, 411 and 415 per Peter Gibson J; *Pfeiffer (E) Weinkellerei-Weineinkauf GmbH & Co v Arbuthnot Factors Ltd* [1988] 1 WLR 150, 160 per Phillips J.
8 See *Re Andrabell Ltd* [1984] 3 All ER 407, 416 per Peter Gibson J; *ICI New Zealand Ltd v Agnew* [1998] 2 NZLR 129, 135-136 per Henry J.
9 See *Borden (UK) Ltd v Scottish Timber Products Ltd* [1981] Ch 25.
10 See *Clough Mill Ltd v Martin* [1985] 1 WLR 111.

Administration orders under the Insolvency Act 1986

S's rights under a Romalpa clause may be inhibited where an administration order is made under the Insolvency Act 1986, Part II, the statutory provisions being based upon many of the recommendations of the Cork Committee.[11] The 1986 Act empowers the court to make such an order directing that an administrator shall manage the business, property and affairs of the company during the period that the order is in force. The purpose of administration is thus to attempt to save the business from insolvency and preserve it as a going concern or achieve a more advantageous realisation of the company's assets than would be effected on a winding up.[12] Sections 10 and 11 of the 1986 Act provide that, during the period between the presentation of a petition for an administration order and the grant of such an order (or dismissal of the petition) and while the order remains in force, no steps may be taken to repossess the goods supplied under a retention of title agreement[13] except with leave of the court (or the administrator during the period of the order) and subject to such terms as the court may impose. The overall effect is that the enforcement of Romalpa clauses is frozen during the periods specified in the Act.[14]

Section 15 of the 1986 Act provides that the administrator may sell the goods supplied under a Romalpa clause provided that the court is satisfied that such a disposal would be likely to promote the purpose, or one of the purposes, of the administration order. A measure of protection is available to S under s 15(5) in that the net proceeds of the disposal must be applied towards discharging the sums payable under the Romalpa clause. Section 15(5)(b) provides that if the proceeds are 'less than such amount as may be determined by the court to be the net amount which would be realised on a sale of the ... goods in the open market by a willing vendor', then such sums as may be required to make good the deficiency shall be applied towards discharging the sums payable under the Romalpa clause. It should be stressed that s 15(5)(b) may be an imperfect safety-net for S as that section refers to the *market* price of the goods and, should that be less than the contract price, S would have only an unsecured claim for the balance.

It is thus apparent that the administrator may overreach S's rights under a Romalpa clause and sell the goods to third parties. Protection is available to such a person dealing with the administrator in good faith and for value in that, under s 14(5) and (6), the administrator is deemed to act as the company's agent and the *bona fide* third party need not inquire whether the administrator is acting within his powers.[15]

---

11 *Insolvency Law and Practice, Report of the Review Committee* (1982, Cmnd 8558), Ch 37.
12 See the Insolvency Act 1986, s 8.
13 Defined widely in the Insolvency Act 1986, s 251. In addition to goods supplied under a Romalpa clause, the restrictions on repossession apply to goods in the company's possession under a hire-purchase, conditional sale or chattel leasing agreement: see s 10(4).
14 See Anderson, *Administrators, Part II of the Insolvency Act 1986* (1987), Ch 4.
15 See also the Insolvency Act 1986, s 232, which provides that the acts of the administrator shall be valid notwithstanding 'any defect in his appointment, nomination or qualifications'.

Proposals for reform of the law

In 1895, the House of Lords[16] considered reservation of title to be a legitimate and unexceptional device within the notion of freedom of contract and this theoretical approach still underpins the use of Romalpa clauses as voluntary mechanisms which control the passing of property between S and B.[17] However, at the start of the 21st century, it is debatable whether Romalpa clauses are the product of genuine agreement between equals or, instead, represent the imposition of unwanted terms by a superior seller upon an inferior buyer. Moreover, Romalpa clauses exist primarily to protect S in the event of B's insolvency and, as third parties may then be affected to a remarkable extent, it is arguable that the emphasis upon freedom of contract should be attenuated. In cases of insolvency, the conspicuous criticism of effective Romalpa clauses is that S is placed in a preferential position without the necessity of having to register the retention of title agreement or, indeed, give it any external publicity whatever. A bank's floating charge must be registered in order to be effective and it can be unearthed by any other creditors if a search is made of the relevant register of charges. In contrast, Romalpa clauses allow S, in effect, to have an invisible security interest which is uniquely available to sellers of goods and is not a privilege which can be enjoyed by suppliers of services, for example.[18] It is thus commonly asserted that S's advantageous position causes the pool of assets available to unsecured creditors (such as the supplier of services to B) to be dissipated further and diminishes the efficacy of the system of credit in that banks are less inclined to lend money to B because an accurate assessment of B's assets cannot be made if goods in his possession are liable to be retaken by S.[19]

The Crowther Committee[20] recommended that Romalpa clauses be treated as security interests and should become registrable, those proposals being supported by the Cork Committee[1] which concluded that 'the absence of any provisions requiring disclosure of reservation of title clauses is unsatisfactory and should be remedied as soon as possible'.[2] The latest proposals are those of the Diamond Review[3] which recommends that Romalpa clauses should be characterised as security interests but the Review emphasises cogently that simple reservation of title clauses are not detrimental to B's other creditors.[4] Simple reservation of title clauses are defined as those by which S retains title to the goods still in B's possession and only until the price of those particular goods is paid *and* the slightly-

---

16 *McEntire v Crossley Bros Ltd* [1895] AC 457 (considered above).
17 See *Clough Mill Ltd v Martin* [1985] 1 WLR 111, 121 per Robert Goff LJ.
18 See *Insolvency Law and Practice, Report of the Review Committee* (1982, Cmnd 8558), Ch 37, para 1619; *Borden (UK) Ltd v Scottish Timber Products Ltd* [1981] Ch 25, 42 per Templeman LJ.
19 Against this, it may be argued that Romalpa clauses encourage the flow of trade in that S may, with increased confidence, allow credit terms to B.
20 *Report of the Committee on Consumer Credit* (1971, Cmnd 4596) paras 4.2.2-4.2.5, Part V and Appendix III.
1 *Insolvency Law and Practice, Report of the Review Committee* (1982, Cmnd 8558), Ch 37.
2 *Insolvency Law and Practice, Report of the Review Committee* (1982, Cmnd 8558), para 1639.
3 *A Review of Security Interests in Property*, A L Diamond (DTI, 1989).
4 *A Review of Security Interests in Property*, A L Diamond (DTI, 1989), paras 17.7-17.8.

augmented clause where S has a claim to receive the price of the goods from the proceeds obtained by B on a re-sale of the goods. These simple reservation of title clauses are regarded as 'purchase money security interests' and are not harmful to other creditors for several reasons. Whereas a security interest granted over *existing* property may effectively remove that property from the debtor's estate, a security interest over goods *newly-supplied* to B to secure simply the price of those goods is, at the very least, neutral in effect. The debt for the price of the goods is counter-balanced by the addition of the new property meaning that other creditors are not affected detrimentally if the property enters the estate subject to a security interest for its price. In fact, as the new property may help to augment the profits of the business, the other creditors may gain thereby and would not seek to discourage such new acquisitions.

The Diamond Review accepts the general principle that non-possessory security interests should be publicised by some form of registration or filing system and, accordingly, the Review recommends the introduction of a new 'notice filing' system of registration. All simple reservation of title clauses amounting to 'purchase money security interests' as defined above, would have to be perfected by the filing of a financing statement and, in the absence of such filing, the security interest would be ineffective against a receiver or administrator. A system for ordering the priority of competing security interests would be instituted and would depend upon the dates of the filing of the financing statements.[5] The criticism that this filing system would place an excessive burden on sellers, thereby diminishing the use of Romalpa clauses, is met by the proposal that the financing statement need not be linked to individual security agreements. Instead, S could file one financing statement for each buyer and, as a measure of protection for B, B would be required to sign the financing statement thus ensuring that he had notice of the Romalpa clause.

In cases of extended reservation of title, ie where S utilises an 'all moneys' or 'all accounts' clause or claims title to manufactured goods, the Diamond Review recommends that the clauses should be regarded as creating a charge which would have to be registered individually for each transaction.

5 See paras 11.7.1-11.7.8.

CHAPTER 18

The transfer of title by a non-owner

Introduction

The position of owner (O) – >seller (S) – >buyer (B)

There are numerous situations where goods may be sold by someone who is not their owner and it must be asked whether such a non-owner might be able to transfer good title in those goods to a buyer. It is natural to assert that this should be impossible on the basis that only an owner (O) should be capable of voluntarily transferring such a good title. In fact, this is the established, general rule of English law,[1] and a seller of goods is thus able to transfer only the title which he possesses, the position being summarised in the Latin maxim *nemo dat quod non habet.* Consider, for example, the situation where a thief steals O's car from his garage and resells it to B, a *bona fide* buyer who pays the market price for the car. The thief has no title and, likewise, B will not obtain any title from the thief. In this context, English law does not consider that the *bona fide* buyer's status warrants any special protection *per se* and his innocence and probity are, consequently, insufficient to deprive O of his vested ownership. Where O has been deprived of his car by a thief in the night, it is clear that he cannot be said, in any shape or form, to have facilitated the loss of his goods but perhaps a different conclusion should be reached where O has participated voluntarily in a transaction which goes awry. Does O still deserve the protection of the law where, for example, he agrees to sell his car to a buyer and is sufficiently lax and imprudent to allow B to drive away in the car before the cheque tendered in payment has been cleared? Many would assert that, when O discovers that his buyer is a swindler and only then regrets his carelessness, it is too late to divest a *bona fide* buyer of title to the car: O's loss of title is the price to be paid for his heedless indifference and, quite naturally, B's title should have paramountcy. It is possible to reach such a conclusion within the exceptions to the *nemo dat* rule but this is not an inevitable outcome because, instead of focusing on the legitimacy of B's claim to protection, the law subjects the initial transaction between O and the swindler to an intimate, technical analysis in order to ascertain whether O might feasibly be divested of his title. It is indisputable that the *nemo dat* rule supports O's *retention* of ownership in preference to B's *acquisition of* it.

---

1   The *nemo dat* rule was also well-known in Roman Law, see Buckland and McNair, *Roman Law and Common Law*, pp 77-78; De Zulueta, *Roman Law of Sale*, p 36.

Theoretically, B should not be prejudiced if he is obliged to return the goods to O or pay damages, as he has redress against his seller (S) for breach of the implied undertaking as to title in the SGA, s 12, but it is obvious that, in practice, this remedy is often valueless where S is a thief or a swindler as he will usually have absconded and/or be insolvent. Here B is often left to carry the loss. The position is the same if the situation is reversed and O loses title to B, in that O has only a potential remedy against the swindler in conversion. Consequently, the struggle between O and B for the right to the goods may well be crucial.

A critique of *nemo dat*

Although the *nemo dat* rule is firmly entrenched in English law, logic by no means dictates its acceptance. The opposite rule, that the rights of the innocent, *bona fide* purchaser merit protection and should have priority over O's vested rights of ownership, is equally tenable. Indeed, many European systems invert *nemo dat* and consider the dominant principle to be protection of the *bona fide* buyer of goods,[2] this approach being exemplified in Art 2279 of the French Civil Code which provides that 'en fait de meubles la possession vaut titre'. It is suggested that this is a rational strategy and that several compelling reasons exist to protect the *bona fide* buyer of goods.

First, in many of the cases of conflict of title between O and B those two parties are set at odds by the acts of a third party, eg a swindler who induces O to part with possession of his goods which are then resold to B. It is often the case that O voluntarily transfers possession to the swindler and he is certainly able to assess the risks inherent in the transaction, eg the swindler's creditworthiness. B, on the other hand, rarely has either the time or the ability to investigate the title to the goods as, unlike real property, there is no certain method of ascertaining such title and he can rely only on the fact of his seller's possession and outward, reasonable appearances. Both the security of transactions and the free-flow of commerce surely demand that, in normal circumstances, B should acquire title from his seller.

Second, B's acquisition of title is often dependent upon the legal nature of the transaction between O and the swindler and O's subjective intent regarding that transaction. This is particularly evident in instances of void and voidable contracts where, for example, B's acquisition of title can hinge on the issue of whether O's mistake as to the identity of the swindler renders the contract void. If this is the case, no title in the goods can transfer to B. Alternatively, the swindler's title might be voidable meaning that B can acquire a good title if he buys the goods from the swindler in the period before his voidable title is avoided by O. It is undeniable, however, that the *bona fide* B has no knowledge of the juridical act which has occurred between O and the swindler and so it is difficult to see why it should affect him. It is beyond doubt that B's appraisal of the transaction between himself and the swindler/seller can turn only on objective, outward appearances. B is surely entitled to protection precisely because he relied upon the seller's possession and the apparent normality of the transaction, yet it is plain that O's error of judgement in parting with his goods is often visited wrongly on the innocent buyer.

2   See the succinct, comparative survey made by the Scottish Law Commission, Memorandum No 27 (1976), *Corporeal Moveables*; Smith, *Property Problems in Sale* (1978), Chs VI and VII.

Third, O is frequently insured against the loss of his goods whereas it is most unlikely that B would be insured against the loss incurred in returning the goods to O. O will thus claim on his insurance policy and the insurer, who is subrogated to O's rights, can in turn commence proceedings against B in those situations where he has not acquired title to the goods. The insurer thus has his cake and eats it: O has paid regular premiums to the insurer against the exact risk of the loss of his goods which has occurred but, after indemnifying O, the insurer may nevertheless recoup this loss from the innocent buyer. It is incontrovertible that this entire scheme represents an inverted allocation of risks.

English law thus approaches the issue of transfer of title by a non-owner with the steadfast protection of O as the primary consideration. As was stressed earlier, instead of emphasising the desirability of B's acquiring title, the law asks whether circumstances might conceivably mean that O has lost title and, as a general rule, it is insufficient for B to rely solely on S's having possession of the goods and unimpeachable evidence of title.[3] Of course, it is obvious that a thief might have both possession and copious evidence of title, and it is often asserted that if such thieves could transfer a good title to B, ownership would become illusory. However, cases of outright theft might easily be exempted from any system which protected the buyer, although some legal systems have not even allowed the theft of O's goods to interfere with the *bona fide* buyer's protection.[4]

Remedies of the owner

Where O has an immediate right to possession of the goods, he is entitled to recover possession from anyone who has not acquired title to the goods. There are several possible remedies. First, he may retake the goods without any court order but such recaption is a dangerous course unless O is absolutely certain of his rights.[5] Second, he may bring an action for delivery up of the goods under the Torts (Interference with Goods) Act 1977, s 3, but this remedy of specific delivery is discretionary. Third, he may commence an action for damages against B under the 1977 Act or seek damages at common law for conversion. Moreover, O is not limited by having to seek a remedy against the party in possession of the goods: any person who has wrongfully converted the goods to his own use or to the use of another will be liable in damages to O for wrongful interference with the goods, provided O had an immediate right to possession at the date of the conversion. Any person who has, for example, sold O's goods will be liable in conversion. It is plain that, although O may lose title under one of the exceptions to *nemo dat*, he will have a remedy for wrongful interference against anyone who converted the goods before O's title was extinguished. Where O sues B and damages are assessed on the basis of compensating O for his entire interest in the goods, s 5 of the 1977 Act provides that payment of all heads of damage will extinguish O's title and, although the section does not expressly provide that O's title will vest in B, this seems the most likely outcome. A contemporary problem in the sale of goods relates to the question of improvements to the goods effected by B in the mistaken belief that he had title

---

3 For recent applications of this emphasis, see *National Employers' Mutual General Insurance Association v Jones* [1990] 1 AC 24; *Debs v Sibec Developments Ltd* [1990] RTR 91 (below).
4 Eg The Italian Civil Code 1942.
5 See the Law Reform Committee, Eighteenth Report (Conversion and Detinue), Cmnd 4774 (1971), paras 116-126.

to them. Under s 6 of the 1977 Act, in an action for wrongful interference (where O sues B for damages or delivery up of the goods) the court may make an allowance in B's favour to the extent of the value of the improvements.[6] This is largely a restatement of the earlier common law,[7] but the Act goes further and s 6(2) extends the availability of the allowance beyond the *actual* improver to a defendant who is a purchaser in good faith deriving his supposed title from the improver, either directly or indirectly.[8]

The exceptions to *nemo dat quod non habet*

Although English law accords primacy to *nemo dat*, it admits numerous exceptions to the rule which detract considerably from its potency. Until recently, a *bona fide* buyer of goods in an open market, or from a shop within the City of London, acquired a good title even if the goods had been stolen from O. The medieval rule of market overt had been much criticised as facilitating the disposal of stolen goods but, in 1966, the Law Reform Committee[9] recommended that the market overt principle should be extended to all *bona fide* purchases from retail premises or public auctions.[10] This radical proposal never seemed likely to be accepted and, in fact, market overt was abolished in 1995[11] but the existence of such a wide rule illustrated the law's desultory approach to the issue of *nemo dat*.[12] The modern law supposedly seeks a balance between the competing interests of O and B[13] but the protection of vested rights of ownership inevitably means that there is an overall bias in O's favour. The basic rule of *nemo dat* is embodied in the SGA, s 21(1):

> 'Subject to this Act, where goods are sold by a person who is not their owner, and who does not sell them under the authority or with the consent[14] of the owner, the

---

6   It is unclear whether B has such a claim for improvements where O simply seizes the goods from B: see *Thomas v Robinson* [1977] 1 NZLR 385 (O is liable for conversion of the components which comprise the improvements unless they have become irretrievably merged in the goods); Matthews, 'Freedom, Unrequested Improvements, and Lord Denning' [1981] 40 CLJ 340.

7   See *Munro v Wilmott* [1949] 1 KB 295; *Greenwood v Bennett* [1973] 1 QB 195.

8   See Ch 19 for more detail on the position in chain transactions.

9   Twelfth Report, *Transfer of Title to Chattels* (1966), Cmnd 2958; for notes on the Report see Diamond (1966) 29 MLR 413; Atiyah (1966) 29 MLR 541.

10 But see Lord Donovan's express reservations on this question, Twelfth Report, *Transfer of Title to Chattels* (1966), Cmnd 2958, pp 18-19.

11 Sale of Goods (Amendment) Act 1994, repealing SGA 1979, s 22(1).

12 For an interesting modern decision on market overt, see *Reid v Metropolitan Police Comr* [1973] QB 551; see also Pease, 'Market Overt in the City of London' (1915) 31 LQR 270; Davenport and Ross, 'Market Overt' in *Interests in Goods* (ed Palmer and McKendrick, 2nd edn, 1998), Ch 14.

13 See Lord Denning's celebrated statement in *Bishopsgate Motor Finance Corpn v Transport Brakes Ltd* [1949] 1 KB 322, 336-337: 'In the development of our law, two principles have striven for mastery. The first is the protection of property. No one can give a better title than he himself possesses. The second is the protection of commercial transactions. The person who takes in good faith and for value without notice should get a good title. The first principle has held sway for a long time, but it has been modified by common law itself and by statute so as to meet the needs of our times'.

14 'Consent' may here refer to the situation where B has not obtained possession of the goods but S assents to a resale from B to B2. Under the SGA, s 47, B2 will obtain a good title, free from S's rights of lien or stoppage in transit. 'Consent' also refers to agency, see below.

buyer acquires no better title to the goods than the seller had, unless the owner of the goods is by his conduct precluded from denying the seller's authority to sell.'

The exceptions to *nemo dat* must now be considered. Overall, the judiciary has upheld vested rights of ownership and the *nemo dat* rule whilst the mercantile community has sought exceptions to the rule which would promote security of transactions.[15] The resultant law is both fractured and fascinating.

Agency

If S sells the goods 'under the authority or with the consent of the owner', it is clear that S will be O's agent and thus, within the common law[16] of agency, S/A will have authority, actual or apparent, to transfer title in the goods to B.

Estoppel

Section 21(1) provides that B will acquire title to the goods if O is 'by his conduct precluded from denying the seller's authority to sell'. The SGA, s 62(2) expressly preserves the common law rules relating to principal and agent and so this wording obviously relates to a separate notion of estoppel and not simply apparent authority in agency. O may create apparent *ownership* in S and B may rely upon the appearance so created thereby gaining a good title to the goods. Equally, an agent (A) may have apparent *authority* to dispose of O/P's goods thereby binding P to the disposition made by A. It is thus clear that S may have 'authority to sell' within s 21(1) when he is either an apparent agent *or* an apparent owner.[17]

It has recently been suggested that it is easier to infer an authority in A to pass property to another than an authority to enter into an obligation on P's behalf[18] and, certainly, more imponderables would seem to be involved in evaluating A's apparent authority to bind P to a contract than in assessing A's authority to sell goods and create a good title in the buyer. Goods are, after all, material objects which are freely transferable without the necessity for an accompanying document of title. It is equally plain, however, that numerous bailees and depositaries can be legitimately in possession of O's goods or documents of title and if the mere entrusting of possession to another were to create an apparent authority in that other to dispose of the goods, ownership would be evanescent.

The single difficulty here is to decide when O might be estopped from denying S's authority to sell. In principle, estoppel could be construed widely in B's favour following the renowned *obiter dictum* of Ashurst J in *Lickbarrow v Mason*[19] that 'wherever one of two innocent persons must suffer by the acts of a third, he who

---

15 See Chorley, 'The Conflict of Law and Commerce' (1932) 48 LQR 51, 64-70.
16 The SGA, s 62(2) preserves the common law of principal and agent.
17 Both notions emanate from the seminal decisions at the end of the 18th and beginning of the 19th centuries, eg *Pickering v Busk* (1812) 15 East 38: see Ch 4.
18 *Shearson Lehman Bros Inc v Maclaine, Watson & Co Ltd* [1988] 1 WLR 16, 28 per Lord Bridge of Harwich.
19 (1787) 2 Term Rep 63, 70.

has enabled such third person to occasion the loss must sustain it'. The modern cases in this context have often considered that this *dictum* is too wide[20] and, in practice, estoppel has been granted such a restricted field of operation that O will lose title by this means in exceptional circumstances only.

Estoppel can now be subdivided, the thread connecting its differing types being that O must make an unequivocal representation of fact which is relied upon by B when he buys the goods from S. As in apparent authority in agency, the representation may be made directly to B, the third party, but this will be rare and, more commonly, O's representation involves instructions given to S to deal with the goods in some way. It is thus clear that the representation can be made under such circumstances of publicity as to justify the inference that B knew of it and acted upon it.[1]

ESTOPPEL BY REPRESENTATION

By words

It is self-evident that estoppel has the greatest chance of being established successfully where O represents by sufficiently unequivocal words that S has authority to sell. In *Henderson & Co v Williams*,[2] for example, bags of sugar belonging to O were stored in the warehouse of W, the defendant. A rogue and a swindler, R, fraudulently induced O to sell the sugar to him and, accordingly, O instructed W to hold the sugar to the order of R, the goods thus being placed at R's disposal. R then sold the goods to an innocent buyer (B) who, being suspicious, obtained a statement from W that he held the goods subject to R's order and, on being pressed further, W confirmed that he held the goods subject to B's order. When R's fraud and his failure to pay were discovered, O ordered W not to deliver the goods to B. It was held that both O and W were estopped from denying B's title to the goods: O had ordered the goods to be held to R's order and had thereby made him appear as an owner and W had attorned to the buyer, B, ie W acknowledged B's rights as a buyer and that he held the goods subject to B's order. Although estoppel is accorded a severely limited field of operation in the setting of the sale of goods, it is difficult to see how any other conclusion could have been reached on these paradigmatic facts.

A vivid illustration of estoppel by representation occurred in *Shaw v Metropolitan Police Comr*.[3] O wished to sell his car and was approached by a car dealer who said he was interested in buying it on behalf of a client.[4] O gave the dealer possession of the car, a letter certifying that he had sold it to the dealer and he also signed the notification of sale and transfer slip in the registration document. The dealer then agreed to sell the car to the plaintiff buyer (B) who gave the dealer a banker's draft in payment. The bank would not cash the draft

---

20 *Farquharson Bros & Co v King & Co* [1902] AC 325, 342 per Lord Lindley; *London Joint Stock Bank Ltd v Macmillan and Arthur* [1918] AC 777, 836 per Lord Parmoor; *Jones (R E) Ltd v Waring & Gillow Ltd* [1926] AC 670, 693 per Lord Sumner; Cf *Commonwealth Trust v Akotey* [1926] AC 72, 76 per Lord Shaw.

1 See eg *Farquharson Bros & Co v King & Co* [1902] AC 325, 341 per Lord Lindley.

2 [1895] 1 QB 521.

3 [1987] 1 WLR 1332.

4 The dealer had not 'bought or agreed to buy' the car from O within the Factors Act 1889, s 9 and the SGA, s 25(1) and was not, therefore, a 'buyer in possession' within those sections (see below).

for the dealer whereupon he disappeared and the price of the car remained unpaid. It then had to be decided whether O or B had the title to the car. The Court of Appeal held that the letter and signed slip given to the dealer were 'the clearest possible representation'[5] that O had transferred ownership to the dealer and that B was clearly entitled to rely on it. However, the court considered that B had not bought the car but, instead, had only *agreed* to buy it, the clear intention of the parties being that title in the car would pass to B only when the dealer was paid. Taking an entirely novel view of the law, the court held that, as the car had not been 'sold' by the dealer within s 21(1),[6] B had not acquired title to it.[7] The outcome was just, for although there was little to be said in support of O's claim, had B succeeded he would have obtained title to the car without paying for it.

Finally, the decision in *Debs v Sibec Developments Ltd*[8] emphasises that, even though O's statement may be an unequivocal representation of S's authority to sell the goods, it will be ineffective unless it is made voluntarily. In *Debs*, armed robbers forced O to sign a detailed receipt purporting to evidence the sale of his car to them and left with the car, the receipt and the car's registration document. It was held that estoppel by representation necessarily implied that the representation should be made voluntarily and thus, on the facts, O was not estopped. This is, of course, cold comfort for the *bona fide* buyer who relies upon unimpeachable evidence of title in the seller but the law's approach again sanctifies vested rights of ownership.[9]

By conduct

It is much more difficult to specify, in the abstract, when O's conduct might amount to a sufficiently clear representation that S has the requisite authority to sell. The decisions vary widely but, overall, conduct has led only rarely to O's being estopped.

The tone was set at the start of the 20th century by the restrictive decision of the House of Lords in *Farquharson Bros & Co v King & Co*.[10] There the plaintiff timber merchants (O) owned timber which was stored with a dock company. O's clerk had authority to send delivery orders to the dock company but only a limited authority to sell timber to well-known customers. The clerk invented an alias and ordered the dock company to hold timber to the order of this fictitious person. Using his alias, he then sold timber to the defendant buyers (B) and instructed the dock company to deliver the goods to B's order. O discovered the

---

5 [1987] 1 WLR 1332 at 1336, per Lloyd LJ.
6 Atiyah (*The Sale of Goods* (10th edn, 2001), pp 368-369) argues that the first part of s 21(1), viz 'where goods are sold by a person', is simply a recital and explanation of the general rule at common law and the *substantive effect* of s 21(1) begins with the words 'unless the owner ...' This view would mean that where B has agreed to buy the goods from S he should be able to rely on estoppel on appropriate facts. In fact, prior to *Shaw*, this interpretation seemed to be accepted tacitly.
7 Although *Shaw's* case stresses that an *agreement* to sell is insufficient for the SGA, s 21(1), it is suggested that estoppel will apply where the goods are pledged by S or there is some other disposition for value. It is likely that the 'dealer' in *Shaw* was not a genuine car dealer but, if he had been such a dealer, *Shaw's* facts might better have been argued on the basis of the Factors Act, s 2(1). But it is also likely that the agreement to sell would not have been within the Factors Act, s 2(1) (see below).
8 [1990] RTR 91.
9 See further Brown, 'Involuntary Estoppel and Transfer of Title in the Sale of Goods' [1990] NILQ 257.
10 [1902] AC 325.

fraud and sued B in conversion. The House of Lords held that the timber still belonged to O and the defence of estoppel failed for two reasons. First, B had not acted on any representation of O's concerning the clerk's authority and knew nothing of any statements made by O to the dock company and, second, the proximate cause of the loss was the clerk's fraud and not any act of O's. The decision thus refused to accept any notion that O owed a duty of care to organise his business so that loss was not caused to innocent purchasers.[11] The Law Lords had dismissed this case tersely[12] but the majority in the Court of Appeal[13] had followed the approach of *Lickbarrow v Mason*[14] and had accepted the arguments on estoppel which involved acknowledging that O had, in the widest sense, *enabled* the fraud to be perpetrated.

A liberal approach was evident in *Commonwealth Trust Ltd v Akotey*[15] where Akotey (O), a grower of cocoa in the Gold Coast, consigned by railway 1,050 bags of cocoa to Laing (S) together with the consignment notes. O had previously sold cocoa to S and was presumably confident that S would buy the goods on this occasion. Before the question of price had been settled between O and S, S sold the goods to the Commonwealth Trust (B) and handed over the consignment notes. In an action in conversion by O against B, the Privy Council held that O was estopped and was precluded from setting up his title against B. *Farquharson's* case was distinguished in that, in *Akotey*, the goods were delivered to S by the direct act of O and there was no intervention of a fraudulent agent, as in *Farquharson*. Lord Shaw considered that 'to permit goods to go into the possession of another, with all the insignia of possession therof and of apparent title, and to leave it open to go behind that possession so given and accompanied, and upset a purchase of the goods made for value and in good faith, would bring confusion into mercantile transactions, and would be inconsistent with law and with the principles so frequently affirmed, following *Lickbarrow v Mason*'.[16]

---

11 See Lord Macnaghten's comments at pp 335-336.

12 'A servant has stolen his master's goods, and the question arises whether the persons who have received those goods innocently can set up a title against the master. I believe that is enough to dispose of this case': [1902] AC 325, 329 per the Earl of Halsbury LC.

13 [1901] 2 KB 697 (A L Smith MR and Vaughan Williams LJ, Stirling LJ dissenting); see notes by Cohen (1902) 18 LQR 18; Ewart (1902) 18 LQR 159. See also *Canadian Laboratory Supplies Ltd v Engelhard Industries of Canada Ltd* (1979) 97 DLR (3d) 1 where, on very similar facts to *Farquharson*, the fraudulent agent was held to have apparent authority. However, in *Engelhard*, the Supreme Court of Canada stressed that (i) in the absence of any act by a responsible corporate official of P's, P was *not* estopped from denying A's authority (ii) in relation to certain transactions, T had made enquiries of such an official who had confirmed A's authority and this was decisive as a holding-out to T.

14 (1787) 2 Term Rep 63 (see above).

15 [1926] AC 72.

16 [1926] AC 72 at 76. See also *Nanka-Bruce v Commonwealth Trust Ltd* [1926] AC 77 which follows *Akotey's* case in the Law Reports and which also involved Laing's dishonest dealings in cocoa. In *Nanka-Bruce*, S consigned 160 bags of cocoa plus a consignment note to Laing (B). B was to resell the cocoa to merchants who were to check the weight and B would pay S according to the weight so checked. On the occasion in question, B sold the cocoa to T and delivered the consignment notes to him. The Privy Council held that the weight check did not suspend the passing of property in the goods to B; rather the sale to B was a *de facto*, completed sale and so T obtained title to the goods. In *Central Newbury Car Auctions Ltd v Unity Finance Ltd* [1957] 1 QB 371, 383, Denning LJ reflected upon the two cases and stressed that: 'In the one case the owner parted with the property to the rogue. In the other case he behaved as if he had. In each case the innocent purchaser was held to be protected. It would be deplorable if in the one case the innocent purchaser was protected and the other not'.

Although both the Court of Appeal in *Farquharson* and the Privy Council in *Akotey* were prepared to extend the scope of estoppel in this context, the general trend has been one of extreme caution in refusing to divest ownership.

It has become a basic axiom of estoppel by conduct that where O merely permits another to have possession of goods or documents of title he is not estopped from denying that other's authority to sell. If the rule were otherwise, any bailment of goods would enable the bailee to transfer title and, in contracts of hire-purchase, O's act of allowing the hirer/debtor to have possession of the goods would enable him to create a valid title in a buyer. Similarly, possession of documents of title may indicate that they have been deposited with the holder for safe keeping only. The decisions thus emphasise that something more than simple possession of goods and/or their documents of title is required for a valid estoppel and this extra dimension would be evident where, for example, O provides S with an acknowledgment or receipt that S has paid for the goods[17] or where O transfers his goods into the name of a broker in a wharfinger's books.[18] The latter examples are arguably definitive of estoppel but, as will be seen later, the cases show little consistency in deciding whether O has unequivocally acted so that an estoppel arises against him. It is clear that, as a general rule, the law draws no distinction between those cases where, on the one hand, S has possession of goods and, on the other, where S has possession of documents of title: both are regarded as insufficient *per se* to estop O. But it must be asked whether the possession of documents of title to goods should be accorded more significance than a simple possession of the goods. A wide range of persons may be in possession of O's goods and it is impossible to construe anything from possession alone but, when a seller has possession of documents of title to goods, it is arguable that they are in his possession purely for the purposes of sale and transfer of title and it is suggested that this fact should be accorded more weight when B's acquisition of title is considered.

The leading decision on the possession of documents of title is *Mercantile Bank of India Ltd v Central Bank of India Ltd*.[19] The Central Bank had advanced money to O on the security of certain railway receipts covering a consignment of goods and, as normal, the Bank returned the receipts to O so that he could obtain delivery of the goods. Instead, O pledged the receipts with the Mercantile Bank in return for an advance from them. The Privy Council held that the Central Bank's prior interest prevailed as possession of the receipts 'no more conveyed a representation that the merchants were entitled to dispose of the property than the actual possession of the goods themselves would have done'.[20]

The corresponding modern decision on the physical possession of goods is *Central Newbury Car Auctions Ltd v Unity Finance Ltd*.[1] A swindler approached the plaintiffs (O) with a view to taking a car owned by them on hire-purchase. It was arranged that (O) would sell the car to a finance company who would then let it on hire-purchase terms to the swindler. O then gave the car's registration book to the swindler and allowed him to take possession of the car. In fact, the finance company refused the hire-purchase proposal. The car was sold to a car

---

17 Eg *Rimmer v Webster* [1902] 2 Ch 163 (below).
18 See *Pickering v Busk* (1812) 15 East 38 (considered in Ch 4).
19 [1938] AC 287.
20 [1938] AC 287 at 303, per Lord Wright.
 1 [1957] 1 QB 371.

dealer (by someone presumed to be the swindler) and then to the defendants who bought the car in good faith. The Court of Appeal held (Denning LJ dissenting) that O was not estopped from denying the swindler's authority to sell the car as merely giving him physical possession of the goods was not a representation that he had authority to sell. Moreover, the court stressed that a car's registration book is not a document of title, this point being accentuated in that the book contains a clear warning that the person in whose name a car is registered may not be the legal owner.

Central Newbury should be contrasted with two other leading decisions which indicate that it is impossible to make generalisations on the outcome of a dispute in this context. In *Lloyds and Scottish Finance Ltd v Williamson*,[2] the plaintiff owner (O) of a Jaguar saloon car delivered it to a car dealer (D) with instructions to sell it at any price D could obtain, with the proviso that D should account to O for £625. D sold the car on terms that the buyer (B) should pay the price to a third party (T), to whom D was indebted. Both B and T were *bona fide* and had no reason to suspect that D was not the owner of the car. The Court of Appeal held that B obtained a good title to the car on the basis that D was authorised to sell as an apparent owner/principal and not as an apparent agent or within the ambit of the Factors Act 1889. Likewise, it was emphasised that the decision did not rest on estoppel. Limiting his judgment to the ground of apparent ownership at common law, Salmon LJ held that O 'did much more than merely put [D] in possession of the motor car. He did what he could to induce any person buying the car from [D] to believe that [D] were the owners of the motor car by authorising [D] to sell it as owners'.[3] Although it is submitted that the decision is just, it is far from clear what O did here to create apparent ownership in D beyond giving him physical possession of the car.

However, in the second decision to be considered, *Eastern Distributors Ltd v Goldring*,[4] the seller of O's van did not obtain even physical possession of it and yet it was held that the buyer acquired a good title to it. In *Goldring*, O wished to buy a new Chrysler car but could not afford the deposit for its hire-purchase. Accordingly, he agreed with a car dealer (D) that D should sell O's existing van to a finance company and apply the proceeds of the sale in paying the deposits on the hire-purchases of both vehicles. To this end, O signed the hire-purchase documents in blank, leaving D to complete them. The hire-purchase on the Chrysler was rejected by the finance company. D had no authority to proceed unless both proposals were accepted but he nevertheless purported to sell the van to the finance company who accepted it as a genuine hire-purchase transaction and sent O the counterpart of the agreement. D told O that neither transaction had gone ahead. One month later, O sold the van to the *bona fide* defendant and the plaintiff finance company sought to recover it from him. The Court of Appeal held that O was precluded from denying D's authority to sell as he had supplied him with the necessary *indicia* of ownership and, accordingly, the finance company acquired a good title to the van that prevailed against any other claimant. Although O never gave physical possession of the van to D, this was clearly not an obstacle to D's appearing to be the owner on the facts of the case. It is suggested that both the *Lloyds* and *Goldring* decisions are correct but

---

2 [1965] 1 WLR 404.
3 [1965] 1 WLR 404 at 410.
4 [1957] 2 QB 600; noted by Goodhart, 'Nature of the Title Passed by a Mercantile Agent at Common Law' (1957) 73 LQR 455; Powell, 'Title to Goods Sold by Owner after Unauthorized Sale by Owner's Agent' (1957) 20 MLR 650.

neither sits happily with the *Central Newbury* case where the swindler obtained physical possession *and* the registration book these being, indisputably, better evidence of title than either the documentation with which the dealer was armed in *Goldring* or the dealer's ungarnished possession of the car in *Lloyds and Scottish Finance.*

Devlin J's judgment in *Goldring* sought to unite apparent authority in agency with apparent ownership under the umbrella of an 'authority to sell' within s 21(1), but it should be stressed that there is one important difference between the two notions. Where the seller is an apparent owner no restrictions can attach to the manner or place of the sale, for an unfettered right to sell under any conditions is a privilege of ownership; a sale outside the normal course of business would thus be material *only if* the sale was made by a dealer/businessman and *only* to the extent that it might cast doubt on B's *bona fides* and whether he was put on enquiry.[5] This reasoning is not applicable to an apparent agent where, in general, an agent's failure to act in the ordinary course of business might mean that the sale was not within the agent's apparent authority.[6]

Overall, the conflicting decisions mean that it is extremely difficult to say with any degree of precision when estoppel might be successfully invoked in this context. Many of the cases in which O has lost his title are situations where there is an initial principal-agent relationship between the parties. For example, P/O may authorise A/S to deal with the property in some way and then deliver a document of title to A/S,[7] or sign a document of title in blank and deliver it to a broker.[8] If A/S disobeys his authority and sells the property or goes beyond a limitation placed on his authority,[9] P may be estopped from asserting his title. Many of the decisions in this group (some of which concern real property) are not justifiable on strict agency principles as A/S has no actual or apparent authority and they are thus closer to cases of apparent ownership. However, in these cases it is often the grant of initial authority between P/O and A/S which is accentuated as the basis of the decision.[10] There is at least as great a divergence

---

5 See *Lloyds and Scottish Finance Ltd v Williamson* [1965] 1 WLR 404.
6 *Motor Credits (Hire Finance) Ltd v Pacific Motor Auctions Pty Ltd* (1963) 109 CLR 87 (Australian High Court held that the sale was not in the ordinary course of business where a sale of cars by a car dealer took place outside business hours, the primary purpose of the transaction being that the buyer wanted the cars as security for a debt owed by the seller (decision reversed on other grounds [1965] AC 867).
7 Eg *Rimmer v Webster* [1902] 2 Ch 163 (O delivered a mortgage bond to a broker (A) and authorised him to sell it. A induced O to execute transfers of the bond to him which also acknowledged receipt of the purchase money by O even though O had received nothing. A submortgaged the bond with the defendant and O was held to be bound by A's acts).
8 See eg *Colonial Bank Ltd v Cady & Williams* (1890) 15 App Cas 267 (see Ch 4); *Fry and Mason v Smellie and Taylor* [1912] 3 KB 282 (O delivered share certificates and a signed, blank transfer to A authorising him to borrow not less than £250 on the shares but A borrowed £100 from T on the security of the certificates. Held that the mortgage was valid); cf *Fox v Martin* (1895) 64 LJ Ch 473 (O authorised A, a stockbroker, to sell shares and entrusted him with share certificates and a blank transfer. A deposited the certificates and transfer with a banker as security for an advance. Held that the banker had no title as against O); *Painter v Abel* (1863) 2 H & C 113 (no estoppel in a client's entrusting a solicitor with title deeds to obtain a loan on a mortgage of property when the solicitor forged the mortgage deed and appropriated the sum obtained).
9 See *Brocklesby v Temperance Permanent Building Society* [1895] AC 173 (O entrusted deeds to A and authorised him to pledge them for a specific sum. A pledged the deeds for a larger sum to a *bona fide* T. Held O could recover the deeds from T only on repayment of the full amount advanced on them).
10 See *Brocklesby v Temperance Permanent Building Society* [1895] AC 173; *Fry and Mason v Smellie and Taylor* [1912] 3 KB 282.

of opinion on estoppel in these agency cases as in those examined above and it is impossible to extract a coherent pattern from the contrasting decisions.[11]

ESTOPPEL BY NEGLIGENCE

It is quite possible for O to be negligent and thereby allow S to appear as an owner or as having O's authority to sell goods but, again, it is hardly ever the case that he might lose title because of such carelessness. Lord Macnaghten's graphic speech in *Farquharson Bros & Co v King & Co*[12] left no room for doubt in its stipulating that O is not estopped by carelessness 'however gross it may have been,' and he went on to say that should O choose to leave his dog unchained or his watch on a seat in the park and, as a result, the goods are subsequently bought by *bona fide* purchasers, O's right to recover his goods must not to be prejudiced. In general, the law considers that carelessness is a privilege of ownership. Consequently, if he is to succeed, B must establish that (i) O owed him a duty of care (ii) in breach of that duty O was negligent, and (iii) the negligence was the proximate cause of B's being induced to buy the goods.

In *Central Newbury Car Auctions Ltd v Unity Finance Ltd*,[13] the potential effect of O's negligence was canvassed in relation to his allowing the swindler to take possession of the car and its registration book, but the majority stressed the need for O to owe a duty of care to B and the manifest absence of such a duty in respect of O's title to his goods. Denning LJ dissented and considered that, on the facts, O should have foreseen that the complete stranger to whom possession was entrusted might dispose of the car for his own benefit.

Despite these difficulties, a duty of care was established in *Mercantile Credit Co Ltd v Hamblin*.[14] The defendant owner (O) of a Jaguar car wished to make arrangements through a car dealer, whom she knew, for the loan of £1,000 on the security of the car. O signed various documents in blank thinking they related to the mortgage of the car and the dealer gave O a blank cheque which he said she could fill in for the amount of the loan when it was finally approved. One of the documents signed by O was the plaintiff finance company's hire-purchase proposal form which the dealer completed himself offering the car for sale to the finance company and containing an offer by O to take the Jaguar on hire-purchase. The company accepted O's purported offer and paid the dealer £800 for the car. Subsequently, the finance company sought to enforce the agreement but O refused to pay any instalments. The Court of Appeal held that O was not bound by the agreement as she had not authorised the dealer to make any offer and was not estopped from denying that fact. However, the court felt that she owed a duty of care in respect of the documents submitted to the company by the dealer as 'she must ... have contemplated ... someone to whom the documents would ultimately go'[15] but she was not in *breach* of that duty because she knew the dealer, who was apparently respectable and solvent, and his blank cheque must have led her to believe that she could rely on his due performance of the arrangement he had made. Moreover, Sellers and Pearson LJJ considered that,

---

11 See *Bowstead & Reynolds on Agency* (16th edn, 1996), Arts 85, 86 and 87.
12 [1902] AC 325, 335-336.
13 [1957] 1 QB 371.
14 [1965] 2 QB 242.
15 [1965] 2 QB 242 at 265, per Sellers LJ.

even if O had been negligent, the proximate cause of the loss would still have been the dealer's fraud and not O's negligence. This is difficult to accept because if O *had* been negligent, it would be nugatory to argue that the proximate cause of the loss was the dealer's fraud, as O would have facilitated that fraud in the first place and, on the facts, the chain of causation leading to O would not have been broken. *Hamblin's* facts are arguably archetypical of estoppel by negligence and, as no estoppel could there be sustained, it is hard to envisage facts where a plea of estoppel by negligence might succeed.

The leading decision on estoppel by negligence is that of the House of Lords in *Moorgate Mercantile Co Ltd v Twitchings*.[16] The plaintiff finance company let a car on hire-purchase terms to a hirer who, before completing payment of the instalments, sold the car to the defendant car dealer. Both plaintiff and defendant were members of Hire Purchase Information Ltd (HPI), a private organisation which operates a register of cars held on hire-purchase terms. Most such cars are registered with HPI and car dealers, when offered a car for sale, normally contact HPI to see if it is the subject of a hire-purchase agreement. On this occasion, the plaintiff finance company had not registered the car with HPI and when the defendant dealer contacted HPI he was told that, according to their records, the car was not registered with them and so he bought the car from the hirer. The plaintiff finance company sued the defendants in conversion, the latter arguing that the plaintiffs were estopped from asserting their title because of their negligence in failing to register the car. The majority in the House of Lords held that the defendant was liable in conversion. As the plaintiffs were under no legal duty to the defendant either to join HPI or take care in registering the agreement with HPI, the plaintiffs were not estopped from pursuing their claim against the defendant.[17] It is clearly arguable that, after *Hamblin* and *Twitchings*, estoppel by negligence is so limited as to be virtually non-existent, particularly as recent decisions have followed this lead and refused to apply the notion on the facts.[18]

THE EFFECT OF ESTOPPEL

There has always been some debate regarding the effect of estoppel. The old view was that estoppel was simply a rule of evidence[19] precluding O from proving certain facts and thus it would not confer a real title, good against the world, but only a metaphorical or negative title binding upon the parties who were privy to the representation. The question was raised in *Eastern Distributors Ltd v Goldring*[20] (above) where the issue was whether the plaintiff finance company, having relied on O's representation, had acquired an

---

16 [1977] AC 890 (reversing [1976] 1 QB 225).
17 Arguments regarding estoppel by representation also failed as (i) the plaintiffs made no direct representation to the defendant (ii) HPI made the representation and, in so doing, was not acting as an agent of the plaintiffs (iii) the statement made by HPI was true as they had said only that the agreement was not *registered*.
18 See *Beverley Acceptances Ltd v Oakley* [1982] RTR 417; *Debs v Sibec Developments Ltd* [1990] RTR 91(Simon Brown J confirmed that there was no initial duty in O to prevent negligent loss of his goods and, on the facts (above), even if O had been under such a duty, the robbers' continuing threats justified his not reporting the robbery sooner than he did).
19 See Spencer Bower and Turner, *Estoppel by Representation* (3rd edn, 1977), pp 7-11 and 16-19.
20 [1957] 2 QB 600.

absolute title or whether the defendant, a *bona fide* purchaser for value without notice from O, might acquire title as he was not privy to the estoppel and not bound by it. If the idea of estoppel as a rule of evidence applied, the plaintiff finance company's title was vulnerable as it was not real and would be defeated on the subsequent sale to the defendant. However, it was held that, under the SGA, s 21(1), a real title was conferred upon the plaintiff and thus O had no title left to pass to the defendant. Devlin J stressed that the principle embodied in s 21(1) was not premised upon orthodox notions of estoppel but was a much broader rule of mercantile convenience based upon apparent authority. Section 21(1) could therefore apply to cases of apparent ownership or apparent agency and was not simply a restatement of the common law's rules on estoppel. Almost certainly, this view is now accepted and a real title is conveyed under s 21(1).[1]

Dispositions under the Factors Act 1889, section 2(1)

HISTORICAL BACKGROUND

The factor was a mercantile agent 'to whom goods are consigned for sale by a merchant, residing abroad, or at a distance from the place of sale, and he usually sells in his own name, without disclosing that of his principal; the latter ... with full knowledge of these circumstances, trusts him with the actual possession of the goods'.[2] It was recognised early in the 19th century that a factor might transfer a good title by virtue of apparent authority or apparent ownership where he effected sales of goods outside the actual authority conferred by the owner/principal, this view being clearly sanctioned in the revolutionary decision in *Pickering v Busk*.[3] It will be remembered from the earlier consideration of that case in the law of agency, that it was revolutionary in engendering a fledgling theory of apparent authority and thus broke free from the established notion of evaluating only the scope of A's actual, internal authority as conferred by P. As the decision also conflicted with the settled notion of *nemo dat,* it is scarcely surprising that its acceptance did not go unhindered.

As previously explained, estoppel and apparent authority at common law were such restrictive notions that a wider and more rational protection was needed for commercial transactions. As commerce rapidly expanded in the late 18th and early 19th centuries, the common law showed a conspicuous inability to recognise the new practices and procedures of the mercantile community. It had, for example, become common practice to leave factors in possession of bills of lading or other documents of title, especially where they were involved in export and import of goods and, furthermore, factors often had to arrange transport

---

1   See also *Mercantile Credit Ltd v Hamblin* [1965] 2 QB 242, 270 per Pearson LJ; *Stoneleigh Finance Ltd v Phillips* [1965] 2 QB 537, 577-578 per Russell LJ; *Snook v London and West Riding Investments Ltd* [1967] 2 QB 786, 803-804 per Russell LJ; *Moorgate Mercantile Co Ltd v Twitchings* [1977] AC 890, 918 per Lord Edmund-Davies.
2   *Baring v Corrie* (1818) 2 B & Ald 137, 143, per Abbott CJ; see Munday, 'A Legal History of the Factor' (1977) 6 Anglo-Am LR 221, 243 et seq.
3   (1812) 15 East 38.

and storage. It was thus imperative that these agents could raise money to pay their immediate expenses and this they often did by pledging the goods or documents of title as security for a loan of money. The common law consistently refused to recognise the factor's apparent authority to pledge and would not extend the principle of *Pickering v Busk*.[4] This conflict between law and commerce led to the enactment of no less than five Factors Acts (1823, 1825, 1842, 1877 and 1889) designed to protect *bona fide* transferees who dealt with factors in the normal course of business. In seeking to protect such *bona fide* purchasers/transferees, the Acts were designed to shift the emphasis towards B's reliance upon reasonable, objective appearances and away from the central tenet of estoppel that O's representation must in some way mislead B. Unfortunately, the wording used in the Acts, that agents had to be 'intrusted' with the goods, was evocative of estoppel reasoning and allowed the judiciary to focus upon facts which might indicate that O had not so intrusted the factor. The ambit of the legislation was thus severely limited by each new decision[5] and these cases led, in turn, to the sequence of amending statutes – the great number of Acts being testimony to the common law's rigid refusal and inability to alter its focus. Moreover, it is ironic that these Acts have had the effect of *limiting* estoppel at common law as the view has often been advanced that the existence of statutory protection indicates that the common law should not readily extend the scope of estoppel.[6]

FACTORS ACT 1889, SECTION 2(1)

Section 2(1) is the heart of the Factors Act (FA):

> 'Where a mercantile agent is, with the consent of the owner, in possession of goods or of the documents of title to goods, any sale, pledge, or other disposition of the goods, made by him when acting in the ordinary course of business of a mercantile agent, shall, subject to the provisions of this Act, be as valid as if he were expressly authorised by the owner of the goods to make the same; provided that the person taking under the disposition acts in good faith, and has not at the time of the disposition notice that the person making the disposition has not authority to make the same.'

Section 2(1) must now be dissected and its workings revealed.

Who is a mercantile agent?

The former factor constituted an established species of agent but the species is now extinct in commerce and the FA has to be applied to 'situations of much more casual agency, such as that of a motor car dealer obtaining offers for a

---

4 See eg *Dyer v Pearson* (1824) 3 B & C 38.
5 See eg *Fuentes v Montis* (1868) LR 3 CP 268; affd LR 4 CP 93 (O/P's withdrawal of A's authority by private communication to A meant that he was no longer 'intrusted' and a subsequent pledge was held to be invalid. This defect was remedied by the 1877 Act but 'intrusted' was abandoned only in the (current) 1889 Act).
6 See *London Joint Stock Bank v Simmons* [1892] AC 201, 215 per Lord Herschell; *Farquharson Bros & Co v King & Co* [1902] AC 325, 343 per Lord Lindley; *Weiner v Gill* [1905] 2 KB 172, 182 per Bray J; cf *Lloyds and Scottish Finance Ltd v Williamson* [1965] 1 WLR 404.

customer'.[7] It is unclear, however, which agents are to be classified as a mercantile agents (MA). The FA, s 1(1) defines a mercantile agent:

> 'The expression "mercantile agent" shall mean a mercantile agent having in the customary course of his business as such agent authority either to sell goods, or to consign goods for the purpose of sale, or to buy goods, or to raise money on the security of goods.'

Although the previous Acts had used the phrase 'agent intrusted', Channell J considered in 1907[8] that the phrase 'mercantile agent' represented a distillation of all the 19th century decisions – these older cases may thus be considered but caution is advised. It is clear that the definition excludes servants,[9] shopmen[10] and clerks.[11] Similarly, carriers,[12] warehousemen,[13] forwarding agents,[14] agents displaying goods in order to obtain offers for sale[15] and other pure bailees,[16] are not mercantile agents. The former group of shopmen and servants is excluded as such persons may not even be agents, let alone mercantile agents, and s 1(1) specifies that the MA must have authority in the customary course of *his* business. The latter group of bailees and custodiers is excluded because these individuals do not customarily perform any of the four functions specified in s 1(1).

Both the problems inherent in defining an MA and the common law's disinclination to divest O of his vested proprietary rights are encapsulated in the facts of *Brown & Co v Bedford Pantechnicon Co Ltd*.[17] There O was a furniture manufacturer who rented rooms in A's offices, in Holborn viaduct, in which to store furniture. A was to use his best endeavours to obtain orders for the sale of the furniture and was paid a 5% commission on sales. O also agreed by letter that A could remove any goods which were sold by him in the ordinary course of business and it was O's name painted over the door of the rooms. A pledged some furniture with the defendants who took possession of it. The Court of Appeal held that O could recover the furniture as (i) A was simply an agent to obtain orders which were 'executed' by O and he was not 'an agent for sale' and (ii) it was doubtful whether the goods were ever in A's possession as they were to remain in O's rented rooms and thus in O's possession. It was thus considered that the letter allowing A to remove goods when sold by him did not alter the character of his agency as one purely for the obtaining of orders. The *raison d'être* of the FA is the protection of *bona fide* third parties who deal with

---

7 *Bowstead & Reynolds on Agency* (16th edn, 1996), Art 89, para 8-142.
8 *Oppenheimer v Attenborough & Son* [1907] 1 KB 510, 514.
9 In *Hyman v Flewker* (1863) 13 CBNS 519, 527, Willes J excluded 'a mere servant or caretaker or one who has possession of goods for carriage [or] safe custody'.
10 See *Lowther v Harris* [1927] 1 KB 393 (below).
11 *Lamb v Attenborough* (1862) 1 B & S 831 (wine merchant's clerk permitted to have dock warrants for the purposes of the business was not an MA).
12 *Oppenheimer v Attenborough & Son* [1908] 1 KB 221, 226, per Lord Alverstone CJ; *Hyman v Flewker* (1863) 13 CBNS 519, 527, per Willes J.
13 *Monk v Whittenbury* (1831) 2 B & Ad 484 (wharfinger); *Cole v North Western Bank* (1875) LR 10 CP 354.
14 *Hellings v Russell* (1875) 33 LT 380.
15 *Brown & Co v Bedford Pantechnicon Co Ltd* (1889) 5 TLR 449.
16 Eg *Staffs Motor Guarantee Ltd v British Wagon Co Ltd* [1934] 2 KB 305 (below); *Kendrick v Sotheby & Co* (1967) 111 Sol Jo 470 (O left his Epstein bronze statuette with A so that A could arrange for it to be photographed and signed by Epsteins's wife. Without any authority from O, A took the statuette to the defendants and instucted them to sell it. Held that A was not an MA as his authority was limited to obtaining the photograph).
17 (1889) 5 TLR 449.

business agents in the normal course of trade, but the *Bedford Pantechnicon* decision is one of many which are insensible to the spirit of the legislation and which consequently diminish its efficacy.

An enduring difficulty of the FA is the determination of the extent to which the phrase 'customary course of his business' in s 1(1) limits the definition to types of agent in *recognised* and *regular* occupations, such as the 19th century factor. Some older decisions took the view that, as with the original factor, the inherent quality of an MA was his general occupation as such[18] but most modern cases indicate that this is not a requirement of being an MA. In *Lowther v Harris*,[19] O wanted to sell a tapestry and stored it in a house, asking A, an art dealer who had a shop nearby, to sell it on a commission basis. A lived in a flat in the house and brought customers to see the tapestry. A pretended that he had sold the tapestry to B1 for £525 and O allowed him to remove it, but A then sold it fraudulently to B2 for £250. It was held that A was an MA dealing in the usual course of business as an art dealer and not as a servant or shopman, even though he acted on an isolated occasion for one owner/principal. It should be stressed that, in *Lowther*, A was an art dealer and, had he not been, the position is unclear.[20]

There are statements in the modern decision in *Rolls Razor Ltd v Cox*[1] which seemingly demand that the MA must have some type of recognised status. There, a travelling salesman who sold washing machines direct to the public by door-to-door calls in a van loaded with the goods, was held not to be an MA. Winn LJ[2] indicated that the 1889 Act applied to the dealings of a 'certain category of persons ... with all the special characteristics, derived from status, not from contract, which appertain to a class of dealers to which it is relatively unlikely in modern times that there will be any additions'. It is clearly arguable that the *Rolls Razor* salesman should have been regarded as an MA and it is unclear what 'category' Winn LJ would have accepted as constituting such agents.

The one principal/one transaction notion promulgated in *Lowther* makes it difficult to know when a person may be an MA. The cases have clearly extended the original idea of the existing, customary authority of the factor to cover other business traders and dealers but the importance to be attached to the business

---

18 See *Hastings Ltd v Pearson* [1893] 1 QB 62 (A sold jewellery from door-to-door and pledged some with T. Mathew J considered he was not an MA as the Act applied only to persons who ordinarily carried on business as mercantile agents and the *pledging* was not a recognised business – the *Hastings* decision was overruled in *Weiner v Harris* [1910] 1 KB 285).

19 [1927] 1 KB 393; see also *Weiner v Harris* [1910] 1 KB 285; *Kendrick v Sotheby & Co* (1967) 111 Sol Jo 470 (held that it was not necessary to show that A had 'any kind of general agency business', per Widgery J); 'It is accepted that it was no bar to Mr Oakley being a mercantile agent that he did not normally deal in motor cars, and that this may have been a "one off" transaction': *Beverley Acceptances Ltd v Oakley* [1982] RTR 417, 431 per Donaldson LJ).

20 In *Hyman v Flewker* (1863) 13 CBNS 519, an insurance agent was held to be an 'agent' within the FA 1842 when he was entrusted with pictures to sell on a commission basis on one occasion only. Willes J considered (pp 527-528) that the agent's employment must correspond 'to that of some known kind of commercial agent' but that the employment of A 'did strictly correspond, though in a small way, to that of a factor'. *Hyman* was considered to be good law in *Lowther v Harris* (see p 398).

1 [1967] 1 QB 552.

2 [1967] 1 QB 552 at 578; Lord Denning MR held that A was not a factor as he did not sell in his own name but on behalf of P as an agent 'pure and simple' (p 568).

status of the agent is far from clear.[3] It can be said with certainty, however, that a person who undertakes to find a buyer for goods out of friendship and without any remuneration is emphatically not an MA[4] as his overall business character is absent. Also, a person who buys and sells goods on his *own behalf* cannot be an MA[5] as here the essence of agency is missing.

The common law has glossed the FA in one fundamental way in that it has been held that a person must be an MA at the date he receives the goods and it is insufficient that he subsequently becomes one, unless there is further consent to his possessing the goods at the date when he has become an MA. In *Heap v Motorists' Advisory Agency Ltd*,[6] O wanted to sell his car and let A have possession of it as A said, untruthfully, that he thought a friend would buy it. A was not an MA at that time but he later obtained a job as a car salesman and sold the car to the defendant. It was held that no title could transfer to the defendant. It is submitted that this decision reaches the wrong conclusion. A had initially been given possession in order to sell the car and, recognising that the Act is designed to protect *bona fide* transferees from mercantile agents, A was an MA at the time of such transfer, his length of service as such being both irrelevant to the transferee and impossible for him to discern.[7]

Finally, provided that it is clear that the person is an MA, it is immaterial that his authority is limited expressly by O[8] and the courts will not allow s 2(1) to be thwarted by a provision that property in the goods is to remain with O until payment.[9]

---

3   Could the Factors Act 1889 have applied to the facts of *Jerome v Bentley & Co* [1952] 2 All ER 114? There A entered O's shop on the pretext of looking for a present and was shown a diamond ring by O. A said he could not afford O's price of £550 but added that in the circles in which he moved he could get up to £1,000 for the ring. O said he only wanted £550 for it and entrusted it to A to sell on terms that (i) A could keep any surplus above £550; and (ii) the ring was entrusted to A for seven days and had to be returned to O thereafter. More than seven days later, A sold the ring to a *bona fide* B. Donovan J held that no title transferred to B as (i) no apparent ownership could be established on the facts by entrusting possession to A; (ii) A had no apparent authority to sell as an agent as O had made no representation to B that A had such authority; (iii) *Watteau v Fenwick* (see Ch 5) could not apply here as A had no usual authority as a 'class' of agent and had no authority at all when he sold the ring whereas, in *Watteau*, A had merely exceeded his existing authority; and (iv) an analogy with *Rimmer v Webster* [1902] 2 Ch 163 (see estoppel, above) failed because when A sold the ring to B his authority as an agent had terminated. It is often asserted that, in *Jerome*, A could not be an MA (see Atiyah, *The Sale of Goods* (10th edn, 2001), p 384) but the FA does not seem to have been pleaded and it is possible that he could be classified as an MA (see Parker, 'Mercantile Agents and the Single Transaction' (1952) 15 MLR 503).
4   *Budberg v Jerwood & Ward* (1934) 51 TLR 99 (A had a doctorate in Russian law and carried on a business as a lawyer advising Russians in this country. One client entrusted him with a pearl necklace for sale but he pledged it. A was not an MA as the transaction was to be performed out of friendship and not in a business capacity).
5   *Belvoir Finance Co Ltd v Harold G Cole & Co Ltd* [1969] 1 WLR 1877 (a car-hire company regularly sold cars which they had held on hire-purchase, lawfully and with the consent of the finance company, the option to purchase under the HP agreement being exercised at the time of sale. Held that they were not mercantile agents and could not transfer title to cars sold without the finance company's consent, since they sold cars on their own behalf and not on behalf of others).
6   [1923] 1 KB 577.
7   Lush J said (p 588) that a man who was entrusted with a car on the pretext of having an urgent mission to fulfil could not subsequently obtain a job as an MA and transfer good title to the car. This is correct, but the example is premised on the *capacity* in which A obtains possession (below) in that, if he *was* an MA at the date he got possession, he could still not transfer good title as he had not been given possession *as* an MA.
8   *Turner v Sampson* (1911) 27 TLR 200.
9   See *Weiner v Harris* [1910] 1 KB 285 (considered in Ch 16).

WITH THE CONSENT OF THE OWNER IN POSSESSION IN THE CAPACITY
OF A MERCANTILE AGENT

Consent

There is no overall definition of 'consent' in the FA but there are important
provisions regarding that notion in the FA, s 2. By s 2(4) the 'consent of the owner
shall be presumed in the absence of evidence to the contrary'[10] and, in summary,
s 2(3) provides that if the MA is in possession of goods with the consent of O
and obtains possession of the documents of title by virtue of his possessing the
goods, he shall be deemed also to have possession of the documents with the
consent of O. This section would apply if, for example, owners of a cargo of
tobacco indorsed the bill of lading relating to the cargo to an MA who was
thereby able to have a dock warrant made out in his name. If the MA then
pledged the goods to B by handing the warrant to him and B honestly believed
the MA was the owner of the cargo, the pledge would be valid because, by s 2
(3), the MA would be deemed to have been in possession of the dock warrant
with the owner's consent.

The question of O's consent has classically caused difficulties where the MA
obtained O's consent to the possession by using fraud or larceny by a trick under
the old rules of theft. Some older decisions took the view that O could not possibly
consent to the MA's possession in this situation and that an MA was 'as capable
of stealing as any other man, and, if he has stolen the goods, there can be no
question … that he must be taken to hold possession of them without the consent
of the owner'.[11] If this view were followed, it would detract substantially from the
bona fide buyer's protection under the FA and it was subsequently rejected in several
decisions[12] but the conclusive change in approach came with the reasoning in
Pearson v Rose & Young Ltd.[13] O, a retail tobacconist, delivered his car to a car
dealer (MA) for display and in order to obtain offers for its sale but the MA had
no authority to sell it. The MA probably intended from the outset to sell the car
and thus, in relation to it, it was likely that he had committed larceny by a trick
but, nevertheless, O clearly consented to the MA's having possession of the car.
However, the MA obtained possession of the car's registration book (log book)
by the ploy of sending O on a bogus errand to visit the MA's wife who had
supposedly been admitted to hospital. As a result of this, O forgot that he had left
the log book with the MA and the circumstances thus indicated that O had definitely
not consented to the MA's having possession of it. The MA then sold the car, with
the log book, to the *bona fide* B. The Court of Appeal stated that the fact that the

---

10 In *Stadium Finance Ltd v Robbins* [1962] 2 QB 664 (considered below), it was considered
    that O's consent to the MA's possession was rebutted where O retained the car's ignition
    key.
11 *Oppenheimer v Frazer and Wyatt* [1907] 2 KB 50, 71, per Fletcher Moulton LJ. See also
    Oppenheimer v Attenborough & Son [1908] 1 KB 221, 232, per Kennedy LJ; *Heap v
    Motorists' Advisory Agency Ltd* [1923] 1 KB 577 (car obtained from O by larceny by a
    trick: O's consent was held to be lacking. *Folkes v King* (below) was distinguished); *Lake
    v Simmons* [1926] 2 KB 51, 72, per Atkin LJ.
12 See *Folkes v King* [1923] 1 KB 282 (the majority (Bankes and Scrutton LJJ) was of the
    opinion that if O in fact consented to the MA's having possession, it was immaterial whether
    the MA committed larceny by a trick); see also *Lake v Simmons* [1926] 2 KB 51 (the
    majority (Bankes and Warrington LJJ; Atkin LJ dissenting) held that a customer was
    'entrusted' (for the purposes of an insurance policy) with goods by a jeweller even though
    she had committed larceny by a trick); *Buller & Co Ltd v T J Brooks Ltd* (1930) 142 LT
    576, 578, per Wright J.
13 [1951] 1 KB 275.

MA had committed larceny by a trick was irrelevant. Denning LJ emphasised that this might seem illogical at first glance but there were many situations where O might consent to a thief's having *possession* of his goods but not to his *stealing* them; the thief's possession of the goods in such a case might nevertheless be with the consent of the owner.[14] However, although this would validate the MA's possession of the car in *Pearson*, O had never consented in any shape or form to the MA's being in possession of the log book. Accordingly, it was held that, within the FA, 'goods' meant car plus log book and that an MA does not act in the ordinary course of business when he sells a car with its log book if either the car or log book has been *obtained* without the owner's consent. Consequently, B did not obtain a good title to the car.

A moment's reflection exposes most of these conclusions as erroneous. First, the FA, s 2(1) speaks of the MA's being in possession of goods *or* documents of title and, in any event, a log book is not a document of title but is, at best, some evidence of title. There can be no justification for artificially extending the meaning of 'goods' to include an extraneous document, particularly when it does not have even the status of a document of title. Second, *Pearson* confuses the first part of s 2(1) regarding O's consent to the MA's possession of the goods, with the later part of that section which provides that the sale, pledge or other disposition by the MA must be 'in the ordinary course of business' of an MA. The court clearly considered that, overall, the MA's business practices were deceitful and far from ordinary but it is plain that, in *Pearson*, the MA sold the car *with* its log book and it is thus impossible to categorise the transaction between the MA and the buyer as anything other than ordinary. The other difficulties caused by *Pearson* will be considered later as each requirement of s 2(1) is evaluated.

After *Pearson*, it is thus beyond doubt that it is sufficient for O intentionally to give possession to the MA and the fact that O's consent is obtained by criminal deception does not defeat the operation of the Act. But might O's consent be vitiated in any other situations? There are *dicta* in *Du Jardin v Beadman Bros Ltd*[15] that an operative mistake of identity might nullify consent and, in *Belvoir Finance Co Ltd v Harold G Cole & Co Ltd*,[16] it was suggested that illegality might be enough, although the latter proposition is contentious as it would seemingly involve O's relying on his own illegal agreement to defeat the rights of the *bona fide* B.

It will be apparent from these situations involving fraud and theft, that O may attempt to *withdraw* his consent to the MA's possession of the goods but the FA has provided for such an eventuality in s 2(2) which stipulates that where the MA has been in possession of the goods or documents of title to goods such a determination of consent will be ineffective, provided that the transfer would otherwise be valid under the Act and the transferee has no notice that the consent has been determined.[17]

---

14 See also *Du Jardin v Beadman Bros* [1952] 2 QB 712 where the *Pearson* view of consent was followed.

15 [1952] 2 QB 712, 718 per Sellers J (S's consent to buyer in possession under the FA, s 9 and the SGA, s 25).

16 [1969] 1 WLR 1877, 1881 per Donaldson J.

17 See *Moody v Pall Mall Deposit and Forwarding Co Ltd* (1917) 33 TLR 306 (a picture dealer in Paris sent pictures to an MA in London, some for sale and some for exhibition. The MA's authority was revoked but he nevertheless pledged the pictures with B who obtained a good title); *Newtons of Wembley Ltd v Williams* [1965] 1 QB 560 (considered below).

In possession

There are several problems relating to the MA's possession. By s 1(2) of the FA 'a person shall be deemed to be in possession of goods or of the documents of title to goods, where the goods or documents are in his actual custody or are held by any other person subject to his control or for him or on his behalf'. It was held in *Beverley Acceptances Ltd v Oakley*[18] that the MA must *actually* be 'in possession' at the time of the transfer to the innocent transferee. There O pledged two Rolls Royce cars with X as security for a loan, the cars being left in X's locked compound. O then sought to obtain another loan from the plaintiff on the security of the cars and, telling X that he wished to arrange insurance on the cars, he obtained from X the keys to the compound and the cars' ignition keys and, in February, showed the cars to representatives of the plaintiff. In March, in order to secure a loan for £25,000, O executed bills of sale in the plaintiff's favour which were duly registered. The Court of Appeal held that, for the purposes of the FA, s 2(1), X was the owner and O was a mercantile agent but that the MA had possession only for a brief time during the visit to the compound and certainly did not have possession in March when the bills of sale were executed. As the Act contemplated that 'possession' and 'disposition' must be simultaneous, the plaintiffs were not protected and, as a prior pledgee, X had priority over the plaintiffs. Lord Denning MR dissented and considered that the ruling would limit dramatically the protection of transferees as formal documents are often executed several days after possession is seen and it is respectfully submitted that this is the preferable view. He also considered that the cars were held by X subject to the control of O, or for him or on his behalf, under the FA, s1(2). This conclusion seems correct, as only O had the power to sell the cars during the four month period of the loan, the period during which he obtained the second loan from the plaintiff.

In possession in the *capacity* of an MA

A related difficulty concerns the nature or character of the MA's possession. It has long been established that the MA must be in possession of the goods in his *capacity* as an MA. In *Cole v North Western Bank*,[19] A carried on business in Liverpool as a sheep's wool broker and also that of a warehouse keeper. In his capacity as a warehouseman he often received from O, a merchant in London, bills of lading for sheep's wool and goats' wool which, when landed, he would value for O but he had no authority to sell it without specific instructions. He usually did sell the sheep's wool for O but he never sold the goats' wool as he was not a broker for goats' wool. On this occasion, A had wool of both types in his warehouse and had received no instruction from O but he pledged the entire consignment with the defendant bankers. It was held that the pledge was invalid as A did not have possession as an MA but as a bailee only and such possession was entirely unconnected with his function as a broker. Blackburn J[20] employed the telling example that, should a house be let furnished to a man who happened to be an auctioneer, it 'never was the common law and could not be intended to be enacted' that he could sell the furniture by auction and give a good title to the buyers. Here the auctioneer is entrusted with the furniture in his capacity as

18 [1982] RTR 417.
19 (1875) LR 10 CP 354.
20 (1875) LR 10 CP 354 at 369.

a tenant in sharp contrast to his capacity as an MA. This approach has been followed in modern cases. In *Staffs Motor Guarantee Ltd v British Wagon Co Ltd*,[1] A, a car dealer, owned a lorry and sold it to the defendant finance company (O), which let it back to him on hire-purchase terms. A remained in physical possession throughout the transaction and, subsequently, he sold the lorry to the plaintiff (B). When A failed to maintain his payments on the hire-purchase, O repossessed the lorry but B asserted that it had title as it had bought the lorry from an MA. It was held that B acquired no title as A was in possession in his capacity as a hirer and bailee but not as an MA. There is no doubt that this is the law in relation to the FA, s 2(1).[2]

Accepting that the MA must have obtained the goods in his business capacity, it is still unclear how this is to be defined. It is plain from the above cases that the MA's possession as a pure bailee is outside his business capacity, and in *Pearson v Rose & Young Ltd*,[3] Denning LJ[4] accepted that if goods were left solely for repair with an MA who was both a dealer and repairer, the MA would not have possession as an MA. However, he went on to explain that the possession would have to be 'for a purpose which is in some way or other connected with his business as a mercantile agent. It may not actually be for sale. It may be for display or to get offers, or merely to put in his showroom: but there must be a consent to something of that kind before the owner can be deprived of his goods'.[5] This is a somewhat nebulous statement but it seems that O need not contemplate that the MA would *dispose* of the goods and thus his having possession for display is sufficient.[6] The present inconclusive state of the law means, however, that it is most unclear where bailment stops and a business capacity starts.[7]

---

1 [1934] 2 KB 305.
2 The *Staffs Motor Guarantee* reasoning was expressly approved as regards the FA, s 2(1), in *Astley Industrial Trust Ltd v Miller* [1968] 2 All ER 36 (a car dealer held a car on sale or return terms from the manufacturer and A, a self-drive car hire firm, took it on hire-purchase terms from the plaintiff finance company. A told the car dealer that he wanted the car for the car hire business but he also had an ancillary business selling cars and duly sold the car to B, the defendant. Held B obtained no title as A did not have possession of the car in the capacity of an MA).
3 [1951] 1 KB 275.
4 [1951] 1 KB 275 at 288.
5 [1951] 1 KB 275 at 288. The delineation in the FA, s 1(1), of the authority of an MA must surely be crucial when his business capacity is called into question viz, 'authority either to sell goods, or to consign goods for the purpose of sale, or to buy goods, or to raise money on the security of goods'.
6 *Turner v Sampson* (1911) 27 TLR 200 (O sent a picture to be hung in the MA's gallery so that he might obtain offers and report to O. Held a sale by the MA was valid); *Moody v Pall Mall Deposit and Forwarding Co Ltd* (1917) 33 TLR 306 (O sent pictures to a gallery owner (MA), some for sale and some for display. Held that the Act applied to all the goods in the custody of the MA whether they were for sale or not); cf *Universal Guarantee Pty Ltd v Metters Ltd* [1966] WAR 74 (A had a refrigerator from O on 'display or return' terms and one of A's employees fraudulently sold it to a hire-purchase company (B). Held that B acquired no title as A was in possession as a bailee only); *Brown & Co v Bedford Pantechnicon Co Ltd* (1889) 5 TLR 449 (above, but there A was clearly held not to be an MA and thus the case does not concern possession in the *capacity* of an MA).
7 It is difficult to accept Willmer LJ's reasoning in *Stadium Finance Ltd v Robbins* [1962] 2 QB 664, 674, that, in withholding the car's ignition key, O did not consent to the MA's having possession of the car in the capacity of an MA. O intended to control the sale himself and had not given the MA authority to sell the car but the MA had possession of the car to receive offers for its sale and was thus surely in possession in the correct capacity. Willmer LJ's analysis also conflicts with the cases cited above on the display of goods by the MA.

Moreover, this requirement regarding the MA's capacity is criticisable for several reasons. First, the FA does not demand that the MA be in possession in his capacity as such and, from B's perspective, provided the MA is *in* possession, his capacity is irrelevant. Second, as capacity is incorporeal, B will have no means of either ascertaining or verifying its existence and it is difficult to see how he might be put on inquiry regarding such an intangible issue.[8] Any concerns that the disposition by the MA might appear abnormal are catered for by the FA requirements that the disposition must be in the ordinary course of business and that B must be in good faith. Third, the decisions on capacity are overly-protective of ownership and, in particular, *Cole v North Western Bank* emphasises the principles of common law estoppel and grafts them illegitimately onto the FA thereby detracting from B's protection under that Act. Finally, the requirement of capacity has been abrogated in the related situation of a seller who is left in possession after a sale to the buyer under the FA, s 8, and the SGA, s 24: the seller's continuing in *physical* possession is sufficient.[9] It is suggested that this should be the position under the FA, s 2(1), but it has been held that the alteration made to the law regarding a seller in possession has not affected the position as regards s 2(1).[10]

GOODS OR DOCUMENTS OF TITLE

The FA, s 1(3) provides that 'goods shall include wares and merchandise' and documents of title are defined in s 1(4) as 'any bill of lading, dock warrant, warehousekeeper's certificate, and warrant or order for the delivery of goods, and any other document used in the ordinary course of business as proof of the possession or control of goods, or authorising or purporting to authorise, either by endorsement or by delivery, the possessor of the document to transfer or receive goods thereby represented'. Documents of title, such as a bill of lading (the receipt by the master of a ship for goods taken on board), in effect represent the goods, and an MA in possession of a document of title can thus pass a good title under the Act.

The courts have had great difficulty in wrestling with the problems caused by car registration books/documents (log books). It is indisputable that a log book is not a document of title[11] but there are implications when, in the sale of a car, it is present or absent. On the basis that a log book is good *evidence* of title, Denning LJ in *Pearson v Rose & Young Ltd*,[12] asserted that, within the

---

8 Cf Blackburn J in *Cole v North Western Bank* (1875) LR 10 CP 354, 371, who, in response to the argument that the defendant could not ascertain A's capacity, thought that 'very little inquiry' would have made the defendants aware that A was not a goats' wool broker, and 'if the plaintiffs knew that the warehouseman whom they trusted was also a wool broker, the defendants were aware that the wool broker whom they trusted was also a warehouseman'.

9 See *Pacific Motor Auctions Pty Ltd v Motor Credits (Hire Finance) Ltd* [1965] AC 867; *Worcester Works Finance Ltd v Cooden Engineering Co Ltd* [1972] 1 QB 210 (considered below).

10 *Astley Industrial Trust Ltd v Miller* [1968] 2 All ER 36.

11 *Joblin v Watkins and Roseveare (Motors) Ltd* [1949] 1 All ER 47; *Pearson v Rose & Young Ltd* [1951] 1 KB 275; *Beverley Acceptances Ltd v Oakley* [1982] RTR 417; *Shaw v Metropolitan Police Comr* [1987] 1 WLR 1332.

12 [1951] 1 KB 275.

FA, 'goods ... means the car together with the registration book'.[13] It will be remembered that, in *Pearson*, it was held that O did not consent to the MA's having possession of the log book and thus one reason for the decision was that the MA did not have possession of the 'goods' with O's consent. This proposition has been criticised as illogical[14] because even if a log book *is* a document of title, the Act would not demand that it be produced with the car (the FA, s 2(1) stipulates for 'goods *or* documents of title') and thus Denning LJ's argument is a non sequitur as it is premised upon the log book as mere evidence of title. Moreover, Denning LJ's approach was not followed by the Court of Appeal in *Stadium Finance Ltd v Robbins*[15] where the argument that 'goods' meant a car plus its ignition key was rejected. It thus seems that a log book is not a vital constituent of a vehicle and it need not be produced by the MA for title in the 'goods' to be transferred, but the log book and *Pearson's* case have connotations for other aspects of s 2(1), considered later.

SALE, PLEDGE, OR OTHER DISPOSITION OF THE GOODS

The effect of a sale is to transfer a good title to B but the wording of the FA, s 2(1) is that the sale, pledge or other disposition 'shall ... be as valid as if [the MA] were expressly authorised by the owner of the goods to make the same' and thus B acquires only such title as was vested in O at the time of the sale. Moreover, it is important to stress that, under the FA, s 12(2), O is not prevented from recovering the goods from the MA or his trustee in bankruptcy at any time before the sale and, by s 12(3), even if O is bound by the MA's sale, he is not prevented from recovering from B the price agreed to be paid for the goods, subject to any right of set-off on the part of B against the MA.

The expression 'pledge' is defined in the FA, s 1(5), to include 'any contract pledging, or giving a lien or security on, goods, whether in consideration of an original advance or of any further or continuing advance or of any pecuniary liability'. Moreover, the FA, s 3 provides that 'a pledge of the documents of title to goods shall be deemed to be a pledge of the goods'. Where goods are pledged by the MA without authority in consideration of an advance in cash, the FA, s 12(2) provides that O has a right to redeem the goods at any time before they are sold on satisfying the claim for which the goods were pledged. A pledge in consideration of an *antecedent* liability is valid although considerably limited by the FA, s 4. This provides that, where an MA pledges goods as security for a debt or liability due from him to the pledgee, the pledgee acquires no further right to the goods than could have been enforced by the MA at the time of the pledge. It follows that, in such a case, the pledgee has no rights against O unless, say, the MA had a lien on the goods at the time of the pledge because O owed him money in which event the pledgee would have the same right of lien against O. Finally, the FA, s 5 deals with the situation where the pledgee does not lend a sum of money to the MA but, instead, gives other goods or a document of title or a negotiable security as the consideration for the pledge. The section provides

---

13 [1951] 1 KB 275 at 290.
14 Hanbury, *The Principles of Agency* (2nd edn, 1960), p 112; see also Goodhart, ' Notes' (1951) 67 LQR 3.
15 [1962] 2 QB 664. The absence of a log book did not prevent B's acquiring title to a car under the FA, s 2(1) in *Folkes v King* [1923] 1 KB 282, but Scrutton LJ suggested (p 300) that its absence might mean that B was *mala fide* (see below).

that the pledgee 'shall acquire no right or interest in the goods so pledged in excess of the value of the goods, documents, or security when so delivered or transferred in exchange' and its purpose is to prevent the pledgee from claiming to retain the pledged goods on the basis that the goods which he gave in consideration have appreciated since the date of the pledge. It follows that O, when redeeming his own goods, need not pay more than the value of the goods given by the pledgee at the date of the pledge.

The consideration necessary for the validity of a sale, pledge, or other disposition is defined in the FA, s 5[16] and the better view is that any form of disposition is protected if it is for valuable consideration. In *Waddington & Sons v Neale & Sons*,[17] O sent a piano to the MA for sale for cash or on hire-purchase terms. The MA sent the piano to an auctioneer for sale by auction and obtained an advance on the goods in anticipation of the proceeds of sale. O sued the auctioneer. It was held that this was not a pledge or other disposition, rather it was a deposit with an instruction to sell and the advance could not amount to consideration. Similarly, although an MA may make a gratuitous disposition by way of sales promotion, which might be in the ordinary course of business, it will nevertheless be invalid as lacking consideration.

Finally, it is suggested that the transaction between the MA and B cannot be merely an agreement but must have a dispositive effect as, unlike the FA, ss 8 and 9, s 2(1) does *not* include the words 'or under any *agreement* for sale, pledge, or other disposition thereof'. If the MA agrees to sell goods to B but, for example, reserves title until payment by B, B will acquire no title and O could recover the goods. However, it should be noted that s 2(1) does not stipulate that *delivery* is necessary for the transfer of title to B.

ACTING IN THE ORDINARY COURSE OF BUSINESS OF A MERCANTILE AGENT

The transferee from the MA must prove that the disposition was made by the MA *or* by his authorised clerk or agent,[18] 'when acting in the ordinary course of business of a mercantile agent'. The leading decision is *Oppenheimer v Attenborough & Son*[19] where O, a diamond merchant, entrusted the MA, a diamond broker, with diamonds to show to potential buyers but the MA pledged the jewels with B. B believed the MA to be an owner/principal in the transaction. It was proved that pledging diamonds was not within the usual or customary authority of diamond brokers and therefore it was argued that 'ordinary course of business' must relate to the trade in which the MA carries on his business and thus this pledge was abnormal and unprotected by the Act. The Court of Appeal held that B obtained a good title. Buckley LJ emphasised that the language in the FA, s 2(1) differs considerably from the phrase 'customary course of *his*

---

16 Section 5 provides: 'The consideration necessary for the validity of a sale, pledge, or other disposition, of goods, in pursuance of this Act, may be either a payment in cash, or the delivery or transfer of other goods, or of a document of title to goods, or of a negotiable security, or any other valuable consideration ...'
17 (1907) 96 LT 786.
18 FA, s 6 provides: 'For the purposes of this Act an agreement made with a mercantile agent through a clerk or other person authorised in the ordinary course of business to make contracts of sale or pledge on his behalf shall be deemed to be an agreement with the agent'.
19 [1908] 1 KB 221.

business' in the FA, s 1(1). He thus held that acting in the ordinary course of business of an MA meant 'within business hours, at a proper place of business, and in other respects in the ordinary way in which a mercantile agent would act, so that there is nothing to lead the pledgee to suppose that anything wrong is being done, or to give him notice that the disposition is one which the mercantile agent had no authority to make'.[20] This is therefore an objective approach to the notion of the ordinary course of business and, in the lower court,[1] Channell J stressed the use of the indefinite article in the FA, s 2(1), viz 'a mercantile agent'. He thought that this meant 'not "the mercantile agent" which the particular man happened to be – in other words, a mercantile agent independently of the particular goods with which he deals'.[2] As regards this requirement of the ordinary course of business, it is also immaterial that the MA acts in his own name as an owner/principal because the object of the Act is to enable the MA in possession of goods to have the same right of dealing with them as if he were the owner.[3]

The facts of *Ceres Orchard Partnership v Fiatagri Australia Pty Ltd*[4] are informative regarding the ordinary course of business of a modern MA. O owned a tractor which the MA, who was in the business of buying and selling tractors, agreed to sell on O's behalf. The tractor was freshly-painted and displayed at the MA's premises. The MA had a dealership arrangement with B who was an importer of Fiat tractors and B was concerned about the level of the MA's indebtedness to him. Accordingly, it was agreed that B would buy O's tractor and a number of others, the purpose of the arrangement being to set-off the price against the debt. B relied on the MA's representation that the tractor belonged to the MA and he did not inspect the MA's stock register which would have disclosed that the tractor was being sold on behalf of O. Eventually, the tractor was sold by another dealer, on behalf of B, and the MA subsequently went into liquidation. The High Court of New Zealand held that B acquired title as the sale was in the ordinary course of business of an MA, this being supported in that the price paid for the tractor was a generous estimate of its market value. Barker J observed that the phrase 'ordinary course of business' is not confined 'to what is done ordinarily in the course of business'.[5]

Transactions have been held to be outside the ordinary course of business of an MA where a diamond broker, without O's authority, asked his friend to pledge diamonds with the defendant,[6] where the price of the goods was paid by B directly to the MA's creditor,[7] where there was a 'forced sale' in which the purchase price was to be set-off against a debt owed by the MA to the buyer[8] and a sale by the

20 [1908] 1 KB 221 at 230-231.
 1 [1907] 1 KB 510.
 2 [1907] 1 KB 510 at 515.
 3 See *Oppenheimer v Attenborough & Son* [1908] 1 KB 221, 229 per Buckley LJ.
 4 [1995] 1 NZLR 112.
 5 [1995] 1 NZLR 112 at 117.
 6 *De Gorter v Attenborough & Son* (1904) 21 TLR 19.
 7 *Biggs v Evans* [1894] 1 QB 88.
 8 *Motor Credits (Hire Finance) Ltd v Pacific Motor Auctions Pty Ltd* (1963) 109 CLR 87 (rvsd on other grounds [1965] AC 867) the MA owed a debt to B and sold some of O's cars to B for £16,510, being the amount of the debt. The sale took place outside normal business hours. The MA then endorsed B's cheque and returned it to B. It was thus clear that B wanted the cars as security for the debt. B considered that the MA was an agent not an owner. The High Court of Australia held that this was not a sale in the ordinary course of business of an MA as an agent could never sell his principal's goods in settlement of his own debt.

MA of an art gallery including all the paintings, furnishings and equipment.[9] Likewise, in *Heap v Motorists' Advisory Agency Ltd*,[10] the sale to B was made by an agent of the MA and B took delivery from the agent and paid the price directly to him, as he was suspicious of the MA. Lush J held that this was not in the ordinary course of business of an MA as it was 'a very peculiar transaction'.[11]

The decision in *Pearson v Rose & Young Ltd*[12] again adds difficulties to this part of the FA. There the MA obtained possession of O's car with his consent, subsequently obtained possession of the car's log book without O's consent, and then sold the car *with* its log book to B. Somervell LJ considered that the *withholding of consent* to the log book meant that the sale was not in the ordinary course of business of an MA. This reasoning was followed in *Stadium Finance Ltd v Robbins*,[13] where O gave the MA/car dealer possession of his car for display in the MA's showrooms so that the MA might tell O of any enquiries or offers made for the car. O kept possession of the car's key but inadvertently left the log book in the locked glove compartment. The MA obtained a key, opened the glove compartment, and sold the car to his own salesman (who was *bona fide*) hire-purchase being arranged through the plaintiffs. The salesman defaulted on the first payment and the plaintiffs sought to recover the car from O who had by then retaken it. The Court of Appeal held that the plaintiffs had not acquired a good title as a sale by an MA who had not been put in possession of the key and log book was not a sale in the ordinary course of business of an MA. It is hardly surprising that these cases have been roundly criticised by commentators.[14] Moreover, Chapman J emphasised cogently in *Astley Industrial Trust v Miller*[15] that the decisions confuse the nature of the possession originally acquired by the MA with the disposition that is subsequently made by him and the second issue, the disposition in the ordinary course of business of an MA, does not depend in any way on the circumstances in which the MA *acquired* possession. Where the car is sold *with* the log book, the sale must be in the ordinary course of business within the principles of *Oppenheimer v Attenborough & Son*. A marginally more convincing justification for *Pearson* would be that O's absence of consent to the MA's possession of the log book meant that he did not have possession of the car in his *capacity* as an MA[16] but, instead, was simply a bailee. But on the *Pearson* facts, where the MA was given possession to obtain offers, this interpretation severely restricts the operation of the FA and appears to countenance O's secret limitation on the MA's usual business authority which is, of course, contrary to the entire rationale of the FA.

Finally, it must be asked whether a sale of a second-hand[17] car without a log book must necessarily be outside the ordinary course of business of an MA. In

9 *Mortimer-Rae v Barthel* (1979) 105 DLR (3d) 289.
10 [1923] 1 KB 577.
11 [1923] 1 KB 577 at 589; s 6 of the 1889 Act was not applied in either *Heap* or *De Gorter*.
12 [1951] 1 KB 275.
13 [1962] 2 QB 664.
14 See Hanbury, *The Principles of Agency* (2nd edn, 1960), pp 111-114; Powell, *The Law of Agency* (2nd edn, 1961), pp 228-232; Goodhart, Notes (1951) 67 LQR 3; Hornby, 'Mercantile Agents and Car Registration Books' (1962) 25 MLR 719; Thornely, 'Sale by Mercantile Agent of Car without Registration Book' [1962] 20 CLJ 139; Schofield, 'The Notionally Absent Registration Book' [1963] JBL 344.
15 [1968] 2 All ER 36, 42.
16 This was in fact one ground of Willmer LJ's decision in *Stadium Finance Ltd v Robbins* (at p 674) as O had not given the ignition key to the MA.
17 It was stressed in *Astley Industrial Trust Ltd v Miller* (above) that a *new* car might not be accompanied by a log book and still be a sale in the ordinary course of business of an MA, as B might reasonably assume that the log book was with the county council for registration.

Pearson, Somervell LJ held that such a sale would not be within the ordinary course of business because 'the price would be substantially reduced thereby'[18] and Vaisey J[19] likened the sale of a car without a log book to the sale of a car with only three wheels. But as Powell[20] rightly emphasised, if an MA chooses to sell defective goods at a cheaper price this is no reason to deny that the sale is in the ordinary course of business of an MA: mercantile agents do not all sell perfect goods. Thus if the MA can give a convincing reason for the log book's absence (eg the car had just been acquired by the last owner and the new log book had not been issued) the sale might well be in the ordinary course of business.

ACTING IN GOOD FAITH AND WITHOUT NOTICE THAT THE MERCANTILE AGENT HAS NO AUTHORITY

The person dealing with the MA must prove[1] (i) that he was in good faith and (ii) that at the time of the disposition he had no notice that the MA lacked authority to make the disposition. In *Heap v Motorists' Advisory Agency Ltd*,[2] Lush J considered these to be separate requirements[3] but did not distinguish the substantive content of each and, indeed, in his judgment the two elements cross and intertwine.[4] It seems clear, however, that if B has actual notice of lack of authority he can hardly claim to be in good faith.

There is no definition of good faith[5] in the FA but, by analogy with the SGA, s 61(3),[6] it would appear to mean 'honestly' and thus negligence in itself should not constitute bad faith. Again, the question of vehicles and their log books is relevant. In *Folkes v King*,[7] Scrutton LJ[8] pointed out that if every purchaser demanded the production of a log book, it would be difficult to find a market for stolen cars and that the courts 'may have to take adverse notice of the conduct of a purchaser who does not require the production of the book of registry'. In *Pearson v Rose & Young Ltd*,[9] Denning LJ[10] said that the courts had adopted this suggestion and now 'view with suspicion any dealing in a second-hand car without a registration book' but it appears that B's failure to ask for the log book in the sale of a second-hand car cannot be conclusive evidence of bad faith.[11] Certainly this issue is better considered primarily within the requirement that B be *bona fide* than as part of the requirement that the sale be in the ordinary course of business.

18 [1951] 1 KB 275, 283.
19 [1951] 1 KB 275 at 291.
20 *The Law of Agency* (2nd edn, 1961), p 231.
 1 The burden of proof is on B: *Heap v Motorists' Advisory Agency Ltd* [1923] 1 KB 577, 590; supported by the Law Reform Committee, Twelfth Report (1966), Cmnd 2958, para 25.
 2 [1923] 1 KB 577.
 3 [1923] 1 KB 577 at 589.
 4 [1923] 1 KB 577 at 590-591.
 5 See generally Jones, *The Position and Rights of a Bona Fide Purchaser for Value of Goods Improperly Obtained* (1921).
 6 The SGA, s 61(3) provides: 'A thing is deemed to be done in good faith within the meaning of this Act when it is in fact done honestly, whether it is done negligently or not'.
 7 [1923] 1 KB 282.
 8 [1923] 1 KB 282 at 300.
 9 [1951] 1 KB 275.
10 [1951] 1 KB 275 at 289.
11 See *Stadium Finance Ltd v Robbins* [1962] 2 QB 664, 675-676, per Willmer LJ.

As was mentioned above, it is plain from *Oppenheimer v Attenborough &*
Son[12] that it does not matter if B thinks he is dealing with an owner/principal
when he is in fact dealing with an MA. However, if B realises that he is dealing
with a specific type of MA and that such an MA notoriously lacks authority to
enter into the particular transaction, B's good faith will be destroyed.[13]

In relation to the SGA and the FA, 'notice' generally means actual knowledge
of a fact and it is commonly said that there is no full doctrine of constructive
notice in commercial transactions[14] and that the buyer of goods has no overall
duty to inquire regarding the right of a seller to dispose of goods.[15] Nevertheless,
it may be impossible for the court to decide whether B had notice of the MA's
lack of authority except by drawing inferences from the facts attendant upon
the transaction and by applying an objective test, ie whether B as a reasonable
man must have known of the MA's lack of authority or knew that he could
ascertain certain facts and deliberately failed to do so.[16]

In the *Ceres Orchard*[17] case, discussed earlier, it was held that B was in good
faith because (i) B's transaction with the MA was a standard arrangement (ii) B
had no reason to doubt the MA's authority (iii) a fair price was paid for the
tractor (iv) the MA's financial problems were not sufficiently serious to make B
suspicious of any fraudulent activity on the MA's part (v) the tractor had been
painted by the MA which would indicate to outsiders that it was the MA's
property, and (vi) there was no way to check the ownership of the tractor apart
from inspecting the MA's private stock book and this would have been an
unjustifiable intrusion into the MA's business.

In conclusion, the facts of *Heap v Motorists' Advisory Agency Ltd*,[18] show
that the same facts may indicate B's bad faith and his notice of the MA's lack of
authority. O had wanted to sell his car for £210 but an agent (A) of the MA
eventually sold it to B for £110. The price was paid directly to A, delivery was
made by A, the log book was never produced and B never asked for it. Lush J
held that 'all these circumstances were, in my opinion, enough to put [B] on
their guard and to fix them with notice. I do not say that they wickedly shut
their eyes to an obvious fraud, but I do say that they did not do what any
reasonable man would have done in this case – namely, decline to buy this car
without knowing more about it'.[19]

Sale under a voidable title

The common law notion of voidable title is preserved by the SGA, s 23 which,
somewhat tersely, provides:

---

12 [1908] 1 KB 221.
13 See *Oppenheimer v Attenborough & Son* [1908] 1 KB 221, 231 per Kennedy LJ.
14 *Manchester Trust v Furness* [1895] 2 QB 539.
15 *Hambro v Burnand* [1904] 2 KB 10; *Feuer Leather Corpn v Frank Johnstone & Sons Ltd*
    [1981] Com LR 251.
16 See *Feuer Leather Corpn v Frank Johnstone & Sons Ltd* [1981] Com LR 251, 253, per
    Neill J.
17 [1995] 1 NZLR 112.
18 [1923] 1 KB 577.
19 [1923] 1 KB 577 at 591. See also *Janesich v George Attenborough & Son* (1910) 102 LT
    605, where Hamilton J suggested that an unusually high rate of interest charged on a
    pledge might be evidence of bad faith on the part of the pledgee, indicating also that he
    had notice that the pledgor lacked authority to make the pledge.

'When the seller of goods has a voidable title to them, but his title has not been avoided at the time of the sale, the buyer acquires a good title to the goods, provided he buys them in good faith and without notice of the seller's defect of title.'

The situation of a voidable title commonly arises where O is induced by the fraud of a swindler to sell goods to the swindler, the goods then being resold promptly by the swindler to an innocent, *bona fide* buyer (B). The swindler might, for example, assert falsely that he is wealthy and creditworthy meaning that O is persuaded thereby to accept a cheque from him in payment for the goods. It is thus apparent that, although the fraud might be very influential in the formation of the original contract between O and the swindler, O nevertheless intends to sell the goods to him at the date the contract is entered into. In the typical scenario encountered, the fraud which is perpetrated will not completely invalidate the contract of sale[20] but, instead, it will render that contract *voidable* at O's option.[1] Upon discovery of the fraud, O may thus choose to rescind the contract. However, if O has not rescinded the contract with the swindler at the time of the sale to B, B will acquire an indefeasible title to the goods, even though the swindler had only a voidable title.[2] Here then, the law does not allow the (undiscovered) fraud to obstruct the transfer of title to a *bona fide* buyer and, in the context of *nemo dat* with its prevalent policy of securing O's vested rights of ownership, the notion of voidable title is uncharacteristically mindful of B's claim to acquire title.

The wording of s 23 can appear somewhat confusing at first glance: it must be emphasised that, in s 23, it is the 'seller' (S) who has the voidable title and, in the archetypal situation, he is also characterised as the swindler. A normal chain of events is thus that the owner (O) sells his goods to the swindler/seller (S) who then resells them to the *bona fide* buyer (B).

O MUST INTEND TO TRANSFER TITLE TO THE SELLER

It is most important to stress that O must intend to transfer *title* to S and S must acquire title, albeit a voidable one. Although this much is clear, the requirements for the creation of a voidable title in S have never been established with absolute certainty.

Provided that O intends to transfer title to S, it seems clear that he need not enter into a contract of *sale*[3] with S and, unusually, s 23 does not demand that S must obtain *possession* of the goods. On the other hand, the mere delivery of possession to a swindler will be insufficient to create a voidable title in him. In *Kingsford v Merry*,[4] O gave a delivery order for goods to S, by which S could obtain possession of the goods, having been induced to do so by the false representation that S had bought the goods from a person (X) to whom O had agreed to sell them. S pledged the goods with a third party (T) but it was held

---

20 Should the fraud induce an operative mistake as to the identity of the swindler, the contract would be void (see below).
 1 The contract may be voidable at O's option because of other factors in the contract's formation, eg duress or undue influence.
 2 See eg *Lewis v Averay* [1972] 1 QB 198.
 3 See *Anderson v Ryan* [1967] IR 34 (contract of *exchange* between O and S induced by S's fraud; S acquired a voidable title).
 4 (1856) 1 H & N 503.

that T could acquire no title as S had no voidable title to transfer. Coleridge J pointed out that there was no privity of contract contract between O and S and no contract for the sale of goods between them which O might affirm or disaffirm. Accordingly, giving the delivery order to S and his obtaining possession of the goods thereby 'would no more pass the property in the goods, than a delivery to an agent or servant of [X] would pass the property to such agent or servant'.[5]

Similarly, there can be no voidable title in S where there is only an *agreement* to sell,[6] a prime example being where a swindler has possession under the agreement but no title is to transfer to him until the goods are paid for.[7] As well as such conditional sales, it is clear that hire-purchase agreements and the delivery of the goods to S on sale or return or similar terms[8] are insufficient to create a voidable title in S and s 23 would thus have no application should S, before he has acquired title, sell the goods to an innocent buyer.[9] The innocent buyer's title may be fed, however, where the swindler acquires the voidable title *after* the sale to the innocent buyer. In *Whitehorn Brothers v Davision*,[10] O delivered a pearl necklace on sale or return terms to a swindler who fraudulently pretended that he had a customer for it. Several days later, the swindler pledged the necklace with the defendant. Although O inquired regarding the necklace, the swindler prevaricated for three weeks. Eventually the necklace was invoiced to the swindler, this transaction being induced by his continuing fraud that he had a customer for it, but the bills the swindler gave in payment were dishonoured and he absconded. It was held that no title transferred to the defendant under the pledge but the subsequent invoicing of the goods to the swindler was a sale which transferred a voidable title to him and thereby fed the defendant's title.

A voidable title must be distinguished from a *void* title, which means a complete absence of any title. This may arise where the contract of sale between O and the swindler is void for a fundamental mistake of identity (eg O thinks that the swindler is X, an existing person, and O can establish that he intended to deal only with X) and, as a consequence, no title can transfer to the swindler and none to B, even if he is *bona fide* and without notice of any defects in the swindler's title. It is obviously advantageous for O if he can establish that the contract with the swindler was void for mistaken identity but, if he is to do so, he must prove that he intended to deal with someone other than the swindler[11]

5 (1856) 1 H & N 503 at 516.
6 See the SGA, s 2(5).
7 There was a written agreement in *Newtons of Wembley Ltd v Williams* [1965] 1 QB 560 (see later), that no property was to pass to the swindler until payment in full was received by O, but both courts proceeded on the basis that his title was voidable. In principle, this is incorrect. Only Sellers LJ thought that 'it may well be' the intent of the parties that no title should transfer until payment (pp 571-572).
8 *Truman (W) Ltd v Robert Attenborough* (1910) 26 TLR 601; *Whitehorn Bros v Davision* [1911] 1 KB 463 (in both cases the same swindler, Bruford (S), had a pearl necklace on sale or return and obtained a voidable title to it *only* when he fraudulently represented that he had a buyer for it and O *invoiced* the necklace to him, this being a sale which transferred the voidable title to S). But see the enigmatic statement by Buckley LJ in *Whitehorn* (p 479) that S might be able to transfer title to a third party where, because of S's fraud, O transfers possession to S and a 'power to pass the property'.
9 It is quite possible that *other* rules or exceptions to *nemo dat* might enable the seller to transfer title in some of these situations. Where there is only an agreement to sell the goods, for example, the SGA, s 25(1)/FA, s 9 (buyer in possession) might apply (see below).
10 [1911] 1 KB 463.
11 See *Cundy v Lindsay* (1878) 3 App Cas 459.

rather than simply being mistaken as to the attributes of the swindler, eg his honesty and creditworthiness.[12] Moreover, it is clear that it will be difficult to prove such a mistake of identity where the parties deal face-to-face for there is then a presumption that O intends to contract with the person who is physically before him.[13] The difference between void and voidable titles is thus crucial for the *bona fide* buyer as he stands some chance of acquiring title in the latter case but the mistake/misrepresentation cases rest on such notoriously fine distinctions that the position is far from satisfactory. Accordingly, it was recommended by the Law Reform Committee[14] that, where goods are sold under a mistake as to the buyer's identity and an apparent contract results, that contract should be regarded as voidable, not void, so far as third parties are concerned.

AVOIDANCE OF A VOIDABLE TITLE

A voidable title is valid unless and until it is avoided by O and so, to prevent the operation of s 23, O must rescind the contract with the seller before the goods are sold to B. The general rule is that O must communicate the rescission to the *seller* but this may be difficult where he is a swindler who has effectively disappeared. Accordingly, it was held in *Car and Universal Finance Co Ltd v Caldwell*[15] that the communication rule is not inflexible. There the defendant, O, had been induced by a fraudulent misrepresentation to sell his car to a swindler and, on discovering that the swindler's cheque was dishonoured, he informed the police and the Automobile Association of the position. Subsequently, the swindler sold the car and it was eventually bought by the plaintiffs who were in good faith and without notice of any defect in title. The Court of Appeal held that O, in informing the police and the AA of the fraud, had clearly evinced an intention to avoid the contract of sale and the plaintiffs acquired no title. It was stressed, however, that here the swindler deliberately intended to disappear and the court left open the question of whether a public act of rescission would suffice where the other party to the contract had made an innocent misrepresentation and then disappeared but without any fraudulent intent.

Caldwell was criticised by the Law Reform Committee[16] as substantially detracting from the operation of s 23, their recommendation being that rescission should require *actual* notice to the other contracting party.[17] *Caldwell's* rule clearly favours the owner but it is difficult to see why even actual notice to the other contracting party should affect the rights of the *bona fide* buyer when, as is normally the case, he is unaware of any such communication.[18] In any event, the harsh effect of *Caldwell* on innocent buyers has been mitigated by the decision

12 See *King's Norton Metal Co Ltd v Edridge, Merrett & Co Ltd* (1897) 14 TLR 98.
13 See *Lewis v Averay* [1972] 1 QB 198; *Phillips v Brooks* [1919] 2 KB 243; cf *Ingram v Little* [1961] 1 QB 31.
14 Twelfth Report, *Transfer of Title to Chattels* (1966), Cmnd 2958, paras 15 and 40(3).
15 [1965] 1 QB 525.
16 Twelfth Report, *Transfer of Title to Chattels* (1966), Cmnd 2958, paras 15 and 40(3).
17 See paras 16, 40(4); see also *MacLeod v Kerr* 1965 SC 253 where, on very similar facts to *Caldwell*, the Court of Session peremptorily dismissed the argument that notifying the police would suffice as a valid rescission.
18 See Smith, *Property Problems in Sale* (1978), pp 168-169. The Diamond Review (*A Review of Security Interests in Property* (HMSO 1989, DTI) recommends (para 13.6.6) that only repossession of the goods should suffice as rescission.

in *Newtons of Wembley Ltd v Williams*[19] which held that the SGA, s 25(1) (buyer in possession) enabled a good title to be transferred to an innocent buyer notwithstanding the fact that O had avoided the swindler's title before the sale took place. The decision is considered in detail later. It should also be remembered that O may lose the right to rescind the contract if any of the bars to rescission apply, eg O's affirmation of the contract.

SALE TO THE BUYER

Section 23 is applicable only to the situation where the 'seller' (S) has a voidable title and the goods are then *sold* to a 'buyer' (B). An actual sale of the goods seems to be contemplated between S and B and an agreement to sell, which attaches some condition to the transfer of the property in the goods to B, is arguably insufficient to transfer title. But it should be noted that there are no requirements (i) that O should give possession of the goods to S (ii) that S should deliver the goods to B or (iii) that the sale from S to B should be made in the ordinary course of business. These factors would be relevant however in deciding whether B is in good faith and without notice. Moreover, although s 23 applies only to a sale to B, the common law encompasses situations where the person with a voidable title pledges the goods with an innocent pledgee.[20]

GOOD FAITH AND LACK OF NOTICE

As in the other exceptions to *nemo dat*, B must be in good faith[1] and without notice of the seller's defective title when he buys the goods. The decision in *Whitehorn Bros v Davison*[2] was remarkable in establishing that O carries the burden of proving that B was *mala fide* and bought with notice. The basis of *Whitehorn* was that a voidable title is valid until avoided and that as O 'comes to displace another from the enjoyment of property'[3] the onus is on O to prove that he should be able retake that property. Although this rule was unquestionably biased in favour of B, the Law Reform Committee[4] recommended that the onus of establishing good faith and want of notice should rest on B, as it does under the other exceptions to *nemo dat*.

Seller in possession

The exception to *nemo dat* provided by the seller in possession relates, in the simplest example, to the situation where S sells goods to B1, property passing to B1 but S remaining in possession of the goods after the sale. If S then resells and delivers the goods to a *bona fide* B2 who has no notice of the first sale, B2 will

---

19 [1965] 1 QB 560.
20 See *Whitehorn Bros v Davison* [1911] 1 KB 463; *Phillips v Brooks* [1919] 2 KB 243.
1   Defined in the SGA, s 61(3).
2   [1911] 1 KB 463.
3   [1911] 1 KB 463 at 481, per Buckley LJ.
4   Twelfth Report, *Transfer of Title to Chattels* (1966), Cmnd 2958, paras 25, 40(13).

acquire a good title to the goods. B1 has a remedy in damages, of course, against his seller (S).

In this situation, there are two reasons to uphold B2's acquisition of title to the goods. First, B1, the owner of the goods, has left S in possession and has thus enabled him to transfer title to B2. Second, the *bona fide* B2 buys the goods from S as an apparent owner. B1 is thus correctly penalised while B2 is justifiably protected. However, as a question of perspective, English law's standpoint does not accord paramountcy to B2's protection; rather, B1 is deemed to accept the risks inherent in leaving his goods in S's possession and so B2 may acquire title as a consequence of B1's actions.

A simple diagram illustrates the position:

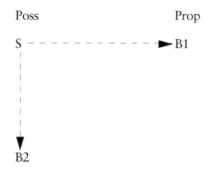

Historically, the seller in possession is connected with the Factors Acts (FA) and the restrictive interpretation of that legislation by the judiciary. In *Johnson v Crédit Lyonnais Co*,[5] S was a tobacco broker and also an independent merchant in tobacco. He received a consignment of tobacco, warehoused it and received the dock warrants and then sold it to the plaintiff (B1). B1 did not want to pay duty on the tobacco and thus he left it in the bonded warehouse, meaning that S was in control of the tobacco and had the dock warrants. S then pledged the goods with the defendants (B2). It was held that B1 must succeed in his action against B2 as (i) the FA 1842 could not apply as S had not been 'intrusted' with the goods as an MA (or any sort of agent) but was only a paid seller remaining in possession of the goods and (ii) the jury had found that B1 was not negligent and estoppel could not apply on these facts. The FA 1877, s 3, was thus passed to give the ordinary seller in possession a power to transfer title to *bona fide* transferees.

The current law is in the FA 1889, s 8, and the SGA 1979, s 24, both sections being almost identical. The FA s 8 provides:

> 'Where a person, having sold goods, continues, or is, in possession of the goods or of the documents of title to the goods, the delivery or transfer by that person, or by a mercantile agent acting for him, of the goods or documents of title under any sale, pledge, or other disposition thereof, [or under any agreement for sale, pledge, or other disposition thereof], to any person receiving the same in good faith and without notice of the previous sale, shall have the same effect as if the person making the delivery or transfer were expressly authorised by the owner of the goods to make the same'.

---

5   (1877) 3 CPD 32.

The bracketed words are inexplicably omitted in the SGA 1979, s 24,[6] and thus it is arguable that s 8 has a wider ambit than s 24. The section(s) must now be analysed.

RELATIONSHIP OF SELLER AND BUYER

The *raison d'être* of ss 8/24 is that S has sold the goods and passed the property in them to B1, but S remains in possession of the goods. If property remains in S, it is self-evident that he can transfer title by virtue of his ownership.[7] Accordingly, ss 8/24 provide unequivocally for the situation of 'a person[8] having *sold* goods' and so the relationship between the two original parties (S and B1) must be that of seller and buyer and the property in the goods must have passed to B1 under a contract of sale.

An agreement to sell does not pass the property in the goods to B1 and a conditional sale to B1, where property remains in S until B1 pays for the goods is not within ss 8/24. This question was raised in the Canadian decision in *Vowles v Island Finances Ltd*.[9] A car dealer (S) agreed to sell a 1932 Plymouth automobile to a buyer under a conditional sale agreement and, on the same day, the dealer assigned his interest in the car and the benefit of the agreement to the appellant finance company. The buyer did not take delivery of the car and the dealer sold it to the respondent, Vowles (B2), who was *bona fide*, paid in cash and took delivery of it. Some three months later, the car was seized by the appellant. The British Columbia Court of Appeal held that, whilst the conditional sale was not an absloute sale, the assignment to the appellant finance company amounted to a sale by S to the company (B1) and so B2 acquired a good title to the car. However, O'Halloran JA considered that the phrase 'having sold goods' should include both absolute and conditional sales and that the conditional sale to the buyer would thus suffice for the operation of the statutory provision (which was identical to ss 8/24) and B2 would thus acquire title without more. There is much force in this argument because, of course, the *bona fide* B2 without notice does not know of the first transaction with B1 and, as he is certainly unaware of the legal *nature* of that transaction, it is arguable that he should not be prejudiced thereby. It remains to be seen whether English law might take this view.

THE NATURE OF THE SELLER'S POSSESSION

S must be in possession of the goods[10] sold *or* the documents of title[11] to the goods and it should be remembered that by the FA, s 1(2), goods are deemed to be in

6 The words were also omitted in the original Sale of Goods Act 1893, s 25(1) and this mystery has never been solved: it seems it was simply an error in transcription. Section 8 is still law because the SGA, s 21(2)(a), provides that 'nothing in this Act shall affect the provisions of the Factors Acts ...' The SGA 1979, s 24, slightly altered the wording of the SGA 1893, s 25(1), by substituting 'has' for 'shall have' in the final phrase.
7 If property *has* passed to B1 but S is an *unpaid seller*, he can transfer a valid title to B2 on exercising his power of resale under the SGA, s 48(2).
8 'Person' is defined in the FA, s 1(6), to include 'any body of persons corporate or unincorporate'.
9 [1940] 4 DLR 357.
10 Different definitions of 'goods' are found in the FA, s 1(3) and the SGA, s 61(1).
11 Defined by the SGA, s 61(1), to have the same meaning as in the FA, s 1(4).

the possession of S where the goods or the documents of title are in his 'actual custody or are held by any other person subject to his control or for him or on his behalf'. This can obviously apply to a warehouseman who stores the goods for S.[12]

It was seen earlier that, under the FA, s 2(1), where the MA remains in possession of the goods but in a changed *capacity*, eg as a hirer/bailee under a hire-purchase agreement, his ability to transfer title is destroyed. Despite the entirely different wording of ss 8/24, the courts applied the same reasoning to a seller in possession, thus demanding that he remain in possession of the goods in his capacity as a seller. This restriction on ss 8/24 left very little room for their operation. In the case considered earlier, *Staffs Motor Guarantee Ltd v British Wagon Co Ltd*,[13] S, a car dealer, owned a lorry and sold it to the defendant finance company (B1), who let it back to him on hire-purchase terms but S remained in physical possession throughout the transaction and, subsequently, he sold and delivered the lorry to the plaintiffs (B2). It was held that B2 acquired no title because the dealer/S was in possession as a bailee and not an MA and, similarly, the dealer could not be a seller in possession as he lacked the capacity of a seller.[14] The first decision which departed from this narrow view was that of the Privy Council in *Pacific Motor Auctions Pty Ltd v Motor Credits (Hire Finance) Ltd*,[15] where it was emphasised that 'continues in possession' in ss 8 and 24 is a neutral expression with no reference to a changed capacity and thus S's continuing in physical possession was all that was necessary.

The *Pacific Motor Auctions* case was followed and extended in *Worcester Works Finance Ltd v Cooden Engineering Co Ltd*,[16] which is now the most important decision on ss 8/24. The defendant sold a car to a dealer (D) who said that he wanted it for a possible customer and D paid for the car by cheque.[17] D and a third party, Millerick (M), then executed documents selling the car to the plaintiff finance company. The finance company considered that they had bought the car from D and had let it on hire-purchase terms to M. In fact, M did nothing further under the agreement, and D remained in possession of the car. Some time later, the defendant repossessed the car from D as his (D's) cheque had been dishonoured. D acquiesced in the repossession by the defendant. D met the hire purchase payments for a while but then stopped paying when £315 was outstanding. The defendants subsequently let the car on hire-purchase terms to a hirer and registered the agreement with HPI. When the plaintiffs discovered

---

12 *City Fur Manufacturing Co v Fureenbond (Brokers) London Ltd* [1937] 1 All ER 799.
13 [1934] 2 KB 305.
14 The *Staffs Motor Guarantee* reasoning on capacity was followed in *Eastern Distributors Ltd v Goldring* [1957] 2 QB 600. See also *Olds Discount Co Ltd v Krett* [1940] 2 KB 117 where the notion was seemingly applied unnecessarily as, on the facts, S lost *physical* possession. A retailer, S, sold furniture to the plaintiff finance company which was then let on HP terms to a hirer who fell into arrears. S repossessed the furniture on behalf of the finance company and resold it to Krett. Held that Krett did not acquire title as the character of S's possession at the time of sale was that of a bailee, not a seller.
15 [1965] AC 867.
16 [1972] 1 QB 210.
17 As the dealer's cheque tendered in payment for the car was dishonoured, it must be asked what title he had to transfer to the plaintiff: (i) if the dealer intended to defraud the defendant, the dealer's title was voidable but had not been avoided at the time of the sale to the plaintiff; (ii) if he did not intend to defraud, his title was unimpeachable until the defendant accepted his repudiation on his failure to pay which, again, was after the sale to the plaintiff; (iii) the dealer could have been a buyer in possession (FA, s 9; SGA, s 25(1)) or an MA under the FA, s 2(1).

the position, they sued the defendants in conversion. The Court of Appeal held that D was a person who had sold goods (to the plaintiff finance company) and had remained in physical possession of them, albeit without the plaintiff's consent. The retaking of the car by the defendants from D amounted to a delivery under a disposition within s 24[18] and the defendants were in good faith. Accordingly, the defendants, the original owners, acquired a good title to the car. It was argued strongly by the plaintiffs that, as the hire-purchase agreement was with M, D should not have been in possession of the car and that, at the very least, s 24 must contemplate a *lawful* possession. The court rejected this argument, emphasising that the seller's continuing physical possession was all that was required and that, unlike the FA, s 2(1), s 24 did not specify that the buyer (B1) of the goods from S should *consent* to S's having possession of those goods.[19] It is thus plain from *Worcester Works* that S can be in possession as a trespasser and it would apparently have been immaterial if the plaintiff finance company had formally revoked their consent to D/S's possession before the disposition to the defendant.[20] It thus seems that nothing short of physical repossession of the car by the plaintiff would have sufficed to defeat D/S's ability to transfer title.

In relation to S's possession, the limits of ss 8/24 are thus clearly defined: the sections will be defeated only by a break in the *physical* possession of S, eg S delivers the goods to B1 but then regains possession as a bailee.[1] However, it is difficult to see why even this restriction should remain as the protection conferred upon B2 is based upon his seeing possession in S and having no reason to suspect any other sale. Where S is *in* possession, what relevance can an earlier break in that possession have for B2? Only rarely might such an interruption in possession put B2 on inquiry regarding B1's prior interest and, in most cases, it will be as irrelevant to him as an earlier change in the character of S's possession. As this latter restriction has been eradicated, it is suggested that the stipulation that S must have unbroken possession[2] should also be eliminated.

Finally, it should be noted that ss 8 and 24 provide not only for the situation where S 'continues' in possession but also where he is 'in possession'. In *Worcester Works*, Lord Denning MR[3] considered that this phrase referred to the situation where S did not have possession when he sold the goods but 'they came into his possession afterwards'.[4]

---

18 Then the SGA 1893, s 25(1).

19 The defendants could not rely on the FA, s 2(1) because: (i) the consent of O (the plaintiff) to the dealer's possession was lacking; (ii) the dealer was not in possession of the car in his *capacity* as an MA (iii) probably the defendant's retaking of the car was not in the 'ordinary course of business' of an MA under s 2(1).

20 The FA, s 2(2) provides that where an MA has been in possession with O's consent, the determination of consent will not affect the disposition by the MA.

1 As in *Mitchell v Jones* (1905) 24 NZLR 932 where S sold and *delivered* a horse to B1 but received it back on hire and sold it to B2. Held B2 obtained no title as S had lost possession and had become a bailee proper (not by attornment as in the *Staffs* case). See also *Olds Discount Co Ltd v Krett* [1940] 2 KB 117 (above).

2 In *Worcester Works*, Lord Denning MR said: 'But there must be continuity of physical possession. If there is a *substantial* break in the continuity, as for instance, if the seller actually delivers over the goods to a purchaser who keeps them for a time, and then the seller afterwards gets them back, then the section *might* not apply' (pp 217-218, emphasis added).

3 [1972] 1 QB 210 at 217.

4 *Benjamin's Sale of Goods* (5th edn, 1997), para 7-058, suggests that this might also cover the situation where S loses possession but lawfully regains it in the capacity of a seller, eg S exercises a right of stoppage in transit, resumes possession and sells the goods.

DELIVERY OR TRANSFER

The act which transfers title to B2 is 'the delivery[5] or transfer[6] ... of the goods or documents of title'.[7] Under ss 8/24 the delivery or transfer must be made by S *or* by an MA[8] acting for him and it is also clear from *Worcester Works* that an acquiescence by S to the goods being taken by B2 is enough as it is 'tantamount to a delivery or transfer by him'.[9]

Sections 8/24 appear to demand that, as a consequence of the sale, pledge or other disposition to B2, there should be an actual delivery or transfer to him, this being reinforced by the sections' reference to B2's 'receiving' the goods or documents of title. The necessity for this chronological symmetry was confirmed by the early decision in *Nicholson v Harper*.[10] S sold to B1 250 dozen bottles of port which were stored in the cellars of a warehouseman and S then pledged the wine with the same warehouseman (B2) as security for an advance. It was held that B1 had title to the goods as there had been no delivery to B2. Instead, B2 had simply remained in possession throughout and, moreover, there had been no transfer to him of any document of title relating to the wine. *Nicholson* is nevertheless criticisable in that the pledge to B2 seemingly involved a delivery of the goods within SGA, s 61(1), ie a 'voluntary transfer of possession from one person to another', or it could be argued that there was a constructive delivery to B2[11] in that he held the goods in his own right as pledgee, but that argument was specifically rejected in *Nicholson*.

However, in a recent decision concerning ss 9/25(1)[12] (buyer in possession), it was stated that delivery could be constructive within those sections: provided there was some positive, voluntary act, which could constitute a constructive delivery of the goods by B1 to B2, it need not entail a *physical* delivery to B2. Moreover, there is now clear authority that S can make a valid constructive delivery to B2 under ss 8/24. In *Michael Gerson (Leasing) Ltd v Wilkinson*,[13] S sold heavy plant and machinery to a finance company (B1) under a sale and leaseback agreement and, consequently, S retained physical possession of the goods and became a seller in possession within ss 8/24. Without the knowledge or authority of B1, S then sold some of the same goods to another finance company (B2) under a second sale and leaseback agreement and, once again, S retained possession of the goods throughout. The issue was thus whether S had 'delivered' the goods to B2 within ss 8/24, an issue which was complicated

---

5 'Delivery' is defined in the SGA, s 61(1) as the 'voluntary transfer of possession from one person to another'.
6 'Transfer' is defined in the FA, s 11: '... the transfer of a document may be by endorsement, or, where the document is by custom or by its express terms transferable by delivery, or makes the goods deliverable to the bearer, then by delivery'.
7 The SGA, s 61(1) provides that 'documents of title' has the same meaning as in the FA, s 1(4).
8 Defined in the SGA, s 26 and the FA, s 1(1).
9 [1972] 1 QB 210, 218 per Lord Denning MR. In *The Saetta* (below), Clarke J held that 'inaction' would not be delivery within ss 9/25(1), but he considered that there was more than 'acquiescence' in *Worcester Works* as there S handed the ignition key to the defendant, B2, thus constituting a voluntary, constructive delivery.
10 [1895] 2 Ch 415.
11 See *Gamer's Motor Centre (Newcastle) Pty Ltd v Natwest Wholesale Australia Pty Ltd* (1987) 163 CLR 236 (a decision on ss 9/25(1), see below).
12 *Forsythe International (UK) Ltd v Silver Shipping Co Ltd and Petroglobe International Ltd, The Saetta* [1993] 2 Lloyd's Rep 268 (see below).
13 [2001] 1 All ER 148.

by the fact that the sale and leaseback amounted to one, synchronous transaction. The Court of Appeal held that, where a seller in possession of goods sold to a buyer, acknowledged that he was holding the goods on account of the buyer in circumstances where he recognised the buyer's right to possess as owner, and S continued thereafter to hold the goods as a bailee with a possession derived from that right, the transaction amounted to a delivery to the buyer immediately followed by redelivery to the seller as a bailee. This was so whether the seller's custody was in the character of a bailee for reward or of a borrower. Clarke LJ emphasised that it was not necessary to identify a precise moment at which S 'delivered' the goods to B2: the sale and leaseback agreement was consistent only with a delivery to B2 for, otherwise, B2 could not have leased the goods back to S. Finally, the entry into the sale and leaseback was a sufficiently voluntary act on S's part to satisfy the definition of 'delivery' in the SGA, s 61(1), viz a 'voluntary transfer of possession from one person to another'. It followed that S delivered the goods under a sale to the *bona fide* B2 who thus acquired title under ss 8/24 and who was, consequently, not liable to B1 in conversion.

It is suggested that, almost certainly, delivery by attornment[14] of a bailee/third party is sufficient for the purposes of ss 8/24 (eg a warehouseman acknowledges that he holds the goods on B2's behalf). However, where S makes two sales to B1 and B2 but retains possession and makes no delivery or transfer of any sort in either sale, it would seem that B1 has the better right and acquires title to the goods.

Finally, as s 8 has a wider wording than s 24 in relation to the delivery or transfer by S to B2 'under any *agreement* for sale, pledge, or other disposition thereof,' it must be asked whether B2 obtains a contractual right to the goods enforceable against B1 when the delivery or transfer by S is consequent upon such an agreement. It is suggested that this is the intention of s 8 but there is no authority on the point. At least in this situation, B2 appears to be immune from an action in conversion at the suit of B1.[15]

SALE, PLEDGE, OR OTHER DISPOSITION

Where there is a completed sale to B2, he acquires title, but where the goods are pledged with B2, B1 still has title to the goods but subject to the rights of the pledgee, B2. The phrase 'other disposition' is more difficult. In *Worcester Works*, it was argued, without success, that the unilateral retaking of the car by the defendant could not be a disposition[16] but Lord Denning MR considered 'disposition' to be 'a very wide word'[17] which extended 'to all acts by which a new interest (legal or equitable) in the property is effectually created'.[18] The two other judges gave a more limited meaning to disposition as a transfer of

---

14 See the SGA, s 29(4).
15 See *Shenstone & Co v Hilton* [1894] 2 QB 452 (a decision on the FA, s 9; see below).
16 As the defendants in *Worcester Works* did not pursue the dealer in regard to the cheque, it is arguable that the retaking of the car was a *resale* by the dealer and 'disposition' need not have been considered: see Phillimore LJ at p 219.
17 [1972] 1 QB 210, 218.
18 [1972] 1 QB 210, 218 citing *Carter v Carter* [1896] 1 Ch 62, 67, per Stirling J.

property, Megaw LJ defining it as 'some transfer of an interest in property, in the technical sense of the word "property", as contrasted with mere possession'.[19]

It remains to be seen whether a gratuitous disposition[20] would suffice but there is nothing in *Worcester Works* which suggests that value is necessary and, unlike the FA, s 2(1), ss 8/24 are not limited by any requirement of a disposition in the ordinary course of business. Other dispositions are also in doubt. What, for example, is the position if S lets the goods on hire-purchase to B2? Here only possession would be transferred to B2 so that S would not dispose of the 'property' in the goods. Until recently, it was arguable[1] that even if B2 exercised the option to purchase under the hire purchase agreement, there might be no delivery of the goods in consequence of the disposition, as in *Nicholson v Harper* (above), but this is now most unlikely in view of the acceptance of constructive delivery in recent decisions.[2]

GOOD FAITH AND LACK OF NOTICE

The person 'receiving' the goods or documents of title (B2) must receive them in good faith[3] and without notice of the previous sale. The burden of proving these facts appears to rest on B2[4] and 'notice' refers to actual notice, that is 'knowledge of the sale or deliberately turning a blind eye to it'.[5] It was argued in *Worcester Works* that the defendant was *mala fide* but Phillimore LJ[6] stressed that when the defendants let the car on hire-purchase, they registered the agreement with HPI, this being cogent evidence of their *bona fides*. Finally, ss 8/24 refer to '*any* person receiving the same in good faith and without notice of the previous sale' and this wording seems to contemplate a sale from B2 to B3 with delivery made by S directly to B3. If so, it is unclear whether B2 or B3, or both, must be in good faith.

Buyer in possession

The exception to *nemo dat* provided by the buyer in possession relates, in the simplest example, to the situation where S agrees to sell goods to B1, title remaining in S but possession being given to B1. B1 will be able to transfer a good title by selling and delivering the goods to a *bona fide* B2 who has no notice of S's prior interest. In principle, S will have a remedy in damages against B1, although this may be illusory in practice as it is obvious that B1 is often a swindler who subsequently disappears without trace.

---

19 [1972] 1 QB 210 at 220.
20 It is unclear whether the FA, s 5 (which defines the consideration necessary for a sale, pledge or other disposition) applies to the FA, s 8, as s 8 is under a different heading in the FA. *Inglis v Robertson* [1898] AC 616, indicates that these two headings in the FA contain separate provisions which do not inter-relate. The SGA, s 24 does not require valuable consideration.
 1 *Benjamin's Sale of Goods* (5th edn, 1997), para 7-062; cf Goode, *Commercial Law* (2nd edn, 1995), p 470.
 2 *The Saetta* [1993] 2 Lloyd's Rep 268 (considered later under ss 9/25(1)); *Michael Gerson (Leasing) Ltd v Wilkinson* [2001] 1 All ER 148.
 3 Defined in the SGA, s 61(3).
 4 See *Worcester Works Finance Ltd v Cooden Engineering Co Ltd* [1972] 1 QB 210, 221, per Megaw LJ
 5 [1972] 1 QB 210 at 218, per Lord Denning MR.
 6 [1972] 1 QB 210 at 219.

It was emphasised when ss 8/24 were considered that, although the *bona fide* buyer's (B2) claim to acquire title could be regarded as paramount, the rationale of the provision relating to the seller in possession is that the buyer/owner of the goods is deemed to accept the risks of leaving his seller in possession of those goods. This reasoning is also applicable to the provisions relating to the buyer in possession in that, here, the seller is penalised for entrusting possession to a person who has only agreed to buy the goods (B1) but who nevertheless appears, from B2's perspective, to be an absolute owner of the goods.

A simple diagram illustrates the position:

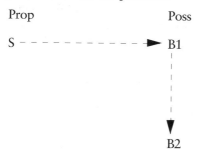

As in the case of a seller in possession, the common law refused to recognise any ability in a buyer in possession to transfer a good title to a third party[7] as he was not an agent intrusted with the goods for sale but was rather a potential owner who held the goods in his own right. The FA 1877, s 4, thus introduced a limited exception to the common law rule. The current law relating to a buyer in possession is found in the FA 1889, s 9 and the SGA 1979, s 25(1), the two sections being almost identical. The FA, s 9 provides:

> 'Where a person, having bought or agreed to buy goods, obtains with the consent of the seller possession of the goods or the documents of title to the goods, the delivery or transfer, by that person or by a mercantile agent acting for him, of the goods or documents of title, under any sale, pledge, or other disposition thereof, [or under any agreement for sale, pledge, or other disposition thereof], to any person receiving the same in good faith and without notice of any lien or other right of the original seller in respect of the goods, shall have the same effect as if the person making the delivery or transfer were a mercantile agent in possession of the goods or documents of title with the consent of the owner'.

The bracketed words are omitted in the SGA, s 25(1)[8] and thus it is arguable that s 9 has a wider ambit. The section(s) must now be analysed.

BOUGHT OR AGREED TO BUY

B1 must have 'bought or agreed to buy' the goods.[9] In most cases, there will be an agreement to sell the goods to B1, such an agreement being defined in the SGA, s 2(5), as a contract of sale where 'the transfer of the property in the goods is to take place at a future time or subject to some condition later to be fulfilled'. Such a condition would be, for example, that no property in the goods is to pass

---

7 *Jenkyns v Usborne* (1844) 7 Man & G 678; *McEwan v Smith* (1849) 2 HL Cas 309.
8 Section 25(1) has slightly altered the wording of s 25(2) of the 1893 Act (which it replaced) by substituting 'has' for 'shall have' in the final phrase.
9 Different definitions of 'goods' are found in the FA, s 1(3) and the SGA, s 61(1).

to B1 before his cheque is cleared. Sections 9/25(1) also apply where B1 has agreed to buy the goods under the terms of a clause reserving title to S until payment is made by B1 (a Romalpa clause). Should B1 sell the goods to B2 within ss 9/25(1), title will pass to B2 and S cannot recover the goods.

However, B1 must be *bound contractually* to buy the goods, so ss 9/25(1) cannot apply to someone who has a mere *option* to purchase which he may or may not choose to exercise, as in a hire-purchase agreement,[10] nor to a person who has simply taken possession of goods on sale or return terms.[11] Similarly, where an agent is given possession of goods in order to sell them on behalf of his principal (O), he is not a buyer in possession within ss 9/25(1) as he has not 'bought or agreed to buy' the goods.[12] Recent cases have also emphasised that if the initial contract between S and B1 is one for work and materials rather than an agreement to sell the goods, ss 9/25(1) have no relevance.[13] On the other hand, it has been held that it does not matter that the original agreement between S and B1 is unenforceable for lack of prescribed form[14] or that it is voidable for fraud at S's option.[15]

Where B1 obtained possession of the goods under a conditional sale,[16] ie the passing of property is conditional upon payment or some other event, he was originally regarded as having agreed to buy the goods within s 9.[17]

10 *Helby v Matthews* [1895] AC 471; *Astley Industrial Trust Ltd v Miller* [1968] 2 All ER 36; *Close Asset Finance Ltd v Care Graphics Machinery Ltd* [2000] 12 LS Gaz R 42.

11 *Percy Edwards Ltd v Vaughan* (1910) 26 TLR 545. But where B1 has possession of goods on sale or return terms and sells them to B2, this is an 'act adopting the transaction' under the SGA, s 18, r 4(a), which operates to pass the property to B1 and thence to B2. However, r 4(a) can be excluded by contrary intention (as it was in *Percy Edwards*: no property to pass to B1 until the goods were paid for in cash), but ss 9/25(1) cannot be thus excluded. In *London Jewellers Ltd v Attenborough* [1934] 2 KB 206, 215, Scrutton LJ opined that, where B has goods on sale or return, although he is not a buyer in possession intially, he might become such a buyer when he exercises his right to sell. This view has not gained acceptance.

12 *Shaw v Metropolitan Police Comr* [1987] 1 WLR 1332 (considered earlier under estoppel). But where an agent sells the goods he might be an MA within the FA, s 2(1), or transfer a good title, at common law, by virtue of apparent authority.

13 *Dawber Williamson Roofing Ltd v Humberside County Council* (1979) 14 BLR 70 (a contract between a a sub-contractor (S) and a building contractor (B1) was for S to tile the roof of a school belonging to the defendants (B2). The slates were delivered to the site by S. The building contractor (B1) went into liquidation and the sub-contractor (S), not having been paid for the slates, tried to recover them from the school (B2). Held there was no agreement for the sale of the goods between S and B1 and so ss 9/25(1) had no application; no title could transfer to B2 who was liable in damages). In this situation, the contract between the main contractor (B1) and the owner of the school (B2) would have to amount to a sale or 'other disposition' if B2 were to acquire title.

14 *Hugill v Masker* (1889) 22 QBD 364.

15 *Newtons of Wembley Ltd v Williams* [1965] 1 QB 560. In *Du Jardin v Beadman Bros Ltd* [1952] 2 QB 712, 718, Sellers J thought that if the agreement between S and B1 was void for mistaken identity, S would not *consent* to B1's possession: this might also mean there could be no agreement to buy.

16 The SGA, s 2(3) provides that 'a contract of sale may be absolute or conditional'.

17 See *Lee v Butler* [1893] 2 QB 318; *Marten v Whale* [1917] 2 KB 480 (B1 agreed to buy a car from S as part of a larger transaction involving the sale of land by B1 to S (subject to S's solicitor's approval of title). B1 was allowed to have possession of the car and sold it to B2. Subsequently S's solicitor disapproved B1's title to the land. Held that there was a conditional contract for the sale of the car and, even though the condition did not materialise, B1 was a buyer in possession and could transfer a good title to B2).

However, changes were introduced by the hire-purchase legislation in the 1960s and now, by the SGA, s 25(2) and the FA, s 9, a buyer under a conditional sale agreement which is a regulated consumer credit agreement within the meaning of the Consumer Credit Act 1974,[18] is *not* to be treated as a person who has bought or agreed to buy the goods.[19] In this sense, the consumer buyer under a conditional sale agreement is equated with the debtor under a hire-purchase agreement. Nevertheless, where B1 is in possession of goods under a conditional sale agreement that is *not* a regulated consumer credit agreement, eg where the financial limits of the Consumer Credit Act have been exceeded or the debtor is a corporation, he can still pass a good title under ss 9/25(1).[20] It should also be stressed that, in the case of motor vehicles, Part III of the Hire-Purchase Act 1964 is applicable to *all* conditional sales irrespective of the consumer or business status of the buyer under the conditional sale and even where the financial limits of the Consumer Credit Act have been exceeded.[1] As the cases in this area frequently concern motor vehicles, Part III of the 1964 Act will confer protection on many *bona fide*, consumer buyers who buy a vehicle from those who have agreed to buy it under a conditional sale.

It will be noticed that ss 9/25(1) refer, somewhat perplexingly, to the situation where B1 has 'bought' the goods: this is curious because if B1 has bought the goods, it is a reasonable assumption that title has passed to him and he can then transfer title to another without restriction. *Benjamin*[2] suggests that 'bought' was inserted to cover situations where, although property and possession may have passed to B1, S still has some right or interest in the goods, eg S may still have a lien over the goods even where they are in B's possession or S may have reserved certain rights under the sale. Even so, these instances will be very rare and the more common situation where B1 is regarded as having 'bought' the goods occurred in *Newtons of Wembley Ltd v Williams*[3] (considered below) where the swindler, B1, had obtained both possession of, and title (albeit voidable) to the goods, but his title was later avoided by S. It was held that B1 could, nevertheless, transfer good title to B2 under ss 9/25(1). Here B1 would seem to be a person who satisfied the requirement of 'having bought' the goods.

---

18 See the Consumer Credit Act 1974, ss 8 and 189(1).
19 A 'conditional sale agreement' which is a consumer credit agreement means an agreement for the sale of goods within the meaning of the Consumer Credit Act 1974 (ie not more than £25,000 is lent otherwise than to a corporate body) under which the purchase price or part of it is payable by instalments and the property in the goods is to remain in the seller (notwithstanding that the buyer is to be in possession of the goods) until such conditions as to the payment of instalments or otherwise as may be specified in the agreement are fulfilled: the SGA, s 25(2)(b) and the FA, s 9.
20 *Forthright Finance Ltd v Carlyle Finance Ltd* [1997] 4 All ER 90 (purchase price outside the financial limits of the CCA). Similarly under the SGA, s 25(2)(b), above, 'the purchase price or part of it is payable by instalments' and so, if this is not the case (as in *Marten v Whale* [1917] 2 KB 480, above) the agreement can be a conditional sale agreement within s 25(1).
1 See below.
2 *Benjamin's Sale of Goods* (5th edn, 1997), para 7-068.
3 [1965] 1 QB 560.

CONSENT OF THE SELLER TO B1'S POSSESSION

S must consent to B1's having possession of the goods or documents of title.[4] By the FA, s 2(4) such consent is presumed in the absence of evidence to the contrary and it is thus clear that the burden is on S to prove lack of consent.[5]

There are the same difficulties here regarding the reality of consent as those considered earlier under the FA, s 2(1). It will be remembered that, under the FA, s 2(1), modern decisions establish that it is immaterial that the MA obtained possession by means of fraud or larceny by a trick provided that O consented in fact to the MA's having possession. This approach was adopted in relation to the buyer in possession in *Du Jardin v Beadman Bros Ltd*.[6] There the fact that B1 obtained possession of a car from S by means of the criminal offence of obtaining by false pretences was held to be immaterial.

Similarly, it is irrelevant that S's consent to possession is given subject to the fulfilment of a condition subsequent on B's part and the condition remains unfulfilled. In *Cahn and Mayer v Pockett's Bristol Channel Steam Packet Co Ltd*,[7] S contracted to sell 10 tons of copper to B1, payment to be by B1's acceptance of a bill of exchange. S sent the bill of exchange for the price together with the bill of lading to B1. B1 was insolvent and did not signify his acceptance of the bill of exchange but indorsed the bill of lading to the plaintiffs, B2, under a contract for the resale of the copper. S stopped the copper in transit. By reason of the SGA, s 19(3),[8] the property had not passed to B1 because he had not satisfied the condition about acceptance, but B1 was treated as a buyer in possession and B2 obtained a good title to the copper.[9]

In relation to car log books and the buyer in possession, the courts have applied the unsatisfactory reasoning adopted in the cases on the FA, s 2(1)[10] and thus

---

4 Documents of title are defined in the SGA, s 61(1) to have the same meaning as in the FA, s 1(4).
5 *Robinson v Restell* (1896) 12 TLR 174. See also the FA, s 2(2) (withdrawal of consent immaterial) and the FA, s 2(3) (where possession of documents of title is gained by virtue of the possession of goods, the documents of title are deemed to be in the MA's possession with the consent of O). Both sub-sections were considered earlier and, although s 9 is not under the same heading in the FA ('Dispositions by Sellers and Buyers of Goods') as s 2 ('Dispositions by Mercantile Agents'), it seems clear that consent under s 9 is subject to s 2: see *Cahn and Mayer v Pockett's Bristol Channel Steam Packet Co Ltd* [1899] 1 QB 643; *Newtons of Wembley Ltd v Williams* [1965] 1 QB 560.
6 [1952] 2 QB 712. But Sellers J suggested that S's consent might be vitiated where the agreement between S and B1 is *void for mistaken identity* (p 718). See also Donaldson J's *obiter dictum* in *Belvoir Finance Co Ltd v Harold G Cole & Co Ltd* [1969] 1 WLR 1877, 1881, that O's consent to the MA's possession under the FA, s 2(1) might be absent if the contract were illegal.
7 [1899] 1 QB 643. See also *Marten v Whale* [1917] 2 KB 480 (condition precedent), facts above.
8 Section 19(3) provides: 'Where the seller of goods draws on the buyer for the price, and transmits the bill of exchange and bill of lading to the buyer together to secure acceptance or payment of the bill of exchange, the buyer is bound to return the bill of lading if he does not honour the bill of exchange, and if he wrongfully retains the bill of lading the property in the goods does not pass to him'.
9 On these facts, B2 is also protected under the SGA, s 47(2) (reproduced in the FA, s 10 which is not repealed). The SGA, s 47(2) provides that where documents of title are lawfully transferred to B1 and then transferred to B2 who takes in good faith and for valuable consideration, then if the transfer to B2 was a sale, the unpaid seller's right of lien and stoppage is defeated and, if the transfer to B2 was a pledge, the unpaid seller's right of lien and stoppage can only be exercised subject to the rights of B2 (see Ch 26).
10 See *Pearson v Rose & Young Ltd* [1951] 1 KB 275.

where B1 obtained possession of a car with S's consent but stole its log book from S, it was held that he could transfer no title in the car to B2.[11] Here B1 is in possession of the goods with S's consent and so it is indisputable that ss 9/ 25(1) should apply, thus enabling B2 to acquire title.

It is very important to consider S's withdrawal of consent to B1's possession. It will be remembered that the FA, s 2(2) provides that where an MA has been in possession of goods or documents of title with O's consent, that consent is deemed to continue even if it has been determined by O, provided that the disponee does not know of the determination. In *Newtons of Wembley Ltd v Williams*,[12] the plaintiff, S, rescinded the contract of sale with B1 when B1's cheque was dishonoured but B1 subsequently sold the car to B2 who then sold it to the defendant. It was held that, by virtue of the FA, s 2(2), S's withdrawal of consent by rescinding the contract did not affect the transfer of title to B2 under ss 9/ 25(1) and, accordingly, the defendant acquired a good title.[13]

POSSESSION OF THE GOODS OR DOCUMENTS OF TITLE

The general rule is that B1 must obtain actual possession of the goods or documents of title and it is insufficient that he has simply bought or agreed to buy the goods. Thus if S retains possession he cannot lose title on a resale from B1 to B2 under ss 9/25(1).[14]

However, it is clear that B1's *constructive* possession may suffice. In *Four Point Garage Ltd v Carter*,[15] the defendant (B2) wanted to buy a Ford Escort XR3i and approached a car dealer (B1) who agreed to supply him with a new car. B2 paid the price in full to B1. As B1 did not have such a car in stock, he agreed to buy the Ford Escort from S, another car dealer, that contract containing a reservation of title clause under which title in the car was to remain with S until payment was made by B1. B1 requested that S should deliver the car direct to B2 and S did so. B1 subsequently went into liquidation without paying S for the car. S sued B2 claiming that (i) the retention of title clause between S and B1 prevented any title transferring to B1 and thus B1 could transfer no title to B2 and (ii) as B1 had never obtained possession of the car and had not delivered it to B2, B2 could not rely on ss 9/25(1). It was held that B1 had obtained constructive possession for the purposes of ss 9/25(1) and S acted as B1's agent in making the delivery; accordingly, B2 obtained a good title.[16]

It will be remembered that, by the FA, s 1(2), a buyer will be deemed to be in possession of goods or documents of title where they are 'held by any other person subject to his control or for him or on his behalf'. This section normally applies

11 *George v Revis* (1966) 111 Sol Jo 51.
12 [1965] 1 QB 560.
13 The Law Reform Committee (Twelfth Report, *Transfer of Title to Chattels*, 1966, Cmnd 2958) recommended that, where the contract has been rescinded, B1 should not be able to transfer title as a buyer in possession under ss 9/25(1) (see paras 24, 40(8)). This is not detrimental to the *bona fide* buyer as the Committee also recommended that, in order to be effective, rescission should be communicated to the other contracting party, ie here S should communicate rescission to B1 (see paras 16, 40(4)).
14 But he could assent to the sale under the SGA, s 47(1) or be estopped as against B2.
15 [1985] 3 All ER 12.
16 Interestingly, but for the (crucial) Romalpa clause between S and B1, the facts of *Four Point Garage* would have involved a *seller* in possession under ss 8/24.

to cases where the goods are in the possession of a third party, eg a warehouseman or carrier[17] who holds them on B1's behalf. In *Capital and Counties Bank Ltd v Warriner*,[18] S sold 12,000 bushels of wheat to B1, issuing transfer-notes in favour of B1 and sending the notes to the warehouseman (W) who stored the wheat. W acknowledged receipt of the notes and issued delivery warrants for the wheat to B1 who then pledged the warrants with B2. B1 then became insolvent without paying S. It was held that B2 was entitled to the goods. It was regarded as immaterial that the wheat was unascertained and this seems to be the position where B2 obtains documents of title to the goods.[19]

It is unclear whether B1 must obtain possession in his *capacity* as a buyer. Suppose that B1 has agreed to buy the goods and, while there is a subsisting relationship of buyer and seller, B1 obtains possession of the goods under some auxiliary arrangement relating to hire or repair of the goods, for example. Might it then be argued that B1's possession is that of a bailee? Although the question of capacity has been evaluated fully in some other exceptions to *nemo dat*, the English courts have never decided the issue conclusively in this context, but the indications are that B1's capacity may be unimportant. In *Marten v Whale*,[20] B1 agreed to buy a car from S as part of a larger transaction involving the sale of land by B1 to S and B1 was allowed to have the car 'on loan'. B1 sold the car to B2 but, subsequently, S's solicitors disapproved B1's title to the land and the projected transaction did not materialise. Nevertheless, it was held that B2 obtained title to the car. The court did not specifically address the question of capacity but considered it sufficient that B1 had agreed to buy the car, albeit under a conditional contract, and had obtained possession with S's consent. The same conclusion was reached in the Australian case of *Langmead v Thyer Rubber Co Ltd*.[1] S began negotiations to sell a car to B1 but it needed painting and thus B1 was given the choice of paying £190 and painting it himself or having S paint it and paying £205. S insisted throughout that payment should be in cash. B agreed to pay £190 but when he came to collect the car, he tendered a cheque which S refused to accept. It was agreed that, pending an arrangement for payment in cash, B1 could take the car to have it painted. B1 took the car and sold it to B2. It was held (Abbott J dissenting) that B2 obtained a good title. The court considered that possession of the car was obtained in connection with the contract of sale and was 'referable to the relationship of seller and buyer'[2] but that possession would be insufficient if 'obtained for a special and temporary purpose which cannot be related to the contractual intention'.[3] It is suggested that *Langmead* reaches the correct conclusion and it is arguable that, as the requirement of capacity has been abrogated in relation to the

---

17 Although s 1(2) was not referred to in *Four Point Garage Ltd v Carter* (above), it seems applicable to those facts, ie S held the goods subject to B1's control.

18 (1896) 12 TLR 216.

19 *Warriner* was followed on this point in *Ant Jurgens Margarinefabrieken v Louis Dreyfus & Co* [1914] 3 KB 40.

20 [1917] 2 KB 480.

1 [1947] SASR 29.

2 [1947] SASR 29 at 42, per Reed J.

3 [1947] SASR 29 at 34, per Napier CJ. The judge considered that possession would be insufficient if, eg, B1's own car had broken down and S had allowed B1 to take the car, which was the subject of the sale, to a garage and bring back a mechanic, or if S had entrusted the car to B1 to take it to a particular paint shop and leave it there, held for S or to his order.

seller in possession under ss 8/24,[4] it would be inapt to *introduce* it as a constituent of the buyer in possession under ss 9/25(1).[5]

Finally, it is unclear *when* B1 must obtain possession of the goods. Sections 9/25(1) indicate a natural chronology that B1 must obtain possession after he has agreed to buy the goods and thus if he has possession and subsequently agrees to buy the goods, the sections might not apply. This could happen, for example, where a car repairer is given possession as a bailee and then agrees to buy the car after he has completed the repairs: but here there may be delivery of possession to B1 as a buyer by the attornment of S and, following the decision in *The Saetta*,[6] this is arguably sufficient for ss 9/25(1) to operate.

DELIVERY OR TRANSFER

The act which passes title is a delivery[7] or transfer[8] of the goods or documents of title by B1 to B2 and, here, the same difficulties arise as those under ss 8/24. Under ss 9/25(1), the delivery or transfer must be made by B1 or by an MA[9] acting for him. However, in *Four Point Garage Ltd v Carter*,[10] discussed above, S delivered the goods direct to B2 on the instructions of B1. S argued that there was no delivery by B1, but the court did not hesitate in holding that there was a constructive delivery to B1 and that S acted as the agent of B1 meaning that the final delivery to B2 was, in effect, made by B1. The decision is patently correct in that it is S's act which allows B1 to have possession in the first place with the consequence that B2 is misled by outward appearances. Where S actively co-operates with B1 by delivering the goods direct to B2, S reinforces B1's apparent ownership.

It has always been assumed, following *Nicholson v Harper*,[11] that an actual delivery or transfer to B2 was required but this approach has been rejected in recent decisions. Constructive delivery to B2 has been endorsed in the High Court of Australia[12] and by Clarke J in *The Saetta*.[13] In the latter case, owners (O) of the vessel *Saetta* let her to charterers on terms that O would accept and pay for all bunkers remaining on board at the time of *Saetta's* redelivery to O. Sellers (S) contracted with the charterers (B1) to supply bunkers to *Saetta*, using a retention of title clause in the contract. B1 did not pay S for the bunkers and

---

4 *Worcester Works Finance Ltd v Cooden Engineering Co Ltd* [1972] 1 QB 210.
5 It is arguable that the cases defining a person who has 'bought or agreed to buy' under ss 9/25(1) militate against this view, eg a buyer on sale or return terms is not a buyer in possession (*Percy Edwards Ltd v Vaughan* (1910) 26 TLR 545).
6 *Forsythe International (UK) Ltd v Silver Shipping Co Ltd and Petroglobe International Ltd, The Saetta* [1993] 2 Lloyd's Rep 268 (see below).
7 See the SGA, s 61(1).
8 See the FA, s 11.
9 Defined in the SGA, s 26 and the FA, s 1(1).
10 [1985] 3 All ER 12.
11 [1895] 2 Ch 415 (see earlier under ss 8/24).
12 *Gamer's Motor Centre (Newcastle) Pty Ltd v Natwest Wholesale Australia Pty Ltd* (1987) 163 CLR 236 (S delivered vehicles to B1 under an agreement for sale by which S reserved property until the price of the vehicles was paid. B1 sold the vehicles to B2, a finance company, but B1 kept possession for the purposes of display. Held that B2 acquired title under the equivalent of ss 9/25(1) and that actual delivery was not required as there was constructive delivery when the character of B1's possession changed and he became a bailee for B2).
13 *Forsythe International (UK) Ltd v Silver Shipping Co Ltd and Petroglobe International Ltd, The Saetta* [1993] 2 Lloyd's Rep 268.

thus no property passed to B1. O subsequently withdrew *Saetta* because of non-payment of hire under the charter and O then consumed the bunkers. O would be liable in conversion to S unless the charterers, B1, had delivered the bunkers to O (as B2). Clarke J held that, under ss 9/25(1), possession has the meaning given to it in the FA, s 1(2), and thus delivery of possession cannot be limited to transfer of actual custody of the goods. Delivery of possession thus included constructive delivery but there had to be some positive, *voluntary* act of transfer by B1.[14] Here O/B2 had gained possession by virtue of the termination of the charterparty for breach of contract and, as B1 had not acquiesced in the withdrawal of the vessel, there could be no voluntary delivery by B1. Accordingly, O/B2 was liable to S in conversion. Following this important decision, it is very likely that delivery by attornment[15] of a bailee/third party would be sufficient (eg a warehouseman acknowledges that he holds the goods on B2's behalf).

Finally, as s 9 has a wider wording than s 25(1) in relation to the delivery or transfer by B1 to B2 'under any *agreement* for sale, pledge, or other disposition thereof,' it must be asked what B2's position is after delivery under such an agreement. The problem arises where, for example, B1 delivers the goods to B2 under a retention of title clause but it has been held recently in *Re Highway Foods International Ltd*[16] that title does *not* transfer to B2 on these facts[17] and S can thus repossess the goods. At least, B2 seems protected from an action in conversion at the suit of S in this situation. In *Shenstone & Co v Hilton*,[18] the plaintiff let a piano to B1 on hire-purchase terms[19] and, before completion of the payments, B1 delivered it to auctioneers (B2) where it was sold by auction. It was held that B2 was not liable in conversion as the delivery to him was an agreement for the disposition of the goods within s 9.

SALE, PLEDGE OR OTHER DISPOSITION

The meaning of a sale, pledge or other disposition has been considered earlier under ss 8/24. In relation to 'other disposition' it has been held that where S delivers building materials to a builder, B1, and B1 has a contract with B2 to incorporate them in a building, although the B1-B2 contract may not be a contract of sale, it can nevertheless be a 'disposition' within ss 9/25(1).[20] As with ss 8/24, it is unclear whether a gratuitous disposition[1] would suffice but it has been held

14 The SGA, s 61(1), defines 'delivery' as the 'voluntary transfer of possession from one person to another'.
15 See the SGA, s 29(4).
16 [1995] 1 BCLC 209.
17 The reasoning in *Re Highway* is that the FA, s 9 is subject to the FA, s 2(1) on the basis that s 9 is said to operate 'as if the person making the delivery or transfer were a mercantile agent in possession of the goods' and, most significantly, s 2(1) applies only to a *sale*. As in the *Newtons* case (see below), this grafting of s 2(1) onto s 9 seems, with respect, to be completely unjustified.
18 [1894] 2 QB 452.
19 The decision was subsequently shown to be wrong in treating a hirer under an HP agreement as a buyer (see *Helby v Matthews* [1895] AC 471).
20 *Archivent Sales & Developments Ltd v Strathclyde Regional Council* (1984) 27 BLR 98 (Court of Session).
1 As mentioned under ss 8/24, the FA, s 5 (which defines the consideration necessary for a sale, pledge or other disposition) may not apply to the FA, s 9, as s 9 is under a different heading in the FA. *Inglis v Robertson* [1898] AC 616 indicates that these two headings in the FA contain separate provisions which do not inter-relate. The SGA, s 25 (1) does not require valuable consideration.

in Scotland that valuable consideration must be given by B2[2] and the requirement in ss 9/25(1) that B1 must act in the ordinary course of business as an MA (see below) would militate against the validity of such a disposition.

GOOD FAITH AND LACK OF NOTICE

The person 'receiving' the goods or documents of title (B2) must receive them in good faith[3] and without notice of any lien or other right of S in respect of the goods. Again, 'notice' means actual notice and the burden of proving good faith and lack of notice appears to rest upon B2.[4] In *The Saetta*,[5] for example, S retained title to the goods under a Romalpa clause until payment by B1. B2 was unaware of the Romalpa clause but he did know that B1 had not paid S. It was argued that B2 must have been aware of the Romalpa clause or some similar right but it was held that B2 had no actual knowledge of the Romalpa clause and there was no evidence that B2 did not receive the goods in good faith.

The reference to S's lien is most unclear. The SGA, s 43(1)(b) provides that an unpaid seller loses his lien[6] over the goods when B 'lawfully' obtains possession of them and it is arguable that 'lawful' posession would have to cover cases where S consents in fact to B1's possession even though that possession has been obtained as a consequence of B1's fraud. Thus one view is that, where ss 9/25(1) are applicable, S will necessarily lose his right of lien as it is based upon physical possession/custody of the goods. The alternative view is that, where B1 has obtained possession by fraud or criminal deception, there can be no question of his possession being 'lawful'[7] so that S might retain constructive possession and his lien even though physical possession has been lost.[8] Much depends upon the significance of physical possession; certainly it appears that S has no right to recover possession from B2 in order to sustain a lien.[9] The question was broached but not answered in *Jeffcott v Andrew Motors Ltd*,[10] the Court of Appeal of New Zealand being content to conclude that, whether or not S's lien survived, B2 will obtain a good title where the requirements of ss 9/25(1) are met. Perhaps the reference to S's lien is intended to apply where S retains possession of the goods but gives possession of documents of title relating to them to B1 and the documents of title are transferred to B2. S might then have a lien on the goods and, if B2 had notice of it, he might acquire title subject to the lien.

THE EFFECT OF DELIVERY OR TRANSFER

The delivery or transfer under ss 9/25(1) has 'the same effect as if the person making the delivery or transfer were a mercantile agent in possession of the goods or documents of title with the consent of the owner'. Prior to 1965, it was assumed

2 *Thomas Graham & Sons Ltd v Glenrothes Development Corpn* 1968 SLT 2.
3 Defined in the SGA, s 61(3).
4 *Heap v Motorists' Advisory Agency Ltd* [1923] 1 KB 577 (FA, s 2(1)).
5 [1993] 2 Lloyd's Rep 268.
6 See also Ch 26 where S's loss of lien is considered.
7 See Smith (1963) 7 JSPTL 225, 226 (review of Atiyah, *The Sale of Goods* (2nd edn, 1963)).
8 See Fridman, *Sale of Goods* (1966), p 262.
9 *Jeffcott v Andrew Motors Ltd* [1960] NZLR 721, 732 per Hutchison J.
10 [1960] NZLR 721.

that these words merely added emphasis to the operation of the sections, this being reinforced by the stipulation that they operated 'as if' the person making the delivery or transfer, B1, were a mercantile agent. Consequently, it was always assumed that a consumer buyer, B1, might transfer a good title to B2, as in *Lee v Butler*,[11] and it was never seriously contended that this wording might mean that B1 should act *literally* as an MA and in the ordinary course of business as such.

This aspect of ss 9/25(1) was examined by the Court of Appeal in *Newtons of Wembley Ltd v Williams*.[12] The plaintiff, S, agreed to sell a car to B1, payment being made by cheque with the proviso that the property in the car was not to pass until the cheque was met. B1 was allowed to take possession of the car. B1's cheque was dishonoured and S took all reasonable steps to trace B1 by informing the police and HPI, thereby rescinding his contract with B1. Later, B1 sold the car to a *bona fide* B2 in Warren Street, London, a well-known street market in used cars. B2 sold the car to the defendant. The court held that (i) B1 had a voidable title to the car but S's rescission was effective in avoiding that title (applying *Car and Universal Finance Co Ltd v Caldwell*[13]); (ii) B1 was a buyer in possession under ss 9/25(1) and the rescission could not affect the operation of those sections because, by virtue of the FA, s 2(2), S's withdrawal of consent was immaterial; and (iii) B1's sale to B2 was effective *only* if made in the ordinary course of business of an MA. As Warren Street was an established market for sales of secondhand cars, the sale by B1 to B2 was made in the ordinary course of business of an MA, so B1 acquired title and, through him, the defendant obtained a good title to the car.[14]

The current position is thus that if B1 is not an MA he must act as if he were one and the transaction between B1 and B2 must comply with the requirements of the ordinary course of business of an MA under the FA, s 2(1). It appears that, if B1 is in fact an MA, he must also act in the ordinary course of business if ss 9/25(1) are to apply.[15] It must be stressed that, although the courts have interpreted the notion of the ordinary course of business of an MA in s 2(1) in a liberal way,[16] the *Newtons of Wembley* analysis severely restricts the operation of ss 9/25(1). The irony of the decision is that, where the person entrusted with the goods *is* in fact an MA, s 2(1) provides adequate protection for *bona fide* transferees, whereas ss 9/25(1) were expressly designed for those cases where B1 is *not* an MA.[17] The

---

11   [1893] 2 QB 318. See also *dicta* to this effect in *Langmead v Thyer Rubber Co Ltd* [1947] SASR 29, 39, per Reed J; *Jeffcott v Andrew Motors Ltd* [1960] NZLR 721, 729, per Gresson P; *National Employers' Mutual General Insurance Association Ltd v Jones* [1990] 1 AC 24, 46-47, per Sir Denys Buckley; *The Saetta* [1993] 2 Lloyd's Rep 268, 280, per Clarke J.
12   [1965] 1 QB 560. See Cornish, 'Rescission without Notice' (1964) 27 MLR 472.
13   [1965] 1 QB 525. When voidable title was considered earlier in this chapter, it was stressed that, in *Newtons of Wembley*, B1 should not have been regarded as possessing a voidable title as S did not intend instantly to pass the property in the goods to B1; instead, he placed a condition on the passing of property to B1, ie payment.
14   In fact, this view had been adopted in the earlier decision in *Lambert v G & C Finance Corpn Ltd* (1963) 107 Sol Jo 666 (B1 agreed to buy S's car, S retaining the log book until B1's cheque was cleared. B1's cheque was dishonoured and the car was eventually sold to the defendant. Havers J held that B1's sale of a car without a log book was not in the ordinary course of business of an MA and the defendant obtained no title. However, the report does not state whether B1 was a private individual or an MA).
15   *Newtons of Wembley Ltd v Williams* [1965] 1 QB 560, 578 per Pearson LJ.
16   *Oppenheimer v Attenborough & Son* [1908] 1 KB 221.
17   Cf *Martin v Duffy* [1985] 11 NIJB 80, where the *Newtons* reasoning was supported on the basis that it would be nonsensical if a buyer from a private seller were to be in a more favourable position than a buyer from an MA. But this argument takes no account of the seller in possession provisions (FA 1889, s 8; SGA 1979, s 24) which can apply to a private seller.

Newtons of Wembley reasoning has not been adopted in other jurisdictions[18] and the Law Reform Committee[19] recommended that the law should be returned to the position which was thought to exist before that decision. It is suggested that the *Newtons of Wembley* stipulation should be discarded leaving the manner of disposal of the goods to be considered under the requirement that B2 must be in good faith.

Finally, there was often speculation that ss 9/25(1) might sanction transfer of title in the situation where O's goods were stolen, the thief selling the goods to B1 who then sold them to B2. The possibility was that, under the wording of ss 9/25(1), B1 had possession with the consent of the *seller*/thief, the sale to B2 then taking effect as if B1 were in possession with the consent of the *owner*. The House of Lords rejected this possibility in *National Employers' Mutual General Insurance Association Ltd v Jones*,[20] emphasising that the policy of the Factors Acts has been to affect only the rights of an owner who has *entrusted* his goods to another and so ss 9/25(1) must be read as meaning that the disposition by B1 has the same effect as if he were an MA in possession of the goods with the consent of the owner who entrusted them to him.

Protection of purchasers of motor vehicles

In 1895, *Helby v Matthews*[1] decided that a person with an option to purchase goods under a hire-purchase agreement was not a buyer in possession within the FA and SGA and consequently unable to transfer title during the currency of the agreement to a *bona fide* purchaser of the goods. In the 20th century, an intransigent problem was that hirers of cars on hire-purchase terms would often sell the vehicles to *bona fide* buyers before completing the instalment payments under the hire-purchase agreement. Consequently, the Hire Purchase Act 1964 enacted a new exception to *nemo dat* in favour of *bona fide*, private purchasers of vehicles from such hirers.

BREADTH OF THE PROVISIONS

Part III of the Hire-Purchase Act 1964 (which was re-enacted with minor changes in terminology in Sch 4 of the Consumer Credit Act 1974) gives special protection to the 'private purchaser' of a motor vehicle which is the subject of a hire-purchase agreement (HP) *or* conditional sale agreement (CS). Sections 27(1) and (2) of the 1964 Act are its core. The person letting the vehicle on HP (or the seller in CS) is referred to as the 'creditor' and the person to whom the vehicle is let on HP (or the buyer in CS) is the 'debtor'. Sections 27(1) and (2) provide:

---

18 See *Langmead v Thyer Rubber Co Ltd* [1947] SASR 29, 39 per Reed J; *Jeffcott v Andrew Motors Ltd* [1960] NZLR 721, 729 per Gresson P. Both statements are to the effect that B1 need *not act* as an MA.
19 Twelfth Report (1966), *Transfer of Title in Chattels*, Cmnd 2958, paras 21-23, 40(7). See also *National Employers' Mutual General Insurance Association Ltd v Jones* [1990] 1 AC 24, 46-47 per Sir Denys Buckley (dissenting). In a powerful, lucid judgment, Sir Denys Buckley stressed the hypothetical nature of the MA provision in ss 9/25(1).
20 [1990] 1 AC 24; see Brown, 'Title to Stolen Goods' (1988) 104 LQR 516.
 1 [1895] AC 471.

'(1) This section applies where a motor vehicle[2] has been bailed or (in Scotland) hired under a hire-purchase agreement, or has been agreed to be sold under a conditional sale agreement, and, before the property in the vehicle has become vested in the debtor, he disposes of the vehicle to another person.[3]

(2) Where the disposition referred to in subsection (1) above is to a private purchaser, and he is a purchaser of the motor vehicle in good faith, without notice of the hire-purchase or conditional sale agreement (the 'relevant agreement'), that disposition shall have effect as if the creditor's title to the vehicle had been vested in the debtor immediately before that disposition.'

There must be an HP or CS agreement for s 27(1) to apply and so credit-sale agreements (where the title in the goods will have passed to B) and simple hiring or leasing agreements are not within its scope. Also, the emphasis upon a completed agreement means that the provisions do not apply where the debtor is given possession of the vehicle on completion of a proposal form which is subsequently not accepted by the creditor.[4] On the other hand, s 27(1) applies even if the HP or CS agreement in question is outside the financial limits prescribed by the Consumer Credit Act 1974 (CCA) and even where the debtor is a body corporate.

Section 29(4) stipulates that the debtor is 'the person who at the material time ... is ... the person to whom the vehicle is bailed' and is still the debtor 'whether the agreement has before that time been terminated or not'. This wording was designed to pre-empt those situations where the agreement provides that if the debtor disposes of the vehicle the agreement is determined but it raises several problems. First, there is no requirement that the debtor be in *possession* of the vehicle at the time of the disposition and thus, theoretically, s 27 could apply where the creditor has re-possessed the vehicle. This is most unlikely however and, if this situation arose, the disponee from the debtor would scarcely be in good faith and without notice. Second, difficulties can be envisaged regarding the validity of the agreement. It seems likely that s 27 will apply where the agreement is unenforceable against the debtor because of failure to comply with the formalities of the CCA.[5] Moreover, where the agreement is voidable, eg for fraud, and has been avoided by the creditor before the disposition by the debtor, it is suggested that the rescission would be regarded as a 'termination' meaning that the Act would apply. If the agreement is void however, eg for mistaken identity, it is likely that the person in possession would not be a 'debtor' thereby excluding the operation of the Act.

THE DISPOSITION BY THE DEBTOR

The debtor must dispose of the vehicle, 'disposition' being defined in s 29(1) as:

'... any sale or contract of sale (including a conditional sale agreement), any bailment ... under a hire-purchase agreement and any transfer of the property in goods in pursuance of a provision in that behalf contained in a hire-purchase agreement, and includes any transaction purporting to be a disposition (as so defined)'.

---

2 Defined in s 29(1) as 'a mechanically propelled vehicle intended or adapted for use on roads to which the public has access'. Are industrial/agricultural vehicles included?
3 'Person' includes a body corporate: see Interpretation Act 1978, s 5 and Sch 1.
4 See *Central Newbury Car Auctions Ltd v Unity Finance Ltd* [1957] 1 QB 371.
5 See *R v Modupe* [1991] Crim LR 530 (failure to comply with formalities did not mean that there was no existing liability under the agreement).

In comparison with the corresponding definitions in the FA and SGA, this is quite narrow and it patently excludes a gift, exchange, mortgage or lien but, on the other hand, no *delivery* is required. The disposition must be by the debtor or his agent and cannot be by a third party such as a bailee of the debtor. In *Keeble v Combined Lease Finance plc*,[6] two partners in an insurance firm acquired a car on HP and were named in the agreement as joint debtors but one partner sold the car to a *bona fide*, private purchaser before all the instalments had been paid. The finance company argued that both partners needed to be parties to the disposition if the private purchaser were to acquire title but the Court of Appeal held that either debtor could transfer a good title. It is clear that, if the finance company's argument had prevailed, the private purchaser's protection would have been significantly diminished.

PRIVATE PURCHASER

On the basis that motor dealers and finance houses have access to HP Information Ltd and sufficient expertise to guard their own interests, only a 'private purchaser' can acquire title under the provisions of Part III and a 'trade or finance purchaser' is excluded. The latter is defined in s 29(2) as:

'... a purchaser who, at the time of the disposition made to him, carries on a business which consists, wholly or partly, –
(a) of purchasing motor vehicles for the purpose of offering or exposing them for sale, or
(b) of providing finance by purchasing motor vehicles for the purpose of bailing ... them under hire-purchase agreements or agreeing to sell them under conditional sale agreements'.

Also in s 29(2), a 'private purchaser' is defined as 'a purchaser who, at the time of the disposition made to him, does not carry on any such business'.

The trade or finance purchaser must thus carry on a 'business' and, in this context, the pursuit of business clearly demands that the transactions involved must be performed with a degree of regularity.[7] Moreover, the specified transactions in which the business must engage are quite restricted in s 29(2) and so many businesses will be classifiable as private purchasers. For example, a company which regularly buys vehicles for *use* in its business would be protected as a private purchaser as would a company which *hires* vehicles to the public as its main business. However, when a purchaser falls within the trade or finance definition, he cannot claim to be a private purchaser merely because he buys a vehicle for his *own use*. In *Stevenson v Beverley Bentinck Ltd*,[8] H, the hirer of a car under an HP agreement, sold it to B. B had a full-time job as a tool-room inspector but he bought and sold cars in his spare time, having entered into some 37 transactions involving cars in the previous 18 months. Notwithstanding that B had bought this car for his own use, he was held to be a trade purchaser and thus he could not acquire title to the car. The court was thus concerned with B's objective business status rather than the subjective capacity in which he bought the goods.

---

6 [1996] CCLR 63.
7 See the CCA, s 189(2): 'A person is not to be treated as carrying on a particular type of business merely because occasionally he enters into transactions belonging to a business of that type'.
8 [1976] 1 WLR 483.

EFFECTS OF SPECIFIED DISPOSITIONS

In s 27(2), (3) and (4), the Act specifies three separate situations where the third party will acquire title. Section 27(2), set-out above, deals with the Act's paradigm of the debtor's disposition to a *bona fide* private purchaser without notice, who acquires a good title. For example, a vehicle owned by O is let to H on hire-purchase and H wrongfully sells it to B, a *bona fide* private purchaser without notice. B acquires a good title.

Section 27(3) provides for the situation where the debtor disposes of the vehicle to a trade or finance purchaser but the *first* private purchaser after that is *bona fide* and without notice. Such a purchaser acquires a good title. This is so even if there are several intermediate trade purchasers. For example, a vehicle owned by O is let to H on hire-purchase and H wrongfully sells it to T, a trade purchaser, who then sells it to B, a *bona fide* private purchaser without notice. B acquires a good title.

Section 27(4) provides for the situation where s 27(3) applies, but the disposition to the first *bona fide* private 'purchaser' without notice is itself a bailment under an HP agreement, and the creditor then transfers the property in the vehicle under the HP agreement to that purchaser (or a person claiming under him). That purchaser acquires a good title, the section also specifying that he nevertheless acquires title if, at the time of his acquiring it, he is no longer *bona fide* and without notice. For example, a vehicle owned by O is let to H on hire-purchase and H wrongfully sells it to F, a finance company, who then lets it on hire-purchase to B who is the first private 'purchaser' and *bona fide*, without notice. The letting to B on hire-purchase is valid and, if in pursuance of the hire-purchase agreement, property in the vehicle is transferred to B, B acquires a good title, even if, by then, he knows of the original HP agreement. It is unclear, however, why the Act arbitrarily limits protection under s 27(3) and (4) to the *first* private purchaser. In the last mentioned example, should F re-possess the vehicle held by B on HP and sell it to B2, a *bona fide* private purchaser, B2 acquires no title as he is not the first purchaser but his claim seems as meritorious as that of B. The first private purchaser restriction does not apply to s 27(2) and thus, should a debtor under an HP agreement wrongfully let the vehicle on HP to B but then re-possess it and sell it to B2, a *bona fide* private purchaser, B2 will acquire a good title.

It is thus clear that the only persons who can claim protection under the 1964 Act are those who are *bona fide*, private purchasers without notice (s 27(2)) or *bona fide*, private, first purchasers without notice (s 27(3) and (4)) or those who claim under them. If the first private purchaser under s 27(3) and (4) is *mala fide*, no subsequent private purchaser can obtain a good title. Moreover, the Act does not absolve either the debtor or the trade purchaser from any liability, civil or criminal, to which they would otherwise be subject (s 27(6)).[9]

---

9 See *Barber v NWS Bank plc* [1996] 1 WLR 641 (the defendant finance company (D) agreed to sell a car to the plaintiff, P, (a *bona fide*, private purchaser) on conditional sale (CS). The CS agreement had an *express* term that D would have title to the car at the date of the agreement. After paying several instalments, P discovered that the car did not belong to D and so he rescinded the agreement and claimed back the instalments which he had paid. CA held that P could do so and, even though he would have acquired title to the car on completion of his payments, s 27(6) preserved the liability of D for breach of the express term in the CS agreement.

It is important to stress that the third party does not acquire an absolute title to the vehicle as s 27(2), (3) and (4) and s 29(5) all specify that the debtor's disposition shall have effect as if the creditor's title to the vehicle had been vested in the debtor immediately before that disposition. If, for example, the finance company who let the vehicle to the debtor had no title, none can be transferred to the *bona fide*, private buyer. Moreover, when such a *bona fide*, private buyer does acquire title under the Act, a related difficulty involves the *quality* of his statutory title. Should he wish to buy a new car and part-exchange the vehicle with the statutory title, the car dealer will discover, from HPI, that there is an existing HP agreement on that vehicle and may well refuse to take it. It is arguable therefore that the buyer should be able to repudiate the contract and sue for breach of the SGA, s 12(1), on the basis that the seller had no right to sell the goods.[10]

GOOD FAITH AND LACK OF NOTICE

The private purchaser must be in good faith *and* without notice of the HP agreement, the burden of proof seemingly resting on the purchaser.[11] 'Good faith' is not defined in the 1964 Act but the test is a subjective one and so it is only necessary that the private purchaser should act honestly.[12] Section 29(3) defines notice as 'actual notice' of the HP agreement and so constructive notice is insufficient, eg an argument that the vehicle was registered with HPI would not, in itself, be notice. Similarly, in *Barker v Bell*,[13] it was held that the buyer did not have notice of the HP agreement where, although he knew of its existence, he was told falsely that all the instalments had been paid.

It is apparent that there may be a long chain of buyers and sellers between the original debtor who wrongfully disposes of the goods and the final, *bona fide* private purchaser and the latter may have considerable difficulty in tracing his title. In order to help him, certain rebuttable presumptions arise under s 28 which mean that, once he establishes that a person (whether a party to the proceedings or not) was a *bona fide* private purchaser without notice (the 'relevant purchaser'), his claim will succeed, unless the creditor who originally supplied the vehicle on HP can prove otherwise.[14] The presumptions are that (i) the disposition to the private purchaser was made by the debtor; (ii) if it is proved that the disposition was *not* made by the debtor, then it is presumed that the debtor disposed of the vehicle to a *bona fide* private purchaser and the relevant purchaser is or was a person claiming under that *bona fide* purchaser; and (iii) if it is proved that the disposition to the relevant purchaser was not made by the debtor but, instead, was a disposition to a trade purchaser, then it is presumed

10 Se Ch 19 on the implied terms relating to title (SGA, s 12(1)) in the sale of goods.

11 *Mercantile Credit Co Ltd v Waugh* (1978) 32 *Hire Trading* (No 2) 16.

12 See *Dodds v Yorkshire Bank Finance* [1992] CCLR 30 (the private purchaser had been suspicious but the agreement specified that the vehicle was not subject to a current HP agreement. Held that the purchaser's suspicions had been laid to rest and she was thus in good faith). The SGA, s 61(3) provides that 'a thing is deemed to be done in good faith ... when it is in fact done honestly, whether it is done negligently or not'.

13 [1971] 1 WLR 983.

14 The presumptions are inapplicable where all the transactions are known, see *Soneco Ltd v Barcross Finance Ltd* [1978] RTR 444.

that the first private purchaser thereafter was *bona fide* and that the relevant purchaser is or was a person claiming under the trade purchaser.

Miscellaneous provisions

There are numerous miscellaneous situations where a non-owner may transfer title in the goods and the SGA, s 21(2)(b) provides that nothing in the Act is to affect 'the validity of any contract of sale under any special common law or statutory power of sale or under the order of a court of competent jurisdiction'.

The most important persons who have a common law power of sale are pledgees of goods or documents of title[15] and agents of necessity, but there is a formidable list of persons with statutory powers of sale.[16] Some of the most significant in the latter category are unpaid sellers of goods,[17] sheriffs, liquidators of companies, trustees in bankruptcy, distraining landlords, pawnbrokers,[18] bailees of uncollected goods,[19] and innkeepers.[20]

Proposals for reform

In 1966, the Law Reform Committee[1] made recommendations for the amendment of the *nemo dat* rules, the individual proposals having been considered in the appropriate places in this chapter. In terms of overall reform, the Committee considered the suggestion of Devlin LJ in *Ingram v Little*[2] that an apportionment of loss might be made between the innocent owner and innocent buyer of goods from a swindler who had disappeared, instead of the law's being forced to opt for one of the two innocent parties. Apportionment was rejected,[3] however, on the basis that it would be difficult to assess in a chain of transactions and the unrestrained judicial discretion involved would engender uncertainty.

The most recent recommendations are those of Professor A L Diamond.[4] His report is concerned principally with reform of the law regarding security over personal property and, building on the foundations laid in the Crowther Committee's Report,[5] he advocates the adoption of uniform treatment for all transactions whereby a security interest is reserved in relation to goods, and the introduction of a system of registration for non-possessory securities. The relevance to *nemo dat* is that a debtor in possession of goods subject to a security interest in favour of a secured creditor might sell the goods to a *bona fide* third party who has no knowledge of the security interest. The Diamond Review

---

15 See Crossley Vaines, *Personal Property* (5th edn, 1973), Ch 23.
16 See *Benjamin's Sale of Goods* (5th edn, 1997), para 7-107.
17 See the SGA, ss 39(1), 48.
18 See the Consumer Credit Act 1974, ss 120, 121.
19 See the Torts (Interference with Goods) Act 1977, ss 12, 13.
20 See the Innkeepers Act 1878, s 1.
 1 Twelfth Report, *Transfer of Title to Chattels* (1966), Cmnd 2958.
 2 [1961] 1 QB 31.
 3 See paras 7-12, 40(1).
 4 *A Review of Security Interests in Property* (HMSO 1989), Department of Trade and Industry.
 5 *Report of the Committee on Consumer Credit* (1971), Cmnd 4596.

considers that, if the law on security interests is reformed, there will be need for a clear statement of the rights of *bona fide* buyers of goods which are subject to a prior security interest as it would be an 'unacceptable hindrance to trade'[6] if buyers from dealers in such goods should have to search the register. The Diamond Report thus makes two separate proposals, the second being more radical than the first. The first proposal is for the minimum protection of the buyer under the new rules and is that innocent buyers of goods would take free of any security interest, except that the present position with motor vehicles should be maintained and trade purchasers would be required to search the register just as they search now with HPI.

The second proposal is more fundamental and would create a principle of 'entrusting', viz, whenever an owner has entrusted his goods to another or acquiesced in their possession by that other ('the possessor') in a wide range of contractual situations, any sale of the goods by the possessor in the ordinary course of business to an innocent buyer would confer a good title on the latter. The requirement of the ordinary course of business would not mean that the possessor should actually carry on such a business but it should appear to a reasonable purchaser that the disposition was in the ordinary course of business, thereby imposing a test analogous to that in *Newtons of Wembley Ltd v Williams.*[7] In the case of a sale by the possessor of *consumer* goods, the requirement of the ordinary course of business would be inapplicable. It is also recommended that the rule in *Car and Universal Finance Ltd v Caldwell*[8] (allowing a public act of rescission) should be abrogated and that even communication to the possessor should be insuffcient as rescission, thus meaning that only repossession of the goods would terminate the consequences of entrusting. These proposals would replace all the technical situations now covered by the SGA, ss 23-25 (and the notion of apparent ownership) with one broad principle of entrusting and, if fleshed out in more detail, they would provide a sound basis for reform of the law.

---

6 Para 13. 5. 2.
7 [1965] 1 QB 560 (considered above).
8 [1965] 1 QB 525 (considered above).

CHAPTER 19

The seller's obligation to transfer title to the goods

Introduction

The 'whole object'[1] of a contract for the sale of goods is that S should transfer the general property[2] in the goods to B, this object being encapsulated in the SGA, s 2(1) which defines a contract of sale as 'a contract by which the seller transfers or agrees to transfer the property in goods to the buyer for a money consideration, called the price'.

The law could not always be stated as authoritatively and decisively as this. In a leading decision[3] in the middle of the 19th century, Parke B held that, at least in a sale of specific goods, there was 'no implied warranty of title on the sale of goods, and that if there be no fraud, a vendor is not liable for a bad title, unless there is an express warranty, or an equivalent to it, by declarations or conduct'.[4] Moreover, there were particular situations where no warranty of title was held to exist, eg sales by sheriffs and auctioneers.[5] Alternatively, there were situations where title would be guaranteed, eg a sale in market overt or 'where articles are bought in a shop professedly carried on for the sale of goods ... [where] the vendor sells "as his own"'.[6] Overall, the general rule was that S did not impliedly warrant title and, of course, this was part of the dominant principle of *caveat emptor*. The general rule was gradually eroded and 'a number of exceptions crept in, till at last the exceptions became the rule, the rule being that the vendor warranted that he had title to what he purported to sell, except in certain special cases, such as that of a sale by a sheriff, who does not so warrant'.[7] However, it was only in the second half of the 19th century that S's undertaking as to title was clearly established as an *implied* term of the sale itself. In 1864, Erle CJ[8] considered that 'in almost all the transactions of sale in

---

1 *Rowland v Divall* [1923] 2 KB 500, 506-507 per Atkin LJ.
2 The SGA, s 61(1) provides that 'property' means 'the general property in goods, and not merely a special property'.
3 *Morley v Attenborough* (1849) 3 Exch 500.
4 *Morley v Attenborough* (1849) 3 Exch 500 at 512.
5 See eg *Peto v Blades* (1814) 5 Taunt 657; *Page v Cowasjee Eduljee* (1866) LR 1 PC 127; *Bagueley v Hawley* (1867) LR 2 CP 625.
6 *Morley v Attenborough* (1849) 3 Exch 500, 513 per Parke B.
7 *Rowland v Divall* [1923] 2 KB 500, 505 per Scrutton LJ.
8 *Eicholz v Bannister* (1864) 17 CBNS 708, 723.

common life, the seller by the very act of selling holds out to the buyer that he is the owner of the article he offers for sale. The sale of a chattel is the strongest act of dominion that is incidental to ownership. A purchaser under ordinary circumstances would naturally be led to the conclusion that, by offering an article for sale, the seller affirms that he has a title to sell, and that the buyer may enjoy that for which he parts with his money'.

The SGA, s 12, contains three implied, contractual obligations of S, thus specifying the nature and extent of the title with which B must be endowed.[9] First, there is an implied condition that S has a 'right to sell' the goods (s 12(1)), second a warranty that B shall acquire the goods free from 'any charge or encumbrance' (s 12(2)(a)) and, third, a warranty that B shall have 'quiet possession' of the goods (s 12(2)(b)). In addition, s 12(3) provides for the situation where S intends to transfer a limited title only. Section 12 provides:

'(1) In a contract of sale, other than one to which sub-section (3) below applies, there is an implied term on the part of the seller that in the case of a sale he has a right to sell the goods, and in the case of an agreement to sell he will have such a right at the time when the property is to pass.

(2) In a contract of sale, other than one to which subsection (3) below applies, there is also an implied term that–

(a) the goods are free, and will remain free until the time when the property is to pass, from any charge or encumbrance not disclosed or known to the buyer before the contract is made, and

(b) the buyer will enjoy quiet possession of the goods except so far as it may be disturbed by the owner or other person entitled to the benefit of any charge or encumbrance so disclosed or known.

(3) This subsection applies to a contract of sale in the case of which there appears from the contract or is to be inferred from its circumstances an intention that the seller should transfer only such title as he or a third person may have.

(4) In a contract to which subsection (3) above applies there is an implied term that all charges or encumbrances known to the seller and not known to the buyer have been disclosed to the buyer before the contract is made.

(5) In a contract to which subsection (3) above applies there is also an implied term that none of the following will disturb the buyer's quiet possession of the goods, namely—

(a) the seller;

(b) in a case where the parties to the contract intend that the seller should transfer only such title as a third person may have, that person;

(c) anyone claiming through or under the seller or that third person otherwise than under a charge or encumbrance disclosed or known to the buyer before the contract is made.

(5A) As regards England and Wales and Northern Ireland, the term implied by subsection (1) above is a condition and the terms implied by subsections (2), (4) and (5) above are warranties.'

The seller's right to sell the goods

Title is a relative concept but it is tolerably clear that when the SGA refers to 'property' it means ownership in the sense of the absolute legal interest in the

---

9 See Bridge, 'The Title Obligations of the Seller of Goods' in *Interests in Goods* (eds Palmer and McKendrick, 2nd edn, 1998), Ch 12.

goods.[10] The overall intent and purpose of s 12(1) is that S should transfer to B the best possible title to the absolute interest and, if a third party can establish a better title to the goods than B's, S will be in breach of s 12(1).

It will be observed, however, that s 12(1) does not demand that S should have either 'title' or 'property' but, instead, it specifies that he must have a 'right to sell' the goods at the appropriate time. The relevant time is specified in s 12(1) as being 'in the case of a *sale*' that 'he *has* a right to sell the goods' and 'in the case of an *agreement to sell* he will have such a right at the time when the *property is to pass*'.[11] The relevant time-permutations can thus be determined with these two rules, eg in a *sale* of specific goods where property passes on contract, S must have the right to sell at the time of contracting with B but, if the passing of property in the specific goods is postponed until some time after contract, this is an *agreement to sell* and S need have the right to sell only at the later time when property is to pass.[12] It follows that 'a contract of sale can perfectly well be performed by a seller who never has title at any time, by causing a third party to transfer it directly to the buyer'[13] because here S will have the right to sell when property is to pass. Moreover, there is no breach of s 12(1) where, for example, S is the agent of the owner and thus authorised to sell the goods to B.

Where S has property in the goods he will normally have a right to sell them but it is clear that these two notions do not always coincide and, even if S is able to transfer a good title, he may be in breach of s 12(1) if he has no right to sell. In *Niblett Ltd v Confectioners' Materials Co Ltd*,[14] S agreed to sell to B a quantity of condensed milk in tins to be shipped from New York to London and some of the tins arrived bearing the brand name 'Nissly'. This label infringed the Nestlé company's trademark and Nestlé obtained an injunction to restrain B's sale of the offending tins. Accordingly, the tins were detained by the Customs and Excise and were released only after the labels had been removed and destroyed. B then sold the tins, without labels, at a loss. The Court of Appeal held that S was liable in damages for breach of s 12(1) as he did not have a right to sell the goods at the time when property was to pass to B. Atkin LJ[15] pointed out that Nestlé had 'a title superior to that of the vendor, so that the possession of the vendee could be disturbed' and Scrutton LJ[16] held that 'if a vendor can be stopped by process of law from selling he has not the right to sell'.[17] In *Niblett*, S did not have the right to sell as Nestlé had a paramount right to stop the performance of the sale but s 12(1) may also be breached where the sale

---

10 See Battersby and Preston, 'The Concepts of "Property", "Title" and "Owner" used in the Sale of Goods Act 1893' (1972) 35 MLR 268.
11 See the SGA, s 2 for the definition of these terms; see also Ch 14.
12 Eg *Anderson v Ryan* [1967] IR 34 (S agreed to sell a specific car and repair it before delivery. S only acquired title to the car *after* the contract was made but, as repairs were to be done to it, property did not pass to B until they were completed and, by then, S had title and had not breached s 12(1)). Having regard to the other rules in the SGA, it is difficult to see why s 12 did not stipulate simply that S should have the right to sell at the moment of the passing of property, ie a 'sale' by definition passes property (s 2(4)) and an 'agreement to sell' does not (s 2(5)).
13 *Karlshamns Oljefabriker v Eastport Navigation Corpn, The Elafi* [1982] 1 All ER 208, 215 per Mustill J.
14 [1921] 3 KB 387.
15 [1921] 3 KB 387 at 402.
16 [1921] 3 KB 387 at 398.
17 Bankes (pp 395-396) and Atkin (pp 403-404) LJJ also held that there was a breach of the SGA 1893, s 14(2) (merchantable quality).

contravenes the criminal law and the goods are seized.[18] Where there is a transgression of the criminal law, it is suggested that there would be no breach of s 12(1) where, for example, S infringes a statutory, administrative requirement but B's rights over the goods are not impaired. If the result were otherwise, B would be provided with a technical means of avoiding a bad bargain.

Nevertheless, it must be questioned whether the notion that S has no 'right' to sell can be extended to other contexts. There are many situations where, although S is not the owner of the goods and does not sell them with the owner's consent, the SGA and other statutes permit him to transfer a good title to B[19] and, at first glance, it is arguable that there is a breach of s 12(1) in this situation in that S may have a *power* to sell but not a *right* to do so. This conclusion is arguably fortified if S has committed a criminal offence in the course of obtaining the goods from the owner and selling them to B, eg obtaining property by deception from the owner. There is no authority directly in point but the orthodox view is that s 12(1) is not breached[20] in this situation as S need not warrant that there is an existing and indefeasible title vested in himself but promises only that he will confer a sound title on B at the appropriate time[1] and B does receive such a title, albeit by virtue of statutory provisions. Alternatively, it can be argued that there is a technical breach of s 12(1) but generally B suffers no identifiable loss[2] and, as he acquires title, the remedy for the breach abates.[3] The view that s 12(1) is breached in this situation seems to be supported by the Court of Appeal's decision in *R v Wheeler*.[4] There B bought goods from S, unaware that they had been stolen from their owner but, as the sale was in market overt, B's title was guaranteed. Nevertheless, B would not have bought the goods had he been aware of the truth. In the course of alluding to B's possible remedies such as rescission for innocent misrepresentation (there was no dishonesty at the time of the sale to B), Stuart-Smith LJ appeared to assume that B could have rejected the goods for breach of s 12(1). It is respectfully suggested that this view is correct: although B may obtain an indefeasible title, it may be stigmatised and barren where it is a protected title conferred upon B by statute. A prime illustration occurs in hire-purchase cases. A private purchaser of a motor vehicle may acquire a good title to it by virtue of Part III of the Hire Purchase Act 1964,[5] even though it was subject to a current hire-purchase agreement, but he may find the vehicle unsaleable as car dealers will discover

---

18 See *Stock v Urey* [1955] NI 71(breach of s 12(1) where a car was seized by Customs as an illegal import, B having to pay tax and duty before he could obtain delivery); see also *Egekvist Bakeries Inc v Tizel and Blinick* [1950] 1 DLR 585; affd [1950] 2 DLR 592 (blueberries were impounded by the Federal authorities in the USA as infringing legislation concerned with food purity and subsequently destroyed. Held S was in breach of the right to sell).

19 See Ch 18.

20 See *Niblett Ltd v Confectioners' Materials Co Ltd* [1921] 3 KB 387, 401-402 per Atkin LJ: 'It may be that the implied condition is not broken if the seller is able to pass to the purchaser a right to sell notwithstanding his own inability'. This was assumed to be the position in *Anderson v Ryan* [1967] IR 34; see also *Benjamin's Sale of Goods* (5th edn, 1997), para 4-004.

1 See *Karlshamns Oljefabriker v Eastport Navigation Corpn, The Elafi* [1982] 1 All ER 208, 215 per Mustill J: '[Section 12] involves no promise about the seller's proprietary rights, only that he will be able to create the appropriate rights in the buyer'.

2 See Atiyah, *The Sale of Goods* (10th edn, 2001), p 104.

3 See Goode, *Commercial Law* (2nd edn, 1995), p 298.

4 (1990) 92 Cr App Rep 279; see Brown, 'The Scope of Section 12 of the Sale of Goods Act' (1992) 108 LQR 221.

5 See Ch 18 on transfer of title by a non-owner.

that it is registered as subject to such an agreement and thus refuse to accept it.[6] Similarly, if antiques have been sold in circumstances where the true owner has not consented to their sale but one of the statutory exceptions to *nemo dat* confers a good title on a *bona fide* buyer, he may find grave difficulty in selling the goods, have to sell them at a loss or be put to expense in attempting to verify his title.[7] It is surely indisputable that B should have a remedy for breach of s 12(1) in these situations where there is a shadow on the title and a provable loss. It is plain that here B's grievance relates to the *quality* of the title conveyed but his claim could not fall within the implied conditions in the SGA, s 14, relating to quality and fitness for purpose of the goods, unless the goods were *physically* defective[8] in some way, as in *Niblett*.

Remedies for breach of s 12(1)

At the outset, it should be stressed that the liability imposed by s 12(1) is strict liability and is thus not dependent on any fault or knowledge of S. Breach of s 12(1) is a breach of condition by S which means that B can treat the contract as repudiated and claim damages for any loss caused by the breach. The general rule is that B cannot retain any benefit under the contract when he repudiates it for breach of condition and thus he must restore the goods to S.[9] Similarly, if B seeks to recover money paid because of a total failure of consideration by S,[10] the failure must be total and B must not have received a partial benefit under the contract.[11] However, English law considers the obligation to transfer title to be so paramount that, where S is in breach of this obligation, B is entitled to recover the whole of the purchase price from S on grounds of a 'total' failure of consideration *even* if B has had considerable use of the goods and has thus obtained a real benefit. Also, the principle that B can accept the goods within s 11(4), thereby losing his right to repudiate the contract for breach of condition and limiting his claim to damages for breach of warranty, does not apply to a breach of s 12(1).

The incomparable superiority of B in this context was established in *Rowland v Divall*.[12] In that case, the defendant (S) bought an 'Albert' motor car in good faith from a thief and resold it to the plaintiff (B), a car dealer, for £334. B repainted the car and displayed it for sale in his showroom, selling it after two months to a Colonel Railsdon for £400. Two months later, the police repossessed the car on behalf of the owner, as it had originally been stolen, and B refunded

---

6 This was accepted by the Crowther Committee, see *Report of the Committee on Consumer Credit* (Cmnd 4596, 1971), Vol I, para 5.7.32. If B's possession is disturbed by the finance company, he should have a remedy for breach of the warranty of quiet possession in s 12(2)(b). See also *Barber v NWS Bank plc* [1996] 1 WLR 641 (considered below).
7 See eg the situation in *Clayton v Le Roy* [1911] 2 KB 1031.
8 See *Harlingdon and Leinster Enterprises Ltd v Christopher Hull Fine Art Ltd* [1991] 1 QB 564.
9 The restoration rule does not apply, however, where the breach of condition itself makes restitution impossible, eg defective goods explode or, as will be seen below, if B is dispossessed of the goods by the true owner because S had no title.
10 The SGA, s 54 provides: Nothing in this Act affects the right of the buyer ... to recover money paid where the consideration for the payment of it has failed.
11 On the question of the totality of the failure of consideration, see *Consensus Ad Idem, Essays on the Law of Contract in Honour of Guenter Treitel* (1996, ed F D Rose), Ch 9, 'Failure of Consideration', Peter Birks.
12 [1923] 2 KB 500.

the £400 to Railsdon. B then claimed the £334 from S. Bray J held that, as B and Railsdon had had four months' use of the car, there had not been a total failure of consideration and B must be limited to his remedy in damages. The Court of Appeal reversed that decision and considered that, despite the four months' use and the fact that the car could not be returned to S, the consideration for the payment had totally failed and B could recover £334. Atkin LJ[13] was emphatic that B had 'not received any part of that which he contracted to receive – namely, the property and right to possession'. Both Atkin and Bankes LJJ also held that the rules regarding acceptance of the goods[14] had no application to a breach of s 12(1)[15] and thus B's sale of the car to Railsdon and/or the lapse of time involved were not acts of acceptance compelling B to sue only for damages. Moreover, in answering the argument that B could not restore the car to S, Scrutton LJ[16] stressed that this was the direct result of S's lack of title and so 'it does not lie in the defendant's mouth to set up as a defence ... his own breach of the implied condition that he had a right to sell'.[17]

Rowland is obviously criticisable in two respects. First, B may recover more loss than he has actually sustained because, in recovering the total price of the goods from S, S is allowed no set-off for depreciation or B's use of the goods before discovery of S's lack of title. On the facts of *Rowland*, however, it was arguably fair that B should recover the full price of £334 as he had paid £400 to the third party, Railsdon[18] and, as Treitel[19] has pointed out, B was a dealer who did not want to use the car but, instead, needed a marketable title in order to sell it. It was thus realistic to assert that B 'did not get what he paid for – namely, a car to which he would have title'.[20] Second, B's right of recovery from S does not depend upon B's possession of the goods being disturbed by the real owner or any claims being made against him by either the real owner or a sub-buyer from B (see eg the *Karflex* case, below).

The effect of decisions after *Rowland*

The extensive consequences of *Rowland* are apparent from later decisions. In *Butterworth v Kingsway Motors*,[1] a Jowett Javelin car was let on hire-purchase terms by a finance company to a hirer who wrongfully (but innocently) sold it before she had completed the payments under the contract. The car was re-sold

13 [1923] 2 KB 500 at 507.
14 Then the SGA 1893, s 11(1)(c), now the SGA 1979, s 11(4).
15 Bankes LJ on the basis that the breach was so serious that 'user of the car by [B] seems to me quite immaterial' (p 504) and Atkin LJ because 'there can be no sale at all of goods which [S] has no right to sell' (p 506). The latter view has been discredited because if every sale *does* transfer title s 12(1) is otiose and, if no title is transferred there is no sale and s 12 cannot apply, leaving B with no remedy. Atkin LJ's reasoning was also advanced by May LJ in *National Employers' Mutual General Insurance Association v Jones* [1990] 1 AC 24, 39-40; see Brown, 'Title to Stolen Goods' (1988) 104 LQR 516.
16 [1923] 2 KB 500 at 505.
17 In the bulk of cases, B will be unable to return the goods to S as he will discover S's defective title only when the goods are repossessed by the real owner.
18 B's claim in *Rowland* seems less meritorious in the light of the fact that the insurers of the real owner sold the car to B for £260 and, not unnaturally, S had argued that this should be the extent of his liability to B: see (1923) 129 LT 757.
19 *The Law of Contract* (10th edn, 1999), p 981.
20 *Rowland v Divall* [1923] 2 KB 500, 504 per Bankes LJ.
 1 [1954] 1 WLR 1286.

several times until, finally, it was sold by Kingsway Motors (S) to Butterworth (B) for £1,275, both parties being in good faith. Almost one year later, the finance company claimed the car from B but, in the alternative, they offered him the choice of acquiring it for £175, this being the outstanding amount under the hire-purchase agreement as the hirer had continued to pay the instalments. By this time the car was worth £800. The day after he heard from the finance company, B claimed the return of £1,275 from S and, eight days later, the hirer paid the £175 to the finance company and thus exercised the option to buy the car. Pearson J considered that B's claim was 'somewhat lacking in merits'[2] but held that he could recover £1,275 from S as money paid upon a consideration which had totally failed.

The important question of 'feeding' the title was raised by the facts of *Butterworth*. This concept means that S may acquire title by, for example, paying-off the true owner, and S's acquisition of title then feeds all the other defective titles in a chain of transactions. It must therefore be decided what effect this has on the right to sell in s 12(1). In *Butterworth*, S had no right to sell either at the time that property was to pass to B or at the time of B's (speedy) repudiation as title had not vested in S at that time, and this fact validated B's claim. But when the hirer paid the final instalment eight days after B's repudiation, she acquired a good title to the car and this fed all the defective titles in the chain, thereby vesting title to the car in S.[3] It is crucial to decide, therefore, what the position would have been if the hirer had paid her final instalment *before* B had sought to repudiate the contract with S. Would B's title then have been fed precluding any breach of s 12(1)? The point was left undecided in *Butterworth* but it seems likely that B's title would have been fed thus preventing his repudiation and disallowing his claim against S for the price.[4] However, the opposite view is that S would still have lacked title and the right to sell at the crucial moment specified in s 12(1), ie the time that property was to pass to B under the contract, and that this fact cannot be altered retrospectively by any artificial notion of feeding the title.[5]

In *Butterworth*, B had used the car for almost a year and it is quite unrealistic to argue that there was a total failure of consideration, but all the leading decisions in this context clearly establish that there is such a total failure if B does not obtain title, even though he obtains *possession*. *Butterworth* thus exemplifies the worst excesses of the *Rowland* principle but there are several decisions concerning hire-purchase agreements which are similarly criticisable. In *Karflex Ltd v Poole*,[6] the plaintiffs were 'hire-purchase dealers' who bought a Riley car from its apparent owner and, describing themselves as 'owners', the plaintiffs then let it on hire-purchase terms to Poole. Poole paid a deposit of £95

---

2   [1954] 1 WLR 1286 at 1291.
3   S could nevertheless recover from his immediate vendor the amount he had been compelled to pay to B (£1,275), minus the value of the car (£800) at the time his title was fed, ie £475.
4   See Pearson J in *Butterworth* at pp 1295-1296 and the persuasive authorities there cited in favour of this result. See also *Lucas v Smith* [1926] VLR 400, 403-404 per Dixon AJ; *Patten v Thomas Motors Pty Ltd* [1965] NSWR 1457 (the facts were very similar to *Butterworth's*, except that the hirer *did* pay off the finance company before B's repudiation and B had used the car for more than two years. Collins J held that B's title had been fed before his repudiation and thus his claim against S failed).
5   See *West (HW) Ltd v McBlain* [1950] NI 144, where Sheil J rejected the notion that B's fed title could affect his remedies against S as it was not possible to revivify something which never had life. A literal reading of s 12(1) ('in the case of a sale [S] *has* a right to sell') supports this view. See also Ellinger, 'Buyer's Remedies when Seller does not have the Right To Sell the Goods' (1969) 5 Vict U Well L Rev 168.
6   [1933] 2 KB 251.

and took possession of the car but then defaulted on the first instalment. The plaintiffs retook the car and commenced proceedings against Poole but it was then discovered that the apparent owner had obtained the car dishonestly and had no title it. The plaintiffs then 'bought out' the real owner and continued their claim against Poole but he argued that it was an express condition of the contract that the plaintiffs should have owned the car at the date that the hire-purchase agreement was *entered into*[7] because he might have wished to exercise the option to purchase immediately after contract. The court agreed with that contention and held that there was a total failure of consideration and so Poole was able to repudiate the contract and recover the deposit.[8] Here Poole had not been dispossessed by the real owner and, indeed, that possibility could not arise at the time of trial because the owner had been bought out.

Karflex was followed recently in *Barber v NWS Bank plc*.[9] B agreed to buy a Honda Accord on conditional sale terms from S, the agreement containing an *express* term that S would have title at the date of the agreement. More than 18 months later, B was in financial difficulties and decided to sell the Honda, pay-off S and buy a cheaper car but he then discovered that the Honda was subject to a prior finance agreement with moneys outstanding and that S had no title to it at the date of the conditional sale to B. No dealer would buy the car from B because of the earlier finance agreement. B then sought to rescind the contract with S and recover all payments made. Some time later, S paid off the earlier claim in full. The Court of Appeal held that B could recover all sums paid despite his unimpeded use of the car for a substantial period of time.[10]

7 Since *Karflex*, the implied condition in s 12(1) has been extended to hire-purchase: see the Supply of Goods (Implied Terms) Act 1973, s 8, re-enacted in the Consumer Credit Act 1974, Sch 4. In hire-purchase agreements, O must have a right to sell, under s 8, at the time that *property is to pass* to H (as in the SGA, s 12(1)) but s 15(4) of the 1973 Act also preserves the common law rule that O must have a right to sell at the time of the *delivery* of the goods to H (see *Mercantile Union Guarantee Corpn Ltd v Wheatley* [1938] 1 KB 490, where Goddard J explained that, in *Karflex*, he had meant to emphasise that the material time was delivery and not the time of the entry into the hire-purchase contract; *Warman v Southern Counties Car Finance Corpn Ltd* [1949] 2 KB 576, below). The result is that O must have a right to sell at *both* times, unless the common law rule is effectively excluded.

8 See the startling decision in *Warman v Southern Counties Car Finance Corpn Ltd* [1949] 2 KB 576 (the hirer (H) had a Hillman car on hire-purchase terms from the defendants and, before payments were completed by H, he received notice of the real owner's (O) claim to the car. H continued payments and exercised the option to buy under the HP agreement on the exact day that O served a writ on him. H then returned the car to O and sued the defendants for damages, claiming all sums paid under the HP contract and the costs of insurance, repairs and legal expenses. H had used the car for eight months. Held that there was an express condition that the defendants were owners of the car and the condition had to be satisfied on *delivery*; it followed that any knowledge gained by H after delivery of the car was immaterial. Finnemore J held that 'if at any stage the option to purchase goes, the whole value of the agreement to the hirer has gone with it' (p 582). In fact, the defendants did not carry the loss in *Warman* as the dealer who had sold the car to them lacked title and was also liable). These hire-purchase decisions have *not* been extended to defects other than title and, once a valid option to purchase has been conferred, there is no total failure of consideration if, for example, a car proves unroadworthy after several months' use: see *Yeoman Credit Ltd v Apps* [1962] 2 QB 508 (no return of instalments paid after six months' use of a seriously defective car).

9 [1996] 1 WLR 641.

10 In *Barber*, S conceded that there was an *express* term of the agreement that he should have property in the Honda at the date of the conditional sale *agreement* and retain it until B paid in full. The effect of the Hire Purchase Act 1964, Part III, was thus not investigated fully but the court concluded that (i) B would have acquired a good title under Part III when he paid S the balance under the agreement, but (ii) s 27(6) of the 1964 Act preserved the trade or finance purchaser's (the defendant, S) civil and criminal liability and so S could still be liable for breach of the express condition regarding title.

Atiyah[11] has suggested that consequences even more calamitous than those above might ensue from the *Rowland* principle: if B buys consumable goods from S and, after consuming them, discovers that S had no title to the goods but had bought them, *bona fide*, from a thief, B may be able to recover the price from S for breach of s 12(1). S might then be sued by the real owner resulting in his having to pay the value of the goods to the owner but B would, consequentially, have received free goods. It seems unlikely, however, that this would occur because B would be unable to satisfy the condition that he should restore the goods to S and this would be due to his *voluntary* act of consumption, whereas the crux of the *Rowland* reasoning was that, although B could not return the car to S, S could not complain as this was the direct result of his own absence of title and breach of condition. Atiyah suggests further that it may be unfair *not* to allow B's right of recovery against S as the real owner may elect to sue B in conversion and then B will, in effect, have paid twice for the goods. The answer to the conundrum may be relatively simple: S is also a tortfeasor and liable in conversion and so B can recover contribution from him under the Civil Liability (Contribution) Act 1978 and this might consist of a total indemnity. This results in a fair risk-allocation as B will have paid the owner for the goods whilst S loses the price of the goods he paid under a *bona fide*, yet hazardous contract, with a thief.

Chain transactions

It is apparent from the cases considered so far that goods may be sold in a chain of transactions before the owner (O) traces the whereabouts of his goods. For example, O's goods may be stolen by a thief who sells them to B and they are then sold to B2, B3 and B4. Each party in the chain is liable in conversion to O, even though innocent, but O will often seek re-possession of the goods or their value from the party in possession, here B4. Each buyer will then join his immediate seller as a party to the action so that, ideally, the loss is borne by the thief. However, the reality of the situation in this example is that the loss will be borne by B because the thief will normally be untraceable and/or insolvent. Another possibility is that the loss might be carried by one party in the middle of the chain if his seller is insolvent, eg B2 is insolvent so the loss is borne by B3. In this example, B3 cannot leap-frog B2 and proceed against B as there is no privity of contract between B and B3.[12]

In such chain contracts it may often happen that one buyer will improve the goods (eg, in *Rowland* the car was repainted) and an exception to the *Rowland* rule, that no allowance is made in S's favour when B recovers the price, is made by the Torts (Interference with Goods) Act 1977, s 6. The overall effect of the section is that, in proceedings by B to recover the price from S for total failure of consideration, then, if S acted in good faith, an allowance shall, where appropriate, be made for improvements to the goods effected by S or by any person from whom S derived his supposed title (whether immediately or not). S must have made the improvements in the mistaken but honest belief that he had good title to the goods. Thus if a thief steals O's car and sells it to S who repaints

---

11   *The Sale of Goods* (10th edn, 2001), p 107.
12   The problem could be overcome by providing that each sale is to operate as an assignment of all S's rights under the sale to B but this possibility was rejected by the Law Reform Committee as the assessment of damages would be difficult (see Twelfth Report *(Transfer of Title to Chattels)*, 1966, Cmnd 2958, para 37).

it in the honest belief that he is the owner and S then sells the car to B, in any action by B to recover the price from S, the amount recoverable may be reduced having regard to the increased value of the improved car. It will be noticed that a party who is sued can claim the allowance despite the fact that the improvements were not carried-out by him personally and thus if the chain is comprised of S–B–B2 and it is B2 who recovers the price from B, B can claim the allowance even though S was the improver' of the car. The reason for this provision is that, where O recovers damages for wrongful interference from any buyer who has made improvements, O's damages will be reduced to the extent of the value of the improvements[13] and thus the allowance is claimable by all the buyers in the chain until it rests with the actual improver.

Finally, the Torts (Interference with Goods) Act 1977, s 5, provides that, where damages are assessed on the basis of compensating O for his entire interest in the goods, payment of all heads of damage will extinguish O's title. The section states this negative effect only but it seems likely that O's title would vest in B. Thus if O obtains damages in conversion from B who bought the goods from S who had no title, B acquires title to the goods which he keeps. If B's title is fed in this way *before* he repudiates the contract with S, it is suggested that his claim to repudiate the contract and recover the purchase price from S should fail (see *Butterworth*, above). However, if B is thus prevented from repudiating, he should nevertheless be able to recover in damages from S the amount he had to pay to O plus the costs of defending the action brought by O.

Suggestions for reform

Rowland has been evaluated by the law reform agencies over a period of twenty years. In 1966, the Law Reform Committee[14] recommended that the buyer in the *Rowland* situation should be allowed to recover from S only his actual loss and that an allowance should be made for any use or benefit he might have obtained from the goods while they were in his possession.

In 1969, the Law Commissions[15] agreed with this in principle but pointed out several obstacles in the path of reform. It was thus questioned (i) whether a dishonest seller who knew that he lacked title should be treated on the same footing as one who is *bona fide*; (ii) whether a *bona fide* seller should be given an opportunity to perfect his defective title (eg by paying-off the real owner) before B could be allowed to repudiate the contract; (iii) how the financial value of the benefit obtained by B from the use of the goods could be valued and whether appreciation and depreciation of the goods should be taken into account; and (iv) how the benefit could be apportioned when the goods had passed through several hands. In view of these difficulties, no reform of the law was recommended.

The matter was considered in 1975[16] and again in 1983 in a working paper,[17] when several possibilities were canvassed. The overall scheme of the 1983 paper

---

13　It is unclear whether B has such a claim for improvements where O simply seizes the goods from B: see *Thomas v Robinson* [1977] 1 NZLR 385; Matthews, 'Freedom, Unrequested Improvements, and Lord Denning' [1981] 40 CLJ 340.
14　Twelfth Report *(Transfer of Title to Chattels)*, 1966, Cmnd 2958, paras 36-38.
15　*Exemption Clauses in Contracts, First Report: Amendments to the Sale of Goods Act 1893* (Law Com No 24; Scot Law Com No 12), 1969, paras 11-19.
16　*Pecuniary Restitution on Breach of Contract* (Law Com WP No 65, 1975), paras 57-78.
17　*Sale and Supply of Goods* (Law Com WP No 85; Scot Law Com CM No 58), 1983, paras 6.1-6.21 and pp 128-129.

was the familiar one that B should not be entitled to the return of the whole price paid under the contract and that the court should be able to consider B's substantial use of the goods but this was balanced by the recommendation that B should be able to terminate the contract in all cases without giving S the opportunity to cure the breach by perfecting his title.[18] It was thought that, unless B was dispossessed by O, a condition of termination should be B's ability to return the goods to S but that the statutory rules on acceptance of the goods should not apply to breaches of s 12. A remedy in damages was thought applicable should B be unable to return the goods. However, the stumbling-block to reform was, again, the difficulty in calculating the monetary entitlement of S on B's termination, not least where no claim had been made by O against S or B at the date of termination.[19] Monetary evaluation proved to be an insuperable obstacle to the Law Commissions in 1987[20] but, this time, an important shift of theoretical emphasis was also evident, arguably bringing the wheel full circle to the reasoning in *Rowland v Divall*: it was stressed that, by definition, a breach of the implied term as to title meant that the goods were not the seller's to sell and it was thus difficult to see why B should have to pay S for his (B's) use of O's goods.[1] Accordingly, no changes are currently recommended to the *Rowland* rule.

It seems indisputable that many of the difficulties of s 12(1) stem from the fact that the 1893 Act made the right to sell a *condition* of the contract: this was not so at common law before 1893 and thus *Rowland* epitomises the inflexibility entailed in classifying the right to sell as a condition.[2] However, it bears repetition that where B has been dispossessed by O or paid damages to him, it is perfectly reasonable that B should be able to recover the price he paid to S. It was also suggested earlier that this outcome was reasonable in *Rowland*. There are, in fact, few situations in the cases where B's recovery of the price has been unreasonable and it is submitted that it is easy to over-accentuate the supposed injustice in this context by focusing upon the handful of buyers who have been sufficiently astute and fleet-of-foot in repudiating their contracts to gain several months' free motoring thereby.

The warranty of freedom from encumbrances: s 12(2)(a)

It is not entirely clear what role the implied warranty of freedom from encumbrances is supposed to perform. The words 'charge or encumbrance' in

---

18 The tenor of the decisions regarding title make it most unlikely that, if B repudiates and S is in time to make a second tender of goods, he would be allowed to cure the defect in title; cf Goode, *Commercial Law* (2nd edn, 1995), p 299. See Ch 23, regarding B's rejection and S's right to cure.

19 See Treitel, *The Law of Contract* (10th edn, 1999), p 983.

20 *Sale and Supply of Goods* (Law Com No 160; Scot Law Com No 104; (1987), Cm 137), paras 6.1-6.5.

1 *Sale and Supply of Goods*, para 6.4; this was the view adopted in *Warman v Southern Counties Finance Corpn Ltd* [1949] 2 KB 576. See also Birks, *An Introduction to the Law of Restitution* (1985), pp 248 and 424; Goff and Jones, *The Law of Restitution* (5th edn, 1998), pp 527-530; Burrows, *The Law of Restitution* (1993), p 264.

2 'Then came the Sale of Goods Act, which re-enacted that rule, but did so with this alteration: it re-enacted it as a condition, not as a warranty ... It being now a condition, wherever that condition is broken the contract can be rescinded, and ... the buyer can demand a return of the purchase money': *Rowland v Divall* [1923] 2 KB 500, 505 per Scrutton LJ. This inflexibility is also apparent in decisions concerning the SGA implied conditions relating to description, quality and fitness for purpose: see Chs 20 and 21.

s 12(2)(a) patently refer to a proprietary right which affects the goods, either legal or equitable, or a possessory right such as a lien.

First, it is clear that a breach of the warranty of freedom from encumbrances will be a rare occurrence as charges or encumbrances over goods are normally enforceable only if the person claiming the right in question has possession of the goods and, if he is not in possession, his right will exist in equity only and will thus be overridden on a sale to a *bona fide* purchaser.

Second, s 12(2)(a) is broader in scope than the original warranty in the SGA 1893, s 12(3). The warranty in the 1893 Act was that the goods 'shall be free' from any charge or encumbrance and this corresponded with the wording in both the previous and the current s 12(1), that S must have a right to sell at the time of the passing of property to B. The current phrasing of s 12(2)(a) is that the goods '*are* free, and will remain free until the time when the property is to pass' and so, in an agreement to sell the goods, there must be no charge or encumbrance on the goods at the date of the agreement[3] and, also, none at the time of the passing of property to B.

Third, it is tolerably clear that there will be a breach of s 12(2)(a) where a charge or encumbrance exists and it is unnecessary for there to be an *assertion* of the encumbrance in the form of a claim made by a third party. It is unclear how damages would be assessed in such a case, but the third party's claim might be asserted in the future and so B should be able to recover the costs attendant upon removing the encumbrance so that the title he acquires is a clean one.

Consequently, in the majority of cases, B will be prejudiced by an encumbrance only where the encumbrancer is in possession of the goods and, in this case, S will be in breach of the duty to deliver the goods. In other cases, where B's possession is disturbed, there will be a breach of the warranty of quiet possession in s 12(2)(b). However, in one decision an express warranty of freedom from encumbrances was regarded as relevant when the encumbrancer was not in possession of the goods. In *Lloyds and Scottish Finance Ltd v Modern Cars and Caravans (Kingston) Ltd*,[4] the defendant dealer (S) bought a caravan from a judgment debtor on whom the sheriff had served a warrant of execution pursuant to a writ of *fieri facias*. S knew of the position but nevertheless sold the caravan to the plaintiff finance company (B) who let it on hire-purchase to a hirer (H). The sheriff seized the caravan from H who repudiated the hire-purchase agreement. S was able to transfer a good *title* to B as the property in the caravan had not left the judgment debtor on service of the warrant, but its execution made the caravan subject to the rights of the sheriff to recover the judgment debt and this encumbrance survived the sale. Edmund Davies J held that S was in breach of the warranties of freedom from encumbrances *and* quiet possession and B could thus recover from S the price of the caravan, the hire-purchase charges which could not be recovered from H, and the costs of asserting title to the caravan. It should be stressed, however, that the warranty of quiet possession would have been sufficient to protect B on these facts and, also, there was arguably a breach of the right to sell in s 12(1).[5]

---

3 In any event, this could apply *only* to an agreement for the sale of specific goods which S owns because unascertained goods might be owned by a third party (or not be in existence) at the date of the *agreement* to sell them.

4 [1966] 1 QB 764; see also *Steinke v Edwards* (unreported, noted at (1935) 8 ALJ 368) (a Government tax levied on a vehicle with a right to distrain on the goods and chattels of the owner was a charge or encumbrance).

5 Following the principle in *Niblett's* case, these facts would appear to involve a breach of s 12(1) as the property rights which S created were subject to the sheriff's right of seizure.

The only other point to stress regarding s 12(2)(a) is that the warranty of freedom from encumbrances will not be implied in relation to any charge or encumbrance which is disclosed or known to the buyer before the contract is made. It is thus expedient for S to disclose any such encumbrances to B although there is no authority on how explicit the disclosure[6] must be if S is to be exonerated from liability. Section 12(2)(a) does not apply to any encumbrances which attach after the passing of property and thus, unlike s 12(2)(b), it is not a continuing warranty. Nothing more need be said regarding s 12(2)(a) as it has not played a leading role in the development of the law; indeed in the *Lloyds* case (above), where s 12(2)(a) could have been crucial, there was an *express* term in the contract that the goods should be free from encumbrances.

The warranty of quiet possession: s 12(2)(b)

The scope of s 12(2)(b)

The warranty in s 12(2)(b) is that B 'will enjoy quiet possession of the goods except so far as it may be disturbed by the owner or other person entitled to the benefit of any charge or encumbrance so disclosed or known'. One immediate possibility is that B might suffer *physical* interference with his possession by the real owner who lawfully repossesses the goods. It may seem an obvious proposition that O's lawful re-possession should amount to a breach of s 12(2)(b) but, in *Niblett Ltd v Confectioners' Materials Co Ltd*,[7] Atkin LJ[8] suggested that the warranty in the SGA resembled the covenant for quiet enjoyment of real property. If this analogy were followed, it would mean that s 12(2)(b) would protect B only from the acts of S and third persons claiming under the seller and would not apply to those claiming by title paramount to S, ie it would not apply where the true owner repossessed the goods. This view, which would substantially restrict s 12(2)(b), was rejected in *Mason v Burningham*.[9] There B bought a typewriter from S for £20 and spent a further £11 10s having it overhauled, but she then learnt that it had been stolen and had to return it to its true owner. In an action for damages for breach of the implied warranty of quiet possession, B recovered both the £20 paid for the typewriter and the amount spent overhauling it. Lord Greene MR[10] emphasised that the wording of the SGA made no reference to the notion of disturbance by title paramount and he was not prepared to import any such gloss. This interpretation has been adopted by the Court of Appeal[11] and is clearly correct.[12]

It is equally clear that there need not be a physical interference with B's possession for there to be a breach of s 12(2)(b). In *Niblett*, the facts of which were considered earlier, Atkin LJ[13] considered that the implied warranty in s 12(2)(b) had also been broken: B could scarcely be said to enjoy quiet possession when he had to remove the labels from the tins before he could gain possession

---

6   The original SGA, s 12(3), had used the word 'declared'.
7   [1921] 3 KB 387.
8   [1921] 3 KB 387 at 403.
9   [1949] 2 KB 545.
10   [1949] 2 KB 545 at 563.
11   *Microbeads AG v Vinhurst Road Markings Ltd* [1975] 1 WLR 218.
12   NB the word 'owner' in s 12(2)(b) refers to the owner of 'any charge or encumbrance so disclosed or known' (ie under s 12(2)(a)) and not to the true owner of the goods.
13   [1921] 3 KB 387, 403.

of them. There was similarly no physical disturbance of B's possession in *Microbeads AG v Vinhurst Road Markings Ltd*,[14] where the issue centred upon the duration of the warranty in s 12(2)(b). There S sold to B some road marking machines which proved to be unsatisfactory and B did not pay the balance of the price. S therefore brought an action against B and B alleged that the goods were unfit for their purpose. Some time later, the patentee of an apparatus for applying road markings commenced an action against B for using the machines in breach of his patent and thus B amended his defence in S's action and set up the patent infringement as a defence and counterclaim. There had not been a publication of the complete specification of the patent at the date of the sale between S and B, the patentee thus being in no position to institute proceedings for infringement at that time and, in fact, neither S nor B had any knowledge of the patent at the time of the sale. S thus argued that there was no breach of s 12(2)(b) as the disturbance in B's possession did not arise from a defect in title which existed at the time of sale (this argument having been accepted at first instance). The Court of Appeal held that there was no breach of s 12(1) as B had obtained a good *title* at the *time of sale* but that B could rely on a breach of s 12(2)(b) as that subsection implied a warranty that B would enjoy quiet possession in the *future* and not merely at the time of sale.

There are two important and inter-connected features of the *Microbeads* decision. First, it is clear that S's liability under s 12(2)(b) is strict and *Microbeads* rejects the possibility that S's liability should be limited to the situation where he either knew, or ought to have known, of the patent. It is unclear, however, how far such strict liability might extend. Although the patentee in *Microbeads* had no *right* to institute proceedings at the date of the sale between S and B, the *risk* of his future interference was present at that time. It remains to be seen if this principle might be extended and whether S might be liable for a disturbance in B's possession when even the possibility of such interference had not arisen at the date of the sale, eg toxic animal feed is withdrawn under legislation but the poisonous constituent was regarded as harmless at the date of sale.

Second, while it is plain that the warranty in s 12(2)(b) is a continuing one, the duration of the obligation is unclear. This issue was broached in *The Playa Larga*,[15] where S contended that liability under s 12(2)(b) should be limited to the 'time of performance' and thus, to render S liable, there should be an actual or potential impediment to quiet enjoyment existing at the time of delivery. This approach would place a time-limit on the section's operation, but Ackner LJ[16] considered S's argument untenable in the light of the *Microbeads* decision. Apart from the situation where the goods have ceased to exist, it is difficult to see how there can be any time-limit on the operation of the quiet possession warranty beyond that imposed by the Limitation Act 1980 under which time will not begin to run against B until the disturbance of possession actually takes place.

The decisions considered thus far establish that B is protected under s 12(2)(b) from disturbance of his possession by the lawful act of O and the lawful acts of third parties (apart from those entitled to a charge or encumbrance disclosed to B before the contract was made). B is also protected against disturbance of his possession by a breach of contract or a tortious act of S, eg S claims to exercise

---

14 [1975] 1 WLR 218.
15 *Empresa Exportadora de Azucar v Industria Azucarera Nacional SA, The Playa Larga* [1983] 2 Lloyd's Rep 171.
16 [1983] 2 Lloyd's Rep 171 at 178-180.

a lien over the goods which is unjustified.[17] However, S cannot be a *guarantor* against every possible disturbance that B might suffer and thus B is not protected from interference caused by the *wrongful* acts of third parties for, otherwise, S's liability would be limitless (eg T's theft of the goods from B's premises; B2's seizure of the goods from B alleging that B sold the goods to him). On the other hand, if S colludes in the wrongful acts of such third parties, he will be liable under s 12(2)(b). In *The Playa Larga*,[18] S was party to discussions with the Cuban Government which led to a decision by the Government to withdraw a vessel from the port of discharge which was loaded with goods already paid for by B. It was held that S was liable for a breach of s 12(2)(b).

Remedies of B for breach of s 12(2)(b)

As the implied term in s 12(2)(b) is a warranty, B is not entitled to treat the contract as repudiated but, instead, he can claim damages, the measure of damages being assessed according to the SGA, ss 53 and 54. Where B is dispossessed of the goods, the normal measure of damages is the value of the goods at the time that he is thus divested of possession.[19] If B has improved the goods or repaired them, as in *Mason v Burningham*,[20] considered earlier, the damages recoverable from S can include the amount so spent. In *Mason*, the court considered that such loss arose 'directly and naturally ... in the ordinary course of events, from the breach of warranty' (s 53 (2)), even though S had no prior knowledge that this damage was likely to result. Where B is not dispossessed of the goods, the measure of damages is the difference between the value of the goods at the time of their delivery to B and the value they would have had but for the adverse claim made upon them. Moreover, B can recover from S any expenses incurred in discharging the adverse claim, legal costs incurred in resisting it and any damages he may have to pay to the claimant. It should be remembered that B must take reasonable steps to mitigate his loss and this could entail discharging the third party's claim on the goods if this course of action involves less expenditure than the value of the goods.

Inter-relationship of s 12(1) and (2)

It is self-evident that, in many disputes, S will be liable for breach of condition under s 12(1) and breach of one or both of the warranties in s 12(2). In *Mason v Burningham*,[1] for example, the implied condition in s 12(1) was not relied upon but S would doubtless have been in breach of that condition as well as being liable for breach of the warranty of quiet possession. However, it will be equally obvious that s 12(1) applies only to breaches at the time of sale whereas the warranty of quiet possession is a continuing warranty protecting B from subsequent disturbance, this point being vividly illustrated in the *Microbeads* decision, considered above.

---

17 See *Gatoil International Inc v Tradax Petroleum Ltd, The Rio Sun* [1985] 1 Lloyd's Rep 350, 360-361 per Bingham J; *Healing (Sales) Pty Ltd v Inglis Electrix Pty Ltd* (1968) 121 CLR 584.

18 *Empresa Exportadora de Azucar v Industria Azucarera Nacional SA, The Playa Larga* [1983] 2 Lloyd's Rep 171.

19 Cf *Lloyds and Scottish Finance Ltd v Modern Cars and Caravans (Kingston) Ltd* [1966] 1 QB 764 (considered earlier) where B recovered the price paid to S.

20 [1949] 2 KB 545.

1 [1949] 2 KB 545.

Sale of a limited title under s 12(3) and exclusion of liability

Section 6(1)(a) of the Unfair Contract Terms Act 1977 provides that 'liability for breach of the obligations arising from section 12 of the Sale of Goods Act 1979 ... cannot be excluded or restricted by reference to any contract term'. This is therefore a *prohibition* on such an exclusion or restriction in domestic sales,[2] applicable to both business and consumer sales.

At the same time, s 12(3) expressly allows that S may transfer a limited title to B where 'there appears from the contract or is to be inferred from its circumstances an intention that the seller should transfer only such title as he or a third person may have'. In either an *express* term of the contract or where the requisite intent can be 'inferred' from the 'circumstances' of the contract, S may thus transfer a limited title only and, in such a case, the implied condition that S has a right to sell the goods does not apply and the implied warranties relating to freedom from encumbrances and quiet possession are modified by s 12(4) and (5) respectively (set out at the start of this chapter). There should be few difficulties where, in an express term, there is clear intent to transfer a limited title, but it is less obvious when S's intention to transfer such a title is to be inferred from the circumstances of the contract. Prior to the SGA 1893, there were a number of decisions in which it was held that no warranty of title was implied, viz where goods where sold by a sheriff,[3] auctioneer[4] or where an unredeemed pledge was sold by a pawnbroker[5] but, although these decisions are a guide regarding the situations contemplated by s 12(3), they can be no more than that. Moreover, in the SGA 1893, the implied terms as to title could be varied, the original s 12(1) commencing with the words 'unless the circumstances of the contract are such as to show a different intention'.[6] In *Payne v Elsden*,[7] for example, the circumstances of an auctioneer's sale of a piano which had been distrained by a bailiff were such that no condition as to title could be implied. Again, it is reasonable to assume that this situation would fall within s 12(3) today.

The striking feature of s 12 is that, at one extreme, the exclusion or restriction of the implied terms contained therein is subject to a universal prohibition (by s 6(1)(a) of the Unfair Contract Terms Act 1977) while, at the other, s 12(3) permits the transfer of a limited title. The juxtaposition of these diametrically opposed notions is, at best, extremely awkward and raises the obvious difficulty of deciding when a clause is to be either banned or approved. Goode[8] asks whether S might attempt to exclude s 12 but then seek to rely on s 12(3) and argue that his real intent was to transfer a limited title. He suggests that this ploy would fail as the core of the contract will be taken to be that which B is

---

2 The prohibition does not apply to international supply contracts: see the Unfair Contract Terms Act 1977, s 26.
3 *Peto v Blades* (1814) 5 Taunt 657.
4 *Bagueley v Hawley* (1867) LR 2 CP 625.
5 *Morley v Attenborough* (1849) 3 Exch 500.
6 See Hudson, 'The Condition as to Title in Sale of Goods' (1957) 20 MLR 236 and 'The Exclusion of Section 12(1) of the Sale of Goods Act' (1961) 24 MLR 690.
7 (1900) 17 TLR 161; see also *Warmings Used Cars v Tucker* [1956] SASR 249; *Niblett Ltd v Confectioners' Materials Co Ltd* [1921] 3 KB 387, 401 per Atkin LJ and 395 per Bankes LJ.
8 *Commercial Law* (2nd edn, 1995), p 302.

'reasonably entitled to assume from the manner in which the contract terms are presented to him' by S. Thus if S 'presents the transaction as one in which he is selling as owner' he will be held to the apparent terms that he is offering and 'the court will not construe the exemption clause as converting a purported transfer of an indefeasible title into a transfer of such title as the seller may possess'. The thrust of this supposition is clear enough but, in assuming that it will not be difficult to draw a clear-cut line between an impermissible exclusion clause and a legitimate clause transferring a restricted title, it does appear, with respect, to state the problem rather than answer it. Goode's example would clearly not be one where it could be inferred from the circumstances that a limited title is on offer under s 12(3) but, in many situations, the boundaries separating a prohibited clause from one that is lawful and permissible will be virtually impossible to map with any degree of precision.

CHAPTER 20

The duties of the seller relating to the description and quality of the goods

Introduction

The common law's strict adherence to the principle of *caveat emptor*[1] (let the buyer take care[2]) in the sale of goods had been on the wane during the 19th century but the Sale of Goods Act 1893 marked the start of that notion's more rapid eclipse by the introduction of statutory implied terms relating to the description, merchantable quality and fitness for purpose of the goods sold. As will be seeen later, a combination of accident and design led to these implied terms being generously interpreted in favour of the buyer.

A significant feature of the 1893 Act was that s 55 permitted the unfettered exclusion or variation of the implied terms. At the end of the 19th century this was an unremarkable illustration of freedom of contract and, indeed, s 55 enabled risks to be allocated and apportioned in contracts between commercial buyers and sellers. However, the 20th century witnessed a growth in inequality of bargaining power which rendered it necessary to protect the weaker party from abuse which was often perpetuated under the guise of a freely bargained-for exclusion clause. There were no statutory controls on exclusion clauses in the sale of goods until the Supply of Goods (Implied Terms) Act 1973 reformed the law significantly. Quite dramatically, the exclusion of the SGA implied terms in 'consumer sales' was prohibited by the 1973 Act and the constraint of a reasonableness test was introduced to gauge the fairness of such an exclusion in sales of goods between commercial buyers and sellers. The consumer buyer had thus truly come of age[3] and the reasonableness test demanded that the substantive issue of fairness be weighed in the balance. This process of interventionism was furthered by the Unfair Contract Terms Act 1977 and, more recently, the Unfair Terms in Consumer Contracts Regulations 1999[4] have enhanced further the buyer's protection.

---

1 See Hamilton, 'The Ancient Maxim Caveat Emptor' (1931) 50 Yale LJ 1133; Atiyah, *The Rise and Fall of Freedom of Contract* (1979), pp 464-479.
2 See *Wallis v Russell* [1902] 2 IR 585, 615 per FitzGibbon LJ: ' "*Caveat Emptor*" does not mean – in law or Latin – that the buyer must "take *chance*"; it means that he must "take *care*"'.
3 Interesting discussions can be found in Borrie, *The Development of Consumer Law and Policy – Bold Spirits and Timorous Souls* (1984); Cranston, *Consumers and the Law* (3rd edn, 2000) Ch 1; Jolowicz, 'The Protection of the Consumer and Purchaser of Goods under English Law' (1969) 32 MLR 1; Atiyah, 'Consumer Protection – Time to Take Stock' (1979) 1 Liverpool LR 20.
4 SI 1999/2083.

The *content* of the implied terms had also been broadened by the 1973 Act and the Sale and Supply of Goods Act 1994[5] further augmented the range of the statutory, implied obligations. The outcome of these developments at the start of the 21st century is that *caveat emptor* has largely transmuted into *caveat venditor*. As early as 1936, Lord Wright[6] considered that the implied conditions of merchantability and fitness for purpose changed the 'old rule' to the rule of *caveat venditor*, such change being 'rendered necessary by the conditions of modern commerce and trade'. Today, the SGA implied terms relating to the description, quality and fitness of the goods provide both consumer and business buyers with a sophisticated level of protection.

The implied terms which relate to the description and quality of the goods may be likened to a pyramidical structure with, at the base, the implied condition that the goods must correspond with their description (s 13), progressing to the obligation that goods must be of satisfactory quality (s 14(2)) and, at the pinnacle, the implied condition that the goods must be fit for the purpose for which they were sold (s 14(3)). A contract for the sale of goods may, of course, contain express terms relating to the quality and fitness of the goods sold, such terms today being frequently construed as innominate in nature, meaning that a buyer may not necessarily reject the goods and repudiate the contract for the breach of such a term but, instead, may only be awarded damages. On the other hand, the SGA implied terms concerning the description, quality and fitness of the goods, are all conditions[7] which, until the SGA, s 15A[8] restricted the non-consumer buyer's right of rejection, meant that the goods could be rejected for even a trivial breach of the statutory conditions. As will be seen later in this chapter, the right of rejection for breach of condition has been somewhat curtailed by s 15A in the case of business buyers, but that right has been re-modelled in favour of consumer buyers. Overall, the SGA implied conditions of quality and fitness remain central to the buyer's protection precisely because they are implied as *conditions* of the contract and their attempted exclusion is subject to stringent statutory control.

Goods may have become infinitely more sophisticated and intricate since 1893 but the problems of determining the rudimentary levels of quality and fitness which must be reached under the implied terms remain both constant and obdurate. On occasion, some decisions have erred in fixing this level but, overall, justice has been done to the majority of buyers and sellers and this stands as testimony to the pragmatic plasticity of the English common law which, all too often, is rebuked unjustifiably for its 'tendency to rely on empirical *ad hoc* rules'.[9]

Section 13: goods must correspond with their description

The SGA 1979, s 13(1), (1A), (2) and (3) provide:

---

5   The Act implemented most of the Law Commissions' recommendations: see *Sale and Supply of Goods*, (Law Com No 160, Scot Law Com No 104, Cm 137, 1987); see also *Sale and Supply of Goods*, Working Paper No 85 (1983).
6   *Grant v Australian Knitting Mills Ltd* [1936] AC 85, 98.
7   See the SGA 1979, ss 13(1A) and 14(6), inserted and substituted respectively by the Sale and Supply of Goods Act 1994, s 7, Sch 2, paras 5(4)(b), 5(5)(b).
8   Inserted by the Sale and Supply of Goods Act 1994, s 4(1).
9   Gow, *The Mercantile and Industrial Law of Scotland* (1964), p 162.

'(1) Where there is a contract for the sale of goods by description, there is an implied term that the goods will correspond with the description.

(1A) As regards England and Wales and Northern Ireland, the term implied by subsection (1) above is a condition.

(2) If the sale is by sample as well as by description it is not sufficient that the bulk of the goods corresponds with the sample if the goods do not also correspond with the description.[10]

(3) A sale of goods is not prevented from being a sale by description by reason only that, being exposed for sale or hire, they are selected by the buyer.'

HISTORICAL BACKGROUND AND DEVELOPMENT OF SECTION 13

Although s 13 now applies to a wide range of sales, this was not the original intention of the SGA 1893 which, based upon the 19th century decisions, sought to draw a distinction between sales of specific goods and goods sold by description.[11] As regards specific goods which were identified and which B might examine, *caveat emptor* was applied strictly, there being no implied term as to quality and, when property passed to B, he would in general lose his right of rejection and be limited to a claim in damages. Conversely, where the sale was by description and B had not seen the goods, they had to correspond with the description given to them and be merchantable[12] and B did not necessarily lose his right to reject the goods when the property in them passed to him.

As the 1893 Act was designed to apply to commercial sales of goods, the definition and rationale of these two divergent types of sale was clear enough, but the dual classification failed to acknowledge those situations where goods were specific but B nevertheless relied upon some description applied to them. In 1900, the decision in *Varley v Whipp*[13] marked a change of approach. There B agreed to buy a second-hand reaping machine which he had never seen, but which was described as 'new the previous year' and as having cut 'only fifty or sixty acres'. In fact, it turned out to be a very old machine which had been mended. These facts were a paradigm for the application of *caveat emptor* but, undaunted, the court held that this was a sale by description such a sale occurring in 'all cases where the purchaser has not seen the goods, but is relying on the description alone'.[14] S thus failed to recover the price.

Some three years later, a significant advance was made in *Wren v Holt*.[15] There a sale of 'Holden's beer' in a tied public house was held to be a sale by description even though B did not ask for the beer by name and, in any event, could be supplied only with Holden's beer. Vaughan Williams LJ expressly denied that such a sale 'over a counter' could be a sale by description[16] but he acceded to the findings of the jury that B went to the beerhouse where Holden's beer was sold and asked to be supplied with beer of that description. The description was thus inferred from the circumstances and it was quite plain that *caveat emptor* did not sit well with these facts where B had no practical

---

10 Section 13(2) is considered in Ch 21, under sales by sample.
11 See Stoljar, 'Conditions, Warranties and Descriptions of Quality in Sale of Goods' (1952) 15 MLR 425 and (1953) 16 MLR 174.
12 See *Jones v Just* (1868) LR 3 QB 197.
13 [1900] 1 QB 513.
14 [1900] 1 QB 513 at 516, per Channell J.
15 [1903] 1 KB 610.
16 [1903] 1 KB 610 at 615.

opportunity to discover the defects in the beer (which contained arsenic) before purchase. B's complaint here was principally that the beer did not meet the required standard of *quality* for consumption and it is important to stress that his claim succeeded under the SGA 1893, s 14(2), which related to merchantable quality. That section applied only where the sale was 'by description' and the need to establish this fact as a preliminary to liability under s 14(2) undoubtedly led to a broadening of the notion of sales by description.[17]

The misgivings expressed in *Wren's* case regarding retail sales of branded goods[18] were bound to come to a head later in the 20th century when mass-produced, brand-name goods with elaborate packaging and labelling became commonplace. It was later established that retail sales of specific goods over a shop's counter were sales by description provided that the goods were sold as corresponding to a description. In *Grant v Australian Knitting Mills Ltd*,[19] B, a doctor, bought a pair of 'Golden Fleece' ankle-length, woollen underpants, from a retail shop. The underpants contained an irritant in the form of excess sulphites and, as a consequence, B developed acute and life-threatening dermatitis which, in an era before anti-biotic drugs, persisted for one year. The sale of the underpants was held to be one 'by description' within the SGA 1893 s 14(2) (merchantable quality) and it was held that the goods did not meet the required standard of merchantability within that section. Lord Wright stressed that a retail sale of a specific thing could be by description 'so long as it is sold not merely as the specific thing but as a thing corresponding to a description, eg, woollen under-garments, a hot-water bottle, a second-hand reaping machine, to select a few obvious illustrations'.[20]

The last stage in the progressive widening of s 13 came when the Supply of Goods (Implied Terms) Act 1973 amended s 13 so that there could be a sale by description even where specific goods on display (eg in a supermarket) were selected by B (now s 13(3)).

The scope of s 13

It is clear from the development of s 13, outlined above, that both sales of unascertained goods, where B relies solely on description, and sales of specific goods in a supermarket, where the only description may be a label, are within the definition of sales by description. This breadth of operation, coupled with the additional facts that the implied term in s 13 applies to private sellers and is classified as a condition, makes it tempting to conclude that virtually every sale must be 'by description' within s 13 thereby providing with B with a potent and almost all-embracing remedy. There is one decision, considered below, which

---

17 See also *Morelli v Fitch and Gibbons* [1928] 2 KB 636.

18 See also *Wallis v Russell* [1902] 2 IR 585, 631, where Holmes LJ rejected the notion that retail sales over the counter could be sales by description because then 'no sale otherwise than by description would be possible'.

19 [1936] AC 85.

20 [1936] AC 85 at 100; see also *Morelli v Fitch and Gibbons* [1928] 2 KB 636 (a sale at an off-licence of a bottle of Stone's ginger wine with a defective neck which cut B when he attempted to draw the cork, was held to be a sale by description); *David Jones Ltd v Willis* (1934) 52 CLR 110 (a pair of 'walking shoes' was sold by description even though B had tried them on).

seems to attribute such a width of operation to s 13 but, unfortunately, the position cannot be encapsulated so effortlessly. In fact, there are two (often inseparable) issues, which make it very difficult to ascertain the scope of s 13. First, it is necessary to ascertain the relationship between s 13 and the orthodox classification of contract terms: where there is a description of the goods, are all such sales 'by description' within s 13? Second, if the sale is one 'by description', it is crucial to ascertain the extent of S's liability under s 13: must S comply with every aspect of the description, no matter how inconsequential?

THE RELATIONSHIP BETWEEN SECTION 13, MERE REPRESENTATIONS AND CONTRACT TERMS

First, it must be asked how s 13 harmonises with the traditional classifications of mere representations and express terms of the contract. It will be apparent that s 13 has the potential to elevate *all* descriptive statements to the status of conditions and, although this would be a startling inference to draw, one prominent case considered below, *Beale v Taylor*, arguably reaches this conclusion and accepts it as being a natural corollary of s 13.

Overall, however, the possibility that the most inconsequential statements are converted into conditions is a remote one and there are, obviously, decisions where such statements have been held to be mere representations. In *Harrison v Knowles & Foster*,[1] S sold two ships to B which, in the particulars of sale, were said to have a deadweight capacity of 460 tons but no mention was made of this in the memorandum of sale. Each ship's capacity was in fact 360 tons but the statements were held to be mere representations and thus not part of the contract at all. The same conclusion was reached in *Oscar Chess Ltd v Williams*,[2] where S described a car as a '1948 Morris 10 saloon' whereas in fact it was a 1939 model. It was held that the statements made gave rise to no contractual liability whatever. It is important to stress, however, that s 13 was not pleaded in either *Harrison* or *Oscar Chess*.

However, assuming that the descriptive statement is a *term* of the contract, there is slightly more credence in the argument that s 13 automatically transforms the statement into a condition, this arguably being the view[3] adopted in *Beale v Taylor*.[4] There B saw an advertisement in *Exchange and Mart* for the sale of a 'Herald convertible, white, 1961, twin carbs, £190'. S was a private motorist and it was his car that was for sale. B took the car for a test drive and noticed a '1200' disc on its rear. B bought the car and subsequently found that it was comprised of two halves from separate cars welded together, the back half being as described but the front half being a much older model with a 948 cc engine. The Court of Appeal rejected the argument which had prevailed in the County Court that this was the sale of a particular car, tried and tested by B, and held

---

1 [1918] 1 KB 608.
2 [1957] 1 WLR 370. See also *Taylor v Combined Buyers Ltd* [1924] NZLR 627, 638, where Salmond J considered that 'there is no sale by description unless the descriptive statement is incorporated in the contract as a term thereof'.
3 In fact, *Beale* could be taken as authority for the proposition that *all* descriptive statements, even mere representations, become conditions within s 13, as Sellers LJ thought that S was 'making no warranties at all and making no contractual terms. But fundamentally he was selling a car of that description' (p 1197).
4 [1967] 1 WLR 1193.

it to be a sale by description within s 13. B was accordingly entitled to damages. In *Beale*, S was a private seller and, as the implied condition of merchantability has always applied only to business sellers, the case could not be argued on the basis that the goods were unmerchantable. A wide interpretation of s 13 may thus have been made in order to fit B's wholly meritorious claim within that section. But at the beginning of the 1970s, the approach taken in *Beale*, particularly when juxtaposed with s 13(3), signalled that it would be difficult to envisage a sale to which s 13 did not apply and the section was seemingly an omnipotent weapon in B's armoury.[5]

Nevertheless, there are many cases before *Beale* which consider that there is inherent validity in the distinction between conditions and warranties and that, quite obviously, there can be a warranty regarding the description of the goods. In the first instance decision in *Harrison v Knowles & Foster*,[6] Bailhache J considered that where there was a sale of a specific, existing chattel, statements as to quality would not be conditions unless the absence of the quality made the thing 'different in kind from the thing as described in the contract'.[7] On that basis, he held that a statement as to the deadweight capacity of two ships was a warranty. This analysis is based upon distinguishing statements regarding the attributes/qualities of goods from statements defining their innate identity/ substance, only the latter being classifiable as conditions. Bailhache J's approach was followed in *Taylor v Combined Buyers Ltd*[8] where, in a carefully reasoned judgment, Salmond J held that 'the sale of a specific article is a sale by description within [s 13] in so far … as the article is expressly sold as being of a certain kind, class, or species; but that statements made as to the quality or other unessential attributes of the article sold are not parts of the description'.[9] With some adjustments in terminology, this approach of limiting the ambit of s 13 to matters of identity/substance has been followed[10] and the modern cases, considered later, also adhere to it.[11]

The recent decision in *Harlingdon and Leinster Enterprises Ltd v Christopher Hull Fine Art Ltd*,[12] substantially restricts s 13 and makes a vivid contrast with *Beale v Taylor*. In *Harlingdon*, S, an art dealer, telephoned B, who was also an art dealer, saying that he had paintings by Gabriele Münter for sale. At S's gallery,

---

5 In 1969, the Law Commission considered s 13 to be 'a valuable instrument for the protection of the buyer' and 'to all intents and purposes comprehensive … this comprehensiveness of the section is further enhanced by the wide construction which the decided cases have given to the word "description"' (*Exemption Clauses in Contracts, First Report: Amendments to the Sale of Goods Act 1893*, Law Com No 24, Scot Law Com No 12 (1969), paras 22 and 25).

6 [1917] 2 KB 606.

7 [1917] 2 KB 606 at 610.

8 [1924] NZLR 627.

9 [1924] NZLR 627 at 644. Salmond J illustrated the distinction: a sale of 'a cask of port wine' could be rejected if it contained beer, as this would be a difference of substance, but a sale of 'a cask of port wine in sound condition' could not be rejected if the port was unsound, as this would be a difference in quality (p 642).

10 See *Couchman v Hill* [1947] KB 554, 559, per Scott LJ: '… every item in a description which constitutes a substantial ingredient in the "identity" of the thing sold is a condition'.

11 In *Ashington Piggeries Ltd v Christopher Hill Ltd* [1972] AC 441, 503, Lord Diplock said that not all statements form part of the description within s 13 but that some may give rise to a breach of warranty. See also *Reardon Smith Line Ltd v Yngvar Hansen-Tangen* [1976] 1 WLR 989, 998, where Lord Wilberforce said that he preferred the innominate term analysis to 'accepting rigid categories'.

12 [1991] 1 QB 564.

B apparently examined the relevant painting in silence but S showed him an auction catalogue which described the picture as being monogrammed 'MÜ', and having the stamp of the estate of Münter. S did not repeat that the artist was Münter but, instead, said that he knew little about the paintings and nothing about the artist. B bought the painting for £6,000, S supplying an invoice which included the artist's name and lifespan. B subsequently discovered that the painting was a forgery and could be resold for only £50 to £100. The Court of Appeal held (Stuart-Smith LJ dissenting) that this was not a sale *by* description as B did not *rely* upon the description given, such reliance being necessary if it were to become a condition of the contract. The reasoning of the majority in *Harlingdon* was based upon distinguishing contract terms from mere representations on the basis of the parties' common intentions[13] and thus the court's conclusion that B relied upon his own judgement rather than that of S, was of paramount importance in the decision. In a powerful and lucid dissenting judgment, Stuart-Smith LJ held that where a statement was a *term*, proof of B's reliance upon it was unnecessary – instead he regarded reliance as a key factor only where B wished to establish a misrepresentation of fact which induced him to enter into the contract.

The *Harlingdon* approach to the question of reliance is particularly controversial. Before the decision there had been an assumption that, where S described the goods, B's reliance upon that description was a natural corollary which would be displaced only in exceptional circumstances. For example, *Benjamin*[14] considers that s 13 would be inapplicable in the rare occurrences where B buys specific goods *as such*, meaning that S makes no promises regarding the goods but, instead, B buys them as seen and exercises his own judgement as regards their condition and value. This rare situation could arise (i) where there is no description at all; (ii) where the description does not relate to the fundamental identity of the goods; or (iii) where it is not relied upon,[15] but it is arguable that *Harlingdon*'s facts could not be shoehorned into any of these categories. First, it is difficult to see how the painting could be any better or more fully described. Second, the dominant view that B did not not rely on S's description is very perplexing: although B's status as an art dealer was a material fact, it surely could not be said to *negate* his reliance upon S's fulsome description. This leaves the issue of whether the description goes to the elemental substance or identity of the goods, a question which was not directly addressed by the majority in *Harlingdon*. The distinction between substance and attributes is discussed more fully below but, while the legal position is far from clear, it is suggested that the identity of the artist must, indisputably, be the defining substance of a contract to buy an authentic painting by that artist.

---

13 See eg, *Oscar Chess Ltd v Williams* [1957] 1 WLR 370; *Dick Bentley Productions Ltd v Harold Smith (Motors) Ltd* [1965] 1 WLR 623.
14 *Benjamin's Sale of Goods* (5th edn, 1997), para 11-011.
15 See *Benjamin's Sale of Goods* (5th edn, 1997), para 11-011 (approved by Nourse LJ in *Harlingdon* (p 574)). See also *Joseph Travers and Sons Ltd v Longel Ltd* (1947) 64 TLR 150 (a sale by sample of war surplus, rubber and canvas boots, described as 'waders' by the parties for convenience. B alleged that this description meant they should be waterproof but it was held that neither party had this facet in mind and there was no sale by description. Again, Sellers J approved *Benjamin's* reasoning holding that '... the buyers bought the goods such as they were and hoped to make a profit out of them' (p 153)). In *Harlingdon*, Stuart-Smith LJ considered that *Travers* was a case where 'both parties knew that the description [was] in fact a misdescription' (p 579).

It is suggested that the best view, and one which was endemic in the law pre-*Harlingdon*, is that, where there *is* a description, B's reliance upon it should be presumed unless disproved by S.[16] However, certainly Nourse LJ's appraisal in *Harlingdon* demands B's reliance on the description as a *positive* requirement if liability is to be imposed under s 13.[17] If this were to become accepted as a pre-requisite of S's liability, s 13 would be seriously disabled in a retrogressive lurch towards the 19th century ideal of *caveat emptor*. Moreover, reliance on S's skill and judgment is the key feature of the implied condition of fitness for purpose under the SGA, s 14(3), but if this requirement of reliance is superimposed on s 13, it is difficult to see what separate role the implied condition of description is expected to play.

Conclusion

It is particularly difficult to discern any overall configuration or guiding principle in the cases considered above. It is tolerably clear that some descriptive statements may have no contractual force whatever and, equally, not all statements are exalted as conditions of the contract within s 13. The categories of mere representations, contractual warranties, conditions, and innominate terms still have validity in the sale of goods and, together with s 13, there is thus considerable room for manoeuvre in resolving any dispute centring upon description. The new s 15A, which provides that the non-consumer buyer is prevented from rejecting the goods for breach of ss 13-15 where 'the breach is so slight that it would be unreasonable to reject them' has added an extra dimension of uncertainty in relation to express terms and s 13. If there is an *express* condition which relates to the essential substance or identity of the goods and this is also classifiable as within the ambit of s 13, it is arguable that a buyer may opt to sue for a slight breach of the express condition and thus circumvent the operation of s 15A, which applies only to the implied conditions in ss 13-15.

This range of possibilities cannot be applauded for introducing coherent flexibility. The law is indeterminate and the decisions haphazard: it is, currently, truly mystifying to predict when a court might adopt either of the polar positions represented by *Beale* and *Harlingdon*.

THE EXTENT OF THE SELLER'S LIABILITY UNDER SECTION 13

Assuming the sale is one by description, the second question is whether a trivial departure from the description of the goods is actionable under s 13 or whether only matters of identity/substance are encompassed by the section. It is scarcely surprising that this issue merges with that on terms of the contract, considered above, and some of the cases make no attempt to separate the fact of a sale by description from the extent of S's liability. Many of the older decisions thus allowed that trifling discrepancies from description could amount to a breach of s 13 and little or no attention was paid to the question of whether or not the descriptive statement was a *condition* of the contract, eg *Re Moore & Co Ltd and Landauer & Co* (below). Again, these decisions came perilously close to

---

16 See Brown, 'Forgery, Fine Art and the Sale Of Goods' (1990) 106 LQR 561.
17 [1991] 1 QB 564, 574; Slade LJ was 'not sure whether that is strictly correct in principle' (p 584).

establishing that s 13 promoted all descriptive statements to the status of conditions or, at least, all terms seemed to be thus converted. On the other hand, the more recent decisions consider that only substantial deviations from description amount to a breach of s 13, this view limiting its operation to those breaches which entail a substitution of goods of a different *kind* for the goods described in the contract.

The older decisions and precise compliance with description

There a numerous decisions which stipulate that, although the goods are substantially what B agreed to buy, a minor deviation from the contract description will nevertheless be a breach of s 13. In fact, the 19th century decisions upon which s 13 was based took this view. In overseas sales, the requirement that goods should correspond with their description was particularly strict as the goods might change hands many times before they could be inspected. Stipulations as to the manner, place, time and date of the shipment have all been held to be part of the description of the goods.

In *Borrowman v Drayton*,[18] there was a contract for the sale of a 'cargo of from 2500 to 3000 barrels' of petrol shipped from New York. S put 300 additional barrels on board but was ready to deliver 3,000 to B or to deliver 2,750 barrels as the mean between 2,500 and 3,000. B refused to take any quantity. It was held that 'cargo' meant the entire load of the vessel and, as 3,300 barrels was in excess of the quantity ordered, B was not bound to accept part of the cargo. Mellish LJ[19] considered this to be 'an unhandsome proceeding on the part of [B]' whose rejection of the goods was patently motivated by a fall in the price of petrol, but that B was still entitled to say 'the thing which you offered me was not the thing I agreed to buy, and, therefore, I will not take it'.

Similarly, in *Bowes v Shand*,[20] a quantity of rice was to be shipped at Madras during the months of March and/or April but most of the rice was shipped in February. It was held that B could reject the consignment as 'rice shipped in February is not the article which has been purchased'[1] and 'if the description of the article tendered is different in any respect it is not the article bargained for and the other party is not bound to take it'.[2]

It is apparent that the decisions after 1893 which adhere to this rigorous approach are part of a continuous pattern. In *Re Moore & Co Ltd and Landauer & Co*,[3] S agreed to sell 3,000 tins of fruit to B to be packed in cases of 30 tins but, although the total quantity was correct, about half of the cases contained 24 tins. B refused to accept any of the goods. The dispute was referred to arbitration, where the umpire found that, packed as they were, there was no difference in the market value of the goods. In the Court of Appeal, S argued that the sale and payment was on the basis of multiples of one dozen tins and

---

18 (1876) 2 Ex D 15.
19 (1876) 2 Ex D 15 at 20.
20 (1877) 2 App Cas 455.
 1 (1877) 2 App Cas 455 at 475, per Lord Hatherley.
 2 (1877) 2 App Cas 455 at 480, per Lord Blackburn. *Bowes v Shand* was approved by the HL in *Bunge Corpn v Tradax Export SA* [1981] 1 WLR 711; see also *Petrotrade Inc v Stinnes Handel GmbH* [1995] 1 Lloyd's Rep 142 (following *Bowes v Shand*, Colman J held that the place of shipment was part of the description of the goods and therefore a condition of the contract).
 3 [1921] 2 KB 519.

that the packing in cases of 30 was not a matter of importance but was only a breach of warranty. It was held that B could reject the entire consignment as the requirement of 30 tins per case was 'part of the description of the goods'[4] and there was thus a breach of s 13.

This exacting approach regarding the description of the goods was adopted wholeheatedly by the House of Lords in *Arcos Ltd v E A Ronaasen & Son*.[5] There the contract was for the sale of wooden staves of ½ inch thick for making cement barrels; approximately 5% conformed with this description but the remainder were nearly all less than 9/16 inch thick. On the facts, this made no difference whatever to the manufacture of cement barrels and, again, the umpire found that the goods were commercially saleable and merchantable under the contract description. The House of Lords held that B could reject all the goods, Lord Atkin stipulating famously that 'a ton does not mean about a ton, or a yard about a yard ... still less does ½ inch mean about ½ inch. If the seller wants a margin he must and in my experience does stipulate for it'.[6] Lord Atkin stressed that deviations which fell within the rule *de minimis non curat lex* could be ignored, but it is clear that this notion excuses only microscopic departures from the contract specification.[7]

Re Moore and *Arcos* have been subjected to particular criticism in that, in both cases, the goods could be used for B's purpose and his motive for rejection was that he wished to avail himself of the falling market in the respective goods and buy more cheaply elsewhere. However, there are many other commercial decisions equally as strict as *Arcos*[8] and the exacting approach which has been adopted can be justified, at least in cases of bulk sales of commodities. First, in terms of general policy, the possibility of there being some notion of commercial equivalence or substantial performance in sales of goods should be resisted: S's obligation to sell goods which match their description is surely not sufficiently arduous to permit such broad excuses for non-compliance with description. Second, the contract is often one for unascertained, future goods where strict compliance is a necessity. Third, B may frequently have a contract to re-sell the

---

4   [1921] 2 KB 519 at 522, per Bankes LJ and p 525, per Atkin LJ. See also *Manbre Saccharine Company Ltd v Corn Products Co Ltd* [1919] 1 KB 198 (starch described as packed in '280 lb bags' but supplied in bags of 220 lb and 140 lb. McCardie J held that the words 'were an essential part of the contract requirements' (p 207).

5   [1933] AC 470.

6   [1933] AC 470 at 479.

7   Two decisions on the quantity of goods delivered (see the SGA, s 30) may be compared: *Margaronis Navigation Agency Ltd v Henry W Peabody & Co Ltd* [1965] 1 QB 300 (deficiency of .09% (12,588 tons 4 cwts instead of 12,600 tons) in a cargo of maize was not *de minimis*); *Shipton Anderson and Co v Weil Bros & Co* [1912] 1 KB 574 (excess of 55 lbs of wheat on an agreed limit of 4,950 tons was within the rule). The *de minimis* rule is considered in more detail in Ch 22.

8   See eg, *Vigers Bros v Sanderson Bros* [1901] 1 KB 608 (sale of timber laths of between 2–4½ feet in length but not more than 3% to be 2 feet long. Under one contract 33% of the laths were 5 feet long and, under the second, 60% were 2 feet long. Held that B could reject the timber, Bigham J stressing (p 610) that laths 2 feet long were 'practically worthless' and those 5 feet long were 'very difficult to sell' and required 'more labour in handling'); *Wimble, Sons & Co v Lillico & Son* (1922) 38 TLR 296 (sale of 'Chilean partly decorticated cotton cake containing approximately 40% protein and 10% oil' did not meet its description with 32.28% protein and 7.78% oil); *Rapalli v K L Take Ltd* [1958] 2 Lloyd's Rep 469 (sale of 15 tons of 'medium onions' with 6%-7% undersized. Held that the entire consignment could be rejected); *Smith Bros (Hull) Ltd v Gosta Jacobsson & Co* [1961] 2 Lloyd's Rep 522 (S's marks on timber which related to its quality were part of the description allowing B to reject the goods).

goods and correspondence with description thus becomes a question of commercial certainty. Fourth, the contract may be completed by third parties on behalf of S and B, eg bankers demanding payment of the price in return for the shipping documents, and a strict rule of compliance is called for as these third parties are in no position to decide whether minor deviations are acceptable.

It should be emphasised, however, that the SGA, s 15A[9] now imposes a restriction on rejection for breach of s 13 (and ss 14 and 15) in *non-consumer*[10] sales 'where the breach is so slight that it would be unreasonable for [B] to reject [the goods]'. In this situation, s 15A provides that the breach 'is not to be treated as a breach of condition but may be treated as a breach of warranty' but it is for S to prove that the breach is a slight one within the section (s 15A(3)). Section 15A(2) allows S and B to exclude expressly the operation of s 15A but, more significantly, s 15A(2) provides that the section's operation can be ousted by an *implied*, contrary intent. The scheme in s 15A undoubtedly introduces a measure of uncertainty to the law[11] and it remains to be seen how a 'slight' breach and the requirement of reasonableness will be interpreted, but it is evident that a prime target of the new section will be cases such as *Arcos*. That being said, the Law Commissions[12] considered that the rule in *Bowes v Shand*,[13] that the date of shipment is part of the description of the goods, would *not* be affected by the new s 15A but it is unclear from the Law Commissions' proposals why this should be so. It is probable that the *Bowes* line of cases is to be regarded as a paradigm of the implied exclusion of s 15A, under s 15A(2), on the basis of the need for certainty in commercial undertakings.[14] It goes without saying that this does not answer the riddle of when B is expected to tolerate 'slight' breaches of contract under s 15A and when, on the other hand, that section is impliedly excluded so that strict compliance with description can legitimately be demanded by the commercial buyer.

Modern decisions: s 13 encompasses only a substantial ingredient of the goods

The technical, exacting approach to description, evident in *Arcos*, has been criticised and re-appraised in recent decisions. In *Reardon Smith Line Ltd v Yngvar Hansen-Tangen*,[15] the dispute related to the charter of a tanker which was in the course of construction. The charter-party referred to the vessel as one to be built at Osaka with the hull number 354 when in fact it was built at Oshima with the number 004 but it complied in every material respect with its specifications. By the time of the vessel's delivery, the charterer sought to reject it arguing that, by analogy with contracts for the sale of goods, the tanker did

---

9 Inserted by the Sale and Supply of Goods Act 1994, s 4(2).
10 Section 15A employs the (troublesome) phrase 'the buyer does not deal as consumer'. The SGA, s 61(5A) provides that this is to be construed in accordance with Part I of the UCTA 1977 (see Ch 25).
11 This was, in fact, the view of the Law Commissions who recommended the introduction of s 15A (see *Sale and Supply of Goods* (Law Com No 160, Scot Law Com No 104, Cm 137 (1987), para 4.23).
12 *Sale and Supply of Goods* (Law Com No 160, Scot Law Com No 104, Cm 137 (1987)), para 4.24.
13 (1877) 2 App Cas 455 (considered earlier).
14 Other possibilities are that the date of delivery was not considered to be within s 13 or that it was regarded as an express condition of the contract.
15 [1976] 1 WLR 989.

not meet its description. The House of Lords held that the vessel's number had no legal significance whatever as the tanker complied in all respects with its physical description in the specifications. Lord Wilberforce criticised *Re Moore* as 'excessively technical and due for fresh examination in this House'[16] and considered that such a technical approach might have validity only in cases of unascertained future goods (eg commodities) where each detail of the description must be assumed to be vital. In other cases, he thought that only a description which constituted a substantial ingredient of the identity of the thing sold should be treated as a condition.

Ascertainment of the substance of the contract was also thought to be crucial in the significant decision in *Ashington Piggeries Ltd v Christopher Hill Ltd*[17] although, most peculiarly, *Reardon* made no mention of this earlier decision. The defendant (S) agreed to make and sell a food compound for mink, the plaintiff mink breeder (B) supplying the formula. S had regularly prepared animal foodstuffs as part of his business but he stressed that he had never before supplied food for mink. S did suggest substituting herring meal for the more expensive constituent of fish meal and, accordingly, S bought Norwegian herring meal from the third party, Norwegian seller (T), under a contract describing it as 'Norwegian herring meal fair average quality of the season'. The herring meal contained a preservative which caused a chemical reaction in the food (generating a chemical called DMNA) rendering it lethal to mink but not to other animals who were, nevertheless, affected detrimentally to a certain extent. If B were to contend that the goods did not meet their contract description, he would be confronted with the obstacle that the food had been prepared according to his own formula. Consequently, B had necessarily to shift the focus onto S's preparation of the food in arguing that the herring meal was no longer herring meal because of the DMNA. The House of Lords held (Viscount Dilhorne dissenting) that s 13 was not breached in either contract of sale (ie T–S; S–B) because, no matter what deficiencies there were in the food, it was still Norwegian herring meal which was supplied in accordance with the description. It was emphasised that no extraneous substance had been added to the herring meal and thus cases such as *Pinnock Bros v Lewis & Peat Ltd*[18] could be distinguished. There castor beans had been added to copra cake which meant that it was poisonous as cattle feed and could no longer be described as copra cake but, in *Ashington*, Lord Guest held that 'herring meal is still herring meal notwithstanding that it may have been contaminated by DMNA'.[19] The same reasoning was applicable to the second sale of the herring meal by the Norwegian seller (T) to S, because the House considered that only the words 'Norwegian herring meal' were part of the description and 'fair average quality of the season' did not form part of the description as these words did not *identify* the subject-matter of the contract.

The *Ashington* decision thus imposes a test of identity: the only descriptive words within s 13 are those which identify the subject-matter of the contract in the sense of defining its essence. The application of this test in *Ashington* meant that the DMNA contamination 'did not result in a different substance ... there was no loss

---

16 [1976] 1 WLR 989 at 998.
17 [1972] AC 441.
18 [1923] 1 KB 690; see also *Munro (Robert A) & Co Ltd v Meyer* [1930] 2 KB 312 (meat and bone meal adulterated with 5% of cocoa husks amounted to a breach of s 13).
19 [1972] AC 441, 472.

of identity'[20] or, as Lord Diplock put it, 'ultimately the test is whether the buyer could fairly and reasonably refuse to accept the physical goods proffered to him on the ground that their failure to correspond with that part of what was said about them in the contract makes them goods of a different kind from those he had agreed to buy'.[1] Essentially therefore, this test entails making the distinction between statements relating to the quality/attributes of the goods and statements regarding their substance/identity and, although Lord Wilberforce discouraged 'metaphysical discussions as to the nature of what is delivered, in comparison with what is sold',[2] this seems to be precisely the ethereal discussion which is called for. Viscount Dilhorne's dissenting opinion accepted the identity test but, after applying it, his conclusion was that *poisonous* herring meal did not merely affect the quality of the herring meal but resulted in a difference *in kind* and this illustrates succinctly the elusive, metaphysical distinction between substance and quality.

It is probable that, in *Reardon Smith* and *Ashington Piggeries*, the Law Lords were influenced by two legal principles which held sway at the time: the notion that there could be a 'fundamental breach' of contract and, second, the development of the innominate term which freed the law from the rigid classification of conditions and warranties. The doctrine of fundamental breach of contract had been resuscitated in the middle years of the 20th century to cope with the recalcitrant problems of all-embracing, 'blanket' exclusion clauses. The courts had arrived at a position where such exclusion clauses were held to be void in cases of fundamental breach in that it was thought impossible to excuse a virtual non-performance of the contract which entailed the substitution of goods different in substance from those described in the contract. The notion of fundamental breach had its beginnings in the notorious statement of Lord Abinger CB in *Chanter v Hopkins*[3] that 'if a man offers to buy peas of another, and he sends him beans, he does not perform his contract ... the contract is to sell peas, and if he sends him anything else in their stead, it is a non-performance of it'.[4] The novel decisions on innominate terms[5] had introduced dramatic flexibility in relation to remedies for breach of contract and the courts were enabled to stand back from the agreement and concentrate on the consequences of the breach rather than the prior classification of terms in the contract itself. Combining the fundamental breach reasoning with that in the decisions concerning innominate terms meant that only a difference in substance was perceived as sufficient to allow B's rejection of the goods and a trivial breach of description was thus ranked as a breach of a term of lesser importance within the overall classification of innominate terms and was to be regarded as sounding in damages only. *Reardon Smith* and *Ashington Piggeries* can be seen as corollaries of these developments but the decisions have circumscribed s 13 so effectively that it has seemingly become otiose: s 13 now implies the obvious in demanding that goods must correspond with their essential identity or substance.

20 [1972] AC 441, 473 per Lord Guest.
 1 [1972] AC 441 at 503-504.
 2 [1972] AC 441 at 489.
 3 (1838) 4 M & W 399, 404.
 4 Eg *Karsales (Harrow) Ltd v Wallis* [1956] 1 WLR 936, 942 per Birkett LJ: 'Clearly it was the duty of the finance company ... to supply the defendant a "car", in the ordinary sense of that term, and not something that needed towing, because in the true meaning of words a car that would not go was not a car at all; and on the evidence before the county court judge that was the kind of article which was supplied'. See Coote, 'Correspondence with Description in the Law of Sale of Goods' (1976) 50 ALJ 17.
 5 Eg *Hong Kong Fir Shipping Co Ltd v Kawasaki Kisen Kaisha Ltd* [1962] 2 QB 26.

In the light of *Ashington Piggeries*, it must be asked how the distinction between identity and attributes is to be determined. If B agrees to buy an oil painting by Picasso, does the fact of its being a forgery denote that it is lacking only a quality or attribute, meaning that the central identity of the contract is 'an oil painting' and that there is compliance with s 13? It is cold-comfort for B to be told that the substance of his contract is nothing more than oils on canvas which can be hung on a wall, but this conclusion seems inevitably to follow from *Ashington Piggeries*. The matter was not broached directly by the majority in *Harlingdon and Leinster Enterprises Ltd v Christopher Hull Fine Art Ltd*[6] but, in his dissenting judgment, Stuart-Smith LJ thought it 'beyond question' that 'the identity of the artist who painted a picture could be a substantial ingredient in the identity of the thing sold'.[7] This is surely the correct approach but, without a doubt it is not representative of English law. It is clear, however, that B's position can be much worse than being saddled with a forgery for he might reasonably assume that he has bought animal food but, under s 13, legitimately be supplied with 'food' which poisons and kills his animals. There is little affinity emotively, logically or practically between forgeries and genuine works of art, and none at all between poison and consumable food. It is a reproach to reason and justice if the worthless or dangerous item can be substituted in each of these examples on the basis that the contract has been complied with in essence by delivering the literal, physical object which was the subject of the undertaking.

One dubious merit of the identity test is that it allows room for manoeuvre. It is possible to say that, in *Arcos*, 'wooden staves for making cement barrels' identified the goods so that s 13 would not be breached on the facts or, alternatively, that 'wooden staves ½ inch thick for making cement barrels' constituted the essential identity of the goods, compliance with this description thus being obligatory under s 13. But this manoeuvrability is also the major criticism of the identity view as B cannot ascertain his rights at the date of contract with any degree of certainty. It is suggested that it is both unrealistic and unfair to apply an ethereal test of identity to practical, commercial descriptions, and that the commercial buyer should be able to demand that goods conform precisely with their contractual description.[8] It has to be said that, while the overall purpose of the new s 15A is clear enough, that section can only aggravate the complications of deciding when a breach of s 13 is sufficiently 'slight' in a non-consumer sale to deny a right of rejection to B or when, on the other hand, s 15A might be impliedly excluded.

---

6   [1991] 1 QB 564.
7   [1991] 1 QB 564 at 578; see also *Nicholson and Venn v Smith Marriott* [1947] 177 LT 189 (table linen described as Carolean in an auction catalogue but which was Georgian and worth much less than genuine, Carolean linen, was held to be a breach of s 13).
8   Proof of trade custom and commercial usage may be admitted so that the literal description of goods may be limited or qualified, see *Grenfell v E B Meyrowitz Ltd* [1936] 2 All ER 1313 (an aviator bought flying goggles described in a catalogue as fitted with 'safety-glass lenses' and could not recover for breach of s 13 when his eye was injured by a splinter from the goggles as they complied with the meaning of 'safety-glass' as then understood); *Steels & Busks Ltd v Bleecker Bik & Co Ltd* [1956] 1 Lloyd's Rep 228 (sale of 'pale crepe rubber, quality as previously delivered' for making suspenders; the rubber caused staining and was found to contain 'PNP', a chemical preservative. Sellers J held that the 'standard generally applied and accepted in the trade' (p 237) meant that the goods complied with their description); *Peter Darlington and Partners Ltd v Gosho Co Ltd* [1964] 1 Lloyd's Rep 149 (50 tons of canary seed sold on a 'pure basis'. It was proved that 98% was the highest standard of purity attainable and B was liable for not accepting the trade standard).

DESCRIPTION AND STATEMENTS RELATING TO THE QUALITY AND
PURPOSE OF THE GOODS

As a general rule, statements relating to the quality and fitness for purpose of
the goods are not part of their description but are the province of the SGA, s 14.
In *Ashington Piggeries*, it was stressed that, in the description 'Norwegian herring
meal fair average quality of the season', only 'Norwegian herring meal' was
part of the description, and the other words related to quality.[9] Thus, although
the goods complied with their description, they were held to be both
unmerchantable and unfit for their purpose.[10] Conversely, it is clear from *Arcos*,
that goods may be of merchantable quality but nevertheless fail to comply with
their description: the wooden staves were perfectly suited to the manufacture of
cement barrels but, nevertheless, they did not comply with their description.

However, the separation of quality and description is not always an obvious
one and, in *Ashington Piggeries*, Lord Hodson[11] acknowledged that words relating
to quality could be part of the description. The difficulties here relate once more
to the separation of identity/substance from quality/attributes, but it is quite possible
for goods to be so deficient in quality that they become goods of a different identity
or kind. In *Pinnock Bros v Lewis & Peat Ltd*,[12] the copra cake sold as animal
food was so contaminated by castor beans that Roche J held that it 'could not be
properly described as copra cake at all'.[13] The fact that quality may be part of the
description is illustrated by *Toepfer v Continental Grain Co*,[14] where the contract
was for 'No 3 Hard Amber Durum Wheat'. An official certificate had been issued
to S in the USA certifying the wheat to be this grade but the inspector had been
negligent and the wheat was of a poorer grade. It had been held that the certificate
was conclusive and that B had no legitimate complaint but B sought damages
arguing that, although the certificate was final as to quality, it was not final as to
description and the error here related to description. It was held that the 'description'
of the wheat also certified its quality and thus the certificate was final. Lord Denning
MR held that 'the word "hard" is a word both of quality and of description ... the
quality and description cannot be separated'[15] and he used the description 'new-
laid eggs' as an example of such inseparability.

It is also possible that the general purpose to which goods will be put may constitute
part of their description. In *Cotter v Luckie*,[16] B bought a bull at auction, which he
had inspected, but which was described as 'a pure bred polled Angus bull'. It was
held that he could reject it when it proved unsuitable for breeding and was thus
unfit for the purpose for which it had been bought, on the basis that this description
indicated that the bull should be a stud bull. Similarly, *Benjamin*[17] suggests that
goods described as 'baby food', 'cough mixture' or 'cold cure' would not conform
with their description if they were totally unsuitable for the purposes indicated.

---

9 [1972] AC 441, 470, 475, 495, 511, per Lords Hodson, Guest, Wilberforce and Diplock
  repectively.
10 See below where these aspects of the decision are considered.
11 [1972] AC 441, 470.
12 [1923] 1 KB 690.
13 [1923] 1 KB 690 at 697.
14 [1974] 1 Lloyd's Rep 11.
15 [1974] 1 Lloyd's Rep 11 at 13. See also *Toepfer v Warinco AG* [1978] 2 Lloyd's Rep 569
  ('fine-ground' was held to relate to description and thus coarse-ground soya bean meal
  could be rejected).
16 [1918] NZLR 811.
17 *Benjamin's Sale of Goods* (5th edn, 1997), para 11-017.

Apart from the situations above, the question of overlap between ss 13 and 14 may have particular relevance where B buys goods from a private seller. As s 14 is inapplicable to private sellers, B may be driven to complain of inferior quality under the guise of s 13, as in *Beale v Taylor*.[18]

Section 14(2): goods must be of satisfactory quality

The SGA 1979, s 14(1), (2), (2A), (2B) and (2C) provide:

'(1)   Except as provided by this section and section 15 below and subject to any other enactment, there is no implied term about the quality or fitness for any particular purpose of goods supplied under a contract of sale.

(2)   Where the seller sells goods in the course of a business, there is an implied term[19] that the goods supplied under the contract are of satisfactory quality.

(2A)   For the purposes of this Act, goods are of satisfactory quality if they meet the standard that a reasonable person would regard as satisfactory, taking account of any description of the goods, the price (if relevant) and all the other relevant circumstances.

(2B)   For the purposes of this Act, the quality of goods includes their state and condition and the following (among others) are in appropriate cases aspects of the quality of goods –

(a)   fitness for all the purposes for which goods of the kind in question are commonly supplied,

(b)   appearance and finish,

(c)   freedom from minor defects,

(d)   safety, and

(e)   durability.

(2C)   The term implied by subsection (2) above does not extend to any matter making the quality of goods unsatisfactory –

(a)   which is specifically drawn to the buyer's attention before the contract is made,

(b)   where the buyer examines the goods before the contract is made, which that examination ought to reveal, or

(c)   in the case of a contract for sale by sample, which would have been apparent on a reasonable examination of the sample.'[20]

It is essential to fit this new provision of satisfactory quality within its historical context if it is to be understood properly.

HISTORICAL BACKGROUND AND EVOLUTION OF THE IMPLIED
CONDITIONS OF MERCHANTABLE QUALITY AND FITNESS FOR PURPOSE

In the 19th century, where B made known to S the purpose for which he required the goods, there was a rule that the goods should be fit for their purpose[1] but the general requirement of merchantable quality stemmed from the *description* given to the goods and in sales by description the goods had thus to comply with the

---

18   [1967] 1 WLR 1193.
19   The SGA, s 14(6) provides that, as regards England, Wales and Northern Ireland, the term implied by s 14 (2) is a *condition* (the new s 14 (6) was substituted by the Sale and Supply of Goods Act 1994, s 7, Sch 2, para 5(5)(b)).
20   Section 14(2C)(c) is considered later under sales by sample.
 1   See *Jones v Bright* (1829) 5 Bing 533.

description and be merchantable.² The two undertakings of fitness and merchantability thus fulfilled similar purposes and both emanated from the description given to the goods, that is either S's description in cases of merchantability or B's description where he made his purpose known to S. The SGA 1893 embodied these two separate conditions but merchantability applied only where the sale was 'by description' which, at the time, did not extend to specific goods, whereas the implied condition of fitness for purpose could apply to both specific and unascertained goods. In fact, as the phrase 'merchantable quality' was not defined in the 1893 Act, there were early doubts as to how it would be interpreted and this apprehension, when coupled with the fact that merchantability did not apply to specific goods, meant that the more accessible and understandable section on fitness for purpose was widely utilised by buyers and was given a broad interpretation by the courts. This process led to an inevitable blurring of the two implied conditions.³

The condition of merchantability was originally designed for the mercantile community indicating that, in sales of unascertained goods by description, the goods should be 'commercially saleable' and its meaning seemed to cause few problems in the 19th century.⁴ The decision in *Gardiner v Gray*⁵ is regarded as pivotal in the early development of this notion of a minimum, core standard of quality which B might legitimately expect from the sale. B agreed to buy 12 bags of 'waste silk' from S, having seen samples of the silk in question which was to be imported from Europe. The written sale note did not refer to the samples or specify any quality for the silk which, on delivery, was found to be inferior to the samples and not saleable as 'waste silk'. Lord Ellenborough held that this was not a sale by sample as the written contract made no such stipulation and parol evidence could not be adduced to vary it. Nevertheless, he held that *caveat emptor* did not apply and B was entitled to 'a saleable article answering the description in the contract' as he 'cannot be supposed to buy goods to lay them on a dunghill'.⁶

Since 1893, the law has tried to steer a middle course between two extremes: first, that the goods be merchantable for *every* purpose for which they could be used (a rule which would be too harsh on every seller) and, second, that they be merchantable for *any one* of those purposes (a rule which would be too detrimental to any buyer). The implied term of merchantability worked satisfactorily in commercial sales as an approximate yardstick of reasonable quality. For example, in *Henry Kendall & Sons v William Lillico & Sons Ltd*,⁷ B bought animal feed which poisoned his pheasants but was suitable and edible food for a wide range of *other* animals. The food was held to have reached the requisite standard of merchantable quality. *Kendall* emphasised that the broad standard of merchantability should not be confused with the narrower implied condition that goods must be fit for the particular purpose for which they are required. A buyer who wished to feed pheasants thus needed to make this purpose known to S for, otherwise, he had to be satisfied with animal food which complied with the less demanding standard of merchantability.

2 See the concise summary in *Jones v Just* (1868) LR 3 QB 197.
3 See Franzi, 'Merchantable Quality and Particular Purpose: Questions of Overlap' (1977) 51 ALJ 298.
4 In *Jones v Just* (1868) LR 3 QB 197, Blackburn J found it unnecessary to give the jury any direction as to its meaning.
5 (1815) 4 Camp 144.
6 (1815) 4 Camp 144 at 145.
7 [1969] 2 AC 31.

At the time of the *Kendall* decision, there was still no statutory definition of merchantable quality but, following the recommendations of the Law Commissions,[8] a definition was introduced in 1973[9] which subsequently appeared as s 14(6) of the SGA 1979.[10] Although the definition in s 14(6) was a broad enunciation of the commercial notion of saleability/merchantability, the stress upon fitness for *purpose* in the subsection was an inappropriate yardstick for measuring quality in sales of consumer goods (see later) and the extent to which s 14(6) broke free from the previous common law was unclear. In *M/S Aswan Engineering Establishment Co v Lupdine*,[11] the Court of Appeal evaluated the earlier authorities in some detail and concluded that the definition had 'not revolutionised the law'.[12] In contrast, at almost the same time, a different panel of the Court of Appeal in *Rogers v Parish (Scarborough) Ltd*[13] considered that s 14(6) was self-sufficient as a definition and that an exploration of the earlier common law was not a practice to be encouraged.

The Law Commissions[14] reported on the issue of merchantable quality just after the decisions in *Rogers* and *Aswan* and recommended that a new definition of 'acceptable quality' should replace 'merchantable quality' in the SGA and that there should be a separate list of pertinent aspects of quality. These recommendations were substantially enacted in the Sale and Supply of Goods Act 1994 which amended the SGA, s 14(2), as set out above, although 'satisfactory quality' is the phrase which appears in the Act. The implied condition of satisfactory quality has replaced that of merchantable quality and, today, provides the central nucleus of B's assurance against the sale of inferior goods. The 1994 Act became law on 3 January 1995 but it is not retrospective in operation[15] and so the merchantable quality provisions will continue to be important for some time as regards contracts entered into before that date. Moreover, it will be virtually impossible to interpret the new provision in a vacuum and much of the old law will thus remain of value.

Section 14(2) applies in sales between a business and a consumer and those between two businesses and the amended section justifiably increases the standard of quality which a consumer buyer can expect of mass-produced goods. However, although the consumer buyer can now reject the goods as against his business seller for a slight breach of s 14(2), the business seller may well be barred, by s 15A, from rejecting those goods as against his own seller.

In theory, the new provisions concerning satisfactory quality revolutionise the law and increase the standard of quality demanded of sellers but the practical

8 *Exemption Clauses in Contracts, First Report: Amendments to the Sale of Goods Act 1893*, Law Com No 24, Scot Law Com No 12, (1969). It was considered that 'it is not satisfactory for an Act which purports to codify a whole branch of the law to use a technical term the meaning of which is far from self-evident and becomes meaningful only when the case law is looked at' (para 42).
9 The Supply of Goods (Implied Terms) Act 1973.
10 Section 14(6) formerly provided: 'Goods of any kind are of merchantable quality within the meaning of subsection (2) above if they are as fit for the purpose or purposes for which goods of that kind are commonly bought as it is reasonable to expect having regard to any description applied to them, the price (if relevant) and all the other relevant circumstances'.
11 [1987] 1 WLR 1. See Brown, 'The Meaning of Merchantable Quality in Sales of Goods: Quality or Fitness for Purpose?' [1987] LMCLQ 400.
12 [1987] 1 WLR 1 at 13, per Lloyd LJ.
13 [1987] QB 933.
14 *Sale and Supply of Goods* (Law Com No 160, Scot Law Com No 104, Cm 137, 1987).
15 See Sale and Supply of Goods Act 1994, s 8.

efficacy of the rules depends upon whether the courts regard 'satisfactory quality' as merely a modified replica of merchantable quality or, instead, see it as a vehicle for meaningful change. Thus far, the only reported case to have considered satisfactory quality is the Scottish decision in *Thain v Anniesland Trade Centre*.[16] *Thain* is considered when the requirement of durability is examined later, but the court took such a disconcertingly constricted view of the new provisions that the decision is strangely reminiscent of old wine in new bottles. So much emphasis was placed on the risk inherent in buying a second-hand car that the court concluded that a major defect which became apparent only *two weeks* after purchase did not render the car unsatisfactory. This decision could easily have been reached under the previous notion of merchantability but, even then, it would have been an extremely restrictive one with nothing to commend it.

THE SCOPE OF SECTION 14(2)

The seller 'sells goods in the course of a business'

The requirement that S must sell the goods 'in the course of a business' is in both s 14(2) and s 14(3)(fitness for purpose). There has been a progressive widening of the notion of the 'business sale' since the SGA 1893, the merchantability provision in that Act stipulating that B should buy goods from S 'who deals in goods of that description'.[17] This narrow definition and that found in the implied condition of fitness for purpose[18] could not apply where B bought goods from S which were not the principal constituent of S's business as a seller, eg the by-products of S's manufacturing process.[19] Nevertheless, a wide interpretation was given to both phrases in *Ashington Piggeries Ltd v Christopher Hill Ltd*.[20] There the House of Lords held that it was immaterial that S had never before made food for mink because he satisfied the definition in the merchantability provision of the SGA 1893 by being a dealer in animal foodstuffs. As he dealt in goods of the *type* or *kind* supplied, it was irrelevant that he did not deal in goods of the exact contract description.[1] Similarly, as S dealt in animal feed, it was held that it was in the course of his business to supply food for mink within the fitness for purpose provision of the 1893 Act.[2]

---

16 1997 SLT (Sh Ct) 102.
17 The SGA 1893, s 14(2).
18 The SGA 1893, s 14(1): 'the goods are of a description which it is in the course of the seller's business to supply'.
19 See eg *Turner v Mucklow* (1862) 6 LT 690 (sale of 'spent madder' which S had used for dyeing purposes); *Ipswich Gaslight Co v WB King & Co* (1886) 3 TLR 100 (sale of surplus tar from S's gas works).
20 [1972] AC 441.
 1 See Lords Guest, Dilhorne and Wilberforce at pp 474, 485 and 495 respectively. Lords Hodson (p 469) and Diplock (p 509) dissented on this point.
 2 See also *Spencer Trading Co Ltd v Devon* [1947] 1 All ER 284 (manufacturers and sellers of glue who were asked to make a glue for fly-paper were liable under the SGA 1893, s 14(1) even though it was the first time they had made such a special glue); *Buckley v Lever Bros Ltd* [1953] 4 DLR 16 (promotional offer by Lever Bros, the well-known soap powder manufacturer, for the sale of clothespegs. Wells J held that the goods were 'of a description which it is in the course of the seller's business to supply' within the (Ontario) SGA because 'by offering these clothespins for sale ... [S] made it part of their business to supply clothespins ... they chose to deal in plastic clothespins' (p 27)).

The current wording in s 14(2), which was inserted originally by the Supply of Goods (Implied Terms) Act 1973, is the culmination of the transformation[3] of the definition into an objective, all-embracing requirement of selling goods 'in the course of a business'. It would be difficult to express this notion in any broader terms and it is clear from the Law Commissions' report[4] which led to the 1973 Act that the new definition was intended to cover a wide spectrum of business sales. It has always been suggested, for example, that S need not operate a business of *selling* goods, eg S could have a car rental business and decide to sell one of the cars,[5] and the phrase should also cover the situation where S regularly sells one type of goods but incidentally sells other goods, eg a coal merchant who sells one of his lorries.[6] Similarly, the definition should encompass the situation where S sells goods in his business for the first time, as there is no requirement that the business be an *established* one.

Until recently, these examples were conjectural as there was no direct authority on the meaning of 'in the course of a business' in s 14(2), but the decision of the Court of Appeal in *Stevenson v Rogers*[7] now establishes emphatically that the conclusions reached above are correct. In *Stevenson*, S had an established business as a fisherman and had purchased his first fishing vessel, *Dolly Mopp*, many years earlier. He bought a new vessel, *Jelle*, in 1983 and operated two boats for a while until he sold *Dolly Mopp* in 1986. In 1988, he sold *Jelle* to B for £600,000, replacing her with another fishing boat, *Marilyn Jane*, which he continued to use in his business. At first instance, it was held that there was an insufficient regularity of dealing to render the sale of *Jelle* 'in the course of a business' within the SGA 1979, s 14(2), and that, accordingly, the implied condition of merchantability in that section did not apply to the sale. The Court of Appeal reversed that decision and ruled that, having regard to the legislative history of the SGA, the wording in s 14(2) of the 1979 Act had been deliberately changed to widen the protection conferred upon a buyer of goods from a business seller. Consequently, it was held that s 14(2) must be construed at face value and the sale of *Jelle* was in the course of a business: the wording of the section did not demand any element of regularity of dealing and so there was no reason 'to re-introduce some implied qualification, difficult to define, in order to narrow what appears to be the wide scope and apparent purpose of the words'.[8]

In *Stevenson*, the court refused to follow and apply the decisions which were established authority on the meaning of 'course of a business' in the Trade Descriptions Act 1968 (TDA) and the Unfair Contract Terms Act 1977 (UCTA).

---

3   A process which began with the Molony Committee (*Final Report of the Committee on Consumer Protection* (1962), Cmnd 1781) which recommended that 'if a retailer sells an article in the course of business he should be answerable for its merchantability ... whether or not he has traded in the same line previously. The test should be whether he sells by way of trade to the particular purchaser and not whether he makes a habit of trading in similar goods, which is a circumstance not necessarily known to the purchaser' (para 443).

4   *Exemption Clauses in Contracts, First Report: Amendments to the Sale of Goods Act 1893* (Law Com No 24, Scot Law Com No 12, 1969), para 31.

5   See *Havering London Borough Council v Stevenson* [1970] 1 WLR 1375 (S had a car hire business and usually sold the cars after two years and paid the proceeds back into his business. He falsely represented a car's mileage and sold it. Held he had committed an offence under the Trade Descriptions Act 1968, s 1(1), as the sale was 'in the course of a trade or business').

6   This example was used by the Law Commissions (Law Com No 24, Scot Law Com No 12, 1969), para 31, n 30.

7   [1999] QB 1028.

8   [1999] QB 1028 at 1039 per Potter LJ.

The House of Lords' ruling in *Davies v Sumner*[9] and that of the Court of Appeal in *R & B Customs Brokers Co Ltd v United Dominions Trust Ltd*[10] established that, unless the transaction is an integral part of the business carried on[11] or is a one-off adventure in the nature of trade and is carried-through to completion, it must have been performed with a degree of *regularity* if it is to be regarded as being in the course of a business (ie the approach adopted by the judge at first instance in *Stevenson*).This different interpretation under the UCTA and the TDA can be explained. The TDA is concerned with criminal offences and it is appropriate that an interpretation be made which is favourable to the defendant/ seller and, likewise, a major function of the UCTA is to protect buyers of goods from the operation of exclusion clauses. Accordingly, the seller in *Davies* would have had to deal regularly if he were to be convicted under the TDA. Similarly, the buyer of goods in *R & B Customs* was a director of a limited company who had bought cars for the company on two or three occasions only and so it was just that, as he did not regularly buy cars in this way, he should be classed as a consumer buyer meaning that the implied conditions of the SGA relating to quality and fitness could not be excluded by his business seller.[12] But if the *Davies* stipulation of regularity had been applied to the *seller* in *Stevenson*, it would have *reduced* the scope of a business sale under s 14(2) and diminished the protection available to the buyer. Accordingly, the phrase 'sells goods in the course of a business' within s 14(2) was interpreted at its wide face value and it is now clear that, for the purposes of s 14(2), it is irrelevant to ask whether the sale of goods in dispute forms an integral part of the business carried on and, likewise, the requirement that peripheral transactions be performed with a degree of regularity is immaterial. Provided that S *has* a business, the last mentioned factors are irrelevant to B.

The *Stevenson* decision furthers the protection of all buyers under s 14(2) but, most particularly, it is helpful for consumer buyers who may often be unable to ascertain with any certainty what specialism S possesses as a seller: such consumer buyers can now rely upon the outward, objective appearance of one sale of goods made in the course of a business. *Stevenson* does mean, however, that there is incongruity between selling in the course of a business for the SGA, s 14(2) (where no regularity of dealing is required) and the buyer's making the contract in the course of a business under the UCTA s 12 (where some regularity of dealing is required if B is to be classified as making the contract in the course of a business).

After the *Stevenson* decision, it is particularly important to focus attention on when S is regarded as having a 'business'. 'Business' is defined in the SGA, s 61(1) as including 'a profession and the activities of any government department or local or public authority' thus indicating that the business need not be carried on for *profit*. In deciding whether an activity amounts to a 'business', the difficulties occur in those situations on the periphery of the definition – a shop in a hospital or a refectory in a university, for example. Although there is no

---

9 [1984] 1 WLR 1301.
10 [1988] 1 WLR 321.
11 It has never been clear what is envisaged by the transaction's being an 'integral' part of the business but, for example, it would arguably be an integral part of a retail business for the retailer to sell his cash tills even though he does not regularly do so.
12 See also *Rasbora Ltd v JCL Marine Ltd* [1977] 1 Lloyd's Rep 645 (powerboat sold to an individual who controlled Rasbora Ltd, the company then being substituted as buyer to avoid payment of VAT. Held this was a consumer sale and so the SGA implied conditions could not be excluded).

case law on the SGA, there are indirect authorities from other contexts but none is conclusive. For example, in *Blakemore v Bellamy*,[13] S, a postman, placed 21 advertisements in newspapers for the sale of eight cars, over a period of 15 months. The court accepted that renovating and selling cars was his 'hobby' and that he was not acting in the course of a business for the purposes of the Business Advertisements (Disclosure) Order 1977.[14] However, the court accepted that 'business' was wider in ambit than 'trade'. In contrast, in *Stevenson v Beverley Bentinck Ltd*,[15] the defendant carried on a part-time business of a car dealer and, on one occasion, he bought a car for private use. It was held that he was *not* a 'private purchaser' for the purposes of Part III of the Hire Purchase Act 1964. It is difficult to draw any accurate conclusions in relation to the SGA but, where an element of profit is discernible and there is some regularity of trading, the enterprise will almost certainly be a business. Accordingly, although it is clearly desirable to define business activity broadly, care must be taken to ensure that the wide definition of 'business' and the *Stevenson v Rogers* ruling do not combine to entangle some amateur sellers, quite unjustly, within the net of business liability in the SGA, s 14.[16]

Finally, the SGA, s 14(5) should be mentioned, its purpose being to make S liable under s 14(2) where he sells goods via an *agent* who acts in the course of a business.[17] Prior to the introduction of s 14(5),[18] a private seller who used a business agent might escape liability for unmerchantable goods as, under the rules of agency, S was the principal with whom the contract was made and, as a private individual, he would thus not be liable. The recent decision of the House of Lords in *Boyter v Thomson*[19] confirms that the private seller will be liable by virtue of s 14(5). It should be noted that s 14(5) contains an exception, viz, S will not be liable where he does not sell in the course of a business and either B 'knows that fact' or 'reasonable steps are taken to bring it to the notice of [B] before the contract is made'. There is, however, no authority on whether B's constructive notice might suffice or what might constitute 'reasonable steps'. For example, B might know of the existence of the agency and, while this alone would be insufficient to exclude s 14(5) as B must know of S's private *status*, it remains to be seen whether B might ever be put on inquiry by knowledge of the agency or by additional facts relating to the agency.

Section 14(2) applies to 'goods supplied under the contract'

This wording is now found in the SGA 1979, s 14(2) and (3)(fitness for purpose). It was first introduced by the Supply of Goods (Implied Terms) Act 1973 in

---

13 [1983] RTR 303.
14 The purpose of this Order is to prevent businesses posing as private sellers and thereby inducing the impression in buyers that the implied terms of the SGA can be excluded, eg by advertising in the small advertisement columns of newspapers, as in *Blakemore*.
15 [1976] 1 WLR 483.
16 See Brown, 'Sales of Goods in the Course of a Business' (1999) 115 LQR 384.
17 Section 14(5) provides: 'The preceding provisions of this section apply to a sale by a person who in the course of a business is acting as agent for another as they apply to a sale by a principal in the course of a business, except where that other is not selling in the course of a business and either the buyer knows that fact or reasonable steps are taken to bring it to the notice of the buyer before the contract is made'.
18 By the Supply of Goods (Implied Terms) Act 1973.
19 [1995] 2 AC 628; see Brown, 'Sale of Goods and Undisclosed Agency' (1996) 112 LQR 225.

confirmation of the decisions under the SGA 1893 which read the words in the preamble to the old s 14 together with the wording in the section itself. The preamble stated that, except as specified in s 14, there was no implied condition or warranty as to quality or fitness of 'goods supplied under a contract of sale' and the courts interpreted this to mean that the condition of merchantability (and fitness for purpose) extended to the goods *supplied* rather than just those that were the subject of the contract of sale.

In *Geddling v Marsh*,[20] S was a mineral water manufacturer who sold mineral water in bottles to B, a retailer. One of the bottles burst in B's hands, injuring her. It was held that S was in breach of the implied condition of fitness for purpose even though the bottles were to be returned to S when empty and, as they remained the property of S, were never sold to B.

Similarly, in *Wilson v Rickett Cockerell & Co Ltd*,[1] B bought a ton of 'Coalite' from S which, although being satisfactory in all other respects, contained an explosive substance which duly exploded in B's fireplace damaging his room and furniture. At first instance, the court followed the grotesque reasoning in a Scottish decision[2] where, on almost identical facts to *Wilson*, except that B lost an eye in the explosion, it was held that the coal was fit for its purpose: the court considered that the defect lay in the extraneous detonator which B had not bought. Fortunately, some respect for English jurisprudence was restored when, in *Wilson*, the Court of Appeal reversed the first instance decision and held that the Coalite was unmerchantable. Denning LJ emphasised that the goods 'supplied' included the explosive and he forcefully rejected S's technical arguments that the goods were sound because the explosive was not embedded in a piece of coal or that there was no contamination of the entire ton of coal. The court thus considered that *Wilson's* facts were indistinguishable 'in principle and logic'[3] from *Chaproniere v Mason*.[4] There B, a solicitor, sent his clerk to buy a bath-bun and meat pie but when B bit the bun one of his teeth, which was decayed, was broken on a stone contained in the bun and an abscess developed on his jaw. Surprisingly, the jury's findings were not in B's favour but the Court of Appeal thought that there should be a fresh trial as the goods were unfit for their purpose.

Other cases reached a similar result to those above by emphasising that the SGA 1893, s 62(1), the Act's interpretation section, defined the 'quality of goods' as including their 'state or condition'.[5] It should be stressed that, in the SGA 1979, s 14(2B), quality is now said to encompass the 'state *and* condition' of the goods, the phrase having been moved forward from the SGA 1979, s 61(1), the Act's interpretation section.

Finally, the Law Commissions[6] considered that decisions such as *Wilson v Rickett Cockerell & Co Ltd* mean that 'free gifts' supplied with the goods sold,

---

20 [1920] 1 KB 668.
 1 [1954] 1 QB 598.
 2 *Duke v Jackson* 1921 SC 362; see the scathing criticism of *Duke* in Gow, *The Mercantile and Industrial Law of Scotland* (1964), p 179.
 3 [1954] 1 QB 598, 609 per Lord Evershed MR.
 4 (1905) 21 TLR 633.
 5 See *Niblett Ltd v Confectioners' Materials Co Ltd* [1921] 3 KB 387 (sale of tins of condensed milk which bore labels infringing the Nestlé trade mark were held to be unmerchantable); *Morelli v Fitch and Gibbons* [1928] 2 KB 636 (a defective glass bottle, containing Stone's ginger wine, cut B when he extracted the cork; it was held to be unmerchantable).
 6 *Exemption Clauses, Second Report* (Law Com No 69, Scot Law Com No 39, (1975), para 35).

as promotional gimmicks, must be of merchantable quality and this reasoning neatly curtails a problem which was, undoubtedly, waiting in the wings.

The meaning of merchantable quality and its replacement by 'satisfactory quality'

As discussed earlier, merchantable quality was concerned with the broad requirement of commercial saleability in the market place and, accordingly, it was a notion applicable primarily to commercial sales of unascertained goods by description. A salient feature of such sales was that the goods could have a wide range of purposes, eg timber or cloth, and could be sold under several different descriptions which would correspond to different qualities. It would be unfair to demand of S that the goods be merchantable for every purpose imaginable and equally unfair on B if S could discharge his obligation by stressing that the goods could be put to some use, because most goods can be used in some way or resold by B, eg a car resold as scrap metal. Merchantability thus sought to establish a standard somewhere between these two polar positions of perfection and virtual worthlessness.

Such a median was arguably reached in the leading modern decision in *Henry Kendall & Sons v William Lillico & Sons Ltd*.[7] Hardwick Game Farm bought foodstuff for their pheasants which turned out to be contaminated by a poisonous substance contained in Brazilian groundnut extraction which was a major ingredient of the food. Many of the pheasant chicks died and others were left stunted and unfit for breeding purposes. The seller, SAPPA, a local compounder of the food, had bought the groundnut extraction from wholesalers who had, in turn, bought it from the fourth parties who had imported it from Brazil. SAPPA admitted liability to Hardwick Game Farm and the litigation then concerned liability under the two other contracts of sale. The House of Lords held that the groundnut extraction was merchantable in both the sales, as it could be sold at the same price and compounded into edible cattle food: it was thus saleable to many buyers under the same description, at a similar price, but for a different *purpose* from that for which it was required in the sales in question. There was liability under both sales, however, for breach of the implied condition regarding fitness for purpose of the goods sold.

Broadly speaking, the tests of merchantability which were advanced in the decisions could be divided into two different formulations with different emphases: *acceptability* to a reasonable buyer and *usability* for at least one purpose to which goods of that description were commonly put.

Acceptability

A version of the acceptability test was suggested by Farwell LJ in *Bristol Tramways etc,Carriage Co Ltd v Fiat Motors Ltd*,[8] as meaning 'that the article is of such quality and in such condition that a reasonable man acting reasonably would after a full examination accept it under the circumstances of the case in performance of his offer to buy that article whether he buys for his own use or

---

7   [1969] 2 AC 31.
8   [1910] 2 KB 831, 841.

to sell again'. This definition was criticised in *Kendall*[9] as being too narrow because goods sold may be merchantable if bought under the same description but for a purpose different from that for which B required the goods, as in *Kendall* itself. A variant of the acceptability test which was approved in *Kendall*[10] was propounded by Dixon J in *Australian Knitting Mills Ltd v Grant*,[11] to mean that the goods 'should be in such an actual state that a buyer fully acquainted with the facts and, therefore, knowing what hidden defects exist, and not being limited to their apparent condition would buy them without abatement of the price ... and without special terms'. This test accentuated price and placed the correct emphasis on whether B would buy the goods rather than whether he would accept them.

Usability and fitness for purpose

Lord Wright suggested in *Cammell Laird & Co Ltd v Manganese Bronze and Brass Co Ltd*,[12] that goods would be unmerchantable where 'in the form in which they were tendered [they] were of no use for any purpose for which such goods would normally be used and hence not saleable under that description'. This test was also criticised by Lord Reid in *Kendall*[13] on the basis that most goods have different descriptions and uses. He emphasised that if the contract description of the goods was so limited that the goods sold would normally have only one purpose, then the goods would be unmerchantable under that description if they were of no use for that purpose. However, a general description of goods would mean that they would normally be used for several different purposes and thus goods would be merchantable under that description if they were fit for any one of those purposes. If B had wanted the goods for one of the purposes for which they were unsuitable he should either have made his particular purpose known to S, or insisted upon a more specific description in the contract.

The acceptability and usability tests were often both approved in the same decisions and Salmon LJ went so far as to suggest that the difference between them was a matter of semantics.[14] However, usability and fitness for purpose tended to dominate the decisions and the old statutory definition of merchantability in the SGA 1979, s 14(6), clearly favoured usability. Although Lord Denning MR was correct in considering the definition in s 14(6) to be 'the best that has yet been devised',[15] the emphasis placed upon functionality in that subsection was restrictive in two ways. First, the utilitarian definition of fitness for purpose was inadequate as a means of testing the quality required of consumer goods, as they might have substantial defects yet still be merchantable as meeting the standard of fitness.[16] A new car might have numerous defects but still be usable and drivable and therefore it would be regarded as fit for its purpose within s 14(6). It is an indictment of the law that, as late as 1982, a judge commented that he 'needed no reminding that it has been said over and over again in the

9 [1969] 2 AC 31, 78-79 and 97 per Lords Reid and Morris respectively.
10 [1969] 2 AC 31 at 79, 108 and 118 per Lords Reid, Guest and Pearce respectively.
11 (1933) 50 CLR 387, 418 (High Court of Australia).
12 [1934] AC 402, 430.
13 [1969] 2 AC 31, 76-77.
14 *Bartlett v Sidney Marcus Ltd* [1965] 1 WLR 1013, 1018.
15 *Cehave NV v Bremer Handelsgesellschaft mbH, The Hansa Nord* [1976] QB 44, 62.
16 See *Millar's of Falkirk Ltd v Turpie* 1976 SLT (Notes) 66 (new car delivered with an oil leak in the power steering system; B sought to reject it but it was held to be merchantable).

Court of Appeal that a second-hand car must not be said not to be of merchantable quality nor fit for the purpose merely because it has a string of defects. Before this can be found, a second-hand car must be shown to be not roadworthy or even unsafe'.[17] Somewhat belatedly, it was becoming clear that the commercial notion of merchantability which assumed that goods which were unsatisfactory for one purpose could either be resold by B or used by him for a different purpose, was badly out-of-step with modern sales to consumers of mass-produced goods. The balancing act which was performed in *Kendall* clearly has no place in the sale to a consumer buyer of a washing machine or refrigerator. At long last, the decision in *Rogers v Parish (Scarborough) Ltd*,[18] broke new ground in holding that a new Range Rover which had defects in its engine, gearbox, oil seals and bodywork was unmerchantable even though it was usable and drivable, having been driven for 5,500 miles in the first six months. Mustill LJ said that the court must consider 'not merely the buyer's purpose of driving the car from one place to another but of doing so with the appropriate degree of comfort, ease of handling and reliability and, one may add, of pride in the vehicle's outward and interior appearance'.[19] This was a bold decision which successfully extended s 14(6) beyond its narrow confines of function and fitness for purpose but the court's reasoning was awkward and artificial in that merchantable quality had to be explained in terms of fitness for purpose. B's *purpose* in buying a car is, clearly, to drive from one place to another, but the other aspects of comfort and appearance etc, mentioned by Mustill LJ, are patently aspects of *quality*.[20] It was thus imperative that, in order to avoid cramped artificiality of reasoning, a statutory definition of quality should emphasise the pertinent aspects of that concept, and this is the aim of the liberated defintion of satisfactory quality.

The second restriction connected with s 14(6) was that the section specified that goods were merchantable 'if they are as fit for the purpose or purposes ... *as it is reasonable to expect*'. These italicised words seemingly signalled a further diminution in the standard of merchantability in that it was arguable that a reasonable buyer could expect to receive goods which passed only some basic test of utility. This was certainly the outcome in *The Hansa Nord*,[1] albeit on an exceptional set of facts. Citrus pulp pellets were sold for £100,000 to B for use as animal feed, an express term of the contract providing that shipment was to be made 'in good condition', but when the ship arrived in Rotterdam about 38% of the cargo was overheated. The market price of pulp pellets had just fallen, a fact which clearly accounted for the subsequent happenings. B rejected the entire consignment and the £100,000 purchase price was repaid, with interest, to B. The pellets were then bought by a Mr Baas, an importer of feeding products, for £30,000, and almost immediately resold to B at the same price. B then used the pellets for the original purpose of cattle food but he used smaller percentages in the food compound than if the pellets had been sound. Mocatta J held[2] that there was a breach of an express condition as the goods were not in 'good condition' and, as they were also unmerchantable, B's rejection was justified. The Court of

17 *Porter v General Guarantee Corpn Ltd* [1982] RTR 384, 393 per Kilner Brown J.
18 [1987] QB 933.
19 [1987] QB 933 at 944.
20 See Brown,'The Meaning of Merchantable Quality in Sales of Goods: Quality or Fitness for Purpose?' [1987] LMCLQ 400.
 1 *Cehave NV v Bremer Handelsgesellschaft mbH, The Hansa Nord* [1976] QB 44.
 2 [1974] 2 Lloyd's Rep 216.

Appeal reversed that decision holding that the stipulation as to 'good condition' was an intermediate or innominate term, breach of which entitled B to damages but not to reject the goods unless the breach went to the root of the contract, which it clearly did not on the facts. It was also held that the goods were of merchantable quality as they were used for their original purpose of feeding to cattle.

The underlying motive of the decision in *The Hansa Nord* was undoubtedly that it was unreasonable for B to reject on the facts and, of course, he could have rejected the goods if they had been held to be unmerchantable. However, the standard of merchantability was lowered by the decision and a potential trap was set for consumer buyers because, if the court considered that B was acting unreasonably in seeking to reject, it might find that the goods were usable and thus merchantable and, in consumer sales, there would rarely be an express term to fall back on, as there was in the *Hansa Nord*. The consumer buyer could thus be left with no remedy whatever for shoddy goods.[3] This sort of artificial reasoning should no longer be necessary with the advent of the SGA, s 15A, which prevents non-consumer buyers rejecting goods where it would be unreasonable to do so for 'slight' breaches of the implied conditions in the SGA, ss 13-15, thus restricting such a buyer to a claim in damages for breach of warranty. Moreover, the new standard of satisfactory quality is considerably higher than that of merchantability and so, in a consumer sale, minor defects can now render goods unsatisfactory thereby allowing B the right of rejection.

Definition and application of the standard of satisfactory quality

The overall impact of the new definition of satisfactory quality is that a markedly higher standard of quality is demanded of sellers than under the previous legislation and the rough-and-ready notion of usability/fitness has been abondoned in favour of a more refined definition of quality. The concept of satisfactory quality in s 14(2A) and (2B) can now perform its correct role, leaving fitness for purpose under s 14(3) to its separate function. The SGA 1979, s 14(2A) provides:

> 'For the purposes of this Act, goods are of satisfactory quality if they meet the standard that a reasonable person would regard as satisfactory, taking account of any description of the goods, the price (if relevant) and all the other relevant circumstances.'

The factors mentioned in s 14(2A) are intended to be 'a basic principle formulated in language sufficiently general to apply to all kinds of goods and all kinds of transaction'[4] and those in s 14(2B) are 'a list of aspects of quality, any of which could be important in a particular case'.[5] The constituents of s 14(2A) will be considered first.

---

3 See *Millar's of Falkirk Ltd v Turpie* 1976 SLT (Notes) 66 (leak in the power-steering of a car which would have cost £25 to repair; the goods were held to be merchantable and so B had no remedy).
4 *Sale and Supply of Goods* (Law Com No 160, Scot Law Com No 104, Cm 137, 1987), para 3.12.
5 *Sale and Supply of Goods* (Law Com No 160, Scot Law Com No 104, Cm 137, 1987), para 3.12.

THE GOODS MUST 'MEET THE STANDARD THAT A REASONABLE PERSON WOULD REGARD AS SATISFACTORY'

As emphasised earlier, the previous definition of quality in s 14(6) demanded that goods be 'as fit for the purpose or purposes ... as it is reasonable to expect,' this test arguably leading to a diminution in the standard of quality as S might establish that cars, for example, could reasonably be expected to possess a number of minor defects on delivery yet still be fit for their purpose. The Law Commissions wanted to avoid this somewhat perverse situation where an increase in the number and frequency of defects could lead to less chance of success in actions for breach of contract[6] and the broad definition of satisfactory quality in s 14(2A) and the specific aspects of quality in s 14(2B) effectively abrogate the previous workmanlike notion of reasonable fitness for purpose.

Similarly, s 14(2A) demands that goods must 'meet the standard that a reasonable person would regard as satisfactory'. It is a reasonable *person* who figures here and not a reasonable *buyer*, so that S cannot argue that a reasonable buyer expects and tolerates minor defects in cars, for example. Moreover, as this test is patently an objective one, it is insufficient that the goods are regarded as unsatisfactory by the *buyer* if they meet the requisite objective standard which a reasonable person regards as satisfactory. Accentuating this objective standard should thus lead, as the Law Commissions envisaged,[7] to a higher overall standard of quality where appropriate (eg new cars) but permit a lower standard where only such a lesser standard could be demanded by a reasonable person (eg second-hand cars[8]).

Finally, the definition in s 14(2A) does not ask whether the reasonable person would find the *goods* to be of satisfactory quality – rather it demands an objective comparison of the state of the goods with the standard which a reasonable person would regard as satisfactory.

'TAKING ACCOUNT OF ANY DESCRIPTION OF THE GOODS'

One of the most significant aspects in any evaluation of quality is the description which is applied to goods. The infinitely variable standards of quality which a reasonable person would regard as satisfactory may be illustrated by, at one end of the spectrum, the description of a car for sale as scrap and spare parts and, at the other, the description applied in the sale of brand new car straight from the showroom. In other words, there must clearly be a sliding-scale of quality relative to the description given to the goods. In *Bartlett v Sydney Marcus Ltd*,[9] S offered to sell a second-hand Jaguar car to B, informing B that the clutch needed repairing and offering B the choice of paying £975 with a repaired clutch or paying £950 and having it repaired at his own cost. B chose the latter option and used the car for a month before the repairs were carried out, the total cost of which came to £84. B sued for damages for breach of the implied condition

---

6 *Sale and Supply of Goods* (Law Com No 160, Scot Law Com No 104, Cm 137, 1987), para 2.11: 'A general deterioration in the standard of manufacture of a particular kind of article would result in a corresponding decline in the standard of merchantable quality for that article'.
7 *Sale and Supply of Goods* (Law Com No 160, Scot Law Com No 104, Cm 137, 1987), paras 3.19-3.27.
8 See *Thain v Anniesland Trade Centre* 1997 SLT (Sh Ct) 102, considered later.
9 [1965] 1 WLR 1013.

of merchantability but the Court of Appeal held that the vehicle was roadworthy and merchantable. Lord Denning MR emphasised that, although the car was far from perfect, it had been sold as a second-hand car with a defective clutch and it thus met the required standard of usability.

The decision in *Business Applications Specialists Ltd v Nationwide Credit Corpn Ltd*,[10] stressed that, after the extended meaning given to merchantable quality in *Rogers v Parish (Scarborough) Ltd*,[11] it was insufficient for a second-hand car simply to be functional in the sense of being roadworthy and usable. There a Mercedes car which was two-and-a-half years old, with a mileage of 37,000, was sold for £14,850. The car broke down after 800 miles because of burnt-out valves and worn valve seals which cost £635 to repair. Parker LJ considered that, should a Rolls-Royce which had covered 1,500 miles be sold at its market value, it would not pass the merchantability test if could merely be driven safely on the road but that, in general, a buyer of a second-hand car must expect *some* degree of wear and tear. Accordingly, the Mercedes was held to be of merchantable quality. In *Shine v General Guarantee Corpn Ltd*,[12] the court also applied *Rogers v Parish* but reached the opposite conclusion on the facts. B bought a two year old Fiat X19 which he subsequently discovered had been submerged in water for 24 hours and had thus been classified as an insurance write-off. Bush J held that the car was unmerchantable as 'no member of the public, knowing the facts, would touch [it] with a barge pole unless they could get it at a substantially reduced price to reflect the risk they were taking'.[13]

It is almost indisputable that the same results would be reached on these facts using the new yardstick of satisfactory quality. In *Rogers v Parish*, for example, the Range Rover was a *new* one and thus a reasonable person would expect it to reach a much higher standard of quality than that of the second-hand car in *Bartlett*.

'THE PRICE (IF RELEVANT)'

The SGA 1979, s 14(2A) provides that one factor to consider in assessing the satisfactory quality of goods is 'the price (if relevant)' and it is self-evident that the price at which goods are sold may be indicative of their quality. Moreover, the description applied to goods is inextricably entangled with the question of their price. The obvious conclusion is that satisfactory quality can legitimately be demanded of a new, 'luxury' car sold at the full market price but a sale of a 'demonstration model' at much less than market price may indicate that a reasonable person should expect a correlative decrease in quality. In the recent Scottish decision in *Thain v Anniesland Trade Centre*,[14] the Sheriff Principal held that 'people who buy secondhand cars get them at less than the original price in large part because secondhand cars have attached to them increased risk of expensive repairs'.[15]

However, it is plain that price may be of no relevance whatever in evaluating quality – it could not be suggested, for example, that the quality of goods sold in the customary January and July retail 'sales' should reflect the reduced price

10 [1988] RTR 332.
11 [1987] QB 933 (see above).
12 [1988] 1 All ER 911; see Brown, 'Merchantable Quality and Consumer Expectations' (1988) 104 LQR 520.
13 [1988] 1 All ER 911 at 915.
14 1997 SLT (Sh Ct) 102.
15 1997 SLT (Sh Ct) 102 at 106.

paid unless, of course, the description indicated that the goods were sub-standard (eg 'seconds'). These factors were illustrated in *Rogers v Parish (Scarborough) Ltd*,[16] where Mustill LJ stressed that the sale of a new Range Rover priced at £16,000 'conjure[d] up a particular set of expectations, not the same as those relating to an ordinary saloon car, as to the balance between performance, handling, comfort and resilience. The factor of price was also significant ... the buyer was entitled to value for his money'.[17]

In commercial sales of commodities, grades of quality are infinite and price arguably plays a more significant role in dictating quality than in sales of standardised, consumer goods. However, the fact that B can resell the goods only at less than the contract price does not necessarily mean that they are of unsatisfactory quality, as prices in a fluctuating market may have to be considered and the fact that B may have made a bad bargain and paid too high a contract price for the goods. It was established in *Brown (B S) & Son Ltd v Craiks Ltd*,[18] that the inference that goods are unmerchantable may be justified only if the goods are saleable at *substantially* less than the contract price. In the Australian case of *Beecham (H) & Co Pty Ltd v Francis Howard & Co Pty Ltd*,[19] B informed S that he wanted spruce timber for making pianos and it was B who selected the timber from S's yard. It was subsequently discovered that much of the spruce was infected with dry rot although it had no external signs of this defect. S argued that the timber was merchantable as it could still be used for making boxes but the price of spruce for box manufacture was 30 shillings per hundred feet whereas B had paid 80 shillings per hundred feet. It was held that the timber was unmerchantable as, although it was saleable, no business man who knew its condition would accept it without a large reduction on the market price.

In contrast, in *Harlingdon and Leinster Enterprises Ltd v Christopher Hull Fine Art Ltd*,[20] there was a sale of a painting for £6,000 which turned out to be a forgery with a resale value of £50-£100 but the Court of Appeal held (Stuart-Smith LJ dissenting) that the painting was not unmerchantable as it was still saleable and not unfit for aesthetic appreciation. Underlying the decision was the perception that B relied on his own judgement and took a calculated risk. Although many sales of fine art are speculative, and here both S and B were fine art dealers, S described the painting as by Münter (see earlier) and B paid a price commensurate with an original work of art. It is therefore difficult to see that B accepted a risk that the painting might not be by Münter and it is suggested that the substantial difference between the contract price of the painting and its resale value was a defect which should have rendered it unmerchantable.

Aspects of satisfactory quality in section 14(2B)

The specific aspects of quality in s 14(2B) are probably the most significant part of the new law in that radical changes have been made to the old rules of merchantability. However, the impact of the changes is softened in that the aspects

16   [1987] QB 933.
17   [1987] QB 933 at 944; see also *Shine v General Guarantee Corpn Ltd* [1988] 1 All ER 911 (above).
18   [1970] 1 WLR 752.
19   [1921] VLR 428.
20   [1991] 1 QB 564.

of quality listed apply only 'in appropriate cases' thus introducing immense room for manoeuvre in that these specific aspects are not part of the *definition* of satisfactory quality in s 14(2A). It is arguable that this renders the notion of satisfactory quality too flexible and, although the Law Commissions wanted the new law to be accessible and of practical utility for 'retailers, consumers and their advisers',[1] there is significant uncertainty here. Nevertheless, the main thrust of the law is clear enough. It would, for example, be quite inapt to suggest, as a general rule, that a second-hand car should be free from 'minor defects' but, on the other hand, all the aspects of quality listed in s 14(2B) could appropriately apply to a *new* car. Each part of s 14(2B) must now be considered.

SECTION 14(2B)(a): FITNESS FOR ALL THE PURPOSES FOR WHICH GOODS OF THE KIND IN QUESTION ARE COMMONLY SUPPLIED

As explained above, the fitness for purpose/usability test which received approval in *Henry Kendall & Sons v William Lillico & Sons Ltd*[2] was that a general description of goods would mean that they would normally be used for several different purposes and thus they would be merchantable under that description if they were fit for any one of those purposes, ie in *Kendall*, the groundnut extraction could have been fed safely to cattle and was thus merchantable. The same result was reached in the decision in *Sumner Permain & Co v Webb & Co*,[3] where S, a manufacturer of mineral waters, sold a quantity of 'Webb's Indian Tonic' to B, knowing that B intended to ship it to Argentina. The water contained salicylic acid which made its sale in Argentina illegal although S did not know that fact. When the tonic water arrived in Argentina, it was seized by the authorities and condemned as unfit for human consumption. It was held that the water could have been sold anywhere but in Argentina and it was therefore merchantable – the fact that the goods were unfit for a particular purpose did not render them unmerchantable.[4]

This approach was confirmed in the modern decision in *M/S Aswan Engineering Establishment Co v Lupdine Ltd*,[5] where the plaintiff, B, bought from the defendant, S, a quantity of waterproofing compound in plastic pails for export to Kuwait where B had a construction company. S had bought the pails from their manufacturer, M. The pails were stacked five or six high in shipping containers and, on arrival in Kuwait, the containers were placed on the quayside in full sunshine with the result that the pails melted and the entire consignment was lost. B successfully sued S in contract (any further detail being absent from the reports) and, in turn, S sought damages from the manufacturer of the pails, M, for breach of s 14(2) and (3). The Court of Appeal held that the pails were of merchantable quality as they were fit for most purposes for which they would be used and were unfit only for being stacked five or six high with

---

1 *Sale and Supply of Goods* (Law Com No 160, Scot Law Com No 104, Cm 137, 1987), para 3.22.
2 [1969] 2 AC 31.
3 [1922] 1 KB 55.
4 B also failed on the ground that the goods were unfit for their particular purpose as, having regard to the fact that B had sold the same tonic water with salicylic acid in Argentina for a number of years, there was no evidence of reliance on S's skill and judgement for the assumption that the sale of the water was not prohibited in that country.
5 [1987] 1 WLR 1.

temperatures inside the pails reaching 70°C (the claim for breach of s 14(3) also failed, as it was held that S had not relied on M's skill and judgement in selecting pails for S's purpose). The court considered the earlier authorities in some detail and concluded that the emphasis in the SGA, s 14(6), on goods being 'as fit for the purpose or purposes for which goods of that kind are commonly bought', did not revolutionise the law and require that goods be fit for *all* the purposes for which they were commonly bought.

The Law Commissions[6] recommended that the law be changed so that goods should be fit for all their common purposes, unless S indicated otherwise, and this reform was embodied in s 14(2B)(a) which demands 'fitness for all the purposes for which goods of the kind in question are commonly supplied'. It must be asked, therefore, whether the new formulation would change the law in the decisions above. Clearly much depends on the interpretation given to '*commonly* supplied'. Almost certainly the outcome would be different in *Kendall*, as there the groundnut extraction was commonly supplied as animal feed and therefore it would be unsatisfactory if it poisoned pheasants. It is likely, however, that the decisions would remain the same in *Sumner* and *Aswan* as it is arguable that, in those cases, the goods were not commonly supplied for the purposes to which they were put.

There are certain other difficulties entailed in s 14(2B)(a). First, there is the notion advocated by the Law Commissions[7] that S 'may ensure that the description of the goods excludes any common purpose for which they are unfit, or otherwise indicate that the goods are not fit for all their common purposes'. The overall intent is clear and thus a wrecked car described as sold for spare parts would still be of satisfactory quality if it were unroadworthy. However, it is most unclear what the relation is between such a limited description (description being relevant in fixing the standard of satisfactory quality) and the controls upon the exclusion of liability for breach of s 14(2),[8] and it seems that a conflict is inherent between these two notions.

Second, there is no indication that the purpose for which the goods are unfit need be the one to which B intended to put the goods. A farmer might thus buy animal feed which he feeds to his pheasants *and* which is fit for that purpose but seek to reject it on discovering that his neighbour's cattle have been poisoned by the same product. An unscrupulous buyer might attempt to reject the goods on this basis where the market price has fallen and then seek to buy replacement goods at a cheaper price elsewhere. This difficulty should be circumvented in non-consumer sales by the SGA, s 15(A), which denies the right of business buyers to reject for slight breaches of the implied conditions in the SGA, ss 13-15, but it should be stressed that s 15A does *not* apply to consumer sales.

SECTION 14(2B)(b): APPEARANCE AND FINISH

This requirement confirms the decision in *Rogers v Parish (Scarborough) Ltd,*[9] which was considered earlier and which stressed that a car's outward and interior

---

6 *Sale and Supply of Goods* (Law Com No 160, Scot Law Com No 104, Cm 137, 1987), para 3.36.
7 *Sale and Supply of Goods* (Law Com No 160, Scot Law Com No 104, Cm 137, 1987), para 3.36.
8 See UCTA 1977 ss 6, 12 and 13 and the Unfair Terms in Consumer Contract Regulations 1999 (SI 1999/2083).
9 [1987] QB 933.

appearance was important as an aspect of its quality. It is now clear that goods which are scratched or dented, for example, may be unsatisfactory even though their literal usability and functioning are not impaired.

SECTION 14(2B)(c): FREEDOM FROM MINOR DEFECTS

Under the old law, there was a conflict between the decisions as to whether minor defects could render goods unmerchantable. In *Jackson v Rotax Motor and Cycle Co Ltd*,[10] B paid £450 for a consignment of motor horns but 364 out of a total of 609 delivered were dented and badly polished. The goods were held to be unmerchantable even though they could have been made merchantable at a cost of £35 because, as Kennedy LJ stressed, the definition of merchantable quality does not mean 'something which can be made merchantable'.[11] Other decisions held that goods which could be repaired easily and cheaply were merchantable. In *Millar's of Falkirk v Turpie*,[12] a new car was delivered with an oil leak in the power steering system which was not dangerous and which would have cost £25 to remedy. Consequently, it was held that the car was merchantable. The dilemma inherent in these decisions is an obvious one: if the goods are held to be unmerchantable B can reject them no matter how easily the defects could be remedied but, if they are held to be merchantable, S is not in breach of contract and need not repair the goods or compensate B at all (as in *Turpie*).

Under the SGA, s 14(2B)(c), it is now clear that the *Jackson* approach is the correct one and the Law Commissions[13] emphasised that freedom from minor defects should be a separate requirement from that of appearance and finish, so that it was beyond doubt that minor malfunctions could render a machine, for example, unsatisfactory. Again, it should be remembered that this raised standard is balanced by the SGA, s 15A, which now prevents a non-consumer buyer from unreasonably rejecting goods for a 'slight' breach of the implied conditions in the SGA, ss 13-15.

SECTION 14(2B)(d): SAFETY

Although there was no requirement of safety in the old merchantability provisions, there were cases which stressed that unsafe cars were also unmerchantable.[14] The Law Commissions[15] thought that the requirement of safety should be included

---

10 [1910] 2 KB 937.
11 [1910] 2 KB 937 at 950; see also *Winsley Bros v Woodfield Importing Co* [1929] NZLR 480 (a new machine for planing boards (price £90) which weighed 1 ton was held to be unmerchantable because of a defect which would have cost 7s 6d to repair or £1 to replace the defective part); *IBM Co Ltd v Shcherban* (1925) 1 DLR 864 (a new 'counting scale' (price $294) was held (Haultain CJS dissenting) to be unmerchantable as the glass dial was broken; the cost of replacement was 25 or 30c).
12 1976 SLT (Notes) 66.
13 *Sale and Supply of Goods* (Law Com No 160, Scot Law Com No 104, Cm 137, 1987), para 3.39.
14 *Lee v York Coach and Marine* [1977] RTR 35 (unsafe and unroadworthy second-hand Morris 1100 car was held to be unmerchantable); *Bernstein v Pamson Motors (Golders Green) Ltd* [1987] 2 All ER 220.
15 *Sale and Supply of Goods* (Law Com No 160, Scot Law Com No 104, Cm 137, 1987), paras 3.44-3.46.

in the SGA because safety is such an important part of many consumer goods, eg electrical appliances and cars. It was also considered that a reference to safety would make it clear that hazardous goods, which can be used safely only when unusual precautions are taken, will not be satisfactory if appropriate warning is not given or if they are more hazardous than they should be.

SECTION 14(2B)(e): DURABILITY

As in the case of safety, above, the previous provisions on merchantability did not include a reference to durability but there was probably a requirement that, to be merchantable, the goods had to be reasonably durable.[16] For example, in *Mash & Murrell Ltd v Joseph I Emanuel Ltd*,[17] S, in Cyprus, sold potatoes c & f Liverpool which, although they were sound at the time of loading, were rotten on reaching their destination. It was held that the potatoes were unmerchantable as they should have been loaded in such a state that they could endure the normal journey.[18]

The new provision puts the matter beyond doubt and the Law Commissions[19] recommended that (i) goods should remain durable for a reasonable period of time; and (ii) the durability requirement should bite at the time of *supply*. There is thus considerable latitude in these recommendations and, under (i), a court will be able to consider durability in relation to differing types and grades of goods and whether they have been well or badly treated after the sale. Under (ii), the defect in the goods must have existed at the date of supply. If, for example, goods eventually fail because of a shoddy design and weak components, the goods would not be durable and the cause of the failure would have been present at the date of supply.

The durability provision is long overdue, particularly in relation to consumer goods, but it may well be difficult to distinguish goods with an initial defect from those which have been treated roughly and/or inadequately maintained by B over a considerable period of time. Moreover, if the goods are held to be unmerchantable because they are not durable, the time lapse involved may well mean that B will have lost his right to reject the goods for breach of the implied condition in s 14 and will be limited to a claim in damages.[20]

The recent Scottish decision in *Thain v Anniesland Trade Centre*[1] considered the question of durability within satisfactory quality. B, a consumer buyer, bought from S, for £2,995, a second-hand Renault 19 car which was five years old and had travelled 80,000 miles. After only two weeks, the car developed an intermittent droning noise which was traced to the gearbox and the car's

16　See *Lexmead (Basingstoke) Ltd v Lewis* [1982] AC 225, 276 per Lord Diplock; *Crowther v Shannon Motor Co* [1975] 1 WLR 30.
17　[1961] 1 WLR 862; revsd on other grounds [1962] 1 WLR 16n.
18　See also *Beer v Walker* (1877) 46 LJQB 677 (sale of rabbits sent by rail from London to Brighton.The rabbits were sound when delivered to the railway at 8 pm but 'putrid and valueless' on arrival at Brighton at 9 am the next day. Held there was an implied warranty that the rabbits should be fit for human food after a normal transit *and* should remain fit until B had a reasonable opportunity of dealing with them).
19　*Sale and Supply of Goods* (Law Com No 160, Scot Law Com No 104, Cm 137, 1987), paras 2.14-2.15 and 3.47-3.61.
20　See *Sale and Supply of Goods* (Law Com No 160, Scot Law Com No 104, Cm 137, 1987), paras 5.12-5.13.
1　1997 SLT (Sh Ct) 102.

performance deteriorated so rapidly that it had to be 'put off the road'. Given the value of the car, it was uneconomic to replace the gearbox. The Sheriff Principal held that there was no evidence that the defect was present when the car was sold[2] and, having regard to the age and mileage of the car, durability was not a quality that a reasonable person would have demanded of it. This is absolutely correct but simply because no reasonable person would consider that a car was or was not *durable* after three or four weeks of use. Durability is a factor within s 14(2B) which might be relevant 'in appropriate cases' and it was, obviously, an inappropriate factor to weigh in the balance on the facts of *Thain*. Rather, when the car broke down after two weeks on the road, a reasonable person would say that it was unsatisfactory and unfit for its purpose without reference to the issue of durability. *Thain's* re-assertion of *caveat emptor* should be contrasted with the new EU Directive.[3] Article 5(3) introduces an important new right for consumers in providing that 'unless proved otherwise, any lack of conformity which becomes apparent within six months of delivery of the goods shall be presumed to have existed at the time of delivery unless this presumption is incompatible with the nature of the goods or the nature of the lack of conformity'. When the Directive is implemented, it will, of course, be possible for a court to accentuate the latter proviso in cases of perishable goods, for example, but it should not be possible to do so on the facts of *Thain*.

Other aspects of quality *not* included in section 14(2B)

SUITABILITY FOR IMMEDIATE USE

The Law Commissions[4] canvassed whether there might be a new requirement that goods should be suitable for immediate use but decided that there were so many goods which were quite properly sold as not suitable for immediate use (eg cooking utensils sold with separate handles; avocado pears which take a few days to ripen after purchase) that to include this requirement within the new legislation would be positively misleading. Also, it was considered that suitability for immediate use was part of fitness for purpose under s 14(3).

However, the Law Commissions envisaged that certain goods would have to be suitable for immediate use and emphasised that such suitability would have to be tested against the background of all other relevant matters, eg self-assembly furniture would not fail the test merely because the object had yet to be assembled but it would have to be in a condition in which it *could* be assembled. In fact, it seems that this is the position at common law. In *Grant v Australian Knitting Mills*,[5] S argued that the underpants containing excess sulphites could have been worn safely after they had been washed by B but the court dismissed that argument on the basis that the underpants had to be fit for immediate use.

---

2 The decision in *Crowther v Shannon Motor Co* [1975] 1 WLR 30 was distinguished on the basis that there the defect was present at the date of purchase (sale of an eight year old Jaguar which seized after three weeks' use, the evidence being that it was 'clapped out' eight months before it was supplied to B).
3 Directive 99/44/EC, 25 May 1999, *Certain Aspects of the Sale of Consumer Goods and Associated Guarantees* (considered later in this chapter).
4 *Sale and Supply of Goods* (Law Com No 160, Scot Law Com No 104, Cm 137, 1987), paras 3.62-3.65.
5 [1936] AC 85.

However a different result was reached in *Heil v Hedges.*[6] B bought a quantity of pork and became ill after cooking it only partially and then eating it. The pork was infected with trichinae but it was proven it would have been harmless had it been cooked thoroughly and thus the goods were held to be of merchantable quality. Here both parties contemplated that something would be done to the goods before their use, ie cooking the meat, and thus *Heil's* facts are equatable with the example above of self-assembly furniture.

SPARE PARTS AND SERVICING FACILITIES

Where goods are defective, they may be rendered useless unless they can be repaired or serviced but the Law Commissions[7] stressed that there was no legal obligation on S to maintain stocks of parts or servicing facilities. It was thought that reform of the law was undesirable as the cost involved in maintaining stocks of parts might entail hardship to the small retailer and such costs would be passed on to B. Moreover, revision of the law would be impracticable as it was unclear whether S's obligation might continue even where the manufacturer had gone out of business and difficulties would arise in stipulating the duration of the obligation and the goods and parts to which it might extend.

IS SATISFACTORY QUALITY CONFINED TO EVALUATING THE *PHYSICAL* QUALITIES OF THE GOODS?

There is, strangely, no direct authority on this question. In *Harlingdon and Leinster Enterprises Ltd v Christopher Hull Fine Art Ltd,*[8] considered earlier, the judge in the County Court considered that merchantable quality did not relate to anything beyond the physical qualities of the goods and that physical qualities would not include the fact that a painting was executed by a particular artist. In the Court of Appeal, Nourse LJ[9] preferred to express no opinion on the point but Stuart-Smith LJ[10] saw no necessity to confine s 14(2) to physical defects. In *Harlingdon,* counsel for S argued that the Scottish decision in *Buchanan-Jardine v Hamilink*[11] established that merchantable quality applied to physical qualities only and, while Nourse LJ thought that *Buchanan* did not support that conclusion, there are certainly statements by Lord Cameron[12] in the decision which appear to limit s 14(2) in this way.

Goode[13] asserts that merchantable quality was not confined to physical qualities and, citing *Niblett Ltd v Confectioners' Materials Co Ltd,*[14] argues that merchantability encompassed any legal impediment which might prevent the

6   [1951] 1 TLR 512.
7   *Sale and Supply of Goods* (Law Com No 160, Scot Law Com No 104, Cm 137, 1987), para 3.66.
8   [1991] 1 QB 564.
9   [1991] 1 QB 564 at 577.
10   [1991] 1 QB 564 at 582.
11   1983 SLT 149.
12   1983 SLT 149 at 153-154: '... merchantable quality relates to the physical quality of the goods themselves and not to external circumstances which might affect their saleability'.
13   *Commercial Law* (2nd edn, 1995), p 326.
14   [1921] 3 KB 387.

goods being used or resold, for example. In *Niblett*, S sold tins of condensed milk under the brand name 'Nissly' and, as the labels bearing this name infringed the Nestlé trade mark, the tins of milk were seized by the Customs and Excise authorities. B had to remove the labels and sold the goods at a loss. Although Bankes and Atkin LJJ held that the goods were unmerchantable, the basis of their decision was that the SGA 1893, s 62(1) defined the 'quality of goods' as including their 'state or condition' and thus the labels were part of the goods. It is arguable that the labels were physically defective and the decision does not appear to be authority for any extension of merchantability to non-physical defects. Moreover, Scrutton LJ's emphatic opinion was that merchantability 'does not touch the title to the goods or the right to sell them'.[15]

Although there are difficulties in defining the boundaries of non-physical defects, it is surely time to recognise that satisfactory quality should encompass qualities other than those which relate purely to physical matters. In *Harlingdon*, it must certainly have been cold-comfort to inform B that the fact that he had paid £6,000 for a forgery 'did not make the painting unfit for aesthetic appreciation [as] it could still have been hung on a wall somewhere and been enjoyed for what it was'.[16]

INSTRUCTIONS, NOTICES AND WARNINGS

Although there is no express reference in s 14(2B) to instructions and warnings supplied with the goods, it is clear that goods sold without any (or with inadequate) instructions/warnings could be unsatisfactory[17] as instructions could be (i) regarded as 'goods supplied' under s 14(2) (ii) within s 14(2B) where 'the quality of goods includes their state and condition', or (iii) where no instructions or defective instructions are supplied the goods may be unsafe under s 14(2B)(d).

The time at which the condition of satisfactory quality must be satisfied

It is not entirely clear exactly when the goods must be of satisfactory quality as some cases on merchantability refer to the time of the passing of property[18] and others to the moment of delivery[19] as being the decisive time. The Law Commissions[20] considered that delivery was the crucial time and this accords

---

15 [1921] 3 KB 387 at 398.
16 [1991] 1 QB 564, 576 per Nourse LJ.
17 This was the view of the Law Commissions, see *Sale and Supply of Goods* (Law Com No 160, Scot Law Com No 104, Cm 137, 1987), para 3.64, fn 52; see also the earlier consultative document (*Sale and Supply of Goods* (Law Com WP No 85, Scottish Law Com Consultative Mem No 58, 1983), para 4.16) where it was suggested that a 'complex self-assembly kit' would be unmerchantable without adequate instructions.
18 *Kemp (A B) Ltd v Tolland* [1956] 2 Lloyd's Rep 681; *Crowther v Shannon Motor Co* [1975] 1 WLR 30.
19 *Jackson v Rotax Motor and Cycle Co* [1910] 2 KB 937; *Henry Kendall & Sons v William Lillico & Sons Ltd* [1969] 2 AC 31; *Lexmead (Basingstoke) Ltd v Lewis* [1982] AC 225.
20 *Sale and Supply of Goods* (Law Com No 160, Scot Law Com No 104, Cm 137, 1987), para 2.14.

with the new requirement of durability in s 14(2B)(e). However, a rule demanding satisfactory quality at the time of delivery would have to be subject to an exception in cases where the property and risk had passed to B but the goods were damaged without the fault of S before delivery.

LATENT DEFECTS AND STRICT LIABILITY OF THE SELLER

It is clear that the duty of S to supply satisfactory goods is strict and it is no defence that he exercised all possible care or that he had not seen or examined the goods before sale. In *Grant v Australian Knitting Mills Ltd*,[1] for example, the underpants containing excess sulphites were unmerchantable even though S could not discover the defect by any reasonable examination because, as Lord Wright[2] stressed, negligence was not relevant to S's liability. This may seem harsh at first glance but, in terms of risk-allocation, the imposition of strict liability on the business seller is not unreasonable. Moreover, if S's liability were to be premised on fault, B would often be deprived of a remedy, as a retailer would normally have the defence that he relied on the manufacturer of the goods to provide goods which were sound.

The state of knowledge of the reasonable person when satisfactory quality is evaluated

When goods are defective and an evaluation is made regarding the possibility of their being of satisfactory quality, the test is whether a reasonable person would consider that the goods reach a standard which is satisfactory. However, problems can arise in fixing the extent of the hypothetical reasonable person's knowledge and the time at which such knowledge is examined. It has long been clear, for example, that where goods have latent defects, S could not argue successfully that the goods *appeared* to be sound and were therefore merchantable – rather, as Dixon J emphasised,[3] the court must impute to the hypothetical buyer a knowledge of the defects and then ask whether, under the contract description and price, the goods would be saleable with those defects. The position regarding latent defects is the same under the new provisions except, as explained earlier, the reasonable *person* is substituted for the buyer. As the Law Commissions stressed,[4] the test involves 'an objective comparison of the state of the goods with *the standard* which a reasonable person would find acceptable. This is intended to require a full comparison of the goods with the standard, not merely a comparison limited to what was visible at the time of sale'.

In the bulk of cases this test should pose no problems but complications arose in *Henry Kendall & Sons v William Lillico & Sons Ltd*.[5] Applying the above

---

1   [1936] AC 85.
2   [1936] AC 85 at 100.
3   *Australian Knitting Mills Ltd v Grant* (1933) 50 CLR 387, 418: on appeal, this test was approved by the House of Lords ([1936] AC 85).
4   *Sale and Supply of Goods* (Law Com No 160, Scot Law Com No 104, Cm 137, 1987), para 3.25.
5   [1969] 2 AC 31.

test to *Kendall's* facts, if the defects had been known at the time of the sale, the goods would have been regarded as poisonous and unsaleable, but *subsequently* it was discovered that limited quantities of the groundnut extraction could be fed safely to cattle. In judging merchantability at the time of sale, the question was thus whether the goods which would have been regarded as unmerchantable, should be regarded as merchantable in the light of the new knowledge available at the time of the trial. The majority in the House of Lords considered that, as after-acquired knowledge of defects was admitted to show that goods were unmerchantable, it would be 'very artificial'[6] to exclude such knowledge which would establish that the goods were merchantable. Lord Pearce and Lord Wilberforce did not subscribe to this view. Lord Pearce[7] explained that, in assessing merchantability, one must assume a knowledge of latent defects and, whilst logic appeared to dictate that all after-acquired knowledge should be admitted, this could not always be the position:

> 'For one is trying to find what market the goods would have had if their subsequently ascertained condition had been known. As it is a hypothetical exercise, one must create a hypothetical market. Nevertheless the hypothetical market should be one that could have existed, not one which could *not* have existed at the date of delivery. Suppose goods contained a hidden deadly poison to which there was discovered by scientists two years after delivery a simple, easy, inexpensive antidote which could render the goods harmless. They would be unmarketable at the date of delivery if the existence of the poison was brought to light, since no purchaser could then have known the antidote to the poison'.[8]

It is respectfully suggested that this incisive reasoning cannot be faulted. It would be unfair to expose B to an action in damages for having originally rejected unsatisfactory goods which later turn out to be satisfactory because of a breakthrough in knowledge. Moreover, the reasoning should also be applicable to the converse situation where goods were thought to be perfectly harmless at the time of delivery but which scientific research subsequently reveals to be toxic, eg goods containing lead or asbestos, neither substance originally being considered as harmful but both having been subsequently proved to be pernicious. It is surely indisputable that after-acquired knowledge should always be disregarded[9] for, otherwise, S and B are unable to ascertain the legal position at the date of delivery of the goods and, if the majority's view in *Kendall* were adopted today, it would clearly detract from the new provision relating to the safety of the goods in s 14(2B)(d).

The exceptions to section 14(2) contained in section 14(2C)

Section 14(2C) specifies that the condition of satisfactory quality will not apply in certain circumstances which must now be considered.

---

6 [1969] 2 AC 31 at 75, per Lord Reid. Lord Guest thought that to exclude such later knowledge would be 'to approach the true situation with blinkers' (p 109).
7 [1969] 2 AC 31 at 118-119.
8 [1969] 2 AC 31 at 118-119.
9 See Henderson, 'Of Merchantable Quality' (1970) 86 LQR 167; Goode, *Commercial Law* (2nd edn, 1995), pp 328-331.

DEFECTS SPECIFICALLY DRAWN TO THE BUYER'S ATTENTION BEFORE
THE CONTRACT IS MADE

Section 14(2C)(a) provides that the implied condition of satisfactory quality 'does
not extend to any matter making the quality of goods unsatisfactory – (a) which
is specifically drawn to the buyer's attention before the contract is made'.

This proviso was introduced by the Supply of Goods (Implied Terms) Act 1973
but, surprisingly, there is no authority relating to it. The difficulties of the proviso
can be categorised. First, the wording introduced in 1973 applied to 'defects'
specifically drawn to B's attention but it is noticeable that new section is broader
in its reference to 'any matter' which is specifically drawn to B's attention. It is
arguable that the 1973 wording might have applied only to defects in the goods
themselves but there is now no such restriction and S may exclude his liability
under s 14(2) by pointing to matters extraneous to the goods.

Second, in demanding that defects are *specifically* drawn to B's attention, the
wording is explicit and indicates that an equivocal, general reference to defects in
the goods would not exempt S. However, even if a defect is specifically pointed
out to B, it remains doubtful how much detail regarding it and its possible
consequences should be made known. It is regrettable that the Law Commissions[10]
rejected the proposal that S should provide written notice of the defects.

Third, there is no requirement that S must draw B's attention to any matter
making the quality of the goods unsatisfactory and so it appears that anyone
may point out defects to B. It does seem, however, that the defects must be *drawn*
to B's attention and this would seem to exclude knowledge of defects culled from
B's own observations (although this situation would be within s 14(2C)(b), below).

Fourth, any defects must be specifically drawn to B's attention *before* the
contract is made and it would thus be too late simply to include a written statement
of defects in the contract itself.

Finally, the burden would appear to be on S to prove facts which would bring
him within the ambit of the exception in s 14(2C)(a).

EXAMINATION OF THE GOODS BY THE BUYER BEFORE THE CONTRACT
IS MADE

Section 14(2C)(b) provides that the implied condition of satisfactory quality 'does
not extend to any matter making the quality of goods unsatisfactory – (b) where
the buyer examines the goods before the contract is made, which that examination
ought to reveal'.

Prior to the SGA 1893, the position at common law was that B could not claim
that the goods were unmerchantable when he could have examined them but
did not take the opportunity, this situation being a paradigm of *caveat emptor*.[11]
The 1893 Act introduced a proviso that B could not complain of defects when
he had *actually examined* the goods and 'such examination' ought to have
revealed the defects. However, the decision in *Thornett and Fehr v Beers & Son*[12]

---

10   *Exemption Clauses in Contracts. First Report: Amendments to the Sale of Goods Act 1893*
     (Law Com No 24, Scot Law Com No 12, 1969), para 50.
11   See *Jones v Just* (1868) LR 3 QB 197, 202 per Mellor J; *Thornett & Fehr v Beers & Son*
     [1919] 1 KB 486, 489 per Bray J.
12   [1919] 1 KB 486.

did much to restore the common law rule as it was held that the proviso applied where, being pressed for time, B made only a cursory examination of the outside of barrels which contained 35 tons of glue. If B had looked inside the barrels he would have discovered the defects in the glue and every facility for such an examination had been provided by S. This latter point seemed a crucial one in the decision[13] and Bray J clearly thought that a full examination could and should have been made by B and that, in its absence, B accepted the risk of the (low-priced) goods being sub-standard. The decision is criticisable, however, as being overly influenced by the earlier common law and the proviso did refer to 'such examination,' meaning the actual examination which B undertook. As there was no evidence in *Thornett* that the defects ought to have been revealed by that examination, it seems that the proviso should not have applied.

The examination provision was amended by the Supply of Goods (Implied Terms) Act 1973 to include the words 'that examination' and this phrase remains in s 14(2C)(b) meaning that the *Thornett* decision is unlikely to be repeated.[14] It follows that, should B make the time-honoured inspection of a car by walking around it and kicking its tyres, he should still be able to complain of any defects in the engine as the cursory examinaton undertaken, ie 'that examination', would not reveal a defective engine. An example of a defect which could not be discovered on examination was the arsenic in beer sold in a public house.[15]

The upshot of the examination proviso is that B is better off if he does not examine the goods at all, a point which is forcefully accentuated by the facts of *R & B Customs Brokers Co Ltd v United Dominions Trust Ltd*.[16] There B bought a car on conditional sale and took delivery of it some six weeks before the contract was completed, during which period B noticed that the car's roof leaked. S tried to cure the leak but without success and eventually B sought to reject the car on the basis that it was both unmerchantable and unfit for its purpose. At first instance, the judge held that B could not rely on the implied condition of merchantability as he had notice of the defect before the contract was completed. The Court of Appeal held that the car was unfit for its purpose but expressed the view that, if the judge's view of the law were correct, the examination proviso was 'something of a trap for a purchaser'.[17] However, Neill LJ was not persuaded that the condition of merchantability was excluded 'if at the time the contract is made the buyer is reasonably of the opinion that the defect can be, and will be, rectified quite easily at no cost to himself'.[18] Although the 1994 Act makes changes to the rules on acceptance of the goods under the SGA, s 35, so that B is not

---

13 Moreover, it appeared that S did not realise that B had failed to avail himself of a full examination (the barrels were stored at a warehouse and S and B managed to miss each other on the day arranged for the examination) and, before the contract was concluded, B said that he had inspected the goods.

14 *Thornett* appears to be inconsistent with the earlier decision of the Court of Appeal in *Bristol Tramways etc, Carriage Co Ltd v Fiat Motors Ltd* [1910] 2 KB 831, where B bought a Fiat omnibus, having inspected it, which turned out to be unsuitable for heavy work in the hilly Bristol district. The bus was held to be unmerchantable. Cozens-Hardy MR said: 'I see no reason to doubt the finding of the learned judge that the slight inspection by the ... plaintiffs of one of the complete omnibuses was not of such a nature as sufficed to disclose the defects' (p 837). See also, to the same effect *Frank v Grosvenor Motor Auctions Pty Ltd* [1960] VR 607.

15 *Wren v Holt* [1903] 1 KB 610.

16 [1988] 1 WLR 321.

17 [1988] 1 WLR 321 at 326, per Dillon LJ.

18 [1988] 1 WLR 321 at 333.

deemed to accept the goods where he asks for or agrees to their repair,[19] the problem encountered in *R & B Customs* has not been confronted.

It would seem that, by virtue of common law principles, B may expressly and voluntarily waive his right to an examination and it is arguable that waiver was the correct basis of the decision in *Thornett*. Similarly, Bray J tentatively suggested in *Thornett*,[20] that B could be estopped from saying that he did not examine the goods (B told S that he had made an inspection) but the point was left open.

Finally, the burden would appear to be on S to prove facts which bring him within the examination proviso.

19 See the SGA 1979, s 35(6).
20 [1919] 1 KB 486, 489.

CHAPTER 21

The duties of the seller relating to fitness for purpose of the goods and sales by sample

The previous chapter considered the seller's duties regarding the description and quality of the goods supplied and it remains to examine the duties of the seller relating to the fitness for purpose of the goods and, also, those concerned with sales by sample. The reform of the law is considered at the end of the chapter.

Section 14(3): goods must be fit for their purpose

The SGA 1979, s 14(3) provides:

> 'Where the seller sells goods in the course of a business and the buyer, expressly or by implication, makes known–
> (a) to the seller, or
> (b) where the purchase price or part of it is payable by instalments and the goods were previously sold by a credit-broker[1] to the seller, to that credit broker,
> any particular purpose for which the goods are being bought, there is an implied term[2] that the goods supplied under the contract are reasonably fit for that purpose, whether or not that is a purpose for which such goods are commonly supplied, except where the circumstances show that the buyer does not rely, or that it is unreasonable for him to rely, on the skill or judgment of the seller or credit-broker.'

There are several features of s 14(3) which are shared with s 14(2) and need be reiterated only briefly as they were considered earlier in detail: (i) under s 14(3), S must sell 'in the course of a business'; (ii) s 14(5) (sale through a business agent) applies to s 14(3); and (iii) s 14(3) extends to 'goods supplied under the contract'.

---

1 The reference to the 'credit-broker' was introduced by the Consumer Credit Act 1974. The SGA, s 14(3)(b) relates to credit-brokers who introduce B to a finance house when B wants to obtain credit. B will thus acquire the goods on conditional sale or credit-sale, ie a dealer (the credit-broker) sells goods to a finance house which then enters into a contract of conditional sale or credit-sale with B, allowing him credit terms. Here the seller/finance house is liable under s 14(3) even though the particular purpose/reliance was made known only to the dealer/credit broker. 'Credit-broker' is defined in the SGA, s 61(1) as a person acting in the course of a business of credit-brokerage carried on by him and 'effecting introductions of *individuals* desiring to obtain credit'. This cannot apply to corporations who must make the purpose known to the finance house (see also the Consumer Credit Act 1974, s 189(1), which excludes corporations from its definition of 'individual').
2 The SGA, s 14(6) provides that, as regards England, Wales and Northern Ireland, the term implied by s 14(3) is a *condition* (the new s 14 (6) was substituted by the Sale and Supply of Goods Act 1994, s 7, Sch 2, para 5(5)(b)).

A consideration of the situations which could potentially fall within s 14(3) may help to clarify both the ambit and operation of the section. First, B might consult an expert manufacturer/seller in order to buy goods which are fitted to his particular purpose in the sense of its being an unusual purpose. Long negotiations may precede the contract which refers expressly to the purpose to which the goods are to be put. Second, B might buy a quantity of animal feed from S, S's state of knowledge being that B is a farmer with livestock. Third, B might ask for and buy a pair of underpants from a large retail, department store. The first situation is arguably paradigmatic of s 14(3), the second situation was drawn within the ambit of the section and, although it was unlikely that s 14(3) was ever intended to apply to the example of the retail sale of underpants, it is indisputable that it is also a sale where the law considers that B makes his particular purpose known to S. In short, the scope of s 14(3) has been widened by the decisions not least because buyers originally chose to sue under this section rather than opting for the more hazardous course of establishing that their purchases were 'unmerchantable'. The particular aspects of s 14(3) must now be considered.

The buyer, expressly or by implication, makes known to the seller any particular purpose for which the goods are being bought

A SPECIALISED PURPOSE

The most obvious situation for the application of s 14(3) is where B wants to buy goods for a *special* or *unusual* purpose and, if so, it is clear that such a purpose must be communicated by B to S, or through their agents. Indeed, the essence of s 14(3) is that, if B has a recondite purpose in mind for the goods, he must be explicit in communicating that purpose to S. There will, of course, always be argument as to whether or not B's purpose is sufficiently unusual to demand that S be *notified* of it expressly or, alternatively, whether S might be regarded as possessing sufficient *knowledge* of B's purpose.

In *Hamilton v Papakura District Council*,[3] B grew tomatoes using the hydroponic method where plants are grown without soil entirely in water, and the defendant council, S, distributed the water supply. S 'knew at the relevant time that its town water supply was used for protected crop growing including the use of soil-less techniques, knew growers preferred that water to bore water because of its high quality and knew that the catchment area was vulnerable to contamination from (inter alia) pesticides'.[4] However, B had never contacted S expressly to discuss any special needs. B's tomatoes showed signs of damage which he attributed to toxic residues of herbicides in the water supplied and, conspicuously, the tomatoes of other growers in the area were similarly affected. The New Zealand Court of Appeal held that B had neither expressly nor by implication made known to S the particular purpose for which the water was required and thus the conditions for invoking the statutory warranty[5] of fitness

---

3   [2000] 1 NZLR 265.
4   [2000] 1 NZLR 265 at 277, per Gault J.
5   The New Zealand Sale of Goods Act 1908, s 16(a).

for purpose had not been fulfilled. Gault J held that 'it is readily to be inferred from the underlying policy of the statutory provision that the communication must be in the general context of the contract to purchase so that seller can elect not to supply or to expressly disclaim responsibility ... general knowledge of horticultural activities in the district acquired in unrelated circumstances was insufficient to amount to the buyers making known by implication the particular purpose for which they required the water they were buying'.[6] This decision thus rests squarely on the fact that B's purpose was unusual in that he grew 'sensitive crops'[7] and 'the special needs purpose of soil-less cherry tomato growing'[8] had not been communicted to S in *any* way.[9]

It is suggested that *Papakura* is an overly-restrictive decision. S was aware that it supplied water to B for horticultural purposes and, as will be seen later in this chapter, the decisions confirm that, provided the buyer's overall purpose is known to the seller, the buyer need not particularise the sub-purposes to which he intends to put the goods. It is arguable, therefore, that because S knew he was supplying water for horticultural purposes, he should have foreseen that the water would be used to grow tomatoes hydroponically.[10] The *Papakura* decision is representative of a group of modern cases which have taken a narrow view of the implied condition of fitness for purpose[11] and which arguably portend a regressive move in the direction of *caveat emptor*.[12]

A PARTICULAR PURPOSE

Where B wishes to use the goods for a particular, as opposed to an obscure or unusual purpose, the law construes the requirement of communication of purpose liberally in B's favour. If the parties have a written contract, it is obviously prudent to specify expressly in the contract itself the particular purpose for which the goods are required. However, even in specialised, commercial contracts, the decisions indicate that this degree of precision is unnecessary where B's purpose is self-evident from the *nature* of the contract. In such a case, B's purpose is made known under s 14(3) 'by implication'. In *Cammell Laird & Co Ltd v Manganese Bronze and Brass Co Ltd*,[13] for example, the House of Lords held that there was a sufficient indication of a particular purpose when B, a shipbuilder, ordered two propellers to be made by S for specific vessels which were being built by B. Lord Wright[14] considered that S 'either knew all that was material to them as propeller makers to know about the vessel and her engines

---

6 [2000] 1 NZLR 265 at 278.
7 [2000] 1 NZLR 265 at 277.
8 [2000] 1 NZLR 265 at 279.
9 See also *Cominco Ltd v Westinghouse Canada Ltd* (1981) 127 DLR (3d) 544 (B bought electrical cable from S which was suitable for use in single strands but there was a fire risk if it was laid in proximity to other cable. Held that B did not inform S of the precise location of the cable in the 'electrical switchroom' but that, if B had thus informed S,'one might imply that [S] should have known other electrical cable would be laid in close proximity to whatever was supplied by it as a seller' (p 561, per Bouck J).
10 See *Ashington Piggeries Ltd v Christopher Hill Ltd* [1972] AC 441, considered below.
11 See also *M/S Aswan Engineering Establishment Co v Lupdine Ltd* [1987] 1 WLR 1; *Slater v Finning Ltd* [1997] AC 473, considered below.
12 See Brown, 'The Swing of the Pendulum from Caveat Venditor to Caveat Emptor' (2000) 116 LQR 537.
13 [1934] AC 402.
14 [1934] AC 402 at 422.

or could have ascertained by enquiry. There is here no need to look beyond the actual terms of the contract to find the particular purpose'.

Moreover, B's purpose may be evident from extrinsic communications, as it was in *Bristol Tramways, etc, Carriage Co Ltd v Fiat Motors Ltd*.[15] There a written contract between S and B for the sale of Fiat buses did not mention the particular purpose for which the buses were required (passenger service in the hilly, Bristol district) but the court found that S was fully aware of B's particular purpose from the negotiations and circumstances surrounding the contract. Likewise, in the leading decision in *Manchester Liners Ltd v Rea Ltd*,[16] B bought 500 tons of coal from S for a particular, named steamship, *Manchester Importer*, which turned out to be unsuitable for the vessel and she had to return to port. The House of Lords held that B had sufficiently communicated the purpose to S in informing him of the particular ship for which the coal was required. Lord Atkinson[17] said:

'It is by no means necessary at common law that the buyer at the time he contracts or proposes to buy should state the purpose for which he requires the goods. If the seller knows from past transactions with the buyer or otherwise what is the purpose for which the buyer requires the goods, it will equally be implied that the seller warrants them to be reasonably fit for that purpose'.

It is thus manifest that, overall, the courts do not demand that B must inform S precisely of his particular requirements. Rather, if the particular purpose is known to S or is apparent from the circumstances, the communication of the purpose will be implied.

The ambit of s 14(3) was broadened considerably, however, when it was recognised that a 'particular' purpose might be nothing more than a *specified* or *stated*[18] purpose. This meant that, where the description of the goods could indicate one purpose only, no further details were required and the goods would have to be fit for that one purpose. It was emphasised earlier, when the notion of merchantability was considered, that many buyers alleged that goods were unfit for their purpose because there were initial doubts as to the meaning and scope of 'merchantability' in 1893, the date of the original Sale of Goods Act. This led to a widening of the meaning of 'particular purpose' but it is also crucial to stress that, at the start of the 20th century, the law was faced with consumer buyers of goods who claimed that goods bought for private use or consumption were unfit for their purpose. Where a consumer buys such goods, there is usually only one purpose to which they can be put and, of course, this became abundantly obvious from the proliferation of mass-produced consumer goods later in the 20th century, eg washing machines and refrigerators.

One of the first and most important decisions to confront this issue was *Preist v Last*.[19] B, a draper, went into a retail chemist's shop and asked for 'a hot-

---

15   [1910] 2 KB 831; see also *Gillespie Bros & Co v Cheney, Eggar & Co* [1896] 2 QB 59 (S liable on a sale of coal for bunkering steamships; the purpose was specified in a letter to S, not in the written contract).

16   [1922] 2 AC 74.

17   [1922] 2 AC 74 at 84; see also *Ashington Piggeries Ltd v Christopher Hill Ltd* [1972] AC 441, 477 per Lord Guest: 'The knowledge of the seller need not be expressly communicated: it may be by implication, as the section provides. If the seller knows the purpose for which the buyer requires the goods, then no express intimation by the buyer is necessary'.

18   See *Henry Kendall & Sons v William Lillico & Sons Ltd* [1969] 2 AC 31, 123 per Lord Wilberforce: '... "particular" ... is not used in contrast to "general" or so as to require a quantum of particularity, but more in the sense of "specified" or "stated"'.

19   [1903] 2 KB 148.

water bottle'. B bought the bottle which, several days later, burst in use. Undoubtedly B was anxious to avoid the difficulty of whether this could be a sale 'by description' in the merchantable quality provision of the SGA 1893 and thus he argued that the bottle was unfit for its purpose. Somewhat unrealistically, counsel for S argued that hot-water bottles were used for many purposes and simply to order one by name was not a distinct communication of the particular purpose for which the article was purchased. The court held that the bottle was unfit for its purpose of warming B in bed and Collins MR rejected the argument that the goods were required only for their ordinary purpose. He emphasised that 'where ... the description of the goods ... points to one particular purpose only, it seems to me that the first requirement of the sub-section is satisfied, namely, that the particular purpose for which the goods are required should be made known to the seller'.[20]

The realistic *Preist v Last* approach was followed in several seminal decisions. In *Grant v Australian Knitting Mills Ltd*,[1] woollen underpants bought in a retail shop contained excess, irritating sulphites and B contracted severe dermatitis from which he almost died. The goods were held to be unfit for their purpose. Lord Wright[2] stressed that 'there is no need to specify in terms the particular purpose for which the buyer requires the goods, which is none the less the particular purpose within the meaning of the section, because it is the only purpose for which any one would ordinarily want the goods. In this case the garments were naturally intended, and only intended, to be worn next the skin'.[3]

After these momentous cases, the original function of the particular purpose provision had become fundamentally transformed so that it came to perform much of the role of merchantability. Moreover, the effect of the decisions is confirmed by the wording of the current s 14(3) which specifies that goods must be reasonably fit for their purpose 'whether or not that is a purpose for which such goods are commonly supplied'.

TO WHAT EXTENT CAN A GENERALISED PURPOSE BE A PARTICULAR PURPOSE?

Although *Preist v Last* extended the concept of particular purpose to cover a specified or known *single* purpose, the extent to which a *general* purpose could be drawn within the particular purpose provisions was unclear for a long time. To put the matter another way, might a general purpose which is communicted to S ever be construed as sufficiently particular to fall within s 14(3)? The decisions establish that B may communicate his overall purpose in sufficiently clear and general terms without any need to particularise the sub-purposes to which he intends to put the goods. Indeed, this approach seems to be a logical continuation of the diminution of the particular purpose notion which commenced

---

20 See also *Wallis v Russell* [1902] 2 IR 585 where the Irish Court of Appeal gave the same interpretation to 'particular purpose' where B bought 'two nice fresh crabs for tea'. The crabs poisoned B and were held to be unfit for their purpose. For an amusing insight on *Wallis*, see Healy, *The Old Munster Circuit* (3rd imp, 1948), pp 198-200.
1 [1936] AC 85.
2 [1936] AC 85 at 99.
3 See also *Frost v Aylesbury Dairy Co Ltd* [1905] 1 KB 608, 613-614 per Collins MR (milk sold to B for drinking and which contained typhoid germs was held to be unfit for its purpose); *Godley v Perry* [1960] 1 WLR 9 (a plastic catapult, bought in a retail shop, was held to be unfit for its purpose when it snapped in use and B lost an eye).

with *Preist v Last*. In *Henry Kendall & Sons v William Lillico & Sons Ltd*,[4] the importers of Brazilian groundnut extraction sold it to the wholesalers knowing that it was to be resold by the wholesalers to animal foodstuff compounders who would make it into cattle and poultry food. The wholesalers sold it to the food compounders knowing that it was to be compounded into poultry food. The food compounders sold the food to game farmers who fed it to their pheasants which were poisoned as a result. In the two sales which were the subject of the litigation viz, (i) the importer's sale to the wholesaler; and (ii) the wholesaler's sale to the food compounder, it was held that the buyers had communicated a sufficiently particular purpose and it was unnecessary for them to specify the precise type of animal to which the substance was to be fed. Lord Morris of Borth-y-Gest said that 'a communicated purpose, if stated with reasonably sufficient precision, will be a particular purpose'[5] and Lord Pearce considered that 'a particular purpose means a given purpose, known or communicated. It is not necessarily a narrow or closely particularized purpose'.[6]

This approach was followed and widened by the House of Lords in *Ashington Piggeries Ltd v Christopher Hill Ltd*.[7] Norwegian suppliers of herring meal sold a quantity of it to a compounder of animal foodstuffs who, in turn, sold food containing it to the mink breeders whose mink were poisoned as a consequence of eating the food. The food compounder knew that the food was for mink and so was liable to the mink breeders on the basis that it was unfit for its purpose. However, the Norwegian seller was also liable to the food compounder for breach of the condition of fitness even though the Norwegian seller knew only that the herring meal was required for *animal food* and did not know its particular sub-purpose as food for mink. Lord Wilberforce[8] emphasised that this purpose as animal foodstuff was wider than that made known in *Kendall* but it was, nevertheless, a sufficiently particularised purpose.[9]

It is suggested that the *Kendall* and *Ashington* decisions must not be seen as imposing too great a liability on S. First, the sub-purposes of feeding the specific animals in question were reasonably foreseeable sub-purposes within the more generalised purpose. Consequently, it was stressed in *Ashington* that the Norwegian seller 'should have realised that if the purpose of the purchase was to feed the meal to animals, it might be fed to mink'.[10] Herring meal can be used as a fertilizer as well as for food and it seems implicit in *Ashington* that if the Norwegian seller had not known whether it was required for food or fertilizer, it would have been impossible to imply the condition of fitness for purpose, for then the seller could not have contemplated that the meal would be used as food, let alone food for mink.[11]

---

4 [1969] 2 AC 31.
5 [1969] 2 AC 31 at 93.
6 [1969] 2 AC 31 at 114.
7 [1972] AC 441.
8 [1972] AC 441 at 496-497.
9 Cf *Hamilton v Papakura District Council* [2000] 1 NZLR 265, considered earlier. There S's 'general knowledge of horticultural activities in the district' acquired in circumstances which the court considered to be unrelated to the contract, was insufficient for B to invoke the statutory implied term relating to fitness for purpose.
10 [1972] AC 441 at 488, per Viscount Dilhorne; see also Lord Guest (p 477-478) and Lord Wilberforce (pp 496-498).
11 Lord Diplock dissented in *Ashington* on the basis that the acceptance of a notion of implied, general purpose meant that S had to supply goods for a purpose to which B *might* (or might not) want to put them. He thought that this was contrary to the essence of the particular purpose notion which involved a combination of B's reliance on S's expertise

Second, there is a difference between a generalised purpose communicated by B to S and B's imprecise statements which could not be classified as a communication of a purpose by even the most charitable observer. In the latter case, a court could state either that s 14(3) was simply not relevant[12] or that the proviso to s 14(3) was applicable, meaning that B could not be said to rely, or that it would be unreasonable for him to rely, on the skill or judgement of S. This issue was relevant in *M/S Aswan Engineering Establishment Co v Lupdine Ltd*.[13] There Lupdine sold waterproofing compound in plastic pails to the Aswan company in Kuwait. Lupdine (B) had bought the pails from the manufacturers (S) and S knew that the pails were wanted for export but not that they were for export to the Gulf. The pails melted in the extreme heat on the quayside in Kuwait but, nevertheless, they were held to be reasonably fit for use as heavy duty pails in export shipment and S was not liable for breach of s 14(3). Lloyd LJ[14] endorsed the observations in *Kendall*[15] and *Ashington*[16] that the wider the designation of purpose by B, the greater the dilution of S's responsibility. He thus considered that, on the facts of *Aswan*, 'the purpose could hardly be wider ... indeed, so wide is the purpose that it could be said that the pails need be little, if anything, more than merchantable'.[17] It is difficult to see, however, that the purpose of 'pails for export' was any wider than the purpose of 'food for animals' in *Ashington* and, consequently, it is suggested that the *Aswan* decision is unduly limiting.

The notion of the generalised, particular purpose meant that the condition of fitness for purpose performed much of the role which would have been better suited to merchantable quality. Under the SGA, s 14(2B)(a), satisfactory quality now encompasses 'fitness for all the purposes for which goods of the kind in question are commonly supplied' and it thus seems that fitness for purpose under s 14(3) need now cover only those situations where B communicates a particular, *uncommon* purpose to S. It remains to be seen how the courts will view this issue.

PARTICULAR PURPOSE WHERE THE BUYER HAS ABNORMAL OR IDIOSYNCRATIC NEEDS

The general rule where B is classifiable as an 'abnormal' buyer is straightforward: B must communicate his abnormality to S for, otherwise, S cannot use skill and

---

and S's ability to exercise that expertise. He thus would not have applied the condition of fitness for a particular purpose in *either* sale (Norwegian seller to Hill; Hill to Ashington Piggeries). In the first sale, he thought it was vital that the Norwegian sellers did not know the food was for *mink* and, in the second, he considered that Ashington Piggeries' provision of their *own* formula for the food meant that they did not rely on Hill's skill or judgement (although he reluctantly acceded to the majority view that there was sufficient reliance in the second sale (see later)). Lord Diplock considered that the 'swing of the pendulum ... from caveat emptor to caveat venditor has now gone far enough' (pp 508-509) and he was, consequently, in favour of arresting it.

12 See Lord Reid's statements in *Henry Kendall & Sons v William Lillico & Sons Ltd* [1969] 2 AC 31, 80, that the purpose must be stated 'with sufficient particularity to enable the seller to exercise his skill or judgment in making or selecting appropriate goods'. See also *Hamilton v Papakura District Council* [2000] 1 NZLR 265, considered earlier.

13 [1987] 1 WLR 1.

14 [1987] 1 WLR 1 at 17.

15 [1969] 2 AC 31, 114-115, per Lord Pearce: 'The less circumscribed the purpose, the less circumscribed will be, as a rule, the range of goods which are reasonably fit for such purpose'.

16 [1972] AC 441, 497, per Lord Wilberforce.

17 [1987] 1 WLR 1, 17.

judgement in providing goods which are suited to B's particular difficulty or sensitivity. In *Griffiths v Peter Conway Ltd*,[18] B bought a bespoke Harris tweed coat from S but she developed dermatitis very soon after after wearing it. Not unnaturally, B argued that the coat was unfit for its particular purpose, namely her personal wearing of it, but she failed in an action for breach of the implied condition of fitness for purpose as she was shown to have an abnormally sensitive skin. The Court of Appeal held that the particular purpose for which the goods were required was the purpose of being worn by a woman with an abnormality and, as this purpose had not been made known to S, he was not liable. B had argued that these facts were equatable with those in *Manchester Liners Ltd v Rea Ltd*,[19] in that, if the ordering of coal for a particular ship meant that B was communicating his purpose to S, the ordering of a coat for a particular individual must, likewise, be a sufficient indication of purpose. However, Sir Wilfred Greene MR stressed that, having regard to the notorious differences between steamships, the naming of the steamship in question was obviously a communication of the particular purpose for which the coal was required but, in *Griffiths*, the facts were abnormal and unknown to S and there was clearly an insufficient indication of purpose by B. This was clearly the correct conclusion because the buyer was unaware of her sensitivity, no seller could have assumed that her skin was abnormal and the coat would not have detrimentally affected the skin of a normal person.

The principle in *Griffiths v Peter Conway Ltd* has always been regarded as a particularly narrow inroad on the seller's liability under s 14(3).[20] In *Griffiths*, Sir Wilfred Greene MR[1] thought that establishing 'where normality ceases and abnormality begins' was not a precise science but he had no doubt that it was 'a question that no judge and jury would have any real difficulty in deciding on the evidence in any particular case'. Furthermore, the argument in *Ashington Piggeries Ltd v Christopher Hill Ltd*[2] was that, as mink were more sensitive than other animals to the poisonous substance (DMNA) in the food supplied, *Griffiths* should have applied to the facts, thereby exonerating the seller. However, the House of Lords emphasised that, to a greater or lesser extent, *all* animals were sensitive to DMNA, whereas the coat in *Griffiths* would not have harmed a normal individual. Lord Guest[3] explicitly categorised *Griffiths* as 'a highly special case'.

The issue of the abnormal buyer was brought to the fore in the recent decision of the House of Lords in *Slater v Finning Ltd*.[4] There the appellant owners (B) of a fishing vessel engaged the respondent marine engineers (S) to repair the vessel's engine when the main bearings failed. S installed a new type of camshaft which its manufacturers claimed would be subject to less wear and have an extended life but the new camshaft failed when the vessel was at sea as did two

---

18 [1939] 1 All ER 685.
19 [1922] 2 AC 74.
20 See also *Ingham v Emes* [1955] 2 QB 366 (the plaintiff, who knew that she was allergic to 'Inecto' hair dye but failed to inform her hairdresser, sued for breach of an implied term in the contract for work and materials alleging that the materials used were unfit for the purpose for which they were required. It was held that she must fail; the implied term extended only to the dyeing of a normal person's hair).
1 [1939] 1 All ER 685, pp 691-692.
2 [1972] AC 441.
3 [1972] AC 441 at 479.
4 [1997] AC 473; see Brown, 'Ship Repairs and Fitness for Purpose' [1997] LMCLQ 193.

further camshafts of identical type fitted by S. Eventually, B had a new engine installed in the vessel and had no further problems; the old engine was sold and fitted in another vessel where, after a thorough overhaul but without a new camshaft, it performed well during extensive fishing trips. B alleged that S was in breach of the implied condition contained in s 14(3), in that the camshaft was unfit for use in their vessel and the particular purpose had been made known to S by the fact that the camshaft was to be fitted in that particular vessel (no claim was made that the contract was one for the supply of services). In dismissing the appeal, the House of Lords held that there was no breach of s 14(3) where the failure of the goods to meet the intended purpose arose from an abnormal feature or idiosyncrasy in the buyer or in the circumstances of the use of the goods, which had not been communicated to S. This was so irrespective of whether or not B was aware of the idiosyncrasy. In the instant case, the House considered that the cause of the failure of the camshafts arose from the vessel's extraordinary tendency to produce excessive torsional resonance, meaning that the camshafts became worn much sooner than was normal. Accordingly, the camshafts were fit for the purpose of installation in a standard vessel and the damage was caused by the external, abnormal factor of resonance.

It is indisputable that S's liability for fitness for purpose should not extend to the facts of *Griffiths*, but it is questionable whether the facts of *Slater v Finning Ltd* ranked as highly special. The *Griffiths* definition of abnormality extends only to those circumstances where the peculiarity in question is wholly latent and either unique to the buyer or shared by an extraordinarily small group. In contrast, most situations within s 14(3) call for B's indication of purpose to be met by a willingness in S to ask relevant questions in the exercise of his skill and judgement.[5] Moreover, it is emphatically this latter requirement which must predominate within s 14(3), as evidenced by the abrogation of the *positive* requirement of the buyer's reliance on the seller's skill and judgement within that section. There is no correlation between those cases where the abnormality in question means that a competent seller *cannot* exercise skill and judgement, as in *Griffiths*, and cases where an inept seller blames his incompetence on an alleged abnormality. It is debatable whether the seller in *Slater v Finning Ltd* acted reasonably in the circumstances by resolutely installing a succession of identical camshafts in the fishing vessel, at least by the time that he fitted the third such camshaft. It surely cannot be an answer for a seller who is confronted by difficulties simply to repeat his mistakes and then abandon his buyer to fate on the basis of a supposed peculiarity which an exercise of the seller's expertise did not disclose. Once it is acknowledged that the seller *can* exercise his skill and judgement, the burden of liability under s 14(3) must fall heavily upon him, and it is thus equally arguable that the seller in *Slater* might have been in breach of the section had he installed only one unsuitable camshaft.

---

5   See *Manchester Liners Ltd v Rea Ltd* [1922] 2 AC 74, considered earlier. The House of Lords held that B had sufficiently communicated the purpose to his seller in informing him of the particular ship for which the coal was required and the fact that the supply of coal was restricted at the time (1919) did not relieve the seller of the obligation to exercise skill and judgement in performing the contract. The seller was thus in breach of the implied condition of fitness for purpose. Lord Atkinson considered that 'when ... the [sellers] purporting to act in the discharge of the obligations imposed upon them by their contract, caused the bunkers of the *Manchester Importer* to be filled with 500 tons of coal ... they must be held to have taken the risk of this coal not being of the kind and character they had warranted that the coal sold should be' (p 89).

B's protection becomes seriously eroded if the courts readily accept the abnormality argument or take the analogous view that B's pupose is extremely unusual and must be communicated expressly and precisely if he is to seek the protection of s 14(3). Certain modern decisions do appear to be moving in this direction,[6] thus arguably beginning to undo cases such as *Ashington Piggeries*, which accepted the notion of the generalised, particular purpose, and thereby making a retrogressive lurch towards *caveat emptor*.[7]

GOODS SUPPLIED UNDER THE CONTRACT ARE 'REASONABLY FIT FOR THAT PURPOSE'

S's duty under s 14(3) is to supply goods that are 'reasonably fit' for the purpose thus indicating that fitness for purpose, like satisfactory quality, is a relative concept. In *Bartlett v Sidney Marcus Ltd*,[8] considered earlier under satisfactory quality, the second-hand car which was the subject of the sale was 'far from perfect'[9] but it was nevertheless held to be reasonably fit for its purpose. The comments of Lord Pearce in *Henry Kendall & Sons v William Lillico & Sons Ltd*[10] summarise succinctly the general rule:

> 'I would expect a tribunal of fact to decide that a car sold in this country was reasonably fit for touring even though it was not well adapted for conditions in a heat wave; but not, if it could not cope adequately with rain. If, however, it developed some lethal or dangerous trick in very hot weather, I would expect it to be found unfit. In deciding the question of fact the rarity of the unsuitability would be weighed against the gravity of its consequences'.

It is plain that reasonable fitness must be considered in tandem with B's specificity of purpose: if B has communicated his purpose precisely and specifically, it is perfectly reasonable that S should supply goods which are suited precisely to that purpose. If, on the other hand, B's purpose is couched in very broad terms, it would be unreasonable to demand of S that he supply goods perfectly fitted for every possible application within the broad purpose stated. This clearly involves a balancing exercise in numerous, differing factual situations. In *M/S Aswan Engineering Establishment Co v Lupdine Ltd*,[11] B required plastic pails in which he intended to export waterproofing compound. The court considered that 'pails required for export' was such a widely stated purpose that, although the pails melted in the extreme heat of Kuwait, they were reasonably fit for the broad purpose which B had specified.

It is thus clear that the notion of reasonable fitness means that S is not a guarantor of perfection and, accordingly, he will not be liable where B has misused

---

6   See *M/S Aswan Engineering Establishment Co v Lupdine Ltd* [1987] 1 WLR 1 (plastic pails required for export which melted in the heat of Kuwait; held that the pails were fit for normal export purposes and were unfit for export only to the Middle East. Consequently, in order to invoke s 14(3) successfully, B should have made his special purpose known to S. Lloyd LJ thought that B's communicated purpose of requiring pails for export could 'hardly be wider ... and the pails needed to be little, if anything, more than merchantable' (p 17); *Hamilton v Papakura District Council* [2000] 1 NZLR 265.

7   In *Slater v Finning Ltd* [1997] AC 473, 488, Lord Steyn concluded that 'to uphold the present claim would be to allow caveat venditor to run riot'.

8   [1965] 1 WLR 1013.

9   [1965] 1 WLR 1013 at 1017, per Lord Denning MR.

10   [1969] 2 AC 31, 115.

11   [1987] 1 WLR 1.

the goods[12] nor does S guarantee suitability for purpose where B has an abnormality which is not communicated to S.[13]

Trivial defects

After the decision in *Parsons (H) (Livestock) Ltd v Uttley Ingham & Co,*[14] it is indisputable that a trivial defect may mean that the goods are not reasonably fit for their purpose. B bought a storage hopper from S for the purpose of storing pig nuts and S delivered and installed the hopper for B. Because S omitted to open the ventilator at the top of the hopper, the pig nuts became mouldy and numerous pigs died as a consequence of eating the food. It would have taken only seconds to open the ventilator but S was nevertheless held to be in breach of the condition of fitness for purpose.

Durability

In order to satisfy s 14(3), it appears that the goods should be durable[15] and here durability must have the same meaning as under s 14(2), ie the durability requirement should bite at the time of supply. In assessing durability, there are the same difficulties here as those under s 14(2) where, it will be remembered, durability is a specific requirement of satisfactory quality under s 14(2B)(e). In summary, the longer the time that B owns and uses the goods, the more difficult it will be to establish that the defect was present at the date of delivery. Moreover, after a lapse of time, S will always seek to establish that the goods have remained fit for a reasonable period of time or that the defect is attributable to B's rough treatment of the goods. These arguments may appear inapt, however, where fitness for purpose is being assessed as, of necessity, B's *purpose* may entail the use or consumption of the goods over a prolonged period of time.

Latent defects and strict liability of the seller

Reasonable fitness is judged objectively and it is clear that liability under s 14(3) is strict in that it extends to latent defects which could not have been detected by S no matter how much care and skill he exercised. In *Henry Kendall & Sons v William Lillico & Sons Ltd,*[16] Lord Reid[17] commented that:

> 'If the law were always logical one would suppose that a buyer, who has obtained a right to rely on the seller's skill and judgment, would only obtain thereby an assurance

---

12 See *Heil v Hedges* [1951] 1 TLR 512 (half-cooked pork chops); *Lexmead (Basingstoke) Ltd v Lewis* [1982] AC 225 (S was not liable under the previous s 14(1) for a defective trailer coupling when B continued to use it knowing of its dangerous state); cf *Shields v Honeywill & Stein Ltd* [1953] 1 Lloyd's Rep 357 (sale of isopropyl alcohol for use by B in blending into syrups for carbonated drinks. S and B had done business for a number of years but, on this occasion, the alcohol had an offensive odour and buyers of the drinks complained. Held S was liable under the previous s 14(1), the Court of Appeal rejecting S's arguments that B should have tested the alcohol or devised methods to mask the odour, but these arguments had prevailed at first instance ([1952] 2 Lloyd's Rep 406)).
13 *Griffiths v Peter Conway Ltd* [1939] 1 All ER 685.
14 [1978] QB 791.
15 See *Lexmead (Basingstoke) Ltd v Lewis* [1982] AC 225, 276 per Lord Diplock; *Lee v York Coach and Marine* [1977] RTR 35, 42 per Stephenson LJ.
16 [1969] 2 AC 31.
17 [1969] 2 AC 31 at 84.

that proper skill and judgment had been exercised, and would only be entitled to a remedy if a defect in the goods was due to failure to exercise such skill and judgment. But the law has always gone farther than that'.

The view of the courts has long been that the exercise of care by S is irrelevant if, in fact, the goods are unfit for their purpose.[18] Consequently, it is no defence that S could not examine the goods before sale[19] or that he took all possible care in the preparation of the goods in an attempt to ensure their fitness for purpose. In *Frost v Aylesbury Dairy Co Ltd*,[20] for example, milk which contained typhoid germs was unfit for its purpose even though the germs could have been discovered by S only in a detailed laboratory analysis. Similarly, in *Grant v Australian Knitting Mills Ltd*,[1] the underpants bought by B which contained excess sulphites were unfit for their purpose even though the defect was not discoverable by S on any reasonable examination. It is thus plain that the imposition of strict liability on S qualifies significantly the emphasis on reasonable fitness, discussed above.

Instructions, notices and warnings

As explained earlier, goods may not be of satisfactory quality if they are supplied with no, or inadequate, instructions, and it is indisputable that this is also the position under fitness for purpose. In *Vacwell Engineering Co Ltd v BDH Chemicals Ltd*,[2] S sold a chemical to B which could explode on contact with water although neither party was aware of this risk. The chemical was supplied in ampoules carrying the warning 'Harmful Vapour' but there was no mention of any other danger. In order to prepare the chemical for use in the manufacturing process, B had to wash the ampoules and, on one such occasion, an ampoule broke and there was a violent explosion in which one of B's employees was killed. It was held that B had relied on the skill and judgement of S to warn him of any unusual hazard and, accordingly, S was liable for breach of the implied condition of fitness for pupose.[3]

Where goods are not inherently or potentially dangerous, they will nevertheless be unfit for their purpose if the instructions supplied with the goods are inadequate. In *Wormell v RHM Agriculture (East) Ltd*,[4] B, a farmer, bought a herbicide to destroy wild oats in his crops but adverse weather conditions prevented his spraying the crops at the correct time. B decided to risk applying the herbicide

---

18 See *Randall v Newson* (1877) 2 QBD 102.
19 See *Bigge v Parkinson* (1862) 7 H & N 955, 959 per Cockburn CJ: 'Where a person undertakes to supply provisions, and they are supplied in cases hermetically sealed, but turn out to be putrid, it is no answer to say that he has been deceived by the person from whom he got them'.
20 [1905] 1 KB 608.
 1 [1936] AC 85.
 2 [1971] 1 QB 88; revsd [1971] 1 QB 111n.
 3 See also *Willis v FMC Machinery & Chemicals Ltd* (1976) 68 DLR (3d) 127 (B bought an insecticide and herbicide from S; the insecticide was manufactured by S but the herbicide was manufactured by a third party and only distributed by S. The two chemicals interacted and damaged B's crop. Held S was liable under the Canadian legislation for breach of the implied condition of fitness for purpose because, although the herbicide was effective, it was unsafe for use with certain insecticides and contained no warning to that effect); cf *Lem v Barotto Sports Ltd* (1976) 69 DLR (3d) 276 (S not liable where B disregarded adequate instructions and warnings).
 4 [1986] 1 WLR 336.

later in the season even though the manufacturer's instructions on the can of herbicide warned that late application might damage the crop. However, the instructions did not warn B that late application could be wholly ineffective and, indeed, this was the eventual outcome. It was held, at first instance, that the instructions were misleading and this rendered the goods unfit for their purpose because 'goods' meant the herbicide together with its instructions. The decision was reversed by the Court of Appeal[5] on the ground that the instructions were not misleading and contained a clear warning that the herbicide should not be used after a certain stage in the crop's growth. B was accordingly put on notice and could not complain that his own misunderstanding rendered the herbicide unfit for its purpose. The Court of Appeal was content with this finding of fact and, regrettably, did not consider the overall legal position of instructions attached to goods. It is arguable that one effect of the decision may be to encourage sellers to use warnings in order to narrow the scope of the statutory implied conditions and thereby 'shrink the core' of their liability rather than seeking to exclude it.[6] Although it is self-evident that warnings are often beneficial for B, it is most undesirable to sanction and legitimise the use of cleverly-designed warnings on poorly-designed, shoddy goods.[7]

The circumstances show that the buyer does not rely, or that it is unreasonable for him to rely, on the seller's skill or judgment

The original s 14(1) in the SGA 1893 provided that B had to make known his particular purpose 'so as to show that [he] relies on the seller's skill or judgment' and thus B had to establish this as a *positive* requirement. Overall, reliance was readily inferred. Two early decisions[8] had taken the view that B's disclosure of purpose normally amounted to sufficient evidence of reliance and, by the time of *Grant v Australian Knitting Mills Ltd,*[9] it was clear that B's choice of a retail shop in which to buy the 'Golden Fleece' underpants amounted to sufficient reliance on the skill and judgement of the retailer in question. Lord Wright[10] stressed that 'reliance will seldom be express: it will usually arise by implication from the circumstances ... to take a case like that in question, of a purchase from a retailer, the reliance will be in general inferred from the fact that a buyer goes to the shop in the confidence that the tradesman has selected his stock with skill and judgment'. This trend was also evident in the later, leading decisons.[11] The culmination of this process was the enactment of the Supply of Goods (Implied

---

5   [1987] 1 WLR 1091.
6   See Ch 25 where this issue is considered.
7   See Brown, 'Liablity for Labelling of Goods and Instructions for Use' [1988] LMCLQ 502; Macleod, 'Instructions as to Use of Consumer Goods' (1981) 97 LQR 550.
8   *Gillespie Bros & Co v Cheney, Eggar & Co* [1896] 2 QB 59, 64 per Lord Russell of Killowen CJ; *Manchester Liners Ltd v Rea Ltd* [1922] 2 AC 74 (see Lord Dunedin, p 81; Lord Atkinson, pp 87-88; Lord Sumner, p 90).
9   [1936] AC 85.
10 [1936] AC 85 at 99.
11 *Henry Kendall & Sons v William Lillico & Sons Ltd* [1969] 2 AC 31, 115 per Lord Pearce; *Ashington Piggeries Ltd v Christopher Hill Ltd* [1972] AC 441, 476-477 per Lord Guest (explaining Lord Reid's apparently restrictive view in *Kendall* (p 81)).

Terms) Act 1973, which introduced the current wording. It is now clear that, where B makes his purpose known, reliance will be presumed unless S proves that there was no reliance by B or that such reliance was unreasonable.

WHEN MIGHT THERE BE NO RELIANCE ON THE SELLER'S SKILL OR JUDGEMENT?

The seller does not purport to exercise skill or judgement

The most obvious example of lack of reliance is where S makes it clear to B that he does not purport to exercise his skill and judgement in selling the goods to B, but it is important to stress that some disclaimers of this nature may be subject to the controls in the Unfair Contract Terms Act 1977.

The facts indicate that there is no reliance on the seller

Apart from such express disclaimers, it may be evident from the facts that there is no reliance on the seller. It is plainly arguable that B does not rely on S where a third party reports favourably to B and B then relies on that third party to the exclusion of S.[12] This might be the case where B relies on statements made by the manufacturer of the goods so that the seller 'is merely a covenient company through which [B] elect[s] to place its orders from time to time'.[13]

Moreover, B may rely exclusively on his own knowledge and expertise. In *Teheran-Europe Co Ltd v S T Belton (Tractors) Ltd*,[14] S sold air compressors to B, a Persian company, after B's managing director had inspected, in England, a machine of the same description that S had for sale. English agents negotiated the contract on B's behalf and, in referring to 'our clients' and the fact that literature was needed for advertising purposes in Persia, the circumstances were such that S had notice that the compressors were for resale in Persia. It was held that B relied on his own skill and judgement in relation to the suitability of compressors for resale in that country because 'it flies in the face of common sense to suppose that he relies on anything but his own knowledge of the market in his own country'.[15]

The seller can supply only one brand of goods

B must also rely on his own judgement where he knows that S can supply only one brand of goods. In *Wren v Holt*,[16] for example, B bought 'Holden's beer' (which contained arsenic) in a tied public house and, although the beer was held to be unmerchantable, B's action failed under the original s 14(1) as he could not be said to rely on S's skill or judgement where S could supply only Holden's beer.

---

12 Where the third party is B's *agent* acting within his authority, B's reliance will normally be established through his agent (see *Ashford Shire Council v Dependable Motors Pty Ltd* [1961] AC 336 (considered in Ch 2) but difficult questions of fact may arise with other third parties.
13 *Cominco Ltd v Westinghouse Canada Ltd* (1981) 127 DLR (3d) 544, 561 per Bouck J.
14 [1968] 2 QB 545.
15 [1968] 2 QB 545 at 560, per Diplock LJ.
16 [1903] 1 KB 610.

The buyer selects the goods from the seller's stock

Might B's selection of goods from S's stock indicate lack of reliance on S? It would be possible to envisage commercial sales where this would indicate that no reliance is placed on S,[17] but it is almost certainly the case that there would be reliance where, for example, B selects goods from a supermarket shelf.

The buyer states a wide, generalised purpose for the goods

As discussed earlier in this chapter, should B state a wide and generalised purpose for goods which might be put to several uses, it may be that he places no reliance on S.[18] Lord Reid's example in *Henry Kendall & Sons v William Lillico & Sons Ltd*,[19] is an excellent illustration of the difficulty S might face. The situation posited was B's purchase of cloth for the purpose of making overcoats. Here S's only clue to the quality which he should supply would be the price of the cloth and he would need more detail in order to exercise his skill and judgement, eg knowledge that B is a Savile Row tailor. In such a situation, S cannot exercise skill and judgement and identify B's particular needs, but it should be stressed that, in some circumstances, S *ought* to enquire further because his specialism is such that he owes a duty to advise B.

This question is one of degree, however, and it is clear that precise and minutely detailed knowledge of B's purpose is not necessary for S to be able to exercise sufficient skill or judgement. In *Henry Kendall & Sons v William Lillico & Sons Ltd*,[20] the first sale of the Brazilian groundnut extraction was made by importers (S) to wholesalers (B) and S knew that B intended to resell the extract to animal foodstuff compounders who would make it into cattle and poultry food. It was held that S had sufficient knowledge of B's purpose and B had relied on S's skill and judgement; he was thus liable when the extract was poisonous to poultry even though it could have been safely compounded into cattle food. Moreover, in *Kendall*, the importer (S) and wholesaler (B) both belonged to the same trade association and, at first instance,[1] it was held that this negated B's reliance on S. The majority in the Court of Appeal[2] and the House of Lords[3] held that, although this was a key factor to consider in assessing reliance, it did not nullify B's reliance on S in *Kendall* and, to decide otherwise, would be 'to convert a decision on fact into a rule of law and to ignore the fact that not all sales, even on a given market ... bear the same character, or involve the same incidents'.[4]

The buyer orders goods from a manufacturer/seller

It has always been assumed that B almost certainly places reliance on S where S is also the manufacturer of the goods. In *Kendall*, Lord Reid[5] suggested that it

---

17 On this point, see *M/S Aswan Engineering Establishment Co v Lupdine Ltd* [1987] 1 WLR 1 (considered below).
18 See *Preist v Last* [1903] 2 KB 148, 153 per Collins MR.
19 [1969] 2 AC 31, 79-80.
20 [1969] 2 AC 31.
 1 [1964] 2 Lloyd's Rep 227; following dicta in *Draper (C E B) & Son Ltd v Edward Turner & Son Ltd* [1965] 1 QB 424.
 2 [1966] 1 WLR 287 (Diplock LJ dissenting on this point).
 3 [1969] 2 AC 31 (Lord Guest dissenting on this point).
 4 [1969] 2 AC 31 at 124, per Lord Wilberforce.
 5 [1969] 2 AC 31 at 82.

would be only in 'unusual circumstances' that B could not be said to rely on the skill and judgement of such a seller/manufacturer. However, in *M/S Aswan Engineering Establishment Co v Lupdine Ltd*,[6] Lloyd LJ[7] emphatically denied that B had relied on the seller/manufacturer's skill or judgement where B saw a description of the plastic pails which he subsequently bought in S's catalogue, was sent a sample by S and wrote to S informing him that he was involved in export sales and thought that S's pails would be more 'suitable and robust' than those which B was currently using. It is most perplexing to see how B could be said not to rely on S on such facts and the conclusion reached by Nicholls LJ[8] was preferable in his finding that B showed at least partial reliance on S, a question which is returned to below.

The buyer has an opportunity to examine the goods

Finally, there is the issue of whether B's opportunity to examine the goods or his actual examination might show that he does not rely on S. At common law, before the SGA 1893, there was no implied warranty of fitness where the 'the goods are in esse, and may be inspected by the buyer ... [because he] has the opportunity of exercising his judgment upon the matter'.[9] Under s 14(3), the fact that such an opportunity to examine was not taken by B might indicate lack of reliance on S on appropriate facts, but the matter must be put in perspective. In *Kendall*, Lord Morris of Borth-y-Gest stressed that there could still be reliance on S where B analysed the goods on delivery. Consequently, it seems that an opportunity to examine which was not taken would certainly be insufficient to exclude B's reliance and an actual examination would have to indicate conclusively that B did not rely on S in any shape or form.

THE BUYER'S PARTIAL RELIANCE ON THE SELLER'S SKILL
AND JUDGEMENT

It is sufficient for B to rely partially on S's skill or judgement, meaning that he relies on him in relation to one aspect of the goods but not as regards another. This notion of partial reliance really involves an enquiry into the relevant specialisms of B and S and the apportionment of responsibility between them. In *Cammell Laird & Co Ltd v The Manganese Bronze and Brass Co Ltd*,[10] B ordered ship propellers which were to be made by S according to B's specifications but certain matters, particularly the thickness of the blades, were left to S. One propeller was unsuitable because of matters outside B's specifications but within the area of expertise left to S. Accordingly, the House of Lords held that S was in breach of the implied condition of fitness for purpose.

A more difficult problem in relation to partial reliance arose in *Ashington Piggeries Ltd v Christopher Hill Ltd*.[11] There B was an expert mink farmer who asked S, an established compounder of animal feed, to make food for mink according to B's formula. S had never before produced food for mink and an

---

6 [1987] 1 WLR 1.
7 [1987] 1 WLR 1 at 17.
8 [1987] 1 WLR 1 at 27.
9 *Jones v Just* (1868) LR 3 QB 197, 202 per Mellor J.
10 [1934] AC 402.
11 [1972] AC 441.

alteration of the formula was agreed between B and S entailing a substitution of herring meal for one of the ingredients. The herring meal contained a preservative which caused a chemical reaction in the food (generating a toxic chemical called DMNA) rendering it lethal to mink but not to other animals which were, nevertheless, affected to a certain extent. The House of Lords held that B relied on S to provide ingredients which were reasonably fit for feeding to animals. Lord Wilberforce[12] said that 'the field thus left to the sellers can be described in terms of their responsibility as merchants, to obtain and deliver ingredients, and relevantly herring meal, not unfit by reason of contamination, to be fed to animals, including mink'. In this way, the areas of expertise of B and S can be delineated. The compounding of the food was held to be within S's area of specialisation but if animals other than mink had been totally unaffected by the DMNA and only mink had been killed, S would not have been liable, as this idiosyncracy of mink would have fallen within B's special competence.[13]

This separation of proficiencies and consequent ascription of responsibility between B and S was also evident in *Venus Electric Ltd v Brevel Products Ltd*,[14] the facts of the case providing an instructive contrast with those of *Ashington*. In *Venus Electric*, S manufactured and sold motors for hair-dryers to B who assembled the hair-dryers for sale to a retailer. The motors were not inherently defective and would have worked satisfactorily in some hair-dryers but B ordered certain modifications to S's design and his assembly of the parts meant that the final product was conceived entirely by him. Many of the hair-dryers failed in use because the design caused excessive stress on all the components. The Ontario Court of Appeal held that S was not liable for breach of the implied term of fitness for purpose as there was insufficient reliance on S's skill and judgement.

In summary, the *Ashington* decision indicates that reliance may be both partial and general in scope but, nevertheless, it must be 'such as to constitute a substantial and effective inducement which leads the buyer to agree to purchase the commodity'.[15]

THE BUYER ORDERS GOODS USING A PATENT OR TRADE NAME

The original s 14(1) in the SGA 1893 contained a proviso that the condition of fitness did not apply where B bought 'a specified article under its patent or other trade name'. As the wording suggested, the proviso was not meant to extend to the sale of raw commodities but, instead, to be applicable to manufactured articles supplied under their established trade names and thus a sale of 'Cyfartha Merthyr coal' for steamships was held not to be an order using such a trade name.[16] In

---

12 [1972] AC 441 at 490.
13 As Viscount Dilhorne put it: 'It is clear that [B] did not rely on [S] to produce a food suitable for mink. He relied on them to produce a food in accordance with the agreed formula and, if they did that, then its suitability for mink was a matter for which he was responsible' (pp 479–480).
14 (1978) 85 DLR (3d) 282.
15 *Medway Oil & Storage Co Ltd v Silica Gel Corpn* (1928) 33 Com Cas 195, 196 per Lord Sumner.
16 *Gillespie Bros & Co v Cheney, Eggar & Co* [1896] 2 QB 59; see also *Cominco Ltd v Westinghouse Canada Ltd* (1981) 127 DLR (3d) 544 (B ordered electric cable described as 'conductor number 12 Teck cable'. Held that 'a sale of Teck cable by itself is not a sale of a specific article under its trade name since there is no one known product called Teck cable. Instead, there is Teck cable manufactured with assorted metal sheeting and with or without a protective jacket' (p 560, per Bouck J)).

contrast, a sale of a quantity of 'Coalite'[17] was within the proviso, as was B's purchase of a bottle of 'R White's Lemonade'.[18]

In fact, the interpretation in two leading decisions meant that the proviso applied in exceptionally limited circumstances. In *Bristol Tramways, etc, Carriage Co Ltd v Fiat Motors Ltd*,[19] B's ordering of 'the 24/40 hp Fiat omnibus' which he had inspected and 'six 24/40 hp Fiat omnibus chassis' was held to be outside the proviso as the order was really for the omnibus and chassis to be made by Fiat. Farwell LJ[20] thus thought that there was a difference between an order for a Fiat omnibus 'which is intelligible only if there be such an article known to the public or the trade' and the order of an omnibus 'to be made by the Fiat Company'. Similarly, in *Baldry v Marshall*,[1] B asked if S could recommend a fast, comfortable car for touring purposes and S suggested a Bugatti. B then ordered 'an eight cylinder Bugatti car' but this was held not to be the use of a trade name within the proviso.

These cases established that the trade name had to be acquired 'by user'[2] and B's order had to be such as to indicate 'that he is satisfied, rightly or wrongly, that it will answer his purpose, and that he is not relying on the skill or judgment of the seller'.[3] The upshot was that the only instance within the proviso would be B's specific *insistence* that S should sell him goods having a trade name. This comparatively rare possibility occurred in *Chanter v Hopkins*,[4] the decision which was thought to have 'inspired'[5] the proviso in s 14(1) of the SGA 1893. There B sent to S, the patentee of an invention known as 'Chanter's smoke-consuming furnace', the following written order: 'Send me your patent hopper and apparatus, to fit up my brewing copper with your smoke-consuming furnace'. When the device turned out to be useless in a brewery, it was held that there was no implied warranty of fitness for purpose and S could recover the full price of the goods. Certainly *Chanter v Hopkins* is still relevant, as there would be no reliance on S if facts closely corresponding to those of the case were to be repeated today.

UNREASONABLE RELIANCE

The notion of unreasonable reliance was introduced into the condition of fitness for purpose by the Supply of Goods (Implied Terms) Act 1973 but it has not been developed by the courts. Often the fact of reliance and the question of whether it is reasonable to rely on S will intertwine: it must often be tempting to conclude that where it is unreasonable to rely on S, there has in fact been no reliance. However, *Teheran-Europe Co Ltd v S T Belton (Tractors) Ltd*[6] and

---

17 *Wilson v Rickett, Cockerell & Co Ltd* [1954] 1 QB 598.
18 *Daniels v R White & Sons Ltd* [1938] 4 All ER 258; Cf *Grant v Australian Knitting Mills Ltd* [1936] AC 85, 99, where Lord Wright did not apply the proviso to the sale of 'Golden Fleece' underpants.
19 [1910] 2 KB 831.
20 [1910] 2 KB 831 at 839.
 1 [1925] 1 KB 260.
 2 *Bristol Tramways, etc, Carriage Co Ltd v Fiat Motors Ltd* [1910] 2 KB 831, 840 per Farwell LJ.
 3 *Baldry v Marshall* [1925] 1 KB 260, 267 per Bankes LJ.
 4 (1838) 4 M & W 399.
 5 *Teheran-Europe Co Ltd v S T Belton (Tractors) Ltd* [1968] 2 QB 545, 563 per Sachs LJ.
 6 [1968] 2 QB 545.

Venus Electric Ltd v Brevel Products Ltd,[7] both discussed earlier, are almost certainly examples of situations where B's reliance on S could be regarded as unreasonable. In the latter case, B's esoteric use of the motors manufactured by S must surely have indicated that, if any reliance had been placed on S originally, B's deployment of the goods supplied meant that it was no longer reasonable to rely on S, and the chain of causation leading to S had thus been broken.

Moreover, where S disclaims any knowledge or expertise in relation to the goods, it may then be unreasonable for B to rely on S's skill or judgement. Such a disclaimer was effective in narrowing S's liability under s 13 in *Harlingdon and Leinster Enterprises Ltd v Christopher Hull Fine Art Ltd*,[8] and this reasoning seems to be even more applicable to s 14(3) where reliance is of direct relevance.

Section 15: sale by sample

The SGA 1979, s 15(1) and (2) provide:

'(1) A contract of sale is a contract for sale by sample where there is an express or implied term to that effect in the contract.
(2)   In the case of a contract for sale by sample there is an implied term[9] –
(a) that the bulk will correspond with the sample in quality;
(b) [repealed][10]
(c) that the goods will be free from any defect, making their quality unsatisfactory, which would not be apparent on reasonable examination of the sample.'

WHAT IS A SALE BY SAMPLE?

Although s 15 is somewhat terse in its definition of a sale by sample, the meaning of such a sale is tolerably clear. In *Drummond (James) & Sons v E H Van Ingen & Co Ltd*,[11] Lord Macnaghten[12] explained that the purpose of a sample 'is to present to the eye the real meaning and intention of the parties with regard to the subject matter of the contract, which, owing to the imperfections of language, it may be difficult or impossible to express in words. The sample speaks for itself'.

Section 15 emphasises that a sale will be *by* sample only when that is the intent of S and B and thus the fact that a sample is exhibited during negotiations does not necessarily bring the sale within s 15 – here the sample may simply be a guide to B of what to expect and the verbal description of the goods will thus remain paramount.[13] This latter possibility occurred in *Gardiner v Gray*,[14] where Lord Ellenborough[15] concluded that the sale was not by sample because the

---

7 (1978) 85 DLR (3d) 282.
8 [1991] 1 QB 564.
9 Section 15(3) provides that the term implied by s 15(2) is a condition.
10 Repealed by the Sale and Supply of Goods Act 1994, s 7; Sch 2, para 5 (6)(a); Sch 3.
11 (1887) 12 App Cas 284.
12 (1887) 12 App Cas 284 at 297.
13 Where the contract is reduced to writing and does not mention the sample, extrinsic evidence may not be allowed to show that the sale is by sample: *Gardiner v Gray* (1815) 4 Camp 144. However, exceptions to this strict adherence to the parol evidence rule have been allowed, see eg *Syers v Jonas* (1848) 2 Exch 111.
14 (1815) 4 Camp 144.
15 (1815) 4 Camp 144 at 145.

sample 'was not produced as a warranty that the bulk correspond with it but to enable the purchaser to form a reasonable judgment of the commodity'. Consequently, in order to be a sale by sample, the parties must intend that the bulk of the goods conforms to the sample, meaning that S expressly or impliedly promises 'that the goods sold should answer the description of a small parcel exhibited at the time of the sale'.[16]

Somewhat surprisingly, s 15 applies to all sales by sample and not just those made in the course of a business but, in reality, selling by sample has always been the exclusive province of business sales and none of the cases concern consumer sales. In a retail sale of goods, where B inspects goods and then receives similar goods in a sealed package, the transaction is undoubtedly analogous to a sale by sample. As it is clear that 'bulk' is given a wide interpretation in sales by sample (see below), there appears to be no objection, in principle, to applying s 15 to a such a consumer sale. That being said, the notion of a sale by sample does seem inapt in such a sale, not least because the rules on examination of the goods and satisfactory quality are modified in sales by sample (see below).

A sale can be both by sample and description and, if so, there must be compliance with s 13(2) because, as that section provides, 'it is not sufficient that the bulk of the goods corresponds with the sample if the goods do not also correspond with the description'.

THE BULK MUST CORRESPOND WITH THE SAMPLE IN QUALITY

There can be a sale by sample where the goods are unascertained[17] or specific[18] and also where they are to be manufactured *after* contract,[19] and so the word 'bulk' may sometimes appear inapt. In fact, it has been suggested that, in certain situations, 'bulk' means little more than 'the contract goods'.[20]

Section 15(2) provides that the bulk must correspond with the sample in quality and there will be no compliance with the section if the goods do not in fact correspond with the sample but could be made to correspond at minimal cost. In *Ruben (E & S) Ltd v Faire Bros & Co Ltd*,[1] rubber sheeting did not match the sample as it was crinkly but it could easily have been warmed and the crinkles could then have been pressed out. Hilbery J held that if an article was delivered which did not accord with sample, it was no defence that it could be made to accord 'by some simple process, no matter how simple'.[2] Sales by sample are analogous to sales by description in that the sample is one way of describing the subject-matter, but the modern cases on s 13, limiting that section's operation to

---

16 *Parker v Palmer* (1821) 4 B & Ald 387, 391 per Abbott CJ.
17 See *Re Walkers, Winser & Hamm and Shaw, Son & Co* [1904] 2 KB 152 (500 tons of St Malo barley, at time of shipment to be 'about as per sample').
18 See *Azémar v Casella* (1867) LR 2 CP 677 (sale of 128 specific bales of cotton to arrive in London per *Cheviot* from Madras, 'equal to sealed sample').
19 See *Heilbut v Hickson* (1872) LR 7 CP 438 (30,000 black army shoes as per sample).
20 See *Benjamin's Sale of Goods* (5th edn, 1997), para 11-095, where it is also suggested that the extended definition of 'bulk' in the SGA, s 61(1), which was introduced to facilitate the new provisions on co-ownership (ss 20A and 20B), will not affect sales by sample, as it is quite unnecessary in sales by sample that the bulk be contained in a 'defined space or area'.
1 [1949] 1 KB 254.
2 [1949] 1 KB 254 at 260.

differences in *substance* or *kind*, have left s 15(2)(a) unaffected. Precise compliance with the sample is demanded subject to the *de minimis* rule and the SGA, s 15A.[3]

That the bulk should correspond with the sample is not as facile a notion as it first appears. Sellers J[4] stressed that 'the extent to which a sample may be held to "speak" must depend on the contract and what is contemplated by the parties in regard to it' but, in general, the comparison of bulk with sample was done by experienced merchants and often a visual evaluation was all that was needed.[5] If the bulk matches the sample on such a visual test, there will be compliance with s 15 even though there are other, major differences between the two. In *Hookway (F E) & Co Ltd v Alfred Isaacs & Sons*,[6] B bought shellac by sample and it was normal practice to check its quality solely by visual examination. B had the sample and bulk analysed and this showed that, in one respect, the shellac was not equal to the sample. Devlin J[7] held that s 15(2)(a) was not breached because the quality of the goods related only 'to such qualities as are apparent on an ordinary examination of the sample as usually done in the trade'. In contrast, it is perfectly possible for the terms of the contract to specify that the goods comply with the sample *and* an analysis,[8] in which case S's obligation is an onerous one.

THE GOODS MUST BE 'FREE FROM ANY DEFECT, MAKING THEIR QUALITY UNSATISFACTORY, WHICH WOULD NOT BE APPARENT ON REASONABLE EXAMINATION OF THE SAMPLE'

The rule at common law was that no condition as to quality was implied in sales by sample because the sample spoke for itself, but there was an implied condition that the goods should be free from any *latent* defects which would render them unmerchantable[9] and it is this obligation which is embodied in s 15(2)(c).

The examination provisions are most important. First, s 15(2)(b) formerly contained an implied condition that B should have 'a reasonable opportunity of comparing the bulk with the sample'. In order to achieve a logical exposition in the SGA, the Law Commissions[10] recommended that s 15(2)(b) should be relocated within the SGA and the substance of this section has accordingly been transferred to s 35(2)(b), although this should entail no material change in the law.

---

3 See *Joe Lowe Food Products Co Ltd v J A & P Holland Ltd* [1954] 2 Lloyd's Rep 71 (sale by sample of 100 tons of dessert powder with one lorry load of 14 tons containing some lumps, this proportion being held to be insufficient to take the case outside the *de minimis* rule).
4 *Steels & Busks Ltd v Bleecker Bik & Co Ltd* [1956] 1 Lloyd's Rep 228, 239.
5 See Lord Macnaghten's emphasis in *Drummond (James) & Sons v E H Van Ingen & Co Ltd* (1887) 12 App Cas 284, 297: 'Pulled to pieces and examined by unusual tests which curiosity or suspicion might suggest, [the sample] would doubtless reveal every secret of its construction. But that is not the way in which business is done in this country'.
6 [1954] 1 Lloyd's Rep 491.
7 [1954] 1 Lloyd's Rep 491 at 511; see also *Steels & Busks Ltd v Bleecker Bik & Co Ltd* [1956] 1 Lloyd's Rep 228 (rubber was sold which caused staining and was found on analysis to contain a preservative ('PNP') not present in the sample. Held that compliance with the sample required visual compliance only and, as PNP was not thus detectable, the rubber was equal to sample).
8 See *Towerson v Aspatria Agricultural Co-operative Society Ltd* (1872) 27 LT 276 (sale of Peruvian guano warranted equal to sample and 'guaranteed analysis').
9 See *Drummond (James) & Sons v E H Van Ingen & Co Ltd* (1887) 12 App Cas 284.
10 Law Com No 160, Scot Law Com No 104, *Sale and Supply of Goods*, Cm 137 (1987), para 6.28.

Second, under s 15(2)(c) there has always been an implied condition that the goods would be free from any defect rendering them unmerchantable which would not be apparent on reasonable examination of the sample. The salient point here was that the condition of merchantability in sales by sample was excluded even where B *did not make such an examination*, if the examination *would* have dislcosed the defects. In contrast, the condition of merchantability under s 14(2) (which extended to sales by sample) was excluded only where B *actually* made an examination and such examination ought to have revealed the defects.[11] There was thus a clash between the provisions in that B might have been able to rely on s 14(2) where he had *not* examined the sample and thus circumvent the policy of s 15(2)(c). The Law Commissions[12] considered that the overall policy of s 15(2)(c) was the correct one and should prevail in sales by sample, as the whole purpose of a sample is that B has an opportunity to examine it and decide upon its suitability for his purposes. Accordingly, the new s 14(2C)(c) makes it clear that s 15(2)(c) is to prevail in sales by sample and, if a reasonable examination of the sample would have revealed the defect, the implied condition of satisfactory quality is excluded as regards that defect even if B has not actually examined the sample.

It is crucial to stress that the implied condition of satisfactory quality is excluded only in relation to defects which would have been revealed on a *reasonable* examination. In *Godley v Perry*,[13] a child lost an eye when a plastic catapult which he had bought snapped in use. The retail seller was liable as the catapult was held to be both unmerchantable and unfit for its purpose. The sales by the importer (S) to the wholesaler (B) and the wholesaler (S) to the retailer (B) were both sales by sample and both buyers had tested a catapult by pulling-back its elastic. It was argued that, by pressing together the catapult's prongs or by holding it down with one's foot, its fragility would have been discovered. Edmund Davies J[14] pointed out, with heavy irony, that 'the potential customer ... might ... have tried biting the catapult, or hitting it with a hammer, or applying a lighted match to ensure its non-inflammability ... but ... none of those tests are called for by a process of "reasonable examination", as that phrase would be understood by the common-sense standards of everyday life'. Accordingly, the defects were not discoverable on the reasonable examination which had been made and both sellers were liable under s 15(2)(c).

Reform of the law

The harmonisation of consumer sales law in the European Union (EU) has been canvassed for a number of years and the earlier reports[15] have now culminated

---

11 This is also the current position in relation to satisfactory quality under s 14(2C)(b).
12 Law Com No 160, Scot Law Com No 104, *Sale and Supply of Goods*, Cm 137 (1987), paras 6.24-6.27.
13 [1960] 1 WLR 9.
14 [1960] 1 WLR 9 at 15.
15 See *Green Paper on Guarantees for Consumer Goods and After-Sales Services*, COM (93) 509; *Proposal for a European Parliament and Council Directive on the Sale of Consumer Goods and Associated Guarantees*, COM (95) 520; *Amended Proposal for a European Parliament and Council Directive on the Sale of Consumer Goods and Associated Guarantees*, COM (1998) 217.

in an EU Directive[16] which must be implemented by Member States no later than 1 January 2002. The new Directive applies *only* where *businesses* deal with *consumers* and, most significantly, the new provisions will add considerably to the range of remedies available to consumers.

The EU Directive on *Certain Aspects of the Sale of Consumer Goods and Associated Guarantees*

ARTICLE 1: THE SCOPE OF THE DIRECTIVE

Consumers, sellers and consumer goods

Article 1 delineates the scope of the Directive and defines the relevant parties. 'Consumer' is defined in art 1(2)(a) as 'any natural person who, in the contracts covered by this Directive, is acting for purposes which are not related to his trade, business or profession'. Clearly limited companies, no matter how small, are outside this definition ('natural person'). Moreover, the implication is that the consumer must be 'acting' *solely* as such, thereby excluding the possibility that a part-time business activity could fall within art 1(2)(a).

'Seller' means 'any natural or legal person who, under a contract, sells consumer goods in the course of his trade, business or profession' (art 1(2)(c)). Clearly limited companies are within this definition ('legal person') but, as with the consumer definition, it is arguable that the emphasis in art 1(2)(c) on 'his' trade, business or profession (in contradistinction to 'a' trade, business or profession) would exclude a part-time business activity. Certainly in *R v Warwickshire County Council, ex p Johnson*,[17] the House of Lords held that the phrase 'in the course of any business of his' in the Consumer Protection Act 1987, s 20(1), meant a business of which the defendant was either the owner or in which he had a controlling interest. Once again, the phrase 'in the *course* of his trade, business or profession' is used in art 1(2)(c) and it remains to be seen whether this will apply to isolated sales in the course of a business (as in *Stevenson v Rogers*[18]), or whether some degree of regularity in selling will be demanded to bring the sale within the course of the business (as in *R & B Customs Brokers Co Ltd v United Dominions Trust Ltd*[19]).

The 'producer' is referred to in various parts of the Directive and is defined in art 1(2)(d) as 'the manufacturer of consumer goods, the importer of consumer goods into the territory of the Community or any person purporting to be a producer by placing his name, trade mark or other distinctive sign on the consumer goods'.

'Consumer goods' are also defined very widely in art 1(2)(b) as 'any tangible movable item' with the exception of water and gas (where 'they are not put up for sale in a limited volume or set quantity'), electricity and 'goods sold by way of execution or otherwise by authority of law'. Article 1(4) provides that 'contracts

---

16 Directive 99/44/EC, 25 May 1999, *Certain Aspects of the Sale of Consumer Goods and Associated Guarantees*. See Beale and Howells, 'EC Harmonisation of Consumer Sales Law – A Missed Opportunity?' (1997) 12 JCL 21.
17 [1993] AC 583.
18 [1999] QB 1028.
19 [1988] 1 WLR 321.

for the supply of consumer goods to be manufactured or produced shall also be deemed contracts of sale for the purpose of this Directive'. It should be stressed that second-hand goods are clearly within the definition of 'consumer goods' in art 1(2)(b).

It is not easy to avoid the difficulties which are inherent in the search for a meaningful, practical definition of a 'consumer' and a 'business' seller. It will be remembered that the UCTA, s 12 prescribes that one party 'makes the contract in the course of a business' while the 'consumer' does not thus 'make' the contract. Although this is abstraction run riot, all the problems which have dogged s 12 lie in wait for the new provisions which employ terminology almost as intangible as that found in s 12. However, s 12 does make some attempt at confinement in stipulating that consumer goods are those 'ordinarily supplied for private use or consumption'. No such limitation is present in the Directive's definition of 'consumer goods' as being 'any tangible movable item' and, indeed, this is so vacuous a formula that it lacks any utility as a demarcation of *consumer* goods: goods which are normally supplied only to tradesmen, eg cement mixers and pantechnicons, are, without a doubt, classified as 'consumer goods' within art 1(2)(b).[20] Consequently, should a consumer buy a cement mixer from a business seller, in order to renovate his home, the sale will be within the provisions of the Directive.

The relationship between the parties

It is somewhat disconcerting that the relationship between the 'seller' and the 'consumer' is not defined or established but it seems that this is deliberate. The paradigm transaction within the Directive is a sale of new, consumer goods made directly between a business seller and a consumer buyer. However, while the definition of a 'seller' demands that he must sell the goods, the 'consumer' who seeks a remedy need not *buy* the goods from that seller. Consequently, the Directive is enigmatic on the question of what rights, if any, are available to consumers who have no privity of contract with the original business seller. The Green Paper had been in favour of extending protection to 'subsequent owners' of the goods and this category would thus include subsequent purchasers and donees from the original purchaser provided that, in both cases, the parties could furnish evidence of the first purchase.[1] Overall, this extension is excluded in relation to the conformity provisions of the Directive in that art 2(1) provides that 'the *seller* must *deliver* goods to the *consumer* which are in conformity with the contract of sale'. However, it is clear that the seller could sell consumer goods to a buyer who is either a consumer or a non-consumer, with a condition that the goods be delivered to a consumer donee who will then have the rights and remedies against the seller which are prescribed under the Directive.

Although this latter possibility broadens the scope of the Directive, it must be stressed that it is only an original sale of consumer goods which activates the new provisions; other contracts of supply, such as hire, hire-purchase or contracts for the supply of services, are *not* drawn within the framework of the Directive.

---

20 Article 1(3) allows Member States the discretion to provide that 'consumer goods' does not apply to 'second-hand goods sold at public auction where consumers have the opportunity of attending the sale in person'.

 1 See *Green Paper on Guarantees for Consumer Goods and After-Sales Services*, COM (93) 509, para 3.3, p 88.

ARTICLE 2: THE NOTION OF CONFORMITY

Article 2 is arguably the central, substantive core of the Directive. Article 2(1) provides that the 'seller must deliver goods to the consumer which are in conformity with the contract of sale'. Article 2(2) then stipulates that 'goods are presumed to be in conformity with the contract' if they meet the four requirements specified, viz:

(a) the goods 'comply with the description given by the seller and possess the qualities of the goods which the seller has held out to the consumer as a sample or model';
(b) the goods 'are fit for any particular purpose for which the consumer requires them and which he made known to the seller at the time of conclusion of the contract and which the seller has accepted';
(c) the goods 'are fit for the purposes for which goods of the same type are normally used';
(d) the goods 'show the quality and performance which are normal in goods of the same type and which the consumer can reasonably expect, given the nature of the goods and taking into account any public statements on the specific characteristics of the goods made about them by the seller, the producer[2] or his representative, particularly in advertising or on labelling'.

Article 2(5) adds a helpful rule regarding the situation where goods are installed by the seller (eg double-glazed windows) or the consumer himself. Providing that installation forms part of the contract of the sale of goods, incorrect installation of those goods by or on behalf of the seller is deemed to be equivalent to lack of conformity of the goods. This also applies where 'the product' is intended to be, and is, installed by the consumer but is installed incorrectly 'due to a shortcoming in the installation instructions'.

Article 2(3) provides one safeguard for the seller in that there will be deemed not to be a lack of conformity if, at the time the contract was concluded, 'the consumer was aware, or could not reasonably be unaware of, the lack of conformity, or if the lack of conformity has its origin in materials supplied by the consumer'.

What is is meant by 'conformity'?

The overall notion of 'conformity' does not appear to pose any novel difficulties for English law and, having regard to the four specific requirements, above, which must be satisfied, the relatively colourless concept of 'conformity' is apt as an organising principle. Many of the Directive's demands will already be realised by the implied conditions in the SGA, ss 13-15, but there are some important changes in the Directive which must be accentuated.

It is unclear what width is to be given to compliance with description in art 2(2)(a). It was stressed in Chapter 20 that English law originally demanded strict compliance with description under the SGA s 13 and this came to be a potent weapon in the consumer buyer's armoury.[3] Later decisions restricted the ambit of s 13 to descriptive words which identified the subject-matter of the contract

---

2 'Producer' is defined in art 1(2)(d), see above.
3 See eg *Beale v Taylor* [1967] 1 WLR 1193.

as distinct from statements relating to its qualities or attributes.[4] As a consumer remedy, it seems apt that art 2(2)(a) be interpreted broadly, meaning that precise conformity with description can be demanded.

Article 2(2)(b) is analogous to the implied condition of fitness for purpose in the SGA, s 14(3). In one respect it is significantly narrower than the common law's interpretation of s 14(3), as it appears to demand that B must expressly communicate his particular purpose to S and that S must 'accept' that purpose. This would indicate that *agreement* must be reached between B and S regarding the particular purpose but, if so, this is an onerous requirement that it is unlikely to be fulfilled in most consumer sales. Article 2(2)(b) is wider than s 14(3), however, in that there are no provisos attached to the new provisions exempting S from liability where B does not rely, or where it is unreasonable for him to rely, on S's skill or judgement.

Article 2(2)(c) and (d) concern the standard of quality which the consumer can demand of the goods and so there is an overlap here with the implied condition of satisfactory quality in the SGA, s 14. In fact, the list of specific aspects of satisfactory quality which are now enumerated in the SGA, s 14(2B)(a)-(e) (eg appearance and finish of the goods; freedom from minor defects) are considerably more demanding than art 2 and, consequently, s 14 confers superior protection on the consumer buyer.

In one respect, however, art 2(2)(d) is revolutionary. In assessing the quality which the consumer can 'reasonably expect', account must be taken of 'any public statements on the specific characteristics of the goods made about them by the seller, the producer[5] or his representative, particularly in advertising or on labelling'. The Directive uses the phrase 'public statements' and this is aimed, principally, at advertisements. The new provisions will enable consumers to rely on advertising produced by a *manufacturer* of the goods when seeking to render the *seller* liable where those goods are not in conformity with the contract of sale. It has always been theoretically possible in English law for a seller to be liable for assertions made in the manufacturer's advertising campaign on the basis of a collateral contract, but the formidable obtsacles of contract formation, consideration, certainty and intent to create legal relations have rendered the possibility a remote one.[6]

The extra liability imposed on a seller by art 2(2)(d) does not seem unreasonable in the light of modern advertising and marketing practices by which consumers are attracted directly to brand-name goods because of the manufacturer's claims. The seller clearly obtains increased business as a consequence of the advertising and it is thus a fair allocation of risk that he is liable where it is incorrect. Moreover, in recent years, advertising has become more precise and factual in its content, often seeking to avoid the extravagant yet meaningless commendation of goods to focus, instead, on declarations as to their value for money and reliability. Undoubtedly difficult issues will have to be confronted in the future regarding which parts of an advertisement or label

---

4   See *Ashington Piggeries Ltd v Christopher Hill Ltd* [1972] AC 441.

5   'Producer' is defined in art 1(2)(d): see above.

6   Where the buyer has bought goods from a retailer, the courts have been reluctant to find a collateral contract between the manufacturer of the goods and the buyer, see *Lambert v Lewis* [1980] 2 WLR 299, CA (denial of collateral contact based on manufacturer's brochures); cf *Wells (Merstham) Ltd v Buckland Sand & Silica Co Ltd* [1965] 2 QB 170 (collateral contract succeeded where the manufacturer gave an *express* assurance to B as to the suitability of the goods for B's purpose).

have a factual content and upon which it is reasonable for the consumer to rely. Whilst this reform is a dramatic innovation for English law, art 2(2)(d) does not go as far as the recommendation in the Green Paper that the seller and manufacturer should be jointly liable.[7]

There are restrictions on the seller's liability for the manufacturer's claims made in advertisements and other 'public statements'. Article 2(4) provides that the seller shall not be bound by such 'public statements' if he (i) 'shows that he was not, and could not reasonably have been, aware of the statement in question'; (ii) 'shows that by the time of conclusion of the contract the statement had been corrected'; or (iii) 'shows that the decision to buy the consumer goods could not have been influenced by the statement'. Again, there are several important issues here.

First, it is difficult to see why the seller's lack of awareness of, for example, an advertising campaign, should exonerate him: it is surely the effect of the advertisment on the *consumer* which is of paramount importance. Equally, will sellers be able to argue successfully that they were unaware of detailed instructions supplied inside sealed goods? Liability should surely be *imposed* on the seller in these situations and he should be deemed to have knowledge of instructions and advertising claims even if he has no actual knowledge of them. The proviso allowing the seller to prove lack of knowledge comes close to demanding that he must *adopt* the advertising or other statement as his own and this approach, if followed, clearly has the potential to excuse the seller in numerous factual situations.

The second limitation on the seller's liability, relating to the correction of the statement, is a reasonable one in principle but surely difficult to apply in practice. On such an important point, it is suggested that the consumer should receive an *express* correction by the seller at the time the contract is concluded. In the absence of such a rule, the perennial, factual difficulties of communication are bound to surface: does a small (or large) notice displayed in a retail shop, for example, suffice to negate claims made in a nationwide advertising campaign?

The third proviso appears to function satisfactorily at a practical level and it is reasonable to exempt the seller from liability where, for example, he proves that a trial advertisement was shown on television for a limited period only and in a restricted area of the country. Alternatively, an advertisement might have been published after the sale was completed. However. the third proviso is criticisable as a consumer protection measure in that it introduces the elusive elements of influence and reliance thus inviting the seller's utilisation of a plethora of fine distinctions regarding these notions.

ARTICLE 3: RIGHTS OF THE CONSUMER

Article 3(1) provides that the seller is liable for lack of conformity which exists at the time the goods are *delivered*. Somewhat confusingly, art 3(2) grants four remedies to the consumer in cases of lack of conformity viz, repair, replacement, price reduction and rescission of the contract. Recital 12 specifies that the seller may offer the consumer any available remedy but that it is 'for the consumer to decide whether to accept or reject this proposal'.

---

7 See *Green Paper on Guarantees for Consumer Goods and After-Sales Services*, COM (93) 509, pp 86–88.

The current remedies available under English law are rejection of the goods and/or damages and so the new reforms will impose a much more elaborate structure which, presumably, is intended to benefit the consumer. Regrettably, it is not at all clear how the four remedies are intended to interrelate and, in relation to the primary remedies of replacement and repair, it is plain that the seller is granted considerable latitude to argue that these remedies are 'impossible or disproportionate'. As will be seen below, an enactment of the Directive in its present form will definitely entail a diminution in the consumer buyer's rights in that the existing, absolute right to reject the goods for minor defects will cease to exist. Instead of this effective and understandable consumer remedy, a system will be substituted which, biased as it is in favour of the seller, can serve only to obscure consumer remedies in a surfeit of enigmatic distinctions. As the Directive is intended to impose a minimum standard of protection and, in view of the fact that English law currently offers superior remedies to the consumer than those proposed, it is hoped that the Directive's diluted reforms are not implemented.

Repair or replacement

Article 3(3) provides that, 'in the first place' the consumer can demand repair or replacement unless these remedies are 'impossible or disproportionate'. There is currently no right in English law to demand that the goods be repaired and this a welcome additional right in cases of trivial defects provided that the consumer has confidence in the seller's ability to effect a repair quickly. 'Repair' is defined in art 1(2)(f) as 'bringing consumer goods into conformity with the contract of sale'.

Article 3(3) goes on to specify that 'a remedy' (presumably repair and replacement) shall be deemed to be disproportionate 'if it imposes costs on the seller which, in comparison with the alternative remedy, are unreasonable, taking into account (i) the value the goods would have if there were no lack of conformity (ii) the significance of the lack of conformity and (iii) whether the alternative remedy could be completed without significant inconvenience to the consumer'. Clearly, this involves a balancing exercise as to which remedy is the most economical and practical in the circumstances. For example, goods may have been made to the consumer's special order with his own unique materials but, if the manufactured goods are not in conformity with the contract, it would be impossible to replace them. Similarly, it may often be both impossible and disproportionate to demand a replacement of second-hand goods – certainly recital 16 stresses that replacement 'is generally not available' for second-hand goods. There will also be situations where both repair and replacement must be regarded as impossible and disproportionate. If second-hand goods are seriously defective, exorbitantly expensive repairs would render this remedy disproportionate and replacement may clearly be impossible. In this event, the remedies of rescission or reduction in the price will be available.

Finally, art 3(3) provides that 'repair or replacement shall be completed within a reasonable time and without any significant inconvenience to the consumer, taking account of the nature of the goods and the purpose for which the consumer required the goods'.

The central difficulty with these remedies is the uncertainty which is introduced by the notion that they may be 'impossible or disproportionate'. Article 3(3) gives priority to the seller's interests in that a remedy shall be deemed to be disproportionate 'if it imposes costs on the seller which, in comparison with the alternative remedy, are unreasonable'. Article 3(3) does provide a counter-balance to this in providing that repair or replacement shall be completed in a reasonable time and without any significant inconvenience to the consumer, taking account of the nature of the goods and the purpose for which the consumer required the goods, but this appears to be a secondary consideration. When faced with the consumer's demand for repair or replacement of non-conformimg goods, it is inevitable that unscrupulous sellers will automatically assert that both these remedies are disproportionate, with the aim of foisting onto the consumer a miniscule reduction in the price of the goods. Undoubtedly many consumers, thus fobbed-off by the seller's assertion, will be saddled with defective goods and an inadequate monetary settlement. The very fact that the seller can avail himself of the disproportionality and impossibility arguments is inapt in the field of consumer protection where remedies should be accessible, intelligible and endow the consumer with superior bargaining power. The Directive's proposals in this context amount to an inversion of these objectives.

Reduction in price or rescission

Article 3(5) deals with the remedies of reduction of the price or rescission which are said to be available (i) 'if the consumer is entitled to neither repair nor replacement'; or (ii) 'if the seller has not completed the remedy within a reasonable time'; or (iii) 'if the seller has not completed the remedy without significant inconvenience to the consumer'. Article 3(6) completes the picture by providing that the consumer is not entitled to have the contract rescinded 'if the lack of conformity is minor'.

Again, the seller has significant room for manoeuvre regarding the 'minor' lack of conformity and, if repair or replacement are not available to the consumer and the defect is classified as 'minor', he is left with the inadequate remedy of a reduction in price. There is a grave danger that many consumers will slip the net of the primary remedies and be left with an insignificant reduction in the price of the goods.

ARTICLE 4: RIGHT OF REDRESS

This article appears to add nothing to a basic understanding of the law in providing that liability can be passed backwards through a chain of sellers. Consequently, art 4 means that, should a retail seller be sued successfully by the consumer for lack of conformity in the goods, that retailer may pursue remedies against his seller (who might be the manufacturer of the goods) under the implied conditions in ss 13-14 of the SGA. Article 4 is explicit that the persons thus liable in the chain 'shall be determined by national law'. Consequently, art 4 states the obvious and does not provide, for example, that liability under the Directive's provisions is transmissible between the parties in the chain.

ARTICLE 5: TIME LIMITS

The period of two years in which non-conformity becomes apparent

Article 5(1) provides that 'the seller shall be liable' where the lack of conformity becomes apparent within two years as from delivery of the goods. If, under national legislation, the rights laid down in art 3(2) are subject to a limitation period, that period shall not expire within a period of two years from the time of delivery.

This provision has caused some consternation[8] but it is not intended to impose a two-year durability requirement for consumer goods. It must be remembered that, under art 3(1), the non-conformity of the goods must exist at the date of *delivery*.

Although a buyer has, under English law, six years in which to pursue a claim for goods which can be shown to have been defective at the time of delivery, in some Member States the consumer can lose his right to complain of defective goods very soon after delivery and, moreover, this conclusion might currently be reached in English law if the consumer is deemed to have accepted the goods under the SGA, s 35. Accordingly, art 5(1) will improve consumer rights in those countries where the lack of conformity was present at the date of delivery but a defect materialises subsequently in the two-year period.

It should also be emphasised that art 5(1) does not impose a limitation period in the sense that the consumer must commence proceedings within the two-year period. Provided that the defects were present at the date of delivery and became apparent within the two-year period, the consumer may commence proceedings at any time within the limitation period prescribed by his national law. Should a Member State have a period of limitation which is less than two years, art 5(1) will, of course, effectively extend that period to two years. The Directive provides that Member States 'may maintain in force more stringent provisions ... to ensure a higher level of consumer protection' (art 8(2)) and so, under English law, should a buyer be able to establish, more than two years after delivery, that a fault existed at the date of delivery, he could commence proceedings at any time within the six-year limitation period.

Finally, art 7(1) provides that Member States 'may provide that, in the case of second-hand goods, the seller and consumer may agree contractual terms or agreements which have a shorter time period for the liability of the seller than that set down in Article 5(1). Such period may not be less than one year.' It is arguable that the one year limit is too long in relation to some types of second-hand goods and it might mean that sellers of such goods could not continue in business (eg charity shops).

The period of two months in which the consumer must inform the seller of non-conformity

Article 5(2) provides that Member States *may* provide that 'in order to benefit from his rights, the consumer must inform the seller of the lack of conformity within a period of two months from the date on which he detected such lack of conformity'.

Some Member States prescribe very short periods during which the buyer must notify the seller of defective goods and so a period of two months might seem generous in those countries. However, there has never been a rule to this effect in English law and it seems an unnecessarily onerous requirement in that a consumer may not be aware of his legal position or unsure as to which party should be contacted regarding the non-conforming goods until the two months

8   See the DTI report *Proposal for a European Parliament and Council Directive on the Sale of Consumer Goods and Associated Guarantees* (September, 1996).

have elapsed. Consequently, it is suggested that this stipulation should not be included in legislation and this is also the view of the DTI.[9]

The six month presumption

Article 5(3) introduces an important new right for consumers in providing that 'unless proved otherwise, any lack of conformity which becomes apparent within six months of delivery of the goods shall be presumed to have existed at the time of delivery unless this presumption is incompatible with the nature of the goods or the nature of the lack of conformity'.

This rebuttable presumption has caused concern amongst many retailers who fear that it will lead to an increase in fraudulent claims being made, but this assertion seems to overlook the fact that the presumption is not applicable where it is 'incompatible with the nature of the goods or the nature of the lack of conformity'. It would be incompatible with the nature of perishable goods, for example, that they should be durable. In short, the six months' presumption will apply only where the nature of the goods means that it would be unusual for defects to appear in six months and the stress on the nature of the lack of conformity means that sellers can establish, where apt, that the goods have been mistreated or maintained inadequately by the consumer.

ARTICLE 6: THE BINDING FORCE OF GUARANTEES

Article 6(1) provides that 'a guarantee shall be legally binding on the offerer under the conditions laid down in the guarantee statement and the associated advertising'. This provision relates to the standard, commercial guarantees offered by sellers or manufacturers of goods and 'guarantee' is defined in art 1(2)(e) as 'any undertaking by a seller or producer to the consumer, given without extra charge, to reimburse the price paid or to replace, repair or handle consumer goods in any way if they do not meet the specifications set out in the guarantee statement or in the relevant advertising'.

The legal status of manufacturers' guarantees has always been in doubt.[10] Where the guarantee is provided by a manufacturer who has no contract of sale with the buyer of the goods, the difficulties of consideration and intent to create legal relations are the hurdles placed in the path of enforceability. If intent is disregarded on the basis that, today, manufacturers patently intend to be legally bound by their guarantees, there is still the problem that consideration may not move from the consumer buyer to the manufacturer. This argument can probably be eliminated where the consumer knows of the guarantee before purchasing the goods so that its presence promotes the sales of the manufacturer's product and benefits him directly, but it is more difficult to reach this conclusion where the consumer discovers the guarantee after he has purchased the goods. It is possible that the guarantee could constitute a collateral, unilateral contract but, as guarantees are commonplace in consumer sales, it is surely inapt to demand that their enforceability should turn on such legal niceties.

In view of these difficulties, art 6(1) is welcome in providing that guarantees shall become legally binding. There are, however, two areas of uncertainty. First,

---

9 See DTI Press Notice P/99/417 (17 May, 1999), p 2.
10 See *Consumer Guarantees* (OFT 1984).

it is unclear what is meant by 'the associated advertising' and whether this may, itself, constitute a guarantee. Second, it is questionable whether the provisions of the guarantee can be invoked by a subsequent consumer/owner of the goods who purchased them from the original consumer purchaser, or by a donee from that original purchaser. The issue here relates to privity of contract in that it is indisputable that a subsequent purchaser or donee has no direct contract with the manufacturer, and the latter might easily seize on the privity argument to deny liability under a guarantee. The Green Paper was in favour of allowing the guarantee to be invoked by anyone in possession of the guarantee who could also furnish evidence of the initial purchase.[11] This is clearly the practice followed by many reputable manufacturers who consider that the guarantee relates to the goods rather than the purchaser and, indeed, there is no exclusion of subsequent purchasers or donees in the broad wording of art 6.

Article 6(2) reinforces art 6(1) in that it provides for the content of guarantees. Accordingly, the guarantee must state that the consumer 'has legal rights under applicable national legislation governing the sale of consumer goods and make clear that those rights are not affected by the guarantee'. This provision is clearly aimed at those guarantees which sought to restrict the consumer's rights by demanding, for example, that defects must be notified in unreasonably short periods of time with the penalty for non-compliance being a loss of the right to reject the goods. This problem is also addressed by the UCTA 1977, s 5 which provides that, in relation to consumer goods, manufacturers' guarantees cannot exclude or restrict liability for loss or damage caused by negligence.

It is now standard for EU Directives to prescribe that the contents of documents must be clear and understandable and this Directive is no exception. Article 6(2) demands that the guarantee must 'set out in plain intelligible language the contents of the guarantee and the essential particulars necessary for making claims under the guarantee, notably the duration and territorial scope of the guarantee as well as the name and address of the guarantor'. Article 6(3) provides that 'on request by the consumer, the guarantee shall be made available in writing or feature in another durable medium available and accessible to him'. Finally, and most usefully, art 6(5) provides that an infringement of the requirements of art 6 shall not affect the validity of the guarantee which will, consequently, remain legally enforceable.

ARTICLE 7: BINDING NATURE AND NON-DEROGATION

An important provision now customarily found in EU Directives is the non-derogation clause. Article 7(1) provides that 'any contractual terms or agreements concluded with the seller before the lack of conformity is brought to the seller's attention which directly or indirectly waive or restrict the rights resulting from this Directive shall, as provided for by national law, not be binding on the consumer'.

---

11 See *Green Paper on Guarantees for Consumer Goods and After-Sales Services*, COM (93) 509, para 3.1.5, p 98.

CHAPTER 22

The seller's duty to deliver the goods

The duty to deliver

The sections of the SGA 1979 which apply to delivery of the goods (ss 27-33) are headed 'Performance of the Contract' and this gives some measure of the relatively utilitarian nature of the rules on delivery. These rules are, nevertheless, of crucial significance to both S and B as delivery and payment are primary, practical obligations of the contract of sale. The SGA, s 27 provides:

> 'It is the duty of the seller to deliver the goods, and of the buyer to accept and pay for them, in accordance with the terms of the contract of sale. '

It is crucial to differentiate the delivery of the goods from the passing of property in them as there is no necessary coincidence between these two concepts: property may pass to B before, on or after delivery. It follows that, even if B owns the goods before delivery has taken place, S or his bailee must nevertheless perform an act of delivery so that B may obtain physical custody of, or control over, the goods. The duty of delivery will necessarily vary with the type of goods being sold and, under s 27, delivery must also be 'in accordance with the terms of the contract of sale'. Accordingly, the parties are at liberty to make whatever contractual arrangements they wish regarding delivery[1] and the SGA will govern the position only to the extent that S and B have not provided for delivery and payment in their contract. Two basic examples may clarify the position regarding the delivery of different types of goods. Where the property in specific goods has passed to B on contract but B has not taken possession of the goods, S's duty to deliver attaches to those specific goods and he will be required to perform some further act in relation to them so that B can obtain either control or custody of the goods. Alternatively, in a contract for the sale of unascertained, generic goods, S must deliver goods which correspond with the contract description but here the passing of property and S's duty to deliver may coincide if the goods are delivered to a carrier for transmission to B (s 32(1)) and are appropriated to the contract (s 18, r 5(2)) at the same time.

---

1 See *Calcutta and Burmah Steam Navigation Co v De Mattos* (1863) 32 LJQB 322, 328 per Blackburn J.

It is important to establish what constitutes delivery because S's failure to deliver the goods renders him liable for non-delivery and, under the SGA, s 28, delivery and payment are concurrent conditions.

MEANING OF DELIVERY

It is extremely difficult to define 'delivery' in concise terms although, quite misleadingly, the SGA attempts to perform that feat: s 61(1) defines delivery as the 'voluntary transfer of possession from one person to another'. At first glance, it might be assumed that this brief definition referred to the familiar, idiomatic meaning of delivery as a physical conveyance of the goods from S to B but, as will be seen later, there is no general rule requiring S to transmit the goods to B. In the vernacular, 'delivery' entails a bilateral act in the sense that S dispatches the goods and B receives them, but delivery in the SGA may be satisfied if the goods are put at B's disposal in a deliverable state. Moreover, delivery need not involve B's acquisition of the physical *custody* of the goods and thus attornment by a bailee, eg a warehouseman, that he holds the goods on behalf of B may suffice as delivery to B. Similarly, there can be a delivery by the transfer to B of the documents of title to the goods or the delivery may be made by S direct to a sub-buyer from B, so that B never has physical custody of the goods.[2] It will be readily apparent that there is no single meaning of 'delivery' but, instead, the law sanctions different methods of delivery and this diversity accounts for the broad, abstract definition in s 61(1). Any attempt at a definition of delivery would thus involve a précis of the above points; instead it is expedient to consider the various ways by which delivery can be effected.

METHODS OF DELIVERY

First, the parties can agree upon any method of delivery and this may often involve an actual dispatch of the goods to B or B may specify that S should deliver the goods direct to a sub-buyer.[3] Second, it is plain that such a dispatch of the goods to B may be commercially impracticable where the goods are afloat, for example, and thus the law permits S to make a *constructive* delivery. The various methods of constructive delivery must now be detailed.

Symbolic delivery

Such a delivery may occur where S delivers to B the symbolic means of acquiring possession, eg the keys to a warehouse where the goods are stored.[4] It is vital, however, for there also to be an implied licence for B to enter the premises and take the goods.[5] Perhaps this mode of delivery is better considered as an instance of actual delivery as the key clearly gives more than symbolic possession of the goods.[6]

---

2 See *Ruben (E & S) Ltd v Faire Bros & Co Ltd* [1949] 1 KB 254; *Four Point Garage Ltd v Carter* [1985] 3 All ER 12.
3 See *Ruben (E & S) Ltd v Faire Bros & Co Ltd* [1949] 1 KB 254; *Four Point Garage Ltd v Carter* [1985] 3 All ER 12.
4 See eg *Jones v Selby* (1710) Prec Ch 300; *Chaplin v Rogers* (1800) 1 East 192.
5 *Wrightson v McArthur and Hutchisons (1919) Ltd* [1921] 2 KB 807, 816-818 per Rowlatt J.
6 See *Ward v Turner* (1752) 1 Dick 170, per Lord Hardwicke.

S becomes a bailee for B after the sale

S may remain in physical custody of the goods after the sale to B but S and B may agree that S shall thenceforth hold the goods as a bailee for B and this may amount to sufficient delivery of the goods to B.[7]

Delivery by attornment

A party attorns to B when he acknowledges that he holds the goods for B. A third party bailee in possession of the goods, eg a warehouseman, may commonly attorn to B and this will amount to a constructive delivery. The SGA, s 29(4) provides that 'where the goods at the time of sale are in the possession of a third person, there is no delivery by seller to buyer unless and until the third person acknowledges to the buyer that he holds the goods on his behalf ...'.

It is important to stress that attornment must be made with the consent of the three parties involved and so, in *Godts v Rose*,[8] an agreement between S and a wharfinger that the goods would be held for B did not amount to a delivery to B. Situations requiring attornment will most frequently occur where the bailee issues a delivery order to S and S then chooses to transfer the document to B. Sometimes the procedure may be reversed and S may give a delivery order to B which is addressed to the bailee. It is thus often the bailee's consent to the arrangement and his actual attornment to B which are pivotal to this mode of delivery and, whilst the attornment may take any form, mere receipt by the bailee of an order or warrant will be insufficient if the bailee does not respond to B in any further way.[9] Moreover, it should be remembered that, even if there is an attornment, no property in unascertained goods can pass to B unless and until they become ascertained.[10]

If B is blameless but cannot obtain the acknowledgment from the bailee, he may be entitled to treat the contract as discharged[11] and, alternatively, S may treat the delivery as having been made correctly if B is at fault in failing to obtain the acknowledgment.[12]

Issue or transfer of a document of title

Section 29(4), above, goes on to state that 'nothing in this section affects the operation of the issue or transfer of any document of title to goods' and this means that there is no need for any attornment by a third party in possession of goods where there is such an issue or transfer to B of a document of title. Certain

---

7 See the decisions on the Statute of Frauds 1677 (later the SGA 1893, s 4(1), repealed in 1954) requirement for the enforceability of contracts for the sale of goods to the value of £10 and above. One stipulation for enforceability was that B must accept and 'actually receive' the goods. B's constructive possession sufficed as an actual receipt: see eg *Elmore v Stone* (1809) 1 Taunt 458 (S, the owner of a livery stable, sold two horses to B but, as B had no stables, he asked S to keep the horses for him. Held this was a constructive delivery); *Castle v Sworder* (1861) 6 H & N 828; Cf *Carter v Toussaint* (1822) 5 B & Ald 855.
8 (1854) 17 CB 229.
9 *Laurie and Morewood v Dudin and Sons* [1926] 1 KB 223; see also *Wardar's (Import and Export) Co Ltd v W Norwood & Sons Ltd* [1968] 2 QB 663 (both considered in Ch 16).
10 Where the new provisions on co-ownership of a bulk are applicable (the SGA, ss 20A and 20B) the definition of delivery in s 61(1) is extended to include 'such appropriation of goods to the contract as results in property in the goods being transferred to the buyer'.
11 *Pattison v Robinson* (1816) 5 M & S 105, 110 per Lord Ellenborough CJ.
12 *Bartlett v Holmes* (1853) 13 CB 630.

documents have become recognised as representing the goods to which they refer. The bill of lading is the paradigm of such a document and, since 1794,[13] it has been acknowledged as a document conferring constructive possession of the goods on the person to whom it is transferred. When S endorses and delivers a bill of lading to B, this operates as a delivery of the goods themselves and no attornment by the carrier is necessary.

Although the SGA, s 61(1) and the Factors Act 1889, s 1(4) provide that documents other than bills of lading are documents of title (eg delivery warrants), as between S and B such other documents do *not* endow B with constructive possession and attornment is still a necessity. Where one of the documents specified in s 1(4) of the Factors Act is transferred to a *bona fide* transferee, however, this disposition may operate to transfer title to the transferee under some of the statutory exceptions to *nemo dat*, eg the Factors Act, s 2(1).[14]

Goods are in the possession of B

If the goods are already in B's possession at the time of the sale, the assent of S to the subsequent passing of property in the goods may also suffice as delivery to B[15] provided there is evidence that the character of B's possession has changed to that of a buyer.

Licence to remove goods

Where S confers a licence on B to remove the goods, B's actual taking of possession constitutes a delivery of the goods.[16]

Delivery to a carrier

Where the SGA, s 32(1) applies, delivery to a carrier is *prima facie* deemed to be delivery of the goods to B. This section was examined earlier[17] and it should be considered together with s 18, r 5(2) on the passing of property to B and s 20, on the issue of risk.

The place of delivery

The general rules regarding the place of delivery are found in the SGA, s 29(1) and (2). Section 29(1) provides:

> 'Whether it is for the buyer to take possession of the goods or for the seller to send them to the buyer is a question depending in each case on the contract, express or implied, between the parties.'

---

13 *Lickbarrow v Mason* (1794) 5 Term Rep 683.
14 See Ch 18.
15 *Edan v Dudfield* (1841) 1 QB 302; *Lillywhite v Devereux* (1846) 15 M & W 285 (both cases on receipt of the goods under the Statute of Frauds/SGA 1893, s 4(1) requirement); cf *Taylor v Wakefield* (1856) 6 E & B 765; *Jennings v Macaulay & Co Ltd* [1937] IR 540.
16 *Congreve v Evetts* (1854) 10 Exch 298, 308 per Parke B; see also *Thomas v Times Book Co Ltd* [1966] 2 All ER 241 (Dylan Thomas had mislaid a manuscript and told the donee that if he found it he could keep it; the donee succeeded in finding it. Held this was sufficient delivery perfecting the gift).
17 See Ch 16 (passing of property) and Ch 24 (risk).

Naturally, the contract may often specify the place of delivery and this may be combined with a specific method of delivery. There is surprisingly little authority in the 19th century regarding the place of delivery but the general rule was that S's obligation was merely to allow B the opportunity of taking possession of the goods at the agreed place of delivery.[18] This rule is embodied in s 29(2) which provides:

> 'Apart from any such contract, express or implied, the place of delivery is the seller's place of business if he has one, and if not, his residence; except that, if the contract is for the sale of specific goods, which to the knowledge of the parties when the contract is made are in some other place, then that place is the place of delivery.'

In the absence of any contrary intent, the general rule is thus that B must collect the goods from S's place of business or residence and S's duty is to have the goods ready for B's collection. An exception is made in the case of specific goods which are at 'some other place' at the time of contract for then the place of delivery is their location at the time of contract.[19] The general rule that S must make the goods available for collection is amplified by s 29(6) which provides that 'unless otherwise agreed, the expenses of and incidental to putting the goods into a deliverable state must be borne by the seller'. This would apply where, for example, the goods have to be dismantled or assembled in order to put them in a deliverable state. Two criticisms are that s 29(2) does not allow for the fact that S may have several places of business and it is unclear whether the place of business or the residence is fixed at the time of contract or may change by the time of delivery. These criticisms apart, the general presumptions in s 29(2) seem curiously anachronistic in modern conditions, particularly in many consumer sales, and it seems that a court might readily infer a contrary intent from the circumstances thus requiring S actually to deliver the goods to B.[20]

Where the contract specifies that S must deliver the goods at B's premises, it was held in *Galbraith and Grant Ltd v Block*[1] that S is discharged if he delivers them at B's premises to someone having apparent authority to receive them, provided that S has not been negligent. In *Galbraith*, S, a wine merchant, sold a case of champagne to B, a licensed victualler, and agreed to deliver it at B's premises. The champagne was delivered at a 'side entrance' to a man who signed the delivery sheet in B's name but B stressed that his premises were shut at the time of the delivery, that he had not authorised anyone to take delivery of the champagne and that, in fact, he had never received it. Lush J nevertheless held that S was entitled to the price of the goods as he had discharged the duty of delivery without any negligence.[2]

---

18 See *Smith v Chance* (1819) 2 B & Ald 753, 755 per Holroyd J; *Wood v Tassell* (1844) 6 QB 234, 236 per Lord Denman CJ; *Wilkinson v Lloyd* (1845) 7 QB 27, 44 per Patteson J.
19 Unascertained goods are not mentioned: might this rule apply to unascertained goods in a particular bulk?
20 See *Wiskin v Terdich Bros Pty Ltd* (1928) 34 ALR 242 (B ordered goods from S asking 'please supply us ...'. Held that it was S's duty to send the goods to B).
1 [1922] 2 KB 155.
2 Cf *Lindon Tricotagefabrik v White and Meacham* [1975] 1 Lloyd's Rep 384 (S agreed to deliver the goods at B's warehouse in Ealing but S's agents wrongly delivered them at B's offices in the City, at 8 am, when no one was there to collect them. The agents promised to re-deliver the goods at the warehouse but, before any collection of the goods, they were stolen. Held S had not fulfilled the terms of delivery and B was not liable for the price).

The time of delivery

The SGA, s 10(1) specifies that, in general, stipulations as to time of payment are not of the essence of the contract, but s 10(2) then provides that 'whether any other stipulation as to time is or is not of the essence of the contract depends on the terms of the contract'. S and B are therefore free to specify in their contract that time is to be of the essence as regards S's obligation to deliver within an agreed time. However, it is now a long-established rule of the common law that, in ordinary commercial contracts for the sale of goods, time is of the essence with respect to delivery[3] even in the absence of any express stipulation to such effect in the contract. This means that if S fails to deliver in the agreed time, B can reject the goods, repudiate the contract for breach of condition and claim damages. Undertakings regarding the time of delivery in the sale of goods are thus regarded as of crucial importance and the strict rule permitting B's rejection for breach of the condition relating to the time of delivery has been left unscathed by the more flexible notion of the innominate term.[4] This does mean that B may often be able to reject goods for a technical breach of the condition relating to the time of delivery even though he has suffered no loss and his motive may be to buy cheaper goods elsewhere, on a falling market. In *Bowes v Shand*,[5] for example, there was a sale of rice to be shipped at Madras during the months of March and/or April but the bulk of the rice (8,150 out of 8,200 bags) was shipped in February. The House of Lords held that B could reject the entire consignment even though there was no material difference between the rice shipped in February and that shipped in March.[6] *Bowes* also illustrates that delivery must be neither late nor *early* because B 'may not be ready with funds ... for payment'.[7] In fact, the time of delivery is often treated as though it were part of the condition relating to the description[8] of the goods and given a correspondingly strict interpretation. It is, however, a separate condition and is 'far more than a mere description of the goods'.[9]

Waiver and time of delivery

The certainty of the rule that B may reject the goods and repudiate the contract for breach of the condition relating to the time of delivery is complicated by the fact that B may waive his rights regarding delivery. Quite often S may request a postponement of the delivery date and only rarely will B seek to repudiate the

---

3 *Bowes v Shand* (1877) 2 App Cas 455, 463 per Lord Cairns LC; *Reuter v Sala* (1879) 4 CPD 239, 249 per Cotton LJ; *Hartley v Hymans* [1920] 3 KB 475, 484 per McCardie J; *Bunge Corpn v Tradax Export SA* [1981] 1 WLR 711, 716 and 729 per Lords Wilberforce and Roskill respectively.
4 The strictness of the rule was preserved by the House of Lords in *Bunge Corpn v Tradax Export SA* [1981] 1 WLR 711; see also *Cie Commerciale Sucres et Denrées v C Czarnikow Ltd, The Naxos* [1990] 3 All ER 64, HL.
5 (1877) 2 App Cas 455.
6 'The non-fulfilment of any term in any contract is a means by which the purchaser is able to get rid of the contract when prices have dropped; but that is no reason why a term which is found in a contract should not be fulfilled': (1877) 2 App Cas 455 at 465-466, per Lord Cairns LC.
7 (1877) 2 App Cas 455 at 463, per Lord Cairns LC.
8 As it was in *Bowes v Shand*: see Lord Cairns LC (p 468), Lord Hatherley (p 475) and Lord Blackburn (p 480).
9 *Aron (J) & Co (Inc) v Comptoir Wegimont* [1921] 3 KB 435, 441 per McCardie J.

contract immediately. Rather, there may be conciliatory negotiations between the parties and, if B acquiesces in a new date for delivery, he may be held to have waived his rights to insist on punctual delivery. The waiver may be operative at common law or, if the necessary conditions are satisfied, it may be effective in equity under the principle of promissory estoppel. Alternatively, the waiver may be justified under the SGA, s 11(2) which provides that 'where a contract of sale is subject to a condition to be fulfilled by the seller, the buyer may waive the condition ...'. The essence of such a unilateral waiver is illustrated in *Hartley v Hymans*.[10] There S agreed to sell 11,000 lb of cotton yarn to B, a yarn merchant in Bradford, with delivery to commence in September at the rate of 1,100 lb per week. Failure to deliver within the stipulated time rendered the contract liable to cancellation by B. Delivery should have been completed by the middle of November but B received no yarn until the end of October and thereafter S delivered various quantities of yarn until the end of February in the following year. During all this period, B wrote letters to S complaining of the delay and asking for better deliveries but, without any notice, B cancelled the contract on 13 March and refused to accept any further yarn. McCardie J held that, although time was of the essence with respect to delivery, B had by his letters waived the right to insist that delivery should have been completed in November. Accordingly, B had no right to cancel in March and S was entitled to damages.

The doctrine of waiver was originally developed to circumvent the difficulties posed by the Statute of Frauds 1677 (and later the SGA 1893, s 4(1)) under which contracts for the sale of goods to the value of £10 and above had to be evidenced in writing. A parol variation of the contract often led to the argument that the earlier contract had been discharged and the new contract was unenforceable as lacking the necessary writing.[11] In order to avoid injustice, the courts began to draw fine distinctions between, on the one hand, a variation of the contract which would necessitate writing and, on the other, a waiver of rights which could be enforceable despite the absence of writing.[12] In 1920, McCardie J[13] referred to these decisions as an 'unhappy confusion of authority' with an 'embarrassing ambiguity of principle' but the notion of waiver is hardly less recondite and elusive today than it was at the start of the 20th century.[14] It is perhaps best regarded as a species of estoppel[15] and, instead of waiving his rights, B might thus be regarded as being estopped from relying on the original delivery date. At its widest, waiver has been described as 'an inchoate doctrine stemming from the manifest convenience of consistency in pragmatic affairs, negativing any liberty to blow hot and cold in commercial conduct'.[16]

---

10 [1920] 3 KB 475.
11 See eg *Cuff v Penn* (1813) 1 M & S 21; *Stead v Dawber* (1839) 10 Ad & El 57; *Plevins v Downing* (1876) 1 CPD 220.
12 See eg *Ogle v Earl Vane* 1868) LR 3 QB 272; *Leather Cloth Co v Hieronimus* (1875) LR 10 QB 140; *Hickman v Haynes* (1875) LR 10 CP 598; *Levey & Co v Goldberg* [1922] 1 KB 688.
13 *Hartley v Hymans* [1920] 3 KB 475, 494.
14 See Dugdale and Yates, 'Variation, Waiver and Estoppel – A Re-Appraisal' (1976) 39 MLR 680.
15 'Whether it be called waiver or forbearance on his part, or an agreed variation or substituted performance, does not matter. It is a kind of estoppel': *Charles Rickards Ltd v Oppenhaim* [1950] 1 KB 616, 623 per Denning LJ.
16 *Panchaud Frères SA v Etablissments General Grain Co* [1970] 1 Lloyd's Rep 53, 59 per Winn LJ.

The requirements of a valid waiver or an estoppel are framed in broad terms and their primary objective is to avert unfairness where one party has relied on a representation made by the other. The central issue is to decide whether B's representation indicates that he has waived his rights or is estopped from asserting them and, in assessing this issue, it is vital to consider the effect of the representation on S, as this is simply the other side of the same coin. First, there is no form required for the waiver which can be in writing, by words or by conduct[17] and no consideration need move from S in support of the new delivery arrangement. There must, however, be a clear and unequivocal representation by B which constitutes the waiver. Second, while it would seem that S need not prove that he has detrimentally altered his position in reliance on the representation, he must show that he has relied upon it so that it would be inequitable for B to renege on his promise.[18] Third, if the postponement is for an unspecified period of time, B may reinstate his rights by giving reasonable notice to S requiring him to deliver the goods in a specified period of time and, if so, delivery on the new date becomes of the essence. In *Charles Rickards Ltd v Oppenhaim*,[19] for example, B agreed to buy from S a Rolls Royce Silver Wraith chassis onto which a body was to be built by 20 March 1948. The car was not completed on time but B continued to press for delivery until, on 29 June 1948, he gave clear notice that if it could not be delivered in four weeks he would be unable to accept it. The car was finally completed on 18 October 1948 but B then refused to take delivery. The Court of Appeal held that, although B was estopped from relying on the original time for delivery being of the essence, his giving reasonable notice to S and stipulating a new delivery date made time of the essence and he was justified in rejecting the car.

No time fixed for delivery

Where the contract does not fix the time for delivery, the SGA, s 29(3) provides:

> 'Where under the contract of sale the seller is bound to send the goods to the buyer, but no time for sending them is fixed, the seller is bound to send them within a reasonable time.'

It should be noted that s 29(3) applies only to the situation where S must *send* the goods to B but the wider common law rule is that, where the contract makes no provision for delivery, the goods must be delivered within a reasonable time.[20] In this context reference should also be made to s 29(5) which provides:

> 'Demand or tender of delivery may be treated as ineffectual unless made at a reasonable hour; and what is a reasonable hour is a question of fact.'

A term of the contract may provide that S should deliver the goods 'as required' or 'on request' and, in such a case, S is not bound to deliver the goods until B has made a request for them.[1] However, after B has requested delivery, S must deliver the goods promptly. It is also clear that S cannot treat the contract as discharged simply because B has not made a request within a reasonable time

---

17   *Bremer Handelsgesellschaft mbH v Vanden Avenne-Izegem PVBA* [1978] 2 Lloyd's Rep 109, 126 per Lord Salmon.
18   *Société Italo-Belge pour le Commerce et l'Industrie SA v Palm and Vegatable Oils (Malaysia) Sdn Bhd, The Post Chaser* [1982] 1 All ER 19.
19   [1950] 1 KB 616.
20   *Ellis v Thompson* (1838) 3 M & W 445, 456 per Alderson B; *Jones v Gibbons* (1853) 8 Exch 920, 922 per Pollock CB
1   *Jones v Gibbons* (1853) 8 Exch 920.

after the contract. Rather, if such a reasonable time has elapsed, S must demand that B notify him of the delivery requirements and, if B fails to do so within a reasonable time, S may treat the contract as discharged.

Delivery of the wrong quantity

The law concerning delivery of the wrong quantity of goods is notoriously strict and remains so even though the Sale and Supply of Goods Act 1994 has amended some of the rules by disallowing the non-consumer's right to reject the goods where the shortfall or excessive delivery is slight (see below).

Insufficient delivery

The SGA, s 30(1) provides:

> 'Where the seller delivers to the buyer a quantity of goods less than he contracted to sell, the buyer may reject them, but if the buyer accepts the goods so delivered he must pay for them at the contract rate.'

This section thus embodies one basic rule that B is not bound to accept an insufficient delivery and S is not exonerated by promising to deliver, or actually delivering, the remainder of the goods at a later date (unless B has agreed to an instalment delivery) because the SGA, s 31(1) provides:

> 'Unless otherwise agreed, the buyer of goods is not bound to accept delivery of them by instalments.'

The general rule is thus that B is entitled to delivery of all the goods at one time. Under s 30(1), B has two options in the case of an insufficient delivery. First, he can reject the amount delivered and sue for any loss caused by S's breach of contract and, if the price has been paid, he can recover it on the basis that the consideration has totally failed. Alternatively, B can accept the quantity of goods delivered, paying for them *pro rata* under the contract, and recover the part of the price which has been overpaid for the undelivered balance. It does seem that B must choose between these two alternatives and he cannot retain *part* of the short delivery and reject the remainder of the goods.[2] Although it might be thought that B's acceptance of the short delivery would amount to a waiver of the breach, it has been held that he can also recover damages for breach of contract in this situation.[3]

The facts of *Behrend & Co Ltd v Produce Brokers' Co Ltd*[4] illustrate the operation of s 30(1). S agreed to deliver to B in London, ex the steamship *Port Inglis*, two different types of cotton seed in parcels of 176 tons and 400 tons. B received 15 tons in one parcel and 22 tons in the other and the vessel then left for Hull to unload other cargo. She returned a fortnight later and the remainder of

---

2   *Champion v Short* (1807) 1 Camp 53 (B ordered half a chest of French plums, two hogsheads of raw sugar and a hundred lumps of white sugar. The plums and raw sugar were delivered but not the white sugar. B sought to accept the plums but reject the raw sugar. Lord Ellenborough held that B could have rejected both the plums and the raw sugar but, as he had accepted the plums, he was also liable for the price of the raw sugar); see also *Tarling v O'Riordan* (1878) 2 LR Ir 82. Cf Hudson, 'Dividing Acceptances in Sale of Goods' (1976) 92 LQR 506.

3   *Household Machines Ltd v Cosmos Exporters Ltd* [1947] KB 217.

4   [1920] 3 KB 530; see also *Harland & Wolff Ltd v J Burstall & Co* (1901) 84 LT 324.

the seed was tendered to B but, in the meantime, B had informed S that the vessel's departure for Hull was a failure to deliver and a breach of contract. It was held that B was entitled to keep the goods actually delivered, reject the remainder and recover so much of the contract price as represented the undelivered seed.

When B 'accepts' the goods under s 30(1) he must pay for them at the contract rate and 'acceptance' presumably has the same meaning as in s 35. One problem could arise where B retains the goods delivered, without rejecting them, on the assumption that a full delivery will be made: if no further goods are delivered, it is possible that B could be deemed to have accepted the short delivery under s 35(4), be precluded from rejecting the goods and thus have to pay for them. This possibility seems unlikely as it deprives s 30(1) of much of its force, inverting its operation and thereby giving an unfair advantage to S.

Where the contract provides for delivery by instalments, a short delivery of one or more instalments does not entitle B to reject all the contract goods unless such short delivery amounts to a repudiation of the whole contract. It is more likely, however, that this will be a severable breach. The question of severable contracts and s 31(2) is considered in more detail in Chapter 23, concerning rejection of the goods.

Excessive delivery

The SGA, s 30(2) provides:

> 'Where the seller delivers to the buyer a quantity of goods larger than he contracted to sell, the buyer may accept the goods included in the contract and reject the rest, or he may reject the whole.'

The SGA s 30(3) then adds:

> 'Where the seller delivers to the buyer a quantity of goods larger than he contracted to sell and the buyer accepts the whole of the goods so delivered he must pay for them at the contract rate.'

As in cases of short delivery, the rule is strict in allowing B to reject all the goods where there is an excessive delivery and S cannot insist that B should carry the cost of selecting the correct quanity from the larger amount.[5] However, there are other possibilities open to B under s 30(2) and (3). First, he may 'accept the goods included in the contract' and reject the excess. As with a short delivery, in cases of an excessive delivery it is arguable that B can neither accept *part* of the correct quantity nor *part* of the excess[6] but the position is unclear.[7] Second, he may keep the 'whole of the goods so delivered' and pay for them at the contract rate.

---

5   *Cunliffe v Harrison* (1851) 6 Exch 903 (S delivered 15 hogsheads of claret instead of 10. B then said he would take 10 only if they proved satisfactory but, on tasting the wine, B disapproved of it and, after several months' delay, rejected all of it. Parke B held that if only 10 hogsheads had been delivered, B's delay would have entailed an acceptance of the wine, but delivery of 15 hogsheads under a contract to deliver 10 was 'no performance of that contract' and S had no claim against B).

6   *Champion v Short* (1807) 1 Camp 53 (*short* delivery, considered above).

7   *Hart v Mills* (1846) 15 M & W 85 (B ordered two dozen bottles of port and two dozen bottles of sherry but was sent four dozen of each. B kept one bottle of port and a dozen of sherry, paid the correct amount of money into court and returned the rest. Held S could recover only the cost of the goods retained by B. The decision would seem to be based on B's acceptance of S's counter-offer but the difficulty is that B did not accept it unequivocally and take the *whole* of the excess, as in the cases considered below); see Hudson, 'Dividing Acceptances in Sale of Goods' (1976) 92 LQR 506.

Where B chooses to keep all of the goods, the excess delivery is regarded as a 'proposal for a new contract'[8] which B accepts by paying for the goods and, if he takes this course, it seems that he is barred from claiming damages for any loss caused by the excess delivery.[9] However, the Law Commissions[10] have questioned whether an excessive delivery should, in all cases, be treated as a counter-offer by S which B may accept. B's acceptance of the counter-offer may be inoffensive where S delivers 85 tons of barley instead of 80 tons but where, for example, one machine of a special type is ordered by B and S delivers two machines by mistake, both of which B accepts, S may face grave difficulties in being unable to supply another buyer with the second machine. As S has delivered the excess goods by mistake, the solution to this problem may lie in the rules of mistake in that B should not be able to take advantage of S's obvious error but, in practice, few difficulties have arisen with this facet of excess delivery.

Minimal discrepancies in delivery and the *de minimis* principle

It is a well-established rule that a minimal deficiency or excess in the quantity of the goods delivered will not entitle B to reject all the goods because *de minimis non curat lex*. The discrepancy must, however, be 'negligible'[11] and thus incapable of 'influencing the mind of the buyer'.[12] In *Shipton, Anderson & Co v Weil Bros & Co*,[13] an excess of 55 lbs of wheat on an agreed limit of 4,950 tons was within the rule and B could not reject all the goods; in terms of money the excess was worth four shillings and the contract price was over £40,000. That the *de minimis* rule is a question of fact is illustrated by the decision in *Margaronis Navigation Agency Ltd v Henry W Peabody & Co Ltd*.[14] There a deficiency of .09 per cent (12,588 tons 4 cwts instead of 12,600 tons) in a cargo of maize was *not* within the *de minimis* rule but it was an important factor in this case that the silo from which the loading took place was able to measure and record the quantity both quickly and precisely.[15]

It is evident that the *de minimis* rule has a limited scope and is somewhat random in application. The Law Commissions[16] were concerned that the exacting standards regarding quantity set by s 30 could be too easily abused by unscrupulous buyers rejecting all the goods for a trivial breach of s 30 and, on a falling market, then buying replacement goods more cheaply elsewhere. Accordingly, it was thought that a restriction should be placed on the non-consumer buyer's right of rejection for breaches of s 30. The recommendation of the Law Commissions has been enacted in the SGA, s 30(2A) and (2B) which

8   *Cunliffe v Harrison* (1851) 6 Exch 903, 906 per Parke B.
9   *Gabriel Wade and English v Arcos Ltd* (1929) 34 Ll L Rep 306. Contrast this position with the acceptance of a shortfall (see above) where B may obtain damages.
10 *Sale and Supply of Goods* (Law Com WP No 85; Scot Law Com CM No 58, 1983), para 6.32.
11 *Arcos Ltd v E A Ronaasen & Son* [1933] AC 470, 480 per Lord Atkin.
12 *Shipton, Anderson & Co v Weil Bros & Co* [1912] 1 KB 574, 577 per Lush J.
13 [1912] 1 KB 574.
14 [1965] 1 QB 300.
15 See also *Wilensko Slaski Towarzystwo Drewno v Fenwick & Co (West Hartlepool) Ltd* [1938] 3 All ER 429 (B could reject when slightly under 1% of the timber delivered failed to conform with its measurements); *Harland & Wolff Ltd v Burstall & Co* (1901) 6 Com Cas 113 (B could reject when 470 loads of timber were delivered instead of 500).
16 Law Com No 160, Scot Law Com No 104, *Sale and Supply of Goods*, Cm 137 (1987), paras 6.17-6.23.

provide that a non-consumer buyer may not reject all the goods in cases of excessive and short delivery where the excess or shortfall is 'so slight that it would be unreasonable for him to do so'. The onus is placed on S to show that the shortfall or excess is 'slight' within this provision. Section 30(2A) and (2B) are thus the mirror image of s 15A which limits the non-consumer buyer's right to reject the goods for 'slight' breaches of the implied terms in ss 13-15.

Express provision for tolerances in quanity

Section 30(5) provides that 'this section is subject to any usage of trade, special agreement, or course of dealing between the parties' and thus S may seek to protect himself in cases of excessive or short delivery by using words of approximation such as 'about' or 'more or less'. Such stipulations allow S a moderate margin as regards the quantity he should deliver but B can utilise the provisions of s 30 if the margin is exceeded.[17] Moreover, such clauses will be unenforceable if they fail to pass the test of reasonableness in the Unfair Contract Terms Act 1977, s 3.

Delivery and payment

SGA, s 28 provides:

> 'Unless otherwise agreed, delivery of the goods and payment of the price are concurrent conditions, that is to say, the seller must be ready and willing to give possession of the goods to the buyer in exchange for the price and the buyer must be ready and willing to pay the price in exchange for possession of the goods.'

Section 28 demands that each party has a *willingness* to perform his side of the bargain but the section does not stipulate that *actual* payment or tender of the price is a condition precedent to S's obligation to deliver the goods. Moreover, s 28 applies 'unless otherwise agreed' and so, for example, where S agrees to give B credit the goods will be delivered before payment is made. Under ss 38 and 41, an unpaid seller who is in possession of the goods is entitled to keep possession of them until payment or tender of the price where the goods have not been sold on credit terms. Similarly S may retain possession where B has been allowed credit but the term of credit has expired or where B becomes insolvent.

It is vital to realise that s 28 allows S to *demand* payment when he is ready and willing to deliver but it does not specify that S can *sue* for the *price*. If B refuses to accept a tender of delivery, S can normally sue for damages for non-acceptance[18] and, likewise, B will have a remedy in damages for non-delivery where S wrongfully neglects or refuses to deliver the goods to him. However, S can maintain an action for the price, under s 49(1), only where *property* in the goods has passed to B and B wrongfully neglects or refuses to pay for the goods according to the terms of the contract.

---

17 See eg *Cross v Eglin* (1831) 2 B & Ad 106 (contract for 300 quarters of rye 'more or less' and a tender of 345 quarters was held to be outside the margin); *Reuter v Sala* (1879) 4 CPD 239; *Payne and Routh v Lillico & Sons* (1920) 36 TLR 569.
18 *Stein Forbes & Co v County Tailoring Co* (1916) 86 LJKB 448.

'Delivery' in s 28 carries the usual meaning in s 61(1) of the 'voluntary transfer of possession from one person to another'. Where goods are shipped, for example, the shipping documents represent the goods and when S is ready and willing to deliver the documents, he is entitled to demand payment of the price from B.[19]

Repudiation of the contract and delivery

Difficulties arise in this context where, before the time for performance arrives, either party indicates to the other that he will not perform the contract, ie B informs S that he will not accept the goods or S tells B that he cannot deliver them at the agreed date. In this situation of an anticipatory breach of contract, the rule is that the innocent party may immediately treat the contract as at an end and claim damages or he may choose to ignore the breach and hold the other party to his obligations. If he chooses the latter course, the innocent party runs the risk that events may turn against him before performance is due because 'he keeps the contract alive for the benefit of the other party as well as his own'.[20] For example, should an event occur before the time of performance which frustrates the contract, both parties are released from their contractual obligations and the innocent party cannot claim damages for the anticipatory breach.[1]

The risk entailed when the innocent party elects to keep the contract alive is well-illustrated in the leading decision in *Fercometal SARL v Mediterranean Shipping Co SA*.[2] A charter-party for the carriage of steel coils from Durban to Bilbao in the vessel *Simona* contained a clause under which the charterers could cancel the contract if the vessel was not ready to load on or before 9 July. On 2 July, the owners of *Simona* asked the charterers for an extension of the cancellation date so that the vessel could load between 13-16 July but the charterers replied that those dates were unacceptable and that they were therefore cancelling the charter-party. They clearly had no right to exercise the cancellation clause in advance and this purported cancellation thus amounted to a repudiation of the contract. On 5 July, the owners telexed the charterers that *Simona* would be ready to load on 8 July and the vessel did arrive in Durban on that date and tendered a notice of readiness to load. In fact, *Simona* was still loading other cargo and was not ready to load the steel on either 8 or 9 July. Accordingly, the charterers commenced the loading of their steel on a substitute vessel and sent a cancellation notice to the owners on 12 July. The House of Lords held that the ship owners' action against the charterers for dead freight must fail. As the owners had not accepted the charterers' repudiation and had continued with the contract, the charter-party survived intact with the right of cancellation unaffected. The cancellation clause thus became operative on 9 July and the charterers actually cancelled on 12 July. The House of Lords held that *two* choices only were available to the innocent party, viz (i) accept the anticipatory breach in which

19 *Horst (E Clemens) & Co v Biddell Bros* [1912] AC 18 (sale of hops under a cif contract to be shipped to Hull, 'terms net cash'. Held that B must pay the price when the shipping documents were tendered instead of waiting for the arrival of the goods); approving the dissenting judgment of Kennedy LJ at [1911] 1 KB 934.
20 *Frost v Knight* (1872) LR 7 Exch 111, 112 per Cockburn CJ.
 1 See *Avery v Bowden* (1855) 5 E & B 714 (the defendant (D) chartered the plaintiff's (P) ship; D committed an anticipatory breach in refusing to load the vessel in the 45 days allowed. P refused to accept the breach but, before the 45 days had elapsed, the Crimean war broke out, frustrating the contract and providing D with a good defence).
 2 [1989] AC 788.

case the contract is finally and conclusively discharged and he is freed from his own duty to perform; or (ii) affirm the contract in which case it remains totally in force and *both* parties must be able and willing to perform at the time of actual performance. Lord Ackner[3] stipulated that 'there is no third choice, as a sort of via media, to affirm the contract and yet to be absolved from tendering further performance unless and until [the other party] gives reasonable notice that he is once again able and willing to perform'.[4]

Although the innocent party's choice either to accept the repudiation or affirm the contract is a plain one, the situation may be somewhat blurred in reality. For example, S may refuse, at least initially, to accept B's repudiation but may also perform other acts such as not arranging for the delivery of the goods to B or not appropriating them to the contract. Unless he does finally accept the repudiation, S runs the risk that B will allege that S was unable to perform the contract at the time of delivery. In the *Fercometal* case, Lord Ackner[5] emphasised that S could be freed from his duty to deliver by the operation of estoppel if B clearly represents to S that he will not accept the goods and S acts on that representation by, for example, not arranging for delivery. If, on the facts of *Fercometal*, the charterers had represented that they no longer required the vessel to arrive on time as they had arranged for the substitute vessel and the owners had then relied on that representation and had given notice of readiness to load only after the cancellation date, the charterers would have been estopped from contending that they could cancel. However, there was no evidence of any such representation in *Fercometal*; the vessel's non-readiness to load was simply the result of the owner's decision to load other cargo first.

The alternative course of action which is open to the innocent party, to *accept* a repudiatory breach, is illustrated in *Berger & Co Inc v Gill & Duffus SA*.[6] S agreed to sell to B 500 tons of Argentinian bolita beans, cif Le Havre, and to provide a certificate of quality. The goods arrived in Le Havre but only 445 tons were discharged, the balance of 55 tons being over-carried to Rotterdam, but the 55 tons were discharged in Le Havre some 12 days later. In the interim, S had presented the shipping documents for the 500 tons but B had rejected them as they did not contain a certificate of quality. S obtained a certificate of quality for the 445 tons and re-tendered the shipping documents and certificate but this tender was also refused. S treated this refusal as a wrongful repudiation of the contract and and thus did not tender a certificate for the remaining 55 tons. In arbitration proceedings, it was found that the 445 tons of beans contained a significant proportion of coloured beans and, as bolita beans are white, the goods did not correspond with the contract description. The Court of Appeal[7] held that,

---

3   [1989] AC 788 at 805.
4   The earlier, controversial decision in *Braithwaite v Foreign Hardwood Co* [1905] 2 KB 543 (see Lloyd, 'Ready and Willing to Perform: The Problem of Prospective Inability in the Law of Contract' (1974) 37 MLR 121) was distinguished and rationalised. *Braithwaite* was often taken as authority for the proposition that the innocent party who refuses to accept the repudiation is absolved from tendering further performance while the repudiatory attitude is maintained and his obligations revive only when the repudiating party gives reasonable notice that he is, once again, able and willing to perform. The owners in *Fercometal* thus argued that they were excused from tendering the vessel ready to load on 9 July. Lord Akner held that *Braithwaite* is not an authority for this proposition or, if it is, it is wrong. This clarifies the law considerably.
5   [1989] AC 788, 805-806.
6   [1984] AC 382.
7   [1983] 1 Lloyd's Rep 622.

as the 55 tons did not conform to the contract, B was entitled to reject all 500 tons under the SGA 1893, s 30(1) and (3). The House of Lords reversed that decision and stressed that B had never contended that the shipping documents did not conform to the contract. Accordingly, B's refusal to accept the re-tendered documents and pay the price was a breach of condition and it was not open to a buyer under a cif contract to justify the rejection of conforming documents by a *subsequent* discovery that the goods shipped did not conform to the contract.[8] As S had elected to treat the contract as repudiated, he was thus released from further performance of the contract and was under no duty to deliver the 55 tons. B was thus liable for non-acceptance of the whole 500 tons.

Most importantly, the recent decision of the House of Lords in *Vitol SA v Norelf Ltd*,[9] emphasises that the innocent party may accept the breach and treat the contract as repudiated by any clear words or conduct. In the *Vitol* case, B agreed to buy a cargo of propane but then wrongfully repudiated the contract. S did not communicate with B but simply failed to perform any further acts in performance of the contract and subsequently resold the cargo. The first communication occurred when S sued B for the loss on the resale of the propane but B argued that S's conduct in reselling the propane amounted to an acceptance of B's repudiation thus discharging B from any further obligations under the contract. The Court of Appeal[10] held that S's failure to perform the contract could not amount to an acceptance of a repudiation of it as the conduct was not clear and unequivocal but, instead, amounted to silence and inaction. This was a most perplexing decision as S's reselling of the goods surely amounted to more than silence and inaction. The decision of the Court of Appeal was, however, reversed by the House of Lords. Lord Steyn[11] stipulated that 'an act of acceptance of a repudiation requires no particular form ... it is sufficient that the communication or conduct clearly and unequivocally conveys to the repudiating party that that aggrieved party is treating the contract as at an end'. In the instant case, if S had opted to keep the contract alive, one of the acts which he would have been obliged to perform was the tender of a bill of lading to B; S's failure to tender the bill was apparent to B and thus constituted sufficient communication of the acceptance of B's repudiation.

---

8 A cif buyer who has accepted the shipping documents can still reject the goods if he discovers that they do not conform to the contract, but here the contract will still be in force.
9 [1996] AC 800.
10 [1996] QB 108.
11 [1996] AC 800, 810-811.

CHAPTER 23

Rejection of the goods

B's right to reject the goods

The buyer's duties under a contract for the sale of goods are to accept and pay for the goods and, if B rejects the goods he is, *prima facie*, in breach of contract. However, this general principle must be qualified as B is justified in rejecting the goods tendered under the contract in several situations. First, B can reject where there is an express term of the contract allowing rejection. Second, a right to reject may be permitted by terms implied by the common law or by custom and usage. Third, B is entitled to reject where S has committed a breach of an express or implied condition of the contract. The modern tendency is to avoid a rigid categorisation of express terms into conditions and warranties but, instead, to consider such terms as innominate in nature, meaning that the consequences of the breach determine whether B may reject the goods. However, where the SGA provides that implied terms are conditions, ie ss 13-15, the general rule is that B may reject the goods if S is in breach of any such condition. The general rule must be qualified, however, by the new provisions in the SGA, s 15A (considered later) which limit the *non-consumer* buyer's right to reject for breach of the implied conditions in the SGA, ss 13-15 where 'the breach is so slight that it would be unreasonable for him to reject' the goods.[1] Moreover, under the SGA, s 11(2), B is not bound to exercise his right to reject the goods for breach of condition and may elect to treat the breach of condition as a breach of warranty, in which case the contract will remain alive and B will be limited to a claim in damages.

A most important aspect of rejection is that, in certain circumstances, B will lose the right to reject the goods under s 35 where he has 'accepted' them before any rejection has occurred and then, under s 11(4), he is limited to a claim in damages for breach of warranty. Should B keep and use the goods, for example, before he attempts to reject them, it is very likely that he will be deemed to have accepted them and it is quite possible that such acceptance may occur even though during the period that he used the goods he was unaware of any defects which constituted a breach of condition.

---

1 See also SGA, s 30 for the restrictions on rejection of the goods where S delivers the wrong *quantity* of goods.

Although the right of rejection has sometimes been equated with the right to repudiate for breach of contract and treat the contract as discharged,[2] the better view is that repudiation and rejection are separate because rejection does not necessarily entail a *termination* of the contract. Support for the latter view can be found in the wording of the SGA, s 11[3] and because s 30 (delivery of the wrong quantity) allows B to reject the goods without there being an automatic termination of the contract. If the contract is not terminated, S may have a right to cure the defective delivery (see later) and re-tender goods which comply with the contract specification, provided that he still has time to do this under the contract. However, if S is unable or unwilling to cure the defective tender, B is then entitled to treat the contract as at an end.

In 1994, the SGA was amended substantially[4] to reflect the Law Commissions' recommendations[5] regarding acceptance and the new provisions are considered later in this chapter. Moreover, an EU Directive[6] which must be implemented by Member States no later than January 2002, will alter fundamentally the *consumer's* right to reject the goods. The provisions of the Directive are considered in detail in Chapter 21.

The mode and consequences of rejection

B may reject the goods either when they are tendered or after their receipt provided, in the latter case, that he has not accepted them within ss 34 and 35. B must exercise the right to reject by an unequivocal notice to that effect given to S and, if the rejection is ambiguous and ineffective, B runs the risk that any subsequent dealing with the goods might amount to an acceptance by him. In *Graanhandel T Vink BV v European Grain & Shipping Ltd,*[7] B's purported notice of rejection referred to a possible resale by him and hinted at an agency of necessity as the goods were 'fastly deteriorating'. S refused the rejection and withheld authority to sell but B nevertheless resold the goods. It was held that the rejection was not final and that B's resale of the goods was unauthorised

---

2 See *Kwei Tek Chao v British Traders and Shippers Ltd* [1954] 2 QB 459, 480 per Devlin J: 'A right to reject is, after all, only a particular form of a right to rescind the contract ... and a rightful rejection ... is a rescission which brings the contract to an end'. Cf Devlin, 'The Treatment of Breach of Contract' [1966] 24 CLJ 192, 194.

3 Section 11(3) describes a condition as a stipulation 'the breach of which *may* give rise to a right to treat the contract as repudiated' (emphasis added). But this arguably refers to the remainder of s 11, viz B may elect to treat the breach of condition as a breach of warranty (s 11(2)) and may be compelled to do so where he has accepted the goods (s 11(4)).

4 By the Sale and Supply of Goods Act 1994.

5 *Sale and Supply of Goods* (Law Com No 160, Scottish Law Com No 104, Cm 137, 1987).

6 *Certain Aspects of the Sale of Consumer Goods and Associated Guarantees* (99/44/EC, 25 May 1999).

7 [1989] 2 Lloyd's Rep 531; see also *Chapman v Morton* (1843) 11 M & W 534; *Vargas Pena Apezteguia y Cia Saic v Peter Cremer GmbH* [1987] 1 Lloyd's Rep 394 (in both cases there was an unequivocal rejection followed by a sale of the goods and B was thus held to have accepted the goods); *Lee v York Coach and Marine* [1977] RTR 35 (B retained a defective car and did not unequivocally reject it until the commencement of the action against S. Held that rejection was too late and B had accepted the car).

and could not be justified by necessity; consequently, the resale constituted an acceptance by B within the SGA, s 35.[8]

Under the SGA, s 36, unless otherwise agreed, B is not bound to return the goods to S and it is sufficient that he 'intimates to the seller that he refuses to accept them'. Where B properly rejects, he may throw the goods on S's hands[9] at the contractual place of examination and the goods continue to be S's property, B's rejection thus being an assertion that property shall not pass to him.[10] Alternatively, if property in the goods has passed to B,[11] it revests in S[12] and the goods are then at S's risk and expense. After an unequivocal rejection, B may no longer deal with the goods unless he has the express or implied authority of S to do so[13] or he is constituted an agent of necessity. Similarly, he does not have a lien over the goods for the repayment of the price.[14] If B does deal with the goods after a clear and proper rejection, eg a resale and delivery of the goods to B2,[15] such dealing may amount to conversion or, alternatively, a court may nevertheless construe B's actions as an acceptance of the goods. This latter question was broached in *Tradax Export SA v European Grain & Shipping Ltd*,[16] where Bingham J held that there was an effective rejection but he also considered the suggestion that B's conduct or communications after a valid rejection might disentitle him from relying on it. He concluded that B might be 'saying one thing and doing another'[17] by purporting to reject and, at the same time, re-selling the goods[18] or B might act in such a way as to create an estoppel against himself. Similarly, B's actions might lead to a new agreement with S involving an express or implied withdrawal of the rejection but that, in all these cases, it would be for S to establish that the effect of B's subsequent conduct destroyed the unequivocal rejection. This type of 'acceptance' by B would result from the principles of the common law and not from the SGA, s 35 which, of course, applies only to acts of acceptance occurring *before* rejection.

8   Evans J suggested (p 533) that S's refusal to accept B's rejection might mean that B's resale could not be conversion but would amount to an acceptance by B. This presumably would apply only where the rejection is equivocal because where B's rejection is unequivocal, property in the goods should remain or revest in S and, despite S's refusal, the resale could still amount to conversion.

9   *Heilbutt v Hickson* (1872) LR 7 CP 438, 455 per Brett J; *Grimoldby v Wells* (1875) LR 10 CP 391.

10   See *Tradax Export SA v European Grain & Shipping Ltd* [1983] 2 Lloyd's Rep 100, 107 per Bingham J.

11   See below where risk and damage to the goods are considered: the modern view is that property in non-conforming goods passes to B.

12   *Kwei Tek Chao v British Traders and Shippers Ltd* [1954] 2 QB 459, 487 per Devlin J who emphasised that B obtained 'only conditional property in the goods'. This reasoning was approved in *Berger & Co Inc v Gill & Duffus SA* [1984] AC 382, 395 per Lord Diplock.

13   See *Laurelgates Ltd v Lombard North Central Ltd* (1983) 133 NLJ 720 (hire-purchase); *Public Utilities Commission of City of Waterloo v Burroughs Business Machines Ltd* (1974) 52 DLR (3d) 481(in both cases B used the goods *after* rejection but this did not affect the right to reject).

14   *Lyons (J L) & Co Ltd v May and Baker Ltd* [1923] 1 KB 685.

15   Title should pass to B2 as B would seem to be a buyer in possession under the SGA, s 25.

16   [1983] 2 Lloyd's Rep 100.

17   [1983] 2 Lloyd's Rep 100 at 107.

18   See also *Chapman v Morton* (1843) 11 M & W 534 (B purported to reject a quantity of oil cake, told S it was at a granary at S's risk and asked S to collect it but this S refused to do. B subsequently sold the cake in his own name and it was held that he had accepted it).

Risk and loss or damage to the goods

If B has custody of the goods *after* a valid rejection, he will owe a duty of care in relation to them as an involuntary, or possibly a gratuitous bailee, and he will thus be liable for deliberate damage to the goods or for gross negligence; he should also be entitled to reimbursement for expenses incurred in the safe keeping of the goods.[19]

An enduring difficulty and one regarding which there is little definite authority is whether B may reject goods which, at the date of rejection, are no longer in substantially the same condition as when he bought them. One rule is tolerably clear: if the goods have deteriorated or perished as a direct result of S's breach of contract, B's right to reject should be unaffected – it is plain that, if the rule were otherwise, the right of rejection would be deprived of its sense and purpose.

It is the position regarding *accidental* loss or damage to the goods between delivery and rejection which is most obscure and it is difficult to find an organising principle which would determine where the loss should fall. Obviously pertinent issues in relation to accidental damage are whether B must be able to make *restitutio in integrum* and the significance of whether property has passed to B or remains in S. Moreover, it is S who has supplied defective goods in the first place and perhaps the natural reaction is to assert that he should be responsible for accidental loss which occurs prior to rejection. A rather mechanical solution to the problem but one which may be assumed by the SGA is that, following the general rule in the SGA, s 20(1) that risk follows property, the risk should remain with S when he has property in the goods (subject, presumably, to B's duties as a bailee) and, conversely, the risk should be on B where property has passed to him. This is certainly the position in sale or return agreements where B is regarded as a bailee until property passes to him and is thus not liable for accidental loss or damage which occurs before that time.[20] Indeed, it is sometimes forgotten that the older cases often inferred that property in goods which did not conform to the contract description did not pass to B.[1] The general thrust thus seemed to be in B's favour and, in fact, the old but only pertinent decision shows a marked reluctance to place the risk of accidental loss on B. In *Head v Tattersall*,[2] B bought a horse at an auction on Monday, said to have been hunted with the Bicester hounds, but the

---

19 See *China-Pacific SA v Food Corpn of India, The Winson* [1982] AC 939 (considered in Ch 6).

20 See *Elphick v Barnes* (1880) 5 CPD 321.

1 The older view was that property in non-conforming goods would not pass to B (see *Wait v Baker* (1848) 2 Exch 1; *Cunliffe v Harrison* (1851) 6 Exch 903; *Vigers Bros v Sanderson Bros* [1901] 1 KB 608; *Taylor v Combined Buyers Ltd* [1924] NZLR 627, 648 per Salmond J; *Hammer and Barrow v Coca-Cola* [1962] NZLR 723,731 per Richmond J) and the SGA, s 18, r 5(1) stipulates that goods of 'that description' must be appropriated to the contract (property in *unsatisfactory* goods which nevertheless conform to description could thus pass to B). However, the better, modern view, is that conditional property vests in B which revests in S on rejection (see *Kwei Tek Chao v British Traders and Shippers Ltd* [1954] 2 QB 459, 487 per Devlin J; *McDougall v Aeromarine of Emsworth Ltd* [1958] 1 WLR 1126; *Rosenthal (J) & Sons Ltd v Esmail* [1965] 1 WLR 1117, 1131 per Lord Pearson; *The Elafi* [1982] 1 All ER 208, 212-213 per Mustill J; *Berger & Co Inc v Gill & Duffus SA* [1984] AC 382, 395 per Lord Diplock).

2 (1871) LR 7 Exch 7; see also *Chapman v Withers* (1888) 20 QBD 824 (horse sold which was warranted 'quiet to ride' with an express condition allowing its return within two days if it did not correspond to the warranty. While being tested by a 'riding master', the horse ran away, fell and broke its collar bone and was in no condition to travel. Held the non-return of the horse (which was eventually destroyed) within the period specified was no bar to B's action for breach of warranty).

contract contained a condition that the horse could be returned on Wednesday if it did not match its description. As it had not been hunted with the Bicester hounds, B returned the horse within the stipulated time but it had been injured without fault on his part. It was held that B could nevertheless return the horse and recover the price and the risk was thus on S even though the property in the horse had passed to B.[3] Although the decision is still referred to extensively in this context, it may be criticised on the basis that it has failed to survive the clear rule in the SGA that risk follows property; similarly, it might correctly be regarded as being based upon an *express* right to reject[4] meaning that the position could be different if B rejected the goods under the general law.

There is, however, considerable support for the opposite view that the risk of accidental loss should fall on B. The Law Commissions' Working Paper in 1983[5] suggested that the right to reject should be lost where B is unable to return the goods in 'substantially the same condition' as at the time of delivery, with important exceptions being made in cases of fair wear-and-tear and where the change in condition was caused by S's breach of contract. This is also the overall stance adopted by *Benjamin*.[6] However, the current report of the Law Commissions stresses that there are situations where rejection should be permitted even where the goods are not in substantially the same condition as at the date of delivery. Thus S may know that B intends to modify the goods in some way or the goods may have to be modified to be installed, examined, fitted or used, and the defect may materialise only after such a process (eg self-assembly goods; carpets that have to be cut in order to be fitted; vacuum packed goods where the seal is broken). The Law Commissions also emphasise that B should be able to reject where it is S's original breach of contract which has caused the goods to deteriorate and that any express statutory provision limiting B's right to reject goods where their condition had changed would be adverse to consumers as it would provide S with

---

3   This was certainly the view of Cleasby B, who thought that the risk of depreciation should fall on S when the property revested in him (see (1871) LR 7 Exch 7 at 13-14).

4   What is the position in the relatively common situation where B buys goods in a retail shop and is expressly allowed to return them if they do not meet his needs, but the goods are damaged with no fault on B's part? If *Head* were followed the risk of any accidental loss would fall on S.

5   *Sale and Supply of Goods* (Law Com WP No 85, Scot Law Com CM No 58, 1983) paras 2.60, 4.76-4.80 (the notion was rejected that, in this context, risk should simply pass with property as it was thought that this would often be dependent solely upon the technical rules as to the passing of property. Similarly, a rule that B should be able to reject goods which were damaged without his fault was thought inapt because, where property had passed to B, it would be difficult to assess fault: an *owner* may be as negligent as he pleases in the treatment of his goods. The positive recommendation was that B should *not* be able to reject the goods unless they were in 'substantially the same condition' at the time of rejection as at the time of delivery, apart from cases where the change was caused by S's breach of contract and those where the goods had been subjected to fair wear-and-tear. This recommendation was considered apt because (i) the goods are in B's control; (ii) B can insure; and (iii) if B chooses to alter the goods, there is no doubt that the risk should be on him.

6   *Benjamin's Sale of Goods* (5th edn, 1997), para 12-059. The decision in *Canterbury Seed Co Ltd v J G Ward Farmers' Association Ltd* (1895) 13 NZLR 96 arguably assumes that the risk is on B. There B's rejection was not absolute and clear and, before S could make any reply, the goods were lost in an accidental fire at B's premises. Held that the risk was on B who was thus liable for the price subject to a reduction for defects in quality. But support for the view that the risk should be on S is found in: Chalmers, *Sale of Goods* (18th edn, 1981), p 157; Sealy, ''Risk' in the Law of Sale' [1972B] 31 CLJ 225, 244; and the Uniform Commercial Code s 2-510. For a review of the position taken in other legal systems see Treitel, *Remedies for Breach of Contract* (1988), pp 388-391.

a clear ground for refusing to take back defective goods.[7] Consequently, although the Law Commissions recognise that this part of rejection is unclear, no reform of the law is currently recommended. In conclusion, the paucity of cases on this topic can undoubtedly be accounted for in that, where goods have changed or deteriorated after delivery to B, B will often be deemed to have accepted the goods within the strict rules of the SGA, s 35 and his right to reject is lost as a consequence.

Recovery of money paid and damages

Where B has justifiably and unequivocally rejected the goods, he may treat the contract as discharged and withhold payment if he has not paid or, alternatively, recover any money he has paid in restitution as upon a total failure of consideration, this right being preserved by the SGA, s 54. A possible bar to such a remedy is that the older cases take a Draconian view in stipulating that the failure of consideration must be total so that any enjoyment of the subject-matter of the contract would prevent recovery.[8] In *Rowland v Divall*,[9] however, it was held that, where S did not transfer any *title* in the goods to B, the consideration had totally failed irrespective of any intermediate use of the goods by B. But *Rowland's* reasoning is that the object of the contract of sale is to transfer title and, without title, B simply does not obtain that for which he bargained. It would thus be difficult to extend this reasoning to rejection for *other* breaches of condition where B's use of the goods might mean that there is not a total failure of consideration.[10] However, it seems unlikely that, today, B's use of the goods immediately after delivery would prevent his claiming upon a total failure of consideration most particularly as his right to reject is lost very soon after delivery and substantial use of the goods will almost certainly mean that he has accepted them within s 35.

As an alternative to the recovery of money paid, B may treat the contract as discharged and seek damages which here would be assessed as damages for non-delivery of the goods.[11] A claim in restitution for money paid may be simpler than claiming damages as, in a claim for damages, B must both prove a loss and take reasonable steps to mitigate that loss. Furthermore, where the market price is falling, recovery of the money paid may be more advantageous to B than seeking damages. However, if B can establish other loss, his claim in damages will be more beneficial than a restitutionary claim.

Does S have a right to cure?

There is limited authority that S has the right to cure a defective tender by re-tendering other goods which are in conformity with the contract on the basis

---

7 See *Sale and Supply of Goods* (Law Com No 160, Scottish Law Com No 104, Cm 137, 1987), paras 5.39-5.40.

8 See *Hunt v Silk* (1804) 5 East 449 (a tenant went into possession under an agreement for a lease but terminated it and vacated the premises several days later because of the landlord's breach. It was held that the tenant's claim for the return of £10 advance payment must fail as he had occupied the premises and could not restore the benefit received).

9 [1923] 2 KB 500.

10 *Yeoman Credit Ltd v Apps* [1962] 2 QB 508 (hire-purchase of a defective car which would have entitled the hirer to reject it but his use of the car for six months prevented his recovering the instalments paid on the ground of total failure of consideration and he was limited to a claim in damages).

11 *Millar's Machinery Co Ltd v David Way & Son* (1935) 40 Com Cas 204.

that the original, defective tender is not necessarily a breach of contract.[12] To the extent that a right of cure exists at common law, it appears to be a precondition of its exercise that the time for delivery under the contract has not expired.[13] Moreover, a corollary of the right would surely be that S should pay B's expenses in relation to the examination and rejection of the original tender. The leading decision on this topic is *Borrowman, Phillips & Co v Free and Hollis*.[14] S agreed to sell a quantity of maize to B and tendered a cargo to arrive by a named vessel but S was unable to tender the shipping documents with the cargo. B refused the tender but S persisted and, the arbitrator having decided against S, S offered the cargo of a second vessel, together with the bill of lading, within the time fixed for tender. B also refused the second tender but it was held that he should have accepted it and S was thus entitled to damages for non-acceptance. Most of the decisions which advert to the right of cure have concerned tenders of goods without the appropriate documents[15] and, in doubting the extent or even the existence of such a right, the Law Commissions[16] emphasised that it would be unlikely to extend to breach of an express or implied term as to quality. The right to cure has, however, recently found favour in the House of Lords[17] and has long been part of the law in the USA.[18]

In support of the right of cure, it must be said that it would substantially reduce the injustice to S where B's rejection of the goods for a trivial and technical breach of condition, on a falling market, is motivated by the desire to buy the goods more cheaply elsewhere. But do the disadvantages attendant upon a right of cure outweigh the advantages? In contracts for the sale of unascertained goods, S could cure the original tender by making the goods conform to the contract or tendering alternative, conforming goods but where the contract is one for the sale of specific goods he could offer only to remedy the defect in the goods, as it would be impermissible unilaterally to substitute other goods for those which have been identified and agreed upon in the contract. This possibility of a re-tender of repaired goods is just one of the many difficulties which militate against a practicable scheme of cure.

In their Working Paper, the Law Commissions[19] had recommended a limited regime of cure in consumer contracts where S could show that the breach was

---

12 See Ahdar, 'Seller Cure in the Sale of Goods' [1990] LMCLQ 364; Apps,'The Right to Cure Defective Performance' [1994] LMCLQ 525; *Termination of Contracts* (eds Birds, Bradgate and Villiers, 1995), Ch 3, Bradgate and White, pp 68-77.

13 See Devlin, 'The Treatment of Breach of Contract' [1966] 24 CLJ 192, 194: 'A tender of a ship (or of goods under a contract for the sale of goods) in a condition that does not comply with the terms of the contract is not a breach of contract. What creates the breach in such a case is the failure to tender within the contract time a ship in a condition that *does* comply with the contract'.

14 (1878) 4 QBD 500; see also *Tetley v Shand* (1871) 25 LT 658; *Smith (E E & Brian) (1928) Ltd v Wheatsheaf Mills Ltd* [1939] 2 KB 302, 314-315 per Branson J.

15 See *Agricultores Federados Argentinos Sociedad Co-operativa Ltda v Ampro SA Commerciale Industriale et Financière* [1965] 2 Lloyd's Rep 157; *Getreide Import Gesellschaft mbH v Itoh & Co* [1979] 1 Lloyd's Rep 592; *SIAT di dal Ferro v Tradax Overseas SA* [1980] 1 Lloyd's Rep 53; *Empresa Exportadora de Azucar v Industria Azucarera Nacional SA, The Playa Larga* [1983] 2 Lloyd's Rep 171.

16 *Sale and Supply of Goods* (Law Com WP No 85, Scot Law Com CM No 58, 1983), para 2.38.

17 *Motor Oil Hellas (Corinth) Refineries SA v Shipping Corpn of India, The Kanchenjunga* [1990] 1 Lloyd's Rep 391, 399 per Lord Goff of Chieveley.

18 See Uniform Commercial Code, s 2-508; Lawrence, 'Cure in Contracts for the Sale of Goods: Looking Beyond Section 2-508' (1989) 21 UCCLJ 333

19 *Sale and Supply of Goods* (Law Com WP No 85, Scot Law Com CM No 58, 1983), paras 4.33-4.62; 4.74-4.75.

slight and that it was thus reasonable for B to accept a repair or replacement of the goods, with the safeguard that B could still reject the goods where the cure was not effected satisfactorily and promptly. The cure regime was rejected as being impracticable in complicated non-consumer transactions however, as here S might be thousands of miles from the point of delivery and the decision to attempt a cure could depend upon detailed examination by experts. Apart from these dominant practical considerations, in principle the right of cure seems apt for non-consumer sales where the commercial buyer is better able than his consumer counterpart to resist pressure from S to accept repairs, for example. That being said, the final report of the Law Commissions[20] discarded the principle of cure completely, emphasising that it would give S a clear ground on which to argue that the consumer buyer was not entitled to reject defective goods and reclaim his money. Moreover, the Law Commissions thought that many disparate questions surrounding the right of cure would need to be answered if it were to be a viable option. For example, would S have to re-deliver repaired goods to B? How quickly should the cure be effected? At whose risk would the goods be while the cure was being effected? It might be added that, if a right of cure were to be limited to minor defects, interminable problems could arise in differentiating major from minor defects. Similarly, the types of cure which S might suggest would be infinitely variable and would have to be subject to a test of reasonableness with regard to both the nature of the cure suggested by S and the chance of its success.

Overall, a broad right of cure seems to pose more problems than it solves and, in terms of general policy, it is vital to preserve an understandable and effective right of rejection in consumer sales so that the consumer buyer's bargaining power is not undermined. Moreover, where a breach is serious, a commercial buyer will often lose confidence in S and he is surely justified in taking a jaundiced view of any attempted cure.

Acceptance of the goods and loss of the right to reject

It is apparent that the right to reject goods for breach of condition is of paramount importance in English law but obviously there must be some fetters on such a right for, otherwise, the goods could be rejected after an indefinite lapse of time and S would simply become B's perpetual guarantor. Ideally, equilibrium should be reached between B's unrealistic claim to reject the goods in perpetuity and S's equally unreasonable assertion that B must lose his right of rejection almost immediately after delivery. There are four principal ways in which B may lose the right to reject the goods.

REJECTION WHERE THERE IS A BREACH OF CONDITION

First, there is the difficulty caused by the consequences of a breach of condition. Broad conditions such as that to supply goods which comply with their description (SGA, s 13) may be breached in a major or minor way, as was amply illustrated

---

20 *Sale and Supply of Goods* (Law Com No 160, Scottish Law Com No 104, Cm 137, 1987), paras 4.9-4.17.

in Chapter 20 on the SGA implied conditions in ss 13-15, and it may sometimes be thought unjust that B should be able to reject the goods because of a trifling breach of an obligation which happens to be classified as a condition. Where there is a slight breach of an *express* term, the courts have preserved flexibility by deploying the notion of innominate terms and the right to reject for breach of such a term is thus dependent upon the consequences of the breach.[1] Many of the SGA implied terms are conditions, however, and the flexibility inherent in the innominate term is lacking: the rule has always been that breach of a condition, however slight, enabled B to reject the goods and claim damages. The courts were sometimes faced with a dilemma as, on the one hand, rejection might be considered unreasonable on the facts but, on the other hand, the court had no power to remedy the situation by deciding that the breach was too slight to allow rejection with, instead, a consequent award of damages. An unsatisfactory resolution of this dilemma is to decide, as in *Millar's of Falkirk Ltd v Turpie*,[2] that there is no breach of contract at all thus denying even damages to B.

The Law Commissions[3] recommended that, in relation to *consumer* buyers, it was of paramount importance to preserve the right of rejection for breach of the implied conditions in the SGA, ss 13-15, even where the breach was slight. Moreover, the possibility that such a consumer buyer might have no remedy at all (as in *Turpie*) seems to be obviated by the high standards now imposed on S by the implied condition of satisfactory quality in the SGA, s 14. However, for *non-consumer* buyers the Law Commissions' recommendation[4] was that the implied conditions in ss 13-15 should remain as conditions but that there should be no right of rejection where the breach of any of those implied conditions was slight and, in this situation, only damages should be available for breach of warranty. This suggested reform has been enacted in the SGA, s 15A,[5] which provides that where B 'does not deal as consumer'[6] and the breach of any of the implied conditions in the SGA, ss 13, 14 and 15 is 'so slight that it would be unreasonable for him to reject [the goods]', the breach 'is not to be treated as a breach of condition but may be treated as a breach of warranty'. Most significantly, s 15A(2) allows S and B to exclude expressly the operation of s 15A but, under s 15A(2), the section's operation can also be ousted by an *implied*, contrary intent. Also, under s 15A(3), it is for S to prove that the breach is a 'slight' one within the section. There is a similar provision in s 30(2A) which applies to delivery of the wrong *quantity* of goods under s 30 and the non-consumer buyer can no longer reject the goods where the shortfall or excess is so slight that it would be unreasonable for him to do so.[7]

It should be stressed that ss 15A and 30(2A) apply *only* to breaches of ss 13-15 and 30 respectively and do not cover any *express* condition in the contract.

---

1 See eg *Cehave NV v Bremer Handelsgesellschaft mbH, The Hansa Nord* [1976] 1 QB 44.
2 1976 SLT (Notes) 66 (considered in Ch 20).
3 *Sale and Supply of Goods* (Law Com No 160, Scottish Law Com No 104, Cm 137, 1987), paras 4.1-4.15.
4 *Sale and Supply of Goods* (Law Com No 160, Scottish Law Com No 104, Cm 137, 1987), paras 4.16-4.25.
5 Inserted by the Sale and Supply of Goods Act 1994, s 4(1). See also the consideration of s 15A in Ch 20 on the SGA implied terms, particularly in relation to s 13.
6 Under the SGA, s 61(5A), references to 'dealing as consumer' are to be construed in accordance with Part I of the UCTA 1977 and the burden of proof is on S to show that B does not 'deal as consumer'.
7 See Ch 22 on delivery of the wrong quantity of goods.

The concept of the innominate term can provide room for manoeuvre and flexibility in relation to many express terms but it remains uncertain as to when rejection will be denied on the basis that the consequences and nature of the breach are slight or, alternatively, when the term will be strictly classified as a condition with concomitant remedies for its breach.[8]

EXPRESS PROVISIONS RELATING TO REJECTION

Second, the contract may make express provision regarding rejection and stipulate that defective goods must be rejected within a fixed time-limit, for example. Such clauses are common in commercial sales and are likely to be classified as exemption clauses and thus subject to the test of reasonableness in the Unfair Contract Terms Act 1977.[9] Moreover, such a contract term restricting a consumer buyer's right to reject goods for breach of the implied conditions contained in the SGA, ss 13-15 is rendered ineffective under the 1977 Act.[10] Also, the Unfair Terms in Consumer Contracts Regulations 1999 impose wide controls on the use of such clauses in consumer sales and may castigate a non-rejection clause as unfair.[11]

THE BUYER TREATS THE BREACH OF CONDITION AS A BREACH OF WARRANTY

Third, under SGA, s 11(2), B is not bound to exercise his right to reject the goods for breach of condition and may elect to treat the breach of condition as a breach of warranty, in which case B will be limited to a claim in damages.

ACCEPTANCE AND LOSS OF THE RIGHT TO REJECT UNDER THE SGA, S 35

Finally and most importantly, under the SGA, s 11(4), where B has 'accepted the goods' before any rejection, he is obliged to treat the breach of condition which has occurred as a breach of warranty which sounds in damages only and 'not as a ground for rejecting the goods and treating the contract as repudiated'.

---

8 See *Maredalanto Compania Naviera SA v Bergbau-Handel GmbH, The Mihalis Angelos* [1971] 1 QB 164; *Bunge Corpn, New York v Tradax Export SA* [1981] 1 WLR 711, 716 per Lord Wilberforce. See also *Sale and Supply of Goods* (Law Com No 160, Scottish Law Com No 104, Cm 137, 1987), para 4.22, fn 25, where the Law Commissions thought that a court should be able to establish, on appropriate facts, that the parties intended the s 15A regime to apply to breach of an *express* term relating to quality.

9 See the UCTA 1977, ss 6 (3) and 13(1)(b); *Green (RW) Ltd v Cade Bros Farms* [1978] 1 Lloyd's Rep 602 (a decision on the Supply of Goods (Implied Terms) Act 1973; sale of seed potatoes requiring B to give notice of rejection within three days of delivery held to be unreasonable in relation to latent defects which could not become apparent until the potatoes started to grow). However, the UCTA's controls do not apply in international sales (see the UCTA, s 26); see further Ch 25.

10 See the UCTA, ss 6 (2), 12; ss 6 and 12 ban clauses which seek to exclude or restrict rejection in relation to the implied conditions in the SGA, s 12 (title) and ss 13-15, but a clause limiting rejection in cases of other breaches of condition, eg late delivery, would be subject to the reasonableness test under the UCTA, ss 3 or 13.

11 See Sch 2, paras (b) and (q).

It is therefore crucial to know when B has 'accepted' the goods. The SGA, s 35 provides that B is deemed to accept in three situations, viz:

(i)   where B intimates to S that he has accepted the goods;
(ii) where the goods have been delivered to B and he does any act in relation to them which is inconsistent with S's ownership; and
(iii) when after the lapse of a reasonable time he retains the goods without intimating to S that he has rejected them.

It is most important to stress that B's acceptance under s 35 is not necessarily linked to his *knowledge* of S's breach of condition and B can thus lose his right to reject defective goods even though he is unaware of the defects. The notion of acceptance is thus not the same as the principle of affirmation where B has knowledge of the breach and of his rights and then elects to affirm the contract.[12] Acceptance in the sale of goods and analogous principles[13] which may have grown from it, are thus based upon a pragmatic notion of deemed acceptance[14] but, of course, in some of the cases B is aware of the breach and then performs an act of acceptance. The concept of the deemed or implied acceptance was carried so far that, under the earlier law, B could accept the goods even though he had neither examined them nor had even an opportunity to examine them, eg where B immediately resold the goods with delivery made by S direct to the sub-buyer.[15]

Section 35 has been amended by the Sale and Supply of Goods Act 1994 and now provides that, before B can accept under heads (i) and (ii) above, he must have a reasonable opportunity to examine the goods, a right which cannot be removed by 'agreement, waiver or otherwise' in a consumer sale but can be thus waived in a non-consumer sale (s 35(3)). Moreover, such an opportunity to examine is now one factor to consider under head (iii) above. The question of the examination of the goods and its effects in relation to acceptance will be considered when each part of s 35 is evaluated, below.

Section 35 applies to both consumer and non-consumer buyers and recognises the need for finality in sales of goods: the general rule is that S must be able 'to close his ledger reasonably soon after the transaction is complete'.[16] The operation of s 35 may thus prevent the unscrupulous, commercial buyer from seeking-out a technical breach of condition in order to reject the goods on a falling market as, irrespective of the SGA, s 15A, he may have accepted the goods by his conduct. Likewise, the capricious, consumer buyer who makes considerable use of the goods but then repents his purchase is similarly precluded from rejecting the goods on a purely frivolous basis. In terms of general policy, it is clearly correct that S should not stand as a perpetual guarantor for B and the Law Commissions recognised that there should be no long-term right of rejection.[17]

---

12   See *Farnworth Finance Facilities Ltd v Attryde* [1970] 1 WLR 1053, 1059 per Lord Denning MR; *Peyman v Lanjani* [1985] Ch 457; *Motor Oil Hellas (Corinth) Refineries SA v Shipping Corpn of India, The Kanchenjunga* [1990] 1 Lloyd's Rep 391, 397-399 per Lord Goff of Chieveley.
13   See *Panchaud Frères SA v Etablissements General Grain Co* [1970] 1 Lloyd's Rep 53.
14   See *Wallis, Son & Wells v Pratt & Haynes* [1910] 2 KB 1003, 1015 where, speaking of acceptance, Fletcher Moulton LJ distinguished express election from 'election statutably implied from acts' (dec revsd [1911] AC 394).
15   *Hardy & Co v Hillerns and Fowler* [1923] 2 KB 490; *Ruben (E & S) Ltd v Faire Bros & Co Ltd* [1949] 1 KB 254.
16   *Bernstein v Pamson Motors (Golders Green) Ltd* [1987] 2 All ER 220, 230 per Rougier J.
17   *Sale and Supply of Goods* (Law Com No 160, Scottish Law Com No 104, Cm 137, 1987), paras 5.16-5.23.

A contract for the sale of goods results in a change of ownership in a physical thing and it cannot be equated with other contracts which may have continuing obligations: it is thus impossible for B to have rights against S which continue *ad infinitum*. However, the commercial buyer has little to fear from the policy that the right to reject is finite. Should he seek to reject, his bargaining strength will frequently be the equal of S's and he is able to withstand any post-contractual threats that he must keep defective goods. At the worst, he should not be afraid of litigation. Similarly, loss of the right of rejection is not catastrophic to the commercial buyer as his assessment of risk should allow for the fact that some goods may be sub-standard and he is able to re-sell such goods, often for some purpose other than that for which they were purchased. Moreover, in commercial sales S's breach is usually measurable satisfactorily in monetary terms. The commercial buyer may thus balance choices and allocate risks in the context of a profit-making transaction.

None of these considerations apply to the consumer buyer who usually has inferior bargaining power in comparison with S and may thus accede to pressure from S to keep defective goods if the alternative is involvement in uncertain and expensive legal proceedings. As consumer goods are bought for private use, defective goods cannot be written-off as a business risk, nor does the consumer buyer normally have the ability to resell such goods. For consumers, rejection is an understandable and effective remedy which means that B may refuse any further contact with a seller in whom he has lost confidence and the preservation of a firm right of rejection has the beneficial long-term effect of keeping product standards high. It is thus essential that the consumer's inequality should not be compromised by a right of rejection which is lost so easily that it becomes illusory. The reform of s 35 by the Sale and Supply of Goods Act 1994 has undoubtedly improved the consumer's position and the Law Commissions' refusal to accept both S's right to cure (see earlier) and S's right, on rejection, to a monetary allowance for B's use of the goods,[18] ensure that the consumer is not further disadvantaged.

The three grounds of acceptance in s 35 must now be considered separately.

Intimation of acceptance by B

Section 35(1)(a) provides that B is deemed to have accepted the goods 'when he intimates to the seller that he has accepted them'. There is no requirement that B should *expressly* intimate his acceptance to S and a valid intimation could be by conduct but, in any event, it seems that the intimation must be clear. In *Varley v Whipp*,[19] the dissatisfied buyer of a reaping machine agreed, in a letter of complaint, to meet S in order to attempt a resolution of their difficulties. It was assumed that this did not amount to an acceptance even though B did not expressly reject the goods. However, where B signs a suitably worded delivery note or acceptance note, it is clear that this amounts to an express intimation of acceptance.[20]

Before the reform of s 35 by the Sale and Supply of Goods Act 1994, B could validly intimate his acceptance *before* he had had a reasonable opportunity to

---

18 *Sale and Supply of Goods* (Law Com No 160, Scottish Law Com No 104, Cm 137, 1987), para 5.7.
19 [1900] 1 QB 513.
20 See *Mechans Ltd v Highland Marine Charters Ltd* 1964 SC 48 (acceptance certificates signed by B constituted acceptance).

examine the goods[1] and concern was voiced that consumer buyers might lose the right to reject on the doorstep when pre-packed goods were delivered and B signed an appropriately-worded delivery note which, for example, provided that he accepted the goods within s 35. This would be most unfair if, as in most consumer cases, B intended only to acknowledge receipt. The problem should be obviated by s 35(2) which applies to consumer *and* commercial buyers and provides that, where goods are delivered to B and he has not previously examined them, he is not deemed to have accepted them under s 35 'until he has had a reasonable opportunity of examining them' to see if they are in conformity with the contract. The effect of s 35(2) is reinforced by both s 34 and s 35(3) which provides that where B 'deals as consumer'[2] he cannot lose his right to a reasonable opportunity to examine by 'agreement, waiver or otherwise'. It follows that the reasonable opportunity to examine can be excluded in a non-consumer sale (see also s 34) and the Law Commissions[3] recommended that such an exclusion should be subject to the controls in the Unfair Contract Terms Act 1977. There is no express reference to the 1977 Act in s 35 and, while a contract *term* restricting or excluding the right of the opportunity to examine in a non-consumer sale would be subject to the test of reasonableness, an exclusion of the right in the acceptance note itself may well be outside the ambit of the 1977 Act which is limited to terms of the contract.[4]

It remains to be seen whether B's opportunity to examine the goods will substantially enhance his position as it is difficult to imagine that anything but the most obvious defects could be discovered when such an examination is made. This is particularly relevant in consumer sales. Where B buys and examines the goods in a retail shop, for example, and then signs a document which is an intimation of acceptance, he would still seem to have lost his right to reject when a defect becomes evident three or four weeks later. This problem is compounded when the third ground of acceptance under s 35 is considered – retention for a reasonable period of time (see below). In this case, assuming that the goods were insufficiently durable under the SGA, s 14(2B)(e), B could obtain only damages.

Acts inconsistent with the ownership of S

Section 35(1)(b) provides that B is deemed to accept the goods 'when the goods have been delivered to him and he does any act in relation to them which is inconsistent with the ownership of the seller'. An obvious difficulty with this phrasing is that, where property and ownership has passed to B, it appears contradictory to speak of B's acts being inconsistent with *S's ownership*. The problem was confronted by Devlin J[5] who explained that, by reason of his right to reject the goods, B has only conditional property in them which may revest in S, and it is with this reversionary interest that B may commit an inconsistent act meaning that he has accepted the goods. Most of the decisions do not articulate clearly the

---

1 *Hardy & Co v Hillerns and Fowler* [1923] 2 KB 490, 498 per Atkin LJ.
2 See the SGA, s 61(5A) which provides that references to 'dealing as consumer' in the SGA are to be construed in accordance with the Unfair Contract Terms Act 1977.
3 *Sale and Supply of Goods* (Law Com No 160, Scottish Law Com No 104, Cm 137, 1987), para 5.24.
4 The Law Commissions *(Sale and Supply of Goods*, Law Com No 160, Scottish Law Com No 104, Cm 137, 1987) also expressed concern on this point (para 2.45, fn 105).
5 *Kwei Tek Chao v British Traders and Shippers Ltd* [1954] 2 QB 459, 487.

principles underpinning this part of s 35 but, as Goode[6] stresses, the notion of the inconsistent act comprises the principles of affirmation, estoppel and B's inability to make *restitutio in integrum* where he has, for example, incorporated the goods in some structure from which they cannot be detached. In the majority of cases, it is perhaps best to acknowledge that this aspect of acceptance is premised upon B's performance of an act in relation to the goods which is an assertion of *his* ownership. In common with the other parts of s 35, B need not necessarily know of the breach at the date he performs the 'inconsistent' act and there is no requirement that S should know that B has performed that act.

Above all other acts, B's resale and delivery of the goods to a sub-buyer has consistently been regarded as an inconsistent act entailing an acceptance within s 35.[7] In *Hardy & Co v Hillerns and Fowler*,[8] S agreed to sell wheat to B, the ship carrying the cargo arriving at Hull on 18 March. On 21 March, the ship commenced discharging and, on that day, B sold and dispatched a quantity of the wheat to sub-buyers. Also on 21 March, B began to have suspicions that the wheat was not in conformity with the contract but he could not be sure until the ship had discharged more of the cargo. B's suspicions were confirmed on 23 March and he rejected the entire cargo and stopped any parcels of wheat which were still in transit to sub-buyers. It was held that B had accepted the goods by the sale and delivery of possession to the sub-buyers and it was irrelevant that B had not had a reasonable opportunity to examine the goods as s 35 was dominant over the right to examine in s 34. This decision was followed in *Ruben (E & S) Ltd v Faire Bros & Co Ltd*,[9] where B ordered S to deliver the goods direct to the sub-buyer who rejected the goods. It was held that B had taken constructive delivery at S's premises and the subsequent re-delivery by S (who acted as B's agent) to the sub-buyer was an act inconsistent with S's ownership of the goods so that B was limited to damages for breach of warranty. These decisions disclosed two difficulties in that, first, B's acceptance could occur before he had had a reasonable opportunity to examine and, second, he was barred from rejecting the goods after a resale even if he could return them to S. The sub-buyer could thus reject as against B but B could not reject as against S, this being the position in *Ruben*.

The SGA, s 35(2) now provides that B (consumer *and* non-consumer) is not deemed to have accepted the goods by an inconsistent act until he has had a reasonable opportunity to examine them. In order for B to accept the goods under this part of s 35, he must thus have a reasonable opportunity to examine the goods at the place contemplated for inspection[10] and then perform an act inconsistent with the ownership of S. Under s 35(3), the right to a reasonable opportunity to examine cannot be taken away by agreement, waiver or otherwise where B 'deals as consumer' but there can be such a waiver in non-consumer sales, a point accentuated by s 34. The reform made by s 35(6)(b) is equally important in providing that B is not deemed to accept 'merely because the goods are delivered to another under a sub-sale or other disposition' – thus remedying

---

6 *Commercial Law* (2nd edn, 1995), pp 371-373; see also the Law Commissions' factual categorisation of inconsistent acts (*Sale and Supply of Goods*, Law Com WP No 85, Scot Law Com CM No 58, 1983, para 2.54).
7 See the decisions referred to earlier, eg *Chapman v Morton* (1843) 11 M & W 534.
8 [1923] 2 KB 490.
9 [1949] 1 KB 254.
10 The place where B must have the opportunity to examine is considered below.

the injustice in *Ruben*. The law is thus much improved and, for example, where a retailer sells defective goods to B who rejects them, the retailer will now be able to reject as against the wholesaler.

In relation to sub-sales and rejection, it must be asked whether it is S's obligation to retrieve the goods and pay the costs. It will be remembered that s 36 provides that, unless otherwise agreed, B is not bound to return the goods to S on rejection and thus if the sub-buyer rejects as against B but does not return the goods to B, S will be obliged to arrange for their return and this may be costly in an international sale. However, it is S who has not complied with the contract and it is unreasonable to impose the burden of returning the goods on B as 'the reason and justice of the thing are against it'.[11] Section 35(6)(b) does specify that B does not lose the right to reject *merely* because the goods are delivered under a sub-sale and it is arguable that, if a non-consumer buyer has an opportunity to examine the goods but does not take it and then resells to the sub-buyer, a court may consider that he has lost his right to reject. This question is connected with the place of the examination (see below) and it may be that the *sub-buyer's* premises are the contemplated place for the inspection of the goods, in which case the goods may be thrown on S's hands at that place.[12]

Another difficulty with sub-sales occurred in international sales where B received the documents representing the goods and made a disposition of those documents by way of sale or pledge before the goods arrived. Here it could be asserted that, by dealing with the documents representing the goods, the goods had been 'delivered' and B had lost his right of rejection. This possibility was rejected in *Kwei Tek Chao v British Traders and Shippers Ltd*,[13] where Devlin J explained that a pledge or sale of the documents is only a disposition of the conditional property which B has received and which will revest in S on rejection and thus transfers of the documents under a string contract did not amount to inconsistent acts within s 35. The reforms made to s 35 now ensure that B is not deemed to have accepted the goods by an inconsistent act until he has had a reasonable opportunity to examine them and so B should be able to reject unless, perhaps, the defective nature of the goods is readily apparent from the face of the documents. Moreover, s 35(6)(b) provides that B is not deemed to accept 'merely because the goods are delivered to another under a sub-sale or other disposition' and it is possible that a court would consider that delivery of the goods, in this context, could apply to delivery of the documents meaning that such a delivery would not amount to acceptance under s 35(6)(b).

Apart from resales, there are many other acts of ownership by B which have been held to disallow his rejection of the goods. Thus, executing a chattel mortgage over the goods,[14] entering the goods for sale at auction even though they remained unsold,[15] entering the goods for auction and 'buying them in' when only low bids were made,[16] and registering ownership of a defective car and advertising it for sale[17] have all been held to be acts of dominion by B over the goods sufficient to bar rejection. In contrast, B's discharge of timber from a ship

---

11 *Grimoldby v Wells* (1875) LR 10 CP 391, 394 per Lord Coleridge CJ.
12 See *Molling & Co v Dean & Son Ltd* (1901) 18 TLR 217, below.
13 [1954] 2 QB 459.
14 *Metals Ltd v Diamond* [1930] 3 DLR 886.
15 *Hitchcock v Cameron* [1977] 1 NZLR 85.
16 *Parker v Palmer* (1821) 4 B & Ald 387.
17 *Armaghdown Motors Ltd v Gray Motors Ltd* [1963] NZLR 5.

followed by his stacking of it into piles of various thicknesses and sorting-out what he considered to be defective timber, were held to be purely administrative acts which did not constitute acceptance.[18] It remains to be seen how far s 35(6)(b) might affect some of these decisions where B has attempted to sell the goods. Atiyah[19] has suggested that 'if resale and delivery to a sub-buyer is not by itself to be treated as an act inconsistent with the ownership of the seller, obviously preliminary steps on the way to this result cannot have this effect either'. This is, with respect, not at all obvious and there is clearly a crucial distinction between those cases where B is unaware of the breach by S and resells the goods (as in *Ruben's* case) and cases where he is cognisant of the breach and elects to affirm the contract (as in the cases above where B attempted to sell[20]). In the latter situation of affirmation, it is surely not unreasonable that relatively trivial acts of dominion should prevent B's rejection of the goods and a court may consider that B's resale or attempted resale, with knowledge of the breach, is a significant act of dominion over the goods.

More substantial acts of ownership in relation to the goods involve B's inability to return the goods in their original condition because they have been consumed by B,[1] incorporated in some other structure[2] or subjected to excessive testing, unless S acquiesces in the testing.[3] In contrast, where a cargo of barley had been delivered in bags and then transferred into a bulk, it was held that B could re-bag the barley in different bags and this did not entail a loss of identity preventing B's rejection.[4] Although B's consumption of the goods, for example, can scarcely be bettered as an act of ownership it must be equally important in these cases that he cannot make *restitutio in integrum*, as he must if property is to re-vest in S.

The position regarding consumer sales and inconsistent acts is rather unclear but it seems that use of the goods with knowledge of the defects would almost certainly be such an act. On the other hand, s 35(6)(b) will mean that B's gift of the goods to another will not necessarily preclude his rejection against S. Concern was voiced that a consumer buyer's acceptance of repairs from S would bar

---

18 *Libau Wood Co v H Smith & Sons Ltd* (1930) 37 Ll L Rep 296.

19 *The Sale of Goods* (10th edn, 2001), p 519.

20 In *Fisher, Reeves & Co Ltd v Armour & Co Ltd* [1920] 3 KB 614, B agreed to buy tinned beef 'ex store Rotterdam' and rejected it on discovering that it was stored in lighters. Scrutton LJ and Eve J thought (*obiter*) that B's *inquiries* about a possible resale, after discovering the true position, would not amount to acceptance. This hardly amounts to an act of dominion by B and, in any event, s 35 could not have applied as it referred (and currently refers) only to those situations 'where the goods have been delivered to [B]' and they were not so delivered in *Fisher*.

1 *Harnor v Groves* (1855) 15 CB 667 (B bought 25 sacks of flour from S and, after using half a sack, he complained of the quality; he then used two more sacks and sold a third. Held that B's dealing with the goods precluded his rejecting them).

2 *Mechan & Sons Ltd v Bow, M'Lachlan & Co Ltd* 1910 SC 758 (shipbuilders (B) fitted tanks into tugs which were not to specification although they could easily have ascertained that fact prior to fitting. Held B was barred from rejection by this act inconsistent with S's ownership).

3 *Lucy v Mouflet* (1860) 5 H & N 229 (B bought a hogshead of cider and told S on 28 May that it was inferior and that if his customers continued to complain he would have to reject it. S did not reply and B complained again on 21 June and on 24 June told S to take it away. About 20 gallons had by then been consumed but it was held that S had acquiesced in B's testing of the cider).

4 *Dower & Co v Corrie, Maccoll & Son* (1925) 23 Ll L Rep 100.

rejection under this part of s 35.[5] The Law Commissions' Working Paper[6] had recommended that the inconsistent act should simply not apply in consumer sales but the SGA, s 35(6)(a) now provides that B (consumer *and* non-consumer) is not deemed to have accepted the goods merely because 'he asks for, or agrees to, their repair by or under an arrangement with the seller'. It should be stressed that s 35(6)(a) applies only to repairs done by S and should B attempt repairs himself or have repairs done by a third party, he may well lose his right to reject.

Retention of the goods for a reasonable period of time

Section 35(4) provides that B is deemed to have accepted the goods 'when after the lapse of a reasonable time he retains the goods without intimating to the seller that he has rejected them'. Section 35(5) adds that the 'questions that are material in determining for the purposes of subsection (4) above whether a reasonable time has elapsed include whether the buyer has had a reasonable opportunity of examining the goods for the purpose mentioned in subsection (2) above,' ie to see if the goods are in conformity with the contract.

As mentioned earlier, the Law Commissions did not subscribe to any long-term right of rejection and also discarded the idea of fixed time periods for the rejection of different types of goods.[7] Accordingly, the question of retention for both consumer and non-consumer buyers is simply a question of fact in determining what is meant by a 'reasonable time'[8] and a reasonable opportunity to examine is simply one factor to consider when assessing the time to be allowed for rejection.

There is little consistency in the decisions but, overall, it is plainly advisable for B to reject unequivocally as soon as defects appear in the goods. It is a perfectly fair rule which specifies that, once B has become *aware* of the defective goods in his possession, lapse of a reasonable period of time will bar his rejection. Here B effectively affirms the contract with full knowledge of the facts. In *Milner v Tucker*,[9] for example, although B was aware that a chandelier was inadequate to light his premises, he retained it for almost six months and, quite reasonably, it was held that he had lost the right to reject it. Opinions may vary, however, as to the meaning of a 'reasonable time' and, as stated above, this is a question of fact. In *Flynn v Scott*,[10] B sought to reject a second-hand van three weeks after it had broken down but it was held that he was too late and it should have been rejected 'within a very few days'[11] after the breakdown.

In the cases considered thus far, B has become aware of the defect and then let time run against him. Does B have an obligation to examine the goods after

---

5 See *Lee v York Coach and Marine* [1977] RTR 35 (B retained and used a defective car and accepted repairs from S. She was held to have lost the right to reject but on the ground that her rejection was too late and communicated only when she commenced proceedings against S).

6 *Sale and Supply of Goods* (Law Com WP No 85, Scot Law Com CM No 58, 1983), para 4.85.

7 *Sale and Supply of Goods* (Law Com No 160, Scottish Law Com No 104, Cm 137, 1987), paras 5.14-5.19.

8 The SGA, s 59 provides that deciding a reasonable time is a question of fact.

9 (1823) 1 C & P 15.

10 1949 SC 442; see also *Lee v York Coach and Marine* [1977] RTR 35.

11 1949 SC 442 at 446, per Lord Mackintosh.

purchase to see if they are defective? There is an immediate and obvious tension here: on the one hand it could be argued that B is entitled to rely on the conditions of the contract which relate to quality, fitness and description and thus not make an examination but, on the other hand, it might be asserted that a prudent buyer would inspect the goods promptly after purchase. Much might turn on the nature of the goods, the scale of the transaction and the status of the buyer as businessman or consumer. Certainly there is authority to the effect that B should make a normal examination of the goods in a relatively short space of time and, if he does not do so, he may have lost his right to reject them. In *Diamond v British Columbia Thoroughbred Breeders' Society*,[12] B bought a racehorse and could have checked its lineage with a certificate of registration which he possessed, but he failed to do so until five months later and it was held that he had lost the right of rejection. Similarly, it might be thought that a prudent buyer should consult expert opinion reasonably soon after purchase in order to ascertain the authenticity of the goods.[13] It may even be sensible to consult an expert as regards possible defects in a car rather than allowing them to develop in use and thus run the risk of losing the right to reject the goods.[14]

If some of the decisions above appear overly-restrictive, there are others which take a more rounded view: the court's decision may be affected by numerous factors which are thought to be in B's favour. In *Hammer and Barrow v Coca-Cola*,[15] S sold Yo-Yos to Coca-Cola (B) which were to be used for promotional purposes and bore the legend 'Drink Coca-Cola Ice Cold'. B complained of defects in the Yo-Yos and some of them were retained by B for 25 days during which time correspondence took place between S and B. Richmond J held that B had not retained the goods for an unreasonable time and stressed that it was important that the Yo-Yos had been made for a special purpose. S was thus not prejudiced by a moderate delay as there could be no suggestion that he would lose an opportunity of reselling the goods – but the judge emphasised that this would normally be of considerable importance in assessing the time for rejection, particularly where S might have to resell on a falling market.

Another factor to consider is that the complex nature of the goods may mean that a longer time should be allowed for B to ascertain whether they are satisfactory. In one decision, where B had resold and delivered the goods to a sub-buyer, a lapse of two to three months spent in trying to ascertain the precise defects and whether the sub-buyer intended to reject was held not to be an unreasonable period of time, particularly as S had threatened that rejection would be a breach of contract.[16] Moreover, where the goods are complex, B's conciliatory approach in allowing S to attempt repairs should not count against

---

12 (1965) 52 DLR (2d) 146.
13 *Hyslop v Shirlaw* (1905) 13 SLT 209 (B retained paintings for 18 months and then sought to reject on the advice of experts. Held that he could have consulted experts immediately and that he had lost the right to reject); cf *Burrell v Harding's Executrix* 1931 SLT 76 (position might be different if paintings are in storage after the sale).
14 *Taylor v Combined Buyers Ltd* [1924] NZLR 627 (three months' use of a car barred rejection, Salmond J holding (see pp 650-652) that B had a duty to entrust the examination of the car to an expert because then the defects might have been discovered immediately). But cars were novelties in 1924: would the *Taylor* view still hold good today? The argument that B should have had an independent check made on a car was rejected in *Freeman v Consolidated Motors Ltd* (1968) 69 DLR (2d) 581.
15 [1962] NZLR 723.
16 *Manifatture Tessile Laniera Wooltex v J B Ashley Ltd* [1979] 2 Lloyd's Rep 28.

him,[17] particularly if any delay in rejecting is caused by S's encouragement that B should have patience with the goods and his assurances that problems can be rectified.[18] Although s 35(6)(a) now provides that B is not deemed to have accepted the goods merely because he agrees to their repair by S, the section does not expressly state that, as regards *retention*, time is suspended during the repairs. This was clearly the intention of the Law Commissions,[19] however, in stating that it would be wrong if the 'clock remained running' during repairs.

Most recently, in *Truk (UK) Ltd v Tokmakidis GmbH*,[20] the court had to consider the question of reasonable time in relation to a contract where goods were bought by B for resale. The decision is also the first to consider the amended provisions of the SGA relating to rejection/acceptance. In *Truk*, B was in the business of buying and selling heavy vehicles which were used to recover other vehicles which had broken down or been involved in accidents and S agreed to supply B with an 'underlift' and fit it to a chassis belonging to B. The terms of the contract were that the underlift would comply with certain requirements as to its construction (the Iveco guidelines) and B would pay the price either six months after delivery or upon the resale of the vehicle, whichever was the earlier. The underlift and chassis were delivered to B in June 1996 and, in December 1996, a potential buyer advised B that the vehicle did not meet the Iveco guidelines. B told S that he could not sell the vehicle unless S supplied stamped documentation from Iveco to the effect that the vehicle complied with their guidelines and he refused to pay for the goods until the documentation arrived. There followed a series of communications between the parties between December 1996 and July 1997. During this period, it was established beyond doubt that the vehicle did not comply with the Iveco assembly regulations. In March 1997, B suggested that S should buy the vehicle from B or that S should remove the underlift, but S did nothing. Eventually, B informed S, in June 1997, that he would have to remove the underlift himself unless the problems were resolved and, in July 1997, B did remove it. S sued for the price of the goods but B counterclaimed that, as they were defective, he had validly rejected them and was entitled to damages.

Judge Raymond Jack QC held that the periods of time involved should be divided into two, viz June 1996 – December 1996 and December 1996 – July 1997. The first difficulty was whether B's right of rejection survived the first six months, thus raising 'in stark form the question of reasonable time'.[1] The judge considered that, if the vehicle had been sold for use by B, a reasonable period for rejection would have been one or two months as B could have inspected the vehicle and asked S, almost immediately after delivery, for proof

---

17   See eg *Barber v Inland Truck Sales Ltd* (1970) 11 DLR (3d) 469 (truck could be rejected after six months' use); *Public Utilities Commission of City of Waterloo v Burroughs Business Machines* (1974) 52 DLR (3d) 481(computer could be rejected after 14 months as B had used his best efforts to make it function and it was 'complex and novel'); *Finlay v Metro Toyota Ltd* (1977) 82 DLR (3d) 440 (car plagued with electrical problems could be rejected after six months' use); *Bernstein v Pamson Motors (Golders Green) Ltd* [1987] 2 All ER 220, 230 per Rougier J: 'What is a reasonable time in relation to a bicycle would hardly suffice for a nuclear submarine'.

18   *Rafuse Motors Ltd v Mardo Construction Ltd* (1963) 41 DLR (2d) 340 (use of a tractor for three to four months did not bar rejection).

19   *Sale and Supply of Goods* (Law Com No 160, Scottish Law Com No 104, Cm 137, 1987), para 5.30.

20   [2000] 1 Lloyd's Rep 543.

 1   [2000] 1 Lloyd's Rep 543 at 549, per Judge Raymond Jack QC.

of compliance with the Iveco guidelines. The vehicle was for resale, however, and the contract envisaged that it might take at least six months to find a buyer. Accordingly, where goods are sold for resale, the judge held that a reasonable time in which to intimate rejection should usually be the time actually taken to resell the goods together with an additional period during which they can be inspected and tried out by the sub-purchaser.[2] Where the price was payable after delivery, as here, the reasonable period of time should last at least until the date for payment. As regards the second period of six months, B was entitled to a reasonable time in which to investigate whether the goods were defective and, in March 1997, he had acted promptly in unequivocally rejecting the vehicle after discovering that it did not comply with the Iveco guidelines. It followed that B had validly rejected the goods, was not liable for the price and was entitled to damages.

Wholly latent defects and retention

The general rule that B may accept the goods under s 35 without having any knowledge of their defects means that time runs against him under this part of s 35 even though the defects are wholly latent. In the much-criticised decision in *Bernstein v Pamson Motors (Golders Green) Ltd*,[3] the court had to consider acceptance by pure lapse of time (there were no attempted repairs by S, for example) in relation to a wholly latent defect. B, a consumer buyer, bought a new Nissan Laurel car from S on 7 December but, as he was ill during the Christmas period, the car made its first journey of any length on 3 January. Some 40 miles into the journey the engine seized and would not restart. B telephoned S the same day and rejected the car and, the following day, he unequivocally rejected the car in writing. It was discovered that a piece of plastic sealant had entered the engine during its assembly and had eventually cut-off the oil supply. In total, the car had been driven for 140 miles. Rougier J held that B had lost the right to reject the car because, as a question of fact, he had retained it for a reasonable period of time and such time was not related to any opportunity for examination of the goods.

Other decisions may be cited which have allowed a much longer period for rejection[4] than *Bernstein* and one which is arguably more restrictive than the latter decision,[5] but this serves only to accentuate the uncertainty of the law. Section 35(5) now specifies that, in assessing the lapse of a reasonable time, it is material to consider whether the buyer has had a reasonable opportunity of examining the goods to see if they are in conformity with the contract, but it must be asked whether this will necessarily alleviate the hardship to B in the

---

2 The judge's reasoning was that, as delivery to a sub-purchaser is no longer deemed to be acceptance (SGA, s 35(6)(b)), it is reasonable to allow an additional trial period by that sub-purchaser.
3 [1987] 2 All ER 220; see Brown, 'Acceptance in the Sale of Goods' [1988] JBL 56, 62-64; Reynolds, 'Loss of Right to Reject' (1988) 104 LQR 16; Hwang, 'Time for Rejection of Defective Goods' [1992] LMCLQ 334.
4 See *Rogers v Parish (Scarborough) Ltd* [1987] QB 933 (B was allowed to reject a Range Rover after six months and 5,500 miles, although here S had attempted futile repairs; acceptance was not pleaded).
5 *Eastern Supply Co v Kerr* [1994] 1 MLJ 10 (Singapore Court of Appeal) (retention of a second-hand car for two weeks barred rejection, *but* here B had knowledge of the defects which appeared during the fortnight he had the car).

Bernstein situation. If B buys goods but does not wish to use them immediately (eg goods bought in January for use on a holiday in July) has he had a reasonable opportunity to examine them such that he loses his right to reject six months later? Moreover, the opportunity to *examine* the goods is only of any utility where the defect *can* be discovered by such an examination and it is valueless where the defect is latent: no reasonable examination which Mr Bernstein could have performed would have disclosed the defect in the engine's interior.

If s 35(5) had emphasised the time which might reasonably be taken for B to *discover the defect*, a suitably extended period would be applicable for latent defects while, at the same time, a court could curtail the period during which other defects could and *should* reasonably have been discovered by B. This approach was evident in the Scottish decision in *Hyslop v Shirlaw*,[6] where B sought to reject paintings more than 18 months after delivery on the basis that they were fakes. It was held that B had lost the right of rejection. Lord Kyllachy considered that 'the onus is on the pursuer to shew that he could not, by any examination reasonably possible, have discovered earlier the disconformity on which his rejection proceeded ... when he did reject – more than eighteen months after delivery – he did so as the result of an examination by experts, whom he might equally have consulted a week after his purchase. He is not, therefore, in the position of a person who has by accident discovered, perhaps years afterwards, something justifying rescission which could not have been discovered except by accident. That is, of course, a different case altogether'.[7] As *Hyslop* was a decision on the SGA 1893, s 35, a court could clearly reach the same conclusion under the amended s 35 but, undeniably, that decision would be more credible if the section had emphasised the nature of the defect and the time which might reasonably be taken for B to discover it.

Reform of the law

The EU Directive, *Certain Aspects of the Sale of Consumer Goods and Associated Guarantees*,[8] which must be implemented by Member States no later than 1 January 2002, will alter the rules on rejection where *consumers* buy goods from *business* sellers. Most particularly, consumer buyers will have two years in which to complain of goods which are not in conformity with the contract, provided that the non-conformity was present at the date of delivery (art 5(1)). Moreover, there is a presumption that defects which materialise within the first six months after delivery existed at the date of delivery (art 5(3)). Clearly these rules will improve the position of consumer buyers. The Directive is considered in detail in Chapter 21.

The place of examination of the goods

As the opportunity to examine is central to B's valid acceptance under s 35, it is vital to know where the place of the examination must be. The general rule is

---

6 (1905) 13 SLT 209.
7 (1905) 13 SLT 209 at 213.
8 Directive 99/44/EC, 25 May 1999.

that the place of delivery is the place of examination. In *Perkins v Bell*,[9] S sold malted barley to B by sample, to be delivered at a railway station and, on the same day, B resold the barley to a brewer. B had a sample of barley sent from the station and then directed that the barley be sent on to the brewer. The brewer rejected the barley and B sought to reject as against S but it was held that he had accepted the barley and the station was the proper place at which he could have inspected it.

However, the general rule may be rebutted by the terms of the contract or the nature of the transaction.[10] In *Saunt v Belcher and Gibbons Ltd*,[11] Bailhache J thought that, if the rule were to be rebutted, S would have to know that the place of delivery was not the final destination and that the place of delivery itself or the nature or packing of the goods would make inspection at that place unreasonable. B's place of business[12] or the sub-buyer's premises may thus be the place where the examination is contemplated. In *Molling & Co v Dean and Son Ltd*,[13] S, a firm of printers in Germany, sold 40,000 books to B in England which S knew were intended for resale in the USA. B did not inspect the books but dispatched them to the USA where they were examined and rejected by the sub-buyer as being defective in quality. It was held that B could reject the non-conforming goods (27,000 books), retain 13,000 books at the contract price and recover from S the costs of transport from the USA on the basis that the sub-buyer's place of business was the contemplated place of inspection. This decision is correct under the new provisions in s 35 as B did not have a reasonable opportunity to examine before the sub-sale which could thus not amount to an acceptance. Similarly, in *Heilbutt v Hickson*,[14] S sold 30,000 shoes to B which S knew were intended for use by the French army, to be delivered at a wharf in London and to be inspected before shipment. As doubts arose regarding the quality of the shoes, S agreed to take them back if they were rejected by the French army. It was held that this amounted to a variation of the place of examination and B could 'throw the shoes upon the [seller's] hands at Lille'[15] when they were rejected by the army on the ground that the soles contained paper. Brett J went further and considered that, because the shoes had a 'secret defect' the inspection in London could be of no practical effect, and France was thus the proper place of examination. Again this decision is clearly correct under the new s 35 and, indeed, Brett J's approach to latent defects and the time taken to discover them might advantageously be applied in the *Bernstein* situation, considered above.

9 [1893] 1 QB 193.
10 Eg it was seen earlier that, in cif contracts, the place of examination is not where the documents are handed to B but is at the port of arrival and acceptance of the shipping documents does not prevent B from rejecting the goods: *Kwei Tek Chao v British Traders and Shippers Ltd* [1954] 2 QB 459.
11 (1920) 90 LJKB 541.
12 *Grimoldby v Wells* (1875) LR 10 CP 391(goods transported part of the way to B's premises in S's cart and then transferred to B's cart. B examined the goods in his barn on the day of delivery and rejected them. Held (i) B had the right to inspect at his barn as it would be unreasonable to do so half way on the journey; (ii) B had no obligation to return the goods to S; and (iii) B's rejection was thus valid).
13 (1901) 18 TLR 217.
14 (1872) LR 7 CP 438; see also *Van den Hurk v R Martens & Co Ltd* [1920] 1 KB 850 (sodium sulphide packed in sealed drums which could not be inspected until opened by sub-B; the sub-B's premises in France were thus the proper place for examination).
15 (1872) LR 7 CP 438 at 455, per Brett J.

Partial rejection of the goods and severable contracts

Before the enactment of the Sale and Supply of Goods Act 1994, the general rule in the SGA, s 11(4) was that, if B accepted *part* of the goods, he would be treated as if he had accepted them all and would be unable to reject any of them. If the goods were partially defective, B therefore had the choice of accepting all of them or rejecting all of them.[16] There were only two exceptions to this all-or-nothing rule. First, where the contract was severable and delivery was made in instalments (see below), B's acceptance of one instalment did not preclude his rejection of another instalment. Second, under the SGA, s 30(4), where S delivered goods of the contract description mixed with goods of a different *description*, B could choose to reject the non-conforming goods and accept the remainder.[17] This meant that fine distinctions were generated between the unwanted goods being of a different description (when B could reject) and their being simply defective in quality (when B could not reject). The distinctions thus drawn were patently illogical, and also caused confusion as regards the requirement that the contract goods be 'mixed' with other goods.[18] Essentially, it was difficult to see why B should not be able to accept 50% of the conforming goods, for example, and reject the other 50%, particularly as such a rule would benefit S as well as B in that S's liability to pay damages would be greater where B was compelled to reject all the goods.[19]

The law has been made to harmonise with both logic and commercial practice: s 11(4) now commences with the words 'subject to section 35A below' and the new s 35A gives B a right of partial rejection in certain circumstances. The idea of the new provision is that B should have a partial right of rejection where some of the goods delivered do not *conform*, by reason of the breach, with the contract requirements and thus the policy of the old s 30(4) has, in effect, been extended to cover all cases of non-conforming goods. Section 35A provides:

'(1) If the buyer –
(a) has the right to reject the goods by reason of a breach on the part of the seller that affects some or all of them, but
(b) accepts some of the goods, including, where there are any goods unaffected by the breach, all such goods,
   he does not by accepting them lose his right to reject the rest.
(2) In the case of a buyer having the right to reject an instalment of goods, subsection (1) above applies as if references to the goods were references to the goods comprised in the instalment.
(3) For the purposes of subsection (1) above, goods are affected by a breach if by reason of the breach they are not in conformity with the contract.
(4) This section applies unless a contrary intention appears in, or is to be implied from, the contract.'

The effect of s 35A is that, if B has a right to reject all the goods by reason of a breach which affects some or all of them but chooses to accept some of the non-

---

16   Cf *Molling & Co v Dean and Son Ltd* (1901) 18 TLR 217, considered above, where B was able to accept part and reject part of the goods on the basis that each of the books had to be up to standard.
17   The SGA, s 30(4) was repealed by the Sale and Supply of Goods Act 1994.
18   See *Levy v Green* (1857) 8 E & B 575; *Barker (W) (Jr) & Co Ltd v E T Agius Ltd* (1927) 33 Com Cas 120; *Re Moore & Co and Landauer & Co* [1921] 2 KB 519.
19   See *Sale and Supply of Goods* (Law Com WP No 85; Scot Law Com CM No 58, 1983), para 6.25.

conforming goods, he does not lose the right to reject the remainder of the non-conforming goods, provided that he accepts *all* the goods which are unaffected by the breach. The possible permutations generated by s 35A can be summarised:

(i) B must have a right to reject *all* the goods by virtue of the breach which has occurred, eg 90% of the goods are defective;
(ii) where, for example, 90% of the goods are defective, B can still elect to reject all the goods or accept all the goods;
(iii) where, for example, 90% of the goods are defective, B can reject that 90% but, if so, he must accept the remaining 10% of conforming goods. Alternatively, B can accept 45% of the defective goods and reject the remaining 45% but, if so, he must still accept the 10% of conforming goods;
(iv) where 100% of the goods are defective, B may reject them all or accept whatever percentage he wishes.

Although s 35A does not provide that it is subject to s 15A (on the loss of the non-consumer buyer's right to reject for slight breaches of ss 13-15) this was the recommendation of the Law Commissions.[20] It thus seems that, where s 15A applies, the non-consumer buyer does not have a right to reject all the goods for a slight breach and thus he cannot have a right to partial rejection under s 35A, because a right to reject all the goods is a pre-condition for the operation of the latter section. A second limitation on s 35A is that, under s 35(7), where B has accepted some of the goods forming part of a 'commercial unit' he is deemed to have accepted all the goods comprised in that unit. The idea here is that B should not be able to pick and choose and thereby accept some parts of a unit which are beneficial to him while rejecting others. The Law Commissions'[1] examples make the position clear: if B accepts one volume from a set of encyclopaedias he is deemed to accept the entire set and, likewise, with one shoe accepted from a pair of shoes. Similarly, it would be most unjust if B could remove sound parts from a defective car and reject what was left. Finally, s 35A applies unless a contrary intention 'appears in, or is to be implied from, the contract' (s 35A(4)).

Severable contracts

Thus far the discussion in this chapter has concerned entire contracts where full and complete delivery by S is a condition precedent to the liability of B to pay the price. The SGA, s 11(4), which provides that B loses his right to reject where he accepts the goods, applies to entire contracts but not where the contract is 'severable'; it is therefore necessary to consider the nature of a severable or divisible contract and B's rights thereunder.

A severable contract classically entails instalment deliveries of goods and its effect is that a breach by one party in relation to a severable obligation may not affect the other obligations. Thus if S should fail to make a delivery of an instalment of goods under such a contract, B will not necessarily be entitled to repudiate the whole contract and, likewise, S may not be able to repudiate if B fails to pay for one instalment; instead there will be a severable breach giving rise to a claim for compensation. The SGA does not define a severable contract but s 31(2) refers to

20 *Sale and Supply of Goods* (Law Com No 160, Scottish Law Com No 104, Cm 137, 1987), para 6.10.
1 *Sale and Supply of Goods* (Law Com No 160, Scottish Law Com No 104, Cm 137, 1987), paras 6.12-6.13.

'a contract for the sale of goods to be delivered by stated instalments, which are to be separately paid for' and goes on to state that, whether the effects referred to above apply, depends on the terms of the contract and the circumstances of the case. Section 31(2) is not an all-embracing definition however, and the courts have been flexible in implying severability thus avoiding the all-or-nothing rule in entire contracts mentioned earlier. In *Jackson v Rotax Motor and Cycle Co*,[2] a contract for the sale of 600 motor horns provided for 'delivery as required' by B and the goods were delivered in 19 cases over two months. On delivery of the last consignment, B sought to reject all but case 2 which he had sold to retailers but it was held that the contract was severable, even though there was no provision for separate payment of instalments. B could thus reject each batch separately and had to pay only for batch 1 (cases 1-4) as he had accepted case 2 of that batch. If this had been regarded as an entire contract, B would have been deemed to accept all the goods under the SGA, s 35.[3]

It is equally clear from s 31(2) that one party can treat *the whole* instalment contract as repudiated if the other party renounces one of his obligations under it, but the pre-1893 authorities on this point were conflicting[4] and thus s 31(2) provides only that 'the terms of the contract and circumstances of the case' must be considered in deciding this issue. It is difficult to ascertain whether the gravity of the breach[5] justifies repudiation of the contract but it was suggested in *Maple Flock Co Ltd v Universal Furniture Products (Wembley) Ltd*,[6] that it is most relevant to consider (i) the ratio quantitatively which the breach bears to the whole; and (ii) the degree of probability or improbability that the breach will be repeated. There, in a contract to sell 100 tons of rag flock in instalments of 1½ tons each, fifteen instalments were accepted but the sixteenth was contaminated by chlorine. Two more deliveries were accepted but then B repudiated because of the contaminated delivery, although a further two deliveries were accepted during the negotiations. It was held that S's breach was not a repudiation of the whole contract but B was in breach of contract and S was entitled to damages. A nice contrast is provided by *Robert A Munro & Co Ltd v Meyer*,[7] where there was a contract for the sale of 1,500 tons of bone meal to be delivered in weekly quantities. After half the total had been delivered, B discovered that it was all adulterated and it was held that this breach by S amounted to a repudiation of the whole contract thus entitling B to treat himself as discharged.

Section 35A, on partial rejection, alters neither the law on severable contracts nor that concerning B's right of rejection. In other words, where B *does* have a right to reject (and for the rule in s 35A to operate he must be entitled to reject *all* the goods) the rules on partial rejection are an *addition* to B's rights. In

---

2   [1910] 2 KB 937.

3   See also *Regent OHG Aisenstadt und Barig v Francesco of Jermyn Street Ltd* [1981] 3 All ER 327 (S agreed to sell 62 suits to B, delivery to be by instalments with the number and size of the consignments being left to S. On one instalment, there was short delivery of one suit and B rejected delivery of all the consignments. Held S was entitled to damages as this was a severable contract which did not entitle B to cancel the whole contract).

4   See Lindley LJ's comments in *Mersey Steel and Iron Co v Naylor, Benzon & Co* (1882) 9 QBD 648, 666.

5   See the general tests proposed in *Freeth v Burr* (1874) LR 9 CP 208 and *Mersey Steel and Iron Co v Naylor, Benzon & Co* (1884) 9 App Cas 434 to the effect that there must be a renunciation or absolute refusal to perform.

6   [1934] 1 KB 148, 157 per Lord Hewart CJ.

7   [1930] 2 KB 312.

severable contracts, therefore, where B has a right to reject one instalment, he may accept some goods from it and reject the rest (see s 35A(2), above). However, the SGA, s 15A (the non-consumer buyer cannot reject for slight breaches of ss 13-15), s 30(2A)(the non-consumer buyer cannot reject for slight breaches of s 30 relating to the quantity of goods delivered) and s 35A have made the law much more flexible than it used to be. It thus seems that the rules on severable contracts will now be superseded by s 35A: B may now reject part and accept part of the goods delivered even where the contract is entire and thus there should be a decreasing need to have recourse to the notion of severability.

CHAPTER 24

Risk, non-existent goods and frustration

Introduction

When a sale of goods has passed the property in them to B and he has taken delivery, it is clear that, normally, any risk of loss or damage would fall on B, the owner of the goods. However, where there is an agreement to sell goods, their accidental loss or damage is not uncommon and it is of primary importance to decide whether S or B should bear the loss: goods are said to be at the risk of either S or B when the cost of their loss, damage or deterioration falls on one or other of those parties.

It is important to stress that the agreement is not *discharged* by the fact that risk is placed on either party. If the risk is on S and he cannot deliver the goods, B cannot be compelled to pay the price but S may nevertheless be liable in damages for non-delivery as he is not discharged from this obligation. Likewise, if the risk is on B he may be liable for the price of the goods even if they are seriously damaged or lost. In short, the rules on risk regulate the rights and liabilities of S and B where the contract is not discharged but the goods are damaged or lost. As S and B remain liable to perform their obligations, it is vital for the party who bears the risk to be insured against the loss or damage to the goods.[1]

On the other hand, where the rules of frustration are operative, both S and B will be automatically discharged from their obligations. Physical damage to the goods may frustrate the contract in certain cases but normally frustration prevents *performance* of the contract by, for example, supervening illegality. Similarly, in cases of mistake, the contract may be rendered void at common law and, in ss 6 and 7, the SGA has rules of extremely limited scope which allow only for the 'perishing' of specific goods before and after contract respectively, in which case the contract is also void.

The transfer of risk

RISK AND THE PASSING OF PROPERTY

The general rule is *res perit domino*, meaning that the risk of loss or damage to goods falls on their owner. This principle is embodied in the SGA, s 20(1):

---

1 Where goods are at one party's risk he has an insurable interest in them even though he does not have property in them: *Inglis v Stock* (1885) 10 App Cas 263.

'Unless otherwise agreed, the goods remain at the seller's risk until the property in them is transferred to the buyer, but when the property in them is transferred to the buyer the goods are at the buyer's risk whether delivery has been made or not'.

It is important to stress that risk is coupled with the passing of property and not physical possession. Specific goods, for example, might be at B's risk from the moment of contract as property in them may pass to him at that time even though he has not taken delivery of the goods. On the other hand, property in unascertained goods cannot transfer to B until, at the earliest, the goods are ascertained and thus risk does not normally transfer to B before that time.[2] Reference should be made to Chapter 16 on the passing of property where many of the decisions considered emphasise the question of risk. The basic rule in s 20(1) is subject to certain qualifications which must now be considered.

Contrary agreement

Section 20(1) applies 'unless otherwise agreed' and thus S and B may make express provision as to where the risk shall lie irrespective of the passing of property or possession. In *The Julia*,[3] Lord Normand said: 'It may be conceded that the parties can agree to some purely artificial allocation of the risk and if they express that agreement in suitable language in the contract it must somehow be given effect'.

A prime illustration of risk passing to B before property occurred in *Martineau v Kitching*.[4] There the contract was for the sale of specific sugar loaves with an express provision that they were to be at S's risk for two months after the contract of sale. B paid the approximate price of four identified lots of sugar and took delivery of some of the goods but some loaves were left with S. The contract terms were that the price paid was subject to adjustment on delivery depending upon the weight of the sugar sold. A fire destroyed S's premises after the expiration of two months from the contract. The majority did not decide whether property had passed to B before weighing/delivery[5] but held that, after the expiry of the two months, it was implied that the risk was on B and that he should also bear the loss (Cockburn CJ held that property, and therefore the risk, had passed to B).[6] B also carries the risk without having property in the goods where there is a retention of title clause in the contract, meaning that property will remain in S until B pays for the goods but that risk will pass to B as soon as the goods are delivered to him. Likewise, the inference from the agreement between S and B, or from usage or a course of dealing, may be that property and risk are to be distinct. In cif contracts, the property in the goods does not generally pass until the shipping documents relating to the goods are handed over to B but the risk passes as soon as the goods cross the ship's rail at the port of shipment. In consequence, when the shipping documents are tendered to B, he is bound to pay for the goods even though they have already been lost at sea.

---

2 But see *Sterns Ltd v Vickers Ltd* [1923] 1 KB 78, below.
3 *Comptoir D'Achat et de Vente Du Boerenbond Belge S/A v Luis de Ridder Ltda, The Julia* [1949] AC 293, 319.
4 (1872) LR 7 QB 436.
5 See now s 18, r 3 (see Ch 16).
6 See also *Castle v Playford* (1872) LR 7 Exch 98 (sale of a quantity of ice with 'risks and dangers of the seas' placed on B from the moment of receipt of the bill of lading. The ship was lost. The court considered that property had probably passed to B but, in any case, the risk was on B and he was liable for the value of the cargo at the date of loss); *Horn v Minister of Food* [1948] 2 All ER 1036.

It is a readily understandable rule that, in the case of specific goods or ascertained goods, the risk may transfer to B before property and it might be thought reasonable that the rule should be limited to those two types of goods. However, provided the goods are identifiable as those which are at B's risk, it is clear that risk in goods which are in an undivided bulk may pass to B. In *Sterns Ltd v Vickers Ltd*,[7] S agreed to sell to B 120,000 gallons of white spirit, being part of a larger quantity of 200,000 gallons owned by S but contained in a storage tank belonging to a third party (T). B obtained a delivery warrant for the spirit, which T had accepted, and B indorsed it to a sub-buyer but, as the sub-buyer did not want to take immediate delivery, he made his own arrangements with T for storage and paid T rent. When the sub-buyer came to take delivery some months later, he discovered that the spirit had deteriorated. As the sub-buyer had claimed damages from B, B in turn claimed damages against S. The Court of Appeal held that the risk had passed to B at the moment that T acknowledged B's rights to 120,000 gallons of the spirit, despite the fact that the quantity sold had not been separated from the bulk. As the risk had passed to B, he had to bear the loss. Scrutton LJ explained that S had done all that he undertook to do and if B had taken delivery of the sprit immediately he would have got all that S had undertaken to sell; as S had no control over the goods it would thus be unfair to put the risk on him.[8] The element of control in B, not S, and the fact that the spirit was left undivided for B's convenience were thus decisive factors in *Sterns* .

Although *Sterns* is clearly good law, it has always been a contentious decision in that the goods were unascertained and risk passed to B on the basis of an implied agreement. In *The Julia*,[9] the House of Lords stressed that *Sterns* was of limited application. Both Lords Porter[10] and Normand[11] considered that *Sterns* applied only where B had an interest in an undivided bulk and a bailee, such as a warehouseman, had attorned to B. The decision could thus not apply to totally unascertained goods and, in *The Julia*, risk was held not to have passed to B in an 'ex ship' contract for the purchase of 500 tons of rye, shipped as part of a larger consignment covered by a single bill of lading which was retained by S, even though B had received a delivery order for the rye. In 'ex ship' contracts, property does not normally pass until the goods cross the ship's rail at the port of *delivery* and thus there were some similarities with *Sterns* where the property could not pass before the goods were separated from the bulk. Lord Normand[12] emphasised that, in *The Julia*, B 'had no more than a promise to deliver a part of the bulk cargo and the case is typically one for the general rule res perit domino'. Moreover, the decision in *Healy v Howlett & Sons*,[13] shows that, in the absence of the exceptional factors in *Sterns*, the courts are unlikely to infer

---

7 [1923] 1 KB 78.
8 Scrutton LJ thought that 'strictly' the property had not passed to B (p 85) and so the case was decided entirely on the question of risk. Of course, there is now no doubt that property cannot pass to B on these facts without *separation* of the 120,000 gallons and, several years after *Sterns*, this matter was put beyond doubt in two seminal decisions: *Laurie & Morewood v Dudin & Sons* [1926] 1 KB 223 and *Re Wait* [1927] 1 Ch 606. Under the SGA, ss 20A and 20B, there can now be co-ownership of an identified bulk (see Ch 16).
9 *Comptoir D'Achat et deVente Du Boerenbond Belge S/A v Luis de Ridder Ltda, The Julia* [1949] AC 293.
10 [1949] AC 293 at 312.
11 [1949] AC 293 at 319.
12 [1949] AC 293 at 320.
13 [1917] 1 KB 337 (see Ch 16).

that the risk is on B where he has agreed to buy unascertained goods which have not been separated from a bulk.

The *Sterns* decision thus has a limited ambit but there are still difficulties with the view that, although property in an undivided bulk cannot pass to B, the risk may transfer to him. In *Sterns*, there had been a uniform deterioration of the white spirit throughout the bulk but it must be asked what the position is if only some of the bulk deteriorates and S can supply B with sound goods, eg S agrees to sell 100 tons of wheat to B from a bulk of 200 tons and only 100 tons are sound. In this example, it seems reasonable that S should carry the primary risk and that B should be supplied with sound goods. This problem is now met under the new ss 20A and 20B[14] of the SGA where, in contracts for the sale of unascertained goods, there can be co-ownership of an identified bulk. Although there is no express reference to the question of risk in the new provisions, it is likely that risk transfers to B when he becomes a co-owner. The Law Commissions[15] had suggested that risk of partial destruction rested with S so long as the quantity destroyed was within the quantity retained by him and so any goods retained by S are deemed to be destroyed first and, thereafter, it seems that the co-owners would suffer a loss proportionately. The question of risk in relation to ss 20A and 20B is considered separately.[16] The same difficulty is faced with the newly-extended definition of 'specific goods' in the SGA, s 61(1) as including 'an undivided share, specified as a fraction or percentage, of goods identified and agreed on as aforesaid' (eg S agrees to sell to B half (or 50%) of the wheat in an identified hopper; S agrees to sell to B a half share in a racehorse).[17] Section 20A does not apply here as these are specific goods but, at common law, the effect is the same as under s 20A: B acquires a proprietary share in the undivided bulk and thus becomes an owner in common. Again, no provision is made in the SGA for the transfer of risk in this situation but it seems likely that the risk in the undivided share will pass to B at the same time as property in the undivided share. The moment when property in the undivided share passes to B will depend upon the intent of S and B.

Most of the discussion above concerned the situation where risk was placed on B even though he had no property in the goods but it is also quite possible for property to pass to B before risk and this will often happen where B pays for specific goods but it is *expressly* agreed that risk will remain with S until actual delivery to B. However, in *Head v Tattersall*,[18] there was no express provision on risk but it was nevertheless held that risk remained with S even though property passed to B. There B bought a horse from S which was said to have been hunted with the Bicester hounds and the contract of sale contained a condition that he could return the horse if it did not answer its description. The horse had not been hunted with the Bicester hounds and B returned it within the stipulated time but it had been injured without fault on his part. It was held that B could nevertheless return the horse and recover the price and the risk was thus on S even though it seems the property in the horse had passed to B. This was certainly the view of Cleasby B who held that damage from the depreciation of a chattel ought to fall on its owner and, as property here revested in S, he was the party

14 Inserted by the Sale of Goods (Amendment) Act 1995.
15 *Sale of Goods Forming Part of a Bulk*, (Law Com No 215; Scot Law Com No 145 (1993)), para 4.14.
16 See Ch 16 where co-ownership of unascertained goods is considered in detail.
17 See Ch 16 where this extended definition of 'specific goods' is considered.
18 (1871) LR 7 Exch 7.

who should bear the loss. The decision is clearly controversial and is considered again where B's right of rejection is examined in Chapter 23.

Delay in the delivery of goods: s 20(2)

The general rule in the SGA, s 20(1) is also qualified by s 20(2) which provides for the situation where delivery is delayed by the fault of S or B. Section 20(2) provides:

> 'But where delivery has been delayed through the fault of either buyer or seller the goods are at the risk of the party at fault as regards any loss which might not have occurred but for such fault.'

It is important to stress that s 20(2) refers to delay in *delivery* and not delay in the passing of property and the section envisages situations where the risk would normally be with one party but, because of the delay, the risk is shifted to the other party. For example, if S sold a new car to B and promised to deliver it to B's office at a certain time the following day then, assuming the car is specific goods, property in it could pass to B on contract – but if S does not deliver it as agreed he is at fault and he carries any loss 'which might not have occurred but for such fault'. The only decision to consider the effect of s 20(2)[19] is that in *Demby Hamilton & Co Ltd v Barden*.[20] S agreed to sell 30 tons of apple juice to B in accordance with a sample, the juice to be delivered to third parties. S crushed the apples, put the juice in casks, and kept it pending delivery. The court found as a fact that it would have been difficult to supply apple juice complying with the sample unless all the apples had been crushed at one time and that the juice was rightly kept for the fulfilment of the contract. Deliveries commenced and would have been completed punctually but for a request from B that S should stop deliveries until further notice. S was ready to deliver at all times and asked for instructions but no further deliveries were made and, some time later, the undelivered juice went putrid and had to be thrown away. The court held that delivery had been delayed through the fault of B and the loss might not have occurred but for his fault. Although the property had not passed to B (presumably because there was no appropriation of the goods) he was liable for the loss under s 20(2) as the risk had passed to him.

There are several other points regarding s 20(2) which should be noted. First, it would be natural to assume that the burden of proof is on the party at fault to show that the delay did not cause the loss but this was not the view taken by Sellers J in *Demby*. Rather, he thought that 'all the facts and circumstances have to be looked at in very much the same way as a jury would look at them in order to see whether the loss can properly be attributed to the failure of the buyer to take delivery of the goods at the proper time'.[1] This would indicate that, where the delay 'might' have caused the loss but it can be shown that such loss would have occurred despite the delay and thus can be attributed to some other cause, the party at fault may avoid liability under s 20(2). Second, Sellers J also stated, in *Demby*,[2] that it was the duty of S to act reasonably and avoid any loss if

---

19 Then, under the SGA 1893, a proviso to s 20.
20 [1949] 1 All ER 435.
 1 [1949] 1 All ER 435 at 437.
 2 [1949] 1 All ER 435 at 438.

possible, eg by selling the goods to another buyer and acquiring other goods to fulfil the first contract. This could not be done in *Demby* because, as stated above, all the apples had to be crushed at one time in order to comply with the sample. Third, although s 20(2) will commonly apply to specific goods, it is clear from *Demby* that it can apply to unascertained goods, Sellers J specifying that 'the goods' referred to in s 20(2) 'must be the contractual goods which have been assembled by the seller for the purpose of fulfilling his contract and making delivery'.[3]

Liability as a bailee: s 20(3)

The general rule in the SGA, s 20(1) is also qualified by s 20(3) which provides:

> 'Nothing in this section affects the duties or liabilities of either seller or buyer as a bailee or custodier of the goods of the other party.'

If property in the goods has passed to B but S remains in possession of the goods, he does so as a bailee for B until the time for delivery and this may often be the position in a sale of specific goods. Thus, even though property has passed to B and the goods are at his risk, S must take reasonable care of them.[4] The positions are reversed if both property in the goods and the risk remain in S but B has possession of them, as would happen in a sale or return contract,[5] and here B must take reasonable care of the goods. A bailee is liable for negligence but is not normally liable for purely accidental loss or damage; the burden of proof is on the bailee, however, to show that he exercised reasonable care. He must abide by the terms of the bailment and becomes strictly liable for any loss if he deviates, eg in failing to store and secure the goods properly. Moreover, a bailee may be vicariously liable where he has entrusted the goods to a servant or agent for loss or damage negligently caused to the goods by that servant or agent, even if the servant or agent is acting for his own benefit.[6]

It is more difficult to ascertain the duties of S *after* the time for delivery has passed and particularly where the delay in delivery is due to B's fault under s 20(2). Where B is at fault, S may be an involuntary bailee only with a lesser standard of care than a voluntary bailee but this seems unlikely after the explicit statement in *Demby Hamilton & Co Ltd v Barden*[7] that, in this situation, it is the duty of S to act reasonably and avoid any loss if possible. Moreover, the SGA, s 37 may apply here allowing S to charge a reasonable amount for care and custody of the goods when B has not taken delivery. That being said,

---

3   [1949] 1 All ER 435 at 437.
4   See *Wiehe v Dennis Bros* (1913) 29 TLR 250 (B agreed to buy from S a Shetland pony called 'Tiny'. The pony was left in the custody of S so that the animal could attract money for 'Our Dumb Friends League' at the International Horse Show at Olympia. 'Tiny' was injured before delivery to B and S was unable to explain how the injuries were caused. Held that S was liable in damages as a gratuitous bailee for failing to take reasonable care of the pony. Scrutton J was 'inclined to think' that property in the pony, as specific goods, had passed to B).
5   See Ch 16.
6   See eg *British Road Services Ltd v Arthur Crutchley & Co Ltd* [1968] 1 All ER 811; *Morris v C W Martin & Sons Ltd* [1966] 1 QB 716.
7   [1949] 1 All ER 435, 438 per Sellers J.

only a lowly standard of care was demanded of a negligent seller in an Australian decision on this issue, where B was also at fault for the delay in delivery.[8]

It is unclear what remedies would be available for a breach of duty by S or B when acting as a bailee in this context but it is arguable that s 20(3) simply preserves the liability of a bailee at common law and such a breach should generate a claim in damages only and not a right in B to reject the goods where S damages them, for example. It is also unclear whether the Law Reform (Contributory Negligence) Act 1945 might apply where both S and B are at fault, eg B neglects to take delivery at the proper time and S negligently damages the goods while they are in his possession as a bailee. If the 1945 Act does apply, the loss would be apportioned between S and B.

Risk where goods are on sale or return; risk where B rejects goods for breach of condition

The question of risk is important in both these situations and is considered where sale or return contracts and B's right of rejection are analysed, viz Chapters 16 and 23 respectively.

CARRIAGE OF GOODS TO THE BUYER

It is now necessary to consider which party bears the loss where the goods are delivered to a carrier or other bailee for transmission to B and they are lost or damaged in transit.

The basic rule: risk passes to B when the goods are delivered to a carrier

The SGA, s 32(1) provides:

> 'Where, in pursuance of a contract of sale, the seller is authorised or required to send the goods to the buyer, delivery of the goods to a carrier (whether named by the buyer or not) for the purpose of transmission to the buyer is prima facie deemed to be a delivery of the goods to the buyer.'

The combined effect of s 32(1) and s 18 r 5(2) (the delivery of *ascertained*[9] goods to a carrier or other bailee/custodier[10] amounts to unconditional appropriation of the goods) means that risk *prima facie* passes with property (s 20(1)) on delivery of the goods to the carrier and the goods are thus at B's risk during transit. In this normal situation, the carrier is regarded as B's agent[11] and particularly so

---

8 *Sharp v Batt* (1930) 25 Tas LR 33 (S had picked 100 cases of apples to meet his contract but delivery was delayed, at B's request, for a month. During that month, the apples developed a fungal disease which would not have occurred if S had wrapped the apples. The Supreme Court of Tasmania held that the property had not passed to B but the apples were at B's risk under s 20(2)(then the proviso to s 20) because the delay was B's fault. Clark J held that S was liable only as a gratuitous bailee after the time for delivery had passed and, as such, he would be responsible only for fraud or gross negligence. While S had been negligent, the court held that he had not been grossly negligent).
9 The goods must be ascertained by the delivery: see *Healey v Howlett* [1917] 1 KB 337 (considered in Ch 16).
10 Note that s 32(1) applies only to a *carrier* and thus if S delivers the goods to any other bailee, eg for pre-delivery inspection, s 32(1) will not apply.
11 *Wait v Baker* (1848) 2 Exch 1, 7 per Parke B.

if B chooses the carrier himself.[12] But this is only the *prima facie* rule and if the terms of the contract or appropriation indicate that the carrier is S's agent, risk and property will not normally pass to B until the goods are actually delivered to B or his agent.[13] The inference that the carrier is S's agent will normally arise where S agrees to deliver the goods at a particular *place* and then property and risk will transfer only on actual delivery at that place.[14]

When the rules on passing of property were considered in chapter 16, it was pointed out that a consumer buyer who orders goods from a mail order catalogue may find that, from the moment of the delivery of the goods to the carrier, both the risk and the property in the goods pass to B and it is arguably time that the SGA was amended to the effect that, in such consumer sales, risk and property pass only on delivery at B's home. The court could, of course, infer that this is the intent of S and B and much might then turn upon whether S is 'authorised or required to send the goods' to B under s 32(1). Where S is contractually bound to arrange a contract of carriage (eg an fob contract) he would be 'required' to send the goods to B but s 32(1) also applies where S is 'authorised' to send the goods and there is very little authority on this point. However, in the Australian case of *Wiskin v Terdich Bros Pty Ltd*,[15] it was held that where B's order commenced with the words 'please supply us', the natural inference was that the goods should be delivered to B's place of business.

The basic rule that risk passes to B on delivery to the carrier is subject to the principle in *Beer v Walker*[16] and *Mash & Murrell Ltd v Joseph I Emanuel Ltd*[17] that the goods should be dispatched to the carrier in such a condition that they can withstand the normal transit and be of satisfactory quality on arrival at their destination and for a reasonable time thereafter. However, it was emphasised in *Mash & Murrell* that B will bear the risk if there is an extraordinary deterioration due to abnormal conditions experienced during the transit.

S must arrange a reasonable contract of carriage

Where s 32(1) is applicable, S's obligation is amplified by s 32(2) which provides:

> 'Unless otherwise authorised by the buyer, the seller must make such contract with the carrier on behalf of the buyer as may be reasonable having regard to the nature of the goods and the other circumstances of the case; and if the seller omits to do so, and the goods are lost or damaged in course of transit, the buyer may decline to treat the delivery to the carrier as a delivery to himself or may hold the seller responsible in damages.'

If S fails to make a reasonable contract of carriage, the risk of loss or damage in transit falls on him, irrespective of whether the property has passed to B or

---

12 *Dunlop v Lambert* (1839) 6 Cl & Fin 600, 620 per Lord Cottenham LC.
13 *Wait v Baker* (1848) 2 Exch 1, 7 per Parke B; *Badische Anilin und Soda Fabrik v Basle Chemical Works, Bindschedler* [1898] AC 200, 207 per Lord Herschell; *Harrison v Lia* [1951] VLR 470.
14 See *Dunlop v Lambert* (1839) 6 Cl & Fin 600, 621 per Lord Cottenham LC; *Calcutta and Burmah Steam Navigation Co v De Mattos* (1863) 32 LJQB 322, 328 per Blackburn J; *Badische Anilin Und Soda Fabrik v Basle Chemical Works, Bindschedler* [1898] AC 200, 207, per Lord Herschell; *Galbraith and Grant Ltd v Block* [1922] 2 KB 155, 156 per Lush J.
15 [1928] 34 ALR 242.
16 (1877) 46 LJQB 677.
17 [1961] 1 WLR 862; revsd on other grounds [1962] 1 WLR 16n.

not. In *Thomas Young & Sons Ltd v Hobson and Partners*,[18] S sold electrical engines to B and it was agreed that S would send them to B by rail. The contract of carriage arranged by S provided that the goods were at B's risk when they could have been sent, at the same cost, at the carrier's risk, in which case the railway would have inspected the goods to ensure that they were safely packed. In fact, the engines were not properly secured in the wagons by wooden battens but were packed closely together and were damaged in transit; B consequently refused to accept the goods. The Court of Appeal held that the contract of carriage was unreasonable in the circumstances and B was justified in refusing to accept the goods. S's duty to make a reasonable contract of carriage does not normally imply a duty to insure the goods during transit.

Section 32(3) allows for the situation where S sends the goods to B by sea and provides that S must give sufficient information to B so that B may insure the goods during the sea transit and, if S does not do so, the goods are at his risk during such sea transit.

Goods sent at S's risk

Section 33 provides:

> 'Where the seller of goods agrees to deliver them at his own risk at a place other than that where they are when sold, the buyer must nevertheless (unless otherwise agreed) take any risk of deterioration in the goods necessarily incident to the course of transit.'

Section 33 applies only where S has expressly agreed to take the risk during transit or this arises by implication, eg 'ex ship' contracts. There are two interconnected points to be made regarding s 33. First, s 33 provides that B is at risk only from deterioration which is 'necessarily incident to the course of transit' and he clearly does not take the risk of abnormal loss. The decision in *Bull v Robison*,[19] one of the 19th century cases upon which s 33 was premised, illustrates what is meant by such ordinary risks of transit. B refused to accept iron which was 'perfectly clean and bright' when dispatched by S but, because of delays and cold weather, had suffered some rusting while in transit to Liverpool by canal. The court considered that, as the deterioration was necessary and unavoidable, B must accept the goods. The determination of what risks are necessarily incident to the transit must be a question of fact and, with the advent of modern transport and packing methods, such risks must be less numerous today than in 1893, when the SGA was enacted. It is, however, obvious that s 33 applies *only* to the ordinary risks of transit and it follows that S is not excused from the consequences of his own negligence, eg failing to pack the goods securely. Second, it is unclear whether the principle in *Beer v Walker*[20] and *Mash & Murrell Ltd v Joseph I Emanuel Ltd*,[1] mentioned earlier, applies to s 33. The rule from these decisions, that goods must be dispatched in such a condition that they can withstand a normal journey and be in a satisfactory condition on arrival and for a reasonable time thereafter, was laid down in the context of S's duty to deliver the goods to a carrier whereupon risk would transfer to B, and not in the s 33 situation. Moreover, the *Mash & Murrell* principle, that S carries the risk

18 (1949) 65 TLR 365.
19 (1854) 10 Exch 342.
20 (1877) 46 LJQB 677.
 1 [1961] 1 WLR 862; revsd on other grounds [1962] 1 WLR 16.

of normal deterioration in transit, seems to be the complete opposite of the rule in s 33. However, the better view is that the *Mash & Murrell* rule should apply to s 33 as it has been cogently emphasised[2] that a distinction must be drawn between two situations. First, those cases where all goods of the contract specification would necessarily deteriorate to a certain extent in transit (the s 33 situation) and, second, those situations where the particular goods have an inherent defect meaning that they cannot withstand a normal transit (the *Mash & Murrell* principle).

THE ARBITRARY NATURE OF THE RULES ON RISK AND THE QUESTION OF INSURANCE

It is apparent that the rules on risk may produce arbitrary results, not least because risk is linked to property rather than possession. The iniquitous results produced in consumer sales have already been alluded to in several places: the fact that specific goods sold to B in a retail shop may be at his risk before delivery to him is matched only by the rule that he may carry the risk where goods are lost in transit. B has an insurable interest in goods at his risk[3] and thus the harshness of the rule is mitigated to a certain extent but it will be an infrequent occurrence that a consumer buyer insures in this way. The best protection for such a consumer buyer is the extra-legal one that few sellers would remain in business if they insisted on their strict legal rights regarding risk but this is hardly a desirable position. Alternatively, there is the hope that a court faced with an unjust issue involving consumers and risk would infer an intent of the parties' which is contrary to both the *prima facie* rules in s 18 regarding the passing of property[4] and those concerned with risk and delivery, outlined in this chapter.

A prudent commercial buyer will realise that risk may be separated from both property and possession and will insure goods at his risk as he has an insurable interest in them. This is because in the event of subsequent loss or damage he may still have to pay the price to S. If neither property nor risk has passed to B, B will still have an insurable interest where he has paid the price, or part of it, on the basis that if the goods are lost and S is insolvent, B might not be able to recover the money paid.

Similarly, S should insure where the goods are at his risk, his insurable interest being based upon the inability to recover the purchase price from B if the goods are lost. Even where risk and property have passed to B, S has an insurable interest while he possesses the goods as he may not be paid if, for example, B becomes insolvent. S thus has an interest in respect of his lien for the purchase price. If S has no lien, while in possession his position as a bailee for B entitles him to insure the goods.

However, the rules on subrogation in insurance may merely move the issue of risk from the insured party to the insurance company. For example, property and risk in the goods may have passed to B but, when S remains in possession of the goods he may insure them. If the goods are lost without S's fault the insurance company will pay S and will then be subrogated to S's rights under

---

2   See Sassoon, 'Damage Resulting from Natural Decay under Insurance, Carriage and Sale of Goods Contracts' (1965) 28 MLR 180, 189-191.
3   *Inglis v Stock* (1885) 10 App Cas 263.
4   See eg *Ward (R V) Ltd v Bignall* [1967] 1 QB 534 (considered in Ch 16).

the policy and may claim the price from B as property in the goods will have passed to him. Subrogation will also apply where the roles are reversed and B has possession and risk but S reserves property in the goods until payment by B. If B insures the goods which are then destroyed without fault on B's part and the insurer pays B under the policy, the insurer is subrogated to any rights B may have against S for non-delivery. But subrogation is dependent upon the risk insured and if S were to insure for both his and B's interest and the insurer were to pay S for the loss of the goods while in his possession, the insurer would not be subrogated to S's rights against B as the reason for insuring was to protect to B. If subrogation were allowed here, it would simply lead to circuity of action in that B would counter-claim against the insurer on the basis that it was precisely against such liability that he had insured in the first place.

The rule coupling risk with the passing of property is arguably inapt in many commercial and most consumer sales and it is suggested that the general rule in the USA, which links risk with delivery,[5] has much to commend it.

Non-existent goods, mistake and frustration

As emphasised at the start of the chapter, the rules concerning risk do not excuse the parties from performance but the rules on mistake and frustration may discharge the contract and free both parties from their obligations. The SGA has two very limited rules contained in s 6 and s 7 which cover only the situations where *specific* goods have *perished* before and after contract respectively and, where the sections apply, the contract for the sale of goods is rendered *void*. It is probable that the sections were originally designed to cope with situations where performance was impossible because the goods had perished in the sense of their having ceased to exist or, at least, having being totally destroyed, although the notion of perished goods has been extended in some later decisions to cover serious deterioration of the goods. It suffices to say at this stage that s 6 relates to *initial* impossibility whereas s 7 deals with *subsequent* impossibility and the doctrine of frustration. Section 6 is sometimes regarded as being premised upon the rules of common mistake in that, if S and B both share the mistaken belief that the goods exist, the contract will be void. As the wording of ss 6 and 7 is identical in many respects, many of the decisions are applicable to both sections, eg those on the meaning of 'perished' goods.

Mistake, the existence of the goods and section 6

The SGA, s 6 provides:

> 'Where there is a contract for the sale of specific goods, and the goods without the knowledge of the seller have perished at the time when the contract is made, the contract is void.'

It will be noticed that s 6 stipulates in absolute terms that the contract is *void* where specific goods have already perished at the date of contract and, unusually for the SGA, the provision does not allow for the contrary intent of S and B.

---

5 See the Uniform Commercial Code, s 2-509(3).

Prima facie, s 6 thus postulates an automatic outcome. Before the ambit of s 6 is considered, it is necessary to examine its rationale and the possibilty that options other than a void contract might exist in this situation.

THE RATIONALE OF SECTION 6: MUST THE CONTRACT BE VOID?

S and B may enter into a contract for the sale of goods which, without their knowledge, have ceased to exist at the date of contract (ie 'perished' as in s 6) or another option is that the goods may never have existed. It is clear that, where there are no goods to be sold to B, there cannot be a *sale* of goods and no property in any goods can pass to him. At first glance, therefore, a reasonable and just solution would seem to be a finding that the contract should be void, thereby freeing both parties from their obligations. S would be excused from the obligation to deliver the goods, B would not have to pay the price for them and any money already paid by B could be recovered. It could be argued, therefore, that s 6 is premised upon impossibility of performance which must necessarily render the contract a nullity. If the matter is viewed as one of common mistake, this is also the most likely outcome as, where the goods have ceased to exist, the case will be one of *res extincta* and S and B will have shared a mistaken belief concerning the most fundamental fact of the obligation.[6] Moreover, irrespective of any abstract notions of mistake, a void contract might correctly result from an examination of the formation and construction of the contract. The existence of the subject matter could thus be construed as an implied condition precedent to the operation of the contract and a failure of the condition would render the contract void. No matter whether the issue is viewed as a question of the construction of the contract, impossibility of performance, or by virtue of an independent doctrine of mistake, a ruling that the contract is void may often be just where the goods do not exist at the date the contract is entered into.[7]

While it may seem obvious to free the parties from the contract, it could equally be asserted that the solution adopted by s 6 is somewhat perverse: having regard to the fact that the contract relates to *specific* goods and there is an implied condition in the SGA, s 12 that S must have *title* to the goods, it might be argued that the general rule should be that S should also impliedly warrant that the goods exist. Overall, however, this not the path which English law has followed.

In opting for the consequence in s 6 that the contract should be void, Chalmers,[8] the draftsman of the SGA 1893, based s 6 on the notorious, but often misinterpreted decision, in *Couturier v Hastie*.[9] In *Couturier*, a cargo of corn had been shipped at Salonica in February for delivery 'to a safe port in the United Kingdom, payment at two months from this date upon handing over shipping documents'. In May, the plaintiff (S) purported to sell the cargo to B through the defendant, a *del credere* agent, who was thus liable as a buyer for the price. Unknown to the parties, the cargo had already been sold by the captain at Tunis before the date of the contract as it had started to deteriorate after storm damage.

---

6 See *Bell v Lever Bros* [1932] AC 161; Lawson, *'Error in Substantia'* (1936) 52 LQR 79; Cheshire,'Mistake as Affecting Contractual Consent' (1944) 60 LQR 175.
7 See *Barrow, Lane and Ballard Ltd v Phillip Phillips & Co Ltd* [1929] 1 KB 574, 582 where Wright J manages to rationalise s 6 on the basis of impossibility of performance, total failure of consideration and mistake.
8 See Chalmers, *Sale of Goods Act 1893* (2nd edn, 1894), p 17.
9 (1856) 5 HL Cas 673, affirming 9 Exch 102.

When he discovered this fact, B repudiated the contract and, as B later went bankrupt, S sued the agent for the price. The central issue was thus whether B would have been liable or, alternatively, whether his repudiation had been justified. The Court of Exchequer[10] held that the correct interpretation of the contract was that B had bought a chance or an adventure and thus the agent remained liable for the price. However, the Court of Exchequer Chamber[11] and the House of Lords[12] held that S must fail in his claim for the price. All the arguments and judgments in *Couturier* focus upon the construction of the contract and throughout there is no mention of either mistake or that the contract should be void: the differences of opinion in the case thus relate to the correct *interpretation* of the contract. S's contention was that B had bought a chance that the cargo would be in existence or such rights as S had under the shipping documents and thus he should be liable for the price even if S did not make delivery. B, on the other hand, claimed that he had agreed to buy a specific parcel of corn and it was this argument which prevailed ultimately. The decision in *Couturier* was thus not that the contract was void but that, as the goods had not been delivered, S could not sustain an action for the price.[13]

It is now widely accepted that the decision in *Couturier* was based upon the intent of the parties and the construction of the contract[14] rather than being premised upon a mechanical rule which prescribes that a contract is void where it lacks subject-matter.[15] Moreover, the decision certainly does not rest upon metaphysical notions of mistake.[16] From the cases cited in the early editions of his book, it seems that Chalmers also regarded the matter as one of the construction of the contract. The common law which he sought to embody in the SGA was thus that the contract should be void where one party promised to do something which without his fault or knowledge was impossible, but that the undertaking would *not* be void if that party promised that performance was possible.[17] It is apparent that, on the true construction of the contract and an assessment of the parties' intentions, there are three clear possibilities in the *Couturier* situation, viz:

10   (1852) 8 Exch 40.
11   (1853) 9 Exch 102.
12   (1856) 5 HL Cas 673.
13   See (1856) 5 HL Cas 673, 681 per Lord Cranworth LC: 'The whole question turns upon the construction of the contract ... The contract plainly imports that there was something which was to be sold at the time of the contract, and something to be purchased. No such thing existing, I think the Court of Exchequer Chamber has come to the only reasonable conclusion on it'.
14   See Atiyah, 'Couturier v Hastie and the Sale of Non-Existent Goods' (1957) 73 LQR 340.
15   See Cheshire, Fifoot and Furmston's *Law of Contract* (13th edn, 1996), p 238: 'The crucial fact was the absence of the contemplated subject-matter, which necessarily emptied the contract of all content'.
16   See Slade, 'The Myth of Mistake in the English Law of Contract' (1954) 70 LQR 385; Shatwell, 'The Supposed Doctrine of Mistake in Contract: A Comedy of Errors' [1955] 33 Can Bar Rev 164.
17   See *Cox v Prentice* (1815) 3 M & S 344 (sale of a silver bar which was incorrectly weighed and valued by a third party assayer. Held that B could 'rescind' the contract and recover the price paid. Lord Ellenborough CJ emphasised that this ruling did not clash with *caveat emptor* as neither party exercised his own judgement, rather this case was one of 'mutual innocence and equal error' (p 348)); *Clifford (Lord) v Watts* (1870) LR 5 CP 577 (a tenant under a mining lease promised to dig at least 1,000 tons of clay each year and to pay a royalty of 2s 6d per ton but there was insufficient clay in the land to meet this figure. Held the tenant was not liable for the deficiency as he had not warranted that 1,000 tons could be dug and so the intent of the parties was that the covenant should not take effect unless there was a sufficient amount of clay in the land. Montague Smith J stressed that 'the

(i)   There may be an implied condition precedent in the contract that the goods exist and, if they do not, the condition is not fulfilled meaning that both parties are freed from obligation.

(ii) S may warrant that the goods exist in which case he would be liable to B for non-delivery, although B would not be liable for the price. This conclusion is surely as obvious and pertinent, in many situations, as possibility (i).

(iii) By the terms of the contract B may have taken the chance that the goods do not exist and he would then be making an *absolute* promise to pay the price, although S would be freed from the obligation to deliver.

The decision in *Couturier* was simply that possibility (iii) was inapplicable on the facts. However, the emphasis in *Couturier* upon the intent of the parties and the construction of the contract arguably indicates that the judges would have sanctioned possibility (ii) in an appropriate situation. Such a construction was certainly placed on the facts which arose in the Australian decision in *McRae v Commonwealth Disposals Commission*.[18] There S had advertised for sale an oil-tanker which was described as 'lying on Jourmaund Reef, which is approximately 100 miles north of Samarai' and had subsequently accepted B's offer to buy it. It was later discovered that no such vessel or reef existed and B had gone to considerable expense in fitting-out a salvage expedition to search for the vessel. B's claim for non-delivery was rejected by the trial judge on the basis that, following *Couturier*, the contract was void, but the decision on that point was reversed by the High Court which stressed that the only proper construction of the contract was that it included a promise by S that there was a tanker in the position specified. B accordingly obtained damages. It seems indisputable that, in cases of non-existent goods, S may be liable on the basis that he has expressly or impliedly promised that the goods do exist and the paramount consideration in determining whether this is the correct outcome is to examine the true construction of the contract.[19]

It must therefore be decided how the *McRae* approach fits, if at all, with the uncompromising rule in s 6 that the contract is void. As the goods in *McRae's* case *never existed* they could not be said to have 'perished' within s 6, as 'perish' naturally assumes that goods have existed and then deteriorated substantially. Following this view, the decision in *McRae* does not clash with s 6 and S's liability for non-existent goods becomes a realistic possibility at common law. More importantly, in cases within s 6, where goods have existed and then perished, it must be decided whether the section embodies an absolute rule of law in declaring the contract void or whether its provisions can be overridden by a contrary intent so that S may be liable where he has expressly or impliedly warranted the existence of the goods or, alternatively, that B may be absolutely liable for the price. Two

covenantor did not undertake to perform an impossibility, but merely to dig and remove such clay as should be found in the land' (p 588)); cf *Marquis of Bute v Thompson* (1844) 13 M & W 487 (tenant of a coal mine agreed in absolute terms to raise a minimum quantity of coal or pay a minimum rent. Held that the tenant was liable to pay the rent as the lessee was bound to perform his covenant whether there was coal to be found or not. Here the risk had been placed on the lessee).

18 (1950) 84 CLR 377.
19 See *Associated Japanese Bank (International) Ltd v Crédit du Nord SA* [1989] 1 WLR 255 where, on facts analogous to non-existent goods, Steyn J's decision was based on the contract's construction with only an *obiter* evaluation of mistake; see Brown, 'Contractual Conditions and Common Mistake' [1989] 40 NILQ 268.

leading authorities[20] advocate the view that contrary intent should prevail and support their argument by giving a liberal interpretation to the SGA, s 55(1).[1] It is suggested that this approach is correct in principle but difficult to sustain in practice in view of the dogmatic wording of s 6.[2] If the contract is necessarily void under s 6, there is a possibility that S might be liable on a collateral contract[3] that the goods do exist or be liable for negligent misrepresentation.[4]

The possibility of S's negligent misrepresentation leads to one possible route for the exclusion of s 6 in that the section applies only where the goods have perished 'without the knowledge of the seller'. The question of S's knowledge and the related issue of fault have received very little attention and it is unclear whether he may seek the protection of s 6 where he is negligent and *ought* to have known that the goods had perished at the time of contract (see below). Section 6 must surely be posited on S's ignorance of the fact that the goods have perished and, at the time of *Couturier* in the mid-19th century, it would be reasonable on such facts to assume that S would not and could not know of the cargo's prior sale. More often than not, this may be an unreasonable assumption in modern conditions with effective, fast communications and, where S's negligence can be established, it must be arguable that s 6 is inapplicable and S is liable.

In conclusion, it must be stressed that there is still no authority that the operation of s 6 can be varied by contrary intent of the parties and the present position is that where the section does apply the contract will be void but, where the common law is applicable, the court's decision will be based on an assessment of the parties' intent, meaning that alternatives other than a void contract are possible.

THE AMBIT OF SECTION 6

Specific goods

Section 6 applies only to specific goods which, it will be recalled, are defined in s 61(1) as 'goods identified and agreed on at the time a contract of sale is made

---

20 See *Benjamin's Sale of Goods* (5th edn, 1997), paras 1-122; 1-131; Atiyah, *The Sale of Goods* (10th edn, 2001), p 96.

1 Section 55(1) provides: 'Where a right, duty or liability would arise under a contract of sale of goods by implication of law, it may (subject to the Unfair Contract Terms Act 1977) be negatived or varied by express agreement, or by the course of dealing between the parties, or by such usage as binds both parties to the contract'. But as Treitel (*The Law of Contract*, (10th edn, 1999), p 272) stresses, the effect of s 6 is that *no* 'right, duty or liability' would arise and there is *no* 'contract of sale of goods'.

2 See Treitel, *The Law of Contract* (10th edn, 1999), p 272.

3 Consideration for S's promise under the collateral contract would have to be B's entry into the main contract. The fact that the main contract is void may be of no significance, see *Strongman (1945) Ltd v Sincock* [1955] 2 QB 525 (main contract was illegal). However, Treitel stresses (*The Law of Contract* (10th ed, 1999), p 273) that 'if nothing had been done under the main contract it would be hard to find any consideration for the seller's promise under the collateral contract. It is just possible that such consideration could be found in the act of purporting to enter into the main contract, especially if it involved the execution of a document. There is even more difficulty in seeing how the buyer's promise to pay can be expressed as a collateral contract, for it seems to be merely a reiteration of his principal obligation under the main contract'.

4 Seemingly this would have to be at common law under *Hedley Byrne*, as the Misrepresentation Act 1967, s 2(1), applies only 'where a person has entered into a contract' and so it may be inapplicable where the contract is void.

and includes an undivided share, specified as a fraction or percentage, of goods identified and agreed on as aforesaid'. The purpose of s 6 is to free S and B from their obligations where the contract is incapable of performance because the goods have perished at the time the contract is made and cannot be replaced and this is obviously the position only with specific goods, as they are unique.

It should be stressed that the definition of specific goods in s 61(1) now also encompasses an undivided share, expressed as a fraction or percentage, of specific goods. This means, for example, that B has a contract for the sale of specific goods when he agrees to buy 20% of the cargo of barley aboard a named vessel and, should the cargo have 'perished' within s 6 at the time of contract, the contract for the sale of the undivided share will be void.

In contrast with specific goods, where the contract is one for the sale of *wholly* unascertained, generic goods, eg 500 tons of wheat, S may have some source of supply in mind which has, unknown to him, perished at the time of contract, but this is immaterial as S simply has an obligation to sell 500 tons of wheat and he must therefore acquire the wheat from some other source. It is plain that there can be no question that goods have perished where the contract is for the sale of wholly unascertained, generic goods, as such goods have no singularity – *genus numquam perit*. The position is no different in contracts for the sale of unascertained, future goods where, for example, S has a third party in mind from whom he intends to buy 500 tons of wheat but the goods have perished at the time of contract.

However, it must be asked whether 'specific goods' can be given an extended meaning for the purposes of s 6 (and s 7) as it may be just to declare the contract void in cases of quasi-specific goods, ie those which have more in common with specific goods but, strictly, fall within the classification of unascertained goods (eg eight bottles of wine from a particular case containing nine bottles in S's cellar, all the bottles having perished at the time of contract). The modern decisions make it clear, however, that no matter what the position was before the SGA 1893, after 1893 a broad meaning cannot be given to 'specific goods' and such goods must, at the date of contract, be in existence and physically identified as the specific goods which form the subject matter of that contract[5] rather than being specifically *described* in the contract. In *Sainsbury (H R & S) Ltd v Street*,[6] the contract was for the sale of 275 tons of barley to be grown on S's farm but only 140 tons were produced because of crop failure. The case was thus one of subsequent impossibility/frustration. Most importantly, MacKenna J emphasised that ss 6 and 7 applied only to 'goods existing'[7] and so a crop yet to be grown could not be specific goods.

However, where the common law applies, S and B could be released from their obligations in appropriate cases by the rules of common mistake[8] or the notion that the existence of the goods is an implied condition precedent to the operation of the contract. This is therefore a possible outcome in cases where (i) S and B agree that unascertained, existing goods are to be drawn from a

---

5 See Ch 16.
6 [1972] 1 WLR 834.
7 [1972] 1 WLR 834 at 837.
8 Section 62(2) expressly provides that the rules of common law, except in so far as they are inconsistent with the Act, shall continue to apply to contracts for the sale of goods, and it refers, *inter alia*, to the common law on the effect of mistake on contracts.

designated bulk[9] or from a designated source,[10] where the bulk has perished or the source has already failed at the time of entering into the contract; and (ii) S and B agree that future, specific goods must be acquired by S from a designated source (eg a specific painting by Picasso to be bought by S from a third party for resale to B) which has perished at the time of contract. It is important to stress that, where the common law applies to the case, the intent of the parties will be paramount and there is scope for more flexibility in the decision than the apparently automatic outcome under s 6 that the contract is void. For example, if the goods have only *partially* perished at the time of contract, is S under an obligation to deliver or offer the remainder of the goods to B? It is plain that if the contract is *void* there can be no such obligation. This problem arose in *Sainsbury (H R & S) Ltd v Street*,[11] above, where only part of the crop materialised and the matter for decision was whether S should have offered that part to B. It was held that, at common law, S was excused from the obligation to deliver that portion of the crop which failed but that he should nevertheless have offered B the barley which was produced (although B need not accept the lesser amount, see s 30(1)) instead of selling it to a third party at a higher price.

When have the goods perished?

There is no definition of 'perish' in the SGA but it is tempting to conclude that, originally, s 6 was aimed only at the situation where goods had been totally destroyed (eg specific bags of corn are consumed by fire) or lawfully sold to a third party (as in *Couturier*) at the time of contract, without S's knowledge or fault, so that the goods could not be delivered to B. It is clear that goods which have physically ceased to exist must have perished but, in other cases, opinions will differ as to whether damage to the goods or their deterioration means that they have perished. The problem is analogous to deciding whether a contract has been frustrated and, of course, the same difficulty regarding perished goods arises under s 7. Accordingly, cases on both s 6 and s 7 can be considered here.

In *Horn v Minister of Food*,[12] S agreed to sell to B a specific lot of 33 tons of potatoes stored in a clamp but, despite all reasonable care by S, the potatoes rotted and were 'useless and could not be delivered'. Morris J considered that s 7 did not apply to relieve B of his liability to pay the price because the potatoes still answered to the description of potatoes 'however grave was the deterioration of their condition'.[13] However, these restrictive remarks were *obiter* as it was held that the risk had passed to B, thereby excluding the operation of s 7. It is virtually certain that the narrow view taken of perished goods in *Horn's* case

---

9   This could apply to situations of co-ownership under the new provisions in the SGA (see ss 20A and 20B). It is unclear what the position will be where *part* of the bulk has perished at the time of contract and there are several co-owners of the bulk. It appears that the buyers' shares will be reduced proportionately and, seemingly, where S is not at fault, he should be excused regarding the short delivery (see s 20A(3) and (4)).

10   In several editions of his book, Chalmers asserted that, although there was no authority at common law, where S agreed to sell to B 'five dozen of the '74 champagne now in my cellar, not knowing that all but three dozen had been destroyed by fire ... probably the contract would be void' (*The Sale of Goods Act 1893*, (6th edn, 1905), p 21). This example was approved by Wright J in *Barrow, Lane and Ballard Ltd v Phillip Phillips & Co Ltd* [1929] 1 KB 574, 583.

11   [1972] 1 WLR 834.

12   [1948] 2 All ER 1036.

13   [1948] 2 All ER 1036 at 1039.

does not represent the law, and several other decisions consider that goods may perish in the sense that they have lost their commercial identity. The decision in *Asfar & Co v Blundell*[14] is often referred to in this context but it should be stressed that it does not concern either s 6 or s 7. A ship carrying a cargo of dates sank in the Thames after being struck by another vessel and, by the time the ship was raised, the dates were 'a mass of pulpy matter impregnated with sewage and in a state of fermentation'.[15] Although the dates were condemned as unfit for human consumption, much of the cargo was resold, transhipped and exported to be used in the distillation of spirit. The matter for decision was whether there had been a total loss of the dates for insurance purposes. The Court of Appeal held that there had been such a total loss and that, while the contrary argument might 'commend itself to a body of chemists'[16] it would not do so to businessmen. The test to be applied was thus whether the nature of the thing was altered so as 'to become an unmerchantable thing, which no buyer would buy and no honest seller would sell'.[17]

The proposition that goods may perish in a commercial sense without their being totally destroyed was accepted recently in New Zealand in the decision in *Oldfield Asphalts Ltd v Grovedale Coolstores (1994) Ltd*.[18] There B agreed to buy from S a large 'blast freezer' which was, in fact, a portable building. Before either property in the goods passed to B or he had taken delivery, the freezer was badly damaged by fire, without the fault of either party, and only its skeletal form remained intact. B contended that S should deliver the building in its original condition but S claimed that the goods had perished and that the contract was consequently void under the New Zealand Sale of Goods Act 1908, s 9, which is identical to the Sale of Goods Act 1979, s 7. Gallen J considered that the building was so changed by the fire that it could no longer be used for the purpose contemplated by the contract and, although it could be restored at immense cost, it would then no longer be possible to describe it as the same building. Accordingly, it was held that the fundamental change to the nature of the building meant that it had perished and it was unacceptable to assert that the term 'perished' was restricted to goods that were perishable in the sense that foodstuffs are – neither the SGA nor its equivalent in New Zealand refer to 'specific perishable goods'.

Both the *Asfar* and *Oldfield* decisions suggest that the destruction of the merchantable character of the goods may well indicate that they have perished and so, as was stressed in *Oldfield*,[19] the description applied to the goods and the purpose to which S and B contemplate that the goods will be put will be crucial factors in arriving at a decision. The notion that goods which have lost their merchantable character may be regarded as having perished was carried to its logical conclusion in the New Zealand decision in *Rendell v Turnbull & Co*,[20] a decision which was influential in *Oldfield*. In *Rendell*, S agreed to sell 'table potatoes' to B but, at the time of the contract, they were suffering from second growth and were unfit for human consumption. Cooper J held that their

14 [1896] 1 QB 123.
15 [1896] 1 QB 123 at 127, per Lord Esher MR.
16 [1896] 1 QB 123 at 127, per Lord Esher MR.
17 [1896] 1 QB 123 at 128, per Lord Esher MR.
18 [1998] 3 NZLR 479; see Brown, 'Perished Goods and the Sale of Goods Act 1979, s 6' [2000] LMCLQ 12.
19 [1998] 3 NZLR 479, 486 per Gallen J.
20 (1908) 27 NZLR 1067.

character as table potatoes had thus been destroyed and the contract was void under the statutory equivalent of the SGA, s 6.[1]

In *Rendell*, S was suing for the price but the decision that the contract was void meant that B's counter-claim for damages on the ground that the potatoes were unmerchantable must also fail. Of course, the underlying assumption and justification for such a decision is that the 'perishing' of the goods is outside S's control and an equitable result is thus to free both parties, as in *Couturier v Hastie*. But if an extended definition of perished goods is accepted, as in *Oldfield*, it is clear that B might take delivery of seriously defective goods. Now, S's liability under the SGA implied conditions in ss 13 and 14 relating to description, satisfactory quality and fitness for purpose is strict and his absence of knowledge that the goods were defective at the date of contract is immaterial. There would thus seem to be a danger lurking in the notion that unsatisfactory goods may be regarded as having perished in that a seller who is unaware of defects which existed before contract might attempt to escape liability under the SGA, s 14 on the basis that the contract is declared void under s 6. If this argument were accepted, S's only liability would be to return the purchase price to B. Furthermore, S's position would, ironically, be improved where the goods were so grossly defective as to have changed their character or identity and so, indisputably, be goods which have 'perished'. The placing of S in such an advantageous position should be avoided and this may be achieved by accentuating and clarifying a number of issues. First, although s 6 applies where goods have perished 'without the knowledge of the seller,' it should be put beyond doubt that s 6 can be pleaded by S only when he is not in breach of contract and is totally unaware that the goods have perished.[2] Second, drawing an analogy with *McRae v Commonwealth Disposals Commission*,[3] goods which have perished must necessarily have been sound originally and deteriorated subsequently and thus goods which have simply been defective from the outset could not have perished within s 6. Third, it is arguable that s 6 should not be available to S where he has 'supplied' the goods under s 14 in the sense of actually delivering them to B or, possibly, where he has parted with possession of them. Apart from these possibilities, the only other option would be to adopt the restrictive view of perished goods which was taken in *Horn's* case, thus meaning that S could rarely plead that the goods had perished.

There are certain other situations were the possibility that the goods might have perished is problematic. In *Barrow, Lane and Ballard Ltd v Phillip Phillips & Co Ltd*,[4] S agreed to sell to B 700 bags of Chinese ground nuts thought to be lying at a wharf. 150 bags were delivered to B but, when B demanded further deliveries, it was discovered that 109 of the bags had been stolen at the date of

---

1 The Sale of Goods Act 1895 (NZ), s 8, which was identical to the SGA, s 6.
2 It is fairly clear that s 6 cannot be pleaded by S where he *knows* that the goods have perished (see *Bell v Lever Bros Ltd* [1932] AC 161, 217 per Lord Atkin) but whether s 6 may be utilised by S when he is negligent and *ought to know* that the goods have perished is most unclear. It is difficult to assert that s 6 is unavailable to S where the goods have perished as a consequence of his own actions but this is arguably the correct position (see the *obiter dicta* in *Tommey v Finextra Ltd* (1962) 106 Sol Jo 1012 per Havers J; *Goodey v Garriock* [1972] 2 Lloyd's Rep 369, 372 per Cusak J). Comparisons with s 7 are unhelpful as that section expressly refers to an absence of fault on the part of S and B.
3 (1950) 84 CLR 377 (see above).
4 [1929] 1 KB 574.

contract and that, during the two months after contract, all but the 150 bags delivered to B had also disappeared. Wright J held that the contract was for an indivisible parcel of goods and 'the position appears to me to be in no way different from what it would have been if the whole 700 bags had ceased to exist'.[5] Accordingly, it was held that the contract was void under s 6. Here the decision that theft of the 109 bags had caused the goods to perish was surely correct as the stolen bags could not 'be followed or discovered anywhere'.[6] But in other cases where stolen goods might be recovered reasonably quickly, eg a car, it would be much more artificial to assert that the goods had perished. The courts would undoubtedly apply a pragmatic rule that, when the goods are unavailable to S at the time for delivery and their prompt recovery is a remote possibility, the goods may be said to have perished. It is also probable that goods which have been requisitioned, eg by the Government in time of war,[7] would be held to have perished and, following *Couturier*, this would seem to be the position where there has been a lawful sale of the goods to a third party.

Part of the goods have perished

It is evident from the decision in *Barrow, Lane and Ballard Ltd v Phillip Phillips & Co Ltd*,[8] above, that where the contract is for the sale of a specific parcel of goods and the contract is indivisible, the fact that part of the goods have perished may be sufficient to avoid the contract under s 6. There are several difficulties here.

First, it was relatively easy in *Barrow* to conclude that 'a contract for a parcel of 700 bags is something different from a contract for 591 bags, and ... to compel the buyer ... to take 591 bags would be to compel him to take something which he had not contracted to take'.[9] Presumably this reasoning could have applied if one bag had been stolen from 700 but, in other cases of specific goods where *quantity* does not predominate and arithmetical certainty is an impossibility, it will not be a simple task to decide whether s 6 should apply where the goods have perished only partially. The court would be driven back to the general question of whether the goods have sufficiently and materially changed in character to qualify as perished goods and this may be a difficult issue where, for example, only a particular yet fundamental component in a machine has perished.

Second, there is a problem regarding the rights of S and B in relation to the portion of the goods which have *not* perished. In *Barrow*, B had paid at the contract rate for the 150 bags of nuts which had been delivered, even though the contract was for an indivisible parcel, and thus the decision meant that he was not liable for the balance of the price. But a decision that the contract is *void* under s 6 must mean that S is not bound to deliver the remainder of the goods to B (eg in *Barrow*, S could have refused to deliver the 150 bags to B if the facts had come to light before delivery) and, equally, it is not open to B to waive his right to a full delivery and insist on taking delivery of the remainder on payment of the

---

5 [1929] 1 KB 574 at 583.
6 [1929] 1 KB 574 at 583, per Wright J.
7 See *Re Shipton, Anderson & Co and Harrison Bros & Co* [1915] 3 KB 676 (Government requisition of a specific parcel of wheat frustrated the contract).
8 [1929] 1 KB 574.
9 [1929] 1 KB 574 at 583, per Wright J.

contract price.[10] It will be recalled that, in *Sainsbury (H R & S) Ltd v Street*,[11] above, there was held to be an implied term that S should offer to B the amount of barley which was produced although S was not liable for the amount of the crop which failed. Although this is a just result, s 6 was not applicable to the facts in *Sainsbury*, and it would seem to be impossible to reach that conclusion where the section does apply.[12]

Third, where B takes possession of the remainder of the goods but refuses to pay any part of the price, a decision that the contract is void would mean that S could maintain only a restitutionary claim on a *quantum meruit*. It would also follow in this situation that B could maintain no action for breach of the implied conditions in s 14 relating to the quality and fitness for purpose of the goods.

Frustration

A contract for the sale of goods can be frustrated[13] at common law or under the SGA, s 7. The common law principles of frustration are preserved by the SGA, s 62(2) and will be considered later. The SGA, s 7 provides:

> 'Where there is an agreement to sell specific goods and subsequently the goods, without any fault on the part of the seller or buyer, perish before the risk passes to the buyer, the agreement is avoided.'

The effect of s 7 is to 'avoid' the contract and, where it applies, both parties will be discharged from their obligations, ie S is not liable for non-delivery and B is not liable for the price. As with s 6, s 7 has a very restricted ambit of operation.

THE AMBIT OF SECTION 7

'An agreement to sell specific goods'

Section 7 applies only to an *agreement* to sell specific goods and not where there is a completed sale. It thus contemplates the situation where specific goods perish after the agreement has been entered into but before property and risk pass to B. Of course, in the absence of contrary intent, the presumption in s 18, r 1 is that property and risk in specific goods pass to B immediately on contract and thus

---

10 In the USA, Williston had argued (*Sales*, 3rd edn, § 162) that such waiver was possible on the basis that impossibility can excuse S no further than the impossibility which in fact exists. His views were adopted in the American Uniform Sales Act 1906, s 7(2) and the UCC s 2-163, which provide that B may avoid the sale or take the remainder of the goods and pay for them.
11 [1972] 1 WLR 834.
12 What is the position where S owns a specific bulk of wheat in a warehouse and enters into two contracts to sell 50% to each of B and B2 but 70% of the wheat has perished at the date of contract? This is now a contract for the sale of *specific* goods as defined in s 61(1). It seems that B and B2 would simply share what is left as this is an inherent risk of contracting in this way (see *Sale of Goods Forming Part of a Bulk*, (Law Com No 215; Scot Law Com No 145 (1993), para 5.2) or might the contracts be void under s 6 meaning that there can be no delivery to either buyer?
13 See generally Treitel, *Frustration and Force Majeure* (1994).

s 7 cannot apply where r 1 does. It follows that s 7 has a very narrow scope and it covers only those situations (i) where S has reserved the 'right of disposal' of specific goods under s 19, eg a condition that no property passes in specific goods until payment by B; (ii) where s 18, rr 2 and 3 apply as those rules govern conditional sales of specific goods; and (iii) in *some* situations within the extended definition of 'specific goods' to be considered next. It is tolerably clear that s 7 may apply even though the goods have been delivered to B, eg in situation (i), above, B might have physical possession of the goods but not the property and risk.

It will be remembered that the newly-extended definition of 'specific goods' in the SGA, s 61(1) includes 'an undivided share, specified as a fraction or percentage, of goods identified and agreed on as aforesaid' (eg S agrees to sell to B half (or 50%) of the oil in an identified tank; S agrees to sell to B a half share in a racehorse). At common law, B thus becomes an owner in common of the identified bulk. It seems indisputable that, once B has *acquired* property in the *undivided share*, he has acquired property in the *specific goods* within the definition in s 61(1) and so this is no longer an 'agreement to sell specific goods' within s 7. Accordingly, if the bulk perishes (in which B had an undivided share) after property in that undivided share has passed to B but before any separation of B's share from the bulk, the contract will not be avoided under s 7. In the examples above, B will frequently wish to separate and take delivery of his 50% of the oil but, of course, he will never want to dissect the racehorse and take delivery of his half share in it. In both situations, however, once B has acquired property in his undivided share, the contract can surely no longer be classified as an agreement to sell specific goods. Alternatively, once B has acquired property in the undivided share, it seems likely that risk will transfer to him at the same time and, if this has occurred before the identified bulk has perished, s 7 will not apply. However, s 7 can apply to an agreement for the sale of such an undivided share in an identified bulk where the bulk perishes before property and risk in that share pass to B, eg a contract for the sale of a half share in a racehorse with property and risk in the share to pass to B on payment but, before payment, the horse dies without the fault of either S or B.

It is clear that a contract for the sale of *wholly* unascertained, generic goods, cannot be frustrated by the fact that the *source of supply* that S has in mind has perished because here S must acquire the goods from elsewhere. Furthermore, 'specific goods' has the same restricted meaning under s 7 as that considered earlier when s 6 was examined. However, it seems that Chalmers, the draftsman of the SGA 1893, based s 7 on *Howell v Coupland*,[14] which allowed an extended meaning to 'specific goods'. In *Howell*, a contract to sell 200 tons of potatoes from a crop to be grown on a particular piece of land belonging to S was held to be one for specific goods to the extent that, when the crop was blighted by disease and only 80 tons could be delivered to B, S was relieved of liability regarding his failure to deliver the 120 tons on grounds of subsequent impossibility of performance. *Howell* had followed the earlier decision in *Taylor v Caldwell*,[15] and was thus part of the fledgling doctrine of frustration. Chalmers[16] thought that s 7 should apply to this situation where goods were *specifically described*

---

14 (1874) LR 9 QB 462; affd 1 QBD 258.
15 (1863) 3 B & S 826.
16 See Chalmers, *Sale of Goods* (18th edn, 1981), p 100.

even if they were not in existence and physically identified at the date of contract, but it is now clear from the decision in *Sainsbury (H R & S) Ltd v Street*[17] that this approach cannot be sustained and 'specific goods' within s 7 cannot be given any wider meaning than the definition of such goods in s 61(1).

In cases of subsequent impossibility and frustration, the issue is not one of the passing of property in goods and and thus there is no objection, in principle, to allowing frustration where there is a contract to sell existing or future, unascertained goods from a particular source which has failed, as in *Howell*. Indeed, there will proably be frustration of the contract at common law in this situation where there is an exclusive source of goods (see later). Thus, while modern orthodoxy denies that an agreement for the sale of 'all the apples to be grown in my orchard next season' can relate to specific goods for the purposes of the rules on the passing of property, there would seem to be no good reason to deny that such a contract might be frustrated if the crop fails.

The goods must have perished

This requirement was analysed earlier when s 6 was considered and it carries the same meaning here. In particular, it may be that English law will adopt the view in *Oldfield's*[18] case, considered earlier, that goods may perish when they have deteriorated so fundamentally that their nature has changed.

Again there are difficulties regarding the situation where goods have partially perished and, following *Barrow, Lane and Ballard Ltd v Phillip Phillips & Co Ltd*,[19] it seems that in cases of partial loss of specific goods before the risk passes to B, the contract is rendered void within s 7. Assuming the price is payable on delivery, B is discharged from the obligation to pay the price and S from the duty to deliver which also means that B has no right to claim the remaining goods from S.[20] This consequence should be compared with the decision in *Sainsbury (H R & S) Ltd v Street*,[1] (considered earlier) the facts of which were outside s 7 as the goods were not specific.[2]

The risk must not have passed to B

As stated above, the paradigm for the operation of s 7 is an agreement to sell specific goods where property and risk are still in S at the time when the goods perish. Alternatively, it is equally clear that s 7 cannot operate when the

---

17 [1972] 1 WLR 834 (considered earlier under s 6). Mackenna J (p 837) thought that *Howell* was probably best considered today as based upon a contingent sale under the SGA, s 5(2) (where both parties are freed when the contingency does not occur) or was preserved by the SGA, s 62(2) (which preserves the rules of common law).
18 [1998] 3 NZLR 479.
19 [1929] 1 KB 574 (see above).
20 In contrast, the USA's Uniform Commercial Code, s 2-613, distinguishes total loss from partial loss: there is automatic avoidance (as in s 7) in the former case but in the latter situation, B has a choice to treat the contract as avoided or accept the goods with an allowance in respect of the partial loss.
1 [1972] 1 WLR 834.
2 As mentioned above, when s 6 was considered, the extended definition of specific goods in s 61(1) includes the purchase of fractions of a specific bulk, eg B and B2 each agree to buy 50% of a specific cargo. Does the fact that 60% of the cargo has perished, before risk or property pass to the buyers, mean that the contracts are avoided under s 7 and no delivery can take place, or do B and B2 have equal shares in the remainder?

agreement has become a sale and property and risk have passed to B at the date the goods perish. This leaves two further permutations. First, the property is in S but risk has passed to B – again s 7 is inapplicable, as emphasised in *Horn v Minister of Food*,[3] considered earlier. There property in the specific potatoes was to pass to B on delivery but it was held that, as S had complied with the storage obligations imposed by the contract, the risk of deterioration was on B. Morris J stipulated that, even if the goods had perished, s 7 would not have applied to the facts. The final possibility is that risk remains with S but the property has passed to B but, again, s 7 would seem to be inapplicable as this would no longer be an agreement to sell. It should thus be stressed again that s 7 has an exceptionally restricted field of operation.

Neither S nor B must be at fault

Section 7 provides that the goods must have perished 'without any fault on the part of the seller or buyer' and 'fault' is defined in s 61(1) as 'wrongful act or default'. The general rule of frustration is that it cannot be pleaded by a party at fault as he is unable to rely on self-induced frustration.[4] If, for example, risk and property in a specific parcel of chemicals are in S prior to delivery of the goods to B and payment by him, and the chemicals explode because of a breach by S of the implied condition as to satisfactory quality in s 14, S could not plead frustration under s 7 and would be liable for non-delivery. Another possibility is that the goods are unsatisfactory under s 14 but perish by reason of some cause *other* than their unsatisfactory quality, such as an accidental fire; here the contract would be avoided under s 7 but B would have a claim for damages for any loss suffered as a consequence of the defective goods before the destruction of those goods.

The question of fault must also be fitted with s 20(2), which was considered earlier, and provides that where delivery is delayed through the fault of either party, 'the goods are at the risk of the party at fault as regards any loss which might not have occurred but for such fault'. Where delivery is delayed through S's fault so that the risk is on him and the goods are then destroyed as a direct[5] result of the delay, it might be thought that s 7 would, in effect, be extended so that S could plead frustration. This would be impossible, however, as S would be at fault in causing the goods to perish. Where the delay in delivery is B's fault, the goods would be at his risk under s 20(2) and thus s 7 could clearly not apply.

The same reasoning regarding fault should apply to s 20(3), also considered earlier, which provides that nothing in s 20 'affects the duties or liabilities of either seller or buyer as a bailee or custodier of the goods of the other party'. Thus, in the above example of the chemicals, if S were storing them for B prior to delivery and they were destroyed as a result of his negligent storage, he would

---

3 [1948] 2 All ER 1036.
4 See also *Howell v Coupland* (1874) LR 9 QB 462, 465 per Blackburn J (first instance, affd (1876) 1 QBD 258): '... if the perishing were owing to any default of the seller, that would be quite another thing. But here the crop failed entirely owing to the blight, which no skill, care, or diligence of the defendant could prevent'; *Lebaupin v Crispin & Co* [1920] 2 KB 714, 717-718 per McCardie J.
5 If S can prove that the loss arose from *some other cause* and thus would have arisen despite the delay, he would not seem to be at fault under s 20(2) (see the earlier consideration of *Demby Hamilton & Co Ltd v Barden* [1949] 1 All ER 435) and could thus plead s 7.

be at fault, unable to argue that the contract should be avoided under s 7 and consequently liable for non-delivery. Equally, B could not utilise s 7 if he negligently destroyed the chemicals in his possession when risk and property remained in S.

Is s 7 an absolute rule?

It is suggested by leading authorities[6] that s 7 can be negated or varied by contrary intent in the same way as s 6, thereby permitting the allocation of the risk that the goods might perish after contract to one of the parties. Treating s 7 as a *prima facie* rule seems correct in principle and would avoid the mechanistic consequences of the section. A court could then decide, for example, that the intent of S and B was that destruction of the goods should not avoid the contract but that, instead, they should remain at S's risk until delivery to B, in which case S would be liable in damages for non-delivery. Alternatively, B might make an absolute promise to pay even if the goods perish.

THE CONSEQUENCES OF SECTION 7

The consequences of frustration of the contract under s 7 are *not* governed by the Law Reform (Frustrated Contracts) Act 1943, which expressly excludes 'any contract to which s 7 of the Sale of Goods Act ... applies'.[7] Instead, the common law rules on the effects of frustration apply and give rise to the notoriously unfair and arbitrary results evidenced in the decisions which occurred before the 1943 Act was law. Overall, frustration at common law can be likened to the fall of a stage curtain in the way that it automatically dictates the rights and obligations of the parties who are left at either side. Although the consequences of the curtain's falling might be characterised as farcical, they can hardly be termed melodramatic, as they clearly lack the strict attention to poetic justice and happy endings characteristic of melodrama. Instead, the curtain cannot be lifted once in place and it is often a question of luck whether one party profits from being on the right side at the right time. In *Chandler v Webster*,[8] for example, a room was hired for the purpose of viewing the coronation procession of 1902, the price being £141 15s payable immediately. The hirer paid £100 deposit and the balance was owed at the date of frustration when the procession was cancelled. It was held that the obligation to pay in full had accrued before the time of frustration and thus the hirer was unable to recover the £100 and, moreover, he remained liable for the balance owing.

---

6 See *Benjamin's Sale of Goods* (5th edn, 1997) para 6-031; Atiyah, *The Sale of Goods* (10th edn, 2001), p 357.
7 Section 2(5)(c) of the 1943 Act. This section also excludes from the Act's operation 'any other contract for the sale ... of specific goods, where the contract is frustrated by reason of the fact that the goods have perished'. It is difficult to see what this enigmatic phrase adds to the words quoted in the text above, but it might refer to cases where s 7 would not apply as the risk has passed to B. But such a contract is almost certainly not frustrated by the fact that the goods have perished. One explanation is that such a situation is exempted from the 1943 Act to emphasise that B is liable for the price and there is no room for apportionment under the 1943 Act: see Atiyah, *The Sale of Goods* (10th edn, 2001), p 361; Treitel, *The Law of Contract* (10th edn, 1999), p 857.
8 [1904] 1 KB 493.

This result ensued despite the fact that the hirer secured no realistic performance under the contract. The roles were reversed in *Krell v Henry*,[9] where, on similar facts, the money did not fall due until after the cancellation and thus the creditor had the misfortune to be on the wrong side of the curtain and unable to recover anything.

The effects of frustration at common law can be summarised with particular reference to the sale of goods and s 7. First, under s 7 the agreement is 'avoided' *only* from the time that the goods perish and thus both parties are released from *future* obligations so that S is excused delivery and B is not liable for the price. The other side of this coin is that obligations which had *accrued* at the date that the goods perished must be performed, eg where the price is payable in advance it remains payable[10] and accrued obligations which have been performed are left undisturbed, eg where the price was paid in advance it is not returned. Nevertheless, because of the exception allowed in the *Fibrosa*[11] case, B does not have to pay the price and can recover any payment made *if* there has been a total failure of consideration, eg no delivery has taken place at all.

Second, unlike the 1943 Act, s 7 contains no provisions for the apportionment of the loss in this situation and if B recovers the whole price from S, S cannot set-off any expenses he may have incurred under the contract before frustration and, if B has paid nothing, S cannot *claim* any expenses. Consider the situation, for example, where S agrees to sell a painting to B and undertakes to restore it and, at the time of the contract, B makes a part-payment towards the price. The painting will not be in a 'deliverable state' at the time of contract and so s 18, r 2 will be applicable meaning that property and the risk in the painting will not pass to B until the work is completed and he has notice of that fact. Suppose that, after S has completed half of the work, the painting is destroyed accidentally by fire. The contract is avoided by s 7 and B is entitled to recover the part of the purchase price he has paid because there has been a total failure of consideration, but S has no right of set-off for expenses he has incurred in carrying out the restoration work.

Third, there are difficulties where partial delivery precedes the perishing of the goods. Here B may have paid the whole price in advance but he cannot recover any of his purchase price, or if payable in advance it remains payable, because there has not been a total failure of consideration, eg any part of a specific parcel of goods has been delivered by S.[12] By the same token, S may have delivered part of the goods and received no advance payment from B, or

---

9 [1903] 2 KB 740.

10 On this point, the effects of *Chandler v Webster* [1904] 1 KB 493 remain good law.

11 *Fibrosa Spolka Akcyjna v Fairbairn Lawson Combe Barbour Ltd* [1943] AC 32. In fact, the rule relating to a total failure of consideration had always applied in the sale of goods: see, eg *Rugg v Minett* (1809) 11 East 210 (considered in Ch 16) *Logan v Le Mesurier* (1847) 6 Moo PC 116 (sale of a raft of red pine timber to be delivered at Quebec but the timber was lost in a storm. Held B could recover back all money paid).

12 Atiyah (*The Sale of Goods*, 10th edn, 2001, p 363) suggests that, where B has paid the full price in advance and received only part of the goods, he may recover 'the amount of the price which is to be attributed to the goods which have perished' on the basis that the *risk* in those goods was on S when they perished (so also if the price is payable in advance, B is only liable for the price of the goods delivered). This attempts an equitable apportionment within the common law but, as Treitel (*The Law of Contract*, 10th edn, 1999, p 856) has cogently stressed, the solution is flawed where the price is not readily apportionable between the delivered and undelivered parts, eg a contract for the sale of specific machinery, to be delivered in parts, is frustrated after payment in full but only partial delivery.

payment is not due in advance, and then S is unable to recover anything for the valuable benefit he has conferred on B.[13]

As the powers of apportionment in the 1943 Act apply to cases of specific goods where the contract is frustrated for some reason other than the fact that the goods have perished, eg Government requisitioning of the goods, it is self-evident that it is extremely difficult to justify the arbitrary consequences which ensue where goods perish within s 7. The 1893 Act singled-out the particular instance of s 7 in sharp contrast with contracts for the sale of wholly unascertained goods which cannot be frustrated and must be decided on the rules of risk. In the light of modern developments in frustration since 1893 and the more complex nature of modern contracts, it is surely time to reform this part of the SGA to cope with the eventualities which are not catered for at present.

INSTANCES OF FRUSTRATION OTHER THAN SECTION 7

A contract for the sale of specific goods may, of course, be frustrated at common law by events other than the destruction of the goods or the fact that they have perished. Frustration of the contract will occur if, after it has been entered into but before the property or risk has passed to B, without the fault of either party, it has become either impossible to perform it legally or it is incapable of performance as the changed circumstances in which it must be performed mean that the undertaking has become a radically different commercial venture from that specified in the contract. In *Re Shipton, Anderson & Co and Harrison Bros & Co*,[14] for example, a contract for the sale of a specific parcel of wheat in a warehouse in Liverpool was held to be frustrated by the Government's requisitioning of the goods thereby excusing S from performance. Again, there seems no reason why, at common law, frustration should not apply to contracts for the sale of future, specific goods where it is agreed, for example, that S will acquire a specific antique from a third party but export restrictions prevent the sale.

The more difficult questions concern the frustration of a contract for the sale of unascertained goods.[15] It was stressed earlier, when ss 6 and 7 were considered, that a contract for wholly unascertained, generic goods, cannot be frustrated by the fact that the goods which S *intends* to supply have perished, as he must simply procure other goods in fulfilment of the contract *(genus numquam perit)* and B is not concerned with the fact that S's intended source of supply has, for example, been accidentally burnt after the conclusion of the contract.[16] The same overall principle applies to agreements to sell future, unascertained goods (eg S agrees to build a ship for B) and if the goods are accidentally destroyed when almost complete, S must simply start work afresh. The leading decision in *Blackburn*

---

13 Here Atiyah (above) considers that, although B could not be liable on the contract, he might be liable in a restitutionary action for as much as he has received. But this would have to be based on a new contract, implied from B's retention of the goods; this might be established where he has the goods in his possession after the time of frustration but difficult to imply if he has sold them, for example, before frustration occurs.
14 [1915] 3 KB 676.
15 Once the unascertained goods have become appropriated to the contract there could be frustration but there is little scope for its application as property and risk will usually pass to B at the time the goods are appropriated.
16 See eg *Jacobs, Marcus & Co v Crédit Lyonnais* (1884) 12 QBD 589; *Re Thornett & Fehr & Yuills Ltd* [1921] 1 KB 219, 227-228 per Lord Reading CJ; *Monkland v Jack Barclay Ltd* [1951] 2 KB 252, 258 per Asquith LJ.

Bobbin Co Ltd v T W Allen & Sons Ltd,[17] emphasises this strict, general rule. S agreed to sell 'seventy standards of Finland birch timber' to B which S intended to import from Finland, although B did not know either that fact or that S had no such timber in stock in England. After the outbreak of war in August 1914, S was unable to obtain timber from Finland because of the paralysis of trade routes and thus contended that the contract was frustrated but, instead, the court held that S was liable in damages for non-delivery. McCardie J[18] concluded that 'in the absence of any question as to trading with the enemy, and in the absence also of any administrative intervention by the British Government authorities, a bare and unqualified contract for the sale of unascertained goods will not (unless most special facts compel an opposite implication) be dissolved by the operation of the principle of [frustration], even though there has been so grave and unforeseen a change of circumstance as to render it impossible for the vendor to fulfil his bargain'. This decision was affirmed by the Court of Appeal,[19] where it was emphasised that B was indifferent regarding the *manner* in which S intended to perform the contract.[20] The stringent rule regarding unascertained goods means that there will also be no frustration where S's sole supplier of goods of the contract description has failed, at least where B is unaware that he is the sole producer of the goods[1] or where the goods are available but there are other, attendant difficulties, which S argues prevent his supplying B with the goods.[2]

In the *Blackburn Bobbin* case, McCardie J left open the possibility that frustration could exceptionally[3] apply to contracts for the sale of unascertained goods and it is plain that it can so apply in certain situations. First, if the contract expressly provides that the goods must come from a particular source, the failure of that source may frustrate the contract, as in *Howell v Coupland,*[4] considered earlier. It does seem that the source must be exclusive and if the contract refers to several sources, the failure of one source only will not frustrate the contract.[5] Second, it is more difficult to decide whether there should be frustration where both S and B *contemplate* that the goods will come from a particular source but there is no express provision to that effect in the contract. In *Re Badische Co*

17 [1918] 2 KB 467.
18 [1918] 1 KB 540, 550.
19 [1918] 2 KB 467.
20 See also *Tsakiroglou & Co Ltd v Noblee Thorl GmbH* [1962] AC 93 (contract for the sale of Sudanese groundnuts to German buyers was not frustrated by the closure of the Suez Canal as the goods could have been shipped round the Cape of Good Hope, entailing a route three times longer than through the Suez canal with consequent increase in the cost of freightage. NB no date had been fixed for delivery of the nuts, which were relatively durable, and there was evidence of sufficient shipping to carry the nuts via the Cape; if the facts had been otherwise, the contract might easily have been frustrated).
 1 *Intertradex SA v Lesieur-Tourteaux SARL* [1978] 2 Lloyd's Rep 509 (breakdown of machinery at the factory of S's sole supplier of goods (replacement parts for the machinery available only from Germany) and interruptions in the supply by rail of raw materials to the factory did not frustrate the contract with B).
 2 See eg *Lebaupin v Crispin & Co* [1920] 2 KB 714 (contract for the sale of 'British Columbia Fraser river salmon' from the 1917 season to be packed in 2,500 ½ lb tins. The packing commenced but (i) many of the tins were found to be defective and before new tins could be obtained the run of salmon had ceased for the season; and (ii) 1 lb tins were filled in priority to ½ lb tins and the salmon run had ceased by the time the latter tins could be filled. Held that the salmon crop was larger than usual, and there was thus no failure of the subject matter of the contract and no frustration).
 3 See also *Carapanayoti & Co Ltd v E T Green Ltd* [1959] 1 QB 131, 146-147 per McNair J.
 4 (1876) 1 QBD 258.
 5 See *Turner v Goldsmith* [1891] 1 QB 544.

Ltd,[6] a contract for the sale of dyestuffs which both parties knew could be obtained only from Germany was held to be frustrated by the outbreak of the 1914–1918 war. Russell J could 'see no reason why, given the necessary circumstances to exist, [frustration] should not apply equally to the case of unascertained goods' and he thought that the dyestuffs had 'almost a specific touch, that is to say, that the goods were in the contemplation of the parties to come from Germany'.[7] This case was arguably dominated by the fact that it would have been *illegal* to allow trade with an enemy in time of war, a rule which is so potent that the contract will be discharged even if it contains an express provision for its suspension during wartime.[8] The contract would thus have been discharged even if S and B had specified a source and it remains unclear what the position might be where a source of supply is mutually contemplated but the alleged frustrating event does not have the prescriptive force of illegality.

Partial failure of a particular source

It is relatively clear from the foregoing discussion that, in a contract to sell unascertained goods from a particular source, the *total* failure of the source may well frustrate the contract but, where the failure is *partial*, it is more difficult to determine the position.

Where only S and B are involved, the effects of a partial failure of a particular source of unascertained goods have been considered earlier, but it may be helpful briefly to restate the position. First, S may be released from his obligation to deliver that part of the source which is unavailable (*Howell v Coupland*[9] – S delivered to B the potatoes which were produced and was excused as regards the amount of the crop which failed). Second, S may be bound to offer the quantity produced to B but, if it is less than he contracted for then, subject to the SGA, s 30, B need not accept it (*Sainsbury (H R & S) Ltd v Street*[10] – S did not deliver to B the barley which was produced but, instead, sold it at more than the original contract price to B2. S was liable to B for failure to deliver the amount of barley which was produced).

Where there are *several* buyers from a particular source[11] and the failure is partial, the law is most unclear. The difficulty posed by a partial failure of

6 [1921] 2 Ch 331.
7 [1921] 2 Ch 331 at 382 and 383. See also *Hulton (E) & Co Ltd v Chadwick and Taylor Ltd* (1918) 34 TLR 230 (contract for S to supply B with paper was frustrated by a wartime Proclamation prohibiting the importation of wood pulp except under licence and regulations which severely restricted the amounts which S could sell. The Court of Appeal held that S and B had contracted on the footing of the continuance of the right to import wood pulp and the contract could not be performed in the changed conditions).
8 *Ertel Bieber & Co v Rio Tinto Co Ltd* [1918] AC 260.
9 (1876) 1 QBD 258.
10 [1972] 1 WLR 834.
11 The new provisions in the SGA, ss 20A and 20B provide that, in a contract for the sale of unascertained goods, there may be co-ownership in an identified but undivided bulk. Similarly, by virtue of the extended defintion of 'specific goods' in s 61(1), there may be co-ownership of specific goods in such a bulk (an agreement to sell such an undivided share thus comes within s 7, see earlier). No express provision has been made in either case for risk and frustration. There would seem to be limited scope for frustration to apply, as risk will probably transfer to B at the same time as property in the undivided share. The contract could thus be frustrated only during the time that the goods are undivided (ie still in bulk) but no property in the undivided share has passed to B because the conditions for its passing have not been complied with (eg B has not pre-paid the price of the goods under s 20A). See Ch 16 on the passing of property.

a particular source is that S will be unable to deliver the full amounts to all his buyers but will be able to deliver in full to some buyers or, alternatively, make a partial delivery to them all. How is S to solve the dilemma facing him? Consider the situation where S agrees to sell the entire bulk of 900 tons of groundnuts stored in a foreign warehouse to three buyers (B, B2 and B3) who each agree to buy 300 tons but, but before the property or risk has passed to the buyers, export controls are introduced meaning that S can obtain only 600 tons. The legal position is unresolved but the various possibilities in this situation are:

(i)   All the contracts are frustrated because S cannot perform them all. This must be an unacceptable solution because, if S has been unable to obtain sufficient goods to satisfy all his buyers, there may well be a general paucity of goods in the market and S would consequently be enabled to resell the goods at inflated prices.

(ii) If S delivers 300 tons to each of B and B2, none of the contracts is frustrated as S's failure to deliver to B3 would be the result of S's election thereby constituting self-induced frustration. B3's contract could thus not be frustrated and S would be liable to B3 in damages. This unattractive resolution of the problem stems from the law's view of frustration[12] and particularly from the recent decision in *The Super Servant Two*.[13] The case concerned a contract to transport a drilling rig in one of two ships, the *Super Servant One* (SS1) or the *Super Servant Two* (SS2), at the carrier's option. The carrier had intended to use SS2 but she sank and it was argued that the contract was frustrated by this loss because SS1 was the subject of another contract and hence not available to carry the rig. The frustration argument was rejected on the basis that the carrier's decision to use SS1 for another contract was his own choice and election thus thwarting his reliance on the loss of SS2 as a frustrating event. This approach is criticisable in that it is the frustrating event which primarily deprives S of the ability to perform all the contracts rather than his voluntary election to perform some of them[14] and it is arguable that, provided that S acts reasonably, his choosing to perform some of the contracts should not preclude his claim that the other undertakings have been frustrated. This argument was, however, expressly rejected in *The Super Servant Two*.[15]

(iii) Only some of the contracts may be discharged, there being two sub-divisions of this possibility. First, S may be able to choose which of the contracts to perform in full, meaning that the other, remaining contracts are discharged. If, for example, S chose to deliver 300 tons to each of B and B2, B3's contract would be discharged. Second and more likely, if an order of priority for the performance of the contracts can be established, eg if the contracts were entered into in chronological order, S would arguably be *justified* in performing both B's and B2's contract and thus only B3's contract would be frustrated. If this solution were adopted, the

---

12 See *Maritime National Fish Ltd v Ocean Trawlers Ltd* [1935] AC 524.

13 *Lauritzen AS v Wijsmuller BV, The Super Servant Two* [1989] 1 Lloyd's Rep 148; affd [1990] 1 Lloyd's Rep 1; see Chandler, 'Self-Induced Frustration, Forseeability and Risk' (1990) 41 NILQ 362.

14 See Treitel, *The Law of Contract* (10th edn, 1999), pp 844-846; Treitel, *Frustration and Force Majeure* (1994), para 5-016.

15 See [1989] 1 Lloyd's Rep 148, 158 per Hobhouse J; [1990] 1 Lloyd's Rep 1, 8-10 per Bingham LJ; 13-14 per Dillon LJ.

fact that S must first deliver to B and B2 would mean that S's failure to perform B3's contract would not be the result of S's election.[16]

(iv) S must offer a *pro rata* delivery of 200 tons to each of B, B2 and B3 which, of course, they are not bound to accept, but S would be discharged from further liability on the contracts.

It is suggested that possibility (iv), *pro rata* delivery,[17] is the most equitable solution. Advanced provisions relating to *pro rata* distribution, sometimes referred to as 'prorating', are accepted in the USA.[18] There the basic notion is that S can allocate the goods in 'any manner which is fair and reasonable' but, in making the distribution, S can consider 'regular customers' who are *not* under contract and his own requirements for further manufacture.[19] S must notify buyers of the amounts available but the buyers may opt either to take the amounts offered or terminate the contracts.[20] The twin obstacles in the path of this solution in English law are that, first, the effect of frustration is to discharge the contract automatically and completely and the courts have no power to adjust or amend the parties' obligations and, second, the notion of self-induced frustration seems firmly embedded in the law after the decision in *The Super Servant Two*. It appears therefore that possibility (ii), above, represents most accurately the current state of the law. This automatic, all-or-nothing approach has little to commend it and accords with the pre-1943 view of frustration in failing to arrive at a fair apportionment under the contracts.

That being said, *pro rata* distribution has been viewed favourably in cases concerning express *force majeure* clauses where S has argued that partial failure of a source should excuse him under the contractual provision.[1] If *pro rata* delivery were to be accepted in English law, it could be achieved by implying a term

---

16 See the (varying) degrees of approval given to this notion in *Tennants (Lancashire) Ltd v C S Wilson & Co Ltd* [1917] AC 495, 508 per Lord Finlay LC; *Intertradex SA v Lesieur-Tourteaux SARL* [1977] 2 Lloyd's Rep 146, 155 per Donaldson J; [1978] 2 Lloyd's Rep 509, 513 per Lord Denning MR; *Continental Grain Export Corpn v STM Grain Ltd* [1979] 2 Lloyd's Rep 460, 473 per Robert Goff J; *Coastal (Bermuda) Petroleum Ltd v VTT Vulcan Petroleum SA, The Marine Star* [1993] 1 Lloyd's Rep 329, 332-333 per Hirst LJ.

17 See Hudson, 'Prorating in the English Law of Frustrated Contracts' (1968) 31 MLR 535 and 'Prorating and Frustration' (1979) 123 Sol Jo 137; Treitel, *Frustration and Force Majeure* (1994), paras 5-015–5-028.

18 See Uniform Commercial Code, s 2-615 (b) and (c).

19 See *Campbell v Hostetter Farms Inc* 380 A 2d 463 (1977) (in making the allocation, S was justified in retaining some corn to feed his own cattle).

20 Uniform Commercial Code, s 2-616.

1 See *Tennants (Lancashire) Ltd v C S Wilson & Co Ltd* [1917] AC 495, 512 per Lord Haldane; Lord Finlay LC (p 508) would have applied *pro rata* distribution only where there were several contracts with the *same* delivery date and his dominant approach was that contracts with earlier delivery dates should rank in priority to those with later dates (see possibility (iii) in the text, above); *Pool Shipping Co Ltd v London Coal Co of Gibraltar Ltd* [1939] 2 All ER 432; *Bremer Handelsgesellschaft mbH v Vanden Avenne-Izegem PVBA* [1977] 1 Lloyd's Rep 133, 161-162 per Mocatta J; [1978] 2 Lloyd's Rep 109, 115 per Lord Wilberforce; *Bremer Handelsgesellschaft mbH v C Mackprang Jr* [1979] 1 Lloyd's Rep 221, 224 per Lord Denning MR; *Bremer Handelsgesellschaft mbH v Continental Grain Co* [1983] 1 Lloyd's Rep 269, 280-281 per Mustill J; 291-294 per Ackner LJ. Cf *Hong Guan & Co Ltd v R Jumabhoy & Sons Ltd* [1960] AC 684, 701-702 per Lord Morris of Borth-Y-Gest (S cannot be 'allowed to excuse their non-performance by reference to their other commitments, or to seek to give those other commitments priority'); *Pancommerce SA v Veecheema BV* [1983] 2 Lloyd's Rep 304, 307 per Sir John Donaldson MR (where S had a legal obligation to deliver to B and a moral commitment to another (a non-contractual first refusal) and he could honour his obligations to either party but not to both, he was not justifed in partially honouring both).

into the contracts which permits such apportionment, in much the same way as the term which was implied in *Sainsbury (H R & S) Ltd v Street*,[2] that S should offer to B the goods which were actually produced. In any event, *pro rata* apportionment can function only where unascertained goods, such as commodities, are capable of infinite divisibility and could not apply, for example, where S agrees to sell three foals to be born from a particular stable to three separate buyers but circumstances outside S's control mean that only two foals are born. Here it would surely be reasonable to discharge one of the contracts but, in the absence of some guide as to priority amongst the buyers, difficulties remain as to which contract should be frustrated.

CONSEQUENCES OF FRUSTRATION UNDER THE LAW REFORM (FRUSTRATED CONTRACTS) ACT 1943

The 1943 Act[3] applies where contracts for the sale of unascertained goods are frustrated or where contracts for the sale of specific goods are frustrated by events other than the fact that they have perished under the SGA, s 7. The 1943 Act aims to avert the iniquitous consequences of the common law (which apply to s 7, see earlier) by seeking to avoid unjust enrichment in the face of frustration. The salient parts of the 1943 Act must be considered with special reference to contracts for the sale of goods and may be divided into two parts.

Recovery of payments made by B and S's set-off for expenses

Section 1(2)[4] provides, first, that a party may recover any payments made in pursuance of a contract, before the time of frustration, even though there has been only a partial failure of consideration. For example, if B pays the whole or part of the purchase price (or any other sums 'in pursuance' of the contract) before the frustrating event occurs, he is entitled to repayment of those sums in full from S and this would still be the position if S had made a delivery of some of the goods under the contract. Second, s 1(2) provides that, if the purchase price or other sums are payable before the frustrating event but have not been paid, they cease to be payable. It is vital to stress that s 1(2) applies only to *money* paid or payable *before* the time of discharge.[5]

The proviso to s 1(2)[6] then improves the position of the party to whom the sums of money, specified above, were paid or payable by allowing him to retain

---

2 [1972] 1 WLR 834.
3 See Glanville Williams, *Law Reform (Frustrated Contracts) Act 1943*.
4 Section 1(2) provides: 'All sums paid or payable to any party in pursuance of the contract before the time when the parties were so discharged (in this Act referred to as "the time of discharge") shall, in the case of sums so paid, be recoverable from him as money received by him for the use of the party by whom the sums were paid, and, in the case of sums so payable, cease to be so payable.'
5 Thus where one party promises to perform some other act before the time of discharge and fails to do so, he is not relieved of that obligation by s 1(2) and would have to pay damages to the other party; nor could he negate his liability under the valuable benefit provisions of s 1(3), as no such benefit would have been obtained by the other party *before* the time of discharge: see Treitel, *The Law of Contract* (10th edn, 1999), p 854.
6 'Provided that, if the party to whom the sums were so paid or payable incurred expenses before the time of discharge in, or for the purpose of, the performance of the contract, the court may, if it considers it just to do so having regard to all the circumstances of the case, allow him to retain or, as the case may be, recover the whole or any part of the sums so paid or payable, not being an amount in excess of the expenses so incurred.'

or recover the whole or any part of such sums of money if he incurred expenses in performing the contract before the time of discharge. Thus where S, before the frustrating event occurs, has incurred expenses in partly-manufacturing the goods, or where he has made costly arrangements for packing or storing the goods, the court may allow him to set-off his expenses against the sums paid or payable by B. It should be stressed that expenses can *only* be set-off against the 'sums so paid or payable' before frustration and thus there must be either an actual payment by B before the time of discharge or a provision for pre-payment in the contract: if S incurs more expenses than the amounts so paid or payable, the sums are irrecoverable. It is clearly advantageous for S to insist on pre-payment where possible but it seems unduly restrictive to deprive him of expenses simply because he has received no payment or a pre-payment provision is absent from the contract.

The court has a discretion in awarding expenses but it is subject to two *upper* limits, viz it cannot award more than the amount paid or payable or more than the actual expenses incurred. There is no authority regarding the assessment of expenses under s 1(2) but, under s 1(4), expenses may include 'overhead expenses' and any 'work or services performed personally'[7] by the party incurring the expenses. In assessing the award, the court will almost certainly take into account the final position after frustration,[8] eg if S is left with partially-completed machinery which could readily be sold to a third party at a considerable profit, he is unlikely to receive anything, but if the goods he has left on his hands were custom-built for B and cannot be sold anywhere, S may receive substantial expenses. This view would mean that the court has regard to S's net loss after making allowance for any goods which he may sell after frustration, rather than simply considering his gross expense.

However, care must be taken in awarding expenses for, otherwise, the position could be as unjust as the old, common law rule, in that 'to shift the whole loss in respect of expenses to the other party would ... be as objectionable as shifting none'.[9] For example, at common law prior to the 1943 Act, if S had made no delivery of the goods to B he would simply have to return to B any pre-payment, no matter how great the expenses incurred by S (thereby shifting the entire loss to S) but, under s 1(2), S could theoretically be allowed to retain the full amount of the pre-payment (thereby shifting the entire loss to B). In exercising its discretion, the court might reach a more equitable result by dividing the loss between S and B. Finally, it should be noted that, in an evaluation of the position between S and B, s 1(2) does not allow the court to assess the 'time value of money,' ie B's payment may have been made or S's expenses incurred well before the frustrating event.[10] Also, s 1(5) provides that money paid under an insurance policy is *not* to be considered when deciding whether any sum ought to be recovered or retained under s 1, unless there was an obligation to insure imposed by an express term of the frustrated contract or any enactment.

---

7   Could S claim as expenses the amounts owed to a carrier or other third party or are such services not 'performed personally'?
8   See Glanville Williams, *Law Reform (Frustrated Contracts) Act 1943*, p 39.
9   Glanville Williams, *Law Reform (Frustrated Contracts) Act 1943*, p 36.
10 See *BP Exploration Co (Libya) Ltd v Hunt (No 2)* [1979] 1 WLR 783; affd [1981] 1 WLR 232, CA. The HL ([1983] 2 AC 352) made no mention of the point. Interest can be awarded on any sum, however.

Payment for valuable benefit obtained

Section 1(3)[11] was intended to reverse the hardship which could arise in relation to entire contracts. Such a contract entails the performance of a completed act and, where nothing was payable in advance, the plaintiff could recover nothing for an incomplete act, even though the cause of the non-completion was an event outside his control. In *Appleby v Myers*,[12] for example, the plaintiff (P) agreed to erect machinery on the defendant's (D) premises but, when the work was almost complete, an accidental fire destroyed both machinery and premises. It was held that P could recover nothing as D's obligation to pay, on completion, had not arisen at the time of the discharge of the contract. In a contract for the sale of goods, where S delivered only part of the goods to B before frustration, he would thus be unable to recover anything but, under s 1(3), B must pay for the valuable benefit received.

In *BP Exploration Co (Libya) Ltd v Hunt (No 2)*,[13] Robert Goff J considered that the major issues in relation to s 1(3) were, first, the identification of the valuable benefit received and, second, the the valuation of the benefit and award of a 'just sum,' not greater than the value of the benefit, having regard to the circumstances of the case and the matters specified in s 1(3)(a) and (b). The decision at first instance in the *BP Exploration* case is crucial as it is the only guide to the application of s 1(3).

Identifying the benefit

In relation to identifying the benefit, Robert Goff J thought that 'valuable benefit' must refer to the end product received by one party and *not* the cost of performance incurred by the other.[14] It is respectfully suggested that this is correct in principle as s 1(3) refers to benefit 'obtained' by one party rather than work done by the other. Where S has delivered part of the goods to B before frustration, the benefit is therefore the actual goods received and this benefit may be worth more or less than S's expenses in manufacturing the goods, for example. However, the insistence on an end product means that, should S deliver goods to B which are then totally destroyed by accident, there is no identifiable benefit left to be assessed because 'section 1(3)(b) makes it plain that [S] is to take the risk of depreciation or destruction by the frustrating event'.[15] Similarly, there is no

---

11 'Where any party to the contract has, by reason of anything done by any other party thereto in, or for the purpose of, the performance of the contract, obtained a valuable benefit (other than a payment of money to which the last foregoing subsection applies) before the time of discharge, there shall be recoverable from him by the said other party such sum (if any), not exceeding the value of the said benefit to the party obtaining it, as the court considers just, having regard to all the circumstances of the case and, in particular –
   (a) the amount of any expenses incurred before the time of discharge by the benefitted party in, or for the purpose of, the performance of the contract, including any sums paid or payable by him to any other party in pursuance of the contract and retained or recoverable by that party under the last foregoing subsection, and
   (b) the effect, in relation to the said benefit, of the circumstances giving rise to the frustration of the contract.'
12 (1867) LR 2 CP 651.
13 [1979] 1 WLR 783; affd [1981] 1 WLR 232, CA; affd [1983] 2 AC 352, HL.
14 But the necessity for an end product does not require the transfer of a tangible object and an end product could be services rendered or advice, for example.
15 [1979] 1 WLR 783, 803 per Robert Goff J.

valuable benefit if the goods delivered are, for instance, of no value without delivery of the remainder. Adoption of this analysis entails an approval of the outcome in *Appleby v Myers* but, with respect, the analysis seems to be an unduly limiting one in view of the court's wide discretion under s 1(3).[16]

Valuing the benefit

As regards the value of the benefit to the party receiving it, where goods are in B's possession at the date of frustration, they must be valued at that date but, if B has disposed of them before frustration, they must be valued at the date of disposal and no allowance can be made in S's favour for the 'time value of money', eg that B had the use of the proceeds from the sale of the goods to a new buyer.[17] This presumably also means that there can be no allowance for B's use of the actual goods before frustration. If the benefit was obtained partly as a result of B's work and partly by S's performance of the contract, Robert Goff J considered that the court must do its best to apportion the benefit between S and B.[18] Moreover, the circumstances specified in s 1(3)(a) and (b) have to be considered in valuing the benefit, eg any expenses of B and any amount which might be retained or recovered by S as expenses under s 1(2) would have to be deducted when the value of the benefit which B obtained was calculated. It seems clear from the judgment of Robert Goff J in *BP Exploration*[19] that, in a contract for the sale of goods, the value of B's benefit will be limited to the price of the goods which have been delivered. This is because B contracted on the basis that he would pay no more than the contract price and it would thus be unfair to compel him to pay more than that price or a proportion of it.

---

16 Glanville Williams had argued (*Law Reform (Frustrated Contracts) Act 1943*, pp 48-50) that, in a case such as *Appleby*, the plaintiff (P) should be able to recover the value of the work done as it could have constituted a benefit prior to frustration, eg if the defendant (D) had sold the factory before the fire, he would have obtained an increased price as a result of P's work or, if D had properly insured the factory, its value for the purposes of a claim under the policy would similarly have been increased.
17 *BP Exploration Co (Libya) Ltd v Hunt (No 2)* [1979] 1 WLR 783, 801-804 per Robert Goff J.
18 [1979] 1 WLR 783 at 802.
19 [1979] 1 WLR 783 at 805-806.

CHAPTER 25

Exclusion clauses and unfair terms in contracts for the sale of goods

Introduction

In contracts for the sale of goods, it is common to find exclusion or exemption clauses which purport to exclude or restrict the rights, duties and liabilities which would otherwise arise.[1] Exclusion clauses are, today, often regarded as objectionable. At a practical level, one party's exclusion or modification of his liability may be unknown to, or not understood by, the other party. At a theoretical level, the contract may be formed in circumstances where there is inequality of bargaining power between seller and buyer so that the weaker of the parties has less ability than the stronger to negotiate the terms of the contract.[2] At worst, the weaker party's only choice is not to enter into the contract but this is hardly a viable option where, for example, S is the sole supplier of the goods in question and, in this situation, the contract terms are effectively dictated by the more powerful party. Alternatively, it is arguable that an imposition of harsh terms may not result from such superior bargaining strength but, instead, might occur where a seller of goods offers a competitive, low price to his buyer and then shifts many of the risks onto the buyer by the use of contract terms of which the buyer may be ill-informed or unconcerned.[3]

Certainly contracts of adhesion, which are formed on a 'take it or leave it'[4] basis, invariably come to light where one party has the whip hand over the other. Well into the 20th century, exclusion clauses were countenanced by the courts in the name of freedom of contract but an espousal of total freedom must necessarily condone an unfettered ability to abuse dominant bargaining strengths. In *Thompson v London, Midland and Scottish Rly Co*,[5] for example, the plaintiff

---

1 See generally Yates and Hawkins, *Standard Business Contracts: Exclusions and Related Devices* (1986); Coote, *Exception Clauses* (1964); Baker, 'The Freedom to Contract Without Liability' [1971] CLP 53.
2 See especially Kessler, 'Contracts of Adhesion – Some Thoughts about Freedom of Contract' (1943) 43 Col L Rev 629; Slawson, 'Standard Form Contracts and Democratic Control of Lawmaking Power' (1971) 84 Harv L Rev 529 .
3 See Goldberg, 'Institutional Change and the Quasi-Invisible Hand' (1974) 17 J Law & Econ 461.
4 See the graphic judgment of Lord Denning MR in *George Mitchell (Chesterhall) Ltd v Finney Lock Seeds Ltd* [1983] QB 284: 'The big concern said, "Take it or leave it". The little man had no option but to take it' (p 297); *Suisse Atlantique Société d'Armement Maritime SA v NV Rotterdamsche Kolen Centrale* [1967] 1 AC 361, 406 per Lord Reid.
5 [1930] 1 KB 41.

was illiterate and so she asked her niece to buy a railway excursion ticket on her behalf. On its face, the ticket bore the warning 'for conditions see back' and the reverse of the ticket carried the statement that it was issued subject to the defendant company's conditions, a copy of which could be purchased for 6d. The conditions contained a clause on page 552 excluding the company's liability for 'injury (fatal or otherwise) ... however caused'. The plaintiff was injured while stepping off the train which had stopped short of the platform but the Court of Appeal held that the defendant had taken reasonable steps to bring the conditions to the plaintiff's notice and so she was bound by them. Lord Hanworth MR considered that, 'having regard to ... the condition of education in this country',[6] the plaintiff's illiteracy was irrelevant and Sankey LJ's unrealistic concession was that, had the conditions been 'printed in Chinese',[7] the plaintiff would 'probably' not have been bound by them. Moreover, the judges saw fit to emphasise that the plaintiff had bought a cheap, excursion ticket (2s 7d as opposed to 5s 4d) and could not therefore expect a high standard of performance from the defendant. This patronising approach undeniably ignored the most important fact in the case – the plaintiff would have had to pay approximately one fifth of the cost of her fare for the dubious privilege of obtaining the defendant's unfair conditions. Patently, statutory intervention was required to ban the exclusion of death or bodily injury caused to passengers travelling by rail and, today, the Unfair Contract Terms Act 1977, s 2(1), places an overall prohibition on the exclusion or restriction of liability for death or bodily injury caused by negligence.

The overriding emphasis upon freedom of contract and *laissez-faire* was epitomised in contracts for the sale of goods. Section 55 of the original SGA 1893 allowed the implied terms of the Act to be freely 'negatived or varied by express agreement' and this remained the position until 1973 when the Supply of Goods (Implied Terms) Act introduced controls on S's ability to exclude the statutory implied conditions of the SGA. Between 1893 and 1973, sellers were quick to take advantage of the ability to exclude the implied terms, a notorious example of blanket exclusion occurring in *L'Estrange v F Graucob Ltd*.[8] B, the owner of a café, bought a cigarette vending machine which proved to be unsatisfactory as it jammed in use but her signature on the contract which excluded 'any express or implied condition, statement, or warranty, statutory or otherwise' was held to bind her, even though she had not read the clause which was in 'regrettably small print'[9] on brown paper.

Where two businesses are approximately equal in terms of bargaining strengths and knowledge of the law, exclusion clauses can be viewed in a different light as here the parties are able to negotiate the terms of their contract and a fair allocation of risks should result. In this situation, it is similarly indisputable that standard form contracts are both apt and legitimate bargaining devices.[10] Standardised contracts are often formulated by trade associations for use between their members in largely standardised transactions and have some conspicuous

6   [1930] 1 KB 41 at 46.
7   [1930] 1 KB 41 at 56.
8   [1934] 2 KB 394; see Lord Denning, *The Family Story* (1981), p 99; Spencer, 'Signature, Consent, and the Rule in *L'Estrange v Graucob*' [1973] 32 CLJ 104 .
9   [1934] 2 KB 394 at 405, per Maugham LJ.
10 See *Photo Production Ltd v Securicor Transport Ltd* [1980] AC 827, 851 per Lord Diplock.

advantages in that they save time, enable an accurate allocation of risks to be achieved (eg in relation to insurance) and minimise disputes.[11]

In many instances, the common law recognised the unfairness of exclusion clauses which were not negotiated by the parties and sought to control exclusions of liability which one party attempted to impose on the other. An array of techniques was amassed which limited the ability of the *proferens* to incorporate such clauses in contracts and exacting rules were developed which demanded that exclusion clauses be interpreted *contra proferentem*. However, the common law was, and is, impeded by the notion of freedom of contract and is thus unable simply to prohibit exclusion clauses which are thought to be unfair. Despite this conceptual difficulty, many decisions came perilously close to banning exclusion clauses outright by applying the notion that a clause could not exclude the consequences of a fundamental breach of contract.[12] It became plain, however, that it was difficult to justify such an approach where the parties had freely negotiated an agreement which contained the exclusion of liability and, in the context of exclusion clauses agreed between equals, the principle of freedom of contract was forcefully re-established by the House of Lords in *Photo Production Ltd v Securicor Transport Ltd*.[13] After that decision it became clear that exclusion clauses should not be subjected to an artificial interpretation in order to vanquish a perceived injustice.

In recent years, the legislature has intervened increasingly to regulate exclusion clauses or, in appropriate situations, to forbid their use completely. The SGA, s 55(1) provides that:

'Where a right, duty or liability would arise under a contract of sale of goods by implication of law, it may (subject to the Unfair Contract Terms Act 1977) be negatived or varied by express agreement, or by the course of dealing between the parties, or by such usage as binds both parties to the contract.'

Exclusion clauses in contracts for the sale of goods are thus, in principle, quite valid but it will be noticed that s 55 is subject to the provisions of the Unfair Contract Terms Act 1977 (UCTA) and that Act imposes substantial restrictions on S's ability to exclude the implied conditions in the SGA, ss 12-15. Also, exclusion clauses relating to other obligations in the contract of sale are subject to a test of reasonableness. Moreover, the Unfair Terms in Consumer Contracts Regulations 1999[14] (UTCCR) subject many terms in consumer contracts for the sale of goods and the supply of services to additional, stringent control on the broad basis that they may be 'unfair terms'. The statutory controls upon exclusion clauses are considered in detail later in this chapter but, first, it is necessary to examine briefly the restrictions on the deployment of exclusion clauses at common law.

---

11 See Prausnitz, *The Standardisation of Commercial Contracts in English and Continental Law* (1937); Isaacs, 'The Standardising of Contract' (1917) 27 Yale LJ 34; Kessler, 'Contracts of Adhesion – Some Thoughts about Freedom of Contract' (1943) 43 Col L Rev 629; Sales, 'Standard Form Contracts' (1953) 16 MLR 318; Wilson, 'Freedom of Contract and Adhesion Contracts' (1965) 14 ICLQ 172; Slawson, 'Standard Form Contracts and Democratic Control of Lawmaking Power' (1971) 84 Harv L Rev 529.
12 See eg *Karsales (Harrow) Ltd v Wallis* [1956] 1 WLR 936; *Charterhouse Credit Co Ltd v Tolly* [1963] 2 QB 683 (see below).
13 [1980] AC 827.
14 SI 1999/2083 The Regulations implement an EC Council Directive (93/13/EEC) and are considered in detail later in this chapter.

The control of exclusion clauses at common law

The basic contractual principles relating to the formation of contracts and the incorporation of exclusion clauses as terms of the contract apply in the sale of goods and the operation of these principles is expressly preserved by THE the UCTA, s 11(2). The rules are considered in the standard textbooks on the law of contract and, while a detailed consideration of such rules is outside the scope of this text, a synopsis of the law is necessary with special emphasis on contracts for the sale of goods.

The common law's control of exclusion clauses can be considered under two broad headings: the first encompasses the specialised rules on the *incorporation* of exclusion clauses as terms of the contract, while the second covers the *interpretation* of such clauses provided they have become integrated as contract terms.

INCORPORATION OF THE EXCLUSION CLAUSE AS A TERM OF THE CONTRACT

Signature

Few problems of incorporation arise where a document containing the exclusion clause is signed, as a party is bound by his signature irrespective of whether or not he has read the clause,[15] unless there has been a misrepresentation as to its effect[16] or *non est factum* can be established.[17]

Notice

In the absence of a signature, the issue will turn on whether reasonable notice[18] of the clause has been given to the party allegedly bound by it[19] and this is a question of fact but unusual or particularly onerous clauses require explicit notice.[20] It should be stressed that this obligation demands that one party must give adequate *notice* of the clause to the defendant rather than ensuring that he has read and understood it.[1]

---

15 *L'Estrange v F Graucob Ltd* [1934] 2 KB 394.
16 *Curtis v Chemical Cleaning and Dyeing Co* [1951] 1 KB 805; *Levison v Patent Steam Carpet Cleaning Co Ltd* [1978] QB 69.
17 *Saunders v Anglia Building Society (No 2)* [1971] AC 1039.
18 *Parker v South Eastern Rly Co* (1877) 2 CPD 416.
19 *Henderson v Stevenson* (1875) LR 2 Sc & Div 470; *Richardson, Spence & Co v Rowntree* [1894] AC 217; *Thompson v London, Midland and Scottish Rly Co* [1930] 1 KB 41.
20 *Thornton v Shoe Lane Parking Ltd* [1971] 2 QB 163; *Interfoto Picture Library Ltd v Stiletto Visual Progammes Ltd* [1989] QB 433; *AEG (UK) Ltd v Logic Resource Ltd* [1996] CLC 265 (see below).
 1 *Thompson v London, Midland and Scottish Rly Co* [1930] 1 KB 41; Cf *Geier v Kujawa, Weston and Warne Bros (Transport) Ltd* [1970] 1 Lloyd's Rep 364 (German passenger in a car who did not see or read a notice in the car that passengers travelled at their own risk. Brabin J held that the defendant (who spoke German) should have translated the notice for his passenger and thus she was not bound by it).

Pre-contractual notice

Reasonable notice must be given before or at the time of contracting and the courts preserve the maximum discretion in fixing the moment of the contract's completion.[2]

Contractual document

If the exclusion clause is contained in a document, the document must be one that a reasonable man would expect to contain the contract terms and an exclusion clause will not be incorporated in the contract if the document in question is not intended to be contractually binding and is a receipt or voucher, for example.[3]

Course of dealing

Two situations can arise here. First, it may be that the parties have regularly dealt with each other in a consistent manner but then notice of the exclusion clauses may be omitted for some reason and the question is whether they may be regarded as *continuing* to contract on the earlier terms. Second, the parties may have regularly and consistently contracted in a manner which would be invalid in the case of a *single* contract and, again, the issue is whether their previous dealings may validate the invalid usage once it is disputed. It is clear that the court may infer that one party has notice of the exclusion clause from a lengthy and consistent course of dealing between the parties even though the normal steps for incorporation have not been followed.[4]

A variation of this principle occurs where both parties are in the same trade or business and may be held to contract on the shared understanding that the standard terms of the business in question are applicable even though they may not be referred to at the time of contract. This principle does not seem to depend on any consistency of dealing and can thus apply to a single contract entered into between businessmen, particularly where they have equality of bargaining power and the terms are reasonable and prevalent in the trade which is involved.[5]

Clause is incorporated but is subject to an overriding oral undertaking or a collateral contract

Even though an exclusion clause is incorporated in the contract, it may be overridden by an express, inconsistent undertaking which is given before, or at

---

2 *Olley v Marlborough Court Ltd* [1949] 1 KB 532.
3 *Chapelton v Barry UDC* [1940] 1 KB 532; *McCutcheon v David MacBrayne Ltd* [1964] 1 WLR 125; *Burnett v Westminster Bank Ltd* [1966] 1 QB 742.
4 See *Spurling (J) Ltd v Bradshaw* [1956] 1 WLR 461(exclusion clause held to be binding when sent consistently to the other party *after* the contract's formation); *Henry Kendall & Sons v William Lillico & Sons Ltd* [1969] 2 AC 31 (oral contract consistently followed by a 'contract note' with exclusion clauses (approximately 100 notes over three years) was held to be binding; see p 113 per Lord Pearce; Cf *Hollier v Rambler Motors (AMC) Ltd* [1972] 2 QB 71 (inconsistent course of dealing (three or four transactions in five years) in a *consumer's* dealings with a garage).
5 See *British Crane Hire Corpn Ltd v Ipswich Plant Hire Ltd* [1975] QB 303; *Chevron International Oil Co Ltd v A/S Sea Team* [1983] 2 Lloyd's Rep 356.

the time the contract is concluded. In *Couchman v Hill*,[6] the written conditions of an auction sale provided that lots were sold 'with all faults, imperfections and errors of description' but, at the time of the sale, B asked both S and the auctioneer if the heifer to be sold was unserved. He received an answer in the affirmative and an overriding collateral warranty was held to exist, the breach of which entitled B to damages.[7] It is debatable how exact the oral promise or collateral contract must be but it seems that only 'an express and specific oral promise'[8] will suffice.

How relevant are the common law rules of incorporation after the UCTA and the UTCCR?

There is still much vigour in the common law principles outlined above. Apart from specific cases where exclusion clauses are rendered ineffective, the statutory controls on exclusion clauses relate to their interpretation as an integral part of the contract whereas the common law hurdles placed in the path of such clauses may prevent their incorporation as contract terms.

The decision in *Interfoto Picture Library Ltd v Stiletto Visual Progammes Ltd*[9] heralded a renaissance of common law powers in establishing that an unusual or onerous condition had to be specifically drawn to the other party's attention. There a clause in a contract of hire which attempted to impose a charge of £5 per day for photographic transparencies retained for more than 14 days (£3.50 per transparency per week would have been reasonable) was held to be ineffective on the basis that the plaintiffs had failed to take adequate steps to draw such a burdensome condition to the defendant's attention.

Interfoto has been followed recently in *AEG (UK) Ltd v Logic Resource Ltd*.[10] There S sold cathode ray tubes to B who exported them to his customer in Iran. S's order-confirmation form stated, on its reverse, that all orders were subject to S's conditions of sale, a copy of which was available on request. Condition 7 in the full conditions excluded the implied terms in the SGA, ss 13-15 and provided, in lieu, a limited guarantee covering faulty parts and bad workmanship. Condition 7.5 provided that B should return any defective parts at his own expense but B had not requested a copy of the conditions and condition 7.5 had not been specifically drawn to his attention. The goods were faulty and were returned to S, the dispute centring upon whether B was liable for the cost of their return. The Court of Appeal held that it was quite possible to incorporate contract terms by reference to other documents but only insofar as the terms were usual or standard in the business in question. Condition 7.5 was held to be extremely onerous and unusual and, in the absence of specific notice to B, it had not been incorporated in the contract and thus did not bind him.

It seems undeniable that *AEG* is generous in its approach to 'onerous' clauses as condition 7 is, arguably, not an *unusual* clause to find in the sale of goods. In *AEG*, Hobhouse LJ considered that *Interfoto* applied only to clauses of an unusual

---

6 [1947] KB 554.
7 See also *Webster v Higgin* [1948] 2 All ER 127; *Harling v Eddy* [1951] 2 KB 739; *Mendelssohn v Normand Ltd* [1970] 1 QB 177 .
8 *George Mitchell (Chesterhall) Ltd v Finney Lock Seeds Ltd* [1983] 1 QB 284, 309 per Kerr LJ (explaining *Evans (J) & Son (Portsmouth) Ltd v Andrea Merzario Ltd* [1976] 1 WLR 1078); *Wake v Renault (UK) Ltd* (1996) Times, 1 August.
9 [1989] QB 433.
10 [1996] CLC 265.

or onerous *type* and condition 7 was usual to the extent that the SGA implied terms were excluded in a business sale and replaced by a limited guarantee. Accordingly, he considered that the material issue was whether the clause was *unreasonable* under the UCTA and that the statutory test of reasonableness provided the legitimate means by which to invalidate the clause rather than doing so by extending the common law rules relating to incorporation. All three judges in the Court of Appeal considered that condition 7.5 failed the the UCTA test of reasonableness. It remains to be seen whether the *Interfoto* reasoning will be limited to clauses which are unusual in *type* or broadened to include those which, although usual in type, are onerous in *content*. Certainly Bingham LJ's judgment in *Interfoto* was premised on broad notions of good faith and, patently, there is no good reason to fetter those principles. A normal type of clause may nevertheless contain extremely harsh conditions and, indeed, this is arguably one good reason to demand that it be accentuated for, otherwise, it might be possible to disguise swingeing, unfair provisions within apparently normal and fair contract terms.[11]

INTERPRETATION OF EXCLUSION CLAUSES AT COMMON LAW

Although an exclusion clause may cross the hurdles of incorporation and become integrated as a term of the contract, the common law insists that such clauses must be expressed unambiguously and adopts a strict interpretation *contra proferentem*. Prior to the inception of statutory controls on exclusion clauses, there were numerous examples of such exacting interpretation. In *Ernest Beck & Co v K Szymanowski & Co*,[12] S sold sewing cotton to B, the length on each reel being stated as '200 yards' but the contract contained the following stipulation:

> 'The goods delivered shall be deemed to be in all respects in accordance with the contract, and the buyer shall be bound to accept and pay for the same accordingly unless the sellers shall within fourteen days after arrival of the goods at their destination receive from the buyers notice of any matter or thing by reason whereof they may allege that the goods are not in accordance with the contract.'

B discovered that the reels only contained 188 yards of cotton 18 months later and he then sued for damages. The Court of Appeal[13] held that the clause purported to limit B's right of rejection but did not affect a claim for damages but the House of Lords went further in stipulating that the clause related only to matters of *quality* and did not apply to a claim in damages for goods which had *not* been delivered.[14] Equally rigorous interpretation was employed in *Wallis,*

---

11 See also the observations of Ratee J in *Nutting v Baldwin* [1995] 2 All ER 321, 329 where the *Interfoto* condition was characterised as 'an unusual term included in usual terms in a contract'.
12 [1924] AC 43.
13 [1923] 1 KB 457.
14 See also *Minister of Materials v Steel Bros & Co Ltd* [1952] 1 All ER 522 (in a contract for the sale of rubber, a clause limited B's right to complain of defects in quality to a period of 60 days after discharge of the goods. The goods were damaged as a consequence of defective *packing*. Held that the defect complained of did not relate to *quality* within the terms of the exclusion clause; Cf *Niblett Ltd v Confectioners' Materials Co Ltd* [1921] 3 KB 387; see Ch 20); *Vsesojwzoje Objedinenije Exportles v T W Allen & Sons Ltd* [1938] 3 All ER 375 (clause that no claim for 'quality and/or condition' of timber would be entertained unless made within 14 days after discharge of the goods. Held that faulty *manufacture* was not a question of quality or condition within the clause).

Son & Wells v Pratt & Haynes[15] where, in a contract for the sale of seed, a clause providing that S gave 'no warranty express or implied as to growth, description, or any other matters' did not absolve him from liability for breach of *condition*.[16] Likewise, in *Andrews Bros (Bournemouth) Ltd v Singer & Co Ltd*,[17] a clause protecting S from liability for breach of implied conditions and warranties in a contract for the sale of a car could not protect him from breach of an *express* term of the contract when he delivered a used car to B instead of a new one.

Statutory restrictions in the UCTA now confine dramatically the ability to exclude liability for negligence but, where it is permissible to attempt an exclusion of such liability, particularly clear wording is needed as it is 'inherently improbable'[18] that one party would release the other from the consequences of his negligence. A distinction has been drawn in the cases between those situations (i) where the defendant might be liable on some ground *other* than negligence, in which case the clause will not normally be construed as extending to, and excluding liability for, negligence[19] and (ii) where the defendant can be liable *only* in negligence, in which case the clause might be interpreted as excluding liability for negligence.[20] These cases are of limited utility in the sale of goods and the UCTA controls the exclusion of liability for negligence but, in those situations where the UCTA does not apply and S could be liable in tort (eg in a sale of harmful chemicals), the decisions are still pertinent.

The interpretation of limitation clauses

It is apparent that the courts used somewhat artificial methods of interpretation to abrogate what were thought to be unreasonably broad and unfair exclusion clauses. However, after the enactment of the UCTA a wide range of exclusion clauses became subject to a test of reasonableness and the courts consequently emphasised that unecessary artifice in interpretation should be avoided and 'one must not strive to create ambiguities by strained construction ... the relevant words must be given, if possible, their natural, plain meaning'.[1] In the decision of the House of Lords in *Photo Production Ltd v Securicor Transport Ltd*,[2] the freedom of parties who bargained on equal terms to formulate their own contract and allocate their own risks was re-asserted to a remarkable extent and this theme was sustained in the decision in *Ailsa Craig Fishing Co Ltd v Malvern Fishing*

15 [1911] AC 394.
16 See also *Baldry v Marshall* [1925] 1 KB 260 (clause in the contract excluded any 'guarantee or warranty, statutory or otherwise'. Held that S's breach of the SGA, s 14 was a breach of a condition and his liability was not excluded by the clause); *Henry Kendall & Sons v William Lillico & Sons Ltd* [1969] 2 AC 31 (clause that 'the goods are not warranted free from defect' did not cover breaches of condition).
17 [1934] 1 KB 17 .
18 *Gillespie Bros & Co Ltd v Roy Bowles Transport Ltd* [1973] QB 400, 419 per Buckley LJ.
19 *Alderslade v Hendon Laundry Ltd* [1945] KB 189; *Canada Steamship Lines Ltd v R* [1952] AC 192; *White v John Warwick & Co Ltd* [1953] 1 WLR 1285 (plaintiff (P) hired a bicycle from the defendant (D), the exclusion clause purporting to exclude liability for personal injury. The saddle tilted forward while P was riding the bicycle and he was injured. Held the clause exempted D from liability in contract but not for liability in negligence).
20 Even so, a very strict interpretation is made, see *Hollier v Rambler Motors (AMC) Ltd* [1972] 2 QB 71.
 1 *Ailsa Craig Fishing Co Ltd v Malvern Fishing Co Ltd* [1983] 1 WLR 964, 966 per Lord Wilberforce.
 2 [1980] AC 827.

Co Ltd.[3] There the House of Lords stated that an interpretation *contra proferentem* was not applicable in its 'full rigour'[4] to limitation clauses (eg a clause limiting liability to damages not exceeding a specific amount or a maximum, calculable sum). The House considered that, while there was an inherent improbability that the innocent party would agree to an exclusion of the other party's liability, there was 'no such high degree of improbability'[5] in his assenting to a limitation of liability. Limitation clauses were thus not to be treated with the 'same hostility'[6] as exclusion clauses and 'must be related to other contractual terms, in particular to the risks to which the defending party may be exposed, the remuneration which he receives, and possibly also the opportunity of the other party to insure'.[7]

While appearing superficially logical, it is suggested that this cleft between exclusion clauses and limitation clauses is not sustainable either in practice or principle. In practical terms, it may be very difficult to separate an exclusion of liability from a clause limiting liability in a contract[8] and, likewise, it is difficult to ascertain precisely which clauses are to be regarded as limitation clauses, eg it is unclear whether a clause imposing a time-limit on claims is to be interpreted leniently. As a matter of principle, it takes little imagination to realise that a clause which drastically limits liability to a trifling sum of money is, in all but name, an effective exclusion of liability. The distinction between the two types of clause was endorsed, nevertheless, in *George Mitchell (Chesterhall) Ltd v Finney Lock Seeds Ltd*,[9] where, on its true construction, the clause was held to limit the liability of S to less than 1% of the loss actually sustained by B (although it was held not to be fair or reasonable to allow S to rely on the clause under the statutory provision which was the forerunner of the UCTA (see below). The *Ailsa Craig* reasoning has, however, been rejected by the High Court of Australia[10] which stressed that both limitation and exclusion clauses were to be interpreted according to their natural and ordinary meaning while construing the clauses *contra proferentem* in cases of ambiguity.

The doctrine of fundamental breach of contract

After the Second World War, the courts developed the concept that certain breaches of contract were so serious and fundamental that exclusion clauses could

---

3 [1983] 1 WLR 964.
4 [1983] 1 WLR 964 at 970, per Lord Fraser of Tullybelton.
5 [1983] 1 WLR 964 at 970, per Lord Fraser of Tullybelton.
6 [1983] 1 WLR 964 at 966, per Lord Wilberforce.
7 [1983] 1 WLR 964 at 966, per Lord Wilberforce; see also the justification of Wright Ct J in the USA decision in *Tessler Bros (BC) Ltd v Italpacific Line and Matson Terminals Inc* [1975] 1 Lloyd's Rep 210, 213: 'This distinction between a limitation on liability and an exemption from liability is crucial A limitation, unlike an exemption, does not induce negligence'.
8 Eg consider the clause in *Pollock (W & S) & Co v Macrae* 1922 SC (HL) 192 where, in a contract to manufacture and install marine engines, a twelve month guarantee for defective parts was followed by the clause 'Apart from the above guarantee the works sell their engines under the condition that they are free from any claims arising through the breakdown of any parts or stoppages of the engines, or from any consequential damages arising from same, direct or indirect'. The House of Lords held that the clause was inapplicable to a congeries of defects which destroyed the workable character of the machine.
9 [1983] 2 AC 803; see Lord Denning MR's criticism of the distinction between exclusion and limitation clauses in the CA: [1983] QB 284, 301.
10 *Darlington Futures Ltd v Delco Australia Pty Ltd* (1986) 161 CLR 500.

not be construed as exonerating the defendant from liability for the consequences of such a breach. The modern fundamental breach doctrine as applied to exclusion clauses sought roots in earlier decisions such as *Chanter v Hopkins*,[11] where the celebrated observation of Lord Abinger CB was that 'if a man offers to buy peas of another, and he sends him beans, he does not perform his contract … the contract is to sell peas, and if he sends him anything else in their stead, it is a non-performance of it'. In 1953, Devlin J[12] thus considered that the supply of pine logs under a contract to sell mahogany logs would be breach of a fundamental term, that being 'something which underlies the whole contract so that, if it is not complied with, the performance becomes something totally different from that which the contract contemplates'. The delivery of mahogany logs of inferior quality and quantity to those contracted for was held, however, not to be a breach of a fundamental term.

The fundamental breach doctrine was extremely effective as a consumer remedy in hire-purchase cases where seriously defective cars were tendered and, in many decisions, wide exclusion clauses purporting to excuse the breaches in question were held to be inoperative.[13] These decisions elevated the notion of fundamental breach into an uncompromising rule of law which *prevented* the application of exclusion clauses in cases of serious breach of contract, thereby adding a formidable weapon to the consumer's armoury. However, such a rule of law was difficult to justify other than in the most nebulous fashion that the weaker party had not truly consented to, or understood, the exclusion of liability or that such clauses were offensive as an abuse of dominant bargaining strength. Equally elusive was the metaphysical notion permeating some of the decisions that there was a definable nucleus of the contract which was beyond the reach of an exclusion clause. In *Karsales (Harrow) Ltd v Wallis*,[14] for example, the Court of Appeal accepted that a car which was in excellent condition when inspected but was incapable of self-propulsion when delivered, was not a car at all.[15] However, this sort of reasoning was incompatible with freely-negotiated contracts made between businesses where exclusion clauses were part of the bargained-for allocation of risks between the parties. In 1964, Pearson LJ took the view that the fundamental breach doctrine was 'not an independent rule of law imposed by the Court on the parties willy-nilly in disregard of their contractual intention. On the contrary it is a rule of construction based on the presumed intention of the contracting parties'.[16] At the first opportunity, in 1967, the House of Lords[17] pronounced that the fundamental breach doctrine amounted

---

11 (1838) 4 M & W 399, 404.
12 *Smeaton Hanscomb & Co Ltd v Sassoon I Setty Son & Co* [1953] 1 WLR 1468, 1470.
13 See eg *Karsales (Harrow) Ltd v Wallis* [1956] 1 WLR 936; *Yeoman Credit Ltd v Apps* [1962] 2 QB 508; *Charterhouse Credit Co Ltd v Tolly* [1963] 2 QB 683.
14 [1956] 1 WLR 936.
15 See [1956] 1 WLR 936, per Birkett LJ at p 942: '… in the true meaning of words a car that would not go was not a car at all'; per Parker LJ at p 943: '… the vehicle delivered in effect is not properly described … as a motor vehicle'. See also *George Mitchell (Chesterhall) Ltd v Finney Lock Seeds Ltd* [1983] 2 AC 803, 813 per Lord Bridge of Harwich. When are goods so defective that there is a difference in substance between the goods promised by S and those which are actually delivered?
16 *UGS Finance Ltd v National Mortgage Bank of Greece and National Bank of Greece* [1964] 1 Lloyd's Rep 446, 453.
17 *Suisse Atlantique Société d'Armement Maritime SA v NV Rotterdamsche Kolen Centrale* [1967] 1 AC 361.

to a rule of construction only and that liability for such a breach could thus be excluded by a lucid clause. Nevertheless, for at least a decade after the House of Lords ruling, several important decisions paid lip-service to the rule of construction while, in effect, applying the rule of law[18] and, by 1976, the latter rule was largely reinstated.[19]

The House of Lords had a second bite of the cherry in 1980 and, in *Photo Production Ltd v Securicor Transport Ltd*,[20] the House clearly resolved to eradicate the fundamental breach doctrine as a rule of law, albeit on the singularly inappropriate facts of the *Photo Production* case.[1] The defendant security firm provided a night patrol service for the plaintiff's factory but one of the defendant's employees deliberately started a fire in the plaintiff's premises (for which he was sentenced to three years' imprisonment) which occasioned a loss to the plaintiff of £615,000. The defendant's standard conditions provided that 'under no circumstances shall the company be responsible for any injurious act or default by any employee' and a sub-clause specifically excluded liability for 'burglary, theft, fire or any other cause'. The House of Lords held (reversing the Court of Appeal[2]) that the fundamental breach doctrine was a rule of construction only and, as the wording of the exclusion clause was clear, its true construction was that it covered deliberate acts as well as negligence so that the defendants were exempted from liability. The House emphasised that the contract was made between businesses of equal bargaining power and that such parties should be free to apportion the risks in their contract. The Law Lords pointed out that there was thus no need for the 'superimposition of a judicially invented rule of law'[3] and that, in commercial contracts negotiated between businessmen capable of looking after their own interests it was 'wrong to place a strained construction upon words in an exclusion clause which are clear and fairly susceptible of one meaning only'.[4] Although the facts of *Photo Production* occurred before the enactment of the UCTA 1977, at the date of the decision the House of Lords underlined the fact that the inception of statutory control of exclusion clauses meant that the fundamental breach doctrine had outlived its usefulness.

If any doubts lingered as to the existence of the fundamental breach doctrine as a rule of law, they were expunged by the decision of the House of Lords in *George Mitchell (Chesterhall) Ltd v Finney Lock Seeds Ltd*.[5] There B, a farmer, ordered a quantity of 'Finney's Late Dutch Special' cabbage seed (a Winter cabbage seed) and was supplied with (inferior) Autumn cabbage seed which, although it germinated and grew, was commercially useless and had to be ploughed in. The cost of the seed was £201.60 and the loss to B was over £61,000. S relied on the conditions of sale which purported to limit his liability to replacement of the seed or a refund of the price paid and also excluded any express or implied conditions or warranties, statutory or otherwise. At first instance,[6]

---

18 See *Harbutt's Plasticine Ltd v Wayne Tank and Pump Co Ltd* [1970] 1 QB 447; *Farnworth Finance Facilities Ltd v Attryde* [1970] 1 WLR 1053; *Mendelssohn v Normand Ltd* [1970] 1 QB 177.
19 See *Wathes (Western) Ltd v Austin's (Menswear) Ltd* [1976] 1 Lloyd's Rep 14.
20 [1980] AC 827.
 1 See Schofield, 'Fundamental Breach – is it really an obituary?' [1981] JBL 49.
 2 [1978] 1 WLR 856.
 3 [1980] AC 827, 843 per Lord Wilberforce.
 4 [1980] AC 827 at 851, per Lord Diplock.
 5 [1983] 2 AC 803.
 6 [1981] 1 Lloyd's Rep 476.

Parker J held that it would make commercial nonsense of the contract to suggest that either party intended the exclusion clause to operate where what was delivered was wholly different in kind from what had been ordered and, in the Court of Appeal, Oliver LJ agreed with this conclusion. In the House of Lords, Lord Bridge of Harwich stressed that this approach came 'dangerously near to re-introducing by the back door the doctrine of "fundamental breach" which this House in *Securicor 1*[7] ... had so forcibly evicted by the front'.[8] The House held that the clause was unenforceable under the SGA, s 55(4)[9] in that it was not fair or reasonable to allow reliance on it but the decision undoubtedly confirmed that *Photo Production* effectively eradicated the fundamental breach doctrine as a substantive rule of law in cases where the parties are businessmen having equality of bargaining power[10] and the clause is clear and unambiguous.[11]

Today, where the UCTA applies, an exclusion clause which seeks to exclude or restrict liability for a fundamental breach is either subjected to the reasonableness test or rendered ineffective in a consumer sale. The facts of *Photo Production* would thus fall within the UCTA, s 3 and those of *George Mitchell* within the UCTA, s 6(3). As mentioned earlier, the controls in the UCTA mean that the rule of law approach is obsolete but this conclusion is reinforced by the UCTA, s 9(1) which provides that the exclusion clause may satisfy the reasonableness test even though the contract has been terminated by breach. Section 9(2) similarly emphasises that, where a contract is affirmed after a breach, the affirmation will not prevent the application of the reasonableness test.

It remains to be seen whether the epitaph of the fundamental breach doctrine has been carved in stone. It is suggested that the doctrine of fundamental breach may still be relevant in consumer contracts where there is clear disparity of bargaining power but, of course, the statutory control of exclusion clauses means that it is largely unnecessary to have recourse to that doctrine. Certainly the notion of the fundamental term is still invoked in order to avoid what might otherwise be a trap for consumers.[12] Consumer cases apart, it is clear that commercial parties are free to exclude the consequences of a fundamental breach of contract by a suitably drafted clause, but there are arguably two intertwined fetters on this freedom. First, Lord Bridge of Harwich stressed in *George Mitchell*[13] that the facts of that case did not make it one of 'peas and beans' as in the *Chanter v Hopkins* example – the clause in *George Mitchell* referred to 'seeds' and seeds had been delivered. It is thus arguable that, as a question of

---

7   Shorthand for *Photo Production Ltd v Securicor Transport Ltd* [1980] AC 827.
8   [1983] 2 AC 803 at 813.
9   Inserted by the Supply of Goods (Implied Terms) Act 1973, s 4.
10   In the CA's decision in *George Mitchell*, Lord Denning MR mourned the passing of fundamental breach as a rule of law and said that such a bold approach had been 'too rude an interference with the idol of "freedom of contract"': [1983] QB 284, 298.
11   In *Glebe Island Terminals Pty Ltd v Continental Seagram Pty Ltd, The Antwerpen* [1994] 1 Lloyd's Rep 213, the New South Wales Court of Appeal held that Glebe Island (terminal operators) were protected by a clause expressly covering 'actions constituting a fundamental breach' even though they had connived in the theft of the defendant's containers of Chivas Regal Scotch whisky. Handley JA dissented on the basis that the exclusion clause rendered performance of the contract an 'illusory promise' (p 226). On the latter point, see *Tor Line AB v Alltrans Group of Canada Ltd* [1984] 1 WLR 48 (below).
12   See *Porter v General Guarantee Corpn Ltd* [1982] RTR 384 (in a hire-purchase contract, the supplier of a defective car was held to be in breach of a fundamental term which thus entitled the plaintiff to repudiate the contract, this approach circumventing the difficulty that, at that date, the car was probably of merchantable quality and fit for its purpose).
13   [1983] 2 AC 803 at 813.

construction, there is a presumption that a clause would not apply to the type of fundamental breach where beans are substituted for peas unless the wording of the clause is absolutely clear and unequivocal. Indeed, the *Suisse Atlantique*[14] decision had earlier subscribed to this view.[15] Second, it is indisputable that the exclusion clause cannot be worded in terms which render the consideration of one party illusory thereby emptying the contract of all content. In the *Photo Production* case, Lord Diplock considered that the 'parties are free to agree to whatever exclusion or modification of all types of obligations as they please within the limits that the agreement must retain the legal characteristics of a contract'.[16] This outer-limit on the deployment of exclusion clauses was illustrated in the recent decision of the House of Lords in *Tor Line AB v Alltrans Group of Canada Ltd*.[17] There a charter-party contained a detailed description of the ship which was to be chartered but the vessel supplied was not of the size specified and the charterer could not load a trailer with containers onto the main deck. The shipowners relied on clause 13 of the Baltime charter which specified in its second sentence that 'the owners not to be responsible in any other case nor for damage or delay whatsoever and howsoever caused even if caused by the neglect or default of their servants'. It was held that the clause did not apply to the eonomic loss suffered by the charterer. Lord Roskill emphasised that, if construed literally, the phrase 'in any other case' would mean that the owners 'would be under no liability if they never delivered the vessel at all ... or delivered a vessel of a totally different description'[18] and, if this approach were tolerated, the charter 'virtually ceases to be a contract for the letting of the vessel ... and becomes no more than a statement of intent'.[19] It is arguable that, *prima facie*, a clause which purports to allow beans to be substituted for peas is a prime example of such a statement of intent.

Statutory control of exclusion clauses

As outlined earlier, the common law had developed an extensive and powerful range of techniques for the avoidance of exclusion clauses but its potency was always subject to freedom of contract and it remained conspicuously unable to declare that a clause was unfair or unreasonable. Businessmen were quick to see the advantages of contracts of adhesion which were endowed with ample and effective exclusion clauses and this abuse of dominant bargaining power led to 'a bleak winter for our law of contract'.[20] Only legislation could curb the worst excesses of exclusion clauses and, when the Supply of Goods (Implied

14 *Suisse Atlantique Société d'Armement Maritime SA v NV Rotterdamsche Kolen Centrale* [1967] 1 AC 361, 398 and 432 per Lords Reid and Wilberforce respectively.
15 On the difficulties of the 'peas and beans' approach as a question of construction and interpretation, see Yates and Hawkins, *Standard Business Contracts: Exclusions and Related Devices* (1986), para 10B(3); Devlin, 'The Treatment of Breach of Contract' [1966] CLJ 192, 210-212.
16 [1980] AC 827, 850; see also *Firestone Tyre Co v Vokins* [1951] 1 Lloyd's Rep 32, 38-39 per Devlin J.
17 [1984] 1 WLR 48.
18 [1984] 1 WLR 48 at 54.
19 [1984] 1 WLR 48 at 58-59.
20 *George Mitchell (Chesterhall) Ltd v Finney Lock Seeds Ltd* [1983] QB 284, 297 per Lord Denning MR.

Terms) Act 1973 was implemented, the law moved 'out of winter into spring'.[1] The 1973 Act introduced statutory control of exclusion clauses in the sale of goods by placing restrictions on S's ability to contract-out of the terms implied by ss 12-15 of the SGA. Several dramatic techniques and concepts were utilised in the 1973 Act which changed the face of the law. First, a clause seeking to exempt S from the provisions of the SGA, s 12 (title) was rendered *void*, thus depriving such a clause of legal validity. Second, the vulnerability of the *consumer buyer* was recognised in that the 1973 Act also rendered void any term of the contract in a consumer sale which sought to exclude the implied terms contained in the SGA, ss 13-15. Finally, in non-consumer sales, the exclusion of the provisions in the SGA, ss 13-15 was impermissible to the extent that it could be shown that it was not *fair or reasonable* to allow reliance on the exclusion clause. Instead of performing 'gymnastic contortions'[2] to evade an exclusion clause, the courts were faced with the challenge of a test of reasonableness and, in other situations where protection for B was needed most, some exclusions of liability in the sale of goods were rendered void.

The overall pattern of the 1973 Act was followed in the Unfair Contract Terms Act 1977 (the UCTA) which also imposed controls on exclusion clauses in contracts other than those for the sale of goods and thus the law finally progressed 'out of spring into summer'.[3]

UNFAIR CONTRACT TERMS ACT 1977

A central difficulty of the UCTA is that it does not define an 'exclusion clause'. Most of the Act's provisions relate to excluding or restricting *liability* and thus apply to the typical exclusion clause which attempts to operate as a defence for breach of an obligation or duty. It is unclear how far the Act encroaches upon duty-defining or 'core shrinking' clauses which purport to exclude or restrict the relevant obligation (eg varying the obligations owed under the SGA, ss 13-15) or prevent a duty from arising in the first place (eg stipulating that no tortious duty of care is owed). Moreover, it may be extremely difficult to differentiate an exclusion clause proper from a core shrinking provision, as will be seen when this topic is discussed below. The provisions of the UCTA may be separated into several compartments in an attempt to clarify this complex statute.

PROVISIONS RELATING DIRECTLY TO THE SALE OF GOODS

The UCTA imposes stringent controls on S's ability to exclude or restrict the implied terms contained in the SGA, ss 12-15 and the Act employs three separate techniques, viz (i) a blanket prohibition on the exclusion or restriction of the implied condition as to title in the SGA, s 12; (ii) a prohibition on the exclusion or restriction in a consumer sale of the implied conditions in the SGA, ss 13-15; and (iii) the permissible exclusion or restriction of the implied conditions in the SGA, ss 13-15 in a non-consumer sale, subject to the test of reasonableness.

---

1 [1983] QB 284 at 298, per Lord Denning MR.
2 [1983] QB 284 at 299, per Lord Denning MR.
3 [1983] QB 284 at 298, per Lord Denning MR.

Prohibition of the exclusion or restriction of the SGA, s 12

The implied condition of title in the SGA, s 12 is regarded as underpinning the entire contract for the sale of goods and thus the UCTA, s 6(1)(a) provides that liability in respect of breach of s 12 '*cannot* be excluded or restricted by reference to any contract term'. This is virtually a blanket provision relating to all sales and, most importantly, it is *not* limited to 'business liability' (the UCTA, s 6(4)). It thus applies in a sale of goods between two private individuals neither of whom makes the contract in the course of a business but it does not apply to 'international supply contracts' (the UCTA, s 26). As discussed in Chapter 19, there is some difficulty reconciling this total prohibition in the UCTA with the provision in s 12 itself that S may transfer a limited interest in the goods and it may be difficult to distinguish a purported exclusion of s 12 from the attempted transfer of a limited title.

Prohibition of the exclusion or restriction of the SGA, ss 13-15 in consumer sales[4]

The strategy of the UCTA is to prohibit the exclusion or restriction of the SGA implied conditions relating to description, satisfactory quality, fitness for purpose and sale by sample (SGA, ss 13-15) in a consumer sale. Accordingly, the UCTA, s 6(2) provides that 'as against a person dealing as consumer', liability for breach of the obligations arising from ss 13-15 of the SGA 'cannot be excluded or restricted by reference to any contract term'.[5] The ability to differentiate a consumer sale from a business sale is clearly crucial and the definition of 'dealing as consumer' is found in the UCTA, s 12 which provides:

'(1) A party to a contract "deals as consumer" in relation to another party if–
(a) he neither makes the contract in the course of a business nor holds himself out as doing so; and
(b) the other party does make the contract in the course of a business; and
(c) in the case of a contract governed by the law of sale of goods ... the goods passing under or in pursuance of the contract are of a type ordinarily supplied for private use or consumption.
(2) But on a sale by auction or competitive tender the buyer is not in any circumstances to be regarded as dealing as consumer.
(3) Subject to this, it is for those claiming that a party does not deal as consumer to show that he does not.'

There are two issues in s 12 which need further investigation: ascertainment of when one party 'makes the contract in the course of a business' and a definition of which goods are 'of a type ordinarily supplied for private use or consumption'.

Making the contract in the course of a business

It is this notion which is used to define simultaneously the business capacity and the consumer capacity – in order to satisfy the UCTA, s 12, one party must

---

4 See Brown, 'Business and Consumer Contracts' [1988] JBL 386; Pearce, 'Acting in the Course of a Business' [1989] LMCLQ 371.
5 It is also a criminal offence, in the course of a business, to purport to display notices and advertisements or use contract terms which are void by virtue of the UCTA: see the Consumer Transactions (Restrictions on Statements) Order 1976 (SI 1976/1813, as amended by SI 1978/27) and cases discussed below.

make the contract in the course of a business and the other party must not. In a sale of goods which are required for private use, made between a business seller and a private, consumer buyer, s 12 clearly prevents the business seller from excluding or restricting the SGA implied conditions in ss 13-15 and this contract is the paradigm for the operation of s 12. Although the precursor to s 12[6] was limited to sales by a business seller to a consumer buyer, there is no such limitation in s 12 and, technically, the section encompasses sales by a consumer to a business, as here the requirement is satisfied that *one* of the parties must make the contract in the course of a business. However, because the basic prohibition in the UCTA, s 6(2) applies only *'as against* a person dealing as consumer' and the operation of ss 6(2) and 12 is necessarily intertwined with the liability imposed by the SGA, ss 13-15, the ban imposed by ss 6(2) and 12 operates only in the case of a sale of consumer goods by a business seller to a consumer buyer.[7]

When does a party make the contract in the course of a business?

When S's liability under the SGA, s 14 was examined earlier in Chapter 20, the notion of the business sale was analysed and, as well as the discussion below, reference should be made to that earlier analysis. It will be remembered that S's liability for satisfactory quality and fitness for purpose under s 14 arises only if he 'sells goods in the course of a business' and that the modern tendency has been to interpret this phrase widely so as not to diminish B's protection.[8] The decision in *Stevenson v Rogers,*[9] has put the issue beyond doubt. There the Court of Appeal held that selling goods 'in the course of a business' must be construed broadly and at face value so that it is immaterial that the goods sold by S do not constitute the principal stock-in-trade of his business and, likewise, no regularity of dealing is required to bring S within s 14. Accordingly, in *Stevenson*, the seller was a fisherman who sold his fishing boat and, although he did not regularly sell fishing boats and his business was that of a fisherman, he nevertheless sold the boat 'in the course of a business' within s 14.

It is vital to emphasise that the *Stevenson* decision applies *only* to the SGA, s 14 and thus it has no effect on the decisions considered below. This means, as will be seen, that there is a fundamental incongruity between selling in the course

---

6 SGA 1893, s 55(7) (inserted by the Supply of Goods (Implied Terms) Act 1973, s 4).
7 The permutations can be collected: (i) **A consumer sells goods to a business**: the SGA, s 14 does not apply at all as this covers only cases where S sells goods 'in the course of a business'. The SGA, ss 13 and 15 do apply to private, consumer sellers but the UCTA, s 6(2) solves the problem as it applies only to exclusion/restriction *'as against'* a consumer. Thus, in a sale by a consumer to a business, the implied terms in ss 13 and 15 may be excluded subject to the test of reasonableness. (ii) **A consumer sells goods to another consumer**: the SGA, s 14 does not apply as there is no sale 'in the course of a business'. The SGA, ss 13 and 15 apply to private sales but s 12 solves the problem as *both* parties 'deal as consumer'. Thus, in a sale between two consumers, the SGA, ss 13 and 15 can be excluded subject to the test of reasonableness. (iii) **A business sells goods to another business**: the SGA, ss 13, 14 and 15 apply but this sale is outside the operation of the UCTA, ss 6(2) and 12 as *neither* party deals 'as consumer'. Thus, in a sale between two businesses, the SGA, ss 13-15 can be excluded subject to the test of reasonableness.
8 See *Ashington Piggeries Ltd v Christopher Hill Ltd* [1972] AC 441; *Spencer Trading Co Ltd v Devon* [1947] 1 All ER 284.
9 [1999] QB 1028.

of a business for the SGA, s 14 (where no regularity of dealing is required) and the buyer's making the contract in the course of a business under the UCTA, s 12 (where some regularity of dealing is required if B is to be regarded as making the contract in the course of a business).

There can arguably be no wider definition than that in the UCTA, s 12, of 'making the contract in the course of a business' and thus a person could, in principle, make the contract in the course of a business even though he does not regularly deal in the goods in question. This view is reinforced by the broad definition of 'business' in the UCTA, s 14 as including 'a profession and the activities of any government department or local or public authority'. It is apt that a wide definition be given to the business sale under the implied terms in the SGA, s 14 for, otherwise, B's protection under those terms becomes eroded. It is this point which is emphasised firmly in the *Stevenson* case, above. Under the UCTA, s 12, S's possible *exclusion* of the SGA implied terms is at issue and thus, as a matter of policy, it is again desirable to favour B's position and protect him from the use of exclusion clauses. Consider the position where a solicitor buys a light bulb or an electric fire for his office from a retail seller: here the solicitor undoubtedly 'makes the contract in the course of a business' and so it should arguably be permissible for S to exclude the SGA implied terms subject only to the requirement of reasonableness. But this would surely be unjust as here the solicitor has no greater knowledge or better bargaining power than if he had bought the light bulb or fire for use in his home, in which case he would certainly be regarded as a consumer for the purposes of s 12 and it would be impermissible for S to exclude the SGA implied terms. Injustice has been avoided thus far by following the approach taken in decisions on the Trade Descriptions Act 1968 in the context of the criminal offence of applying a false trade description 'in the course of a trade or business'.[10] The decisions stipulate that an offence is committed only where the transaction in question is either an integral part of the business or, if it is an ancillary activity, it must have been performed with a degree of *regularity*.[11] The leading decision regarding exclusion clauses and s 12 is *R & B Customs Brokers Co Ltd v United Dominions Trust Ltd*.[12] There the plaintiff company (B Ltd) was in the business of freight forwarding and shipping brokerage. One of its directors decided to buy a Colt Shogun car to be used for personal and company purposes, trading in an existing company car in part exchange. The car was bought in the company's name but it proved to be defective. The Court of Appeal held that B Ltd had not made the contract in the course of a business within the UCTA, s 12 as the purchase of the car was 'only incidental to the carrying on of the relevant business'[13] and, as this was only the second or third car bought by B

10 Trade Descriptions Act 1968, s 1(1).
11 See *Havering London Borough Council v Stevenson* [1970] 1 WLR 1375 (owner of a car hire business regularly sold the cars after two years' use. Held this was 'normal practice' and 'an integral part of the business' (p 1377, per Lord Parker CJ); *Davies v Sumner* [1984] 1 WLR 1301 (self-employed courier who used his own car to transport films for a television company sold it in part exchange for a new car but falsely represented the car's mileage. The House of Lords held that this sale did not have the requisite 'degree of regularity' (p 1305, per Lord Keith of Kinkel) to bring it within 'the course of a trade or business' in the Trade Descriptions Act 1968 s 1).
12 [1988] 1 WLR 321; see Brown, 'Business and Consumer Contracts' [1988] JBL 386.
13 [1988] 1 WLR 321 at 331, per Dillon LJ.

Ltd, the requisite degree of regularity was lacking.[14] In view of the broad wording of s 12, the decision in *R & B Customs* reaches an awkward yet desirable conclusion.

Finally, s 12(1)(a) provides that, in order to 'deal as consumer', the party in question must neither make the contract in the course of a business *nor hold himself out* as so doing. The question of holding-out was raised in *R & B Customs Brokers* in that there both the contract and the application for finance were made in the plaintiff company's name and full details of the company were given in the section of the application headed 'Business Details'. The Court of Appeal concluded that these facts did not constitute a holding-out but this conclusion seems untenable: it is patently arguable that these facts show that the contract was made in the course of a business but, if not, there was surely a holding-out that it was so made. Certainly where a contract is entered into in a corporate name and the cost of the goods is debited as a company expense or where a private individual pretends to be a business purchaser in order to obtain a trade discount, it is irrefutable that there would be sufficient evidence to establish a holding-out that the contract was made in the course of a business.

The goods are 'of a type ordinarily supplied for private use or consumption'

There is no authority regarding the interpretation of this somewhat enigmatic phrase in s 12. There is no requirement that the goods be exclusively for private use and so many multi-purpose goods could be supplied either for private or business use (eg cars, boats, furniture and food) and the legal position would be dependent upon whether the transaction fell within the business or consumer category, as already explained.

It is tolerably clear that the purpose of the words 'type' and 'ordinarily' is to exclude from the consumer category goods which are normally and regularly supplied exclusively for business use, eg a pantechnicon or a cement mixer. This leaves an indeterminate category of goods such as decorating materials (eg ceramic tiles or ladders) which were once regarded as trade goods but are now increasingly sold to consumers. There are serious difficulties, however, in deciding which 'type' of goods are ordinarily supplied for private use or consumption and whether the *size* of the transaction is relevant. Scotch whisky in a 70cl bottle is clearly a type of goods within the consumer category but would a consumer buyer who chose to buy a cask of whisky direct from a distillery obtain the protection of the UCTA, s 12? Once other facts are added to the illustrations above the position is clearer. Should the consumer buyer of the cask of whisky obtain a trade discount, for example, this might be regarded as a holding-out that he acts in the course of a business but this does not solve the difficulties of interpreting this part of s 12 in isolation.

---

14   See also *Rasbora Ltd v JCL Marine Ltd* [1977] 1 Lloyd's Rep 645 (the defendant boatbuilders agreed to build a power boat for the individual who controlled Rasbora Ltd (R Ltd). R Ltd was then substituted as buyer, the purpose of this transaction being to avoid payment of VAT. The boat sank on her maiden voyage. Lawson J held that (i) the original sale was a consumer sale within the SGA 1893, s 55(7) (ii) the novation to R Ltd did not change the character of the sale to a business sale (iii) even if the original sale had been to R Ltd, it would have been a consumer sale as the boat was to be used by the majority shareholder and not chartered to third parties); *Peter Symmons & Co v Cook* (1981) 131 NLJ 758 (firm of surveyors who bought a Rolls Royce car to be used only on special occasions was held to be a consumer buyer).

The UCTA, s 12 and agency difficulties

There is no provision in s 12 concerning contracts entered into by agents, the obvious difficulty being the situation where a business agent sells goods on behalf of a consumer/principal. Normal agency reasoning demands that the principal is liable and, for example, where a consumer buys goods from a business agent who is acting for a consumer/principal, the consumer buyer could be misled into assuming that he has the protection of the UCTA, ss 6 and 12 when, in fact, it seems that he does not. It was for this reason that the SGA, s 14(5)[15] was enacted (viz, the provisions of s 14 apply to a sale in the course of a business by an agent acting for a private seller unless the buyer knows, or reasonable steps have been taken to inform him, that the seller is private seller) but s 14(5) applies only to 'the preceding provisons' of the section and cannot be extended to the UCTA, s 12. If the business agent sells goods on behalf of an *undisclosed* consumer/principal, the normal rules of agency stipulate that the contract is formed with the agent and so it would clearly be made in the course of a business, thereby affording the protection of the UCTA, ss 6 and 12 to the consumer buyer who deals with the business agent.

Exclusion or restriction of the SGA, ss 13-15 in non-consumer sales

In relation to *non-consumer sales*, a contract term purporting to exempt the seller from all or any of the provisions in ss 13–15 of the Sale of Goods Act is not automatically void. The UCTA, s 6(3) provides:

'As against a person dealing otherwise than as consumer, the liability specified in subsection (2) above can be excluded or restricted by reference to a contract term, but only in so far as the term satisfies the requirement of reasonableness.'

The reasonableness requirement in relation to the exclusion, by a contract term, of the SGA, ss 13-15 in non-consumer sales, is found in the UCTA, s 11(1) and (2). Section 11(1) specifies:

'In relation to a contract term, the requirement of reasonableness for the purposes of this Part of this Act ... is that the term shall have been a fair and reasonable one to be included having regard to the circumstances which were, or ought reasonably to have been, known to or in the contemplation of the parties when the contract was made.'

It is important to stress the *time* at which the term must be assessed in order to ascertain whether it is 'fair and reasonable': under s 11(1) the term must have been a fair and reasonable one *to be included in the contract*. The statutory provisions which were the forerunner of the UCTA[16] provided that the test was whether it was reasonable *to allow reliance* on the term and the difference between these two tests is a significant one. In *Stewart Gill Ltd v Horatio Myer & Co Ltd*,[17] the Court of Appeal stressed that, under s 11(1), the term itself must pass the reasonableness test and that, consequently, it must be evaluated as a whole meaning that there can be no severance of the unreasonable parts of the

---

15 See Ch 20.
16 Prior to the UCTA, see the SGA 1893 s 55, as inserted by the Supply of Goods (Implied Terms) Act 1973, s 4 .
17 [1992] QB 600; see Brown and Chandler, 'Unreasonableness and The Unfair Contract Terms Act' (1993) 109 LQR 41.

clause in order to render the remainder reasonable. The moral for draftsmen is thus to separate omnibus clauses into their component parts. The test imposed by s 11(1) is clearly a strict one and, as the courts have to assess reasonableness at the time of contract, they are placed in the difficult position of having to consider the range of possible breaches of contract which could occur without considering the breach which *has* occurred.[18]

The application of the reasonableness test

The central question as to how the reasonableness test is applied must now be considered. The UCTA, s 11(2) provides:

'In determining for the purposes of section 6 or 7 above whether a contract term satisfies the requirement of reasonableness, regard shall be had in particular to the matters specified in Schedule 2 to this Act; but this subsection does not prevent the court or arbitrator from holding, in accordance with any rule of law, that a term which purports to exclude or restrict any relevant liability is not a term of the contract.'

The 'guidelines' in the UCTA, Sch 2 are thus paricularly important and show the balancing act which the court must perform in assessing reasonableness. It will be noticed that the guidelines apply only to sale and supply of goods under ss 6 and 7. The guidelines appeared in virtually the same form in the forerunner to the UCTA[19] but the Law Commissions had not intended that they be incorporated in any Act and, by the time of the report which led to the UCTA, it was thought that guidelines might be misleading in that they could never be comprehensive.[20] Accordingly, the list was not augmented in content or ambit in the UCTA. In fact, the guidelines appear to have been helpful and have been regarded as relevant to the other provisions of the UCTA.[1] Schedule 2 provides:

The matters to which regard is to be had, in particular for the purposes of section 6 (3) ... are any of the following which appear to be relevant –

(a) the strength of the bargaining positions of the parties relative to each other, taking into account (among other things) alternative means by which the customer's requirements could have been met;

(b) whether the customer received an inducement to agree to the term, or in accepting it had an opportunity of entering into a similar contract with other persons, but without having to accept a similar term;

(c) whether the customer knew or ought reasonably to have known of the existence and extent of the term (having regard, among other things, to any custom of the trade and any previous course of dealing between the parties);

(d) where the term excludes or restricts any relevant liability if some condition is not complied with, whether it was reasonable at the time of the contract to expect that compliance with that condition would be practicable;

(e) whether the goods were manufactured, processed or adapted to the special order of the customer.

---

18 See Adams and Brownsword, 'The Unfair Contract Terms Act: A Decade of Discretion' (1988) 104 LQR 94, 114-118.

19 See the SGA 1893, s 55(5).

20 See *Exemption Clauses, Second Report* (Law Com No 69, Scot Law Com No 39, 1975), paras 184-196.

 1 See *Singer Co (UK) Ltd v Tees and Hartlepool Port Authority* [1988] 2 Lloyd's Rep 164, 169 per Steyn J; *Flamar Interocean Ltd v Denmac Ltd, The Flamar Pride and Flamar Progress* [1990] 1 Lloyd's Rep 434, 438-439 per Potter J.

Section 11(4) should be emphasised in that it relates to the situation where 'by reference to a contract term or notice' a person 'seeks to restrict liability to a specified sum of money'. Section 11(4) provides that, in deciding whether the term or notice satisfies the requirement of reasonableness, 'regard shall be had in particular ... to (a) the resources which he could expect to have available to him for the purpose of meeting the liability should it arise; and (b) how far it was open to him to cover himself by insurance'.

Finally and very importantly, s 11(5) provides for the burden of proof: it is for those claiming that a contract term or notice satisfies the requirement of reasonableness to show that it does.

Decisions regarding the reasonableness test

Decisions on the reasonableness test are still comparatively rare. *George Mitchell (Chesterhall) Ltd v Finney Lock Seeds Ltd*[2] is an important decision of the House of Lords but it should be stressed that the case did not concern the UCTA but applied the earlier controls on exclusion clauses in the SGA, the most important difference being that, as mentioned earlier, under the old provisions the time for judging reasonableness was at the date of *breach*. The facts of *George Mitchell* were considered earlier and it will be recalled that seed merchants (S) sold late cabbage seed to farmers (B) on terms which purported to limit the liability of S, should the seed prove to be defective, to replacing the defective seed or refunding the purchase price (£201.60). The seed delivered was not late cabbage seed at all and the crop planted by B was a failure resulting in a loss of £61,000. The House of Lords held that, on its true construction, the limitation clause did apply to the facts *but* that it would not be fair or reasonable to permit S to rely on the clause which was, accordingly, unenforceable. In reaching this conclusion, the House attempted to balance several factors. *In S's favour*: (i) B knew of, and understood, the conditions and had dealt with S for many years; similarly, the damages claimed were out of proportion to the price of the seed. *In B's favour*: (ii) a similar limitation of liability was universally embodied in contracts between seedsmen and farmers which had never been negotiated between representative bodies but, equally, had not been the subject of protest; certainly B had no opportunity to buy seeds without the limitation; (iii) S had been negligent in supplying the wrong seed; (iv) S could insure against the risk of crop failure without materially increasing the cost of seeds; (v) S admitted that their practice had always been to negotiate settlements of claims and this indicated, decisively, that S considered that reliance on the limitation clause was not fair or reasonable. It must be asked how the position in *George Mitchell* might differ under the UCTA. In deciding the question of reasonable reliance, the House was able to 'entertain a whole range of considerations, put them in the scales ... and decide at the end of the day on which side the balance comes down'.[3] This meant that events at the date of breach could be considered, eg S was negligent in supplying the seed; the fact and extent of the crop's failure. The extent of the crop's failure points up one crucial difference between the old and new law: in the case of a trifling failure/loss it might be reasonable, under the old law, for S to *rely* on the clause but, under the UCTA test the minimal loss could not be considered and, consequently, it might well be unreasonable to *include* the clause in the contract.

---

2 [1983] 2 AC 803.
3 [1983] 2 AC 803 at 816 per Lord Bridge of Harwich.

By the same token, if it is decided that the clause was a reasonable one to include in the contract, it cannot be impugned by the size of the subsequent loss.

The facts of *Green (R W) Ltd v Cade Bros Farms*,[4] provide an instructive contrast with *George Mitchell*. S, a seed potato merchant, sold 'uncertified' seed potatoes to B, a farmer with a substantial farming business. The contract sought to limit S's liability to repayment of the price and required B to give notice of 'rejection, claim or complaint' within three days of delivery of the seed potatoes. The potatoes were planted and it subsequently materialised that they were infected with a virus which could not be detected by looking at the seeds but which became obvious when the potatoes started to grow. Crucial differences between the *George Mitchell* facts and those of *Cade* were that, in the latter case, the potatoes were 'uncertified' and so cheaper than 'certified' potatoes which were guaranteed free from the virus and, also, S had not been negligent. Applying the pre-UCTA test, Griffiths J held that the clause limiting S's liability to repayment of the price was reasonable in relation to both patent and latent defects as S and B were businessmen with equal bargaining power and S's conditions were based upon the long-standing, standard form conditions of the national trade association. As such, they were 'not conditions imposed by the strong upon the weak'[5] but were the terms upon which both S and B were content to do business. On the other hand, the judge held the three day time limit on claims to be unreasonable[6] as regards latent defects which could not possibly be discovered until the potatoes began growing.[7] The same conclusion would almost certainly be reached under the UCTA criterion that it must be fair and reasonable to include the term in the contract.

There are now decisions on the UCTA reasonableness test and, although few concern the sale of goods, they are important nevertheless. In *The Zinnia*,[8] Staughton J considered that a provision would be unreasonable in a ship repair contract if, in the case of defective repairs, it required the vessel to be returned to the yard where it had been repaired. He thought that, having regard to the UCTA Sch 2, para (d), the result of the clause would be 'capricious ... [as] the apportionment of risk is made to depend upon where a casualty happens to occur'.[9] In the same case, he also expressed the view that the conditions could be unreasonable if they were 'convoluted and prolix' and in such small print that they could barely be read or understood.[10]

In *Smith v Eric S Bush*,[11] the House of Lords held that a disclaimer of liability for negligence in a surveyor's report shown to a house buyer failed the reasonableness test (the test for *non-contractual* notices, under the UCTA, s 11(3), is whether it is reasonable to *rely* on the clause having regard to the circumstances

---

4 [1978] 1 Lloyd's Rep 602.

5 [1978] 1 Lloyd's Rep 602 at 607, per Griffiths J.

6 It is clear that, after *Stewart Gill Ltd v Horatio Myer & Co Ltd* [1992] QB 600, it is not possible, under the UCTA, to sever the clause into reasonable and unreasonable parts in this way. The *Cade* analysis turns upon reasonable *reliance* where severance was (more) acceptable.

7 See also *Rees-Hough Ltd v Redland Reinforced Plastics Ltd* (1984) 2 Con LR 109 (in a sale of piping, a provision excluding liability unless the supplier was notified of complaints within three months was held to be unreasonable under the UCTA).

8 *Stag Line Ltd v Tyne Shiprepair Group Ltd, The Zinnia* [1984] 2 Lloyd's Rep 211.

9 [1984] 2 Lloyd's Rep 211 at 223.

10 [1984] 2 Lloyd's Rep 211 at 222; in relation to sale of goods, see also the UCTA, Sch 2, para (c).

11 [1990] 1 AC 831.

when liability arose). Lord Griffiths considered that, in assessing reasonableness, it was 'impossible to draw up an exhaustive list of the factors that must be taken into account when a judge is faced with this very difficult decision'[12] but he posed the questions which should 'always be considered'[13] viz:

(1) Were the parties of equal bargaining power? Reasonableness is more easily discharged in a one-off contract between equals than where, as was the case in *Smith v Eric S Bush*, the disclaimer was imposed upon a purchaser who had no effective power to object.

(2) Would it have been possible to obtain the advice from an alternative source taking into account considerations of cost and time? On the facts it was considered unreasonable for a first-time buyer to find the extra resources for an independent survey. It also appeared that some building societies offered buyers the choice between a survey with liability and one without liability but the former was so costly that few buyers opted for it; Lord Templeman[14] seemed to doubt whether the additional charge could be justified and it may thus be a general rule that, where such alternatives are offered, the extra *charge* must be justifiable if the reasonablness test is to be met.

(3) How difficult is the task being undertaken for which liability is excluded? Where a difficult or dangerous undertaking was involved, the high risk of failure would be a pointer to the reasonableness of excluding liability. On the facts, the valuation presented no difficulty as the valuer was required to show only that basic degree of care and skill which the law demands and the work was at the lower end of the surveyor's field of expertise.

(4) What are the practical consequences of the decision on the question of reasonableness? On the facts, the risk was not one which would involve significant hardship for the valuer as he could cover it by professional indemnity insurance at modest cost, but the loss to the purchaser could be a financial catastrophe and purchasers were unlikely to insure or unable to afford insurance. The resulting imposition of liability on the surveyor might result in his increased insurance premiums which cost would be passed on to the public but it would not be anything like the figures involved in the difference between a valuation with liability and one without liability, as mentioned in Lord Templeman's speech.

Most of the above questions and the UCTA, s 11(4), concerning the restriction of liability to a specific sum of money, were considered in *St Albans City and District Council v International Computers Ltd*.[15] The defendants supplied the plaintiff council with a computerised database for the purposes of calculating the community charge. The software was defective and the population in the area was overstated with the result that the community charge was set too low, the resultant loss to the council being over £1.3 million. The contract contained a clause limiting the defendant's liability to £100,000. In a lucid judgment, Scott Baker J held[16] that the clause was subject to the reasonableness test under the UCTA, s 3 *or* ss 6 and 7, thus indicating that the contract could be one for the

---

12 [1990] 1 AC 831 at 858.
13 [1990] 1 AC 831 at 858.
14 [1990] 1 AC 831 at 853.
15 [1995] FSR 686; affd [1996] 4 All ER 481, CA.
16 The judge's decision regarding the exclusion of liability was affirmed by CA: [1996] 4 All ER 481.

sale or supply of goods.[17] Taking into account the Sch 2 reasonableness guidelines and s 11(4), the judge considered that (i) the parties had unequal bargaining power, (ii) the defendants had not justified the figure of £100,000 which was small in relation to the potential risk and actual loss, (iii) the defendants were insured in an aggregate sum of £50 million worldwide, and (iv) the practical consequences were that the defendant could insure and was insured and could thus pass on the premium to its customers whereas if the loss were to fall on the council it would ultimately be borne by the local population. It was not unreasonable that the party who made the profit should carry the risk. These factors outweighed the other considerations that the parties should be free to make their own bargain and that the council contracted with its eyes open, that limitations such as this were commonplace in the computer industry and that the software involved was an area of developing technology. Accordingly, the defendants had not discharged the burden of proof under s 11(5) and had failed to establish that the clause was a fair and reasonable one to have been included in the contract.

OTHER RELEVANT PROVISIONS IN THE UCTA

The UCTA, s 2

The UCTA, s 2(1) provides:

> 'A person cannot by reference to any contract term or to a notice given to persons generally or to particular persons exclude or restrict his liability for death or personal injury resulting from negligence.'

Negligence is defined in the UCTA, s 1(1), and s 1(3) provides that s 2 is limited to 'business liability'. Provided the liability is such a business liability, it does not matter whether the other party is a consumer or a business. 'Personal injury' is defined in the UCTA, s 14. In the sale of goods, an obvious application of s 2(1) would be where S sells machinery to B and, in a contract term, seeks to exclude liability in negligence for personal injury caused by it. However, by its referring to 'notices', s 2(1) covers a broad range of situations, the majority of which are not directly pertinent to this text, where there could be tortious liability but there is no contractual relationship between the parties, eg a manufacturer of goods who has no contract with the buyer cannot exclude liability for death or bodily injury caused by defective goods which the negligent manufacturer has put into circulation.

The UCTA, s 2(2) provides:

> 'In the case of other loss or damage, a person cannot so exclude or restrict his liability for negligence except in so far as the term or notice satisfies the requirement of reasonableness.'

Section 2(2) applies to loss or damage caused to property and subjects the relevant contract term to the reasonableness test. An example in the sale of goods would be a term whereby S seeks to exclude liability in negligence for damage caused by the goods to B's property both real and personal.

---

17 See Ch 14 for a consideration of Sir Iain Glidewell's comments in the CA ([1996] 4 All ER 481, 493) that a computer disk containing a program was within the definition of 'goods' in the SGA 1979, s 61(1), but that the program *itself* was not goods.

The UCTA, s 3

The provisions of the UCTA which were considered earlier apply only to the exclusion or restriction of the implied conditions in the SGA, ss 12-15. Other exclusion clauses in contracts for the sale of goods, eg relating to the time and place of delivery, may be caught by the UCTA, s 3 which subjects terms within its ambit to the requirement of reasonableness. Section 3 provides:

'(1) This section applies as between contracting parties where one of them deals as consumer or on the other's written standard terms of business.
(2) As against that party, the other cannot by reference to any contract term –
(a) when himself in breach of contract, exclude or restrict any liability of his in respect of the breach; or
(b) claim to be entitled –
(i) to render a contractual performance substantially different from that which was reasonably expected of him, or
(ii) in respect of the whole or any part of his contractual obligation, to render no performance at all,
except in so far as ... the contract term satisfies the requirement of reasonableness.'

The reasonableness test for the purposes of s 3 is found in the UCTA, s 11(1) and has been considered above, the only difference being that the guidelines in Sch 2 do not expressly apply to s 3.

It will be noticed that s 3 is restricted to business liability as it applies in two situations only, viz (i) where one party 'deals as consumer' and the other does not (the meaning of dealing as consumer within the UCTA, s 12 was considered earlier, ie one party is a consumer and the other is a business), and (ii) where one party deals on 'the other's written standard terms of business'.

It is thus plain that, within s 3, both parties can be businesses provided that one business deals on the other's 'written standard terms of business'. Where both parties use standard form contracts, an immediate problem is thus to decide which party deals on the other party's terms and an analysis of the contract's formation may have to be made.[18] This difficulty apart, the UCTA does not define 'written standard terms', the Law Commissions[19] having deliberately decided against a prescriptive definition. Moreover, there is no direct authority but much conjecture regarding the phrase. The overall purpose of stipulating for 'written standard terms' is to exclude terms which are individually *negotiated* between the parties[20] but this obvious fact does not help in fixing the ambit of s 3. Does the contract have to be *exclusively* in writing? Are terms 'standard' when used for the first time or only when they have been employed for a period of time? If the former construction applies, must the terms be *intended* for indefinite use? How great a deviation from the standard terms is permissible before such terms cease to be 'standard'? It seems likely that the courts will take a robust approach to these questions if only to prevent a party from making trivial and regular alterations to written contracts in order to argue that his terms are not standardised.

---

18 See *Butler Machine Tool Co v Ex-Cell-O Corpn (England) Ltd* [1979] 1 WLR 401.
19 See *Exemption Clauses, Second Report* (Law Com No 69; Scot Law Com No 39, 1975), paras 151-157.
20 *Flamar Interocean Ltd v Denmac Ltd, The Flamar Pride and Flamar Progress* [1990] 1 Lloyd's Rep 434, 438 per Potter J (where a standard agreement was subject to 'a number of alterations' it ceased to be standard). See also *McCrone v Boots Farm Sales Ltd* 1981 SLT 103 (consideration of 'standard form contract' in the UCTA, s 17 (Scotland only)); Jacobs, 'Written Standard Terms of Business' [1983] JBL 226; *Chester Grosvenor Hotel Co Ltd v Alfred McAlpine Management Ltd* (1991) 56 BLR 115, 131 per Judge Stannard.

Section 3(2)(a) applies to clauses which seek to exclude or restrict liability for breach of contractual undertakings but it should be stressed that it assumes the existence of a *breach* of contract and an attempt to exclude or restrict attendant *liability*. It cannot extend to core-shrinking clauses which seek to define the obligations owed rather than excluding liability in the event of a breach (see below).

Section 3(2)(b)(i) and (ii) can apply to core-shrinking clauses, however. Section 3(2)(b)(i) would apply, for example, to a term by which a tour operator reserves the right to substitute one holiday destination for an inferior alternative[1] or, in the sale of goods, a provision under which S claims to be entitled to deliver inferior, substitute goods. It is vital to stress that s 3(2)(b)(i) turns upon the *reasonable expectations* of the other party but it is most unclear how these can be gauged. The Law Commissions had in mind that a duty-defining clause might mislead one party regarding the extent of the other party's obligations[2] but if a clause clearly defines the obligations owed it is difficult to see how it might be established that the aggrieved party could *reasonably* expect anything other than the performance which was stipulated. A further possibility might be to assess the reasonable expectations of one party without reference to the clause but this would impose a solution based upon notions of public policy and is redolent of the rule of law approach to fundamental breach. It is equally unclear how a 'substantially different' performance is to be assessed but, again, this is reminiscent of fundamental breach in the implication that it is possible to identify a level of acceptable performance. A clause might pass the reasonableness test where the aggrieved party's expectations are totally unreasonable and, in many cases, would certainly do so where the substantially different performance on offer is *superior* to that which one party is obliged to provide under the contract (eg in a pleasure cruise, a term that the passenger might be moved from economy to first class accommodation at no extra charge). It would not necessarily follow that, in commercial contracts for the sale of goods, a term which allowed for the substitution of more valuable goods for the contract goods would pass the reasonableness test.

Section 3(2)(b)(ii) applies where there is a contractual obligation but the clause gives one party a discretion not to perform the whole, or any part of, the obligation. It seems likely that *force majeure* clauses under which S claims to be entitled to cancel the contract or suspend it because of events outside his control will be supervised by s 3(2)(b)(ii) but, in a commercial contract for the sale of goods, such a clause would often pass the reasonableness test. It is more difficult to decide whether a clause would be within the section which entitles S to cancel the contract in the event of B's non-payment by a specified date but, again, such an innocuous commercial provision would frequently pass the reasonableness test.

The UCTA, s 4

Under s 4, a person who 'deals as consumer' cannot, by any contract term, be made to indemnify another person in respect of liability that may be incurred

---

1   See *Anglo-Continental Holidays Ltd v Typaldos Lines (London) Ltd* [1967] 2 Lloyd's Rep 61 (considered below); see also Package Travel, Package Holidays and Package Tours Regulations 1992, reg 12 (SI 1992/3288).
2   See *Exemption Clauses, Second Report* (Law Com No 69; Scot Law Com No 39, 1975), para 143.

by the other for negligence or breach of contract, except in so far as the contract term satisfies the requirement of reasonableness. Section 4 does not apply to indemnity clauses in business contracts and, indeed, such clauses do not appear to be within the ambit of the UCTA.

The UCTA, s 5

Section 5 renders ineffective clauses in manufacturers' guarantees which seek to exclude or restrict the manufacturer's liability in negligence for 'loss or damage' in respect of goods of 'a type ordinarily supplied for private use or consumption' and which prove 'defective while in consumer use'. A 'guarantee' is defined widely in s 5(2)(b) but it must be in writing and s 5(2)(a) provides that goods are in 'consumer use' when a person is using them or has them in his possession for use 'otherwise than exclusively for the purposes of a business'. This latter phrase is a wide one and would cover goods which are used partly for business and partly for private use, eg a company car used on private holidays.[3] It is important to stress that s 5 applies *only* where the parties are not in a contractual relationship (ie manufacturer/distributor and consumer; see s 5(3)) but, unlike the UCTA, s 2, s 5 does not distinguish between injury to the person and damage to property but instead covers *all* loss or damage.

The UCTA, s 10

The purpose of s 10 is to curb evasion of the UCTA's provisions by means of a secondary contract containing exclusion clauses which, if inserted in the primary contract, would be prevented by the Act. The rationale of s 10 is thus to prevent what cannot be done directly being done indirectly. For example, in a retail sale of goods to a consumer buyer, a secondary contract made between buyer and retailer for the servicing or repair of the goods might attempt to restrict the buyer's rights against the retailer under the primary contract of sale. Alternatively, the secondary contract might exist between the buyer and a third party and purport to affect the buyer's rights against the seller, eg a term in a manufacturer's guarantee (amounting to a binding contract) which attempts to deprive the buyer of rights under the main contract of sale. It had always been canvassed whether s 10 might apply, quite inappropriately, where parties to a contract subsequently reached a *bona fide* compromise of a dispute under the first contract. However, it was decided in *Tudor Grange Holdings Ltd v Citibank NA*,[4] that s 10 was never intended to apply to such settlements which are not consonant with the *evasion* of the UCTA and, moreover, that the section had no application where the parties to both primary and secondary contracts were the same. By itself the latter conclusion effectively removes compromises from the ambit of s 10 but also means that the section has no relevance to the above example of two separate contracts of sale and repair made between retailer and consumer buyer and it is here that the preventive and deterrent effect of s 10 is arguably needed most. That being said, the UCTA, ss 3 and 6 operate in relation to '*any* contract term' and those sections might thus be applicable to a term in a secondary contract without the necessity to resort to s 10.

---

3 Cf 'dealing as consumer' under the UCTA, s 12 (considered above).
4 [1992] Ch 53; see Brown, 'Secondary Contracts and Section 10 of the Unfair Contract Terms Act' (1992) 108 LQR 223.

Apart from these difficulties, the ambit of s 10 is unclear as it refers to a term in the secondary contract 'prejudicing or taking away rights' under another contract. The emphasis upon 'rights' makes it uncertain whether s 10 would apply, for example, to an onerous term such as a time limit on B's communicating defects to S. Moreover, the rights which are thus prejudiced or taken away by the secondary contract must relate to 'the enforcement of another's *liability* which this ... Act prevents that other from excluding or restricting' and it is arguable that s 10 cannot control a core-shrinking clause which seeks to define the duties owed rather than excluding liability. Again, these difficulties might be avoided by applying the catch-all provisions in the UCTA, s 13 but, overall, s 10 seems to be stripped of much of its efficacy illustrating that this provision, introduced late in the Act's progress through Parliament, was always an over-cautious one.

The UCTA, s 13

Section 13 attempts to draw several varieties of exclusion clause within the ambit of the UCTA rather than simply those which seek to exclude or restrict liability. It is important to stress that s 13 must be cross-referenced with the other sections of the UCTA and, in this sense, it is not a self-standing provision. For example, an onerous condition within s 13(1)(a), in a sale of goods between two businesses and relating to the SGA, ss 13-15, would be subject to the reasonableness test by virtue of ss 6(3), 11(1) and (2) and Sch 2. Section 13 provides:

> '(1) To the extent that this Part of this Act prevents the exclusion or restriction of any liability it also prevents –
> (a) making the liability or its enforcement subject to restrictive or onerous conditions;
> (b) excluding or restricting any right or remedy in respect of the liability, or subjecting a person to any prejudice in consequence of his pursuing any such right or remedy;
> (c) excluding or restricting rules of evidence or procedure;
> and (to that extent) sections 2 and 5 to 7 also prevent excluding or restricting liability by reference to terms and notices which exclude or restrict the relevant obligation or duty.
> (2) But an agreement in writing to submit present or future differences to arbitration is not to be treated under this Part of this Act as excluding or restricting any liability.'

Examples within s 13 would be: s 13(1)(a) – provisions requiring B to make a claim for defective goods within a time-limit, demanding that B furnish several copies of such a claim or stipulating that B must commence proceedings against S in a shorter period than that specified by the Limitation Acts; s 13(1)(b) – clauses which eliminate or restrict B's right to reject[5] defective goods, stipulate that B is totally responsible for redelivery of defective goods to S, forbid B's recovery of damages for consequential loss, or provide for the loss of a deposit if B commences proceedings against S for defective goods; s 13(1)(c) – a term providing that receipt of the goods by B is conclusive evidence that they are satisfactory.[6]

---

5 See also the controls on the loss of B's right to reject the goods in the SGA, s 35 (considered in Ch 23).

6 See *Howard Marine and Dredging Co Ltd v A Ogden & Sons (Excavation) Ltd* [1978] QB 574 (held not fair or reasonable to allow reliance on a term in the contract for the hire of barges which provided that their acceptance was conclusive evidence of fitness for their intended use).

It is unclear whether liquidated damages clauses are within s 13(1)(b)[7] as they differ from normal limitation clauses in that they are a genuine pre-estimate of loss and are inserted for the benefit of both parties[8] but certainly the Law Commissions thought that they should be subject to control.[9]

The final part of s 13(1) which refers to 'excluding or restricting liability by reference to terms and notices which exclude or restrict the relevant obligation or duty' relates to duty-defining clauses or 'core-shrinkers' and this topic is considered next.

CLAUSES WHICH SHRINK THE CORE OF THE OBLIGATION

In general, English law views exclusion clauses as providing a possible defence[10] to an action for breach of contract, these devices thus being regarded exclusively as a shield to a claim in damages. Looking from a different perspective, it is possible to see such clauses as terms of the contract which, along with the other terms of the bargain, define and delimit the obligations which are undertaken by the parties. The latter view, originally propounded by Coote,[11] was thus that 'exclusion' clauses are in fact consensual terms which specify the inherent content and scope of the bargain, but this theory has been criticised for failing to take sufficient account of the development of standard form contracts and thus being inapt where exclusion clauses are clearly imposed by the stronger party.[12] Certainly the UCTA is drafted largely in terms that exclusion clauses are defensive devices and the Act does not directly confront the issue of the duty-defining or 'core-shrinking' clause. In the light of the controls in the UCTA, a controversial issue is the extent to which it is permissible for S to employ a duty-defining term to 'shrink the core' of the obligation which he owes to B instead of seeking to exclude or restrict his *liability* in the event of a breach of contract. A consideration of a range of possible clauses illustrates the inherent difficulty in categorising contract terms as either exclusionary or definitional. At one extreme, a sale of 'all the horses in my paddock except for the palomino' would be regarded as legitimately defining the ambit of the contract. More controversially, a term might stipulate that B should not rely on S's description of the goods but should make his own examination of them thereby arriving at, and relying upon, his own evaluation of the goods. Similarly, S might warn B that he is unsure as to the suitability of the goods for B's particular purpose or inform B that he has no expertise in B's area of trade and that B must therefore satisfy himself as to the suitability of the goods for his purpose. Finally, edging ever closer to exclusion clauses, a one-year

---

7   Such clauses are probably within the UCTA, s 3(2)(a).
8   *Suisse Atlantique Société d'Armement Maritime SA v NV Rotterdamsche Kolen Centrale* [1967] 1 AC 361, 420 per Lord Upjohn.
9   See *Exemption Clauses, Second Report* (Law Com No 69, Scot Law Com No 39, 1975), paras 164-166.
10 See *Rutter v Palmer* [1922] 2 KB 87, 92 per Scrutton LJ.
11 *Exception Clauses* (1964); Coote, 'Unfair Contract Terms Act 1977' (1978) 41 MLR 312; see also Yates, *Exclusion Clauses in Contracts* (2nd edn, 1982).
12 See Adams,'An Optimistic Look at the Contract Provisions of the Unfair Contract Terms Act 1977' (1978) 41 MLR 703; Adams and Brownsword, 'The Unfair Contract Terms Act: A Decade of Discretion' (1988) 104 LQR 94, 95-96.

warranty given with the sale of a used car might cover 'all parts and labour costs' but qualify this later in the contract by providing that B must pay the first £50 of any claim under the warranty, or a warning on the packaging of mass-produced consumer goods might state that they should be used only in a certain way, eg an 'all-purpose' household cleaner with a warning that it should not be used on certain surfaces. Core-shrinking clauses are important as regards business and consumer sales but have particular significance in consumer sales because of the UCTA, s 6, under which S *cannot* exclude or restrict his liability for breach of the implied conditions in the SGA, ss 13-15: it is thus imperative to decide when a core-shrinking clause might infringe s 6.

On the one hand it is arguable that core-shrinking devices entail simply a reasonable definition of risks under the contract, this view being supportable in relation to the implied conditions in the SGA, s 14, as those conditions have an intrinsic capacity for modification, eg under s 14(2C)(a) S is not liable for defects which are specifically drawn to B's attention before the contract is made. Indeed, core-shrinking clauses should arguably not be regarded in an unfavourable light in non-consumer sales where two businesses bargain on an equal footing. On the other hand, such clauses are clearly offensive if they succeed in negating the protection conferred by the SGA implied terms and circumvent the controls in the UCTA. This would be the case in consumer sales where B might consider his protection to be watertight only to find that he has been duped by a skilfully drafted clause. The report of the Law Commissions upon which the UCTA was based sought to distinguish between objectionable and unobjectionable duty-defining clauses and recommended that the former category be subjected to control where the effect of the clause might mislead a promisee regarding the extent of the promisor's obligation.[13]

As emphasised earlier, the difficulty in drawing core-shrinking clauses within the UCTA is that most of the Act's provisions are drafted in defensive terms of 'excluding or restricting *liability*' whereas core-shrinking clauses seek to define the relevant obligation or duty which is owed and allocate responsibilities rather than seeking to renounce liability. As will be seen, this obstacle might not be allowed to thwart the UCTA if the decisions are followed which take a rugged approach to the issue of duty-defining clauses. The relevant provisons of the UCTA which could apply to core-shrinking clauses are ss 3 and 13.[14] Section 3 contains the overall reasonableness requirement for liability arising in contract and, of particular relevance here, s 3(2)(b)(i) and (ii) provide that one party cannot, by reference to any contract term, claim to be entitled (i) 'to render a contractual performance substantially different from that which was reasonably expected of him' or (ii) 'in respect of the whole or any part of his contractual obligation, to render no performance at all', except in so far as the term satisfies the reasonableness requirement. Section 3 could thus apply to core-shrinking clauses in business and consumer sales which do not relate to the implied conditions in the SGA, ss 13-15,[15] eg an express term concerning

---

13   See *Exemption Clauses, Second Report* (Law Com No 69, Scot Law Com No 39, 1975), paras 143-146.
14   See Palmer and Yates, 'The Future of the Unfair Contract Terms Act 1977' [1981] 40 CLJ 108, 123-130.
15   In fact, there should be no objection to applying s 3 to core-shrinking clauses which *do* relate to the SGA, ss 13-15.

delivery of the goods. The UCTA, s 13 may be more helpful in this context as it extends the scope of the UCTA, s 2 and ss 5-7 by defining exclusion clauses widely and thus s 13(1) seeks to control 'terms and notices which exclude or restrict *the relevant obligation or duty*'. The operation of s 13 could thus prohibit core-shrinking clauses in relation to the implied conditions in the SGA, ss 13-15 in consumer sales (where the UCTA would otherwise be usurped) and subject such clauses which relate to the SGA implied conditions in non-consumer sales to the test of reasonableness.

It seems that the common law has taken its usual pragmatic approach to core-shrinking clauses, relying on innate good sense to distinguish the acceptable clause from its unacceptable counterpart. Some decisions have thus regarded duty-defining clauses as legitimate bargaining devices which do not seek to exclude liability, at least in situations where the qualified obligation which arises amounts to a genuine allocation of risks between equals.[16] Other cases have condemned such clauses as shams and poorly-disguised exclusions of liability, consequently drawing them within the UCTA's controls. In *Anglo-Continental Holidays Ltd v Typaldos Lines (London) Ltd*,[17] a contract for the hire of a vessel for a pleasure cruise in the Mediterranean provided that 'steamers, sailing dates, rates and itineraries are subject to change without prior notice'. The Court of Appeal held that the defendants could not substitute an older, smaller and generally inferior vessel for that named in the contract as this would be a radical departure from the bargain. Russell LJ recognised that this was a clause 'under which the actual contractual liability may be defined' but that it could not be allowed 'to alter the substance of the arrangement'.[18] Likewise, in *Cremdean Properties Ltd v Nash*,[19] sellers of an office block in Bristol sought to rely on a clause which provided that the particulars of sale were believed to be correct but that 'their accuracy is not guaranteed and any error, omission or misdescription shall not annul the sale'. At the date of the decision, the Misrepresentation Act 1967, s 3, subjected a provision which sought to 'exclude or restrict' liability for misrepresentation to a test of reasonableness.[20] It was argued that the clause in the contract would simply nullify any representation which had been made but it was held that the clause, on its true construction, did not have this effect. Bridge LJ concluded that, even if the clause had been framed in terms that the seller was conclusively deemed to have made no representation, it would still have been an attempt to exclude or restrict liability and the courts would not allow 'such ingenuity ... to defeat the plain purpose at which section 3 is aimed'.[1] Scarman LJ added that 'Humpty Dumpty would have fallen for this argument. If we were to fall for it, the Misrepresentation Act would be dashed to pieces which not all the King's lawyers could put together

---

16 See *Renton (G H) & Co Ltd v Palmyra Trading Corpn of Panama* [1957] AC 149 (clause valid which permitted discharge of cargo at ports other than London and Hull); *Kenyon, Son & Craven Ltd v Baxter Hoare & Co Ltd* [1971] 1 WLR 519, 522 per Donaldson J; *Trade and Transport Inc v Iino Kaiun Kaisha Ltd, The Angelia* [1973] 1 WLR 210, 230-231 per Kerr J; *Photo Production Ltd v Securicor Transport Ltd* [1980] AC 827, 851 per Lord Diplock.
17 [1967] 2 Lloyd's Rep 61.
18 [1967] 2 Lloyd's Rep 61 at 67.
19 (1977) 244 Estates Gazette 547.
20 The current s 3 was substituted by the UCTA, s 8(1).
 1 (1977) 244 Estates Gazette 547, 551.

again'.[2] In the sale of goods, duty-defining terms were given short shrift in *Lutton v Saville Tractors (Belfast) Ltd*.[3] There B was a consumer buyer of a used Ford Escort XR3 which was plagued with defects but the contract provided that (i) the car was sold on the 'understanding' that B entered into the agreement relying on his own judgment, and (ii) a 'purchaser's declaration' purported to contain an acknowledgment that B had not relied on the 'skill, judgment or opinion of the seller, its servants or agents in relation to the goods'. Carswell J held that the car was unmerchantable and that these clauses were 'transparent attempts to escape the operation of section 6(2)(a) of the 1977 Act, which should not be permitted to operate successfully'.[4] Similarly, many of the decisions concerning duty-defining clauses in the law of tort have taken a robust approach and deemed them to be exclusion clauses. In *Phillips Products Ltd v Hyland*,[5] the argument was firmly rejected that the clause in question did not exclude or restrict liability within the UCTA, s 2(2) but merely allocated responsibility by transferring liability for the acts of a JCB driver from the owner of the excavator to the plantiff hirer of it. Slade LJ stressed that 'a transfer of liability from A to B necessarily and inevitably involves the exclusion of liability so far as A is concerned ... there is no mystique about "exclusion" or "restriction" clauses. To decide whether a person "excludes" liability by reference to a contract term, you look at the effect of the term. You look at its substance'.[6] This reasoning was approved by the House of Lords in *Smith v Eric S Bush*,[7] in what is undoubtedly the principal decision on core-shrinking clauses. There a building society instructed the defendant surveyor to report upon and value a house but the surveyor's report contained a disclaimer of liability regarding its accuracy. The chimneys were not adequately supported and one of them subsequently collapsed. The plaintiff purchaser/mortgagor of the house claimed damages in negligence against the defendant surveyor. It was held that the disclaimer of liability was a notice which purported to exclude liability for negligence and would be ineffective by virtue of the UCTA, s 2(2) unless it satisfied the test of reasonableness in s 11(3) which test, on the facts, the

---

2 (1977) 244 Estates Gazette 547, 551; clauses were also held to be unreasonable under s 3 in *Walker v Boyle* [1982] 1 WLR 495 ('no error, mis-statement or omission ... shall annul the sale') and *South Western General Property Co Ltd v Marton* (1982) 263 Estates Gazette 1090 ('all statements ... are made without responsibility ... any intending purchaser must satisfy himself ... as to the correctness of each statement'); cf *Overbrooke Estates Ltd v Glencombe Properties Ltd* [1974] 1 WLR 1335 where it was held that a sale catalogue specifying that the auctioneer (A) lacked authority to make or give any representations or warranties in respect of the property negated any apparent authority in A to make such statements and was not subject to the Misrepresentation Act 1967, s 3 (see Coote, 'Limitation of Authority by Common Form' [1975] 34 CLJ 17). *Overbrooke* was followed by the CA in *Collins v Howell-Jones* (1980) 259 Estates Gazette 331 (see Murdoch, 'Excluding Liability for Misrepresentation' (1981) 97 LQR 522). In *Cremdean*, Bridge LJ saw a difference between P's 'publicly giving notice limiting the ostensible authority of his agents' (ie *Overbrooke*) and P's circumventing s 3 'by a clause excluding his own liability for a representation' (p 551). Might a shop thus publish an effective notice that the sales staff lack authority to make any statements regarding the goods sold?
3 (1986) 12 NIJB 1.
4 (1986) 12 NIJB 1 at 19.
5 [1987] 1 WLR 659 (Note).
6 [1987] 1 WLR 659 at 665-666 See also *Photo Production Ltd v Securicor Transport Ltd* [1980] AC 827, 850 per Lord Diplock: '... an exclusion clause is one which excludes or modifies an obligation ... that would otherwise arise under the contract by implication of law'.
7 [1990] 1 AC 831.

disclaimer failed to satisfy. The House rejected the notion that the UCTA should not apply to disclaimers which sought to prevent a duty of care from coming into existence and Lord Griffiths postulated the pragmatic 'but for' test. Speaking of both the UCTA, s 11(3) and s 13(1), he considered that those provisions 'indicate that the existence of the common law duty to take reasonable care ... is to be judged by considering whether it would exist "but for" the notice excluding liability'.[8] *Smith v Eric S Bush* was concerned only with tortious liability but it is very likely that the same reasoning would apply in *consumer* sales of goods where the contract would contain the implied conditions in the SGA, ss 13-15 but for the clause in question.[9] However, in contrast to the vigorous approach in *Smith v Eric S Bush*, there have been recent indications in tort cases concerning *Hedley Byrne* liability that, in accord with the decision in *Hedley Byrne* itself, an assumption of responsibility may be negated by an appropriate disclaimer.[10]

Also very relevant in this context are two divergent decisions on the Consumer Protection (Restriction on Statements) Order 1976[11] which, *inter alia*, makes it a criminal offence to purport to display notices or use contract terms which are void under the UCTA, s 6 (eg 'no return of goods after sale' or 'no money refunded'). The necessity for criminal sanctions arose because sellers continued to employ such notices which, although void if challenged in court, could nevertheless be *displayed* in shops; the 1976 Order thus sought an effective means to prevent consumers being misled. In *Hughes v Hall*,[12] S, a second-hand car dealer, sold a car to B, a consumer buyer, and gave him a document which provided that the car was 'sold as seen and inspected'. The Divisional Court of the Queen's Bench Division held that this phrase was a clause purporting to exclude liability for breach of the SGA, s 13 and thus an offence had been committed. In contrast, in *Cavendish-Woodhouse Ltd v Manley*,[13] the Divisional Court held that a suite of furniture sold by a retailer to a consumer with an invoice providing that it was 'bought as seen' did not purport to exclude liability under the SGA, s 14 but indicated simply that, in a sale of specific goods such as this, B had in fact seen them. Accordingly, no offence was committed. Although Ackner LJ deemed *Hughes* to be a 'puzzling decision'[14] it is respectfully suggested that the conclusion reached in *Cavendish-Woodhouse* fails to acknowledge the mischief which the 1976 order sought to suppress.

Overall, the only pattern which emerges from the decisions above is the elusive, unsatisfactory formulation that the UCTA must not be flouted by duty-

8 [1990] 1 AC 831 at 857; cf the pre-UCTA decision in *Hurley v Dyke* [1979] RTR 265 where the HL accepted that a seller of a second-hand Reliant three-wheeler car, knowing of its potentially dangerous state, was not liable in negligence to a passenger in the car who was left as a paraplegic after the chassis collapsed, because the car had been sold at auction subject to the warning that it was 'as seen with all its faults and without warranty'.
9 The Law Commission accepted (*Fiduciary Duties and Regulatory Rules*, Law Comm CP No 124, 1992, para 33.28) that the *Smith v Eric S Bush* reasoning is appropriate in relation to clauses which seek to define fiduciary duties. See also *Johnstone v Bloomsbury Health Authority* [1991] 2 All ER 293, 300-301 per Stuart-Smith LJ (strongly supporting Slade LJ's reasoning in *Hyland*). .
10 See *Henderson v Merrett Syndicates Ltd* [1995] 2 AC 145, 181 per Lord Goff of Chieveley; *McCullagh v Lane Fox & Partners Ltd* [1996] 1 EGLR 35, 45 per Hobhouse LJ; *First National Commercial Bank plc v Loxleys* [1997] PNLR 211, CA.
11 SI 1976/1813 as amended by SI 1978/27.
12 [1981] RTR 430.
13 (1984) 82 LGR 376.
14 (1984) 82 LGR 376 at 382.

defining clauses. Equally unsatisfactory is the nebulous proposition that, as the implied terms in the SGA, ss 13-15 are not absolute and contain an inherent ability for modification, it must be possible to arrive at a modified bargain in some cases. The abiding difficulty lies in differentiating a clause which is an attempt to evade the UCTA from a permissible term which delineates the duties owed under the contract. What is the position, for example, in a retail sale to a consumer buyer when a bin of goods is labelled 'Slightly imperfect goods at reduced prices, bought as seen with all faults'? It might be thought that this should be a permissible re-definition of S's duties under the SGA implied terms but where is the line to be drawn when other, interminable facts could be posited?

The recent decision in *Harlingdon and Leinster Enterprises Ltd v Christopher Hull Fine Art Ltd*,[15] exemplifies the difficulties of fixing the legitimate boundaries of such a modified bargain. There both S and B were art dealers and S telephoned B saying that he was in a position to sell a painting by an artist named Gabriele Münter. At S's gallery, B was shown an auction catalogue which described the picture as being monogrammed 'MÜ.' and having the stamp of the estate of Münter. However, S did not repeat that the artist was Münter but, instead, indicated that he knew little about the paintings and had never heard of the artist. B bought the painting for £6,000, S supplying an invoice which included the artist's name and lifespan. B subsequently discovered that the painting was a forgery. The Court of Appeal held that this was not a sale by description within the SGA, s 13, as B did not *rely* upon the description given by S but rather upon his own judgement.[16] The court's analysis was thus that the operation of s 13 was nullified because (i) the pre-contractual representations of S made on the telephone were not relied upon by B and did not become terms of the contract; and (ii) the vague, non-contractual statements of S made at the gallery indicated that S's judgement should not be relied upon. It is (ii) which is controversial in that this reasoning permits a statutory implied condition to be negated by an oral, non-contractual representation. The startling conclusion is thus that the UCTA does not apply to such a representation which, in effect, excludes the implied condition.[17] In a forceful dissenting judgment, Stuart-Smith LJ warned that it would be 'a serious defect in the law if the effect of a condition implied by statute could be excluded by the vendor's saying that he was not an expert in what was being sold or that the purchaser was more expert than the vendor. That is not the law; it has long been held that conditions implied by statute can only be excluded by clear words. There is nothing of that kind in this case'.[18] *Harlingdon* does appear both to expose and tolerate such a defect in the law: if the conclusion reached by the court is ameliorated by the fact that this was a manifest business sale entered into between equals, in a notoriously speculative market, the application of the *Harlingdon* reasoning to a consumer sale of goods would be objectionable and unacceptable.

Finally, there is the question of warnings and instructions regarding the use of goods. It does appear that clear warnings as to the manner in which goods

---

15 [1991] 1 QB 564.
16 See Ch 20 where this aspect of the decision is considered.
17 This approach is most evident in the judgment of Slade LJ: 'I do not say that in the present case section 13 has been excluded by any contract term; my analysis of the position is that the contract was not one for the sale of goods by description' (p 586).
18 [1991] 1 QB 564 at 580.

should be used or not abused may define S's duty under the SGA implied conditions. In *Wormell v R H M Agriculture (East) Ltd*,[19] the Court of Appeal held that B, a farmer, chose to ignore clear warnings and instructions on a container of herbicide which specified the times at which it should be applied to crops and, accordingly, he could not complain that the goods were unfit for their purpose within the SGA, s 14(3). Again, this notion must be treated with caution in consumer sales so that elaborate and obscure instructions are not permitted to annul B's protection under the SGA and the UCTA.[20]

THE UNFAIR TERMS IN CONSUMER CONTRACTS REGULATIONS 1999

The original Regulations[1] came into force on 1 July 1995 in order to implement an EC Council Directive[2] but the 1999 Regulations[3] (UTCCR), which came into force on 1 October 1999, revoke and replace the original Regulations and reflect more closely the wording of the Directive.

The wording of the Regulations has been clarified and the powers of enforcement granted by them have been extended considerably. In terms of substance, there is one significant change from the position under the 1994 Regulations. Previously, the UTCCR applied only to the business supply of goods and services to consumers under the terms of a standard-form contract, and there was doubt as to whether interests in land were covered. However, the amended definition of a 'supplier' in the 1999 Regulations omits any reference to goods and services. It is thus clear that standard-form business contracts for the supply to consumers of goods, services and interests in land, are within the 1999 Regulations.

The purpose of the Directive was to harmonise the laws of Member States of the EC and ensure that contracts with consumers do not contain unfair terms but, regrettably, no attempt was made to dovetail the UTCCR with the UCTA. The result is a complex, overlapping set of rules which is most undesirable in the sphere of consumer protection where remedies should be accessible and understandable. A contract term can thus be subject to both the UTCCR and the UCTA and this means that a term might satisfy the requirements of the UCTA and yet fail the requirements imposed by the UTCCR and vice versa. The overall effect of the UTCCR is that an 'unfair term' in a contract concluded between a consumer and a seller or supplier 'shall not be binding on the consumer' (reg 8(1)).

---

19 [1987] 1 WLR 1091.
20 See Brown, 'Liability for Labelling of Goods and Instructions for Use' [1988] LMCLQ 502.
1 SI 1994/3159; see Brandner and Ulmer, 'The Community Directive on Unfair Terms in Consumer Contracts: Some Critical Remarks on the Proposal Submitted by the EC Commission' (1991) 28 CML Rev 647; Hondius, 'EC Directive on Unfair Terms in Consumer Contracts: Towards a European Law of Contracts' (1994) 7 JCL 34; Collins, 'Good Faith in European Contract Law' (1994) 14 OJLS 229; Beale, 'Legislative Control of Fairness: The Directive on Unfair Terms in Consumer Contracts' in *Good Faith and Fault in Contract Law* (1995, eds Jack Beatson and Daniel Friedmann), Ch 9; Brownsword and Howells, 'The Implementation of the EC Directive on Unfair Terms in Consumer Contracts – Some Unresolved Questions' [1995] JBL 243.
2 93/13/EEC.
3 SI 1999/2083.

It is important to stress that, ultimately, it is the Directive which is paramount and thus, in interpreting the UTCCR, the court must have regard to the purpose and wording of both the Directive and its recitals.[4]

SCOPE OF THE REGULATIONS

The UTCCR, reg 4(1), broadly defines the scope of the regulations:

> '... these Regulations apply in relation to unfair terms in contracts concluded between a seller or supplier and a consumer.'

This generalised statement of the scope of the UTCCR plainly needs further elaboration and, overall, a comparison must be made with the controls in the UCTA.

It is vital at the outset to stress that the UTCCR apply only to contract *terms*, written or oral,[5] whereas parts of the UCTA apply to notices, which do not form part of any contract, and seek to exclude liability in tort.[6] It will be apparent that, overall, the UCTA has a much broader scope than the UTCCR.[7]

Regulations 4(2)(a) and (b) provide that the Regulations do not apply to contractual terms incorporated in order to comply with statutory or regulatory provisions of the UK[8] or the provisions of international conventions to which the Member States or the Community are party. Moreover, the fact that the UTCCR applies only to consumer contracts would, of necessity, exclude most international sales.

Certain other contracts were expressly exempted from the operation of the 1994 Regulations, viz 'any contract relating to employment ... succession rights ... rights under family law ... and the incorporation and organisation of companies or partnerships'.[9] It is striking that this list of excluded contracts has been *deleted* from the 1999 Regulations. It must be assumed that the rationale underpinning the deletion is that, in the recitals to the Directive,[10] this group of contracts is said to be excluded from the ambit of the Directive itself and the 1999 Regulations have sought better to embody the wording of the Directive. It must be asked, therefore, whether these contracts are within or without the

---

4 *Marleasing SA v La Comercial Internacional de Alementacion SA*, Case C-106/89 [1990] ECR I-4135; *Lister v Forth Dry Dock and Engineering Co Ltd* [1990] 1 AC 546.
5 Oral contract terms are within the UTCCR (to the extent that they are not 'individually negotiated': see reg 5(1)) as the Directive demands the consumer's equal protection under oral and written contracts (93/13/EEC, recital 11). The UTCCR refer throughout to 'a contractual term' without further qualification.
6 See the UCTA, ss 2(1), 5(1), 11(3) and 11(4).
7 Certain contracts are exempted from the ambit of the UCTA (see Sch 1). Most significantly, contracts of insurance are totally excluded from the UCTA but, to a certain extent, insurance contracts are within the UTCCR: the *premium* charged could not be challenged as unfair as this would fall within reg 6(2) (see below) as a term concerning the adequacy of consideration/main subject-matter of the contract (see also 93/13/EEC, recital 19) but other terms, eg a short time-limit on making claims under the policy, can be within the UTCCR.
8 Eg the Package Travel, Package Holidays and Package Tours Regulations 1992 (SI 1992/3288). The DTI considered that the rules established by self-regulatory bodies (eg OFGAS) should be excluded as such rules derive from statute, see *Unfair Terms in Consumer Contracts Regulations 1994, Guidance Notes* (DTI, 1995), para 3.16.
9 The UTCCR 1994, Sch 1.
10 93/13/EEC, recital 10.

Regulations. The purposive construction which must be adopted when interpreting the Directive dictates that full consideration must be given to the recitals and, consequently, it seems that this group of contracts will continue to be excluded from the operation of the UTCCR. Alternatively, but more improbably, it is arguable there is now nothing to prevent the 1999 Regulations from applying to this cluster of contracts. Employers might be perturbed to think that contracts of employment are within the 1999 Regulations and will argue that it is difficult, if not impossible, to envisage situations where the employer would be regarded as either a 'seller' or a 'supplier' and the employee cast as a 'consumer'. However, employers regularly supply goods such as tools, equipment and materials to employees in the course of their employment and, an employer's provision of training contracts for his employees might easily be regarded as a supply of services. If onerous, unfair conditions were to be be attached to these undertakings for the supply of goods or services to employees, it is difficult to see, at least in principle, why the UTCCR should not render them unenforceable.[11]

Seller or supplier

'Seller' and 'supplier' are defined in reg 3(1) as 'any natural or legal person who, in contracts covered by these Regulations, is acting for purposes relating to his trade, business or profession, whether publicly owned or privately owned'. The 1994 Regulations previously defined a 'seller' as 'a person who sells goods and a 'supplier' as 'a person who supplies goods or services'. Most significantly, the new definition in reg 3(1) omits any reference to selling goods and supplying services. It is thus plain that, while the selling of goods and the supply of services are still the most significant targets at which the UTCCR are aimed, the Regulations do now cover the creation or transfer of interests in land,[12] eg terms contained in tenancy agreements. There is no definition of either 'goods' or 'services' within the UTCCR.[13]

There is, likewise, no definition of a 'trade, business or profession' in the UTCCR[14] and no further delineation of when the seller or supplier will be regarded as 'acting for purposes relating to' his trade, business or profession. It remains to be seen how this latter phrase will be defined but its counterpart in the UCTA, s 12 ('makes the contract in the course of a business') has been interpreted by the common law as requiring a *regularity* of business dealings.[15]

11 There is recent authority that the UCTA, s 3, can apply to contracts of employment, see *Brigden v American Express Bank Ltd* [2000] IRLR 94 Morland J had no doubt that, within the UCTA, s 12(1)(a) and (b), the employee was a 'consumer' in that he did not make the contract in the course of a business while the employer did make the contract in the course of a business.

12 This is also the view of the OFT, see *Unfair Contract Terms*, Bulletin No 8, Dec 1999, para 16, and Case Report No 19, p 28.

13 The SGA 1979, s 61(1) defines goods as 'all personal chattels other than things in action and money'. It is also noteworthy that the UTCCR Sch 2, para 2(c), assumes that certain transactions in securities and contracts for the purchase or sale of foreign currency are within the Regulations. It would be difficult to classify these as sales of *goods* (a coin sold as an *object* could be a sale of goods, for example) but they could be regarded as contracts for the supply of services.

14 See the definition of 'business' in the UCTA, s 14, which does not include 'a trade'.

15 See *R & B Customs Brokers Co Ltd v United Dominions Trust Ltd* [1988] 1 WLR 321. Alternatively, in relation to the UTCCR, a court might adopt the approach in *Stevenson v Rogers* [1999] QB 1028, that no regularity is required (both decisions were considered above).

Consumer

'Consumer' is defined in reg 3(1) as 'any natural person who, in contracts covered by these Regulations, is acting for purposes which are outside his trade, business or profession'.

There are five striking differences between the UCTA and the UTCCR regarding 'consumers'. First, it is apparent that the UTCCR apply only where the contract is made between a business and a consumer but, within the UCTA, both parties can be businesses (eg under s 3) or both can be consumers (eg between two consumers, exclusion of the SGA, s 13 is subject to the reasonableness test). Second, the the UTCCR definition of 'consumer' applies only to 'natural' persons and does not include limited companies, but companies can be regarded as consumers under the UCTA.[16] Third, where one party is 'dealing as consumer' in a contract for the sale or supply of goods under the UCTA, the *goods* must be 'of a type ordinarily supplied for private use or consumption' (s 12(1)(c)) but no such restriction applies within the UTCCR and a consumer might thus buy a reaping machine, for example, and still be within the Regulations. Fourth, the UCTA, s 12(2) provides that 'on a sale by auction or competitive tender the buyer is not in any circumstances to be regarded as dealing as consumer' but, again, this limitation does not apply to the UTCCR. Finally, the UCTA notion that a consumer may be transformed into a business buyer by holding-out that he acts in the course of a business (s 12(1)(a)) is absent from the UTCCR.

UNFAIR TERMS WITHIN THE UTCCR

When is a contract term unfair?

An 'unfair term' is defined in reg 5(1) as:

'A contractual term which has not been individually negotiated shall be regarded as unfair if, contrary to the requirement of good faith, it causes a significant imbalance in the parties' rights and obligations arising under the contract, to the detriment of the consumer.'

There are thus four crucial elements in the operation of the the UTCCR unfairness test, viz (i) the contract term must not have been 'individually negotiated'; (ii) an absence of good faith; (iii) a significant imbalance in the parties' rights and obligations under the contract; and (iv) detriment to the consumer. Viewed in isolation, reg 5(1) is, at best, somewhat nebulous, but the notion of unfairness is given more definition elsewhere in the UTCCR and attention must now be focused on how the court would decide whether a term which is not individually negotiated is unfair.

The contract term must not have been 'individually negotiated'

It is central to the UTCCR that contract terms must *not* have been 'individually negotiated' if they are to be within the Regulations. Regulation 5(2) provides:

'A term shall always be regarded as not having been individually negotiated where it has been drafted in advance and the consumer has therefore not been able to influence the substance of the term.'

16   See *R & B Customs Brokers Co Ltd v United Dominions Trust Ltd* [1988] 1 WLR 321.

Most standard-form contracts are thus subject to the UTCCR and there is no necessity for the term in question to be drafted by the seller or supplier (eg a trade association's standard terms would thus be within the UTCCR). In this respect, the UTCCR is narrower than the UCTA because most of the UCTA's provisions can apply to individually negotiated contracts (with the exception of the UCTA, s 3). The phrase 'drafted in advance' in reg 5(2) is somewhat unclear but the intent must be that the term in question has been drafted in advance of the negotiations which precede the contract.

It will be remembered that the scope of 'written standard terms' in the UCTA, s 3 is somewhat unclear, but the UTCCR at least make some attempt to clarify the meaning of 'individually negotiated' terms. Regulation 5(3) provides that, even if a 'specific term or certain aspects of it in a contract has been individually negotiated', the UTCCR can nevertheless apply to the rest of the contract 'if an overall assessment of it indicates that it is a pre-formulated standard contract'.

Most importantly, the burden of proving that a term is individually negotiated and thus outside the Regulations is placed upon the seller or supplier (reg 5(4)) whereas the UCTA contains no rule as to the burden of proof regarding 'written standard terms'.

Assessing unfairness

Regulation 6(1) provides that:

> 'Without prejudice to regulation 12, the unfairness of a contractual term shall be assessed, taking into account the nature of the goods or services for which the contract was concluded and by referring, at the time of conclusion of the contract, to all the circumstances attending the conclusion of the contract and to all the other terms of the contract or of another contract on which it is dependent.'

It is under reg 6(1) that the court must assess the factors leading to the contract's conclusion and, having regard to the goods or services themselves, weigh in the balance the contract terms which seek to favour the seller/supplier against those which are advantageous to the consumer. In this way, the court might conclude that there is a significant imbalance in the parties' rights and obligations to the detriment of the consumer.

First, the reference to 'the nature of the goods or services' means that, for example, a term which might be unfair in a contract for the sale of new goods could be quite fair in the sale of second-hand goods. Second, the court must consider 'all the circumstances attending the conclusion of the contract' which could encompass, for example, any pre-contractual duress by the seller or supplier. Equally, in the seller's favour, it could be relevant that the consumer had examined the goods before contract and was fully aware of their condition. Third, 'all the other terms of the contract or of another contract on which it is dependent' must be assessed and thus a term might seem unfair if extracted from the contract and viewed in isolation but could be fair within the matrix of rights and liabilities created by the contract. Finally, it is vital to stress that the assessment of the term's unfairness is made at 'the time of conclusion of the contract' and this test is the same as that for reasonableness under the UCTA, meaning that post-contractual events cannot be taken into account in assessing fairness.

The Court of Appeal has recently considered the question of unfairness under the UTCCR[17] in *Director General of Fair Trading v First National Bank plc*.[18]

---

17 The court applied the UTCCR 1994.
18 [2000] 2 All ER 759.

The agreement under scrutiny was a standard form loan agreement regulated by the Consumer Credit Act 1974 (CCA). Clause 8 of the agreement provided that, should the borrower default on his repayments, interest continued to be payable at the contract rate on the outstanding principal plus accrued interest unpaid, until any judgment obtained by the bank was discharged. Interest thus continued to be payable before and after judgment until that judgment was discharged by payment. The Director General sought an injunction to restrain the bank from further use of the contract term and contended that it would operate unfairly where (i) judgment was obtained against the borrower; (ii) an order was made to pay the debt by instalments, eg a time-order under the CCA, s 129; but (iii) no order was made under the CCA, s 136 to amend the agreement, with the result that interest would continue to accrue notwithstanding the due payment by the borrower of the instalments ordered. Peter Gibson LJ concluded that, where an order is made for payment by instalments which are tailored to meet what the borrower can afford, it would be unfair then to inform him that he had to pay further sums by way of interest under clause 8. The bank's clause had not been specifically drawn to the borrower's attention at or before the conclusion of the contract and he would not be given notice of it at any later time prior to the making of an order nor in the order itself. Accordingly, it would come as a 'disagreeable surprise'[19] to the borrower to find that compliance with an order for payment by instalments did not discharge the debt but left him owing further substantial sums to the bank. The Court of Appeal thus held that clause 8 was unfair because (i) the bank had a superior bargaining position as against the relatively weak position of the consumer/borrower and it had not adequately considered the consumer's interests; (ii) clause 8 created 'unfair surprise'[20] and did not satisfy the test of good faith; (iii) a significant imbalance was created in the rights and obligations of the parties; and (iv) clause 8 clearly operated to the detriment of the consumer.

Schedule 2: the indicative list of unfair terms

An important feature of the UTCCR is that reg 5(5) refers to Sch 2 as providing 'an indicative and non-exhaustive list of the terms which may be regarded as unfair' and Sch 2 contains a copious list of 17 potentially unfair terms. It must be stressed that these are merely *examples* of terms which *might* be unfair and, here, it is not possible to list and analyse all the examples in Sch 2. The Office of Fair Trading produces regular bulletins on unfair contract terms with abundant examples of such terms and the amendments ordered by the Director General of Fair Trading under his powers of enforcement. Indeed, these bulletins are an indispensable aid to understanding the practical operation of the UTCCR.

The illustrative range of possible unfair terms in Sch 2 is a broad one. For example, Sch 2, para 1(i) suggests unfairness in 'irrevocably binding the consumer to terms with which he had no real opportunity of becoming acquainted before the conclusion of the contract'. This is analogous to the common law rules for the successful integration of exclusion clauses as contract terms but it goes conspicuously beyond the mechanistic common law rules concerning notice of exclusion clauses. Under the common law, a claimant may be bound by an

---

19   [2000] 2 All ER 759 at 770, per Peter Gibson LJ.
20   [2000] 2 All ER 759 at 770, per Peter Gibson LJ.

exclusion clause of which he has notice or which he has signed, despite his lack of *understanding* of its content but, in consumer contracts within the UTCCR, Sch 2, para 1(i) makes significant inroads on the common law rules.[1] Likewise, if a term is drafted obscurely or in very small print it can be said that there is no opportunity to become 'acquainted' with it before contract.

Sch 2 also contains many terms which are currently within the control of the UCTA. In several cases, better protection is available under the UCTA as some of the Sch 2 examples of *prima facie* unfairness are subjected to an absolute ban under the UCTA. There are are *no* such clear-cut prohibitions in the UTCCR. For example, the UCTA, s 2(1) prohibits the exclusion/restriction of liability for death or bodily injury caused by negligence but, under the UTCCR, such a term is *prima facie* regarded as unfair.[2] Again, the UCTA, ss 6 and 12 contain a prohibition on the exclusion/restriction of the implied conditions in the SGA, ss 13-15 in a consumer sale. In such cases of divergence, the consumer will obviously choose the provision which is most advantageous to him but, in other cases, he is free to plead both unfairness under the UTCCR and unreasonableness under the UCTA and this may lead to considerable uncertainty in the law.

There are, however, several terms in the UTCCR which would neither fall within the UCTA nor be subject to the common law's control. Most importantly, the UTCCR clearly apply to terms which confer *rights* on the seller or supplier rather than terms which seek to exclude or restrict a *liability* or shrink the core of an *obligation or duty*. The UTCCR, Sch 2, para 1(d) provides one such example of unfairness where a term confers on S the right to retain a deposit where B decides not to proceed with the contract without providing correlative compensation for B where S cancels the contract. Even the wide-ranging UCTA, s 13 covers only onerous clauses (such as loss of a deposit) which relate to the exclusion or restriction of S's *liability* (eg, s 13(1)(b): '... subjecting a person to any prejudice in consequence of his pursuing any such right or remedy') and the loss of deposit example in the UTCCR Sch 2, para 1(d), would be outside the UCTA's control.

Other striking examples of unfair terms within Sch 2 which are not covered by the UCTA and which are particulary relevant to the sale of goods include (i) providing for the price of goods to be determined at the time of delivery or allowing S to increase the price of the goods without, in both cases, giving the consumer the right to cancel if the final price is too high in relation to the price agreed under the contract;[3] and (ii) automatically extending a contract of fixed duration where the consumer does not give notice to terminate it and the deadline fixed for the consumer to express his desire not to extend the contract is unreasonably early.[4]

Strangely, the UTCCR make no provision for the burden of proof in relation to unfairness[5] whereas, under the UCTA, the onus is placed squarely on the person

---

1 See *Thompson v London, Midland and Scottish Rly Co* [1930] 1 KB 41; *L'Estrange v F Graucob Ltd* [1934] 2 KB 394; (considered above).
2 Sch 2, para 1(a).
3 Sch 2, para 1(l); see also Sch 2, para 2(c) and (d) which qualify this potentially unfair term in cases where price is linked to Stock Exchange fluctuations or where the contract contains other, lawful price indexation clauses, or in contracts for the sale of foreign currency.
4 Sch 2, para 1(h).
5 The DTI is 'content' that the burden of proof should lie on the party alleging unfairness, see *Unfair Terms in Consumer Contracts Regulations 1994, Guidance Notes* (DTI, 1995), para 53.

seeking the protection of the clause to show that it satisfies the test of reasonableness or for those claiming that a party does not 'deal as consumer' to show that he does not so deal.[6]

Terms concerning adequacy of the price or defining the subject matter of the contract

One crucial limitation on the scope of the test of unfairness in the UTCCR is contained in reg 6(2) which stipulates that:

> 'In so far as it is in plain, intelligible language, the assessment of fairness of a term shall not relate –
> (a) to the definition of the main subject matter of the contract, or
> (b) to the adequacy of the price or remuneration, as against the goods or services supplied in exchange.'

Para (a)

Fundamental to the operation of reg 6(2) is the stipulation in para (a) that no assessment shall be made of the fairness of a term which 'defines the main subject matter of the contract'. While para (b) represents an indisputable facet of freedom of contract in allowing the parties to fix the price of goods or services, para (a) is the fundamental embodiment of that notion in that it grants to the parties the liberty to define clearly the subject matter of their contract. An example of such a core term, referred to by the Office of Fair Trading,[7] is that retail 'gift vouchers' may, plainly and intelligibly, state the date upon which they expire and thus become invalid.

It is also clear that many definitional or 'core-shrinking' provisions which are clear and intelligible will fall, correctly, outside the control of the UTCCR and be regarded as fair and legitimate. For example, in a consumer sale of a second-hand car, S might provide a clearly-worded, intelligible list of defects, both the list and the defects having been drawn to B's attention before contract, with the car's price being commensurate with a car in that defective state. Undoubtedly, S would be regarded as having, quite fairly, defined the subject-matter of the contract and the contract terms would not fall foul of the UTCCR. Again, as Sir Guenter Treitel[8] points out, Lord Devlin's celebrated example of the anxious hostess who asked her seller to 'send me peas or if you haven't got peas send me beans, but for heaven's sake send something' would seem to be within para (a). This term would not be *prima facie* unfair as one enabling S unilaterally to alter the characteristics of the product to be provided[9] because, as Lord Devlin emphasised, the contract would be for 'peas, beans or anything else *ejusdem generis* and is a perfectly sensible contract to make'.[10]

There is more difficulty once the line is crossed into the realms of unfair core-shrinking terms. It may not be an easy task to locate that line but the UTCCR certainly makes no attempt at differentiating permissible, definitional terms from such terms which are impermissible and unfair.

---

6   The UCTA, ss 11(5) and 12(3).
7   See *Unfair Contract Terms*, Bulletin No 6, April 1999, para 124 and Case Report 56, p 49.
8   *The Law of Contract* (10th edn, 1999), p 249.
9   See Sch 2, para 1(k).
10   See 'The Treatment of Breach of Contract' [1966] CLJ 192, 212.

Para (a)[11] was considered recently by the Court of Appeal in *Director General of Fair Trading v First National Bank plc*,[12] the facts of which are given above. The bank argued that the core terms of a credit agreement extended beyond the rate of interest payable to cover both the period during which interest was payable and the sum on which it was payable. However, the Court of Appeal rejected that argument and accepted the Director General's contention that clause 8 consisted of default provisions which were applicable where a *breach* of contract occurred and it followed that such terms did not define the 'main subject matter of the contract'. Accordingly, the default provision relating to interest was not exempted from the operation of the UTCCR and its fairness fell to be assessed by the court.[13]

Para (b)

Para (b) enunciates the familiar rule that adequacy of consideration will not be challenged *per se* and thus the price charged for the goods or services remains within the central core of freedom of contract. Even though the UTCCR are the apotheosis of *caveat venditor* in consumer contracts, an undertaking cannot be impugned simply because the consumer has, voluntarily and openly, made a bad bargain. Nevertheless, the notion that the quality/price ratio is not subject to interference must be treated with caution and there are clearly cases where price is a significant factor in assessing unfairness. It is plain from the decision in *Director General of Fair Trading v First National Bank plc*,[14] above, that sellers and suppliers are not to be allowed shelter in the argument that contract terms relate to the adequacy of consideration when, in fact, those terms are unfair within the UTCCR. In *First National Bank*, the Court of Appeal stressed that, if the default provisions under consideration were regarded as relating to the adequacy of consideration, 'almost any provision containing any part of the bargain would be capable of falling within the reach of reg 3(2)'[15] and this would, obviously, be an unacceptable conclusion as the UTCCR would be rendered ineffectual.

First, just as price can be important in the evaluation of satisfactory quality under the SGA, s 14, it must be a relevant factor in assessing unfairness under the UTCCR in some situations. For example, S might sell defective goods purporting to exclude liability for such defects and charging a price which is commensurate with goods which are *not* defective. Here the inflated price would surely be a factor to consider in castigating the contract terms as unfair under reg 6(1).

Second, price-escalation clauses which purport to allow S to increase the price of goods without giving B a right to cancel the contract if the final price is too high in relation to the price agreed, are potentially unfair.[16] Similarly, onerous terms of the type in *Interfoto Picture Library Ltd v Stiletto Visual Programmes Ltd*,[17] which stipulate for exorbitant fines if goods are retained longer than the

---

11 The UTCCR 1994, reg 3(2), para (a). The UTCCR 1999, reg 6(2), para (a), replaces reg 3(2) but is, in substance, identical to reg 3(2).
12 [2000] 2 All ER 759.
13 This aspect of the decision is considered above.
14 [2000] 2 All ER 759.
15 [2000] 2 All ER 759 at 768, per Peter Gibson LJ.
16 See the UTCCR Sch 2, para 1(l).
17 [1989] QB 433.

original contract period, would almost certainly be unfair in consumer contracts.[18]

Third, reg 6(2) itself provides that term will not be be impugned where it is expressed in 'plain intelligible language' and so, for example, a term is undoubtedly unfair if, quite unnecessarily, the price of the goods can be ascertained only by a difficult calculation involving a cross-referencing of terms.

As mentioned above, para (b) was evaluated in *Director General of Fair Trading v First National Bank plc*.[19] The default provisions regarding the payment of interest were held not to be terms concerned with 'the adequacy of the price or remuneration' within para (b). Instead, terms relating to the adequacy of the price or remuneration were held to be those which defined the parties' rights and obligations in the due *performance* of the contract. Moreover, the default provisions did not relate to the *rate* at which interest was payable but, instead, provided for the continuation of the contractual rate after judgment.

Assessing good faith

The 1994 Regulations[20] contained a list of four factors to be taken into account in making an assessment of good faith, viz (a) the strength of the parties' bargaining positions; (b) whether the consumer had an inducement to agree to the term; (c) whether the goods or services were sold/supplied to the special order of the consumer; and (d) the extent to which the seller/supplier had dealt fairly and equitably with the consumer. These four factors have been deleted from the body of the 1999 Regulations because they are contained in recital 16 to the Directive[1] and the 1999 Regulations sought to reflect more accurately the wording of the main text of the Directive. Accordingly, these four factors remain crucial as reference must be made to the recitals in interpreting the Regulations and, of course, reg 5(1) stipulates that the absence of 'the requirement of good faith' is crucial in assessing the unfairness of a contract term.

The first three factors above closely resemble three of the five guidelines on reasonableness in the UCTA, Sch 2.[2] However, the reference to 'good faith' in reg 5(1) and the statement in the recitals to the Directive that 'the requirement of good faith may be satisfied by the seller or supplier where he deals fairly and equitably with the other party whose legitimate interests he has to take into account'[3] are a remarkable departure from the narrower notion of reasonableness in the UCTA. Potentially, the scope of the good faith requirement is immense. Undoubtedly it can apply to matters in the negotiation and formation of the contract such as misrepresentation and duress and it can also encompass the notion that contract terms must be legible and understandable. Similarly, the Office of Fair Trading[4] has accentuated that, in assessing good faith, it takes account of the availability and use of explanatory pre-contractual brochures and whether, having signed a contract, consumers are given a reasonable 'cooling-off' period in which they may cancel the contract without penalty. Although these are fundamental factors to consider,

---

18 See eg, the UTCCR Sch 2, para 1(e),(h),(i) and (l).
19 [2000] 2 All ER 759.
20 Sch 2.
 1 93/13/EEC.
 2 See Sch 2, paras (a), (b) and (e).
 3 93/13/EEC, recital 16.
 4 *Unfair Contract Terms*, Bulletin No 2, Sept 1996, para 222.

they are not uniquely redolent of *good faith*. For example, reg 7 provides expressly that written terms must be expressed in 'plain, intelligible language',[5] the common law retains sufficient vigour to control pre- contractual duplicity[6] and the UCTA oversees the narrower notion of reasonableness. Is it not time to acknowledge that the inauguration in English law of the Civil law's concept of 'good faith' demands a radical transformation of the existing law?

It is hoped that English law will begin to develop a modern, positive[7] formulation of good faith or refine established concepts of equity in order to ensure fulfilment of the consumer's reasonable expectations and demand conscionable, fair dealing on the part of the business supplier and seller.[8] Certainly recital 16 to the Directive refers in broad terms to 'making an overall evaluation of the different interests involved' and that the 'legitimate interests' of the consumer must be taken into account. Alternatively, a sceptical view is that the more accessible guidelines in recital 16, mentioned above, might be those which are accentuated and, after balancing the easily understandable, pragmatic factors specified in reg 6(1), the court might consider that there is a significant imbalance to the detriment of the consumer which is thereby contrary to good faith. In this way, the requirement of good faith might not develop as a *substantive* test of fairness but would, instead, be subjugated to the more accessible, *procedural* tests of fairness in contract formation.[9] The very existence of reg 6(2), proscribing interference with the adequacy of the price/remuneration and the definition of the main subject matter, arguably invites the courts to follow this latter route – clearly, there will be no substantive investigation regarding the reasonableness of the price paid by the consumer. If it is to avoid being the outcast in Europe, English law must begin to consider good faith as a substantive element and heed the warning that 'prohibiting unfair terms, and creating a positive duty of good faith in the performance of contracts, are very different things'.[10]

Director General of Fair Trading v First National Bank plc[11] is, as yet, the only decision to consider the UTCCR and good faith but the reasoning employed augurs well for the development of that notion. The Court of Appeal stressed that, in order to comply with the requirement of good faith, 'terms must be reasonably transparent and should not operate to defeat the reasonable

---

5 See below.
6 See also the UTCCR, reg 6(1): 'all the circumstances attending the conclusion of the contract' must be considered when assessing the unfairness of a contract term.
7 There are encouraging signs in a later OFT report, where it is recognised that 'the requirement of good faith does not in our view equate to an absence of "bad faith", in the narrow English sense of dishonest or deceptive conduct' (*Unfair Contract Terms*, Bulletin No 4, Dec 1997, p 23).
8 See Summers, 'Good Faith in General Contract Law and the Sales Provisions of the Uniform Commercial Code' (1968) 54 Va L Rev 195; Waddams, 'Unconscionability in Contracts' (1976) 39 MLR 369; Forte, 'Unfair Contract Terms: evaluating an EEC perspective' [1985] LMCLQ 482; Brownsword, 'Two Concepts of Good Faith' (1994) 7 JCL 197; Brownsword, 'Good Faith in Contracts Revisited' [1996] 49 CLP 111 .
9 On the distinction between substantive and procedural unfairness see Leff, 'Unconscionability and The Code – The Emperor's New Clause' (1967) 115 U Pa L Rev 485; Ellinghaus, 'In Defense of Unconscionability' (1969) 78 Yale LJ 757; Spanogle, 'Analyzing Unconscionability Problems' (1969) 117 U Pa L Rev 931; Epstein, 'Unconscionability: A Critical Reappraisal (1975) 18 J Law & Econ 283; Gordley, 'Equality in Exchange' (1981) 69 Cal LR 1587; Eisenberg, 'The Bargain, Principle and its Limits (1982) 95 Harv L Rev 741.
10 The Hon Mr Justice Steyn, 'The Role of Good Faith and Fair Dealing in Contract Law: A Hair-Shirt Philosophy?' (1991) Denning LJ 131, 136.
11 [2000] 2 All ER 759.

expectations of the consumer'.[12] The relevant term relating to the payment of interest was held to create 'unfair surprise' in the consumer and thus it did not satisfy the test of good faith.

The effects of an unfair term

The UTCCR, reg 8(1) specifies that an 'unfair term in a contract concluded with a consumer by a seller or supplier shall not be binding upon the consumer'. It should be noted that the unfair term ceases to bind only the *consumer* and thus, should he so wish, the consumer may enforce the contract containing the unfair term. Regulation 8(2) allows for severance of the unfair term and then 'the contract shall continue to bind the parties if it is capable of continuing in existence without the unfair term'. It thus seems that the unfair term, eg an exclusion of liability, might thus cease to bind the consumer but leave him liable for the price of the goods. However, the contract would clearly not be capable of 'continuing in existence' if the unfair term went to the root of the contract, but this raises the unanswered question of when such a fundamental, unfair term, might have this dissolutive effect on the entire undertaking.

In *Director General of Fair Trading v First National Bank plc*,[13] the Court of Appeal ordered that the defendant bank should amend the unfair term and incorporate the new term in its standard form contract.

Prevention of the continued use of unfair terms

Regulations 10-15 relate to the machinery for challenging unfair terms and the prevention of their continued use. Under reg 10(1), it is the duty of the Director General of Fair Trading to consider complaints made to him regarding unfair terms and, under reg 12(1), he may apply for an injunction against the person using such a term. In deciding whether or not to apply for an injunction, the Director may have regard to any undertakings given to him by the person as to the continued use of the term in question (reg 10(3)).

The negotiations between the Office of Fair Trading and traders/trade associations regarding unfair terms is almost certainly a more effective method of regulating the use of such terms than private and costly consumer litigation. Regulation 13(3) provides that the Director General and the specified regulatory bodies[14] can require traders to produce copies of their contracts and give information as to their use. This power thus facilitates the investigation of complaints and, moreover, ensures that sellers and suppliers are complying with court orders and abiding by any undertakings that they may have given regarding the contract terms. The administrative pattern of control is furthered by reg 15 which expressly provides for the Director General to disseminate information to the public regarding the Regulations[15] and publicise those terms which have been castigated as unfair. It is, however, regrettable that there are no criminal sanctions

---

12   [2000] 2 All ER 759 at 769, per Peter Gibson LJ.
13   [2000] 2 All ER 759.
14   See below.
15   The OFT produces regular and informative material on unfair contract terms which have been referred to the Director General, see *Unfair Contract Terms Bulletins*.

for contravening the UTCCR, as the provisions which allow for criminal prosecution for the contravention of the UCTA[16] act as a deterrent to rogue traders.

Regulation 11 extends the power to seek an injunction to other regulatory bodies which are specified in Sch 1, eg the Data Protection Registrar and the Directors General of Electricity, Gas and Water, provided such bodies have notified the Director General of their intention to apply for an injunction at least 14 days before the application is made, unless the Director consents to the application being made within a shorter period (reg 12(2)(a) and (b)). Most importantly for consumers, this power to seek injunctions extends to every weights and measures authority in Great Britain and the Consumers' Association.

Intelligibility in written contracts

Regulation 7 provides that 'a seller or supplier shall ensure that any written term of a contract is expressed in plain, intelligible language' and that, 'if there is doubt about the meaning of a written term, the interpretation which is most favourable to the consumer shall prevail'. Although the common law[17] might achieve this result by a combination of the rules on reasonable notice and interpretation *contra proferentem*, the express articulation of principle in reg 7 is most welcome.

The Office of Fair Trading[18] has stressed that recital 20 to the Directive couples the plain and intelligible language requirement with the demand that consumers should be given 'an opportunity to examine all the terms' and that, consequently, there is a single requirement that before entering into a contract, consumers must be able to read and understand all its written terms. Moreover, there is clearly a distinction to be drawn between *plain* language and *intelligible* language: a plainly-worded clause may nevertheless be woefully unintelligible. The Office of Fair Trading has pointed out that 'references to statutes and to consumer rights under them are not normally intelligible, and are potentially unfair where consumers need to understand the reference to know where their rights and interests lie. Accordingly we invariably challenge excessively wide exclusions of liability even when they are qualified by saving provisions ... to the effect that ... consumers' statutory rights are unaffected. Indeed, the phrase "this does not affect your statutory rights" is a prime example of plain language that is not intelligible'.[19]

Although reg 7 appears to be uncomplicated, it does pose problems. First, it is unclear to whom the language must be plain and intelligible: terminology which may appear convoluted to a consumer may be crystal-clear to a seller, lawyer or judge. Undoubtedly the thrust of reg 7 is that the term should be comprehensible to a consumer but, again, does this mean one who is credulous and careless or is the standard that of the circumspect and cautious?[20] Second,

---

16 See the Consumer Transactions (Restrictions on Statements) Order 1976 (SI 1976/1813, as amended by SI 1978/27).
17 See also the UCTA, Sch 2, para c.
18 *Unfair Contract Terms*, Bulletin No 2, Sept 1996, paras 2.6-2.7; 2.21-2.22.
19 *Unfair Contract Terms*, Bulletin No 2, Sept 1996, paras 2.17-2.18.
20 See generally Ramsay, *Consumer Protection Text and Materials* (1989), pp 215-231; Ramsay, 'Consumer Law and Structures of Thought: A Comment' (1993) 16 Journal of Consumer Policy 79. Although the OFT considers that 'contract terms must normally be within the understanding of ordinary consumers *without legal advice*' (*Unfair Contract Terms*, Bulletin No 2, Sept 1996, para 2.13), this is not overly-helpful in defining such an 'ordinary' consumer.

the remedies available to the consumer where reg 7 is contravened are left unresolved. If, under reg 6(2), the price or main subject matter are not expressed in plain, intelligible language, the seller or supplier runs the risk that the term may be declared unfair but no such penalty attaches to reg 7. The intent here may well be that a term which is not expressed plainly and intelligibly is *prima facie* unfair,[1] but it is surely difficult *always* to yoke ambiguity and uncertainty with unfairness. In conclusion, there seems to be a danger that reg 7 may be regarded as little more than an enactment of the *contra proferentem* rule of interpretation.

---

1 The OFT considers that 'the use of terms which consumers find difficult to read and understand is a potential source of unfairness in its own right that fully deserves attention and action' (*Unfair Contract Terms*, Bulletin No 2, Sept 1996, para 2.10).

CHAPTER 26

The seller's real remedies

Introduction

Where S has not been paid for the goods, his most obvious remedies are either to sue B for the price or maintain an action in damages for non-acceptance of the goods. These are *personal* actions[1] on the contract itself and may clearly be apt where B can pay for the goods but refuses to do so.

An unpaid seller also has several remedies in respect of the goods themselves meaning that, in effect, the goods are a form of security which ensure payment of the price. These *real* remedies, so called because they depend upon the actual goods, are most useful in cases of insolvency where B cannot pay as it is plain that, in such cases, a personal action for the price will often be fruitless. The real remedies comprise, first, the seller's lien, which is the right to retain possession of the goods until payment is made by B and, second, the right to stop the goods which are in transit to B. Principally, these remedies protect the unpaid seller where the goods have not been delivered into the physical possession of B. The third real remedy, resale of the goods, is greatly facilitated once S's lien has attached to the goods or they have been successfully stopped in transit, but the right to resell is separate from the first two real remedies.

The risk that S might become simply an unsecured creditor of B's in the event of the latter's bankruptcy is thus considerably reduced by the existence and exercise of the real remedies. However, it must be stressed that the decreasing importance of the real remedies coincides with the increased use of bankers' commercial credits, the essence of this device being that S can obtain payment from a bank in his own country upon presentation of the shipping documents, meaning that he is rarely an unpaid seller who needs to invoke the real remedies. Moreover, modern developments have meant that S may seek more extensive rights by using a Romalpa clause, ie an express term of the contract whereby S reserves *property* in the goods until he has been paid in full, even where the goods have been delivered into B's physical possession. Romalpa clauses have become increasingly technical and so they are considered separately in Chapter 17.

The real remedies are intricate and care is needed in deciding upon their applicability in various factual situations; moreover, as the three remedies interlock, they can truly be understood only as a whole.

---

1 See Ch 27.

The unpaid seller's real remedies against the goods

The three rights of the unpaid seller against the goods themselves are (i) a lien for the price (ii) a right to stop the goods which are in transit to B, and (iii) a right of resale of the goods. Accordingly, the SGA, s 39 provides:

'(1) Subject to this and any other Act, notwithstanding that the property in the goods may have passed to the buyer, the unpaid seller of goods, as such, has by implication of law –
(a) a lien on the goods or right to retain[2] them for the price while he is in possession of them;
(b) in case of the insolvency of the buyer, a right of stopping the goods in transit after he has parted with the possession of them;
(c) a right of re-sale as limited by this Act.
(2) Where the property in goods has not passed to the buyer, the unpaid seller has (in addition to his other remedies) a right of withholding delivery similar to and co-extensive with his rights of lien or retention and stoppage in transit where the property has passed to the buyer'.

It will be noticed that these real remedies arise 'by implication of law' and thus they can be excluded or varied by express agreement or by a course of dealing between the parties. The first two remedies, lien and stoppage in transit, are applicable primarily in situations where the goods have not been physically delivered to B or his agent and it will be noticed that s 39(1) provides that it is immaterial that *property* in the goods may have passed to B – here it is the fact that B has not obtained actual possession which is crucial. Lien and stoppage are frequently the precursors to the exercise by S of the right of resale, the third real remedy.

Section 39(2) confers rights upon the unpaid seller where property has *not* passed to B and, although the section seems somewhat superfluous where S is the owner of the goods, it confirms that S's rights where he still has property in the goods should be no less than in the situation where property has passed to B. The essence of a lien is the right to retain possession of goods which belong to another and so s 39(2) was said by Chalmers, the draftsman of the SGA, to be necessary 'because it would be a contradiction in terms to speak of a man having a lien upon his own goods'.[3] Under s 39(2), S will thus claim to retain goods in which he has property until payment is made by B. One situation in which this can occur is in a contract to sell unascertained goods in instalments where property will not pass until the goods are appropriated to each instalment and, provided the contract is not severable, S may refuse to deliver future instalments until he is paid for deliveries which have already been made to B.[4]

In contrast with s 39(1), there is no specific right of resale in s 39(2) and this was omitted, presumably, on the basis that such a right was unnecessary where S retained property in the goods. However, a literal interpretation of the provisions could lead to the wholly unacceptable conclusion that an unpaid seller could resell the goods where property had passed to B under s 39(1) but that no

---

2 The 'right to retain' and 'retention' are, here, terms of Scottish law.
3 Chalmers, *Sale of Goods* (18th edn, 1981), p 202; see also *Nippon Yusen Kaisha v Ramjiban Serowgee* [1938] AC 429, 444 per Lord Wright.
4 *Re Edwards, ex p Chalmers* (1873) 8 Ch App 289 (see below, when possession and S's lien are considered); *Longbottom & Co Ltd v Bass, Walker & Co* [1922] WN 245.

right of resale would be available where property had not passed under s 39(2). It does seem, however, that the right of resale is available whether or not property has passed to B.[5]

Before the three real remedies can be considered separately, it is necessary to examine the meaning of two important concepts in s 39, viz the 'unpaid seller' and 'insolvency'.

THE UNPAID SELLER

First, a wide meaning is given to 'seller' in s 38(2):

> 'In this Part of this Act "seller" includes any person who is in the position of a seller, as, for instance, an agent of the seller to whom the bill of lading has been indorsed, or a consignor or agent who has himself paid (or is directly responsible for) the price.'

The general definition of 'seller' in the SGA, s 61(1) is 'a person who sells or agrees to sell goods' and so s 38(2) grants remedies to a wider range of persons who have not been paid and are 'in the position of a seller', eg S's agent who has himself paid the price to S .[6] However, the expanded definition in s 38(2) does not extend to a buyer who has a claim against the seller for repayment of the price. Thus where B paid the price to S but then lawfully rejected the goods, he could not claim a lien over the goods in order to oblige S to repay the price to him.[7] In this situation, B's rejection of the goods revests the property in S leaving B with only a personal claim against S[8] – B should thus reject the goods and claim the return of the price only if he is convinced as to S's solvency for he is clearly dependent on this. This is criticisable as it is difficult to see why B should not have a lien for the price where his rejection of the goods is justifiable and lawful.

Second, an 'unpaid seller' is defined in the SGA, s 38(1):

> 'The seller of goods is an unpaid seller within the meaning of this Act –
> (a) when the whole of the price has not been paid or tendered;
> (b) when a bill of exchange or other negotiable instrument has been received as conditional payment, and the condition on which it was received has not been fulfilled by reason of the dishonour of the instrument or otherwise.'

There are two crucial points in relation to the unpaid seller. First, it seems that S can be 'unpaid' despite the fact that payment is not *due* under the contract, because the right of lien or stoppage is available to S where B becomes *insolvent* even though the date of payment has not arrived. Second, during a period of credit allowed by S or during the currency of a negotiable instrument, S is deemed to have waived his right to a lien, but S will be 'unpaid' where, for example, B's cheque is dishonoured and he becomes insolvent and here S's right to a lien revives. Similarly, where B is obliged to pay by opening a banker's commercial credit in favour of S, the opening of the credit is regarded as conditional payment and, if the banker defaults, S may claim the price from B and his real remedies against the goods are renewed.

---

5 See *Ward (R V) Ltd v Bignall* [1967] 1 QB 534, 545 per Diplock LJ.
6 See *Imperial Bank v London and St Katharine Docks Co* (1877) 5 Ch D 195.
7 *Lyons (J L) & Co Ltd v May and Baker Ltd* [1923] 1 KB 685.
8 See Ch 23.

INSOLVENCY

The SGA, s 61(4) defines insolvency:

> 'A person is deemed to be insolvent within the meaning of this Act if he has either
> ceased to pay his debts in the ordinary course of business or he cannot pay his debts
> as they become due.'

The definition is important because stoppage in transit can only be exercised
when B becomes insolvent and, likewise, B's insolvency is one of several incidents
which justify S's lien over the goods. There is, in fact, some uncertainty regarding
the precise meaning of insolvency in this situation as there is minimal authority.
It is clear that neither B's insolvency nor bankruptcy necessarily amounts to a
repudiation of the contract[9] because, for example, the trustee in bankruptcy may
tender the price to S within a reasonable time of B's default and claim delivery
of the goods.[10] Although insolvency itself is not a repudiation of the contract,
an unequivocal intimation that B will not proceed with the contract may amount
to a repudiation and so where B states that he is insolvent so as to indicate that
he does not intend to, or cannot, perform the contract, S may regard this as a
repudiation and terminate the contract.[11]

The unpaid seller's lien

The SGA, s 41(1) provides:

> 'Subject to this Act, the unpaid seller of goods who is in possession of them is entitled
> to retain possession of them until payment or tender of the price in the following
> cases: –
> (a) where the goods have been sold without any stipulation as to credit;
> (b) where the goods have been sold on credit but the term of credit has expired;
> (c) where the buyer becomes insolvent.'

THE NATURE AND EFFECT OF THE SELLER'S LIEN

The essence of a lien is the right to retain possession of goods which belong to
another until certain demands of the party in possession are met. The unpaid
seller's lien is a *particular* lien which arises only in the circumstances prescribed
by the SGA and is not *general* lien for all debts due from B: S's lien is thus a
right to retain possession of the goods until B has paid or tendered the whole of
the price. Moreover, the lien covers only the price of the goods and does not
extend to the expenses involved in keeping or storing the goods, the reason for
this being that S retains the goods for his own benefit thereby ensuring the
continuation of the lien.[12]

---

9 See *Re Edwards, ex p Chalmers* (1873) 8 Ch App 289.
10 See *Re Nathan, ex p Stapleton* (1879) 10 Ch D 586.
11 See *Re Phoenix Bessemer Steel Co* (1876) 4 Ch D 108, 120-121 per James LJ; *Re Nathan,
    ex p Stapleton* (1879) 10 Ch D 586, 590 per Jessel MR.
12 *Somes v British Empire Shipping Co* (1860) 8 HLC 338; *China-Pacific SA v Food Corpn
    of India* [1982] AC 939. S might be able to establish a claim in damages for expenses: see
    Bloxam v Sanders (1825) 4 B & C 941.

The SGA, s 48(1) provides that the exercise of S's lien (or stoppage in transit) does not rescind the contract of sale and thus there is still an obligation on S to deliver the goods on payment of the price by B or, for example, by his trustee in bankruptcy. Moreover, although S's exercise of his lien will often be the forerunner of the right of resale, the lien itself does not give S any *property* in the goods and the right to resell must be sought elsewhere, eg under the SGA, s 48(3) or by virtue of an express term of the contract. However, the SGA, s 48(2) provides that, where S has exercised his lien and then resold the goods, the new buyer acquires a good title to them as against the original buyer. It should be emphasised that, although the new buyer will acquire title to the goods in this situation, there is nothing in the statutory provisions which exonerates S from liability in breach of contract to the original buyer. This question is returned to when S's right of resale is considered as a separate topic.

As mentioned earlier, it is immaterial to the exercise of S's lien that property in the goods has passed to B but, of course, for the lien to arise S must have physical possession of the goods. It should also be remembered that s 39(2) (considered earlier) allows S rights which are co-extensive with a lien in cases where property in the goods has not passed to B.

CONDITIONS FOR THE OPERATION OF THE SELLER'S LIEN

There are three conditions for the valid exercise of S's lien, viz:

(1) S must be unpaid;
(2) the goods have been sold without any stipulation as to credit *or* the period of credit has expired *or* B has become insolvent (these are the conditions in s 41(1));
(3) S must be in possession of the goods or part of them.

The definition of an 'unpaid seller' in condition (1) was considered earlier. It should also be stressed in relation to condition (2), that the unpaid seller is given a lien in a simple sale of goods where no credit is allowed to B, and this clearly harmonises with the general rule in the SGA, s 28, which provides that delivery and payment are concurrent conditions. If S does grant credit to B, he is deemed to waive his lien for the agreed credit period but the lien revives after expiry of the period, whether or not B is insolvent. Often, however, S will have delivered the goods to B before the period of credit has expired and he will thus have no lien. Likewise, where B is allowed credit during the period of a negotiable instrument, the lien is waived for that period of time but will revive if the negotiable instrument is dishonoured. The meaning of 'insolvency' in condition (2) was also considered earlier but it bears repetition that, where B has become insolvent, S is entitled to a lien even though any period of credit has not expired. S can thus retain the goods and see whether full payment is made by B or his trustee in bankruptcy and this conveniently avoids the necessity for S to prove in the bankruptcy for the price of the goods.

Condition (3), that S must be in possession of the goods, demands further analysis. As a general rule, S's lien is a right to *retain* possession but not to regain it once it has been lost.[13] The central difficulty is that possession is a notoriously

---

13 *Jeffcott v Andrew Motors Ltd* [1960] NZLR 721, 732 per Hutchison J: 'a lien ... is a shield, not a sword, giving a defence not a right of action'.

pliable concept[14] and, throughout the differing types of lien which the law acknowledges,[15] there is no single, cohesive definition of the nature and extent of the possession which suffices as the foundation of a lien: the law may consider actual, constructive or symbolic possession to be acceptable.[16] By and large, the unpaid seller's possession is sufficient if he has overall control of the goods even though he allows B access to them and a degree of control, provided that this does not amount to exclusive possession.[17] In *Milgate v Kebble*,[18] S sold a quantity of apples to B and, with S's permission, B was allowed to store them in a kiln in S's outhouse. S gave B the key of the kiln but S retained the key of the outhouse. As B did not pay for the apples, S resold them. It was held that, although property in the goods had passed to B, he had neither actual possession nor the immediate right to possession; instead S was in possession and had a valid lien upon the goods. Likewise, S was held not to have relinquished possession to B where B bought cigars in S's shop which were packed in boxes supplied by B and left in S's shop, to be paid for before being removed.[19] Moreover, it was held in *Miles v Gorton*,[20] that B's payment of warehousing charges to S whilst the goods remained on S's premises was insufficient to confer possession upon B.[1] In *Paton's Trustees v Finlayson*,[2] B bought a growing crop of potatoes on S's land and was allowed to lift them and store them on the land in pits. It was a term of the contract that S would arrange for the carting of the potatoes to a railway station but B became bankrupt while the potatoes were in the pits and the price had not been paid to S. It was held that, although property in the goods passed to B on lifting, the handling of the potatoes by B did not amount to a delivery of the goods to him; on the contrary, S retained physical possession and his right of lien. Ultimately, the court must decide whether the extent of the control which B has over the goods means that possession has shifted from S to B. Thus, where oak timber lying at a wharf was sold to B who was allowed to measure the timber, number and mark each tree with his initials and spend money on squaring the timber, it was held that possession had passed to B.[3] Likewise, where S placed the goods in two locked rooms within his premises but gave the keys to B and conferred on him an irrevocable licence to enter the premises and

---

14   See Pollock and Wright, *Possession in the Common Law.*

15   See generally Crossley Vaines, *Personal Property* (5th edn, 1973), Ch 7; Silvertown, *The Law of Lien* (1988); Bell, *Modern Law of Personal Property in England and Ireland* (1989), Ch 6.

16   See especially the valuable discussion in *Great Eastern Rly Co v Lord's Trustee* [1909] AC 109 (on the carrier's lien) and Fletcher Moulton LJ's (dissenting) judgment in the CA: [1908] 2 KB 54.

17   See *Great Eastern Rly Co v Lord's Trustee* [1909] AC 109; [1908] 2 KB 54, CA: in a leading decision on the carrier's lien, the G E Rail Co's lien on coal was held to continue even though a coal merchant was permitted to stack the coal on land let to him by the company. The land was within the railway yard, the gates of which were kept closed at certain times.

18   (1841) 3 Man & G 100.

19   *Boulter v Arnott* (1833) 1 Cr & M 333.

20   (1834) 2 Cr & M 504.

 1   See the SGA, s 41(2) which provides that S's lien is not lost by the fact that S holds the goods as agent or bailee for B.

 2   1923 SC 872.

 3   *Cooper v Bill* (1865) 3 H & C 722; cf *Holderness v Shackels* (1828) 8 B & C 612 (separation of whale oil into casks marked with the initials of a part-owner of a ship and stored in a warehouse of a third party was held to be a 'qualified appropriation' only. The part-owners could inform the warehouseman not to deliver the goods until the disbursements of the ship had been met and thus they had a lien on the casks).

remove the goods, it was held that possession had passed to B.[4] At common law, S lost his lien if he attorned to B and thereby acknowledged that he held the goods as a bailee for B and on account of B. The position was altered in the SGA 1893 and the SGA, s 41(2) now provides that S may 'exercise his lien or right of retention notwithstanding that he is in possession of the goods as agent or bailee or custodier for the buyer'. Nevertheless, the fact that S has changed his capacity from a seller to a bailee or agent might mean that S has waived his lien (see below).

The situation where S has made a partial delivery of the goods is covered by the SGA, s 42:

> 'Where an unpaid seller has made part delivery of the goods, he may exercise his lien or right of retention on the remainder, unless such part delivery has been made under such circumstances as to show an agreement to waive the lien or right of retention.'

The general rule is thus clearly expressed that part delivery does not involve a loss of S's lien but it is possible that partial delivery is intended by both parties to be delivery of the whole[5] and if B claims that S has lost his lien by such a partial delivery, the onus is on B to prove it.[6] Where there is a contract for the sale of a specific quantity of goods in instalments, the presumption is that an entire contract exists and thus S may exercise a lien over any part of the goods which have not been delivered if any part of the total price is unpaid.[7] This is not the case where the contract is severable with separate instalment deliveries and separate payment made for each delivery, because each instalment is treated as a separate contract. Thus, if S has delivered one instalment which has not been paid for, he cannot refuse to deliver and claim a lien over an instalment of goods which has been paid for, because he would then have, in effect, a general lien and the SGA contemplates only a particular lien.[8] In severable contracts, therefore, a lien can only be claimed over goods forming part of an instalment which has not been paid for.

TERMINATION OF THE LIEN

The SGA, s 43(1) specifies the three principal situations in which S will lose his lien:

> '(1) The unpaid seller of goods loses his lien or right of retention in respect of them—
> (a) when he delivers the goods to a carrier or other bailee or custodier for the purpose of transmission to the buyer without reserving the right of disposal of the goods;
> (b) when the buyer or his agent lawfully obtains possession of the goods;
> (c) by waiver of the lien or right of retention.'

---

4 *Wrightson v McArthur and Hutchisons (1919) Ltd* [1921] 2 KB 807.
5 *Kemp v Falk* (1882) 7 App Cas 573, 586 per Lord Blackburn. Section 42 demands an 'agreement to waive the lien' which, strangely, mixes agreement with the unilateral notion of waiver.
6 *Re McLaren, ex p Cooper* (1879) 11 Ch D 68, 73 per Brett LJ.
7 See *Re Edwards, ex p Chalmers* (1873) 8 Ch App 289 (goods were sold on terms of instalment deliveries each month, payment to be made 14 days after each delivery. After the November delivery, B did not pay for it and became insolvent. Held S could withhold delivery of the December instalment until the price of both the November and December instalments was tendered to him).
8 An express term of the contract could confer a general lien over any of B's goods in S's possession.

It should be stressed that s 43 is not a comprehensive statement of how S's lien may be lost: the lien will terminate, for example, where the whole of the price of the goods is paid or tendered to S as he will then no longer be an 'unpaid seller' within the SGA, s 38(1).

S delivers the goods to a carrier

Paragraph (a) of s 43(1) provides that S's lien will terminate when the goods are delivered to a carrier for transmission to B and this dovetails with the basic rule in the SGA, s 32(1) that delivery to a carrier is, *prima facie*, deemed to be a delivery to B.[9] However, this is only the *prima facie* rule and so if there are any special circumstances, eg S agrees to deliver the goods to B at a particular location/destination, the carrier may be regarded as S's agent meaning that the lien will remain in force. If the goods are shipped under a bill of lading, possession is deemed to transfer to B or his agent when the bill has been endorsed and delivered to B. However, providing the goods are still in transit to B, S may be able to exercise the right to stop the goods in transit but it should be stressed that stoppage in transit is limited in that its operation depends upon B's being *insolvent*. Section 43(1), para (a) also refers to the power of S to reserve the right of disposal. This power is contained in the SGA, s 19 and was considered earlier,[10] its normal meaning being that S reserves *property* in the goods until some condition is fulfilled. In the context of a lien, the most relevant situation where S may reserve the right of disposal is that given in s 19(2) where S takes a bill of lading which makes the goods deliverable to the order of S or his agent (instead of to the order of B). Property *and* possession in the goods shipped then remain in S, as possession of the bill of lading is regarded as constructive possession of the goods themselves. Constructive possession of the goods is transferred to B only when S indorses and delivers the bill of lading to B.

B or his agent lawfully obtains possession

Paragraph (b) of s 43(1) specifies that S's lien is lost when B or his agent lawfully obtains possession of the goods. Again property and possession must be distinguished and, although property in specific goods and the right to possess them can pass to B on contract, some form of *delivery* is needed before B obtains possession. An exception to this rule occurs where B was in possession of the goods before the sale as a bailee for S; in this situation S's assent that B holds the goods on his own account from the moment of the contract's formation or the passing of property may be sufficient to amount to delivery to B.[11]

The meaning of 'possession' in s 43(1)(b) is again somewhat indeterminate but guidance can be sought from the cases considered earlier on the question of the degree and nature of S's possession which is required for the acquisition and operation of his lien. Similarly, the decisions on the issue of the termination of transit under the right of stoppage in transit (see later) may be helpful. The

9   The question of delivery was considered in Ch 22; see also Ch 16 (passing of property) and Ch 24 (risk).
10 See Ch 16 on the passing of property and Ch 17 on reservation of title.
11 See Ch 22 on delivery. Note that, under the SGA, s 41(2), S may exercise his right of lien where he is in possession of the goods as bailee for B.

decision in *Tansley v Turner*[12] is, however, directly relevant. There S sold to B a quantity of felled ash timber on land belonging to a third party, at a price of 1s 7½d per cubic foot. B measured and took away much of the timber and the remaining trees were marked and measured but the cubic contents had not been ascertained precisely at the date of B's bankruptcy. It was held, first, that property in the timber had passed to B as the incomplete calculation was too trifling an incident to suspend the passing of property and, second, that S did not have a lien on the remaining timber for the whole of the price as there was 'a complete delivery'[13] to B. Where S has completely delivered the goods to B, S's later resumption of possession for some extraneous purpose, eg re-packing[14] or repair[15] of the goods, will not cause the lien to revive.

It will be noticed that s 43(1)(b) provides that B or his agent must 'lawfully' obtain possession of the goods. There are three possibilities to consider here. First, if S voluntarily transfers physical possession of the goods to B and has not been misled in any way, his lien will be lost. Second, an unlawful removal of the goods which deprives S of possession against his will and without his consent will not terminate the lien but it is unclear whether S must resume physical possession and how it can be restored. In *Wallace v Woodgate*,[16] S kept a livery stable and sold horses to B but he had an agreement with B for a lien over the horses for the costs of continuing to stable them. B was allowed to use the horses but he fraudulently removed them to another stable. It was held that S could retake the horses (without using force) and his lien revived when he resumed possession. Third, there is the situation where S consents in fact to B's physical possession of the goods but the consent has been induced by fraud or criminal deception. In these circumstances, it may be that S's lien will be lost thereby ensuring consonance with the SGA, s 25(1) (buyer in possession) where, it will be remembered, S's *de facto* consent suffices for the operation of that section. Alternatively, S's lien might survive as possession and title are separate notions but much depends on the weight accorded to physical possession; certainly it appears that a court cannot order a return of the goods to S[17] and so there are inherent difficulties here regarding the enforcement of the lien.

S will lose possession and thus his lien where a third party in possession of the goods as S's bailee attorns to B,[18] ie acknowledges that he holds the goods on behalf of B.[19] There must however be an attornment and, where goods are stored in a warehouse, simply handing a delivery order to B will be insufficient unless and until the warehouseman attorns to B.[20]

Where S has made a *partial* delivery of the goods, the SGA, s 42 (considered earlier) provides that he may still exercise his lien on the remainder unless the partial delivery amounts to a waiver of the lien.

---

12 (1835) 2 Bing NC 151.
13 (1835) 2 Bing NC 151 at 154, per Tindal CJ.
14 *Valpy v Gibson* (1847) 4 CB 837.
15 *United Plastics Ltd v Reliance Electric (NZ) Ltd* [1977] 2 NZLR 125.
16 (1824) Ry & M 193 (followed in *Jeffcott v Andrew Motors Ltd* [1960] NZLR 721).
17 *Jeffcott v Andrew Motors Ltd* [1960] NZLR 721, 732 per Hutchison J; see Ch 18 where s 25(1) is considered.
18 See the SGA, s 29(4), considered in Ch 22 on delivery.
19 *Harman v Anderson* (1809) 2 Camp 243; *Hawes v Watson* (1824) 2 B & C 540 (S sold to B who resold to sub-B. Warehousemen attorned to sub-B who then paid B. Held that the right to possession passed to the sub-B and S's lien for the price was lost despite B's bankruptcy).
20 *M'Ewan and Sons v Smith* (1849) 2 HL Cas 309.

Waiver of the lien

Section 43(1)(c) refers to waiver of the lien and this can occur either at the date of contract or during its performance. Examples of (implied) waiver of the lien at the time of contract are provided by s 41(1)(b), ie where S has allowed credit to B the lien is waived until the period of credit has expired, and s 38(1)(b), ie the lien is waived during the currency of a bill of exchange which S has taken for the price. It is tolerably clear that, as s 43 covers cases where the lien terminates, s 43(1)(c) refers to instances where the lien has been in existence and is waived during performance of the contract.

A waiver can occur in several differing situations. Perhaps most obviously, S's lien will be waived where he deals with the goods in a manner which is inconsistent with his right simply to retain possession of them, eg where he wrongfully consumes[1] the goods or resells[2] them. If S is then sued by B for wrongful interference with the goods he cannot justify his actions by setting-up his lien. A waiver can also result where S makes a new arrangement with B which is inconsistent with the lien's continuation, eg taking an alternative security from B for the price of the goods[3] or if S refuses to deliver the goods to B on some ground other than B's failure to pay or tender the price.[4] However, where S obtains a judgment for the price he does not waive his lien (s 43(2)) as only a fully satisfied judgment for the price ends the lien.[5]

Sub-sales and waiver of the lien?

It is most important in this context to consider the effect of a resale to a sub-buyer. The general rule in the SGA, s 47(1) is that the unpaid seller's right of lien (or stoppage in transit) is not affected by any sale, or other disposition of the goods (such as a pledge) which B may have made *unless* the seller has 'assented' to such a sub-sale or disposition, in which case his lien will be lost. Section 47(1) relates to the situation where B is *not* in possession of the goods but resells them to a sub-buyer[6] and S assents to that sub-sale. The notion of S's assent is analogous both to a waiver of his rights and an estoppel as, when it occurs, the sub-B will obtain a title free from S's lien (or right of stoppage) but it differs from waiver proper in that the assent here can be communicated to B rather than the sub-B. *Knights v Wiffen*[7] was a leading decision upon which s 47(1) was premised. There S sold barley to B and retained possession of it in his own warehouse as he was an unpaid seller. B sold a quantity of the barley to the sub-buyer and he paid B for it; the sub-buyer was then given a delivery order by B which was addressed to a station master. The sub-buyer then forwarded the order to the station master asking him to hold the goods for the sub-buyer. Upon being shown the delivery order by the station master, S agreed

---

1 *Gurr v Cuthbert* (1843) 12 LJ Ex 309.
2 *Chinery v Viall* (1860) 5 H & N 288.
3 See *Bank of Africa Ltd v Salisbury Gold Mining Co Ltd* [1892] AC 281.
4 See *Boardman v Sill* (1808) 1 Camp 410n.
5 Should S allow the goods to be taken in execution by the sheriff, he will lose his lien on giving possession to the sheriff.
6 Section 47 commences with the words 'subject to this Act', thereby referring, principally, to s 25(1) (buyer in possession).
7 (1870) LR 5 QB 660; see also *Merchant Banking Co v Phoenix Bessemer Steel Co* (1877) 5 Ch D 205.

to put the barley on rail when it was required by the sub-buyer. When B became insolvent, it was held that S was estopped from denying the sub-buyer's title and had no lien against the sub-buyer.

The concept of 'assent' has been considered in more modern cases and it is clear that S cannot be said to have assented to a resale merely because he has been informed of it and has raised no objections to it. In *Mordaunt Brothers v British Oil and Cake Mills Ltd*,[8] the normal practice of S, a seller of oil, was to retain possession until he received a delivery order from B. B then resold the oil and signed a delivery order in favour of the sub-buyer who delivered it to S with the indorsement 'please wait our orders'. Sometimes S did not comment on this procedure but, at other times, he stated that the delivery orders were 'in order'. On this occasion, B fell into arrears in paying S and S refused to make further deliveries; he then returned some unexecuted orders to the sub-buyer and claimed a lien on the oil. It was held that S had not assented to the sub-sales and thus retained his lien. Pickford J stressed that S could not be said to assent merely because a sub-sale had been brought to his notice and he was in receipt of that information but, instead, the assent must indicate that he 'intends to renounce his rights against the goods'.[9]

Assent was again considered in *Mount (D F) Ltd v Jay and Jay (Provisions) Co Ltd*.[10] There S sold to B 250 cartons of tinned peaches which were deposited at a wharf, S and B agreeing that the price should be paid by B out of the money received from the sub-buyer. S made out a delivery order in favour of B and delivered it to B who then indorsed it 'please transfer to our sub-order' and sent it to the wharfinger. B sold some of the cartons to the sub-B and gave him a new delivery order. The sub-buyer paid B but B refused to pay S. S then contacted the wharfinger, cancelled the delivery order and claimed a lien on the 225 cartons still remaining at the wharf. Salmon J held that S had assented to the sub-sale and had lost his lien. The judge emphasised that S knew that B could pay for the peaches only out of money obtained from the sub-buyer and the true inference was that S assented to the resale, in the sense that he intended to renounce his rights against the goods and take the risk of B's honesty. Salmon J also held that s 47(1) could apply to sales of both unascertained and specific goods but that it might be easier to infer assent in the latter case in the sense that S could hold specific goods for the sub-buyer.

Finally there is the question of assent and attornment. Where the unpaid seller in possession of the goods attorns to the sub-buyer and thus acknowledges that he holds the goods on his behalf or to his order, it is clear that this is a prime example of assent to the sub-sale within s 47(1).[11] As mentioned earlier, the same principle applies where a third party in possession of the goods as S's bailee (eg a warehouseman) attorns to B.

Under s 47(2), the unpaid seller will also lose his lien (or right of stoppage) if a sub-buyer or pledgee receives in good faith and for value a document of

---

8 [1910] 2 KB 502.
9 [1910] 2 KB 502 at 507.
10 [1960] 1 QB 159.
11 *Pearson v Dawson* (1858) EB & E 448; see also *Knights v Wiffen*, above. S's knowledge of the sub-sale or his simply informing the bailee of it will *not* amount to an assent: *Poulton and Son v Anglo-American Oil Co Ltd* (1910) 27 TLR 38, 39 per Channel J.
12 The SGA, s 61(1) provides that 'document of title' has the same meaning as in the Factors Act 1889 (see the FA, s 1(4)).

title[12] to goods which has been lawfully transferred[13] to B. For example, in *Ant Jurgens Margarinefabrieken v Louis Dreyfus & Co*,[14] S agreed to sell to B 2,640 bags of seed from a shipment of 6,400 bags and B paid by cheque. S gave B delivery orders for the 2,640 bags and B sold the seed to the sub-buyer and indorsed the delivery orders to him. When B's cheque was dishonoured, S told his warehouse to withhold delivery. Pickford J held that the transfer of the delivery orders (which were regarded as documents of title) terminated S's lien. It should also be noted that the person who transfers the document of title can create it himself, eg the delivery order in *Dreyfus*, and it is unnecessary that he should have received it from a third party before it can be 'transferred' within s 47(2). There is clearly an overlap between s 47(2) and s 25(1)(buyer in possession). In *Cahn and Mayer v Pockett's Bristol Channel Steam Packet Co Ltd*,[15] S contracted to sell 10 tons of copper to B, payment to be by B's acceptance of a bill of exchange. S sent the bill of exchange for the price together with the bill of lading to B. B was insolvent and did not signify his acceptance of the bill of exchange but indorsed the bill of lading to the plaintiff sub-buyers, under a contract for the resale of the copper. S stopped the copper in transit. By reason of s 19(3), the property had not passed to B but the sub-buyer obtained a good title under s 25(1). The court also held that, by virtue of the proviso to s 47 (now s 47(2)), S's right of stoppage in transit, which arose because B was insolvent and the goods were still in the course of transit, was defeated. Finally, Salmon J said, *obiter*, in *Mount (D F) Ltd v Jay and Jay (Provisions) Co Ltd*,[16] that s 47(2) could apply only if the *same* document which is handed to B is transferred by him to the sub-buyer and therefore s 47(2) did not apply to the facts in *Mount's* case as there B created the document himself.[17]

The unpaid seller's right of stoppage in transit

The right of stoppage in transit is stated succinctly in the SGA, s 44:

> 'Subject to this Act, when the buyer of goods becomes insolvent the unpaid seller who has parted with the possession of the goods has the right of stopping them in transit, that is to say, he may resume possession of the goods as long as they are in course of transit, and may retain them until payment or tender of the price.'

Although S's right of stoppage is an old remedy[18] which was potent when international sales involved a long transit, it is now largely archaic because of the use of bankers' commercial credits whereby S is paid by a bank in his own country. The remedy still has some relevance where the sale is on credit terms but an extensive and detailed coverage of stoppage is somewhat inapt in modern conditions. It will be noticed that s 44 prescribes that three conditions must be

---

13 See the SGA, s 61(1) on 'delivery' and the Factors Act 1889, s 11.
14 [1914] 3 KB 40.
15 [1899] 1 QB 643; see also Ch 18.
16 [1960] 1 QB 159, 168.
17 The judge considered (p 169) that the wording of s 25(1) was less rigorous and was not limited to cases where B1 transfers the same document to B2; see Borrie, 'Documents of Title' (1960) 23 MLR 100.
18 See *Lickbarrow v Mason* (1793) 4 Bro Parl Cas 57 where the remedy was recognised by the House of Lords; Blackburn, *Contract of Sale* (2nd edn, 1885), pp 311-414.

met before S may stop the goods in transit, viz S must be unpaid, B must be insolvent and the goods must still be in the course of transit.

THE NATURE AND EFFECT OF THE RIGHT OF STOPPAGE

The general rule is that when S delivers the goods to a carrier he loses his right of lien (s 43(1)(a)) but, by validly stopping the goods in transit, his lien is restored and S may thus gain priority over the creditors of the insolvent B when B becomes bankrupt. When the goods are stopped in transit, S puts the carrier under an obligation to redeliver the goods to him (s 46(4)) so that he regains the right to possession of the goods. It is irrelevant to the exercise of stoppage that property in the goods has passed to B (s 39(1)), this fact emphasising the extent of S's right of recaption. In fact, stoppage has real significance only in those cases where property has vested in B because, where S is the owner of the goods, he may withhold delivery until B is prepared to pay the price. S must, of course, be an unpaid seller in order to exercise the right of stoppage but, as stated above, this remedy arises only upon B's *insolvency* (s 39(1)(b); s 44). The meaning of both 'insolvency' and the 'unpaid seller' were considered at the start of this chapter but there is one particular problem with stoppage. If S stops the goods in transit, he takes the risk of being unable to prove B's insolvency[19] but it appears that if B becomes insolvent before the end of the transit, the stoppage will be valid even if he was not insolvent at the date of stoppage.[20] The right of stoppage is available to S in his capacity as a seller and, because s 61(1) defines a 'seller' as someone who sells or *agrees* to sell, the remedy is available to B when, before property is vested in B, he resells the goods to a sub-B.[1]

DURATION OF THE TRANSIT

It is central to the right of stoppage to determine when the goods are in transit so that S may exercise this remedy or, conversely, whether they have reached their destination meaning that it is too late for S to intervene. The nature of transit is that 'the goods should be in the custody of some third person, intermediate between the seller who has parted with and the buyer who has not yet acquired actual possession'.[2] The SGA, s 45(1) provides:

> 'Goods are deemed to be in course of transit from the time when they are delivered to a carrier or other bailee or custodier for the purpose of transmission to the buyer, until the buyer or his agent in that behalf takes delivery of them from the carrier or other bailee or custodier.'

If the carrier is the agent of S, it is plain that S retains possession and may exercise his lien without recourse to the right of stoppage. If, on the other hand, the carrier is B's agent, the transit ends when S delivers the goods to the carrier but, if so, the

---

19 *The Tigress* (1863) 32 LJPM & A 97.
20 *The Constantia* (1807) 6 Ch Rob 321, 326 per Sir William Scott.
 1 See also s 38(2) which extends the meaning of 'seller' to any person 'who is in the position of a seller', eg S's agent to whom a bill of lading has been indorsed.
 2 *Gibson v Carruthers* (1841) 8 M & W 321, 328 per Rolfe B; see also *Schotsmans v Lancashire and Yorkshire Rly* (1867) LR 2 Ch App 332, 338 per Cairns LJ.

agent must be authorised to take *actual* delivery on B's behalf rather than being simply an agent to transport the goods to B.[3] Thus the fact that the carrier is nominated by B does not mean that the transit ends when the goods are delivered to that carrier.[4] In short, s 45 is premised on the carrier's being independent of both S and B.

As s 45(1) provides, the transit continues 'until the buyer or his agent in that behalf takes delivery' of the goods. The transit thus ends when B takes delivery personally or when an agent authorised by B receives the goods which are to be held at B's disposal and it is then irrelevant that the goods are sent, on B's instructions, to a further destination.[5] It is clear that B does not 'take delivery' simply when the goods *arrive* at their destination and it seems that much may turn upon B's intent. In *James v Griffin,*[6] B often used a particular wharf as a warehouse but, on one occasion, he ordered goods to be landed at the wharf but did not intend this to be a delivery to himself. He did not inform the wharfinger of that fact and he appeared to consider himself to be B's agent. It was held that the goods were not in B's constructive possession as he had not assented thereto and thus the transit had not ended. Constructive delivery may suffice under s 45(1), as where the carrier attorns to B (see s 45(3), below), but B does not normally obtain constructive possession by marking or inspecting goods which are in the carrier's physical possession[7] nor by taking delivery of part of the goods (see s 45(7), below). Beyond the general rule in s 45(1), the remaining subsections of s 45 detail particular circumstances relating to the termination of the transit. These can now be considered.

Delivery before the appointed destination: s 45(2)

Section 45(2) provides that:

> 'If the buyer or his agent in that behalf obtains delivery of the goods before their arrival at the appointed destination, the transit is at an end.'

At first sight, it seems puzzling that B or his agent[8] may take delivery of the goods *before* they arrive at their designated destination and thereby deprive S of the right of stoppage. The rule is said to acknowledge, however, that the carrier and the consignee (B) can agree to a different destination from that agreed between the carrier and the consignor (S).[9] It is possible that S could then seek redress against the carrier but it is indisputable that the transit is terminated by B's

---

3 It will be remembered that s 32(1) provides that delivery of goods to a carrier is *prima facie* deemed to constitute delivery to B. This delivery will always be subject to s 45(1) unless the agent is authorised to take *actual* delivery: *Re Cock, ex p Rosevear China Clay Co* (1879) 11 Ch D 560; see also the judgments in *Kendal v Marshall, Stevens & Co* (1883) 11 QBD 356.

4 *Bethell v Clark* (1888) 20 QBD 615, 617 per Lord Esher MR. Transit normally ends when the goods are shipped by S on a ship belonging to B. See s 45(5), below, for the position where B charters a ship.

5 *Bethell v Clark* (1888) 20 QBD 615; *Kendal v Marshall, Stevens & Co* (1883) 11 QBD 356.

6 (1837) 2 M & W 623.

7 *Whitehead v Anderson* (1842) 9 M & W 518, 535 per Parke B (B merely inspected and touched a cargo of timber on board ship).

8 The agent must be authorised to take delivery at some place other than the appointed destination and authority to do so will not be readily implied: *Mechan & Sons Ltd v North Eastern Rly Co* 1911 SC 1348.

9 *Whitehead v Anderson* (1842) 9 M & W 518; *London and North Western Rly Co v Bartlett* (1861) 7 H & N 400; *Reddall v Union Castle Mail Steamship Co Ltd* (1914) 84 LJKB 360; *Johann Plischke und Söhne GmbH v Allison Bros Ltd* [1936] 2 All ER 1009.

agreement with the carrier for delivery at a different destination. The rule may be even more potent as there is old authority that B can end the transit by wrongfully taking possession of the goods without the carrier's consent, even though the carrier might then have recourse against B.[10] This seems anomalous and inconsistent with the rule that S's lien is lost when B lawfully obtains possession of the goods (s 43(1)(b)) but, against this, s 45(2) excludes any reference to the lawfulness of B's acquisition and, instead, pointedly refers to the situation where B '*obtains* delivery'.[11] Moreover, it has been logically asserted that, if B's agreement with the carrier ends the transit, B's taking possession of the goods without consent should have the same effect because the wrongfulness of the act is *vis-à-vis* the carrier, not S.[12]

Carrier attorns to B: s 45(3)

Section 45(3) provides:

> 'If, after the arrival of the goods at the appointed destination, the carrier or other bailee or custodier acknowledges to the buyer or his agent that he holds the goods on his behalf and continues in possession of them as bailee or custodier for the buyer or his agent, the transit is at an end, and it is immaterial that a further destination for the goods may have been indicated by the buyer.'

Under s 45(3), the carrier attorns to B and a relationship of bailment is created between them 'by virtue of some contract or course of dealing between them, that ... the character of the carrier shall cease, and that of warehouseman supervene'.[13] It is essential that *both* B and the carrier should *consent* to the latter's change of character from carrier to bailee/warehouseman[14] and so attornment cannot be inferred simply from the fact that the carrier has notified B that he is ready to deliver the goods.[15]

Goods rejected by B: s 45(4)

Section 45(4) provides:

> 'If the goods are rejected by the buyer, and the carrier or other bailee or custodier continues in possession of them, the transit is not deemed to be at an end, even if the seller has refused to receive them back.'

---

10 *Whitehead v Anderson* (1842) 9 M & W 518, 534 per Parke B; see Blackburn, *Contract of Sale* (2nd edn, 1885), pp 371-379.
11 The general rule in the SGA, s 45(1) is that transit ends when B 'takes delivery'; 'delivery' is defined in s 61(1) as 'voluntary transfer of possession ...'
12 Greig, *Sale of Goods* (1974), p 303; cf Todd, 'Stoppage in Transitu: The Course of Transit' [1978] JBL 39, 43, who argues that B could not seize the goods in this way as consent would be absent but that, where he obtains possession by fraud, this might amount to voluntary transfer of possession within s 61(1).
13 *Bolton v Lancashire and Yorkshire Rly Co* (1866) LR 1 CP 431, 438 per Erle CJ.
14 Clear consent of the carrier seems to be required: see *Whitehead v Anderson* (1842) 9 M & W 518 (B claimed to take constructive possession of goods on board ship but the master remained silent and did not consent to deliver immediate possession to B. Held B did not acquire constructive possession); *Coventry v Gladstone* (1868) LR 6 Eq 44. But it seems that consent may be inferred from silence/delay on B's part: *Taylor v Great Eastern Rly Co* (1901) 17 TLR 394 (defendant carrier sent B a notice that he would hold the goods as warehouseman and charge B rent; Bigham J held the transit ended after 'a reasonable time had elapsed for [B] to elect whether he would take the goods away or leave them in the defendant's depôt on rent' (p 394).
15 *Mechan & Sons Ltd v North Eastern Rly Co* 1911 SC 1348.

This rule is justified in that if B rejects the goods he cannot be said to have taken either actual or constructive possession of them.[16] The relationship between s 45(3) and (4) is somewhat in doubt since, if the carrier attorns to B under s 45(3) and then B inspects the goods and rejects them, it is unclear whether the transit has ended or not. One view is that the transit has ended by the attornment but it is arguable that, as attornment is effective only with B's consent, his rejection of the goods renders the attornment inoperative and thus S's right of stoppage continues.

Delivery to a ship chartered by B: s 45(5)

Section 45(5) provides:

> 'When goods are delivered to a ship chartered by the buyer it is a question depending on the circumstances of the particular case whether they are in the possession of the master as a carrier or as agent to the buyer.'

The general rule is that transit ends when the goods are shipped on a vessel *owned* by B[17] but whether a ship which is chartered by B is to be treated as his ship depends upon the intent of the parties shown by the terms of the charter party and the bill of lading.[18] Ordinarily, where the ship has been chartered by B, the master is an employee and agent of the shipowner and, the goods being in the possession of the master as agent for the shipowner, they are liable to stoppage by an unpaid seller. However, a charter party by demise is analogous to a lease of the ship to B and, as the master and crew are then treated as B's employees, delivery of goods to the ship ends S's right of stoppage.

Carrier's wrongful refusal to deliver to B: s 45(6)

Section 45(6) provides:

> 'Where the carrier or other bailee or custodier wrongfully refuses to deliver the goods to the buyer or his agent in that behalf, the transit is deemed to be at an end.'

When the general rule in s 45(1) was considered, above, it was stressed that B must 'take delivery' and that this entails much more than the arrival of the goods at their destination. It follows that, under s 45(6), B must be ready and willing to take delivery but the carrier then wrongfully refuses to deliver the goods to him or his agent.[19] If the carrier has a valid reason to refuse delivery, eg he has a lien over the goods for unpaid freight, his refusal will not be 'wrongful'.

Partial delivery of the goods: s 45(7)

Section 45(7) provides:

> 'Where part delivery of the goods has been made to the buyer or his agent in that behalf, the remainder of the goods may be stopped in transit, unless such part delivery has been made under such circumstances as to show an agreement to give up possession of the whole of the goods.'

---

16 *Bolton v Lancashire and Yorkshire Rly Co* (1866) LR 1 CP 431.
17 *Schotsmans v Lancashire and Yorkshire Rly Co* (1867) LR 2 Ch App 332.
18 *Berndtson v Strang* (1868) 3 Ch App 588.
19 This was the rule before the SGA 1893 and s 45(6) was based upon the decision in *Bird v Brown* (1850) 4 Exch 786 (see Ch 3).

This rule is analogous to that in s 42 concerning the possible loss of S's lien by partial delivery of the goods to B: both s 42 and s 45(7) emphasise the general rule that partial delivery does not normally entail the surrender of S's lien or his right of stoppage. In many commercial contracts, it will clearly be difficult to establish an 'agreement' between the parties that partial delivery is intended to be delivery of the whole.[20] Thus, in *Re McLaren, ex p Cooper,*[1] delivery of 30 tons of miscellaneous iron castings from a cargo of 114 tons did not prevent S from stopping delivery of the remainder but the cogent example given by Cotton LJ[2] was that, if the whole cargo comprised one entire machine, delivery of one essential part of it might amount to possession of the whole.

EXERCISE OF THE RIGHT OF STOPPAGE

Section 46(1), (2) and (3) provide:

'(1) The unpaid seller may exercise his right of stoppage in transit either by taking actual possession of the goods or by giving notice of his claim to the carrier or other bailee or custodier in whose possession the goods are.
(2) The notice may be given either to the person in actual possession of the goods or to his principal.
(3) If given to the principal, the notice is ineffective unless given at such time and under such circumstances that the principal, by the exercise of reasonable diligence, may communicate it to his servant or agent in time to prevent a delivery to the buyer.'

Where goods were carried by sea in the 19th century, it is obvious that S might have difficulty in taking actual possession of the goods or, because of poor methods of communication, it might be an arduous task for S to give notice of stoppage to the carrier. Accordingly, notification to the carrier's principal assumed significance (now s 46(2)) meaning that the shipowner could be contacted[3] and was under a duty to communicate with the master of the ship with reasonable diligence. Section 46(3) emphasises that S's notice is only effectual if given under such circumstances that the principal can communicate with his agent in time to prevent delivery to B and suggests that, following the common law, the principal is under a duty to communicate with his agent with reasonable diligence and would be liable to S in conversion if, in breach of duty, the goods were delivered to B.

Duties of the parties after notice of stoppage is given

Section 46(4) provides:

'When notice of stoppage in transit is given by the seller to the carrier or other bailee or custodier in possession of the goods, he must re-deliver the goods to, or according to the directions of, the seller; and the expenses of the re-delivery must be borne by the seller.'

The carrier must act on the notice of stoppage and if he disregards it and delivers the goods to B he will be liable in conversion because, under s 44, notice of stoppage

---

20 See *Tanner v Scovell* (1845) 14 M & W 28; *Kemp v Falk* (1882) 7 App Cas 573.
1 (1879) 11 Ch D 68.
2 (1879) 11 Ch D 68 at 75-76.
3 See *Whitehead v Anderson* (1842) 9 M & W 518.

means that S resumes the right to possession of the goods.[4] Although the SGA does not delineate the rights and duties of S and the carrier after stoppage, the leading decision in *Booth Steamship Co Ltd v Cargo Fleet Iron Co Ltd*[5] does so. The Court of Appeal established that the exercise of S's power of stoppage means that (i) S is under an obligation to the carrier either to take delivery himself or give directions for delivery; (ii) in order to regain actual possession of the goods, S must pay any unpaid freight to the carrier and, if he does not, he will be liable in damages to the carrier; the carrier's lien for freight has priority over S's right of stoppage;[6] (iii) if S fails to give instructions to the carrier after stoppage, S will be liable to the carrier in damages for any expenses incurred by the carrier, eg landing charges; and (iv) S cannot compel the carrier to deliver physical possession of the goods to him during the transit: it is delivery of the goods at their destination which may be stopped but *not the transit* of the goods to their destination.

Under s 48(1), the contract of sale is not rescinded by S's exercise of stoppage in transit (or lien) and property in the goods does not revest in S. Instead, S resumes the right to possession of the goods (s 44) and thus regains his lien as an unpaid seller. However, where S is unpaid and has possession of the goods, he has more than a possessory lien in that he may be able to resell the goods under the provisions of s 48, considered below.

The unpaid seller's right of resale

The SGA, s 48(1) provides:

> 'Subject to this section, a contract of sale is not rescinded by the mere exercise by an unpaid seller of his right of lien or retention or stoppage in transit.'

The reason for this provision is that, unless the time of payment is a condition precedent to the operation of the contract, B's delay in paying the price does not 'rescind' (in modern terminology 'terminate') the contract. Moreover, in exercising his right of lien or stoppage, S takes the preliminary steps toward enforcing the contract in that he is seeking a security to ensure B's payment of the price. The contract between S and B thus remains operative – it is not 'rescinded' and property in the goods does not revest in S. However, as S is unpaid he obviously has an eye to reselling the goods and the consequences of such a resale, both between S and the first buyer and S and the second buyer, have to be assessed in the light of further considerations.

The SGA does not distinguish explicitly between S's *power* and *right* to resell the goods but it is important to separate and clarify these notions before the remedy of resale and its consequences can be understood. There are several situations, considered presently, where S has a power to resell the goods and confer a good title on the second buyer to the exclusion of the first buyer but S may nevertheless be liable in breach of contract to the first buyer. In contrast, where S has a right to resell the goods he can transfer a good title to the second buyer and will *not* be liable to the first buyer.

---

4 See *Litt v Cowley* (1816) 7 Taunt 169 (goods were sent to Pickfords in Manchester for delivery in London. S gave notice of stoppage to the Manchester premises but in good time for it to be relayed to London. The goods were delivered by mistake and it was held that S could maintain trover against the assignees of the bankrupt B).
5 [1916] 2 KB 570.
6 See also *United States Steel Products Co v Great Western Rly Co* [1916] 1 AC 189.

THE SELLER'S POWER OF RESALE

S has the power to resell the goods and confer a good title on the second buyer in three situations.

First, where S still has the property in the goods he has the power to resell to the second buyer by virtue of his ownership but, where he had agreed to sell the goods to the first buyer, he may nevertheless be liable to that first buyer in breach of contract. Section 48 does not refer to this situation where S retains property but, under s 48(2)(see below) confers an express power of resale on the unpaid seller where property has passed to B. It seems that the draftsman thought it unnecessary to state the obvious: S patently has a power of resale where he still owns the goods.[7]

Second, where S is left in possession of the goods after a sale to the first buyer, S is empowered to transfer good title to the second buyer where the requirements of the SGA, s 24/Factors Act 1889, s 8[8] are complied with. Again, the resale will be wrongful as against the first buyer and S will be liable to him in contract and, where property had passed to the first buyer, S may be liable in tort.

Third, in those situations where property has passed to the first buyer, an unpaid seller who has exercised his right of lien or stoppage has the power to resell the goods and confer a good title on the second buyer. Without the addition of any other facts, eg S has expressly reserved a right of resale in the contract, S will still be liable here to the first buyer for breach of contract and conversion. Thus, the SGA, s 48(2) provides:

> 'Where an unpaid seller who has exercised his right of lien or retention or stoppage in transit re-sells the goods, the buyer acquires a good title to them as against the original buyer.'

The main purpose of s 48(2) is to protect the second buyer who does not know what the legal position is between S and the first buyer: the second buyer thus acquires title to the goods whether or not S has a *right* of resale against the first buyer. Without the protection of s 48(2), the second buyer would acquire title at common law only if S had retained or re-acquired property in the goods at the time of resale. A normal application of s 48(2) will occur whenever S has exercised his right of lien or stoppage and has actual possession of the goods. However, s 48(2) does not demand that S be in actual possession and thus he should be able to resell within s 48(2) whenever he has a right to possession of the goods as against the first buyer.[9] Thereafter, under s 48(2) no delivery of the goods to the second buyer is required as a condition of his acquiring a good title and he need not be in good faith – in fact, he may know of the first sale and his title is nevertheless valid. It will be apparent that, although the operation of ss 48(2) and 24 may coincide in many situations, s 48(2) is free of the restrictive limitations imposed upon the 'seller in possession' under s 24.[10]

---

7 See *Ward (R V) Ltd v Bignall* [1967] 1 QB 534, 545 per Diplock LJ.
8 See Ch 18.
9 This could occur where S stops the goods in transit but the carrier has a lien for the freight which S must discharge in order to regain actual possession of the goods. S would still be entitled, as against the first buyer, to immediate possession.
10 See Ch 18. Under s 24, S must be in possession of the goods or documents of title and there must be a delivery to the *bona fide*, second buyer: none of these requirements apply to s 48(2).

THE SELLER'S RIGHT TO RESELL

There are certain instances where S has not only a power of resale but also the right to resell and is under no duty to anyone to refrain from exercising it. S's right to resell as against the first buyer arises in several situations.

First, if B repudiates the obligations he owes under the contract, S may accept the repudiation, treat the contract as terminated and resell the goods.[11] Under the general principles of contract law, B's repudiation must show an intention to abandon or put an end to the contract but when such an abandonment occurs is not necessarily easy to determine. Failure to pay the price may often be insufficient to amount to repudiation, particularly if delivery is made in instalments and B has failed to pay for one instalment only[12] but, as mentioned earlier, if B is insolvent and informs S of that fact in circumstances which indicate his unwillingness or inability to perform the contract, S may treat the contract as repudiated.[13] Somewhat surprisingly, it is unclear at common law what precise effect the termination of the contract has on S's right to resell the goods and confer title on a second buyer. Following the rule in sales of land, it is arguable that, after B's repudiation, S should be entitled to resell as an unfettered owner.[14] Moreover, the rule that, at common law, property in goods revests in S on his acceptance of B's repudiation so that he may resell without restriction, forfeit any deposit paid by the first buyer[15] and is not liable to account to him for any profit, has been adopted in New Zealand in the decision in *Commission Car Sales (Hastings) Ltd v Saul*.[16] There B voluntarily returned to S the Plymouth sedan which he had agreed to buy and Turner J appeared to consider that S's physical possession of the goods was important. It seems that when S lawfully terminates the contract, he should have the right to resell whether or not property in the goods has passed to B. More particularly, where S retains property he clearly has a power to resell as owner and confer a title on the second buyer and the first buyer's repudiation will give S the right to resell as against that first buyer.[17] Where property has passed to the first buyer before his repudiation, S's termination of the contract revests the property in S[18] and he should then be entitled to resell without restriction. Where property revests in S in this way, he has the immediate right to possession and it is suggested that he should have the right to resell whether or not he has recovered physical possession from the first buyer,[19] but the extent to which S is entitled to retake possession of the goods on B's repudiation is most unclear.[20]

---

11 See *Compagnie de Renflouement v W Seymour Plant Sales* [1981] 2 Lloyd's Rep 466.
12 See the SGA, s 31(2) and s 10; *Mersey Steel and Iron Co Ltd v Naylor, Benzon & Co* (1884) 9 App Cas 434.
13 *Re Phoenix Bessemer Steel Co* (1876) 4 Ch D 108.
14 See *Howe v Smith* (1884) 27 Ch D 89; *Cornwall v Henson* [1900] 2 Ch 298.
15 Unless S sues for damages for loss occasioned by the breach, in which case he would have to bring the deposit into account and give credit for it.
16 [1957] NZLR 144.
17 This is supported by the view of Robert Goff LJ in *Clough Mill Ltd v Martin* [1985] 1 WLR 111 that, where S retains title under a Romalpa clause until the full price is paid but B repudiates the contract and S accepts it, S may then resell as an owner uninhibited by any contractual restrictions and keep any profit made.
18 *Ward (R V) Ltd v Bignall* [1967] 1 QB 534, 550 per Diplock LJ.
19 But where the first buyer has physical possession of the goods, he could transfer a good title to a third party under the conditions specified in the SGA, s 25.
20 If S has property in the goods but B has possession, it seems that S may be able to recover physical possession of the goods upon B's repudiation and, indeed, this proposition is

Second, the unpaid seller has a statutory right of resale where the goods are perishable. The SGA, s 48(3) provides:

'Where the goods are of a perishable nature, or where the unpaid seller gives notice to the buyer of his intention to re-sell, and the buyer does not within a reasonable time pay or tender the price, the unpaid seller may re-sell the goods and recover from the original buyer damages for any loss occasioned by his breach of contract.'

It is now beyond doubt that s 48(3) gives S a right of resale against the first buyer: the first contract is terminated and property revests in S so that S may resell the goods as owner without restriction.[1] It will be noticed, however, that s 48(3) is limited to the 'unpaid seller' and it therefore does not extend as far as the common law rights on repudiation, considered above, where S may terminate the contract for breaches other than non-payment of the price. The underlying rationale of the first part of s 48(3) is that, as S is in possession of perishable goods, delivery and payment by B must be simultaneous. It thus seems that, with perishable goods, S has the right to resell immediately upon B's failure to pay the price on the agreed date.[2] In general, 'perishable' goods are those which will, in time, deteriorate physically[3] although in an early case,[4] Best CJ[5] seemed prepared, somewhat unconventionally, to include within this category goods whose value was likely to decrease.

Third, under the second part of s 48(3), the unpaid seller can give notice to B and thereby make payment within a reasonable time of the notice of the essence of the contract.[6] If B then fails to pay within a reasonable time, S may treat the contract as repudiated and has the right to resell the goods. This part of s 48(3) can apply to any type of goods and, under the SGA, s 59, the question of what is a 'reasonable time' is a question of fact. It seems that the draftsman of the SGA assumed that S's right of resale under s 48(3) might only be exercised where S was in possession of the goods at the time of resale and there is some authority, albeit tenuous, to support this view[7] – certainly a normal resale under s 48(3) occurs after S has exercised his right of lien or stoppage and is thus in actual possession of the goods. As with the right of resale at common law following B's repudiation of the contract, considered above, S may lose his statutory right to resell after both property and possession have passed to B but, as with the

---

accepted in the Romalpa cases even where there is no express term in the contract permitting S's retaking of the goods. But where both property *and* actual possession have passed to B, S will commit conversion (see *Stephens v Wilkinson* (1831) 2 B & Ad 320; *Page v Cowasjee Eduljee* (1866) LR 1 PC 127) and a probable breach of s 12(2)(b) should he re-take the goods (see *Healing (Sales) Pty Ltd v Inglis Electrix Pty Ltd* (1968) 121 CLR 584). Here S must pursue a personal action as the outer-limits of the real remedies have been reached. Indeed, if S could terminate the contract and re-possess the goods in this way, the complicated apparatus of the real remedies would be virtually otiose.

1 See *Ward (R V) Ltd v Bignall* [1967] 1 QB 534 (considered below).
2 See the SGA, s 10(1): stipulations as to time of payment are not of the essence *unless a different intention appears* from the contract.
3 *Sharp v Christmas* (1892) 8 TLR 687 (resale of potatoes as a 'perishable commodity'); see, by analogy, the notion of goods which have perished within the SGA, s 6: *Asfar & Co v Blundell* [1896] 1 QB 123.
4 *Maclean v Dunn and Watkins* (1828) 4 Bing 722.
5 (1828) 4 Bing 722 at 728.
6 See *Ward (R V) Ltd v Bignall* [1967] 1 QB 534 (considered below).
7 *Ward (R V) Ltd v Bignall* [1967] 1 QB 534, 545 per Diplock LJ (who appears to assume that S would be in possession); *Commission Car Sales (Hastings) Ltd v Saul* [1957] NZLR 144 (*obiter* that the equivalent provision to s 48(3) applied only where S had not lost possession).

common law rules, there appears to be no definitive rule that S must be in physical possession of the goods in order to exercise the right of resale under s 48(3). There would, nevertheless, be practical difficulties militating against such a resale where S does not have possession of the goods: S might be unable to make delivery of the goods at the relevant time and, likewise, many second buyers would be reluctant to agree to buy the goods where the first (perhaps insolvent) buyer retains possession. Moreover, where the first buyer has actual possession of the goods but S terminates the contract for breach, that first buyer still has the power as against S to transfer good title to a third party if the conditions in the SGA, s 25 (buyer in possession) are complied with.

Fourth, S may have an express, contractual right to resell the goods. The SGA, s 48(4) provides:

> 'Where the seller expressly reserves the right of re-sale in case the buyer should make default, and on the buyer making default re-sells the goods, the original contract of sale is rescinded but without prejudice to any claim the seller may have for damages.'

When S resells under an express provision in the contract with the first buyer, that contract is terminated and, if property in the goods had passed to B, it revests in S who may then sell as an unfettered owner.[8] Obviously a resale under an express right to do so in the first contract means that S will not be in breach of contract to the first buyer. The express right to resell may be very wide as it is broadly based upon situations where B 'makes default' but the meaning of 'default' must depend on the construction of the contract containing the right of resale. Furthermore, in contrast with s 48(3), under s 48(4) S need not be an 'unpaid seller' and there is no requirement that he should give any notice to B of his intention to resell.

EFFECTS OF THE TERMINATION OF THE FIRST CONTRACT UNDER SECTION 48(3) AND (4)

Section 48(4) expressly provides that a resale in the exercise of a contractual right rescinds the original contract of sale meaning, in modern terminology, that it is 'terminated', but there is no corresponding provision to that effect in s 48(3). Accordingly, in *Gallagher v Shilcock*,[9] Finnemore J held that a resale under s 48(3) did not rescind the original contract with the result that, if on the facts the property had passed to the first buyer, any profit made on a resale belonged to that first buyer. The judge's reasoning was that S sold the goods 'in a capacity analogous to that of a pledgee, or in some limited capacity'[10] and this notion that S did not sell as an absolute owner was, in fact, the rule which had been adopted in the 19th century (see below). However, the *Gallagher* decision was overruled by the Court of Appeal in *Ward (R V) Ltd v Bignall*.[11] There B agreed to buy two cars from S for £850 (a Standard Vanguard and a Ford Zodiac) and paid a deposit of £25. Almost immediately, B repudiated the contract and refused to pay or take delivery of the cars. S

---

8 *Ward (R V) Ltd v Bignall* [1967] 1 QB 534.
9 [1949] 2 KB 765.
10 [1949] 2 KB 765 at 773.
11 [1967] 1 QB 534.

demanded that B should pay and take delivery failing which S stated that he would resell the cars and claim damages in respect of any loss. As B still refused to pay, S resold the Vanguard for £350 but could not resell the Zodiac. Accordingly, S sued for the price of the Zodiac and the loss incurred on the sale of the Vanguard. It was held that the resale of the Vanguard had rescinded the contract with B and that S was not entitled to the price of the Zodiac. B was thus liable only for damages for non-acceptance.

The Court of Appeal in *Ward (R V) Ltd v Bignall* considered that both s 48(3) and (4) were intended to have the same effect in terminating the first contract but, as only s 48(4) expressly provides for such termination, some dexterity of reasoning was needed to justify this outcome. The basic rule in the SGA, s 10(1) is that stipulations as to time of payment are not of the essence and B's failure to pay is not necessarily a breach which justifies S in treating the contract as repudiated. In *Ward*, the Court of Appeal held that the purpose of s 48(3) is, however, to make time of payment of the essence in cases of perishable goods or where S gives notice of his intention to resell, and B's failure to pay then amounts to repudiation which S accepts by reselling the goods. The resale thus terminates the first contract, property in the goods revests in S[12] and, although B is no longer liable to pay the price, he becomes liable to pay damages for non-acceptance. In contrast, if the contract expressly provides for resale, S could resell without acting inconsistently with the contract; resale would simply be the exercise of a contractual right and not the acceptance of B's repudiation. Accordingly, the Court of Appeal considered this to be the reason why s 48(4) provides expressly that a resale terminates the first contract.

The practical result of the decision in *Ward (R V) Ltd v Bignall* is that whenever S resells under s 48(3) and (4) he sells as an unfettered owner and may keep any profit made on the resale. At first glance, this rule seems rational and Atiyah[13] asserts that it would be 'absurd' if S had to account to a defaulting buyer for profits made as a result of his labours in reselling the goods. However, s 48(3) and (4) were based on the common law prior to the SGA 1893 which, when understood, discloses the rationale of both subsections. Section 48(4) was based upon the decision in *Lamond v Davall*,[14] that a resale by virtue of an express condition in the first contract had the effect of terminating that first contract. However, s 48(3) was based upon different principles and considerations from the *Lamond* decision. First, it was clear that B's punctual payment was not of the essence of the contract.[15] Second, when property in the goods had transferred to B, it remained vested in him and S could not treat the contract as rescinded simply because of B's failure to pay on time.[16] Third, this meant that S did not resell the goods as an unfettered owner but, instead, he resold in the 'limited capacity' described by Finnemore J in the *Gallagher* case. In 1885, Lord Blackburn's treatise[17] thus explained that S's resale 'interferes not only with the

---

12 Diplock L J considered that this was 'well-established' (p 550) although no authority was cited in support of such a rule. Presumably it could be substantiated on the basis of an implied condition subsequent.
13 *The Sale of Goods* (10th edn, 2001), p 468.
14 (1847) 9 QB 1030.
15 See *Martindale v Smith* (1841) 1 QB 389. The SGA, s 10(1) currently provides that stipulations as to time of payment are generally not of the essence.
16 See *Maclean v Dunn and Watkins* (1828) 4 Bing 722; *Page v Cowasjee Eduljee* (1866) LR 1 PC 127, 145 per Lord Chelmsford.
17 *Contract of Sale* (2nd edn, 1885), pp 445-446.

purchaser's right of possession, but also with his right of property; but that the vendor's right does not ... amount to a right to resume a complete right of property, so as to devest totally the purchaser's right of property; or in other words, that the vendor cannot treat the contract of sale as rescinded, so as to resume his property as if the sale had never been made'. Accordingly, this meant that 'if the resale produced a sum greater than the unpaid portion of the price, the purchaser would be entitled to the surplus; if there was a deficiency, he would still remain indebted to the vendor for that amount'.[18] The SGA rules concerning resale of the goods thus fall into place: s 48(1) specifies that a contract of sale is not rescinded by the mere exercise by an unpaid seller of his right of lien or stoppage, ie property does not revest in S, and s 48(2) then ensures that the second buyer acquires a good title to the goods when S exercises his *power* of resale in the situations specified in s 48(3).

With this scheme in mind, there is much plausibility in Greig's[19] argument that s 48(3) left the question of termination of the first contract and S's *right* to resell to be decided upon whether or not B had repudiated the contract. As explained earlier, at common law S could treat the contract as terminated and had the right to resell the goods only where B had repudiated his obligations under the contract. An equitable result is reached if B is allowed to retain any profit on a resale where his conduct was not repudiatory (as in *Gallagher v Shilcock*) and the contract thus remains intact and, likewise, justice is done if S has the unfettered right to resell following B's obvious repudiation (as in *Ward (R V) Ltd v Bignall*). This approach arguably allows more fluidity than the unbending rule of the current law. Furthermore, this notion of accounting to B on a resale finds (indirect) support in the context of Romalpa clauses. It was suggested by the Court of Appeal in *Clough Mill Ltd v Martin*[20] (without any reference to s 48(3) or (4)) that only where B had repudiated the contract could S recover and resell the goods without restriction thus keeping any profits; in contrast, where the contract was still subsisting, it was implicit that S would resell sufficient goods to meet the outstanding purchase price but would then account to B for any surplus profit.

Forfeiture of deposits

Where the first contract is terminated, as in *Ward (R V) Ltd v Bignall*, it remains to consider the question of deposits paid by B. Where S resells and makes no claim for damages, it seems that he may forfeit B's deposit as well as keeping any profit on the resale[1] although there is no watertight authority to this effect as the deposit was not considered in the *Ward* case. Following general principles, it is clearer that if S sues for damages he must bring the deposit into the reckoning and thus allow B credit for the amount paid, and this would also apply if S resold

---

18 *Contract of Sale* (2nd edn, 1885), p 446.
19 See the valuable analysis in Greig, *Sale of Goods* (1974), pp 312-316; see also Fridman, *Sale of Goods* (1966), pp 277-279.
20 [1985] 1 WLR 111.
 1 *Commission Car Sales (Hastings) Ltd v Saul* [1957] NZLR 144(the court treated the Oldsmobile car which was traded-in in the same way as a monetary payment by way of deposit and thus S kept the car); *Howe v Smith* (1884) 27 Ch D 89 (sale of land); Cf *Gallagher v Shilcock* [1949] 2 KB 765 (B was entitled to recover the deposit on the basis that the contract was not terminated).

at a loss and then sued B for damages.[2] Where S considers a resale he is thus placed in a favourable position in that, if he can resell at a profit he may do so thereby terminating the contract and retaining both profit and any deposit paid but, if he cannot secure a profit on a resale, he should affirm the contract and sue B for damages.

2 *Commission Car Sales (Hastings) Ltd v Saul* [1957] NZLR 144.

CHAPTER 27

The personal remedies of the seller

Introduction

In addition to the real remedies discussed in Chapter 26, S has personal remedies for breach of contract by B. S may thus either commence proceedings for the *price* of the goods or sue B for *damages for non-acceptance* of the goods. A crucial difference between these two remedies is that, where property in the goods has passed to B and S is entitled to claim the price, S is suing for a fixed debt and it follows that none of the rules on damages apply to the claim. S must show simply that the price is due under the contract but he need not prove any loss, and the rules on remoteness, mitigation and penalties are inapplicable. If S can maintain an action for the price, he will often be placed in a secure and favourable position. Should S sue B for damages, however, the normal principles of the law relating to damages apply and so, for example, S must take reasonable steps to mitigate his loss. In very general terms, the SGA envisages that S may sue for the price where property has passed to B (s 49) or, alternatively, that he may maintain an action against B for damages (s 50) where property has not passed. Clearly this general scheme must be subject to some overlap in that, if the property has passed to B *and* he wrongfully neglects or refuses to accept the goods, S can sue under either s 49 or s 50. S often faces a dilemma as to which remedy he should pursue to best advantage, this question being considered after the action for the price has been examined.

The seller's action for the price

The SGA provides that S can sue for the price in two situations, viz (i) where property has passed to B, and (ii) where the contract specifically provides that payment is to be made on a fixed date irrespective of the passing of property or S's obligation to deliver the goods.

Where property has passed to B

The SGA, s 49(1) provides:

> 'Where, under a contract of sale, the property in the goods has passed to the buyer and he wrongfully neglects or refuses to pay for the goods according to the terms of the contract, the seller may maintain an action against him for the price of the goods'.

It cannot be stressed enough that S's entitlement to sue for the price is limited to cases where *property* in the goods has passed to B and does not arise simply because B's obligation to pay falls due. Thus, although s 28 provides that delivery of the goods and payment of the price are concurrent conditions, the fact that *delivery* of the goods has been made to B does not, in itself, permit a claim for the price. The cardinal rule that S cannot maintain an action for the price where property has not passed applies even where it is the wrongful act of B which prevents the passing of property. In *Colley v Overseas Exporters*,[1] S agreed to sell leather belting to B on fob terms and the contract obliged B to nominate a ship onto which the goods were to be loaded by S. The price was to be paid when delivery was made to the ship. S sent the goods from Sheffield to Liverpool but, owing to B's failure to name an effective ship (after five attempts), S was unable to load the goods. It was held that S could not sue for the price even though it was solely B's default which meant that property did not pass to him.[2] S had argued that B's default was crucial[3] and should have enabled him to sue for the price but McCardie J stressed that adoption of this view would lead to unacceptable results. B would equally have been in default had he repudiated the contract before the goods had left Sheffield and so, in every case where B's default prevented S from passing the property to B, S would have a right to sue for the price. This could happen even in situations where B refused to take delivery of goods which were unascertained. It follows that S's correct remedy in the *Colley* situation is to sue for damages for non-acceptance under s 50(1). Nevertheless, where S is entirely innocent this seems to impose a heavy burden on him and it must be asked how the *Colley* rule fits with the decision in *White and Carter (Councils) Ltd v McGregor*.[4] There the House of Lords held that, in the face of one party's repudiation, the innocent party may complete his side of the performance (provided there need be no co-operation with the party in breach) and then sue for the sum agreed to be paid for his performance. The contract in *White and Carter* was not one for the sale of goods and Lord Keith[5] considered that the rule concerning anticipatory breach did *not* apply to a sale of unascertained or future goods. Thus if B repudiates his obligations before property passes to him (eg the goods have not been appropriated to the contract), S can maintain only an action for damages; he cannot ignore B's repudiation, press on with his performance and claim the price.

Colley distinguished the decision in *Mackay v Dick*[6] on the ground that there was a condition subsequent in the latter case. In *Mackay*, a digging machine had been delivered to B who was bound to keep and pay for it unless it failed a stipulated test. B neglected to test the machine and it was held that S could recover the price. But here property had passed to B and his failure to co-operate meant that property did not revest in S. There is thus a decisive distinction to be made between cases where B defaults before property passes (*Colley*) and those where he defaults after it has passed (*Mackay*).

---

1 [1921] 3 KB 302.
2 See also *Stein, Forbes & Co v County Tailoring Co* (1916) 86 LJKB 448 (under a cif contract, B wrongfully refused to take up the shipping documents when S tendered them. It was held that S could not sue for the price).
3 It had also been argued that B's failure to nominate a ship meant that he was estopped from denying that property had passed to him. This argument failed. McCardie J stressed (pp 311-312) that, while estoppel by conduct could prevent B from disputing that property had passed to him, his breach of contract would not, without more, lead to such an estoppel.
4 [1962] AC 413.
5 [1962] AC 413 at 437.
6 (1881) 6 App Cas 251.

It is insufficient that property alone has passed to B since an action for the price lies under s 49(1) only if the buyer 'wrongfully neglects or refuses to pay for the goods according to the terms of the contract'. This question depends upon B's duty or obligation to pay. The terms of the contract will specify when payment is due and thus 'wrongful' must be interpreted having regard to those terms. It follows that B's neglect or refusal will not be wrongful if the price is not due under the contract (eg B has been allowed credit and the credit period has not expired), or if S is in breach of certain obligations (eg S is unwilling to deliver the goods, delivery and payment normally being concurrent conditions under s 28). Likewise, B could show that his failure to pay the price is not wrongful where the time for payment under the contract has been waived by S.

Where the price is payable on a fixed date irrespective of the passing of property

The SGA, s 49(2) provides:

> 'Where, under a contract of sale, the price is payable on a day certain irrespective of delivery and the buyer wrongfully neglects or refuses to pay such price, the seller may maintain an action for the price, although the property in the goods has not passed and the goods have not been appropriated to the contract. '

Under s 49(2), S may sue for the price even though property has not passed to B and despite the fact that the goods have not been delivered to him. The link established in s 28 between S's duty to deliver and B's duty to pay the price is thus broken by s 49(2) and the section is based upon the decision in *Dunlop v Grote*.[7] There B had agreed to buy 1,000 tons of iron to be delivered before the end of April, the contract providing that 'if the delivery of the said iron should not be required ... on or before 30 April', payment was to be made on that date. B paid a portion of the price and refused to pay the balance but Cresswell J held that S could recover the whole sum once 30 April had arrived.

The major difficulty with s 49(2) lies in the interpretation of 'a day certain' and whether this must be a fixed date or, instead, might cover those cases where provision has been made for *ascertaining* the date of payment. A restrictive view was taken in *Shell-Mex Ltd v Elton Cop Dyeing Co Ltd*.[8] The contract was for the sale of 1,000 tons of oil to be delivered in instalments, at the request of B, up to June 22 1927. Payment was to be made within 14 days of the delivery of each instalment. B repudiated the contract with 466 tons left to be delivered and the property in the goods had not passed to B. A clause in the contract provided that the 'sellers have the right at any time to invoice the buyers the due quantities of oil not taken up, and to demand payment of the invoice amounts'. After June 22 1927, S sued for the price. Wright J held that S's claim for the price must fail as the clause was not sufficiently specific in providing for payment on a day certain: he considered that s 49(2) applied only where the price is payable *on* a day certain and could not be extended to cases where the price is payable *by* a day certain. S's remedy thus lay in damages. The same view was taken in *Stein, Forbes & Co v County Tailoring Co*,[9] where a contract for the sale of a quantity of sheepskins provided that payment was to

---

7 (1845) 2 Car & Kir 153; the rule is traceable to *Pordage v Cole* (1669) 1 Wms Saund 319.
8 (1928) 34 Com Cas 39.
9 (1916) 86 LJKB 448.

be made by 'net cash against documents on arrival of the steamer'. It was held that S could not claim the price when B refused to accept the shipping documents: Atkin J stressed that the price was not payable on 'a day certain irrespective of delivery' but, instead, the price was payable *expressly against* delivery.[10] The bulk of authority thus establishes that 'a day certain' must be a concluded, precise date which is pre-determined by the contract and which can be ascertained without reference to the parties or any third party.

Nevertheless, in *Workman, Clark & Co Ltd v Lloyd Brazileño*,[11] it was held that, in a shipbuilding contract, S could sue for instalments of the price as they became due, even though the date on which they fell due was ascertained by reference to the various stages reached in the construction of the vessel. The underlying rationale of *Workman* is undoubtedly that S should be able to sue for instalments during the performance of the contract when property in the goods has not passed to B for, otherwise, S will have a partially-completed ship on his hands and no recourse to any cash from B in order to continue the ship's construction. In *Workman*, S could not have maintained an action in damages and would thus have had no remedy (apart from suspension of work under the terms of the contract) had the instalments of the price been unenforceable. Likewise, in an Australian decision,[12] S let premises to B which contained S's machinery and B was permitted to use it while negotiations were proceeding for its sale to B. The subsequent contract provided that property was not to pass before delivery but that payment of the price was to be 'net cash before delivery'. The purchase price was never paid. Here it was unclear exactly when B had to pay but it was held that 'net cash before delivery' imposed a condition that the goods were to be paid for before the property should pass by delivery; B came under an obligation to pay in a reasonable time and failure to do so meant that S could sue for the price even though no delivery[13] had been made and the property had not passed to B. Having regard to the strict interpretation of s 49(2) discussed above, an English court faced with these facts could hardly hold that the price was payable 'on a day certain'[14] and, as property had not passed to B, s 49(1) would also be inapplicable. It is arguable that this sort of contractual provision seeks to give S total protection against B's failure to pay the price and the orthodox view is that a claim for damages for non-acceptance is apt where property has not passed to B. However, Chalmers[15] considered that, where B has accepted delivery of the goods, payment to be 90 days after delivery with a provision that property does not pass until payment, there 'seems no good reason why [S] could not claim the price'. In this example, it is clear that s 49(1) cannot apply as no property has passed to B and, as B has accepted the goods, S is

---

10 See also *Muller, Maclean & Co v Leslie and Anderson* (1921) 8 Ll L Rep 328 (goods were sold c & f to be paid for by cash against documents but B refused to pay against the documents. Held S could not sue for the price as it was not payable 'on a day certain'); *Henderson and Keay Ltd v A M Carmichael Ltd* 1956 SLT (Notes) 58 (terms were 'prompt cash against invoice': held this was not 'on a day certain'. The date of the receipt of the invoice left it open to S to make the price payable at any time either before or after delivery and B thus had no certainty as to when the price might be required).
11 [1908] 1 KB 968.
12 *Minister for Supply and Development v Servicemen's Co-operative Joinery Manufacturers Ltd* (1951) 82 CLR 621.
13 Here 'delivery' would entail a change in the character of B's possession from bailee to owner.
14 This was, in fact, the view of Webb J in the *Servicemen's Co-operative Joinery* case, above.
15 *Sale of Goods Act 1979* (18th edn, 1981), p 225.

unable to claim damages for non-acceptance under s 50. It is, consequently, difficult to disagree with Chalmers's conclusion on these facts. Certainly it appears that many of the provisions commonly in use, eg 'price to be paid 30 days after invoice', are not within the definition of payment 'on a day certain' in s 49(2).

S's claim to interest on the price

Where S is entitled to sue for the price, may he claim interest from B for any delay in making payment? The House of Lords[16] has recently upheld the general rule at common law that damages are not awarded for delay in paying a fixed sum of money and a claim for interest has always been regarded as equivalent to a claim for damages in this situation.[17] It is, however, possible for the contract to provide for the payment of interest. Moreover, a plaintiff might obtain special damages by bringing himself within the second rule of remoteness of damage in *Hadley v Baxendale*,[18] if he had to obtain finance from a third party and thus pay interest as a consequence of the defendant's failure to pay.[19] In the High Court and County Court, in proceedings for the recovery of a debt or damages, the court now has a discretion to include simple interest in any sum for which judgment is given, but if S makes provision in the contract with B for the payment of interest on the price, he is not dependent on the court's discretion.[20]

Payment by instalments

An enduring difficulty in contracts where the price is payable in instalments concerns S's right to retain payments which have been made or have accrued prior to the termination of the contract by reason of B's breach. The modern view is that the consequences of the termination of a contract for breach must be sharply differentiated from the situation where there is rescission *ab initio* in cases of misrepresentation, for example. Where the innocent party is entitled to treat himself as discharged because of the other party's breach, only the *future* obligations of both parties come to an end but the discharge does not operate retrospectively and thus does not affect vested rights under the contract.[1] In cases of hire and hire-purchase, for example, it is clearly established that instalments which fall due before termination for the hirer's breach are recoverable in an action for debt[2] and, in a time charter party of a vessel, the shipowner can recover the arrears of hire due but still unpaid at the date of his acceptance of the repudiation.[3]

In contracts for the sale of goods the decision in *Hyundai Heavy Industries Co Ltd v Papadopoulos*[4] raises some important issues. There shipbuilders agreed to 'build, launch, equip and complete' a vessel at a price of US $14.3m with instalment payments representing specified percentages of the total price. The

---

16 *President of India v La Pintada Compania Navigacion SA* [1985] AC 104.
17 *London, Chatham and Dover Rly Co v South Eastern Rly Co* [1893] AC 429.
18 (1854) 9 Exch 341.
19 See *Wadsworth v Lydall* [1981] 1 WLR 598.
20 See *Economic Assurance Society v Usborne* [1902] AC 147.
 1 *Heyman v Darwins Ltd* [1942] AC 356; *Johnson v Agnew* [1980] AC 367.
 2 See eg *Chatterton v Maclean* [1951] 1 All ER 761.
 3 *Leslie Shipping Co v Welstead* [1921] 3 KB 420.
 4 [1980] 1 WLR 1129; see Beatson, 'Discharge for Breach: The Position of Instalments, Deposits and Other Payments Due Before Completion' (1981) 97 LQR 389.

contract contained express terms permitting the shipbuilder to terminate the contract if an instalment was not paid when due. A valid notice of termination was given on 6 September for non-payment of the second instalment which had fallen due on 15 July and which represented 2.5% of the price. The issue was whether the July instalment remained payable after the termination of the contract. The House of Lords held that the shipbuilder should succeed against the buyer's guarantor for the amount which was unpaid. The House differentiated shipbuilding contracts from straightforward contracts for the sale of goods in that, in a shipbuilding contract, the shipbuilder must necessarily perform work and incur expenses in constructing the vessel and should therefore be entitled to accrued instalments of the price. Accordingly, the decision in *Dies v British and International Financing and Mining Corpn Ltd*[5] was distinguished. There B was allowed to recover a pre-paid instalment of the price where, in breach of contract, he failed to take delivery of rifles and ammunition under a simple contract for the sale of goods, the court emphasising the general rule that recovery was possible in the absence of any contractual intent that the sum should be forfeited. In this situation, payment is regarded as conditional on delivery.

The *Hyundai* reasoning was applied by the House of Lords in *Stocznia Gdanska SA v Latvian Shipping Co*.[6] The Law Lords re-emphasised that, in a shipbuilding contract, there is not a total failure of consideration in a contract to design and build a vessel to a certain specification simply because B has not received the finished ship and property in it has not been transferred to him. Accordingly, instalments of the purchase price which have accrued before termination can be retained or recovered by S. This analysis would also indicate that, where the contract is one for payment of the price in instalments and B has obtained delivery of the goods and used them before gaining property in them, he will be in no position to recover instalments paid before termination as there is not a total failure of consideration. It is thus clear that, in a sale of existing goods where there are no expenses to be incurred by S in reliance on an advance payment, there will be a total failure of consideration if there is no delivery of the goods and B cannot then be compelled to pay the price or, if he has paid it, he may recover it from S.[7] It is less clear, however, whether the *Hyundai* view of failure of consideration may extend to contracts other than shipbuilding where S is both a manufacturer and seller of the goods. It was argued in *Stozcnia* that the *Hyundai* reasoning was inconsistent with the earlier *Fibrosa*[8] case. It will be remembered that, in *Fibrosa*, S had partially completed the manufacture of machinery at the date the contract was frustrated and yet B was able to recover instalments paid to S before the frustrating event on the basis that, in the absence of any delivery of the goods to B, there was a total failure of consideration. In *Stozcnia*, the two Law Lords who expressed a view considered that *Fibrosa* was correctly regarded as a simple contract of sale and that 'the manufacture of the goods by the supplier does not necessarily mean that the manufacture constitutes part of the contract consideration'[9] and, moreover, that 'the distinction between a simple contract of sale, in which the only consideration is the transfer of title,

5 [1939] 1 KB 724.
6 [1998] 1 WLR 574.
7 See also *Rover International Ltd v Cannon Film Sales Ltd (No 3)* [1989] 1 WLR 912, 930-932, where Kerr LJ explained *Dies* as a case of total failure of consideration.
8 *Fibrosa Spolka Akcyjna v Fairbairn Lawson Combe Barbour Ltd* [1943] AC 32.
9 [1998] 1 WLR 574, 590 per Lord Goff of Chieveley.

and a contract of sale which also includes the provision of services prior to delivery, may sometimes be a fine one'.[10] It is, with respect, very difficult to ascertain the fine distinction between the *Fibrosa* facts and those of *Stozcnia* but this slender and elusive distinction will, no doubt, be disputed time-and-again in future disputes. Finally, the position where there is not a total failure of consideration, as in *Hyundai*, but the *entire* price has been paid or is payable before termination is also contentious but, in principle, the current rules would indicate that the price cannot be recovered by B or, alternatively, that it remains payable by him.

S's quandary: should he sue for the price or for damages?

It was stressed in the introduction to this chapter that if the property in the goods has passed to B *and* he wrongfully neglects or refuses to accept and pay for the goods, S can sue either for the price under s 49 or for damages for non-acceptance under s 50. This is not a straightforward choice, however, and S may be placed in an invidious position when he has to make a decision regarding possible remedies. Much may depend upon whether the goods have been delivered to B or not and the practical question of resale will often loom large but, in general, several basic issues are clear. An action for the price has the advantage that S is not concerned with the rules relating to damages: he is thus under no duty to mitigate his loss and the issue of remoteness of damage is inapplicable. It may thus seem prudent for S to sue for the price, arguing that property has passed to B, but the outcome might be that property had not passed to B and that S's remedy lies in damages for non-acceptance. When S sues for the price, he must have the goods available for delivery to B and it follows that, in choosing not to resell the goods, S would have failed to mitigate his loss meaning that his damages would be substantially curtailed. Alternatively, S might take steps to mitigate his loss by reselling the goods but he cannot then perform the contract with B as he is unable to deliver the goods and thus he loses any claim to the price. In addition, S's resale or attempted resale might be regarded by the court as evidence of S's acceptance of B's repudiation; the contract would then be terminated and property would revest in S, consequently eliminating any possibility of his claiming the price.

It is obviously desirable to have rules which stipulate exactly when S may sue for the price but it is doubtful whether a rule based upon the passing of property always achieves this objective: passing of property may be divorced from physical delivery in principle but, in practice, delivery is often regarded as decisive. Moreover, it is surely crucial to decide which of the two parties should have the reponsibility of disposing of the goods and, again, ascertaining whether S or B has the property in the goods may be inconclusive. It might thus be apt to confine S to a claim in damages where he can resell the goods with ease but permit him to claim the price whenever resale could be accomplished more easily by B. Many of these pragmatic issues have been addressed in the USA's Uniform Commercial Code (UCC)[11] which frees the law from the overall restraint of the passing of property. Under the UCC, s 2-709, the basic principle is that S can sue for the price only where B has 'accepted' the goods and this

---

10   [1998] 1 WLR 574 at 600, per Lord Lloyd of Berwick.
11   See also the discussion of these questions in the Ontario Law Reform Commission's *Report on the Sale of Goods* (1979).

notion is not necessarily connected to the passing of property but means that B has obtained control/possession of the goods. As B has possession, it is regarded as unfair to limit S to damages and impose the burden on S of disposing of the goods. On the other hand, S cannot normally claim the price of unaccepted goods as the UCC recognises that he is usually better placed to dispose of them than B. Two exceptions are admitted to this general scheme. First, S can recover the price when risk of loss has passed to B and the goods have been lost or damaged within a reasonable time after risk has passed. Second, he can sue for the price where the goods are 'identified to the contract' (ie earmarked) *and* he is unable, after reasonable efforts, to resell them at a reasonable price or the circumstances reasonably indicate that such efforts will be unavailing. If B refuses to accept the goods, S is thus obliged to attempt to resell them. Should his efforts prove fruitless, S can sue for the price even though property has not passed to B. If S *can* resell before judgment, under s 2-709(2) he does not lose his right to sue for the price but his claim is then for the contract price minus the resale price and is not a claim in damages.

The seller's action for damages for non-acceptance of the goods

In those cases where property in the goods has not passed to B, S's normal remedy is damages for non-acceptance of the goods under s 50(1). Section 54 provides for consequential losses or expenses and s 37 for S's loss incurred in storing the goods.

The SGA, s 50(1) provides:

'Where the buyer wrongfully neglects or refuses to accept and pay for the goods, the seller may maintain an action against him for damages for non-acceptance.'

The question of B's wrongful neglect or refusal to pay for the goods was investigated earlier when S's action for the price was considered. The normal rules relating to a claim in damages apply to s 50(1) and thus S must prove a loss, take reasonable steps to mitigate his loss and cannot recover losses which are too remote. Moreover, s 50(2) and (3) lay down the basic rules for the measure of damages:

'(2) The measure of damages is the estimated loss directly and naturally resulting, in the ordinary course of events, from the buyer's breach of contract.
(3) Where there is an available market for the goods in question the measure of damages is prima facie to be ascertained by the difference between the contract price and the market or current price at the time or times when the goods ought to have been accepted or (if no time was fixed for acceptance) at the time of the refusal to accept.'

Section 50(2) is merely a statutory endorsement of the first rule in *Hadley v Baxendale*[12] while s 50(3) reiterates the normal measure of damages under that first rule and 'is an obvious deduction from sub-s(2), applicable in general to the ordinary goods of commerce for which there is more or less ready sale'.[13] Section 50(2) operates where there is no 'available market' within s 50(3) or

---

12 (1854) 9 Exch 341.
13 Chalmers, *Sale of Goods Act 1979* (18th edn, 1981), p 228.

where the '*prima facie*' rule in s 50(3) is regarded as inappropriate for some reason. Accordingly, it is apt to consider the principles of the available market rule before any analysis of the position under s 50(2). In the analysis which follows, a basic knowledge of the general principles relating to damages is assumed and further guidance on those principles should be sought in the texts on the law of contract.

THE 'AVAILABLE MARKET' RULE UNDER SECTION 50(3)

The normal measure of damages, as stated in s 50(3), is the difference between the contract price of the goods and their market price at the time stipulated in the contract for their acceptance. This represents the amount that S requires in order to be placed in the position he would have been in had the contract been performed.

The available market rule in s 50(3) is designed to bring certainty and objectivity to the assessment of damages and the section envisages a hypothetical resale by S at the time of B's non-acceptance of the goods. The section is also premised upon the general principle that S must take reasonable steps to mitigate his loss and thus, where there is an available market, it is presumed that S will go into that market and resell the goods. However, under s 50(3), S does not actually have to resell the goods in the market but, instead, his loss is crystallised at the date of breach using the market rule. Under the market rule, it follows that where there is an available market for the goods, S will be entitled to substantial damages only if the market price of the goods is lower than the contract price. If S can readily dispose of the goods on the market to a substitute buyer at a price equal to or higher than the contract price, he has suffered no loss.

The meaning of an 'available market'

It is clearly vital that 'available market' be defined as s 50(3) applies only where such a market exists.[14] It has been cogently asserted that 'in attempting to define "market" the courts have been distracted from the relatively simple proposition of mitigation that a substitute should be reasonably available to the plaintiff, and instead concentrated on the more technical aspects of the word'.[15] An early definition of a market centred upon a *place* where goods can be sold,[16] eg an official exchange where goods are quoted and sold, but it is clear that this is far too limiting a notion.[17] More modern definitions tend to state the obvious in that an available market must have 'buyers and

---

14   See Waters, 'The Concept of Market in the Sale of Goods' (1958) 36 Can Bar Rev 360; Lawson, 'An Analysis of the Concept of 'Available Market'' (1969) 43 ALJ 52 (Part I) and (1969) 43 ALJ 106 (Part II).

15   Ogus, *The Law of Damages* (1973), p 326.

16   *Dunkirk Colliery Co Ltd v Lever* (1878) 9 Ch D 20, 25 per James LJ.

17   In *Charrington & Co Ltd v Wooder* [1914] AC 71, 82, Lord Dunedin denied any fixed legal significance to 'market'; *Heskell v Continental Express Ltd* [1950] 1 All ER 1033, 1050 per Devlin J: 'A market for this purpose means more than a particular place. It means also a particular level of trade'; *ABD (Metals and Waste Ltd) v Anglo Chemical and Ore Co Ltd* [1955] 2 Lloyd's Rep 456, 466 per Sellers J: 'It is not necessary to establish a market that it should have a fixed place or building, but that there must be sufficent traders who are in touch with each other to evidence a market ...'

sellers'[18] and that the goods can 'freely be sold, and that there was a demand sufficient to absorb readily all the goods that were thrust on it, so that if a purchaser defaulted, the goods in question could readily be disposed of'.[19]

It must be asked, however, what is meant by an *available* market. An 'available market' carries with it the connotation that there must be immediate access to buyers within a reasonable distance of the place where the breach of contract occurred. There are thus three inter-connected issues here in the definition of an available market, viz (i) the time when such a market must be 'available'; (ii) its geographical location; and (iii) its size.

First, the question of time and market availability must be considered. It is suggested that, having regard to differing types of goods and businesses, there should be access to substitute buyers in a reasonable period of time if there is to be an available market. Certainly it has been held, in a case concerning S's non-delivery, that there is no available market if there will be an eight or nine months' delay before substitute goods can be obtained.[20] A most realistic approach was taken in *Shearson Lehman Hutton Inc v Maclaine Watson & Co Ltd (No 2)*.[1] There it was held that, if S actually offered the goods for sale, there was no available market unless there was one actual buyer on that day at a fair price. If, on the other hand, there was a hypothetical sale only, there was no available market unless there were sufficient traders potentially in touch with each other to evidence such a market in which S might resell the goods. Moreover, it was held that the market price of the goods in a hypothetical resale in the available market was assessed at the date of breach but it was also permissible to take into account the price which might be negotiated within a few days with other potential buyers who were not part of the market on the relevant date only because of difficulties in communication.[2]

The second issue relates to whether there can be a 'market' anywhere other than the place of delivery. Again, this is important in relation to S's duty to act reasonably in order to mitigate his loss but he cannot be expected to search far and wide for a market. There is a vast difference between the situation where a contract can be entered into for the *resale* of the goods (eg on an international market but S is not normally involved in international trade and there might be a delay of several months before he could physically dispose of the goods) and the situation where the market for their resale is *available*. In *Dunkirk Colliery Co v Lever*,[3] B refused to accept a quantity of coal and James LJ[4] assumed that S might have to send it in wagons to a different location but, again, it seems that the test must be one of reasonableness having regard to the time and expense involved in seeking a market elsewhere.[5] In *Thompson (W L) Ltd v Robinson*

---

18 *The Arpad* [1934] P 189, 191 per Bateson J.
19 *Thompson (W L) Ltd v Robinson (Gunmakers) Ltd* [1955] Ch 177, 187 per Upjohn J.
20 *Lesters Leather & Skin Co Ltd v Home & Overseas Brokers Ltd* (1949) 82 Ll L Rep 203.
 1 [1990] 3 All ER 723.
 2 In *Charter v Sullivan* [1957] 2 QB 117, 133-134 Sellers LJ considered that the resale of a car some seven to ten days after B's breach of contract meant that there was 'no immediate buyer' and thus no available market but this seems too strict a test.
 3 (1878) 9 Ch D 20.
 4 (1878) 9 Ch D 20 at 25.
 5 *Kwei Tek Chao v British Traders and Shippers Ltd* [1954] 2 QB 459, 499 per Devlin J; see also *Lesters Leather & Skin Co Ltd v Home & Overseas Brokers Ltd* (1949) 82 Ll L Rep 203 (in a case of S's non-delivery (in the UK) of snake skins, it was held that there was no available market where B would have had to buy substitute goods in India with an eight or nine months' delay after breach).

(Gunmakers) Ltd,[6] S was a car dealer in the East Riding of Yorkshire and the court assumed that he should seek a substitute buyer in that part of Yorkshire.

The third factor, the size of the market, may also be crucial in deciding whether there is an available market, as intermittent buying and selling of small quantities of goods cannot satisfy the immediacy inherent in the definition of an available market.[7] If the goods were to be sold in one consignment under the terms of the original contract, the fact that the entire consignment could be resold immediately in smaller lots would be immaterial as there would clearly be an available market. Indeed, if S cannot find a substitute buyer for one large parcel of goods, he may be under an obligation to divide the goods into smaller quantities in fulfilment of his duty to mitigate his loss.[8] However, it would be difficult to establish that there was an available market if S could resell the goods in small parcels only and during an unreasonably lengthy period of time.[9] It is also clear that price *may* have an effect on the question of an available market: a very high or very low price may denote that there is either a scarcity or surplus of the goods in question and so no available market.[10]

Fixed retail prices and an available market

The meaning of 'available market' has been considered in two leading cases where the goods could be sold only at a fixed retail price. In *Thompson (W L) Ltd v Robinson (Gunmakers) Ltd*,[11] B agreed to buy a new Standard Vanguard car from S, a car dealer, at a retail price fixed by the manufacturer, but subsequently B refused to take delivery of the car. S persuaded the wholesaler to take back the car. B contended that the measure of damages was the difference between the contract price and the market price and, since these prices were the same, the damages should be purely nominal. Upjohn J held that, as the supply of Vanguard cars at this time exceeded the demand for them, there was no 'available market' in that a substitute buyer could not readily be found. Accordingly, s 50(3) was inapplicable to the facts: S had sold one less car than he would have done had B completed the purchase and he was thus entitled to damages representing the lost profit on the sale. In contrast, in *Charter v Sullivan*,[12] B refused to accept a new Hillman Minx car which he had agreed to buy from S at a fixed retail price but here the market was reversed in that demand for such cars outstripped supply and S was able to resell the car to another buyer within ten days of B's repudiation. Since the contract price and the market price

---

6   [1955] Ch 177.
7   *Kwei Tek Chao v British Traders and Shippers Ltd* [1954] 2 QB 459, 498 per Devlin J.
8   *Tredegar Iron and Coal Co v Gielgud* (1883) Cab & El 27.
9   See *Garnac Grain Co Inc v H M Faure and Fairclough Ltd* [1968] AC 1130n (in the case of S's breach, the HL was prepared to accept that there was an available market in which to buy 15,000 tons of lard where the purchases could be made only in small parcels (up to 2,000 tons each) over a period of time, but there is no consideration of the reasonableness of the time period).
10 *Kwei Tek Chao v British Traders and Shippers Ltd* [1954] 2 QB 459, 498 per Devlin J; Cf *Bradley & Sons Ltd v Colonial and Continental Trading Ltd* [1964] 2 Lloyd's Rep 52, 64 per Willmer LJ: 'You do not do away with an existing market merely by proving that prices fall, even if they fall disastrously'; *Campbell Mostyn (Provisions) Ltd v Barnett Trading Co* [1954] 1 Lloyd's Rep 65.
11 [1955] Ch 177.
12 [1957] 2 QB 117.

were the same, and B's breach did not affect the number of such cars sold by S over any given period, S was held to be entitled to nominal damages only. It was thus clear that S made the same number of sales that he would have done if B had accepted the car and the new sale was a *substituted* sale rather than an *additional* sale: S could make only one sale and therefore only one profit. Jenkins LJ[13] emphasised that s 50(3) depended upon differences existing between the contract and market prices based upon supply and demand and such a situation was not attainable where the goods could be sold only at fixed retail prices. As resale price maintenance has largely disappeared in England, it will usually be possible to ascertain a market price having regard to the prevailing market conditions.

Goods made to order and an available market

There may be no available market if goods are to be specially made to B's order or where the contract is for goods which are not kept in stock and thus have to be specially ordered.[14] If B refuses to accept goods which have been specifically manufactured for him, S is entitled to damages representing the costs incurred in making them (if work has already been done) and the loss of profit incurred. In *Re Vic Mill Ltd*,[15] S contracted to manufacture and sell certain machines to B but, as B went into liquidation, the contract was discharged by breach at a time when S had manufactured only some of the machines. S made minor changes to those machines which had already been manufactured and sold them to a third party at marginally less than the original contract price. It was held that S was nevertheless entitled to the profit he would have made on the sale to B. Hamilton LJ stressed that, had both contracts been in existence at the same time, S would have had room in his works to perform both of them. It followed that S had an opportunity to make two separate sets of profit and had lost that opportunity through B's default: the second buyer was an additional, not a substitute buyer.

The reasoning in *Re Vic Mill Ltd* could not apply where the goods are unique and, if S resells at the contract price or above he suffers no loss whatever, as it is evident that S could not have made more than one set of profit from unique goods. In *Lazenby Garages Ltd v Wright*,[16] the Court of Appeal held that a second-hand BMW 2002 motor car was unique goods and thus there was no available market. As S resold to B2 at a price higher than he had agreed with B, S suffered no loss from B's breach of contract and was thus not entitled to damages.

THE TIME FOR ASCERTAINING THE MARKET PRICE

Provided that there is an available market, s 50(3) provides that the time for assessing the difference between the contract price and the 'market or current price' is at 'the time or times when the goods ought to have been accepted or (if no time was fixed for acceptance) at the time of the refusal to accept'.

---

13 [1957] 2 QB 117 at 128.
14 See *Borries v Hutchinson* (1865) 18 CBNS 445; *Hinde v Liddell* (1875) LR 10 QB 265.
15 [1913] 1 Ch 465.
16 [1976] 1 WLR 459.

The time when the goods ought have been accepted

The contract will usually stipulate an exact time for acceptance. Where the contract provides for instalment deliveries at particular times, damages for B's failure to accept an instalment must be calculated according to the market price prevailing at the time stipulated for delivery of that instalment.[17] Also, where the contract specifies a period of time during which delivery and acceptance is to be made, the time at which the goods ought to be accepted by B is the time of *actual tender* by S.[18] It is also clear that the time for acceptance can be fixed by reference to the happening of an event such as the arrival of a ship.[19]

No time fixed for acceptance

Section 50(3) also deals with the situation where B refuses to accept the goods under a contract which does not fix the time for acceptance and here s 50(3) stipulates that the calculation of damages must be based upon the market price at the time of B's 'refusal to accept' the goods. This has caused some confusion and controversy in its radical departure from the normal rule of assessment set-forth in the first part of s 50(3). When might this part of the section apply? It was held in *Millett v Van Heek & Co*[20] that, where there is an anticipatory breach of contract (see later), the assessment of damages is *not* made at the time of S's refusal to deliver the goods (*Millett* concerned S's anticipatory breach) but the relevant time remains the date fixed for delivery; it is almost certain that the same reasoning would apply to s 50(3) and B's refusal to accept the goods. Moreover, in *Millett*, the Divisional Court held[1] that a contract for delivery of the goods within a reasonable time is not a contract with a fixed time for acceptance within s 51(3) (S's breach) but, in the Court of Appeal,[2] opinions on this point were expressly reserved. Atkin LJ[3] considered that 'meaning could be given to the words, "if no time was fixed", by reading them as referring to a contract such as to deliver goods on demand or to deliver goods as required by the purchaser'. Even in these situations, it is difficult to see how the second part of s 50(3) can have any application. For example, in a contract to deliver goods within a reasonable period of time, B may refuse to accept the goods at the end of that period but then the date for the assessment of damages is at *that* time, ie when the goods ought to have been accepted. The same conclusion seems irresistible where the delivery must be on demand because, once the demand is made and refused, the time when the goods ought to be accepted/delivered is fixed and damages are thus assessed at that date. The apparent superfluity of the second part of s 50(3) is why, more recently, the Privy Council concluded that (in relation to s 51(3) and S's breach) it may well be that 'the enactment was introduced into the subsection without consideration in depth of the juristic

---

17 See *Brown v Muller* (1872) LR 7 Exch 319 (damages for S's non-delivery) considered in Ch 28.
18 See the corresponding rule where B sues for non-delivery in Ch 28: the last possible time at which S may tender delivery is the time for the assessment of damages (*Leigh v Paterson* (1818) 8 Taunt 540).
19 *Melachrino v Nickoll and Knight* [1920] 1 KB 693 (a decision on the SGA 1893, s 51(3) and B's damages for S's non-delivery).
20 [1920] 3 KB 535; affd [1921] 2 KB 369.
 1 [1920] 3 KB 535.
 2 [1921] 2 KB 369.
 3 [1921] 2 KB 369 at 378.

position, and that on analysis it proves, exceptionally, to have no content whatever'.[4] It does seem that any theoretical or practical significance is denied to this portion of s 50(3). Although most of the decisions here concerned S's breach under s 51(3), it is tolerably clear that the same rule would apply to cases of B's breach under s 50(3) and the courts do not distinguish the two situations.

ACTUAL RESALE BY S IN THE AVAILABLE MARKET

As the available market rule is premised upon a hypothetical sale by S and the loss which he would have sustained had he resold the goods in that market,[5] there can be difficulties where S has *actually* resold the goods in the available market.

No problems ensue where the sale is at the prevailing market price but where S has resold at *less* than the market price he may attempt to claim damages based upon the difference between the contract price and the actual resale price instead of the market price. It seems clear that if S resells immediately at less than the market price, he will be unable to recover the difference between the contract price and the actual resale price because here the mitigation principle dictates that the reasonable seller could and should have obtained the market price.

The position is less clear where S resells at a price *higher* than that prevailing in the market and thus does more than he is obliged to do under the mitigation principle. Can B capitalise on this position to reduce the damages which are payable or, alternatively, can the enterprising S claim that he should be able to retain the profit made by reselling above the market price? In a leading decision of the House of Lords[6] concerning mitigation, Viscount Haldane LC[7] emphasised that where the plaintiff has successfully diminished the loss caused by the defendant's breach, the actual diminution of the loss he has suffered may be taken into account even though there was no duty on him to act in the way he did. However, Viscount Haldane added that, in order to be taken into account in this way, the plaintiff's subsequent action must arise 'out of the transaction'[8] or 'out of the consequences of the breach and in the ordinary course of business'.[9] Consequently, where S has only *one* batch of goods which B has refused to accept and he resells that batch immediately, it is argued cogently[10] that the higher price which he receives is a direct consequence of B's breach and should be taken into account in calculating S's damages so that he would recover only his actual loss, ie the difference between the contract price and the actual resale price. This should apply only where S resells the identical goods immediately for, if S had

---

4 *Tai Hing Cotton Mill Ltd v Kamsing Knitting Factory* [1979] AC 91, 104 per Lord Keith of Kinkel.
5 *Shearson Lehman Hutton Inc v Maclaine Watson & Co Ltd (No 2)* [1990] 3 All ER 723,726 per Webster J: '... where as in this case the seller did not in fact sell or offer the goods for sale on the date of the breach, the subsection contemplates a hypothetical sale by a hypothetical seller of the amount in question of the goods in question'.
6 *British Westinghouse Electric and Manufacturing Co Ltd v Underground Electric Railways Co of London Ltd* [1912] AC 673.
7 [1912] AC 673 at 689-692.
8 [1912] AC 673 at 689.
9 [1912] AC 673 at 690.
10 See *Benjamin's Sale of Goods* (5th edn, 1997), para 16-069; Atiyah, *The Sale of Goods* (10th edn, 2001), pp 490-492.

further stock at the date of B's breach, a subsequent resale of only *some* of that stock at higher than market prices would not necessarily flow directly from B's breach and, in this event, S should be entitled to the difference between the contract and market prices under s 50(3). This reasoning is supportable by analogy with the situation where S does *not* resell the goods immediately but, instead, opts to retain them for a while before a resale occurs. In *Campbell Mostyn (Provisions) Ltd v Barnett Trading Co*,[11] it was held that if S subsequently resells the goods at a profit because their market price has risen, his damages are not thereby diminished but are nevertheless assessed as the difference between the contract price and market price at the date of breach. In *Campbell*, the Court of Appeal accepted the view of Lord Wrenbury in a case concerning the sale of shares[12] that S is regarded as shouldering the risk of market fluctuations so that, if the market prices fall, B cannot be liable for the additional loss and, likewise, S is entitled to any fruits of his speculation if the market rises. Where S does not speculate in this way but instead resells the goods immediately, it thus seems correct that any price obtained which is higher than that prevailing in the market should be taken into account meaning that S can recover only his actual loss.

ANTICIPATORY BREACH, DAMAGES AND THE MARKET RULE

If B announces in advance of the agreed delivery date that he will not take delivery of the goods, he commits an anticipatory breach of contract. As with any anticipatory breach of contract, the innocent party has the option of (i) accepting the repudiation and treating the contract as discharged; or (ii) affirming the contract and thus continuing to treat it as binding, thereby refusing to accept the repudiation as a breach.[13]

Acceptance of B's anticipatory repudiation

If S accepts B's anticipatory repudiation, he may sue immediately for damages for breach of contract and, if there is an available market for the goods, the date for ascertaining the market price is the date fixed for *delivery* because that remains the date when the contract ought to be performed.[14] If the trial is heard before the date of delivery, the court must do its best to speculate and estimate the correct market price at the future delivery date. The fact that damages are assessed at the date of delivery means that S cannot attempt to fix the date of his acceptance of B's repudiation as the relevant time for the assessment of the market price and he might wish to do this if the market price was substantially less than

---

11 [1954] 1 Lloyd's Rep 65.
12 *Jamal v Moolla Dawood Sons & Co* [1916] 1 AC 175, 179.
13 See *Frost v Knight* (1872) LR 7 Exch 111; *Fercometal SARL v Mediterranean Shipping Co SA* [1989] AC 788. It may be that, once S has elected to affirm the contract, he cannot revert to the right to treat the contract as terminated. This is because the guilty party needs to know whether the contract has been ended or kept alive as, in the latter case, he will still have the opportunity of performance, see *Stocznia Gdanska SA v Latvian Shipping Co* [1997] 2 Lloyd's Rep 228, 234-237 per Colman J (the point was left open in the HL in *Stocznia*, see [1998] 1 WLR 574, 594 per Lord Goff of Chieveley); Treitel, 'Affirmation after Repudiatory Breach' (1998) 114 LQR 22.
14 *Frost v Knight* (1872) LR 7 Exch 111, 113 per Cockburn CJ; *Melachrino v Nickoll and Knight* [1920] 1 KB 693 (S's breach); *Millett v Van Heek & Co* [1921] 2 KB 369 (S's breach).

the contract price at that time.[15] If the rule were otherwise, S would receive more as a result of the breach than he would have obtained if the contract had been performed.

Nevertheless, a vital qualification must be added to this *prima facie* rule in that the doctrine of mitigation must be considered: once S has accepted B's repudiation he comes under a duty to take reasonable steps to mitigate his loss by, most obviously, reselling the goods in the available market. The burden of proof is on B to show that S ought reasonably to have resold the goods before delivery. Accordingly, if S should have mitigated his loss by reselling the goods, the relevant market price is that prevailing at the time when he should have resold and not the market price at either the date of B's repudiation or the date of S's acceptance of that repudiation. If the market price is falling between the date of S's acceptance of the repudiation and the date fixed for delivery, it is clearly reasonable that S should resell at once and thus he cannot make B liable for any more than the difference between the contract price and the market price at the date of repudiation. This is illustrated in *Roth & Co v Taysen, Townsend & Co*.[16] On 24 May, B agreed to buy a cargo of maize which was to be shipped from Argentina on 15 July. The market was falling and B repudiated on 28 May; if S had resold then his loss would have been £680. S commenced proceedings on 24 July but, on the falling market, his loss on that date would have been £1,557. S eventually resold when the cargo arrived on 5 September, at a loss of £3,807. It was held that S had accepted the repudiation on 24 July and, as this was the date at which he should have resold the goods, he was entitled only to the loss which he would have incurred on that date. This rule demanding that S must recognise a falling market in advance undoubtedly places him in an invidious position as 'in general one can only sensibly speak of a falling (or rising) market with reference to what has happened in the past rather than to what will happen in the future'.[17] It is thus unclear whether S's damages would be reduced if, on a falling market, he correctly resold the goods in mitigation of his loss but then found that the market price rose rapidly before the date fixed for delivery.

Refusal to accept B's anticipatory repudiation

Where S refuses to accept B's repudiation, he may continue to treat the contract as binding and wait until the stipulated date for delivery before he tenders the goods. Here B's anticipatory but, unaccepted repudiation, is regarded as a nullity.[18] If B refuses to accept the goods on the date fixed for delivery he is, of course, then in breach of contract and, consequently, S must take reasonable steps to mitigate his loss by attempting to resell the goods. The market price will be that which prevails at the date fixed for delivery and the market price at any earlier date is immaterial. Similarly, in this case where S refuses to accept the repudiation, it should be stressed that S has no duty to mitigate his loss during the period *before* delivery as the mitigation principle applies only where there is an *actual* breach of contract. On a falling market, S is fully entitled to wait for the date of delivery

---

15 *Melachrino v Nickoll and Knight* [1920] 1 KB 693.
16 (1895) 73 LT 628; affd 12 TLR 211.
17 *Lusograin Comercio Internacional De Cereas Ltda v Bunge AG* [1986] 2 Lloyd's Rep 654, 663 per Staughton J.
18 *White and Carter (Councils) Ltd v McGregor* [1962] AC 413, 444 per Lord Hodson.

even though he can see that it is probable that the damages payable by B may increase in the interval. This rule can engender startling consequences. In *Tredegar Iron and Coal Co Ltd v Hawthorn Bros & Co*,[19] B agreed to buy coal from S at 16s per ton to be delivered during February. On 16 February, B repudiated the contract but informed S of an offer from T to buy the coal at 16s 3d per ton. S declined that offer and insisted that B should perform the contract. When B failed to take delivery at the end of February, S sold the coal at 15s per ton in early March. The Court of Appeal allowed S's claim for damages against B for the 1s per ton he had lost on the original contract price, the damages thus being assessed at the date at which B should have taken delivery.[20]

It is equally important to emphasise that, in the situation where S refuses to accept B's repudiation, the contract subsists for the benefit of *both* parties[1] and thus B may change his mind and take delivery as originally agreed. It is then clear that B is not in breach of contract and is under no liability to pay damages to S.[2] Alternatively, S may decide to accept the repudiation in which case he has an immediate duty to mitigate and his damages will be assessed by reference to the market price at the date when S, acting reasonably, ought to have resold the goods.

DAMAGES UNDER SECTION 50(2) WHERE THERE IS NO 'AVAILABLE MARKET'

In defining an 'available market', earlier, several situations were identified where there is no such market for the goods, eg where the goods were specially made to B's requirements[3] or where supply exceeds demand so that willing buyers are unobtainable.[4] Where there is no available market and thus s 50(3) is inapplicable, the basic rule is that enunciated in s 50(2), viz 'the measure of

---

19 (1902) 18 TLR 716.
20 In *White and Carter (Councils) Ltd v McGregor* [1962] AC 413, P supplied local authorities with litter bins in return for the right to place advertisements on the bins. P and D agreed that D's business would be advertised on the bins for three years but D repudiated the contract on the same day that it was entered into. P refused to accept the repudiation: he prepared the advertisements, displayed them for three years and then claimed the sum due under the contract. The House of Lords held that P should succeed. It seems that *White and Carter* is limited to recovery of a specific debt and to cases where D's collaboration is not needed for the completion of P's contractual obligations. It will, therefore, have a very limited application in the sale of goods. If property in the goods can pass to B without any act or consent on his part, S should be able to proceed with the contract so that property does pass to B and S can then sue for the *price* which is, of course, a debt. Similarly, the price may be payable by B under the contract terms *before* property passes to B (under s 49(2)) and, again, S might be able to press on with performance without B's concurrence. But in a contract for the sale of unascertained or future goods, B's anticipatory repudiation would nullify his assent to S's later appropriation of the goods to the contract. This would also be true if the property's passing were dependent on B's acceptance of the goods and/or his taking delivery of them (this was the view of Lord Keith (dissenting) at p 437). However, S could, for example, continue with the manufacture of goods and, in an action for *damages*, he could recover the difference between the contract price and the market price at the date fixed for delivery to B without any obligation to mitigate his loss.
1   The risks involved may thus favour either party: see the consequences which ensued in *Fercometal SARL v Mediterranean Shipping Co SA* [1989] AC 788.
2   *White and Carter (Councils) Ltd v McGregor* [1962] AC 413, 444 per Lord Hodson.
3   See *Re Vic Mill Ltd* [1913] 1 Ch 465 (considered earlier).
4   See *Thompson (W L) Ltd v Robinson (Gunmakers) Ltd* [1955] Ch 177 (considered earlier).

damages is the estimated loss directly and naturally resulting, in the ordinary course of events, from the buyer's breach of contract'. Following general principles, S is thus entitled to be placed in the position in which he would have been had the contract been performed and the general rule is that the measure of S's loss is the difference between the contract price of the goods and the *value* of the goods to S at the time and place of B's breach. Where there is no ready market in which S can resell the goods, this 'value' clearly has to be assessed by some yardstick other than a simple appraisal of the market price. In *Harlow & Jones Ltd v Panex (International) Ltd*,[5] B repudiated a contract for the sale of 10,000 tons of Russian steel and S made 'desperate efforts' to sell the goods which were 'hawked round the world'.[6] The Russian suppliers took back 1,500 tons at cost price and S managed to sell the remaining 8,500 tons to German buyers three months after B's breach of contract. There was clearly no available market for the goods during the three month period and Roskill J held that S's loss was the difference between the contract price and the value of the goods to S at the time and place of the breach. Accordingly, as regards the 8,500 tons of steel S's loss was the difference between the price at which the goods were sold and the contract price and, in relation to the 1,500 tons, the measure of damages was the difference between the price at which S bought the goods from the Russian suppliers and the price S would have obtained from B.

It is thus clear that, if S does succeed in finding a substitute buyer even though there is no available market, the resale price may provide evidence of S's loss. In *Robbins of Putney Ltd v Meek*,[7] B refused to accept a Bentley 'T' series saloon from S at the contract price of £7,150 and, after advertising it for sale on sixteen occasions in the motoring press, S sold it to a motor dealer for £5,750. It was held that there was no available market for the Bentley at the date of breach and, as S had acted reasonably in mitigating his loss, the measure of damages was the difference between the contract price and the price obtained on the resale. It will be apparent that, even in the absence of an available market, S comes under a duty to take reasonable steps to mitigate his loss. He may be able to persuade his seller to take back the goods, as in *Harlow & Jones Ltd v Panex (International) Ltd*,[8] above, but it was stressed in *Harlow* that S need not 'nurse the interests of the contract breaker'[9] and accept his offer to buy the goods at a reduced price. Where there is no available market for the goods, S is entitled to deal with them 'in any reasonable way'[10] and an obvious course of action would be for S to adapt the goods in some way to make them saleable and suitable for another buyer. His damages will then include the cost of the adaptations as well as the lost profit on the first sale.[11] S does not have to take risks and incur speculative expenditure in an attempt to minimise his loss[12] but it is relatively clear that it would be reasonable for S to incur limited expenditure in order to make the goods saleable.

Finally, it should be remembered that although there is no available market, S may be entitled to the profit that he would have made on the first sale even

5 [1967] 2 Lloyd's Rep 509.
6 [1967] 2 Lloyd's Rep 509 at 529 per Roskill J.
7 [1971] RTR 345.
8 [1967] 2 Lloyd's Rep 509.
9 [1967] 2 Lloyd's Rep 509 at 530, per Roskill J.
10 *Re Vic Mill Ltd* [1913] 1 Ch 465, 473 per Hamilton LJ.
11 *Re Vic Mill Ltd* [1913] 1 Ch 465.
12 *Jewelowski v Propp* [1944] KB 510.

though he does succeed in reselling the goods: this is because he may be able to prove, as S did in *Re Vic Mill Ltd*,[13] that he would (but for B's breach) have made two sales instead of one[14] and thus the second buyer is an additional buyer rather than a substituted buyer.

CONSEQUENTIAL LOSSES AND EXPENSES INCURRED

Section 54 preserves the right of both parties to recover special damages. Section 54 provides:

> 'Nothing in this Act affects the right of the buyer or the seller to recover interest or special damages in any case where by law interest or special damages may be recoverable, or to recover money paid where the consideration for the payment of it has failed.'

Claims for consequential losses and expenses are more commonly made by B than S but it is clear that, where B has refused to accept the goods and S resells the goods in the market, S may claim expenses which are reasonably incurred in making the resale, eg advertising costs.[15] Such a claim must, of course, be justified within the rules of remoteness and mitigation. S's claim for consequential losses is not dependent upon whether or not property has passed to B and, indeed, S may claim such damages in addition to his claim for the price, provided he can satisfy the remoteness and causation rules, eg special damages would be available if S had been obliged to obtain a loan from a third party and pay interest on it as a direct consequence of B's failure to pay. Moreover, where S has resold the goods as an unpaid seller under s 48(3), the section expressly preserves his right to 'recover from the original buyer damages for any loss occasioned by his breach of contract' and this would presumably also be the position in the case of an express right of resale under s 48(4) as that section refers to S's claim for 'damages'.

Arguably s 37 is more important for S in that, where B does not take delivery, the section enables S to make a claim for charges for storage of the goods and other loss occasioned by B's neglect or refusal to take delivery. Section 37 provides:

> '(1) When the seller is ready and willing to deliver the goods, and requests the buyer to take delivery, and the buyer does not within a reasonable time after such request take delivery of the goods, he is liable to the seller for any loss occasioned by his neglect or refusal to take delivery, and also for a reasonable charge for the care and custody of the goods.
> (2) Nothing in this section affects the rights of the seller where the neglect or refusal of the buyer to take delivery amounts to a repudiation of the contract.'

Special damages are thus available to S for loss which is the consequence of B's failure to take prompt delivery, eg S's storage costs,[16] transportation costs or

---

13   [1913] 1 Ch 465.

14   The burden of proof is on the defaulting buyer to prove that S could not have made the second profit as well: *Hill & Sons v Edwin Showell & Sons Ltd* (1918) 87 LJKB 1106.

15   See *Ward (R V) Ltd v Bignall* [1967] 1 QB 534.

16   See *Greaves v Ashlin* (1813) 3 Camp 426; *Somes v British Empire Co* (1860) 8 HL Cas 338. In *Penarth Dock Engineering Co Ltd v Pounds* [1963] 1 Lloyd's Rep 359, B did not take delivery of a floating pontoon in a reasonable period of time and was held liable in trespass. The measure of damages was not any loss to S (there was none) but the benefit obtained by B, ie free storage.

the cost of extended insurance. It could be argued that s 37 is limited to the situation where property has passed to B, this being suported by the reference to S's 'charge' for the 'care and custody' of the goods. Certainly if property has passed to B and S sues for the price, s 37 allows S to claim the costs of such care and custody and 'any loss occasioned by [B's] neglect or refusal to take delivery', eg the goods have gone bad and harmed other goods in S's possession.

Where S sues for damages for non-acceptance of the goods under s 50, the losses and expenses specified in s 37 will be included in his claim for damages and, in this respect, the courts have not separated ss 37 and 50. Moreover, loss resulting from accidental destruction of the goods after B's failure to take delivery will be considered as part of the transfer of risk transfer under s 20(2).

CHAPTER 28

The remedies of the buyer

The remedies to be considered in this chapter are damages for non-delivery, delayed delivery and for the defective quality of the goods.

The buyer's action for damages for non-delivery of the goods

Section 51 provides B with a remedy in damages for non-delivery where S wrongfully neglects or refuses to deliver the goods to B. It is the counterpart to the seller's remedy, in s 50, for damages for non-acceptance, already considered. Section 51 provides:

'(1) Where the seller wrongfully neglects or refuses to deliver the goods to the buyer, the buyer may maintain an action against the seller for damages for non-delivery.
(2) The measure of damages is the estimated loss directly and naturally resulting, in the ordinary course of events, from the seller's breach of contract.
(3) Where there is an available market for the goods in question the measure of damages is prima facie to be ascertained by the difference between the contract price and the market or current price of the goods at the time or times when they ought to have been delivered or (if no time was fixed) at the time of the refusal to deliver'.

The provisions of s 51 reflect those in s 50 and reference should be made to Chapter 27 where s 50 is examined: on all the major issues the reasoning in the cases is applicable to both S's remedy for non-acceptance and B's remedy for non-delivery. Section 51(3) is the normal rule to be applied where there is an available market whereas s 51(2) applies in the absence of such a market. Moreover, s 54 allows B to claim special damages, eg loss resulting from special circumstances known to S. B may claim damages for non-delivery even though the property in the goods has passed to him and his damages should be assessed on the same basis whether or not property has passed.

THE 'AVAILABLE MARKET' RULE UNDER SECTION 51(3)

Section 51(3) is a replica of s 50(3), the latter section providing for S's remedy in damages for B's non-acceptance of the goods. Accordingly, the normal measure of damages when S fails to deliver the goods is set-forth in s 51(3) as the difference between the contract price of the goods and their market price at the time stipulated in the contract for the delivery of the goods. This represents the amount that B requires in order to be placed in the position in which he would have been had the contract been performed. If the market price is lower than the contract price, B is entitled to nominal damages only as he can buy substitute goods in the market without incurring any extra cost. Section 51(3) assumes that B has not paid the price of the goods to S but, if he has, B is entitled to recover it, with interest, together with the difference between that price and the market price at the time when the goods ought to have been delivered.[1] Most of the difficulties associated with s 51(3) are similar to those which arise under s 50(3) and, to avoid repetition, reference should be made to Chapter 27 where S's remedy in damages is considered.

The meaning of an 'available market'

The issues here are the same as those which were examined under s 50(3) and an 'available market' has largely the same meaning no matter whether it is B who fails to accept the goods or S who fails to deliver them except, of course, where S does not deliver the goods, B is concerned with the availability of sellers so that he may buy substitute goods. An available market demands that B has access to sellers who are willing and able to supply substitute goods quickly and the stress on the *availability* of the market involves a consideration of those elements considered in Chapter 27 viz (i) the time when such a market must be 'available'; (ii) its geographical location; and (iii) its size.

THE TIME FOR ASCERTAINING THE MARKET PRICE

Section 51(3) specifies that the time for ascertaining the market price is 'the time or times when [the goods] ought to have been delivered or (if no time was fixed) at the time of the refusal to deliver'.

The time when the goods ought to have been delivered

The same rules apply here as those considered under s 50(3). First, the contract terms should be examined to determine whether an exact time has been fixed for delivery. The question of instalment deliveries was considered in *Brown v Muller*[2] where 500 tons of iron was to be delivered in about equal portions in September, October and November. S refused to deliver in August and B claimed as damages the difference between the contract and market prices on 30 November, this being £237. If B had bought iron in August the difference would have been £25, and if he had bought one third of the iron at the end of each of the three months, the sum of the differences would have been £109. The court held that the last figure was the true measure of damages. Where the contract specifies a period of time during which S may deliver the goods, the time for assessing the market price in the case of non-delivery is the last moment at which S is entitled to tender delivery.[3] Likewise, if S must deliver the goods on a fixed

---

1 *Startup v Cortazzi* (1835) 2 Cr M & R 165.
2 (1872) LR 7 Exch 319.
3 *Leigh v Paterson* (1818) 8 Taunt 540 (contract to sell tallow 'in all next December'; 31 December was the date for the assessment of damages for non-delivery).

day, he has the whole of the business hours of that day in which to make delivery.[4] B thus acts reasonably in discharge of his duty to mitigate if he attempts to buy replacement goods the next day and it follows that this should be the time at which the market price is taken for assessment purposes.[5] It is also clear that the time for delivery of the goods can be fixed by reference to the happening of an event such as the arrival of a ship in the future.[6]

No time fixed for delivery

Again, the same difficulties arise here as those under s 50(3) and it is difficult to find any application for this second part of s 51(3). It was held in *Tai Hing Cotton Mill Ltd v Kamsing Knitting Factory*[7] that, in the case of an anticipatory repudiation by S, the market price of the goods is *not* to be assessed at the time of S's refusal to deliver (see below). The situation where no time is fixed for delivery is discussed more fully in chapter 27, in the context of s 50(3), and it now seems clear that the second parts of both s 50(3) and s 51(3) are otiose.

ANTICIPATORY BREACH, DAMAGES AND THE MARKET RULE

The rules relating to S's anticipatory repudiation follow closely those where B repudiates before the date of delivery. Where S announces his refusal to deliver the goods before the time for delivery arrives, he commits an anticipatory breach of contract. As with any anticipatory breach of contract, the innocent party has the option of (i) accepting the repudiation, treating the contract as discharged and suing immediately for damages; or (ii) affirming the contract and thus continuing to treat it as binding, thereby refusing to accept the repudiation as a breach.[8]

Acceptance of S's anticipatory repudiation

If B opts for the first alternative and accepts S's anticipatory repudiation, the date for assessing the market price is the date fixed for *delivery*, not the date of S's repudiation nor the date that B accepts it.[9] The rule is justified in that B should not be able to increase the amount of damages payable by fixing a date earlier than the delivery date as the relevant one for assessing the market price; if this were possible it would put B in a better position than if the contract had

---

4 *Roper v Johnson* (1873) LR 8 CP 167.
5 *Gainsford v Carroll* (1824) 2 B & C 624; *Bremer Handelsgesellschaft mbH v Vanden Avenne-Izegem P V B A* [1978] 2 Lloyd's Rep 109; *Kaines (UK) Ltd v Osterreichische etc* [1993] 2 Lloyd's Rep 1.
6 *Melachrino v Nickoll and Knight* [1920] 1 KB 693.
7 [1979] AC 91.
8 See *Frost v Knight* (1872) LR 7 Exch 111; *Fercometal SARL v Mediterranean Shipping Co SA* [1989] AC 788. It seems that once B has elected to affirm the contract, he cannot revert to the right to treat the contract as terminated. This is because the guilty party needs to know whether the contract has been ended or kept alive as, in the latter case, he will still have the opportunity of performance, see *Stocznia Gdanska SA v Latvian Shipping Co* [1997] 2 Lloyd's Rep 228, 234-237 per Colman J.
9 *Frost v Knight* (1872) LR 7 Exch 111, 113 per Cockburn CJ; *Melachrino v Nickoll and Knight* [1920] 1 KB 693, 699 per Bailhache J; *Millett v Van Heek & Co* [1921] 2 KB 369; *Tai Hing Cotton Mill Ltd v Kamsing Knitting Factory* [1979] AC 91, 102 per Lord Keith of Kinkel.

been duly performed. B may thus claim as damages the difference between the contract price and the (higher) market price at the time when the goods ought to have been delivered. If the trial is heard before the date of delivery, the court must do its best to estimate the correct market price at the future delivery date.

However, the theoretical principle above is dominated by the pragmatic rule that once B has accepted S's repudiation, B has a duty to mitigate his loss by, for example, buying substitute goods in the market. He cannot simply let the market price of the goods rise and then seek to take advantage of it at the date of delivery, but the onus of proof is on S to show that B ought reasonably to have purchased such goods before delivery.[10] Where the market is rising between the date of B's acceptance of S's repudiation and the date fixed for delivery, it is clearly reasonable that B should buy substitute goods at the date he accepts the repudiation and thus he cannot make S liable for any more than the difference between the contract price and the market price at the date of repudiation. If S is able to prove that B could have mitigated his loss, the relevant market price is that prevailing at the date on which he could and should have bought the substitute goods. This rule is illustrated in *Kaines (UK) Ltd v Osterreichische etc.*[11] B agreed to buy 600,000 barrels of crude oil from S on 3 June for delivery in September but S repudiated the contract on 18 June. B accepted the repudiation and bought substitute oil on 29 June. The dispute was as to whether B should have bought the oil earlier in mitigation of his loss. The Court of Appeal held that, having regard to the volatile market in crude oil and allowing B a little time to assess the impact of the breach, it would have been reasonable for B to have bought oil on 19 June. Accordingly, 19 June was the date for the assessment of B's loss irrespective of what B did or failed to do at that time. The court stressed that, had market prices risen after that date, B's failure to buy would not have increased the damages payable by S and, likewise, had the price fallen steadily, B's failure to buy would not have reduced the damages.

In the situation where B accepts S's anticipatory repudiation but does *not* buy in the market in mitigation of his loss, the market may fall between the date when he could have mitigated and the date of delivery. This occurred in *Melachrino v Nickoll and Knight*,[12] where it was held that B's loss must be fixed by reference to the lower price at the date of delivery and this resulted in B's obtaining nominal damages only. Where the market falls in this way B's damages will thus be reduced and, where the market rises, B's damages will be assessed according to the lower price existing at the date when he should have mitigated by buying substitute goods.

When S's remedies were evaluated in the face of B's anticipatory repudiation, it was stressed that S is placed in an invidious situation in having to recognise that a market is falling in advance of its fall, and then choose the correct moment to resell in mitigation of his loss. It is equally clear that B is placed in a difficult position when an anticipatory breach occurs and an astute buyer would assess the market position carefully before accepting S's repudiation. However, there are also unresolved issues regarding B's remedies. For example, it is unclear whether B's damages would be reduced if, on a rising market, B correctly and reasonably buys goods in order to mitigate his loss only to discover that the market price tumbles before the date fixed for delivery.

10 *Roper v Johnson* (1873) LR 8 CP 167.
11 [1993] 2 Lloyd's Rep 1.
12 [1920] 1 KB 693.

Refusal to accept S's anticipatory repudiation

Where B refuses to accept S's repudiation, he may continue to treat the contract as binding and wait until the stipulated date for delivery to see if S tenders the goods. S's anticipatory repudiation is then nugatory[13] but S will, of course, be in breach of contract if he fails to deliver on the agreed delivery date. When S refuses to deliver the goods on the date fixed for delivery, B must take reasonable steps to mitigate his loss by attempting to buy substitute goods. The market price will be that which prevails at the date fixed for delivery and the market price at any earlier date is immaterial. Similarly, in this case where B refuses to accept the repudiation, it should be stressed that B has no duty to mitigate his loss during the period *before* delivery as the mitigation principle applies only where there is an *actual* breach of contract. On a rising market, B is fully entitled to refuse to accept S's repudiation and wait for the date of delivery even though he can foresee the probability that the damages payable by S may increase in the interval. In *Tai Hing Cotton Mill Ltd v Kamsing Knitting Factory*,[14] S agreed, on 23 March 1971, to deliver 1,500 bales of cotton yarn to B and it was agreed that B could call for deliveries on giving reasonable notice, this being accepted as one month's notice. S made some deliveries but wrote to B on 31 July 1973 repudiating the contract. B refused to accept this and continued to press for delivery but, on 28 November 1973, B issued a writ claiming damages. The Privy Council held that B could call for delivery up to 28 November 1973 on giving reasonable notice and thus 28 December 1973 was the date on which the goods ought to have been delivered and the damages were to be assessed on the basis of the difference between the contract price and market price on 28 December 1973.

It is equally important to emphasise that, in the situation where B refuses to accept S's repudiation, the contract subsists for the benefit of *both* parties[15] and thus S may change his mind and deliver the goods to B as originally agreed. In this situation, it is clear that S is not in breach of contract and is under no liability to pay damages to B.[16] Alternatively, B may decide to accept the repudiation in which case he has an immediate duty to mitigate and his damages will be assessed by reference to the market price at the date when B, acting reasonably, ought to have bought substitute goods.

ACTUAL PURCHASE BY THE BUYER IN THE AVAILABLE MARKET

It must be asked here whether B's damages are affected where he buys substitute goods in the market at more or less than the market price and this is the mirror image of the problem, considered in Chapter 27, of S's actual resale in the market where B refuses to take delivery of the goods.

No problems ensue where B buys goods at the prevailing market price but where B buys substitute goods at *more* than the market price he may attempt to claim damages based upon the difference between the contract price and the actual purchase price instead of the market price. It seems clear that if B buys goods immediately at more than the market price, he will be unable to recover

---

13   *White and Carter (Councils) Ltd v McGregor* [1962] AC 413, 444 per Lord Hodson.
14   [1979] AC 91.
15   The risks involved may thus favour either party: see the consequences which ensued in *Fercometal SARL v Mediterranean Shipping Co SA* [1989] AC 788.
16   *White and Carter (Councils) Ltd v McGregor* [1962] AC 413, 444 per Lord Hodson.

the difference between the contract price and the actual purchase price because here the mitigation principle dictates that the reasonable buyer could and should have bought the goods at the market price.

Where there is an available market and thus a market price which can be ascertained at the date of S's non-delivery, it is logical that damages should be assessed by reference to that price even though B has bought substitute goods at much less than the market price. This is because it could not be argued that B's opportunity to buy at the low price arose *solely* as a consequence of S's breach; if, in fact, S had delivered the contract goods, B would *still* have been able to buy the low-priced goods in the available market.[17]

If B chooses to speculate and does not buy substitute goods in the market immediately, then it is suggested that his damages should be assessed by reference to the market price at the date of S's non-delivery even though B has subsequently bought substitute goods at less than the market price. Here B runs the risk that the market may rise or fall and thus a rise in the market prices should not mean that B could claim the extra amount from S and, likewise, where the market falls B should be entitled to reap the benefits from such a fall: acceptance of a risk in this way means that B may either gain or lose from the gamble.[18] However, this may not be the case in the unusual circumstances where B subsequently buys the *same* goods from S at less than the market price. In *Pagnan and Fratelli v Corbisa Industrial Agropacuaria Ltda*,[19] B, after having lawfully rejected the goods because of their defective quality, agreed to buy the same goods from S at a reduced price and B then resold them at a profit. It was held that, as the sale was of the same goods and between the same parties, it was part of a continuous dealing[20] between S and B and B had suffered no loss since he obtained the goods at less than their market price at the date of S's breach of contract.

DAMAGES UNDER SECTION 51(2) WHERE THERE IS NO 'AVAILABLE MARKET'

Where there is no available market for the goods at the time of S's failure to deliver and thus s 51(3) is inapplicable, the basic rule is that enunciated in s 51(2), viz 'the measure of damages is the estimated loss directly and naturally resulting, in the ordinary course of events, from the seller's breach of contract'.

There may be no available market in which B could buy substitute goods in the situation where demand for goods exceeds their supply or where the goods were to have been made to B's special order or design and no reasonable substitute goods are available. Following general principles, B is entitled to be placed in the position in which he would have been had the contract been performed but, as the basic market rule cannot apply, some other method of

---

17 See the correlative argument in Ch 27 regarding B's non-acceptance: if S resells the *identical* goods at a higher price than the market price, this is *solely* attributable to B's breach and should be taken into account in calculating S's damages so that S would recover only his actual loss, ie the difference between the contract price and the actual resale price.

18 See Ch 27 where the same rule applies to the calculation of S's damages in the case of B's non-acceptance of the goods.

19 [1970] 1 WLR 1306.

20 This view of 'continuous dealing' is best illustrated in *British Westinghouse Electric and Manufacturing Co Ltd v Underground Electric Railways Co of London Ltd* [1912] AC 673 (see below).

assessment must be used. The general rule is that B is entitled to recover the difference between the *value* of the goods at the time and place of the breach and the contract price and thus 'value' must be substituted for the ascertainment of the market price. It is evident that this may entail difficult and elusive calculations. Subject to the principle of remoteness, much may depend on the *purpose* for which B required the goods. Vital indicators of B's loss may thus be the price of the goods which B would have obtained on their resale or the profits that B would have made had he received the contract goods and, as S knew that he intended to do, manufactured new products from them.[1] Again, S may refuse to deliver goods to B which B intends to use or hire-out in the course of his business (eg machinery) and, if so, the court must attempt to assess the income which B could have expected to receive from the goods during their working life. The decisions concerning B's loss of user-profits have arisen in the context of delayed delivery and are considered later but they are also valid authorities in the situation of non-delivery.

Resale price of the goods as evidence of value

If there is no available market but a business buyer has resold the goods, the price in the resale contract may be advanced as *evidence* of the true 'value' of the goods 'although not brought to the knowledge of [S]'.[2] In *France v Gaudet*,[3] B had a contract with a sub-buyer for the sale to him of 100 cases of champagne at 24s per dozen. S then agreed to sell champagne of the requisite quality to B at 14s per dozen but S subsequently refused to deliver the wine. Champagne of that quality could not be procured in the market to supply the sub-buyer and thus it was held that B was entitled to recover as damages the difference between 14s and 24s. As a *bona fide* sale had taken place, the champagne had acquired an actual value of 24s per dozen.

Using this assessment of loss, B is thus able to recover his loss of profit on the resale but it is clear that the court is not bound to accept the resale price as conclusive evidence of the value of the goods. In *The Arpad*,[4] B was a consignee under a bill of lading who had bought Roumanian wheat in August 1930 from S. B sued the shipowner as regards a short delivery of the cargo shipped under the bill of lading and delivered at Hull in January 1931. There was no market at Hull for Roumanian wheat in conformity with the sample which B had seen and thus he could not buy this type of wheat and was unable to fulfil the resale contracts with sub-buyers which he had entered into in August. The price of Roumanian wheat had fallen considerably between August and January. The Court of Appeal treated the case as analogous to one where S fails to deliver the goods and held that, in the absence of an available market, the value of the goods must be ascertained by other evidence which could include the price at which B had resold the goods, but that a resale price in contracts 'made at a date far removed from the date of the breach of contract have to be neglected'[5] as being unsatisfactory evidence of the value of the goods at the time of breach. Accordingly, in arriving at an estimate of B's damages, the price fixed in the August contract had to be disregarded.

---

1 *Leavey (J) & Co Ltd v George H Hirst & Co Ltd* [1944] KB 24.
2 *Grébert-Borgnis v J & W Nugent* (1885) 15 QBD 85, 89 per Sir William Brett MR.
3 (1871) LR 6 QB 199.
4 [1934] P 189.
5 [1934] P 189 at 212, per Greer LJ.

Purchase of substitute goods from another seller

Even though there is no available market, B is nevertheless under a duty to take reasonable steps to mitigate his loss and thus he *might* be able to buy suitable substitute goods from another seller.[6] If B does find an alternative supplier, the price at which he bought the substitute goods can provide evidence for the calculation of damages and, provided B's steps in mitigating his loss were reasonable ones to take, he may obtain as damages the difference between the contract price and the price paid for the substitute goods.[7]

Where B can obtain substitute goods he should buy goods which are the nearest available equivalent to the contract goods. The *nearest* equivalent goods may, however, be of superior quality and thus higher in price than the contract goods but, provided the disparity is not too great, B can recover the extra amount. Thus, in *Hinde v Liddell*,[8] where S failed to deliver 2,000 grey shirtings according to sample and B immediately bought the nearest equivalent shirtings costing £137 10s more than the contract price, he was held able to recover that amount in damages. Likewise, provided B's actions are reasonable, he may recover the extra expense of adapting the substitute goods to meet his requirements.[9]

It must be asked whether it might ever be reasonable for B to order the *manufacture* of substitute goods where none are readily available for purchase in the market. The general rule demanding that B should mitigate his loss means that, normally, this would be unreasonable[10] but this rule can produce surprising results. In *The 'Alecos M'*,[11] S agreed to sell a 14-year-old ship to B and, although the contract expressly provided that there would be a spare propeller, none was delivered. At first instance,[12] Steyn J awarded as damages the cost of replacement of the propeller ($121,000) but the Court of Appeal upheld the decision of the arbitrator that the commercial value of the spare propeller on the ship was no

---

6 *Benjamin's Sale of Goods* (5th edn, 1997), para 17-024 asserts that B cannot be under a *duty* to buy substitute goods where there is no available market and his damages should not be assessed on the basis that he ought reasonably to have bought goods corresponding as closely as possible to the contract description. The accuracy of this assertion is substantiated in that (i) B need not accept goods which do not match the contract description and thus his damages should not be assessed on the basis that he ought to have bought roughly equivalent goods; and (ii) a sub-buyer from B could reject non-conforming goods and it would thus be unfair to make B accept such goods under the main contract. Cf *Sharpe (C) & Co Ltd v Nosawa & Co* [1917] 2 KB 814 (in a non-delivery of Japanese peas of a certain quality, Atkin J held that B could and should have bought the nearest equivalent Japanese peas as the difference in the goods 'was not so great as to amount to a difference of kind or character' and a difference in quality was 'a matter which [could] be adjusted when assessing damages' (p 821).
7 *Hinde v Liddell* (1875) LR 10 QB 265.
8 (1875) LR 10 QB 265; see also *Diamond Cutting Works Federation Ltd v Triefus & Co Ltd* [1956] 1 Lloyd's Rep 216 (S failed to deliver industrial diamonds at the contract price of 24s 6d per carat; B was found to have acted reasonably in paying 40s per carat and was entitled to recover the difference in price).
9 *Blackburn Bobbin Co Ltd v T W Allen & Sons Ltd* [1918] 1 KB 540 (S failed to deliver Finnish timber and B was held entitled to claim the extra cost of buying English timber even though this involved 'far more expense and also far more waste in cutting' (p 554 per McCardie J; affd [1918] 2 KB 467 on the issue of frustration without considering the assessment of damages).
10 *Elbinger AG v Armstrong* (1874) LR 9 QB 473 (considered below).
11 *Sealace Shipping Co Ltd v Oceanvoice Ltd, The Alecos M* [1991] 1 Lloyd's Rep 120.
12 [1990] 1 Lloyd's Rep 82.

more than its scrap value ($1,100) and, accordingly, that was the value which B had lost and to which he was entitled as damages. The Court of Appeal and the arbitrator justified this approach in two principal ways. First, the decision was much influenced by the age of the vessel and the arbitrator's finding that the provision of spare propellers had 'gone out of fashion' in the construction of new ships. It was therefore considered unreasonable for B to have a new, spare propeller manufactured for an older vessel when the likelihood of using the spare was remote. Second, the arbitrator stressed that B had not bought a spare propeller and there was doubt as to whether he genuinely intended to do so in the future. Both these justifications are criticisable. There can be little doubt that B's damages were assessed on the basis of his scrapping the vessel but, as Steyn J pointed out, there was 'no suggestion that the vessel was bought in order to scrap her immediately'.[13] His reasoning thus acknowledged B's interest in having the propeller for potential *use* even though the chance of such use was remote. Moreover, Steyn J considered that B's genuine intent to buy a new propeller must be irrelevant as such a test introduces subjective elements into an objective enquiry of the value of what has not been delivered. He emphasised that when the market value measure is adopted, it is immaterial whether or not B intends to replace the missing goods, and this must surely be the correct rule. Finally, as Treitel[14] pointed out, if a cautious buyer had made an independent contract for the purchase of a spare propeller it would have been hard to resist his claim for the cost of a substitute and, furthermore, that the scrap value of the propeller could be relevant as a measure of damages only if propellers had been available for *purchase* in scrap yards. Despite these convincing criticisms, the decision was recently accepted as correct by one of the Law Lords.[15] If the presence of a substitute propeller in *The Alecos M* was thought to be insignificant, what would be the position if, for example, S failed to deliver an essential component of a machine and as a consequence B's business came to a standstill? If no such components were readily available for purchase in the market, it might well be reasonable for B to order the manufacture of a new component.[16]

If B has bought better quality substitute goods, which are later resold by him at a profit, must some adjustment be made so that the profit is set-off against the cost of buying the substitute goods when B claims that cost as damages from S? In *Hinde v Liddell*,[17] where B obtained as damages the difference between the contract price and the higher price which he paid for substitute goods, Field J[18] considered that 'had [B] derived any benefit from the advance in price, I should hesitate before I said that he could recover the whole of the difference'. This approach was followed in *Erie County Natural Gas and Fuel Co Ltd v Carroll*.[19] B held several leases which entitled him to sink wells and seek quantities of natural gas. He assigned the leases to S on terms that S would supply him with all the gas he needed for his lime works and quarry but S failed to supply the gas. As B could not obtain gas from any alternative source, he spent $58,297 and obtained new leases, drilled new wells and thus established a substitute gas supply. Later

---

13   [1990] 1 Lloyd's Rep 82 at 84.
14   'Damages for Non-Delivery' (1991) 107 LQR 364.
15   *Ruxley Electronics and Construction Ltd v Forsyth* [1996] AC 344, 371-372 per Lord Lloyd of Berwick.
16   See *Bacon v Cooper (Metals) Ltd* [1982] 1 All ER 397.
17   (1875) LR 10 QB 265.
18   (1875) LR 10 QB 265 at 270.
19   [1911] AC 105.

B sold his entire business for $225,000, $75,000 of which represented the substituted gas supply. When B sued to recover as damages the cost of procuring the substitute gas supply, the Privy Council held that the price obtained by B from the sale of the substituted supply should be deducted from this cost. As S had to pay for the cost of the substituted source, he was entitled to be credited with the amount for which the substituted source was sold and, accordingly, B obtained only nominal damages. The *Erie* decision is rational and is part of the principle that the subsequent transaction which is in dispute (here the substituted gas supply) must arise out of the consequences of the breach if it is to be taken into account.[20] The rule seeks to prevent B from profiting at S's expense but it is relatively clear that it should apply only to cases of a profit made on B's resale of the goods or where B profits from the use of the goods in a manufacturing process,[1] for example. It should not operate to reduce B's damages where, acting reasonably, B buys substitute goods for his own use which are the closest equivalent he can obtain but which possess some inherent bonus.[2]

Finally, it should be asked whether B might ever be under a duty to mitigate his loss by accepting the original seller's offer to supply substitute goods. This is obviously a controversial issue as, on the one hand, it can be argued that B should not have to trust to the guilty party's *bona fides* and assurances of performance while, on the other hand, it can be asserted that mercantile disputes are impersonal and S's reasonable offer should be accepted on the basis that there should be no inclination to allow 'an unhappy indulgence in far-fetched resentment'.[3] Certainly where B lawfully rejects the goods because of their defective *quality*, he is not bound to accept them if S offers them to B in mitigation of the breach of contract.[4] This rule is founded upon the notion that if B had to accept defective goods offered in mitigation his right of rejection would, in effect, be rendered otiose.[5] Moreover, in most cases of an available market, it must be assumed that B intends to buy substitute goods in the market and thus it would be unjust to force him to accept goods from S which do not conform with the contract. However, might the position be different where the goods are of the requisite quality under the contract but S offers to deliver them later than agreed or on different terms relating to

---

20 This principle is best illustrated in *British Westinghouse Electric and Manufacturing Co Ltd v Underground Electric Railways Co of London Ltd* [1912] AC 673 (where *Erie* was approved); see also the criticism in Greig, *Sale of Goods* (1974), p 278.

1 See *British Westinghouse Electric and Manufacturing Co Ltd v Underground Electric Railways Co of London Ltd* [1912] AC 673.

2 See *Harbutt's Plasticine Ltd v Wayne Tank and Pump Co Ltd* [1970] 1 QB 447 (P's factory was destroyed as a consequence of D's breach of contract. P obtained modern, replacement buildings but his damages were not reduced to take account of this bonus in the form of more valuable buildings. The decision is probably best explained in that P's rebuilding was done in mitigation of his loss; a reduction in damages would have been in order only for buildings which were more extensive than the old factory).

3 *Payzu Ltd v Saunders* [1919] 2 KB 581, 586 per McCardie J.

4 *Heaven and Kesterton Ltd v Etablissements François Albiac et Cie* [1956] 2 Lloyd's Rep 316; cf *Pagnan and Fratelli v Corbisa Industrial Agropacuaria Ltda* [1970] 1 WLR 1306, where B accepted the defective goods at a *reduced price*.

5 See also *Strutt v Whitnell* [1975] 1 WLR 870 (P bought a house from D with 'vacant possession' but a sitting tenant had protection and refused to leave. P wished to claim damages based upon the difference in value between the house as described and the house with its tenant but D then offered to buy back the house from P. The Court of Appeal held that the rules of mitigation could not compel P to resell the house to D as this would reverse P's decision to keep the property). In *The Solholt* [1983] 1 Lloyd's Rep 605, *Strutt* was said to turn on its own special facts (see below).

payment? In this situation, there is authority to the effect that B is under a duty to accept S's reasonable offer of performance. In *Payzu Ltd v Saunders*,[6] S agreed to sell to B 200 pieces of crêpe de chine to be delivered over a nine-month period with payment to be made within one month of each delivery less a discount of 2½%. Delivery commenced in November 1917 but B's cheque drawn in payment on December 21 went astray and was not received by S. Early in January 1918, S asked B why he had not paid and B drew another cheque which, owing to a delay in obtaining the signature of one of B's directors, was not sent to S until 16 January. On that day, B ordered a second delivery of goods but S believed that B's financial position was such that B could not meet the cheque which allegedly had been drawn in December and, accordingly, S refused to make any further deliveries unless B paid in cash (seemingly without the 2½% discount). B refused to do this and, due to the war-time conditions, B could not obtain similar goods from another seller. Subsequently, B brought an action claiming damages based upon the difference between the contract price and market price at the date of S's failure to deliver. It was held that S had repudiated the contract in unequivocally demanding payment in cash for future deliveries but that B had not repudiated the contract by failing only to make punctual payment. However, in awarding B damages for 'serious and substantial business inconvenience',[7] both the judge at first instance and the Court of Appeal held that B should have accepted S's cash offer and thereby mitigated his loss. The market price of the goods had risen by the date of S's failure to deliver but B was thus prevented from recovering damages for the increased loss which was caused by his failure to mitigate.[8] It is clear, however, that B does not have to accept S's offer where there is doubt surrounding S's *bona fides* and ability to perform under the contract,[9] but there were no such doubts in *Payzu*.

In fact, the *Payzu* view of mitigation was adopted and extended in *The Solholt*.[10] There, S sold a ship to B for $5m with delivery to be no later than 31 August but the ship was tendered on 3 September. At the end of July, S had twice sought an extension of the delivery date but this was refused by B and, on 3 September, B rejected the vessel under a contract term. After cancellation of the contract, B offered to buy the ship for $4.75m but that offer was refused and there were no further negotiations between the parties. B subsequently claimed damages for non-delivery. The market value of the ship had risen to $5.5m on 31 August and there was no other suitable vessel available which B could buy: B could thus have expected to recover half a million dollars in damages as the difference between the contract price and the value of the ship at the date of breach. It was held that B could not recover any damages as he had failed to mitigate his loss: S would have accepted B's offer to purchase the ship at the

---

6 [1919] 2 KB 581; see also *Houndsditch Warehouse Co Ltd v Waltex* [1944] KB 579.
7 [1919] 2 KB 581 at 587, per McCardie J.
8 See Bridge, 'Mitigation of Damages in Contract and the Meaning of Avoidable Loss' (1989) 105 LQR 398, 411-423. The author criticises *Payzu* on the basis that S was enriched by B's failure to mitigate: on the rising market S was free to resell the goods at more than the contract price agreed with B *and* S would not have obtained the higher market price if B had accepted S's offer of mitigation.
9 *Payzu Ltd v Saunders* [1919] 2 KB 581, 586 per McCardie J and 588-589 per Bankes LJ; *ABD (Metals and Waste) Ltd v Anglo Chemical & Ore Co Ltd* [1955] 2 Lloyd's Rep 456 (held that B was justified in refusing S's offer as S would not guarantee a delivery date; Sellers J (p 463) doubted 'whether at any time [S was] ready and willing to deliver').
10 *Sotiros Shipping Inc and Aeco Maritime SA v Sameiet Solholt, The Solholt* [1983] 1 Lloyd's Rep 605.

original price without prejudice to B's claim for damages for the delay and it would have been reasonable for B to take the initiative in making that offer. This is a startling decision in that it imposes an obligation on B to open negotiations with S immediately after he has lawfully rejected the goods and it is difficult to resist the conclusion that B's right of rejection is thereby rendered nugatory. Moreover, as in *Payzu*, the outcome was that S made a profit of half a million dollars as a result of his own breach of contract but this fact was dismissed curtly in the decision as 'wholly irrelevant'.[11]

DAMAGES FOR LOSS OF PROFITS UNDER A SUB-SALE MADE BY THE BUYER

Where there is a market price at the date of S's breach, the normal measure of damages under the available market rule is not affected by the fact that B has resold an equivalent quantity of the goods to a sub-buyer at either *more* or *less* than the market price. In both cases, B's damages are still assessed as the difference between the contract price and market price at the date and time of S's failure to deliver the goods.[12] Consequently, if there is a sub-sale of the goods at less than the market price, S cannot claim that B's damages should be reduced because of this fact. This is justified in that B must still buy substitute goods in the market in order to fulfil his obligations under the sub-contract and his loss is thus assessed by reference to the market price. In *Williams Bros v Ed T Agius Ltd*,[13] S agreed to sell a quantity of coal to B for delivery in November, the contract price of which was 16s 3d per ton. At the date of S's failure to deliver, the market price for such coal was 23s 6d per ton. In October, B had contracted to resell coal of the same desciption and amount to the sub-buyer at 19s per ton. B claimed as damages the difference between the contract price (16s 3d) and the market price at the date of breach (23s 6d), this being 7s 3d. S argued that B was entitled only to the difference between the contract price and the resale price of 19s, this being 2s 9d. The House of Lords held that B should be awarded as damages 7s 3d per ton, that being the sum which would enable him to buy similar goods in the market; the obligations under the sub-contract were thus irrelevant to B's rights under the first contract with S. Conversely, the sub-sale will not increase B's damages if it was made above the market price and here the rule can be justified in that B could and should have mitigated his loss by buying goods at the market price to fulfil the contract with his sub-buyer.

There are, however, exceptional situations where B may be able to claim loss of profits on the sub-sale and here S's liability is based upon the principles in *Hadley v Baxendale*[14] and the parties' reasonable contemplation of the consequences of a breach: the state of S's knowledge at the time of the original contract of sale, whether actual or imputed, thus becomes crucial.

---

11 [1983] 1 Lloyd's Rep 605 at 608, per Sir John Donaldson MR.
12 *Rodocanachi v Milburn* (1886) 18 QBD 67; *Williams Bros v Ed T Agius Ltd* [1914] AC 510, 522-523 per Lord Dunedin: '... barring special circumstances, the defaulting seller is neither mulct in damages for the extra profit which the buyer would have got owing to a forward resale at over the market price ... nor can he take benefit of the fact that the buyer has made a forward resale at under the market price'; *James Finlay & Co Ltd v N V Kwik Hoo Tong H M* [1929] 1 KB 400, 411 per Scrutton LJ; *Kwei Tek Chao v British Traders and Shippers Ltd* [1954] 2 QB 459, 489-490 per Devlin J.
13 [1914] AC 510.
14 (1854) 9 Exch 341.

When might B recover loss of profits under the sub-sale?

Loss of profits on the sub-sale even though there is an available market

Even though there is an available market for the goods, there are two situations where B cannot avoid the loss under a sub-sale. The first is where B has contracted to sell to his sub-buyer the selfsame, specific goods which he has bought from S. The second is where the contract of sub-sale has the same delivery date as in the original contract of sale. In these cases, although there may be an available market in the same type of goods, the terms of the sub-sale mean that it is not available to B.[15] However, even in these situations B cannot recover the loss under the sub-sale unless S should have contemplated at the time of the original contract of sale that B was, or was probably, buying the goods for the purposes of resale and that B could fulfil his obligations under the sub-sale by delivering only the selfsame goods to the sub-buyer. It should be stressed that this degree of knowledge is demanded of S if B is to recover the loss under the sub-sale and it is insufficient that sub-sales are within S's reasonable contemplation. This is because in a commercial sale of goods to a business buyer, a resale to a sub-buyer will often be in S's reasonable contemplation but here S will also reasonably contemplate that B will be able to buy substitute goods in the market to fulfil his obligations under the sub-sale should S fail to deliver under the original contract.[16]

The leading, controversial decision on this topic is *Re R and H Hall Ltd v W H Pim (Junior) & Co's Arbitration*.[17] B bought an unascertained cargo of 7,000 tons of Australian wheat of a certain quality and description at 51s 9d per quarter. The contract provided that S should give a notice of appropriation to the contract of a specific cargo in a specific ship and thus the House of Lords treated this as 'the sale of the cargo of an individual ship which is either specifically identified or is to be so identified'.[18] Moreover, the contract contained clauses which expressly recognised that B might resell the goods during the course of the voyage. After the contract was made, the market rose and B resold at 56s 9d a quarter. When the ship arrived S failed to deliver, having earlier sold the cargo to a different buyer, and the market price of similar wheat was then 53s 9d per quarter. S was prepared to pay as damages the difference between the contract price and market price at the date of the ship's arrival (2s) but B claimed the difference between the contract price and the price at which he had resold the goods (5s). The House of Lords held that the latter figure was the correct measure of damages as the contract terms showed that 'it was contemplated that the cargo might be passed on by way of sub-sale'[19] and it was also contemplated that the resale would be of the named, identifiable cargo so that, of necessity, B would be in default to his sub-buyer if S failed to deliver that specific cargo.[20] Accordingly, the market price had to be disregarded because B could not obtain on the market the particular cargo which he had agreed to resell.

---

15 See *Williams Bros v Ed T Agius Ltd* [1914] AC 510, 523 per Lord Dunedin; *Patrick v Russo-British Grain Export Co Ltd* [1927] 2 KB 535, 541 per Salter J; *The Arpad* [1934] P 189, 215 per Greer LJ: 'If the Court is dealing with a case in which the sub-sale is a sale of the selfsame thing, that involves the fact that there is no market in which the thing can be be bought, but only a market in which it can be sold'.

16 *Kwei Tek Chao v British Traders and Shippers Ltd* [1954] 2 QB 459, 489 per Devlin J.

17 [1928] All ER Rep 763.

18 [1928] All ER Rep 763 at 765, per Viscount Haldane.

19 [1928] All ER Rep 763 at 765, per Viscount Haldane.

20 [1928] All ER Rep 763 at 765 (Viscount Haldane); p 766 (Viscount Dunedin); p 768 (Lord Shaw); p 771 (Lord Phillimore); p 772 (Lord Blanesburgh).

The principal difficulty emanating from *Hall v Pim* relates to ascertaining the reasonable contemplation of the parties regarding a sub-sale of the identical goods. When does S have actual or imputed knowledge of such a sub-sale? First, B may be able to prove that S had *actual* knowledge at the date of the original contract that B intended to resell the goods or that they were bought to fulfil 'an already existing special contract',[1] in which case the loss of profit on the resale is recoverable.[2] Second, in *Hall v Pim*, three of the Law Lords accentuated forcefully that the original contract expressly provided for B's right of resale so that S *contracted* to put B in a position to fulfil his sub-contracts.[3] Third, it is also clear from *Hall v Pim* that neither S's actual knowledge of the sub-sale nor a contract term providing expressly for B's right to resell are necessary: B is able to claim his lost profits on a sub-sale of the identical goods which, at the time of the original contract, the parties *ought* reasonably to have contemplated will *probably* be made.[4] On this basis, it was regarded as common business practice to resell cargoes which were afloat and for there to be standard-form resales along 'a string' of contracts. The chances of the identical cargo being resold or, alternatively, of B's taking actual delivery of it were found to be 'about equal' and thus an 'even chance'[5] that the sub-sale would happen was sufficient for the probability test. A further facet of *Hall v Pim* was that S's liability was limited to loss of *normal profits* under a sub-sale made on *usual terms*. Viscount Dunedin thus emphasised that there was a practical check on S's liability in that 'the contracts must have been entered into before the time of delivery, and they must be contracts in accordance with the market, not extravagant and unusual bargains'.[6] It thus seems that B will receive the actual loss of profits on the sub-sale only where the sub-sale is of a usual type and the profit is not exorbitant.[7]

1 *Aryeh v Lawrence Kostoris & Son Ltd* [1967] 1 Lloyd's Rep 63, 68 per Willmer LJ.

2 *Frank Mott & Co Ltd v Wm H Muller & Co (London) Ltd* (1922) 13 Ll L Rep 492; *Household Machines Ltd v Cosmos Exporters Ltd* [1947] 1 KB 217.

3 [1928] All ER Rep 763 – Viscount Haldane: 'Whether [B] was likely to enter into such sub-contracts and pass the cargo down a chain of re-sales is not material. It is enough that the contract contemplated by its terms that he should have the right to do so if he chose' (p 765); 'I do not think that the real question is one of probability or of circumstances foreseen by the seller. It is to my mind a pure question of the terms of the contract itself ...'. (p 766); Lord Shaw: 'My principal reason is that I think that the two parties had actually provided for the very case of sub-sales, which has caused these extra losses' (p 768); Lord Phillimore: 'But if the tribunal ... comes to the conclusion that [S] contracted to sell ... on terms that he should be responsible for damage which might accrue ... then he must be held liable. He has contracted on those terms, and there is an end of it' (pp 770-771).

4 [1928] All ER Rep 763 – Viscount Haldane: '... the principle is not to be confined to a sub-contract already actually made at the date of the original contract, but applies also to the case of a sub-contract which will probably be made' (p 766); Viscount Dunedin: 'I do not think that "probability" ... means that the chances are all in favour of the event whatever its happening. To make a thing probable, it is enough, in my view, that there is an even chance of its happening. That is the criterion I apply ... I think there was here in the contemplation of parties the probability of a re-sale' (p 767); Lord Shaw: 'What has happened was ... that that very damage was a reasonable contemplation of both parties as the probable, by which I think is truly meant the not unlikely, result of the breach of the bargain' (p 769).

5 [1928] All ER Rep 763 at p 767, per Viscount Dunedin.

6 [1928] All ER Rep 763 at 767, per Viscount Dunedin; Lord Shaw stressed that 'it is not suggested that these prices were out of the ordinary course of business' (p 768).

7 *Household Machines Ltd v Cosmos Exporters Ltd* [1947] KB 217 (there was no available market for the goods but the damages were less than the actual profit (10% profit awarded but resale price had 12% profit) which was held by Lewis J to be 'too high' (p 219); see also *Coastal International Trading Ltd v Maroil AG* [1988] 1 Lloyd's Rep 92.

The decision in *Hall v Pim* was criticised almost immediately by the Court of Appeal[8] on the basis that it was difficult to reconcile with the decision in *Williams Bros v Ed T Agius Ltd*,[9] considered earlier. However, the facts and the decisions in these two cases are as alike as chalk and cheese. In *Williams*, B could reasonably buy substitute goods in the market in order to fulfil his sub-contract whereas, in *Hall v Pim*, the original contract contemplated that B might resell the selfsame goods and the default of S in the original sale was thus bound to produce an enforced default on the part of the original buyer under the terms of his sub-sale.[10] It is suggested that *Hall v Pim* correctly defines the principles relating to the probability of a resale of the identical subject matter of the original contract so that such a resale can be within the reasonable contemplation of the parties and is not dismissed as being too remote.[11]

Loss of repeat orders from sub-buyers?

When the question of damages for the delivery of defective goods is considered below, it is clear that where it is within the reasonable contemplation of S and B that S's supply of defective goods might lead to B's customers withdrawing their business from B meaning that no 'repeat orders' are given, damages may be awarded for the resultant loss in profits. There would appear to be no obstacle to applying this principle in cases of non-delivery.

Loss of profits on the sub-sale where there is no available market

Where S fails to deliver but there is no available market in which B can buy substitute goods in order to fulfil the sub-sale, B is entitled to his loss of profit on the sub-sale where S had actual knowledge[12] that the goods were bought with a view to resale or ought to have contemplated the resale as probable. The second situation, where S ought to have contemplated the resale, is illustrated by *Patrick v Russo-British Grain Export Co Ltd*.[13] S sold 2,000 tons of Russian wheat to B, a merchant, as per sealed sample at 56s 9d per 480 lb. Several days later, B sold a similar parcel of 2,000 tons of Russian wheat to the sub-buyer on identical terms except as to price, this being 60s 6d per 480 lbs. S failed to deliver the

---

8   *James Finlay & Co Ltd v N V Kwik Hoo Tong H M* [1929] 1 KB 400 (where *Hall v Pim* was famously said by counsel to have 'astonished the Temple and surprised St Mary Axe' (see Sankey LJ at p 417)).
9   [1914] AC 510.
10 A distinction made by Lord Dunedin in *Williams* (p 523) and thus applied by him in *Hall v Pim*.
11 See *James Finlay & Co Ltd v N V Kwik Hoo Tong H M* [1929] 1 KB 400, 415 where Greer LJ was the only judge who thought *Hall v Pim* to be 'reasonable and sound'. In *Koufos v C Czarnikow Ltd, The Heron II* [1969] 1 AC 350, the speeches in the House of Lords refer to *Hall v Pim* with no note of dissent.
12 *Grébert-Borgnis v J & W Nugent* (1885) 15 QBD 85; *Frank Mott & Co Ltd v Wm H Muller & Co (London) Ltd* (1922) 13 Ll L Rep 492 (S failed to deliver wire rods which (i) could be obtained only from S as the sole selling agent; and (ii) S knew that B required the rods for resale. Held that B could recover the loss on the resale); *Leavey (J) & Co Ltd v George H Hirst & Co Ltd* [1944] KB 24 (sale of material which S knew was required for making overcoats. S failed to deliver and B could not obtain substitute goods because of a wartime Order limiting supplies. Held B could recover his loss of profits); *Household Machines Ltd v Cosmos Exporters Ltd* [1947] KB 217.
13 [1927] 2 KB 535; see also *Coastal (Bermuda) Petroleum Ltd v VTT Vulcan Petroleum (No 2), The Marine Star* [1994] 2 Loyd's Rep 629.

wheat and it was impossible for B to obtain Russian wheat conforming or approximately conforming to the sample. Salter J held that B was entitled to recover as damages his loss of profit on the resale as, at the date of the original sale, 'the resale [was] contemplated by both parties as a thing that [would] probably occur in the ordinary course of business'.[14] It is thus clear that it is not necessary that S should have known that B 'was buying to implement a contract already made, or that the buyer would certainly resell; it is enough if both parties contemplate that the buyer will probably resell and the seller is content to take that risk'.[15]

As with the rule in *Hall v Pim*, it is clear that if B is to be successful in claiming his loss of profits on the sub-sale, the terms of the sub-sale must be usual and the profit must not be exorbitant.[16]

Damages payable by B to the sub-buyer?

Wherever B can recover loss of profits on the sub-sale, (ie within the rule in *Hall v Pim* or where there is no available market) he is *also* entitled to recover any damages he may have paid to his sub-buyer for breach of the terms of the sub-sale: in *Hall v Pim* this was said to be on the basis that 'the one is the corollary of the other'.[17] The case cited in *Hall v Pim* in support of this proposition was *Grébert-Borgnis v J & W Nugent*.[18] There S had actual knowledge at the date of the original contract that B had already sold the goods on the same terms (except as to price) to a sub-buyer in France and that B was buying the goods in order to fulfil that sub-contract. The Court of Appeal held that B was entitled to recover as damages the amount of profit he would have made on the sub-sale and also damages in respect of his liability to that sub-buyer.[19]

CONSEQUENTIAL LOSSES AND EXPENSES INCURRED

As a general rule B should be able to avoid consequential losses where there is an available market for the goods as he is able to buy substitute goods in the market either for his use or for resale. B may nevertheless incur expenses in transporting the goods, for example, and these are recoverable as 'special damages' within the SGA, s 54.

Where there is no available market the position is different and B may often want to claim for consequential losses and expenses, eg adapting the nearest equivalent goods to meet his needs or the profits which he would have made under a sub-sale. Many of these types of loss may flow directly from the breach

---

14 [1927] 2 KB 535 at 541.
15 [1927] 2 KB 535 at 540, per Salter J.
16 *Household Machines Ltd v Cosmos Exporters Ltd* [1947] KB 217; *Coastal International Trading Ltd v Maroil AG* [1988] 1 Lloyd's Rep 92 ('Not only was the provision unusual but the result which it would have produced in the way of profit to [B] was unreasonable', at p 96, per Leggatt J).
17 *Re R and H Hall Ltd v W H Pim (Junior) & Co's Arbitration* [1928] All ER Rep 763, 767 per Viscount Dunedin.
18 (1885) 15 QBD 85.
19 Where B can recover damages from S in respect of compensation paid to his sub-buyer, he can also recover costs *reasonably* incurred in defending an action by that sub-buyer, eg where the sub-buyer's claim was exorbitant.

of contract but, to the extent that they are classified as consequential losses, B may claim under s 54. These claims were discussed earlier when the question of damages and the lack of an available market was considered.

The buyer's action for damages for delay in delivery of the goods

Where B lawfully refuses to accept S's late tender of the goods, the situation will be one of non-delivery, as discussed earlier. It should be borne in mind, however, that if B fails to act reasonably in mitigating his loss, his damages nay be reduced to nil.[20] Damages for delay in delivery arise where B elects to accept S's late tender of the goods. The SGA contains no provisions which deal with the case of S's late delivery but it should be stressed that there are several differences between a claim for damages for late delivery and such a claim in cases of non-delivery. First, where B accepts the late delivery of the goods, the contract still subsists and, as there is a defective performance under the contract, the measure of damages is analogous to that applicable in cases of breach of warranty; in contrast, in cases of non-delivery B treats the contract as repudiated by reason of S's non-performance and thus damages are measured on the basis of a breach of condition. Second, in cases of non-delivery B's complaint is that he has to buy substitute goods at more than he agreed to pay under the contract with S but, with late delivery, B obtains the goods but they are either less valuable or less advantageous to him at the date of actual delivery than they would have been at the date fixed for delivery under the contract. Where there is an available market and B requires the goods for resale, it is thus the market price at the time fixed for delivery which must be taken (not the contract price) and B's measure of damages is the difference between the market value of the goods at the due date for delivery and their market value at the actual date of delivery. It should follow that neither the contract price nor the price agreed under a resale with a sub-buyer at the time of actual delivery should be material in assessing B's loss, but this question is considered more fully later. Third, in instances of non-delivery, B is expected to mitigate his loss by buying substitute goods in the market immediately after S's failure to deliver. This should not apply in cases of delayed delivery where S promises to deliver the goods and tenders them at a later date as he will then be estopped from asserting that B should have *bought* replacement goods. However, in suitable situations B could reasonably be expected to *hire* goods in mitigation of his loss during the period before delivery, eg where S is to deliver machinery to be used in B's manufacturing process. However, if S constantly reassures B that the goods are to be delivered, it would be unreasonable to expect B to hire goods in the face of such promises.[1]

It is thus evident that the measure of damages in cases of late delivery depends upon whether the goods were bought for resale or for use by B and much may

---

20 See *Sotiros Shipping Inc and Aeco Maritime S A v Sameiet Solholt, The Solholt* [1983] 1 Lloyd's Rep 605 (considered above).
1 See *Smeed v Foord* (1859) 1 E & E 602 (S was late in delivering a threshing machine and the evidence was that B could have hired another machine but was prevented from doing so by S's assurances of delivery. B recovered damages for having to dry his corn and its consequential loss of value).

turn upon whether S should have contemplated the purpose for which B had bought the goods, eg the profit to be made on a resale by B.

WHERE THE GOODS ARE BOUGHT FOR RESALE

Where there is an available market for the goods, the measure of damages when B has bought the goods for resale is the difference between the market value of the goods at the time and place fixed for delivery and their (lower) market value at the time and place of actual delivery to B. This means that B is entitled to recover as damages any fall in the market price of the goods between the contractual date of delivery and the actual date of delivery and this should put B in the same position as if the goods had been delivered punctually by S.[2]

Where there is no available market, the court must attempt to ascertain the fall in 'value' of the goods between the date fixed for delivery and the actual date of delivery by any relevant means. In *Borries v Hutchinson*,[3] for example, S contracted to deliver 75 tons of caustic soda to B at Hull and, as S knew, B had agreed to sell the goods to a sub-buyer 'on the continent'. S was one month late in making a delivery of only 26 tons and the rates for freight and insurance to St Petersburg, the ultimate destination of the goods, had risen in the interim. Moreover, there was no available market for the purchase of caustic soda. It was held that B could recover as damages the increased freight and insurance and also the loss of profit on the resale of the undelivered portion of the goods.

As in cases of non-delivery, it does seem that, correctly, where there *is* an available market the price in a resale of the goods to a sub-buyer should be ignored when assessing market value. B's damages should thus be assessed as the difference between the market price at the date fixed for delivery and the actual date of delivery irrespective of whether the resale price is higher or lower than the market price at the date of actual delivery. This is because B could have bought other goods in the available market to fulfil his obligations under the sub-contract and then the market price would be relevant to the goods which are delivered late by S. A resale by B at below the market price prevailing at the date of actual delivery would not increase S's liability and thus, by the same token, a resale at higher than the market price at that date should not reduce B's damages. However, this view was not followed in *Wertheim v Chicoutimi Pulp Co.*[4] S was late in delivering a quantity of wood pulp which B had bought at 25s per ton. The market price of the pulp was 70s per ton at the date and place fixed for delivery but when the goods were actually delivered the market price had fallen to 42s 6d per ton. Under several sub-sales, some of which B entered into before the original contract and some of which were later than that but before the actual delivery by S, B resold the goods at 65s per ton. B delivered the goods under his sub-contracts and, although the report does not say how this occurred, the most likely reason is that the date of delivery under the sub-contracts was later than the date of S's actual delivery. B argued that his loss was 27s 6d per ton but the Privy Council allowed the buyer only 5s per ton as damages, assessed

---

2 Most peculiarly, there is no direct authority to support this 'rule' but see *Borries v Hutchinson* (1865) 18 CBNS 445 and *Koufos v C Czarnikow Ltd, The Heron II* [1969] 1 AC 350 where this measure was accepted by the HL for delayed delivery in a contract of carriage.

3 (1865) 18 CBNS 445.

4 [1911] AC 301.

as the difference between the market value at the date and place fixed for delivery and the price which B obtained under the sub-sales. Lord Atkinson confirmed the general rule that the market value at the date of actual delivery was presumed to be the true value of the goods to B but that this presumption was rebutted where B obtained the goods and sold them at a much higher price than their prevailing market value. In this case, the real value of the goods to B 'is proved by the very fact of this sale to be more than the market value ... unless he is, against all justice, to be permitted to make a profit by the breach of contract [and] be compensated for a loss he never suffered'.[5] This reasoning followed almost inevitably from Lord Atkinson's view that the overall purpose of damages was 'to secure only an indemnity'.[6]

Wertheim was criticised and distinguished in *Slater v Hoyle & Smith Ltd*[7] where the price in a sub-sale was not taken into account in measuring damages. Scrutton LJ stressed that, on the facts of *Wertheim*, B was under no obligation to deliver to the sub-buyer the selfsame goods which he received under the original contract and so 'if he had bought other goods and used them for the sub-contract, he would have been left with goods delivered at a time when the market price was 42s 6d, instead of when it was 70s, and would have recovered 27s 6d'.[8] Scrutton LJ further emphasised that 'all the English decisions[9] show that [B] cannot measure the real value of what he has lost by reference to a contract peculiar to himself, for which [S] is not responsible'.[10] It is, of course, this contract 'peculiar to himself' which means that B makes a profit as result of his business acumen in securing an advantageous sub-sale and, as Treitel[11] points out, it is incorrect to assert that B profits from the *breach* of contract. Nevertheless, *Slater* was itself criticised in a recent decision of the Court of Appeal[12] concerning damages for defective quality and, while the *Wertheim* decision has met with relatively limited approval in the past,[13] it may find favour in future decisions. In any event, *Wertheim* is limited to cases of delayed delivery where the goods are actually obtained by B and 'the amount of prejudice [is] no longer a matter of speculation' because 'it [has] been put to the test by the goods being actually sold'.[14]

WHERE THE GOODS ARE BOUGHT FOR USE

Where B buys the goods for use rather than resale, his complaint is that he has been deprived of the use of the goods during the period when delivery was delayed and thus he may recover damages for loss of use based upon the normal use of

5 [1911] AC 301 at 308, per Lord Atkinson.
6 [1911] AC 301 at 307.
7 [1920] 2 KB 11 (a decision on defective quality and damages).
8 [1920] 2 KB 11 at 23-24.
9 See principally *Rodocanachi v Milburn* (1886) 18 QBD 67 and *Williams Bros v Ed T Agius Ltd* [1914] AC 510, considered above.
10 [1920] 2 KB 11 at 24.
11 *The Law of Contract* (10th edn, 1999), p 885.
12 *Bence Graphics International Ltd v Fasson UK Ltd* [1998] QB 87 (considered below).
13 *Williams Bros v Ed T Agius Ltd* [1914] AC 510, 522 and 529 per Lords Dunedin and Atkinson respectively; *British Westinghouse Electric and Manufacturing Co Ltd v Underground Electric Railways Co of London Ltd* [1912] AC 673, 690 per Viscount Haldane LC; see also Greig, *Sale of Goods* (1974), pp 289-291.
14 *Williams Bros v Ed T Agius Ltd* [1914] AC 510, 522 per Lord Dunedin.

such goods but not for any unusual use which is unknown to S. Where there is an available market for the goods, B should be able to mitigate his loss either by buying substitute goods or hiring other goods until delivery of the contract goods.

If the goods to be delivered are profit-earning chattels, B may recover the loss of profits that he would have made during the period between the date fixed for delivery and the actual date of delivery. In *Victoria Laundry (Windsor) Ltd v Newman Industries Ltd,*[15] B was a launderer and dyer who wanted to expand his business and S agreed to sell B a large boiler to be delivered on 5 June 1946. In fact, the boiler was not delivered until 8 November 1946 and no substitute boiler had been available in the market during that period. B sued for damages claiming the loss of profits from (i) the increased business in which he could have engaged had the boiler been delivered on the due date; and (ii) the profits which he would have earnt from certain highly lucrative dyeing contracts which he could have obtained with the Ministry of Supply. The Court of Appeal held that, as S knew that B was a launderer who wanted the boiler for immediate business use, he ought to have anticipated that B would lose business from the delay and thus losses under (i), above, were recoverable. However, in the absence of special knowledge, S could not reasonably have foreseen the additional losses from B's failure to obtain the dyeing contracts and so losses under (ii), above, could not be recovered. The *Victoria Laundry* case was significant in the development of the law for two principal reasons. First, previous decisions which allowed recovery for loss of profits had concerned delayed delivery of goods which were manifestly intended to secure profits, viz profit-earning ships,[16] and so the decision recognised that loss of trading profits could be claimed where the profit-earning potential of the goods was less obvious. Second, *Victoria Laundry* acknowledged that delayed delivery of *part* of a profit-earning chattel could be just as significant as delayed delivery of the entirety of such a profit-earning chattel.[17]

It does seem that loss of profits are recoverable in relation only to the normal or obvious use of the goods which S can contemplate at the date of contract. In *Cory v Thames Ironworks and Shipbuilding Co Ltd,*[18] B, a coal merchant, bought a floating boom derrick from S, a shipbuilder, which was the first vessel of its kind to be built in England and was fitted with heavy machinery for raising sunken vessels. B intended to fit hydraulic cranes and machinery to the vessel for the purpose of transhipping coal from colliers to barges without the need for any intermediate landing but this was an entirely novel use of the vessel. S knew that the derrick was required for B's business but had no notice or knowledge of this special purpose; instead, S considered that the hull was to be used as a coal store. The existing equipment in the hull proved so difficult to remove that S was six months late in making delivery and, as a consequence, B had to pay for the machinery supplied by a third party which was to be fitted into the hull, and

---

15 [1949] 2 KB 528.
16 See *Cory v Thames Ironworks and Shipbuilding Co Ltd* (1868) LR 3 QB 181 (below); *Re Trent and Humber Co, ex p Cambrian Steam Packet Co* (1868) 4 Ch App 112 (delayed delivery of a ship after repair; the plaintiff recovered as damages the net profit which he would have made from chartering the vessel had she been delivered on time); *Steam Herring Fleet Ltd v V S Richards & Co Ltd* (1901) 17 TLR 731.
17 See Asquith LJ, [1949] 2 KB 528, at pp 543-544: 'The fact that a part only is involved is only significant in so far as it bears on the capacity of the supplier to foresee the consequences of non-delivery'.
18 (1868) LR 3 QB 181.

two tugs which B had bought for towing the coal barges to and from the hull were 'comparatively useless' during the time in which the hull was undelivered. It was held that B could recover only those profits which would have been made through using the hull in the way which S could reasonably have contemplated, ie as a coal store, and the loss of profits from the specialised use of the derrick were irrecoverable as not being within S's reasonable contemplation.

There are several features of *Cory* which call for comment. First, the decision clearly establishes that if the goods have an obvious purpose, B must inform S of any special purpose to which he intends to put the goods if S is to be liable for loss arising from that special purpose. Also, it appears that if there are, for example, two *normal* purposes to which B can put the goods, *x* and *y*, he may recover damages even though S contemplated *x* when in fact B intended the goods for *y* and claims loss arising from *y*. It is less clear what the position is where the goods have *no* obvious purpose but here it would surely be difficult for S to allege that B's intended purpose was special and so that purpose should not be regarded as being too remote. Second, in *Cory* B did not claim as damages the profits that he would have made from the novel use of the hull (this being his actual loss) but, instead, claimed only £420 which would have been the loss of profits if the hull had been used as a coal store. The difficulty here was that this latter loss had not actually been suffered by B but Cockburn CJ considered that B had 'lost the larger amount, and there can be no hardship or injustice' in making S liable for the (lesser) loss of profits which were within S's reasonable contemplation. In *Cory*, the loss which B actually suffered was the same *type* as the loss which would have occurred in the normal use of the hull and for which B obtained damages, ie a loss of trading profits. It is unclear, however, whether damages can be recovered if the loss actually suffered is different in kind or type from that which would have occurred in the ordinary course of things.[19]

LOSS OF PROFITS ON A SUB-SALE MADE BY THE BUYER

Where S makes a late delivery of the goods, the general rule is that B cannot recover his loss of profits made under a sub-sale and, in this respect, the rule in relation to late delivery follows that of non-delivery. Where there is market in which goods are readily available to B, S cannot reasonably contemplate loss of profits under a sub-sale as the ordinary consequence of late delivery. In *Portman v Middleton*,[20] B agreed to repair a threshing engine for its owner (who was aptly named Sheaf) by the beginning of August and B then contracted with S for S to make a new fire-box for the engine, but B did not inform S of the contract with Sheaf. As a consequence of S's delay, B had to buy a fire-box from T and so he could not deliver the repaired engine to Sheaf until November. Having settled Sheaf's claim of £20 for breach of contract, B sought to recover that sum from S but it was held that he must fail as the loss was not within S's reasonable contemplation.

The position is different where S actually knows of the resale or ought reasonably to have contemplated it as probable at the date of the original contract,

---

19 Treitel (*The Law of Contract*, 10th edn, 1999, p 903) asks (but does not answer) the following question: 'Suppose A sells poisonous cattle-food to B, who eats it himself in the course of an unforeseeable nutritional experiment, and dies. Can his executor sue A for the loss of a cow?'

20 (1858) 4 CBNS 322.

as here he will be liable for B's loss of profits. In *Hydraulic Engineering Co Ltd v McHaffie Goslett & Co*,[1] S agreed to sell part of a machine to B having been told that the machine (a 'gun powder pile driver') was to be resold to a sub-buyer. Due to S's delay, the sub-buyer refused to take delivery of the machine. It was held that B could recover from S his loss of profits on the sub-sale and the expenditure he had uselessly incurred, less the value of the incomplete machine which was left in his possession. Moreover, where S contemplated the sub-sale or ought reasonably to have done so, he will be liable to B for damages which B is obliged to pay to his sub-buyer as a consequence of S's delay. In *Elbinger AG v Armstrong*,[2] S agreed to supply B with 666 sets of wheels and axles, S having actual knowledge that (i) B was under a contract to deliver wagons to a Russian railway company and that the wheels and axles were to be part of the completed wagons; and (ii) B's sub-contract with the Russian buyer contained a liquidated damages clause which applied in the event of B's delay in delivery. S did not know, however, the exact delivery dates of the wagons as specified in the sub-contract nor the precise amounts payable under the liquidated damages clause. S delivered the first 100 sets late, no substitute wheels and axles were available in the market and thus B was in default to his Russian buyer and had to pay damages for delay. As S did not know the detailed terms of the liquidated damages clause, Blackburn J did not think it apt, as a general rule, for B to recover from S the exact amount of the liquidated damages paid to the sub-buyer but, on the facts, he upheld the award of that sum by the jury.

As in cases of non-delivery, where B can recover damages from S in respect of compensation paid to his sub-buyer, he can also recover costs *reasonably* incurred in defending an action by that sub-buyer. Where the sub-buyer makes an extravagant claim for damages, it is clearly also in S's interests that B defend the action.[3]

Loss of repeat orders from sub-buyers?

When the question of damages for the delivery of defective goods is considered later, it is clear that where it is within the reasonable contemplation of S and B that S's supply of defective goods might lead to B's customers withdrawing their business from B meaning that no 'repeat orders' are given, damages may be awarded for the resultant loss in profits. There would appear to be no obstacle to applying this principle in cases of delayed delivery.

OTHER LOSSES IN RELATION TO DELAYED DELIVERY

It is possible to recover other losses apart from those concerned with user-profits or the resale of the goods and thus B may claim damages for extra expenses incurred as a consequence of the late delivery and which are in the reasonable contemplation of the parties as not unlikely to result or which arise from special circumstances[4] actually contemplated by the parties. Everything will thus depend on S's knowledge of B's circumstances and the purpose to which B intended to

---

1 (1878) 4 QBD 670.
2 (1874) LR 9 QB 473.
3 *Agius v Great Western Colliery Co* [1899] 1 QB 413.
4 See eg *Aruna Mills v Dhanrajmal Gobindram* [1968] 1 QB 655.

put the goods. For example, in one case[5] where S, a shipbuilder, failed to deliver fishing vessels on time, it was held that B could recover the wages paid to fishermen whose services had been rendered superfluous during the delay. In *John M Henderson & Co Ltd v Montague L Meyer Ltd,*[6] S was late in delivering a crane to B for use in B's timber yard and B recovered as damages the extra labour costs of moving and loading the timber by hand but he failed to recover other losses as being too remote, viz (i) the extra demurrage on barges which were waiting to be unloaded; (ii) rent for the storage of some timber; and (iii) the costs relating to congestion on the wharf and of diverting some ships elsewhere.

The buyer's action for damages for the defective quality of the goods

It is useful at this stage to draw together B's remedies where S tenders goods which do not conform to the contract description under the SGA, s 13 or fail to meet the standards of quality demanded of S under the SGA, ss 14 and 15. First, B can reject the goods for breach of condition,[7] thereby treating the contract as discharged, and claim damges for non-delivery. Second, B could reject the goods and seek a restitutionary remedy for the recovery of the price paid. Third, B could accept the goods or be deemed to accept them under the SGA, s 35, meaning that the breach of condition must be treated as a breach of warranty under the SGA, s 11(4): here B can no longer reject the goods but is confined to a claim for damages for breach of warranty. There may, of course, be other contractual undertakings relating to the condition of the goods which may be classified either as warranties or as innominate terms and which do not permit B to reject the goods but restrict him to an action in damages. The section which follows is thus concerned with the situation where B sues for damages for a breach of a warranty or an innominate term relating to the quality, state or condition of the goods.[8]

The SGA, s 53 prescribes the measure of damages for breach of warranty as follows:

'(1) Where there is a breach of warranty by the seller, or where the buyer elects (or is compelled) to treat any breach of a condition on the part of the seller as a breach of warranty, the buyer is not by reason only of such breach of warranty entitled to reject the goods; but he may –
(a) set up against the seller the breach of warranty in diminution or extinction of the price, or
(b) maintain an action against the seller for damages for the breach of warranty.
(2) The measure of damages for breach of warranty is the estimated loss directly and naturally resulting, in the ordinary course of events, from the breach of warranty.
(3) In the case of breach of warranty of quality such loss is prima facie the difference between the value of the goods at the time of delivery to the buyer and the value they would have had if they had fulfilled the warranty.
(4) The fact that the buyer has set up the breach of warranty in diminution or extinction of the price does not prevent him from maintaining an action for the same breach of warranty if he has suffered further damage.'

---

5 *Steam Herring Fleet Ltd v V S Richards & Co Ltd* (1901) 17 TLR 731; see also *Waters v Towers* (1853) 8 Exch 401.
6 (1941) 46 Com Cas 209.
7 Subject to (i) S's possible right to cure the breach and re-tender the goods; and (ii) the SGA, s 15A; see Ch 23.
8 Damages for breach of s 12 (S's title) are not within the ambit of s 53 (see Ch 19).

Section 53(1)(a) and (4) are based upon the decision in *Mondel v Steel*,[9] to the effect that B can make a counter-claim for damages which is allowed to be set-off in diminution or extinction of the price, thereby avoiding circuity of actions. But s 53(4) goes further in providing that B is not prevented from bringing another action for the same breach of warranty if he has suffered 'further damage'. The meaning of this is unclear but it probably refers to the case where B's claim for damages exceeds the price (ie it is in 'extinction' of the price) so that he may bring a separate action for the additional loss he has suffered. It should be stressed that B does not have to set-up the breach of warranty by way of defence and thus, if he has paid the price, he may still maintain a later, separate action for breach of warranty[10] and this would be very important where defects manifest themselves only at a later date.

It will be noticed that s 53(2) sets-out the first rule in *Hadley v Baxendale*[11] while s 53(3) states the *'prima facie'* measure of damages, but a recent and significant decision of the Court of Appeal,[12] which is considered later, has stressed that s 53(2) should be the starting point in assessing damages and s 53(3) should not be applied if it means that B would recover more than his true loss. Moreover, although s 53(3) refers expressly to breach of warranty of 'quality' it is widely thought that a similar measure of damages would apply to breaches of the SGA, ss 13, 14(3) and 15.

DAMAGES FOR DIMINUTION IN VALUE OF THE GOODS: SECTION 53(3)

The normal measure of damages as prescribed by s 53(3) is the difference between the value of the goods if they had complied with S's warranty, assessed at the time and place[13] of delivery, and the actual value of the goods at the time and place of delivery. If B recovers a sum of money which amounts to this difference, he will be put in the position he would have been in if there had been compliance with the warranty. If the goods are valueless at the date of delivery, B is entitled to recover the full value which the goods should have had. This measure compensates B for the value of the inferior goods only and B's right to recover damages for other, consequential losses, eg personal injury caused by the goods, is considered later. It is thus clear that there are two values to be ascertained at the date of delivery: the value of the goods as warranted at that date and, secondly, the value of the goods in their defective state at that date.

Ascertaining the value of the goods as warranted

Normally, where there is a market price for goods of the same contractual description and quality, this will establish the 'value' of the goods in the contract between S and B.

Where there is no available market, any relevant evidence may be admitted to prove the value of the goods. As a general rule, the contract price is irrelevant

---

9 (1841) 8 M & W 858.
10 See *Davis v Hedges* (1871) LR 6 QB 687.
11 (1854) 9 Exch 341.
12 *Bence Graphics International Ltd v Fasson UK Ltd* [1998] QB 87.
13 The place of delivery is not mentioned in s 53(3) but, by analogy with non-delivery and delayed delivery, the place of delivery is probably a factor to consider (although Diplock LJ did not think so, see *Aryeh v Lawrence Kostoris & Son Ltd* [1967] 1 Lloyd's Rep 63, 72-73).

as it is the value of the goods as warranted at the time of *delivery* to the buyer which must be assessed; accordingly, if there is a marked discrepancy between the contract price and the value of the goods at the time of delivery, the contract price should be disregarded.[14] Likewise, the price at which B had agreed to resell the goods is immaterial and so a resale price which is higher than the value of the goods as warranted should not increase the damages and, similarly, where the resale price is lower than the value as warranted, the damages should not be decreased.[15] Nevertheless, in the absence of other evidence, both the contract price and resale price may be *evidence* of value as may the price at which a third party offered to buy the goods.[16]

Ascertaining the value of the goods in their defective state

The obstacles placed in the path of this valuation were considered by Devlin J in *Biggin & Co Ltd v Permanite Ltd*.[17] First, it was stressed that there is 'rarely any market for damaged goods' and so 'one can rarely arrive at an accurate figure of unsound value'.[18] Second, Devlin J thought that the price at which B has sold the goods may be a sound guide where the sub-buyer has full knowledge of the defective state of the goods but the evidence of hypothetical sub-buyers as to what they would have paid for goods 'which they never saw and of whose defects they learnt only at secondhand'[19] is unlikely to be of use. Finally, the judge accentuated the common commercial practice of dealing with this type of case by the fixing of a price allowance by an adjuster or a person skilled in the relevant trade, and such a reduction in price was made in *Biggin*. It should be mentioned that the above considerations apply only to damaged/defective goods and there will clearly be a market for goods which are, for example, unfit only for B's particular purpose.

Where the actual value of the goods cannot be ascertained

If there is simply no market for the defective goods, it will obviously be impossible to fix a market value and so the court may award damages based on the cost of the repairs which are necessary for the goods to reach the standard under the contract and thus become saleable.[20] However, although the decision of the House of Lords in *Ruxley Electronics and Construction Ltd v Forsyth*[1] was not concerned with a sale of goods, it seems clear that if the difference in value between the goods as described in the contract and the defective goods supplied is only slight, but the cost of repairs needed to bring the goods up to the warranted standard

---

14   *Loder v Kekulé* (1857) 3 CBNS 128; *Slater v Hoyle & Smith Ltd* [1920] 2 KB 11, 17 and 18 per Warrington LJ.
15   See *Clare v Maynard* (1837) 6 Ad & El 519; Cf *Bence Graphics International Ltd v Fasson UK Ltd* [1998] QB 87 (see below).
16   *Cox v Walker* (1835) 6 Ad & El 523n.
17   [1951] 1 KB 422; revsd on a different ground: [1951] 2 KB 314.
18   [1951] 1 KB 422 at 438.
19   [1951] 1 KB 422 at 439.
20   *Minster Trust Ltd v Traps Tractors Ltd* [1954] 1 WLR 963.
 1   [1996] AC 344 (construction of a swimming pool which should have had a diving area 7 feet 6 inches deep. On completion, the pool was suitable for diving but was only 6 feet deep. The cost of rebuilding the pool was £21,560. P was awarded £2,500 for 'loss of amenity'); see Chandler, 'Defective Performance of Building Contracts: Expectations in a Straitjacket' [1996] ICLR 255.

would be exorbitant, the measure of damages will normally be based upon the difference in value rather than the cost of the repairs.[2]

B may be entitled to claim as damages the cost of buying substitute goods to perform the intended function of the defective, contract goods but, if B makes an extra profit from the new goods, his damages may be reduced to take this into account. In *British Westinghouse Electric and Manufacturing Co Ltd v Underground Electric Railways Co of London Ltd*,[3] S sold turbines to B which were deficient in power and economy and not in accordance with the contract. B used the turbines for a time (whilst reserving his right to damages) but eventually replaced them with improved turbines of a different design from another manufacturer. The arbitrator found that the new turbines were so superior in efficiency and economy that it would have been to B's advantage to replace the old turbines with the new machines even if the old turbines had complied with the contract specification in the first place. The House of Lords held that B's replacement of the turbines was a 'natural and prudent course followed by those whose object was to avoid further loss, and that it formed part of a continuous dealing with the situation in which they found themselves, and was not an independent or disconnected transaction'.[4] However, even though B had not been under a duty to mitigate his loss in this way, his actions had actually lessened his loss and, in the claim for damages for the cost of installing the new turbines, the extra profit which resulted had to be taken into account. As this profit exceeded the cost of the new machines, B could not recover that cost. B had nevertheless suffered loss before replacing the turbines because the cost of their operation was greater than it would have been had they complied with the contract; this loss was recoverable and had not been lessened by the replacement turbines.

Other decisions which are based on the same notion as *British Westinghouse* have been noted earlier in the consideration of different aspects of damages[5] but it should be stressed that the principle does raise difficult issues of causation in deciding whether or not[6] the benefit in dispute forms part of a 'continuous dealing' and thus arises directly from B's attempts to mitigate the potential loss resulting from the breach.

The time when value is to be ascertained: the time of delivery to B

It is clear that, under s 53(3), the general rule is that the time of delivery to B is the material time for the valuation of the goods,[7] but the section also specifies

---

2 It seems likely that, where a *consumer* buys defective goods, the court will be flexible and consider B's subjective satisfaction which should result from the goods thus awarding damages for 'loss of amenity' or the notion of the 'consumer surplus': see *Ruxley*, above, at pp 360-361 per Lord Mustill; Harris, Ogus and Phillips, 'Contract Remedies and the Consumer Surplus' (1979) 95 LQR 581.
3 [1912] AC 673.
4 [1912] AC 673 at 692, per Viscount Haldane LC.
5 See eg *Erie County Natural Gas and Fuel Co Ltd v Carroll* [1911] AC 105.
6 See *Hussey v Eels* [1990] 2 QB 227 (B was induced to buy a house by a misrepresentation that there had been no subsidence. Over two years later, B demolished the house and resold the site at a considerably higher price than he had paid, having obtained planning permission for two houses to be built on it. Held this was not to be taken into account in assessing damages as the resale was *not* part of a continuous transaction of which the original purchase was the inception).
7 See *Jones v Just* (1868) LR 3 QB 197 (the market rose after contract so that B was able to resell damaged hemp at a price 'very nearly equal' to the contract price. It was held, nevertheless, that damages should be measured by the difference between the value of the damaged hemp at the time of *delivery* and the value *at that time* of hemp as warranted under the contract. B was thus given the benefit of the rise in the market).

that this is merely the '*prima facie*' rule and it may occasionally be apt to make a valuation at a later date. Most obviously, there may be a reasonable lapse of time after delivery before the defect is discovered: in the sale of a racehorse, for example, its defective performance might be manifest only after its first race.[8] Likewise, where goods are sold in sealed packages and S knows that they are for resale, the valuation should be made at the time when the goods are delivered to the sub-buyer as this is the time and place when it is reasonable to expect the packages to be opened and examined.[9] A warranty of quality may also have relevance only as to the future and so B will be unable to discover the defect until long after delivery; here the valuation should be made at that later date. In *Ashworth v Wells*,[10] an orchid was sold for 20 guineas and warranted as being white but, after two years' cultivation, it flowered as a mundane purple orchid which was worth about 7s 6d. The Court of Appeal held that B was not limited to recovering the loss that he had suffered at the date of delivery and damages were assessed on the basis of the resale value of a white orchid at the date when the plant flowered (£50).

WHAT IS THE POSITION IF THE BUYER PERFORMS UNDER A SUB-SALE DESPITE THE SELLER'S BREACH?

The general rule where S delivers defective goods but B is nevertheless able to deliver the goods under a sub-sale is that B's damages should not be reduced by taking the sub-sale into account. The leading decision is *Slater v Hoyle & Smith Ltd*,[11] which was discussed briefly in the context of delayed delivery. There B bought a quantity of unbleached cotton from S in order to fulfil a sub-sale, which he had made earlier, of bleached cotton. The sub-sale was thus not of the selfsame, identical goods which were the subject of the principal sale and S knew nothing of the sub-sale. The cotton delivered by S was not up to the contractual standard but B was able to perform the sub-sale by delivering at least some of the cloth to his sub-buyer. The sub-buyer paid the full price under his contract with B and did not reject the goods, probably because he used the cloth to make shirts and 'the test of merchantable character [was] entirely different from [that] in the principal contract'.[12] B refused to take the remainder of the goods from S and, when S sued B for non-acceptance, B counterclaimed for damages for breach of warranty of quality. S argued that the resale prices realised by B should be taken into account instead of the market price and, as the resale prices were equal to the price in the main contract of sale, B had suffered no loss and was in the same position as if the cloth delivered by S had not been inferior. The Court of Appeal ignored the prices under the sub-sales and awarded B damages based

---

8 See *Naughton v O'Callaghan* [1990] 3 All ER 191 (damages for misrepresentation regarding a horse's pedigree).
9 *Van den Hurk v R Martens & Co Ltd* [1920] 1 KB 850 (sodium sulphide packed in sealed drums which could not be inspected until opened by sub-B at his premises in France several months after the original delivery to B). See also ss 34 and 35 on examination and acceptance of the goods: the place of delivery is the normal place for the examination of the goods but the general rule may be rebutted by the terms of the contract or the nature of the transaction, as in *Van den Hurk*.
10 (1898) 14 TLR 227.
11 [1920] 2 KB 11.
12 [1920] 2 KB 11 at 19, per Scrutton LJ.

upon the normal measure of the difference between the market price of cloth as warranted at the time of delivery and the market price of the inferior cloth at the time of delivery. The court stressed that (i) B was under no obligation to deliver the *identical* goods of the principal contract to the sub-buyer; (ii) B might thus have bought goods in the available market to fulfil his profitable sub-contract and he would then be left with the inferior goods so that the normal measure of damages of the difference between the two market prices would then apply; and (iii) if B was 'lucky enough, for reasons with which the seller has nothing to do, to get his goods through on the sub-contract without a claim against him, this on principle cannot affect his claim against the seller any more than the fact that he had to pay very large damages on his sub-contract would affect his original seller'.[13]

The Court of Appeal has, however, recently criticised *Slater* and chosen not to follow its approach. In *Bence Graphics International Ltd v Fasson UK Ltd*,[14] B was in the business of selling self-adhesive decals to manufacturers of containers used in the carriage of goods by sea who, in turn, sold the containers marked with the decals to shipping lines. B bought vinyl film from S for making the decals, it being a condition of that contract that the film would survive in good, legible condition for at least five years. The vinyl film was defective because too little ultraviolet stabiliser had been used in its manufacture with the result that some of the decals became illegible and there were extensive complaints from the end-users of the containers. Only one such complaint led to a claim against B who settled it at his own expense and B was then indemnified by S. Also, B returned defective film to S which was worth £22,000 and S conceded that he was liable for that amount, but the contract price which B had paid was £564,328. At the time of the trial, there was no possibility of any claims being made against B in the future as the limitation period had expired. Morland J held that B could recover the latter sum under s 53(3) on the basis of the difference in value of the film as warranted at the time of delivery and its actual value at that time (meaning that he considered the film to be valueless). The Court of Appeal reversed that decision (Thorpe LJ dissenting) and held that the *prima facie* measure in s 53(3) was displaced where both parties contemplated that B would manufacture a product from the goods sold which would, in turn, be sold to others. In such a case, the measure of damages for defects in the goods sold should be the extent of B's liability to the subsequent or ultimate users of the product and that this measure would apply whether or not the resultant liability in damages was higher or lower than that which would have resulted from the *prima facie* measure in s 53(3). Accordingly, on the facts, a judgment for £22,000 was substituted plus damages to be assessed on the basis of B's liability to the subsequent users of the product.

Bence has been criticised convincingly by Treitel[15] on the basis that the Court of Appeal treated the case as one of remoteness when in fact that principle was not an issue to be considered. He stresses that, where S delivers goods which are not in conformity with the contract, B may suffer loss in two separate ways viz, (i) the inferior goods may have less value than goods which conform with the contract; or (ii) B may have intended to put the goods to some particular use for which, by reason of the non-conformity, they are unsuitable. In *Bence*, B suffered

---

13 [1920] 2 KB 11 at 23, per Scrutton LJ.
14 [1998] QB 87.
15 'Damages for Breach of Warranty of Quality' (1997) 113 LQR 188.

the loss in (i) and this should not be subject to the test of remoteness whereas, clearly, the loss in (ii) is so subject. Second, the author prefers the reasoning in *Slater's* case, above, and points out that, in *Bence*, B was under no obligation to use the vinyl supplied by S in performance of the sub-contracts and could have used material supplied by another manufacturer. In this event, B would have been left with the defective material supplied by S and the normal measure of damages for diminution in value would have applied. Third, Treitel emphasises that *Bence* was not a case where B's use of the vinyl in performance of the sub-contracts resulted in any benefit to B which mitigated his loss in fact and thus ought to be considered, as it was in the *British Westinghouse*[16] case considered earlier. The line of cases where B's loss is in fact avoided, stress that the benefit thus accruing to B must arise directly from the breach rather than being a collateral benefit and, in *Bence*, it appears that any benefit fell into the latter category as arising from the forbearance of B's customers to make claims against him. Finally, although it is tempting to conclude that the first instance decision in *Bence* would allow B a windfall in terms of his being awarded more than he had lost, it was the aforementioned forbearance of B's customers which led to such a gain and it is difficult to see why S, the party in breach, should reap the benefit of this windfall having supplied worthless goods but having received the price of perfect goods.

Technically, *Bence* may be distinguished from *Slater* principally on the grounds that, in the latter case, no claim was made against B and S knew nothing of the sub-sale, but the law is now left in an uncertain state; it is submitted that the reasoning in *Slater* is preferable to that in *Bence*.

LOSSES OTHER THAN DIMINUTION IN VALUE WHERE THE SELLER DELIVERS DEFECTIVE GOODS

It goes without saying that, where defective goods are supplied by S, it will not be uncommon for those goods to cause physical damage to other goods or real property, or injury to the person may result. This may often occur because B is unaware of a latent defect in the goods and thus further damage ensues from the faulty goods. Moreover, there is the familiar problem of whether B may recover profits which are lost on a sub-sale or which would have accrued from the use of the goods. These heads of loss and others can now be considered.

The time at which B discovers the defect in the goods

B has actual knowledge of the defect

First, if the goods are *patently* defective, B cannot continue to use the goods and then recover from S the loss which results from such obvious defects.[17]

Second, it may be reasonable that B does not discover immediately that the goods are defective but it is clear that, once B does know of the defect, he cannot make S liable for any further loss which could have been avoided by B's taking

---

16 [1912] AC 673.
17 In *British Oil and Cake Co Ltd v Burstall & Co* (1923) 39 TLR 406, 407, Rowlatt J said that 'if a buyer received from his seller an article which was "patently" not the article contracted for, he could not use it at the risk of the seller'. See also *Hammond & Co v Bussey* (1887) 20 QBD 79, 86 per Lord Esher MR.

reasonable steps to remedy the defect and thereby mitigate his loss. In *Lambert v Lewis*,[18] B bought a coupling for a trailer from S (a retail seller), which had a defectively designed locking system and B was involved in a road accident with a third party when the trailer broke loose from its coupling. B knew that the locking mechanism was damaged but he continued to use it for several months without having it repaired or ascertaining whether it was safe to use in that state. The House of Lords held that, once B discovered the damage, he could no longer rely on S's warranty that the goods were fit for their purpose as an excuse for his own failure to remedy the breach. Accordingly, B could not recover from S the damages that he had paid to the third party. The Court of Appeal had held that there was no break in the chain of causation between the breach of warranty and the accident and thus S was liable to B. Although this view is superficially attractive in that S is prevented from easily sloughing-off his liability under the SGA, further reflection reveals that it imposes too great a liability on S. The Court of Appeal's analysis meant that, in effect, S became an insurer of B's negligence until the moment that B's gross carelessness snapped the chain of causation. Consequently, S's liability would *increase* in direct proportion to the severity of B's negligence until the point at which the chain of causation broke: this amounts to an inversion of the proper allocation of both risk and liability and so it must be unacceptable.

Third, it is clear that once B knows that the goods are defective, he cannot increase S's liability by reselling the goods to a sub-buyer and then making S liable for B's liability to that sub-buyer. Here the duty to mitigate his loss demands that B should inform the sub-buyer of the defects. Moreover, if B acquires knowledge of the defects after the sale to the sub-buyer and passing on that knowledge would decrease B's liability to the sub-buyer, B is under a duty to inform the sub-buyer of the position.[19]

Must B examine the goods?

The question broached above, as to whether defects are patent or latent, goes hand-in-glove with the issue of B's examination of the goods. Must B examine the goods thoroughly or is he entitled to rely on S's warranty of quality and fitness under the contract? Certainly where the defect is not immediately obvious, B is not prevented from claiming damages on the basis that he did not make a meticulous inspection of the goods.[20] If B were denied damages because of his failure to inspect the goods, S could readily escape liability and, accordingly, the general rule is that B is entitled to rely on S's undertakings as to quality and fitness for a reasonable period after the delivery of the goods.[1] In *Pinnock Bros v Lewis and Peat Ltd*,[2] B bought from S a quantity of East African copra cake for the purpose of feeding to cattle and resold it to sub-buyers without examining it. The copra cake was so contaminated with castor beans that it was poisonous and the cattle became ill. It was held that B could recover from S the compensation which he had paid to the sub-buyer. Roche J considered that the defect could

---

18 [1982] AC 225.
19 *Biggin & Co Ltd v Permanite Ltd* [1951] 1 KB 422, 435 per Devlin J.
20 *British Oil and Cake Co Ltd v Burstall & Co* (1923) 39 TLR 406, 407 per Rowlatt J (where the defect is not patent, B has no duty to examine the goods and can use them on the assumption that they are the goods contracted for).
 1 *Lambert v Lewis* [1982] AC 225, 276 per Lord Diplock.
 2 [1923] 1 KB 690.

have been discovered only by an expert analyst and, as it would be unreasonable to expect that B should undertake such an analysis, he was entitled to rely on the contract with S 'rather than to rely on any precautions of [his] own'.[3]

Furthermore, in both *Mowbray v Merryweather*[4] and *Scott v Foley, Aikman & Co*,[5] the defendant (D) supplied goods for the use of the plaintiff (P) and his employees and the employees were physically injured by the defective goods. P paid damages to his employees and, although P had not examined the goods before they were used, he recovered from D damages for D's breach of warranty that the goods were reasonably fit for use. These decisions are potent in that P was negligent *vis-à-vis* his employees in not examining the goods and an inspection would have disclosed the defects, but it was held, nevertheless, that P owed no duty *to D* to inspect the goods and could thus rely on D's warranty that they were sound.[6] In *Lambert v Lewis*,[7] above, only the *Mowbray* decision was considered by the House of Lords and it was distinguished on the facts. Delivering the only speech, Lord Diplock approved Winn LJ's limitation upon the *Mowbray* principle which he enunciated in *Hadley v Droitwich Construction Co Ltd*.[8] This is that *Mowbray* applies only if S warrants the quality or fitness for purpose of the goods in such terms that there is no necessity for B to take certain precautions with the goods and it is B's failure to take those same precautions which has made him liable to the third party. Accordingly, this reasoning could not apply to the facts of *Lambert v Lewis* as, once B knew that the coupling was damaged and it was not in the same state as when it was delivered, the only warranty which would justify his failure to get it repaired would be a warranty that it was safe to continue to use it with a trailer on the roads. This was similarly the position in the *Droitwich Construction* case, above, where the defendant (D) hired a crane to the plaintiff (P) but D did not promise to maintain it; instead, P undertook to put a competent man in charge of it and service it properly. In fact, P put a 16-year-old youth in charge of the crane and it was never serviced. When one of P's employees was injured by the defective crane and obtained damages from P, it was held that D was not liable to indemnify P because D had not warranted that the crane need not be serviced – the position was quite the reverse and there was thus no warranty upon which P could rely.

Is B ever on enquiry? *Ought* B to know of the defect?

In all the cases considered above where B has succeeded against S on the warranty, it is implicit that B has acted reasonably either in not inspecting the goods or not discovering the defect. There is no direct authority as to whether B might ever be

---

3   [1923] 1 KB 690 at 698. The same decision was reached on very similar facts in *British Oil and Cake Co Ltd v Burstall & Co* (1923) 39 TLR 406 and *Dobell (G C) & Co Ltd v Barber and Garratt* [1931] 1 KB 219. See also *Smith v Johnson* (1899) 15 TLR 179 (S, a builder, sold mortar to B which so defective that the building in which it was used had to be demolished and rebuilt. Bruce J held that B could not, by reasonable diligence, have discovered the defects in the mortar in its wet state before it was used and thus the costs of demolition and rebuilding were recoverable from S).
4   [1895] 2 QB 640.
5   (1899) 16 TLR 55.
6   In *Mowbray*, P was a stevedore who agreed to discharge a cargo from D's ship and D agreed to provide the equipment to do so. D supplied a defective chain which broke in use injuring one of P's workmen. In *Scott*, P chartered a ship from D which had a defective iron ladder leading to the hold; the ladder gave way injuring an employee. Here it was said that the 'slightest inspection' would have disclosed the ladder's dangerous condition.
7   [1982] AC 225.
8   [1968] 1 WLR 37, 43.

put on enquiry and *ought* to discover the defect but, if this notion exists in this context, it must be limited severely for, otherwise, S has a ready means to escape liability for his warranty. The point was raised in *Dobell (G C) & Co Ltd v Barber and Garratt*,[9] where S sold to B a quantity of linseed cake from India which was contaminated with poisonous castor seed. S knew that the linseed cake was to be re-sold as cattle food. B resold the cakes to dealers and there was a further sub-sale to buyers whose cattle were poisoned after eating the feed. It was well known that, in India, the same presses were used to crush linseed and castor seed and they were not always cleaned thoroughly after the crushing of castor seed. S had made a futile attempt to disclaim responsibility[10] for the analysis of the cake but he argued that the disclaimer, and B's knowledge that castor seed could find its way from the presses into the linseed cakes put B on enquiry, meaning that he should have conducted his own analysis before reselling the goods. This argument was accepted by Roche J at first instance and, although he held that B was entitled to damages based on the defective quality of the linseed cake, he disallowed B's claim against S for the amount of damages which B had paid to his sub-buyer. The Court of Appeal rejected the notion that B should have tested the goods and held that B was entitled to rely on S's warranty of fitness without any further analysis. B thus recovered from S the amount of damages which B had paid to his sub-buyer. Greer LJ dissented, however, and considered that B should have had the cake analysed before reselling it as B had 'reason to doubt the soundness of the goods and [did not] take the appropriate steps to resolve that doubt'.[11]

In *Lambert v Lewis*, above, B had *actual* knowledge that the locking mechanism of the coupling was damaged and this put him on enquiry so that he should have inspected the coupling to ascertain whether or not it was safe to use. The decision thus does not broach directly the issue of when B might reasonably be put on enquiry but it is arguably implicit from Lord Diplock's speech that circumstances may arise where B is on enquiry such that S will not be liable for further loss which, under the rules of mitigation, B might reasonably have avoided.

The defect in the goods can be discovered only by using them

There can be no argument that B failed to discover a defect in the goods where such a defect can be revealed only by the use of the goods by B, his sub-buyer or the ultimate buyer. In *Hammond & Co v Bussey*,[12] S, a coal merchant, sold 'steam coal' to B, a shipping agent, knowing that B intended to resell the coal for use in steamships. B resold the coal under substantially the same description to the sub-buyer, the owner of steamships, but it was not reasonably fit for use as steam coal. S admitted his liability to pay B the damages which B had paid to the sub-buyer and it was held that B could also recover from S the costs of defending an action by the sub-buyer. The court stressed that the fact that the coal was unfit for its purpose 'was not a fact which would be patent to [B] on inspection of the coal; it could only be found out when it came to be used'.[13]

---

9 [1931] 1 KB 219.
10 The sale was regulated by the Fertilisers and Feeding Stuffs Act 1926, s 2(2) of which prevented contracting-out of the warranty.
11 [1931] 1 KB 219 at 247.
12 (1887) 20 QBD 79.
13 (1887) 20 QBD 79 at 86, per Lord Esher MR; see also *Kasler and Cohen v Slavouski* [1928] 1 KB 78 (presence of antimony in a rabbit fur collar could be discovered only when it was worn by a sub-buyer who contracted dermatitis); *George Mitchell (Chesterhall) Ltd v Finney Lock Seeds Ltd* [1983] 2 AC 803.

CLAIMS FOR THE BUYER'S LOSS OF PROFIT

If, at the date of contract, S knew or ought reasonably to have contemplated that B intended to use the goods to make a profit, and S's breach of his undertaking as to quality or description thwarts B's profit-making activities, B may recover damages from S for those lost profits. Where B could put the goods to several different uses, it is unclear whether S must know or reasonably contemplate the exact category of use from which B has lost profits or whether it is sufficient that B's use of the goods is within a range of possible uses, the entire range being within S's reasonable contemplation. The question here is one of remoteness. In *Bunting v Tory*,[14] B, a farmer, bought a Friesian bull at an auction of pedigree cattle and intended that the bull would be used for breeding purposes, although S was not informed of that fact. The auction catalogue, which provided that all statements therein were the responsibility of S, stated that the butter fat content of the milk of the bull's dam was 4.5% whereas it was 3.5%. B discovered the error three years later and claimed that there was a blot on the pedigree of every calf sired by the bull; accordingly he sought to recover the loss in value of the bull's progeny during the three years after the sale. Hilbery J held that B was entitled only to the normal measure of damages in s 53(3), viz the difference between the value of the bull at the time of delivery and the value it would have had if the statement in the catalogue had been correct. B was not entitled to damages corresponding to the lost value of the progeny as the judge held that S did not know that B intended to use the bull for breeding and B might have bought the bull, for example, to make 'a quick profit on resale'.[15] *Bunting* is criticisable in that Hilbery J considered that a person buying a bull of 14 or 15 months old was 'likely to be buying it for breeding purposes'[16] and, consequently, the decision does not harmonise with one decision in which B recovered damages (for physical loss) where the use to which he put the goods was only one from a range of ordinary, possible uses[17] and another leading decision where B's use was not regarded as the principal use of the goods.[18] The latter view must surely be preferable: in *Bunting*, B could presumably use the pedigree bull for two purposes only, viz breeding or resale, and both of these must have been within S's reasonable contemplation at the date of contract.

Perhaps the commonest case where B claims loss of profits is where he intends to manufacture something from the goods which he has bought and, at the date of contract, S knew or ought reasonably to have contemplated that fact. In *Richard Holden Ltd v Bostock & Co Ltd*,[19] B, a firm of brewers, bought sugar from S for brewing beer but the sugar suplied contained arsenic and B had to

---

14   (1948) 64 TLR 353.
15   (1948) 64 TLR 353 at 354.
16   (1948) 64 TLR 353 at 354.
17   *Bostock & Co Ltd v Nicholson & Sons Ltd* [1904] 1 KB 725 (sale of sulphuric acid warranted free from arsenic from which B made brewing sugar which was sold to brewers; the presence of arsenic rendered the beer poisonous. Although suphuric acid was used for a 'great variety of purposes', its use in food products was regarded as 'a well-recognised and ordinary use' (p 736 per Bruce J) and S was liable for the price of the acid and the other spoilt ingredients (but not the amount of damages which B paid to the brewers, see below)).
18   *Henry Kendall & Sons v William Lillico & Sons Ltd* [1969] 2 AC 31 (foodstuff for cattle or poultry which B used for pheasants); see also *Ashington Piggeries Ltd v Christopher Hill Ltd* [1972] AC 441.
19   (1902) 18 TLR 317.

destroy large quantities of beer which had been brewed using the sugar. S's argument that damages should be limited to the costs of making an equivalent amount of fresh beer was rejected and the Court of Appeal held that B could recover the market value of the beer which had to be destroyed, this value being held to include the profit that B would have made on its sale.[20]

It is apparent from the facts of the *Holden* case, above, that B may recover the profits that he would have made under a sub-sale (or potential sub-sale) provided that S knew that B intended to resell the goods and it was within his reasonable contemplation that delivery of defective goods would be not unlikely to cause B to lose the profit on the sub-sale.[1]

It is also important to consider B's loss of general business profits where the sale is one of defective, profit-earning goods. In *Cullinane v British Rema Manufacturing Co Ltd*,[2] B purchased a clay pulverising plant from S who warranted that it would pulverise B's clay at a specified rate. When it failed to do so, B claimed damages for (i) the capital expended in installing the plant; and (ii) the loss of business profits for a period of three years from the date of installation until the date of trial (the estimated useful life of the plant was, however, ten years). The Court of Appeal held (Morris LJ dissenting) that B could not recover damages for both these heads of loss even though the claim for loss of profits was for three years only and not for the full ten years' life of the plant. Consequently, it was held that B must elect between the two claims and thus either be restored to a pre-contractual position (ie recover the capital outlay, his reliance interest) or be put forward as if the contract had been properly performed (ie recover the lost profit, his expectancy interest). The court was at pains to ensure that B did not obtain a double recovery[3] but all the judgments assume that, as a general principle, B is entitled to claim for the loss of business profits where it is in the contemplation of the parties that the goods sold will be used to yield a profit.[4] Such a claim for loss of profits is, of course, subject to B's duty to take reasonable steps to mitigate his loss. It may often be reasonable for B to use a defective machine, for example, for a reasonable period after delivery in order to see if it performs in accordance with its warranty. Once it is apparent that the machine does not match its warranty, a reasonable course of action in mitigation of loss might be the purchase of a replacement machine and, if B fails to follow such a course, his claim for any further loss of profits will be denied. Moreover, should the replacement machine prove superior to the existing machine thereby generating greater profits, these must be taken into account in quantifying B's damages.[5] In *Cullinane*, the argument that B should have bought other machinery to mitigate his loss was rejected: this would have been unreasonable as B would have had to buy more than two machines to obtain a

---

20 See also *Wagstaff v Shorthorn Dairy Co* (1884) Cab & El 324 (sale of inferior seed potatoes which resulted in an inferior crop. B's damages were assessed as the difference between the market value value of the crop which would have resulted had the seed answered to its warranty and the inferior crop which actually resulted); *Ashworth v Wells* (1898) 14 TLR 227 (considered above).
1 See also *Molling & Co v Dean and Son Ltd* (1901) 18 TLR 217 (considered in Ch 23 on rejection) where B recovered the loss of profit on the sub-sale.
2 [1954] 1 QB 292.
3 See Macleod, 'Damages: Reliance or Expectancy Interest' [1970] JBL 19; Stoljar, 'Normal, Elective and Preparatory Damages in Contract' (1975) 91 LQR 68.
4 See [1954] 1 QB 292, Evershed MR (p 303), Jenkins LJ (p 308) and Morris LJ (p 316).
5 See *British Westinghouse Electric and Manufacturing Co Ltd v Underground Electric Railways Co of London Ltd* [1912] AC 673.

product at the rate warranted by S and he would have incurred the expense of dismantling the existing plant and, probably, having to enlarge his premises to accommodate the new machinery.

Finally, where it is within the reasonable contemplation of S and B that S's supply of defective goods might lead to B's customers withdrawing their business from B meaning that no 'repeat orders' are given, damages may be awarded for the resultant loss in profits. In *GKN Centrax Gears Ltd v Matbro Ltd*,[6] S sold defective drive axle assemblies to B who fitted them in fork lift trucks and sold them to customers. The trucks regularly broke down and this led to a loss of of repeat orders. The Court of Appeal was unanimous in holding that damages were recoverable for the loss of these repeat orders from existing customers.[7] Moreover, damages are not limited in amount to the loss of custom actually proved by customers who give evidence that they would not give repeat orders; instead, the court can 'draw inferences from the evidence called as to the probable extent of the total loss of business resulting from the original seller's breach of contract and must make its own moderate estimate without attempting perfect compensation'.[8]

PHYSICAL INJURY CAUSED TO THE BUYER OR HIS PROPERTY

In accordance with general principles, B may recover damages for injury to his person or property caused by the defective goods if it was in the parties' reasonable contemplation at the date of contract that breach of S's obligations was not unlikely to cause such loss. Also, B does not have to prove that S ought to have contemplated the details of the loss if he can contemplate that damage of the *kind* or *type* that has occurred was not unlikely and, if this requirement is satisfied, S need not have contemplated the *extent* of the loss. The application of these principles in the sale of goods means that B may recover substantial damages for personal injury where the intrinsic value of the goods is minimal. In *Godley v Perry*,[9] for example, the child who lost an eye when a defective catapult costing 6d snapped in use, recovered £2,500 in damages and, in *Grant v Australian Knitting Mills Ltd*,[10] B recovered substantial damages from S for the life-threatening dermatitis which developed and was caused by the excess sulphites in the woollen underpants which he had bought. The damages for personal injury or death may include compensation for loss of earnings, pain, suffering, discomfort and the loss of faculty, such as the destruction of B's eye in *Godley*.[11]

---

6 [1976] 2 Lloyd's Rep 555.
7 See [1976] 2 Lloyd's Rep 555, Lord Denning MR (pp 573-574), Stephenson LJ (p 577) and Bridge LJ (p 580).
8 [1976] 2 Lloyd's Rep 555 at 578, per Stephenson LJ; see also *Aerial Advertising Co v Batchelor's Peas Ltd (Manchester)* [1938] 2 All ER 788 (the defendants (D) employed the plaintiff (P) to fly an aeroplane trailing an advertising banner which read 'Eat Batchelor's Peas'. In breach of contract, P managed the incredible feat of flying with the banner over the crowded town square of Salford during the two minutes' silence on Armistice Day. Hardly surprisingly, this resulted in a vigorous denunciation of D's products and a marked drop in their sales. Although Atkinson J had difficulty in putting a figure on lost sales, he awarded damages for loss of profits).
9 [1960] 1 WLR 9.
10 [1936] AC 85; see also *Geddling v Marsh* [1920] 1 KB 668; *Morelli v Fitch & Gibbons* [1928] 2 KB 636.
11 [1960] 1 WLR 9, 13 per Edmund Davies J.

If it is in the reasonable contemplation of S and B that the goods will be used by members of B's family and it is not unlikely that the defective goods would injure them, B may recover damages for pecuniary loss caused to him by the injuries. In *Jackson v Watson & Sons*,[12] B bought tinned salmon from S, a grocer, which was unfit for human consumption and, as a consequence of eating it, B became ill and his wife died. B recovered damages for the medical and funeral expenses he had paid and for the loss of his wife's services which, particularly as B had a family of seven small children, meant that he had been obliged to hire servants to perform such services.[13] Although these decisions concern injury and death to the buyers' wives, it also seems that damages may be recovered for injury caused to other members of B's 'household'.[14]

Where the defective goods cause damage to B's other property, his damages may include compensation for such a loss provided that it was within the reasonable contemplation of both S and B that it was not unlikely that the defective goods would cause loss of the type or kind which has occurred. In *Borradaile v Brunton*,[15] for example, B bought from S a chain cable for an anchor. The chain cable was defective and snapped in use causing the loss of both cable and anchor. It was held that, in addition to the value of the cable, B could recover the value of the lost anchor. There are numerous other cases in which it has been held that B may recover damages for loss of, or damage to, his other property caused by the defective goods.[16] In these cases, B was adopting either the ordinary use of the goods or one use from a range of ordinary uses[17] even if it was not the predominant use,[18] and damages would thus be within the first rule in *Hadley v Baxendale*.[19] But if B puts the goods to some *special* use and damage to other property results, S will be liable only if, before contract, he has been informed of B's intended use.

---

12 [1909] 2 KB 193.
13 See also *Preist v Last* [1903] 2 KB 148 (defective hot-water bottle which burst in use scalding B's wife. B recovered the medical expenses incurred in the treatment of his wife); *Frost v Aylesbury Dairy Co Ltd* [1905] 1 KB 608 (typhoid germs in milk; B recovered the expenses in relation to the illness and death of his wife).
14 See *Square v Model Farm Dairies (Bournemouth) Ltd* [1939] 2 KB 365 (typhoid germs in milk; B, a solicitor, seemingly recovered expenses for 'assistance' rendered to his wife, children, niece and the children's governess while they were ill: see pp 367, 371 and Slesser LJ at p 374).
15 (1818) 8 Taunt 535.
16 See *Smith v Green* (1875) 1 CPD 92 (cow sold to B, a farmer, with a warranty that it was free from foot and mouth disease. B placed the cow in his herd. B recovered the value of the cows which died); *Randall v Newson* (1877) 2 QBD 102 (S, a coach builder, supplied B with a pole for his carriage which broke in use and the horses were injured. B recovered compensation both for the value of the pole and the injury to the horses); *Bostock & Co Ltd v Nicholson & Sons Ltd* [1904] 1 KB 725 (sale of sulphuric acid warranted free from arsenic which was used by B in making brewing sugar which was then sold to brewers. The acid contained arsenic and B recovered the price of the (worthless) acid and the value of the other spoilt ingredients); *Wilson v Rickett Cockerell & Co Ltd* [1954] 1 QB 598 ('coalite' containing a detonator exploded in B's fireplace damaging the room and furnishings); *Henry Kendall & Sons v William Lillico & Sons Ltd* [1969] 2 AC 31 (animal feed containing a toxic substance sold to game farmers and fed to pheasants. Many of the pheasants died and others grew up stunted. B recovered the value of the lost birds and the reduced value of the surviving birds).
17 As in *Bostock & Co Ltd v Nicholson & Sons Ltd* [1904] 1 KB 725 (above) where making brewing sugar was one ordinary use of the acid.
18 As in *Henry Kendall & Sons v William Lillico & Sons Ltd* [1969] 2 AC 31 (above) where the food could be fed to cattle, poultry or pheasants.
19 (1854) 9 Exch 341.

A somewhat difficult decision concerning damage to B's other property occurred in *Parsons (H) (Livestock) Ltd v Uttley Ingham & Co Ltd*.[20] B, a pig farmer, bought from S a storage hopper for pig nuts which were to be fed to his top-grade pig herd. B's requirements were known to S at the date of contract and S agreed to install the hopper. When S supplied the hopper, he failed to open the ventilator on the top but this was not noticed later as the top of the hopper was 28 feet above the ground. The result was that the nuts dispensed by the hopper were mouldy but, as B did not think that the mouldy nuts would be harmful, he continued to feed them to the pigs. In fact, pigs fed with the nuts became ill with a rare intestinal infection and 254 of them subsequently died, causing loss to B of between £20,000 and £30,000. Swanwick J held that S was in breach of the SGA implied condition of fitness for purpose and, as this was an 'absolute warranty', S was liable for all loss resulting from the breach whether or not this was within the parties' reasonable contemplation. In case he was wrong on this point, the judge added that neither party could reasonably have contemplated at the date of contract that there was a serious possibility that feeding mouldy nuts to the pigs would cause illness. Under this second finding, the loss suffered by B would be too remote and thus irrecoverable.

The Court of Appeal did not agree with the judge's view of the 'absolute warranty' theory and thus the crucial issue was whether the loss was too remote. The majority of the Court of Appeal ruled that damages were recoverable for breach of contract where, at the date of contract, the parties would have contemplated as a serious possibility[1] the type of consequence, not necessarily the specific consequence, that ensued upon breach of contract. It was thus unnecessary for B to establish that S ought reasonably to have contemplated the serious possibility that the pigs would die from eating mouldy nuts. Instead, it was held that it must have been within the contemplation of S and B that injury to the pigs was a serious possibility if the *hopper* was unfit for storing pig nuts and so S was liable for the whole of the loss even though the quantum was greater than the parties might have contemplated. Scarman LJ stressed that the correct enquiry was 'what is likely to happen to the pigs if the hopper is unfit for storing nuts suitable to be fed to them' rather than 'what is likely to happen if the nuts are mouldy'.[2] There are two controversial aspects of this decision. First, it must be asked whether the rare intestinal infection (E coli) which the pigs contracted was of the type or kind which could reasonably have been contemplated as a serious possibility or whether it was different in type. Although it is not easy to make this distinction, it is respectfully submitted that the decision is correct: once it is acknowledged that serious illness could be contemplated, it is plain that the illness which resulted was different in gravity and extent but not type. Second, as Goode[3] points out, S's breach was defined in the broadest possible terms as being the sale of a hopper which was unfit for its purpose within the SGA. Faced with Swanwick J's finding that neither party could reasonably have contemplated

20   [1978] QB 791.
 1   Lord Denning MR considered that the higher degree of foreseeability postulated by the majority (Orr and Scarman LJJ) and based upon *Koufos v C Czarnikow Ltd, The Heron II* [1969] 1 AC 350, applied only where the claim was for purely financial loss and, where the claim was for physical damage, it was enough if S could have foreseen a 'slight possibility' (p 804) that eating mouldy pig nuts would cause illness to the pigs. He thus agreed that S was liable but via the application of this test.
 2   [1978] QB 791 at 812.
 3   *Commercial Law* (2nd edn, 1995), p 408.

at the date of contract that there was a serious possibility that feeding mouldy nuts to the pigs would cause illness, the Court of Appeal's reasoning shifts the emphasis from the particular breach (closed ventilator) to the indefinite breach of condition (goods not reasonably fit for their purpose) when deciding upon the consequences which flow naturally from that breach. It is thus arguable that this is too imprecise a yardstick for determining S's liability. It does seem, however, that the Court of Appeal's analysis ought to lead to the same conclusion as that reached by Swanwick J in that the supply of a hopper which was unfit for its purpose would lead naturally to the nuts within it being mouldy: in this way the Court of Appeal simply deletes the second, and arguably crucial, stage of the enquiry. It is clear that, when the *Parsons* analysis of remoteness is combined with the onerous duties which S owes under the SGA implied conditions relating to fitness and quality, B is placed in an extremely advantageous position.

COMPENSATION PAID TO A SUB-BUYER

The problem envisaged here is that S may be in breach of his undertakings relating to the condition of the goods and B may resell the goods on the same terms to a sub-buyer. If B has paid damages to the sub-buyer, may he recover that amount from S? It is tolerably clear from the cases on 'string contracts' (considered later) and the decision in *Hammond & Co v Bussey*[4] (the facts of which were considered earlier) that B may do so but, in *Hammond*, S admitted his liability to pay B the damages which B had paid to his sub-buyer. Nevertheless, the judgment of Bowen LJ in *Hammond* supports the view that B may recover from S the damages paid to the sub-buyer provided that, at the date of contract, the parties could reasonably contemplate that (i) B would, or probably would, resell the goods; (ii) the resale would, or probably would, contain the same or similar undertakings relating to condition; and (iii) it was not unlikely that S's breach would cause B to be in breach to his sub-buyer who would consequently claim damages from B.

Likewise, if these conditions are met and B has reasonably incurred costs in defending the claim brought by the sub-buyer, B may recover from S the costs paid to the successful sub-buyer and also the costs of his own defence. It is thus essential to decide when it is reasonable for B to incur costs in defending the sub-buyer's claim. In *Hammond*, B's invidious position between S and the sub-B was accentuated – as the defect in the goods could be discovered only in use (coal for steamships), B was in no position to ascertain whether the goods met their description. Should B accept the sub-buyer's assertion that the goods were defective and submit to the claim or, on the other hand, was it reasonable for B to defend the claim? It was stressed that, on these facts, it would not have been reasonable for B to submit to judgment and the reasonableness of B's position was reinforced in that he informed S of the impending claim and S insisted that the coal supplied was in accordance with the contract. Accordingly, it was held that B could recover from S the costs reasonably incurred in defending the (successful) sub-buyer's claim.[5]

---

4 (1887) 20 QBD 79.
5 See also *Sydney Bennett Ltd v Kreeger* (1925) 41 TLR 609 (B obtained as damages from S the costs incurred in B's defending the sub-B's successful claim for physical injury caused by a coat sold by B. Again, B's defence was reasonable as, when he was informed of the position, S denied liability but did not suggest that B would have no defence to the action).

It would, however, be unreasonable for B to defend the claim if he was told by S that such a defence was pointless[6] or if the goods were returned to B by the sub-buyer so that B might himself ascertain whether or not they complied with the contract.[7]

Finally, it is clear from the Court of Appeal's decision in *Biggin & Co Ltd v Permanite Ltd*,[8] that if litigation between B and the sub-buyer should have been in the reasonable contemplation of S and B at the date of contract, it 'would be unfortunate if they were not also held to contemplate reasonable settlements'.[9] In *Biggin*, B acted on legal advice and settled the sub-buyer's claim for £43,000 and it was held that B could recover that amount from S in damages. The onus is on B to establish a *prima facie* case that the settlement is reasonable and the fact of legal advice is relevant in this respect but S may also attempt to establish that B was not liable to pay anything to the sub-buyer or adduce evidence that the settlement was unreasonable.

Compensation paid to sub-buyers in 'string contracts'

The situation to be considered here is one where S is in breach of his contract with B as regards the description or condition of the goods and B resells the goods on the same terms to a sub-buyer, who then resells to another sub-buyer, so that eventually a lengthy 'string' of contracts results for the sale of the selfsame, defective goods. Here each sub-buyer will sue his immediate seller in the string so that, finally, B will pay damages and costs to the first sub-buyer for breach of B's undertaking. May B then recover that amount from S? It is clear that B may do so provided that it was within the reasonable contemplation of S and B at the date of contract that (i) B intended to resell or would probably resell and that, in turn, his sub-buyer would probably resell so that a string of contracts is established of the same goods; (ii) each sub-sale would, or probably would, contain the same or similar terms as to the description or condition of the goods; (iii) it was not unlikely that S's breach would cause B and each sub-buyer to be in breach of his obligations; and (iv) it was not unlikely that liability would be passed up the string of contracts. In *Pinnock Bros v Lewis and Peat Ltd*,[10] for example, S sold a quanity of East African copra cake to B. B resold it to sub-buyers who sold it to dealers and they, in turn, sold it to farmers who fed it to cattle. Roche J's finding of fact was that it was within the contemplation of the parties that the copra cake would be used only for cattle food. The copra cake was so contaminated with castor beans that it was poisonous and the cattle became ill. Each party, starting with the farmer, sued his immediate seller and it was held that, at the end of the string, B could recover from S the damages and costs which he had been obliged to pay to his sub-buyer. Provided the conditions referred to above are met, it does not matter how many sub-sales occur in the string.[11]

---

6 *Hammond & Co v Bussey* (1887) 20 QBD 79, 90 per Lord Esher MR.
7 See *Wrightup v Chamberlain* (1839) 7 Scott 598 (horse returned to B by sub-B). Also, it was stessed earlier that, when B knows that the goods are defective *before the resale*, he cannot increase S's liability by reselling the goods to a sub-B and then making S liable for B's liability to that sub-B. Here B should inform the sub-buyer of the defects either before the resale or after it, if it is only then that he gains knowledge of the defects.
8 [1951] 2 KB 314.
9 [1951] 2 KB 314 at 321-322, per Somervell LJ.
10 [1923] 1 KB 690; see also *Dobell (G C) & Co Ltd v Barber and Garratt* [1931] 1 KB 219 (considered above).
11 See *Kasler and Cohen v Slavouski* [1928] 1 KB 78, 85 per Branson J; *Biggin & Co Ltd v Permanite Ltd* [1951] 1 KB 422, 432 per Devlin J.

When B is liable to the sub-buyer in this way, B may also recover from S the *total* costs incurred by himself and all the other sub-buyers in the string, provided that the sub-buyers acted reasonably in incurring the costs. The cumulative costs in a long string can be substantial, as illustrated by *Kasler and Cohen v Slavouski.*[12] S sold dyed rabbit skins to B, a wholesale furrier, knowing that B intended to make them into fur collars. There were then four sub-sales, (viz, B–>C, C–>D, D–>E, E–>F) and the final buyer of a coat (F) contracted dermatitis from the fur collar which contained antimony. The skins were thus unfit for the purpose of being made into fur collars. B recovered from S (i) the damages and costs which E paid to F; and (ii) the costs of each of the intervening parties in the string. Thus, although the damages recovered by F were £67, B succeeded in his claim against S for over £650. The buyers in the string must act reasonably in incurring the costs and this is a question of fact which depends on the circumstances at the time that each party must make a decision, but it is clearly wise to seek legal advice. In *Kasler*, only the draper (E) who sold the coat to F contested the claim, the other parties in the string paying the respective claims but incurring small non-action costs. It thus had to be decided whether E's defence of the action was reasonable. F was prepared to settle for £50 but then an analyst's report stated that the collar was free from any harmful substance. It was thus held to be quite proper and reasonable for E to fight the case.

A difficult issue of causation in string contracts is whether, in order to keep the string intact, the warranties in all the sub-sales must be identical to that in the first sale between S and B. If the warranty is varied materially, there may be a claim for damages which could not be contemplated by the original seller and for which he should not be liable. In *Dexters Ltd v Hill Crest Oil Co (Bradford) Ltd,*[13] Scrutton LJ considered that the undertakings in the contracts should be the same for, otherwise, the sum recovered in the last contract in the string could not be regarded as the measure of damages for breach of the first contract. There the goods were described in the first contract as 'dark cotton seed grease as per sample No 9536' but in the last contract the description had changed to 'black cotton seed grease', the latter being more valuable and thus commanding a higher price. Scrutton LJ's *dictum* is regarded as being overly-restrictive and, in an earlier decision,[14] B recovered against S even though the goods were described differently in a sub-sale. The matter was broached by Devlin J in *Biggin & Co Ltd v Permanite Ltd,*[15] who, adopting Scrutton LJ's basic principle, went on to consider what degree of variation in description would break the chain of contracts. He stressed that Scrutton LJ was dealing with a chain of contracts between merchants where one might expect the same specification to be used but, for example, a builder when making a contract for repair with a householder will not recite all the warranties which he may have received from his supplier in respect of materials which he may use. Accordingly, the principle might be applied very differently according to whether the injury for which the defendant is being asked to pay is a market loss or physical damage. In the former case, any variation which is more than a matter of words is likely to be fatal because

---

12 [1928] 1 KB 78.
13 [1926] 1 KB 348.
14 *British Oil and Cake Co Ltd v Burstall & Co* (1923) 39 TLR 406 (in a string contract for the sale of copra cake, the fact of its being resold as 'free from castor' did not preclude the recovery of damages as copra cake which is not free from castor cannot be described as copra cake and so nothing was added by the description).
15 [1951] 1 KB 422, 433-434.

there is no way of telling its effect on market value but, in the latter case, the nature of the physical damage will show whether the variation was material or not. The upshot would appear to be that, if a sub-buyer in the string alters the description of the goods or varies the original warranty, the original seller should still be liable provided that the loss or injury sustained by the buyer at the end of the chain was caused by a defect which was within both the scope of the original seller's warranty and the variations superimposed in the sub-sales. Devlin J's illustration was of an original warranty that goods could safely be used for one year after manufacture with a sub-buyer's additional warranty that they could safely be used for two years: if the injurious consequences occurred within one year, the additional warranty ought not to bar the claim.[16]

Finally, in string contracts where sub-sales are within the contemplation of the parties, Devlin J held in the *Biggin*[17] case, above, that B's damages must be assessed by reference to the sub-sales 'whether [he] likes it or not'.[18] Thus, although the measure of damages in s 53(3) (the difference between the value of the defective goods and their value if they had complied with the warranty) might yield substantial damages for B, if it is B's 'liability to the ultimate user that is contemplated as the measure of damage and if in fact [the goods are] used without injurious results so that no such liability arises, [B] could not claim the difference in market value, and say that the subsale must be disregarded'.[19] This approach was followed in *Bence Graphics International Ltd v Fasson UK Ltd*,[20] where it was held that S and B contemplated the measure of damages for defects in the goods should be the extent of B's liability to subsequent users of the defective goods (£22,000) rather than the decreased market value of the defective goods (£564,328).

COMPENSATION PAID TO STRANGERS

It may have been within the reasonable contemplation of S and B at the date of contract that, if the goods delivered by S were defective, it is not unlikely that personal injury to a third party (T) or damage to his property could result from the defect. If it was also not unlikely that B would be held liable to compensate T for his loss, B can recover from S the damages and costs which he has had to pay to T together with B's own costs incurred in reasonably defending T's claim. Surprisingly, there are no decisions which are direct authority for this rule but it was approved by the House of Lords in *Lambert v Lewis*[1] and, if that case had not been dominated by B's discovery of the damage to the goods, it would undoubtedly have applied on the facts. The other significant decisions[2] in support of this rule were considered earlier but they concern a supply of goods to be used by the plaintiff and his employees rather than a sale of goods. B's liability

---

16 Devlin J's approach was approved by Auld LJ in *Bence Graphics International Ltd v Fasson UK Ltd* [1998] QB 87 where, on the facts, there were no material differences in the contracts in the chain which would have put damage claimed at any point in the chain outside the imputed contemplation of the original S and B.
17 [1951] 1 KB 422.
18 [1951] 1 KB 422 at 436.
19 [1951] 1 KB 422 at 436.
20 [1998] QB 87.
 1 [1982] AC 225 (considered above).
 2 *Mowbray v Merryweather* [1895] 2 QB 640; *Scott v Foley, Aikman & Co* (1899) 16 TLR 55.

to T in this situation will usually be in tort but the liability could be contractual (under a contract of employment, for example). Also, there is little doubt that the rule would apply to a reasonable out-of-court settlement made with T.[3]

CLAIMS FOR ADDITIONAL EXPENSES, INCONVENIENCE AND DISAPPOINTMENT

If it was within the reasonable contemplation of the parties at the date of contract that B was not unlikely to incur additional expenses if S delivered defective goods, B may recover from S the reasonable amount of such expenses which he has incurred, or have been wasted, as a result of S's breach. There are numerous examples of B's recovery of such expenses in the decisions considered earlier. In *Smith v Johnson*,[4] S, a builder, sold mortar to B which was so defective that the building in which it was used was condemned and so it had to be demolished and rebuilt. Bruce J held that the costs of demolition, rebuilding and loss of ground rent were recoverable from S. Similarly, where S supplied defective steam turbines, B recovered damages for the extra coal which was consumed during the period when they were used.[5]

It is probable that B may recover *pre-contractual* expenditure if it was in the reasonable contemplation of the parties at the date of contract as not unlikely to be wasted in the event of S's breach in delivering defective goods, but neither of the decisions on this issue concerns the sale of goods.[6]

In one case, where it was within the reasonable contemplation of the parties at the date of contract that B might be prosecuted if S supplied B with defective goods, it was held that B could recover both the fine and costs of his defence.[7] There B was not negligent but it was said that if he had been even partly negligent, damages would not have been recoverable. Later cases have introduced the question of public policy, ie if B is punished, it is contrary to public policy to allow him to recover an indemnity against the consequences of such punishment and, if damages are recovered, the purpose of the law is defeated.[8] It is thus likely that, provided B is neither negligent nor has *mens rea*, he should recover damages against S for the fine.

---

3 A settlement was made in *Mowbray v Merryweather* (above) and in *Biggin & Co Ltd v Permanite Ltd* [1951] 2 KB 314, B recovered from S the amount of a settlement made with the sub-B (see above).
4 (1899) 15 TLR 179.
5 *British Westinghouse Electric and Manufacturing Co Ltd v Underground Electric Railways Co of London Ltd* [1912] AC 673; see also *Molling & Co v Dean & Son Ltd* (1901) 18 TLR 217 (sale of books which S knew were to be shipped to a sub-buyer in the USA. The sub-B rejected the defective goods and B recovered the costs of the shipment to and from the USA: the outward voyage was wasted expense and the return voyage was an additional expense caused by the breach).
6 See *Anglia Television Ltd v Reed* [1972] 1 QB 60 (plaintiffs recovered the whole of the wasted expenditure in relation to the preparation of a television play when the defendant/actor repudiated the contract and no substitute could be found); *Lloyd v Stanbury* [1971] 1 WLR 535 (S wrongfully refused to convey land to B and B recovered the costs of removing a caravan from the land which, under the contract, B had provided for S until a bungalow could be built for S on the land).
7 *Cointat v Myham & Son* [1913] 2 KB 220 (food unfit for human consumption in B's shop); revsd on another ground (1914) 30 TLR 282.
8 *Leslie (R) Ltd v Reliable Advertising and Addressing Agency* [1915] 1 KB 652; *Askey v Golden Wine Co Ltd* [1948] 2 All ER 35; *Payne v Ministry of Food* (1953) 103 L Jo 141. This does not apply if B is acquitted, see *Proops v W H Chaplin & Co* (1920) 37 TLR 112.

Finally, in sales of defective goods to consumers, where the goods are intended for use and enjoyment, B may recover damages for inconvenience and disappointment. In *Jackson v Chrysler Acceptances Ltd*,[9] B took a new Chrysler Hunter car on hire-purchase terms from the defendants after informing them that he intended to use it for a forthcoming holiday in France. The car broke down on numerous occasions and needed many new parts including a clutch, camshaft and radiator. The car was found to be unmerchantable and B recovered damages both for the defective car and the spoilt holiday. Likewise, in *Bernstein v Pamson Motors (Golders Green) Ltd*,[10] B bought a new Nissan Laurel car from S and, some 40 miles into its first significant journey, the engine seized and would not restart. It was beyond doubt that the car was unmerchantable and Rougier J held that B could recover the cost of wasted petrol, the costs incurred by B and his wife who had to return home by alternative transport, an amount for the loss of the use of the car while it was being repaired and damages for 'a totally spoilt day comprising nothing but vexation'.[11]

---

9 [1978] RTR 474.
10 [1987] 2 All ER 220.
11 [1987] 2 All ER 220 at 231. See also *Gascoigne v British Credit Trust* [1978] CLY § 711 (damages obtained for expense and frustration caused by a car's breakdown in domestic use).

CHAPTER 29

Specific performance

Although an action for damages is B's principal remedy should S refuse to deliver the goods, the court has a *discretion* to award a decree of specific performance[1] to B, provided the goods are specific or ascertained. If the court orders that the contract be specifically performed, B will receive the goods which are the subject of the contract of sale.[2] The SGA, s 52 provides that specific performance is available only to B and no correlative right is given to S[3] but, of course, the performance which S usually wishes to enforce is B's payment of the price under s 49. It does seem, however, that specific performance may be ordered at the suit of S in appropriate circumstances.[4] The SGA, s 52 provides:

'(1) In any action for breach of contract to deliver specific or ascertained goods the court may, if it thinks fit, on the plaintiff's application, by its judgment or decree direct that the contract shall be performed specifically, without giving the defendant the option of retaining the goods on payment of damages.
(2) The plaintiff's application may be made at any time before judgment or decree.
(3) The judgment or decree may be unconditional, or on such terms and conditions as to damages, payment of the price and otherwise as seem just to the court.'

Specific or ascertained goods

Specific performance is available under s 52(1) only where the goods to be delivered are 'specific or ascertained'. 'Specific goods' are defined in the SGA, s 61(1) as 'goods identified and agreed on at the time a contract of sale is made and includes an undivided share, specified as a fraction or percentage, of goods

---

1 See Treitel, 'Specific Performance in the Sale of Goods' [1966] JBL 211; Sharpe, *Injunctions and Specific Performance* (1983); Jones and Goodhart, *Specific Performance* (2nd edn, 1996), pp 143-154.
2 B may be estopped from seeking specific performance after he has elected to accept damages from S: *Meng Leong Development Pte Ltd v Jip Hong Trading Pte Ltd* [1985] AC 511.
3 *Re Wait* [1927] 1 Ch 606, 617 per Lord Hanworth MR; *Shell-Mex Ltd v Elton Cop Dyeing Co Ltd* (1928) 34 Com Cas 39, 46-47 per Wright J.
4 See *Astro Exito Navegacion SA v Southland Enterprise Co Ltd (No 2)* [1982] QB 1248 (in the sale of a ship, documents to be presented by S under a letter of credit included a notice of readiness to be signed by B. B refused to sign and S commenced proceedings for specific performance. The CA upheld a mandatory injunction directing B to sign. In effect, S obtained specific performance as the order that B must perform an act which enabled S to obtain the price amounted to the same thing as specific performance. The decision was affirmed by the HL without reference to this point: [1983] 2 AC 787).

identified and agreed on as aforesaid'. The meaning of 'specific goods' was considered in some detail in Chapter 16. The latter reference in s 61(1) to the 'undivided share' is a recent addition to that section[5] and was introduced at the same time as the reform of the law relating to ownership in common of unascertained goods in an identified bulk.[6] This extended defintion of specific goods means that specific performance could be ordered in a contract to sell a *fraction or percentage* from a bulk of goods provided that the bulk is identified and agreed on at the date of contract (eg half the cargo of wheat aboard a specific, named ship). It should be stressed that, where there is contract to sell a specified *quantity* from an identified bulk (eg 300 tons of wheat from the cargo aboard a specific, named ship), the new rules on co-ownership may apply but there can be no order for specific performance as the goods are not specific goods within s 61(1). This is confirmed by the new sections of the SGA concerned with co-ownership, ie s 20A(1) refers to 'a specified quantity of unascertained goods'.

There is no definition of either 'unascertained' or 'ascertained' goods in the SGA but, working by inference from the definition of 'specific goods' in s 61(1), unascertained goods are those which are *not* identified and agreed on at the time a contract of sale is made. It follows from this that 'ascertained goods' refers to those goods which were unascertained at the date of contract but have become 'identified in accordance with the agreement after the time a contract of sale is made'.[7] It will be recalled from the consideration of the rules on the passing of property that the law demands that the individuality of the goods must be established before they can be regarded as ascertained. In *Thames Sack and Bag Co Ltd v Knowles & Co Ltd*,[8] the contract was for the sale of ten bales of Hessian bags and an invoice was sent to B, after contract, which gave the specific numbers and marks of the bales from which the ten were to be taken. Sankey J held that the goods were not ascertained for the purposes of s 52 as there had been no separation of the ten bales from the remainder. The later decision in in *Re Wait*[9] conclusively established that a contract for the sale of 500 tons of wheat which had not been separated from 1,000 tons aboard a specific vessel was a contract for the sale of unascertained goods. The goods could not possibly be classified as specific goods nor were they 'ascertained' and thus specific performance was refused.[10]

Section 52 applies whether or not the property in the goods has passed to B[11] but, where property has passed, in any proceedings for wrongful interference with the goods,[12] B may ask for an order for delivery of the goods although this remedy is within the discretion of the court.

5 Added by the Sale of Goods (Amendment) Act 1995, s 2(d).
6 See the SGA, ss 20A and 20B.
7 *Re Wait* [1927] 1 Ch 606, 630 per Atkin LJ.
8 (1918) 88 LJKB 585.
9 [1927] 1 Ch 606.
10 The new co-ownership provisions in the SGA, ss 20A and 20B would now apply to the facts of *Re Wait*. Note that the extended definition of 'specific goods' in s 61(1) does not apply to *Re Wait* as the contract was one to sell a specified *quantity* (500 tons), not a 'fraction or percentage' of the goods as specified in s 61(1).
11 *James Jones & Sons Ltd v Earl of Tankerville* [1909] 2 Ch 440, 445 per Parker J; *Re Wait* [1927] 1 Ch 606, 617 per Lord Hanworth MR; *Cohen v Roche* [1927] 1 KB 169, 180 per McCardie J.
12 Under the Torts (Interference with Goods) Act 1977, s 3.

When might specific performance be decreed?

Before the SGA, specific performance was an equitable remedy and the orthodox principle which permeates the decisions is that specific performance of a contract for the sale of goods will be refused if damages are an adequate remedy. Damages would be sufficient, of course, in 'contracts for the sale of commodities which could be ordinarily obtained in the market'[13] and, in this situation, B has a duty to make a substitute purchase of the commodities in the market and thereby mitigate his loss. Moreover, the courts have refused to allow specific performance where its decree would mean the circumvention of B's duty to mitigate his loss: if B has failed to mitigate, he will not be allowed to *profit* by being awarded specific performance when market prices have risen after the date of breach.[14] The courts have also denied specific performance to B where S is insolvent on the basis that, if B were to obtain specific performance, he would also obtain an undeserved priority over S's other creditors. It was for this reason that B sought specific performance of the contract in *Re Wait*,[15] as there S went bankrupt after B had paid the price but before the goods had become ascertained under the contract. The combination of these factors means that, in contracts for the sale of goods, specific performance is regarded as an exceptional remedy.

An important feature which may influence the court to order specific performance is the fact that the goods are 'of peculiar and practically unique value'[16] to B. In *Behnke v Bede Shipping Co Ltd*,[17] B, a German shipowner, agreed to buy a ship whose engines and boilers satisfied German regulations and which he could put into immediate service. There was only one other comparable ship in existence which would satisfy B's requirements and the evidence was that it had probably been sold. Wright J held that damages would not be an adequate compensation for B and he ordered specific performance of the contract.[18] Likewise, in *Phillips v Lamdin*,[19] the contract was for the sale of leasehold premises required for residential and professional use by B, a naturopath. S had removed from the building, some time between contract and completion, an ornate door designed by Adam, the celebrated architect. Croom-Johnson J held that damages would not be an adequate remedy and thus it was apt that the door should be reinstated 'as you cannot make a new Adam door'.[20]

In contrast, specific performance will be refused where 'the chattel is an ordinary article of commerce and of no special value or interest ... and where damages would fully compensate.'[1] In *Cohen v Roche*,[2] B failed to obtain specific performance of a set of Hepplewhite chairs bought at auction and was limited to damages for breach of contract, but the salient facts were that this was 'ordinary Hepplewhite furniture'[3] and B was a dealer who bought the chairs for

13 *Re Wait* [1927] 1 Ch 606, 630 per Atkin LJ.
14 *Buxton v Lister* (1746) 3 Atk 383, 384 per Lord Hardwicke LC; *Re Schwabacher* (1907) 98 LT 127, 128 per Parker J (sale of shares).
15 [1927] 1 Ch 606.
16 *Behnke v Bede Shipping Co Ltd* [1927] 1 KB 649, 661 per Wright J.
17 [1927] 1 KB 649.
18 On the sale of ships, see also *Marine (C N) Inc v Stena Line A/B, The Stena Nautica (No 2)* [1982] 2 Lloyd's Rep 336; *Eximenco Handels AG v Partrederiet Oro Chief, The Oro Chief* [1983] 2 Lloyd's Rep 509.
19 [1949] 2 KB 33.
20 [1949] 2 KB 33 at 41.
 1 *Whiteley Ltd v Hilt* [1918] 2 KB 808, 819 per Swinfen Eady MR.
 2 [1927] 1 KB 169.
 3 [1927] 1 KB 169 at 179, per McCardie J.

resale at a profit with no special customer in view. An overly-restrictive approach was followed in *Société des Industries Métallurgiques SA v Bronx Engineering Co Ltd*.[4] S agreed to manufacture and sell to B, a Tunisian company, an unusual machine for cutting metal which would take nine to twelve months to complete at a cost of £287,000, and would weigh 220 tons. S did not complete the machine on time and eventually told B that he had found a Canadian buyer for it. The Court of Appeal held that the machine was definitely not an ordinary article of commerce but it was not unique and thus damages would be an adequate remedy. This seems to be a particularly rigid decision in view of the fact that a replacement machine could not be obtained for another nine to twelve months, B could not effectively mitigate his loss and damages would be very difficult to quantify as the machine was required for B's business in Tunis.

The *Bronx Engineering* case does raise the question of whether the courts should be more open to the possibility of specific performance and thereby draw the remedy within the mainstream instead of its remaining within a narrow backwater. The *Bronx Engineering* decision emphasises that damages are regarded as the primary and sufficient remedy and specific performance as execeptional yet it is difficult to see why specific performance should not have been ordered on the *Bronx* facts. B was placed in an intolerable position of hardship as there could hardly be said to be an available market for the purchase of a substitute machine and, moreover, S would not have been prejudiced by an order of specific performance.

Furthermore, Treitel[5] cogently pointed out that there are cases (undoubtedly outside the scope of s 52) where specific performance might well be appropriate either because damages can be assessed but the calculation must necessarily be conjectural and elusive or where B would suffer excessive hardship if specific performance were denied. First, there are those cases where S repudiates a long-term contract to deliver goods by instalments at a price fixed at the beginning of the term and, secondly, there are 'requirement contracts' where S is in breach of an agreement to supply B with, for example, all the raw materials which B needs for a manufacturing process. In the former instalment example, it will be very difficult to forecast before the end of the period how much it will cost B to obtain a substitute and, in the case of a requirement contract, S's repudiation may leave B in a virtually helpless position. The narrow interpretation given to 'specific or ascertained goods' would mean that this type of contract would usually fall outside s 52: in *Dominion Coal Co Ltd v Dominion Iron and Steel Co Ltd*,[6] for example, the Privy Council held that specific performance could not be ordered in a contract for S to supply B with 'all the coal that [B] may require for use in its works'.

There is, however, modern authority that a court may order specific performance where damages are inadequate even where the facts are clearly beyond the scope of s 52. In *Sky Petroleum Ltd v VIP Petroleum Ltd*,[7] B agreed to buy from S his 'entire requirement' of petroleum and diesel fuel for B's filling stations, the contract to operate for ten years with a stipulation that minimum yearly quantities be supplied. At a time when the supply of petrol was restricted and B had no prospect of finding an alternative source of supply, S purported to

4 [1975] 1 Lloyd's Rep 465.
5 See Treitel, 'Specific Performance in the Sale of Goods' [1966] JBL 211, 224-229.
6 [1909] AC 293; see also *Fothergill v Rowland* (1873) LR 17 Eq 132.
7 [1974] 1 WLR 576.

terminate the contract on the basis that B had exceeded the credit provisions in the contract. B applied for an injunction to restrain S from withholding supplies of petrol. Goulding J emphasised that to grant an injunction in the terms sought would be to order specific performance of a contract to sell unascertained goods and that, normally, such an order would be refused as damages would be an adequate remedy. On the (unusual) facts, however, S was B's sole supplier and the only means by which B might continue in business and, as damages would patently be an inadequate remedy, an injunction was granted.[8] Similarly, in *Howard E Perry & Co Ltd v British Railways Board*,[9] during a steel strike in 1980 the defendant refused to allow a quantity of steel belonging to the plaintiff to be moved as it feared further industrial action by workers. The court ordered the specific delivery of the steel because, during the strike, steel was not readily available on the open market and damages would thus not compensate the plaintiffs for the difficulty in continuing with their business. Sir Robert Megarry V-C[10] stressed that damages would be a 'poor consolation if the failure of supplies forces a trader to lay off staff and disappoint his customers (whose affections may be transferred to others) and ultimately impels him towards insolvency'.

In the USA, the Uniform Commercial Code, s 2-716 (1), provides that specific performance may be ordered where the goods are unique or 'in other proper circumstances'. The comment to the section states that its object is to further 'a more liberal attitude than some courts have shown in connection with contracts of sale ... output and requirement contracts involving a particular or peculiarly available source or market present today the typical commercial specific performance situation.'

---

8 In *Re London Wine Co (Shippers) Ltd* [1986] PCC 121,149-150, Oliver J doubted that there was any power to order specific performance beyond s 52 and thought that *Sky Petroleum* did not involve a sale of goods but was 'a long-term supply contract under which successive sales would arise if orders were placed and accepted'.
9 [1980] 1 WLR 1375.
10 [1980] 1 WLR 1375 at 1383.

PART THREE

Consumer credit

CHAPTER 30

Introduction to hire-purchase and consumer credit

Historical introduction: the emergence of hire-purchase and other forms of consumer credit

It has always been common to sell goods on credit terms with the price payable by the buyer in instalments and allowing credit in this way enables businesses to sell goods which the buyer could not otherwise afford to buy outright. It is not surprising that the provision of modern consumer credit developed at the same time as the mass production of goods and, in England, hire-purchase dates principally from the second half of the 19th century. Singer sewing machines were amongst the first goods to be offered on hire-purchase terms and were particularly suited to the transaction in that the sewing machine was an asset with a long life against which money could be advanced with safety and, from the hirer's perspective, it generated income for him while he was paying-off the instalments. Unsurprisingly, traders were quick to see the advantages of hire-purchase to their businesses; other consumer durables quickly followed in the wake of sewing machines and were taken on hire-purchase terms by eager customers.[1]

Today, a hire-purchase transaction commences when a customer approaches a dealer in order to obtain goods on credit and the dealer suggests that the customer should obtain hire-purchase. The dealer and customer complete forms which amount to an offer of the dealer to sell the goods to a finance company and an offer of the customer to take back the goods on hire-purchase terms. When the finance company accepts such an offer, property in the goods passes to the finance company and, in turn, the contract of hire-purchase is completed with the customer. The customer then *hires* the goods from the finance company and the price is payable in instalments. The customer is given an *option* to purchase the goods at the end of the period of hire but he can return the goods before exercising the option and, if he defaults in paying the instalments, the goods can be re-possessed by the owner.

---

1 'The process of persuading people to incur debt, and the arrangements for them to do so, are as much a part of modern production as the making of the goods and the nurturing of wants' (J K Galbraith, *The Affluent Society* (3rd edn, 1976), p 148). For an historical account of the development of consumer credit, see *Report of the Committee on Consumer Credit* (Cmnd 4596, 1971), Vol 1, Ch 2.

The dealer is thus able to sell goods which he might not otherwise have sold outright to a buyer and, likewise, the customer is able to have possession of goods which he could not have afforded to buy on cash terms. The advantage from the finance company's point of view is that, as it retains title throughout the period of the hire-purchase agreement, it has a measure of security in the case of default by the customer but the drawback for the finance company is that it usually never sees the goods which are the subject of the hire-purchase contract and yet it is liable should those goods prove defective. It is thus plain that the finance company places great reliance on the dealer who instigates the hire-purchase.

The emergence of hire-purchase from other forms of instalment credit

Although the tripartite transaction outlined above has proven to be popular, it was quite feasible that other forms of granting credit could have performed the role which hire-purchase came to play so effectively. Various factors intervened, however, to curtail the utility of some of these other means of furnishing credit.

First, the simple form of the conditional sale could easily have accomplished the function of hire-purchase if it had taken root. In a conditional sale, the contract provides that property in the goods will not pass to the buyer unless some condition is fulfilled, the condition most frequently being that the price must be paid in full. However, in *Lee v Butler*,[2] it was held that a person who was in possession of furniture under a conditional sale agreement had 'agreed to buy' the goods within the Factors Act 1889, s 9[3] and, by virtue of that section, he could transfer a good title to a *bona fide*, third party buyer, thus defeating the seller/owner's title. The format of the conditional sale thus failed to provide the seller with effective security for the unpaid price.[4]

Second, there could have been a widespread scheme of chattel mortgage which would have functioned in much the same way as a mortgage of real property. The buyer of the goods would be allowed credit terms and have physical possession of the goods but property in the goods would be transferred to the seller with the intention that it would be re-conveyed to the buyer once the debt had been paid. The seller would thus have effective security for the debt and could seize the goods if the buyer defaulted in repaying the loan. In England, the stumbling block to the development of chattel mortgages was the Bills of Sale Acts 1878 and 1882.

A bill of sale is simply a document by which property in goods is transferred from A to B and it is used principally is in those situations where B does not obtain posession of the goods yet clearly requires some documentary evidence of title. This will obviously be the case in a chattel mortgage where a creditor lends money to a debtor on the security of the goods but the creditor has no physical possession of them. The Bills of Sale Acts 1878 and 1882 demand that,

---

2 [1893] 2 QB 318.
3 A virtually identical provision is contained in the SGA, s 25(1) (see Ch 18).
4 In *Newtons of Wembley Ltd v Williams* [1965] 1 QB 560, it was held that the buyer in possession must act *as if* he were a mercantile agent if a good title is to be transferred under the Factors Act, s 9. If this point had been taken in *Lee v Butler*, the case would have been decided differently and, as the Law Reform Committee stressed (Twelfth Report, *Transfer of Title to Chattels* (Cmnd 2958, 1966), fn to para 23), there might have been no need for the development of the system of hire-purchase as private individuals would not have been able to transfer good title as buyers in possession.

where the debtor remains in possession of the goods, such a bill of sale should be executed in a certain form and then registered. In the case of a bill of sale given by way of security for the payment of money, the 1882 Act stipulates that failure to comply with its provisions relating to form and registration renders the bill of sale void as against all creditors *and* the parties to the mortgage.[5] One significant purpose of the legislation, which is still in force, is thus to ensure that a person cannot defraud and defeat his creditors by effecting a secret mortgage of his goods to another. Being left in possession of the goods, the debtor might thus obtain credit by virtue of his apparent ownership and the mortgage would then be set up against the creditors when they sought satisfaction from the debtor. Consequently, those who extend credit to persons who have apparent ownership of goods are protected in that the Act demands the registered visibility of bills of sale which must show that the debtor has assigned the goods described therein under the mortgage with the creditor. The function of the later Act, in 1882, was to protect *debtors* from the consequences of imprudent loans at swingeing rates of interest and this protection was secured by requiring both a certain form for the bill and its registration but also by imposing restrictions on the creditor's right to seize the goods for default in payment. The 1882 Act thus performed a role analogous to that of modern consumer credit legislation.[6] Nevertheless, the rigorous formalities of the Bills of Sale Acts inhibited the growth in this country of any widespread and popular use of chattel mortgages as devices for granting credit.

However, an ingenious form of transaction was beginning to materialise as a means of eluding the Bills of Sale Acts – the contract of hire-purchase. The landmark decision in *McEntire v Crossley Bros Ltd*[7] was crucial to the development of hire-purchase in that the then novel hire-purchase transaction was freed from the shackles of the Bills of Sale Acts. There B agreed to buy a gas engine from S with payments to be made in instalments. The property in the goods was to remain in S until full payment had been made but B was allowed to have possession of the engine. If B defaulted in payment, S could seize the engine. When B became bankrupt, S claimed the engine but B's trustee in bankruptcy argued that the transaction was a void bill of sale. The House of Lords held that S must succeed and explained that the Bills of Sale Acts applied only where an *owner* of goods granted to another party a charge over goods and a right to seize them. In *McEntire*, B had never become an owner and was thus unable to grant a bill of sale. The agreement in *McEntire* was a conditional sale but, of course, the principles explained in the decision but would apply with equal force to hire-purchase as there the hirer/debtor of the goods is clearly not the owner and similarly cannot grant a bill of sale. In view of the ruthless practices

---

5 Nevertheless, the lender of the money could recover the loan, with reasonable interest only, in an action for money had and received: see *Davies v Rees* (1886) 17 QBD 408 (58% interest claimed by the lender but, as the bill of sale was unregistered and void, so was the covenant for repayment at 58%, and the court awarded interest at 5%); *North Central Wagon Finance Co Ltd v Brailsford* [1962] 1 WLR 1288.

6 This might, in one sense, have had a negative effect as the 1882 Act prohibited the use of bills of sale for loans under £30, such bills being absolutely void. This arguably led to much higher rates of interest being charged on such small loans as debtors could not grant security over their goods. In *Carringtons Ltd v Smith* [1906] 1 KB 79, 90, Channell J considered it a 'notorious fact that the Bills of Sale Act, 1882 ... had the effect ... of raising the normal rate of interest on moneylenders' bills of sale from 25 per cent. or 30 per cent., which had been about the highest before, to 60 per cent., which became the regular rate'.

7 [1895] AC 457.

of moneylenders which the Bills of Sale Act 1882 had sought to control, the *McEntire* decision was a hollow triumph for the common law's ideal of freedom of contract. The hire-purchase contract was, of course, a newly-developing device and there was little evidence at the end of the 19th century of consumers being abused at the hands of this innovative transaction. In fact, it was only in 1938 that legislation controlling hire-purchase was enacted but, by then, it was long overdue.

The *McEntire* development apart, the decision in *Lee v Butler* still meant that a buyer under a conditional sale agreement could transfer title to a *bona fide* third party, but *Lee v Butler* was distinguished in *Helby v Matthews*[8] – the seminal decision which established hire-purchase as a functional reality. There the House of Lords ruled that a hirer under a hire-purchase agreement was not a person who had 'agreed to buy' the goods as, whilst he had an *option* to buy, he was not under an *obligation* to do so. In *Helby*, the owner of a piano agreed to let it on hire, the bailee agreeing to pay monthly instalments. The terms of the agreement provided that the bailee might terminate the hiring by delivering up the piano to the owner, the bailee remaining liable for all arrears of hire charges. It was also agreed that if the bailee should punctually pay all the monthly instalments, the piano would become his sole property and that until such full payment the piano should continue to be the sole property of the owner. The bailee was given possession of the piano and he paid a few of the instalments but then he pledged it with a pawnbroker as security for an advance. The House of Lords held that on the true construction of the agreement the bailee was under no legal obligation to buy, but merely had an option either to return the piano or to become its owner by payment of all the instalments. In consequence, the bailee was not someone who had 'agreed to buy' the goods within the meaning of the Factors Act, s 9. He could not, therefore, pass any rights in the piano to a pledgee under s 9 and the owner was entitled to recover the piano from the pawnbroker. As the bailee could not transfer good title to a third party, the owner's security remained intact. *Helby* ensured the popularity of hire-purchase with businessmen and this form of trading thus began to flourish.

Abuse by traders and statutory control of hire-purchase

In *Helby v Matthews*,[9] Lord Macnaghten[10] had few doubts regarding the utility of hire-purchase:

> 'The learned counsel for the respondents spoke of dealings of this sort with an air of righteous indignation as if they were traps for the extravagant and impecunious – mere devices to tempt improvident people into buying things which they do not want and for which at the time they cannot pay. I think that is going too far. I do not see why a person fairly solvent and tolerably prudent should not make himself the owner of a piano or a carriage ... by means of periodical payments on such terms as those in question in the present case. The advantages are not all on one side. If the object of desire loses its attractions on close acquaintance – if faults are developed or defects discovered – if a coverted treasure is becoming a burthen and an incumbrance it is something, surely, to know that the transaction may be closed at once without further liability and without the payment of any forfeit. If these agreements are objectionable on public policy grounds it is for Parliament to interfere.'

---

 8 [1895] AC 471.
 9 [1895] AC 471.
10 [1895] AC 471 at 482.

This somewhat idealistic and naïve view of hire-purchase could not foresee the abuse which some traders would later seek to perpetrate. It was not uncommon for the goods to be re-possessed for a trivial default on the hirer's part when the larger part of the hire-purchase price had been paid[11] and, at common law, there was no relief against such forfeiture. There was thus no question of allowing the hirer a longer time in which to pay nor could he recover any portion of the instalments he had already paid. Moreover, the 'minimum payment' clause was a common feature of the early agreements whereby the hirer had to pay a fixed or calculable sum on the determination of the agreement. The nominal justification for such clauses was to compensate the owner for the rapid depreciation of the goods but often the true purpose was to allow the owner to recover the loss of future instalments which he had expected to receive under the agreement. The sums claimed under such clauses became extortionate but, eventually, the courts began to control this abusive practice by striking down minimum payment clauses on the basis that they were penalties.[12]

However, a conceptual difficulty lay in the path of justice: where the hirer committed no *breach* of the agreement but, instead, voluntarily exercised his option to determine the contract and return the goods, it had been held that the minimum payment clause could not be a penalty.[13] The asinine position in which the law found itself could not be disguised and the injustice emanating from it could never be condoned, but it took the bold acuity of Lord Denning[14] to draw attention to this lamentable state of affairs:

> 'Let no one mistake the injustice of this. It means that equity commits itself to this absurd paradox: it will grant relief to a man who breaks his contract but will penalise the man who keeps it. If this be the state of equity today, then it is in sore need of an overhaul so as to restore its first principles.'

Accordingly, the hirer who could not meet his obligations should have been advised to wait until the finance company commenced proceedings against him rather than, as an honest man, seeking lawfully to terminate the agreement. Ultimately, the House of Lords was driven to employ grossly artificial reasoning in the quest for justice. In *Bridge v Campbell Discount Co Ltd*,[15] the hirer wrote to the finance company apologising for the fact that he could not afford to maintain payments on a Bedford Dormobile and, in order to bring the facts within the law on penalties so that the minimum payment clause could be invalidated, the House of Lords concluded that the hirer's letter indicated that, albeit reluctantly, he felt obliged to break his contract.[16]

In an attempt to thwart these various abuses by traders and curb the unfairness of one-sided contracts, Parliament intervened in 1938 with the first Hire-Purchase

---

11 See *Cramer v Giles* (1883) Cab & El 151; *Reynolds v General and Finance Facilities* (1963) 107 Sol Jo 889.
12 See *Cooden Engineering Co Ltd v Stanford* [1953] 1 QB 86 (the whole of the unpaid balance (excluding only 10s payable on the exercise of the option to purchase) became payable under the term in question. CA held the clause was a penalty); *Lamdon Trust Ltd v Hurrell* [1955] 1 WLR 391.
13 *Associated Distributors Ltd v Hall* [1938] 2 KB 83.
14 *Bridge v Campbell Discount Co Ltd* [1962] AC 600, 629.
15 [1962] AC 600; see Ziegel, 'The Minimum Payment Clause Muddle' [1964] 22 CLJ 108.
16 See also the approach in *United Dominions Trust (Commercial) Ltd v Ennis* [1968] 1 QB 54 (CA held that the debtor must voluntarily and consciously exercise the option to terminate. On the facts, the finance company was held to have terminated the contract for breach and so the minimum payment clause was void as a penalty).

Act which, for its time, was a far-reaching and revolutionary measure. Restrictions were imposed on the owner's power to repossess the goods after one third of the hire-purchase price had been paid and, in such an action for repossession, the court was given wide powers to relieve the hirer against forfeiture. Moreover, certain statutory conditions were implied into the contract relating to the quality and fitness for purpose of the goods which could either not be excluded or excluded subject to certain conditions. The 1938 Act was the first piece of legislation to prevent the exclusion of the implied terms relating to quality and fitness for purpose of the goods and, until the enactment of the Supply of Goods (Implied Terms) Act 1973 which controlled exclusion clauses in the sale of goods, the hirer under hire-purchase was better off in this respect than the cash purchaser of goods. Equally important were the 1938 Act's provisions which sought to ensure that the hirer was informed of the cash price of the goods and was therefore able to calculate the cost of the credit extended to him, and the fact that the main terms of the financial arrangements had to be in writing with the provision that the hirer must receive a copy.

There were later statutes regulating hire-purchase agreements in 1954 and 1964, followed by a consolidating Hire-Purchase Act 1965. The 1964 Act enlarged the hirer's protection considerably and the Act and regulations made thereunder prescribed the *physical* form in which the agreement had to be cast.[17] An attempt was also made to curb forceful, 'doorstep selling' of hire-purchase by allowing the hirer an unqualified right to cancel the agreement within a limited period (the 'cooling-off' period) where it had been signed at a place other than trade premises.

The design and philosophy of the Consumer Credit Act (CCA)

The report of the Crowther Committee

At the time of the Crowther Committee's report[18] in 1971, hire-purchase had become merely one of several forms of granting credit to consumers. The Crowther Committee made several criticisms of the existing law, many of which the CCA sought to remedy.

It was emphasised that consumers who wish to obtain goods or services on credit terms might do so under several, disparate transactions with differing legal configurations. The consumer might thus acquire goods under hire-purchase, conditional sale or credit sale and pay the price of the goods in instalments (ie vendor credit). Alternatively, he might obtain a loan of money from a bank, for example, purchase the goods outright and then repay the loan in instalments (ie lender credit). The Crowther Committee considered that the central feature of such transactions was, however, the granting of credit. The consumer's concern is to acquire immediate possession of goods while being granted time to pay for them and he is usually unconcerned whether credit is provided by a seller or a third party and creditors who advance the price of the goods think of the

---

17 This effective policy was continued with regulations made under the 1965 Act: see the Hire-Purchase (Documents) (Legibility and Statutory Statements) Regulations 1965, SI 1965/1646.

18 *Report of the Committee on Consumer Credit* (Cmnd 4596, 1971).

transaction as a loan irrespective of its legal form. The Committee thus considered that the various credit transactions should be grouped according to substance rather than form: the aim of the CCA is thus to provide uniform protection to individuals who are advanced credit irrespective of the legal form of the transaction.

In fact, the Crowther Committee recommended the repeal of a wide range of statutes and their replacement with two statutes which would distinguish between rules of general application and rules applicable to consumer credit agreements. The CCA was the product of the latter recommendations but the former statute has never materialised.

How effective is the CCA?

The CCA did not set out to revolutionise the law of hire-purchase as, overall, the protective measures of the Hire-Purchase Acts of 1964 and 1965 were thought to have worked well in practice. Moreover, in the 1960s, those Acts contained important consumer protection measures which could readily be understood by the public at large. The overall approach of the Crowther Committee was that the provision of credit was beneficial to consumers and that, as defaulting debtors were a recalcitrant minority, the best approach was one of minimal interference 'with the consumer's freedom to use his knowledge of the consumer credit market to the best of his ability and according to his judgement of what constitutes his best interests'.[19] Although the Committee's favourable view of the role of consumer credit was balanced by an acknowledgment of the necessity for consumer protection, the overall *laissez-faire* attitude of the Crowther Report has been criticised in that the consumer protection measures in the CCA could have been stricter.[20]

A conspicuous feature of the CCA is that it lays down a mosaic of rules, in the most abstract terms, which demand much internal cross-referencing before any overall pattern can be discerned.[1] Furthermore, despite the formidable length of the CCA, it is principally a skeletal form providing for regulations and orders to be made by statutory instrument and there can also be 'determinations' and directions issued by the Director General of Fair Trading which are quasi-judicial in nature. The innate complexity of the Act when coupled with the regular outpouring of regulations mean that it can be difficult to keep abreast of the law and, without a doubt, the law of consumer credit is incomprehensible to the average consumer.[2] This view of the law relating to consumer credit was shared

19 *Report of the Committee on Consumer Credit* (Cmnd 4596, 1971), para 3.9.1.
20 See Cranston, *Consumers and the Law* (3rd edn, 2000), p 238.
 1 See the trenchant criticism of Aubrey L Diamond (*Commercial and Consumer Credit: An Introduction* (1982)) in the context of the classification of agreements recognised by the CCA: 'The words can be read. They can even be understood. But it is extremely difficult to visualise the precise situations they are intended to deal with' (p 52). See also the book's Preface: 'Despite [the Act's] skilled drafting and masterly arrangement, I sometimes felt that, like Herman Melville in *Moby Dick*, I could claim that "The classification of the constituents of a chaos, nothing less is here essayed"' (p vii). Cf Ramsay, *Consumer Protection, Text and Materials* (1989), pp 367-368: 'The Act has been criticised by business and enforcement officers because of its detailed requirements ... lawyers steeped in the glories of the common-law tradition of individualized decision-making may dislike the style of the Act. But it is those sections of the Act based on this tradition – the extortionate-credit-bargain provisions – which are most irrelevant to the general regulation of the market.'
 2 See Lindgren, 'The Consumer Credit Act 1974: Its Scope' (1977) 40 MLR 159, 173.

by Robert Goff LJ[3] when he opined that the CCA was 'an Act of extraordinary length and complexity, which must raise very considerable problems for those officials whose task it is to see that it is enforced and for those citizens, whether corporate or individual, who are affected by its terms and seek conscientiously to abide by them'. Almost certainly, the obsessive and interminable division and sub-division of agreements which are recognised within the CCA detracts from its efficacy as a consumer protection measure. Schedule 2 of the Act attempts to offset this intricacy with explanatory examples of the Act's application but, regrettably, even that Schedule is a masterpiece of obfuscation. It is striking that the contemporary law is as fragmented as it ever was and, indeed, in many cases it may be more difficult to locate the relevant rules than before the enactment of the CCA.[4] It is true that better substantive rules exist today than formerly but even the most functional rules are rendered nugatory if they are secreted in a labyrinth of impenetrable obscurity.

At least the overall aspirations of the CCA were admirable in seeking to integrate the disparate forms of credit provision according to substance rather than form and separate consumer credit from commercial credit. Furthermore, the Act's administrative system for the licensing of businesses engaged in the provision of credit must rank as one of the most significant consumer protection measures of recent years. It is now indisputable that the threat of cessation of business is a more efficacious control on business malpractice than isolated, private actions instituted against rogue traders or, indeed, even the occasional threat of prosecution.

Many of the concepts which were introduced by earlier hire-purchase legislation remain intact in the CCA but they have been refined and enlarged and a major effect of the Act has been to extend statutory control to the other types of consumer credit agreement apart from hire-purchase. As mentioned earlier, the CCA introduces the terminology of debt to consumer credit and the consumer who is granted credit is referred to as the *debtor* and the provider of credit is the *creditor*. Moreover, the *supplier* is the person supplying goods or services under a consumer credit agreement. The Act sometimes refers to a *credit-broker* and this designation could apply, for example, to a dealer who arranges a hire-purchase transaction. The terms *owner* and *hirer* should now be restricted to consumer hire agreements, the owner being the party who hires out the goods to the hirer under such an agreement.

---

3 *Jenkins v Lombard North Central plc* [1984] 1 WLR 307, 313.
4 Eg, the conditional sale is now a hybrid between the sale of goods and consumer credit and straddles no less than six major statutes: the Factors Act 1889; the Hire-Purchase Act 1964, Part III; the Supply of Goods (Implied Terms) Act 1973; the UCTA 1977; the SGA 1979 and the CCA 1974.

CHAPTER 31

The classification of agreements in the Consumer Credit Act

Any evaluation of the CCA must begin with the overall classification of the agreements which are recognised by the Act. The examination of this classification is, in itself, quite daunting. First, the central category of *regulated agreements* must be sub-divided into *consumer credit agreements* and *consumer hire agreements*. Second, there is a host of smaller categories which cling to the coat tails of the larger group, and these must also be delineated, viz exempt agreements, small agreements, non-commercial agreements, multiple agreements, linked transactions, and credit-token agreements.

It is equally important to understand how the CCA charts the different *categories of credit* which are available to a debtor. Once the broad definitions of the types of agreement and the overall notion of credit and its sub-divisions are understood, each specialised variety of *credit agreement* can be examined (eg hire-purchase; credit-sale), a task undertaken in Chapter 32. It will be apparent that the CCA contains expansive categories which are divided and then sub-divided, and the road to eventual mastery of the Act begins with an appreciation of these unremitting classifications and definitions.[1] Some repetition and extensive cross-referencing are inevitable in any exposition of the CCA.

Regulated agreements

It has been said that 'the regulated agreement is the key to an understanding of the scope of the Act'[2] in that (i) all regulated agreements are governed by the requirements and restrictions of the Act; (ii) transactions linked to regulated agreements (eg a maintenance contract) are affected by the Act; (iii) security provided in relation to a regulated or linked agreement is controlled by the Act; (iv) businesses which wish to grant credit under regulated agreements must be licensed by the Director General of Fair Trading; and (v) those wishing to carry on an ancillary credit business (eg credit-brokerage), the definition of which is tied closely to that of the regulated agreement, must also be licensed by the Director.

---

1 See Lord Hoffmann's opening comments on the CCA in *Dimond v Lovell* [2000] 2 All ER 897.
2 Goode, *The Consumer Credit Act; A Students' Guide* (1979), p 49.

The regulated agreement is thus at the heart of the CCA and is defined in s 189(1) as a consumer credit agreement *or* a consumer hire agreement which is *not* an exempt agreement.[3] Exempt agreements are not regulated by the Act except that they can be re-opened if they are regarded as extortionate credit agreements. It is, consequently, of prime importance that the broad categories of consumer credit agreements and consumer hire agreements are examined and defined first. This chapter is concerned principally with the classification of the agreements recognised by the CCA but there is, unavoidably, some overlap into the substantive content of such agreements. Moreover, the recent decision of the House of Lords in *Dimond v Lovell* must be considered as this ruling has profound implications for both 'credit hire' agreements and the meaning of 'credit' generally.

Consumer credit agreements

The CCA, s 8, specifies the three broad requirements of a 'consumer credit agreement', viz:

(i)   a personal credit agreement[4] between an individual (the debtor) and any other person (the creditor);
(ii) the creditor provides the debtor with credit not exceeding £25,000;[5]
(iii) the agreement is not an exempt agreement.

The introduction of '*personal* credit agreement' serves only to confuse at this stage in the definitional structure of the Act and adds nothing to the demarcation of a 'consumer credit agreement' in s 8. It has been emphasised,[6] however, that the reference to a 'personal credit agreement' is principally a drafting device in that the CCA occasionally needs to refer to an agreement as having the characteristics of a consumer credit agreement but without the financial limitation imposed by the CCA (eg ss 10 and 11).

Section 9(1) adds tersely, yet significantly, that '"credit" includes a cash loan, and any other form of financial accommodation'. In the midst of such a laboriously technical Act concerned exclusively with the provision of credit, it is anomalous that 'credit' is defined so succinctly. Goode[7] has stressed consistently that the key to the meaning of 'credit' is that there must be a contractual deferment of the time when the debt would ordinarily be paid. The emphasis here is on *contractual* deferment meaning that the creditor must receive consideration for agreeing to the delayed payment by, for example, stipulating for interest. This requirement serves to distinguish the grant of credit proper from those situations where the debtor takes it unilaterally in the form of dilatory

---

3   Exempt agreements are defined in the CCA, s 16, or in orders made under that section, see below.
4   It should be stressed that, following general principles, there must be a binding contract with, for example, certainty of terms: see *Scammell v Ouston* [1941] AC 251. If there is no binding contract then, *a fortiori*, the provisions of the CCA regarding formalities of the agreement cannot apply.
5   The credit limit was raised to £25,000 in 1998, see the Consumer Credit (Increase of Monetary Limits) (Amendment) Order 1998, SI 1998/996.
6   Goode, *Consumer Credit Law* (1989), para 7.5.
7   See *Consumer Credit Law* (1989), Ch 8.

payment or the creditor is equally lackadaisical in sending his bill. The position where the creditor simply allows the debtor time to pay will also not amount to an agreement for credit unless some consideration is received by the creditor.

Similarly, care must be taken with the notion of *deferment*: where a newsagent's bill for newspapers is paid, under the contract, at the end of each month, there is no deferment of a debt as the newsagent is not entitled to payment until the end of the month. There will often be one date fixed in the contract for payment and a second, later date, stipulated as the time for the deferred payment and so, for example, the holder of a credit card is given the option to settle his account immediately or to defer payment and incur interest charges, and here there is no doubt regarding the provision of credit. However, although the contract may provide for one method of payment only, it is incorrect to suppose that no credit is granted in the absence of an express date for the deferred payment. In an agreement for the sale of goods in the configuration of a credit-sale, the parties agree initially that payment can be made in instalments and yet there is clearly an extension of credit as, under the SGA, s 28, the buyer comes under an obligation to pay for the goods when he takes delivery of them. It follows that there must always be an evaluation of when payment would be *earnt* under the contract in order to determine whether credit has been extended in the contractual deferment of the debt.

The concept of the consumer credit agreement is designed to encompass all types of credit and so, as well as hire-purchase, there are numerous other credit transactions within the broad scope of the consumer credit agreement. These forms of credit are outlined in Chapter 32 and include conditional sales, credit-sales, personal loans, overdraft facilities, credit card transactions, mortgage transactions, pledges and check trading. Furthermore, the definition is not limited to the supply of goods or land on credit terms – the provision of services on credit terms, for example, is also within its ambit.

As s 8 refers to a personal credit agreement between an 'individual' (the debtor) and 'any other person' (the creditor), it is important to understand which parties are comprised within these definitions. An 'individual' is defined in s 189(1) as including 'a partnership or other unincorporated body of persons not consisting entirely of bodies corporate'. As the creditor is 'any other person', this encompasses an individual or a body corporate, but the debtor *must* be an individual as defined. It is immediately apparent that the CCA draws unincorporated traders and businessmen within its protection as well as private individuals and so, for example, a partnership which obtains a photo-copying machine on hire-purchase is a debtor under a consumer credit agreement within the Act.

Somewhat ironically, there is no definition of a 'consumer' in the Consumer Credit Act. The CCA neither draws elaborate distinctions between 'business' and 'consumer' transactions nor asks the *purpose* for which the credit is supplied and it thus avoids the definitional problems encountered in many other consumer protection statutes. In seeking to establish the parameters of consumer and business contracts, the Unfair Contract Terms Act 1977, s 12, asks the enigmatic question whether or not the contract has been made 'in the course of a business' and adds that the goods must be 'of a type ordinarily supplied for private use or consumption' if one party is to be regarded as 'dealing as consumer'. In contrast, the two tests utilised by the CCA, a financial upper-limit and the exclusion of corporate debtors, have the merit of clarity and leave no room for dispute regarding the outer-limits of an abstract definition such as that in s 12. The Crowther Committee sought this degree of simplicity and rejected the *purpose* for which the credit was supplied as a controlling test on the basis that it was too elusive and incapable of verification by the creditor.[8]

Consumer hire agreements

Prior to the CCA, there was no legislative protection for an individual who took goods on simple hire as distinct from hire-purchase and it was possible to evade the hire-purchase legislation by couching the agreement in terms of a straightforward hiring of goods. A consumer hire agreement is a regulated agreement within the Act but it is *not* within the definition of a consumer credit agreement as it does not involve credit; instead the payments made are *rent* for the use of the goods and are thus not payments which go towards the price of the goods or the repayment of a loan. Moreover, there are no sub-divisions in the definition of consumer hire as the hiring of goods can take only one legal configuration.

A consumer hire agreement is defined in the CCA, s 15, and comprises the following elements:

(i)   an agreement made by a person with an individual (the hirer) for the bailment[9] of *goods*;[10]
(ii) the agreement is not a hire-purchase agreement;
(iii) the agreement is capable of subsisting for more than three months;
(iv) the agreement does not require the hirer to make payments exceeding £25,000;
(v) the agreement is not an exempt agreement.

The CCA thus clearly applies to domestic rental agreements and, having regard to the definition of 'individual' considered earlier, it also applies where partnerships or sole traders hire equipment for use in their businesses, for example.

The idea underlying the 'three months rule' in s 15 is that certain short-term contracts for the hiring of goods should be excluded from the CCA definition of consumer hire, eg where a consumer hires 'do it yourself' equipment for one week. On the other hand, it is apt that a lease of expensive, heavy equipment, for one year, for example, should be included within the control of the CCA because such an agreement performs a function analogous to a credit agreement proper. In the Act, this policy is couched in terms that, in order to be within the s 15 definition of consumer hire, the agreement must be '*capable* of subsisting for more than three months'. The position at the time the agreement is entered into must thus be evaluated. If the agreement is for a fixed term which does not

---

8   See *Report of the Committee on Consumer Credit* (Cmnd 4596, 1971), paras 6.2.17–6.2.19. See also *Consumer Credit* (United Kingdom Comparative Law Series, Vol 3, ed Goode, 1978), Ch 2, pp 28-35.
9   The draftsman's choice of 'bailment' rather than 'hiring' is unfortunate and unnecessary. In principle, the Act could apply to bailments other than hire, eg where possession of goods is delivered to another for repair and payment is made *to* the bailee/repairer. It seems clear that s 15(1) must be restricted to hire agreements where payment is made *by* the bailee rather than to the bailee, see Palmer and Yates, 'The Application of the Consumer Credit Act to Consumer Hire Agreements' [1979] 38 CLJ 180.
10 The CCA, s 189(1) (as amended by the SGA 1979, Sch 4, para 18) provides that 'goods' has the same meaning as in the SGA, s 61(1). It will be recalled that, in the sale of goods, there can be difficulties in deciding whether goods are part of the land/building or are to be regarded as separate. The same considerations apply here in considering whether goods and chattels are hired for separate use and enjoyment.

exceed three months and *neither* party has an option to renew the period of hire, the agreement is clearly incapable of subsisting more than three months. However, this would appear to be the only situation where it can be asserted unequivocally that the agreement cannot extend beyond its three months' duration. Where the agreement is for an indeterminate period of time, as it could be where the hiring is from week to week with a prescribed period of notice to terminate the agreement, it is clearly to be treated as one which can subsist for more than three months. Similarly, an agreement made initially for three months with an option given to either party to extend it for a longer period must be considered as capable of subsisting for more than three months.

Section 15 provides that a consumer hire agreement is for 'the *bailment* ... of goods to the hirer' being 'an *agreement* which is capable of subsisting for more than three months'. It is thus somewhat ambiguous as to whether the actual hire of the goods (ie the bailment) must be capable of subsisting longer than three months or, alternatively, whether an agreement which subsisted for longer than that period would be within the section in the sense that the hirer might have the option to pay the charges at a date later than three months from the commencement of the actual hire of, say, two months only. This point was raised in the recent decision in *Dimond v Lovell*,[11] the detailed facts of which are considered below. The car hire agreement in question provided, in clause 19, that the 'maximum rental period of this rental agreement must not exceed 28 days'. The agreement was capable of lasting more than three months in the sense that the hirer might pay the hire charges more than three months after the agreement was signed, ie credit was allowed until such time as the claim for damages was concluded against the third party. The Court of Appeal accepted[12] that it was the actual period of hire which must be examined when ascertaining whether the agreement was capable of subsisting for more than three months and, as the period of the car hire could not exceed 28 days, the agreement in *Dimond* was not a consumer hire agreement within s 15. The decision in *Dimond* is thus in accord with the purpose of s 15, that is to ensure that only those hiring agreements for lengthy periods are within the Act.

In calculating whether the hirer is within the financial ceiling of £25,000 or whether he is 'required to pay' more than £25,000, his *minimum* contractual liability must be examined, having regard also to his right to terminate the agreement. Moreover, 'payments' here mean all sums payable under the agreement, eg payments for maintenance of equipment and VAT.[13] Consequently, if an agreement of three years' duration provided for rental of £9,000 per annum with a right to terminate[14] at the end of the second year, the agreement would still be a consumer hire agreement within s 15(1), but it would *not* be if there were no such 'break clause'.

'Credit hire' and the decision in *Dimond v Lovell*

In recent years, 'credit hire' firms have begun to materialise, these being businesses which are prepared to hire replacement cars to motorists whose own cars have

---

11 [2000] 1 QB 216, CA; affd [2000] 2 All ER 897, HL.
12 [2000] 1 QB 216, 232 per Sir Richard Scott V-C.
13 See *Apollo Leasing Ltd v Scott* [1986] CCLR 1.
14 The statutory right of termination in s 101 must be ignored in calculating the hirer's minimum liability as that section applies only where the agreement is *first* established as a consumer hire agreement: see the CCA, Sch 2, example 20.

been damaged in accidents. It is often the case that the innocent driver's insurance company does not offer a replacement car under the terms of the policy and so these credit hire firms fill a gap in the market: they are prepared to offer car hire only in those instances where the motorist /hirer was totally blameless and the other driver was entirely at fault in causing the accident. The assumption is that the innocent motorist /hirer will not pay the hire charges but, instead, the cost of the hire will be charged to the driver who was at fault in causing the accident as part of the damages which are payable by him. Consequently, the replacement car is hired to the innocent motorist on credit terms and the credit hire firms effectively take control of the motorist's claim in negligence against the blameworthy driver. The cost of hiring the car is approximately twice the normal rate (the 'spot rate') for such a car hire and thus the credit hire companies have prospered with this method of doing business. It is, of course, the blamewothy driver's insurance company which ultimately has to foot the bill and the artificially exaggerated hire charge is eventually reflected in the augmented insurance premiums which are charged to the generality of motorists. The scheme is, self-evidently, popular with the innocent driver who does not have to worry about hiring a car, paying in advance, and then seeking to claim the cost from the driver at fault. That being said, if things do not go to plan, the innocent driver is liable for the excessive hire charges and legal costs of the failed action, and many consumers will not realise their potential liability when committing themselves to credit hire agreements. However, the financial burden of credit hire has fallen on the insurance companies and has proved to be very costly for them. It is hardly surprising that, in recent years, insurers have tried to find a means of thwarting the burgeoning credit hire firms but they have had no success[15] until the recent litigation in *Dimond v Lovell*.[16]

In *Dimond*, the plaintiff (P) was driving home from work in her Suzuki Vitara when a car driven by the defendant (D) ran into P's car from behind. On the advice of her insurance broker, P hired a replacement car from 1st Automotive Ltd, the agreement providing that 'the lessor will allow the hirer credit on the hire charges until such time as a claim for damages has been concluded against the party that the hirer alleges is liable for damages arising out of the said accident'. The agreement signed by P did not specify the hire charge and these details were to be inserted only at the end of the period of hire. The daily rate of hire was was almost double the spot rate and the total rental charge for eight days was £346.63. D's insurer admitted liability and paid the repair costs but disputed the £346.63 hire charge and so 1st Automotive Ltd began proceedings, in P's name, to recover that sum from D's insurance company. P succeeded at first instance in the Sheffield County Court on the basis that the agreement was not a regulated consumer hire agreement within the CCA but that, even if it was such an agreement and was unenforceable, P could still recover as damages the cost of hiring the replacement car. That decision was reversed by the Court of Appeal on the ground that the agreement was one under which credit was provided and so it was within the CCA's definition of a regulated consumer credit agreement. It followed that there had been a total failure to comply with the formalities and documentation required by the CCA and, under ss 65(1) and 127(3), the agreement was improperly executed and unenforceable by 1st Automotive Ltd against P, the hirer. This meant

---

15 See the failed attempt in *Giles v Thompson* [1994] 1 AC 142 to have such agreements invalidated as being champertous.
16 [2000] 1 QB 216, CA; affd [2000] 2 All ER 897, HL.

that, as P could not be liable to pay the hire charge to 1st Automotive Ltd, she could not recover that amount in damages against D.

P appealed to the House of Lords arguing that (i) the agreement was not one under which credit was advanced and so it was not regulated under the CCA; or (ii) the agreement was a 'multiple agreement' within the CCA, s 18[17] such that the credit provision was a regulated agreement within the CCA but the hiring provision was outside the Act and was, therefore, an enforceable agreement; or (iii) even if P, the hirer, was under no liability to pay the hire charges, she could nevertheless recover those charges from D. The House of Lords dismissed the appeal.

The primary issue in the House of Lords was whether 'credit' had been granted to P, the hirer. The argument advanced by 1st Automotive was that this was not simply an agreement for the hire of a car because the agreement also entailed the pursuit of the hirer's claim against the motorist at fault. Viewed this way, these obligations would constitute an entire contract and so 1st Automotive would not be able to recover any part of the consideration until P had had the use of the car and the claim for damages was brought to a conclusion. This argument was rejected by the House of Lords on the basis that it would involve an artificial construction of the contract in the light of the fact that there was no express contractual *duty* on 1st Automotive to pursue the claim. Furthermore, there could be no implied term to that effect, not least because P was not concerned whether 1st Automotive pursued her claim or not, as long as she did not have to pay the hire charges. The House emphasised that the terms of the hiring agreement stated unequivocally that 'the lessor will allow the hirer credit on the hire charges' and so, as the hirer's obligation to pay the hire charges was deferred, credit was granted to the hirer. The agreement was thus held to be a 'personal credit agreement' under s 8(1), a 'consumer credit agreement' under s 8(2) and, as it was not an exempt agreement, it was a regulated consumer credit agreement. As the agreement had been improperly executed it was, under s 65(1), unenforceable against the hirer.

The second, alternative argument was that the agreement was a multiple agreement under s 18, in that one part was the hiring of the car and the other part the pursuit of the claim. The credit provisions would thus belong only to the latter part of the agreement concerned with the pursuit of the claim. This argument was also dismissed by the House as there was a single contract: the provisions creating a debt (ie the hiring of the car) could not be divorced from the provisions under which the debt was payable (ie the credit allowed to the hirer). Accordingly, s 18 had no relevance to the agreement.

Finally, there was the contention that even if P, the hirer, was under no liability to pay the hire charges, she could nevertheless recover those charges from D. The House of Lords held that, as P could could not be liable to pay the hire charges, she could not recover them as damages from D. Most importantly, the Law Lords expressed their views, as *obiter dicta*, on the measure of damages which would have been available had the agreement been enforceable against the hirer, P. This is arguably the most significant aspect of the decision because, assuming (as did the House of Lords) that credit hire companies can re-draft their agreements to correct the deficiencies disclosed in *Dimond* and render the agreement enforceable against the hirer (see below), the principles upon which damages are calculated is vital to the future profitability of the credit hire business. The view adopted in all

---

17 See below where multiple agreements are considered.

three courts was that P had acted reasonably in using the services of 1st Automotive and had not failed to mitigate her loss. However, the decision in the House of Lords emphasised that the two lower courts had failed to consider the rule that requires additional benefits obtained as a result of taking reasonable steps to mitigate loss to be brought into account in the calculation of damages.[18] Consequently, P had obtained not only the use of the car but additional benefits, viz relief from the anxiety and financial risk in pursuing the claim. The value of the additional benefits obtained was represented by the difference between what P was willing to pay 1st Automotive and what she would have been willing to pay an ordinary hire company for the use of the car. Accordingly, in credit hire cases the equivalent 'spot rate' of hire will ordinarily be the net loss after allowance has been made for the additional benefits.

As mentioned earlier, credit hire firms must now alter their terms of business if credit hire agreements are to become enforceable. This could be done in a number of ways. First, a costly option is to ensure that credit hire agreements comply with the provisions of the CCA relating to the formalities/documentation of regulated agreements. Second, the credit hire firms could apply to the Director General of Fair Trading for a 'waiver or variation' under s 60(3) where it appears 'impracticable for the applicant to comply with any requirement' relating to the form and content of documents embodying regulated agreements. There is no good reason, however, why such an exemption should be allowed and, in any event, the Director can grant a waiver 'only if he is satisfied that to do so would not prejudice the interests of debtors or hirers' (s 60(4)). Finally, the most plausible and least expensive option is to ensure that credit hire agreements fall within the classification of 'exempt agreeements' in s 16 and Regulations made under it.[19] Thus, debtor-creditor-supplier agreements for fixed-sum credit where the credit is repayable in *four payments or less* within a period *not exceeding 12 months* beginning with the date of the agreement, are exempt agreements. It is already apparent, however, that the courts are adopting a strict interpretation of the Regulations relating to exempt agreements[20] and, moreover, the 12 months during which the credit must be repaid may well be too short a period for the credit hire firms to resolve the claim against the motorist at fault. However, it is the House of Lords' ruling on the correct measure of damages which is likely to be the undoing of the credit hire firms and many have already gone into liquidation.

What are the wider implications of *Dimond v Lovell*?

After the House of Lords' decision in *Dimond* and, having regard to the definition of 'credit' in the the CCA s 9(1) as including 'a cash loan, and *any other form of financial accommodation*', many agreements which include an express term giving the consumer the option to pay at a time later than that at which the obligation to pay would otherwise have arisen, will be agreements which extend credit to the consumer. There are numerous such agreements where the total price can be paid in instalments over a period of time, eg insurance premiums, students' fees, and agreements for mobile telephones. Although these types of

---

18 See *British Westinghouse Electric and Manufacturing Co Ltd v Underground Electric Railways Co of London Ltd* [1912] AC 673.
19 See below for a consideration of exempt agreements.
20 See *Ketley v Gilbert* [2001] 1 WLR 986; *Zoan v Rouamba* [2000] 2 All ER 620, considered below.

agreement have not been regarded as advancing credit in the conventional sense, they are now almost certainly classifiable as regulated consumer credit agreements and so they must comply with the requirements of the CCA if they are to be enforceable. Alternatively, the safest and most economical course of action is for the providers of such services to ensure that their agreements comply with the requirements of exempt agreements, ie the credit must be repayable in four payments or less within a period not exceeding twelve months beginning with the date of the agreement.

In *Dimond*, clause 19 of the agreement (limiting the period of hire to 28 days) prevented it from being a consumer hire agreement within the CCA, s 15. Until the decision in *Dimond*, it had been assumed that consumer hire and consumer credit were mutually exclusive categories but, in the Court of Appeal, Sir Richard Scott V-C[1] accepted that credit hire agreements of the type at issue fell within *both* categories. This conclusion was, of course, *obiter dictum*, but it means that many hire agreements, such as equipment leasing, must comply with the CCA requirements relating to both of these categories.

Exempt agreements

There are certain agreements which would be within the ambit of regulated agreements if they were not specifically isolated as being exempt agreements. Consequently, exempt agreements are not subject to the CCA at all, with the important exception of the provisions relating to extortionate credit bargains (ss 137-140) which do apply to exempt agreements.

The CCA, s 16, and orders and regulations made under it enumerate a range of exempt agreements. The largest category of exempt agreements in s 16 comprises certain consumer credit agreements for house purchases which are secured by a mortgage and where the creditor is a recognised lender, viz local authorities, banks, building societies and certain bodies specified in the Schedule to the Consumer Credit (Exempt Agreements) Order 1989,[2] as amended. Also within this exempted group of mortgage lending, are those agreements where the recognised lenders make additional loans to customers who already have mortgages with them, for certain types of insurance against loss or damage to the buildings and contents, and mortgage protection and indemnity insurance.

There are other important exemptions in the 1989 Order which recognise that small-scale, 'trade credit', is not within the CCA. The first exempted group are debtor-creditor-supplier agreements for fixed-sum credit *other* than hire-purchase, conditional sale and agreements secured by a pledge or agreements financing the purchase of land,[3] where the credit is repayable in *four payments or less* within a period not exceeding twelve months beginning with the date of the agreement. Within this category would be, for example, a credit-sale agreement with a retailer where the buyer/debtor pays a deposit on goods and agrees to pay the remainder in three equal monthly instalments. As mentioned earlier when 'credit hire' agreements were considered, the courts have been very strict in the interpretation of the 1989 Order which applies to this category of exempt

---

1 [2000] 1 QB 216, 232.
2 SI 1989/869.
3 See the separate exempt category in relation to land, considered below.

agreement. In *Ketley v Gilbert*,[4] a credit hire agreement of the type in *Dimond v Lovell*, provided that the hire charge should be met by 'a single payment on the expiry of 12 months starting with the date of this agreement'. The 1989 Order specifies that the payments must be made '*within* a period not exceeding twelve months beginning with the date of the agreement'. The Court of Appeal held that 'on the *expiry* of twelve months' meant *after* twelve months have been exceeded and the Order clearly demanded that payment be within the twelve month period. Accordingly, the agreement did not fall within the exempt category.[5] Instead, it was a regulated agreement within the CCA. The agreement was thus unenforceable as there had been no compliance with the formalities of the CCA relating to regulated agreements.

Second, the 1989 Order exempts debtor-creditor-supplier agreements for running-account credit under which the whole of the credit is to be repaid in one instalment, provided the agreement is not one for hire-purchase, conditional sale or an agreement secured by a pledge or one financing the purchase of land. This exemption applies to the 'charge card' facility offered by card issuers such as American Express and, also, some retail shops, under which the cardholder is required to repay the full amount owing each month, but the exemption would not apply to credit cards under which the debtor can choose the amount he wishes to pay each month in settling the debit balance. Also exempted in this category is the normal 'trade credit' granted by a supplier of domestic goods, such as a milkman, grocer or newsagent, where the debtor pays each periodical account in one lump sum.

Third, certain debtor-creditor agreements are exempted by the 1989 Order where the cost of the credit is low. In order to qualify for this exemption, the debtor-creditor agreement must be of a type offered to 'a certain class or classes of persons' (eg employees) and 'not offered to the public generally' and, second, the only charge included in the total charge for credit is interest which cannot exceed 1% above the highest of any base rates published by the English and Scottish Clearing Banks, being the rate that was in operation 28 days before the making of the agreement

Fourth, any debtor-creditor-supplier agreement to finance the purchase of land where the debtor is obliged to repay the credit and any charges falling within the total charge for credit in four instalments, or less, is exempt.

Fifth, an exemption is made in the case of consumer hire agreements entered into with a corporate body authorised by statute to supply gas, water or electricity, for the hire of equipment for metering gas, water or electricity.

Small agreements

The CCA, s 17 defines a small agreement[6] as either (a) a regulated consumer credit agrement for credit not exceeding £50,[7] *other than* a hire-purchase or

---

4   [2001] 1 WLR 986.
5   The same conclusion was reached in *Zoan v Rouamba* [2000] 2 All ER 620.
6   See the illustrations of small agreements in the CCA, Sch 2, examples 16, 17 and 22.
7   The figure was increased to £50 by the Consumer Credit (Increase of Monetary Limits) Order 1983 (SI 1983/1878). The figure is decreased to £35 if the agreement is within the Consumer Protection (Cancellation of Contracts Concluded away from Business Premises) Regulations 1987, reg 9 (SI 1987/2117, as amended by SI 1988/958; SI 1998/3050).

conditional sale agreement;[8] or (b) a regulated consumer hire agreement which does not require the hirer to make payments exceeding £50. Moreover, in either case the agreement must be one that is unsecured or secured[9] by a guarantee or indemnity only. Section 17(3) and (4) contain anti-avoidance provisions designed to prevent the splitting-up of agreements into two or more agreements which are below the £50 limit. The purpose of defining small agreements is to enable certain sections of the Act to exclude such agreements. Thus, small debtor-creditor-supplier agreements for restricted-use credit enjoy exemption from the provisions in Part V of the CCA relating to formalities of the agreement, supply of copies etc, nor do the rules on withdrawal and cancellation of the agreement apply to small agreements.

Non-commercial agreements

The provisions of the CCA are directed fundamentally at commercial/professional lending and so many of the Act's provisions (eg relating to formalities of the agreement and its cancellation) do not apply to 'non-commercial agreements' which are defined in s 189(1) as consumer credit or consumer hire agreements 'not made by the creditor or owner in the course of a business carried on by him'. With the stress on *a* business in s 189(1), it is likely that the legislature intended that non-commercial agreements would be those which were not carried on in the course of *any* business. This would mean that an isolated loan in the course of a business, irrespective of its nature, should not qualify as a non-commercial agreement. On the other hand, s 189(1) employs the abstract, troublesome phrase 'in the *course* of a business', thus arguably indicating the necessity for regular business activity.[10] Just as enigmatically, s 189(2) provides that 'a person is not to be treated as carrying on a particular type of business merely because occasionally he enters into transactions belonging to a business of that type'.

In *Hare v Schurek*,[11] the plaintiff carried on a business as a car salesman and he did not normally extend credit to his customers nor was he licensed to carry on a consumer credit business under the CCA, although he did have a licence to conduct ancillary credit business, especially that of credit brokerage. On one occasion, he agreed to supply a Ford Orion car on hire-purchase terms to his step-son's friend and, subsequently, he commenced proceedings to recover the balance owed under the agreement. The Court of Appeal held that the words 'a business' in the definition of a non-commercial agreement meant a consumer credit or consumer hire business, these being the only types of business regulated by the CCA and, second, that a person who enters into occasional regulated agreements in the course of his business is not carrying on a consumer credit or hire business by virtue of the CCA, s 189(2). It followed from this reasoning that the plaintiff did not need a consumer credit licence and, accordingly, the agreement was enforceable against the defendant.

---

8 No matter how small the credit provided, these agreements cannot qualify as small agreements.
9 See the definition of 'security' in the CCA, s 189(1).
10 Cf *Stevenson v Rogers* [1999] QB 1028.
11 [1993] CCLR 47.

Multiple agreements

Mutiple agreements are defined in the CCA, s 18, in somewhat confusing terms.[12] Some agreements covered by the Act fall within two or more of its sub-divisions and, where this occurs, the agreement is treated as within each of the categories concerned. A credit card, for example, is a restricted-use debtor-creditor-supplier agreement if it is used to buy goods, and an unrestricted-use debtor-creditor agreement when it is utilised to withdraw cash.[13] Section 18 has twin objectives in ensuring that (i) the formal requirements of the CCA (eg relating to cancellation and copies of the agreement) apply to *each* part of the agreement; and (ii) the financial limits of the Act are not evaded by combining two separate agreements (each of which would be below the financial ceiling of £25,000) into one agreement whch exceeds the £25,000 upper monetary limit for regulated agreements and would thus be outside the Act's protection.[14]

In *National Westminster Bank plc v Story*,[15] the bank agreed to lend money to the defendants under three separate credit facilities (an overdraft and two loans amounting to £20,000 of £5,000 and £15,000 respectively). The overdraft complied with the CCA but the the issue was whether the loans were to be regarded as separate agreements. The bank had not treated the loans as regulated agreements and, if there was a *single* agreement, the CCA would not apply as the financial limit was then £15,000. If, on the other hand, this was a multiple agreement, the CCA would apply and the loans would be unenforceable. The Court of Appeal held that the credit facility amounted to one agreement and so it was not unenforceable under the CCA. Auld LJ considered that the facilities were agreed as part of one package, not only as to the total level of credit but also as to the common conditions for the provision of all the three facilities.

Linked transactions

It is not uncommon for ancillary contracts to be entered into at the same time that goods are procured on credit, eg maintenance and insurance contracts, and these ancillary transactions are defined in the CCA, s 19, as 'linked transactions'. There are potential hazards to the debtor in such linked transactions. First, they may be used as a means of imposing additional charges on the debtor and, second, the Act's provisions relating to the debtor's right to cancel the credit agreement would be seriously weakened if the debtor were able to cancel that credit agreement but nevertheless remained bound by the linked transaction – the continuation of the linked transaction might thus be a major disincentive to the debtor's exercise of his right of withdrawal or cancellation. Consequently, the CCA provides that if the debtor withdraws from

---

12 See *Multiple Agreements and Section 18 of the Consumer Credit Act 1974, A Discussion Paper* (OFT, June 1995).

13 Illustrations of multiple agreements can be found in the CCA, Sch 2, examples 16 and 18 (it has been suggested that the latter example is wrong, see Goode, *Consumer Credit Law* (1989), para 9.48).

14 See *Dimond v Lovell* [2000] 2 All ER 897, considered above, where a strained interpretation as to the meaning of mutiple agreements was rejected by the House of Lords.

15 [1999] 20 LS Gaz R 41.

or cancels the principal credit agreement, there will be a withdrawal from the linked transaction or it will be automatically cancelled (see below).

A linked transaction is defined in s 19(1) and (2)[16] as a transaction[17] (other than one for the provision of security, eg a contract of guarantee) entered into by the debtor or hirer, or a relative[18] of his, with any other person, in relation to an actual or prospective regulated agreement (the 'principal agreement') of which it does not form part, provided that it falls within one of the three categories (a), (b) or (c) in s 19(1). It is thus plain that the parties to the linked transaction can be, and often are, different parties from those to the principal credit agreement and might comprise, for example, a relative of the debtor and a contractor who agrees to maintain the goods which are the subject of the principal agreement. The three categories in s 19 must now be considered.

The first category of linked transaction in s 19(1)(a) is one entered into 'in compliance with a term of the principal agreement'. For example, a hire-purchase agreement in relation to goods or a consumer hire agreement might demand that the debtor or hirer enter into a contract of maintenance regarding the goods; here the maintenance contracts are linked transactions and it does not matter that the other party to the linked transactions has no connection with the creditor and, likewise, it is irrelevant that the debtor or hirer is at liberty to choose a maintenance contractor. The position would be the same should a relative of the debtor have entered into the linked transaction. The linked transactions within category (a) must be made *after* the principal, regulated agreement has been entered into but a transaction made before the principal agreement can be a linked transaction within category (b) or (c).

The second category of linked transaction in s 19(1)(b) is one where the principal agreement is a debtor-creditor-supplier agreement and the linked transaction 'is financed, or to be financed, by the principal agreement'. A prime example within this category is where a finance house has a pre-existing relationship with a seller of goods and grants a loan to the debtor so that he may buy goods from that seller. The loan is clearly the principal agreement and the sale of goods to the debtor is a linked transaction. At first glance it might be thought that a hire-purchase agreement, where the finance house/creditor is the supplier of the goods or services, might entail a linked transaction within this category, but this is not so as s 19(1) specifies that the linked transaction cannot be part of the *regulated agreement itself* and, in hire-purchase, credit-sale and conditional sale, the supply of the goods and the provision of credit are merged in one agreement.

The third category of transaction in s 19(1)(c) is, in fact, sub-divided into three categories which share in common the notion that a person (*not* necessarily the creditor himself: see s 19(2)) initiates the linked transaction by 'suggesting it' to the debtor, hirer or his relative, who enters into the linked transaction (i) to induce the creditor to enter into the principal agreement (eg a contract for the maintenance of the goods suggested by the creditor); or (ii) for another purpose related to the principal agreement (eg in a contract for a holiday on credit terms, a policy of insurance against the risk of cancellation taken out at the creditor's suggestion); or (iii) where the principal agreement is a resticted-use credit

---

16 See also the CCA, Sch 2, example 11.
17 'Transaction' clearly has a wider meaning than 'agreement': see *Greenberg v IRC* [1972] AC 109, where Lord Simon considered it to be a 'business deal'. It is plain from s 96(2) that the linked transaction may itself be a regulated credit or hire agreement.
18 See ss 189(1) and 184 for the definition of 'relative'.

agreement, for a purpose related to a transaction financed or to be financed by the principal agreement (eg where the debtor agrees to take a freezer on credit and a supplier of frozen foods calls on the debtor and agrees to sell him frozen food with which to stock the freezer). Under s 171(2), there is a rebuttable presumption that the person who initiated the linked transaction by suggesting it to the debtor knew that the credit agreement had been made or contemplated that it might be made.

There are several crucial provisions in the CCA which define the relationship between the principal agreement and the linked transaction. First, s 19(3) provides that a linked transaction entered into before the making of the principal agreement has no effect until such time (if any) as that agreement is made. Second, a withdrawal from a prospective, principal agreement operates as a withdrawal from the linked transaction (ss 57(1) and 69(1)) and, likewise, a cancellation of the agreement operates to cancel the linked transaction and to withdraw any offer to enter into a linked transaction (s 69(1)).[19] In the event of cancellation of the linked transaction, s 70 provides that any sum which has been paid by the debtor is repayable and any sum which but for the cancellation would have been payable, ceases to be payable.[20] Moreover, if there is a cancellation of a linked transaction which concerns goods, s 72 imposes a duty on the debtor to surrender the goods[1] to the other party and, until surrender, to retain possession of the goods and take reasonable care of them. Third, if for any reason the debtor's indebtedness is discharged before the time fixed by the agreement, he is at the same time discharged from liability under the linked transaction, apart from debts which have already accrued (s 96(1)).

Certain types of linked transaction are exempted from the three foregoing provisions by Regulations[2] made in 1983, viz (i) contracts of insurance; (ii) written guarantees relating to goods; and (iii) agreements relating to the operation of a savings, deposit or current account. The rationale of excluding certain linked transactions from the cancellation provisions was to avert possible hardship to the debtor in the event of cancellation and this could arise, for example, should motor insurance be cancelled retrospectively. Nevertheless, the exemption of all classes of insurance is very controversial as insurance, in one guise or another, is a routine linked transaction and the fact that it is not automatically cancelled when the principal agreement is cancelled considerably detracts from the rationale and force of the CCA provisions. The Regulations relate only to insurance contracts as linked transactions and, of course, there might well be a right to cancel the insurance at common law or under statute.[3]

The second exemption concerning written guarantees relating to the goods is equally controversial. A guarantee is defined as anything in writing which contains a promise or assurance that defects in goods will be made good by complete or partial replacement, or by repair, monetary compensation or otherwise.[4] The

---

19   Rescission of the principal agreement at common law, eg for misrepresentation, does not seem to affect the linked transaction. Also, rather surprisingly, there is no provision in the CCA that the linked transaction is cancelled where the principal agreement has been improperly executed and is thus enforceable only by order of the court.
20   See the exception in s 70(5).
1   See the exceptions in s 72(9).
2   Consumer Credit (Linked Transactions) (Exemptions) Regulations 1983, SI 1983/1560.
3   See eg the Insurance Companies Act 1982, ss 75-77.
4   Consumer Credit (Linked Transactions) (Exemptions) Regulations 1983 (SI 1983/1560), reg 1(2).

upshot of this regulation is that, for example, the debtor may have cancelled a credit agreement relating to a home computer and returned it to the supplier, but nevertheless be saddled with a linked guarantee for the computer's maintenance and repair. From the debtor's perspective, this is clearly inapt.

The final type of linked transaction whch is excluded from the cancellation provisions is an agreement relating to the operation of a deposit or current account, including a savings account. This exception is more plausible and so, for example, a bank may stipulate that the debtor must open a current account as a condition of his obtaining a bank loan. In this event, the current account would be unaffected should the debtor cancel the loan or discharge his indebtedness before the time fixed by the loan agreement.

Credit-token agreements

A credit-token agreement is defined, somewhat tersely, in the CCA, s 14(2) as a 'regulated agreement for the provision of credit in connection with the use of a credit-token'.

Section 14(1) is more forthcoming and defines a credit-token as:

'... a card, check, voucher, coupon, stamp, form, booklet or other document or thing given to an individual by a person carrying on a consumer credit business, who undertakes –
(a) that on production of it (whether or not some other action is also required) he will supply cash, goods and services (or any of them) on credit, or
(b) that where, on the production of it to a third party (whether or not any other action is also required), the third party supplies cash, goods and services (or any of them), he will pay the third party for them (whether or not deducting any discount or commission), in return for payment to him by the individual.'

Paragraph (a) relates to two-party credit cards where the issuer is also the supplier (eg a large department store's credit card) and paragraph (b) applies to the three-party situation where the issuer of the card (eg a bank) is the party who agrees to pay the supplier for goods or services obtained by the debtor. As will be seen below, the definition of a credit-token is not dependent upon the existence of a regulated agreement, but a credit-token agreement is a regulated agreement.

Examples of credit-tokens include credit cards issued by a shop for use by customers to buy goods and have their accounts debited on credit terms, credit cards proper such as Access, Visa and Barclaycard, and 'checks' issued by check trading companies with which the holder can buy goods from approved suppliers.[5] There is some controversy as to whether bank cards used to obtain cash from automated cash dispensers (ATMs) and debit cards by which a supplier (eg a retailer) can claim reimbursement from the issuer (eg a bank) are within the classification of credit-tokens.[6] Certainly a cheque guarantee card by which a bank agrees to honour cheques drawn by its customers up to a stated limit is

---

5 A typical check trading arrangement is where on payment of, say, £5, C issues D with a trading check under which D can spend up to £100 at any shop which has agreed, or in future agrees, to take C's trading checks. The face value of the checks is paid by D to C in instalments. The trading check is a credit-token under s 14(1)(b).
6 See Ch 32, where this matter is discussed.

not a credit-token because payment by the bank to the retailer who supplied the goods, for example, is payment of the cheque and not payment for the goods.[7]

It has been held that a document can be a credit-token even where the creditor's promise to supply goods on production of the token is not binding contractually and thus there is no credit-token agreement in existence. In *Elliott v Director General of Fair Trading*,[8] a retailer of shoes instigated a promotional campaign whereby cardboard cards covered in plastic and thus closely resembling actual credit cards, were posted to members of the public. The cards, which were unsolicited, carried on their face the wording 'the Elliott Account ... valid September 1, 1977–August 30, 1978' and the reverse of the cards had a box for the customer's signature and stated that 'this credit card is valid for immediate use, the sole requirement is your signature and means of identification'. In fact, this was untrue as other conditions had to be satisfied in order to obtain credit such as signing forms and completing a direct debiting mandate to a bank. The retailer was charged with the offence of issuing unsolicited credit-tokens contrary to the CCA, s 51. At best, the issue of the card was an offer to enter into a credit-token agreement or, more likely, it was nothing more than an invitation to treat and so the defence argued that, until the other conditions had been satisfied, there was no credit-token agreement and the card was not a credit-token within s 14. Despite this argument, the Divisional Court upheld the conviction of the retailer. Lord Lane CJ stressed that the CCA, s 14(1), specified that the issuer of the card had only to *undertake* to provide credit and, consequently, there was no need for the existence of a contract or even the possibility of a contract. Second, it was held that the card was, both on its face and its reverse, a credit-token. Moreover, the Lord Chief Justice gave an alternative reason for his decision: even assuming that the necessary undertaking could not be established on the basis that other particulars had to be completed before credit would be granted, those other particulars fell within the wording of 14(1)(a), viz 'whether or not some other action is also required'.

Liability for misuse of credit-tokens

Although in some respects possession of a credit card is safer than carrying cash, there is clearly a grave risk if the card is used by a stranger without the debtor's permission. In the first place, the card might be stolen when it is first issued but before the debtor receives it and so the CCA, s 66 provides that the debtor is not liable for use made of a credit-token by another person unless (i) the debtor had previously accepted the token; or (ii) its use constituted an acceptance of it by him. By s 66(2), the debtor accepts a credit-token when he or a person authorised by him to use it under the terms of the agreement (a) signs it; or (b) signs a receipt for it; or (c) it is first used. No doubt problems lie in wait regarding (b) and whether the debtor must sign a receipt for the credit-token itself or whether it is sufficient simply to sign a receipt for the letter/package containing it.

The CCA, s 84, limits the debtor's liability for loss of the credit-token or its misuse by someone else. At the heart of s 84 is the notion that the debtor should give notice of the loss or misuse of the credit-token as quickly as possible and, in furtherance of this policy, the credit-token agreement must contain legible details of the name, address and telephone number of the person to whom notice

---

7   See the CCA, Sch 2, example 21.
8   [1980] 1 WLR 977.

can be given.[9] If the agreement does not contain this information, the debtor is not liable for misuse of the credit-token by others (s 84(4)). Once notice has been given to the creditor, either orally or in writing, that the credit-token has been lost or stolen or is for any other reason liable to misuse, the debtor is not liable for any loss arising subsequently (s 84(3)).[10]

Subject to these dominant provisions, if the credit-token is misused by someone who has acquired possession of it with the debtor's *consent*, the debtor is liable, under s 84(2), without limit. In cases of loss or theft, the debtor's liability is limited, under s 84(1), to £50[11] (or the credit limit if lower) for misuse during the period beginning when the credit-token ceased to be in the possession of an authorised person and ending when it is once again in the possession of an authorised person.[12] Finally, s 171 (4)(a) and (b) provide that, in any proceedings brought by the creditor under a credit-token agreement, it is (i) for the *creditor* to prove that the credit-token was lawfully supplied to the debtor, and was accepted by him (see s 66, above); and (ii) if the debtor alleges that any use made of the credit-token was not authorised by him, it is for the *creditor* to prove either that the use was so authorised or that the use occurred before the creditor had been given notice under s 84(3).

The EC Directive on 'distance selling'[13] demanded reform of some of the rules concerning the misuse of credit-tokens[14] in this type of distance contract. The Directive has now been implemented by the Consumer Protection (Distance Selling) Regulations 2000[15] which apply to contracts for goods or services to be supplied to a consumer by a supplier where the contract is made exclusively by means of distance communication, ie any means used 'without the simultaneous physical presence of the supplier and the consumer' (reg 3).[16] There are extensive provisions allowing the consumer to cancel such distance contracts and reg 21 provides that, where 'fraudulent use' has has been made of the consumer's 'payment card'[17] by 'another person not acting, or to be treated as acting, as his agent', the consumer can cancel the payment. If the payment has already been made, the consumer will be entitled to be recredited or to have all sums returned by the card issuer. As under the CCA, where the consumer alleges that the use of his card was not authorised by him, the burden is on the card issuer to prove otherwise (reg 21(3)).

---

9 See the Consumer Credit (Credit-Token Agreements) Regulations 1983 (SI 1983/1555).
10 Under s 84(5), notice takes effect when received but if it is given orally, and the agreement so requires, it shall be treated as not taking effect if not confirmed in writing within seven days.
11 See the Consumer Credit (Increase of Monetary Amounts) Order 1983 (SI 1983/1571) which increased the amount from £30 to £50.
12 See also the *Code of Banking Practice* (subscribed to by all leading banks and building societies) which is to similar effect in relation to 'payment cards', such cards *not* being limited to those which are 'credit-tokens' as defined by the CCA. This (voluntary) code provides that the card issuer will bear the full costs for all unauthorised use of the card once the card holder has told the issuer that it has been stolen or lost, and imposes a maximum liability of £50 in the event of misuse before the card holder has informed the issuer. The code applies only to 'personal customers' (ie private individuals) and excludes sole traders, partnerships and societies.
13 *Protection of Consumers in Respect of Distance Contracts* (Directive 97/7/EC, May 1997).
14 See art 8.
15 SI 2000/2334.
16 Schedule 1 provides an indicative list of distance communication, eg letter, telephone, electronic mail, catalogue, radio or television.
17 Regulation 21(6) defines 'payment card' as including 'credit cards, charge cards, debit cards and store cards'.

It will be apparent that these rules are premised on the fact that the consumer should be under *no liability* at all where there has been fraudulent use of his credit card. Consequently, reg 21(5) amends the CCA, s 84(1) and (2) by removing both the (potential) liability of the debtor for the unlimited liability posited by s 84(2), and his liability for the first £50 of loss to the creditor under s 84(1), where there has been misuse of a *credit-token* in connection with a *distance contract*. It should be stressed that this amendment is restricted to distance contracts and to the misuse of credit tokens, as defined by the CCA, and does not extend to 'payment cards' as defined in the Regulations.

Calculating the amount of credit provided

Agreements which exceed the credit limit specified above, currently £25,000, are not within the Act's control and so it is vital to know how the credit limit is calculated. In deciding whether an agreement is within the financial ceiling, it is necessary to separate 'fixed-sum credit' from 'running-account credit' as these classifications are crucial as regards the calculation of the credit limits.

FIXED-SUM CREDIT

The notion of 'fixed-sum credit'[18] is straightforward and comprises, for example, a personal loan of a fixed sum from a bank, building society or moneylender, hire-purchase agreements and both credit-sales and conditional sales. Fixed-sum credit is therefore a single advance and it will still be fixed-sum credit where the total amount is made available in instalments and even where the creditor makes a second loan to the debtor before the first is repaid – here there will simply be two fixed-sum credit agreements.

The amount of credit is here relatively ease to calculate: in the case of the loan it is the capital amount to be lent and in the case of hire-purchase, credit-sale and conditional sale of goods, it is the cash price less any deposit which is paid. It cannot be stressed enough that interest charges are *not* within the amount of *credit* allowed even though, of course, interest will be paid by the debtor and time will be allowed for its payment. Consequently, if a loan of £25,000 is made by the creditor, this is the amount of credit provided and, for the purposes of computing the credit, other fees and charges are disregarded. The CCA, s 9(4), thus provides that 'an item entering into the total charge for credit shall not be treated as credit even though time is allowed for its payment'.

RUNNING-ACCOUNT CREDIT

The matter is slightly more complicated where 'running-account credit'[19] is involved as this means that a fluctuating amount of credit is provided but with, normally, an upper-limit, eg bank overdrafts, credit cards, charge cards and retail shop accounts.[20] This type of credit is often referred to as 'revolving credit'

---

18 Defined in the CCA, s 10(1)(b).
19 Defined in the CCA, s 10(1)(a).
20 See the CCA, Sch 2, Part II, examples 15, 16, 18 and 23.

in that the debtor can draw on the account up to an agreed limit and each payment that the debtor makes in reduction of the debt restores the credit level by the amount of the payment. In relation to running-account credit, the CCA, s 10(2) specifies that 'credit limit' means 'as respects any period, the maximum debit balance which, under the credit agreement, is allowed to stand on the account during that period, disregarding any term of the agreement allowing that maximum to be exceeded merely temporarily'. The latter exception, relating to the maximum debit balance being temporarily exceeded, was inserted to elucidate the position where a bank honours a cheque drawn by its customer which goes beyond an agreed credit limit. Accordingly, if there is an agreed credit limit of £25,000 with a term permitting that amount to be exceeded temporarily, the agreement will nevertheless be within the CCA.

The CCA, s 10(3)(a) and (b) provide that running-account credit accounts will be taken to be within the £25,000 limit in four situations. First, and quite obviously, the agreement will be within the £25,000 limit where the credit limit does not exceed £25,000, eg an agreement providing that the debtor's total indebtedness shall not at any one time exceed £25,000. However, s 10(3)(b) then sets forth three situations where running-account credit is deemed not to exceed £25,000 whether or not there is a credit limit and, if there is, notwithstanding that it exceeds £25,000. These three situations are easily understood when it is appreciated that they are anti-avoidance measures in that, without them, it would be easy for a creditor to take the agreement outside the Act's protection by fixing an illusory, upper-credit limit or no credit limit at all.

The first situation, in s 10(3)(b)(i), is where the debtor cannot draw at any one time more than £25,000, no matter how high the credit limit is. If, for example, a bank provides an overdraft facility of £200,000 *or* a facility without limit, but qualifies this by a provision that the debtor can draw no more than £20,000 in any one month, the agreement will be within the CCA.

The second situation, in s 10(3)(b)(ii), is also designed to block the creditor's attempted avoidance of the Act. The creditor might set a high credit limit but seek to discourage high levels of borrowing by having a scale of increasing charges, eg a credit limit of £35,000 with interest charges being doubled at amounts above £10,000. In this way the creditor might hope to avoid the Act's provisions by setting the high credit limit but know that the debtor is effectively thwarted from borrowing more than £10,000. Consequently, where the increased charges commence (or any other conditions favouring the creditor are imposed, eg the debtor must provide security) at a level *below* the Act's financial ceiling of £25,000, the agreement will be a consumer credit agreement within the Act (as in the above example of doubled interest charges at £10,000).

The third situation, in s 10(3)(b)(iii), is formulated to cope with those situations where the credit limit imposed is unrealistic in the particular situation or no limit is imposed. Accordingly, if it is 'probable' at the date of the agreement that the amount of credit granted will not 'at any time' exceed the statutory limit of £25,000, the agreement will be a consumer credit agreement within the Act. The example of this situation in the Act[1] is that C agrees to provide D, a small shopkeeper who carries a stock of about £1,000, with short-term finance to enable him to acquire stock needed for the shop from time to time. Although there is no credit limit, it is probable that D's indebtedness will not at any time rise above [£25,000] and so the agreement is a consumer credit agreement within the Act.

---

1 Schedule 2, example 7.

There is clearly a degree of uncertainty in s 10(3)(b)(iii). Example 7, above, is tolerably clear but there is potential difficulty where, in long-term arrangements, the debtor will require finance which is close to the Act's credit limit.The uncertainty is lessened in that the probability of the credit's exceeding £25,000 is tested at the date of the agreement and thus subsequent events are disregarded and, similarly, s 171(1) allows the parties to agree that s 10(3)(b)(iii) does not apply to the agreement.

DIFFERENTIATING THE *AMOUNT* OF THE CREDIT FROM THE TOTAL *CHARGE* FOR THE CREDIT

Prior to the CCA, there were very few statutory controls on the calculation of interest in credit agreements[2] and, in those situations where no controls existed, there was no standardised method by which interest was calculated and expressed. In an area where abuse of the debtor has always been rife, it is not surprising that attempts have been made consistently to disguise the true costs of finance. At one extreme, it was not uncommon for a false hire-purchase price to be stated, eg that a fictitious deposit had been paid by the debtor, in a crude attempt to take the agreement outside the statutory financial limits.[3] Less obvious practices concerned the imposition of hidden, extra charges on the debtor and the rate of interest was usually stated as a 'flat rate' so that the actual amount which was payable by the debtor was grossly distorted.[4] In *Reading Trust Ltd v Spero*,[5] Scrutton LJ's telling example was that 'to pay sixpence for the loan of a pound for a week does not sound harsh and unconscionable, but it is at the rate of 130 per cent. per annum'.[6]

As well as seeking to control the disreputable and dishonest creditor, a central tenet of the Crowther Report was that there should be standardised rules for stating the cost of credit thus enabling debtors to compare the costs of borrowing offered by the numerous lenders vieing for custom in the market place. Consequently, a crucial distinction is drawn in the CCA between the *amount* of the credit which is provided and the total *charge* for that credit and it must be stressed that these are mutually exclusive terms. There are two crucial issues which emanate from this distinction.

First, the CCA, s 9(4) provides that 'an item entering into the total charge for credit shall not be treated as credit even though time is allowed for its payment' and so, in calculating whether or not the credit exceeds the £25,000 financial ceiling, the charge made for that credit must be disregarded (eg interest, credit charges and certain fees).[7] The CCA, s 20, defines the total charge for credit as

---

2   See the Moneylenders Acts 1900-1927 and the Hire-Purchase Act 1965.
3   See *Menzies v United Motor Finance Corpn Ltd* [1940] 1 KB 559 (the instalments to be paid amounted to £37 but the agreement stated that a further £25 had been paid as a deposit, bringing the total price to £62. The financial limit at the time was £50. The £25 had never been paid and, as the real price of the car was £37, the agreement was held to be within the hire-purchase legislation).
4   The flat rate is applied to the original credit advanced and takes no account of the fact that the outstanding capital is *reducing* during the agreement; the actual annual rate (APR) is about double the flat rate.
5   [1930] 1 KB 492.
6   [1930] 1 KB 492 at 503.
7   See the CCA, Sch 2, example 10 (the figures given are outdated but the method of calculation is, of course, correct).

'the true cost to the debtor of the credit provided or to be provided under an actual or prospective consumer credit agreement'.

Second, s 20 provides for the making of regulations prescribing the method of calculating both the *total charge for credit* and the *rate of the total charge for credit* (ie its expression as an annual percentage rate, referred to as the APR), and also by providing for regulations which ensure that the charge for credit and the APR are disclosed in advertisements, quotations and the agreement itself.[8] It is apparent that the calculation/disclosure of these charges and rates is vitally important and the issue of charges is also significant in the performance of the agreement where, for example, the debtor makes an early settlement or exercises his right to cancel the agreement.

The Consumer Credit (Total Charge for Credit) Regulations 1980[9] prescribe which items are to be treated as entering into the total charge for credit. Regulation 4 provides that the total charge for credit must include:

(i) the total of the interest payments, and
(ii) 'other charges' at any time 'payable under the transaction' by or on behalf of the debtor or a relative of his whether to the creditor or any other person, notwithstanding that the whole or any part of the charge may be repayable at any time. The date for determining the total charge for credit is the date of the agreement (reg 3).

It is self-evident why category (i), the interest payments, are within the total charge for credit, but category (ii) deliberately extends the reach of the regulations to 'other charges' made, for example, under subsidiary contracts such as repair or maintenance. The Crowther Committee[10] stressed that, if the rules were limited simply to charges made under the credit agreement itself, the creditor could quote an attractively meagre rate of interest but impose charges for other ancillary services, eg documentation fees. Accordingly, if the debtor is *required* to pay any of the following, they are 'other charges' within the total charge for credit: legal costs, surveyors' fees, stamp duties, insurance premiums or charges for guarantees required by the creditor for the sole purpose of ensuring that all or part of the credit, interest and other charges is repaid in the event of the debtor's death, invalidity, illness or unemployment, installation/maintenance charges and fees payable to a credit broker for negotiating the credit. This statement must be qualified immediately, however, in that certain charges are excluded by reg 5.

There are numerous charges which are excluded under reg 5, and the categories must be understood in order to appreciate the rationale of this part of the CCA. Arguably the most important point is that default charges payable in the event of the debtor's failure to comply with the contract are excluded. For example, the agreement might provide that higher rates of interest become payable on payments that are overdue, but the stipulated higher rates are excluded. Again, should the debtor agree to keep the goods in good working order but fail to do so with the consequence that the creditor pays repair charges to a third party and then seeks indemnity from the debtor under the terms of the credit agreement, the amount claimed does not figure in the total charge for credit.

---

8 See the CCA, ss 44, 52 and 60. Regarding consumers' understanding of APR, see *Consumers' Appreciation of 'Annual Percentage Rates'*, OFT Research Paper 4 (OFT 104, 1994); *Consumer Credit Deregulation* (OFT 103, 1994), Ch 7.
9 SI 1980/51 as amended by SI 1985/1192; SI 1989/596; SI 1999/3177.
10 *Report of the Committee on Consumer Credit* (Cmnd 4596, 1971), para 6.5.17.

Although the additional items which are excluded in reg 5 cannot be exhaustively classified here, the principal categories of excluded charges can be outlined and the reasons for their exclusion explained, viz:

(i) charges that would be payable if the same goods/services were bought for cash rather than on credit terms, eg delivery charges;

(ii) maintenance or repair charges which become *necessary* and therefore arise only spasmodically, eg the debtor agrees to maintain the goods and enters into a contract of maintenance where charges would be payable *only* where the goods need repairing;

(iii) bank charges levied on current accounts which accrue upon the debtor's use of the credit arrangement – here the creditor cannot know how often the debtor may use his account and so he is unable to calculate the charges;

(iv) incidental charges incurred by the debtor prior to the application for the credit agreement which provide him with benefits other than access to credit, eg membership subscription of the RAC or AA motoring clubs where the debtor/member might have access to credit facilities at a preferential rate – if this were not excluded, the membership fee would have to be included in the total charge for credit;

(v) all insurance premiums apart from those specified above as included, eg premiums under insurance taken out before the debtor applies for a credit agreement but covering the goods under that agreement (an existing home contents policy, for example); premiums under a voluntary contract of insurance which the debtor takes out but which is not required as a condition of the making of the agreement by the creditor.

Provided that the total charge for credit has been ascertained, it is possible to determine the annual percentage rate (APR) of the total charge for credit. The rules for calculating the APR have recently been amended by Regulations[11] which implement the latest EC Directive.[12] The old methods of calculation have been replaced by a single method and the resulting rate is required to be rounded to one decimal place.

The consequences of failing to separate the amount of the credit from the cost of the credit were illustrated recently in *Wilson v First County Trust Ltd (No 2)*.[13] The debtor wished to raise a six-month loan of £5,000 on the security of her car and the creditor charged her a document fee of £250 but, as the debtor could not pay the fee immediately, it was added to the amount of the loan which was recorded as £5,250. The debtor argued that the £250 document fee was an item entering into the total charge for credit which, under s 9(4), should not be taken into account in ascertaining the amount of the credit. The Court of Appeal held that the agreement contravened the Consumer Credit (Total Charge for Credit) Regulations 1980 and, as it lacked a 'prescribed term', it was totally unenforceable under s 127(3). However, most significantly, it was also held that the absolute prohibition on enforceability in s 127(3) infringed Article 6.1 of the European Convention on Human Rights. This startling aspect of the decision is considered in more detail in Chapter 37.

---

11 The Consumer Credit (Total Charge for Credit, Agreements and Advertisements) (Amendment) Regulations 1999 (SI 1999/3177).

12 Directive 98/7/EC.

13 (2001) Times, 16 May; see also [2001] QB 407 (interim judgment).

Restricted-use and unrestricted-use credit

A further distinction in the CCA is made between restricted-use credit, defined in s 11(1), and unrestricted-use credit which is defined negatively in s 11(2) as not being restricted-use credit. These categories cross and intertwine with those previously considered.

RESTRICTED-USE CREDIT

As its name suggests, a restricted-use credit agreement is a regulated consumer credit agreement under which credit is provided to finance a *particular* purchase or transaction and the *creditor* can *control*[14] how the finance is to be applied. Three categories of restricted-use credit are recognised in s 11.

The first categorisation, in s 11(1)(a), is the most obvious one and comprises, for example, hire-purchase, credit-sale, conditional sale and retail shop accounts, and here the creditor is also the supplier of the goods, services or land to the debtor.[15] Credit hire agreements are also within this classification following the decision of the House of Lords in *Dimond v Lovell*.[16]

Second, in s 11(1)(b), there are situations where, for example, the supplier of goods to the debtor is a third party and the creditor provides the finance by paying the supplier, eg the creditor/finance company makes a personal loan to a debtor for the purpose of buying goods but the creditor pays the supplier for those goods directly.

Third, s 11(1)(c) recognises that there can be circumstances where there is an agreement to refinance any *existing* indebtedness of the debtor to the creditor *or* to another person. Two situations are thus envisaged within this third category, viz (i) the debtor is in difficulties and so the creditor makes a new advance of money to the debtor to be used to pay-off the existing loan, or (ii) the debtor's indebtedness to third parties is discharged by the creditor's payment to those third parties.

Finally, it is important to stress that, under s 11(3), an agreement is *not* one for restricted-use credit if the credit is provided in such a way that the debtor is free to use it as he chooses, even though 'certain uses' would contravene the credit agreement. This presumably covers the case where a bank loan to buy a car is paid *directly to the debtor* with a stipulation that he must buy the car from a particular supplier but the debtor chooses to buy the car from a different supplier.[17]

UNRESTRICTED-USE CREDIT

An unrestricted-use credit agreement is defined negatively in s 11(2) as not being a restricted-use credit agreement, as defined in s 11(1). In unrestricted-use credit,

---

14 See the CCA, s 11(3), considered below.
15 See also the CCA, Sch 2, example 10.
16 [2000] 2 All ER 897.
17 But see the CCA Sch 2, example 12, where this permutation of the facts is not used to illustrate s 11(3).

the *debtor* has control over the application of the finance which is provided instead of that control being exercised by the creditor. If the debtor has this element of control and is at liberty to use the credit as he chooses, the credit will be within the unrestricted-use classification *even* if the debtor has agreed with the creditor to use the loan for a particular purpose. Examples of unrestricted-use credit include a bank's personal loans and overdrafts, and pawnbrokers' loans.

Debtor-creditor-supplier agreements and debtor-creditor agreements

WHAT ARE 'DEBTOR-CREDITOR-SUPPLIER' AND 'DEBTOR-CREDITOR' AGREEMENTS?

These inelegant, confusing appellations have, in fact, relatively straightforward meanings which inter-relate with the two definitions of credit considered above, ie restricted-use credit and unrestricted-use credit. Once it is realised that the debtor-creditor-supplier agreements and debtor-creditor agreements relate principally to the *nature of the transactions* involved and are *not* a delineation of three-party and two-party transactions respectively, the issues become clearer.

Debtor-creditor-supplier agreements denote that there is a close connection between the credit agreement and the supply of goods or services, whereas debtor-creditor agreements indicate that there is no such connection. The nature of this connection must be considered first. The Crowther Committee[18] considered that there were good reasons to separate 'connected loans' from 'unconnected loans' in the sense that, where a loan is advanced to a debtor who decides to use it to buy goods on cash terms, the purchase of the goods is nothing more than a straightforward sale of goods and the loan provided in order that the debtor may buy the goods is simply a normal loan of money. The two transactions of sale and loan are thus *separate* and *unconnected*. This description thus contains the elements of a debtor-creditor agreement, an example of such an agreement being a loan of money from a bank or finance house which the debtor decides to use to buy a car from a second-hand car dealer.

If, on the other hand, the price of the goods is advanced by the seller himself or by a connected lender in the sense that the lender has a business connection with the seller which consists of providing loans to debtors for the purchase of goods from that seller, the sale of the goods and the loan of the money are *connected* and *entwined*. Where a seller of goods allows the buyer to have credit terms (eg credit-sale), there is thus an immediate, linear connection between the parties. Moreover, in those instances where the lender and supplier/seller are separate parties, they are nevertheless connected in the sense of being engaged in a joint venture with mutual benefits. These are descriptions of debtor-creditor-supplier agreements. Where the supplier of the credit and the supplier of the goods are the same person, the agreement is definitely a debtor-creditor-supplier agreement, eg a credit-sale between seller and buyer or a hire-purchase agreement. Equally, where the creditor and the supplier are distinct and separate parties but are connected by business arrangements, the agreement is always a debtor-creditor-supplier

18   See *Report of the Committee on Consumer Credit* (Cmnd 4596, 1971), paras 6.2.22-6.2.24.

agreement, eg a restricted-use credit agreement within s 11(1)(b) where, for example, the creditor/finance company and the supplier have an existing business connection and the creditor makes a personal loan to the debtor for the purpose of buying a car from the supplier/seller with payment being made by the creditor directly to the supplier/seller of the car. Here it is apparent that the creditor and the seller are committed to a symbiotic, business relationship.

It will be immediately apparent from these examples that it is *not* the number of parties which is the central feature of the these definitions; in a debtor-creditor-supplier agreement, for example, there might be only two parties to the agreement (eg credit-sale) and not three parties as the designation 'debtor-creditor-supplier' implies.

THE DEFINITION OF DEBTOR-CREDITOR-SUPPLIER AGREEMENTS IN THE CCA

A debtor-creditor-supplier agreement is defined in the CCA, s 12, as a regulated consumer credit agreement falling into one of three categories recognised in that section. As stressed above, the essence of the debtor-creditor-supplier agreement is that there is a close connection between the creditor and the supplier of the goods or services and the loan which is advanced is thus what the Crowther Committee categorised as a 'connected loan'.

The first category, in s 12(a), is a restricted-use credit agreement which falls within s 11(1)(a). The latter section applies to a regulated consumer credit agreement 'to finance a transaction between the debtor and the creditor'. This covers, for example, hire-purchase, credit-sale, conditional sale, retail shop accounts, and 'credit hire'[19] agreements. It must be stressed that, in these situations, the creditor and supplier are the *same person* and so the supply of the goods/services and the granting of credit to the debtor are amalgamated in one agreement. Section 12(a) thus applies exclusively to two-party debtor-creditor-supplier agreements. Consequently, in hire-purchase transactions, the 'supplier' refers to the creditor who is the legal supplier[20] and not the dealer who physically supplies/delivers the goods to the debtor.

Second, s 12(b) acknowledges a restricted-use credit agreement which falls within s 11(1)(b), meaning one to finance a transaction between a debtor and a person (the supplier) other than the creditor provided that it is made by the creditor under 'pre-existing arrangements', or in 'contemplation of future arrangements', between himself and the supplier. It is plain that this has to be a three-party arrangement. Within this category is the situation, for example, where the debtor wants to buy a car from a seller/supplier and the finance is provided by the creditor who has an existing business relationship with the seller, the price of the car being paid directly to that seller. Similarly, s 12(b) applies to transactions where the debtor uses a credit card (eg a Visa or Access card) to buy goods as here arrangements will have been made between the creditor and the supplier of the goods. It should be stressed that, under s 12(b), the credit agreement can be made in circumstances where the creditor and supplier have *pre-existing* arrangements or where it is made in contemplation of *future* arrangements. These 'arrangements' will be examined in more detail later.

---

19   See *Dimond v Lovell* [2000] 2 All ER 897.
20   See the CCA, s 189(1) for the definition of 'supplier'.

The third category, in s 12(c), is an unrestricted-use credit agreement which is made by the creditor under pre-existing arrangements between himself and a person (the supplier) other than the debtor in the knowledge that the credit is to be used to finance a transaction between the debtor and the supplier. An example within s 12(c) would be where a supplier of goods and a creditor/finance company have an existing, business relationship and the supplier will deal with customers on cash terms only. Consequently, the supplier always directs a debtor/customer to the creditor so that the debtor can obtain a loan. Even where the loan is advanced by the creditor directly to the debtor and can be applied by the debtor for any *purpose* that he chooses, the agreement will be within s 12(c) if the creditor knows that the loan will be used to finance a transaction between the debtor and the supplier.[1] Under s 12(c), there *must* be 'pre-existing arrangements' between the creditor and supplier and this difference between s 12(b) and s 12(c) is explainable because, where the agreement relates to unrestricted-use credit, as in s 12(c), an agreement made merely in contemplation of future arrangements would not amount to a sufficiently close connection between the creditor and supplier for the purposes of the debtor-creditor-supplier agreement.

What are the 'arrangements' referred to in s 12?

The CCA, s 187, expands on the meaning of such arrangements between the creditor (C) and supplier (S) thereby shedding some light on the nature of the joint venture in which these two parties must be engaged, although the wording is elusive at best.

Pre-existing arrangements

Section 187(1) and (4) define 'pre-existing arrangements' as 'arrangements previously made' between C and S (or their associates) and so these arrangements must have been made between C and S *before* the debtor applies for credit from C. They will include prior arrangements between retailers and banks who supply customer/debtors with cheque cards such as Visa, under which retailers agree to accept the use of the cards in their shops[2] and arrangements where S is supplied with proposal forms from C and C always pays S a commission for introducing customer/debtors to C.[3] Section 187(3)(a) and (b) reinforce the fact that the arrangements must be pre-existing by excluding arrangements made in 'specified circumstances' for payments by C to S and those arrangements where C merely 'holds himself out' as willing to make such payments to S, eg C introduces a cheque card scheme and advertises it by writing to major retailers.[4]

Section 187(5) provides that where C is an associate of S, eg where they are part of the same group of companies, there is a (rebuttable) presumption that there are pre-existing arrangements between the two companies.

Future arrangements

Section 187(2) provides that 'a consumer credit agreement shall be treated as entered into in contemplation of future arrangements between a creditor and a

---

1 See the CCA, Sch 2, example 8.
2 See the CCA, Sch 2, example 21.
3 See the CCA, Sch 2, example 8.
4 See the CCA, Sch 2, example 21.

supplier if it is entered into *in the expectation that arrangements will subsequently be made* [between C and S] for the supply of cash, goods and services ... to be financed by *the* consumer credit agreement'. It is clear that the contemplated future arrangements referred to do not mean a nebulous, equivocal prospect of business arrangements between C and S regarding the extension of credit in relation to further, future agreements. The matter is complicated, however, by the reference in s 187(2) to the somewhat indeterminate 'expectation' that arrangements will subsequently be made between C and S. This must indicate that there is no need for an *agreement* between C and S relating to the future arrangements. Thus, at the date of the consumer credit agreement, there need only be an expectation of C's arrangement with S for S to supply goods, for example, to the debtor pursuant to C's granting of credit under *that* consumer credit agreement with the debtor. This would apply to the situation where, for example, a creditor issues a credit card to a customer/debtor in the expectation that arrangements will be made between creditor and supplier for the supplier to accept the cards, or where there is an expectation that arrangements will be made between creditor and supplier for the supplier to join that credit card scheme and accept the cards when presented.

Debtor-creditor-supplier agreements and the CCA, s 75

Where there is a debtor-creditor-supplier agreement within s 12(b) or (c), the claim available to the debtor under the CCA, s 75 is of great significance as the section provides that, if the debtor has a claim against the *supplier* for misrepresentation or breach of contract, he shall have a 'like claim' against the creditor.[5] However, s 75 does *not* apply to debtor-creditor agreements.

THE DEFINITION OF DEBTOR-CREDITOR AGREEMENTS IN THE CCA

A debtor-creditor agreement exists where there is no connection between the creditor and supplier of the goods or services and the loan is thus what the Crowther Committee referred to as an 'unconnected loan'. The debtor-creditor agreement is defined in the CCA, s 13, where three types of this regulated consumer credit agreement are recognised but this is rather a laboriously obsessive exercise in that the Act might just as well have defined the debtor-creditor agreement as one which was *not* a debtor-creditor-supplier agreement.

First, under s 13(a), the debtor-creditor agreement can be a restricted-use credit agreement which falls within s 11(1)(b) but is not made under pre-existing arrangements nor in contemplation of future arrangements between the creditor and a supplier. This covers the situation where, for example, the enterprising debtor uses his own initiative to locate a creditor to finance the purchase of goods from a supplier but the creditor insists on direct payment to the supplier.

Second, under s 13(b), the debtor-creditor agreement can be one for restricted-use credit which falls within s 11(1)(c) as an agreement to refinance any existing indebtedness of the debtor's whether to the creditor or another person. This applies to the grant of *new* credit to discharge, wholly or in part, an existing indebtedness of the debtor to the creditor who provides that new credit or to discharge debts owed to a third party.

---

5 Section 75 is considered in detail in Ch 35.

Third, s 13(c) recognises a debtor-creditor agreement which is one for unrestricted-use credit which is not made under pre-existing arrangements between creditor and supplier. This covers all personal loans where there is no connection between the creditor and the supplier and the loan is paid directly to the debtor who is free to apply it in whatever way he pleases. In this latter example of a personal loan, the agreement would still be a debtor-creditor agreement for unrestricted-use credit where, *vis-à-vis* creditor and debtor, the loan is advanced for a particular purpose but the debtor breaches his contract with the creditor and uses the loan for a different purpose from that stipulated (see s 11(3), above).

CHAPTER 32

The different types of credit available to the debtor

Introduction

A striking feature of English law in the larger part of the 20th century was the distinction that was drawn between loan credit ('lender-credit') and sale credit ('vendor-credit'). The category of lender-credit comprised those cases where the debtor obtained a loan of money from a bank, for example, and then utilised the loan to buy goods or pay for services. The latter classification of vendor-credit comprised principally hire-purchase, conditional sale and credit-sale. Loans of money had always been subject to the usury laws and, from 1900, loans came under the control of the Moneylenders Acts. However, the transactions which fell within the vendor-credit category were not regarded as loans of money and, consequently, were outside the control of those Acts.[1] Indeed, Diplock LJ stressed in *Premor Ltd v Shaw Bros*[2] that the economic function of the transaction, viz providing credit to a purchaser of goods, should not be confused with the legal nature of the transaction and 'the whole object of a hire-purchase transaction is to avoid performing that economic function by means of a loan of money on the security of goods'. As outlined in Chapter 30, in the 20th century hire-purchase slowly became subject to control both at common law and under statute.

By the mid 1960s, hire-purchase was becoming less popular with the larger finance companies because it was subject to tight controls under the Hire Purchase Act 1965 and, at that time, regulations also demanded minimum deposits on goods in order to restrain consumer spending. Consumers increasingly wanted loans of money to pay for holidays abroad and the provision of services such as the installation of double-glazing, but the hire-purchase format was suited to financing only sales of goods. In the 1960s, a customer's creditworthiness could be more easily verified than before because credit reference agencies had become an established feature of the credit market and so it was less important for finance houses to have a security interest in the goods supplied on credit terms. Consequently, finance houses began to provide personal loans to consumers for the purchase of goods and services direct from third party retailers with whom the finance houses were 'connected'.

---

1 See *Olds Discount Co Ltd v John Playfair Ltd* [1938] 3 All ER 275; *Olds Discount Co Ltd v Cohen* [1938] 3 All ER 281n.
2 [1964] 1 WLR 978, 985.

In the 'connected lender' situation, the retailer directs the consumer to a particular finance house in order to obtain a loan and the finance house, in turn, stipulates that the loan must be employed to purchase goods or services from that particular retailer. In some instances the loan is paid direct to the retailer for the goods supplied. Moreover, the retailer is paid a substantial commission by the finance house on credit business introduced thus giving the retailer a positive incentive to procure a credit transaction as opposed to a cash sale. This method of doing business clearly had advantages for the finance house and the retailer but there were serious drawbacks for the consumer/debtor. First, as finance houses furnished a loan of money and did not sell the goods to the consumer, they carried no liability under the Sale of Goods Act 1893 for defective goods supplied, for example. This was in sharp contrast to hire-purchase where the finance house was liable by virtue of statutory implied terms in Hire-Purchase legislation relating, for example, to merchantable quality and fitness for purpose of the goods supplied. Second, although the retailer would be directly liable on the contract with the consumer (eg a sale of goods), if the retailer became insolvent the debtor would have no practical recourse against him and would, nevertheless, be bound to maintain the repayments under the loan contract.

This form of connected lending arguably had wider ramifications which emanated from the connected, yet strangely impersonal structure, of the tripartite relationship which was created. The retailer was almost certainly less concerned with customer satisfaction if the finance house effectively supported his business by generating customers for whom he did not have to compete and, likewise, if the finance house was not liable for defective goods or services, it had little interest in supervising the retailer's business standards. The Crowther Committee's Report differentiated between connected lenders who were involved in a 'joint venture'[3] as described above, and wholly independent lenders. While it was thought that there was no justification to make the latter group liable for defects in the goods supplied with the aid of the loan, it was strongly recommended that the connected lender should be liable for misrepresentations made by the retailer in antecedent negotiations *and* for breaches of the agreement between the customer and the retailer relating to defective goods, for example. This suggested reform was clearly a radical one. Most significantly, the Consumer Credit Act 1974 embodies the Crowther recommendations in ss 75 and 56 and in the concept of the 'linked transaction', all of which are considered in detail in later chapters. Under s 75, for example, where a debtor has a claim against the supplier for breach of contract he has a 'like claim' against the creditor.

It is thus apparent that, although hire-purchase had proven to be a popular method of granting credit, many other forms of credit had begun to develop and overtake it in the 20th century. In 1971, the Crowther Committee on Consumer Credit[4] criticised robustly the anomalies in the varying kinds of legal restriction imposed on different types of lenders and traders. The Crowther Committee's view was that the law was concerned with form rather than substance[5] and that, in order to remedy this state of affairs, credit transactions should be consolidated so that the essence of the transaction – the granting of credit – would thus be accentuated and controlled appropriately. As a result, the CCA was passed by Parliament but implementation of the Act was slow. Following the Act, various

---

3   See *Report of the Committee on Consumer Credit* (Cmnd 4596, 1971), para 6.6.22 *et seq.*
4   *Report of the Committee on Consumer Credit* (Cmnd 4596, 1971).
5   *Report of the Committee on Consumer Credit* (Cmnd 4596, 1971), para 4.2.2.

Regulations were made to amplify and implement it and parts of the Act were brought into effect on different dates, but the CCA only became fully effective in May 1985. Much of the protection previously accorded to hirers who took goods on hire-purchase is given by the Act to individuals who obtain goods (or services) through other types of credit transaction, while those taking goods on hire-purchase receive additional protection.

It had always been customary in hire-purchase to refer to the customer as the 'hirer' and the other two parties as the 'dealer' and the 'finance company' and these terms are obviously still used when discussing the earlier law. However, the CCA introduced an array of new terminology: in particular, the *debtor* is the customer who has to repay the loan and the *creditor* is the person who provides the finance, eg the finance company. Although it is common to find that the term 'dealer' is still used in hire-purchase, the dealer is often characterised in the CCA as a *credit-broker*.[6] Strictly speaking, the terms 'owner' and 'hirer' should now be confined to hiring or leasing of goods under the CCA, s 15. The CCA does perpetuate, however, the reference to goods being 'bailed' under the hire-purchase agreement.[7]

The principal methods of granting credit

The CCA 1974 covers a very wide range of credit agreements. It applies to hire-purchase, conditional sales and, with some modifications, credit-sale agreements but it also governs moneylending transactions and pledges and the legislation dealing with these transactions, the Moneylenders Acts 1900–1927 and the Pawnbrokers Acts 1872–1960, have been repealed. Furthermore, the 1974 Act covers a wide range of other credit transactions such as check trading, credit card transactions, bank overdrafts and other types of running-account credit. Finally, the CCA applies also to hire or rental agreements.

It is now important to delineate the principal methods of granting credit, dissect the legal structure of the various arrangements and examine the parties involved. The CCA is a remarkably technical piece of legislation which formulates numerous categories of credit transaction and yet, paradoxically, the technical categories which are created are often framed in somewhat intangible terms. This amalgam of the technical and the abstract is somewhat alarming and, moreover, very little sense can be derived by advancing through the sections of the Act in chronological order. Consequently, any exposition of the CCA is dogged by the need to make extensive cross-references within the Act.

HIRE-PURCHASE

The essential features of a hire-purchase agreement are that (i) the debtor hires the goods from the creditor/finance company under a contract of bailment; (ii) the creditor/finance company retains property in the goods during the period of hire; (iii) the debtor/customer makes instalment payments of the price and is granted an option to purchase after payment of the instalments; and (iv) a contract

---

6 See the definitions of these terms in the CCA, ss 189(1) and 145.
7 See the definition of 'hire-purchase agreement' in the CCA, s 189(1).

of sale of goods is formed if the debtor/customer decides to exercise the option and buy the goods. These elements are included in the CCA, s 189(1), which provides that:

> '"hire-purchase agreement" means an agreement, other than a conditional sale agreement, under which –
> (a) goods are bailed or (in Scotland) hired in return for periodical payments by the person to whom they are bailed or hired, and
> (b) the property in the goods will pass to that person if the terms of the agreement are complied with and one or more of the following occurs –
>   (i)   the exercise of an option to purchase by that person,
>   (ii) the doing of any other specified act by any party to the agreement,
>   (iii) the happening of any other specified event.'

When a customer/debtor wishes to take goods from a dealer/owner on hire-purchase, the dealer himself often does not have the resources to provide credit and, consequently, the common form of hire-purchase transaction is that the dealer sells the goods to a finance company and the finance company, now the owner of the goods, enters into the hire-purchase agreement with the customer. The dealer will retain the deposit paid by the customer and receive the balance of the purchase price from the finance company.

Under this method of contracting, the rights and obligations under the hire-purchase agreement exist between the customer and the finance company and the dealer will not be a party to that agreement. The Supply of Goods (Implied Terms) Act 1973, ss 9-11, apply to every[8] hire-purchase agreement and terms relating to the description and quality of the goods and their fitness for purpose are implied into the agreement. The Unfair Contract Terms Act 1977 controls the attempted restriction or exclusion of these implied terms which correspond very closely to those in the SGA 1979, ss 13-15. The sale by the dealer to the finance company will, of course, be subject to the SGA 1979 except insofar as the obligations implied by that Act have been excluded or varied in the sale which has taken place between the two businesses involved.

The CCA extends to hire-purchase agreements by virtue of s 9(3) which provides that 'the person by whom goods are bailed ... to an individual under a hire-purchase agreement shall be taken to provide him with fixed-sum credit to finance the transaction of an amount equal to the total price of the goods less the aggregate of the deposit (if any) and the total charge for credit'. A regulated hire-purchase agreement is a debtor-creditor-supplier agreement for restricted-use credit.

The basic mechanics of the hire-purchase transaction, described above, involve 'direct collection' as the finance company collects the payments direct from the customer but there is an alternative method of operation known as 'block discounting'. Here the dealer enters into hire-purchase agreements directly with customers and then *assigns* his rights under them, together usually with the ownership in the goods, to a finance company. The dealer normally continues to collect instalments as they become due from the customer but does so under the block discounting scheme as agent for the finance company. This system considerably reduces administration and attendant costs for the finance company but its disadvantage is that the finance company is vulnerable should the dealer be fraudulent or inept.

---

8   The implied terms apply to every hire-purchase agreement and they are *not* restricted to regulated agreements within the CCA: they are thus implied into the agreement irrespective of the amount financed and even where the debtor is not an individual but is, instead, a body corporate.

Recourse and re-purchase agreements

The finance company often enters into a 'recourse agreement' with the dealer, meaning that the dealer agrees to be liable to the finance company in the event of the customer's default. In this way, the finance company attemps to minimise some of the obvious risks it runs in hire-purchase.

The recourse agreement may take the form of a re-purchase agreement. Here the dealer agrees to re-purchase the goods from the finance company if the customer defaults and the hire-purchase agreement is terminated. This may not be as advantageous to the finance company as it appears at first glance. The drawback of this undertaking is that, if it is to enforce the obligation, the finance company must be in a position to deliver the goods to the dealer for, otherwise, there is a total failure of consideration. Where the customer has absconded with the goods, for instance, it is clear that the dealer cannot be compelled to re-purchase them.[9] Similarly, if the finance company wishes to enforce the agreement against the dealer, it must do so within a reasonable time of repossessing the goods. In *United Dominions Trust (Commercial) Ltd v Eagle Aircraft Services Ltd*,[10] the plaintiff finance company (P) supplied an aircraft on hire-purchase to the hirer, Orion Airways Ltd (H), and the defendant dealer (D) agreed to re-purchase it from P, at a price equal to the outstanding balance plus expenses, if the hire-purchase agreement should be terminated by either party before payment of the full hire-purchase price. The recourse agreement also provided that P would notify D within seven days of every default by H in payment. When H had defaulted and gone into liquidation, P terminated the hire-purchase agreement but did not give D notice of the default within seven days and allowed five months to elapse before asking D to re-purchase the aircraft. The Court of Appeal held that the re-purchase undertaking was unilateral in nature and thus involved D's irrevocable offer to P to re-purchase the aircraft if the conditions specified in it were adhered to by P. Accordingly, the offer was subject to an implied condition precedent that P should give reasonable notice to D to buy back the goods and this condition had not been fulfilled. This analysis meant that D's obligation to re-purchase the goods never came into existence.

Because of these difficulties, it is more common for the finance company to have a recourse agreement with the dealer under which he agrees to indemnify the finance company in the event of the customer's default. The distinct advantage of the indemnity from the finance company's perspective is that, unless there is an express obligation to deliver the goods to the dealer,[11] there is no duty to do so before claiming on the indemnity. It is a matter of interpretation whether the agreement is an indemnity or a guarantee but the agreement is usually cast in the form of an indemnity and there is no doubt that such an undertaking is more advantageous from the finance company's point of view than a contract of guarantee. First, an ancillary, contract of guarantee is enforceable only if the main contract is valid. Thus, if the hire-purchase agreement is void or the customer is released from liability for any reason,[12] the finance company has a claim against the dealer only if the recourse agreement is one of indemnity. Second, the indemnity may be claimed even where the finance company lawfully

---

9 See *Watling Trust Ltd v Briffault Range Co Ltd* [1938] 1 All ER 525.
10 [1968] 1 WLR 74.
11 See *Bowmaker (Commercial) Ltd v Smith* [1965] 1 WLR 855.
12 See *Unity Finance Co Ltd v Woodcock* [1963] 1 WLR 455.

terminates the agreement on the customer's default.[13] Third, under an indemnity the dealer is liable to the finance company for the company's actual loss and not just the amount of instalments by which the customer was in arrears at the date of default.[14] Once the dealer compensates the finance company, he is subrogated to the rights of the latter but, if the goods have been destroyed or are lost, there is no question of there being a failure of consideration and, in such a case, the dealer does not have a right of set-off against the amount claimed by the finance company.

Refinancing arrangements

The Bills of Sale Acts 1878 and 1882 have been discussed elsewhere in this text.[15] The overall aim of the legislation is that, where an owner of goods passes the property in the goods to another as security for a loan but remains in possession of the goods, the bill of sale transferring title to that other should be in a cerain form and registered. A secret mortgage in favour of another will be void against creditors and the lender himself will have no rights against the goods, although he may recover the loan with reasonable interest only, as money had and received.[16] An important function of the Acts is thus to protect creditors who extend credit to those who have apparent ownership of goods.

It is thus plain that the parties must not be allowed to use the hire-purchase format as a cloak for what is, in effect, a loan of money on the security of goods, thereby evading the Bills of Sale Acts. Accordingly, the courts examine the true intent of the parties and some agreements which are ostensibly hire-purchase agreements may be held to be void as unregistered bills of sale. This is apt to be the case where an *existing owner* of goods sells them and then immediately hires them back from the purchaser, giving the purchaser a right to seize the goods if the instalment payments under the contract are not met. If, irrespective of the *form* used, the substance of the arrangement is a loan of money on the security of goods, the hire-purchase contract may be held to be a deliberate attempt to avoid the Bills of Sale Acts and, consequently, it will be void as an unregistered bill of sale, it will not bind creditors and the lender himself will have no rights against the goods.[17]

Overall, the courts have adopted a generous approach and, if the agreement is to be struck-down there must be a clear intent to evade the Acts by concocting a bogus arrangement. Thus, where *all*[18] the parties to the transaction (including the finance company) are aware that the true nature of the transaction is to provide a loan on the security of the customer's goods, the hire-purchase agreeement is a sham and it will be void as an unregistered bill of sale.[19] Consequently, even though the customer intends to deceive the finance company, the agreement may be upheld as a genuine hire-purchase agreement if the latter is completely unaware of any irregularity. In *Snook v London and West Riding Investments Ltd*,[20] A, who wanted to raise £300 on the security of his car, arranged to sell it to B for £800 and take

---

13 *Goulston Discount Co Ltd v Clark* [1967] 2 QB 493.
14 See *Financings Ltd v Baldock* [1963] 2 QB 104; *Goulston Discount Co Ltd v Clark* [1967] 2 QB 493.
15 See Chs 15 and 30.
16 *Davies v Rees* (1886) 17 QBD 408.
17 See the facts of *Re Watson* (1890) 25 QBD 27 (considered in Ch 15).
18 *Snook v London and West Riding Investments Ltd* [1967] 2 QB 786, 802 per Diplock LJ.
19 *Polsky v S and A Services Ltd* [1951] 1 All ER 1062n.
20 [1967] 2 QB 786; see also *Stoneleigh Finance Ltd v Phillips* [1965] 2 QB 537.

it back on hire-purchase terms. The Court of Appeal held that the transactions of sale and hire-purchase were genuine and that, therefore, B could exercise the rights of re-possession given to him by the hire purchase agreement. The majority of the court were not disposed to label the hire purchase agreement as a sham merely because it recorded that a deposit of £500 had been paid when the *only* money that had been transferred was £300 from B to A. Russell LJ explained that if A wanted to raise £300 on a car worth £800, he could agree to sell it for £800 on terms that it be hired back for a deposit of £500 and instalments of, say, £350. The finance company could draw a cheque for £800 in favour of A and A could draw a cheque for the finance company for £500. Instead, as here, one cheque was drawn by the finance company in favour of B for £300.

In what is often referred to as a refinancing arrangement, the owner of goods genuinely sells them to a dealer who, in turn, resells them to a finance company and the finance company then hires the goods to the owner on hire-purchase terms. It is plain that, when the goods never leave the owner's possession and property in the goods is transferred to the finance company, the overall effect of the scheme is that the owner has received a loan on the security of goods which remain in his possession and subject to his control. Where the transactions are genuine from the outset, the arrangement will be upheld and will not contravene the Bills of Sale Acts and be void as an unregistered bill of sale. In this situation, the finance company's position is a strong one as it does not buy the goods directly from the owner, as in some of the instances already discussed, and it may not even realise that the hire-purchaser was the original owner. However, the arrangement would be a sham if, for example, the dealer's name on the documentation submitted to the finance company was used to hide the fact that the owner was the true seller of the goods and the finance company knew this to be the position. The arrangement would then almost certainly be void as an unregistered bill of sale and the finance company could not acquire title to the goods.

In an authentic and orthodox hire-purchase agreement where the hire-purchaser has no *prior* interest in the goods and is thus not an existing owner, there should not be any contravention of the Bills of Sale Acts. The paradigm hire-purchase agreement does not involve a bill of sale given as security for money lent since the property in the goods is not vested in the hire-purchaser during the subsistence of the hire-purchase agreement and thus it is not a case of an *owner* of goods granting a bill of sale and a right of seizure to another.[1] A genuine hire-purchase agreement grants credit facilities to a hire-purchaser in order that he may be supplied with goods and ultimately purchase them and it is not designed to be a loan of money to him on the security of goods.

Likewise, 'block discounting', referred to earlier, does not seem to be affected by the Bills of Sale Acts. Here the dealer enters into hire-purchase agreements directly with customers and then *assigns* his rights under them, together usually with the ownership in the goods, to a finance company. The assignment by the dealer of not merely his contractual rights under hire purchase agreements but also of his interests in the goods is a bill of sale, but as block discounting normally consists of absolute assignments and the dealer retains neither possession of the goods nor the right to possession, the Bills of Sale Acts will not apply.[2]

---

1 *Re Robertson, ex p Crawcour* (1878) 9 Ch D 419; *McEntire v Crossley Bros Ltd* [1895] AC 457 (see Ch 30); see Diamond, 'Hire-Purchase Agreements as Bills of Sale' (1960) 23 MLR 399 (Part I) and 516 (Part II).
2 See Guest, *The Law of Hire-Purchase* (1966), paras 128; 680-683.

CONDITIONAL SALE

In a conditional sale, the buyer agrees to buy the goods at the outset and obtains possession but the agreement expressly provides that property in the goods will not pass to the buyer until he has paid all the instalments of the price – a conditional sale is therefore an agreement to sell goods[3] subject to this condition regarding the passing of property. A buyer under a conditional sale agreement is thus bound to buy the goods and this fact distinguishes conditional sale from hire-purchase where the hirer has merely an option to purchase the goods. Accordingly, the CCA, s 189(1) defines a 'conditional sale agreement' as:

> 'An agreement for the sale of goods or land[4] under which the purchase price or part of it is payable by instalments, and the property in the goods or land is to remain in the seller (notwithstanding that the buyer is to be in possession of the goods or land) until such conditions as to the payment of instalments or otherwise as may be specified in the agreement are fulfilled.'

Although the conditional sale is principally an agreement for the sale of goods, it is equally plain that conditional sales resemble hire-purchase agreements in that the owner/seller will retain property in the goods, with concomitant security, during the currency of the agreement. The conditional sale agreement usually makes express provision for the termination of the agreement and S's resumption of possession on B's default but it has been held that, in the absence of a term to the contrary, S's repossession terminates the agreement and S consequently forfeits his right to arrears of instalments of the price,[5] although here S should be able to recover an equivalent sum as damages for breach of contract.

Under the CCA, s 8, a conditional sale agreement is a consumer credit agreement where the debtor/buyer is an 'individual' and the creditor provides the debtor with credit not exceeding £25,000. As such, it is a regulated agreement under the CCA and it is not an 'exempt agreement' under the CCA, s 16.[6] A regulated conditional sale agreement is a debtor-creditor-supplier agreement for restricted-use credit.

Regulated conditional sale agreements are treated by the CCA in the same way as regulated hire-purchase agreements. The debtor under a regulated conditional sale agreement has the same right as the debtor under a regulated hire-purchase agreement in that he can terminate the agreement under s 99 before the final payment is due. However, by s 99(4), although the debtor may terminate even after the property has passed to him, this does not apply if he has already sold the goods to another who does not become the debtor under the agreement. Moreover, by s 99(5), if the debtor does properly terminate after the property has passed to him, the property at once revests in the previous owner and this is normally the creditor.

A regulated conditional sale agreement is subject to the same requirements as to default and s 76 and s 98 notices, the same restrictions on repossession once one-third of the total price has been paid and the special powers of the court. Also applicable are the provisions of the Act governing entry into agreements, the position of the dealer (credit-broker), the right of cancellation,

---

3   See the SGA 1979, s 2(3) and 2(5).
4   Conditional sales of land have begun to appear undoubtedly to avoid the law relating to mortgages.
5   *Hewison v Ricketts* (1894) 63 LJQB 711; *A-G v Pritchard* (1928) 97 LJKB 561.
6   Consumer Credit (Exempt Agreements) Order 1989, art 3(2)(b) (SI 1989/869).

the obligations of the creditor and debtor to give information, appropriation of payments, variation of agreements, death of the debtor, early payment by the debtor, extortionate agreements, security, and advertisements. Moreover, the licensing provisions in Part III of the CCA apply to finance companies who make conditional sale agreements just as they apply to companies making hire-purchase agreements. Similarly, the licensing provisions in s 147 apply to dealers who negotiate conditional sale agreements.

In other respects, conditional sales are governed by the Sale of Goods Act 1979 and the implied terms relating to title, quality and fitness for purpose of the goods, for example, are those in the SGA, ss 12-15. Similarly, the Unfair Contract Terms Act 1977 and the Unfair Terms in Consumer Contracts Regulations 1999 apply to conditional sales. Most importantly, the Supply of Goods (Implied Terms) Act 1973, s 14(1) specifies that the SGA 1979, s 11(4) (which relates to the loss of the right to reject the goods and provides that a breach of condition in a contract of sale is, in certain circumstances, to be treated as a breach of warranty), shall *not* apply to conditional sale agreements that are 'consumer' sales within s 12 of the UCTA 1977. It follows that a buyer under a conditional sale agreement which is a consumer sale does not lose his right to reject the goods for breach of a condition (express or implied) of the contract merely because he has 'accepted' them, eg by keeping them after he has had a reasonable opportunity to examine them without giving notice of rejection. Moreover, by s 14(2) of the 1973 Act, a breach of condition by the seller under such a conditional sale agreement is to be treated as a breach of warranty and not as grounds for rejecting the goods 'if (but only if) it would have fallen to be so treated had the condition been contained or implied in a corresponding hire purchase agreement ...' The significance of these provisions is that the elaborate and sometimes unjust rules in the SGA relating to the buyer's deemed acceptance of the goods and his consequent loss of the right to reject them do not apply to conditional sales. Instead, the less stringent rules of hire-purchase are relevant and so the buyer must *affirm* the contract if he is to lose the right to reject the goods and be limited to a claim in damages. Consequently, only where the buyer evinces an intention to continue with the agreement (eg by continuing to pay instalments of the price) after he has become aware of the seller's breach of condition, will he be limited to a claim in damages.[7]

As stated earlier, the decision in *Lee v Butler*[8] was that a person in possession of goods under a conditional sale agreement had 'agreed to buy' the goods within the Factors Act 1889, s 9 (and the SGA, s 25(2)) and could thus transfer a good title to the third party by virtue of those sections. In contrast, the decision in *Helby v Matthews*[9] stressed that the customer/hirer under a hire-purchase agrement had only an option to buy and was thus not a person who had *agreed* to buy the goods. The position is now clarified by statute: where the conditional sale agreement is defined as a 'consumer-credit agreement' in the CCA 1974,[10] the Factors Act, s 9 and the SGA, s 25(2)(a) provide that the buyer under a conditional sale agreement is *not* a person who has bought or agreed to buy the goods.[11] In other words, in

---

7 See Ch 35.
8 [1893] 2 QB 318.
9 [1895] AC 471.
10 See CCA, ss 8 and 189(1).
11 The buyer under a conditional sale agreement can, nevertheless, be a buyer in possession where the CCA does *not* apply.

this situation the debtor/buyer is treated in the same way as a debtor/customer under a hire-purchase agreement and he has no power to pass a good title to a third party. Nevertheless, where the CCA does *not* apply (eg the financial limits of the CCA have been exceeded), the buyer under a conditional sale may still be able to transfer a good title as a buyer in possession under the Factors Act, s 9 and the SGA, s 25(2).[12]

It should also be stressed that some of the other exceptions to the rule *nemo dat quod non habet*[13] are applicable to *all* conditional sales, ie whether or not the CCA is applicable. The conditional seller's title might thus be defeated at common law by virtue of estoppel, ie if he has held-out the buyer as an apparent owner or agent. Similarly, the conditional seller might be precluded from denying the buyer's 'authority to sell' the goods under the SGA, s 21(1). Likewise, the Factors Act 1889, s 2, (the provisions relating to possession by mercantile agents) and Part III of the Hire-Purchase Act 1964 (concerning dispositions of motor vehicles) are both applicable to all conditional sales.

CREDIT-SALE

Where there is a credit-sale, the price of the goods is paid in instalments and so credit is extended to the buyer, but there is *no* condition suspending the passing of property in the goods to the buyer and so the sale is absolute within the SGA, s 2(3). The CCA, s 189(1) defines a 'credit-sale agreement' as:

> 'An agreement for the sale of goods, under which the purchase price or part of it is payable by instalments, but which is not a conditional sale agreement.'

As such, property passes to the buyer *immediately* under the SGA, s 18, r 1, and it follows that the buyer, as the owner of the goods, can transfer a good title to third parties. Credit-sale is a form of unsecured credit as the creditor has no direct rights against the goods and, should the debtor default, the creditor's only remedy is to sue for the unpaid instalments of the price.

Under the CCA, s 8, a credit-sale agreement is a consumer credit agreement where the debtor/buyer is an 'individual' and the creditor provides the debtor with credit not exceeding £25,000 and it is a regulated agreement if it is not an 'exempt agreement' within s 16 and orders made under it. Apart from the provisions relating to extortionate credit, exempt agreements are not subject to the CCA. For example, many domestic transactions on account are credit-sales, eg the newsagent's delivery of the newspapers, and they will also be exempt agreements where, for example, the account is settled every month.[14] Moreover, the requirements of the CCA relating to the form and content of the agreement do not apply to 'small agreements'[15] which are defined in the CCA, s 17. Credit-sale agreements for credit not exceeding £50 are within the definition of small agreements.

Regulated credit-sale agreements are governed by the provisions of the CCA concerning default and s 76 and s 98 notices, the special powers of the court, entry into agreements, the position of the dealer (credit-broker), the right of cancellation, the obligations of the creditor and debtor to give information,

---

12 See *Forthright Finance Ltd v Carlyle Finance Ltd* [1997] 4 All ER 90.
13 See Ch 18 where *nemo dat* is considered.
14 See the Consumer Credit (Exempt Agreements) Order 1989, SI 1989/869 (as amended).
15 See Ch 31.

appropriation of payments, variation of agreements, death of the debtor, early payment by the debtor, and security. Even 'small agreements' are covered by the statutory provisions concerning extortionate agreements and advertisements. Moreover, the licensing provisions of the CCA apply to finance companies and dealers engaged in credit-sale transactions. On the other hand, the nature of the credit-sale agreement means that the buyer/debtor has no right to terminate the agreement under the CCA, s 99, and the restrictions on repossession under s 90 are also inapplicable.

In credit-sale agreements the implied terms relating to title, quality and fitness for purpose of the goods are those in the SGA, ss 12-15. Similarly, the Unfair Contract Terms Act 1977 and the Unfair Terms in Consumer Contracts Regulations 1999 apply to conditional sales.

FIXED-SUM CREDIT AGREEMENTS

A fixed-sum credit agreement is one where a specific sum is advanced to the debtor for a specified period and which will be utilised for a specific or non-specific purpose. An agreement is classified as one for fixed-sum credit even though the amount of the loan is payable to the debtor in instalments. 'Fixed-sum credit' is distinguished from running-account credit (see below) and the former is defined in the CCA, s 10(1)(b) as 'any other facility under a personal credit agreement wherby the debtor is enabled to receive credit (whether in one amount or by instalments)'.

Fixed-sum loans may be obtained from an array of sources and examples include banks, finance houses, building societies, and insurance companies. A conventional, fixed-sum loan is repayable over an agreed period of time with interest charged on the balance which is outstanding and the loan will frequently be unsecured, a fact which will be reflected in the rate of interest which is paid by the debtor. Alternatively, the loan might be secured by, for example, the assignment of a life asssurance policy, and less interest would then be charged by the creditor. It should be stressed that pawnbroker's loans, hire-purchase, credit-sale, conditional sale and check trading are all within the classification of fixed-sum credit.[16]

With a standard, fixed-sum loan (eg a bank loan) the debtor will often have control over the application of the finance and use it for any purpose that he wishes. However, a modern and very significant development is that of the purchase-money loan and the notion that the creditor/lender of the money is connected in a business sense with the retailer who supplies goods or services to the debtor. In this situation, there is a loan agreement between the creditor and the debtor and a separate contract for the sale of goods or supply of services between the debtor and a retail supplier. The salient feature of the relationship is, however, the business connection between the creditor and the supplier and the fact that the *creditor* controls the application of the loan and makes the payment for the goods or services direct to the supplier. This method of finance is often used as an alternative to hire-purchase or credit-sale and the business relationship of the parties is almost identical to that found in hire-purchase in that the supplier recommends that the debtor should seek finance from the creditor who, in turn, pays a commission to the supplier and pays the supplier directly.

---

16 See also the CCA, Sch 2, Part II, examples 9, 10, 17 and 23.

The debtor then repays the loan in instalments which combine the principal sum plus interest. Whilst the business realtionship between the parties is analogous to that of hire-purchase, the legal relationship is entirely different – in the connected loan situation the debtor buys the goods from the retail supplier with the loan which is advanced by the creditor. If there is thus a connected, tripartite arangement between the parties, the loan is categorised as a debtor-creditor-supplier agreement. If, on the other hand, the loan is not a connected loan of this type and the creditor is wholly independent and not linked to any supplier, the agreement is categorised as a debtor-creditor agreement. The implications of connected and unconnected lending in relation to the CCA are examined in more depth in the next chapter.

RUNNING-ACCOUNT CREDIT

In contrast to fixed-sum credit, the notion of running-account credit (sometimes referred to as 'revolving credit') must now be considered. Running-account credit means that, instead of receiving a fixed sum of money which is to be repaid in instalments, the debtor is given a credit limit and can draw on his account at any time provided that his indebtedness does not exceed the prescribed limit. As the debtor need not use the amount of credit which is available and interest is charged only when the debtor draws on the facility, it is apparent that the amount of credit to be advanced is not fixed. Every time the debtor draws on the account the amount of credit which is available is reduced but each repayment that is made by him necessarily restores that available credit. In contrast to fixed-sum credit which will end when the loan is repaid at the conclusion of a fixed-term, running-account credit may continue without limit, this flexible arrangement thus having undoubted advantages for both parties. The CCA, s 10(1) defines running-account credit as:

> ' ... a facility under a personal credit agreement whereby the debtor is enabled to receive from time to time (whether in his own person, or by another person) from the creditor or a third party cash, goods and services (or any of them) to an amount or value such that, taking into account payments made by or to the credit of the debtor, the credit limit (if any) is not at any time exceeded'.

The phrase 'credit limit' in s 10(1) is defined by s 10(2). Under s 10(2) it means 'as respects any period, the maximum debit balance which, under the credit agreement, is allowed to stand on the account during that period, disregarding any term of the agreement allowing that maximum to be exceeded merely temporarily'.[17]

Under s 10(3)(a), where the running-account credit does not exceed £25,000 it will be a regulated agreement under the CCA. Section 10(3)(b) sets out three situations where running-account credit is deemed not to exceed the £25,000 limit whether or not there is a credit limit, and if there is, notwithstanding that it exceeds the specified amount. The first situation is where the debtor is not enabled to draw at any one time an amount which exceeds £25,000 (eg a bank agrees an overdraft with the debtor of £50,000 (or without limit) but provides that he cannot draw more than £15,000 in any one month). The second situation

---

17 See the CCA, Sch 2, Part II, examples 6, 7, 19, 22 and 23. The stipulation that the maximum debit balance can be exceeded temporarily is to allow a bank, for example, to honour cheques drawn on it which will cause the agreed overdraft to be exceeded temporarily.

is where the agreement provides that if the debit balance rises above a given amount (not exceeding £25,000) the rate of the total charge for credit increases or any other term favouring the creditor or his associate comes into operation (eg the agreement provides for an increased rate of interest if the debit balance exceeds £15,000). The third situation is where, at the time the agreement is made it is probable, having regard to the terms of the agreement and any other relevant considerations, that the debit balance will not at any time rise above £25,000 (eg the creditor cannot avoid the CCA by agreeing to provide running-account credit up to £35,000 when it is probable that the debtor will not require more than £25,000).

Running-account credit may take many different forms. As in the case of fixed-sum credit, running-account credit may be purchase-money credit (eg a retail shop's credit account; credit cards such as Access and Barclaycard) or it may not be linked necessarily to purchases of goods or services (eg a bank overdraft). Many people have running-account credits with shops which are known as 'budget accounts'. In this situation, a retailer agrees with the debtor (D) to open an account in D's name and, in return for D's promise to pay a specified minimum amount each month into the account and to pay a monthly charge for credit, agrees to allow to be debited to the account, in respect of purchases made by D from the retailer, such sums as will not increase the debit balance at any time beyond the credit limit. The credit limit is defined in the agreement as a given multiple of the specified minimum sum paid each month (eg 24 times the monthly payment). Provided the credit limit is not over £25,000, this is a regulated agreement for running-account credit.

An alternative to the budget account is the 'option account'. Here the the credit limit is not fixed as a multiple of the monthly payments but, instead, it is agreed in advance. The account holder is given the option of making regular monthly payments with interest charged on the debit balance which is unpaid or, alternatively, he can repay the balance owing in full.

With a bank overdraft, the debtor is given an agreed credit limit so that he may overdraw his account up to that limit and interest is payable on the balance outstanding at any particular time. Unlike a retail shop's credit account, the debtor will not usually have to make regular payments to reduce the overdraft although the bank may demand that the debtor acts swiftly to decrease the amount which is outstanding if it considers it to be too high.

The popularity of running-account credit lies in its flexibility and this type of credit has overtaken fixed-sum credit largely because many different transactions can be comprised within one agreement whereas, with fixed-sum credit, a separate agreement is needed for each transaction. Today, arguably the commonest form of running-account credit is the credit card issued by a bank (eg Access or Barclaycard) or other card issuer and credit cards are considered below.

CHECK TRADING

Check trading is the system whereby vouchers ('checks') of stated denominations are issued by the check trader to customers for use in designated shops/outlets. The customer makes an initial payment to the check trader, usually 5% of the check's face value, and pays the remainder in instalments. The shop accepts the check from the customer and is paid by the check trader less a discount. The check trader's profit thus comes from (i) the charge made to the customer;

(ii) the discount allowed by the shop; and (iii) the delay between the issue of the check to the customer and payment for the goods to the shop. The system was originally for small amounts repayable by weekly payments made to a collector of the check trader who called at the customer's home and this method of granting credit remains popular today.

The credit granted is fixed-sum credit and check trading is classified as a debtor-creditor-supplier agreement within the CCA, s 12(b), for restricted-use credit. The principal significance of the check trading agreement being a debtor-creditor-supplier agreement is that, under the CCA, s 75, where the customer has a claim in damages against the shop for misrepresentation or breach of contract, he has a like claim against the check trader and both the latter and the shop are jointly and severally liable. It should also be noted that the check is a credit-token under the CCA, s 14(1)(b) and the agreement is a credit-token agreement under s 14(2).

CREDIT CARDS AND OTHER PAYMENT CARDS

The term 'credit card' is neither employed nor defined in the CCA as such cards were not in widespead use in 1974 but, nevertheless, the Act's structure copes perfectly well with credit card arrangements. It is unhelpful that, in practice, a confusing nomenclature is applied to the range of payment cards in existence without much regard for the card's function, eg 'credit cards', 'charge cards' and 'debit cards'. In commerce, 'credit cards' usually denote tokens which allow the cardholder access to *extended* credit with an *instalment payment facility* and, most significantly, such cards should be contrasted with debit cards where the cardholder's account is debited and money transferred to the supplier of goods or services in approximately the same time that a cheque would take to be cleared. The various types of card, the parties involved in payment card transactions and the legal status of those transactions must now be considered separately.

Credit cards

Credit card arrangements may involve either two or three parties. In a two-party transaction the creditor is also the supplier of goods or services to the debtor and, commonly, this is the situation which occurs with credit cards issued by large retail stores. On production of the card the cardholder is allowed to make a purchase on credit terms which have been established by agreement between the shop and the cardholder. Here the shop will be directly liable to the cardholder if the goods or services prove to be defective and, certainly where there is a sale of goods on credit terms, the contract will be one of credit-sale.

In a typical three-party credit card arrangement, a bank (or any other finance company/card issuer) issues the debtor with a credit card under which he can spend up to a specified amount at any shop or supplier of services which has agreed, or in future agrees, to accept the Bank's credit cards. The bank pays the shop or supplier of services direct (normally after deducting a discount) and, in due course, the debtor repays the bank.[18] In *Re Charge Card Services Ltd*,[19] the Court of Appeal stated that the three-party credit card transaction

18 It is common for a fourth party to be added to this scheme, viz the 'merchant acquirer' who pays the supplier and recovers the amount owing from the card issuer.
19 [1987] Ch 150; affd [1989] Ch 497.

involves three separate bilateral contracts, viz (i) between the cardholder and the card issuer; (ii) between the card issuer and the supplier; and (iii) between the supplier and the cardholder for the sale of goods or supply of services. Moreover, in contrast to payment by cheque which is a conditional payment only, it was held that payment by credit card is an absolute, unconditional payment. In *Re Charge Card Services Ltd*, various cardholders had used their cards to pay for petrol before the card issuer became insolvent. Several garages were owed money by the card issuer and, being unable to obtain the money from the insolvent company, they commenced proceedings against the cardholders. As some cardholders had paid the card issuer for the petrol it would have been unfair to make them pay again and this outcome was avoided by the finding that payment by means of the card was absolute, not conditional. The court also considered that, as between the cardholder and card issuer, the latter had the right to claim payment from the cardholder even if the card issuer had not paid the garages and thus those cardholders who had not paid the card issuer for the petrol remained liable to do so. It is thus clear that it is the supplier who is deemed to run the risk where the card issuer becomes insolvent, not the cardholder.

It is also crucial to stress that the CCA, s 75, is applicable to the three-party card arrangement. Consequently, the card issuer/creditor is jointly and severally liable with the supplier in respect of any claim that the cardholder/debtor has against the supplier for misrepresentation or breach of contract in relation to the supply of goods or services. It is thus prudent for the cardholder to pay for goods and services with his credit card instead of paying by cash or cheque because the liability imposed by s 75 is clearly a bonus for the cardholder.

Credit card agreements are examples of running-account credit and the 'budget account' and the 'option account' were considered when running-account credit was explained earlier. Most of the major credit cards are in the form of option accounts, eg Access and Barclaycard, and it is also very common for cards issued by retail stores to adopt this format. Almost all credit cards used by individuals will be within the £25,000 credit ceiling and will thus be regulated agreements within the CCA and both two-party and three-party cards are classified as debtor-creditor-supplier agreements[20] for restricted-use credit. Both two-party and three-party cards also fall within another classification in that they are 'credit tokens'[1] within s 14(1)(a) or (b) and the agreements are classified as credit-token agreements within s 14(2).

Some credit cards permit cash to be obtained on the presentation of the card and so, for example, the cardholder might obtain a cash loan from a bank and the card issuer would immediately pay the amount of the loan to the bank; the cardholder would then repay the card issuer in instalments. In the case of such a cash loan, the arrangement will be categorised as a debtor-creditor agreement for unrestricted-use credit.

Charge cards

The designation 'charge card' should be restricted to those cards which require the cardholder, under the terms of his account with the card issuer, to settle the outstanding balance in full within a prescribed period after a statement is issued,

---

20 See the CCA, s 12(a) (two-party cards) and s 12(b) (three-party cards).
1 See Ch 31 where credit-token agreements are considered.

eg American Express and Diner's Club. The cardholder thus obtains interest-free credit for a limited period of time but no extended credit is available. As in the case of credit cards proper, a charge card may be either a two-party (eg a retail department store's card) or a three-party transaction (eg an American Express card used to pay for goods supplied by shop). If payment is not made by the specified date, default interest becomes payable.

All charge card agreements will be classified as exempt agreements within the CCA where the card may be used to obtain goods and services and the whole amount of the credit provided in any period has to be repaid by a single repayment;[2] as such, these agreements are not regulated by the CCA. One important consequence of this is that, as s 75 applies only to regulated agreements,[3] it does not apply to three-party charge card arrangements and so liability under that section is not imposed on the card issuer as creditor. Similarly, the CCA's provisions on credit-tokens are inapplicable to charge cards.

However, should the cardholder be able to obtain cash with a charge card it will be classified as a debtor-creditor agreement and, as such, it will not be an exempt agreement unless the low-cost credit exemption applies to it.[4] Moreover, the card will then be a credit-token within s 14(1)(a) or (b) and the agreement classified as a credit-token agreement within s 14(2).

Debit cards

Debit cards enable the cardholder to buy goods and services from suppliers with whom arrangements have been made with the issuer of the card, usually a bank or Building Society, for the card's acceptance. The cardholder will have a current account with the bank and, under the terms of the agreement between the cardholder and the bank, the cardholder authorises the bank to debit his account in payment for the goods or services supplied. The debit card is primarily a means of debiting directly the cardholder's account in payment and serves much the same function as a cheque except that it is more convenient and can be used for much greater amounts than those guaranteed by cheque cards.

There has always been controversy as to the precise legal status of a debit card. A debit card is 'in essence a vehicle for cash payment'[5] and where there is no agreement between the bank and the cardholder allowing the latter to overdraw on his account, there is no credit agreement within the CCA. However, where the cardholder has an overdraft facility with a credit limit not exceeding the £25,000 financial limit of the CCA, there is a regulated agreement within the Act but it is not a debtor-creditor-supplier agreement by virtue of the CCA, s 187(3A).[6] The purpose of this section is to indicate that the EFTPOS transaction (electronic funds transfer at point of sale) is a debtor-creditor agreement meaning that the bank is *not* liable under the CCA, s 75 for misrepresentations and breaches of contract by the supplier.

It seems that the debit card will be a 'credit-token' within the CCA, s 14(1)(b) because the creditor must reimburse the supplier and this is the position whether

---

2 See the Consumer Credit (Exempt Agreements) Order 1989, SI 1989/869, art 3(1)(a)(ii).
3 See the juxtaposition of ss 75 and 12, the latter section defining the regulated debtor-creditor-supplier agreements to which s 75 applies.
4 See the Consumer Credit (Exempt Agreements) Order 1989 (SI 1989/869), art 4.
5 Goode, *Consumer Credit Law* (1989), para 9.34.
6 Inserted by the Banking Act 1987, s 87.

or not there is an overdraft facility; where there *is* such a facility, there will be a regulated credit agreement *and* a credit-token agreement.

Finally, if the debit card allows the cardholder to obtain cash, it will be a debtor-creditor agreement for unrestricted-use credit and will be exempted from the documentation requirements of Part V of the CCA under s 74(1)(b) (ie a debtor-creditor agreement enabling the debtor to overdraw on a current account).

Cheque guarantee cards

Cheque cards are entirely different from credit cards proper. When a cheque card is given by a bank to a customer, the bank undertakes to honour cheques drawn by the customer up to a specified amount (currently £100) whenever a payee/supplier of goods or services takes the cheque in reliance on the cheque card, whether or not the customer has funds in his account to meet the cheque. The use of the card gives the supplier a direct contractual right *vis-à-vis* the bank to have the cheque paid when he presents it.[7]

Since a customer is entitled to draw a cheque and use his cheque card even if there is no money in his current account, the agreement between the bank and the customer is a consumer credit agreement[8] whether or not an overdraft facility has been agreed. As the cheque card has no express credit limit, the customer may use the cheque card any number of times and so the agreement is an agreement for running-account credit under the CCA, s 10.

If the debit balance does not exceed £25,000 it will be a regulated agreement but it is *not* a credit-token agreement under s 14(1)(b) because payment by the bank to a retailer, who takes the customer's cheque in reliance on the cheque card, is payment of the cheque, not payment for the goods supplied by the retailer.

The bank will have no obligations with regard to the quality of goods bought or otherwise in respect of any breaches of contract by the retailer under the CCA, s 75 because the consumer credit agreement is *not* a debtor-creditor-supplier agreement – the bank and retailer are not treated as having made 'pre-existing arrangements' provided that the bank is willing to make payments of cheques 'to suppliers generally' (s 187(3)(b)). Accordingly, the agreement is a debtor-creditor agreement for unrestricted-use credit under s 13(c) and will be exempted from the documentation requirements of Part V of the CCA under s 74(1)(b) (ie a debtor-creditor agreement enabling the debtor to overdraw on a current account).

Cash cards

Cash cards are issued by banks and building societies to enable the cardholder to obtain cash by using the card in an automatic teller machine (ATM). The cardholder's account is debited electronically and the ATM is programmed to accept the cardholder's personal identification number (PIN) and to refuse payment unless the account is in credit or an overdraft facility has been

---

7 Whether such a right exists where the cardholder's signature has been forged depends on the conditions printed or referred to on the card. In *First Sport Ltd v Barclays Bank plc* [1993] 1 WLR 1229, there was a forged signature, copied from the cheque card, on a stolen cheque. Held that the bank was liable to the retailer as the card did not state (as it could have done) that the bank would incur liability to the retailer only if the card was presented by the authorised signatory.
8 See CCA, Sch 2, Part II, example 21.

agreed. Many cash cards can be used in the machines of other banks and building societies who have arranged to accept the card.

If the ATM is programmed to refuse the card unless the account is in credit, there is no agreement to provide the cardholder with credit and thus no regulated credit agreement. Here the bank owes money to the customer who is, in fact, a creditor not a debtor. If, on the other hand, there is an agreed overdraft facility with the cardholder, the agreement will be a debtor-creditor agreement for unrestricted-use credit. The position is less clear in those cases where the cardholder may obtain cash from the ATMs of banks other than the bank with which he has an account. It seems most likely that the bank dispensing the cash will be acting as an agent for the cardholder's bank, but it is possible that a deemed extension of credit might arise under the CCA, s 14(3) and then it is irrelevant that the cardholder's bank has not agreed to provide the cardholder with credit.

Where cash is obtainable only from the ATM of the cardholder's bank and only when the account is in credit, the cash card is not a credit-token (see s 14(1)(a)) but, again, if cash can be obtained from the ATMs of banks other than the cardholder's bank, the card may be a credit-token within s 14(1)(b) and the agreement a credit-token agreement within s 14(3).

To the extent that cash cards are debtor-creditor agreements for unrestricted-use credit, they are exempted from the documentation requirements of Part V of the CCA under s 74(1)(b) (ie a debtor-creditor agreement enabling the debtor to overdraw on a current account).

CHAPTER 33

The formation of the agreement, withdrawal and cancellation

Introduction

The law relating to the formalities of the agreement, its specified content and its possible cancellation is contained in Part V of the CCA. The object of this part of the Act is to ensure that the debtor is aware of his rights and obligations and the pattern of control is similar to that found in the earlier hire-purchase legislation. That legislation set new standards of consumer protection with both the substantive rights granted to the hirer (eg the right of cancellation of the agreement) and the Draconian regulations which prescribed, in minute detail, the physical form of the hire-purchase agreement (eg the minimum, permissible size of the print and the colour of the lettering).

The provisions relating to formalities in Part V of the CCA apply to all regulated agreements apart from four categories of agreement which are exempted under s 74, viz (i) small DCS agreements for restricted-use credit;[1] (ii) non-commercial agreements;[2] (iii) DC agreements enabling the the debtor to overdraw on a current account (as determined by the Director General of Fair Trading); and (iv) certain agreements to finance payments on death[3] (as determined by the Director General of Fair Trading).

The formalities of the agreement

Pre-contract disclosure

Regulations may be made under the CCA requiring specified information to be disclosed to the debtor before an agreement is made (s 55). Failure to comply with such regulations before the making of an agreement means that the agreement is not properly executed (s 55(2)) and enforceable only on an order of the court. At present, no regulations have been made under s 55.

---

1 See Ch 31 for the definition of 'small' agreements (ss 55 and 56 apply to this category).
2 See Ch 31 for a definition of 'non-commercial' agreements (s 56 applies to this category).
3 See the Consumer Credit (Payments Arising on Death) Regulations (SI 1983/1554).

Form and content of the agreement

The CCA, s 60(1) requires the Secretary of State to make regulations as to 'the form and content of documents embodying regulated agreements'. The regulations are intended to ensure that the debtor is made aware of his rights and duties, the amount and rate of the total charge for credit, the protection and remedies available to him under the Act, and other matters it is considered by the Secretary of State desirable for him to know in connection with the agreement. Under s 60(3), the Director General of Fair Trading has certain powers to waive or vary any requirement of such regulations.

The Consumer Credit (Agreements) Regulations 1983[4] specify, in immense detail, the requirements of form, legibility and contents of regulated agreements. The policy of dictating the physical form of a standardised, statutory agreement, which figured so radically in the Hire-Purchase legislation in the 1960s, has been continued in these Regulations. For example, the agreement has to contain prominent boxes in which the debtor must sign and the regulations prescribe the form of words which must be featured in such signature boxes. Likewise, the financial information and related particulars must be 'shown together as a whole' and 'not interspersed with other information',[5] a requirement which has come to be known as the 'holy ground' rule. Although it is impossible to summarise all the regulations here, there are, broadly, five categories of information which must be contained in documents embodying regulated agreements:

(i)   a descriptive heading which is appropriate for the legal nature of the agreement, eg 'Conditional Sale Agreement regulated by the Consumer Credit Act 1974';

(ii) the names and addresses of the parties;

(iii) the financal particulars, viz the cash price, the amount of any deposit, the amount of the credit, the APR, the total amount payable, the amount of each payment and when each is payable, and details of default charges;

(iv) details of any security provided by the debtor;

(v)   notices informing the debtor or hirer of certain stautory rights, viz his right of cancellation and early termination, statutory protection in the event of his losing a credit-token and his right of early settlement.

Signatures

The CCA, s 61(1) provides that a regulated agreement is not properly executed and, therefore, not enforceable against the debtor except on an order of the court (s 65) unless it satisfies the requirements set out in s 61(1). Section 61(1) specifies three requirements:

(a)   there must be a document in the prescribed form, itself containing all the prescribed terms and conforming to regulations under s 60(1), which is signed in the prescribed manner both *by* the debtor or hirer and *by or on behalf of* the creditor or owner,[6] and

(b)   the document must embody all the terms of the agreement, other than implied terms, and

---

4   SI 1983/1553 (as amended).

5   Consumer Credit (Agreements) Regulations 1983, reg 2(4).

6   Under s 61(4), where the debtor is a partnership or an unincorporated body of persons, the requirement as to the signatures is that the agreement be signed *by or on behalf of* the debtor and *by or on behalf of* the creditor.

(c) the document when presented or sent to the debtor or hirer for signature must be in such a state that all its terms are readily legible.

These are important requirements and, most particularly, they prevent a re-occurrence of the practices of fraudulent dealers who, having induced debtors to sign hire-purchase forms in blank, then completed the forms with inflated figures. At common law, it had been held that the debtor was bound by the terms of the document he signed in this way on the basis that he had not acted carefully and was thus estopped from denying the agreement's validity[7] and, as the general rule was that the dealer was not regarded as the agent of the finance company, the debtor had no direct remedy against the latter company in the event of the dealer's fraud.[8] The overall strategy of the CCA provisions is that the agreement must be complete and in the form prescribed at the time of signature and, as stressed above, an improperly executed agreement is not enforceable against the debtor except on an order of the court (s 65). However, s 127 permits a measure of judicial discretion regarding enforcement orders in cases of infringement of the regulations. While s 127(3) stresses the general rule that an enforcement order shall not be made if s 61(1)(a) is not complied with, s 127(3) permits the the court a discretion and, accordingly, the section provides that non-conformity with the prescribed form will not necessarily be fatal *provided* that, as a minimum requirement, the document contains all the prescribed terms and was signed by the debtor or hirer.

Copies of the agreement

The CCA, ss 62 and 63, contain the provisions pertaining to the supply of copies of the agreement by the creditor or owner. The reference in these sections to the 'unexecuted agreement' means simply that the agreement is prospective: s 189(1) defines an 'unexecuted agreement' as a 'document embodying the terms of a prospective regulated agreement'. When both the debtor and creditor have signed the agreement it becomes executed.[9]

In the commonest situation, the prospective debtor will sign the agreement first and the creditor will sign later, thereby executing agreement. The agreement signed by the prospective debtor or hirer constitutes an offer to the prospective creditor but, in the typical situation, some time may elapse before the creditor accepts the offer and signs the agreement. The agreement may provide that it comes into existence when it is signed by or on behalf of the creditor but, in the absence of such a provision, communication of acceptance will be required at common law. Consequently, in the familiar situation which is encountered, the

---

7 *United Dominions Trust Ltd v Western* [1976] QB 513 (held that the debtor owed a duty to the finance company to take care in signing the documents and so he was bound by the figures inserted by the dealer; only a successful plea of *non est factum* would relieve the debtor and this could not be established).

8 See *Campbell Discount Co Ltd v Gall* [1961] 1 QB 431 (the dealer inserted the wrong figures and it was held that there was no *consensus ad idem* in the terms of the offer and acceptance between the debtor and the finance company. The finance company did not succeed against the debtor but, unsatisfactorily, the debtor's claim for the return of money paid under the agreement lay against the dealer alone); *Branwhite v Worcester Works Finance Ltd* [1969] 1 AC 552 (debtor could recover the deposit from the finance company on the basis of a total failure of consideration).

9 See the definition of 'executed agreement' in s 189(1).

moment that the copy of the executed agreement (see below) is given or posted to the debtor or hirer will be the moment that the contract is completed.

The copy provisions of the CCA turn on the question of when the agreement becomes executed and they can best be understood if the three situations which are encountered in the formation of the agreement are separated.

Unexecuted agreement is 'presented personally' or 'sent' to the debtor and has not been signed by the creditor

The commonest situation encountered is where the prospective debtor or hirer is 'presented personally' (s 62(1)) with an unexecuted agreement to sign. The dealer or representative of the creditor will have prepared the agreement in accordance with the regulations, but it will not have been signed by the prospective creditor and so here the debtor's signature on the unexecuted agreement constitutes an offer to the creditor. In this situation, s 62(1) provides that a copy of the unexecuted agreement signed by the debtor or hirer, and of any other document referred to in it, must 'there and then' be delivered to the debtor or hirer. Alternatively, the position might be as above but the unexecuted agreement will have been sent to the debtor or hirer for him to sign and, in this case, s 62(2) provides that a copy of it, and of any other document referred to in it must be sent to him at the same time.

In both these situations of personal presentation or sending of the unexecuted agreement to the debtor, s 63(2) specifies that a copy of the *executed* agreement and any other documents referred to in it must be 'given' to the debtor or hirer 'within the seven days following the making of the agreement'. This must mean that the debtor should actually *receive*[10] the copy of the executed agreement within the seven days after the 'making of the agreement'. Typically, the agreement will be 'made' at the moment when the copy of the executed agreement is posted to the debtor and so that copy must be received within seven days after it has been posted.[11] If the agreement is a cancellable one, s 63(3) provides that the copy of the executed agreement must be sent *by post*.

Unexecuted agreement is 'presented personally' or 'sent' to the debtor and has been signed by the creditor

In the rarer situation, an unexecuted agreement may be presented personally to the debtor or hirer for his signature but the document will become an executed agreement *when he signs it*. This will happen in those cases where the agreement has already been signed by or on behalf of the creditor. In this event, s 63(1) provides that a copy of the *executed* agreement, and of any other document referred to in it, must be 'there and then' delivered to the debtor or hirer. This is achievable, of course, because the agreement is 'presented personally' to the debtor and executed immediately on the debtor's signature and so the executed agreement is available instantly. If, on the other hand, the unexecuted agreement is sent to the debtor or hirer for his signature and it becomes an executed

---

10 'Give' is defined in s 189(1) as 'deliver or send by post to'.

11 In the case of a credit-token agreement where a copy is required according to these rules, the period is relaxed somewhat and, under s 63(4), the copy of the executed agreement need not be given within the seven days following the making of the agreement 'if it is given before or at the time when the credit-token is given to the debtor'.

agreement when he signs it, s 62(2) is applicable and a copy of the *unexecuted* agreement, and of any other document referred to in it, must be sent to him at the same time. However, in both these cases where the agreement becomes executed on the debtor's signature, *no further copy is required* because the creditor or owner has already signed the agreement before presenting it or sending it to the debtor and the debtor will ultimately have two copies of the executed agreement in his possession – one copy which was delivered 'there and then' with the original or one copy which was sent through the post with the original.[12] As no further copy is required, an extra safeguard is imposed in this situation where the agreement is a cancellable one: s 64(1)(b) specifies that a notice of cancellation rights must be sent separately, by post, to the debtor or hirer wthin seven days following the making of the agreement, which here will be the date that the debtor signs the agreement.

The debtor completes an unexecuted agreement which he has selected from a dispenser

The debtor or hirer might, for example, simply select an unexecuted agreement from a display stand or cut out an agreement from a magazine and then sign it and send it to the creditor. Here there is no duty to supply a copy of the unexecuted agreement[13] but, under s 63(2), the creditor must supply a copy of the *executed agreement* within seven days of the date it was made.

Form and content of copies

The Consumer Credit (Cancellation Notices and Copies of Documents) Regulations 1983,[14] specify the form and content the copies to be supplied and so, for example, the copy supplied must a true copy[15] and easily legible.[16] It will be noticed that ss 62 and 63 provide that the debtor or hirer has to be supplied with copies not only of the unexecuted/executed agreements but also with 'any other document referred to' in the agreements and this would comprise, for example a mortgage or other security referred to in the agreement. It was realised that there had to be some limit on the duty to provide documents which are referred to in the agreement for, otherwise, the creditor might have to supply a copy of the CCA itself. Section 180(3) allows for regulations to be made which exclude certain classes of document from the supply requirement and, in fact, the regulations exclude eight specific types of document.[17]

If the requirements of ss 62 and 63 are not observed, a regulated agreement is not properly executed and, therefore, not enforceable except on a court order

---

12 In the situation of the posted, unexecuted agreement which becomes executed on the debtor's signature, the debtor will be sent a copy of the unexecuted agreement which, of course, lacks only his signature. It seems that no further copy of the agreement is required even where the contract provides that it becomes operative at a later date, eg when the debtor's credit-rating is approved.
13 Often this type of form or leaflet contains a copy of the unexecuted agreement for the debtor to keep.
14 SI 1983/1557 (as amended).
15 Regulation 3.
16 Regulation 2.
17 See the Consumer Credit (Cancellation Notices and Copies of Documents) Regulations 1983 (SI 1983/1557), reg 11.

(s 65). Section 127(4) provides that the court will not make an enforcement order *in the case of a cancellable agreement* if ss 62 or 63 are contravened unless a copy of the agreement and any other document referred to in it were given to the debtor before proceedings commenced.

Copies and notice of cancellation rights

In the case of an agreement which is cancellable under s 67, s 64(1) provides that a notice in the prescribed form indicating the right of the debtor to cancel the agreement, how and when that right is exercisable and the name and address of a person to whom notice of cancellation may be given, must be included in every copy given to the debtor under ss 62 or 63. The Consumer Credit (Cancellation Notices and Copies of Documents) Regulations 1983[18] have prescribed the various forms of notice which are required for the different types of regulated agreement.

Where a copy of the executed agreement must be 'given' to the debtor 'within the seven days following the making of the agreement' under s 63(2) then, if the agreement is a cancellable one, s 63(3) provides that the further copy must be sent *by post*.

Moreover, as stressed earlier, in those cases where only one copy of the agreement is required because the agreement becomes executed when the debtor or hirer signs it, notice of cancellation rights must be sent *separately* by post to the debtor within seven days following the making of the agreement (s 64(1)(b)).

Section 64(5) provides that a cancellable agreement is not properly executed if the requirements of s 64 are not observed and, in such a case, s 127(4)(b) specifies that the court will *not* make an enforcement order under s 65(1).

Withdrawal and cancellation

Withdrawal

It was stressed above that, in the archetypal situation, the prospective debtor signs an unexecuted agreement which is sent to the creditor and, when it is signed by the creditor, it will become an executed agreement. In signing the agreement, the debtor makes an offer to the creditor to enter into the credit agreement and the general rule of contract law is that an offeror may revoke his offer at any time before its acceptance by the offeree. Accordingly, the prospective debtor may revoke his offer in the interval before the creditor accepts it, the creditor's posting of the completed agreement to the debtor being the moment of such acceptance where the post is used.[19] At common law, the general rule is that the offeror must communicate his revocation to the offeree or his agent if it is to be effective.[20] Most sensibly, in *Financings Ltd v Stimson*,[1] the court regarded the dealer in a hire-purchase transaction as an agent of the creditor for the purpose of communicating such a revocation of an offer. There

---

18 SI 1983/1557 (as amended)
19 *Adams v Lindsell* (1818) 1 B & Ald 681.
20 *Byrne & Co v Leon van Tienhoven & Co* (1880) 5 CPD 344.
 1 [1962] 1 WLR 1184.

the debtor completed the hire-purchase proposal form for a car at the dealer's premises and was allowed to drive away in it. Four days later, the debtor returned the car to the dealer informing him that he no longer wanted it. The car was stolen from the dealer's premises and, although it was recovered, it was badly damaged. The following day the creditor purported to accept the debtor's offer. The Court of Appeal held that no contract existed between the debtor and creditor because (i) the return of the car to the dealer amounted to a revocation of the debtor's offer to the creditor and the dealer was the agent of the creditor for receiving the communication of revocation; and (ii) the debtor's offer was conditional on the goods remaining in the same condition at the date of acceptance as at the date of offer and, as the car was damaged and obviously not in its original condition, the debtor's offer had lapsed and was incapable of acceptance. It is doubtful that many prospective debtors realise that they have such a right of withdrawal and, while the CCA follows the rule at common law, outlined above, the Act modifies and clarifies the common law rules on withdrawal in favour of the prospective debtor.

WITHDRAWAL UNDER THE CCA

At common law, an offeror may bind himself to keep his offer open absolutely or for a specific period of time either by a document under seal or by contract with consideration furnished by the offeree, eg an owner of land grants an option to purchase under seal or in consideration of an option fee. However, under the CCA, s 59(1), a prospective debtor cannot bind himself to enter into a prospective regulated agreement and an agreement which purports to do so is void. Section 59(2) provides that regulations may exclude certain agreements from the operation of s 59(1).[2]

As stressed earlier, the general rule at common law is that the revocation of an offer takes effect only when it is communicated to the other party or his agent and, if the post is used as the means of revocation, receipt of the letter is thus required for a valid revocation. Somewhat uncharitably in the context of the CCA, the latter rule on communication and receipt of letters *does* apply to withdrawal under the CCA if notice of withdrawal is communicated to, or served in writing, on the creditor, owner or either their actual agents or deemed agents under s 57(3).[3] The rule demanding actual communication is softened somewhat by the CCA, s 57(2) which provides that 'the giving to a party of a written or oral notice which, however expressed, indicates the intention of the other party to withdraw from a prospective regulated agreement operates as a withdrawal from it'. It is thus put beyond doubt that the debtor's failure to use formal language will not detract from the withdrawal provided that the intent to withdraw is plain and is communicated to the other party.

---

2 The Consumer Credit (Agreements to enter Prospective Agreements) (Exemptions) Regulations 1983 (SI 1983/1552) exempt agreements to enter into prospective hire agreements or prospective restricted-use credit agreements for fixed-sum credit to finance the purchase of goods, where the the goods are required by the hirer or debtor for the purpose of a business carried on by him. This exemption is principally for equipment leasing agreements where the lessor may require an undertaking of the lessee not to withdraw his offer once the lessor has ordered goods from a supplier.
3 *Cancellation* takes effect on *posting* under s 69(7) but this does not apply to withdrawal as s 57(1) applies only the same *consequences* to withdrawal as to cancellation.

However, most significantly, the debtor or hirer need not necessarily give notice of withdrawal to the creditor or owner or their actual agents because, under s 57(3), a wide range of persons is 'deemed to be the agent' of the creditor or owner for the purpose of receiving a notice of withdrawal, viz:

(i)   a credit-broker or supplier who is the negotiator in 'antecedent negotiations' (s 57(3)(a)); and

(ii) 'any person' who, in 'the course of a business carried on by him', acts on behalf of the debtor or hirer in 'any negotiations for the agreement' (s 57(3)(b)).

Such a deemed agent is also deemed to be under a contractual duty to the creditor or owner to transmit the notice to him forthwith (s 175).[4]

Under category (i) above, the prospective debtor can give notice of withdrawal to the dealer who conducted the antecedent negotiations in a hire-purchase, credit-sale or conditional sale agreement. Likewise, notice of withdrawal can be given to a supplier of goods who similarly conducted the antecedent negotiations in the connected loan situation of a debtor-creditor-supplier agreement within s 12(b) or (c). Category (ii), outlined above, is very broad. 'Any person' who 'in the course of a business carried on by him' has acted on behalf of the debtor in 'any negotiations for the agreement' means that the debtor can communicate withdrawal to his *own* solicitor, provided that he has negotiated on the debtor's behalf. Moreover, the Citizens' Advice Bureau (CAB) might be within this category if it can be said to act 'in the course of a business' in negotiating with a creditor or owner on behalf of the debtor. There is no indication that profit is an essential requirement of 'business' as defined in s 189(1) and (2) and so it seems likely that, if negotiations have taken place on behalf of the debtor, notice of withdrawal could be made to the CAB. It should be noted that there is no definition of 'negotiations' in the CCA nor, for that matter, is there an indication of what is meant by a 'prospective regulated agreement' from which the debtor is seeking to withdraw. It is tolerably clear that 'negotiations' are to be understood in a more informal way than 'antecedent negotiations' which are designated and defined in s 56.[5] Moreover, the draftsman has assumed that, where the debtor wishes to withdraw from a *prospective* agreement, something substantive has occurred from which he needs to withdraw, most particularly that he has made an offer to the creditor or owner.

Withdrawal from a prospective land mortgage

The CCA, s 58 contains special provisions for the opportunity of withdrawal from a prospective land mortgage.[6] Under s 67(a), the right of cancellation

---

4   It is not clear what effect s 175 may have on communication of withdrawal to a deemed agent. It is suggested that, in the context of the CCA, notice of withdrawal given orally or sent by post to an agent (actual or deemed) will take effect when it is received by him, whether or not it is received by the creditor or owner as principal. The purpose of s 175 must be to *establish* the creditor's or owner's right to sue the *deemed* agent for breach of contract, ie if the creditor or owner suffers a loss as a consequence of the deemed agent's failure to act promptly, the latter can be liable for breach of this deemed contractual duty.

5   See Ch 35 where s 56 is considered.

6   Certain land mortgage transactions are exempt agreements under the CCA, s 16 and Consumer Credit (Exempt Agreements) Order 1989 (SI 1989/869). Most first mortgages from building societies or local authorities, for example, will be exempt agreements and the special provisions on withdrawal are aimed principally at second mortgages.

under s 67 is not available where 'the agreement is secured on land, or is a restricted-use credit agreement to finance the purchase of land or is an agreement for a bridging loan in connection with the purchase of land'. If cancellation were allowed, there would be considerable administrative difficulties for the Land Registry and so, instead of the right of cancellation, ss 58 and 61(2) and (3) provide for a special right of withdrawal in relation to land mortgages.

The overall notion is that the debtor must be allowed a pre-contractual period of isolation and consideration during which he may choose to withdraw from the agreement and, so that no pressure can be placed upon him, he must not be approached by the creditor in any way during this consideration period. It follows that there are special procedures to be observed in relation to land mortgages. First, the creditor or owner must give[7] the debtor or hirer an advance copy of the unexecuted agreement which contains a notice in the prescribed form[8] indicating the right of the debtor or hirer to withdraw from the prospective agreement, and how and when the right is exercisable. This copy must be given to him before the unexecuted agreement is sent to him for signature and it must be accompanied by any other document referred to in that unexecuted agreement (s 58(1)). Second, not less than seven days after the advance copy was given to him, the unexecuted agreement must be sent by post to the debtor or hirer for signature (s 61(2)(b)). Third, the debtor or hirer must be allowed the consideration and isolation period which starts with the giving of the advance copy and ends on the expiry of seven days after the day on which the unexecuted agreement is sent to him for signature, or on its return by him after signature, whichever occurs first (s 61(3)). Fourth, the creditor or owner must not contact the debtor or hirer in any way during the consideration period, except in response to a specific request made by the debtor or hirer after the beginning of the consideration period (s 61(2))c)). Finally, no notice of withdrawal must have been received by the creditor or owner before the sending of the unexecuted agreement (s 61(2)(d)). These special provisions do not apply, however, to a restricted-use credit agreement to finance the purchase of the mortgaged land or an agreement for a bridging loan in connection with the purchase of the mortgaged land or other land (s 58(2)).

It should be stressed that the rules relating to copies of the agreement in ss 62 and 63 *also* apply to land mortgages and, as copies must be sent to each debtor (s 185), an extremely elaborate procedure is set in motion.

Consequences of withdrawal

The CCA, s 57(1) provides that the withdrawal of a party from a prospective regulated agreement has the same consequences as if the agreement had been made and then cancelled under s 69. This means that not only the offer to enter into the agreement is terminated but also that the consequences of *cancellation* apply as stipulated in ss 69-73, discussed below. This is the position *even* where the agreement, if made, would not have been a cancellable agreement (s 57(4)). The principal consequences of the withdrawal are the cancellation of any linked

---

7 'Give' is defined in s 189(1) as 'deliver or send by post to'.
8 As prescribed by the Consumer Credit (Cancellation Notices and Copies of Documents) Regulations 1983 (SI 1983/1557), as amended.

transaction,[9] withdrawal of any offer to enter into a linked transaction, repayment of deposits and the return of part-exchange goods or the repayment of the part-exchange allowance.

Cancellation

The unique right to cancel the *concluded* credit agreement was first introduced by the Hire-Purchase Acts of 1964 and 1965 following the recommendations of the Molony Committee in 1962.[10] At that time, there was considerable evidence of high-pressure sales techniques by door-to-door salesmen with the result that debtors were often persuaded to commit themselves to more credit agreements and/or more extensive agreements than they could sensibly afford. Additionally, doorstep sellers and their employers cannot always be relied upon to have permanent business premises at which a wronged consumer might complain and seek redress. With these considerations in mind, the Molony Committee recommended a 'cooling-off period' for such doorstep selling and this was enacted in the Hire-Purchase Acts. The hirer who signed the hire-purchase agreement at a place other than trade premises was thus allowed four days in which to cancel the agreement, commencing with the day of the receipt by post of the copy of the agreement.

The right of cancellation and its effects are particularly wide under the CCA and it has been said that 'the excessively complicated provisions run to several pages of statutory text, and virtually have the effect that any cancellable agreement is not worth the paper it is written on: it provides a nightmare for the trade, who must provide separate documentation for – and ensure that that is only but always used for – cancellable agreements; and this has in some cases led to a blank refusal to undertake this type of business. It is for consideration whether there is a technically simpler method of achieving the generally acceptable statutory objective, eg it is a common precaution not to perform the agreement until the cooling-off period has expired, so why not simply make this mandatory in all cases?'[11] This is cogent criticism but it overlooks the fact that, if this attractively simple rule were adopted, disputes would nevertheless have to be resolved in those cases where there had been some performance under the agreement prior to cancellation. The draftsman of the CCA therefore sought to formulate all-embracing provisions which would anticipate, regulate and, often, determine the outcome of any disputes.

WHEN IS AN AGREEMENT CANCELLABLE UNDER THE CCA?

The general policy of curbing doorstep selling continues in the CCA but the fledgling notion of cancellation in the earlier hire-purchase legislation has now

---

9 Certain types of linked transaction are exempted from the withdrawal/cancellation provisions by the Consumer Credit (Linked Transactions) (Exemptions) Regulations 1983 (SI 1983/1560), viz (i) contracts of insurance; (ii) written guarantees relating to goods; and (iii) agreements relating to the operation of a savings, deposit or current account. See Ch 31 where linked transactions are considered.
10 *Final Report of the Committee on Consumer Protection* (1962), Cmnd 1781.
11 J K Macleod and M Cronin in *Consumer Credit* (United Kingdom Comparative Law Series, Vol 3, ed Goode, 1978), Ch 22, p 294.

truly come of age in an extensive, potent remedy, available to debtors and hirers. A cursory glance at the right of rescission reveals that the statutory right to cancel bears no resemblance to the remedy of rescission at common law. The debtor's inability to restore the goods through loss or because he has consumed them, for example, does not impede his right of cancellation. Even where the debtor is in breach of duties imposed by the CCA, such as the duty to take care of the goods during the cancellation period, he may be liable in damages for breach of statutory duty but he is not barred from cancelling the agreement. Indeed, the only obvious situation in which the right of cancellation is unavailable to the debtor is where he has failed to serve the notice of cancellation within the statutory time-limits.[12]

The right of cancellation under the CCA is given by s 67 which provides:

'A regulated agreement may be cancelled by the debtor or hirer in accordance with this Part[13] if the antecedent negotiations included oral representations made when in the presence of the debtor or hirer by an individual acting as, or on behalf of, the negotiator, unless –

(a) the agreement is secured on land, or is a restricted-use credit agreement to finance the purchase of land or is an agreement for a bridging loan in connection with the purchase of land, or
(b) the unexecuted agreement is signed by the debtor or hirer at premises at which any of the following is carrying on any business (whether on a permanent or temporary basis) –
 (i) the creditor or owner;
 (ii) any party to a linked transaction (other than the debtor or hirer or a relative of his);
 (iii) the negotiator in any antecedent negotiations.'

There are several broad requirements of s 67 which must now be dissected under three headings.

Antecedent negotiations and oral representations

First, the *antecedent negotiations* must have included *oral representations*. It is obvious that some communication is necessary before a regulated agreement can come into existence and the negotiations involved are thus 'antecedent negotiations' as defined in s 56(1).[14] The 'negotiator' referred to in s 67 and s 56(1) is the person who conducts such antecedent negotiations.

Typically, a dealer who sells goods to the creditor to be let to the debtor on hire-purchase conducts the antecedent negotiations in his capacities as 'negotiator', 'credit-broker' and deemed agent of the creditor under s 56(1)(b).[15] The creditor or owner might himself conduct such negotiations (s 56(1)(a)) or a supplier/seller who sells goods against a credit-card issued by a third party can be such a negotiator under s 56(1)(c). Again, a familiar occurrence within s 56(1)(c) is where the supplier in a connected loan, debtor-creditor-supplier agreement, introduces the debtor to the creditor so that finance becomes available to the debtor, eg a supplier/installer of kitchen equipment who

---

12 Less obviously, the creditor may have commenced proceedings against the debtor and obtained judgment before the debtor attempts to cancel. Here the debtor's purported cancellation cannot have the effect of nullifying the judgment which is valid until set aside, see *Skuce (V L) & Co v Cooper* [1975] 1 WLR 593.
13 This means Part V of the CCA.
14 See also s 189(1); see Ch 35 where s 56 is considered.
15 See *UDT v Whitfield* [1987] CCLR 60.

introduces the debtor to a finance house with whom the supplier has pre-existing business arrangements. Here the supplier is a negotiator within s 67.

When section 56 is considered in chapter 35, it is emphasised that, by an unfortunate oversight, antecedent negotiations (as defined in s 56) do not cover the case of negotiations conducted by a *dealer* in relation to goods which are then sold to a lessor/owner to be *hired* on lease or rental to the hirer. It follows that such a dealer in a consumer hire agreement cannot be a 'negotiator' for the antecedent negotiotions which are conducted within s 67. Moreover, there is a presumption at common law, that the dealer is not considered to act as the agent of the owner[16] unless exceptional circumstances point to such an agency.[17] The owner himself[18] can conduct antecedent negotiations or *his* agent or employee[19] can qualify as negotiators, but it is rare that the owner (or his staff) and the prospective hirer will deal face-to-face and, of course, the cancellation provisions demand that oral representations must be made in the presence of the debtor. The startling conclusion which must be reached is that, in the majority of situations, the cancellation provisions do not apply to consumer hire agreements conducted through the medium of a dealer[20] even where he makes oral representations in the presence of the hirer and the hirer signs the agreement at his home (see below).

'Representation' is defined so widely in s 189(1) that it would seem to cover any statement but, in *Moorgate Property Services Ltd v Kabir*,[1] Staughton LJ considered that this apparent width was not what Parliament had intended. The judge held that the 'oral representations' in s 67 need not be misrepresentations but must be statements of fact or opinion or an undertaking as to the future which was capable of inducing the debtor to enter into the agreement, eg statements as to the suitability of the goods for the debtor's purpose. Moreover, Staughton LJ held that the statements need not actually induce the debtor to enter into the contract nor need the maker of the statement intend them so to induce the debtor.

Oral representations made in the presence of the debtor or hirer

Second, the oral representations must be be made by an individual acting as, or on behalf of, the negotiator, when *in the presence of the debtor or hirer*. Representations made over the telephone, by post, telex or electronic mail will thus be outside s 67. However, it does not matter *where* the antecedent negotiations take place, provided that oral representations are made in the presence of the debtor. It will be noted that the representations need not be made *to* the debtor and s 67 is satisfied if they are made in his presence, but 'presence' arguably indicates the debtor's physical presence rather than that of his agent or employee. The oral representations can, of course, be made by an agent or employee of the negotiator and, indeed, this is a physical necessity where the negotiator is a limited company.

---

16 *Branwhite v Worcester Works Finance Ltd* [1969] 1 AC 552; *Woodchester Equipment (Leasing) Ltd v BACFID* [1995] CCLR 51.
17 See *Woodchester Equipment Leasing Ltd v Clayton and Clayton* [1994] CCLR 87 (an agency was established at common law in a consumer hire agreement, meaning that there were antecedent negotiations within s 56 and the agreement was cancellable under s 67).
18 See s 56(1)(a) (antecedent negotiations can be conducted by the creditor or owner).
19 See s 67 (the oral representations can be made 'by an individual acting as, or on behalf of, the negotiator').
20 See Goode, *Consumer Credit Law* (1989), paras 15.34-15.35; 15.45.
1   [1995] CCLR 74.

Agreement signed somewhere other than specified business premises

Third, under s 67(b), the right of cancellation is *not* available if the agreement is signed at the *business premises* of (i) the creditor; (ii) a party to a linked transaction; or (iii) a negotiator in any antecedent negotiations. This is justified on the basis that the debtor will usually have visited the trade premises voluntarily and will not be subject to the innate pressures and temptations which arise where a salesman visits his home unsolicited.[2] If a hire-purchase agreement is signed at the dealer's showroom, for example, the right of cancellation does *not* apply.

Section 67(b) provides that the business is 'any' business which is carried on at premises and the business can be pursued 'on a permanent or temporary basis'. This is designed to encompass the numerous temporary 'businesses' which can be encountered, eg a mobile caravan outside a supermarket or a stand at an exhibition. However, s 67(b) is somewhat ambiguous. Under s 67(b), it is the *business* which can be permanent or temporary and so it must be asked whether a mobile caravan, for example, falls within the definition of 'premises'. Might a court decide that temporary locations are not 'premises' and that the debtor or hirer may cancel the agreement on the basis that, where he signs the agreement at such locations, he signs off trade premises? There is considerable authority on the meaning of 'premises' but in contexts other than consumer credit. As a general rule, 'premises' undoubtedly indicate 'some degree of permanency'[3] and use of the word 'implies some definite place with metes and bounds'.[4] However, the word has been held to take 'colour and content from the context in which it is used' and to have 'no recognised and established primary meaning'.[5] Certainly a cave formed as a result of quarrying[6] and the forecourt of a shop[7] have been held to be 'premises' but the public highway has been held not to constitute 'premises'.[8] It remains to be seen whether an established street market, eg Warren Street market, would be regarded as within the definition of 'premises'.

It should also be stressed that, under s 67(b), the debtor or hirer does not have the right of cancellation where the agreement is signed by him 'at' the

---

2 Should cancellation also be available where the debtor signs at business premises? It is arguable that the pressure to sign the agreement can be applied with equal force in the dealer's showroom and the debtor's living room, but the suggestion to extend cancellation rights to agreements signed at trade premises was rejected by the OFT: see *Consumer Credit Deregulation* (1994), paras 6.34-6.35.

3 *West Mersea UDC v Fraser* [1950] 2 KB 119, 124 per Lord Goddard CJ (a house-boat had been moored on mud flats for six years and its position rose and fell with the tide only. Held that there was a sufficient element of permanency to constitute the boat 'premises' within the Water Act 1945 thus entitling its owner to a supply of water for domestic purposes).

4 *Andrews v Andrews and Mears* [1908] 2 KB 567, 570 per Buckley LJ.

5 *Maunsell v Olins* [1975] AC 373, 383 per Viscount Dilhorne.

6 *Gardiner v Sevenoaks RDC* [1950] 2 All ER 84 (films were stored in an underground chamber, formed artificially as result of quarrying and excavations and closed by a wooden door. The appellant had a lease of the cave for a term of 14 years. Held that the cave was 'premises' under the Celluloid and Cinematograph Film Act 1922 and so the appellant was obliged to comply with statutory safety requirements).

7 *Grandi v Milburn* [1966] 2 QB 263 (a petrol-tanker on the forecourt of a shop dispensed petrol direct to the fuel tanks of cars for a period of four hours. Held that the tanker was *not* 'premises' but that the forecourt did constitute 'premises' upon which petrol was being kept without a licence).

8 *Andrews v Andrews and Mears* [1908] 2 KB 567 (a workman employed to cart rubbish from the Albert Hall was killed in an accident in a public street, two miles from the site of the work. Held that the accident had not occurred 'on, or in, or about premises' on which the work was to be executed).

business premises which are specified, rather than 'in' or 'on' those premises. Consequently, there would be no right of cancellation where, for example, the debtor or hirer signed the agreement outside a car dealer's showroom after the inspection of a car.

Finally, in order to deprive the debtor of the right of cancellation under s 67, the agreement must be signed at the business premises of those parties listed in s 67(b), and so the agreement *can* be cancelled if the signature is made at the premises of some disparate trader,[9] at the debtor's own business premises, or at the office of his solicitor. It also follows that, should the debtor take the agreement home to sign it at his leisure, the agreement is definitely cancellable under s 67.[10]

NOTICE OF CANCELLATION RIGHTS

This question of the special requirements in relation to the notification to the debtor or hirer of the right of cancellation, was covered when the copy provisions were considered earlier.

THE COOLING-OFF PERIOD

The cooling-off period during which the debtor or hirer may serve a notice of cancellation is laid down by the CCA, s 68. The period commences at the date the debtor signs the unexecuted agreement and ends five days after he *receives* the copy of the executed agreement. He must receive that copy within seven days following the 'making of the agreement' (s 63(2)), the agreement typically being 'made' when the creditor posts the executed agreement to the debtor and thus that executed agreement must be received within seven days of its posting. Alternatively, the unexecuted agreement may be presented personally or sent to the debtor and on his signature it becomes an *executed* agreement: here no copies of the executed agreement are sent *at a later date*. In this case, it will be remembered that a notice, informing him of his right of cancellation, must be sent *separately* by post to the debtor within seven days following the making of the agreement (s 64(1)(b)) and the debtor has until the end of the fifth day following the date of receipt of this separate notice in which to serve his notice of cancellation. This seems complex at first glance but, in fact, it is relatively simple. For example, if the debtor signs the agreement on Saturday 1 May and he receives the copy of the executed agreement *or* the separate notice of cancellation on Friday 7 May,[11] the cooling-off period lasts until midnight on Wednesday 12 May.

There is one other possibility. The Director General of Fair Trading has power (s 64(4)) to dispense with the separate notice of cancellation (s 64(1)(b)). Where

---

9 Cf Hire-Purchase Act 1965, s 58(1).

10 The OFT has recommended that the agreement should *not* be cancellable where the debtor signs at home after visting trade premises in that the pressures of doorstep selling do not apply in these circumstances: see *Consumer Credit Deregulation* (1994), para 6.36.

11 Where the agreement is cancellable, the second copy or notice must be sent by post and *received* within the seven days following the making of the agreement: see s 63(3) (second copy) and s 64(1)(b) (separate notice of cancellation).

this occurs,[12] the cooling-off period extends to the end of the fourteenth day following the day on which he signed the unexecuted agreement (s 68(b)). For example, if the debtor signs the agreement on Saturday 1 May he has until midnight on Saturday 15 May to cancel the agreement.

It will be apparent that the cooling-off period is premised upon the *receipt* by the debtor of the copy of the executed agreement or the separate notice of cancellation and, here, complications seem to abound. First, there seems nothing to stop the dishonest debtor from extending the cooling-off period by claiming falsely that the copy or notice was delayed in the post, but the CCA arguably accepts this risk as a consequence of making the right of cancellation available to honest debtors. Second, if the creditor discovers that the copy or notice has been lost in the post, he can presumably rectify matters by sending a second copy or notice *provided* it is received by the debtor in the seven days after the making of the agreement. Third, the position is most unclear if the creditor complies with the copy or notice provisions by posting them in the seven day period but they are (a) not received within that period or (b) never received at all. After the lapse of the seven days, it is arguable that it would be impossible to allow the cooling-off period to commence from the moment of the actual receipt of the late copy or notice in situation (a) or allow the creditor to send a fresh copy or notice in situation (b) and permit the cooling-off period to commence from the moment of its receipt. In both these circumstances, the copy or notice would simply be out of time within the limits prescribed by s 63(2) or s 64(1)(b), and s 68(a) provides that the cooling-off period commences on the receipt of the copy or notice 'under' s 63(2) or s 64(1)(b). Consequently, the possibilities here are (i) the debtor has lost his right to cancel; (ii) his right to cancel is available indefinitely; or (iii) the cooling-off period would be allowed to commence from the date of the receipt of the late copies. None of these options is in the least desirable but justice would seem to be served by the adoption of (ii). Some credence is lent to this view in that the right of cancellation is not dependent upon the receipt of the copy or notice: s 68 allows the debtor to cancel immediately after signing the unexecuted agreement.[13]

METHOD OF CANCELLATION AND ITS COMMUNICATION

The CCA, s 69 provides that a 'notice of cancellation' can be served on:

(a) the creditor or owner, or
(b) the person specified in a separate cancellation notice given under s 64(1), or
(c) a person who is an agent of the creditor or owner.

Most importantly, s 69(6) adds that (i) the credit-broker or supplier who is the negotiator in antecedent negotiations, and (ii) any person who, in the course of a business carried on by him, acted on behalf of the debtor or hirer in any negotiations for the agreement, are both deemed to be the agent of the creditor

---

12 See Consumer Credit (Notice of Cancellation Rights) (Exemptions) Regulations 1983 (SI 1983/1558) (the exemption applies to certain mail order consumer credit agreements).

13 Typically, after the debtor has signed the unexecuted agreement, he will have a right of withdrawal. Alternatively, the creditor may have signed first so that the document is executed on the debtor's signature and then the debtor's right of cancellation becomes operative.

or owner for the purpose of receiving a notice of cancellation. 'Notice' means 'notice in writing' under the CCA, s 189(1).

The persons who are deemed to be agents and upon whom notice of cancellation may be served are identical to those persons who are deemed to be agents for receiving a notice of withdrawal under s 57(3). In hire-purchase, for example, the debtor can serve the notice of cancellation on the dealer who negotiated the transaction. As in the withdrawal provisions, the debtor can serve the notice of cancellation on his *own* agent who acted on the debtor's behalf in the negotiations, eg his own solicitor. Once again, this provision ensures that debtors are not prejudiced by informing someone who they may think is the agent of the creditor but who is, in fact, their own agent. The persons who are deemed to be agents for receiving the notice of cancellation are also deemed to be under a contractual duty to transmit the notice to the creditor forthwith (s 175).

There are further provisions which are ultra-protective of the debtor. First, under s 69(1), apart from the fact that it must be in writing, a notice of cancellation does not have to be in any particular form and, provided that it indicates the debtor's intention to withdraw from the agreement, it operates to cancel the agreement. Consequently, the debtor need not complete the cancellation form sent in the second copy of the agreement or the form in the separate notice of cancellation. Second, under s 69(7), a notice of cancellation sent by post is deemed to be served at the time of *posting*, whether or not it is actually received.[14]

THE EFFECTS OF CANCELLATION

The general effects of the service of a notice of cancellation are enunciated in s 69(1) as (i) cancellation of the agreement and any linked transaction and (ii) withdrawal of any offer by the debtor or hirer, or his relative, to enter into a linked transaction. Section 69(4) adds that the general effect of cancellation is that the agreement is treated 'as if it had never been entered into'.[15] The general rule under s 70 is that, on cancellation, sums which were payable cease to be payable and sums which were paid prior to cancellation must be repaid. Under s 72, there is a duty to restore the goods to the other party on cancellation. These are the overall effects of cancellation but the detailed consequences must now be investigated.

Cancellation in relation to emergencies and installations

The general rule that the agreement is treated 'as if it had never been entered into' is subject to two important exceptions. Section 69(2) limits the consequences

14 What is the connection between s 175 and s 69(7)? Section 175 provides that a person who is deemed 'to receive a notice or payment as agent of the creditor or owner ... shall be deemed to be under a contractual duty to the creditor or owner to transmit the notice, or remit the payment, to him forthwith'. It cannot be intended that s 175 should alter the rule under s 69(7) and demand that notice of cancellation sent to a deemed agent be received rather than posted. Moreover, the reference to payment is puzzling as there is no provision in the CCA deeming any person an agent of the creditor or owner for the receipt of money. It seems that the purpose of s 175 is to *establish* the creditor's or owner's right to sue the *deemed* agent for breach of contract, ie if the creditor or owner suffers a loss as a consequence of the deemed agent's failure to act promptly, the latter can be liable for breach of this deemed contractual duty.
15 It has been held that this means void *ab initio* and not merely voidable until the date of cancellation, see *Colesworthy v Collmain Services Ltd* [1993] CCLR 4.

of cancellation in the situation of a debtor-creditor-supplier agreement for restricted-use credit which finances:

(a) the doing of work or supply of goods to meet an emergency, or
(b) the supply of goods which, before service of the notice of cancellation, had by the *act of the debtor or his relative* become incorporated in any land or thing *not comprised* in the agreement or any linked transaction.

In these two special circumstances, s 69(2) provides that the provisions of the agreement and any linked transaction relating to credit and credit charges are cancellable, but the debtor remains liable to pay the cash price of the services or the cash price of the goods. It should be stressed that these two instances apply *only* to debtor-creditor-supplier agreements for restricted-use credit where the supplier extends the credit himself (eg hire-purchase; credit-sale), or where there is a connected loan and the supplier is paid directly.

An example within the emergency category would be a contract for work and materials to help with the resolution of a domestic catastrophe such as fire or flood. It would clearly be unfair if the debtor could use the goods or services which had been supplied and, once the emergency had passed, seek to cancel the agreement. An example within the category of incorporation of the contract goods in land or other goods would be a domestic installation which cannot readily be detached, eg the fitting of new kitchen equipment. The reason underlying the installation exception is that unfettered cancellation should be impossible once the goods have become integrated in real property or other goods. It cannot be stressed enough that it is only where the installation has 'by the act of the *debtor* or his *relative*' become incorporated in land or goods that the debtor is liable for the cash price and, should the *supplier or creditor* install the goods, the normal rules on cancellation apply but with the Draconian consequences that the creditor or supplier cannot recover the goods and the debtor does not have to pay for them.[16] It is clearly prudent for the trader to wait until the cooling-off period has expired before installing goods such as double-glazed windows in the debtor's house.

As stressed above, in these two special cases cancellation extinguishes the *credit* obligations of the debtor under the principal agreement and any linked transaction but he remains liable for the *cash* price of the goods or services supplied (s 69(2)). When he has paid the cash price, the debtor can keep the goods which were supplied to meet the emergency or incorporated in the land or other goods, and title to them will pass to him (s 72(9)(c) and (d)).

Finally, it is a startling omission from the CCA that the emergency exception applies only to consumer *credit*[17] and does not apply to the *hire* of goods.[18] Goods are, of course, frequently supplied on hire to meet an emergency, eg equipment to deal with the consequences of fire or flood. In such a case, provided that the hirer has the right of cancellation, he can cancel the agreement, refuse to pay the hire charges or recover any payment made (see below), and he is *not* under a duty to return the goods. The hirer need not return the goods because, although

---

16 See the CCA, s 72(9)(d), considered later. If an independent contractor installs the goods, the dispute can be resolved by asking which party has employed the contractor. If he is a contractor employed by the debtor, the agreement cannot be cancelled.

17 See the definition, in s 12, of the debtor-creditor-supplier agreement as a 'consumer *credit* agreement'.

18 The supply of goods which have become incorporated in land etc, within s 69(2)(b), would not be the subject of a hire agreement.

hire agreements are not within s 69(2), they have not been excluded from s 72(9). Accordingly, s 72(9)(c) relieves the 'possessor' of the duty to return goods 'supplied' to meet an emergency, and this is clearly broad enough to cover hire.

Money paid by the debtor prior to cancellation is repayable and/or ceases to be payable

There are several, common situations where the debtor might make a payment prior to cancellation, eg payment of a deposit to a dealer in a hire-purchase transaction, payment of the first instalment to the creditor under the repayment terms in hire-purchase, payment under a linked transaction for goods or services supplied, or a payment to a credit-broker as a fee for arranging the credit.[19]

Section 70(1)(a) provides that, on cancellation of a regulated agreement and of any linked transaction, any sum paid by the debtor or hirer, or his relative, under or in contemplation of the agreement or transaction (including any item in the total charge for credit) is *repayable*. If, under the terms of the cancelled agreement, the debtor or hirer, or his relative, is in possession of any goods, he has a lien[20] on them (s 70(2)) for any sum payable to him under s 70(1). Any sum repayable is, by virtue of s 70(3), 'repayable by the person to whom it was originally paid'.[1] Section 70(1)(b) completes the picture by providing that any sum (including any item in the total charge for credit) which but for the cancellation is, or would or might become, payable by the debtor or hirer, or his relative, under the agreement or transaction, *ceases to be so payable*.

The general rule in cancellation is that the debtor's claim for repayment must be made against the person to whom the sum was paid (s 70(3)) but, in the case of a debtor-creditor-supplier agreement under s 12(b), s 70(3) places an extra, extended obligation on the creditor in that the creditor and the supplier are jointly and severally liable for the repayment to the debtor, or his relative, of sums paid under the agreement or under a linked transaction within s 19(1)(b). It will be recalled that a cardinal application of s 12(b) is in the connected-lending situation where, for example, the debtor wants to buy a car from a seller/supplier and the finance is provided by the creditor who has an existing business relationship with the seller (or such relations are contemplated in the future), the price of the car being paid directly to that seller. Linked transactions within s 19(1)(b) are those where there is a principal debtor-creditor-supplier agreement and the linked transaction is financed by the principal agreement. Thus the linked transaction is the purchase of the car in the example above. If the debtor has paid a deposit to the seller/supplier in such a case, it is recoverable on cancellation either from that seller/supplier or from the creditor or from both of them together.

---

19   The effect of s 70(6) is that, on cancellation, the credit-broker can retain no more than £3 in respect of 'a fee or commission charged' by him (the amount was originally £1 but it was raised to £3 by the Consumer Credit (Increase of Monetary Amounts) Order 1983 (SI 1983/1571). This is the total amount that a credit-broker can charge and, under s 70(7), if the total charge for credit includes any sum payable or paid by the debtor to the credit-broker otherwise than in respect of a fee or commission charged by him, that sum shall for the purposes of s 70(6) be treated as if it were such a fee or commission.

20   The money might be repayable under a linked transaction, for example, but the lien will nevertheless attach to the goods in the debtor's possession.

 1   See *Colesworthy v Collmain Services Ltd* [1993] CCLR 4.

Section 12(b) also applies to transactions where the debtor uses a credit card (eg a Visa or Access card) to buy goods, as here arrangements will have been made between the creditor and the supplier of the goods. Such agreements will rarely fall within the cancellation requirements and, in any event, money will probably have been paid to the creditor only. However, such a credit-token agreement is cancellable under s 67 and the joint and several liability in s 70(3) is applicable to creditor and supplier. Section 70(5) does provide, however, that the debtor is not entitled to repayment of a sum paid (or release from the obligation to pay) for the *issue* of the credit-token until it has been returned to the creditor or surrendered to a supplier. This provision relates only to this amount paid for the issue of the credit-token and does not apply to the amounts paid or payable for the goods or services obtained with that token. The purpose of s 70(5) is arguably to give the debtor an incentive to return the credit-token and thus reduce the risk of fraud where it has not been returned and is lost. Moreover, in check-trading agreements the debtor often has to pay an amount to receive the checks and s 70(5) is thus also aimed at these agreements.

The rationale of s 70(3) is that the debtor might encounter substantial difficulties in recovering any deposit paid from the supplier of the goods or services whereas the creditor should be solvent and more reliable as regards repayments. Under s 70(4), the creditor may, in turn, claim an indemnity from the supplier (subject to any agreement between them) for loss incurred in discharging the liability of the supplier, including any costs reasonably incurred in defending proceedings instituted by the debtor.[2]

It is important to emphasise that this joint and several liability applies *only* to a s 12(b) debtor-creditor-supplier agreement. In the case of a s 12(a) debtor-creditor-supplier agreement which is limited to two parties, eg hire-purchase, credit sale and conditional sale, the creditor and the supplier are the same party and so the s 70(3) joint and several liability cannot apply. In the case of a deposit paid to a dealer in hire-purchase, the starting point for recovery must now be the dealer himself under s 70(3), which provides that money is repayable by the person to whom it was originally paid. However, the debtor also has a right at common law[3] to recover from the *finance company* such a deposit paid to the dealer; the basis of the claim is not that the dealer is the agent of the finance company but rather that the finance company is deemed to have received the deposit since the company will have paid the dealer the agreed sale price less the amount of the deposit. The deposit must thus be returned on cancellation because of a total failure of consideration.

Finally, in this context of recovery of sums paid by the debtor on cancellation, some consideration must be given to s 70(1)(c) which provides for the situation where money has been paid on the debtor's behalf. Where the creditor makes payments (on behalf of the debtor) to the supplier before cancellation occurs under a debtor-creditor-supplier agreement within s 12(b), s 70(1)(c) provides that the supplier must repay the amount to the creditor on cancellation. It is strange that there is no equivalent provision in the CCA relating to payments made by the creditor to a dealer in hire-purchase.

---

2 This could occur if the supplier falsely informed the creditor that the agreement had been signed at his business premises and thus was not cancellable.
3 *Branwhite v Worcester Works Finance Ltd* [1969] 1 AC 552.

Linked transactions and cancellation

Under s 69(1), cancellation of the principal regulated agreement operates to cancel any linked transaction[4] and, if the linked transaction has not been concluded at the time of cancellation, the offer by the debtor or hirer, or his relative, to enter into the linked transaction is withdrawn. Linked transactions are defined in the CCA, s 19 and were considered in some detail earlier.[5] For example, in a hire-purchase agreement for a computer system, the debtor might enter into a contract with a third party for the maintenance of the computers, but that contract is a linked transaction and so will be cancelled if the principal hire-purchase agreement is cancelled.

The consequences of cancellation on the principal agreement apply with equal force to the linked transaction where the debtor has paid money or received goods under it (see ss 70 and 72). If the debtor had paid any sums under the maintenance agreement in the computer example, above, he would be entitled to the return of that money and, should he receive any goods under the linked transaction, their return is controlled by s 72.

A striking feature of cancellation in relation to linked transactions is that the linked transaction can be cancelled even though the other party to that transaction was totally oblivious that a requirement of the credit agreement was that the debtor should enter into the linked transaction. In the computer example, above, the maintenance contract may be obligatory under the hire-purchase agreement but the maintenance contractor may have no reason to suspect that there is hire-purchase agreement in existence. The maintenance contract is, nevertheless, a linked transaction under s 19(1)(a). Similarly, in the situation where the debtor obtains a loan from a credit company and uses the loan to buy a car from a car dealer, the purchaser/debtor having been introduced to the credit company pursuant to arrangements between dealer and credit company, the cash sale is a linked transaction. There is no reason for the car dealer to be aware of the loan and, furthermore, although on cancellation the debtor will normally have asked the dealer for the return of the purchase price, there is no statutory requirement that the dealer be made aware of the cancellation. Despite this, the sale of the car is cancelled when the loan is cancelled. The dealer then comes under an obligation to collect the goods from the debtor and he will have to commence proceedings against him should any balance of the purchase price be outstanding.

Return of goods received by the debtor prior to cancellation

The debtor or hirer might be allowed to take possession of the goods comprised in the principal agreement or, in a connected-loan situation, the supplier might deliver goods to the debtor under a linked transaction before cancellation occurs. In this situation, s 72 governs the rights, duties and liabilities in relation to the goods. Broadly, on cancellation the debtor or hirer is bound to surrender the goods and, in the interim, he must both retain possession and take reasonable care of them.

---

4 Apart from the three categories of linked transaction which are not cancelled under the Consumer Credit (Linked Transactions) (Exemptions) Regulations 1983 (SI 1983/1560); see Ch 31.
5 See Ch 31.

Section 72 is said to apply to (i) a restricted-use debtor-creditor-supplier agreement; (ii) a consumer hire agreement; (iii) a linked transaction to which the debtor or hirer is a party; or (iv) a linked transaction to which a relative of the debtor or hirer is a party, and these seem to be a comprehensive list of the situations where possession might be obtained before cancellation. The statutory rules concerning the restoration of the goods must now be examined. Section 72 refers to the 'possessor' and this is 'the person who has acquired possession' and 'the other party' is 'the person from whom the possessor acquired possession'.

The duty to restore the goods

On cancellation the possessor must restore the goods he has in his possession to the person from whom he acquired possession, ie 'the other party' (s 72(4)). Under s 72(5), the possessor is not bound to re-deliver the goods to the other party's premises but, instead, his duty is to make them available for collection at his *own* 'premises'. Where the possessor's address is specified in the executed agreement, s 72(10) provides that it is that address 'and no other' where the goods must be available.

The goods have to made available to 'the other party' who is 'the person from whom the possessor acquired possession' but it is unclear who this is: it could mean the legal supplier (eg the finance house in hire-purchase) or the physical supplier of the goods (eg the dealer in hire-purchase). This point is purely conjectural, however, because the duty to restore the goods is discharged by the possessor's having them available at his own premises or, under s 72(6), by delivering them (at his own premises or elsewhere) or sending them at his own expense, to any person on whom a notice of cancellation could have have been served under s 69, but *not* the person who acted for the debtor or hirer in negotiations (eg his solicitor). If the possessor chooses to send the goods to a person on whom notice of cancellation could be served then, under s 72(7), he is under a duty 'to take reasonable care to see that they are received by the other party and not damaged in transit'.

The possessor's duty to surrender the goods does not arise until he has received a 'request in writing signed by or on behalf of the other party' and served on him either before or at the time when the goods are collected from his premises (s 72(5)). Strangely, no regulations have been made prescribing the form of such a written request and so the other party need not specify a time for collection, for example. More significantly, the other party need not state that the possessor's duty is simply to surrender the goods. Failure by the possessor to restore the goods under the statutory provisions is actionable as a breach of statutory duty for which damages are available (s 72(11)).

Under s 70(2), the possessor has a lien on the goods for any sums which are repayable to him on cancellation under s 70, and so the duty to restore the goods is subject to this lien. The person who should repay the money to the possessor need not be the other party to whom the goods should be surrendered but could be a supplier under a linked transaction, for example.

Classes of goods exempted from the duty to restore

Most significantly, certain classes of goods are exempted from s 72 by s 72(9) and need not, or cannot, be surrendered by the possessor, viz:

(a) perishable goods, or
(b) consumable goods which were consumed before cancellation, or

(c)   goods supplied to meet an emergency, or
(d)   goods which before cancellation had become incorporated in any land or thing not comprised in the cancelled agreement or a linked transaction.

Categories (c) and (d) were considered earlier under s 69(2). It will be remembered that, on cancellation, the debtor is liable only for the cash price of the goods in these categories and, having paid for them, it follows logically that the goods need not be restored. Note, however, that the juxtaposition of s 69(2)(b) and s 72(9)(d) mean that the debtor/possessor is liable to pay the cash price for goods which have been installed/incorporated under para (d) and does not have to return them *only* when he, or a relative of his, has performed the act of installation. If the *supplier or creditor* rashly and impulsively performs the installation before cancellation, the debtor does not have to pay and he comes under no obligation to restore the goods. Moreover, when s 69(2) was considered, it was stressed that the combined effect of s 69(2) and s 72(9)(c) is that a *hirer* of goods supplied for use in an emergency does not have to return to them and is freed from obligations relating to payment.[6]

In relation to categories (a) and (b), perishable goods and consumable goods, the cancellation provisions of the Act apply but the possessor has no duty to restore the goods and so he may dispose of them or consume them without restriction. Under s 70(1), he can recover any sums paid in respect of them or obtain release from liability for sums remaining payable. This appears, at first glance, to be an astonishing oversight, but there is a reason underpinning this generous rule. The supply of food on credit as a principal agreement is rare but one of the agreements at which these provisions were aimed was the supply of a freezer stocked with food. The rationale of the CCA is thus that the debtor/possessor must not be deterred from cancelling the contract for the freezer through fear of incurring liability to pay for the food. The creditor can solve the problem posed by paras (a) and (b) simply by postponing delivery of the goods until after the expiration of the cancellation period.

If the goods supplied are consumable goods within category (b), it should be stressed that, under the wording of s 72(9)(b), the debtor is released from his obligation to return the goods only where they are 'goods which by their nature are consumed by use' and, moreover, they must actually have *been* consumed prior to cancellation. A prime example of a contract which meets these requirements is one for a car supplied on credit with a tank full of petrol.

The duty to take care of the goods

Section 72(3) provides that, during the pre-cancellation period,[7] the possessor 'shall be treated as having been under a duty throughout the pre-cancellation period to retain possession of the goods and to take reasonable care of them'. The object of this provision is to ensure that the debtor who cancels the agreement does not escape liability by the assertion that it had become impossible to restore the goods or they had been damaged prior to cancellation. In this way, cancellation does not absolve him from liability.

---

6   The remaining categories of perishables, consumables and goods incorporated in land etc, would not be the subject of hire.
7   Defined in s 72(2)(c) as 'the period beginning when the possessor acquired possession and ending with the cancellation'.

It will be noticed that this duty is imposed retrospectively and so, on cancellation, the possessor will be liable for loss of possession or damage which occurred before cancellation even where the acts in question were lawful when performed. Consider, for example, the situation where the possessor has goods on credit-sale terms and either sells them or damages them before cancellation. Here the goods will belong to the possessor at the the date of disposition or damage as, in credit-sale, the passing of property in the goods is not suspended until the instalment payments are completed. Nevertheless, on cancellation, the buyer will, in both cases, be liable in damages for the value of the goods.

After cancellation, the possessor has a duty to retain possession and take reasonable care of the goods until they are surrendered (s 72(4)) but, if he has not received the written request to restore the goods within 21 days of his cancellation notice, the possessor's duty to take reasonable care ceases at the end of this period[8] unless he 'unreasonably refuses or unreasonably fails to comply' with the request in which case his duty continues until surrender (s 72(8)). The aim of s 72(8) is to ensure that the duty to look after the goods is not visited on the possessor indefinitely in those cases where the other party is lax in seeking their collection, but the section does not altogether succeed in its aim. What is the position if the other party serves the request in the 21 day period but does not collect the goods until well after the 21 days have expired? There is no obligation placed upon the other party actually to collect the goods in the 21 day period and so it is impossible to ascertain how long the possessor's duty to take care subsists once the request has been served. Arguably, the thrust of the provision is that request and collection both occur within the 21 days, but this is not enunciated in s 72(8). Moreover, the duration of the possessor's duty to look after the goods is complicated by the existence of the possessor's lien for sums repayable to him on cancellation (s 70(2)), particularly as the sums need not be repayable by the party to whom the goods must be surrendered but may be owed by a supplier under a linked transaction, for example. Consequently, the other party's right to restoration of the goods may be deferred during the continuance of the lien and that other party may be unaware of the existence of the lien. This uncertainty, on such a crucial issue, should be resolved as soon as possible.

It is clear that the possessor's duty to take reasonable care ends on the delivery of the goods (whether at the possesor's premises or elsewhere) to any person on whom a notice of cancellation could have been served or, alternatively, when the possessor has sent the goods to such a person (s 72(6) and (7)).

Recovery of part-exchange goods or allowance

It is not uncommon, particularly in hire-purchase agreements for cars, for the dealer to take goods in part-exchange and this operates as a part-payment by the debtor. Section 73 details the consequences of cancellation in relation to part-exchange and the section applies where 'in antecedent negotiations, the negotiator agreed to take goods in part-exchange … and those goods have been delivered to him'.

Section 73(2) provides that, unless the part-exchange goods are returned to the debtor or hirer before the end of ten days beginning with the date of cancellation 'in a condition substantially as good as when they were delivered

---

8 On the expiry of the 21 days the possessor presumably becomes an involunatary bailee with an obligation not to cause wilful damage to the goods.

to the negotiator', the debtor or hirer is entitled to recover from the negotiator 'a sum equal to the part-exchange allowance'. The 'part-exchange allowance' is defined in s 73(7)(b) as 'the sum agreed as such in the antecedent negotiations or, if no such agreement was arrived at, such sum as it would have been reasonable to allow[9] in respect of the part-exchange goods if no notice of cancellation had been served'. Consequently, if the cancellation notice is served on Monday, the part-exchange goods must be returned on or before Wednesday of the following week. If the part-exchange goods are tendered after the ten days have expired, the debtor can demand the part-exchange allowance and is under no obligation to accept the goods. It will be remembered that, under s 69(7), the debtor's posted notice of cancellation is deemed to be served at the time of *posting*, and if it is delayed in the post so that the ten days have expired, the negotiator must necessarily pay the part-exchange allowance.

In the case of a restricted-use debtor-creditor-supplier agreement falling within s 12(b) (eg a connected lending transaction with the creditor's providing a loan for the debtor to buy a new car from a dealer/negotiator, the latter having introduced the debtor to the creditor pursuant to arrangements with the creditor), the negotiator and the creditor are jointly and severally liable[10] for payment of the part-exchange allowance to the debtor (s 73(3)). The creditor is, however, entitled to be indemnified by the supplier (subject to any agreement between them) as the principal liability is clearly that of the supplier (s 73(4)).

If the debtor or hirer is in possession of goods to which the cancelled agreement relates, he has a lien on those goods (s 73(5)) for re-delivery of the part-exchange goods or the part-exchange allowance (during the ten days) or for the part-exchange allowance only (after the ten days).

In those cases where the part-exchange allowance is paid to the debtor, s 73(6) provides that title to the goods shall vest in the negotiator. If the creditor has to repay the part-exchange allowance to the debtor because of joint and several liability in the debtor-creditor-supplier situation, the creditor may be prejudiced if the supplier/negotiator has gone into liquidation: the latter has title to the goods which will remain his property for the benefit of his creditors while the creditor receives nothing.

Money paid to the debtor before cancellation

Should the debtor receive a loan during the cancellation period he might be tempted to spend it straightaway and, if he were then to cancel the agreement and be obliged to repay the loan with interest immediately, he could be financially embarrassed. Alternatively, if he could refuse lawfully to repay the loan under the cancellation provisions on the basis that money ceased to be payable on cancellation (s 70(1)(b)), there would be obvious injustice to the creditor. Accordingly, s 71 was devised to discourage the lender from making a

---

9   No guidance is offered on such a reasonable allowance.
10   Note that, in hire-purchase, the debtor can recover the part-exchange allowance only from the dealer/negotiator under s 73(2) and the dealer does not act as the creditor's agent in taking the part-exchange goods. It is difficult to see why joint and several liability was restricted to the debtor-creditor-supplier situation. In hire-purchase, the creditor is liable however, at common law, to account to the debtor for the value of the goods given in part-exchange on the basis that the creditor is deemed to have received that amount as it will have paid the dealer the agreed sale price less the amount allowed in part exchange: *Branwhite v Worcester Works Finance Ltd* [1969] 1 AC 552.

cash loan to the debtor before the cancellation period has expired and to provide for the situation where a loan has been advanced during that cancellation period.

Section 71(1) provides that, notwithstanding the cancellation of the credit agreement (other than a debtor-creditor-supplier agreement for restricted-use credit), 'the agreement shall continue in force so far as it relates to repayment of credit and payment of interest'. Section 71 is thus confined to unrestricted debtor-creditor-supplier and debtor-creditor agreements where the loan is paid direct to the debtor and he is free to apply it as he wishes, even though the loan may have been provided for a specific purpose. It is tolerably clear that the section relates only to cash loans actually received before cancellation and, moreover, it is only this primary agreement to provide the loan which continues to exist, subject to modifications prescribed by s 71. Collateral undertakings such as insurance or agreements for maintenance of the goods to be purchased with the loan are extinguished[11] and, similarly, any guarantee, indemnity or security[12] given in connection with the loan also become inoperative, the intent of s 71 thus being to ensure that the debtor incurs no liability apart from repayment of the loan with interest.

Section 71 allows the debtor who cancels an agreement for a cash loan several choices. First, under s 71(2), he may repay the loan in full *without interest* before the expiry of one month following service of the notice of cancellation or, in the case of a credit repayable by instalments, before the date on which the first instalment is due. If the debtor chooses this option he will, in effect, have had an interest-free loan. Second, if the whole of a credit repayable by instalments is not repaid on or before the date specified above, the debtor is not liable to repay any of the credit except on receipt of a request in writing in the prescribed form[13] signed by or on behalf of the creditor. This request must state the amounts of the remaining instalments which must be 'recalculated by the creditor as nearly as may be in accordance with the agreement and without extending the repayment period, but excluding any sum other than principal and interest' (s 71(3)). The effect of s 71(3) is that, where the loan is not repaid in full within the time limits dictated by s 71(2), it must be repaid in the period between the request for repayment and the contractual date for the payment of the final instalment. While the instalments will be paid at the frequency specified in the agreement, the payments will necessarily be larger during the shortened repayment period.

Finally, s 71(4) provides that the debtor can repay the money to any person on whom he could have served a notice of cancellation under s 69, apart from the debtor's own agent who acted for him in the negotiations for the agreement, eg the debtor's solicitor.

The effects of cancellation on security provided

Section 113(3)(a) provides that, on the cancellation of a regulated agreement, s 106 shall apply to any security provided by the agreement. In turn, s 106 specifies that (i) the security 'shall be treated as never having effect', ie it is nullified retrospectively; and (ii) the debtor or hirer is entitled to the return of

---

11 See the CCA, ss 69(1) and (4).
12 See the CCA, s 113(3) and s 106.
13 The form is prescribed in the Consumer Credit (Repayment of Credit on Cancellation) Regulations 1983 (SI 1983/1559).

any property lodged with the creditor or owner by way of security, eg deeds to land, indemnities or bonds.[14]

Under s 113(5), the debtor or hirer cannot be made to repay money advanced prior to cancellation (s 71) or restore goods (s 72) until the duties imposed on the creditor under s 106 have been discharged.

Exceptions to the cancellation provisions

Only regulated agreements can be cancelled under s 67 and so exempt agreements are not cancellable. Section 67(a) provides its own exception in that it does not apply where 'the agreement is secured on land, or is a restricted-use credit agreement to finance the purchase of land or is an agreement for a bridging loan in connection with the purchase of land'.[15]

In addition to the above categories, s 74 lists further exemptions from Part V (apart from s 56) of the CCA and thus from the cancellation provisions:

(i)   a non-commercial agreement defined in s 189(1) as a consumer credit or consumer hire agreement 'not made by the creditor or owner in the course of a business carried on by him';
(ii) a debtor-creditor agreement enabling the debtor to overdraw on a current account;
(iii) a debtor-creditor agreement to finance the making of such payments arising on, or connected with, the death of a person as may be prescribed by regulation where the Director General of Fair Trading has so determined;
(iv) a small debtor-creditor-supplier agreement for restricted-use credit, eg a credit-sale agreement for credit not exceeding £50.

OTHER RIGHTS OF CANCELLATION RELEVANT TO CONSUMER CREDIT AGREEMENTS

Consumer Protection (Cancellation of Contracts Concluded Away From Business Premises) Regulations 1987[16]

Doorstep selling is also controlled under these Regulations which implemented an EC Directive.[17] Broadly, 'consumers'[18] have a seven-day cooling-off period during which there is a right to cancel an agreement for the supply of goods or services costing more than £35 and entered into during an unsolicited visit by a 'trader'[19] to the consumer's home (or that of another person) or his place of work.

14 See the definition of 'security' in s 189(1).
15 If cancellation were permitted, administrative difficulties would be caused for the Land Registry. These agreements are subject to a *pre*-contractual right of consideration and reflection: see s 58(1) and s 61(2), considered earlier in this chapter.
16 SI 1987/2117; as amended by SI 1988/958; SI 1998/3050. See also the cancellation rights in the Timeshare Act 1992, but the right of cancellation conferred by the 1992 Act does not extend to any agreement which may be cancelled under the CCA.
17 Council Directive 85/577/EEC, dated 20.12.1985.
18 Defined in reg 2(1) as a person 'other than a body corporate, who, in making a contract to which these Regulations apply, is acting for purposes which can be regarded as outside his business'.
19 'Trader' is defined in reg 2(1) as 'a person who, in making a contract to which these Regulations apply, is acting for the purposes of his business, and anyone acting in the name or on behalf of such a person'. 'Business' is defined in reg 2(1) as including 'a trade or profession'.

Credit and hire agreements are within the 1987 Regulations along with a wide range of other contracts.[20] The trader must deliver a notice in writing informing the consumer of his right to cancel but it is clear that these 1987 Regulations and the right of cancellation under the CCA are intended to be mutually exclusive because, under reg 4(2), the obligation to give written notice under the Regulations is dispensed with when the agreement is cancellable under the CCA. Agreements which are cancellable within the CCA will thus remain exclusively subject to the provisions of the CCA.

Nevertheless, the 1987 Regulations can apply to those credit and hire agreements which are *not* cancellable under the CCA because (i) they exceed the £25,000 financial ceiling of the CCA (no upper monetary limit is specified under the 1987 regulations); (ii) they are agreements excluded from the cancellation provisions by the CCA, s 74; or (iii) they are exempt agreements under the CCA, s 16, other than certain agreements connected with land.

Consumer Protection (Distance Selling) Regulations 2000[1]

These Regulations, which implement the EC Directive on 'distance selling'[2] apply to contracts for goods or services to be supplied to a 'consumer' by a 'supplier' where the contract is made exclusively by means of distance communication, ie any means used 'without the simultaneous physical presence of the supplier and the consumer' (reg 3(1)).[3] As a general rule,[4] the Regulations allow the consumer a 'cooling-off' period for cancellation of up to seven working days after the delivery of the goods or, in the case of services, up to seven working days from the date of the contract.[5] It will be apparent that the right of cancellation in distance contracts is the antithesis of cancellation under the CCA where, of course, the antecedent negotiations must have included oral representations made by the negotiator when in the *presence* of the debtor or hirer.

Article 6(4) of the Directive demands that, where the price of the goods or services is fully or partly financed by credit, and the consumer has exercised his right to cancel the distance contract, the credit agreement shall also be cancelled 'without any penalty'. Accordingly, under reg 15, where a notice is given cancelling the distance contract, that notice also has the effect of cancelling 'any related credit agreement', the latter being defined in reg 15(5) as 'an agreement under which fixed sum credit[6] which fully or partly covers the price under a contract cancelled under regulation 10 is granted – (a) by the supplier, or (b) by another person, under an arrangement between that person and the supplier'. Where a related credit agreement is cancelled, if the supplier is not the same person as the creditor, the supplier must inform the creditor of the notice of cancellation (reg 15(2)). Moreover, under reg 15(4), if any security has been provided under the related credit agreement, it must be treated as 'never having had effect' and any property lodged with the creditor solely for the purposes of the security must be returned by him.

---

20 See Ch 14 where the Regulations are considered in more detail.
1 SI 2000/2334.
2 *Protection of Consumers in Respect of Distance Contracts* (Directive 97/7/EC, May 1997).
3 Schedule 1 provides an indicative list of distance communication, eg letter, telephone, electronic mail, catalogue, radio or television.
4 See Ch 14 where the Distance Selling Regulations are considered in more detail.
5 See regs 11 and 12.
6 Regulation 15(6)(b) provides that 'fixed sum credit' has the same meaning as in the CCA, s 10.

Following cancellation, the related credit agreement continues in force so far as it relates to repayment of the credit and interest but this general rule is subject to reg 16. Under reg 16, following the cancellation of the related credit agreement, if the consumer repays the whole or a portion of the credit – (a) before the expiry of one month following the cancellation of the credit agreement; or (b) in the case of a credit repayable by instalments, before the date on which the first instalment is due, no interest is payable on the amount repaid. If the whole of a credit repayable by instalments is not repaid on before the date specified in para (b), above, the consumer is not liable to repay any of the credit except on receipt of a request in writing, signed by the creditor, stating the amounts of the remaining instalments, but excluding any sum other than principal and interest. Moreover, this duty to repay the credit and interest is not enforceable before the creditor has discharged the duty to return any property lodged with him as security.

CHAPTER 34

Matters arising during the currency of the agreement

Introduction

A dominant feature of the CCA is that various rules ensure that the debtor is provided with information at all stages of the credit agreement. The rules considered in earlier chapters seek to protect the debtor from abuse both before contract and at the stage of the contract's completion but the debtor also has a right to be kept informed of certain matters during the currency of the credit agreement. The type of information to be provided depends upon the character of the agreement but the central tenet of the information provisions is that the debtor must be enabled to make an informed choice regarding options which are open to him. Arguably the most important features to be considered here are (i) the debtor's statutory right to discharge his obligations prior to the contractual termination date by making an early settlement; and (ii) the statutory right to voluntary termination of the agreement in hire-purchase, conditional sale and consumer hire.

Creditor's or owner's duty to provide information

Fixed-sum credit

Under s 77, if the creditor under a regulated agreement for fixed-sum credit (other than a non-commercial agreement (s 77(5)) receives a request in writing from the debtor and payment of a fee of 50p,[1] the creditor must within the prescribed period of twelve working days[2] give the debtor a copy of the executed agreement (if any) and of any other document referred to in it, together with a statement signed by or on behalf of the creditor showing, 'according to the information to which it is practicable for him to refer', the following:

(a) the total sum paid by the debtor;
(b) the total sum which has become payable but remains unpaid, and the various amounts comprised in that total sum, with the date when each became due; and

---

1 Increased from 15p to 50p by the Consumer Credit (Increase of Monetary Amounts) Order 1983, SI 1983/1571.
2 See the Consumer Credit (Prescribed Periods for Giving Information) Regulations 1983, SI 1983/1569. 'Working day' is defined in s 189(1).

(c) the total sum which is to become payable under the agreement by the debtor, and the various amounts comprised in that total sum, with the date, or mode of determining the date, when each becomes due.

As with much of the CCA, the consequences are grave if the creditor fails to comply with these requirements. First, he is not entitled to enforce the agreement while the default continues and, if the default continues for one month, he commits an offence (s 77(4)(a) and (b)). Second, the statement provided by the creditor 'is binding on him' (s 172) meaning that, should the creditor state the balance which is outstanding incorrectly, eg £500 rather than £5,000, he is bound by that figure and, upon tendering £500, the debtor would be entitled to a termination statement under s 103. In such a case, however, the creditor may request the court to give 'such relief ... as appears to the court to be just' (s 172 (3)) but, if relief were granted in the example above, it is likely that the creditor would have to pay all the costs of such an application to rectify his own error. It should also be noted that, under s 77, the creditor need give only information 'to which it is practicable for him to refer' and so the provision of information that was incorrect or inaccurate might be excused on this ground.

Running-account credit

Section 78(1) imposes an identical duty to supply information on request (in the same period of time and for the same fee) in an agreement for running-account credit (other than a non-commercial agreement (s 78(7)) except that the information to be supplied is different. Here the creditor must indicate:

(a) the state of the account;
(b) the amount, if any, currently payable under the agreement by the debtor to the creditor; and
(c) the amounts and due dates of any payments which, if the debtor does not draw further on the account, will later become payable under the agreement by the debtor to the creditor.

The factors considered above in relation to s 77, eg the consequences for non-compliance, apply also to s 78.

In an agreement for running-account credit (other than a non-commercial agreement or a small agreement (s 78(7)) there is, in addition, a duty under s 78(4) and (5) to provide periodic statements of account *automatically*, and in the prescribed form and with the prescribed contents[3] showing the state of the account at regular intervals of not more than twelve months. These statements of account are, of course, the familiar, periodic statements produced by credit-card companies and banks. It would be wasteful to send separate statements to every debtor who is party to a joint account and so, in the case of joint accounts, s 185(2) allows one or more debtors to sign a 'dispensing notice' releasing the creditor from his duty to send statements to that person.

Surprisingly, there is no sanction for failure to send periodic statements of account under s 78. However, the Director General of Fair Trading could suspend or revoke the creditor's licence (s 170(2)) or the debtor could apply to the High Court for a mandatory injunction directing that a statement be provided (s 170(3)) but the court has no power to award damages (s 170(1)).

---

3 See the Consumer Credit (Running-Account Credit Information) Regulations 1983, SI 1983/1570.

Consumer hire

Section 79(1) imposes an identical duty to that in ss 77 and 78 in relation to consumer hire agreements (other than non-commercial agreements (s 79(4)) and here the owner must indicate (a) the total sum which has become payable under the agreement by the hirer but remains unpaid; and (b) the various amounts comprised in that total sum, with the date when each became due.

Again, the time limits for providing the information and consequences in the event of non-compliance etc, are the same as under ss 77 and 78.

Information to surety

Sections 107-109 are virtual mirror images of ss 77-79 in that they provide for the creditor under a regulated agreement for fixed-sum credit or running-account credit, and the owner under a regulated consumer hire agreement to give information to a surety, ie a person by whom any security is provided. Again, the creditor or owner, within twelve working days after receiving a request in writing from the surety and payment of a fee of 50p, must provide the surety with the same statement as could have been called for by the debtor or hirer under ss 77-79. Additionally, the creditor or owner must give to the surety a copy of the executed agreement (if any) and of any other document referred to in it, and a copy of the security instrument (if any).[4] There are the same sanctions for non-compliance under these sections as those under s 77.

Information as to settlement figure

Section 97 provides that a creditor under a regulated agreement must, within twelve working days after he has received a written request from the debtor, give the debtor a statement in the prescribed form indicating the amount of the payment required to discharge the debtor's indebtedness under the agreement, together with the prescribed particulars showing how the amount is arrived at.[5] If the creditor fails to comply, he is not entitled, while the default continues, to enforce the agreement (s 97(3)(a)) and, if the default continues for one month, he commits an offence (s 97(3)(b)). It is important to note that this settlement figure is not the same as that required under ss 77 and 78 (the total sum remaining to be paid under the agreement) because the settlement figure under s 97 must take into account any statutory rebate to which the debtor is entitled under s 95. The rebate is not available in consumer hire and this accounts for the omission of such hire agreements from s 97.

Termination statement

The unsatisfactory position which formerly prevailed in many hire-purchase and conditional sale contracts was that the debtor was rarely given any documentary evidence of the completion of payments under the agreement. A written confirmation of the discharge of the obligations under the contract would clearly be valuable *vis-à-vis* the creditor but, as regards third parties, it would also be invaluable

---

4   See also s 110 which provides for the debtor or hirer to rceive a copy of any security
    instrument executed in relation to the agreement after the making of the agreement.
5   See the Consumer Credit (Settlement Information) Regulations 1983, SI 1983/1564.

evidence that title to the goods had vested in the debtor. Under s 103, the debtor or hirer under a regulated agreement (other than a non-commercial agreement) has the right, on request, to obtain a termination statement confirming that he has discharged his indebtedness under the agreement and that, accordingly, the agreement has ceased. The debtor or hirer must serve a notice which complies with s 103(1) and then the creditor or owner must, within twelve working days of receipt of the notice, either comply with it by confirming the accuracy of the debtor or hirer's notice or serve on the debtor or hirer a counter-notice stating that he disputes the correctness of the notice or asserts that the debtor or hirer is not indebted to him under the agreement. The creditor's or owner's default in complying with s 103, which continues for one month, is an offence (s 103(5)).

The debtor's right of early settlement

A debtor under a regulated consumer credit agreement may wish to settle his indebtedness ahead of time, not least because he may want to become the owner of goods held on hire-purchase terms in order to sell them at a profit. Equally important is the fact that the debtor may find a cheaper source of credit elsewhere and seek to discharge his existing indebtedness by a refinancing arrangement.

An important, non-excludable right[6] under the CCA, s 94 is thus that the debtor under a regulated consumer credit agreement is entitled, at any time, to give notice to the creditor and pay all amounts due under the agreement, less any rebate of charges for credit allowable under s 95, thereby discharging his indebtedness. The right of early settlement together with a rebate of charges for credit is not available in consumer *hire* as the nature of the agreement precludes such a right: there are no additional charges to be levied in consumer hire and, at the end of the period of hire, the owner's right to possess the goods revives. There is the right to *terminate* a consumer hire agreement under s 101, however, and this right is considered later.

The debtor must give written notice[7] to the creditor for the early settlement to be effective under s 94 and this can be given 'at any time'. It must be stressed that, in contrast with some other provisions of the CCA such as those concerned with cancellation, *no* individuals are deemed to be agents of the creditor for the purposes of receiving a notice of early settlement. For example, a negotiator who is certainly a deemed agent of the creditor in conducting antecedent negotiations under s 56, is *not* such a deemed agent to receive the notice of early settlement.

There is no form prescribed for the debtor's notice and, provided that it clearly indicates his intent to settle ahead of time, it should be effective. Section 94(2) adds that the notice need not be concerned solely with the question of early settlement but may embody the exercise by the debtor of any option to purchase goods conferred on him by the agreement and 'deal with any other matter arising on, or in relation to, the termination of the agreement'. Section 94 clearly envisages that the debtor might choose to calculate the amount necessary to settle the agreement himself (including the rebate) and pay that amount at the same time that he gives his written notice to the creditor to settle early, but this must be a rare eventuality and, more commonly, the debtor will first request settlement information under s 97 (see below).

---

6   See s 173(1).
7   'Notice' in s 189(1) is defined as 'notice in writing'.

Under s 96(1), early settlement also means that, as a general rule, the debtor (or any relative of his[8]) is discharged from any liability under a linked transaction but there are three important exceptions to this general rule. First, s 96(1) provides that early settlement shall not discharge liabilities which have already accrued and this would mean, for example, that should a charge have been incurred for the installation of goods under a linked transaction, that debt remains payable. Second, linked transactions which provide the debtor with credit remain valid (s 96(2)) and, third, the linked transactions detailed in the Consumer Credit (Linked Transactions) (Exemptions) Regulations 1983[9] are unaffected by early settlement.

Rebate on early settlement

It is obvious that where the debtor settles his indebtedness early he benefits the creditor financially in that interest can be earnt on the amount which the debtor pays in settlement and thus, in recognition that the debtor should not be treated unfairly, s 95(1) provides that regulations can be made for the allowance of a rebate of charges to the debtor as compensation for early payment. It should be noted that s 95(1) stipulates that regulations may provide for a rebate in a wide variety of situations and not just those envisaged by s 94, viz 'under s 94, on refinancing, on breach of the agreement, or for any other reason, his indebtedness is discharged or becomes payable before the time fixed by the agreement'.

The Consumer Credit (Rebate on Early Settlement) Regulations 1983[10] entitle the debtor to a rebate in the circumstances specified in s 95(1) and furnish the detail concerning the calculation of rebates. The terms of the regulations are such that a rebate may be claimed only when the debtor actually *pays* the sum required for early settlement. Consequently, in *Forward Trust Ltd v Whymark*[11] it was held that, where the debtor pays only part of his indebtedness, the creditor may obtain judgment for the balance of the instalments due without any deduction of a rebate, but the debtor can claim the rebate when satisfying the judgment.

The debtor's first step in obtaining a rebate for early settlement will usually be to ascertain his outstanding liabilities and s 97(1) provides that, within twelve working days[12] of the receipt of the debtor's written request for information, the creditor must give the debtor a written statement[13] indicating the amount of the payment required to discharge his indebtedness under the agreement toegether with the prescribed particulars showing how the amount is arrived at. A creditor who fails to comply with s 97(1)[14] is not entitled, while the default continues, to enforce the agreement and, if the default continues for one month, he commits

---

8 It is only the debtor's liability which is said to be discharged under s 96(1) but, presumably, a supplier's liability under a linked transaction would also be discharged where he has not supplied goods or services under the contract.

9 SI 1983/1560; see Ch 31.

10 SI 1983/1562.

11 [1990] 2 QB 670.

12 See the Consumer Credit (Settlement Information) Regulations 1983, SI 1983/1564.

13 The format of the statement and its particulars are prescribed by the Consumer Credit (Settlement Information) Regulations 1983, SI 1983/1564. In an agreement for running-account credit, the supply of a statement of account under s 78 will suffice, and so the amount required to discharge the debtor's indebtedness is the amount shown in the debit balance at the end of the period covered by the statement.

14 The creditor need not provide a statement where the debtor's request is made within one month of sending a previous statement (s 97(2)).

an offence (s 97(3)). Moreover, should the creditor give an incorrect statement of the amount payable on early settlement which is in the debtor's favour, he may be estopped from claiming the true amount where the debtor has altered his position in reliance on that incorrect statement.[15]

Calculating the rebate

There are two crucial factors to evaluate in the calculation of the rebate which mean that it is difficult to arrive at a precise and fair estimate of the sum to which the debtor is entitled. First, it is logical to assert that the interest charges should be spread over the contract period actuarially, so that the rate of interest charged at the end of each repayment period on the principal sum outstanding remains constant. An accurate estimate of the rebate would thus be the interest which still remains to be earnt at the date of settlement. Second, the creditor incurs costs and expenditure in relation to the agreement at an uneven rate and the actuarial assessment would be fair only if such costs were not incurred, meaning that interest alone was earnt, or were incurred perfectly evenly throughout the period of the agreement. In fact, the costs are incurred unevenly and comprise those which are foreseeable at the start of the contract (eg legal costs; payment of commission to a dealer) those which persist throughout the agreement (eg rent and wages) and costs which arise from imponderables (eg defaults by the debtor and expenses in relation to legal proceedings and repossesssion of the goods). It is thus apparent that, in contrast to the calculation of the pure *cost* of the credit to the debtor which is assessed and disclosed at the commencement of the agreement, the creditor's expenses must be considered when evaluating the rebate if equilibrium is to be reached between the parties.

The arithmetical calculations of the rebate in the regulations[16] attempt to embody the factors outlined above and there five different formulae which can be applied depending upon the type of agreement in question, eg the credit is repayable in a single lump sum at the end of a specified period or is repaid by equal or unequal instalments. Moreover, in order to allow the creditor to recoup the costs incurred, the regulations permit the settlement date to be deferred thus reducing the rebate which is payable.[17] The maximum deferment is two months for loans of up to five years' duration and one month for loans over five years' duration.

There has been considerable criticism of the methods used in calculating the rebate and the Director General of Fair Trading[18] has stressed that, in certain instances, debtors may be penalised for settling early in that the cost of such a settlement can be greater than simply continuing to pay the instalments until the end of the agreement. Accordingly, the Director recommends that the rebate should be calculated on the basis of an 'actual reducing balance' rather than the 'rule of 78'[19] which is currently adopted in the regulations. Two further criticisms were made in the OFT review. First, it was thought that the deferment of settlement dates was over-generous in that the return to lenders was often greater

---

15 See *Lombard North Central v Stobart* [1990] CCLR 53.
16 Consumer Credit (Rebate on Early Settlement) Regulations 1983, SI 1983/1562.
17 See regs 5 and 6.
18 *Consumer Credit Deregulation* (OFT, June 1994), Ch 8, paras 8.1-8.16.
19 For a detailed explanation of this rule see Goode, *Consumer Credit Law* (1989), Ch 20, para 20.16.

than their costs and that the charging of a fixed fee would be more appropriate. Second, the review stressed that consumers complained that no information was provided regarding early settlement at the time of entry into the credit agreement and, indeed, the only legal requirement is that there be a notification in the agreement of the right to settle early. The Director concluded that full details of early settlement and the proposed fixed fee should be clearly stated in credit agreements. The Department of Trade and Industry[20] has agreed with the OFT recommendations except that reservations were expressed regarding the idea of a fixed fee, the DTI preferring a rule that lenders should state if such a fee were to be levied, with licensing powers being utilised to ensure the fairness of charges.

The debtor's right of voluntary termination in hire-purchase and conditional sale

If the debtor does not discharge his indebtedness ahead of time, he may opt for the alternative course of action and exercise his right to terminate the agreement without completing the payments. This right is given *only* to the debtor under a hire-purchase agreement or a debtor/buyer under a conditional sale agreement by the CCA, ss 99 and 100, and it must be emphasised that these sections do *not* apply to other credit agreements such as credit-sale or where the debtor takes a personal loan.

Section 99(1) provides that, at any time before the final payment under a regulated hire-purchase or regulated conditional sale agreement falls due, the debtor shall be entitled to terminate the agreement by giving notice in writing to any person entitled or authorised to receive the sums payable under the agreement. The written notice could thus be given directly to the creditor or to a dealer if payments are made through him and he has authority to receive them, but there are *no* deemed agency provisions in this context. Once again, this right of termination cannot be excluded.[1]

It will be noticed that the right of termination must be exercised 'before the final payment falls due'. The contract may contain an accelerated payment clause which allows the creditor to demand the outstanding balance in full if the debtor defaults in paying one instalment and, provided that the clause is not regarded as an unenforceable penalty,[2] it must be asked what effect it has on termination and the 'final payment' to be made by the debtor. Acceleration clauses are recognised in the CCA as having validity,[3]

---

20 *Deregulation of United Kingdom Consumer Credit Legislation* (DTI, August 1995), Ch 5.
 1 See s 173(1).
 2 An acceleration clause is subject to the rules on penalties provided it is activated by, and exercisable on, the debtor's *breach* of contract (see *Wadham Stringer Finance Ltd v Meaney* [1981] 1 WLR 39). In order to escape the rules on penalties at common law, there would have to be some rebate of charges under an acceleration clause and so, if the rebate on offer is much less than that permitted under the Regulations on early settlement and, certainly if the balance outstanding is repayable with interest thereon for the full term (here the creditor would be placed in a better position than if the agreement had simply run its course), the clause will fall foul of the rules on penalties. If the clause is void, the debtor's right of termination will still be valid. See Ch 36 where accelerated payment clauses are considered in more detail.
 3 See ss 76(1)(a), 86(1) and 87(1)(b).

but such clauses cannot be enforced unless a default notice has been served under s 87[4] giving the debtor not less than seven days' notice, and the seven days have elapsed without the default having been remedied. Consequently, the debtor can terminate the agreement after the default notice has been served but, if he has not exercised that right within the seven days or remedied the default, the acceleration clause will be activated meaning that, once the final payment has fallen due at the end of the seven days, the right of termination is lost.[5]

LOSS OF THE RIGHT OF TERMINATION IN CONDITIONAL SALES: SECTIONS 99(3), 99(4) AND 99(5)

Under the definition in s 189(1), a 'conditional sale agreement' can apply to land as well as goods but, by s 99(3), the debtor cannot terminate a conditional sale agreement relating to land once title to the land has passed to the debtor. Similarly, under s 99(4), the debtor's right to terminate a conditional sale agreement relating to goods is lost 'where the property in the goods, having become vested in the debtor, is transferred to a person who does not become the debtor under the agreement'. These provisions are intended to apply to those (rare) situations where title to land or property in goods has vested in the debtor before he has completed all the payments under the conditional sale contract but, of course, most conditional sales are designed to transfer title only when the payments have been completed.

Under s 99(4), the right of termination is lost only where property in the goods has become *vested* in the debtor and the goods have then been *transferred* (by sale or otherwise) to the third party. The section would thus be inapplicable where title to the goods passes from the debtor to the third party under Part III of the Hire-Purchase Act 1965 (which applies to conditional sale) or any other exception to the rule *nemo dat quod non habet*, and s 99(4) does not apply where the debtor assigns his rights under the condtional agreement.[6] It is possible for property in the goods to vest in the debtor under a hire-purchase agreement before he has paid all the instalments, but it should be noted that s 99(4) is restricted to conditional sale agreements.

Apart from the rule in s 99(4), the debtor under a conditional sale agreement relating to goods may nevertheless terminate the agreement after property in the goods has become vested in him. Should this occur, s 99(5) provides that the property in the goods thereupon revests in the person (the 'previous owner') in whom it was vested immediately before it became vested in the debtor. The proviso to s 99(5) permits title to be vested in the previous owner's successor in interest if, for example, the previous owner has died (ie his personal representative) or become bankrupt (ie his trustee in bankruptcy).

---

4   Or a notice under s 76(1) where the event activating the acceleration of payments is not a *breach* of contract (see Ch 36).
5   *Wadham Stringer Finance Ltd v Meaney* [1981] 1 WLR 39 (a decision on the Hire-Purchase Act 1965, s 27(1) which was, in substance, identical to the CCA, s 99(1)).
6   Under s 189(1), 'debtor' includes the person to whom rights and duties under the agreement have been assigned and so, if the third party under s 99(4) is an assignee, he becomes the debtor meaning that s 99(4) does not apply and the first debtor can terminate the agreement.

THE LIABILITY OF THE DEBTOR ON TERMINATION

Financial consequences

Termination of the agreement operates only as regards the future and 'does not affect any liability under the agreement which has accrued before the termination' (s 99(2)). This means that the debtor will remain liable for arrears of instalments and he will also be liable in damages if there has been a breach of the agreement.

It was common in hire-purchase ageements to allow the debtor a right of termination before the expiration of the contract but he was often penalised by having to make payments under a 'minimum payment' clause. Such clauses were justified ostensibly on the basis of compensating the creditor for the depreciation in the goods, but often the creditor's real object was the recovery of future instalments and the sums payable were often exorbitant. Moreover, the common law rules on penalties could not (and still cannot) be invoked where the debtor voluntarily terminated the agreement, as he had not committed a breach of contract.[7] Clearly reform was necessary and the Hire-Purchase Act 1965 introduced controls on the minimum payment clause. This pattern of control has been followed in the CCA, s 100. Under s 100(1), where the debtor terminates the agreement under s 99, he 'shall be liable, unless the agreement provides for a smaller payment, or does not provide for any payment, to pay the creditor the amount (if any) by which one-half of the total price exceeds the aggregate of the sums paid and the sums due in respect of the total price immediately before the termination'. Consequently, unless the agreement provides for a payment of less than 50% or no payment at all, the debtor's minimum liability is to pay 50% of the total price. However, if the debtor has paid, or becomes liable to pay, more than 50% before termination, on termination he is not entitled to recover the excess which he has paid nor is he relieved of the (accrued) obligation to pay.

To this basic rule, there are several additions and qualifications. First, the amount payable by the debtor might be reduced. Under s 100(3), if in any action the court is satisfied that a sum less than the amount specified in s 100(1) would be equal to the 'loss sustained' by the creditor in consequence of the termination by the debtor, the court may make an order for the payment of that sum. It is not clear how the 'loss sustained' by the creditor would be calculated[8] but the court will presumably be guided by the principles established in *Yeoman Credit Ltd v Waragowski*.[9] Suppose, for example, that the total price of a car is £1,000, the debtor has paid £260 by way of a deposit and instalments and one instalment of £40 is due. The debtor then determines the agreement and returns the car which has been properly maintained (see s 100(4), below). The creditor sells it for £600. *Prima facie*, the creditor is entitled to claim the £40 due plus the difference between £500 and £300, ie, £200. But the court may on these facts, allow only the £40 due plus £100, ie, the difference between the total price of £1,000 and the total of the sums received from or owed by the debtor and the sale price obtained for the car, this being the loss sustained by the creditor. That being said, it does seem that s 100(3) will only rarely be applied as, having regard

---

7 *Associated Distributors Ltd v Hall* [1938] 2 KB 83. See Ch 36 where the minimum payment clause is considered in more detail.
8 For contrasting views see Goode, *Hire-Purchase Law and Practice* (2nd edn, 1970), pp 406-407; Guest, *The Law of Hire-Purchase* (1966), para 609.
9 [1961] 1 WLR 1124 (see Ch 36).

to the rapid depreciation of many second-hand goods, a reduction of the amount payable by the debtor to under 50% of the price would mean that the creditor was recovering goods on termination which were worth 50% of the hire-purchase or conditional sale price, or more than that. This could happen, of course, if the debtor terminated the agreement after paying only one or two instalments and a reduction in the 50% payable would also be apt where goods such as antiques had *appreciated* in value.

Second, the amount payable by the debtor might be increased, under s 100(4), if the debtor has contravened an obligation to take reasonable care of the goods or land, on the basis that such an augmented sum would 'recompense the creditor for the contravention'.

Third, under s 100(2), the rule on payment of 50% of the price is qualified if there is an installation charge in the total price to be paid. The rationale of s 100(2) is that it is fair that the creditor be paid the installation charge in full. Accordingly, s 100(2) provides that the reference to one-half of the total price in s 100(1) 'shall be construed as a reference to the aggregate of the installation charge and one-half of the remainder of the total price'. An example clarifies this wording. If the total price is £1,000 of which £200 is an installation charge, the installation charge is first deducted, leaving £800. This figure is then halved, ie £400, and the installation charge is then added in full, leaving a total of £600 to be paid by the debtor.

Return of the goods on termination

Having determined the agreement, the debtor must allow the creditor to retake the goods and s 100(5) provides that, if the debtor wrongfully retains possession of the goods after termination then, in any action brought by the creditor to recover possession, the court, unless it is satisfied that having regard to the circumstances it would not be just to do so, shall order the goods to be delivered to the creditor without giving the debtor an option to pay the value of the goods. In denying the option to the debtor to pay the value of the goods, s 100(5) ensures that the debtor cannot terminate the contract and seek to obtain the goods more cheaply than if he had continued with the agreement.

Concurrent rights available to the debtor

It will be apparent that the debtor may have several concurrent rights regarding the termination of the agreement and, indeed, it is possible for the rights of cancellation, early settlement and voluntary termination to exist concurrently. The average consumer will have no knowledge of the significance of these rights nor of the consequences attendant upon their exercise but he may frequently inform the creditor that, for example, he wishes 'to end the agreement'. There are patently two forms of 'termination' possible under the CCA, ie early settlement under s 94, and voluntary termination in hire-purchase and conditional sale under s 99. Under s 99, the debtor must return the goods to the creditor and the financial consequences are dictated by s 100. If early settlement is a possibility, it will clearly be in the debtor's long term interest to opt for such a settlement, obtain a rebate under the Regulations on early settlement, and have title to the goods vested in him (s 94(2)).

If, however, the debtor wishes to return the goods there is simply no comparison between the right of cancellation under s 67 (where money paid is refunded to the debtor) and that of voluntary termination under s 99 (where the 50% payment rule applies). At the point where the debtor has simultaneous rights to end the agreement, all the complex, regulatory apparatus of the CCA ceases to help him, as everything pivots on the honesty and integrity of the creditor to inform the debtor of the options open to him. It is arguable that the debtor in this situation is in no worse a position than many other consumers who might be subject to fraudulent practices in that there are limits on the extent to which the law can protect against blatant abuse. But it is somewhat ironic, in the context of the CCA and its welter of regulations, that here the debtor's rights must ultimately depend on the good faith of the other party. It would thus be desirable for regulations to impose a duty on the creditor to inform the debtor of his rights when the latter evinces an intent to end the agreement without more specificity.

Termination of consumer hire agreements

The CCA, s 101 confers a right on the hirer under a regulated consumer hire agreement to terminate the agreement by giving notice to any person entitled or authorised to receive the sums payable under the agreement. The earliest termination date is 18 months after the making of the agreement (s 101(3))[10] and the idea underpinning s 101 is that hirers might wish to be alleviated from burdensome, long-term contracts, where the rental payments vastly exceed the value of the goods which have been hired. Subject to the minimum period of 18 months, the periods of notice which must be given by hirers are prescribed by s 101(4), (5) and (6) (unless the agreement provides for a shorter period) as follows:

(a) If the agreement provides for the making of payments by the hirer at equal intervals, the length of one interval or three months, whichever is less.
(b) If the agreement provides for the making of such payments at differing intervals, the length of the shortest interval or three months, whichever is less.
(c) In any other case, the minimum period of notice is three months.

Termination under s 101 does not affect any liability which has accrued before termination (s 101(2)) and so the hirer is liable for any rental payments which are outstanding at the date of termination. Moreover, should the owner seek to impose an additional liability on the hirer (eg an additional payment for loss of future rental payments), the provision will be void (s 173(1)).

Section 101(7) provides that the statutory right to terminate does not apply to certain agreements. The exemptions reflect the complications inherent in the hiring of goods and particularly the difficulties of finance leasing. In finance leasing, the right to early termination can cause hardship to the owner where he buys the goods solely to lease them to the hirer. The owner, a financial institution, bases the costs on a minimum period of hire of four to five years, this length of time being necessary in order to make the agreement feasible and give the desired return on the capital outlay in purchasing the equipment which is to be leased. For the owner, such a finance lease is a purely financial operation where he provides the finance to purchase the equipment but retains minimal interest in the equipment itself, having transferred the practical advantages and

---

10 Note that this is not the date of the commencement of the period of hire.

disadvantages of ownership to the hirer. Moreover, the hirer's position must be considered in that, rental payments compressed into a period of 18 months would mean that the reason for hiring goods, ie the ability to spread the capital cost of the equipment over four to five years, would be lost, with the consequence that few hirers would wish, or could afford, to do business on such terms. Consequently, s 101(7) and (8) provide that the following agreements are exempt from the termination provisions:

(a) Any agreement which provides for the making by the hirer of payments which in total (and without breach of the agreement) exceed £900[11] in any year. This will exempt most finance leases from s 101.

(b) Any agreement where (i) goods are bailed for the purposes of a business carried on by the hirer or the hirer holds himself out as requiring the goods for those purposes; and (ii) the goods are selected by the hirer and acquired by the owner for the purposes of the agreement at the request of the hirer from any person other than the owner's associate. This exemption applies to most equipment leasing where the owner 'acquires' the goods and then leases them to the lessee.

(c) Any agreement where the hirer requires or holds himself out as requiring, the goods for the purpose of bailing them to other persons in the course of a business carried on by him.

(d) Any agreement made by a person carrying on a consumer hire business specially exempted by the Director General of Fair Trading (s 101(8)). Under this exemption, the owner has to convince the Director that hirers would benefit from the exclusion of s 101 and this would be the case where more taxing financial terms would have to be imposed on the hirer if the exemption were not granted or, alternatively, that the goods could not be hired at all in the absence of an exemption.

---

11 Increased from the £300 stipulated in the CCA by the Consumer Credit (Increase of Monetary Amounts) Order 1983, SI 1983/1571.

CHAPTER 35

Liability of the creditor, owner and supplier for defective goods and services

Introduction

When classifying the liability of the creditor for defective goods or services supplied, the distinction between the credit agreement and the contract of sale or supply must constantly be kept in mind. Sometimes, of course, the creditor both advances the credit and supplies the goods under the agreement and this occurs in hire-purchase, conditional sale and credit-sale. Alternatively, the creditor may be entirely separate from the supplier and this would occur, for example, where a bank or finance house makes a personal loan to the debtor so that he can can buy goods from a supplier. In this latter situation, the creditor is not party to the supply contract but the transaction will be classified as either a debtor-creditor-supplier agreement which involves a *connected* loan or a debtor-creditor agreement where there is an *unconnected* loan, and this distinction is crucial as regards the debtor's rights.[1] Most significantly, it will be necessary to consider those situations where the debtor may have a remedy against both the creditor and the separate supplier under the CCA, ss 56 and 75.

The terms implied by the Supply of Goods (Implied Terms) Act 1973 (relating to the description, quality and fitness for purpose of the goods) into hire-purchase agreements are considered separately, not least because hire-purchase is still a significant form of consumer credit. Finally, mention must be made of the hirer's remedies under a contract for the leasing or hire of goods.

Unconnected loans and debtor-creditor agreements

If the debtor obtains a loan from a creditor and uses it to buy goods from a seller or services from a supplier neither of whom has any connection with the creditor, the credit agreement is a *debtor-creditor agreement* as defined by ss 11 and 13. For example, in agreements under s 13(a), the debtor seeks out a creditor to finance the purchase of goods from a supplier but, even though there are no business 'arrangements' between the creditor and the supplier, the creditor insists on direct payment to the supplier making this an agreement for restricted-use

---

1 See the explanations and definitions of debtor-creditor-supplier and debtor-creditor agreements in Ch 31.

credit. Alternatively, under s 13(c), there may be an agreement for unresricted-use credit and this covers all personal loans where the loan is paid directly to the debtor who is thus free to apply it in whatever way he pleases. In this latter example of a personal loan, the agreement would still be a debtor-creditor agreement for unrestricted-use credit where the loan is advanced for a particular purpose but the debtor breaches his contract with the creditor and uses the loan for a different purpose from that stipulated (see s 11(3)).

The essential feature which connects these debtor-creditor agreements is that there are no business arrangements between the creditor and the supplier and so the loan is an 'unconnected loan'. As no such arrangements exist between creditor and supplier, the credit agreement and the contract of supply are separate and distinct. If the debtor wishes to buy goods with the loan advanced by the creditor, there will be a contract for the sale of goods between the buyer (debtor) and the seller. The Sale of Goods Act 1979 (SGA) thus governs that sale and, most particularly, the SGA implied terms relating to description, quality and fitness for purpose of the goods are the main source of the buyer's remedies where the goods prove to be defective. Should the debtor enter into a contract for the supply of services with the supplier, the Supply of Goods and Services Act 1982 implies terms which are virtually identical to those in the SGA. The Unfair Contract Terms Act 1977 and the Unfair Terms in Consumer Contracts Regulations 1999 apply both to contracts for the sale of goods and those for the supply of services.

It will thus be apparent that, in a debtor-creditor agreement, the creditor carries no liability for goods or services which prove to be unsatisfactory and this is a perfectly reasonable allocation of risks where the creditor and supplier are entirely separate and unconnected.

Connected loans and debtor-creditor-supplier agreements

The debtor-creditor-supplier agreement is defined in the CCA, ss 11 and 12. It will be remembered that, in such an agreement, the creditor and the supplier are either one and the same, eg hire-purchase agreements, or the arrangements between the creditor and the supplier are such that they are involved in a joint business venture, eg a seller of goods sends potential customers to a finance house with whom he has arrangements in order that the debtor can obtain a loan to pay for the goods. Here the seller generates business for the finance house which, in turn, keeps the seller's business afloat by providing him with an abundance of buyers who are able to pay for the goods in cash. The 'connected loan' situation is thus the paradigm of a symbiotic, business relationship. Another example of a debtor-creditor-supplier agreement is that between a credit-card issuer and the recognised suppliers of goods and services who agree to accept the card as the means of payment.

In the situation of a connected loan, debtor-creditor-supplier agreement, where the creditor advances a loan to the debtor so that he may buy goods from a seller, the debtor (buyer) will have a separate contract of sale with the seller and, in this respect, the position is exactly the same as under a debtor-creditor agreement. Equally, if the debtor uses his credit card to pay for goods bought from a seller or to pay for services to be supplied, there is a direct contract of sale between the debtor (buyer) and the seller of the goods or a direct contract between the debtor (buyer) and the supplier of the services. Accordingly, either the Sale of Goods Act 1979 (SGA) or the Supply of Goods and Services Act 1982 apply to these direct contracts. Likewise, the debtor under a hire-purchase agreement has a direct contract with his creditor/finance house and terms are implied into that contract by the Supply of Goods (Implied Terms) Act 1973 which are very close to those of the SGA and are considered later in this chapter.

It has been emphasised that debtor-creditor-supplier agreements share the characteristic that the connection between the credit agreement and the supply agreement is either direct (as in hire-purchase) or indirect yet connected (as in a connected loan or a credit-card transaction). It will also be realised that the dealer in a hire-purchase transaction, the seller of goods in a connected loan situation or the shopkeeper who accepts the debtor's credit card in payment for goods, may all make promises and assurances in relation to the goods or services which are to be supplied. In these situations, should the *creditor* be liable for such promises and assurances if they amount to misrepresentations or breaches of contract? The CCA enacts the recommendations of the Crowther Committee[2] that, in cases of connected loans, the creditor and supplier are involved in a joint venture and thus joint and several responsibility is apt. Moreover, the Committee considered that a 'negotiator' in 'antecedent negotiations' (eg a car dealer in a hire-purchase transaction) should be deemed to be the agent of the creditor and so, for example, any misrepresentations made by the dealer/negotiator would be attributed to the creditor as having been made by an agent of the creditor. The Crowther Committee also stressed that, assuming the seller/supplier is worth pursuing, the creditor is better placed than the debtor to put pressure on him to deal with the debtor's complaint, not least by threatening to withdraw future finance facilities unless the seller/supplier attends to the debtor's complaint and takes greater care in the conduct of his business.

Under the provisions of the CCA, the creditor thus frequently incurs liability for the acts of a negotiator or supplier of goods or services. This liability may be in addition to the creditor's existing, direct liability to the debtor (eg in hire-purchase where the creditor is directly liable for breach of the implied terms in the Supply of Goods (Implied Terms) Act 1973) or it may be a liability imposed on the creditor for defective goods or services supplied where none existed otherwise (eg in a connected loan transaction or where the debtor pays with a credit card – in both situations only the seller/supplier is *directly* liable under his contract with the debtor if defective goods or services are supplied). The creditor's liability is established by two, overlapping sections of the CCA. First, s 56 deems that certain individuals are agents of the creditor when conducting 'antecedent negotiations' and, second, s 75 imposes joint and several liability on the creditor and supplier in debtor-creditor-supplier agreements. These two sections must now be set in context and considered in detail.

The Consumer Credit Act, section 56 and deemed agency

INTRODUCTION: THE LIABILITY OF THE DEALER IN
HIRE-PURCHASE AGREEMENTS

In the typical hire-purchase agreement, the dealer sells the goods to the creditor/ finance company and the finance company then lets those goods on hire-purchase to the customer/debtor. The contract of hire-purchase is between the creditor

---

2 *Report of the Committee on Consumer Credit* (Cmnd 4596, 1971), paras 6.6.20-6.6.29.

and the debtor and, as the dealer is not privy to that contract, the general rule is that he cannot be liable in any way to the debtor on the hire-purchase contract. Likewise, there is no contract for the sale of goods between the debtor and the dealer and so the latter is not liable for breach of the implied terms of the SGA.[3]

Nevertheless, the dealer clearly has an important managerial task in the formation of the hire-purchase agreement and virtually all the negotiations are arranged through him, the finance company remaining an impersonal entity in the background. An enduring problem in hire-purchase agreements has always been the extent to which the dealer who negotiated the transaction might (i) be liable directly and personally for representations made; and (ii) might be regarded as the agent of the creditor/finance company, thus rendering the creditor liable for his statements or acts.

Representations made by the dealer

At common law, a collateral contract can exist between the dealer and the debtor[4] and the paradigm of such a collateral undertaking occurred in *Andrews v Hopkinson*.[5] There the plaintiff debtor was considering the possibility of taking a second-hand car on hire-purchase when the defendant dealer told the plaintiff: 'It's a good little bus. I would stake my life on it; you will have no trouble with it'. The car was sold to a finance company which let it to the plaintiff on hire-purchase terms. A week after delivery of the car to the plaintiff, he was injured in a collision while driving the car owing to the failure of the steering which was seriously defective. There was an exclusion clause in the hire-purchase agreement which successfully deprived the plaintiff of any remedy against the finance company, but McNair J held that a collateral contract existed between the dealer and the plaintiff. The plaintiff was thus entitled to damages against the dealer for breach of the express warranty in that collateral contract that the car was sound.[6] The consideration supporting this collateral contract is that, in return for the dealer's promise, the debtor suffers a 'detriment' in entering into the main contract with the finance company. Correctly therefore, the undertaking is also unilateral in nature as the debtor is not bound to enter into the main contract but the collateral contract is crystallised if he does form a binding contract with the finance company. The courts steadily extended the ambit of the collateral contract during the 20th century[7] but, nevertheless, if the dealer is to be liable for breach of such a contract, his statements must be certain and unequivocal[8] and made with the necessary intent[9] to be bound contractually.

---

3 *Drury v Victor Buckland Ltd* [1941] 1 All ER 269. The dealer could, of course, enter into an agreement with the debtor for the installation of the goods, for example, and then he could be liable directly for breach of the terms implied by the Supply of Goods and Services Act 1982.
4 See *Webster v Higgin* [1948] 2 All ER 127; *Brown v Sheen and Richmond Car Sales Ltd* [1950] 1 All ER 1102.
5 [1957] 1 QB 229.
6 Although it is sometimes said that a collateral *warranty* existed, it is more accurate to categorise this notion as a separate, collateral *contract*. See Wedderburn, 'Collateral Contracts' [1959] CLJ 58.
7 See eg *City and Westminster Properties (1934) Ltd v Mudd* [1959] Ch 129; *Evans (J) & Son (Portsmouth) Ltd v Andrea Merzario Ltd* [1976] 1 WLR 1078; *Esso Petroleum Co Ltd v Mardon* [1976] QB 801.
8 *Astley Industrial Trust Ltd v Grimley* [1963] 1 WLR 584, 596 per Pearson LJ; *Garbett v Rufford Motor Co Ltd* (1962) Guardian, 12 March
9 *Alicia Hosiery Ltd v Brown Shipley Ltd* [1970] 1 QB 195; *Independent Broadcasting Authority v EMI Electronics* (1980) 14 BLR 1.

The measure of damages for breach of the collateral contract depend upon the effect that the breach has on the main contract of hire-purchase but the general rule is that the debtor can recover damages in respect of loss which directly and naturally results in the ordinary course of events from the breach of warranty. In *Yeoman Credit Ltd v Odgers*,[10] the brakes on a car were so defective that it was unroadworthy and, consequently, it was returned to the finance company. The Court of Appeal held the debtor could recover from the dealer the whole sum which the debtor was liable to pay to the finance company under the hire-purchase agreement by way of instalments together with the costs incurred by the debtor in reasonably defending the action brought against him by the finance company for falling into arrears.

Finally, it should be noted that the dealer can also be liable in deceit, in the tort of negligence[11] and, undoubtedly, for negligent misstatement at common law which causes financial loss. At common law, in hire-purchase agreements, the dealer cannot be liable under the Misrepresentation Act 1967 as that Act applies only where the misrepresentation induces the representee to enter into a contract with the *representor* and, of course, no contract results with the dealer.[12] The dealer could employ an exclusion clause which seeks to exclude his liability under a collateral contract and such an exclusion will be subject to the reasonableness test under the UCTA, but it is unlikely that the controls in the Unfair Terms in Consumer Contracts Regulations 1999 would be applicable between dealer and debtor as the dealer is neither a 'seller' nor a 'supplier' within the Regulations.

The dealer's liability under a collateral contract is undoubtedly less significant today than it was at the date of *Andrews v Hopkinson* because there are now effective controls in the Unfair Contract Terms Act 1977 on the finance company's ability to exclude the implied terms relating to the quality and fitness for purpose of the goods supplied[13] and, under the CCA, the dealer is deemed to be the agent of the finance company when conducting the preliminary negotiations relating to the hire-purchase agreement.

The dealer as agent at common law

At common law, the question of whether the dealer might be the agent of either the debtor or the creditor/finance company has always been a vexed one.[14] In *Financings Ltd v Stimson*,[15] Lord Denning MR considered that 'if we take, as we should, a realistic view of the position, the dealer is in many respects and for many purposes the agent of the finance company'. Having regard to the perception of the average debtor and the totality of the operations that the dealer performs

---

10 [1962] 1 WLR 215.
11 McNair J held that the dealer was liable in negligence in *Andrews v Hopkinson* [1957] 1 QB 229.
12 It is tempting to argue that a collateral contract is formed with the dealer/representor, but the dealer's statement is the totality of such a collateral contract and the Misrepresentation Act 1967 envisages a misrepresenation followed by a contract.
13 The dealer's obligations may still be significant (i) in relation to non-consumer agreements; (ii) where the finance company is for any reason not worth suing; and (iii) if the dealer gives express undertakings going beyond the obligations of the creditor which are implied by the Supply of Goods (Implied Terms) Act 1973 Act, eg an express promise to effect repairs free of charge in certain eventualities.
14 See Guest, 'Hire-Purchase and the Dealer' (1963) 79 LQR 33; Hughes, 'Agency in Hire-Purchase Transactions' (1964) 27 MLR 395.
15 [1962] 1 WLR 1184.

in arranging the hire-purchase, apparently on behalf of the finance company, it is difficult to disagree with the statement by the Master of the Rolls. From the inception of the negotiations, when the dealer produces the finance company's form and completes it, to the conclusion of the contract when the dealer receives a commission from the finance company, all the indications are those of an established principal-agent relationship.

Somewhat perversely, the common law has invariably considered that, while the dealer can be the agent of the finance company for some limited purposes,[16] there is no overall presumption of such an agency.[17] The matter was put beyond doubt by the majority decision of the House of Lords in *Branwhite v Worcester Works Finance Ltd*.[18] In that case the debtor signed in blank an agreement to take a car on hire-purchase and was allowed £130 on the part-exchange value of his existing car, that being his deposit. The dealer fraudulently inserted figures in the proposal form contrary to those agreed with the debtor. The finance company purported to accept the offer to sell the car and sent the sale price to the dealer less £130 which the debtor had paid the dealer as a deposit. When the customer saw the discrepancy in the figures in his copy of the agreement, he relied on the dealer to get them corrected and, in the meantime, he paid no instalments. The dealer did nothing and shortly afterwards he disappeared. Eventually the finance company repossessed the car and the customer then sued for the return of the £130 'deposit'. The House of Lords held unanimously that the finance company had received from the debtor £130, albeit only in account and not in notes or by cheque, for a consideration which had wholly failed. Accordingly, they were bound to repay £130 to him on the basis of a total failure of consideration. Second, the House decided that the dealer did *not* receive the deposit as agent of the finance company and the finance company would thus not have to account for it to the debtor under agency reasoning. While acknowledging that the dealer can be the agent of the finance company in specific situations, the Law Lords emphasised that there is no general agency relationship between the parties and the dealer acts first and foremost on his own behalf. The debtor would thus not succeed in recovering the deposit from the finance company if, for example, the dealer absconded with the money before the sale from the dealer to the finance company was arranged. Lords Reid and Wilberforce dissented and considered that 'the established mercantile background of hire-purchase transactions'[19] whereby the dealer has a standing relationship with the finance company, led to the conclusion that the dealer was the finance company's agent. In hire-purchase, the practical consequences of the *Branwhite* decision

16   At common law, the dealer has been regarded as agent for the finance company for (i) the purpose of receiving notice from the debtor of the revocation of his offer to take the goods on hire-purchase (*Financings Ltd v Stimson* [1962] 1 WLR 1184); (ii) the receipt of offers from the debtor but not offers subject to a condition precedent or other qualification (*Northgran Finance Co Ltd v Ashley* [1963] 1 QB 476); and (iii) delivering the goods to the debtor after the agreement has been completed (*Mercantile Credit Co Ltd v Hamblin* [1965] 2 QB 242, 269 per Pearson LJ).

17   'There is no rule of law that in a hire-purchase transaction the dealer never is, or always is, acting as agent for the finance company or as agent for the customer. In a typical hire-purchase transaction the dealer is a party in his own right, selling his car to the finance company, and he is acting primarily on his own behalf and not as a general agent for either of the other two parties': *Mercantile Credit Co Ltd v Hamblin* [1965] 2 QB 242, 269 per Pearson LJ; see also *Campbell Discount Co Ltd v Gall* [1961] 1 QB 431.

18   [1969] 1 AC 552.

19   [1969] 1 AC 552 at 586, per Lord Wilberforce.

have been nullified by the CCA, s 56 which deems that the dealer in hire-purchase agreements is the agent of the creditor. However, s 56 does not apply to consumer hire agreements and, as will be seen below, the restrictive *Branwhite* reasoning has meant that it is very difficult to establish an agency in such hiring agreements.

Reform of the law and the rationale of s 56

From the consumer's point of view, the position as described above was clearly both unrealistic and, often, unjust. Reform of the law came with the Hire-Purchase Act 1965, s 16(1), which provided that the dealer was regarded as the agent of the finance company in pre-contractual negotiations and this policy was continued and extended in the CCA, s 56. The overall intent of s 56 is that, in several situations, certain individuals will be *deemed* to be the statutory agent of the creditor in conducting the 'antecedent negotiations' of the credit transaction. Should the dealer in a hire-purchase transaction, for example, misrepresent the quality of the goods, he now makes the misrepresentation as agent of the finance company/creditor under s 56(1)(b). In such a case, the debtor can either commence proceedings against the creditor or stop his payments and when sued, make a counterclaim. It should be stressed that s 56 extends well beyond hire-purchase agreements and so, for example, a supplier in a connected loan, debtor-creditor-supplier agreement, is also deemed to be the agent of the creditor under s 56(1)(c). In fact, three types of agreement are within s 56 and these must be examined first but it should be emphasised that s 56 applies only to *regulated* agreements. In accordance with s 56, the deemed agent is referred to as the 'negotiator'. This appellation could be attached, for example, to the supplier in a debtor-creditor-supplier agreement within s 12(b) or (c), or the credit-broker who negotiates hire-purchase agreements within s 12(a) and who is usually the 'dealer' in such a transaction.

TO WHICH AGREEMENTS DOES SECTION 56 APPLY?

The CCA, s 56(1)(a)

The first situation within s 56 is where, under s 56 (1)(a), antecedent negotiations are 'conducted by the creditor or owner in relation to the making of any regulated agreement'.

First, it should be noted that s 56(1)(a) applies to '*any* regulated agreement' and this includes debtor-creditor agreements and consumer hire, unlike s 56(1)(b) and (c) which have a limited ambit.

Second, it is crucial to realise that this part of s 56 is *not* concerned with a deemed agency but would apply, for example, to negotiations conducted by a trader who finances the transaction himself, the creditor in hire-purchase who might lead the negotiations himself or the owner who himself negotiates a consumer hire agreement. It would also apply to negotiations conducted by an employee of the creditor or owner acting in the course of his employment and those conducted by an *authorised* agent of the creditor or owner who is thus, indisputably, such an agent at common law. In these situations, the negotiations conducted by the employee or agent would be considered to be conducted by the creditor or owner himself within s 56(1)(a).

The *Branwhite* case, discussed above, put it beyond doubt that the dealer who arranges hire-purchase transactions does not normally act, at common law, as an agent for the creditor/finance house and so he does not fall within s 56(1)(a) as the authorised agent of the creditor – but this is now unimportant as such a dealer is drawn within the deemed, statutory agency of s 56(1)(b), below.

Similarly, in a consumer hire/leasing transaction, a dealer who arranges the transaction and sells goods to a lessor/owner to be let to a hirer on lease or rental, will not normally be the agent of the lessor/owner at common law. Several cases concerning consumer hire/leasing have followed the *Branwhite* case, discussed earlier, and have denied that the dealer is the agent of the owner[20] except where the facts have indicated unequivocally that an agency relationship existed.[1] Moreover, it is vital to stress that the dealer who negotiates a leasing transaction is *not* deemed to be the agent of the owner within s 56(1)(b) (see below). Consumer hire is not drawn within s 56(1)(c) as no *credit* is involved in granting hire and, consequently, the startling conclusion is that hiring/leasing transactions arranged by dealers slip the net of deemed agency in s 56. This means that the debtor under a hire-purchase agreement who negotiates with a dealer is in markedly a better position than the hirer under a leasing agreement which is negotiated by such a dealer.

The CCA, s 56(1)(b)

Section 56(1)(b) applies to the situation where a 'credit-broker'[2] conducts negotiations 'in relation to goods sold or proposed to be sold by the credit-broker to the creditor before forming the subject-matter of a debtor-creditor-supplier agreement within s 12(a)'.

Only two-party, debtor-creditor-supplier agreements are within s 12(a). The commonest situation within s 56(1)(b) is where the credit-broker conducts the antecedent negotiations of a hire-purchase agreement with the prospective debtor, the goods then being sold to the creditor/finance company and let on hire-purchase to the debtor or, alternatively, supplied on conditional sale or credit-sale terms to him.[3] Section 56(2) provides that s 56(1)(b) is a case of deemed, statutory agency.

It must be stressed that there are two situations to which s 56(1)(b) is inapplicable. First, s 56(1)(b) does not apply to a credit-broker engaged in negotiations for *debtor-creditor* agreements, but here the credit-broker is normally an agent of the creditor at common law and so the situation will fall within s 56(1)(a).

Second, s 56(1)(b) refers only to goods 'sold by the credit-broker to the *creditor* before forming the subject-matter of a debtor-creditor-supplier agreement within s 12(a)' and so s 56(1)(b) does not cover consumer hire/leasing where the credit-

---

20 See *Mynshul Asset Finance v Clarke* [1992] CLY 487; *Williams (J D) & Co v McCauley, Parsons and Jones* [1994] CCLR 78, CA; *Woodchester Equipment (Leasing) Ltd v BACFID* [1995] CCLR 51, CA.

1 See *Woodchester Equipment Leasing Ltd v Clayton and Clayton* [1994] CCLR 87 (*Branwhite* was distinguished on the basis that *Clayton* concerned a leasing agreement whereas *Branwhite* was hire-purchase. An agency was thus established at common law. It may be that, after the *BACFID* decision (above) in the CA, the *Clayton* decision (County Court) must be considered to be incorrect); *Purnell Secretarial Services Ltd v Lease Management Services Ltd* [1994] CCLR 127 (the agreement was such that the owner was estopped from denying the authority of the dealer and was thus liable for the dealer's misrepresentation).

2 Credit brokerage is simply the business of introducing individuals who require credit to those whose business it is to grant credit. See the CCA, ss 145(2)-(4) and s 189(1) which defines a 'credit-broker' as 'a person carrying on a business of credit brokerage'.

3 See the CCA, Sch 2, examples 2 and 4.

broker sells the goods to an *owner* who then lets them on simple hire to the hirer. In *Moorgate Mercantile Leasing Ltd v Isobel Gell & Ugolini Dispensers (UK) Ltd*,[4] Mrs Gell ran a newsagent and confectionery shop and was visited by a representative of Ugolini Dispensers who sought to interest her in hiring an 'ice shake dispensing machine'. The representative left an advertising pamphlet and wrote on it that Mrs Gell could buy the machine for £25 at the end of the agreement. This was untrue as the prospective agreement was a leasing agreement and not a hire-purchase agreement. The representative returned next day and told Mrs Gell that, should she agree to take the machine, she could return it at any time and would be responsible only for accrued instalments and the costs of its removal. On the faith of these statements, Mrs Gell signed a leasing agreement with the plaintiff which, in fact, contained no right of termination but did embody a liquidated damages clause. The machine proved to be unprofitable and Mrs Gell asked the plaintiffs to remove it. She was then told that there was no right of termination and, in fact, the plaintiff claimed £1,200 in damages under the agreement. It was held that, although misrepresentations had been made by Ugolini, the plaintiff was not liable for them as this was a consumer hire agreement and so Ugolini was not deemed to be the agent of the plaintiff within s 56. If this had been a hire-purchase agreement, the plaintiff would have been liable under s 56, and there is no good reason to exclude consumer hire from the ambit of that section. The only way to avoid the conclusion reached in the *Gell* case would be a finding that Ugolini was an agent of the plaintiff at common law but, as emphasised above, the unrealistic *Branwhite* decision effectively thwarts such a finding in the majority of situations. The law is patently in need of reform.

The CCA, s 56(1)(c)

The final situation in which s 56 is relevant is where, under s 56(1)(c), antecedent negotiations are 'conducted by the supplier in relation to a transaction financed or proposed to be financed by a debtor-creditor-supplier agreement within section 12(b) or (c)'.

This covers, for example, the connected loan arrangement where negotiations are conducted by a supplier of goods or services (eg double-glazing) who supplies them to the debtor with finance being provided by the creditor, the supplier and creditor having pre-existing business arrangements. Also within s 56(1)(c) is the situation where a shopkeeper/negotiator discusses the quality of goods with a customer who intends to buy them using a credit-card issued by a bank or other credit-card issuer.[5] Again, s 56(2) provides that s 56(1)(c) is a case of deemed, statutory agency.

Once more, it must be stressed that consumer hire is not within s 56(1)(c), as that subsection applies only to consumer *credit* agreements as defined in s 12(b) and (c) and hiring does not entail the provision of credit.

THE LIABILITY OF THE CREDITOR UNDER SECTION 56

Under s 56(2), the antecedent negotiations are 'deemed to be conducted by the negotiator in the capacity of agent of the creditor as well as in his actual

4 [1988] CCLR 1.
5 See the CCA, Sch 2, example 3.

capacity'. Section 56(4) provides that 'antecedent negotiations' are 'taken to begin[6] when the negotiator and the debtor ... first enter into communication (including communication by advertisement), and to include any representations made by the negotiator to the debtor ... and any other dealings between them'.

The personal liability of the dealer at common law under *Andrews v Hopkinson*, considered above, is thus preserved by s 56(2), viz 'in his actual capacity' and, of course, the 'negotiator' will remain liable directly on any contract of supply to which he is party, eg in a connected loan, debtor-creditor-supplier agreement under s 56(1)(c), where the negotiator/supplier sells goods to the debtor, the finance being provided by the creditor.

However, it is plain that the creditor is now liable under s 56 for representations and promises made by the supplier or dealer who acts as the 'negotiator' in the agreement. During the antecedent negotiations the negotiator may make statements relating to the credit agreement (eg the cost of the credit and the number of instalments) or he may assure the debtor as to the condition, age or quality of the goods to be supplied. He might also act in a negligent way by delivering dangerous goods to the debtor before the credit agreement is completed. In all these situations, the negotiator is deemed to act as the agent of the creditor and his statements and acts will generate a wide range of possible claims which can be pursued by the debtor.

The statements made in the negotiations may be relevant in assessing the creditor's liability for breach of the statutory implied conditions of description, quality and fitness for purpose, eg the debtor makes the particular purpose for which he requires the goods known to the negotiator/dealer in a hire-purchase transaction. By a process of elimination this is a possibility under s 56 only where the negotiator's statements are made on behalf of the creditor under 56(1)(b), ie where a credit-broker conducts negotiations in relation to goods sold or proposed to be sold by the credit-broker to the creditor before forming the subject-matter of a debtor-creditor-supplier agreement within s 12(a). This would cover hire-purchase, conditional sale and credit-sale where the implied terms of the SGA 1979 or the Supply of Goods (Implied Terms) Act 1973 are implied into the creditor's agreement with the debtor.[7]

Most importantly, as the negotiator acts as the agent of the creditor under s 56, the negotiator's statements may become terms of the credit agreement itself and, in this event, the debtor has the right to sue for breach of contract.

Almost as significant as the two previous possibilities, is the fact the negotiator's misrepresentations are attributed to the creditor in agreements within ss 56(1)(b) and 56(1)(c) and so the remedies for misrepresentation can be pursued by the debtor. Here the Misrepresentation Act 1967, s 2(1), would be available to the debtor with the added attraction that, under s 2(1), the burden is on the creditor to disprove negligence.

Finally, the creditor could be liable in tort for the negotiator's negligence in delivering dangerous goods to the debtor in the period before the credit agreement has been concluded. These are the overall consequences of the deemed agency under s 56. However, a closer examination of the section supports these conclusions and underscores the extent of the creditor's liability.

---

6   The CCA does not say when antecedent negotiations *end* but it is a reasonable assumption that, being *antecedent* negotiations, they end once the regulated credit agreement is concluded. Post-contractual communications are thus not within s 56.
7   These implied terms are considered later in this chapter.

What is the *extent* of the creditor's liability under s 56?

First, it is striking that, under s 56(4), antecedent negotiations are taken to begin with communication by advertisements, and any sales literature which the debtor reads at the dealer's premises or any such literature distributed by the dealer, for example, would be within the negotiations. Consequently, the creditor can be liable for any misrepresentations in an advertisement, poster or leaflet distributed by the negotiator/dealer.

Second, it will be noticed that s 56 *deems* that the negotiator's negotiations are conducted in the *capacity of agent* of the creditor and so this statutory imposition of agency is freed from the common law's restrictions as to whether or not the dealer/agent has any actual or apparent authority from the creditor/principal. Consequently, it could not be argued that the negotiator's representations are immoderate and not normally made by a person in his position, nor that the debtor should be put on enquiry in any circumstances regarding the extent of the negotiator's authority.

Third, the reference in s 56(4) to 'representations' of the negotiator/dealer indicates that the statements do *not* necessarily have to be made with the intent of becoming terms of the credit agreement. Instead, they can be misrepresentations[8] and, indeed, there is no requirement that the representations be made *expressly*.

Fourth, for good measure, s 56(4) refers to 'any other dealings' between the negotiator and the debtor. This safety net should thus catch promises relating to any ancillary arrangements such as the installation or repair of the goods. Moreover, 'dealings' could encompass, for example, a pre-delivery inspection of the goods which has been performed negligently by the negotiator or the pre-contract delivery of dangerous goods to the debtor which injure him thus rendering the creditor liable in tort for negligence, even where no (actual) representation has been made by the negotiator.

Last but not least, it is arguable that s 56 may be operative even though no *concluded* agreement between the debtor and creditor results from the antecedent negotiations. There is certainly no specific requirement in s 56 that such a contract must result and, indeed, s 56(1)(b) and (c) refer respectively to 'goods sold or *proposed* to be sold' and a 'transaction financed or *proposed* to be financed'. This would clearly be relevant in the situation mentioned above, where the debtor seeks to render the creditor liable in tort for dangerous goods which have injured the debtor, even though no regulated agreement has been formed between the debtor and creditor.[9]

Although these contentions have not all been confirmed by decisions at common law, the width of the statutory agency was illustrated recently in *Forthright Finance Ltd v Ingate*.[10] There the dealer, a licensed credit-broker, agreed to take a car from the debtor in part-exchange for a replacement car to be supplied on conditional sale by a finance company, Carlyle Finance Ltd, and he also agreed to settle the balance outstanding on the conditional sale agreement with the plaintiff finance company relating to the existing, part-exchange car. The dealer subsequently went into liquidation without having discharged the

---

8 The CCA, s 189(1) defines 'representation' as including 'any condition or warranty, and any other statement or undertaking, whether oral or in writing'.

9 Cf Goode, *Consumer Credit Law* (1989), para 17.12, who argues that a regulated agreement must result if s 56 is to be operative.

10 [1997] 4 All ER 99; following *UDT v Whitfield* [1987] CCLR 60.

balance owing on the part-exchange car. The plaintiff finance company then obtained judgment against the debtor for the balance outstanding on the part-exchange car. The Court of Appeal held that Carlyle Finance Ltd must indemnify the debtor in relation to her outstanding liability on the part-exchange car on the basis that the dealer's promise was made as the deemed agent of Carlyle Finance Ltd under s 56(1)(b). The court rejected the Scottish decision in *Powell v Lloyds Bowmaker Ltd*[11] which had limited s 56(1)(b) to its wording of negotiations conducted 'in relation to goods sold or proposed to be sold by the credit-broker to the creditor', ie only negotiations as to the new, replacement car and not those regarding the existing, part-exchange car. Staughton LJ held that 'the law is plain enough: one simply has to inquire whether all the negotiations form part of the one transaction as a matter of fact'.[12] Henry LJ[13] added that the reference in s 56(4) to 'other dealings' would certainly apply to the promises made regarding the existing, part-exchange car.

There are two final points regarding the creditor's liability. First, it must be emphasised that the creditor's liability under s 56 is non-excludable as s 56(3) provides that an agreement is void, if and to the extent that, it purports to provide that the negotiator (or someone acting on his behalf) is to be treated as the debtor's agent or to relieve the creditor from liability for the dealer's acts or omissions.[14] Second, unlike the position under s 75, the creditor is *not* given any statutory right of indemnity under s 56 against the negotiator/dealer for the acts performed by the latter in the course of his deemed agency and any such rights will hinge on the agreement, if any, between the creditor and the negotiator/dealer. At common law, an agent is normally under a duty to indemnify his principal for loss caused while acting in breach of duty or without authority and there seems to be no reason why this should not also be the position under the statutory agency created by s 56.

The Consumer Credit Act, section 75: joint and several liability of creditor and supplier

Where there is a debtor-creditor-supplier agreement within s 12(b) or (c), the claim available to the debtor under the CCA, s 75 is of great significance as the section provides that, if the debtor has a claim against the supplier for breach of contract, he shall have a 'like claim' against the creditor. Assuming that the debtor has a direct claim against the supplier, eg in a connected loan situation, for breach of the terms implied by the SGA in the contract of sale between the supplier and debtor (buyer), s 75 permits that claim for breach of contract to be pursued against the creditor who advanced the loan. This remedy is thus of immeasurable importance to the debtor, particularly where the supplier is insolvent or has disappeared.

---

11   [1996] CCLR 50.
12   [1997] 4 All ER 99, 105.
13   [1997] 4 All ER 99 at 106-107.
14   If the creditor has a clause in the contract with the debtor which seeks to exclude liability for misrepresentations, including those made by the dealer, it is unclear whether it is (i) automatically void under s 56(3); or (ii) subject to the reasonableness test under the Misrepresentation Act 1967, s 3.

TO WHICH AGREEMENTS DOES SECTION 75 APPLY?

Before the substance and scope of the 'like claim' is investigated, it is necessary to stress that, in comparison with s 56, s 75 is relatively limited in scope. Section 75 applies *only* to debtor-creditor-supplier agreements falling within s 12(b) or (c) which must, necessarily, be *regulated* agreements. Consequently, s 75 has no application to exempt agreements or those agreements which are outside the CCA, eg where the debtor is a company.

There is much confusion regarding the agreements which are within s 75 but the key to an overall understanding of the scope and purpose of the section is that it is limited to those situations where the creditor and the supplier are *distinct and separate* parties. The paradigm of s 75 is thus the three-party, connected loan agreement where the creditor and supplier have business arrangements and the creditor finances a contract of supply between the debtor and the third party supplier, eg a contract for the installation by the supplier of double-glazing in the debtor's home. It cannot be stressed enough that the nature of that *supply* contract is irrelevant to the operation of s 75 (apart from the exceptions in s 75(3), considered below) and it could thus take the form of, for example, a hire/leasing agreement, credit-sale, conditional sale or cash sale.[15] Moreover, it is also immaterial that the supply contract is itself not a regulated agreement or is totally outside the ambit of the CCA: it is the primary, credit agreement, which must be a regulated agreement, not the contract of supply which is financed by the credit.

With the overall design of s 75 in view, it is possible to categorise the principal agreements within s 12(b) and (c) and thus within s 75. First, at the core of s 75 is the connected loan where the creditor makes a loan to the debtor to finance a transaction between the debtor and a third party supplier, the supplier having 'arrangements' in the form of a business relationship with the creditor and having introduced the debtor to the creditor. Second, three-party credit card transactions are within s 75, ie where the debtor uses his card to obtain goods or services form a third party supplier with whom the card-issuer/creditor has pre-existing business arrangements. Likewise, check trading is within s 75 as being a debtor-creditor-supplier agreement for restricted-use credit within the CCA, s 12(b). It should be stressed, however, that transactions using debit cards and cheque guarantee cards are *not* within s 75. The CCA provides that, in both these cases, such 'arrangements' as exist, ie the business relationship between creditor and supplier, are to be disregarded.[16]

It will now be plain that s 75 has no application to hire-purchase agreements, which are two-party, debtor-creditor-supplier agreements within s 12(a), because in hire-purchase the creditor/finance company is also the legal

---

15 It is often said that s 75 does not apply to credit-sale or conditional sale agreements but, without more, this is misleading. The section does not apply to credit-sales or conditional sales within s 12(a) and s 11(1)(a) as being agreements 'to finance a transaction between the debtor and the creditor' ie when they are *two-party* agreements. But s 75 can apply in three-party, debtor-creditor-supplier agreements where the contract of *supply* is a credit-sale or conditional sale.
16 In relation to cheque guarantee cards, see the CCA, s 187(3)(b). Transactions using cheque guarantee cards are debtor-creditor agreements for unrestricted-use credit under s 13(c). As regards debit cards, see the CCA, s 187(3A).

supplier[17] and, for the same reason, s 75 does not apply to two-party conditional sale or credit-sale. Where, as in these transactions, the creditor is also the supplier, the debtor has a direct claim against the creditor on the contract of supply made between them and so s 75 is superfluous in such a situation.[18]

Two sets of circumstances are excluded from the operation of s 75 by s 75(3). The first exemption, in s 75(3)(a), is where the supply contract under which the debtor can claim is a non-commercial agreement.

Second, s 75(3)(b) provides that s 75 does not apply 'so far as the claim relates to any single item to which the supplier has attached a cash price not exceeding £100 or more than £30,000'.[19] As the *cash price* of the goods or service supplied must be between £100 and £30,000, both small and large agreements are outside the scope of s 75. Small agreements are excluded to relieve creditors of an abundance of trivial claims and, where the cash price is over £30,000, the debtor may often be a business or certainly of sufficient means to fend for himself and, likewise, the supplier will often be reputable and so less likely to become insolvent. It should be stressed that these figures are cash prices and not *credit* limits. Should the cash price of the goods be £120, for example, and a deposit of £10 be paid to the supplier by means of the debtor's credit card, the agreement will be within s 75 even though the credit advanced is only £10. Alternatively, if the cash price of a car is £35,000, for example, and the credit advanced is £25,000 with the debtor's supplying £10,000 in cash, the agreement is not within s 75. However, should the cash price be £30,000 with £26,000 credit extended to the debtor and £4,000 paid in cash, the overall financial ceiling of the CCA (£25,000) would be exceeded and the credit agreement would not be a regulated agreement within s 75. Finally, under s 75(3)(b), it is most unclear when s 75 does not apply on the basis that the claim relates 'to any single item' to which the supplier has attached a cash price not exceeding £100 or more than £30,000.[20]

Section 75(4), which should not be confused in any way with s 75(3), provides that s 75 applies notwithstanding that, in entering into the supply contract, the debtor 'exceeded the credit limit or otherwise contravened any term of the [credit]

---

17   See *Porter v General Guarantee Corpn Ltd* [1982] RTR 384, where this point was overlooked. The debtor under a hire-purchase agreement successfully sued the creditor/ finance company for breach of contract and it was held that the creditor could obtain an indemnity from the dealer under s 75, on the basis that the dealer was the *supplier*. This is, with respect, incorrect: the creditor is the supplier in hire-purchase. On the facts, it is likely that the creditor (as buyer of the goods from the dealer) should have been able to sue the dealer (as seller) for breach of the implied terms in the contract of sale between them and thus be (correctly) placed in the same position as under s 75.

18   The CCA, s 56(1)(b), considered above, applies to hire-purchase and so the creditor/finance company will be liable, for example, for misrepresentations made by the dealer in antecedent negotiations.

19   The amounts stated in the CCA were increased by the Consumer Credit (Increase of Monetary Limits) Order 1983, SI 1983/1878 .

20   'Single item' seems designed to apply principally to the supply of goods but, as s 75 applies to contracts for services and work and materials as well as contracts for the supply of goods, a 'single item' may be difficult to define with precision. For example, what is the position where (i) a machine costs £25,000 but one crucial part of it is defective and is sold separately at a cash price of £50, with the consequence that the entire machine is defective; (ii) in a contract for the installation of double-glazing at a cash price of £8,000, one component costing £50 is faulty, or an inspection of the work, costing £50, is made incorrectly, with the consequence that the debtor has to pay a further £2,000 to cure the defects; and (iii) an agreement for the installation of kitchen equipment costing £500 is subdivided into ten instalments of £50 as work progresses or, alternatively, ten computers are sold to a partnership at a price of £3,500 each but paid for in a lump sum of £35,000?

agreement'. This provision relates, therefore, to a breach of the *credit agreement* between the debtor and creditor. Take, for example, the situation where the debtor has a credit card issued by the creditor/card issuer and, using the card, the debtor buys goods from the supplier/seller. If the goods prove to be defective, the debtor can claim against the creditor under s 75 even where the purchase of the goods takes the debit balance on his credit card over the 'credit limit'[1] agreed with the creditor/card issuer.

THE SCOPE OF LIABILITY UNDER SECTION 75

Section 75 provides that, if the agreement is a debtor-creditor-supplier agreement within s 12(b) or (c) and the debtor has a claim in damages against the supplier for 'misrepresentation or breach of contract' (eg breach of the terms implied by the SGA in the contract of sale of goods between debtor and supplier/seller), he 'shall have a like claim against the creditor, who, with the supplier, shall accordingly be jointly and severally liable to the debtor' for the damages. Only claims which lie against the supplier for misrepresentation or breach of contract can be pursued against the creditor and so no claim could be sustained in tort for negligence or for duress or undue influence, for example. Moreover, it should be remembered that s 75 limits the creditor's liability to 'a transaction financed by the agreement'. If, for example, there is a breach of a subsidiary contract for the supplier to service the goods, which is *not* financed by the creditor, the creditor will not be liable under s 75.

Subject to any agreement between the creditor and supplier, the creditor is entitled to be indemnified by the supplier for loss suffered by the creditor in satisfying this liability including costs reasonably incurred by him in defending proceedings instituted by the debtor (s 75(2)). The risk for the creditor is obviously that the supplier will be insolvent and, if so, the creditor will be solely responsible for the supplier's misrepresentation or breach of contract.[2]

At first sight, it might seem harsh to impose this liability on the creditor under s 75, but closer inspection reveals that this is not the case. If the contract is one of hire-purchase, the creditor is directly liable for breach of the terms implied into the agreement by the Supply of Goods (Implied Terms) Act 1973, and so s 75 imposes the same liability on the creditor if, instead of hire-purchase, he chooses to finance the transaction by a loan of money in the setting of a debtor-creditor-supplier agreement. Section 75 is thus the practical embodiment of the ethos of the connected loan in that the creditor and supplier are regarded as being engaged in a joint venture to their mutual advantage. The connected lender will invariably offer inducements to a supplier to direct customers to the lender and so it would be unfair to insist that the supplier should shoulder all the responsibility. Plainly, in view of the liability under s 75, the creditor must choose with care those suppliers with whom he has business arrangements or, alternatively, advance loans without attaching pre-conditions as to the use of the money and without making arrangements with suppliers, thereby taking himself outside the scope of s 75. Certainly the debtor in a debtor-creditor-supplier agreement is placed in an

---

1 See the definition of 'credit limit' in s 189(1) and s 10(2).
2 The creditor's right of indemnity does not give him any rights over the goods if they are rejected by the debtor. If the supplier is insolvent and the creditor's right of indemnity is valueless, the creditor carries full liability under s 75 and yet has no rights over the goods which can be claimed by the supplier's trustee in bankruptcy.

advantageous position in being able to sue the usually solvent creditor/finance company – the debtor who has obtained an unconnected loan under a debtor-creditor agreement or a straightforward buyer of goods for cash who has not obtained any credit, might find that their only claim is against an insolvent seller. The astute buyer of goods or services will obviously seek to pay with a credit card in order to obtain the bonus of joint and several liability of the creditor and supplier.

While the creditor should patently carry a measure of liability when he and the supplier are involved in a joint venture, as described, it must be asked whether that liability is currently too exacting. First, while it is clear that the creditor is not the supplier of goods or services to the debtor, whenever additional liabilities are imposed on the supplier the creditor's liability increases correlatively. For example, the recent changes to the condition of satisfactory quality implied by the SGA, s 14 into contracts for the sale of goods, are automatically replicated in the creditor's augmented liability. The expanded liability of the seller may be justified in any number of ways but, without any consideration of the creditor's position, that increased range of liability is deemed to apply to him. Second, there is no requirement that the debtor should first pursue his remedies against the supplier under the contract of supply; instead, his first choice may be to commence proceedings against the creditor. This question is considered in more detail when s 75 is considered in relation to credit cards, but suffice to say that the Crowther Committee and the latest OFT report both reject the argument that the creditor should have only a confirming liability in cases where the debtor cannot obtain satisfaction from the supplier. Third, there is no correlation betweeen the *amount advanced* by the creditor and the extent of his liability: the creditor might lend only a fraction of the purchase price of expensive and complex goods bought by the debtor but his liability is not commensurate with the amount of the loan and, when consequential losses are considered, his ensuing liability could be immense. Again this question is discussed more fully when s 75 is considered in relation to credit cards, below. Fourth, the creditor's liability under s 75 is incurred no matter what promises have been given by the supplier and irrespective of the nature of the contract of supply. In a contract for the sale of a computer system to a small business, for example, the buyer may have paid for an extended guarantee regarding the goods. The loan advanced to pay for the computers may have been repaid after two years and the seller may have gone out of business, but the creditor will nevertheless be liable should the goods fail during the period of the guarantee several years later.[3] Here the creditor's role is undeniably that of a long-term insurer. As a retort to these assertions, however, it must be stressed that the creditor shoulders *vicarious* liability and thus the risks outlined above, although far-reaching, must surely be regarded as inherently acceptable where liability is imposed on one party for the acts of another.

CREDIT CARDS AND SECTION 75

Both s 75 and s 56(1)(c) apply to goods which are paid for by credit cards such as Access or Visa,[4] as such debtor-creditor-supplier agreements are within s 12(b)

---

3   Alternatively, the supplier may have gone out of business but the debtor will, of course, have to continue to make payments to the creditor for the price of the goods or services, this being a powerful argument for the existence of s 75 and the creditor's liability.
4   Provided the debtor's agreement with the bank *for the use of the card* was entered into after 1 July 1977 (Consumer Credit Act 1974 (Commencement No 3) Order 1977, SI 1977/ 802). Under pressure from the Office of Fair Trading, Access and Barclaycard (the only

or (c). Accordingly, the consumer who pays by credit card is afforded incomparable remedies but credit card issuers have resisted the imposition of liability under s 75 as far as possible, arguing that the debtor should first proceed against a solvent supplier. The finance houses have always argued that their liability should be secondary and confined to cases where the debtor is unable to obtain redress against a seller because of his insolvency. However, at the outset the Crowther Committee rejected this argument on the basis that (i) it imposes a heavy burden on the consumer in initiating litigation; and (ii) the obligation to pay the loan instalments while pursuing his claim against the seller might substantially diminish his ability to prosecute his claim.[5]

Moreover, the credit card issuers have suggested that there are no 'arrangements' between themselves and the supplier for the purposes of s 12(b) or (c) in view of the relatively new, intervening role of separate merchant acquirers.[6] But it is the *arrangements* between the parties which are crucial in determining the existence of a debtor-creditor-supplier agreement rather than the *number* of parties to the transaction, and it is suggested that this intervention of a fourth party does nothing to alter such arrangements for the purposes of the debtor-creditor-supplier agreement.

Wider arguments which have been pressed by the card issuers are, first, that the extensive use of credit cards as a normal method of payment was not envisaged by the Crowther Committee in 1971 and that, second, s 75 was originally premised on the relationship between a finance house and a supplier where inducements were offered by the finance house to the supplier to promote credit-based transactions, but that this is not a realistic appraisal of the modern credit card transaction. Third, the card issuers assert that most debtors do not distinguish between credit cards proper and debit cards (which are exempt from s 75) in that they pay their credit balances in full each month and do not want to obtain extended credit.[7]

All these arguments have been censured and refuted by the Office of Fair Trading,[8] the overall view of the OFT being that s 75 is a valuable consumer protection measure. The current recommendation of the OFT[9] is that there should be no requirement under s 75 that the debtor should first proceed against the supplier as this stipulation would detract substantially from consumer protection, particularly in overseas transactions. However, the OFT report suggests that the creditor's liability should be limited to the *amount charged to the card* in

relevant cards for pre-1977) agreed to accept liability for cards issued before July 1977 but *only* to the extent of the amount of credit used on the transaction in question. It is thus sound advice for holders of cards issued before July 1977 to cancel them and enter into a new agreement with a card-issuer.

5 *Report of the Committee on Consumer Credit* (Cmnd 4596, 1971), paras 6.6.26-6.6.29.
6 The normal practice with a credit card transaction is for the debtor/cardholder to sign a voucher proffered by the supplier instead of paying for the goods or service supplied by other means. The supplier sends the voucher to a merchant acquirer who reimburses the supplier for the price less a commission. The merchant acquirer then passes the voucher to the creditor/card issuer who reimburses the merchant acquirer less a commission. The creditor then sends a monthly statement to the debtor/cardholder who pays the creditor for the goods or service, together with any interest due on earlier unpaid amounts.
7 The fact remains, however, that debtors have the option of obtaining such extended credit under a credit card and, if the card issuers wish to be free of liability under s 75, they can invite debtors to convert their cards to monthly payment cards which thereby become exempt agreements under the CCA; see Chs 31 and 32.
8 See *Connected Lender Liability* (OFT 097, March 1994).
9 See *Connected Lender Liability* (OFT 132, May 1995).

respect of the purchase in question instead of the present position where the debtor may claim for all the loss which flows from the misrepresentation or breach of contract of the supplier. The OFT accepts that the extent of the liability currently imposed on the creditor is unreasonable as consequential losses could be immense in certain areas, eg in travel contracts with claims arising from death in an air crash. Moreover, the creditors' exposure to such losses does not reflect their involvement in, or the profit they derive from, the transaction. In order to harmonise with the reduced level of liability recommended, it is further suggested that the monetary limits in s 75 be amended and expressed in terms of the amount of credit granted rather than the purchase price of the item. The upper limit would thus be £25,000 as the maximum amount that can currently be obtained under a regulated agreement.

The credit card issuers have always contended that s 75 does not apply where the card has been used to make a purchase overseas, arguing that there are no 'arrangements' in relation to the foreign supplier. There are indications, however, that this is now an untenable argument. In *Jarrett v Barclays Bank plc*,[10] the debtor entered into an agreement to buy an annual timeshare in property in Portugal and paid the deposit with his Barclaycard, the balance of the price being financed by a loan from the Royal Bank of Scotland. Both credit agreements were alleged to be debtor-creditor-supplier agreements within the CCA, s 12(b). Subsequently, the debtor claimed that the vendor of the property was guilty of misrepresentation and breach of contract and commenced proceedings in the county court against the bank as creditor, under the CCA, s 75 and s 56. On a preliminary application, the proceedings were struck out on the basis that article 16 of the Brussels Convention established that the courts of the country in which the property was situated had exclusive jurisdiction over the claims. The debtor appealed against that striking out. The Court of Appeal held that, although the contract with the timeshare seller was governed by foreign law, the debtor-creditor-supplier agreement between the debtor and the bank was governed by English law and was thus subject to s 75. Accordingly, it was held that the action should proceed to trial in the county court.

In *Jarrett*, the Court of Appeal stressed that the 'like claim' under s 75 did not have to incorporate all the features of the claim against the supplier and, indeed, it could not be an identical claim as many of the debtor's remedies against the supplier, such as injunctions or specific performance, could not lie against the creditor. *Jarrett* does not, of course, decide the issue of whether 'arrangements' exist with foreign suppliers and, moreover, the decision leaves open the question as to whether the bank could obtain an indemnity against the foreign supplier under s 75(2). It is suggested, however, that 'arrangements' exist between the creditor and the foreign supplier as the card networks are international. Indeed, there is a stronger case for s 75 to operate with foreign suppliers as, assuming a claim is possible against the supplier, there are clearly immense difficulties for the debtor should he seek to pursue that claim overseas.

There remain two areas of concern in relation to s 75 and credit cards. First, many consumers now pay for holidays with credit cards but it is not always clear whether the travel agent is the agent of the debtor or the agent of the tour operator whose services the debtor wishes to buy. In the context of the debtor-creditor-supplier agreement, this may be crucial. Where payment is made direct to the tour operator or where the travel agent is clearly the agent of the tour

10 [1999] QB 1.

operator, the tour operator is the supplier and s 75 applies. If, on the other hand, the travel agent is the debtor's agent, it is he, not the tour operator who is taken to be the supplier and so, if the tour operator is in breach of contract in failing to provide a holiday, it is not the supplier/travel agent who is in breach of contract and s 75 will be inapplicable. The OFT has recognised that s 75 may not apply in the latter case[11] and, at present, it is clearly prudent for consumers to pay the tour operator directly and thus remove any doubt that the creditor will be liable for breaches by the tour operator/supplier.

Second, there is the difficulty caused by two credit cards being issued on a single account, eg to a husband and wife, where it seems that only the principal cardholder can be regarded as a debtor under s 75. The OFT considers that the second cardholder acts as an agent of the principal cardholder[12] and so claims under s 75 in relation to purchases made by the second cardholder should be pursued by the principal cardholder, but the matter is not free from doubt.

WHAT IS THE EXTENT OF THE 'LIKE CLAIM'?

Section 75 provides that, if the debtor has a claim against the supplier for misrepresentation or breach of contract 'he shall have a like claim against the creditor, who, with the supplier, shall accordingly be jointly and severally liable to the debtor'. The extent of the 'like claim' is somewhat in doubt as the Act does not define this notion but the decision in *Jarrett v Barclays Bank plc*,[13] above, stresses that the claim against the creditor cannot be *identical* to that against the supplier.

It is tolerably clear that the debtor has the same claim against the creditor that he has against the supplier and so s 75 is intended to make the creditor vicariously liable for the supplier's default under the contract of supply. It follows that a claim for damages for misrepresentation or breach of contract against the supplier is sustainable against the creditor and, if the debtor rejects the goods, he should be able to claim the return of the price from the creditor. But if the debtor can rescind the contract of supply, does he have a right to rescind the credit agreement itself? In the Scottish case *United Dominions Trust Ltd v Taylor*,[14] a finance company lent money to Taylor for the purchase of a car from a motor dealer, the contract being a debtor-creditor-supplier agreement within the CCA, s 12(b). Taylor claimed to have rejected the car for breach of contract and misrepresentation by the dealer and he refused to pay any instalments under the finance agreement. The finance company sought to enforce the contract of loan against Taylor but the Sheriff Principal held that, as Taylor had a claim to rescind the contract of sale, he had a 'like claim' to rescind the credit agreement even though 'the creditor has given no grounds for rescission of the loan contract'.[15]

Taylor's case has met with much criticism and it is strange that s 56(1)(c) and (2) were not argued by Taylor, ie the supplier's misrepresentations which induced the credit agreement were deemed to be made by the supplier as agent

---

11 See *Connected Lender Liability* (OFT 097, March 1994), paras 5.11-5.17.
12 See *Connected Lender Liability* (OFT 097, March 1994), paras 5.19-5.20.
13 [1999] QB 1.
14 1980 SLT (Sh Ct) 28; followed in *Forward Trust Ltd v Hornsby* [1996] CCLR 18.
15 1980 SLT (Sh Ct) 28 at 31, per the Sheriff Principal (R Reid QC).

of the creditor thus allowing the debtor to rescind the credit agreement or giving him a complete defence when sued by the creditor. As regards s 75, Davidson[16] stresses that the word 'claim' is indicative that the debtor's rights are limited to monetary compensation whereas 'right' or 'remedy' would be apposite if the conclusion reached in *Taylor* had been intended by the CCA. Moreover, as Goode[17] points out, the liability of the creditor is joint and several with the supplier but a claim to rescind the credit agreement is not one for which any joint and several liability on the part of the supplier can arise. Although the outcome in *Taylor's* case is questionable, Diamond[18] emphasised that the same result could have been achieved under s 75 by the debtor's claiming against the creditor for the return of the price (ie the claim available against the supplier) and an indemnity against any liability to interest or other charges for credit.

SECTION 75 DOES NOT APPLY TO A DEBTOR-CREDITOR AGREEMENT

It is plain that s 75 is a potent remedy for the debtor under debtor-creditor-supplier agreements within s 12(b) or (c). In contrast, where there is a debtor-creditor agreement there are no arrangements between the creditor and any supplier and s 75 has no application. For example, the creditor might lend the debtor £15,000 and hand the money directly to the debtor. If he then uses the money to buy a car from the supplier/seller and there are no arrangements between the creditor and the supplier, there is no question of the creditor's being liable to the debtor should the car prove not to be of satisfactory quality. Here the agreement between debtor and creditor is a debtor-creditor agreement and it would make no difference if the creditor paid the amount of the loan direct to the supplier, provided that there were no pre-existing arrangements between the creditor and the supplier and no contemplation of any future arrangements between them.

OVERLAP AND INTER-RELATION BETWEEN SECTION 75 AND SECTION 56

Sections 75 and 56 function in different ways. In a three-party, debtor-creditor-supplier agreement, s 75 simply shifts the supplier's liability under the supply contract onto the creditor. In the situations where s 56 applies (a much wider range of situations than those within s 75), the section provides that the negotiator's statements and acts are made as the deemed agent of the creditor. It follows that s 56 is important primarily as regards statements made by the negotiator in relation to the credit agreement, in that they may become terms of that agreement or render the creditor liable in misrepresenation. In this latter situation, should the negotiator/supplier have misrepresented the position under the credit agreement *only*, the creditor would not be liable under s 75, as there would be neither a breach of the *supply* agreement nor any misrepresentation regarding that supply agreement.

There is, however, some overlap between s 75 and s 56(1)(c) as both sections apply to three-party, debtor-creditor-supplier agreements within s 12(b) and

16 'The Missing Linked Transaction' (1980) 96 LQR 343.
17 See Goode, *Consumer Credit Law* (1989), para 16.51.
18 *Commercial and Consumer Credit: An Introduction* (1982), p 269.

(c). Consider the example of a three-party, debtor-creditor-supplier agreement for the sale of a car to the debtor by a car dealer/supplier, the cost being financed by the creditor in this connected loan situation where the creditor and supplier have existing business arrangements. Assume that the seller induced the debtor to enter into the credit agreement by falsely representing the car's age, mileage and its fitness for the debtor's purpose and, not long after the conclusion of the contract, he became insolvent. Here the debtor would have concurrent claims against the creditor under s 56 and s 75 because (i) the misrepresentation has certainly induced the credit agreement (s 56); and (ii) there is also a misrepresentation or breach of contract as regards the supply contract, ie the sale of the car (s 75). It is thus clear that, with connected loans and credit card transactions, the debtor has access to unrivalled and all-encompassing remedies.

EXCLUSION OF LIABILITY AND SECTION 75

Any attempt by the parties to contract-out of s 75 is void under s 173 but, of course, if the supplier is able effectively to exclude or restrict his liability to the debtor for misrepresentation or breach of contract in the contract of supply, the exclusion or restriction can be utilised by the creditor if the 'like claim' is made against him under s 75. The creditor could not insert a term in the credit agreement attempting to restrict the rights of the debtor under the supply contract, because this ploy is prevented by the Unfair Contract Terms Act 1977, s 10.

The liability of the creditor for defective goods in hire-purchase agreements

It will be remembered that, in hire-purchase, the dealer sells the goods to the creditor/finance company which lets them on hire-purchase terms to the debtor. There is no direct contract between the debtor and the dealer but, as discussed earlier, there might be a collateral contract or the dealer might incur personal liability in tort for deceit or negligence and, undoubtedly, for negligent misstatement at common law which causes financial loss. Additionally, the dealer is a 'credit-broker' or 'negotiator' within the CCA, s 56 and so representations made while negotiating the hire-purchase agreement are deemed to be made by him as the agent of the creditor. Section 75 does not apply to hire-purchase, however, as the debtor has direct remedies against the creditor/supplier under the hire-purchase contract.

It is with the obligations owed by the creditor/supplier to the debtor in hire-purchase that this part of the text is concerned. The principal obligations of the creditor as to title, quality and fitness for purpose of the goods depended, originally, on the rather uncertain common law. Although terms were implied into hire-purchase agreements at common law, many of the older decisions on bailments and simple hire were unclear as to the nature and extent of the duties owed. There was, for example, no authority at common law as to whether a term regarding the merchantability of the goods could be implied into a contract of hire-purchase and, likewise, the development of the implied condition as to fitness for purpose in hire-purchase was hindered by the common law's emphasis upon *laissez-faire* ideals and *caveat emptor*.[19] Statutory implied terms were introduced in the Hire-Purchase Act 1938 and this policy was continued in the later Acts concerned with hire-purchase but not all agreements were within the Acts and so there were no statutory terms implied into some agreements – the Hire Purchase Act 1965, for example, applied only where the hire-purchase price was not more than £2,000 and the bailee was not a body corporate.

The Supply of Goods (Implied Terms) Act 1973, ss 8-11,[20] import into *every*[1] hire-purchase agreement a range of implied terms relating to title, satisfactory quality and fitness for purpose of the goods and their correspondence with description and sample. These statutory obligations are almost identical to those in ss 12-15 of the SGA 1979.[2] Moreover, the controls on the exclusion of the implied terms (UCTA 1977, ss 6 and 12)[3] apply to both the sale of goods and hire-purchase. It should be re-emphasised that the debtor's claim for breach of the implied terms which are analysed below must be pursued against the creditor/finance company and not against the dealer who arranged the hire-purchase transaction.

Finally, it is quite possible that the creditor could agree to perform a service in relation to the goods, eg install the goods in the debtor's premises, and then the Supply of Goods and Services Act 1982 imports certain terms into that contract which are also very similar in content to the implied terms in the SGA.

IMPLIED TERMS AS TO TITLE

The Supply of Goods (Implied Terms) Act 1973, s 8 provides:

'(1) In every hire-purchase agreement, other than one to which subsection (2) below applies, there is –
(a) an implied condition on the part of the creditor that he will have a right to sell the goods at the time when the property is to pass; and
(b) an implied term that –
  (i) the goods are free, and will remain free until the time when the property is to pass, from any charge or encumbrance not disclosed or known to the person to whom the goods are bailed or (in Scotland) hired before the agreement is made, and
  (ii) that person will enjoy quiet possession of the goods except so far as it may be disturbed by any person entitled to the benefit of any charge or encumbrance so disclosed or known.
(2) In a hire-purchase agreement, in the case of which there appears from the agreement or is to be inferred from the circumstances of the agreement an intention

---

19 See eg *Robertson v Amazon Tug and Lighterage Co* (1881) 7 QBD 598 where there were *obiter dicta* to the effect that, in the hire of a specific chattel, there was no implied condition of fitness, even though the owner knew the purpose of the hire. It was not until 1962 that this notion was finally excised from the common law in the decision in *Yeoman Credit Ltd v Apps* [1962] 2 QB 508.

20 Re-enacted with minor amendments by the CCA 1974 (see s 192 and Sch 4, para 35) and amended by the Sale and Supply of Goods Act 1994 to keep the implied terms in harmony with those in the SGA 1979.

1 These implied terms apply irrespective of the amount which is financed, whether or not the debtor is a corporation and are *not* limited to hire-purchase agreements which are regulated agreements within the CCA 1974.

2 See Chs 19-21.

3 See Ch 25.

that the creditor should transfer only such title as he or a third person may have, there is –

(a) an implied term that all charges or encumbrances known to the creditor and not known to the person to whom the goods are bailed or hired have been disclosed to that person before the agreement is made; and

(b) an implied term that neither –
   (i) the creditor; nor
   (ii) in a case where the parties to the agreement intend that any title which may be transferred shall be only such title as a third person may have, that person; nor
   (iii) anyone claiming through or under the creditor or that third person otherwise than under a charge or encumbrance disclosed or known to the person to whom the goods are bailed or hired, before the agreement is made; will disturb the quiet possession of the person to whom the goods are bailed or hired.

(3) As regards England and Wales and Northern Ireland, the term implied by subsection (1)(a) above is a condition and the terms implied by subsections (1)(b), (2)(a) and (2)(b) above are warranties.'

It will be noticed that, under s 8(1)(a), the creditor need have a right to sell the goods *only* at the time that property is to pass to the debtor but, at common law, there is an implied condition in hire-purchase that the creditor should be capable of conferring title both at the time of the *delivery*[4] of the goods to the debtor *and* at the time of the exercise of the option to purchase when *property is to pass* to the debtor.[5] The common law rule was sometimes criticised as being too stringent in that the debtor acquires ownership only on the exercise of the option to purchase and it is thus unnecessary for the creditor to have title before that time[6] but in a continuing contract such as hire-purchase, it is obviously reasonable for the debtor to have an assurance on delivery of the goods that the creditor has title and that he may therefore make instalment payments with a degree of confidence. Moreover, the debtor might wish to exercise the option to purchase immediately after the goods have been delivered to him. In any event, the common law rule is preserved by s 15(4) of the 1973 Act[7] and so the debtor can invoke the wider common law rule *unless* it is excluded in the agreement. However, any contract term seeking to exclude or restrict the statutory implied condition in s 8 is void under s 6 of the UCTA.[8]

It is also necessary to refer to common law for the remedy available to the debtor if the creditor is in breach of the statutory or common law implied condition as to title. If, at either of the times specified above, the creditor's title is defective, the debtor is entitled to repudiate the agreement and recover from the creditor any money paid by way of deposit and/or instalments as money had and received for a consideration that has wholly failed. In such a case, the law's view of the

---

4 In *conditional sale* agreements, the SGA, s 12 governs the position regarding title and so the seller need have title *only* at the time that property is to pass; there is no term implied at common law that title be vested in the seller at the date of delivery to the purchaser.

5 *Mercantile Union Guarantee Corpn Ltd v Wheatley* [1938] 1 KB 490; *Warman v Southern Counties Car Finance Corpn Ltd* [1949] 2 KB 576.

6 See Dugdale, 'Hire-Purchase Agreements – Implied Condition as to Title' (1959) 35 NZLJ 45.

7 Section 15(4) provides: 'Nothing in sections 8 to 13 ... shall prejudice the operation of ... any rule of law whereby any term, other than one relating to quality or fitness, is to be implied in any hire-purchase agreement'.

8 The incorporation of such a term in a hire-purchase agreement may also be a criminal offence, see the Consumer Transactions (Restrictions on Statements) Order 1976, SI 1976/1813.

position is that the basis of the hire-purchase agreement, the option to purchase, has gone. As in the decisions on the sale of goods, this breach has Draconian consequences[9] and the money paid by the debtor may still be recovered even though, after discovering the defective title, he continues to pay the instalments or seeks to exercise the option to purchase, thereby affirming the transaction. Moreover, the creditor is not entitled to set-off an amount for the use of the goods that the debtor has had and so the rule here is the same as that in the sale of goods.[10] In *Warman v Southern Counties Car Finance Corpn Ltd*,[11] the plaintiff (P) had taken a car on hire-purchase from the defendants (D) who were described in the contract as owners. P paid four out of twelve monthly instalments and then learnt that someone else was the true owner of the car. He did, however, pay the balance of the instalments and purported to exercise his option to purchase. After the true owner demanded the return of the car, P surrendered it to him and then claimed damages from D, these being all the payments he had made to D in respect of the car and the cost of insurance and repairs done to it. Finnemore J upheld the claim and disallowed D's counterclaim for 'hire rent' for the period (8 months) during which the plaintiff had used the car.

In some cases, the creditor may acquire title to the goods by purchasing them from their true owner before the debtor exercises the option to purchase. In *Karflex Ltd v Poole*,[12] this acquisition of title was held not to prevent the debtor from recovering all the sums which he had paid, this being justified because the creditor had been unable to confer a good title at the start of the contract. In *Karflex*, a dominant fact was that the creditor acquired title *after* the action was commenced against the debtor for default and the agreement had been terminated. In most cases where the creditor subsequently acquires title, this will feed the defective title and so it is logical that a debtor would have to exercise his right to repudiate for breach of condition *before* title is fed to him and his defective title is rectified.[13] This question remains undecided, however, and reference should be made to Chapter 19 where the issue is covered in more detail.

Finally, it should be noted that there are implied warranties in s 8 relating to freedom from encumbrances, quiet possession and transfer of a limited title by the creditor. As in the sale of goods, the scope of the warranties of freedom from encumbrances and quiet possession is unclear[14] but, in any event, it is apt that the debtor under a hire-purchase contract should be granted the same protection as the buyer or hirer[15] of goods.

IMPLIED CONDITION AS TO DESCRIPTION

The Supply of Goods (Implied Terms) Act 1973, s 9, provides:

'(1) Where under a hire purchase agreement goods are bailed or (in Scotland) hired by description, there is an implied condition that the goods will correspond with the

---

9   See Ch 19 where the cases on sales of goods and hire-purchase are considered.
10   As established in *Rowland v Divall* [1923] 2 KB 500.
11   [1949] 2 KB 576.
12   [1933] 2 KB 251.
13   *Butterworth v Kingsway Motors Ltd* [1954] 1 WLR 1286 (see Ch 19).
14   See Ch 19.
15   There is ancient authority that the warranty of quiet possession exists in simple hire (see *Lee v Atkinson and Brooks* (1609) Cro Jac 236) and such a warranty is implied by the Supply of Goods and Services Act 1982, s 2(2).

description, and if under the agreement the goods are bailed or hired by reference to a sample as well as a description, it is not sufficient that the bulk of the goods corresponds with the sample if the goods do not also correspond with the description.

(1A) As regards England and Wales and Northern Ireland, the term implied by subsection (1) above is a condition.

(2) Goods shall not be prevented from being bailed or hired by description by reason only that, being exposed for sale, bailment or hire, they are selected by the person to whom they are bailed or hired.'

There is every reason to suppose that the principles which are pertinent to sales by description under the SGA 1979, s 13,[16] are equally applicable to hire-purchase and s 9 of the 1973 Act. The dominant, modern theme which permeates the decisions in the sale of goods is that the implied condition of description in the SGA, s 13 will only be breached if the goods which are delivered are different in kind or substance from those promised under the contract. Indeed, this notion is evident in some of the decisions on hire-purchase. In *Astley Industrial Trust Ltd v Grimley*,[17] Upjohn LJ[18] said that 'the lender must lend that which he contracts to lend and not something which is essentially different' and so delivery of a defective Bedford tipping lorry was held not to amount to a breach of the implied term as to description as the thing delivered was still a lorry, albeit a defective one.

IMPLIED CONDITIONS AS TO QUALITY AND FITNESS FOR PURPOSE

The Supply of Goods (Implied Terms) Act 1973, s 10 provides:

'(1) Except as provided by this section and section 11 below and subject to the provisions of any other enactment ... there is no implied term as to the quality or fitness for any particular purpose of goods bailed or (in Scotland) hired under a hire-purchase agreement.

(2) Where the creditor bails or hires goods under a hire-purchase agreement in the course of a business, there is an implied term that the goods supplied under the agreement are of satisfactory quality.

(2A) For the purposes of this Act, goods are of satisfactory quality if they meet the standard that a reasonable person would regard as satisfactory, taking account of any description of the goods, the price (if relevant) and all the other relevant circumstances.

(2B) For the purposes of this Act, the quality of goods includes their state and condition and the following (among others) are in appropriate cases aspects of the quality of goods –
  (a) fitness for all the purposes for which goods of the kind in question are commonly supplied,
  (b) appearance and finish,
  (c) freedom from minor defects,
  (d) safety, and
  (e) durability.

(2C) The term implied by subsection (2) above does not extend to any matter making the quality of goods unsatisfactory –
  (a) which is specifically drawn to the attention of the person to whom the goods are bailed or hired before the agreement is made,
  (b) where that person examines the goods before the agreement is made, which that examination ought to reveal, or

16 See Ch 20.
17 [1963] 1 WLR 584.
18 [1963] 1 WLR 584 at 597.

(c) where the goods are bailed or hired by reference to a sample, which would have been apparent on a reasonable examination of the sample.

(3) Where the creditor bails or hires goods under a hire-purchase agreement in the course of a business and the person to whom the goods are bailed or hired, expressly or by implication, makes known –

(a) to the creditor in the course of negotiations conducted by the creditor in relation to the making of the hire-purchase agreement, or

(b) to a credit-broker in the course of negotiations conducted by that broker in relation to goods sold by him to the creditor before forming the subject matter of the hire-purchase agreement,

any particular purpose for which the goods are being bailed or hired, there is an implied term that the goods supplied under the agreement are reasonably fit for that purpose, whether or not that is a purpose for which such goods are commonly supplied, except where the circumstances show that the person to whom the goods are bailed or hired buyer does not rely, or that it is unreasonable for him to rely, on the skill or judgment of the creditor or credit-broker.

(4) An implied term as to quality or fitness for a particular purpose may be annexed to a hire-purchase agreement by usage.

(5) The preceding provisions of this section apply to a hire-purchase agreement made by a person who in the course of a business is acting as agent for the creditor as they apply to an agreement made by the creditor in the course of a business, except where the creditor is not bailing or hiring in the course of a business and either the person to whom the goods are bailed or hired knows that fact or reasonable steps are taken to bring it to the notice of that person before the agreement is made.

(6) In subsection (3) above and this subsection –

(a) 'credit-broker' means a person acting in the course of a business of credit brokerage;

(b) 'credit brokerage' means the effecting of introductions of individuals desiring to obtain credit –

(i) to persons carrying on any business so far as it relates to the provision of credit, or

(ii) to other persons engaged in credit brokerage.

(7) As regards England and Wales and Northern Ireland, the terms implied by subsections (2) and (3) above are conditions.'

It will be noticed that s 10 is, in substance, identical to the SGA, s 14 and the alterations in the wording are simply to make the section applicable to hire-purchase, eg 'creditor' and 'credit-broker'. It is astonishing that, at common law, there was no authority as to whether an implied term of merchantability existed in hire-purchase. It is now clear that the debtor's position is equated with that of the buyer in a sale of goods and he thus has a sophisticated level of protection under the two implied conditions of satisfactory quality and fitness for purpose in s 10.

It should be stressed that, for the condition of fitness for purpose in s 10 to apply, s 10(3) provides that the debtor can inform *either* the creditor *or* the credit-broker in the course of negotiations and so it is sufficient if, in hire-purchase, the debtor informs the dealer of his particular purpose. The requirement that either party could be notified was introduced by the Hire-Purchase Act 1964 to avoid the trap that only notification to the finance company or its agent would suffice and, at common law, the dealer was not the finance company's agent for that purpose.[19]

---

19 *Astley Industrial Trust v Grimley* [1963] 1 WLR 584.

However, it will be noticed that s 10(6)(b) defines 'credit brokerage' as 'the effecting of introductions of *individuals* desiring to obtain credit' and so where the debtor is a corporation, the particular purpose will have to be made known to the creditor and thus, inadvertently, the CCA (see Sch 4, para 35) has returned the corporate debtor to the position before the 1964 Act.[20]

IMPLIED CONDITION AS TO SAMPLE

The Supply of Goods (Implied Terms) Act 1973, s 11, provides:

'(1) Where under a hire-purchase agreement goods are bailed or (in Scotland) hired by reference to a sample, there is an implied term –
(a) that the bulk will correspond with the sample in quality; and
(b) that the person to whom the goods are bailed or hired will have a reasonable opportunity of comparing the bulk with the sample; and
(c) that the goods will be free from any defect, making their quality unsatisfactory, which would not be apparent on reasonable examination of the sample.
(2) As regards England and Wales and Northern Ireland, the term implied by subsection (1) above is a condition. '

Again, s 11 approximates very closely to the SGA, s 15.[1]

IMPLIED TERM AS TO DELIVERY

There is no implied term in the 1973 Act relating to delivery in hire-purchase but it is undoubtedly an implied term at common law that the creditor must deliver the goods to the debtor and, moreover, it seems that the rules on the manner, place and time of delivery are broadly similar to those in the sale of goods. The hiring commences only when the goods are delivered to the debtor and he accepts delivery and, if the debtor wrongfully refuses to accept delivery, it follows that the creditor cannot recover instalments due under the contract but, instead, his remedy lies in a claim for damages.[2]

The duty of delivery is a fundamental one so that breach of the duty entitles the debtor to repudiate the contract.[3] In *Bentworth Finance Ltd v Lubert*,[4] the debtor acquired a car on hire-purchase from the plaintiff finance company and, after taking delivery of it, she did not use it as it was unlicensed and the log book had not been delivered to her. By that stage, the dealer had disappeared. The debtor did not pay any instalments and, when the finance company sued for arrears, the Court of Appeal held that the agreement was subject to the suspensive condition that the log-book should be delivered and thus the debtor was not liable as the agreement had never come into operation. If the creditor fails to deliver the goods, the debtor's remedy lies in damages and, unless the goods are unique or special, he will not obtain specific performance. The measure of damages for non-delivery is presumably determined in the same way as in the sale of goods where the seller fails to deliver.

---

20 See also the CCA, s 189(1), which excludes corporations from its definition of 'individual'.
1 See Ch 21.
2 *British Stamp and Ticket Automatic Delivery Co Ltd v Haynes* [1921] 1 KB 377; *National Cash Register Co Ltd v Stanley* [1921] 3 KB 292.
3 *Charterhouse Credit Co Ltd v Tolly* [1963] 2 QB 683, 708 per Upjohn LJ.
4 [1968] 1 QB 680.

EXCLUSION CLAUSES

At common law, the implied obligations of the creditor could be excluded or modified by the express terms of the hire-purchase agreement but the courts developed various principles by which they sought to limit the effect of exclusion clauses. Indeed, many hire-purchase decisions were pivotal in developing the potent common law rule that exclusion clauses could not absolve a defendant from the consequences of a fundamental breach[5] and this was a valuable weapon for the consumer. It is now clear, however, that there is no common law rule preventing absolutely a suitably drafted exclusion clause from excluding liability for fundamental breach.[6]

All the Hire-Purchase Acts contained restrictions on contracting-out of the statutory implied terms and this policy was continued in the Supply of Goods (Implied Terms) Act 1973. The present law is contained in the Unfair Contract Terms Act 1977 (UCTA) and, just as the statutory implied terms in hire-purchase are virtually identical to those in the sale of goods, the controls on exclusion clauses in hire-purchase mirror those which apply in the sale of goods.[7] By the UCTA, s 6(1)(b), the implied terms as to title in s 8 of the 1973 Act *cannot* be excluded or restricted by any contract term: as in the sale of goods, this is an all-embracing prohibition. As regards the terms implied by ss 9–11 of the 1973 Act, the UCTA, s 6(2) provides that they cannot be excluded or restricted by reference to any contract term as against a person 'dealing as consumer' and this latter notion is defined in the UCTA, s 12.[8]

In relation to non-consumer agreements, ie where the debtor does not 'deal as consumer', the UCTA, s 6(3) provides that liability under ss 9-11 of the 1973 Act can be excluded or restricted by reference to a contract term but only in so far as the term satisfies the requirement of reasonableness.

It should also be noted that the Unfair Terms in Consumer Contracts Regulations 1999 are drawn in very wide terms and certainly apply to exclusion clauses in contracts of hire-purchase between creditor and debtor; reference should be made to Chapter 25 where the Regulations are considered.

Remedies of the debtor

In most respects, the debtor's remedies approximate to those of the buyer in a sale of goods. Accordingly, if the creditor is in breach of an express or implied warranty, the debtor is limited to a claim in damages, but breach of an express or implied condition of the contract entitles the debtor to treat the contract as repudiated and claim damages. Where the goods delivered are so defective that they are worthless or their failure to correspond with description is so fundamental

---

5 See *Karsales (Harrow) Ltd v Wallis* [1956] 1 WLR 936; *Yeoman Credit Ltd v Apps* [1962] 2 QB 508; *Charterhouse Credit Co Ltd v Tolly* [1963] 2 QB 683; *Unity Finance Ltd v Hammond* (1965) 109 Sol Jo 70; *Farnworth Finance Facilities v Attryde* [1970] 1 WLR 1053.
6 *Photo Production Ltd v Securicor Transport Ltd* [1980] AC 827; see Ch 25 for a consideration of fundamental breach.
7 See Ch 25 for detail on exclusion clauses.
8 See also the Consumer Transactions (Restrictions on Statements) Order 1976 (SI 1976/1813; as amended by SI 1978/127) which makes it an offence for a business to attempt to exclude the hire-purchase implied terms in a consumer transaction.

that they differ in identity from the goods which were promised, there is authority that the debtor can recover all sums paid as upon a total failure of consideration.[9] More often than not, the debtor will have received some benefit from the contract so that there will not be a total failure of consideration and then, as stated, he will be able to treat the contract as discharged and claim damages.

It will be recalled that the SGA, s 15A now limits the non-consumer buyer's right to reject the goods for breach of the implied terms in the SGA, ss 13-15 where the breach is 'so slight that it would be unreasonable for him to reject them' and a corresponding provision is now found in s 11A of the Supply of Goods (Implied Terms) Act 1973. Accordingly, the non-consumer debtor[10] can no longer reject the goods for slight breaches of the terms implied by ss 9-11 of the 1973 Act.

LOSS OF THE DEBTOR'S RIGHT TO REJECT THE GOODS

In hire-purchase agreements, there are no rules equivalent to those in the SGA on the buyer's loss of the right to reject the goods once he has accepted them.[11] Most particularly, this means that the technical rules on deemed acceptance do not apply in hire-purchase but, instead, the debtor must *affirm* the contract if he is to lose the right to reject the goods and be limited to a claim in damages.[12] Affirmation differs from acceptance in that affirmation requires *knowledge* of the defects and a subsequent *election* to proceed with the contract[13] whereas acceptance in the sale of goods can occur where the buyer is unaware of latent defects in the goods but, for example, retains the goods for an unreasonable period of time.[14]

Affirmation in hire-purchase will occur where the debtor evinces an intention to continue with the agreement after he is aware of a breach of condition on the part of the creditor and, for example, continues to pay instalments under the agreement. In *Jackson v Chrysler Acceptances Ltd,*[15] for example, the debtor was held to have affirmed the contract after using a defective car between April and November 1975, paying instalments on it, driving it for 6,000 miles and agreeing to have it repaired.[16] That being said, there are several decisions where the notion of affirmation has been construed liberally in the debtor's favour and

---

9   *Karsales (Harrow) Ltd v Wallis* [1956] 1 WLR 936; *Yeoman Credit Ltd v Apps* [1962] 2 QB 508;*Unity Finance Ltd v Hammond* (1965) 109 Sol Jo 70.
10 Section 11A(4) of the 1973 Act provides that 'dealing as consumer' is to be construed in the same way as in the UCTA 1977, s 12.
11 See the SGA, ss 11(4) and 35, considered in Ch 23.
12 The Law Commissions recommend no change to the existing law that there are different rules in sale and hire-purchase: see *Sale and Supply of Goods* (Law Com No 160, Scot Law Com No 104, Cm 137 (1987)), paras 5.6-5.9; 5.43-5.46.
13 *Farnworth Finance Facilities Ltd v Attryde* [1970] 1 WLR 1053, 1059 per Lord Denning MR.
14 The rules on affirmation in hire-purchase apply also to conditional sale agreements provided that the buyer 'deals as consumer' within the meaning of the UCTA, s 12. See below where the terms implied in conditional sale are considered.
15 [1978] RTR 474.
16 See also *Charterhouse Credit Co Ltd v Tolly* [1963] 2 QB 683 (affirmation between December and April even though the car was used on only two occasions); *UCB Leasing Ltd v Holtom* [1987] RTR 362 (affirmation where a new Alfa Romeo had been driven for 8,000 miles during seven months).

the indulgence shown by the courts bears no resemblance to the strict approach taken in some cases on the sale of goods. In *Farnworth Finance Facilities Ltd v Attryde*,[17] a motor cycle which the debtor held on hire-purchase proved to be defective and although (i) he used it for four months during which he drove it for 4,000 miles; (ii) repeated attempts were made to repair it; and (iii) he maintained his instalment payments, the Court of Appeal held that he had not affirmed the contract and could reject the motor cycle when, finally, its chain broke. In an interesting twist of logic, the court considered that, instead of amounting to affirmation, his conduct showed that he was prepared to affirm the contract *only* if the motor cycle were put right.[18]

Moreover, after the startling decision in *Yeoman Credit Ltd v Apps*,[19] the law appeared to be that the debtor might affirm the contract and nevertheless reject the goods if they were later found to be defective. There the car which was the subject of the hire-purchase agreement had a conglomeration of latent defects and, although the debtor complained to the finance company, he continued to pay instalments in the hope that he could persuade the finance company to pay for some of the repairs. Subsequently, the debtor rejected the car and paid no further instalments. The Court of Appeal held that (i) the debtor had affirmed the contract by paying instalments after delivery; (ii) there had not been a total failure of consideration and the finance company could thus retain all sums paid and recover the amounts that were owing at the date of rejection; but (iii) at the date of the debtor's rejection the finance company was still in breach and this 'continuing breach' rendered the rejection lawful meaning that the debtor did not have to pay any further instalments and could recover £100 in damages. Holroyd Pearce LJ considered that hire-purchase was 'more analogous to a simple hiring than to a purchase'.[20] While a contract of hire or a lease of goods may impose a continuing obligation on the owner to maintain and repair the goods, for example, it has always been difficult to see how a right of rejection can exist after a valid affirmation of the contract and how a 'continuing breach' can possibly be justified in hire-purchase in the absence of a continuing obligation or duty.[1] When the finance company *is* in breach of condition, the debtor has his choice of remedies, but the finance company does not act as a perpetual guarantor of the quality and fitness for purpose of the goods supplied. The later decision of the Court of Appeal in *UCB Leasing Ltd v Holtom*,[2] stressed that the right of rejection is lost once affirmation has occurred and Holroyd Pearce LJ's statement regarding continuous breaches was criticised and characterised as *obiter dictum*. *Holtom's* case thus correctly re-establishes that affirmation bars any subsequent rejection, the debtor then being limited to a claim in damages for breach of warranty, and effectively banishes the 'continuing breach' theory.

This may not, however, place the debtor in too detrimental a position. Where the debtor wrongfully rejects the goods, as in the *Yeoman* case, and is sued by the finance company for damages, he can nevertheless counterclaim for damages for

---

17 [1970] 1 WLR 1053.
18 See also *Porter v General Guarantee Corpn Ltd* [1982] RTR 384 (no affirmation in continuing negotiations for two months regarding the repair of a Ford Granada car); *Laurelgates Ltd v Lombard North Central Ltd* (1983) 133 NLJ 720 (no affirmation during eight months of continuing repairs to a Daimler Sovereign car).
19 [1962] 2 QB 508.
20 [1962] 2 QB 508 at 522.
 1 See Goode, *Hire Purchase Law and Practice* (2nd edn, 1970), pp 456-461.
 2 [1987] RTR 362.

the finance company's breach of contract in supplying the defective goods. In the *Yeoman* case, the basis of the debtor's £100 damages was also criticisable as it was based on the cost of putting the car into good working order but this could have no significance when he had *rejected* the car[3] and, as he had not actually done any repairs, he appeared to recover damages for a loss which he had not suffered. The measure of damages in this context is not easy to formulate but in *Charterhouse Credit Co Ltd v Tolly*,[4] the Court of Appeal considered that the correct measure was 'the cost of hiring a similar [chattel] on similar terms as to the eventual option to purchase'.[5] There the debtor had elected to affirm the contract after discovering that the vehicle delivered was unroadworthy and the finance company terminated the contract for default in payment. The debtor counterclaimed for breach of contract and his measure of damages was the amount paid by him under the contract and the expenses he actually incurred in attempting to repair the goods, minus the value of the benefit received by him while the goods were in his possession.[6] This measure of damages thus coincided with what would have been awarded had the debtor himself treated the contract as discharged.

The buyer's remedies in credit-sale and conditional sale

It will be remembered that, in a conditional sale, the buyer agrees to buy the goods at the outset and he also obtains possession, but the agreement expressly provides that property in the goods will not pass to the buyer until he has paid all the instalments of the price. In credit-sale, the price of the goods is paid in instalments and so credit is extended to the buyer, but there is *no* condition suspending the passing of property in the goods to the buyer and so the sale is absolute within the SGA, s 2(3).

In both conditional sale and credit-sale, the statutory implied terms relating to title, description, quality and fitness for purpose are those contained in the SGA 1979, ss 12-15. Reference should be made to Chapter 32 where both these types of sale are considered in more detail and also to Chapters 19-21 where the SGA implied terms are analysed.

There are several points concerning conditional sale and credit-sale which might helpfully be reiterated here. First, the SGA, s 14(3)(b) allows the buyer in both these types of sale to communicate any particular purpose for which the goods are required to the *credit-broker* who sold the goods to the seller who, in turn, sold them to the conditional sale or credit-sale buyers. Second, the rules on *affirmation* (as in hire-purchase, considered above) apply to the conditional sale buyer who 'deals as consumer' within the UCTA, s 12, and such a buyer is thus not bound by the rules in the sale of goods relating to acceptance of the goods and the correlative loss of the right to reject.[7] In this respect, conditional sale is thus equated with hire-purchase as the two types of agreement fulfil very similar

---

3 It would, of course, be relevant where the debtor *affirms* the contract and here the measure of damages would be the amount required to put the goods into a good state of repair together with damages for loss of use while they were being repaired: see *Charterhouse Credit Co Ltd v Tolly* [1963] 2 QB 683, 711-712 per Upjohn LJ.
4 [1963] 2 QB 683.
5 [1963] 2 QB 683 at 706, per Donovan LJ
6 This measure was followed in *UCB Leasing Ltd v Holtom* [1987] RTR 362, except that the debtor was also awarded £500 for 'inconvenience and stress'.
7 See the Supply of Goods (Implied Terms) Act 1973, s 14(1) and (2).

purposes. No such generosity is extended to the credit-sale buyer as such a buyer is comparable to a normal purchaser of goods who pays in cash in a single payment: no condition suspends the passing of property to either the cash or credit-sale buyer. Third, the statutory implied terms in the SGA apply to both conditional sale and credit-sale even though the agreements may not be regulated consumer credit agreements within the CCA, eg where more than £25,000 credit is extended or where, in a credit-sale agreement (*not* a conditional sale) with a retailer, the buyer/debtor pays a deposit on goods and agrees to pay the remainder in three equal, consecutive monthly instalments.[8] Fourth, the statutory rules concerning the exclusion or restriction of the statutory implied terms in the SGA, are those in the UCTA 1977 and the Unfair Terms in Consumer Contracts Regulations 1999.

The hirer's remedies in consumer hire

The Supply of Goods and Services Act 1982 implies certain obligations into all contracts for the hire of goods (including consumer hire agreements) which bear a close resemblance to the obligations of sellers under the Sale of Goods Act 1979 and creditors in hire-purchase under the Supply of Goods (Implied Terms) Act 1973.

In s 7, there is an implied condition that the bailor has a right to transfer possession of the goods by way of hire for the period of the hire and an implied warranty of quiet possession. Section 8 implies a condition that, if the goods are hired by description, the goods will correspond with the description. Sections 9 and 10 imply conditions of satisfactory quality and fitness for purpose and an implied term, where goods are hired by reference to sample, that the bulk shall correspond with the sample. In harmony with the SGA 1979, s 15A, and the Supply of Goods (Implied Terms) Act 1973, s 11A, there is a newly-inserted s 10A in the Supply of Goods and Services Act 1982. Section 10A limits the non-consumer hirer's right to treat the contract as repudiated where it would be unreasonable to do so for 'slight' breaches of ss 8, 9 and 10 of the 1982 Act. Such a slight breach is now to be treated as a breach of warranty, not a breach of condition.

Under the UCTA 1977, s 7, liability for breach of ss 8–10, above, cannot be excluded or restricted by reference to any contract term as against a person 'dealing as consumer'. As against a person dealing 'otherwise than as consumer', liability for breach of ss 8–10 can be excluded or restricted in so far as the term satisfies the reasonableness test in the UCTA. Liability for breach of s 7 of the 1982 Act can be excluded or restricted in both consumer and business contracts subject to the reasonableness test. Consumer hire is also subject to the Unfair Terms in Consumer Contracts Regulations 1999.

Rescission of the regulated agreement and the Consumer Credit Act, section 102

At common law, the general rule concerning rescission of a contract is that the injured party must communicate the rescission to the other party. This might

---

8 See the Consumer Credit (Exempt Agreements) Order 1989, SI 1989/869 (as amended).

prove difficult for a debtor in that he might not know with whom he should attempt to communicate and so the CCA, s 102, which applies to all regulated agreements, simplifies the process of rescission. Section 102(1) provides that certain persons are deemed to be the agent of the creditor or owner for the purpose of 'receiving any notice' rescinding the agreement which is 'served' by the debtor or hirer, viz (i) a credit-broker or supplier who was the negotiator in antecedent negotiations; and (ii) any person who, in the course of a business carried on by him, acted on behalf of the debtor or hirer in any negotiations for the agreement. These are exactly the same persons who are deemed to be agents for receiving notices of withdrawal (s 57(3)) and cancellation (s 69(6)) and the persons who are deemed agents within the specified categories were considered when the rights of withdrawal and cancellation were examined.[9]

Section 102(1) refers to the deemed agents' 'receiving' a 'notice' which is 'served' by the debtor or hirer. 'Notice' is defined in s 189(1) as 'notice in writing' and thus it is clear that a verbal communication of rescission will not suffice for s 102(1). It will be remembered that the deemed agents are also deemed to be under a contractual duty to the creditor or owner to transmit the notice to him forthwith (s 175) but it is suggested that the notice of rescission under s 102(1) will take effect upon receipt by the deemed agent.[10]

There is no definition of 'rescind' in s 102 but s 102(2) provides that 'rescind' does not include (a) service of a notice of cancellation; or (b) termination of an agreement under ss 99 or 101, or by the exercise of a right or power in that behalf expressly conferred by the agreement. It is suggested that 'rescission' under s 102 must encompass more than simply the remedy which is available in cases of fraud, misrepresentation, duress and undue influence. It should thus extend to the situation where the debtor or hirer rejects defective goods and seeks damages, ie where the debtor accepts a repudiatory breach by the other party.

9 Sections 57(3), 69(6) and 102(1) are the only provisions in the CCA which deem certain persons to be the agent of the creditor or owner for the receipt of notices.
10 The purpose of s 175 must be to *establish* the creditor's or owner's right to sue the *deemed* agent for breach of contract, ie if the creditor or owner suffers a loss as a consequence of the deemed agent's failure to act promptly, the latter can be liable for breach of this deemed contractual duty.

CHAPTER 36

Remedies of the creditor and owner

The creditor's remedies for breach of contract are still largely drawn from the common law and most have remained unaltered by the CCA although, as will be seen below, the Act has placed formidable barriers in the path of *enforcement* in order to protect the debtor and hirer. The restrictions on enforcement imposed by the CCA can be appreciated better when the substantive remedies available to the creditor are understood.

The creditor's remedies on the debtor's default in hire-purchase and conditional sale

A hire-purchase or conditional sale agreement will be terminated if the debtor commits a repudiatory breach of contract which is accepted by the creditor and, clearly, this occurs where the debtor renounces the agreement and refuses to comply with it.[1] Similarly, there is a repudiatory breach where the debtor wrongfully disposes of the goods to which the agreement relates.[2] If the breach does not amount to a renunciation of the contract, the creditor cannot treat the contract as repudiated and this could be the case where there is simply a failure to pay one or two instalments.[3] However, the agreement will usually make prompt payment of instalments of the essence and, in such a case, any default in payment will entitle the creditor to treat the contract as repudiated.[4] Indeed, the terms of the agreement invariably provide that the creditor can terminate the agreement for any breach by the debtor even though that breach does not constitute a repudiation of the agreement. It should be stressed, however, that the creditor need not terminate the contract for breach and, in the event of non-payment of instalments (undoubtedly the most frequently encountered breach), the creditor may always sue for arrears. In such a case, the creditor need not serve a default notice under s 87 (see later) where the agreement is regulated

---

1 *Overstone Ltd v Shipway* [1962] 1 WLR 117; *Yeoman Credit Ltd v Waragowski* [1961] 1 WLR 1124.
2 *Union Transport Finance Ltd v British Car Auctions* [1978] 2 All ER 385.
3 *Financings Ltd v Baldock* [1963] 2 QB 104.
4 *Lombard North Central plc v Butterworth* [1987] QB 527.

but, under s 93, he cannot claim interest on arrears which is higher than that payable under the contract generally, ie the contractual rate of interest.[5]

Consequences of termination on breach

On the termination of the agreement for breach of contract in hire-purchase and conditional sale, the general rule at common law is that the creditor may repossess the goods and is entitled to damages.

REPOSSESSION OF THE GOODS

It is a basic rule of bailment that any act which is inconsistent with that bailment, eg a sale or pledge of the goods, determines the bailment and the right to possession reverts to the bailor even if there is no express term in the contract to that effect.[6] Although the general rule is that the creditor may retake his goods where he has an immediate right to possession, this is a hazardous course of action which may open the creditor to an action in trespass or conversion unless he is absolutely sure of his ground. The circumspect creditor will commence proceedings to recover the goods and, in an action for wrongful interference with goods under the Torts (Interference with Goods) Act 1977, s 3, the court may make an order for delivery up of the goods, with or without the option to pay their value, and for payment of any 'consequential damages'. Alternatively and more likely, there can be a claim for damages alone. The measure of damages is normally the value of the goods but where the balance of payments outstanding is less than the value of the goods, the correct measure of damages is that outstanding balance at the date of conversion.[7] Moreover, if an award of damages means that the creditor obtains payment of the price earlier than he would otherwise have received it, a reduction is apt to take account of the accelerated payment.

It should be stressed that, where the agreement is regulated under the CCA, the goods may have become 'protected goods' under s 90 and, if the goods have achieved this status, the creditor has several obstacles to overcome should he seek to re-possess them.[8] Moreover, under s 92, the creditor cannot enter premises to retake possession of the goods without a court order, and s 92 applies whether or not the goods are 'protected'.

DAMAGES FOR BREACH OF CONTRACT BY THE DEBTOR

Any breach of the hire-purchase or conditional sale agreement entitles the creditor to sue for damages but the *measure* of the damages recoverable will depend upon whether or not the breach is repudiatory in nature.

5 If the agreement provides 'interest-free' credit, it seems that the debtor cannot be made to pay *any* default interest.
6 See *Bowmakers Ltd v Barnet Instruments Ltd* [1945] KB 65; *North Central Wagon and Finance Co Ltd v Graham* [1950] 2 KB 7; *Union Transport Finance Ltd British Car Auctions Ltd* [1978] 2 All ER 385.
7 *Wickham Holdings Ltd v Brooke House Motors Ltd* [1967] 1 WLR 295.
8 Protected goods are considered later in this chapter.

Repudiatory breach

Where the breach amounts to a repudiation, the measure of damages is in accordance with the principle established in *Yeoman Credit Ltd v Waragowski*.[9] There the plaintiffs let a van to the defendant on hire-purchase, the terms being an initial payment of £72 and 36 monthly instalments of £10 0s 9d with a further £1 to be paid on exercising the option to purchase. The total hire-purchase price was £434 7s 0d. The debtor paid the deposit and took delivery but paid none of the instalments. Six months later, in accordance with the terms of the agreement, the plaintiffs retook possession and then sold the van for £205. In an action against the debtor, the Court of Appeal held that the plaintiffs were entitled to arrears of instalments amounting to £60 4s 6d and, as damages for breach of contract, the difference between the total price less the £1 'option money' and the sum of the sale price obtained and the deposit and instalment arrears. The damages allowed, therefore, were £434 7s 0d (less £1) less (£205 plus £72 plus £60 4s 6d) = £96 2s 6d. It is apparent that, even though the agreement was terminated after only six months and judgment was obtained within one year, the creditor recovered damages which put him in the position that he would have been in had the agreement run its intended course. *Waragowski* was followed in *Overstone Ltd v Shipway*[10] but with one crucial alteration in approach: the Court of Appeal adopted the *Waragowski* measure of damages but held that, in an action of this kind, the finance company obtains accelerated receipt of its capital outlay and so, in order to put the creditor in the same position as if the contract had been performed, the damages should be reduced by an appropriate amount. Moreover, the creditor is under a duty to mitigate his loss and so he must obtain the best price which can reasonably be obtained should he, for example, repossess the goods and sell them.

Non-repudiatory breach

If the debtor has not repudiated the agreement but is merely in arrears with, say, two or three instalments, and the creditor exercises a contractual right to terminate the agreement, the creditor may claim against the debtor only the amount of instalments in arrears, damages for any failure on the part of the debtor to take reasonable care of the goods, and the cost of repossessing them. The creditor cannot, however, claim damages for loss of profit as he may do in a case of repudiation. In *Financings Ltd v Baldock*,[11] the plaintiffs let a truck under a hire-purchase agreement, the terms being an initial payment of £100 and 24 monthly instalments of £28 10s 3d. The total price was £772 16s 0d. The debtor paid the deposit and took delivery but failed to pay the first two instalments. He did inform the creditor, however, that he hoped to pay off the arrears. The creditor subsequently exercised the contractual right to end the agreement and repossess the truck. The Court of Appeal held that mere failure to pay two instalments did not constitute a repudiation of the agreement and that the plaintiffs were entitled to damages amounting to the two instalments in arrears only. The reason for this rule is that termination is due to the *creditor's* election to determine the contract rather than the debtor's breach and, consequently, the debtor reaps the corresponding benefit.

---

9   [1961] 1 WLR 1124.
10   [1962] 1 WLR 117.
11   [1963] 2 QB 104.

It is clearly to the debtor's advantage to state that he intends to pay off the arrears rather than repudiate the contract and, overall, there has been a distinct tendency for the courts to hold that the debtor's conduct is not repudiatory, thereby avoiding the swingeing consequences of the *Waragowski* decision. It is clear, for example, that the creditor cannot push the debtor into a corner and compel him to repudiate the contract. In *Eshun v Moorgate Mercantile Co Ltd*,[12] the debtor had paid £115 out of the total hire-purchase price of £405 17s 3d and, while the default notice stated, accurately, that he was £23 3s 6d in arrears, it added that 'unless we do hear from you with payment within the course of the next nine days ... we shall have no alternative but to assume that you do not wish to continue the hiring ... and are, in effect, terminating by repudiation'. The Court of Appeal held that the creditor could not force a repudiation on the debtor in this way, the notice was invalid and the creditor had no right to re-possess the goods. Accordingly, the creditor was liable in damages to the debtor.[13]

However, it does seem that creditors can readily avoid the decision in *Financings Ltd v Baldock* by skilled drafting of their contracts. According to the Court of Appeal in *Lombard North Central plc v Butterworth*,[14] if the contract states that prompt payment is of the essence of the agreement this indicates that such punctual payment is a condition of the contract. Consequently, any delay in making payments can be treated as a repudiation of the contract even if it does not actually amount to repudiatory conduct. The creditor can then accept the repudiation, terminate the contract and claim as damages the loss of the whole of the transaction, as in *Waragowski*. In *Lombard*, Nicholls LJ[15] viewed this outcome with 'considerable dissatisfaction' in that it 'emasculated' the decision in *Financings Ltd v Baldock*. This does seem to be the position, however, and it is plain that creditors commonly frame all the debtor's obligations, or as many as possible, as conditions.

Measure of damages and the CCA

It is curious that the CCA neither imposes any limits on, nor seeks to control, the measure of damages available to a creditor, as discussed above. One criticism of the *Waragowski* measure of damages is that it pays no regard to the debtor's option to terminate the agreement, eg by making payments up to one-half of the price. Suppose the price is £3,000 and the debtor pays £750 before defaulting. He is in arrears for a further £750 and then the goods are repossessed and sold for, say, £750. The court will award the £750 in arrears so that the creditor will now have received in all £2,250. As the debtor could lawfully have terminated the agreement by paying £1,500, it is curious that on breach he should be required by the *Waragowski* decision to pay, on these facts, a further £750.[16] It is arguable that, as the debtor has a right to terminate the agreement under the CCA, s 99, and s 100 provides for his liability in the

---

12 [1971] 1 WLR 722.
13 See also *Brady v St Margaret's Trust Ltd* [1963] 2 QB 494; *Kelly v Sovereign Leasing* [1995] CLY 720 (in an unregulated hire-purchase agreement it was held that a failure to make two payments was not a repudiatory breach and the creditor was liable in conversion for wrongfully re-possessing the goods).
14 [1987] QB 527.
15 [1987] QB 527 at 546.
16 See *Financings Ltd v Baldock* [1963] 2 QB 104, 113–114 per Lord Denning MR; Ziegel, 'Damages for Breach of a Hire-Purchase Contract' (1961) 24 MLR 792.

event of such voluntary termination,[17] he should be under no greater liability than this when the creditor terminates the agreement for default. If this approach were to be followed, the court would consider the debtor's right to terminate when assessing unliquidated damages or invalidate as a penalty a liquidated damages clause which sought to impose a greater liability than that prescribed by s 100. Moreover, s 173(1) provides that 'a term contained in a regulated agreement ... is void if, and to the extent that, it is inconsistent with a provision for the protection of the debtor ... contained in this Act or in any regulation made under this Act'. It is is tempting to conclude, therefore, that a liquidated damages clause would be declared void if it sought to impose a liability greater than that specified in s 100.

THE OPERATION OF MINIMUM PAYMENT CLAUSES

It has always been commonplace for hire-purchase agreements to provide that, on the termination of the agreement, the creditor shall be entitled to claim a minimum payment from the debtor. The minimum payment clause becomes operative in three principal circumstances, viz (i) on breach of contract by the debtor; (ii) on the exercise by the debtor of a voluntary right to terminate the contract; and (iii) on the death or bankruptcy of the debtor. Whether a minimum payment clause is effective depends on the nature of the event which activates it. Also, the position under the CCA and other statutes must be considered.

Breach of contract and the common law relating to penalties

A minimum payment clause is intended to compensate the creditor for the depreciation in the goods and the original view was that it could be enforced simply as one of the terms of the agreement. The possibility that a minimum payment clause might be invalidated as a penalty did not therefore arise. However, in *Cooden Engineering Co Ltd v Stanford*[18] the Court of Appeal held that, where there was a *breach* of contract, the issue of liquidated damages and penalties was pertinent and fell to be considered. In that case, a hire-purchase agreement relating to a 1935 Ford car provided that the creditor could terminate the contract if the debtor failed to make any payment on the day it fell due. Thereupon the whole of the unpaid balance of the hire-purchase price became payable (excluding only a 10s option fee). When the debtor fell into arrears, the creditor terminated the agreement, recovered possession of the car and sued for the unpaid balance under the minimum payment clause. The Court of Appeal held that the creditor's claim was based on the debtor's breach of contract and thus it was necessary to discover whether the sum payable was recoverable as liquidated damages or, alternatively, was irrecoverable as amounting to a penalty. The court concluded that the payment constituted a penalty and, consequently, the creditor was limited to a claim for damage actually suffered. The *Stanford* case was followed in *Landom Trust Ltd v Hurrell*,[19] where a clause requiring the debtor to pay 75% of the hire-purchase price on breach and repossession of the goods was invalidated as a penalty.

17 The debtor's voluntary termination was considered in Ch 34.
18 [1953] 1 QB 86.
19 [1955] 1 WLR 391.

It was the debtor's breach which led to the minimum payment clause being struck down in both the *Stanford* and *Lamdon* cases. The earlier Court of Appeal decision in *Associated Distributors Ltd v Hall*,[20] to the effect that the law relating to penalties had no application where the debtor voluntarily terminated the agreement, was thus left unscathed. This led to the unacceptable paradox that a debtor who voluntarily terminated the agreement would be worse off than his counterpart who was in breach of contract, as only the latter was at liberty to invoke the rules concerning penalties. It was the decision of the House of Lords in *Bridge v Campbell Discount Co Ltd*[1] which sought to remedy this injustice and alleviate the hardship caused to the debtor. In *Bridge*, the debtor took a second-hand Bedford Dormobile on hire-purchase terms, the total price being £480 payable by an initial deposit of £105 followed by monthly intalments over a period of three years. He paid the first instalment but, two weeks later, he wrote to the creditor that 'owing to unforeseen personal circumstances I am sorry but I will not be able to pay any more payments ... will you please let me know when and where I will have to return the car. I am very sorry regarding this but I have no alternative'. Clause 9 of the agreement provided that if it was terminated for any reason, the debtor should pay all arrears and 'by way of agreed compensation ... such further sum as may be necessary to make the rentals paid and payable hereunder equal to two-thirds of the hire-purchase price'. Clause 6 further stipulated that the 'hirer may at any time terminate the hiring ... and thereupon the provisions of clause 9 hereof shall apply'. The creditor thus claimed £206 (two-thirds of the price was £321 but the debtor had paid £115). The Court of Appeal viewed the debtor's letter as voluntarily terminating the agreement and thus held that the rules on penalties had no application. That decision was reversed by the House of Lords on the basis that the letter was not a notice of termination but was a breach of contract, albeit a reluctant one. Accordingly, the law relating to penalties did apply to the facts and the minimum payment clause was held to be a penalty.[2] It was emphasised that the clause could not possibly be a genuine pre-estimate of loss as a car depreciates the longer it remains in the debtor's possession but the sum to be paid under the agreement was at its largest when the car was returned after a short period of time and got progressively *smaller* with the passage of time. Unfortunately for the creditor, this was a sliding-scale of compensation which slid in the wrong direction. It was also stressed that the sum claimed was expressed as a proportion of the hire-purchase price, even though this comprised a large amount of interest. Moreover, having regard to the realisable value of the re-possessed goods, the minimum payment clause would almost certainly have allowed the creditor more than 100% of the hire-purchase price.

It follows from *Bridge v Campbell Discount Co Ltd* that a minimum payment clause must (i) provide a sliding-scale of compensation which increases as the period of the bailment progresses; (ii) provide for the particular nature, condition and value of the goods at the date of the breach and permit the debtor an allowance for the value of the re-possessed goods;

---

20 [1938] 2 KB 83.
 1 [1962] AC 600.
 2 The reluctance to hold that the debtor had terminated the contract was also evident in *United Dominions Trust (Commercial) Ltd v Ennis* [1968] 1 QB 54 (debtor who wrote an unequivocal letter of termination but was *unaware* of the minimum payment clause was held not to have exercised his option to terminate. As the creditor had terminated the contract on the debtor's breach, the minimum payment clause was invalidated as a penalty).

and (iii) provide the debtor with a discount for the accelerated payment to be received by the creditor. All these requirements were met in *Anglo-Auto Finance Co Ltd v James*,[3] with the exception of (iii), and in consequence the clause was struck-down as a penalty.

Finally, the fact that the House of Lords decided in *Bridge v Campbell Discount Co Ltd* that the debtor was in breach of contract, meant that no decision was reached as to whether the rules concerning penalties were available to the debtor where he voluntarily terminated the agreement or where it was terminated by an event stipulated in the agreement which did not entail a breach of contract, eg death or bankruptcy. Nevertheless, the Law Lords expressed their opinions on the matter and revealed a marked difference of opinion. Lord Simonds and Lord Morton of Henryton did not wish to see the rules on penalties applied to voluntary termination and both considered that *Associated Distributors Ltd v Hall*, above, was correctly decided. Lord Denning and Lord Devlin both agreed that *Associated Distributors Ltd v Hall* was wrongly decided and Lord Denning added that the courts had a broad power to grant relief against a penal sum irrespective of the reason for the termination of the agreement. Lord Devlin's reasoning was somewhat narrower than this in that he considered relief to be apt where the clause stated falsely that the sum in question was payable as compensation for depreciation. Lord Radcliffe refused to express a decisive opinion but it is tolerably clear that he preferred the views of Lord Simonds and Lord Morton of Henryton. Although the point thus remains open in the House of Lords, the Court of Appeal has subsequently considered that *Associated Distributors Ltd v Hall* was correctly decided[4] and so the common law relating to penalties does not currently apply to a voluntary termination by the debtor or a termination on some ground other than breach of contract.

Minimum payment clauses under the CCA and other controls on their operation

First, where the agreement is regulated hire-purchase or regulated conditional sale agreement under the CCA, the debtor has a right to terminate the agreement under s 99 and, if that right is exercised, s 100 imposes strict controls on the debtor's liability. Voluntary termination and its consequences were considered in Chapter 34.

Second, a minimum payment clause might mean that the agreement could be re-opened as an extortionate credit bargain under the CCA, s 137. This power applies to *all* credit agreements, whether or not they are regulated agreements[5] and regardless of the amount financed under the agreement. The rules on extortionate credit are considered in Chapter 37.

Third, the Unfair Terms in Consumer Contracts Regulations 1999[6] could invalidate a minimum payment clause in an agreement for credit entered into between a 'consumer' and a 'seller or supplier' on the basis that it is an 'unfair term'. The Regulations are very broadly based and were analysed in depth in Chapter 25. Schedule 2 of the Regulations provides an indicative and non-exhaustive list of terms which may be unfair and, in particular, para (e) designates

---

3 [1963] 1 WLR 1042.
4 See *Goulston Discount Co Ltd v Harman* (1962) 106 Sol Jo 369; Cf *United Dominions Trust (Commercial) Ltd v Ennis* [1968] 1 QB 54, 64 per Lord Denning MR.
5 See the CCA, s 140.
6 SI 1999/2083.

as potentially unfair a term which requires 'any consumer who fails to fulfil his obligation to pay a disproportionately high sum in compensation'. It may be that para (e) is restricted to cases of breach of contract, and it is unclear whether the Regulations can apply to unfair minimum payment clauses in those instances where there is a voluntary termination by a 'consumer' debtor.

Fourth, where the agreement is regulated, the creditor must serve a notice on the debtor or hirer under either s 76 or s 87 where he wishes to 'demand earlier payment of any sum' under a term of the regulated agreement (s 76) or by reason of any breach (s 87) and, after the service of such a notice, the debtor can apply for a time order under s 129.

ACCELERATED PAYMENT CLAUSES

It is common in conditional sale, credit-sale, and loan agreements which are repayable in instalments, to provide that the future instalments can be called-in immediately on the debtor's default. Such an accelerated payments clause would be advantageous to the creditor where the debtor's breach is non-repudiatory in character because, as seen earlier in *Financings Ltd v Baldock*,[7] it may be difficult to recover the outstanding instalments from the debtor in this situation. Moreover, where the goods have depreciated to such an extent that termination of the agreement and re-possession are fruitless and/or impracticable, an acceleration of payments is a desirable remedy for the creditor.

As in the case of minimum payment clauses, acceleration clauses are subject to the rules on penalties where they are activated by, and exercisable on, the debtor's *breach* of contract. As a (very) general proposition, the acceleration clause will not be penal if it specifies that the whole balance becomes due immediately because this accelerates the repayment by the debtor rather than increasing his liability.[8] In most cases, the creditor will want to recover the interest due for the period of credit and it is here that the difficulties arise regarding the penal nature of an acceleration clause. It is plain from the decision in *The Angelic Star*[9] that a clause which permits recovery of the principal sum together with *accrued* interest is not a penalty, but that if the balance and interest thereon for the full term of the agreement are payable immediately, the clause is penal in effect as 'a payment of money stipulated as *in terrorem* of the offending party'.[10] If the clause were enforceable in such a case, the creditor would also be markedly better off than if the agreement had run its full course. Accordingly, in order to escape the rules on penalties at common law, there would have to be some rebate of charges under an acceleration clause[11] and so, if the rebate on offer is significantly less than that permitted under the Regulations on early settlement[12] the clause will fall foul of the rules on penalties.

---

7 [1963] 2 QB 104.
8 See *Protector Endowment Loan & Annuity Co v Grice* (1880) 5 QBD 592; *Wallingford v Mutual Society* (1880) 5 App Cas 685; *Oresundsvarvet Aktiebolag v Marcos Diamantis Lemos, The Angelic Star* [1988] 1 Lloyd's Rep 122.
9 *Oresundsvarvet Aktiebolag v Marcos Diamantis Lemos, The Angelic Star* [1988] 1 Lloyd's Rep 122.
10 *Dunlop Pneumatic Tyre Co Ltd v New Garage and Motor Co Ltd* [1915] AC 79, 86 per Lord Dunedin.
11 See *Wadham Stringer Finance Ltd v Meaney* [1981] 1 WLR 39 (a rebate, calculated in accordance with 'the rule of 78', prevented the clause from being classified as a penalty).
12 The Consumer Credit (Rebate on Early Settlement) Regulations 1983, SI 1983/1562.

Somewhat surprisingly, the effect of an accelerated payments clause in a hire-purchase agreement is unclear. In *Wadham Stringer Finance Ltd v Meaney*,[13] a decision on a conditional sale agreement, Woolf J seemed to assume that such a clause would, subject to the rules on penalties in cases of breach, be valid in a hire-purchase agreement. However, a debtor/buyer under a conditional sale agreement is contractually bound to buy the goods whereas a debtor under a hire-purchase agreement is not bound to pay the total price. In hire-purchase agreements, the acceleration clause would, however, lead to an automatic exercise of the debtor's option to purchase and so the legal position is unclear.

Accelerated payment clauses under the CCA and other controls on their operation

In the case of regulated agreements under the CCA, the creditor cannot enforce an accelerated payments clause without first serving a non-default notice under s 76 or a default notice under s 87 (see later). The debtor could then apply for a time order under s 129 and the court could, in effect, reverse the accelerated payments clause by ordering that the balance be paid in appropriate instalments.

Alternatively, in cases of hire-purchase and conditional sale, the debtor could exercise the right of termination under s 99, provided that he does so before the expiry of the non-default or default notice. Under s 99, the debtor must thus exercise the right of termination 'before the final payment ... falls due' and the acceleration clause locks into position.[14] On termination, s 100 provides for the debtor's liability to be capped[15] and the right of termination would be advantageous to the debtor where the goods have severely depreciated in value.

As in the case of minimum payment clauses, both the provisions of the CCA regarding extortionate credit and the Unfair Terms in Consumer Contracts Regulations 1999 could apply to accelerated payment clauses.

Restrictions on the termination or enforcement of the agreement under the Consumer Credit Act

Some of the restrictions on enforcement in the CCA have already been referred to, above, and it will be apparent that the CCA has not introduced a new array of substantive remedies available to the creditor nor has it sought to codify the relevant common law regarding breach of contract. Instead, the Act's contribution has been to control tightly the enforcement of the existing remedies and ensure that adequate formalities and notice attend such enforcement. Moreover, the CCA acknowledges that there are disparate reasons why a debtor may fall into arrears and this is reflected in the division between default notices and non-default notices.

NON-DEFAULT NOTICES

The debtor may have neither defaulted on payment nor be in breach of any term of the agreement but, instead, an event may have occurred which causes the

13   [1981] 1 WLR 39.
14   See *Wadham Stringer Finance Ltd v Meaney* [1981] 1 WLR 39.
15   See Ch 34 where the right of termination is considered.

creditor to enforce one of the terms of the agreement. This might be the case where, for example, the debtor has been declared bankrupt or has become unemployed and, in consequence, the agreement permits the creditor or owner to repossess the goods.

Where the agreement enables the creditor or owner to pursue a course of action if certain events occur, the CCA, s 76 imposes a duty on him to give notice before taking that action. Section 76(1) provides that the creditor or owner must give not less than seven days' notice, in the prescribed form,[16] of his intention to enforce a term of the regulated agreement by which he seeks to:

(a) demand earlier payment of any sum (eg under an accelerated payments clause), or
(b) recover possession of any goods or land, or
(c) treat any right conferred on the debtor or hirer by the agreement as terminated, restricted or deferred.[17]

Section 76(2) provides that the requirement of notice applies only where a period for the duration of the agreement is specified in the agreement and that period has not ended when the creditor or owner does an act mentioned in s 76(1). Section 76 still applies, however, where either party is entitled to terminate the agreement before the end of the fixed period. Where, for example, an overdraft has been granted to the creditor for six months subject to a condition that the amount outstanding must be repaid on demand, a notice under s 76 is required if that demand is made before the six months have expired, but the s 76 notice would *not* be needed if the loan were repayable on demand with no period fixed for the duration of the agreement. Most importantly, s 76(4) provides that s 76(1) does not prevent a creditor from treating the right to draw on any credit as restricted or deferred and taking any such steps to make the restriction or deferment effective, eg no notice is necessary to suspend an overdraft or to withdraw a credit-card (or cheque book) from the debtor and inform suppliers that the card should not be accepted.

The twin purposes of a non-default notice under s 76 are to warn the debtor or hirer of the imminent action to be taken and, if he has difficulty in making any payment under the agreement, to allow him to apply for a time order under s 129. The notice must thus inform the debtor of his right to apply for a time order and that the court can extend the time for payment of any sums due. It must be stressed, however, that s 76 does *not* apply to a right of enforcement arising by reason of any *breach* (s 76)(6)) and so the section is not designed to enable the debtor or hirer to take *remedial* action in curing any such breach. Similarly, s 76 is not applicable to termination of the *entire* agreement by the creditor for specified events other than a breach by the debtor or hirer, as notice of termination in such a case is governed by s 98.

Notice of termination in non-default cases

Where the creditor or owner wishes to *terminate* the agreement for specified events *other* than a breach, s 98 governs the position. Section 98(1) provides that the

---

16 See the Consumer Credit (Enforcement, Default and Termination Notices) Regulations 1983, SI 1983/1561, as amended by SI 1984/1109. Immense detail is prescribed in the Regulations in terms of substance and form.
17 The 1983 regulations, above, provide that s 76 does not apply in the case of non-commercial agreements in relation to which no security has been provided (reg 2(9)).

creditor or owner is not entitled to terminate a regulated agreement except by or after giving the debtor or hirer not less than seven days' notice of the termination. As under s 76, s 98(1) applies only where the agreement is for a specific period and that period has not ended when the creditor or owner wishes to terminate the agreement. Section 98(1) still applies, however, where either party is entitled to terminate the agreement before the end of the fixed period. Section 98(4) also mirrors s 76(4) in allowing a creditor to suspend an overdraft or to withdraw a credit card from the debtor without having to give a notice of termination under s 98(1).

A notice of termination under s 98(1) is ineffective if it is not in the prescribed form (s 98(3)).[18] Most significantly, in contrast to default notices under s 87, there is no need to specify any remedial action by the debtor or hirer in a s 98 notice and, indeed, any such action cannot prevent the notice from operating. The proper course of action for a debtor or hirer who seeks to avoid the consequences of termination is to apply for a time order under s 129, and the notice must inform him that he has such a right and that the court can extend the time for payment of any sums due.

DEFAULT NOTICES

In contrast to ss 76 and 98, which oversee the exercise of remedies where events have occurred which are not technical breaches of contract, the CCA, s 87 governs the exercise of remedies where the debtor or hirer is in default and there is a breach of the regulated agreement. Typical breaches occur where there is a failure to pay money due under the agreement or where the debtor neglects to take care of the goods and fails to insure them. Similarly, in hire-purchase it is not uncommon for the debtor to sell the goods, in breach of contract, to a third party.

By s 87(1), the creditor or owner must serve a 'default notice', in accordance with s 88, on the debtor or hirer before he is entitled, by reason of any breach by the debtor or hirer, to do any of the following:

(a) terminate the agreement, or
(b) demand earlier payment of any sum (eg under an accelerated payments clause), or
(c) recover possession of goods, or
(d) treat any right conferred on the debtor or hirer by the agreement as terminated, restricted or deferred, or
(e) enforce any security.

Section 87(1) refers to 'any breach' and so it applies to breaches of the regulated agreement other than a default in payment and, it seems, the section applies to the exercise of the remedies listed in it which could arise from the common law as opposed to the agreement itself, eg the right to terminate the agreement (s 87(1)(a)) by reason of a repudiatory breach by the debtor. However, s 87(1) does *not* require the service of a default notice before the creditor or owner is entitled to claim damages or arrears of payments, as distinct from the other remedies specified in the section.[19] Similarly, it appears that no default notice is needed if the creditor or owner seeks to rescind the agreement for misrepresentation.

18 See the Consumer Credit (Enforcement, Default and Termination Notices) Regulations 1983, SI 1983/1561, as amended by SI 1984/1109.
19 Unless he proceeds against a surety, in which case s 87(1)(e) would apply.

As in s 76(4), considered above, s 87(2) does not prevent a creditor from treating the right to draw on any credit as restricted or deferred and taking any such steps to make the restriction or deferment effective.[20] Where, for example, the debtor's breach consists of overdrawing on the credit facilities available to him, the creditor can take immediate steps to restrain further use of the credit facility without serving a default notice. Moreover, s 87(3) emphasises that the doing of an act by which a floating charge beccomes crystallised, eg the appointment of a receiver, is not the enforcement of a security under s 87(1)(e) and so, in this event, no default notice is required.

Form and content of default notices

The earlier statutory provision requiring service of a default notice (Hire-Purchase Act 1965, s 25) omitted to specify the precise details that the notice ought to contain and the consequences of the debtor's not complying with it, although the Court of Appeal valiantly endeavoured to remedy the omission of the legislature.[1] The CCA, s 88 has now put the matter beyond doubt.

Section 88(1) provides that the notice must be in the prescribed form[2] and must specify:

(a) the nature of the alleged breach;
(b) if the breach is capable of remedy, what action is required to remedy it and the date before which that action is to be taken;
(c) if the breach is not capable of remedy, the sum (if any) required to be paid as compensation for the breach, and the date before which it is to be paid.

Under s 88(2), a date specified under s 88 (1) must not be less than seven days after the date of service of the default notice and the creditor or owner may not pursue any of the remedies mentioned in s 87 before the specified date or, if no requirement is made under s 88(1), before those seven days have elapsed.

The default notice must contain information in the prescribed terms about the consequences of failure to comply with it (s 88(4)). It may include a provision terminating the agreement, or for the taking of other action as specified in s 87(1) at any time after the seven days (or more specified in the notice) have elapsed, together with a statement that the provision will be ineffective if the breach is duly remedied or the compensation duly paid (s 88(5)). By s 89, if before the seven days or more specified in the default notice the debtor or hirer takes the action required in the notice, the breach must be treated as 'not having occurred'.

Breach of the agreement may activate other rights of the creditor or owner under a separate provision in the agreement and so, for example, an accelerated payments clause may come into operation in the event of a default in paying an instalment. In order to avoid the necessity for two default notices in this situation, s 88(3) provides that it is sufficient for the creditor to serve one default notice only in respect of the original breach which activates the separate provision of the agreement.

---

20 As in the case of s 76, the Consumer Credit (Enforcement, Default and Termination Notices) Regulations 1983, SI 1983/1561, provide that s 87 does not apply in the case of non-commercial agreements in relation to which no security has been provided (reg 2(9)).
1 *Eshun v Moorgate Mercantile Co Ltd* [1971] 1 WLR 722 (facts considered above).
2 See the Consumer Credit (Enforcement, Default and Termination Notices) Regulations 1983, SI 1983/1561, as amended by SI 1984/1109.

In the recent decision in *Woodchester Lease Management Services Ltd v Swain & Co*,[3] the Court of Appeal stressed that the requirements of s 88 must be construed strictly. There the defendant firm of solicitors hired a photocopier from the plaintiffs under a regulated consumer hire agreement. In breach of the agreement, rental payments stopped and the plaintiffs served a default notice in which the amount needed to remedy the breach was incorrectly stated as £879 whereas the arrears of payments amounted to £634. As the defendants made no payments, the plaintiffs claimed the arrears due and damages for breach of contract. The Court of Appeal held that the default notice was invalid and so the plaintiffs could not recover damages and were entitled to the arrears only. Kennedy LJ pointed out that the CCA was enacted to protect consumers who entered into complex, standard form contracts with large financial organisations. The consumer was thus often at a disadvantage and would not necessarily know the correct amounts which were outstanding under the agreement. The creditor or owner, on the other hand, could easily calculate the correct sum which was due and, as the CCA, s 88 demanded that the nature of the alleged breach and the action required to remedy it should both be specified in the default notice, it was incumbent on the creditor or owner to perform that task accurately.

When is a breach 'capable of remedy'?

It will be apparent that ss 88 and 89 are designed to give the debtor or hirer a second bite of the cherry and so, if the breach of contract is remediable, he is allowed to remedy it. It is thus crucial to decide when the 'breach is capable of remedy' within s 88(1)(b).

At one end of the spectrum, breaches involving the non-payment of money are always remediable by paying the amount due. In the middle, it is a more difficult question of fact to decide whether damage to goods entails a breach which can be remedied and, at the opposite end of the spectrum, a sale of the goods by the debtor under a hire-purchase contract to a *bona fide* buyer who acquires title,[4] must surely be irremediable as the debtor has no right to demand the return of the goods from the buyer.[5] Similarly, if bankruptcy is specified in the agreement as constituting a breach, it is also irremediable.[6]

If the breach can be remedied, s 88(1)(b) specifies that the creditor or owner must state in the default notice what action is needed in order to remedy it and the date before which that action is to be taken. Regarding the time in which the breach must be remedied, it should be stressed that the seven days specified in s 88(2) is a *minimum* requirement, but what is the position where the creditor or owner fixes a time limit which the debtor or hirer considers to be unreasonably short? The debtor or hirer can apply to the court for a time order under s 129 and seek to have the period extended and, almost certainly, the court would ask whether the breach is remediable within a reasonable period of time.

---

3 [1999] 1 WLR 263.
4 Under Part III of the Hire-Purchase Act, 1964.
5 This would not necessarily be the case where, for example, the hirer in a leasing agreement sub-lets the goods to a third party. No title would be transferred and, assuming that the hirer can regain possession of the goods, the breach is remediable.
6 See *Civil Service Co-operative Society Ltd v McGrigor's Trustee* [1923] 2 Ch 347, 356 per Russell J.

The position where the breach is irremediable

If the breach is not capable of remedy, the creditor or owner has a right to claim compensation under s 88(1)(c) although, as the section refers to 'the sum (if any) required to be paid as compensation' he need not make such a claim. If compensation is sought, a date for its payment must be given and it must be not less than seven days after the date of service of the default notice (s 88(2)). If the compensation is duly paid, the creditor or owner can do no more and is prevented from terminating the agreement as s 89 provides that, if the debtor or hirer 'takes the action specified', the breach must be treated as 'not having occurred'.

It follows from this that, if the creditor or owner wishes to terminate the agreement, he would be wise not to demand compensation but rather to proceed with the action specified in the default notice after the minimum seven day period has elapsed. The debtor or hirer can, nevertheless, apply for a time order under s 129.

Effects of an invalid notice under sections 76, 87 and 98

There can be a transgression of the notice provisions where (i) no notice is given at all; (ii) where the notice is defective in some respect; or (iii) where the creditor or owner takes steps to enforce the notice too soon after its service.

First, it is clear that a transgression of the notice provisions will provide a complete defence to an action which the creditor or owner pursues under the aegis of such an invalid notice.[7]

Second, it is striking that the CCA provides no sanction where the creditor or owner actually proceeds to enforcement under an invalid notice and, consequently, the rights of the debtor or hirer are not as conclusive as they might be. An injunction might be granted to prevent the enforcement of the agreement but this remedy is of little practical value to a consumer debtor. Where the creditor or owner repossesses goods under an invalid notice, the debtor or hirer may sue in conversion. The measure of damages in such a case is unclear and the normal rule in conversion, that the true measure is the value of the goods converted, must be modified where the debtor has only a partial interest in the goods.[8] In *Eshun v Moorgate Mercantile Co Ltd*,[9] the creditor repossessed a Ford Anglia car under an invalid default notice[10] and, although the Court of Appeal held that the debtor could recover all the payments which he had made, the legal basis of the decision was left in doubt. This was not an unjust assessment on the facts of *Eshun* but, in those situations where the debtor has almost completed the instalments, such an award would clearly be inapt as the amount recovered would invariably exceed the value of the repossessed goods.

Protected goods in hire-purchase and conditional sale

In hire-purchase agreements, the creditor's right to repossess the goods on default by the debtor lies at the heart of the hire-purchase transaction, but this drastic

---

7 *Woodchester Lease Management Services Ltd v Swain & Co* [1999] 1 WLR 263.
8 *Brierly v Kendall* (1852) 17 QB 937.
9 [1971] 1 WLR 722.
10 Issued under the Hire-Purchase Act 1965, s 25.

step is a recognition that there is no life left in the agreement and so it is a remedy of last resort. Another facet of the right to repossess the goods is that it may be used as a threat to rouse the debtor into making payments under the agreement. Clearly, this potent right of re-possession must be controlled, especially in those situations where the debtor has paid a large proportion of the price of the goods and his default is minimal. The notion that goods can become 'protected' recognises that, after the debtor has made substantial payments under the contract, he acquires a proprietary interest in the goods which is worthy of protection.

The current provisions of the CCA curtail the creditor's right to repossess protected goods without a court order and are modelled on ss 33 and 34 of the Hire-Purchase Act 1965[11] which sought to protect debtors from the iniquitous 'snatch-back' of goods. The restrictions on the repossession of protected goods are in addition to the rules on default notices in s 87 and thus the creditor cannot seek repossession without first complying with those rules.

WHEN DO GOODS BECOME 'PROTECTED'?

Sections 90 and 91 of the CCA prevent the creditor under a hire-purchase or conditional sale agreement from recovering possession of protected goods without a court order and, if the creditor recovers the goods in contravention of s 90, the debtor is released from all liability and may recover all payments made under the agreement (s 91).

Section 90(1) furnishes the basic definition of 'protected goods' and prescribes three conditions which must exist if the goods are to fall wthin this category, namely:

(a) the debtor must be in breach of a regulated hire-purchase agreement or regulated conditional sale agreement relating to goods;
(b) the debtor must have paid to the creditor one-third or more of the total price of the goods; and
(c) the property in the goods remains in the creditor.

If these conditions are satisfied, s 90(1) provides further that 'the creditor is not entitled to recover possession of the goods from the debtor except on an order of the court'.

The scope of s 90

First, ss 90 and 91 apply *only* to hire-purchase and conditional sale agreements where the 'property in the goods remains in the creditor'. A hirer under a consumer hire agreement can apply for a time order under s 129 or, if the goods are repossessed by the owner, he may seek repayment and release from liability under s 132. In a credit-sale agreement property in the goods passes to the buyer on contract and, if the goods were to be repossessed by the seller, he would be liable in conversion.

Second, s 90 operates to protect the debtor only when he is in breach of the agreement. This means that, despite the fact that the debtor has paid one-third or more of the total price of the goods, they can be repossessed if the debtor is

---

11   See Goode, *Hire-Purchase Law and Practice* (2nd ed, 1970), Ch 19, pp 412-433; Guest, *The Law of Hire-Purchase* (1966), paras 532-558.

not then in breach of the agreement but the contract stipulates that certain *other* events, apart from breach, entitle the creditor to repossess the goods. Such an event might be, for example, the levy of execution by a third party against the debtor's assets. Provided that one-third of the price had been paid, goods were protected under the Hire-Purchase Act 1965, s 33, no matter how the agreement terminated, and so it is very surprising that the debtor's protection was *decreased* by the CCA. It has been pointed out, however, that the debtor is unlikely to be prejudiced by this as 'it is extremely unusual for a non-breach ground of possession to arise where the debtor is not already in default of some obligation under the agreement'.[12]

Third, the debtor must have paid one-third or more of the total price of the goods if they are to be classified as protected goods and, under s 189(1), 'payment' includes tender of payment. This would almost certainly include payment or tender by a surety, but there is no express provision to that effect. It is thus necessary to make an addition of the amounts paid by the debtor including any deposit, the instalments paid and the option fee. If the amount comes to more than one third of the total price of the goods, they are protected goods. If the creditor has insisted upon a large cash deposit or there is a substantial part-exchange allowance, it is plain that the goods may achieve the status of protected goods almost immediately. However, s 90(2) amends the basic rule where a charge has been made for installation. Section 90(2) provides that, if the debtor has paid an installation charge to the creditor and that amount is specified as part of the total price, the amount so specified is to be deducted from the amount paid by the debtor and is not to be regarded as part of the total price of the goods. It follows that the debtor must have paid the installation charge plus one third of the balance of the total price if the goods are to become protected. If, for example the debtor takes goods on hire-purchase for a total price of £600 of which £60 is an installation charge and he has made payments amounting to £220, the goods are not protected. Here the goods would become protected once the debtor had paid £60 plus one third of £540, ie £240. It should be stressed that s 90(2) applies only where 'the *agreement specifies*' that the creditor must install the goods and so the normal one third rule is applicable if there is no contractual *obligation* on the creditor to undertake an installation but, for example, he has told the debtor what the charge will be if he does thus install the goods.

PROTECTED GOODS IN RELATION TO SUCCESSIVE AND MODIFIED AGREEMENTS: SECTION 90(3) AND 90(4)

One common way in which a creditor could seek to avoid the the provisions relating to protected goods would be to transfer goods upon which the debtor had paid more than one third of the total price to a new agreement, perhaps with additional goods being taken on hire-purchase, payments under the original agreement then being credited to the new agreement. For example, if the debtor has a microwave oven on hire-purchase for £300 of which £100 has been paid and he approaches the same creditor in order to take a dishwasher on hire-purchase for £500, the creditor might induce the debtor to cancel the original agreement and make a new one for both items totalling £800, with a

12 Goode, *Consumer Credit Law* (1989), para 30.34.

credit of £100 for sums already paid under the original agreement. If the debtor acceded to this new arrangement he would, in the absence of any statutory control, lose the accrued protection on the microwave oven and would have no protection whatever under the new agreement as he has not paid one third of the total price.

Section 90(3) avoids this consequence by providing that, once one third of the total price has been paid under the original agreement, any goods comprised in both the original and the new agreement will be protected goods if the debtor is in breach of the new agreement, irrespective of the fact that he has not paid one third of the total price under the new agreement.

The debtor need not have defaulted under the original agreement in order to gain the protection of s 90(3). Moreover, there need be no goods added to the agreement as in the example above, ie the dishwasher. If, for example, the debtor had binoculars and a telescope on hire-purchase in one agreement and had made payments of more than one third of the total price, the creditor might suggest that the binoculars be regarded as paid-up and that a new agreement be entered into in relation to the telescope. Should the debtor default under the new agreement, the telescope would be classified as protected goods under s 90(3), even though the debtor had not paid one third of the total price under that new agreement.

The notion that the provisions relating to protected goods must not be evaded also applies, by virtue of s 90(4), to the situation where the later agreement is a 'modifying agreement' as defined in s 82(2). Such a modifying agreement 'varies or supplements an earlier agreement' rather than, as in the examples above, terminating that agreement and replacing it with a new agreement. Modification would thus occur where goods are *added* to the original agreement. In the case of a modifying agreement, s 90(1) applies to both the agreements. Consequently, provided that the original goods had acquired protected status under the one third payment rule, the goods which have been added under the modifying agreement become protected goods as well, without having to satisfy the one third payment rule in relation to the combined agreements.

APPROPRIATION OF PAYMENTS BETWEEN TWO OR MORE AGREEMENTS: SECTION 81

In the context of protected goods and the one third payment rule, it is crucial to consider the rules on appropriation of payments where there are two or more agreements between the same parties. Where a payment is made by the debtor in such a situation, the rule at common law is that he may appropriate the payment between the agreements in any way he chooses[13] but, if he does not do so, the creditor may make whatever appropriation he thinks fit. There is a consequent risk of the creditor's appropriating all the payment to one agreement so that, for example, less than one third is paid on the other agreement and the goods comprised in it do not become protected goods.

The CCA, s 81 provides for this situation by, first, preserving and codifying the debtor's common law right to appropriate payment as he thinks fit (s 81(1)) and by providing, unlike the position at common law, that this statutory right cannot be excluded (s 173(1)). Second, should the debtor fail to make an

---

13   See *Peters v Anderson* (1814) 5 Taunt 596.

appropriation, the creditor's common law right to do so is replaced by a statutory rule as to appropriation under s 81(2), viz 'the payment shall be appropriated towards the satisfaction of the sums due under the several agreements respectively in the proportions which those sums bear to one another'. Consider the situation where, for example, instalments of £20 are due under the first agreement and instalments of £10 are due under the second agreement. Should the debtor pay £15 without appropriation to either agreement then, under s 81(2), £10 is appropriated to the first agreement and £5 to the second agreement.

GOODS ARE NOT PROTECTED WHERE THE DEBTOR TERMINATES THE AGREEMENT: SECTION 90(5)

Section 90(5) provides that s 90(1) does not apply, or ceases to apply to an agreement, if the debtor has terminated, or terminates the agreement. Where the debtor exercises a right of termination either under the agreement or under the CCA, the creditor is entitled to recover possession without obtaining an order of the court, although the debtor could still apply for a time order under under s 129(1).

If the debtor is to be deprived of protection under s 90(1), it is clear that his act of termination must be a voluntary and informed act. In *United Dominions Trust (Commercial) Ltd v Ennis*,[14] the debtor had a Jaguar car on hire-purchase terms and, because his earnings were affected by a strike, he could not afford to pay the first instalment on the car. He told the finance company that he 'would like to get rid of the worry of the car' and the latter's representative dictated a letter to the debtor which he subsequently sent to the finance company stating that he wished to 'terminate' the agreement. The finance company claimed £271 under a minimum payment clause. The Court of Appeal held that the debtor's letter was not an exercise by him of the option to determine the agreement; rather, the finance company must be taken to have terminated the contract and the minimum payment clause was a penalty and thus unenforceable. Lord Denning MR considered that 'a hirer is not to be taken to exercise such an option unless he does so consciously, knowing of the consequences, and avowedly in exercise of the option. If this were not so, the document would be an absolute trap set to catch him.'[15]

GOODS CAN BE REPOSSESSED WHERE THE DEBTOR CONSENTS TO REPOSSESSION OR HAS ABANDONED THE GOODS

Under the Hire-Purchase Acts of 1938 and 1965, the creditor was prohibited from *enforcing* any right to recover possession of protected goods 'otherwise than by action'. This meant that it was only the enforcement of the right which was strictly controlled and the creditor was not precluded from accepting a *surrender* of the goods from the debtor. The decision in *Mercantile Credit Co Ltd v Cross*[16] established that there must be full and free consent to repossession given by the

---

14 [1968] 1 QB 54.
15 [1968] 1 QB 54 at 64.
16 [1965] 2 QB 205; see also *Chartered Trust plc v Pitcher* [1988] RTR 72 (CA held that the debtor did not know of the court's powers under the Hire-Purchase Act 1965 to refinance the transaction and he had not given unqualified and informed consent to the repossession of the goods).

debtor after he had received all the information concerning his rights although, on the facts, it was a rather strained interpretation to view the debtor's consent as informed and voluntary.[17]

The CCA, s 90(1) provides that 'the creditor is not entitled to recover possession of the goods from the debtor except on an order of the court' and although this would seem, initially, to deny any recovery of possession apart from the situation where a court order is obtained, s 173(3) specifies that the debtor's 'consent' given at the time when possession is recovered is equivalent to a court order for possession. Accordingly, *Mercantile Credit Co Ltd v Cross* remains good law but it should be stressed that, under s 173(3), the debtor's informed consent to repossession must be 'given at that time' and so a provision in the contract that the debtor is deemed to give consent to repossession in *advance* would not secure any protection for the creditor should he recover possession without a court order.

It is possible, of course, that the debtor might abandon all rights to possession of the goods as in *Bentinck Ltd v Cromwell Engineering Co.*[18] There the debtor took an MGB sports car on hire-purchase and his employer, the defendant, signed a contract of guarantee. The debtor fell into arrears when the goods had become protected goods under the Hire-Purchase Act 1965, s 33. Thereafter the car was badly damaged in an accident and the debtor left it in the custody of a garage but, not long after that, he disappeared without trace. Eventually, the finance company took possession of the car with the consent of the garage owner, sold it for £50 and claimed the outstanding balance from the defendant under the guarantee. The Court of Appeal held that the debtor had abandoned all rights to his possession of the goods and so the repossession was not enforcement of a right to repossess from the hirer otherwise than by action. Accordingly, the finance company had acted lawfully and could enforce the guarantee.[19]

As mentioned above, the CCA, s 90(1) omits any reference to 'enforcing' a right to recover possession and so the issue of abandonment has to be considered in the light of s 173(3) and the debtor's consenting to repossession. If the goods are truly abandoned, it seems likely that a court would conclude that the debtor has consented to their repossession. The matter is not free from doubt, however, in view of the fact that the consent to the repossession must be '*given* at that time' and the nature of abandonment means that a court would have to conclude that the debtor impliedly consented to repossession by the creditor.

REPOSSESSION OF THE GOODS FROM A THIRD PARTY

Where the debtor has lawfully entrusted physical possession of the goods to a third party (eg a repairer) but the debtor has retained control of the goods, the

---

17 In *Cross*, the debtor's consent was regarded as voluntary and informed despite the fact that Willmer LJ (delivering the judgment of the court) considered that it was 'unwillingly given' (p 214) and that the debtor had failed to read the statement of his rights in the hire-purchase contract which the judge considered to be in 'language about as simple as could be devised' (p 214). This is clearly an outmoded view of what, in the sphere of consumer protection, constitutes voluntary, informed consent and *Cross* conflicts with the (contemporaneous) approach taken in *United Dominions Trust (Commercial) Ltd v Ennis* [1968] 1 QB 54 (considered above).

18 [1971] 1 QB 324.

19 See also *United Dominions Trust (Commercial) Ltd v Kesler* (1962) 107 Sol Jo 15; *Lombank Ltd v Dowdall* (1973) 118 Sol Jo 96

repossession of the goods from that third party without a court order or the consent of the debtor is clearly a contravention of s 90(1). In *Bentinck Ltd v Cromwell Engineering Co*,[20] Lord Denning MR[1] was emphatic that the creditor could not recover possession from a repairer or a garage[2] to whom the debtor had bailed the goods.

This reasoning would not apply, of course, where the debtor wrongfully sells the goods to a third party who does not acquire title to the goods by reason of an exception to the *nemo dat* rule. In this situation, it is arguable that the debtor has abandoned the goods, as in the *Bentinck* case, and recovery of possession from the third party would definitely not be recovery of possession 'from the debtor' within s 90(1). Here repossession without a court order would thus be lawful and it has also been suggested[3] cogently that no default notice need be served on the debtor under s 87(1) because (i) s 87(1) is limited to rights exercisable 'by reason of any breach ... of a regulated agreement' and the creditor has a distinct, non-contractual cause of action, ie conversion; and (ii) s 87(1) presupposes that the debtor has actual or constructive possession of the goods and it cannot apply where the debtor has wrongfully disposed of the goods.

DEATH OF THE DEBTOR AND PROTECTED GOODS

Section 90(6) provides that, where goods are protected goods 'at the death of the debtor', they shall remain as protected goods until the grant of probate or administration. Consequently, until this time, the goods cannot be recovered from the person in possession of them without a court order or the consent of the 'debtor'. Where the debtor dies testate, his executor becomes the 'debtor' immediately when the death occurs[4] and may give consent to the repossession of the goods from a third party such as a bailee/repairer. Should the debtor die intestate, his administrator becomes the 'debtor' upon the grant of letters of administration. Before that, the debtor's rights are vested in the President of the Family Division of the High Court.[5]

As the 'debtor', the executor can consent to the repossession of the goods but, should such consent be given by anyone else, it will be ineffective. In *Peacock v Anglo-Auto Finance Co Ltd*,[6] the debtor died intestate and his mother consented to the creditor's repossession of the goods. Subsequently, the debtor's widow became administratrix of the estate and was held to be entitled to repayment of all monies paid by the debtor on the basis that, when the debtor died, there was no one who could lawfully consent to the return of the goods.

---

20 [1971] 1 QB 324.
 1 [1971] 1 QB 324 at 328.
 2 Lord Denning MR approved the decision in *F C Finance Ltd v Francis* (1970) 114 Sol Jo 568 (debtor took the car to a garage and informed the finance company of its location; held the repossession was unlawful).
 3 Goode, *Consumer Credit Law* (1989), para 30.18.
 4 See the definition of 'debtor' in the CCA, s 189(1).
 5 See the Administration of Justice Act 1925 and 1970.
 6 (1968) 112 Sol Jo 746.

NO ENTRY ON PREMISES TO REPOSSESS GOODS

Except under an order of the court, the creditor is not entitled to 'enter any premises' to take possession of goods subject to a regulated hire-purchase agreement[7] and any such entry is actionable as a breach of statutory duty (s 92(1) and s 92(3)). Under s 173(1), any term in an agreement purporting to give the creditor permission to enter premises will be void. As the creditor cannot enter *any* premises, he will be unable to enter the premises of a third party. Again, s 173(3) is applicable here and so the creditor may enter premises with the full and free consent of the debtor given at the time. It should be stressed that s 92(1) applies whether or not the goods are protected goods.

'Premises' are not defined in the CCA. The very wide definition of 'premises' was discussed when the debtor's right of cancellation was considered[8] and, once again, the question is of considerable practical importance in the context of repossession. It is clearly apt to adopt a broad definition of 'premises' in relation to repossession, thereby curtailing the creditor's rights. It is thus suggested that the creditor should be able to repossess goods without a court order *only* from public property and that every other location (including the premises of a third party) should properly be regarded as 'premises'.

CONSEQUENCES OF THE CONTRAVENTION OF SECTION 90

If goods[9] are recovered by the creditor in contravention of s 90, s 91 provides that (a) the agreement, if not previously terminated, shall terminate and (b) the debtor shall be released from all liability under the agreement and shall be entitled to recover from the creditor all sums paid under the agreement.[10] Likewise, a surety is entitled to recover any money he has paid.[11] If the debtor wishes to be certain that the agreement has terminated under s 91 he can apply for a declaration to that effect (s 142(2)).

Section 170(1) emphasises that these are the only rights of the debtor. He is not entitled to have the goods returned to him nor does he have a right to a claim for damages in conversion[12] because, as the agreement is terminated, the debtor does not have a right to possession but the creditor does have such a right even though it can legitimately be enforced by court order only. Nevertheless, the debtor can hardly be regarded as disadvantaged under s 91 because he may have used the goods for a considerable period of time before repossession and, of course, as all sums paid are returned to him, he will have had that use free of charge.

---

7 Note that s 92(1) also applies to conditional sale and consumer hire agreements.
8 See Ch 33.
9 Section 91 refers to 'goods' not 'the protected goods' and so the consequences of contravening s 90, which are specified in s 91, apply even where the creditor repossesses some of the goods. As the agreement *terminates* automatically when the creditor wrongfully repossesses some of the goods, he can, presumably, repossess the remainder without any court order.
10 Return of the goods to the debtor does not satisfy this obligation, see *Capital Finance Co Ltd v Bray* [1964] 1 WLR 323.
11 See the CCA, s 113(3)(b) and s 106 (a) and (d).
12 *Carr v James Broderick & Co Ltd* [1942] 2 KB 275.

Other restrictions on enforcement

DEATH OF THE DEBTOR OR HIRER

It was, formerly, not uncommon for creditors to terminate hire-purchase agreements on the death of the debtor and repossess the goods, with resultant distress and hardship to the debtor's family. In principle, the death of the debtor need not prejudice the creditor as the debtor's estate will remain liable under the agreement. Consequently, there is no inherent need to terminate the agreement and repossess the goods. This is recognised by the the CCA, s 86(1), which restricts the rights of the creditor or owner on the death of the debtor or hirer. Section 86(1) provides that 'the creditor or owner under a regulated agreement is not entitled, by reason of the death of the debtor or hirer, to do an act specified in paras (a) to (e) of s 87(1) if at the death the agreement is fully secured'. The acts thus specified in s 87(1) paras (a) to (e) which must not be performed are: (a) termination of the agreement; (b) demanding earlier payment of any sum; (c) recovering possession of any goods or land; (d) treating any rights of the debtor conferred by the agreement as terminated, restricted or deferred; and (e) enforcement of any security.

The creditor or owner is prevented from taking these steps only where the agreement is 'fully secured' at the time of death and, although this is not defined in the CCA, the intent is clearly that the security must be sufficient to cover the obligations which are outstanding under the agreement at the time of death. Section 86(2) further provides that, if at the death of the debtor or hirer the agreement is only 'partly secured or is unsecured', the creditor or owner is entitled to do an act specified in paras (a) to (e) but only on an order of the court.

It is thus crucial to know what is meant by full and partial security and how these two notions are differentiated. The definition of 'security' in the CCA, s 189(1), covers both real security (eg a mortgage or charge) and personal security (eg a contract of guarantee or indemnity) but there is no indication as to which type of security is required for s 86(1). This difficulty apart, the valuation of the security at the date of death is a question of fact and, while this should not pose insuperable difficulties in the case of real security, it may not be easy to decide whether a personal contract of guarantee means that the agreement is 'fully secured'. Almost certainly it would be necessary to consider the actual financial status of the surety rather than the theoretical value of the guarantee.

The creditor must thus be sure that the security is deficient before he commences proceedings under s 86(2). Furthermore, s 128 provides that the court shall make an order under s 86(2) only if 'the creditor or owner proves that he has been unable to satisfy himself that the present and future obligations of the debtor or hirer under the agreement are likely to be discharged'. In attempting to discover whether or not the terms of the agreement will be observed, it is clear that the creditor must make positive enquiries of those managing the deceased debtor's affairs in order to ascertain their ability and willingness to make the payments under the contract.

The scope of s 86

Section 86 applies to all regulated agreements but there are certain restrictions on its operation. First, under s 86(3), s 86 applies in relation to the termination of an agreement only where (a) a period for its duration is specified in the agreement; and (b) that period has not ended when the creditor or owner purports to terminate the agreement, nothwithstanding that, under the agreement, any party is entitled to terminate it before the end of the period so specified. This means, for example, that if the debtor had an account of indefinite duration at a retail department store, the retailer can demand that the outstanding balance on the account be settled at once on the death of the debtor.

Second, under s 86(4), s 86 does not prevent the creditor 'from treating the right to draw on any credit as restricted or deferred, and taking such steps as may be necessary to make the restriction or deferment effective'. In other words, a creditor can end a line of credit, such as an overdraft, on the debtor's death and he may take practical steps to ensure that the credit is withdrawn, eg withdrawing a credit card.

Third, under s 86(5), s 86 does not affect the operation of any agreement providing for payment of sums due under the regulated agreement, or becoming due under it on the death of the debtor, out of the proceeds of a policy of life assurance on the debtor's life.

Finally, under s 173(3), the creditor or owner can take action without an order of the court under s 86(2) if the informed, voluntary consent of the personal representatives has been obtained. This does *not* apply to s 86(1), however, as that section *prohibits* certain acts on the death of the debtor or hirer in the case of a fully secured agreement.

ENFORCEMENT OF SECURITY

Frequently a contract of indemnity or guarantee is entered into to provide the creditor or owner with some security[13] for the performance of the debtor's or hirer's obligations. Section 111(1) provides that when a default or non-default notice (under ss 76, 87 and 88) or a notice of termination (under s 98) is served on the debtor or hirer, a copy of the notice must be served by the creditor or owner on any surety.[14] If the creditor or owner fails to comply with s 111(1), s 111(2) provides that the security is enforceable against the surety on an order of the court only.

The CCA also contains important provisions regarding the realisation and enforcement of securities. Section 112 empowers the Secretary of State to provide by regulation for any matters relating to the sale or other realisation of property over which any right has been provided by way of security but, as yet, no regulations have been made under this section.

Section 113 seeks to ensure that the creditor or owner cannot enforce a security and recover more than he would be entitled to under the regulated agreement, and so this section prevents evasion of the CCA by the use of a security. Section 113(1) states that, if a security is provided in relation to an actual or prospective regulated agreement, it shall not be enforced so as to benefit the creditor, directly or indirectly, to an extent greater than would be the case if the security were not provided, and any obligations of the debtor were carried out to the extent to which they would be enforced under the Act. Section 113(2) adds that, where a

---

13 'Security' is defined in s 189(1).
14 'Surety' is defined in s 189(1).

regulated agreement is enforceable on an order of the court or the Director only, any security provided in relation to the agreement is enforceable where such an order has been made in relation to the agreement, but not otherwise. For example, if an agreement is enforceable only on a court order made under s 65(1) because the agreement is improperly executed, any security provided is, likewise, enforceable only where such an order has been made. These rules also apply where a security is provided in relation to an actual or prospective linked transaction (s 113(8)).

Section 113, sub-ss (3)-(6) provide for the effect of s 106 upon securities in various circumstances and so, for example, if an agreement is cancelled under s 69 or terminated under s 91, the security shall, so far as it is so provided, be treated as never having effect.

Section 113(7)[15] provides an important exception to the overall scheme of s 113. Where an indemnity or a guarantee is given in a case where the debtor or hirer is a minor, or is otherwise not of full capacity, s 113(1) shall be read as if he were of full capacity. This means that guarantees or indemnities given by an adult are not valueless in the case of minors and, if the agreement is unenforceable against the debtor or hirer solely because he is under 18, the creditor or owner can nevertheless enforce the security.

15 As amended by the Minors' Contracts Act 1987, s 4.

CHAPTER 37

Judicial control

In the previous chapter consideration was given to the stringent requirements imposed by the CCA[1] regarding default notices and non-default notices where a creditor or owner wishes to enforce his rights. There are, however, situations where a creditor or owner is unable to exercise his rights without a court order. Also of great significance is the fact that the debtor or hirer may apply to the court for a time order which might, for example, extend the period during which the payment of instalments can be made. Equally important is the power given to the court to re-open extortionate credit bargains, even where the agreement is not regulated under the CCA. This chapter considers these wide, special powers which the court possesses under the CCA.

Enforcement orders

The CCA draws a distinction between those cases where (i) the creditor or owner has *infringed* the provisions of the Act and, consequently, must obtain a court order before he is able to proceed further; and (ii) there is no such infringement but, nevertheless, a court order is required before the creditor or owner can proceed further.

ENFORCEMENT ORDERS IN SITUATIONS OF INFRINGEMENT

Section 127 draws a distinction between minor and major infringements. A minor infringement may not necessarily render the agreement unenforceable and the court is endowed with a broad discretion to consider whether or not it would be just to make an enforcement order. An example of such a minor infraction would be a failure to supply the requisite copies of the agreement under ss 62 and 63.

In the case of major infringements (as specified in s 127(3) and (4)) the policy of the CCA was to place a total ban on enforceability by the creditor and, with this aim in view, the court was *prevented* from making an enforcement order in such cases. However, s 127(3) has recently been held to infringe Article 6.1 of the European Convention on Human Rights and Article 1 of the First Protocol

---

1 See ss 76, 87 and 98.

thereto. This important and controversial issue is examined in more detail when the major infringements are considered, below.

Minor infringements

First, it is necessary to consider the position regarding minor infringements. Section 127 grants to the court a wide discretion as to whether it will make an enforcement order and the terms which it may impose if it does make such an order. Section 127(1) provides that in the case of an application for an enforcement order under:

(a) s 65(1) (improperly executed agreements), or
(b) s 105(7)(a) or (b) (improperly executed security instruments), or
(c) s 111(2) (failure to serve copy of notice on surety), or
(d) s 124(1) or (2) (taking of negotiable instrument in contravention of s 123),

the court shall dismiss the application if, but only if, it considers it just to do so having regard to (i) prejudice caused to any person by the contravention in question, and the degree of culpability for it; and (ii) the powers conferred on the court by s 127(2) and ss 135 and 136. Section 127(2) permits the court, if it appears just to do so, to reduce or discharge any sum payable by the debtor or hirer, or any surety, so as to compensate him for prejudice suffered as a result of the contravention in question.

The emphasis in s 127(1) and (2) is that an enforcement order will be made unless there has been 'prejudice' suffered (ss 127(1)(i) and (2)) as a consequence of the contravention. Consequently, if there has been a minor, technical infringement but the debtor or hirer is none the worse off as a result, the court may waive the breach and not award any compensation to the debtor or hirer.[2] On the other hand, there will be clear evidence of prejudice if, had he been provided with the correct information in the first place, the debtor could have obtained a better rate of interest elsewhere, and this may justify a substantial reduction in the interest payable under the agreement.[3]

Major infringements

Second, there are the situations involving major infringements. The original intent of the CCA was that, under s 127(3) and (4), three situations were singled-out for special treatment and, here, the court was *precluded* from making an enforcement order. In the event of such major infringements, the debtor or hirer could thus retain possession of the goods and was not liable for instalments or other payments.

First, under s 127(3), the court cannot make such an order if s 61(1)(a) (signing of agreements) was not complied with unless a document (whether or not in the prescribed form and complying with regulations under s 60(1)) itself containing all the prescribed terms of the agreement was signed by the debtor or hirer

<hr>

2 See *Nissan Finance UK v Lockhart* [1993] CCLR 39.
3 See *National Guardian Mortgage Corpn v Wilkes* [1993] CCLR 1 (failure to supply the pre-contract copy (CCA, s 58) justified a substantial reduction of interest); *Rank Xerox Finance Ltd v Hepple and Fennymore* [1994] CCLR 1 (failure to provide information on accelerated payments in the event of default, meaning that the agreement was not properly executed under s 61, led to a claim for such payments amounting to £5,444 being reduced to £500).

(whether or not in the prescribed manner).[4] The upshot of this provision is that the creditor must make sure that the debtor or hirer has *signed* a document containing all the *prescribed* terms[5] – if the document is unsigned or does not contain the prescribed terms, it cannot be enforced in any circumstances. This Draconian provision was intended (see the *Wilson* decision, below) to ensure a basic, minimum level of protection for the debtor or hirer. It is not fatal to enforcement if terms *other* than the prescribed terms are omitted and s 127(5) provides that, where an enforcement order is made 'in a case to which subsection (3) applies' the order may direct that the agreement is to have effect 'as if it did not include a term omitted from the document signed by the debtor or hirer'.

The recent decision in *Wilson v First County Trust Ltd (No 2)*,[6] has examined s 127(3) in detail and reached a remarkable conclusion. In *Wilson*, the debtor wished to raise a six-month loan on the security of her BMW car and she approached the defendant creditor, a pawnbroker, who charged her a 'document fee' of £250 in respect of the loan of £5,000. The fee was added to the amount of the loan as the debtor could not afford to pay it immediately. The £250 was thus part of the total *charge* for credit which, by the CCA, s 9(4), could not be taken into account in ascertaining the *amount* of the credit. It followed that, by specifying the amount of the loan as £5,250, the agreement incorrectly stated the amount of credit and infringed the Consumer Credit (Agreements) Regulations 1983 (SI 1983/1553) because it did not include a term prescribed in those Regulations, viz a statement as to the correct, total amount of credit. The Court of Appeal accepted the debtor's argument that, under s 127(3), the court was precluded from enforcing the agreement. Moreover, under the CCA, s 113, the security over the debtor's car was unenforceable. However, the Court of Appeal also held that s 127(3) infringed Article 6.1 of the European Convention on Human Rights and Article 1 of the First Protocol thereto to an extent which was disproportionate. This was so because the *absolute* bar to enforcement in the case of an agreement which did not contain the prescribed terms was a disproportionate restriction on the right of the creditor to have the enforceability of his loan determined by the court. At first glance this seems to be an inversion of logic, as the punitive effect of s 127(3) was designed expressly to protect the rights of the *debtor* and shield him from abuse by the creditor in an area where the exploitation of debtors has always been rife. However, the Court of Appeal stressed that, although the original policy aim of s 127(3) was legitimate, it did not follow that the *method* by which that aim was to be achieved was also legitimate. An inflexible prohibition was not needed in order to achieve the legitimate policy aim of s 127(3), as this could be accomplished by empowering the court to do what was just and reasonable in a particular case. This conclusion was fortified as the courts were given a discretion to reach a just result in very similar circumstances under s 127(1), above. It is unclear what effect this finding will have on s 127(4)(a) and (b), considered below. Moreover, it remains to be seen what impact the human rights legislation may have on statutory provisions which impose absolute bans on the exclusion or restriction of liability (eg the Unfair Contract Terms Act 1977, s 6(2)) rather than subjecting such exclusion clauses to a test of 'reasonableness', thereby investing the court with an inherent discretion to reach a just outcome. Total prohibitions on the enforcement of rights

---

4 See *Wilson v First County Trust Ltd* (2001) Times, 16 May; [2001] QB 407.
5 See the Consumer Credit (Agreements) Regulations 1983 (SI 1983/1553), Sch 6.
6 (2001) Times, 16 May; see also [2001] QB 407 (interim judgment).

or the exclusion of liability which are encountered in consumer legislation were designed to endow the weaker party with a core level of protection which is immune from both the stronger party's interference and the common law's conspicuous desire to promote *laissez-faire* ideals during a large part of the 20th century. There will always be attempts by dishonest, stronger parties to exploit their dominance and tests based upon 'reasonableness' are both innately uncertain and necessarily demand litigation and judicial interpretation before their meaning and scope are divulged. On the other hand, absolute bans on the enforcement of rights equalise consumers' bargaining power, act as powerful disincentives to corrupt trading practices and are both easily understood by, and accessible to, consumers. Section 127(3) embodied all these aspirations and the wisdom of replacing its robust inflexibility with an amorphous test which directs the court to do justice in the circumstances must, therefore, be doubted.

Second, under s 127(4)(a), an enforcement order cannot be made in the case of a cancellable agreement if a provision of s 62 or s 63 (relating to copies of the agreement) was not complied with, and the creditor or owner did not give a copy of the executed agreement, and of any other document referred to in it, to the debtor or hirer before the commencement of the proceedings in which the order is sought. Once again, s 127(4)(a) is not cast in absolute terms and a failure to supply a copy under under s 62 or s 63 can be remedied provided that a copy of the executed agreement is given to the debtor or hirer before the commencement of proceedings.

Third, under s 127(4)(b), the court cannot make an enforcement order in the case of a cancellable agreement if s 64(1) (notice of cancellation rights) was not complied with. Here there is no room for manoeuvre and the infringement simply cannot be remedied, leaving the agreement permanently unenforceable.[7]

ENFORCEMENT ORDERS WHERE THERE IS NO INFRINGEMENT

In four circumstances, the CCA demands that the creditor or owner must obtain an order of the court even though he has not infringed any of the Act's provisions, viz:

(i)   under s 86(2), where an agreement is only partially secured or is unsecured, and the creditor or owner wishes to exercise rights arising as a result of the death of the debtor or hirer;

(ii) under s 90(1), where the goods are 'protected goods' and the debtor does not consent to their recovery by the creditor;

(iii) under s 92(1), where there is entry onto premises to take possession of goods subject to a regulated agreement and, under s 92(2), where there is recovery of the possession of land under a conditional sale agreement; and

(iv) under s 126, where there is enforcement of a land mortgage.

In relation to (i), above, s 128 states that the court shall make an order under s 86(2) only if 'the creditor or owner proves that he has been unable to satisfy himself that the present and future obligations of the debtor or hirer under the agreement are likely to be discharged'. As regards (ii)-(iv), above, the CCA contains no special provisions regarding the approach which the court should adopt when dealing with actions for the recovery of protected goods or for the

---

7   See *Moorgate Property Services Ltd v Kabir* [1995] CCLR 74.

enforcement of a land mortgage. However, the court has a broad discretion under ss 129-131 and ss 133-136 as regards orders which it might make and on what terms, these being considered later.

THE EFFECT OF ENFORCEMENT WITHOUT A COURT ORDER

Only two of the sections of the CCA which demand a court order before a regulated agreement can be enforced provide their own sanctions in the event that enforcement occurs without the mandatory court order, viz s 91 (consequences of the wrongful repossession of protected goods) and s 92(3) (wrongful entry onto premises to repossess goods and wrongful repossession of land). It seems that the consequences which are set-out in s 91 are all-embracing[8] but that an injunction may be available for breach of statutory duty under s 92(3).[9]

Where the sections of the CCA demand that the creditor or owner must obtain a court order to enforce the agreement but do not provide their own sanctions for enforcement without such an order,[10] s 170(1) appears to thwart any remedy other than an injunction (s 170(3)) although, under s 170(2), the Director General of Fair Trading has the power to treat the breach as a ground, for example, to suspend or revoke a licence.

Time orders

Arguably the most important power of the court is that provided under s 129 – the making of a 'time order'. There are three situations in s 129(1) where a time order can be made:

(a) on application by the creditor or owner for an enforcement order;
(b) on an application made by the debtor or hirer, under s 129(1)(b), after service on him of a default notice under s 87, or a notice under s 76(1) or s 98(1);
(c) in an action brought by a creditor or owner to enforce a regulated agreement or any security, or recover possession of any goods or land to which a regulated agreement relates.

The court thus has power to intercede and make a time order in virtually every situation[11] where the creditor or owner is attempting to enforce a regulated agreement or security. The importance of this latter requirement must be stressed in that the creditor or owner must take steps to enforce the agreement, in the circumstances defined in s 129(1), before the debtor or hirer can seek a time order. The debtor's independent right to ask for a time order exists only within the framework of s 129(1), ie when he is served with a default or enforcement notice. Moreover, in those agreements where the debtor or hirer has possession of goods (hire-purchase, conditional sale and consumer hire) he should apply to the County Court[12] for a time order as soon as possible after receiving a default

---

8   These are considered in Ch 36.
9   See the CCA, s 170(1) and 170(3).
10   See ss 65, 86(2), 105(7), 111(2), 113(2), 124 and 126.
11   Cf s 130(3).
12   Under s 189(1), 'court' means the County Court.

notice under s 87 for, otherwise, the goods might be lawfully repossessed in the meantime without a court order (eg the goods are not 'protected goods' or they are not on 'premises' within s 92) and the making of a time order cannot reverse the position.

THE COURT'S POWERS REGARDING THE TERMS OF TIME ORDERS

Under s 129(2), the court has a broad discretion to vary the terms of the agreement or security regarding payment. The subsection stipulates that the time order must provide for one or both of the following 'as the court considers just':

(a) payment by the debtor or hirer or any surety of any sum owed under a regulated agreement or a security by such instalments, payable at such times, as the court, having regard to the means of the debtor or hirer and any surety, considers reasonable;
(b) the remedying by the debtor or hirer of any breach of a regulated agreement (other than non-payment of money) within such period as the court may specify.

Section 130 contains supplementary provisions concerning time orders under s 129.

Time orders under s 129(2)(a)

In most applications for time orders, the debtor seeks time to pay and, if it considers it just to do so, the court may adjust the rate and timing of the instalments. Under s 129(2)(a), the court must have regard 'to the means of the debtor or hirer and any surety' and it is only where the debtor or hirer makes an offer to pay by instalments, which is accepted by the creditor or owner, that the court need not hear evidence of means (s 130(1)). The balancing exercise which the court must perform was illustrated in *First National Bank plc v Syed*.[13] There the Court of Appeal looked at the position of both the debtor and the creditor in deciding whether it was just to make a time order. In *Syed*, there was a history of default, merely sporadic payments by the debtor and no realistic possibility that his finances would improve. Consequently, the court considered it unjust to make the creditor accept instalments which would not even keep pace with the interest which was accruing on the account. A time order was thus refused and a possession order was granted.

As s 129(2)(a) applies to 'any sum owed', it is clear that the debtor or hirer can always ask for time to pay the arrears under the agreement. There are, however, certain situations where a time order may extend to *future* instalments. First, in relation to hire-purchase and conditional sale agreements, s 130(2) provides expressly that the court may consider future instalments when making a time order, thereby giving the court a discretion to re-draft the terms of the agreement regarding payment.

Second, if an accelerated payments clause in an agreement has been activated so that all remaining instalments have become due immediately, the debtor can ask for time to pay those instalments as here the creditor is calling in the entire loan. The conjoined appeals in *Southern and District Finance plc*

13 [1991] 2 All ER 250.

v Barnes[14] concerned possession proceedings brought by creditors to enforce mortgages granted by debtors as security for loans which had been advanced to them. The Court of Appeal held that, where possession proceedings are brought by the creditor, he demands payment of the whole sum which is outstanding under the charge, whether or not the loan has actually been called in. Accordingly, as the sum owed would comprise the total indebtedness, the court could make a time order in respect of the entire debt.[15]

After several conflicting decisions,[16] it is now clear that a time order which re-schedules a debt is *not* limited to extending the *time* during which the instalments must be paid. In *Southern and District Finance plc v Barnes*,[17] Leggatt LJ stressed that s 136 permits the court to include such provision as it considers just for amending any agreement or security in consequence of a term of the order. Consequently, the court can reduce the contractual rate of interest which is charged because, otherwise, the interest which accrues over the extended period of time for repayment would render the time order futile and ineffectual.[18]

It will be seen, below, that when a time order is made under s 129(2)(b), s 130(5) stops the creditor or owner from enforcing his rights under the agreement but there is no such provision in relation to time orders made under s 129(2)(a). Consequently, allowing the debtor or hirer an extension of time in which to pay does not preclude the enforcement by the creditor or owner of his remedies for default. This means that, unless controls elsewhere in the CCA prevent it (eg the goods have become protected goods) the creditor might be able to seize the goods or commence proceedings for their recovery. This position is criticisable as default in payment is patently the most frequent breach which is encountered. However, ss 133, 135 and 136 allow the court considerable room for manoeuvre when making an order and, in *Southern and District Finance plc v Barnes*,[19] where the Court of Appeal was dealing with an agreement secured on land, it was stated that where justice requires the making of a time order, the court should suspend any possession order that it also made, provided that the terms of the time order are complied with.

Time orders under s 129(2)(b)

Under s 129(2)(b), the time order relates to 'the remedying by the debtor or hirer of any breach of a regulated agreement (other than non-payment of money) within such period as the court may specify'. These breaches are rarer than those relating to non-payment of money and most commonly arise in hire-purchase, conditional sale or hire agreements where, for example, the debtor or hirer has failed to maintain the goods properly or has lost possession of them. In both these examples, the breach might be remediable. The creditor or owner will serve a default notice under s 87 which must specify the time during which the breaches must be remedied (a minimum of seven days from the date of receipt of the notice), and so a time order under s 129(2)(b) can extend the time allowed for remedying the breach.

14 (1995) 27 HLR 691.
15 See also *Director General of Fair Trading v First National Bank plc* [2000] 2 All ER 759, 765-766 per Peter Gibson LJ.
16 *Cedar Holdings Ltd v Jenkins* [1988] CCLR 34; *Ashbroom Facilities v Bodley* [1992] CCLR 31; *Cedar Holdings Ltd v Thompson* [1993] CCLR 7.
17 (1995) 27 HLR 691.
18 See also *Director General of Fair Trading v First National Bank plc* [2000] 2 All ER 759, 765-766 per Peter Gibson LJ.
19 (1995) 27 HLR 691.

Section 130(5) is crucial to the operation of time orders under s 129(2)(b) and applies only in cases of non-monetary breaches under the latter subsection. In effect, s 130(5)(a) immobilises the creditor during the period of the time order and prevents him from exercising remedies which would otherwise be available. Accordingly, he cannot enforce the agreement by exercising any of the rights mentioned in s 87(1) (terminating the agreement; demanding earlier payment of any sum; recovering possession of goods or land; treating any right conferred on the debtor or hirer by the agreement as terminated, restricted or deferred; and enforcing any security). Not only is the creditor or owner prevented from taking such steps in relation to a breach which the time order has expressly addressed, he cannot pursue these rights in relation to new breaches of contract which occur during the period of the time order. Constrained in this way, the remaining, proper course of action, is for the creditor to apply (under s 130(6)) for a revocation or variation of the time order.

Moreover, under s 130(5)(b), a distinction is drawn between 'primary' and 'secondary' provisions of the agreement. The essence of the subsection is that, where a time order has been granted so that remedial action can be taken in relation to a breach of a primary provision, a secondary provision which would normally be activated on that breach is not activated and remains inoperative during the period of the time order. If, for example, the agreement provides for payment of compensation (secondary provision) where the debtor fails to repair the goods (primary provision), the creditor cannot invoke the provision as to compensation while the time order relating to the failure to repair remains in force.

If the breach is remedied during the period of the time order, s 130(5)(c) provides that it 'shall be treated as not having occurred'. If it has not been remedied, the creditor may proceed to enforce his rights at the end of the period prescribed in the time order.

Section 130(4) and the statutory bailment

Section 130(4) provides that, where, following the making of a time order in relation to a hire-purchase, conditional sale or consumer hire agreement, the debtor or hirer is in possession of the goods, he shall be treated as a bailee under the terms of the agreement, notwithstanding that the agreement has been terminated. Consequently, subject to the terms of the time order, the obligations under the agreement endure (eg an obligation to insure the goods) and the debtor or hirer is constituted a statutory bailee. As stated above, in relation to time orders under s 129(2)(b) (non-monetary breaches), s 130(5) prevents the creditor from exercising remedies under the contract and, provided the breach is remedied during the period of the time order, s 130(5)(c) provides that it 'shall be treated as not having occurred'.

Protection orders

There is a distinct possibility that a debtor or hirer might hide, damage or dispose of the goods if he knows that there is a likelihood of repossession by the creditor or owner. Accordingly, s 131 provides that, on the application of the creditor or owner under a regulated agreement, the court may make 'such orders as it thinks just for protecting any property of the creditor or owner, or property subject to any security, from damage or depreciation pending the determination of any proceedings under this Act, including orders restricting or prohibiting use of the property or giving directions as to its custody'.

Special powers of the court in relation to hire-purchase and conditional sale agreements

Under s 133, the court has special powers in relation to a regulated hire-purchase or conditional sale agreement (i) where there is an application for an enforcement order or a time order; or (ii) where an action is brought by the creditor to recover possession of goods to which the agreement relates. In these situations, if it 'appears to the court just to do so', it may make a return order or a transfer order.

RETURN ORDERS

As the name suggests, a return order is, under s 133(1)(i), an order 'for the return to the creditor of goods to which the agreement relates'. Such an order may be unconditional or, more commonly, it will be either conditional or suspended by virtue of the court's powers under s 135. The return order may thus be suspended on condition that the debtor pays the unpaid balance in instalments which the court considers just, pursuant to a time order. If the debtor complies with the order, completes the instalments and fulfils any other conditions then, under s 133(5), the creditor's title to the goods vests in the debtor. It should be noted that s 135(1)(b)(i) and (ii) provide for the supension in differing ways, viz (i) 'until such time as the court subsequently directs'; or (ii) 'until the occurrence of a specified act or omission'. If the debtor defaults under the suspended order then, under (i), the creditor must apply to the court for the suspension to be lifted but, under (ii), the creditor can immediately proceed to execute the return order.

Most importantly, under s 135(2), the court cannot suspend an order for delivery up of the goods by the debtor or 'any person' unless satisfied that the goods are in his possession or control.

TRANSFER ORDERS

The hire-purchase or conditional sale agreement may relate to separate, divisible goods and a transfer order, under s 133(1)(b)(ii), may provide for the transfer to the debtor of the creditor's title to certain goods to which the agreement relates and the return to the creditor of the remainder of the goods. Under the earlier hire-purchase legislation this was referred to as a 'split order', but it was always rare.

Where a transfer order is made, the transferred goods are such of the goods to which the agreement relates as the court thinks just, but such an order shall be made only where the paid-up sum exceeds the part of the total price referable to the transferred goods by an amount equal to at least one-third of the unpaid balance of the total price (s 133(3)). The purpose of this somewhat obscure provision is to compensate the creditor where he is obliged to accept the return of used goods under the transfer order. An example makes this more accessible. Suppose the total price of the goods is £3,000, then, assuming the goods to which the agreement relates can physically be separated, a transfer order may be made in respect of goods to which £1,000 of the total price is referable provided the debtor has paid up at least £1,500. £500 is one-third of the unpaid balance of the total price and the paid-up sum (£1,500) does exceed the part of the total price referable to the transferred goods (£1,000) by £500. The part of the total price referable to the transferred goods is the part assigned to those goods by the agreement or (if no such assignment is made) the part determined by the court to be reasonable (s 133(7)).

Notwithstanding the making of a return order or transfer order, the debtor may at any time before the goods enter the creditor's possession, claim the goods ordered to be returned to the creditor on payment of the balance of the total price and the fulfilment of any other necessary conditions (s 133(4)).

If, in contravention of a return order or a transfer order, any goods to which the order relates are not returned to the creditor, the court may (on the creditor's application) revoke the order so far as it relates to those goods and order the debtor to pay the unpaid portion of so much of the total price as is referable to those goods (s 133(6)).

Section 133(5) applies to transfer orders as well as return orders, and so the creditor's title to the goods will vest in the debtor when the total price is paid and any other necessary conditions are fulfilled under the transfer order.

Power to vary agreements and securities

Section 136 provides that the court 'may in an order made by it under this Act include such provision as it considers just for amending any agreement or security in consequence of a term of the order'. In *Southern and District Finance plc v Barnes*,[20] it was argued that s 137 gives wide powers to the court to re-write loan agreements where the rate of interest is extortionate and these powers would be otiose if all agreements could be re-written using a combination of ss 129 and 136. Leggatt LJ stressed that there was a difference between ss 136 and 137: the court could invoke the provisions as to extortionate credit bargains at any time, irrespective of default, but s 136 did not stand alone because the court could not amend an agreement unless it had been persuaded to make an order under the Act. Furthermore, the judge considered that the key phrase in s 136 was 'in consequence of a term' and so, unless the contemplated amendment was truly a consequence of an order and the making of that order was also just, there was no power to make the amendment. It followed that, in consequence of a term of a time order under s 129, the court was empowered under s 136 to adjust the contractual rate of interest which was charged.

Orders in relation to consumer hire agreements

Section 133 does *not* apply to consumer hire agreements but many of the provisions considered earlier do apply to such agreements. The court can make a protection order under s 131 if it thinks that the goods may be damaged or destroyed. After a default notice or a s 76 or s 98 notice is served on the hirer, he may apply to the court and a time order might be made under s 129. There are wide powers in s 135 for conditional or suspended orders to be made by the court but, most importantly, under s 135(3), a suspended order may *not* extend the contractual period during which the hirer is entitled to possession of the goods.

These orders are essentially no different from those made in hire-purchase or conditional sale but, under s 132, the court has one power which is unique to consumer hire and is expressed in very broad terms. Where the owner recovers possession of the goods otherwise than by action *or* where in proceedings relating to the hire agreement the court makes an order for delivery of the goods to the owner, the hirer may apply to court for an order that (i) the 'whole or part of any sum' paid by the hirer in respect of the goods shall be repaid; and (ii) the obligation to pay the 'whole or part of any sum' owed in respect of the goods shall cease. The court may grant the application in full or part where it 'appears just to do so, having regard to the extent of the enjoyment of the goods by the hirer'. These extensive provisions are designed to mitigate hardship to the hirer where, for example, a large deposit has been taken at the start of the contract which is then terminated for default after only a short period of time. In *Galbraith v Mitchenall Estates Ltd*,[1] the plaintiff (P) entered into a contract for the hire of a caravan which was intended to be a home for his wife and family. He paid a deposit of £550.10s and incurred an obligation to pay 60 rental instalments of £12.10s each month for five years. As P paid no instalments, the defendants (D) terminated the agreement after five months and sold the caravan for £775, a sum which would have been greater but for the damage caused by the repossession agents. As the original retail price of the caravan was £1,050, D had received £275 more than that price after five months (£550.10s deposit + £775 sale price = £1,325.10s). P, on the other hand, had paid £550.10s for five months' occupation of the caravan. As there was no unconscionable conduct at the date the agreement was entered into, Sachs J considered that he was unable to grant any relief to the hirer at common law even though the terms of the agreement were 'hideously harsh'. Clearly the court now has power, under s 132, to alleviate the hardship caused in such agreements, a power which is particularly necessary in view of the fact that goods can become 'protected goods' only in hire-purchase and conditional sale agreements and the court's power to re-open extortionate credit bargains does not extend to consumer hire agreements.

Extortionate credit bargains

The Moneylenders Acts 1900–1927 (repealed by the CCA, 1974) empowered the courts to reopen a moneylending transaction where the interest was 'excessive' and the transaction was 'harsh and unconscionable'. The 1927 Act created a rebuttable presumption that the interest was excessive and the transaction harsh and unconscionable if the interest charged exceeded 48% per annum but, where the interest was under that threshold, the onus was on the borrower to prove that the interest was excessive. The Acts were not always successful in that the moneylender could often justify the rate of interest having regard to the small amount of the loan and the inherent risk of unsecured lending. Furthermore, the Moneylenders Acts did not apply to hire-purchase agreements and, if the lender was not in the business of moneylending, the Acts had no application at all.

SCOPE OF THE CONSUMER CREDIT ACT, SECTIONS 137-140

The CCA, ss 137-140 contain broad provisions empowering the court to re-open extortionate credit agreements and these sections were the model for similar

---

1   [1965] 2 QB 473.

provisions in the Insolvency Act 1986. Under the CCA, s 137(1), if the court 'finds a credit bargain extortionate it may re-open the credit agreement so as to do justice between the parties'.

This power applies to *all* credit agreements, whether or not they are regulated agreements.[2] Section 137(2)(a) provides that 'credit agreement' means 'any agreement between an individual[3] (the "debtor") and any other person (the "creditor") by which the creditor provides the debtor with credit of any amount'. For example, a loan to an individual of £500,000 is within ss 137-140. The court's power also extends to the classifications of 'exempt agreements', 'small agreements' and 'non-commercial agreements'. It follows that any form of credit or financial accommodation is within ss 137-140, eg hire-purchase, credit-sale, cash loans and trading checks, and the creditor does *not* have to be in the business of providing credit. The only restriction on the operation of ss 137-140 is that the debtor must be an individual. However, the power to re-open the agreement does *not* apply to consumer hire but, as discussed above, the court can provide relief within the terms of s 132.[4]

WHAT IS A 'CREDIT BARGAIN' IN THIS CONTEXT?

In deciding whether a credit agreement should be re-opened, the court is not limited simply to an investigation of the terms of the credit agreement itself. The court may make a much wider examination of the 'credit bargain' and thus look at any ancillary agreement or linked transaction which must be taken into account when calculating the total charge for credit,[5] eg a maintenance contract which must be entered into pursuant to the main credit agreement where the debtor is not allowed to nominate the contractor or a fee paid under a credit-brokerage contract.

Section 137(2)(b) defines a 'credit bargain' as (i) 'where no transaction other than the credit agreement is to be taken into account in computing the total charge for credit, means the credit agreement; or (ii) where one or more other transactions are to be so taken into account, means the credit agreement and those other transactions, taken together'. The notion of the 'credit bargain' is thus an anti-evasion measure which prevents the creditor from keeping the credit charges under the actual credit agreement at a low level while fixing the credit charges under the ancillary contracts at an extortionate level. Section 137(2)(b)(ii) emphasises that the court can examine the total charge for the credit under all the agreements at issue.

THE STATUTORY DEFINITION OF AN EXTORTIONATE CREDIT BARGAIN

The meaning of an extortionate credit bargain is delineated in s 138(1) which provides that:

2 See the CCA, s 140.
3 Defined in s 189(1) as including a partnership or other unincorporated body but *not* a body corporate.
4 If the agreement is not within the CCA's definition of consumer hire (see s 15), the hirer can invoke only equity's jurisdiction to set aside unconscionable bargains.
5 See the CCA, s 20(1) and the Consumer Credit (Total Charge for Credit) Regulations 1980 (SI 1980/51) as amended by SI 1985/1192, SI 1989/596.

'(1) A credit bargain is extortionate if it –

(a) requires the debtor or a relative of his to make payments (whether unconditionally, or on certain contingencies) which are grossly exorbitant, or

(b) otherwise grossly contravenes ordinary principles of fair dealing.'

The reference to payments made 'on certain contingencies' allows the court to consider charges made on default or on voluntary termination of the agreement, for example. It would be an insuperable task for the CCA to attempt a definition of payments which are 'grossly exorbitant' and so, instead, s 138(2) provides that, in determining whether the credit bargain is extortionate, 'regard shall be had to such evidence as is adduced concerning':

'(a) interest rates prevailing at the time it was made,

(b) the factors mentioned in subsection (3) to (5), and

(c) any other relevant considerations.'

Subsections (3) to (5) list particular factors relevant to the debtor, creditor, and linked transactions which are a mixture of objective and subjective criteria.

Factors listed in s 138(3) as applicable to the debtor are:

'(a) his age, experience, business capacity and state of health; and

(b) the degree to which, at the time of making the credit bargain, he was under financial pressure, and the nature of that pressure.'

Factors listed in s 138(4) as applicable to the creditor are:

'(a) the degree of risk accepted by him, having regard to the value of any security provided;

(b) his relationship to the debtor; and

(c) whether or not a colourable cash price was quoted for any goods or services included in the credit bargain.'

Section 138(5) adds that factors applicable to a linked transaction include the question 'how far the transaction was reasonably required for the protection of debtor or creditor, or was in the interest of the debtor'.

THE DECISIONS ON EXTORTIONATE CREDIT BARGAINS

Under the Moneylenders Acts, the court could reopen the agreement where the interest charged was 'excessive' and the transaction was 'harsh and unconscionable'. Under the CCA, the credit bargain is 'extortionate' where the debtor is required to make payments which are 'grossly exorbitant' or where the bargain 'contravenes ordinary principles of fair dealing'.

Overall, the decisons concerned with the CCA have stressed the fact that, although the transaction may be 'unwise', this does not render the credit bargain extortionate under the Act[6] and, by and large, the courts have adopted a restrictive interpretation of the Act's provisions. Moroever, there have been admonitions to the effect that, as the provisions of the CCA are both novel and comprehensive, decisions on the Moneylenders Acts should not be

---

6 See *Wills v Wood* [1984] CCLR 7, 15 per Sir John Donaldson MR; *Davies v Directloans Ltd* [1986] 1 WLR 823, 836-838 per Edward Nugee QC (sitting as a deputy High Court judge); *Coldunell Ltd v Gallon* [1986] QB 1184.

consulted[7] and, in one decision,[8] the judge stressed that the test for re-opening a credit bargain had been made *more* stringent under the CCA as 'exorbitant' replaced 'excessive' and was also qualifed by the word 'grossly'.

In 1991, the then Director General of Fair Trading, Sir Gordon Borrie QC, expressed concern that 'the extortionate credit bargain provisions of the Act have not effectively dealt with the problems to which they were addressed'.[9] The Director General considered that there were particular difficulties where 'the costs of credit ... substantially exceed levels which would be generated by a fully competitive market and/or are so oppressive or exploitive that no sensible person, independently advised, would find them acceptable'.[10] Moreover, the Director General's report stressed that 'non-status' lenders (ie those with poor creditworthiness) are often 'induced to borrow on excessive or oppressive terms against the security of their homes without regard to their ability to repay the loan' and, in cases of unsecured loans, 'a series of short-term cash loans, each one usually paying off existing indebtedness to the same lender, can trap borrowers ... into extremely expensive cycles of debt'.[11]

Payments which are 'grossly exorbitant': s 138(1)(a)

The debtor is most likely to allege that interest, charges under the agreement and any sums payable under a linked transaction are 'grossly exorbitant'. Under the Moneylenders Acts, the decision of the House of Lords in *Samuel v Newbold*[12] established that an excessive rate of interest could, in itself, be sufficient to re-open the agreement on the basis that the rate was 'excessive' and the transaction 'harsh and unconscionable'.[13] Lord Macnaghten emphasised that 'the rate of interest may be so monstrous' as to show, by itself, that the agreement contravened 'ordinary rules of fair dealing'.[14] However, the judiciary has frequently warned that some varieties of agreement will, necessarily, carry higher interest than others and all the circumstances of the credit bargain must be considered. This reasoning leads to the conclusion that, for example, a rate of interest which would be extortionate under a long-term hire-purchase agreement might be justifiable in the case of a short-term, small loan, granted to the debtor immediately. In *Blair v Buckworth*,[15] for example, Lord Alverstone CJ cautioned that the rate of interest might, on its own, be a fallacious test as to whether a transaction was harsh and unconscionable because '1s. interest for a

---

7 *Ketley (A) Ltd v Scott* [1981] ICR 241, 245 per Foster J; *Davies v Directloans Ltd* [1986] 1 WLR 823, 831 per Edward Nugee QC (sitting as a deputy High Court judge); cf *Castle Phillips Finance Co Ltd v Khan* [1980] CCLR 1, 3 per His Honour Judge Perks.

8 *First National Securities Ltd v Bertrand* [1980] CCLR 5 (Judge White, Wandsworth County Court).

9 *Unjust Credit Transactions* (OFT, Sept 1991), para 1.7.

10 *Unjust Credit Transactions* (OFT, Sept 1991), para 1.5.

11 *Unjust Credit Transactions* (OFT, Sept 1991), para 1.6. See the example at para 4.12 of a couple who borrowed £50 and, in order to pay off the loan at the end of the agreement, they were offered a further loan at a higher rate of interest. At the end of the second year the same thing happened and, after 25 years, the couple owed £2,500 and were paying £10 per week.

12 [1906] AC 461.

13 See p 467 per Lord Loreburn LC; p 470 per Lord Macnaghten; p 473 per Lord James of Hereford, and p 477 per Lord Atkinson.

14 [1906] AC 461 at 470.

15 (1908) 24 TLR 474.

week on £1 or 5s. interest on £1 for a short period, though an enormous rate of interest, ought not to be set aside'.[16] More recently, in *Woodstead Finance Ltd v Petrou*,[17] a loan was advanced to pay off mortgage arrears but the rate of interest of 42% (APR) was not disturbed because this was the normal rate for short-term loans of this type.

One solution to these problems would have been for the CCA (or a new statutory provision) to follow the scheme of the earlier Moneylenders Acts and impose an absolute ceiling on rates of interest but, today, this is regarded as unworkable having regard to the wide range of differing credit transactions within the CCA.[18] While this may be justifiable as an abstract proposition, it does little to exculpate extortionate and oppressive rates of interest: one case encountered by the Office of Fair Trading involved interest of £37.50 charged on a three week loan of just over £100, this being an APR of just under 400,000%.[19]

An ethereal, yet narrow definition of an extortionate credit bargain (in tandem with the need for the court to re-open such bargains) does not deter the corrupt practices of loansharks and thus miscarries as an efficacious consumer remedy. The consumer/debtor is frequently ignorant of his rights but the creditor always knows that, in the improbable event of the bargain's being re-opened, a reasonable rate will be fixed and so there is no reason for him not to stipulate an exorbitant rate in the first place. A system of absolute ceilings on rates of interest is, undeniably, an understandable consumer remedy which would eradicate the worst cases of abuse, particularly if contracts which contravened the interest rate ceilings were also to be rendered unenforceable. It has to be acknowledged, however, that fixed ceilings tend to encourage a black market of illegal lending thus exacerbating abusive practices. Moroever, there is a tendency for the fixed ceilings to acquire an air of respectability with the consequence that interest rates move upwards and so average market rates increase. The Moneylenders Acts contained a rebuttable presumption that interest was excessive and the transaction harsh and unconscionable where the rate of interest exceeded 48% per annum. In fact, the Crowther Committee had recommended that the 48% presumption should remain,[20] but this was not enacted in the CCA. It is suggested that a presumption of this nature should be revived as it does not harbour the dangers of the absolute, fixed ceiling. The menace of black market credit should be lessened, as honest creditors could charge higher rates of interest in high-risk loans and seek legitimately to justify those rates and, if different thresholds of permissible interest existed throughout differing credit transactions, rate flexibility would be preserved.

The decisions on s 138(1)(a)

The decisions which have interpreted s 138(1)(a) must now be examined. In *Ketley (A) Ltd v Scott*,[1] the defendants (D) had agreed to buy a house but needed to

---

16 (1908) 24 TLR 474 at 476.
17 [1986] CCLR 107.
18 See *Reform of the Law on Consumer Credit* (Cmnd 5427, 1973), para 68. Interest rate ceilings are also rejected by the OFT (see *Unjust Credit Transactions* (Sept 1991), Annex C, pp 41-43).
19 *Unjust Credit Transactions* (OFT, Sept 1991), para 2.17.
20 *Report of the Committee on Consumer Credit* (Cmnd 4596, 1971), para 6.6.9.
 1 [1981] ICR 241.

raise a loan quickly in order to complete the purchase. The plaintiff company (P) lent £20,500 to D, the rate of interest being expressed as 12% over three months (equivalent to 48% per annum) and the contract was signed in the presence of solicitors for both sides. D did not tell P that he had granted a legal charge on the house to his bank to cover an overdraft and was liable under other guarantees to third parties, nor did he disclose that a professional valuation of the house was less than the value he was claiming for it. As the loan had not been repaid, P claimed payment of the sums due and possession of the property. P obtained judgment but the order directed an inquiry as to whether the interest was extortionate. Foster J held that, for various reasons, the credit bargain should not be re-opened. First, P had lent 82% of the value of the property with such 'extraordinary speed' that it was impossible to make the necessary inquiries as to D's financial position and thus the degree of risk accepted by P was high (see s 138(4)(a)). Second, having regard to that degree of risk, the rate of interest charged was not extortionate (see s 138(2)(a)). Third, D had his solicitor with him when the agreement was entered into and he was not inexperienced in business matters. Moreover, he was not under any financial pressure and 'knew exactly what he was doing' (see s 138(3)(a) and (b)). Fourth, D's 'deceitful acts' in not telling P of the charge on the house and the non-disclosure of the other financial commitments meant that it would not be just to re-open the credit agreement (see s 139(1)). Accordingly, it was held that the credit bargain was not extortionate within s 138(1) and should not be re-opened.

The same conclusion was reached in *Davies v Directloans Ltd*,[2] where the mortgage agreement in question was not regarded as an extortionate credit bargain for several reasons. Edward Nugee QC (sitting as a deputy High Court judge) considered that the test was not whether a creditor had acted in a morally reprehensible manner but, instead, 'the starting and ending point in determining whether a credit bargain is extortionate must be the words of section 138(1)'.[3] Accordingly, although the plaintiffs were naive and trusting, they were advised by an independent solicitor that the mortgage was expensive and any financial pressure that they were under was the inevitable consequence of their original decision to buy the property and no advantage was taken of it by the defendant. Having regard to the security offered, the degree of risk accepted by the defendant was significant and the advance amounted to 83.3% of the purchase price. This justified the rate of interest charged, which was more than that charged by building societies but, at 21.7% APR, it was not grossly exorbitant in comparison with the prevailing rates of interest (a building society rate of 17.5% APR and some finance houses charging 26%-35% APR).

In contrast with these cases, bargains have been re-opened in some decisions, but many of the cases were in the County Court and have been left unreported. In *Barcabe Ltd v Edwards*,[4] the debtors borrowed £400 in order to buy a car and the flat rate of interest was nearly 100% (APR 319%). One of the debtors was illiterate and the other had a low level of literacy. It was held that it was *prima facie* extortionate to charge 100% interest when other lenders were charging 20% and the court substituted a rate of 40% which would have given an APR of 92% under the original terms. Likewise, in *Devogate v Jarvis*,[5] a

2 [1986] 1 WLR 823.
3 [1986] 1 WLR 823 at 831.
4 [1983] CCLR 11 (Birmingham County Court).
5 (16 November 1987, unreported); Sevenoaks County Court.

loan of £10,000 was well-secured on the debtors' property and was advanced to pay off existing debts at an APR of 39%. The court substituted an APR of 30% and stressed that, although the rate of interest was not unusual in the non-status sector (ie debtors with poor creditworthiness), the loan was well-secured and so the degree of risk involved justified a lower rate of interest. In *Prestonwell Ltd v Capon*,[6] the debtors' mortgage of £18,000 at flat rate of 42% was halved to 21%, the judge taking into account that the debtors (i) could have obtained a cheaper loan elsewhere; (ii) had little business capacity; (iii) were under financial pressure; (iv) had no access to proper legal advice; and (v) the risk to the creditor was low. The decision in *Shahabinia v Giyahchi*[7] backfired on the debtor who took loans for business purposes with flat rates of interest between 78% and 156%. In the High Court, the judge re-opened the bargain and substituted a rate of 15%, but the Court of Appeal considered that this did not do justice between the parties as 15% was less than the bank rate during some of the relevant period. Accordingly, the court replaced the rate of 15% with a flat rate of 30% on each loan. Finally, in *Castle Phillips & Co Ltd v Wilkinson*,[8] the debtors took a bridging loan secured by a mortgage on their home and were required to pay interest (4% per month) which was more than three times the rate charged by building societies. The interest was reduced to 20% per annum which reflected the short-term loan which had been advanced.

The credit bargain 'grossly contravenes ordinary principles of fair dealing': s 138(1)(b)

Section 138(1)(b) provides that the credit bargain is extortionate if it 'grossly contravenes ordinary principles of fair dealing' and so, even if the payments required are *not* 'grossly exorbitant' under s 138(1)(a), the credit bargain can be re-opened under the alternative formulation in s 138(1)(b).

Under the Moneylenders Acts, the court could re-open the agreement where the transaction was 'harsh and unconscionable' and this was held to be the case where, for example, the moneylender exercised misrepresentation on the borrower. In *Carringtons Ltd v Smith*,[9] Channell J considered that the Act was meant to 'hit' the 'moneylender's traps for the unwary' and so the judge insisted that, although a rate of interest of 60% per annum was not, in itself, necessarily excessive or harsh and unconscionable, if it were to be disguised as 1s in the pound per month in order to deceive the borrower, he would 'then hold that the interest was both excessive and harsh and unconscionable'.[10] Equally, the harsh and unconscionable criterion was used to re-open agreements where there was necessity on the part of the borrower known to the lender and used to his advantage,[11] where the borrower

---

6 (1988) unreported; Corby County Court.
7 (5 July 1989, unreported), CA.
8 [1992] CCLR 83.
9 [1906] 1 KB 79.
10 [1906] 1 KB 79 at 91; see also *Victorian Daylesford Syndicate Ltd v Dott* [1905] 2 Ch 624.
11 See *Blair v Buckworth* (1908) 24 TLR 474 (the agreement was re-opened because the plaintiff moneylender (P) knew of the urgent necessity of the borrower for money within a few days, and that it was essential for him to leave for Russia with the money in order to protect his assets there. The rate of interest was 44% even though the loan was secured on land worth some three times the amount of the loan. It was held that P took advantage of the borrower's necessitous situation and the fact that the *borrower* appreciated the significance of the transaction was only one element to consider); see also *Bonnard v Dott* (1906) 21 TLR 491; *Part v Bond* (1906) 22 TLR 253.

did not understand the terms of the agreement[12] and, significantly, when the borrower had been unfairly tempted to take a loan. The latter point was raised in *Lewis v Mills*,[13] where the borrower had refused a loan from a moneylender but, a few days later, wrote to him asking his terms for a loan of £100. The moneylender replied enclosing banknotes for £100 and a promissory note with a swingeing default clause which had not been explained to the borrower. The borrower signed the note but defaulted on the second instalment. Rowlatt J observed that the borrower had the cash in his hands when 'his other creditors were clamouring at the gate, and the temptation was very great'.[14] Accordingly, as the terms of the loan had never been negotiated, it was held that the agreement could be re-opened.

Many of these situations under the Moneylenders Acts could not arise today as the the CCA and its welter of regulations prescribe, for example, the formalities of the credit agreement and demand the disclosure of rates of interest which show the true cost of the loan. However, it is regrettable that the courts have shown a marked reluctance to develop any principles relating to 'fair dealing' under s 138(1)(b), preferring to emphasise that improvident or unwise transactions are not extortionate and, thereby, ignoring the wider connotations of unfairness.[15]

The Court of Appeal had to consider the ambit of s 138(1)(b) in *Coldunell Ltd v Gallon*.[16] The defendants were an old couple aged 86 and 91 who took a loan of £20,000 in order to support a business venture of their son. The loan was secured on their home, their only capital asset, and the creditors knew the purpose of the loan and that it would be repaid by the son. No survey was undertaken, no enquiries were made as to the father's age, status or income and the contract was drafted by the creditor's solicitors. The solicitors advised the couple to take independent legal advice but this advice did not reach them, possibly because it was intercepted by the son. The money was paid to the son but he was very soon in default and the creditors sought repayment of the principal and interest or, failing that, possession of the property. The Court of Appeal held that neither the creditors nor their solicitors had authorised the son to be their agent in the transaction and they were thus not liable for his undue influence or dishonesty. Moreover, the fact that the loan was for the son's benefit did not mean that there was a duty on the creditor to *ensure* that the couple had independent advice, instead there was only a duty to warn of the desirability of such advice. As the rate of interest was not excessive, the parents sought refuge in the CCA, s 138(1)(b), and argued that the transaction contravened 'ordinary principles of fair dealing'. The court held that the burden on the creditors to prove that the bargain was not extortionate was discharged once they had shown that they were not tainted by the son's undue influence and that this bargain 'was on its face a proper and not extortionate commercial bargain and that the plaintiffs acted in a way that an ordinary commercial lender would be expected to act'.[17] Purchas LJ added that, had there been any evidence of the creditors' involvement in the deceitful behaviour of the son, he would have decided without hesitation that their conduct fell within s 138(1)(b), but there was no such evidence.

With respect, these generalisations are most unhelpful, limited as they are to a superficial consideration of procedural unfairness viewed in terms of manifest

---

12 See *Stirling v Rose* (1913) 30 TLR 67.
13 (1914) 30 TLR 438.
14 (1914) 30 TLR 438 at 439.
15 See *Wills v Wood* [1984] CCLR 7.
16 [1986] QB 1184.
17 [1986] QB 1184 at 1202, per Oliver LJ.

deceit and dishonesty. Moreover, the judgments circumvent the factors in s 138 which the court must consider in determining whether a credit bargain is extortionate. In *Coldunnel*, the relevant issues were the age, experience and business capacity of the debtor and the degree of risk accepted by the creditor. The county court judge had applied these factors in deciding that the creditors had failed to discharge the burden upon them and prove that the bargain was not extortionate, but the Court of Appeal held that, in the face of the evidence, the judge was not entitled to draw that conclusion.

THE BURDEN OF PROOF AND NATURE OF THE RELIEF AVAILABLE

Under s 171(7), if the debtor or any surety alleges that a credit bargain is extortionate, the creditor has the onus of proving the contrary. This should be helpful to the debtor but the burden on the creditor was discharged with minimal effort in *Coldunell Ltd v Gallon*, above. It is significant that, under s 139(1)(a), an application that the credit agreement be re-opened may be made by the debtor or surety even though the creditor has not instituted proceedings, although few consumers will be likely to initiate an action in this way thus accentuating the inutility of private law in this area. A credit agreement may also be re-opened at the instance of the debtor or any surety in any proceedings to enforce the agreement, any security relating to it or any linked transaction (s 139(1)(b)) or at the instance of the debtor or a surety in other proceedings where the amount paid or payable under the credit agreement is relevant (s 139(1)(c)).

In re-opening the agreement, the court's powers to relieve the debtor or a surety from payment of any sum in excess of that fairly due and reasonable are to make one or more of the orders specified in s 139(2), viz:

(a) direct accounts to be taken;
(b) set aside the whole or part of any obligation imposed on the debtor or a surety by the credit bargain or any related agreement;
(c) require the creditor to repay the whole or part of any sum paid by the debtor or a surety under the credit bargain or any related agreement, whether paid to the creditor or any other person;
(d) direct the return to the surety of any property provided for the purposes of the security; or
(e) alter the terms of the agreement or any security instrument.

In particular, it should be noted that s 139(2)(c) may require the creditor to repay sums which have been paid to a person other than himself. Section 139(3) adds a specific rule to the general rule in s 139(2)(c) by providing that an order may be made under s 139(2) 'notwithstanding that its effect is to place a burden on the creditor in respect of an advantage unfairly enjoyed by another person who is a party to a linked transaction'.

Section 139(4) provides that no order made under s 139(2) shall alter the effect of any judgment and so, once the creditor has obtained judgment against the debtor or a surety for recovery of the loan or enforcement of a security, the debtor or surety must comply with the judgment and cannot seek relief under s 139(2). In the recent decision in *Rahman v Sterling Credit Ltd*,[18] a loan was secured by a legal charge on the debtor's property, the rate of interest being 32%. On the debtor's default, the creditor had obtained a possession

---

18 [2001] 1 WLR 496.

order but warrants of execution had not been obtained and the debtor continued to make last-minute payments to forestall the creditor. The debtor applied to the county court to set aside the possession order and for leave to file a defence and counterclaim alleging, for the first time, that the loan was an extortionate credit bargain and thus seeking an order under s 139. The judge dismissed the application on the gound that, under s 139(4), any order under s 139(2) could not alter a judgment such as a possession order. The Court of Appeal held that (i) the action was not at an end as the creditor continued to accept payments from the debtor and warrants of execution had not been obtained, and (ii) the eight-year delay did not mean that the claim was barred; no limitation period was stipulated in the CCA and, as the action was based upon a specialty, the Limitation Act 1980, s 8(1) was applicable, meaning that the debtor's claim was not barred as the cause of action arose in 1989 and so the prescribed period of twelve years had not elapsed.

Sections 137-140 do not expressly provide that past transactions can be re-opened but this was certainly the position under the express wording of the Moneylenders Act 1900, s 1. Almost certainly the court can re-open past transactions because, otherwise, the extortionate credit provisions might be circumvented by closing an extortionate bargain and then refinancing it on reasonable terms. In *Lyle (B S) Ltd v Pearson*,[19] Goddard LJ stressed that the Moneylenders Acts could not be evaded 'by this patent and almost shameless device, by which the moneylender, having lent money at a harsh and unconscionable rate of interest, seeks to escape any difficulty into which that may put him by embodying all the previous loans and interest in a new promissory note at some low rate of interest and then suing the defendant on that as soon as he has made default'.[20] Moreover, in *Davies v Directloans Ltd*,[1] the court assumed that past transactions could be re-opened under the CCA.

PROPOSALS FOR REFORM REGARDING EXTORTIONATE CREDIT

The Crowther Committee considered that 'there is a level of cost above which it becomes socially harmful to make loans available at all'.[2] It is indisputable that the CCA provisions have not succeeded in controlling such socially harmful extortionate credit, particularly in short-term, small cash loans advanced to poor consumers, where the need to obtain credit and the ignorance of the consequences of accepting it are at their most conspicuous.[3]

The dominant, *laissez-faire* attitude of the courts when yoked with a severely restricted, 19th century definition of an extortionate credit bargain in the CCA, s 138, has proven to be a recipe for failure. Overall, the courts have felt constrained to abide by market forces in the credit market with a consequent inability or unwillingness to investigate inequality of bargaining power and resultant oppression. This approach leads inevitably to the conclusion that, provided there has been no fraud or procedural irregularity in the formation of

19 [1941] 2 KB 391.
20 [1941] 2 KB 391 at 396-397.
1 [1986] 1 WLR 823.
2 *Report of the Committee on Consumer Credit* (Cmnd 4596, 1971), para 6.6.6.
3 See Caplovitz, *The Poor Pay More: Consumer Practices of Low Income Families* (1963); Caplovitz, *Consumers in Trouble: A Study of Debtors in Default* (1974); *Consumers and Credit* (National Consumer Council, 1981).

the credit bargain, that 'bargain' cannot be re-opened.[4] It is ironic that the extortionate credit provisions should be confined in this way, as there are ample controls on such procedural irregularities elsewhere in the CCA. Moreover, the CCA extortionate credit provisions now look cramped and archaic in comparison with, for example, the Unfair Terms in Consumer Contracts Regulations 1999.

In 1991, the Office of Fair Trading (OFT) reported on extortionate credit practices[5] and made several important recommendations, viz:

(a) The concept of an 'unjust credit transaction' should replace that of an extortionate credit bargain in ss 137-140.
(b) 'Excessive payments' should be substituted for 'grossly exorbitant' payments in s 138(1)(a).
(c) A new test of 'deception, oppression, impropriety or unfairness' (using the same statutory wording as is used to assess the fitness of a trader to hold a credit licence) should supplant the current reference to 'ordinary principles of fair dealing' in s 138(1)(b).
(d) The factors to be taken into account in assessing whether a credit bargain is unjust should remain as they are in s 138 but with one important addition, ie 'the lender's care and responsibility in making the loan, including steps taken to find out and check the borrower's creditworthiness and ability to meet the full terms of the agreement'.
(e) The courts should have the power to re-open agreements of their own motion.
(f) The Director General (and other enforcement authorities) should be given the power to apply to the court for a declaration that a credit transaction is unjust.
(g) The courts should be required to notify the Director General of all cases where an unjust credit transaction has been re-opened.
(h) Stronger penalties should be introduced for the unlicensed provision of credit.

Overall, the 'unjust credit transaction' would be a less rigid definition than the current formulation and be better suited to modern credit transactions which have both increased in volume and changed in form since the report of the Crowther Committee in 1971. The OFT considered that 'extortionate' was too strong a word to identify agreements which should be re-opened in that it conveys a sentiment which is excessively narrow, focuses obdurately on the level of payments, and may also have connotations of violence. Likewise, it was thought that 'grossly exorbitant' was too restrictive a phrase which pitched the test too far in the creditor's favour. Accordingly, the new, less restrictive test of the 'unjust credit transaction' would be closely aligned with the Act's provisions dealing with the revocation of credit licences.

Perhaps the most significant recommendation was (d), above. The OFT has revoked licences where, in the case of secured loans, the creditor knew, or ought to have known, that the debtor would be able unable to meet the payments, with the consequence that the creditor took possession of the debtor's home. Similarly, in short-term, unsecured lending it is rare for the creditor to undertake any checks on the debtor's creditworthiness and, to cover the cost of default, interest rates are set at high levels. The new recommendation that checks should be made on creditworthiness would deter the deceitful practices in secured lending. It should also mean that, with unsecured loans, such checks would reduce the risk of default

---

4 See *Coldunell Ltd v Gallon* [1986] QB 1184, considered earlier.
5 *Unjust Credit Transactions* (OFT, Sept 1991).

which, in turn, should be reflected in lower interest rates for the generality of borrowers and higher rates for borrowers who are more likely to default. However, it is arguable that any reform in this area should also include a *statutory duty* on the creditor to ensure that the debtor *receives* independent advice.

The Law Commission also considered extortionate credit in a report in 1991 concerned with mortgages.[6] The recommendation[7] was that there should be a new statutory jurisdiction for the court to set aside or vary the terms of a land mortgage (the CCA being amended so that it would no longer apply to credit bargains secured by a land mortgage) with a view to doing justice between the parties if (a) principles of fair dealing were contravened when the mortgage was granted; or (b) the effect of the terms of the mortgage is that the mortgagee has rights substantially greater than, or different from, those necessary to make the property adequate security for the liabilities secured by the mortgage; or (c) the mortgage requires payments to be made which are exorbitant; or (d) the mortgage includes a postponement of the right to redeeem. In deciding whether to exercise its powers under (b) or (d), it was thought that the court should not consider the fact that the terms were freely negotiated between the parties but, if the terms were freely negotiated and the offending term was set aside or varied, the court should have a discretion to order the mortgagor to compensate the mortgagee for any loss. Otherwise, the powers of the court under the new jurisdiction and the factors to be taken into account should be analogous to those contained in the CCA, ss 137-140.

Overall, these are insipid proposals for reform. It is imperative that there be a new definition of extortionate credit and the formulation proposed by the OFT introduces elements of unfairness and oppression which are, potentially at least, less confining than those currently employed in the CCA. However, as discussed earlier, it is suggested that a new definition of extortionate credit should be combined with a rebuttable presumption of the credit bargain's being extortionate where the rate of interest charged exceeds a certain level. Moreover, a statutory duty should be imposed on creditors to ensure that debtors receive independent advice.

---

6 *Transfer of Land – Land Mortgages* (Law Com No 204, 1991).
7 See paras 8.1-8.8.

CHAPTER 38

The regulation of business activities

The licensing system under the Consumer Credit Act

Prior to the CCA 1974, moneylenders and pawnbrokers required licences in order to trade, the licence being authorised by the magistrates' court and then obtained from the local authority. There was thus no central agency to enforce the legislation and prosecutions were very rare.[1] Moreover, there was no licensing system for finance houses which provided hire-purchase and the hire-purchase legislation in the 20th century failed to provide a licensing framework. The Crowther Committee recognised that an improvement in the substantive rights of debtors was insufficient *per se* and, if consumer rights were to have any bite, it was vital that such rights be underpinned by effective administrative control of those who advance credit. Consequently, an extensive licensing regime was imposed by the CCA.

The initial introduction of licensing should act as a sieve through which undesirable traders are purged from the system because they do not apply for a licence and, once in place, it is arguable that many businesses will strive to comply with the law in order to obtain a licence. Moreover, licensing provides an effective means of controlling rogue traders in that, instead of the ineffectual threat of an occasional prosecution, the offender runs the risk of being denied the right to continue in business. Indeed, the threat of losing his livelihood may often be enough to deter malpractice on the part of the creditor. Finally, an important consequence of the licensing system is that accurate and regular information becomes available to the Office of Fair Trading (OFT) and emergent credit practices, both good and bad, can thus be monitored.

All that being said, some would assert that there are disadvantages to licensing. It could be argued that a corrupt lender may realise all too well that he will not obtain a licence and so he may simply pursue illegal lending practices in the first place. Viewed this way the licensing system could be said to encourage a recalcitrant, black market in credit. Moreover, a frequent criticism of the licensing system is that it can become overly-expensive in terms of administration costs and it is sometimes argued that a positive licensing system is simply too costly. Instead, it is often suggested that a negative system would be a better alternative.

---

1 See Goode, 'The Legal Regulation of Lending', Ch 3 in *Instalment Credit* (ed Diamond, 1970).

Under a negative system, traders are allowed to function without a licence but swindlers who are shown to be unfit to grant credit are banished from trading.[2]

It is indisputable, however, that the positive licensing system has distinct advantages and it is the option favoured by the OFT.[3] Above all else, positive licensing has a preventive effect in identifying those who are unfit to operate in the first place while a negative system would, necessarily, have to operate retrospectively in attempting to banish undesirable traders from the system. Moreover, the OFT considers that negative licensing is as expensive and burdensome in terms of administration as its positive counterpart yet, by definition, a negative system yields no income. A good case can be made, however, for reducing the complexity of the current licensing regime.[4]

The Director General of Fair Trading is responsible for the administration of the stringent, regulatory licensing system[5] introduced by the CCA.

Which businesses need a licence?

The CCA, s 21 provides that 'a licence is required to carry on a consumer credit business or consumer hire business'. In addition, s 147(1) provides that an 'ancillary credit business', as defined in s 145(1), also requires a licence.[6] It is thus necessary to analyse these types of business in some detail.

Consumer credit businesses and consumer hire businesses

Section 189(1) defines a 'consumer credit business' as 'any business so far as it comprises or relates to the provision of credit under regulated consumer credit agreements' and the same section defines 'consumer hire business' as 'any business so far as it comprises or relates to the bailment ... of goods under regulated consumer hire agreements'. These definitions make it clear that the only businesses which require a licence are those concerned with the provision of credit under a *regulated* consumer credit agreement, or the bailment of goods under a *regulated* consumer hire agreement. Conseqently, licences are not required by businesses which provide credit only in excess of £25,000 or bail goods to hirers who pay only in excess of £25,000. Because regulated consumer credit and consumer hire agreements apply only where the debtor or hirer is an 'individual',[7] businesses which provide credit or hire goods only to companies do not need a licence. Also excluded from the licensing provisions are businesses which provide

---

2 See generally *Report of the Committee on Consumer Credit* (Cmnd 4596, 1971), Vol I, p 255; see also Borrie, 'Licensing Practice under the Consumer Credit Act' [1982] JBL 91; Cranston, *Consumers and the Law* (3rd edn, 2000), pp 464-469; Ramsay, *Consumer Protection, Text and Materials* (1989), pp 322-327.

3 See *Consumer Credit Deregulation* (OFT, 1994), Ch 9, paras 9.9-9.21; Sir Gordon Borrie, *The Development of Consumer Law and Policy – Bold Spirits and Timorous Souls* (1984), pp 78-90.

4 See *Consumer Credit Deregulation* (OFT, 1994), Ch 9, paras 9.22-9.51.

5 See the CCA, Part III, ss 21-42; Borrie, 'Licensing Practice under the Consumer Credit Act' [1982] JBL 91.

6 See the informative booklet produced by the Office of Fair Trading, *Do you need a credit licence?* (OFT 147).

7 See ss 8(1), 15(1) and 189(1).

credit or hire under exempt agreements only, local authorities[8] and any body corporate empowered by a public general Act naming it to carry on a business.[9]

Ancillary credit businesses

An 'ancillary credit business', defined in the CCA, s 145(1), is:

> 'any business so far as it comprises or relates to –
> (a) credit brokerage,
> (b) debt-adjusting,
> (c) debt-counselling,
> (d) debt-collecting, or
> (e) the operation of a credit reference agency.'

It is thus clear that 'ancillary credit business' is defined broadly and, unlike the definitions of consumer credit and consumer hire businesses, above, it is not restricted by the concept of the *regulated agreement*. The remainder of s 145 specifies in more detail the constituents of the five types of ancillary credit business and so these individual businesses must now be considered separately.

Credit brokerage

First and most commonly, under s 145(2)(a)(i) and s 145(3)(a) and (b), credit brokerage consists of the effecting of introductions of individuals desiring to obtain credit to persons carrying on a consumer credit business or a business which comprises or relates to consumer credit agreements being, otherwise than by virtue of s 16(5)(a), exempt agreements. These sections thus cover the obvious cases of the finance broker and the mortgage broker. Another example of credit brokerage within these sections is the retailer (eg a car dealer) who does not directly enter into credit agreements but introduces customers who want credit (in any form) to finance companies. However, it was held in *Brookes v Retail Credit Cards Ltd*,[10] that a retailer who merely displayed application forms for a credit company's credit cards was not a credit-broker and did not introduce persons to the credit company.

Second, under s 145(2)(a)(ii), in the case of an individual desiring to obtain credit to finance the acquisition or provision of a dwelling occupied or to be occupied by himself or his relative, credit brokerage is the effecting of introductions to any person carrying on a business in the course of which he provides credit secured on land. For example, an estate agent who introduces clients who want to obtain a mortgage to a building society will thus need a licence as a credit-broker, even though the amount of credit involved will normally exceed the £25,000 limit in the CCA.

Third, under s 145(2)(b) and s 145(4), credit brokerage is the effecting of introductions of individuals desiring to obtain goods on hire to persons carrying on a consumer hire business.

Fourth, under s 145(2)(a)(i), s 145(2)(b), s 145(3)(c) and s 145(4)(b), credit brokerage is the effecting of introductions of individuals desiring to obtain credit, or to obtain goods on hire, to persons carrying on a business which comprises

8   See s 21(2).
9   See s 21(3); eg the Agricultural Mortgage Corporation.
10 [1986] CCLR 5.

or relates to unregulated agreements where the law applicable to the agreement is the law of a country outside the United Kingdom, and if the law applicable to the agreement were the law of part of the United Kingdom it would be a regulated consumer credit agreement or a regulated consumer hire agreement.

Fifth, under s 145(2)(c), credit brokerage is the effecting of introductions of individuals desiring to obtain credit, or to obtain goods on hire, to other credit-brokers. In *Hicks v Walker*,[11] Walker was a car dealer who had failed to obtain a licence under the CCA. He introduced customers to another car dealer, Purchase, who worked for R & Co Ltd which had a licence and to which Walker had sub-let part of his premises. Purchase also worked for Walker in that, when Walker's customers wanted credit, Purchase would inform his employer, R & Co Ltd, and the company would make the necessary arrangements with a finance company. The finance houses thought that they were dealing with R & Co Ltd but Walker's customers thought they were dealing with either Walker or Purchase acting on behalf of Walker. It was held that Walker was carrying on the business of credit brokerage by introducing individuals to another credit-broker (R & Co Ltd) through the agency of Purchase. Walker was thus convicted, under s 39(1), of carrying on the business of credit brokerage without a licence and both Purchase and R & Co Ltd were guilty of aiding and abetting that offence.

Finally, it should be noted that s 146 excludes certain categories of person from the statutory definition of a credit-broker. First, under s 146(1)-(4), solicitors and barristers engaging in contentious business are not to be treated as carrying on the business of credit brokerage or any ancillary credit business. Second, s 146(5) admits certain exceptions to limited forms of business. Introductions effected by an individual by canvassing off trade premises either debtor-creditor-supplier agreements falling within s 12(a) or regulated consumer hire agreements shall be disregarded if (a) the introductions are not effected by him in the capacity of an employee; and (b) he does not by any other method effect introductions falling within s 145(2). This means, for example, that housewives who act as part-time agents (paid on a commission basis for concluded sales) for mail-order companies and canvass applications from those who wish to buy goods on credit-sale are not credit-brokers, and neither are agents who are authorised by check trading companies to canvass trading check applications.

Debt-adjusting

Under s 145(5), debt-adjusting is defined to mean, in relation to debts due under consumer credit agreements or consumer hire agreements (a) negotiating with the creditor or owner, on behalf of the debtor or hirer, terms for the discharge of a debt, or (b) taking over, in return for payments by the debtor or hirer, his obligation to discharge a debt, or (c) any similar activity concerned with the liquidation of a debt.

Once again, this is a broad definition. It would seem that an example falling within (a) or possibly (c), above, is the car dealer who negotiates a settlement figure with the finance company when a customer has a car on hire-purchase and wishes to part-exchange it for a new car. Paragraph (b) speaks for itself and there are those in business who engage in this practice. Solicitors,[12] accountants

---

11 (1984) 148 JP 636.
12 Section 146(2)-(4), considered above, applies only to contentious business. Barristers who negotiate settlements for clients do not act as debt-adjusters (see s 146(1)).

and consumer advice agencies who negotiate on behalf of clients regarding debts owed to third parties are within the definition of debt-adjusters but, all three of these categories have been issued with 'group' licences.

It should be noted that the definition in s 145(5) applies to 'debts due under consumer credit agreements or consumer hire agreements' and so this covers exempt agreements. However, should the amount of credit advanced or hire paid exceed the statutory limit of £25,000, this will not fall within the s 145(5) definition as the agreement would not be within the classification of a consumer credit or consumer hire agreement (see ss 8 and 15).

Debt-counselling

Under s 145(6), debt-counselling is the giving of advice to debtors or hirers about the liquidation of debts due under consumer credit agreements or consumer hire agreements. This definition applies to any debt-counsellor who regularly gives advice for reward, solicitors (advising on non-contentious business), accountants, bankers and consumer advice agencies. Debt-counselling relates only to the 'liquidation of debts due' and so cannot apply to advice given to a prospective debtor or hirer. As with debt-adjusting, the definition of debt-counselling applies to 'consumer credit agreements or consumer hire agreements' (see above).

Debt-collecting

Under s 145(7), debt-collecting is the taking of steps to procure payment of debts due under consumer credit agreements or consumer hire agreements. Again, this broad definition is not confined to debt-collecting agencies but also embraces solicitors and accountants, for example. As with the two previous classifications, it relates to 'consumer credit agreements or consumer hire agreements'.

Credit reference agencies

Under s 145(8), a credit reference agency is a person carrying on business comprising the furnishing of persons with information relevant to the financial standing of individuals, being information collected by the agency for that purpose. In contrast to the broad definitions considered above, it seems that there is a limited meaning ascribed to the credit reference agency. Many people provide information on 'the financial standing of individuals' and so, for example an employer or a bank might furnish such information to a building society which is considering the advance of a loan to an individual. It could not be said, however, that the bank or employer carried on a business 'comprising' the furnishing of such information, as this word suggests that the business must be devoted *entirely* to such furnishing of information. Moreover, the bank or employer would not have 'collected' the information for the 'purpose' of furnishing it to other persons. In short, the definition in s 145(8) seems limited to businesses which comprise nothing other than the collection and dissemination of information relevant to the financial standing of individuals.

Exceptions in relation to debt-adjusting, debt-counselling and debt-collecting

Under s 146(6)(a)-(e), it is not debt-adjusting, debt-counselling or debt-collecting for a person to do anything in relation to a debt arising under an agreement if he is, first, the creditor or owner under the agreement, otherwise than by virtue of an assignment (s 146(6)(a)). This exception is necessary because, otherwise, the creditor or owner would be carrying on the business of debt-collecting by collecting debts due to himself. It should be noted that this exception does not apply to an assignee, unless the assignment is made in connection with the transfer to the assignee of any business other than a debt-collecting business (s 146(6)(b)).

Second, it is not debt-adjusting, debt-counselling or debt-collecting for the 'supplier in relation to the agreement' or a credit-broker who has acquired the business of the person who was the supplier in relation to the agreement to do anything in relation to a debt arising under an agreement (s 146(6)(c) and (d)) This would seem to cover *only* the situation where a loan has been advanced and so the supplier and creditor are different parties – where the creditor and supplier are the same parties (as in hire-purchase), s 146(6)(a) would apply.

Finally, s 146(6)(e) refers to the exception admitted by s 145(5), and referred to earlier, that housewives acting as part-time agents of mail-order companies, for example, are not classified as credit-brokers.

What is the meaning of 'carrying on a business' in this context?

It will be recalled that s 21 provides that 'a licence is required to *carry on* a consumer credit business or consumer hire business' and that s 147(1) provides that the licensing rules in the CCA apply to an 'ancillary credit business'. It is consequently crucial to know when such a business is being carried on.

The CCA, s 189(1) provides that 'business' includes a 'profession or trade' and s 189(2) adds that 'a person is not to be treated as carrying on a particular type of business merely because occasionally he enters into transactions belonging to a business of that type'. The courts have accentuated the word 'occasionally' and so, in *Hare v Schurek*,[13] a car salesman who, on one occasion, supplied a car on hire-purchase to a friend, was held not to be carrying on a consumer credit business and did not need a licence. The same approach has been adopted in relation to 'carrying on' a business of moneylending under the Moneylenders Acts 1900 and 1927. In *Wills v Wood*,[14] a retired hotelier gave his solicitors £11,000 to lend to their clients and £3,000 was advanced to the defendant, a client of the solicitors, secured by legal charges over her real property. The Court of Appeal accepted that the hotelier was not carrying on the business of moneylending but was engaged in investment, there being a fundamental difference between carrying on a business and merely investing savings.[15]

---

13 [1993] CCLR 47; see also *R v Marshall* (1989) 90 Cr App Rep 73 (the appellant entered into six credit transactions over a period of 16 months and was convicted of acting as a credit-broker without a licence contrary to s 39(1). The CA considered that the judge had misdirected the jury and the appellant's conviction was quashed. The decision is thus unsatisfactory although the court clearly considered that these would be 'occasional' transactions within s 189(2) and would not have sufficient regularity for the carrying on of a business).
14 [1984] CCLR 7.
15 See also *Litchfield v Dreyfus* [1906] 1 KB 584 (the plaintiff carried on a business as an art dealer and lent money to friends, about ten in total; he did not advertise as a moneylender. Farwell J held that the Moneylenders Act 1900 applied to those 'carrying on the business of money-lending as a business, not to persons who lend money as an incident of another business' (p 590)); *Kirkwood v Gadd* [1910] AC 422 ('What is carrying on a business? It imports a series or repetition of acts': p 423, per Lord Loreburn LC); *Edgelow v MacElwee* [1918] 1 KB 205 (the plaintiff solicitor was held to be an unregistered moneylender as he was 'systematically engaging in ordinary money-lending transactions, and the appellation of "clients" was given (if at all) to needy and adventitious borrowers … his vocation as a

The provision of consumer credit, consumer hire or ancillary credit services need not be the *sole*, or even *primary* activity, of the business. This fact is emphasised by the definitions in the CCA of the three types of business (ie consumer credit, consumer hire and ancillary credit businesses), all of which stress 'any business *so far as* it comprises or relates to' the provision of credit, the bailment of goods or the types of ancillary credit business which are specified.[16] For example, a company which manufactures goods but also regularly lends money to its employees clearly needs a licence, as would a solicitor who regularly lends money to his clients. The only exception to this general rule appears to be the definition of credit reference agencies, considered above, where the furnishing of information on the financial standing of individuals must seemingly constitute the *sole* activity of the business rather than being a secondary activity in some other business.

Administration of the licensing system

The CCA, s 22 provides that licences may be either 'standard' or 'group' licences. A licence is normally a 'standard' one granted to the particular applicant for the prescribed period[17] but 'group' licences are obtainable in certain circumstances, eg the Law Society, the various accountancy bodies and Citizens' Advice Bureaux have obtained such group licences. The standard licence is issued to 'a person named in the licence' and, under s 22(2), is not assignable. Except in the case of a partnership or an unincorporated association, a standard licence shall not be issued to more than one person (s 22(3)). Moreover, s 24 permits the licensee with a standard licence to carry on business under the name or names specified in the licence, but not under any other name.

The Director General of Fair Trading is given wide powers in relation to the issue, renewal, variation, suspension and revocation of licences.[18] Under s 25(1), the applicant for a licence must satisfy the Director that 'he is a fit person to engage in activities covered by the licence' and s 25(2) delineates a (non-exhaustive) list of factors to which the Director shall have regard, these factors embracing issues other than criminal conduct (eg oppressive or deceitful business practices).[19] This monitoring of traders is a most important source of consumer protection and any criminal conduct[20] or undesirable practices which come to the Director's attention may mean that a licence will not be granted or that it may be suspended or revoked.[1]

---

solicitor ... was used as a mere disguise' (p 209, per McCardie J)); *Skelton Finance Co Ltd v Lawrence* (1976) 120 Sol Jo 147 (two isolated loan transactions did not import the necessary element of system, repetition and continuity to constitute a moneylending business); Cf *Conroy v Kenny* [1999] 1 WLR 1340 (CA held that it was not necessary to establish a number of loans over a period of time; if the business was that of moneylending it was unnecessary to look any further).

16 See ss 189(1) and 145(1).
17 The period is now five years: see Consumer Credit (Period of Standard Licence) Regulations 1975 (SI 1975/2124, as amended by SI 1991/817).
18 CCA, ss 27-33.
19 See the CCA, s 25(2)(d).
20 See the CCA, s 166 (notification of convictions and judgments to the Director General); see also *Quinn v Williams Furniture Ltd* [1981] ICR 328.
 1 See *Credit Default Register Ltd v Secretary of State* [1993] CCLR 59.

The consequences of unlicensed trading

Under s 39(1), it is an offence to engage in unlicensed trading. In *R v Curr*,[2] the appellant ran a 'mobile greengrocery and drapery business' and, although he had no licence under the CCA, he lent money to customers at rates of interest of approximately 800% per annum. The appellant had told the police that he had no time to carry on his business within the law. He must have had, no doubt, ample time to reflect on this attitude, as he was sentenced to twelve months' imprisonment and fined £2,400.

At least as important a deterrent to unlicensed trading is the fact that agreements entered into may be rendered unenforceable. It should be stressed that the agreements which are discussed below are unenforceable against the debtor or hirer, but they can be enforced by the latter parties against the creditor or owner, ie the agreements are not rendered *void*.

The CCA, s 40(1) provides that, if a regulated agreement (other than a non-commercial agreement) was made when the creditor or owner was unlicensed, it is enforceable against the debtor or hirer *only* where the Director has made an order under s 40 that regulated agreements made by the creditor during a certain period are to be treated as if he were licensed. Without such an order, any security is also unenforceable.[3] Relevant factors listed in s 40 that the Director must take into account are how far, if at all, debtors were prejudiced by the creditor's conduct, whether the Director would have been likely to grant a licence had one been applied for and the degree of culpability for failure to obtain a licence.

It is significant that the creditor or owner also runs a grave risk if the credit-broker with whom he transacts business is unlicensed. The CCA, s 149 provides that if a regulated agreement made by a debtor or hirer results from an introduction effected by an *unlicensed credit-broker*, the agreement is enforceable against the debtor or hirer *only* where an order has been made by the Director General. Without such an order, any security is also unenforceable.[4] Again the factors referred to in s 40, above, are relevant to the Director's determination. It is plain that s 149 encourages all creditors to be vigilant regarding credit-brokers and dealers who introduce debtors to them and the section applies whether or not there are pre-existing arrangements between the creditor and the credit-broker.

Section 148 completes the picture regarding licensing and enforceability of agreements by providing that the agreement for the services of a person carrying on an ancillary credit business, if made when he is unlicensed, is enforceable against the other party only where the Director General has made an order which applies to the agreement. The general purpose of this provision is clear in precluding an unlicensed trader from recovering fees or commission without an order from the Director. However, it is unclear whether 'an agreement for the services of a person carrying on an ancillary credit business' extends only to his business activities in the capacity of a credit-broker, for example, or whether it might extend to *all* the services provided by him. An estate agent who also acts as a credit-broker might thus be precluded from recovering not

---

2 (1980) 2 Cr App Rep (S) 153.
3 See s 113(2).
4 See s 113(2).

only the fee payable by the debtor for the introduction to the creditor but also the commission payable by the seller of the property.

Seeking business: advertising and canvassing

Part IV of the CCA (ss 43-54) and ss 151-154 seek to control the advertising of credit facilities and the canvassing off trade premises for certain regulated agreements, thereby acknowledging that the consumer is vulnerable to the attractions of obtaining credit and needs protection at the stage *before* any agreement is completed.[5] The objective of the controls in the CCA is to ensure that, when they are seeking business, traders provide prospective debtors with full and clear information about the nature and price of the services they are offering.

This aspect of the regulation of business activity is not new. The Betting and Loans (Infants) Act 1892 made it an offence to write to persons under 21 years of age offering loans, and the controls on seeking business which existed under the Moneylenders Act 1927 were arguably more effective than the statutory provisions concerned with the licensing of moneylenders. The moneylender was prohibited from employing canvassers or agents to elicit business and had to conduct his business activities in his authorised name and at his authorised address. Moreover, he could not issue unsolicited circulars inviting applications for loans and the content of newspaper advertisements was controlled strictly. The hire-purchase legislation in the 1960s contained limited controls on advertisements for credit and the disclosure of the cash price of goods, but there was no coherent, overall control until the CCA in 1974. The three areas of control in the CCA relate to advertising, quotations and canvassing.

ADVERTISING

Under s 189(1), 'advertisement' is given a comprehensive definition so that, quite literally, every *form* of advertising is drawn within it. For example, the definition clearly covers advertising by post in specifying 'distribution of ... circulars, catalogues, price lists or other material' and it is also sufficiently broad to draw electronic mail within it. Moreover, 'advertiser' in relation to an advertisement is defined in s 189(1) as 'any person indicated by the advertisement as willing to enter into transactions to which the advertisement relates'. The latter definition indicates that the 'advertiser' need not be the person who has published the advertisement and so, for example, where a retailer places an advertisement stating that credit is available from a finance company, the latter is the advertiser, although he may have a defence under s 168 if the advertisement was published without his knowledge.

Infringement of the advertising provisions is a criminal offence[6] but the CCA does not invalidate the agreement which the consumer is induced to enter into as a result of the false or misleading advertisement.

---

5   See the informative booklet produced by the Office of Fair Trading, *Credit Advertising* (OFT 016).
6   See the CCA, s 167 and Sch I; ss 45 and 46.

Scope of the control on advertising

Sections 43 and 151 provide the basic framework of the scope of the advertising controls. Section 43(1) provides that Part IV of the CCA applies 'to any advertisement, published for the purposes of a business carried on by the advertiser, indicating that he is willing (a) to provide credit, or (b) to enter into an agreement for the bailment ... of goods by him'. Section 151 extends the controls on advertising to 'advertisement[s] published for the purposes of' businesses which provide the ancillary credit services of credit brokerage, debt-adjustment or debt-counselling. It should be stressed that it is not simply the advertising of regulated agreements which is controlled. The advertising provisions apply also to businesses providing credit to individuals which is secured on land and, for example, the advertising of mortgages from building societies and banks is within the controls even where the credit advanced far exceeds the £25,000 statutory ceiling.[7] There are two crucial points to be made regarding the nature and scope of the advertising controls.

First, s 43(1) refers to 'any advertisement, published for the purposes of a business carried on by the advertiser' and so it is abundantly clear that the provision of credit need not be the main business of the advertiser. Indeed, the nature of the advertiser's business is irrelevant as it is the nature of the services which are advertised which is crucial. For example, should a car dealer advertise that he will advise on the liquidation of existing debts as an incentive to customers to buy goods from him, the advertisement is a debt-counselling advertisement within s 151(2).

Second, s 43(1) refers to an advertisement which is 'published' but it does not say to whom it must be published. It has been suggested that the advertisement 'must be issued or displayed either to the public at large or to an individual or individuals as members of the public, not in some other capacity'.[8] There is no authority on the question of publication but the meaning of 'indicating that he is willing to provide credit' in s 43(1) was considered in *Jenkins v Lombard North Central plc*.[9] There a price sticker supplied by the respondent finance company was attached to a car on a dealer's premises. The stickers were divided vertically and gave the cash price of the goods on the right hand side while the left hand side contained the name and logo of the finance company, this being a stylised £ sign. The appellant alleged that the price sticker was an advertisement indicating the finance company's willingness to provide credit as the finance company was well-known and the main purpose of the display was to show that credit was available. The Divisional Court held that this was insufficient to 'indicate' that the company was willing to provide credit and so the advertisement was not within the Act's provisions. The court took the view that the proper test was whether the advertisement *itself* expressed a willingness to provide credit rather than whether an ordinary person would *conclude* that the advertisement indicated a willingness to provide credit by, for example, relying on extrinsic factors such as his own knowledge. The price stickers were thus a form of corporate advertising and did not refer to any specific services which could be provided.

---

7 See *Scarborough Building Society v Humberside Trading Standards Department* [1997] CCLR 47.
8 Goode, *Consumer Credit Law* (1989), para 12.13.
9 [1984] 1 WLR 307.

Certain advertisements are exempted from the control of the CCA, Part IV, by s 43 and the Consumer Credit (Exempt Advertisements) Order 1985[10] as follows:

(i)   Under s 43(3)(a), an advertisement which indicates that the credit *must* exceed the statutory ceiling of £25,000 *and* that no security is required or the security is to consist of property other than land.

(ii) Under s 43(3)(b), an advertisement which indicates that the credit is available only to a body corporate.

(iii) Under s 43(4), an advertisement of leasing, hire or rental, which indicates that the advertiser will not enter into a consumer hire agreement; if this exemption is to apply, the advertisement must exclude *all* types of consumer hire agreement, whether regulated or exempt.

(iv) Under s 43(2)(c), where the advertiser's business comprises or relates to unregulated agreements and the proper law is a foreign law.

(v)   Under the 1985 Regulations, an advertisement which indicates that the credit is payable in four instalments or less within a period of twelve months and is for a debtor-creditor-supplier agreement (NB the Regulations do apply to agreements financing the purchase of land).

(vi) Under the 1985 Regulations, an advertisement where a trader allows customers to charge their purchases to an account and settle the account at the end of fixed period, eg the milk bill payable at the end of every month.

Form and content of advertisements

The CCA, s 44 empowers the Secretary of State to make regulations regarding the form and content of advertisements within Part IV. Section 44 states that the overall object of the regulations is to ensure that 'the advertisement conveys a fair and reasonably comprehensive indication of the nature of the credit or hire facilities offered by the advertiser and of their true cost to persons using them'.

The form and content of advertisements are prescribed by the Consumer Credit (Advertisements) Regulations 1989[11] which are lengthy and very intricate. 'Advertisement' and 'advertiser' have the same meaning as in s 189(1), considered above, and the Regulations apply to every advertisement within s 43(1) and s 151, also considered above. At the outset, it is important to stress that the decision in *Jenkins v Lombard North Central plc*,[12] considered earlier, means that certain advertisements are outside the control of both the CCA and the Regulations but, as will be seen, it is only in the most limited of circumstances that this could occur.

The overall scheme of the Regulations is that advertisements are divided into three categories: *simple*, *intermediate*, and *full*. It is not practicable to give the detail of the Regulations here but an outline of the major provisions is desirable. The simple advertisement is very limited and is designed to keep the name of the trader in the public eye as one willing to provide credit or hire out goods. Accordingly, it may include all or any of the trader's name, postal address, telephone number, logo and occupation, but the simple advertisement cannot give *information* on credit or specify *prices*. The Office of Fair Trading considers simple advertisements to be the sort of material found on 'bookmatches, business

10   SI 1985/621.
11   SI 1989/1125, as amended by SI 1999/2725; SI 2000/1797.
12   [1984] 1 WLR 307.

cards and note pads'.[13] Beyond this is the intermediate advertisement which allows the trader a measure of choice in the amount and type of information which can be included and it prescribes a minimal level of information which *must* be included. The full advertisement must contain detailed information regarding deposits, repayments, and the APR which must be calculated to within fine tolerances and rounded to one decimal place.[14]

If a flat rate of interest is shown, the APR must be given greater prominence than the flat rate in the advertisement. The upshot of all this detail is that the prospective debtor should not be misled but, instead, should be able to make an informed comparison of the cost of credit which is available from different traders. Moreover, infringement of the Regulations is a criminal offence[15] but, as mentioned earlier, the CCA does not invalidate an agreement entered into as result of a misleading advertisement.

The Office of Fair Trading[16] has suggested that the advertising rules are 'unsatisfactory in their present detailed and prescriptive form'[17] in that the costs in enforcing and administering the system are not matched by positive advantages to the consumer. Moreover, the OFT considered that minor infringements of the detailed rules were not uncommon, even amongst reputable traders, and that over-emphasis on the enforcement of such detail could lead to a neglect of the broader issues of seriously misleading or deceptive advertising. Accordingly, as with the licensing rules, it was recommended that the advertising regulations be simplified so that, instead of seeking compliance with minute detail, the greatest significance would be attached to demanding a minimum of required information in advertising copy and ensuring that the advertisement was not false or misleading.

Availability of cash terms: s 45

Section 45 provides that where an advertisement, to which Part IV applies, indicates that the advertiser is willing to provide credit under a restricted-use credit agreement relating to goods or services to be supplied by any person, but at the time when the advertisement is published that person is not holding himself out as prepared to sell the goods or provide the services (as the case may be) for cash, the advertiser committs an offence.

The purpose of s 45 is to prohibit advertisements which give the impression that a debtor will not be charged for credit or charged only a meagre amount when, in fact, the advertiser does not sell the goods or provide the services on cash terms so that, consequently, the debtor cannot determine what the cash price is and compare it with the rate of the credit to be charged.

False or misleading advertisements

Section 46 provides that if an advertisement, to which Part IV applies, conveys information which in a material respect is false or misleading the advertiser

---

13 *Credit Advertising* (OFT 016), p 5. This booklet provides an excellent guide to credit advertising with ample, visual illustrations of the correct and incorrect form to adopt in the advertisements.

14 In accordance with The Consumer Credit (Total Charge for Credit) Regulations 1980 (SI 1980/51, as amended by SI 1985/1192, SI 1989/596, SI 1999/3177).

15 See the CCA, s 167 and Sch I; ss 45 and 46.

16 See *Consumer Credit Deregulation* (OFT, 1994), Ch 5.

17 *Consumer Credit Deregulation* (OFT, 1994), para 5.9.

commits an offence. Section 46(2) adds that information 'stating or implying an intention on the advertiser's part which he has not got is false'. It need not be an aspect of the *credit* which is misleading: provided that the advertisement falls within Part IV, s 46 applies if *any* aspect of it is misleading. In *Rover Group Ltd and Rover Finance Ltd v Sumner*,[18] the advertiser was guilty of an offence under s 46 when the advertisement for a Rover Metro indicated the cash price of £5,995 and, only in very small print in a footnote, indicated that an extra cost was payable for road tax, delivery to the dealer and number plates.[19]

QUOTATIONS

Following the recommendations of the Director General of Fair Trading in *Consumer Credit Deregulation*,[20] the Consumer Credit (Quotations) Regulations 1989 (SI 1989/1126) were revoked.[1] The regulations relating to quotations were not thought to be particularly helpful to consumers and it was also considered that the costs associated with them outweighed any benefit which might have resulted. The information which previously had to be included in a quotation was very similar to that which must be included in a full credit or hire advertisement, but there is no longer a legal requirement for traders to give a quotation in a specific *form*.

New Regulations[2] have provided, however, that clear and legible warnings, as prescribed, must be given in quotations in certain circumstances. The Regulations apply to persons who carry on consumer credit businesses, consumer hire businesses, businesses which provide credit to individuals seucured on land, and credit-brokers. If such businesses provide a quotation[3] to a prospective customer in connection with a prospective credit agreement, or prospective hire agreement, which will or may be secured by a mortgage or charge on the customer's home, that quotation must include a statement that that such security is or may be required and, in addition, the warning that 'Your home is at risk if you do not keep up repayments on a mortgage or other loan secured on it'. This warning, with suitable amendments, must also be included in quotations provided in connection with a prospective hire agreement which will or may be secured on the prospective customer's home (reg 5). Warnings are also prescribed where a quotation is provided in connection with a prospective credit agreement which will be secured by mortgage, charge or standard security on land and require repayments to be made in currency other than sterling, ie 'The sterling equivalent of your liability under a foreign currency mortgage may be increased by exchange rate movements' (reg 4). Regulation 6 contains the same requirements where the quotation is provided by a credit-broker.[4]

18　[1995] CCLR 1.
19　See also *Metsoja v H Norman Pitt & Co Ltd* [1990] CCLR 12; *Ford Credit plc v Normand* 1994 SLT 318.
20　OFT, 1994, paras 5.20-5.28.
1　See SI 1997/211.
2　The Consumer Credit (Content of Quotations) and Consumer Credit (Advertisements) (Amendment) Regulations 1999 (SI 1999/2725) which add special warning statements in quotations for particular types of mortgage loan.
3　Defined in reg 2(1) as 'any document by which a person gives a prospective customer information about the terms on which he is prepared to do business'.
4　See also the Consumer Credit (Advertisements and Content of Quotations) (Amendment) Regulations 2000 (SI 2000/1797)

CANVASSING AND SOLICITING

The CCA is particularly concerned with the control of 'doorstep selling' of credit and it will be remembered that the debtor or hirer has a right of cancellation where the agreement has been signed at premises other than business premises and the requirements of s 67 are complied with.[5] In addition, ss 48-51 control the canvassing of applications for credit 'off trade premises'. There is, however, neither inter-dependence nor correlation between the cancellation and canvassing provisions.

Canvassing under s 48

Before the criminal offences connected with canvassing and soliciting (s 49) can be considered, it must first be decided what is meant by 'canvassing'. The CCA, s 48, provides:

'(1) An individual (the "canvasser") canvasses a regulated agreement off trade premises if he solicits the entry (as debtor or hirer) of another individual (the "consumer") into the agreement by making oral representations to the consumer, or any other individual, during a visit by the canvasser to any place (not excluded by subsection (2)) where the consumer, or that other individual, as the case may be, is, being a visit –
(a) carried out for the purpose of making such oral representations to individuals who are at that place, but
(b) not carried out in response to a request made on a previous occasion.
   (2)   A place is excluded from subsection (1) if it is a place where a business is carried on (whether on a permanent or temporary basis) by –
(a) the creditor or owner, or
(b) a supplier, or
(c) the canvasser, or the person whose employee or agent the canvasser is, or
(d) the consumer.'

The substance of 'canvassing' under s 48 is thus that (i) oral representations are made to the prospective debtor, hirer or any other individual, (ii) in the course of an unsolicited visit devised for the purpose of making such representations, (iii) to any place other than a place where a business is carried on by the creditor, owner, supplier, canvasser (or his employer or principal) or the prospective debtor or hirer. These three points must now be investigated in more detail.

Oral representations

While oral representations[6] must be made, they can be made to the 'consumer' (ie the prospective debtor or hirer) or to 'any other individual'. Oral representations could thus be made, for example, to the consumer's wife or brother, provided they are made to induce the *consumer*, rather than his wife or brother, to enter into the agreement. Although the oral representations will usually be made face-to-face, they need not be made in such a personal and direct manner. Thus oral communications which take place on an intercom system, internal telephone, door answer-phone or even a pre-recorded audio tape, video tape or CD played to the consumer, would all amount to canvassing within s 48 provided that these communications take place at the consumer's home, for example.

---

5 See Ch 33.
6 Canvassing by mail or electronic mail is beyond the scope of s 48.

It also clear that both the canvasser and the consumer or other individual must be physically present at the premises in question when the oral representations are made, as s 48(1) specifies that the oral representations must be made 'during a visit by the canvasser to any place ... where the consumer, or that other individual, as the case may be, is'. For example, both a telephone call made by the canvasser from his business premises to the consumer at his home, and a telephone call made by the canvasser from the consumer's home to the consumer at his business premises, would *not* amount to canvassing within s 48.

There is every reason to suppose that 'oral representations' would be given the same, broad meaning, as that under the right of cancellation in s 67.[7]

Unsolicited visit

Canvassing occurs within s 48 only where the visit is unsolicited. Consequently, under s 48(1)(b), it is *not* canvassing if the visit is 'carried out in response to a request made on a previous occasion'. There are several uncertainties here.

First, it is not clear how far apart in time the request on the 'previous occasion' must be from the visit: can minutes separate the two or must there be a substantial lapse of time between the previous occasion and the visit? The salient words 'previous occasion' and 'visit' indicate that, while these two elements must necessarily be separated in time, the most crucial aspect is that they be separated in terms of their *objective*, eg the canvasser telephones the consumer and requests permission to visit him at his home the next day.[8]

Second, no form is prescribed for the 'request' that the visit be made and so it appears that a request made in any form will mean that the visit does not amount to canvassing within s 48. It should also be stressed that the request can come from either the consumer *or* the canvasser.[9]

Third, in order to amount to canvassing within s 48, the visit must be 'carried out for *the purpose of making such oral representations* to individuals who are at that place' (s 48(1)(a)). This 'purpose' requirement is rather elusive. Does the *sole* purpose have to be that of making the oral representations and soliciting business or does it suffice that this is *one* of the purposes of the visit? If the former interpretation is correct, there will be many situations which are not within the scope of 'canvassing'. Where, for example, the canvasser calls at the consumer's home regarding an issue connected with an existing agreement, but then persuades the consumer/debtor to enter into a new loan agreement, this would not be canvassing within s 48 as the visit would not have been made for the sole purpose of soliciting the new loan. However, it would clearly not amount to canvassing, under either interpretation, where the canvasser visited the consumer's home on a purely social visit and an agreement was then concluded, because the visit would not have been even partly for the purpose of making oral representations and soliciting business.

---

7   See s 189(1) for the definition of 'representation'; *Moorgate Property Services Ltd v Kabir* [1995] CCLR 74.

8   Note that this telephone call does not amount to canvassing within s 48, although this is arguably too lenient. Perhaps it would have been better, as the Crowther Committee had wanted, to prohibit such a call unless the consumer had made a prior request to the canvasser.

9   See also the consideration of s 49(2), below.

Visit to any place other than one where a business is carried on by those persons specified in s 48

As with the right of cancellation, the idea underpinning s 48 is that the consumer comes under greatest pressure to enter into an agreement where the canvassing takes place at his home. Neither the likelihood of intimidation nor the prospect of temptation are so great where the canvassing takes place at the business premises of the canvasser, for example, particularly where the consumer has visited those premises voluntarily and is able to leave them without hindrance. Consequently, it is only canvassing which takes place 'off trade premises' which is controlled and so it does *not* amount to canvassing within s 48 if the soliciting occurs at 'a place' where 'a' business is carried on by one of the four categories of person listed in s 48(2)(a)-(d), above.

It is significant that, under s 48, the business can be conducted at 'a place' (not 'premises' as in s 67[10]) on a 'temporary basis'. It is thus beyond doubt that, should the consumer be solicited at a mobile caravan used by the creditor for business purposes temporarily at trade fairs or outside a supermarket, this does not amount to canvassing within s 48 as it occurs at, not off, trade premises. It is equally significant that it is not canvassing, within s 48, if the soliciting of the consumer occurs at the *consumer's own place of business*, provided that he does actually carry on a business there rather than using it exclusively as a home, for example (s 48(2)(d)). Nevertheless, this is balanced by the fact that the right of *cancellation*, under s 67, *is* available to the debtor or hirer where the agreement is signed at the debtor's or hirer's own business premises.

OFFENCES IN RELATION TO CANVASSING UNDER SECTION 49

It is striking that s 48 defines what is meant by 'canvassing' but the section is passive in the sense that it neither prohibits certain actions nor creates any criminal offences in relation to canvassing. Two criminal offences are created, however, by s 49.

Section 49(1)

Section 49(1) provides that it is 'an offence to canvass debtor-creditor agreements off trade premises'. Debtor-creditor loans are what the Crowther Committee referred to as 'unconnected loans', ie credit which is not extended in connection with the arrangements between creditor and supplier. Typical examples of debtor-creditor agreements are loans by moneylenders or pawnbrokers and an ordinary bank loan. Section 49(1) is thus aimed at controlling those who importune for straightforward cash loans by making unsolicited visits at places other than trade premises. This is, of course, the habitual practice of 'loansharks'.

However, it must be stressed that, in deciding whether the offence of canvassing under s 49(1) has been committed, it is necessary to refer to s 48 for the definition of 'canvassing'. For example, even in relation to debtor-creditor agreements, a request in any form that the visit be made to the consumer's home means that the visit is not canvassing within s 48 and, consequently, an offence has not been committed under s 49(1).

10 See Ch 33.

It will also be evident that it is permissible to canvass *debtor-creditor-supplier* agreements either off trade premises or at trade premises. It follows that, for example, persons offering hire-purchase, conditional sale, credit-sale, and rental/hire agreements may canvass for business, as may credit card issuers[11] and check traders. However, an important qualification to add is that, under s 23(3), a specific licence is required for the canvassing off trade premises of debtor-creditor-supplier agreements or regulated consumer hire agreements and a group licence cannot suffice for this purpose.

Section 49(2)

While it is clear that a visit made after a prior request in any form cannot constitute canvassing under s 48, and such a request would mean that no offence was committed under s 49(1) in relation to debtor-creditor agreements, s 49(2) creates the separate offence of soliciting. Section 49(2) provides:

> 'It is also an offence to solicit the entry of an individual (as debtor) into a debtor-creditor agreement during a visit carried out in response to a request made on a previous occasion, where –
> (a) the request was not in writing signed by or on behalf of the person making it, and
> (b) if no request for the visit had been made, the soliciting would have constituted the canvassing of a debtor-creditor agreement off trade premises.'

Consequently, even if the visit follows a previous request, it will still be an offence for a canvasser, without a *signed request in writing*, to canvass the consumer within the definition in s 48, and attempt to persuade him to enter into a debtor-creditor agreement[12], ie the mischief against which this provision is aimed is the canvassing by 'loansharks' of debtor-creditor agreements off trade premises without a signed request in writing.[13]

It is tempting to assume that it will be the debtor who makes this signed request in writing and, if so, the section would achieve its aim. However, as the signed request in writing can emanate from *either* party, both the mechanics and utility of this section are questionable. Is it sufficient for the canvasser to send the signed request in writing to the debtor specifying a date for the visit? Section 49(2) does not specify that such a 'request' must be met with a correlative assent and so it seems all too easy for the canvasser to intimidate the debtor by presenting him on the doorstep with the formal, signed request in writing while simultaneously covering his tracks for the purposes of s 49(2). In order to function effectively, the exception in 49(2) should be limited to those situations where the debtor has made a signed request in writing to the canvasser.

Section 49(3)

Section 49(3) provides a limited exception to the offences created by s 49(1) and (2) in that it is permissible to solicit 'for an agreement enabling the debtor to

---

11   But see s 51 in relation to unsolicited credit-tokens.
12   See *R v Chaddha* [1984] CCLR 1.
13   But it is baffling that the legislature created the two, quite separate offences in ss 49(1) and 49(2), as the s 49(1) offence is completely subsumed by the more explicit s 49(2) offence, ie it is irrelevant that the canvasser visits in response to a prior request in some form (exonerating him under s 49(1)) because that request must be a signed request in writing to escape criminal liability under s 49(2).

overdraw on a current account of any description kept with the creditor' provided that the Director General of Fair Trading has made a determination that such current accounts are to be excluded from s 49(1) and (2). The Director made a determination[14] excluding existing, current accounts, but only where the canvasser is the creditor or an employee of the creditor. A bank manager may thus visit an existing customer/debtor at his home and solicit the possibility of the debtor's taking an overdraft on his current account.

CANVASSING AND ANCILLARY CREDIT SERVICES

Sections 153 and 154 control the canvassing off trade premises by those engaged in ancillary credit services, ie where the canvasser solicits the consumer to enter into an agreement for the provision to the consumer of such ancillary services. Canvassing here is defined in terms analogous to those in s 48 and most of the requirements are the same as in that section. The salient features of canvassing under s 153 are:

(i) The canvasser makes oral representations to the consumer, or any other individual, during a visit by the canvasser to any place (not excluded by subsection (2)) where the consumer, or that other individual as the case may be, is, being a visit (a) carried out for the purpose of making such oral representations to individuals who are at that place, but (b) not carried out in response to a request made on a previous occasion.

(ii) A place is excluded, under s 153(2), from the canvassing provisions if it is a place where (whether on a permanent or temporary basis) – (a) the ancillary credit business is carried on, or (b) any business is carried on by the canvasser or the person whose employee or agent the canvasser is, or by the consumer.

Under s 154, it is an offence to canvass off trade premises the services of a *credit-broker, debt-adjuster or debt-counsellor*. It is only these three providers of ancillary credit services who are prohibited from canvassing – canvassing by a debt-collector or a credit reference agency is thus permissible.

CIRCULARS SENT TO MINORS

Under s 50(1), it is an offence to send any document to a minor, with a view to financial gain, inviting him to (i) borrow money; or (ii) obtain goods on credit or hire; or (iii) obtain services on credit; or (iv) apply for information or advice on borrowing money or otherwise obtaining credit, or hiring goods. Section 50(2) adds that, in any proceedings under s 50(1), it is a defence for the person charged to prove that he did not know, and had no reasonable cause to suspect, that the individual was a minor. However, s 50(3) provides that, where a document is received by a minor at any school or other educational establishment for minors, a person sending it to him at that establishment knowing or suspecting it to be such an establishment shall be taken to have reasonable cause to suspect that he is a minor.

It should be noted that the offence here is to *send* any document to a minor and so there is no prohibition on giving such a document to the minor in person.

14 1 June 1977.

However, provided that the document is sent, there is no requirement that it be received. Moreover, it is the sender who must send the document to the minor rather than a third party, eg no offence is committed where a circular sent to a minor's home is then posted to the minor, at a different address, by his father. Section 50 was considered recently in *Alliance and Leicester Building Society v Babbs*[15] where the Divisional Court held that an offence is *not* committed if (i) the circular states that loans are not available to persons under 18 as, in this event, the circular does not amount to an *invitation* to obtain credit; and (ii) the advertiser/sender has a policy and system to ensure that applications from minors are rejected (here a computer program which barred loans to minors) as then the circular would not be sent 'with a view to financial gain' under s 50.

UNSOLICITED CREDIT-TOKENS

Section 51 is aimed at controlling the unsolicited dispatch of credit cards on the scale which occurred with the launch of the 'Access' card, before the enactment of the CCA. It will be remembered that credit cards fall within the, now rather quaint classification, of 'credit-tokens'. The definition of credit-tokens and credit-token agreements was considered in Chapter 31.

Section 51(1) provides that it is an offence 'to give[16] a person a credit-token if he has not asked for it' and subsection (2) adds that 'to comply with subsection (1) a request must be contained in a document signed by the person making the request, unless the credit-token agreement is a small[17] debtor-creditor-supplier agreement'. Exceptions are admitted to this general rule by s 51(3) in that subsection (1) does not apply 'to the giving of a credit-token to a person – (a) for use under a credit-token agreement already made; or (b) in renewal or replacement of a credit-token previously accepted by him under a credit-token agreement which continues in force, whether or not varied'. There was a successful prosecution under s 51 in *Elliott v Director General of Fair Trading*,[18] a case which is considered in detail in Chapter 31.

15 [1993] CCLR 77.
16 'Give' is defined in s 189(1) as 'deliver or send by post to'.
17 That is a debtor-creditor-supplier agreement which, under s 17, is classifiable as 'small' (currently credit not exceeding £50).
18 [1980] 1 WLR 977.

Index